THE ESSENTIAL WHOLE EARTH CATALOG

Doubleday NEW YORK LONDON TORONTO SYDNEY AUCKLAND

PURPOSE

WE ARE AS GODS and might as well get good at it. So far remotely done power and glory — as via government, big business, formal education, church — has succeeded to the point where gross defects obscure actual gains. In response to this dilemma and to these gains, a realm of intimate, personal power is developing — the power of individuals to conduct their own education, find their own inspiration, shape their own environment, and share the adventure with whoever is interested. Tools that aid this process are sought and promoted by the *Essential Whole Earth Catalog*.

FUNCTION

The *Essential Whole Earth Catalog* is an evaluation and access device. It can help a user discover what is worth getting and how to get it. We're here to point, not to sell. We have no financial obligation or connection to any of the suppliers listed. We only review stuff we think is great. Why waste your time with anything else?

An item is listed in this *Catalog* if it is deemed:

1. Useful as a tool,
2. Relevant to independent education,
3. High quality or low cost,
4. Easily available by mail.

The listings are continually revised and updated according to the experience and suggestions of *Catalog* users and staff. Latest news can be found in our magazine, *Whole Earth Review* (see inside front cover).

PROCEDURE

Order items in this Catalog directly from the supplier or publisher. Books can also be ordered from the Whole Earth Access Company if the access is marked "or Whole Earth Access."

ORDERING FROM SUPPLIERS

Consider these points of mail order etiquette essential. They'll make shopping by mail more pleasant for you and the companies you're dealing with. This advice is distilled from the requests of hundreds of the firms listed in this Catalog, plus our own experience over the past 18 years.

1. Include payment with your order. Use a money order or personal check. Cash or stamps won't do. If you're buying an expensive product like a music synthesizer, their catalog will usually describe credit terms, if any. Don't send U.S. money orders or personal checks overseas.

Staff

Editor Emeritus
Stewart Brand

Editor
J. Baldwin

Managing Editor
Jeanne Carstensen

Assistant Editors
Art Kleiner
Richard Nilsen
Peter Warshall
Jay Kinney
Tom Ferguson, M.D.

Publisher
Kevin Kelly

Research Manager
Cindy Craig

Research
David Finacom
Dorothy Houser
Don Baker
Michael Hoekstra
Ken Conner

Research/Proofreading
Lori Woolpert

Designer
Kathleen O'Neill

Production Manager
Susan Erkel Ryan

Camera
Donald Ryan

Typesetting
James Donnelly
Joan Gill
M. Alan Born

Proofreading
Hank Roberts
Jonathan Evelegh
William Ryan

Layout/Pasteup
Jerri Linn

Pasteup
Steve Lipke
"Captain" Bruce Walker
Rebecca Wilson
Catherine Courtenaye
Alex Gubanov

Far-Ranging Factotum
Dick Fugett

Index
David Burnor
Ted Schultz

Office
Christina Sponseller

Controller
Cliff Figallo

WELL
(Whole Earth 'Lectronic Link)
Matthew McClure
John Coate

Carpenter
Liz Fial

Office Beasts
Sally
Borderline collie/McNab
Tesla
Border collie/Australian shepherd
Fifi
Irish Black rat (R.I.P.)
Jason and Amelia
Goldfish (R.I.P.)
Hive
Approximately 15,000 honey bees (*Apis melliferae*)

POINT Foundation Board
Paul Hawken
Huey Johnson
Doug Carlston
Stewart Brand
Kevin Kelly

Stats and Halftones
Marinstat
Mill Valley, CA

Color Separations
Pro Graphics
Clearwater, FL

Film
Progressive Graphics
Oregon, IL

Literary Agent
John Brockman Associates

Doubleday
Les Pockell
Karen Johnston

THE ESSENTIAL WHOLE EARTH CATALOG

Published by Doubleday, a division of Bantam Doubleday Dell Publishing Group, Inc., 666 Fifth Avenue, New York, New York 10103.

Doubleday and the portrayal of an anchor with a dolphin are trademarks of Doubleday, a division of Bantam Doubleday Dell Publishing Group, Inc.

Library of Congress Cataloging-in-Publication Data.
The Essential Whole earth catalog.

Includes index.
1. Manufaturers — Catalogs.
2. Handicraft — Equipment and supplies — Catalogs.
I. Whole earth catalog.
TS199.E77 1986 338.47'6029
86-16630 ISBN 0-385-23641-7

6 8 9 7 5

BG

2. Include sales tax if the supplier is in the state you are ordering from.

3. Expect prices to rise. The prices shown in this catalog are accurate as of August 1986. Most firms will write you back if you don't send enough money. Some will bill you for the extra amount.

4. Use International Money Orders (IMOs) to send money abroad. They're available from your post office. To send money to the U.S. from abroad, use IMOs or a bank draft in U.S. dollars.

5. Expect prices to be higher if you live outside the U.S. It's best to write for the price and shipping costs by enclosing an International Reply Coupon (available at your post office). Be sure to ask about the price and time difference between shipment by sea (months sometimes, with high possibility of damage and theft) and by air (secure and quick, but very expensive for heavy items).

6. Write legibly. If you do much mail ordering, it's worthwhile to get address labels and stick them on everything. If your writing can't be read, at least folks will know where it came from.

7. Say what you want on the outside of the envelope. Writing "mail order" or "catalog request" or "subscription order" under the address will help prevent the loss of your order.

8. Use stock numbers where we've listed them, especially if ordering from the U.S. Government Printing Office.

9. Some companies have an 800 number for ordering. Call 1-800-555-1212 to find out. Some of these companies will accept credit card orders. You may be charged extra for credit card service.

10. Don't order from the excerpts of catalogs we've reviewed. Send for their brochure or catalog to get latest specifications and prices, and order from that.

11. Be patient. It takes *at least* two weeks for your goods to arrive; four to six weeks' wait is normal, especially if you've paid by personal check. Don't worry unless it's taken more than two months. Keep a record of date of purchase, and a photocopy or other record of your check, so if your order is lost you can give them specific details. Include your full name and address (with zip code) every time you write.

12. Be gentle. When complaining, remember that your goal is resolution, not revenge. If you are polite, calm, and specific, the person you're talking with will likely be more cooperative.

13. Be considerate. Don't send away for catalogs just to keep your mailbox full. Some businesses we've listed in past Catalogs have been so swamped by frivolous inquiries that they had to shut down. If you write for free information, send a stamped, self-addressed envelope (SASE).

DON'T FORGET LIBRARIES! Most libraries can get you most any book if you're willing to wait for the interlibrary loan network to work its magic. If it's a book, you probably don't have to buy it.

And don't forget your local bookstore. You can order most of the books in this Catalog through them, thus supporting a local business, and probably saving you postage and handling charges.

DO NOT ORDER ANYTHING FROM US AT THE WHOLE EARTH CATALOG

ORDERING BOOKS FROM WHOLE EARTH ACCESS

The phrase "or Whole Earth Access" that appears under most book access information in this Catalog means that you can order the book from the Whole Earth Access Company, an outfit inspired by the *Whole Earth Catalog* but not connected with us in any way. They offer this service as a convenience to our readers, especially for multiple book orders from various publishers.

Whole Earth Access Company has a catalog of their own (see p. 245) plus stores in San Francisco, Berkeley, and San Rafael, California. They keep thousands of titles in stock and can get many others. In addition to books, they carry a selection of tools, hardware, housewares, clothing, electronics, and computers, often at bargain prices.

Here's how to order from Whole Earth Access (be sure to send the order to THEM and not to us, or hellish confusion will result).

1. Print the name, telephone number, and address to which you want the order shipped.
2. Print the titles and quantity of the books you want, the page number they appear on in this Catalog, and the list prices. When only a postpaid price is given, that IS the list price. (Some companies don't charge for postage and handling.)
3. Total the prices of the books you are ordering.
4. For delivery in California, add 6 percent tax (6½ percent in BART counties).
5. Add $3 to each order of up to five books, and 50¢ for each additional book for postage and handling. Orders of over 20 books will be charged actual UPS shipping rate.
6. Orders are shipped UPS unless you indicate otherwise.
7. For rush orders, specify UPS Blue Label (2nd Day Air). This costs $6.50 for up to five books (instead of the $3 mentioned above).
8. For foreign orders, shipping is $4 for the first two books and 50¢ for each additional book. For orders to developing countries, International Registry Insurance is recommended. That costs an extra $3.60 per order. Please remit bank draft in U.S. dollars.
9. Enclose payment in full with check or money order. VISA/MasterCharge customers print name from card, account number, expiration date, and sign your name.
10. VISA/MasterCharge cardholders can order by phone. Call toll-free 800/845-2000 (or locally, 415/845-3000) between 10 a.m. and 6 p.m. Pacific time.

Send orders to:

Whole Earth Access
2990 Seventh Street
Berkeley, CA 94710
800/845-2000 • 415/845-3000

Whole Earth Access Statement:
"We will do our best to get your books to you as soon as we can. If for any reason you are dissatisfied with our products or service, please return the books to us and we will promptly refund your money.

"Publishers' prices are subject to change. We will adjust your order accordingly, issuing a refund if necessary. Current booklists and prices are available on request."

INTRODUCTION

by Stewart Brand

ON PAGE 152 of *The Essential Whole Earth Catalog* is an essay by editor J. Baldwin titled "One Highly-Evolved Toolbox." It could have been the title of the whole book. In an earlier printing of the essay (it itself has evolved through four editions), J. wrote:

"Our portable shop has been evolving for about twenty years now. There's nothing very special about it except that a continuing process of removing obsolete or inadequate tools and replacing them with more suitable ones has resulted in a collection that has become a thing-making system rather than a pile of hardware."

Just so with the *Whole Earth Catalog*. Though the book has been made wholly new five times now since I started the process in 1968, it was the constant daily research for our magazine *Whole Earth Review* (formerly *CoEvolution Quarterly*) that kept and keeps us current. What started as a kind of precocious-kid operation has had maturity thrust upon it — partly through the hard knocks of business survival, partly through the maturing of its audience and its makers, partly through the refining of the fields it reports on.

We've seen enthusiasms like communes come and go, enthusiasms like solar energy come and 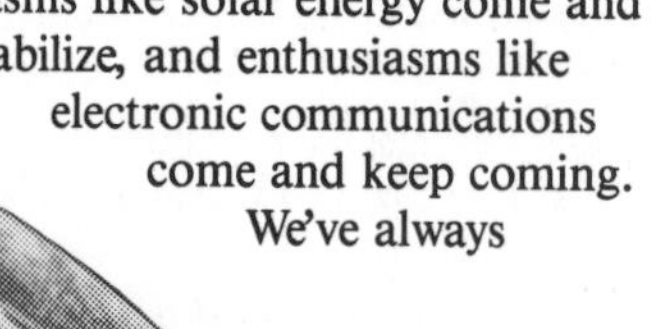stabilize, and enthusiasms like electronic communications come and keep coming. We've always pushed self-publishing; now we can push desktop publishing (p. 316). Right up to the 1981 *Whole Earth Catalog*, all the how-to books we reviewed were books. Now there are 1,000 how-to video cassettes on the market (see p. 331). The original *Whole Earth Catalog* got a somewhat inaccurate reputation as a back-to-the-land bible. All this edition has to offer rural life is primarily urban tools. The prevalence of satellite dishes on the countryside suggests that urbanity has less and less to do with clusters of tall buildings and ever more to do with global perspective.

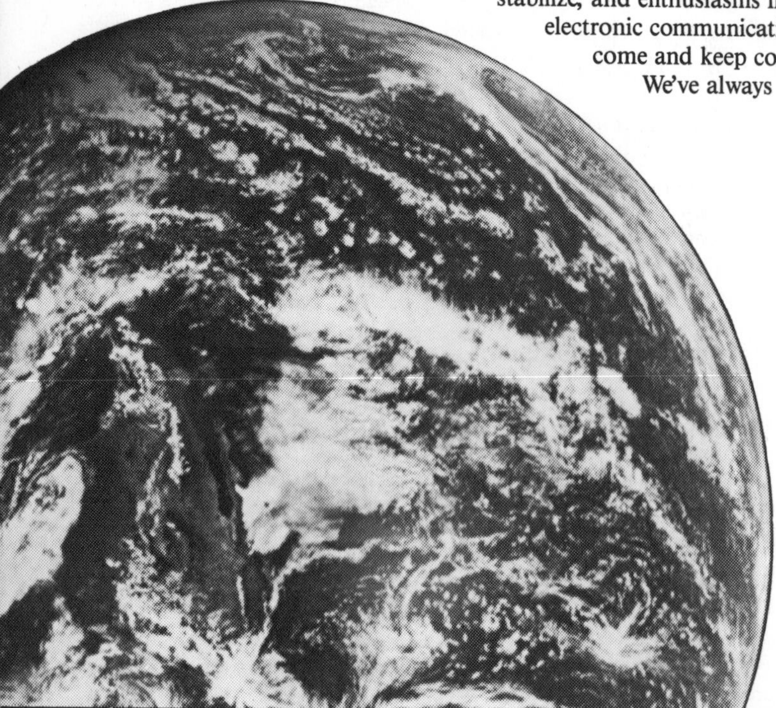

My name is on the cover mainly as an indication of continuity. I had a hand in selecting items to repeat from previous *Catalogs* and participated in renaming the sections, but my role with Whole Earth these days is one of richly enjoyed *emeritus*. Kevin Kelly runs the place with a far more capable hand than mine, and J. Baldwin made production on this *Catalog* sing like none before. You can see the ever-growing skill of old hands like naturalist/reviewer Peter Warshall and designer Kathleen O'Neill. You can also see the fresh perspective brought by a generation of newcomers. The production and research crews are about half and half of each.

The original core idea is intact. Instead of trying to review everything that exists, the *Whole Earth Catalog* only recommends what it finds to be the best available across the widest spectrum of usefulness it can discover. The reviews are written and excerpts selected as if they were advertising written by customers, the way you tell a friend about something you found that you've come to love. We know we haven't identified everything wonderful, but since excellence leads to excellence we can trust the reader to keep up the search beyond these pages.

The "Whole Earth" in the title refers to planetary perspective, not to the range of our coverage. Some day maybe, but I hope not — the world might gain by seeing itself whole, but it should forever elude coverage by anybody.

Of the 1962 items recommended here, 1086 are books, 297 are magazines, 579 are mail order suppliers. Each is an opportunity to learn a skill. In times even more in transition than the times that were a-changin' in the '60s, there is no safer and more rewarding strategy than the routine acquiring and use of new skills.

"Live and learn" is a redundancy. Live is learn. ■

Photos by Kevin Kelly

PREFACE

by
J. Baldwin

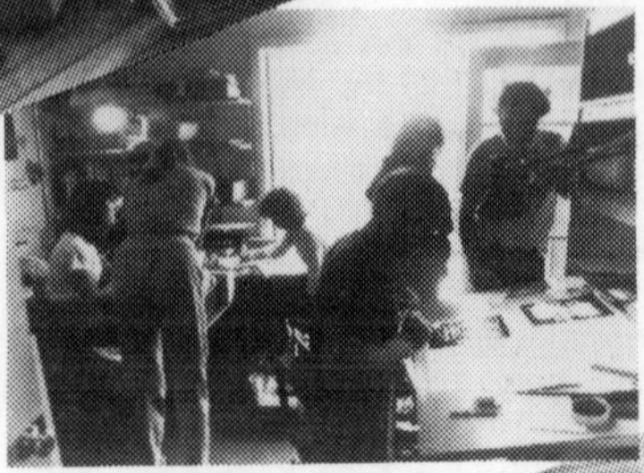

OUR OFFICE looks like a kicked-over anthill. Always. A succotash of books, catalogs, letters and strange hardware litters the place — some of it sent to us at our request, some sent by readers who think we've missed something. (We greatly encourage you to join the fray; see inside front cover for how.) We never know when we're going to meet someone or something we've never heard of before.

With such diverse input, it's no surprise that just about anyone can find things in this *Catalog* that'll make them mutter something like, 'Hm, I'd better read up on this," "I always wondered where you got those," or (as we often do ourselves), "Hey, check *this!*" Much of the information we've gathered is difficult or annoying to find, let alone with an opinion from an experienced reviewer. We'll look at most anything, old or new, wild or straight. We're the only publication we know of where such a melange is gathered into one place so you can mix and match your way into uncharted territory.

Of the 1,086 books recommended here, 652 are dated 1982 or newer. (The most recent *Catalog* came out in 1981.) Yet we acknowledge that newest is not necessarily best. You'll find classics whose excellence has let them endure despite a lack of current review or popularity. On the other hand, many of our favorite oldies are missing — out of print. Some have been replaced by books we think are inferior.

Out-of-prints were a bother in the production of previous *Catalogs,* but they were a pestilence in this one. Over and over, we'd get a page built around a famous and wonderful book, only to have one of our researchers sigh, "It's OOPed."

Several forces are causing this unhappy state of affairs. First is a change in how books are sold. Bookstore chains are taking over the retail book trade, and they want every foot of shelf to pay its way. Such stores concentrate on fast-selling, well-publicized books rather than the slow-and-steady-selling classics. A recent spate of publishers taking over publishers hasn't helped; in a typical takeover, heads roll, taking enthusiasm for certain books with them. In 1981, the IRS made things worse by instituting a tax on unsold inventory (IRS vs. Thor Power Tools). That ruling gave publishers incentive to dump warehoused books rather than pay the inventory tax on them, which means disaster to books that find their niche slowly and settle to steady but unspectacular sales. To the IRS, books are mere products like electric drills. To us, books are sources of information. It's dumb to make information harder to find.

Even reference books aren't immune: the massive and authoritative *Rodale's Encyclopedia of Indoor Gardening* is gone. We mourn the passing of gems like Sir John Russell's *The World of Soil.* Our policy is to only present things that can be obtained by mail, but sometimes we recommend out-of-print books anyway because they're irreplaceable. Thus we feature the influential and disturbing *Architecture Without Architects* (p. 115) and the peerless *How to Find and Buy Your Place in the Country* (p. 140). You might be able to make a modest living reprinting books like these.

Of course, heh heh, *Whole Earth Catalogs* go out of print, too. But we do replace 'em with new ones now and then. Old friends can see that we've shrunk a bit physically — down from an unwieldy 5½-pound megabook that wouldn't fit shelves (especially bathroom shelves) to a relatively svelte and handy 2½ pounds. The table of contents remains about the same length, but the number of items reviewed has been limited to those our editors and consulting specialists deem to be the best introduction to a subject: the *essential* in our new title.

Metaphorically, previous *Catalogs* were like jungles. This edition is more like a garden, the result of 18 years of cultivation by us and our millions of readers. But it's not a formal garden; we encourage hybrids. Always have. Reviewers of our *Catalogs* have often missed the point by calling us a "wishbook." Not at all. You can grab ahold of nearly anything in here and make it a part of your life. Use the book like a huge key ring — select a key from one of our pages and use it to open the door to something new to you. Access to tools and ideas, just like it says on the cover. We use it ourselves. ■

6 WHOLE SYSTEMS

UNDERSTANDING WHOLE SYSTEMS means looking both larger and smaller than where our daily habits live and seeing clear through our cycles. The result is responsibility, but the process is filled with the constant delight of surprise. Neither the Earth nor our lives are flat. What happened in the 20th century? The idea of self — the thing to be kept alive — expanded from the individual human to the whole Earth.

—Stewart Brand

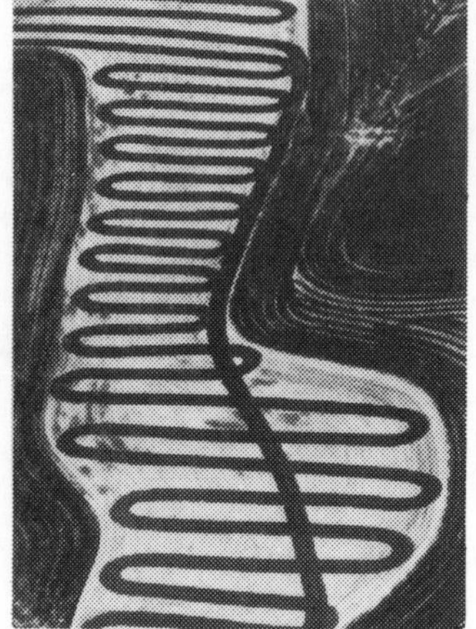

Below From Above

The best book of aerial photographs ever (133 — in color). What is unique is the captioning — Gerster knows what he is floating over, or he studies it until he does. He knows the history of places, and why the farmers do odd things, and what the tribe is after, and how to keep sand dunes from covering the oasis. The book is a tour de force of form and content.

The range is so worldwide and culturally rich that no reader-flier can escape wanting to try things differently. That's the yield of perspective. I've seen no other book — not even the space satellite ones — with perspective like this.

—Stewart Brand

◄

Battling wind erosion on a field near Wichita, Kansas. A sudden May wind spurred the farmer into action. He roughened up the soil with a spring-tooth harrow by driving haphazardly over the field. He simply wanted to secure the largest possible amount of land against the wind in the shortest possible time and with the least fuel consumption. Uncultivated fields lack sufficient protective surface cover of crop residue. The dry, whitish crust indicates just how vulnerable they are when bare. In Kansas every year the wind blows away an average of three tons of soil per acre — only about four-fifths of a ton less than what is lost through water erosion.

►

The village of Labbezanga, on an island in the Niger River, Mali. The granaries wind through the village like strings of beads. In them, millet and rice keep for up to three years, though in the recent past, during the seemingly endless droughts, the harvest has rarely been sufficient to maintain full capacity. The amphora-shaped mud containers, some as high as the houses, are filled and emptied through an opening at the top. Stone slabs and fragments, jutting out from the body of the granaries like spikes, make them easier to climb. The villagers, settled, non-nomadic members of the Songhai tribe, live mainly in the traditional round mud huts with domed thatched roofs. In Labbezanga, however, terrace-roofed square houses of Islamic-Arabic origin are on the increase. Owning one boosts a family's social standing.

I have explained in the introduction why I felt like Columbus when I found Labbezanga. Beyond being "the most beautiful village in Africa," it is also, according to the cyberneticist Frederic Vester, a shining example of an inter-connected system. For the unassuming Labbezangans almost too much praise.

Below From Above
Georg Gerster
1986; 133 plates
$35
($37 postpaid) from:
Abbeville Press
505 Park Avenue
New York, NY 10022
or Whole Earth Access

Powers of Ten

Like the famous film of the same name by Ray and Charles Eames, ***Powers of Ten*** *takes you on a photographic journey from quasars to quarks — 10^{25} to 10^{-16} — in 42 incremental steps, each one ten times the next. The changes in scale are provocative and truly mind-expanding, because you can't comprehend such matters without the aid of sensitive instrumentation (and some imagination). It's both jarring and inspiring to see how much of what is really going on is invisible to our five senses.*

—JB

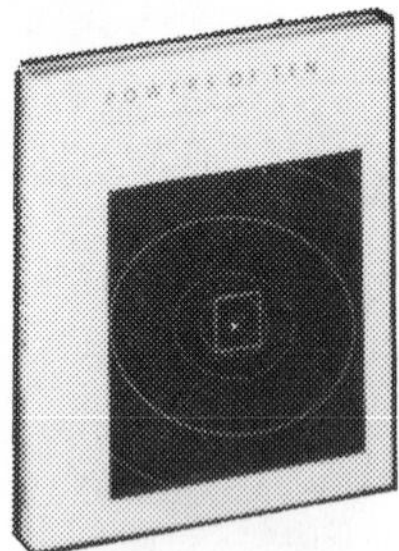

Powers of Ten
Philip and Phylis Morrison and The Office of Charles and Ray Eames
1982; 150 pp.
$19.95
($21.45 postpaid) from:
W. H. Freeman & Co.
4419 West 1980 South
Salt Lake City, UT 84104
or Whole Earth Access

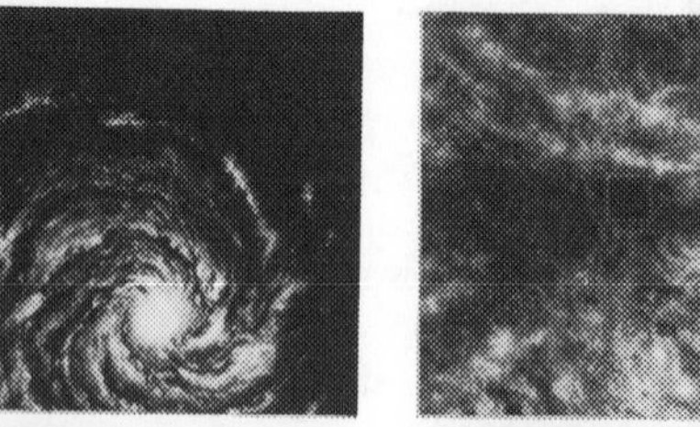

10^{21} meters

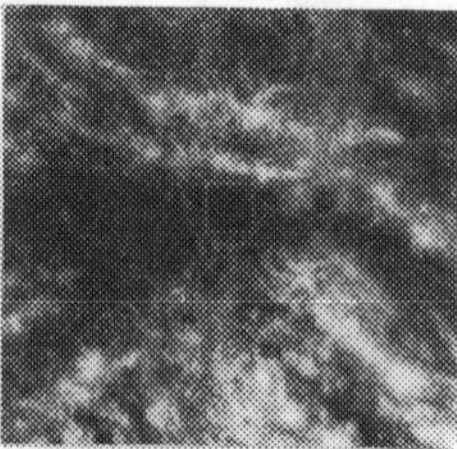

10^{20} meters

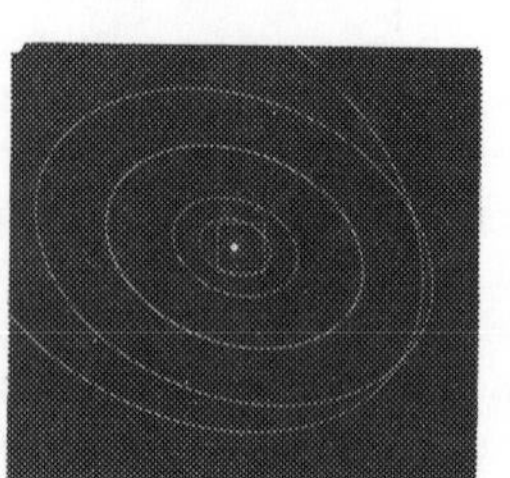

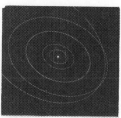

10^{13} meters

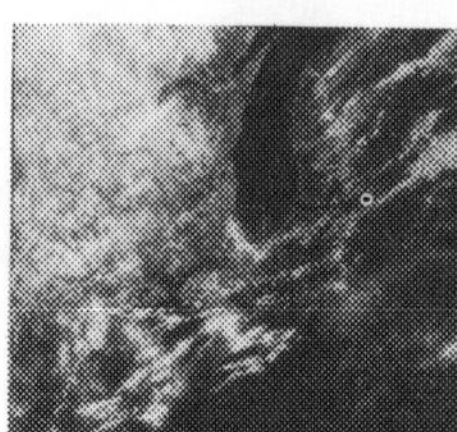

10^{6} meters

10^{0} meters

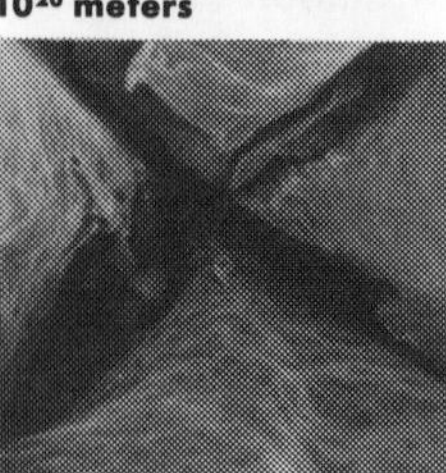

10^{-3} meters

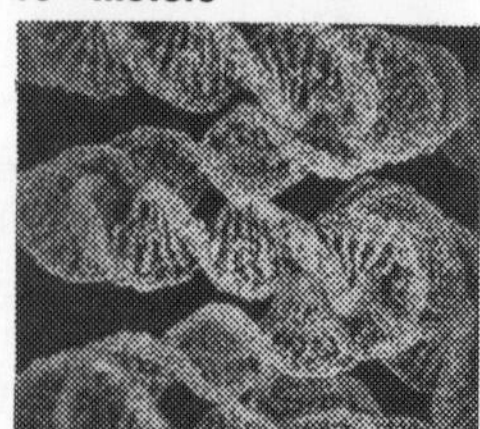

10^{-8} meters

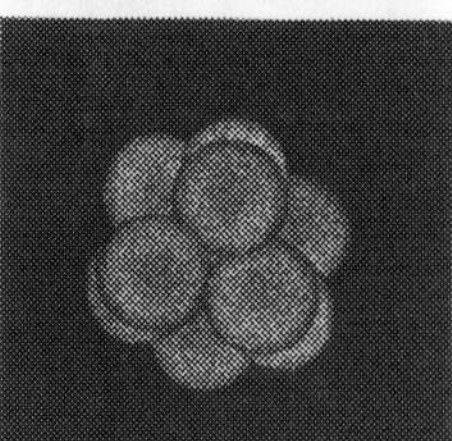

10^{-14} meters

"THERE IS NOTHING like astronomy to pull the stuff out of man. His stupid dreams and red-rooster importance: let him count the star-swirls."
—"Star Swirls" by Robinson Jeffers

Cosmos

Human knowledge used to be divided into: 1) our people; 2) everything else. In the last decade or so, it's started to divide differently: 1) Earth; 2) everything else. This new book is now the best introduction to understanding everything in the context of Earth, and Earth in the context of everything else.

It's a personal view — Carl Sagan's — derived from his public television series of the same name. I liked those programs far less than this book, but clearly the necessarily graphic research for video yielded a rich inventory of images for the book. (They are mostly new and mostly highly illuminating and knowledgeably captioned. That's rare in the field of popular astronomy, where half-decent images are recycled forever.) Carl is opinionated as well as insightful; both characteristics give the book its life. Both are invigorating. You might well wind up on another planet just to refute his preference for robots in space.
—Stewart Brand

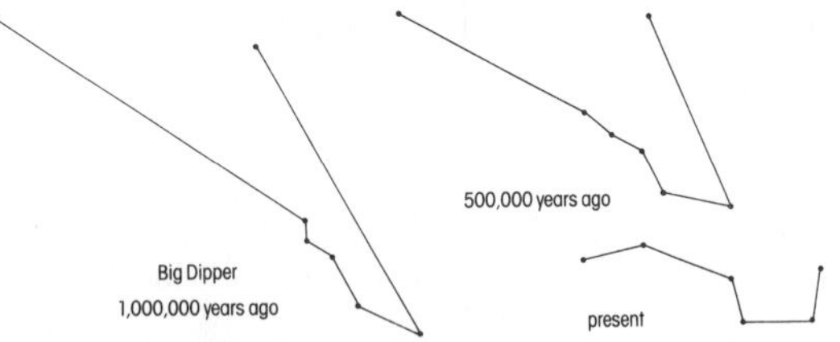

Computer-generated images of the Big Dipper as it would have been seen on Earth one million years ago and half a million years ago. Its present appearance is shown at bottom.

•

Neutron star matter weighs about the same as an ordinary mountain per teaspoonful — so much that if you had a piece of it and let it go (you could hardly do otherwise), it might pass effortlessly through the Earth like a falling stone through air, carving a hole for itself completely through our planet and emerging out the other side — perhaps in China. People there might be out for a stroll, minding their own business, when a tiny lump of neutron star plummets out of the ground, hovers for a moment, and then returns beneath the Earth, providing at least a diversion from the routine of the day. If a piece of neutron star matter were dropped from nearby space, it would plunge repeatedly through the rotating Earth, punching hundreds of thousands of holes before friction with the interior of our planet stopped the motion.

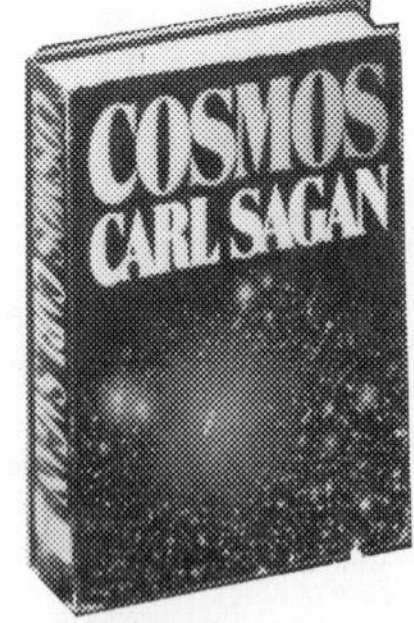

Cosmos
Carl Sagan
1980; 365 pp.
$15.95
($16.95 postpaid) from:
Random House
Order Dept.
400 Hahn Road
Westminster, MD 21157
or Whole Earth Access

The New Astronomy

Astronomers don't look through telescopes. (The eye isn't very good at star-watching.) Moreover, a lot of what is going on out there is happening "invisibly." Infrared, ultraviolet, x-ray, radio and gamma radiation can be detected and the images captured on film. This book explains how it's done and shows what has been found in startling color images of cosmic activity. The author fortunately speaks normal English and makes the phenomena comprehensible without recourse to intricate math. The book gives new meaning to the word fascinating. —JB

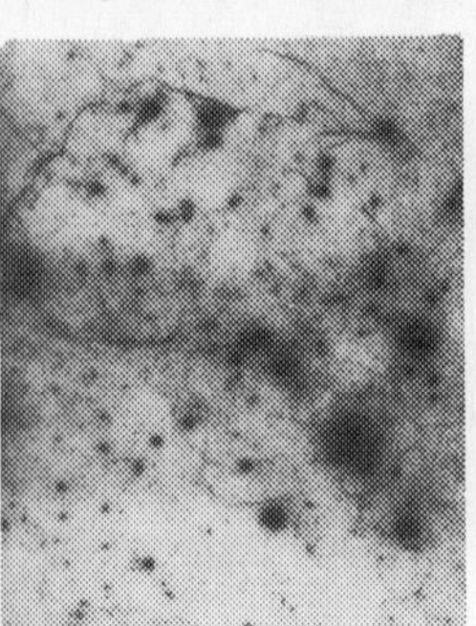

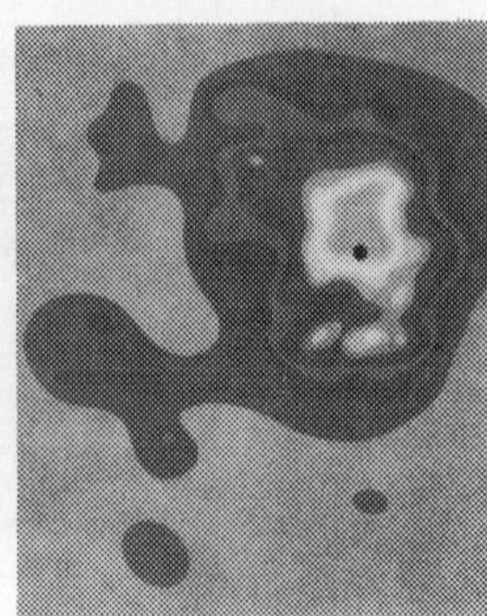

Left: Optical, 501 nm oxygen line, negative print, 1.2 m UK Schmidt Telescope.
Right: Radio, 11 cm, 64 m Parkes Telescope.

•

Like other supernova remnants, the Vela remnant is far more striking when observed at radio and X-ray wavelengths. At radio wavelengths it is one of the brightest sources in the sky, as strong as the Crab Nebula. The radio picture (right) covers the same area of sky as the optical photograph (left), and is color coded so that the faintest outer regions are pink, with successively brighter parts in shades of blue, green, orange and red. (The pulsar is too weak to show up here; its position is shown by the black spot.) The radio picture shows the total extent of the gases and shockwaves from the explosion much more clearly. The radio-emitting remnant is 4^0 (about 100 light years) across.

Echoes of the Ancient Skies

A great work of connection is done here. The Earth's sky is connected to the Earth's dwellings, temples, and cities. The present, in this perspective sadly impoverished, is connected to our deepest past at its most perceptive and intelligent. Here are the sun daggers striking to the middle of labyrinths on certain days, the horizon points that connect the whole world to the whole year to the whole life, the lines drawn on the land to match the lines found between the sky and the passage of time. Richly told, richly illustrated.

How have our modern architects remained so blissfully ignorant of these findings? All we seem to know in our constructions these days is the crudities of north, east, south, west. The solar energy crowd also appears devoid of art, subtlety, or science compared to our primitive ancestors. —Stewart Brand

The pyramid was carefully oriented and proportioned to let the profile of its northwest corner create first one inverted triangle of light and then another below it in a descending image of a diamondback serpent. At the bottom are serpent heads. The serpent heads argue well that the alignment and effect were intended. It seems reasonable that the display played a dramatic part in a ceremony timed by the equinox. This serpent of sunlight matches the markings of the indigenous rattlesnake of Yucatan, and the many sculptured feathered serpents of Chichen Itza can be identified, by their rattles, as rattlesnakes, too. This links the equinox serpent to rattlesnake symbolism that involves the year, the passage of time, and the idea of renewal.

The New Astronomy
Nigel Henbest and Michael Marten
1983; 240 pp.
$29.95 postpaid from:
Cambridge University Press
510 North Avenue
New Rochelle, NY 10801
or Whole Earth Access

Echoes of the Ancient Skies
Dr. E. C. Krupp
1983; 380 pp.
$19.45
($20.95 postpaid) from:
Harper & Row
2350 Virginia Avenue
Hagerstown, MD 21740
or Whole Earth Access

Sunsets, twilights, and evening skies: Aden and Marjorie Meinel, 1983; 163 pp. **$32.50** postpaid from Cambridge University Press, 510 North Avenue, New Rochelle, NY 10801.

or Whole Earth Access

Sunsets, twilights, and evening skies

Is it intimations of a gorgeous death, or revelling in the seamless gradation of blazing horizon to a starry dark, or the lifelong scout for the green flash that keeps us going and gazing on sunsets? Part of the attraction surely is the spectacular variety. This book's color photos and clear explanations can serve as a sort of field guide of twilight special effects — green flashes, noctilucent clouds, zodiacal light, volcanic dust leading to Bishop's rings and blue suns, and the Earth's own shadow climbing the fading eastern sky. Is there a more universal ceremony of planethood than watching the sun set and, by profound implication, rise? —Stewart Brand

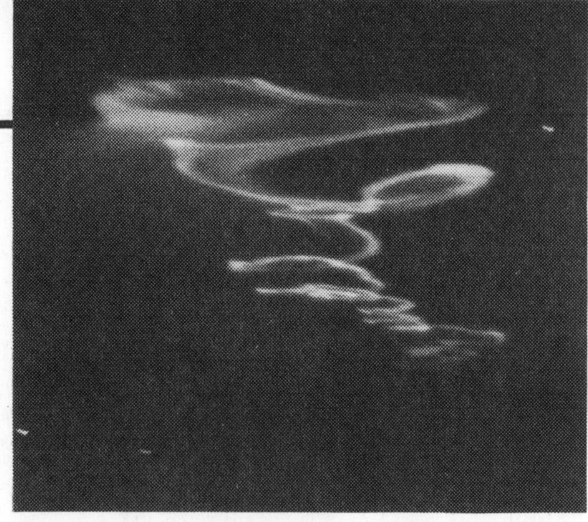

Convoluted rocket trail seen from El Centro, California.

Sky Watching

Learning the identity of those uncountable twinkling points in the night sky can be a daunting task without a guide. Books are a good place to start. That's where you'll find out the names of the constellations (and how they got them), where and when to look, and what you're really looking at (e.g., that "star" is actually an enormous galaxy comprising billions of stars). ***Skyguide*** *is a good one, done in the usual Golden Field Guide manner. It's concentrated in northern midlatitudes but is useable south of the equator, too. The charts are big enough to see at night by flashlight.*

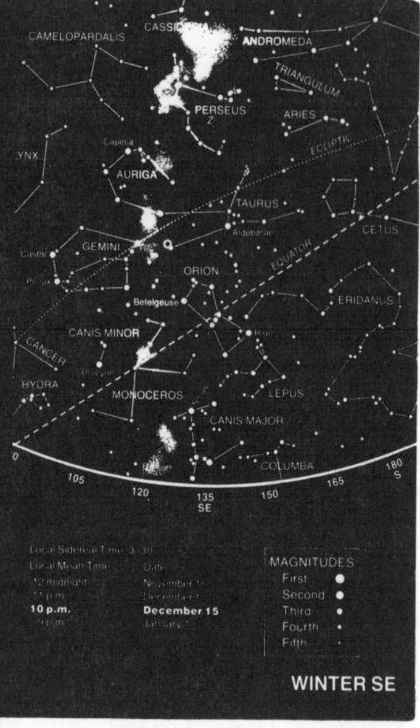

—Skyguide

Guidebooks are a bit awkward when you're actually outdoors looking; there are a number of adjustable charts that can help. The Night Sky Star Dial has won praise from astronomy buffs because its two-sided design manages to reduce distortion and look more like the real sky. Sky Challenger is a star finder with six interchangeable dials designed to interest children: an introduction, "Binocular Treasure Hunt," "Where Are The Planets?," "Native American Constellations," and "Star Clock." Night Star is an eight-inch flexible plastic dome that can be set to your exact location anywhere on earth. Minimal distortion and the accompanying booklet make it exceptionally easy to use.

If you'd like a zoo-guide voice in your Walkman telling you what you're looking at, try Tapes Of The Night Sky. The two tapes give four 25-minute tours of the sky — one for each season — with pauses built in to give you a chance to follow the instructions. Comes with maps.

And there is software. Tell Star II is the most popular one. It gives you a planetarium view without having to look at the real thing — an advantage if the weather is bad or you wish to investigate the skies over where you aren't. Good for beginners. You can get a four-page annotated list of astronomy software for the most popular home computers from Astronomical Society of the Pacific.

So what's happening in the sky this month? The constellations change seasonally, but there are events such as meteor showers and comets that aren't shown on charts. A good way to keep current is with the ***Abrams Planetarium Sky Calendar*** *or with the calendar published monthly in the excellent* ***Sky and Telescope*** *magazine.*

Stunning slides and posters of celestial objects are available from Hansen Planetarium and the Astronomical Society of the Pacific. —JB

[All the above suggested by Andrew Fraknoi, Executive Officer of the Astonomical Society of the Pacific]

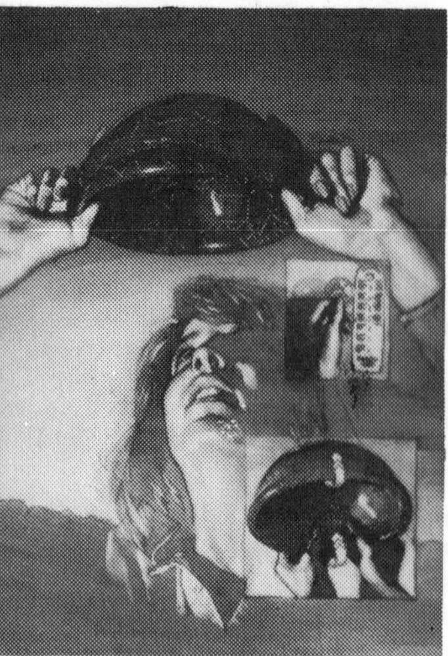

Night Star.

Skyguide: Mark R. Chartrand III, 1982; 280 pp. **$7.95** ($8.95 postpaid) from Western Publishing Company/ Dept. M, P. O. Box 700, Racine, WI 53401.

The Night Sky Star Dial: $3.25 (information **free**) from David Chandler Company, P. O. Box 309, LaVerne, CA 91750.

Sky Challenger: $8.95 postpaid from Discovery Corner/ Lawrence Hall of Science, University of California, Berkeley, CA 94720.

Night Star: $47.50 (information **free**) from Night Star Company, 1334 Brommer St., Santa Cruz, CA 95062.

Tapes Of The Night Sky: $15.45 (information **free**) from Astronomical Society of the Pacific/Catalogue Dept., 1290 24th Avenue, San Francisco, CA 94122

Tell Star II: $79.95 (information **free**) from Spectrum Holobyte, 1050 Walnut Street, #325, Boulder, CO 80302.

Abrams Planetarium Sky Calendar: $5/year (4 issues) from Sky Calendar / Abrams Planetarium, Michigan State University, East Lansing, MI 48824.

Sky and Telescope: Leif J. Robinson, Editor. **$20**/year (12 issues) from Sky and Telescope, 49 Bay State Road, Cambridge, MA 02238-1290.

Hansen Planetarium: Catalog **free** from 1098 South 200 West, Salt Lake City, UT 84104.

Astronomical Society of the Pacific: Astronomy Software Annotated List **$1** (information **free**); both from A.S.P., 1290 24th Avenue, San Francisco, CA 94122.

Questar Telescope —*Sky and Telescope*

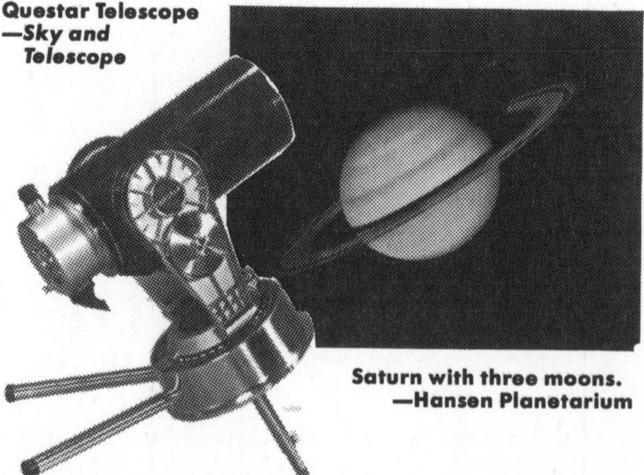

Saturn with three moons. —Hansen Planetarium

Buying a Telescope

Buying a good telescope is similar to buying a good camera or car: it's worth doing some research. There are many different types of telescopes and even within the same type, quality and price can vary widely. The November 1985 issue of ***Consumer Reports*** *had an excellent evaluation of amateur telescopes, giving specific brand names (check your library).*

Another helpful source with more information about what each type of telescope does best is the nontechnical pamphlet ***Selecting Your First Telescope:*** *Sherwood Harrington, 1982; 12 pp.,* ***$2*** *donation from A.S.P./Info Packets Dept., 1290 24th Ave., San Francisco, CA 94122.*

—Andrew Fraknoi

Entering Space

This book is quite simply the best and most attractive introduction to manned space exploration that I have seen. Written by one of the Space Shuttle astronauts (before the Challenger tragedy), it is an upbeat, behind-the-scenes look at the U.S. space program. Over 215 dramatic color illustrations, many unique to the book, provide a visual feast for the space enthusiast. —Andrew Fraknoi

◄
While I idly watched a trail of ash and smoke spread out over the Pacific from the cone of a Nicaraguan volcano, Dale began to secure the A-frame.

Entering Space
Joseph P. Allen
with Russell Martin
1985; 240 pp.
$16.95
($18.10 postpaid) from:
Workman Publishing Co.
Stop Order Dept.
1 West 39th Street
New York, NY 10018
or Whole Earth Access

Planetary Landscapes

Access to planets! Pictures and text show and explain radically different geological processes in a way that makes other planetary bodies more familiar and our own more fantastic. This is exciting stuff. It's a lot like anthropological archaeology, where a mix of careful observation and creative detective work is needed. What's presented is both the what (discovered) and the how (it was discovered). Greeley is contagiously fascinated with his subject. Everything is explained with an attention to a type of detail necessary for scientists but often neglected for laymen — such as an explanation of "things that go wrong with pictures sent from space." The mountains of Mars to the moons of Jupiter — come alive.
—David Finacom

►
Oblique Viking orbiter view across Gangis Chasma in the canyonlands of Mars. The landslide on the far wall extends as far as 50 km from the canyon wall and is one of several landslides that have enlarged the canyon. Visible in the lower right is a dark deposit which consists of sand dunes, demonstrating aeolian activity.

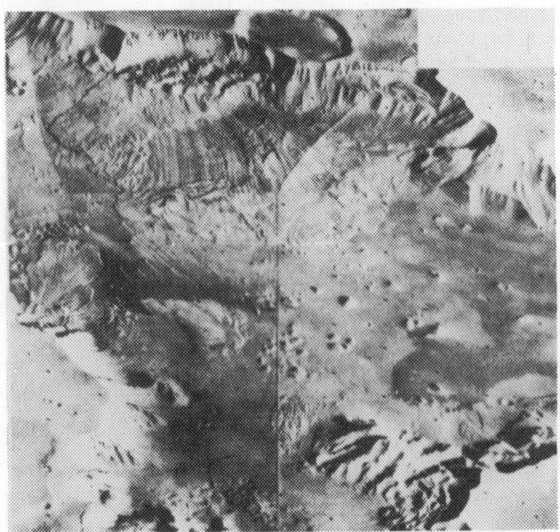

Planetary Landscapes
Ronald Greeley
1985; 265 pp.
$44.95
($46.95 postpaid) from:
Allen & Unwin, Inc.
8 Winchester Place
Winchester, MA 01890
or Whole Earth Access

The Greening of Mars

British scientist James Lovelock, the co-author of the Gaia Hypothesis — which suggests how Earth's life uses the atmosphere to regulate the planet — has co-authored a novel on how to do something similar with Mars. Lovelock's credentials to devise such a scheme are impressive. Back before the Viking probe of Mars' surface, he was hired by NASA to analyze the chances for life on Mars by studying the Martian atmosphere. His conclusion — no life on Mars because its atmosphere is so chemically stable it shows nothing is fiddling with it — was hushed up by NASA, but there was a nice byproduct: because Earth's atmosphere is so chemically unstable that the presence of life is required to explain it, Lovelock's Mars research led directly to the Gaia Hypothesis (see next page).

What is particularly appealing about his plan to green Mars is its low-cost, nongovernmental, realistic, unromantic, even somewhat tawdry approach. He would gather up the world's obsolete solid-fuel missile rockets (available to anyone who can reasonably dispose of them), lash them together, and fire them in the general direction of Mars. For payload they carry the world's warehoused and outlawed chlorofluorocarbons (remember when spray deodorant threatened our precious ozone?), which are released on collision with Mars. As a greenhouse gas the chlorofluorocarbons are 100 times more potent than the CO_2 that worries us on Earth — frozen Mars starts rapidly warming toward livability. Throw in a few Antarctic lichens to multiply and darken Mars' albedo (reflectivity). Within 11 years humans can begin to arrive in semi-comfort and accelerate the process.

I find the book mildly interesting as a novel but riveting as a proposal. A number of young scientists have been intrigued enough by the British edition of this book to call a meeting in Canada to discuss the implications of its ideas. One term that came out of that meeting I just love — "ecopoieses" — "the process of a system making a home for itself." —Stewart Brand

•
On Earth, the weight of the organisms living in the top few centimetres of a field of grass is much greater than the weight of the cows feeding on that grass. You might stock five cows, weighing say 2.5 tonnes, on one hectare of very good pasture. Depending on the soil, the population in the top few centimetres may weigh between 11 and about 22 tonnes per hectare, or around 1.6 kg per cubic metre, and of that total, more than 1.4 kg consists of nothing but bacteria, fungi, and protozoa. On Earth, the total weight of all the organisms that are too small to be seen by the unaided human eye exceeds by a huge margin the weight of those you can see.

When you add together the effect on the environment of each of these tiny organisms it amounts to a major alteration in the chemistry of the entire planet. It is this alteration that allows us to distinguish between a planet that supports life and one that does not.

The Greening of Mars
James Lovelock and
Michael Allaby
1984; 215 pp.
$3.50
($4.50 postpaid) from:
Random House
Order Dept.
400 Hahn Road
Westminster, MD 21157
or Whole Earth Access

• Folks interested in furthering the cause of space exploration and space colonies get together to chat in the L5 Society. Membership includes their magazine, **L5 News** (not available separately).
L5 Society: Membership **$30**/year from 1060 Elm Street, Tucson, AZ 85719.

The Living Planet
David Attenborough
1985; 320 pp.
$17.95
($19.45 postpaid) from:
Little, Brown & Co.
200 West Street
Waltham, MA 02254
or Whole Earth Access

The Biosphere Catalogue
Tango Parrish Snyder, Editor
1985; 240 pp.
$12.95
postpaid from:
Synergetic Press
P. O. Box 689
Oracle, AZ 85623
or Whole Earth Access

The Biosphere
Scientific American Editors
1970; 134 pp.
$10.95
($11.95 postpaid) from:
W. H. Freeman
4419 West 1980 South
Salt Lake City, UT 84104
or Whole Earth Access

Gaia

This may turn out to be one of the epochal insights of this century: that the entire life of Earth, through its atmosphere and ocean, functions effectively as one self-regulated organism: Gaia (after the Greek Earth goddess).

Free-lance British scientist James Lovelock writes a winning prose. This is a brief, personal, convincing performance. It even overcomes my lifelong aversion to chemistry, making fascinating sense of the difference between the chemical equilibrium of a dead planet and the chemical steady state of a live one.

Along the way, he notes that from Gaian perspective we are over-concerned with industrial pollution and under-concerned with protecting the integrity of the all-important tropical jungles and continental shelves of the sea.

As science and as poetry, Gaia (pronounced "guy - a") is a major planetary self-discovery. It's likely that all our thinking will be reoriented to accommodate the goddess.
—Stewart Brand

Gaia
J. E. Lovelock
1979; 157 pp.
$6.95 postpaid from:
Oxford University Press
16-00 Pollitt Drive
Fair Lawn, NJ 07410
or Whole Earth Access

•

If we are a part of Gaia it becomes interesting to ask: "To what extent is our collective intelligence also a part of Gaia? Do we as a species constitute a Gaian nervous system and a brain which can consciously anticipate environmental changes?"

•

By now a planet-sized entity, albeit hypothetical, had been born, with properties which could not be predicted from the sum of its parts. It needed a name. Fortunately the author William Golding was a fellow-villager. Without hesitation he recommended that this creature be called Gaia, after the Greek Earth goddess also known as Ge, from which root the sciences of geography and geology derive their names. In spite of my ignorance of the classics, the suitability of this choice was obvious. It was a real four-lettered word and would thus forestall the creation of barbarous acronyms, such as Biocybernetic Universal System Tendency/Homeostasis. I felt also that in the days of Ancient Greece the concept itself was probably a familiar aspect of life, even if not formally expressed. Scientists are usually condemned to lead urban lives, but I find that country people still living close to the earth often seem puzzled that anyone should need to make a formal proposition of anything as obvious as the Gaia hypothesis. For them it is true and always has been.

Fire-weed on Mount Saint Helens, four years after eruption.

The Living Planet

In the Attenborough style of a long anecdote and a short but pithy summary conclusion, ***The Living Planet*** *introduces the larger biological communities (biomes or biogeographical regions): tundra, jungles, grasslands, oceans, deserts, sweet waters, etc. A breezy book with gripping color photographs that will entice the reader into more appreciation of how this little spinning sphere got to have so much happening.* *—Peter Warshall*

•

So the wounds inflicted on the land by volcanoes eventually heal. Although volcanoes may seem, on the short scale by which man experiences time, the most terrifyingly destructive aspect of the natural world, in the longer view they are the great creators.

The Biosphere Catalogue

A wide-ranging book of adventurous intellect. You can find everything from the best botanical gardens to shields against cosmic particles. From the Gaian point of view, this is the only publication to consider all aspects of materially closed, energetically opened systems — from hermetically sealed test tubes to "bio-regenerative life support systems" that might be used for space colonization. The cutting edge of the world as it is.
—Peter Warshall

An "Ecosphere" is a materially closed, energetically open ecosystem. This one includes microbes, algae and shrimp. Some simpler systems have lived, totally closed, for 17 years. They are being used to understand the Earth's biosphere and how to build a living space on Mars.

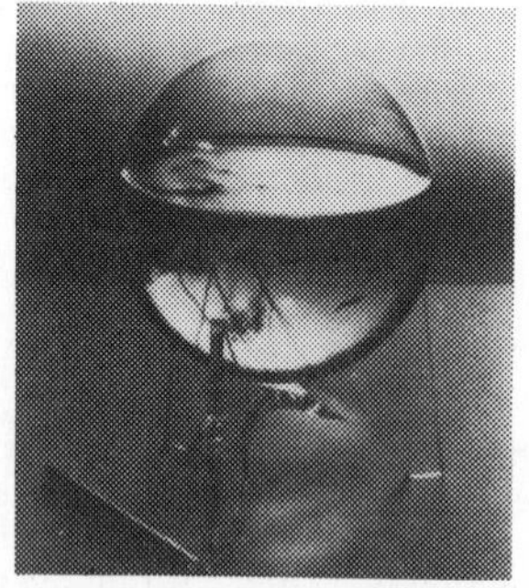

The Biosphere

"The earth's thin film of living matter is sustained by grand-scale cycles of energy and chemical elements." Learning the long term rules and delicate equilibriums of life as this book can teach them explains why man's activities of the past 150 years are having such an effect on the planet. *—David Finacom*

Biosphere exchanges water vapor, oxygen and carbon dioxide with the atmosphere and hydrosphere in a continuing cycle, shown here in simplified form.

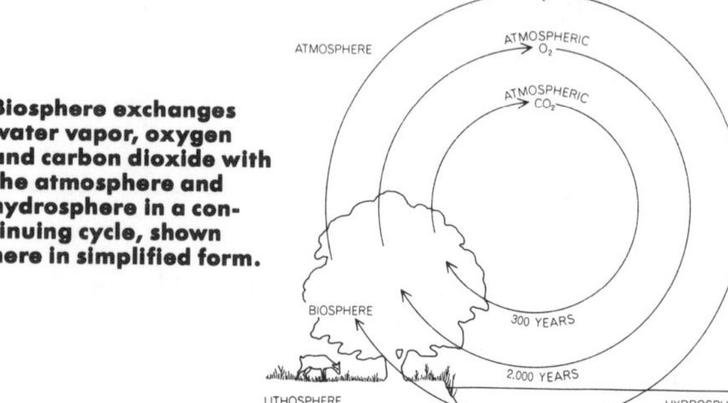

Snow "igloos" form when a heavy snow covers warm ground, as in the geyser areas of Yellowstone Park. After the storm, heat from the earth causes the snow to shrink in this way.
—Field Guide to the Atmosphere

A Field Guide to the Atmosphere

"It was a dark and stormy night." Most fiction seems to begin with a weather report. For good reason — nothing so quickly establishes a locale and mood. Also nothing so connects a place with everywhere else on Earth, and with the grand procession of the year and years, as the daily weather. Observe it and you observe them.

This lovely guide is the most detailed of all weather books. The captions not only tell you what clouds those are but how they got that way, and pretty quickly you catch on how they fit in the grand scheme of things — jet streams, various crystal effects, and such. Any window becomes a cure for boredom. —Stewart Brand

A Field Guide to the Atmosphere
Vincent J. Schaefer
and John A. Day
1981; 359 pp.
$10.70
($11.70 postpaid) from:
Houghton Mifflin Co.
Mail Order Dept.
Wayside Road
Burlington, MA 01803
or Whole Earth Access

•

The ordinary soap bubble is a valuable tool for measuring certain features of the atmosphere.

A most interesting phenomenon can be observed when large bubbles are made in temperatures colder than -10°C (14°F). Shortly after a large bubble starts floating in the cold air, one or more ice crystals are likely to start growing on its surface; this is caused by the presence of ice nuclei or tiny ice crystals in the air. The crystals in the bubble film grow rapidly until the bubble either breaks or becomes completely frozen. Quite often, when a number of crystals form and the bubble breaks, the crystals fall separately, and by counting them it is possible to ascertain roughly the number of ice nuclei in a given volume of air. Large differences are often encountered.

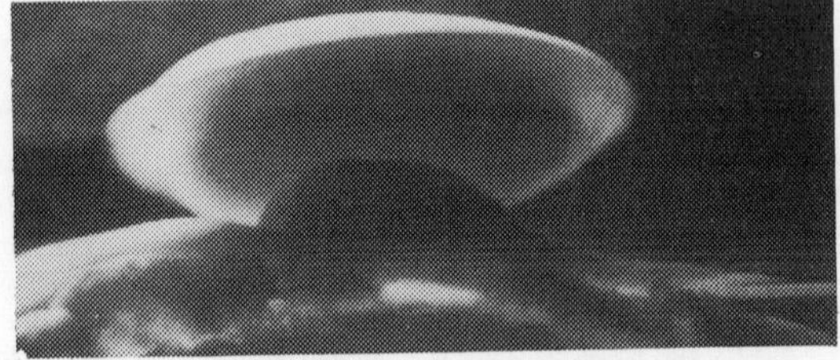

Unusually symmetrical lenticular altocumulus gives the appearance of a flying saucer. . . . The remarkable symmetry of this cloud, its resemblance to a flying saucer, and the fact that such clouds may form and disappear in less than a minute, often gives rise to fanciful tales of mysterious objects that appear in the sky.

The Coevolution of Climate and Life

Ah weather. It can irritate us so . . . being beyond our control. Yet, in one lifetime, we get so little feel for its true extremes — little Ice Ages, Greenhouse Effects, el Nino. These are but the passing children of biospheric evolution or rather a coevolution in which life itself helps steer the fickle unknown forces of climate. This tome analyzes the speculations of "new primitive" scientists trying to understand the sun god's spots or the heavens' and oceans' affinity for dancing carbon molecules. It covers four billion years and focuses on the I'm-going-to-scare-you issues of aerosols, nuclear winter, overheating, acid rains and droughts. It is, at times, tainted by a humorless, clawing "humanism" and a college-sophomore attitude toward topics it cannot fully comprehend (history, Marxism, capitalism, the Gaia hypothesis). But there is no other book so readable and complete. You leave it linked — by each breath, each eddy current created by your waving arm, each belch of your automobile — to the huge involvement of atmosphere, planet spin, and life.
—Peter Warshall

The Coevolution of Climate and Life
Stephen H. Schneider
and Randi Londer
1984; 576 pp.
$25
($29.50 postpaid) from:
Sierra Club Bookstore
730 Polk Street
San Francisco, CA 94109
or Whole Earth Access

►

The climatic system of the earth consists of many interacting subsystems: the atmosphere, the oceans, the cryosphere (ice and snow), the biosphere (biota and their environment plus humans and their activities), the bottoms of the oceans, and some of the solid material below land and oceans. The interacting components of these subsystems are called the *internal* climate system, whereas those forces that drive the climate system, but are not an internal part of that system, are known as *external* forcing or *boundary* conditions.

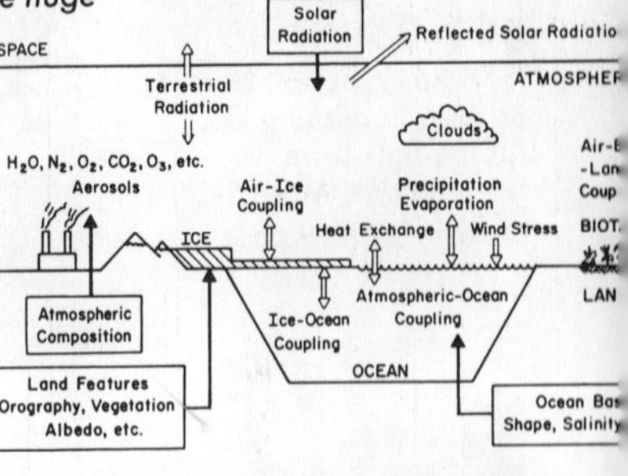

►

For many years people have attempted to correlate events on earth with variations in sunspot numbers. The variation of the Dow Jones stock market averages or the quality of wine vintages are just two such examples. . . . Although no reliable mechanism has ever been identified to connect sunspot activity with such earthly behavior, more careful research has been undertaken in recent years to examine the possibility that such fundamental changes on the sun could be related to events at the earth's surface.

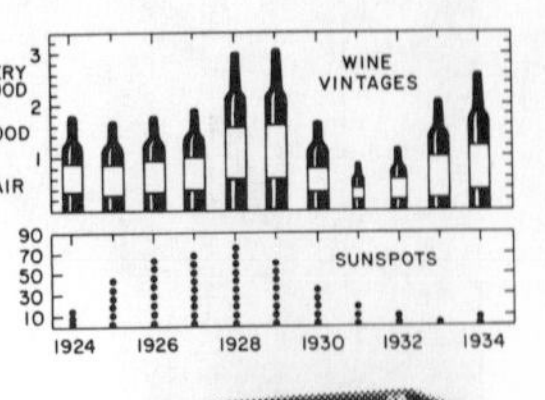

Weather Instruments

"For many years I was self-appointed inspector of snowstorms and rainstorms, and did my duty faithfully, though I never received one cent for it." —Thoreau

Browse this catalog. Choose what you need or can afford. Do it. —Peter Warshall

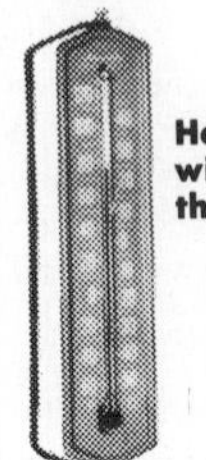

Home/office window thermometer.

Certified relative humidity and temperature indicator.

Garden rain gauge.

Instrument shelter.

Science Associates
Catalog **free** from:
Science Associates
Box 230-34
Princeton, NJ 08542

• Best mag for world weather watchers.
Weatherwise: Linda Dove, Editor. **$20**/year (6 issues) from Heldref Publications, 4000 Albemarle Street NW, Washington, DC 20016.

• See **Weather for Mariners** (p. 290) for best predictions.

EOSAT/Landsat

EOSAT Satellite Images
$50 - $3,300
Information **free** from:
EOSAT
4300 Forbes Boulevard
Lanham, MD 20706

In 1984, the U.S. Congress decided to turn the Landsat program over to the private sector. The still-functioning Landsat 4 and 5 satellites, and the huge archive of data accumulated since 1972, have been transferred to the Earth Observation Satellite Company (EOSAT).

Prices range from $50 for a black and white photo on paper with 80-meter ground resolution (image size 7.3 inches on an edge, showing approximately 115 miles square), up to $3,300 for a computer-compatible tape of a scene from the Thematic Mapper (TM) on Landsat 5. TM scenes have a ground resolution of 30 meters — less than SPOT (see review next page) provides, but the TM's primary sensor has seven spectral filters, compared with SPOT's three. This finer spectral discrimination makes it possible to identify different plant species or types of rock by detecting subtle differences in the color of the sunlight they reflect, even when they're not identifiable by shape or texture.
—Robert Horvitz

EOSAT/Landsat view of center-pivot irrigated cropland south of Garden City, Kansas.

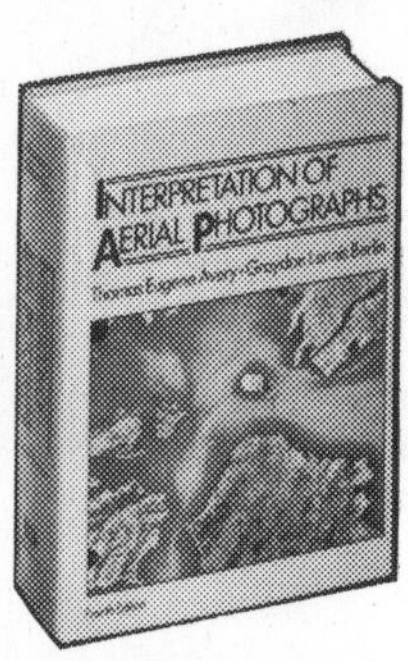

Interpretation of Aerial Photographs
Thomas E. Avery and Graydon L. Berlin
1985; 554 pp.
$37.35
($38.85 postpaid) from:
Burgess Publishing Co.
7108 Ohms Lane
Minneapolis, MN 55435
or Whole Earth Access

Interpretation of Aerial Photographs

Rural area photographed before and after an interval of 16 years. Among changes evident on the right exposure are: (A) a new pond; (B) a cleared right-of-way; (C) a new residential area; (D) a pine plantation; and (E) reversion of an abandoned field to forest land. Scale is about 1:32,000. (Courtesy U.S. Department of Agriculture.)

Learn how to read aerial and satellite photos for tree species, geological trends, camouflaged missile sites, industrial pollution, and the peculiar configuration of your yard. The best book.
—Stewart Brand

Characteristics and Availability of Data from Earth Imaging Satellites
C. Scott Southworth
1985; 102 pp.
$6.50 postpaid from:
Public Inquiries
U. S. Geological Survey
169 Federal Building
Denver, CO 80294

Characteristics and Availability of Data from Earth Imaging Satellites

This handsome booklet is a useful guide to five research collections managed by federal agencies (including Seasat, Nimbus-7, and the Shuttle Imaging Radar-A).
—Robert Horvitz

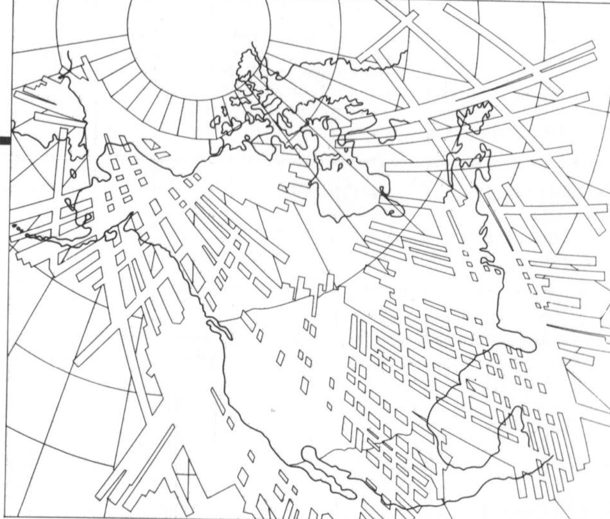
►
General coverage of Seasat synthetic aperture radar over the North American continent from the June 26, 1978, launch until the October 10, 1978, termination of the mission. United States coverage portrays ascending (southeast to northwest) and descending (northeast to southwest) satellite tracks.

SPOT 1

On February 21, 1986, the French space agency launched the first satellite specifically designed for remote sensing on a commercial basis: SPOT 1. Its high-resolution images are marketed through an international network of subsidiaries and affiliates. Because of SPOT's sidelooking capability, it can view a site without passing directly overhead. Thus, it can re-view ground areas more often than Landsat — every few days, if necessary.

Prices for a scene showing 60 x 60-85 km of surface range from $370 for a 19'' x 19'' color transparency (20 meters ground resolution), to $2550 for a computer-compatible tape with geometric corrections. ''Panchromatic'' images can attain a ground resolution of ten meters — three times finer than Landsat's best — with prices starting at $400 for a photoprint on paper. But the boost in clarity comes with a loss of color: panchromatic images are only available in black and white.

Thus, the two systems have different strengths that make them suited to somewhat different purposes. SPOT's sharper images make it more useful for investigations where human activity and constructions are the focus, while Landsat's superior spectral filtering gives it advantages in resource identification and surveys.

—Robert Horvitz

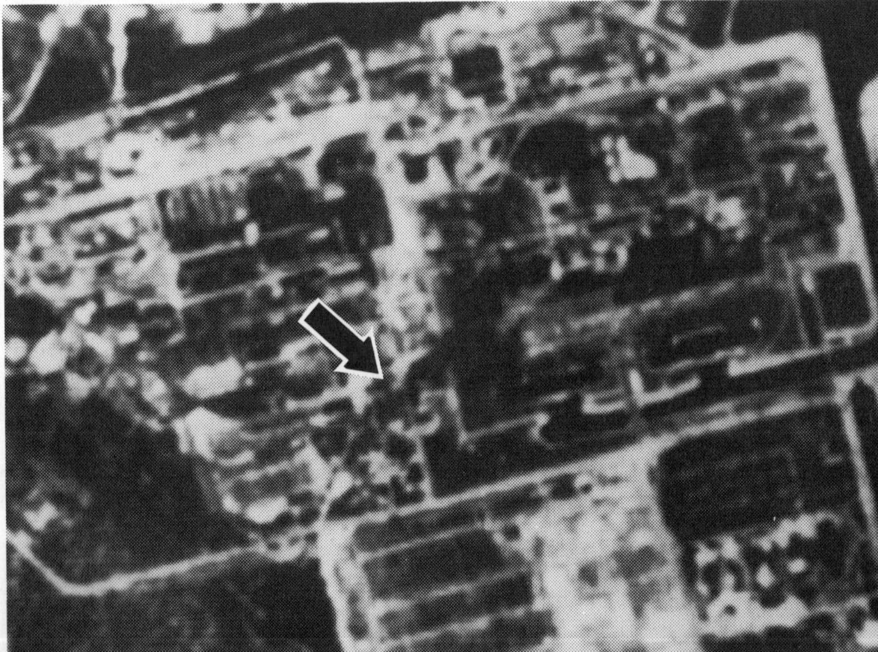

The SPOT 1 image that gave the civilian world one of the first glimpses of the damaged Russian nuclear reactor at Chernobyl in 1986. Arrow points toward a dark squiggly diagonal line — thought to be scorched ground resulting from an explosion.

SPOT 1
Information **free** from:
SPOT Image Corporation
1897 Preston White Drive
Reston, VA 22091

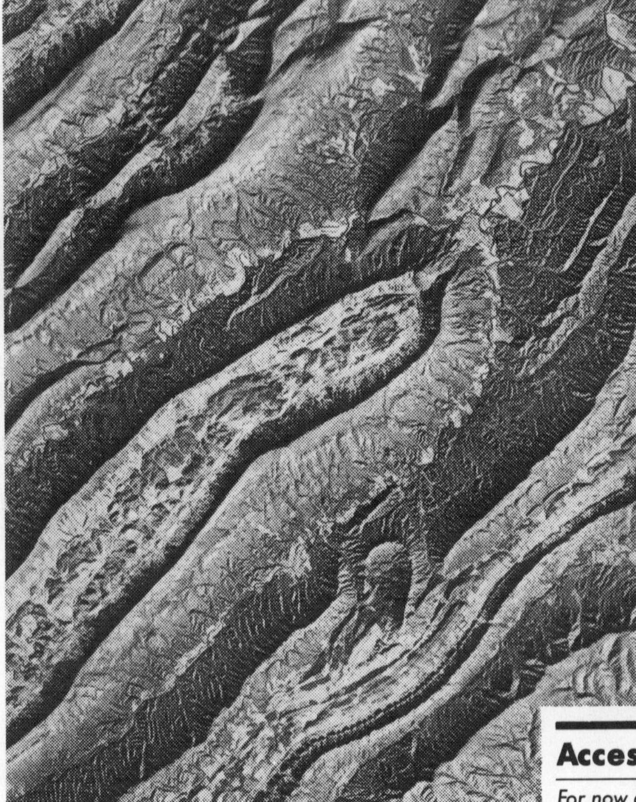

Atlas of North America

With a level of quality readers have come to expect from **National Geographic**, *this book is a wondrous display of what must be the quintessence of space-based photography. Set in a context of text, maps, and illustrations, it is the color photographs — from satellites, shuttle crews, and aircraft — that make this atlas unique. Though nominally North American, the coverage slights Canada to the benefit of Mexico, Central America, and the Caribbean. This book may be the forerunner of a more mature exploitation of space imagery at work.*

—Don Ryan
[Suggested by David Burnor]

◄ **Valleys and ridges northwest of Roanoke, Virginia, stand out in sharp relief in this enhanced false-color Landsat image. To sharpen the relief, a computer has exaggerated tonal contrasts between eastern, illuminated slopes and the shaded western sides.**

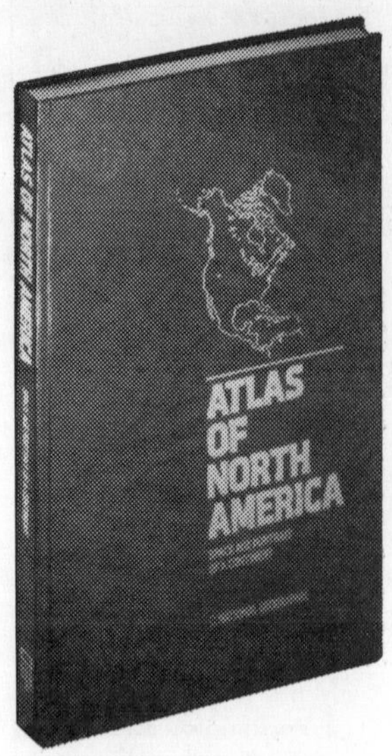

Atlas of North America
Wilbur E. Garrett
1985; 264 pp.
$29.95
($34.20 postpaid) from:
National Geographic Society
Washington, DC 20036
or Whole Earth Access

Access to Public Space Images

For now at least, oceanographic and meteorological satellites continue to be operated by the U.S. Government as a public service. The Satellite Data Services Division of NOAA's National Environmental Satellite Service maintains an archive of over 8 million images from some 30 satellites going back more than 20 years, and their prices are much lower than their commercial cousins'. Prices start at $9 for a black and white print from a negative (plus $4 handling per order), and range up to $100.

—Robert Horvitz

Satellite Data Services Division: Information **free** from SDSD, World Weather Building, Room 100, Washington, DC 20233.

• Satellite photographs are one of the best tools for developing reliable data on worldwide problems such as drought and deforestation. Data of this sort is critical to organizations attempting large-scale corrections of human folly.

Goode's World Atlas

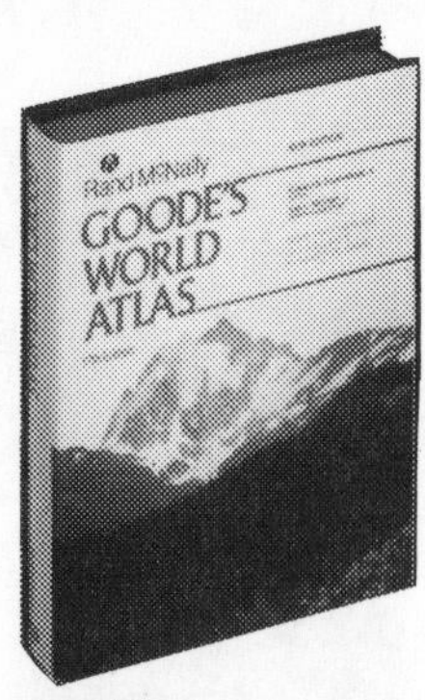

Per buck, this atlas has the most and best — 372 pages of locational maps (from continent right down to city), landforms, climate, weather, vegetation, soil, population, agriculture, trade, language, resources, ocean floor, topped off with a fine pronouncing index. When something in the newspaper puzzles you, check here. Well, well: about ten languages are spoken in different regions of the Soviet Union.

—Stewart Brand [Suggested by David Brooks]

Goode's World Atlas
Edward B. Espenshade, Jr., Editor
1986; 367 pp.
$22.50
($27.50 postpaid) from:
Rand McNally Map Store
23 East Madison Street
Chicago, IL 60602
or Whole Earth Access

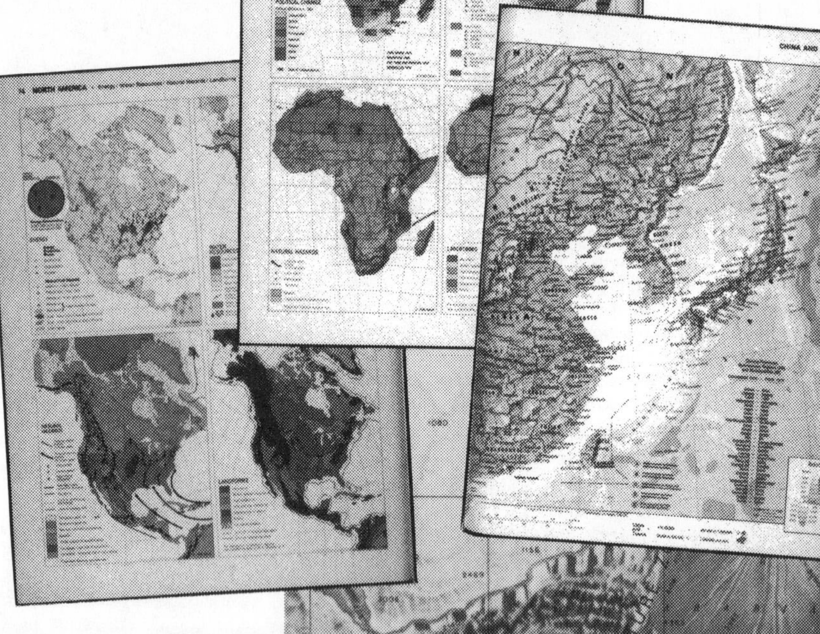

(Top) Africa — Political Change/Peoples/Natural Hazards/Landforms. (Right) China and Japan. (Left) North America — Energy/Water Resources/ Natural Hazards/Landforms.

Ocean floor panorama (24" x 38") section shown full size.

Two-thirds of the Planet: A Wall Map and Atlas

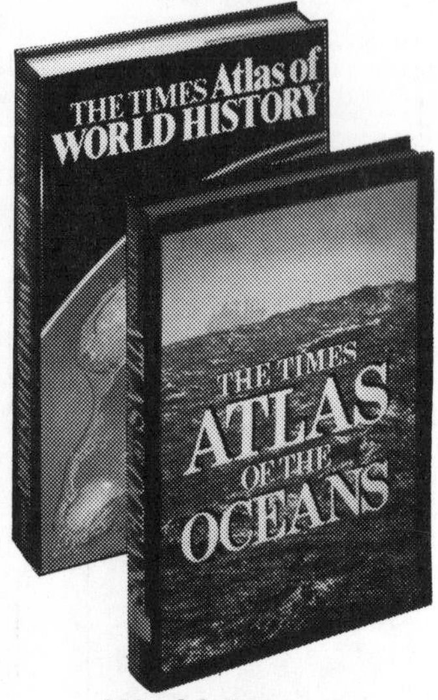

The great explorers of the twentieth century have been the oceanographers. Their maps have confirmed the theory of floating continents, exposed mountain ranges taller than the Himalayas, located the deepest communities of living creatures, opened the last great caches of Earth's resources, and made me feel, once again, reverent toward our birthplace. The ***World Ocean Floor Panorama*** *wall map cheaply and beautifully displays the earth surface of the planet for the first time in history. —Peter Warshall*

The ***Times Atlas of the Oceans*** *is a pure joy to behold. A comprehensive understanding of the ocean environment has become critical as we learn more about the limits of the once-boundless sea. The* ***Times Atlas*** *is well-written, graphically pleasing, and logically organized — it includes weather patterns, fisheries and resource exploitation, ship-borne commerce, shoreline development, pollution sources, military strategy, sea law, etc. —David Burnor*

World Ocean Floor Panorama
Bruce C. Heezen and Marie Tharp, 1977
$50 postpaid
(44" x 76");
$18.50 postpaid
(24" x 38") from:
Marie Tharp
1 Washington Avenue
South Nyack, NY 10960

The Times Atlas of the Oceans
Alastair Couper, Editor
1983; 268 pp.
$79.95
($81.45 postpaid) from:
Van Nostrand Reinhold Co.
Order Dept.
7625 Empire Drive
Florence, KY 41042
or Whole Earth Access

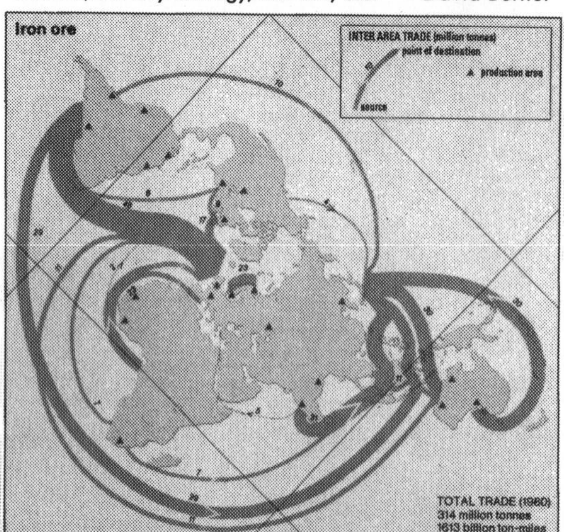

Iron ore is the most important dry cargo in world seaborne trade. In 1980 about 314 million tonnes were transported, representing around 35 per cent of world production. *—The Times Atlas of the Oceans*

The Times Atlas of World History

Most engrossing new reference book in decades. Six hundred color maps ingeniously present historical periods from the perspective of the time and people involved. Praise be, the volume corrects generations of Europe-centered versions of history. —Stewart Brand

The Times Atlas of World History: (Revised Edition) Geoffry Barraclough, 1985; 360 pp. **$75** ($78 postpaid) from Hammond, Inc./Sales Dept., 515 Valley Street, Maplewood, NJ 07040 (or Whole Earth Access).

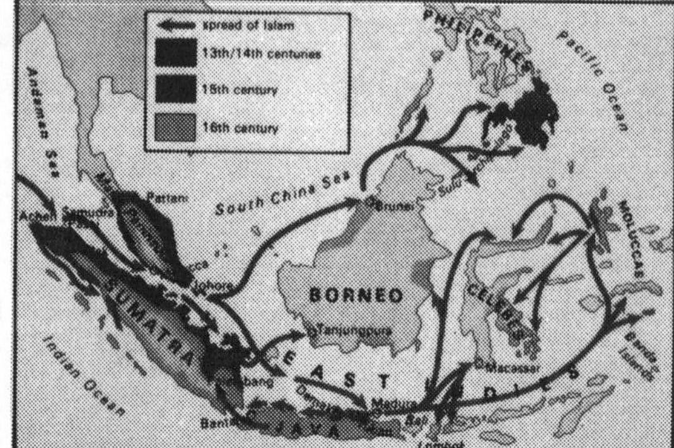

Map size 22″ x 39″.

World Biogeographical Provinces

*This map is the gem of 15 years of thought and work on the **Whole Earth Catalog**. It is the map of how the Earth itself has simultaneously produced variety and parallels during its long evolution . . . how water, soils, plants, animals, and locations near or far from the oceans create provinces of similar life. Besides its beauty, it's being used to insure that every biogeographic region of the planet will have at least one representative ecological community preserved. It is a meditative map.*

By scanning similar provinces I understand why Australian eucalyptus do so well in California; why the "Mediterranean" regions have similar heritages and can look to each other for advice on wine, sunlight in art, fire, grasses, and erosion management. —Peter Warshall

World Biogeographical Provinces Map
Miklos D. F. Udvardy, S. Brand, T. Oberlander
1975, 1976, 1978
$5
postpaid from:
Whole Earth Access
2950 7th Street
Berkeley, CA 94710

World Political Map
National Geographic Society
1983
$6
($8.40 postpaid)
order #02690

World Map Index
$1.50
($2.75 postpaid)
order #02495

Both from:
National Geographic Society
17th and M Streets NW
Washington, D.C. 20036

National Geographic World Political Map

Like it or not, this is how the Earth has been subdivided. From Burkina Faso to Tasmania, each political bloc is displayed in full color on heavy paper. A best buy. Index available for an extra buck and a half. —Peter Warshall

Section shown ½ lifesize. Full map size 48″ x 68″. ►

Map Use

If I had to limit myself to one book about mapmaking and map use, this would be it. The illustrations show cartographic concepts very well. The authors do an excellent job, reminding the reader that the map is not the territory, and that maps can be used to abuse as well as to enlighten. —Ron Hendricks

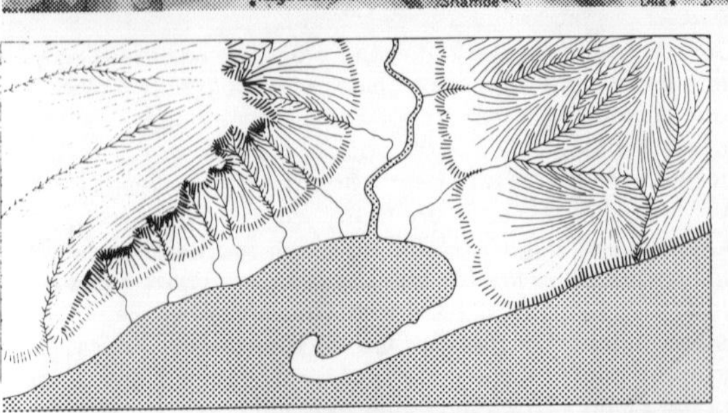

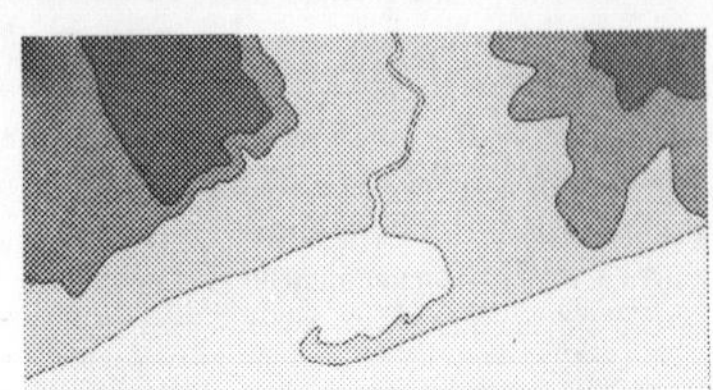

(Above) The hachure method of relief portrayal.

(Right) The hypsometric (or layer tint) method.

Map Use
Phillip C. Muehrcke
1978; 474 pp.
$21.95
($23 postpaid) from:
J. P. Publications
P. O. Box 4173
Madison, WI 53711
or Whole Earth Access

• For excellent maps and atlases of particular regions:
National Geographic maps and atlases: catalog **free** from National Geographic Society, 17th and M Streets NW, Washington, D.C. 20036.
Maps, posters and charts: catalog **free** from Superintendent of Documents, U.S. Government Printing Office, Washington, D.C. 20402.

The Structures of Everyday Life
Volume 1
1981; 623 pp.

The Wheels of Commerce
Volume 2
1982; 670 pp.

The Perspective of the World
Volume 3
1984; 699 pp.
All by Fernand Braudel

$16.95 each volume
($18.45 postpaid)
All from:
Harper and Row
2350 Virginia Avenue
Hagerstown, MD 21740
or Whole Earth Access

The Shorter Science and Civilisation in China
Joseph Needham and Colin A. Ronan
1978; 326 pp.
Vol. 1

$18.95
($19.95 postpaid)

Volume 2

$42.50
($46.50 postpaid)
Both from:
Cambridge University Press
510 North Avenue
New Rochelle, NY 10801
or Whole Earth Access

Technics and Civilization

I first read this book in 1957, and twice since then.

Here are the first lines of the book.

> *During the last thousand years the material basis and the cultural forms of Western Civilization have been profoundly modified by the development of the machine. How did this come about? Where did it take place?*

Lewis Mumford is an unusual man. He is not an engineer or a scientist, he isn't an historian or sociologist, you can't identify him as a business man or a literary man or an academic. He seems beyond all those roles. This made him especially attractive to me when I was 19 because his style smelled of the place I wanted to go. He is profound, poetic, knowledgeable. He takes care of the large and small things in his books.

***Technics and Civilization** is a good book to start with; if you like it, there are many others of his to turn to, **Myth of the Machine, Arts and Technics, The City in History, Transformation of Man, The Pentagon of Power,** etc.*

How I have used him; all through my twenties I used him as my guide. —*Steve Baer*

•

Most of the important inventions and discoveries that served as the nucleus for further mechanical development did not arise, as Spengler would have it, out of some mystical inner drive of the Faustian soul: they were wind-blown seeds from other cultures. . . . Taking root in medieval culture, in a different climate and soil, these seeds of the machine sported and took on new forms: perhaps, precisely because they had *not* originated in Western Europe and had no natural enemies there, they grew as rapidly and gigantically as the Canada thistle when it made its way onto the South American pampas.

Modern cotton spinning. During the paleotechnic period the textile industries were the pattern for advanced production, and the term factory was at first applied solely to textile factories. Today the worker has a smaller part than ever to play in them: he lingers on as a machine-herd.

Technics and Civilization
Lewis Mumford
1934; 1963; 495 pp.

$8.95
($9.95 postpaid) from:
Harcourt Brace Jovanovitch
1250 6th Ave., 4th Floor
San Diego, CA 92101
or Whole Earth Access

Civilization and Capitalism

*The first book in this three volume set, **The Structures of Everyday Life**, is divided into sections: rice, corn, beer, furniture, alcohol, iron and many many others. I found that I paid close attention to Braudel; most history books make my mind wander. He turns the usual history upside down — many details of everyday life but perhaps no mention of the King. All his discussions are filled with quotes from first hand.*

There are no chapters of theories concerning why this or that happened. Instead piece by piece you hear about furniture in China and Europe, alcohol in France, England and America. The details pour out of the book. One of the nicest qualities of the book is that it can be opened anywhere and read for 20 minutes. Braudel has enough respect for life and the past to be immensely puzzled by it — so he never imposes some kind of false structure that you have to pay attention to.

—*Steve Baer*

*Braudel's cleverness is to pay attention to the "weight of numbers" in history: the price of eggs, the amount of wine a family consumed, the number of times goods changed hands during trade. The measurements add up to understanding. These observations are explored in full by the further two volumes, **The Wheels of Commerce** and **The Perspective of the World**. You won't find the breadth of civilization fit into a smaller bundle.*

—*Kevin Kelly*

Science and Civilisation in China

*Joseph Needham is a renowned biologist who travelled into unexplored regions of Chinese technological history and became a yet more renowned historian and interpreter of what is for most of us the back of the planet. His series is awesome in size and depth; he's done the mining, but you've got to refine the ore to suit your own purposes. One purpose might be learning about Taoism and how its influence helped the Chinese discover and utilize some technology long before the West and also overlook or never utilize other stuff that the West seized on. Another purpose might be taking some of the mechanical inventions of old China — from man-kites to waterwheels — and applying them to your own hand technology of intentional communities. There's no source like the source in these matters. If you're timid, you should try **The Shorter Science and Civilisation in China** in two abridged volumes. Or you could blow $1,100, get all nine full volumes, and then wait anxiously for the next one to rumble down the chute from Cambridge.*

Awesome books. —*Stewart Brand*

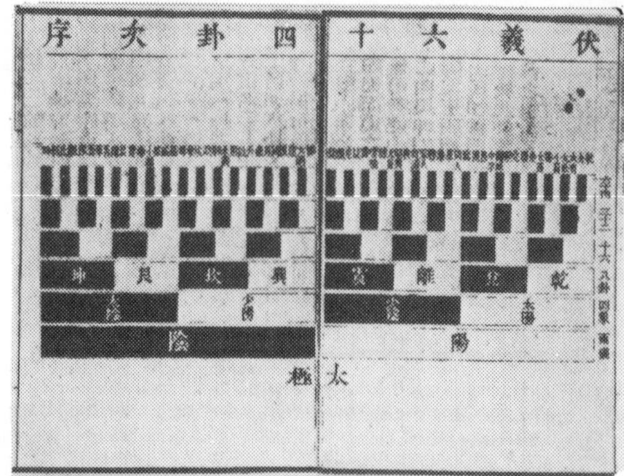

Segregation Table of the symbols of the Book of Changes . . . . Yin and Yang separate, but each contains half of its opposite in a 'recessive' state, as is seen when the second division occurs. There is no logical end to the process but here it is not followed beyond the stage of the 64 hexagrams.

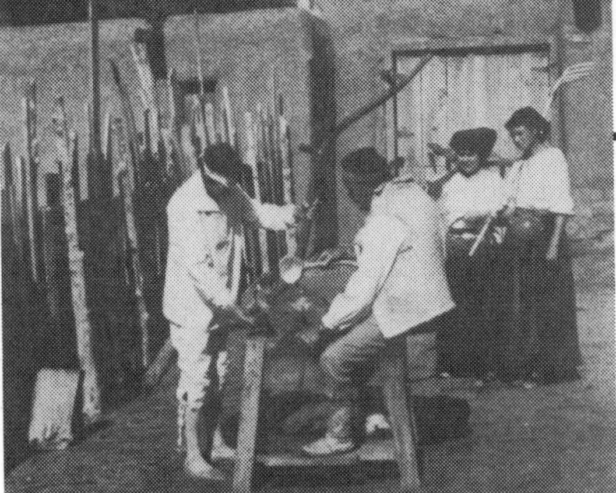

Preparing for the wheat harvest in colonial New Mexico.
—The Living History Sourcebook

The Living History Sourcebook

Living history is a curious blend of grassroots obsessiveness and radical academia. It started out with history buffs getting dressed up to act out bygone battles. They discovered no one really knew very much about what happened back then because when they tried things the way the professors said they were, it didn't work. The buffs kept getting dressed up, having fun and living out the roles, rediscovering new things as a pastime, and finally the experts got interested. Eventually when some museums found out that the only way you could get TV-numbed Americans to visit a museum was to have people dress up in costume and demonstrate old-timey ways, a veritable movement got rolling. There are now several magazines, hundreds of active sites, festivals, mock battles, rendezvous, and a whole new science. This sourcebook will lead you to them all. —Kevin Kelly

—Living History Sourcebook

Candle dipping in an authentic, nineteenth-century New England context. Old Sturbridge Village. ***—The Living History Sourcebook***

The Living History Sourcebook
Jay Anderson
1985; 469 pp.
$19.95
($21.45 postpaid) from:
American Association for State and Local History Press
172 2nd Avenue North
Suite 102
Nashville, TN 37201
or Whole Earth Access

Practicing History

To get to any depth in a complex story, secondary sources — other people's histories — aren't good enough; you have to go to primary sources: letters, diaries, maps, journals, newspaper accounts, photographs, and memoirs. Nothing will help introduce you to the craft of history-writing as well as this book of essays by Barbara Tuchman. (She wrote the Pulitzer Prize winning history of the fourteenth century, **A Distant Mirror***.) Ms. Tuchman's methods: discard the unnecessary, write like a storyteller, invent nothing, and use mainly primary sources.*

You could be a historian with nothing more than this book of advice and examples, access to a good research library (with interlibrary loan), a little travel, and the devotion of a year or two. —Art Kleiner

•

Selection is what determines the ultimate product, and that is why I use material from primary sources only. My feeling about secondary sources is that they are helpful but pernicious. I use them as guides at the start of a project to find out the general scheme of what happened, but I do not take notes from them because I do not want to end up simply rewriting someone else's book. Furthermore, the facts in a secondary source have already been pre-selected, so that in using them one misses the opportunity of selecting one's own.

Practicing History
Barbara W. Tuchman
1959; 306 pp.
$7.95
($8.95 postpaid) from:
Random House
Order Dept.
400 Hahn Road
Westminster, MD 21157
or Whole Earth Access

Old Glory

Your town has origins. So does your family. This is a splendid book about how to find and preserve and parade them. There is such a thing as cultural good ecology. Savor your own peculiar community's weirdness. Savor some other people's. —Stewart Brand

•

Every town should have at least one great old building to show off to visitors, and there certainly ought to be at least one amazing story that goes along with it.

•

There probably isn't another project we know of that is at one time as useful and as much fun as doing a history survey.

What information does a town history survey include? A successful town history survey should (1) provide a comprehensive list of all historically-significant properties in or near the town; (2) give an explanation for each property — plus a sketch of its history; (3) provide information as to who owns each property; and (4) mention the owner's plans for the future of the property.

Old Glory
James Robertson, Editor
1973; 191 pp.
$4.95
($5.95 postpaid) from:
Warner Books, Inc.
666 5th Avenue
New York, NY 10103
or Whole Earth Access

The Tape-Recorded Interview

Some of your local history is in records, but a lot more of it is in minds. Here's how to ensure it's in both. When you're an old geezer, wouldn't you like to be asked what really happened back in 1985? —Stewart Brand

•

I remember one young girl, interviewing an old woodsman, who asked what they cut down the trees with. "Well, girlie," he said with a kind of amused contempt, "we used an ax, that's what we used!" Girlie looked him right in the eye: "Poll or double-bit?" she said. You could feel his attitude change. "Well, mostly poll axes, but later on . . . ." It comes down to this: The more you know about your informant's life, work, and times, the better equipped you will be to carry on the interviews — and the more you will enjoy your work!

The Tape-Recorded Interview
Edward D. Ives
1980; 130 pp.
$5.50
($7 postpaid) from:
University of Tennessee Press
Attn.: Order Dept.
740 Cascadilla Street
Ithaca, NY 14850
or Whole Earth Access

• A free catalog of books about how to find, appreciate and show other people artifacts and history.
American Association for State and Local History Press: AASLH, Catalog Order Dept., 172 5th Avenue North, Suite 102, Nashville, TN 37201.

• See also **The Times Atlas of World History** (p. 14).

Patterns of Culture
Ruth Benedict
1934, 1959; 291 pp.
$8.70
($9.70 postpaid) from:
Houghton Mifflin Co.
Mail Order Dept.
Wayside Road
Burlington, MA 01803
or Whole Earth Access

Patterns of Culture

*Years go by and still no book replaces **Patterns of Culture**. The graceful contrasts of human life. The reminder to reflect on our cultural prejudices before judging another tribe. Unique anthropology by a unique woman.*
—*Peter Warshall*

•

Later, traditionally when the boy is about fourteen and old enough to be responsible, he is whipped again by even stronger masked gods. It is at this initiation that the kachina mask is put upon his head, and it is revealed to him that the dancers, instead of being the supernaturals from the Sacred Lake, are in reality his neighbours and his relatives. After the final whipping, the four tallest boys are made to stand face to face with the scare kachinas who have whipped them. The priests lift the masks from their heads and place them upon the heads of the boys. It is the great revelation. The boys are terrified. The yucca whips are taken from the hands of the scare kachinas and put in the hands of the boys who face them, now with the masks upon their heads. They are commanded to whip the kachinas. It is their first object lesson in the truth that they, as mortals, must exercise all the functions which the uninitiated ascribe to the supernaturals themselves.

The Savage Mind
Claude Levi-Strauss
1968; 290 pp.
$10.95 postpaid from:
University of Chicago Press
11030 South Langley Ave.
Chicago, IL 60628
or Whole Earth Access

The Savage Mind

The formidable Levi-Strauss parses the logic of totemism — native science based on deepest familiarity with fellow species and ritual celebration of mutual dependency. He gestures in detail at the dramatic life awaiting souls willing to bear totemic relation to the life around them.
—*Stewart Brand*

***The Savage Mind** is uncanny: revealing our primitive thought as much as tribal peoples'. You end up wondering who's the dunce.* —*Peter Warshall*

•

A native thinker makes the penetrating comment that "All sacred things must have their place." (Fletcher) It could even be said that being in their place is what makes them sacred for if they were taken out of their place, even in thought, the entire order of the universe would be destroyed. Sacred objects therefore contribute to the maintenance of order in the universe by occupying the places allocated to them. Examined superficially and from the outside, the refinements of ritual can appear pointless. They are explicable by a concern for what one might call "micro-adjustment" — the concern to assign every single feature, object or creature to a place within a class.

•

The natives themselves are sometimes acutely aware of the "concrete" nature of their science and contrast it sharply with that of the whites:

"We know what the animals do, what are the needs of the beaver, the bear, the salmon, and other creatures, because long ago men married them and acquired this knowledge from their animal wives. Today the priests say we lie, but we know better. The white man has been only a short time in this country and knows very little about the animals; we have lived here thousands of years and were taught long ago by the animals themselves. The white man writes everything down in a book so that it will not be forgotten; but our ancestors married the animals, learned all their ways, and passed on the knowledge from one generation to another." (Jenness)

Cultural Survival Quarterly
Jason Clay, Ph.D., Editor
$20/year
(4 issues) from:
Cultural Survival, Inc.
11 Divinity Avenue
Cambridge, MA 02138

Cultural Survival

Homogenization is consuming even the most isolated indigenous cultures on the planet. Can the languages of threatened cultures be saved? Can indigenous people share game parks where white men come to play? Is the drug trade crucial to some tribal people's cultural survival? Does "education" really mean loss of identity?

***Cultural Survival** is an organization of concerned anthropologists and other citizens trying to preserve threatened cultures and explore ways in which native peoples can accommodate to the twentieth century without too great a loss of their own uniqueness. Their magazine, **Cultural Survival Quarterly**, provides thorough coverage of their efforts.* —*Peter Warshall*

•

It is difficult for an Eskimo who has spent his entire life surviving in the Arctic to understand the motives of someone who has traveled thousands of miles to float down a river in a rubber boat. Some recreational users cannot understand why hundreds of caribou are killed each fall on a very short stretch of river (Onion Portage) in a National Park. There are many subsistence activities that are critical enough or sensitive enough that recreationists blundering through or a research helicopter flying over could easily disrupt the activity and possibly result in a serious reduction of the winter's food supply for a village. Sport hunting methods and purposes don't usually coincide with subsistence hunting practices.

•

When David and Pia Maybury-Lewis visited the Shavante Indians in 1956, they had only just established peaceful contact with Brazilian society. They were hunters and gatherers who spent little time in their slash-and-burn gardens where beans, squashes and maize were planted. Children learned without formal schooling, by watching their elders. There were no doctors or nurses.

When the Maybury-Lewises revisited the Shavante in 1982 they found dramatic changes. The Indians were no longer nomadic. Their lands had been guaranteed after a bitter fight and they were dependent upon agriculture, practicing tractor-driven rice farming. Yet their villages maintained their traditional layouts: beehive huts arranged in a semicircle or in concentric semicircles. Most of their villages had schools with several teachers. Two villages had infirmaries and smaller ones were visited regularly by a nurse.

Ice fishing with nets, Kobuk Valley National Park.
©National Park Service

• See **The Forest People** (p. 58) and **The Mountain People** (p. 59).

• For an excellent introduction to kinship and marriage patterns (more diverse and careful than you'd believe) see:

Kinship and Marriage: Robin Fox, 1984; 228 pp. **$8.95** postpaid from Cambridge University Press, 510 North Avenue, New Rochelle, NY 10801.

Before 1800: Slender, square sandstone or slate slabs with or without elaborate carvings.

•

If your ancestor lived in an urban area after 1800, check utility records: sprinkling systems, sidewalk widening, sewer, water, power, gas, garbage pick-up records. These are especially valuable for identifying addresses for immigrants who move from one part of the city to another as their economic conditions improve. Second, third, and fourth-class cities also keep these records.

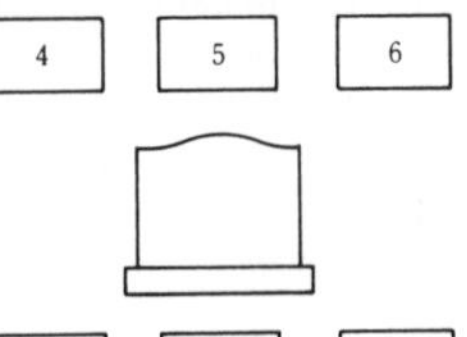
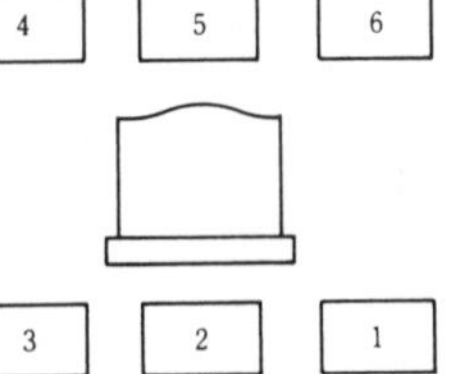

Sketch of Scandinavian grave arrangement.

•

In family plots, it is frequently possible to determine family relationships from the relative positions of the graves. Usually the dominant couple or parents are in the center with a large stone while children have smaller stones. Positioning of graves can also indicate national origins. Scandinavians seem to position plots with the father in the lower right-hand corner (1), the mother next to him (2), with children and spouses (3-6) placed in order of death clockwise around a large stone bearing the family name.

The Source

Simply the best genealogy book to get if you want to buy only one. This mammoth handbook is the best all-purpose reference manual for both hobbyists and professional genealogists. It goes into great detail about where to look for records, and even where not to look. For instance, it tells you not to count on finding military records from 1912 to 1959 because a disastrous fire destoyed 80 percent of them in 1973. **The Source** *tells which files are left intact. The 16 experts who compiled the book also include specifics for the increasing numbers of racial minorities doing ancestral research, such as blacks and Asian-Americans.* —Bob Mitchell

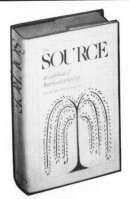

The Source
Arlene Eakle and Johni Cerny, Editors
1984; 786 pp.
$32.95
postpaid from:
Ancestry, Inc.
P. O. Box 476
Salt Lake City,
UT 84110-0476

Archaeology

A rare specimen: a textbook that is a joy to read for its own sake. **Archaeology** *ably puts across the science and practice of discovering the past, with a twist I've not seen before: co-author Rathje's study of contemporary garbage in Tucson, Arizona, is used to demonstrate how archaeologists treat data and test hypotheses. I found myself painlessly learning something new on nearly every page.*
—Jay Kinney [Suggested by Jim Heidke]

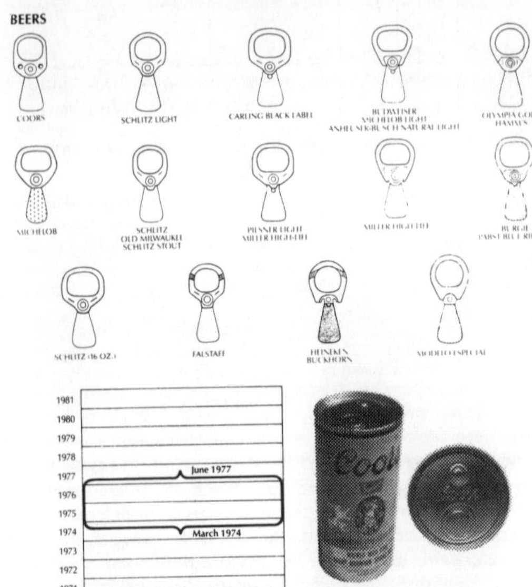

Because of its short life, the Coors punch-top can — manufactured between 1974 and 1977 — is a very effective horizon marker. Levels in modern landfills that contain this type could be precisely dated.

Archaeology
William L. Rathje and Michael B. Schiffer
1982; 434 pp.
$25.95
($26.95 postpaid) from:
Harcourt Brace Jovanovich
1250 6th Avenue, 4th Floor
San Diego, CA 92101
or Whole Earth Access

• Start here at the beginning of your search for your family's history. They've got the tools — books, software, and indexes. You bring the persistence.
Ancestry's Catalog: free from Ancestry, P.O. Box 476, Salt Lake City, UT 84110.

Archaeology Magazine

One of the few remaining sciences that embraces amateur participation is archaeology. An awful lot of fantastic research is carried out (literally) by eager bands of students and volunteers sifting through old layers of silt. There's another kind of field work going on these days, too: Experimenters shed their modern habits and by taking up ancient tools reconstruct the past by living it for a while. The findings of both these kinds of research are given colorful play in this classy journal, which might be mistaken for an enticing travel magazine. Between the ads and the magazine's biannual listing of excavations in progress, it's the best place to find a dig to work on.
—Kevin Kelly [Suggested by Thor Conway]

•

Tunisia Dig: Kerkouane/Kelibia. The only completely preserved Punic town, abandoned in the 3rd century B.C., this site is unique in the Mediterranean. It features domestic architecture, including a temple, baths and a necropolis. On-site museum will open July 1986. Caves and other sites in the area. *Getting there:* From Tunis take the road to Korba Kelibia. No appointment necessary for admission or guide; accessible by train; hotel and Florida restaurant in Kelibia 12 kilometers; camping 10 kilometers; site accessible to persons in wheelchairs. Volunteers accepted. Contact: Mohammed Fantar, Institut National d'Archeologie et d'Art, 4 Place du Chateau, Tunis, Tunisia 1008 (tel) 261-693.

This complete skeleton was the first of the Christian burials excavated at Tipu, Belize, and is typical of those found under the church floor.

Archaeology
Phyllis Pollak Katz, Editor
$20/year
(6 issues) from:
Archaeology
Subscription Service
P.O. Box 928
Farmingdale, NY 11737

Engines of Creation
K. Eric Drexler
1986; 298 pp.
$17.95 postpaid from:
Doubleday & Co.
Direct Mail Order
501 Franklin Avenue
Garden City, NY 11530
or Whole Earth Access

Engines of Creation

The Last Technological Revolution is upon us: "nanotechnology" — the science of building molecules to order. What this might mean for good or bad is enthusiastically examined in this lively book. There is some gee-whizzing; how could there not be when the potentials include cell repair, disease reduction, and life extension? Ebullience is balanced by a serious discussion of the potential for horrifying weaponry, and the social disorder that could result from thoughtless incorporation of nanotechnology into an unprepared populace. The book is remarkably wide-visioned and comprehensively based: most unusual for this sort of thing. Future-reading at its best. —JB

•

Not human whims but the unchanging laws of nature draw the line between what is physically possible and what is not — no political act, no social movement can change the law of gravity one whit. So however futuristic they may seem, sound projections of technological possibilities are quite distinct from predictions.

•

The simplest medical applications of nanomachines will involve not repair but selective destruction. Cancers provide one example; infectious diseases provide another. The goal is simple: one need only recognize and destroy the dangerous replicators, whether they are bacteria, cancer cells, viruses, or worms. Similarly, abnormal growths and deposits on arterial walls cause much heart disease; machines that recognize, break down, and dispose of them will clear arteries for more normal blood flow. Selective destruction will also cure diseases such as herpes in which a virus splices its genes into the DNA of a host cell. A repair device will enter the cell, read its DNA, and remove the addition that spells "herpes."

World Future Society
Membership
$25/year
(includes *The Futurist*)
Future Survey
Michael Marien, Editor
$49/year (12 issues)
All from:
World Future Society
4916 St. Elmo Avenue
Bethesda, MD 20814

The World Future Society

More interested in possibilities than predictions, the World Future Society conducts ongoing discussions amongst its 25,000 members. Their magazine, **The Futurist**, *works over ideas both nasty and nice, not mere pie-in-the-sky stuff. The editor fortunately avoids academic dead-serious essays, preferring to look at subjects with an open mind and unafraid of controversy. You'll probably find the same attitude in the World Future Society chapter near you.*

The Society also publishes **Future Survey**, *a monthly abstract of matters futurist from books, articles, and other sources. The book reviews are particularly good. I find that I keep up with futurist thought a lot more easily in this publication than in any other, including* **The Futurist**. —JB

•

Is owning a telephone and a computer a right or a privilege? This question will be at the center of one of the most critical issues of the next 10 years. The resolution of it will answer an impending question the government and the private sector are anxious to have answered: Which will contribute more to public militance — greater access to information or more restricted access to information?
—The Futurist

•

Age Wars: The Coming Battle Between Young and Old, Phillip Longman (Americans for Generational Equity, Washington), *The Futurist*, 20:1, Jan-Feb 1986, 8-11.

Today's prosperity is being purchased at the eventual expense of today's younger citizens and those yet unborn. The early decades of the next century may bring a war between the generations, as tomorrow's elderly attempt to compel the young to honor the compounding debts of the present era: 1) the delayed repairs to the physical infrastructure (roads, bridges, etc.); 2) the postponed safe disposal of toxic wastes; 3) running down supplies of topsoil, energy, and clean water; 4) the massive Federal deficit (financing the interest charges alone on this year's deficit will cost the average citizen now entering the work force an extra $10,000 in taxes over his or her lifetime); 5) failing to save for the retirement of the baby boom generation (by 2035, there could be fewer than two workers for each retiree). The baby boomers will pass an impossible encumbrance on to their children, and/or face an impoverished old age. Indeed, the baby boomers are already in the grip of real downward mobility: between 1973 and 1983, real after-tax income of households headed by a person 25-34 declined by nearly 19%. Concludes that younger Americans must encourage government to institute reforms in their own and the nation's long-term interest. —*Future Survey*

• Professional futurists have it out in this academic journal. **Futures:** David Green, Editor. **$60**/year (12 issues) from Quadrant Subscription Services Limited, Oakfield House, Perrymount Road, Hayward Heath, RH 3DH England.

• Requisite reading for serious predictors. International, accurate, and witty.
The Economist: Rupert Pennant-Rey, Editor. **$85**/year (51 issues) from The Economist, Subscription Service Dept., P. O. Box 904, Farmingdale, NY 11737.

Yesterday's Tomorrows
Joseph J. Corn and
Brian Horrigan, Editors
1984; 158 pp.
$17.95 postpaid from:
Simon & Schuster
Mail Order Sales
200 Old Tappan
Old Tappan, NJ 07675
or Whole Earth Access

Yesterday's Tomorrows

It's hard to say which is most salient in these visions of how we were going to be living today: prescience, hubris, or naivete. In any case, a look at this book should induce a certain humility in our own prognostications of the future, despite the "advances" we enjoy. —JB

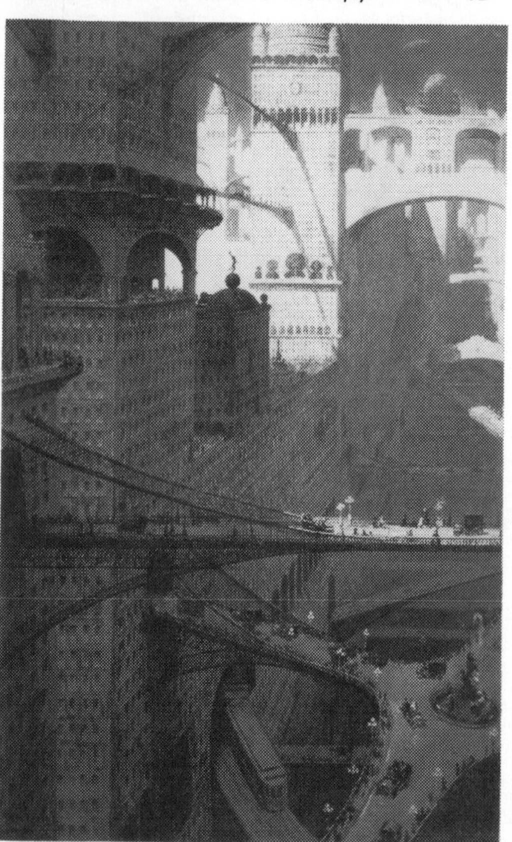

William Robinson Leigh, "Visionary City," 1908. The dizzying pace of growth in Manhattan around the turn of the century was clearly the inspiration for Leigh's exquisite drawing, published as a magazine illustration in 1908.

Back in 1967, the insights of Buckminster Fuller initiated The Whole Earth Catalog. —*Stewart Brand*

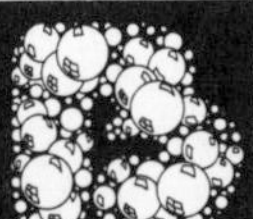ACK IN 1951, when I was 18, the insights of Buckminster Fuller initiated my education. I was particularly impressed by his assertion that if a person is sensitive enough to identify "as-yet-unattended-to human-environment-advantaging physical evolutionary tasks," and is disciplined and committed enough to attend to them, there is no need to worry about earning a living. (I've found this to be true — I've never looked for a job since then.)

Fuller contended that it is easier to reform the built environment than reform people, that the world's resources can be distributed better by doing more with less ("ephemeralization") than by war. To demonstrate this principle, he developed a number of resource-efficient artifacts, including his famous geodesic domes, which shelter a space with 1/50th of the material required by conventional construction. He referred to himself as "Guinea Pig B" (for Bucky), living his life as an experiment showing what one person might accomplish.

Bucky's everything-is-connected-to-everything vision and highly detailed language make some of his writing and lecturing hard to follow if you're new to it. I'd start with a book *about* him, the autobiographical *Buckminster Fuller*, or *The Dymaxion World of Buckminster Fuller* (now out of print, but still available from his Institute; see below). Next try *Critical Path*, a book that chronicles human evolution right up to the present, then brilliantly outlines the path we must take for species survival. Many people think it's his best, most easily understood book. For the details, you'll have to work hard reading *Synergetics 1* and *2*. In them, Bucky's philosophy is set out complete with the math, geometry, and physics backing it. A recent doctoral dissertation, *The Educational Philosophy of R. Buckminster Fuller*, neatly consolidates Bucky's views on dealing with ignore-ance.

All of Bucky's books plus an extensive selection of maps, video tapes, and other artifacts are available from The Buckminster Fuller Institute (directed by his daughter, Allegra Fuller Snyder). The Institute manages his archives and coordinates those continuing Fuller's work. Their newsletter, *Trimtab*, keeps you up to date with what's new, of which there is plenty. Guinea Pig B has left us lots to do. —JB

•

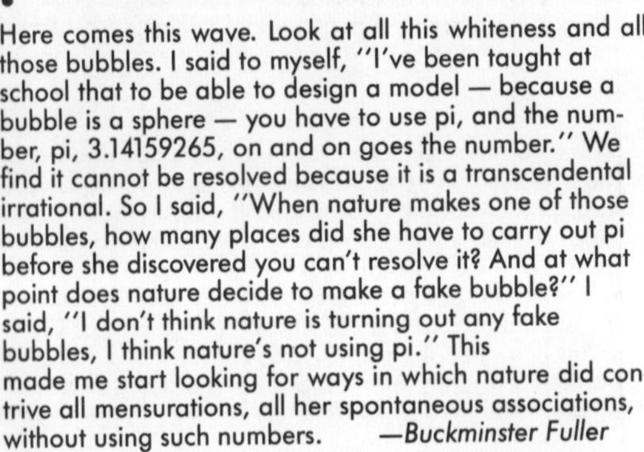

Here comes this wave. Look at all this whiteness and all those bubbles. I said to myself, "I've been taught at school that to be able to design a model — because a bubble is a sphere — you have to use pi, and the number, pi, 3.14159265, on and on goes the number." We find it cannot be resolved because it is a transcendental irrational. So I said, "When nature makes one of those bubbles, how many places did she have to carry out pi before she discovered you can't resolve it? And at what point does nature decide to make a fake bubble?" I said, "I don't think nature is turning out any fake bubbles, I think nature's not using pi." This made me start looking for ways in which nature did contrive all mensurations, all her spontaneous associations, without using such numbers. —*Buckminster Fuller*

•

Physics has found no solids! So to keep on teaching our children the word solid immediately is to drive home a way of thinking that is going to be neither reliable nor useful.

There are no surfaces, there are no solids, there are no straight lines, there are no planes. —*Buckminster Fuller*

•

There comes a time, however, when we discover other ways of doing the same task more economically — as, for instance, when we discover that a 200-ton transoceanic jet airplane — considered on an annual round-trip-frequency basis — can outperform the passenger-carrying capability of the 85,000-ton *Queen Mary*. —*Critical Path*

• Also see World Game and A Dymaxion Map (p. 89).

• You can make geodesic models with the kits in Edmund's Scientific catalog (p. 389).

•

I am not a thing — a noun. I am not flesh. At eighty-five, I have taken in over a thousand tons of air, food, and water, which temporarily became my flesh and which progressively disassociated from me. You and I seem to be verbs — evolutionary processes. Are we not integral functions of the Universe? —*Critical Path*

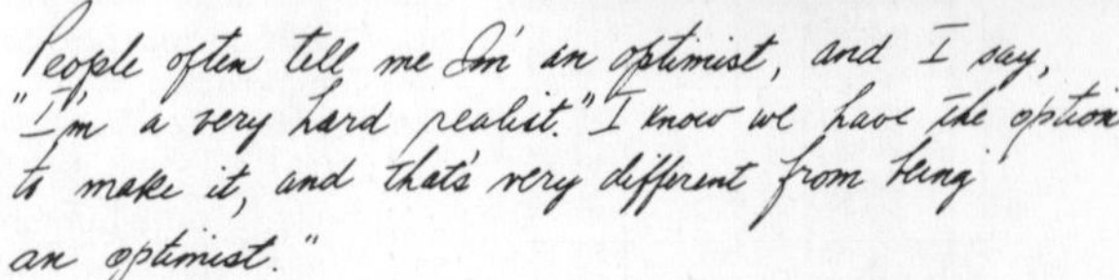

"People often tell me I'm an optimist, and I say, "I'm a very hard realist." I know we have the option to make it, and that's very different from being an optimist."

•

1053.832 Radiation outcasts. Radiation does not broadcast; broadcast is a planar statement; there are no planes. *Out* is inherently omnidivergent. Radiation omnicasts but does not and cannot *incast*; it can only go-in-to-go-out. *In* is gravity.

1053.833 If radiation "goes through" a system and comes out on the other side, it does so because (1) there was no frequency interference — it just occurred between the system's occurrence frequencies — or (2) there was tangential interference and deflection thereby of the angle of travel, wherefore it did not go through; it went by. —*Synergetics*

Buckminster Fuller (An Autobiographical Monologue / Scenario): Documented and Edited by Robert Snyder, 1980; 218 pp. **$18.95** postpaid.

The Dymaxion World of Buckminster Fuller: Buckminster Fuller and Robert Marks, 1960; 246 pp. **$11.95** postpaid.

Critical Path: Buckminster Fuller, 1981; 471 pp. **$11.95** postpaid.

Synergetics: Buckminster Fuller, 1975; 876 pp. **$16.95** postpaid.

Synergetics 2: Buckminster Fuller, 1979; 592 pp. **$16.95** postpaid.

Trimtab Bulletin: Allegra Fuller Snyder and Janet Brown, Editors. **$8**/year (6 issues); information **free.**

All from Buckminster Fuller Institute, 1743 South La Cienega Blvd., Los Angeles, CA 90035 (or Whole Earth Access).

The Educational Philosophy of R. Buckminster Fuller: Alex Gerber, Jr., 1985; 351 pp. **$42** postpaid from University of Southern California, Library Photo Duplication Service, University Park, Los Angeles, CA 90089.

GREGORY BATESON IS RESPONSIBLE for a number of formal discoveries, most notably the "Double Bind" theory of schizophrenia. As an anthropologist he did pioneer work in New Guinea and (with Margaret Mead) in Bali. He participated in the Macy Foundation meetings that founded the science of cybernetics but kept a healthy distance from computers. He wandered thornily in and out of various disciplines — biology, ethnology, linguistics, epistomology, psychotherapy — and left each of them altered with his passage.

Steps to an Ecology of Mind chronicles that journey. It is a collection of all his major papers, 1935-1971. In recommending the book I've learned to suggest that it be read backwards. Read the broad analyses of mind and ecology at the end of the book and then work back to see where the premises come from.

Bateson has informed everything I've attempted since I read *Steps* in 1972. Through him I became convinced that much more of whole systems could be understood than I had thought, and that much more existed wholesomely beyond understanding than I thought — that mysticism, mood, ignorance and paradox could be rigorous, for instance, and that the most potent tool for grasping these essences — these influence nets — is cybernetics.

Mind and Nature: A Necessary Unity addresses the hidden, though unoccult, dynamics of life — the misapprehension of which threatens to unhorse our civilization. Bateson doesn't have all the answers, he just has better questions — elegant, mature, embarrassing questions that tweak the quick of things.

One of the themes that emerges is the near identity between the process of evolving and the process of learning, and the ongoing responsibility they have for each other which includes our responsibility, which we have shirked. We shirked it through ignorance. *Mind and Nature* dispels that.

Bateson's previous writing — *Naven; Communications: The Social Matrix of Psychiatry; Balinese Character* and *Steps to an Ecology of Mind* — has been addressed to various audiences of specialists. *Mind in Nature* is addressed to a general readership. It is new thought in an old virtue — the use of fine original writing to express ideas whose excellence is embedded in the clarity of their expression. Stong medicine.

—Stewart Brand

Steps to an Ecology of Mind
Gregory Bateson
1972; 541 pp.
$4.95
($5.95 postpaid) from:
Random House
Order Dept.
400 Hahn Road
Westminster, MD 21157
or Whole Earth Access

Mind and Nature
Gregory Bateson
1979; 259 pp.
$4.95
($6.45 postpaid) from:
Bantam Books
414 East Golf Road
Des Plaines, IL 60016
or Whole Earth Access

•

It is a nontrivial matter that we are almost always unaware of trends in our changes of state. There is a quasi-scientific fable that if you can get a frog to sit quietly in a saucepan of cold water, and if you then raise the temperature of the water very slowly and smoothly so that there is no moment *marked* to be the moment at which the frog should jump, he will never jump. He will get boiled. Is the human species changing its own environment with slowly increasing pollution and rotting its mind with slowly deteriorating religion and education in such a saucepan?

•

Human sense organs can receive *only* news of difference, and the differences must be coded into events in *time* (i.e. into *changes*) in order to be perceptible. Ordinary static differences that remain constant for more than a few seconds become perceptible only by scanning.

•

Ross Ashby long ago pointed out that no system (neither computer nor organism) can produce anything *new* unless the system contains some source of the random. In the computer, this will be a random-number generator which will ensure that the "seeking," trial-and-error moves of the machine will ultimately cover all the possibilities of the set to be explored.

•

I do not believe that the original purpose of the rain dance was to make "it" rain. I suspect that that is a degenerate misunderstanding of a much more profound religious need: to affirm membership in what we may call the *ecological tautology*, the eternal verities of life and environment. There's always a tendency — almost a need — to vulgarize religion, to turn it into entertainment or politics or magic or "power."

—*Mind and Nature*

•

No organism can afford to be conscious of matters with which it could deal at unconscious levels.

—*Steps to an Ecology of Mind*

•

Mere purposive rationality unaided by such phenomena as art, religion, dream, and the like, is necessarily pathogenic and destructive of life; its virulence springs specifically from the circumstance that life depends upon interlocking *circuits* of contingency, while consciousness can only see such short arcs as human purpose may direct.

•

When you narrow down your epistemology and act on the premise "what interests me is me, or my organization, or my species," you chop off consideration of other loops of the loop structure. You decide that you want to get rid of the by-products of human life and that Lake Erie will be a good place to put them. You forget that the eco-mental system called Lake Erie is part of *your* wider eco-mental system — and that if Lake Erie is driven insane, its insanity is incorporated in the larger system of *your* thought and experience.

•

My father, the geneticist William Bateson, used to read us passages of the Bible at breakfast — lest we grow up to be *empty-headed* atheists.

•

In no system which shows mental characteristics can any part have unilateral control over the whole. In other words, *the mental characteristics of the system are immanent, not in some part, but in the system as a whole.*

—*Steps to an Ecology of Mind*

•

It seems to puzzle psychologists that the exploring tendencies of a rat cannot be simply extinguished by having the rat encounter boxes containing small electric shocks.

A little empathy will show that from the rat's point of view, it is not desirable that he learn the general lesson. His experience of a shock upon putting his nose into a box indicates to him that he did *well* to put his nose into that box in order to gain the information that it contained a shock. In fact, the "purpose" of exploration is, not to discover whether exploration is a good thing, but to discover information about the explored. The larger case is of a totally different nature from that of the particular.

—*Mind and Nature*

I and Thou

*You can read **I and Thou** in two hours and not get over it for the rest of your life. Buber tells you how you stand, either in a dialogical relationship with the Creative Force or in a position of "havingness" where you are a thing bounded by other things.* —Ken Kesey

A discovery more prime than Einstein's Relativity is Buber's distinction between the "experience" of I-It and the "relation" of I-You. It can cure at once the twin pathologies of Transcendent God and Controllable Nature. In "I-You" is the possibility of love that does not possess, as well as the realest perception of learning, which is coevolution. Martin Buber's original German torrent is well served by the translation and prologue by Walter Kaufmann. —Stewart Brand

•

A man's relation to the "particular something" that arrogates the supreme throne of his life's values, pushing eternity aside, is always directed toward the experience and use of an It, a thing, an object of enjoyment. For only this kind of relation can bar the view to God, by interposing the impenetrable It-world; the relationship that says You always opens it up again.

•

Whoever says You does not have something for his object. For wherever there is something there also another something: every It borders on other Its; It is only by virtue of bordering on others. But where You is said there is no something. You has no borders.

Whoever says You does not have something; he has nothing. But he stands in relation.

•

Throughout all of this the tree remains my object and has its place and its time span, its kind and condition.

But it can also happen, if will and grace are joined, that as I contemplate the tree I am drawn into a relation, and the tree ceases to be an It. The power of exclusiveness has seized me.

•

I perceive something. I feel something. I imagine something. I want something. I sense something. I think something. The life of a human being does not consist merely of all this and its like.

All this and its like is the basis of the realm of It.

But the realm of You has another basis.

•

When I confront a human being as my You and speak the basic word I-You to him, then he is no thing among things nor does he consist of things.

He is no longer He or She, limited by other Hes and Shes, a dot in the world grid of space and time, nor a condition that can be experienced and described, a loose bundle of named qualities. Neighborless and seamless, he is You and fills the firmament. Not as if there were nothing but he; but everything else lives in *his* light.

•

In truth language does not reside in man but man stands in language and speaks out of it.

•

Extended, the lines of relationships intersect in the external You. Every single You is a glimpse of that. Through every single You the basic word addresses the eternal You.

I and Thou
Martin Buber
1958; 137 pp.
$4.95 postpaid from:
Macmillan Publishing Co.
Order Dept.
Front and Brown Streets
Riverside, NJ 08075
or Whole Earth Access

The Amy Vanderbilt Complete Book of Etiquette

I used to think that to have manners was to be mannered; that etiquette was affectation. Now I see that discipline of any sort is a lot more comfortable than its absence, and that is quite as true of consideration for others as it is of daily exercise or meditation. Comfortable, yes; effortless, no. There's inborn grace and learned grace, and in a world of constant change and conflict, what's inborn may soon be eroded.

All you have to do is follow a few hundred simple suggestions. The essence of them is consideration for others, whether that is made manifest as tact, promptness in thanking people, being organized enough not to confound everybody else, or making a proper introduction. The point of all the information, commonplace (how to make a bed) or esoteric (what sort of gift to give a nun), is "to help people make it through life just a little more easily and be a little more sure of themselves." —Stephanie Mills
[Suggested by Edith G. Mills]

•

Some bachelors become truly bored by having to attend parties every night and always having to take care of whatever single woman is present. If this is the case, the man should be frank with his friends. "Look, I'd love to come over some night to have a hamburger with you and the kids and to relax a bit, but I'm tired of parties." Frankness in social relationships never has to be rude; well-stated frankness is always for the best.

•

A very nice gesture to make before the dinner party is to ask a recovered alcoholic if there is some drink he or she particularly likes, such as iced tea or a special kind of juice. Some like to drink tea or coffee during the cocktail hour. A recovered alcoholic who doesn't want to be "different" might ask for ginger ale because it "looks like scotch and soda."

•

For a dinner party, the table should be set the same for all guests. You do not set the recovered alcoholic's place at the dinner table with the wineglasses conspicuously missing. When wine is served, this guest will simply make a "no, thank you" gesture when the wine is offered to him. He might also accept wine in his glass in order not to distract, but will, of course, leave it untouched. You are not putting temptation in his way by offering him wine, because a recovered alcoholic has to train himself with a fine-edged will power to refuse liquor of all kinds in all circumstances.

Recessional, ► Christian ceremony, optional arrangement. Reading from top down: Groom and bride; flower girl or page, or pages, if any, or second honor attendant, if any; best man and maid or matron of honor; ushers and bridesmaids paired.

▲ Formal dinner setting as guest approaches the table. The butter plate is optional. Glasses for four wines — sherry, white, red, and champagne — are included, as well as a water goblet.

The Amy Vanderbilt Complete Book of Etiquette
Revised by Letitia Baldrige
1978; 879 pp.
$17.95 postpaid from:
Doubleday and Company
Direct Mail Order
501 Franklin Avenue
Garden City, NY 11530
or Whole Earth Access

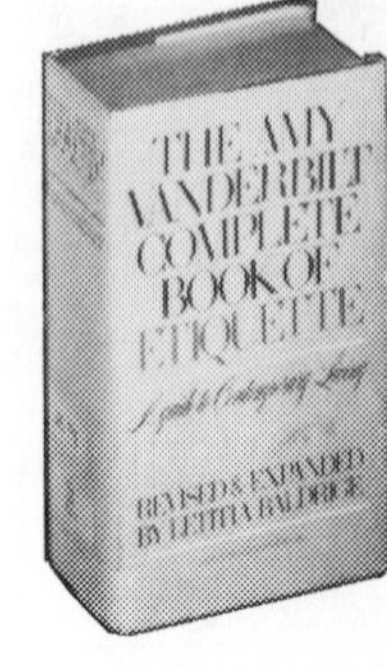

CYBERNETICS IS THE DISCIPLINE of whole systems thinking. For a field of such importance it is shocking there are so few introductory books. The ones here, like the Bateson books on p. 22, introduce the cybernetic frame of mind. They instill habits of minds that lead to on-going health effectiveness in all your dealings becuase they become self-adjusting. A whole system is a living system is a learning system.

—Stewart Brand

Systemantics
John Gall
1986; 297 pp.
Write for price to:
The General Systemantics Press
3200 West Liberty, Suite A
Ann Arbor, MI 48103-9794
or Whole Earth Access

Systemantics

The pun in the title carries the important message that systems have "antics" — they act up, misbehave, and have their own mind. The author is having fun with a serious subject, deciding rightly that a sense of humor and paradox are the only means to approach large systems. His insights come in the form of marvelously succinct rules of thumb, in the spirit of Murphy's Law and the Peter Principle. This book made me 1) not worry about understanding a colossal system — you can't, 2) realize you CAN change a system — by starting a new one, and 3) flee from starting new systems — they don't go away.

—Kevin Kelly

•

We begin at the beginning, with the Fundamental Theorem: New systems mean new problems.

•

The system always kicks back — Systems get in the way — or, in slightly more elegant language: Systems tend to oppose their own proper functions.

•

Systems tend to malfunction conspicuously just after their greatest triumph. Toynbee explains this effect by pointing out the strong tendency to apply a previously successful strategy to the new challenge. The army is now fully prepared to fight the previous war.

•

A complex system that works is invariably found to have evolved from a simple system that worked. The parallel proposition also appears to be true: A complex system designed from scratch never works and cannot be made to work. You have to start over, beginning with a working simple system.

The Recursive Universe
William Poundstone
1985; 252 pp.
$7.95
($8.95 postpaid) from:
Contemporary Books
180 North Michigan Ave.
Chicago, IL 60601
or Whole Earth Access

The Recursive Universe • Life

*You are God in the game of **Life**, a computer game. Let there be a grid. And you create all in it. You design not only the creatures but the rules of their universe. Let the cells live (a black dot) or die (emptiness) in each generation. And then there is time, a thousand generations a minute. Let there be graphic patterns of your cells' growth, as they pulse in expansion, or flicker into extinction. Their destiny is fixed by the original premises that you, God, choose. Mathematically there is no way to tell where the system is going until you try it. That you can TRY it is heavenly.*

*Invented in 1970 by mathematician John Conway, **Life** is no longer played as a mere game. Run on large mainframe computers, this game, and others like it, have proved to be a fertile field of scientific research, the first hands-on cybernetics laboratory. (The discipline is called Cellular Automata.) Some of the curious results and startling implications of running these simple worlds are clearly presented in **The Recursive Universe**. To be a part-time God yourself, you only need a home version of **Life**, which is available in the public domain for Apple, IBM and Macintosh computers.*

—Kevin Kelly

Life
John Conway
$15 (Macintosh)
$10 (Apple IIe)
$8 (IBM PC)
Public Domain
Software Copying Co.
33 Gold Street, #13
New York, NY 10038

•

When *Life* was first introduced, three of the biggest questions *Life* players wondered about were these: Is there any general way of telling what a pattern will do? Can any pattern grow without limit (so that the number of live cells keeps getting bigger and bigger)? Do all patterns eventually settle down into a stable object or group of objects?

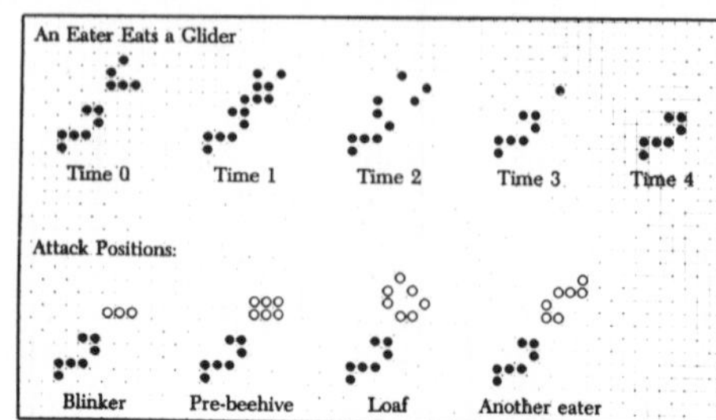

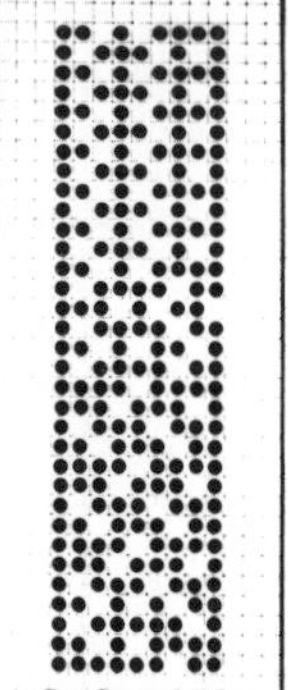

A Garden-of-Eden Pattern

Actually, Conway chose the rules of *Life* just so that these sorts of questions would be hard to answer.

•

[One kind of pattern] does not even have itself for a predecessor. It is an unstable pattern with no predecessors. The only way it can possibly turn up on the *Life* screen is for someone to use it as a starting configuration. The name for such a configuration is a "Garden-of-Eden" pattern.

This is a pattern with no past. It can never appear in *Life* except in the initial state.

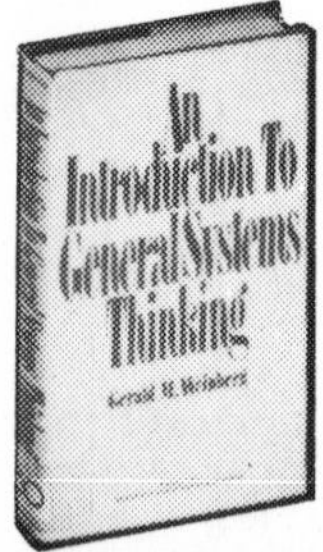

An Introduction to General Systems Thinking
Gerald M. Weinberg
1975; 279 pp.
$42.95
postpaid from:
John Wiley & Sons
Order Dept.
1 Wiley Drive
Somerset, NJ 08873
or Whole Earth Access

An Introduction to General Systems Thinking

Viewed from just about any perspective this book is an exemplary introduction to a complex subject. The fascinating observations are well organized and are stated in a consciously informal tone. Thoughtful questions for research and additional readings are provided for those who want to go beyond the scope of the book. Over a hundred wide-ranging quotes add to the fun.

—William Courington

•

Discriminating too many states is what we have previously called *undergeneralization*. The popular image of science envisions the scientist making the maximally precise measurements as a basis for his theories, but, in practice, scientists are lucky that measurements are not overly precise. Newton based his Law of Universal Gravitation on the elliptical orbits of Kepler, but Kepler abstracted these ellipses from the observations of Tycho Brahe. Had those observations been a bit more precise (as precise as we now can make) the orbits would not have been seen as ellipses, and Newton's work would have been much more difficult. With *more precise* observations, the simplifications we discussed in Chapter 1 would have been left for Newton to make *explicitly* — thus immensely compounding his difficulties.

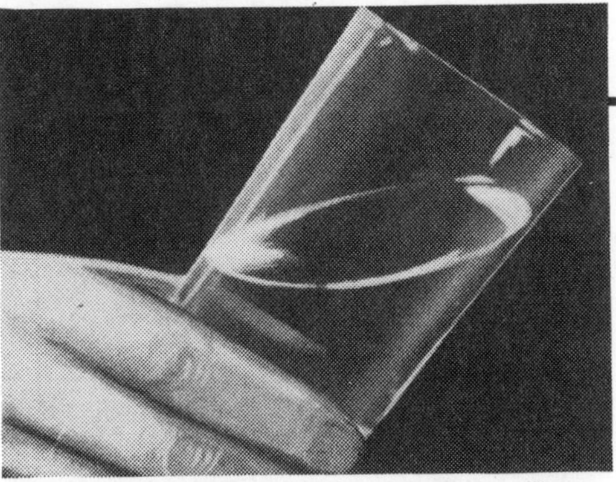

When we cut a cylinder by a plane, we get an ellipse.

Mathematical Snapshots

The most graphically insightful math book in print. Most math feeds proof; this lovely stuff feeds understanding, and is no less rigorous. If someone were going to see only one mathematics book in their life, this would be the best.
—*Stewart Brand*

•

To determine the centroid of a stick, we place it horizontally on the edges of our palms and then we bring our hands closer together; finally they meet in the center of gravity. The stick never loses its equilibrium because when the centroid, which is initially between the palms, approaches one of them, the pressure on the nearer palm becomes many times greater than the pressure on the other palm; its product by the coefficient of friction must finally surpass the analogous product for the other palm; when this happens, the relative movement of the first palm ceases and the relative movement of the other one starts. This play continues alternately until both palms meet; the centroid is always between them and it is there at the final stage. The trick is done automatically without any conscious effort.

Mathematical Snapshots
Hugo Steinhaus
1969; 311 pp.
$8.95 postpaid from:
Oxford University Press
16-00 Pollitt Drive
Fair Lawn, NJ 07410
or Whole Earth Access

How to Solve It

This is the best book I know of for lining up a problem for a logical solution. The emphasis is on math, but it is simple logic and can easily be applied to all forms of problem identification and analysis. Better yet is that the methods shown really work even on personal decision-making binds. Essentially it's a head-straightener. —*JB*

UNDERSTANDING THE PROBLEM

What is the unknown? What are the data? What is the condition?
Is it possible to satisfy the condition? Is the condition sufficient to determine the unknown? Or is it insufficient? Or redundant? Or contradictory?
Draw a figure. Introduce suitable notation.
Separate the various parts of the condition. Can you write them down?

DEVISING A PLAN

Have you seen it before? Or have you seen the same problem in a slightly different form?
Do you know a related problem? Do you know a theorem that could be useful?
Look at the unknown! And try to think of a familiar problem having the same or a similar unknown.
Here is a problem related to yours and solved before. Could you use it? Could you use its result? Could you use its method? Should you introduce some auxiliary element in order to make its use possible?
Could you restate the problem? Could you restate it still differently? Go back to definitions.
If you cannot solve the proposed problem try to solve first some related problem. Could you imagine a more accessible related problem? A more general problem? A more special problem? An analogous problem? Could you solve a part of the problem? Keep only a part of the condition, drop the other part; how far is the unknown then determined, how can it vary? Could you derive something useful from the data? Could you think of other data appropriate to determine the unknown? Could you change the unknown or the data, or both if necessary, so that the new unknown and the new data are nearer to each other?
Did you use all the data? Did you use the whole condition? Have you taken into account all essential notions involved in the problem?

CARRYING OUT THE PLAN

Carrying out your plan of the solution, *check each step.* Can you see clearly that the step is correct? Can you prove that it is correct?

LOOKING BACK

Can you *check the result?* Can you check the argument?
Can you derive the result differently? Can you see it at a glance?
Can you use the result, or the method, for some other problem?

• Lots of folks think learning math is a hopeless task. There are some books on p. 389 that can help you grasp math, calculus, and geometry.

How to Lie with Statistics

In these days of polls and "proof" furnished by testing by "independent laboratories," it might be well to bear in mind the lessons given by this simple book. It's been around a long time, but it's still deadly. —*JB*
[Suggested by Roger Knights]

•

Simply change the proportion between the ordinate and the abscissa. There's no rule against it, and it does give your graph a prettier shape. All you have to do is let each mark up the side stand for only one-tenth as many dollars as before. That *is* impressive, isn't it? Anyone looking at it can just feel prosperity throbbing in the arteries of the country. It is a subtler equivalent of editing "National income rose ten per cent" into ". . . climbed a whopping ten per cent." It is vastly more effective, however, because it contains no adjectives or adverbs to spoil the illusion of objectivity. There's nothing anyone can pin on you.

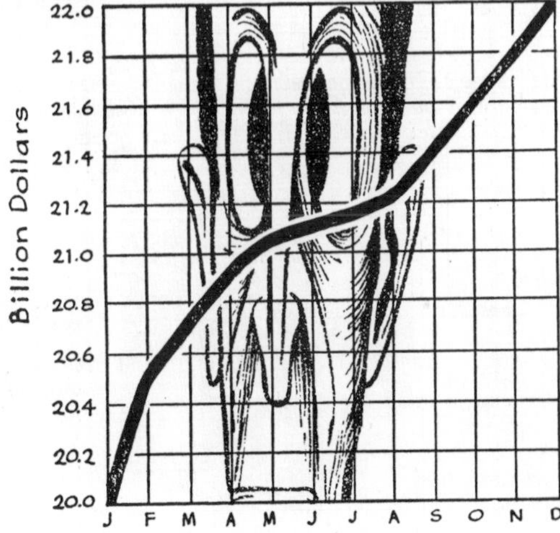

How to Solve It
Gyorgy Polya
1973; 253 pp.
$6.95
($8.05 postpaid) from:
Princeton University Press
3175 Princeton Pike
Lawrenceville, NJ 08648
or Whole Earth Access

How to Lie with Statistics
Darrell Huff
1954; 142 pp.
$2.95 postpaid from:
W. W. Norton
500 Fifth Avenue
New York, NY 10110
or Whole Earth Access

Science 86
Allen L. Hammond, Editor
$18/year
(10 issues) from:
Science 86
Subscription Dept.
P. O. Box 10790
Des Moines, IA 50340

New Scientist
Michael Kenward, Editor
$99/year
(52 issues) from:
Business Press International
Subscription Dept.
205 East 42nd Street
New York, NY 10017

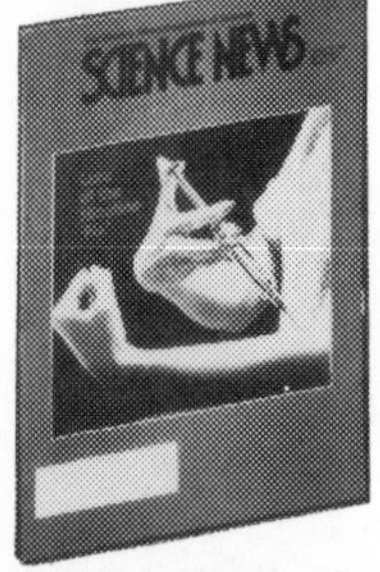

Science News
Joel Greenburg, Editor
$29.50/year
(52 issues) from:
Science News
231 West Center Street
Marion, OH 43305

Science 86

__Science 86__ changes its number each year, but not its excellent popularized science reporting. It's the layperson's version of __Science__ (they're both published by the august American Association for the Advancement of Science); no footnotes or jargon. It's the best magazine of its kind.
—JB

New Scientist

My primary source of scientific and technical information is the wide-ranging reporting in this weekly. It's very British: droll wit abounds, and the criticism (some of it rather nasty) spares nobody, including the U.S.A., giving an unusual political aspect not found in other science magazines. You should have heard the shrieks around this office when it was suggested we cut our subscription as an economy measure.
—JB

•

Although the seed of most crops has already been sown worldwide, wild and exotic species provide insurance and new genes to regenerate cultivars. Commercial crops are many times as vulnerable to pests and disease as their wild brethren, and plant biologists are ever watchful for new species that confer resistance, higher productivity, or useful traits such as tolerance to high salinity in water.

Jack Kloppenburg, assistant professor of rural sociology at the University of Wisconsin, has enlightened the North-South debate with an analysis of where plant species originated. In general, the North is indeed "gene-poor" and the South "gene-rich". But no region is genetically independent, and no region can afford to isolate itself through a "genetic OPEC", an option some gene-rich countries are considering.

Rice comes from the East — but there is no way to keep it there.

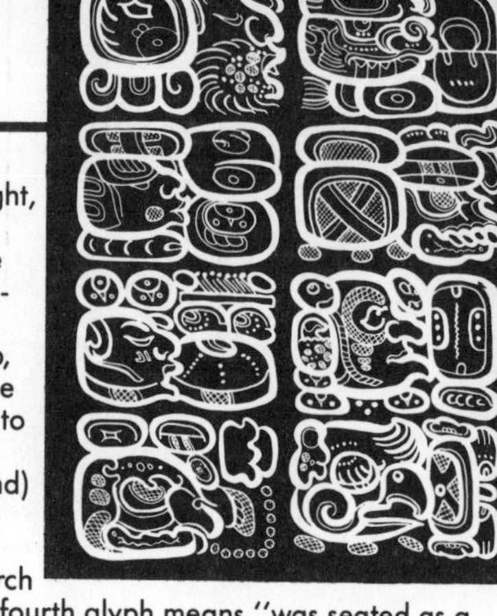

► The inscription, right, from a tablet at Palenque tells the story of a coronation. Read left to right from the top, its first glyph is the phrase, "it came to pass." The next (containing a hand) and third (a skull) signify the date equivalent to March

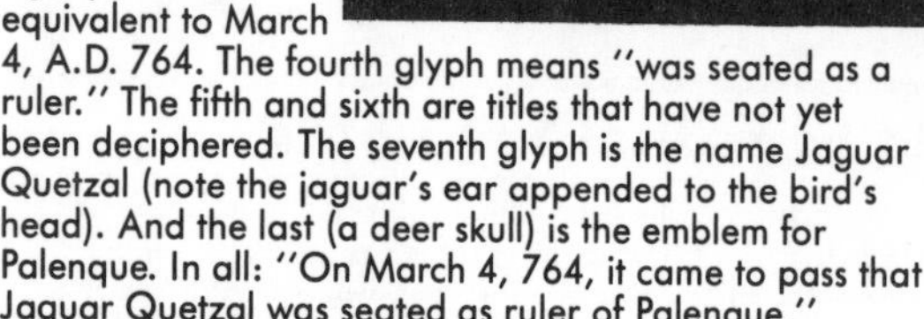

4, A.D. 764. The fourth glyph means "was seated as a ruler." The fifth and sixth are titles that have not yet been deciphered. The seventh glyph is the name Jaguar Quetzal (note the jaguar's ear appended to the bird's head). And the last (a deer skull) is the emblem for Palenque. In all: "On March 4, 764, it came to pass that Jaguar Quetzal was seated as ruler of Palenque."

Science News

A highly palatable digest of current top stories in science. The least demanding in terms of technical background, it's a quick read — only about ten pages of editorial material per issue, with adequate pictures. Sometimes it has by far the best coverage of fast-breaking stories.
—Stewart Brand

•

The unresolved issue of dependency is made even more worrisome, several researchers told *Science News*, by tobacco's availability, its low cost relative to illegal drugs and its social acceptability. "You can say nicotine is in the category of heroin and stimulants," Henningfield notes, "but there are very few offices where you can shoot heroin."

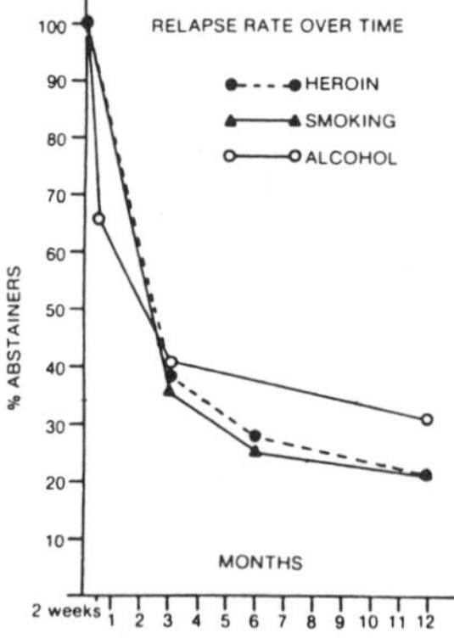

Relapse rates for individuals treated for heroin, smoking and alcohol addiction are very similar.

Science

Top of the line. Possibly the best science magazine in the world (the major challenge would be from England's __Nature__). This is where you can really watch news taking shape. Often pretty technical, but it's the real goods.
—Stewart Brand

Science
Daniel E. Koshland, Jr.
Editor
$65/year
membership included
(51 issues) from:
AAAS
1333 H Street NW
Washington, DC 20005

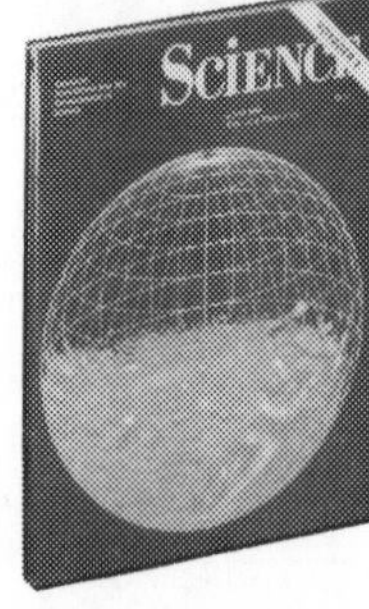

•

Air entrapped in bubbles of cold ice has essentially the same composition as that of the atmosphere at the time of bubble formation. Measurements of the methane concentration in air extracted by two different methods from ice samples from Siple Station in western Antarctica allow the reconstruction of the history of the increase of the atmospheric methane during the past 200 years.

Measured CH^4 concentration plotted against the estimated mean gas age.

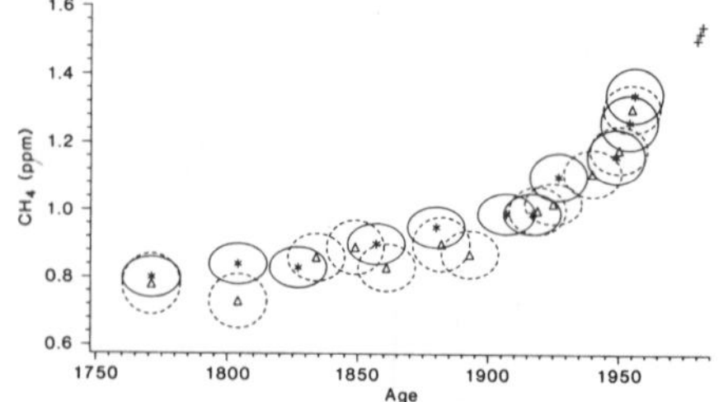

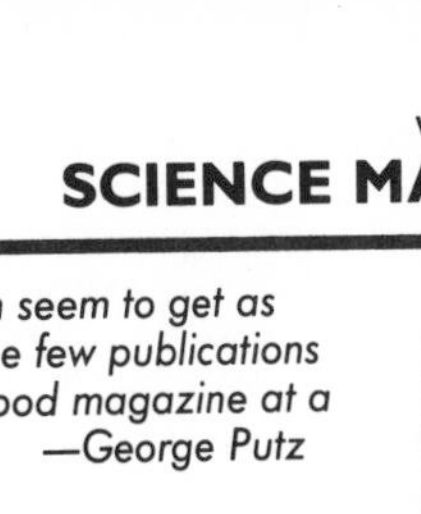

Natural History Magazine

I use it two ways: The monthly column "This View of Life" by Stephen Jay Gould, who teaches Biology, Geology and History of Science at Harvard, regularly contributes to (or at least soundly reaffirms) my understanding of how the world works. He explains fundamental issues clearly and always sets them against a background of why anyone ever thought differently. Second, it is written and edited in such a way that our children seem to get as much out of it as we do. It is one of the few publications we've found that has this quality. A good magazine at a good price from a great institution. —George Putz

◄

Every July in southwestern Alaska, the chum salmon migrate up the McNeil River to spawn, and every brown bear for miles around shows up to catch them. The short northern summer is ending, and the bears are putting on the poundage to carry them through their hibernations. They converge on the McNeil and they eat, and they eat, and they eat.

It is the largest known gathering of brown bears in the world. As many as fifty may be in sight at any given time, eating, sleeping, or walking around. Dominant bears take the best fishing spots; when they've had their fill, lower-ranked bears can come in. Coastal brown bears belong to the same species as upland grizzlies, but bears living near the water tend to be larger — up to a thousand pounds.

Natural History
Alan Ternes, Editor
$20/year
(12 issues) from:
Natural History
P. O. Box 5000
Harlan, IA 51537

To create their winter larder, acorn woodpeckers drill out storage cells in trees and poles. One pine tree contained 50,000 imbedded acorns.
—Audubon

The Ecologist

Edited by the ebullient Teddy Goldsmith, this British mag is a nice mix of careful and radical. It has a strong point of view, lots of good ideas, and considerable effect.
—Stewart Brand

•

Since the late 1970s, and with increasing severity, a new phenomenon leading to the dying and death of its forests has been sweeping across Europe. Although some species appear to be more resistant than others, one by one they are succumbing — spruce, pine, fir, beech, oak, ash, rowan — and if the pace of death continues large tracts of once forested areas will soon be virtually denuded of trees.

Whether the phenomenon of forest death — waldsterben as the West Germans call it — will spread to all woodlands and forests throughout Europe is a moot point. The rapidity with which the disease has struck trees first in one forested area and then another is extremely disturbing, and a forest that shows few signs of damage one year may present a very different picture one or two years later when as many as half the trees may be suffering die-back. . . . The political ramifications of a disease pattern that appears to correspond to atmospheric pollution fall-out are clearly very great.

***Is this the future?* The hill top of the Hornisgrinde in the Black Forest littered with dead fir and spruce.**

The Ecologist
Edward Goldsmith, Nicholas Hildyard, and Peter Bunyard, Editors
$20/year
(6 issues) from:
The Ecologist
Subscription Dept.
Worthyvale Manor Farm
Camelford, Cornwall
PL32 9TT U.K.

Audubon

It's for the birds, but not just — protection of all life is now the official business of the Audubon Society *(see p. 87)**. The magazine is slick and well-produced with gorgeous photographs and graphics enhanced by a high editorial standard. Like other upscale nature publications, Audubon is having an interesting time balancing nature conservation with the conservative nature of many Society members.*
—JB

Audubon
Les Line, Editor
$30/year
(membership included)
(6 issues) from:
National Audubon Society
Membership Data Center
P. O. Box 2666
Boulder, CO 80322

Scientific American

The patriarch of science magazines is more into explanation and less into news. Article difficulty is about max for a nonprofessional reader in whatever subject (almost anything!) is being discussed. Book reviews and drawings are exceptional.
—JB

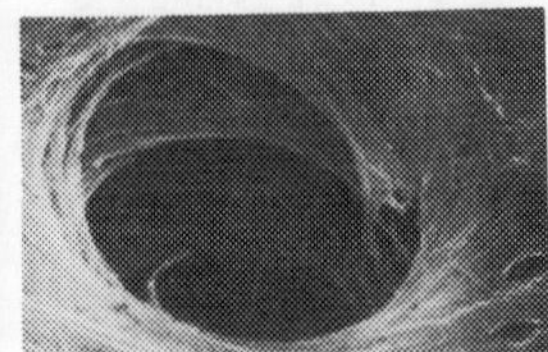

DERMAL GLAND DUCT *(dark circle)* is surrounded by chitin fibers in this micrograph of the endocuticle of the scorpion *Hadrurus arizonensis*, photographed from the underside and enlarged roughly 4,500 times. The helicoid arrangement of fibers allows the cuticle to withstand stress that might otherwise lead to cracking. The micrograph is from Barry K. Filshie of the Commonwealth Scientific and Industrial Research Organization in Australia.

Scientific American
Jonathan Piel, Editor
$24/year
(12 issues) from:
Scientific American
P. O. Box 5919
New York, NY 10164-0411

• As we go to press, there seems to be vigorous corporate takeover action affecting several of the science magazines, and we can't tell yet whether the information on these two pages is still valid as you read it. Our apologies.

• **Discover** is another layperson's explain-it science magazine that enjoys a wide following.
Discover: Gil Rogin, Editor. **$24**/year (12 issues) from Time Inc., 541 North Fairbanks Court, Chicago, IL 60611.

Microcosmos
Lynn Margulis
and Dorion Sagan
1986; 301 pp.

$17.95 postpaid from:
Simon & Schuster
Mail Order Sales
200 Old Tappan Road
Old Tappan, NJ 07675
or Whole Earth Access

Microcosmos

The prose is at times raucous, joyful, teasing, even catty — the tone of two good friends going out to the local bar on Friday and living it up. But, as one reads, it becomes clear that this book is also brilliant science.

This is by far the best book written on human prejudice and evolutionary history. It carefully tracks the evolution of life on earth from one-celled life into today's mind-boggling variety of cell conglomerates. This book makes clear the importance of symbiosis, mutual dependence, cooperation, and cohabitation in evolution, thus delightfully shoving "species competition" and Spencerian "survival of the fittest" into the back seat ashtray.

An excellent companion to ***Microcosmos*** *is* ***Five Kingdoms*** *. . . A field guide that achieves the proper balance of microbes and mammals; it is the reference book for the study of planetary life.* —*Peter Warshall*

Five Kingdoms: Lynn Margulis and Karlene V. Schwartz, 1982; 338 pp. **$28.95** ($29.95 postpaid) from W. H. Freeman & Co., 4419 West 1980 South, Salt Lake City, UT 84104 (or Whole Earth Access).

•

So significant are bacteria and their evolution that the fundamental division in forms of life on earth is not that between plants and animals, as is commonly assumed, but between prokaryotes — organisms composed of cells with no nucleus, that is, bacteria — and eukarotes — all the other life forms. In their first two billion years on earth, prokaryotes continuously transformed the earth's surface and atmosphere. They invented all of life's essential, miniaturized chemical systems — achievements that so far humanity has not approached. This ancient high biotechnology led to the development of fermentation, photosynthesis, oxygen breathing, and the removal of nitrogen gas from the air. It also led to worldwide crises of starvation, pollution, and extinction long before the dawn of larger forms of life.

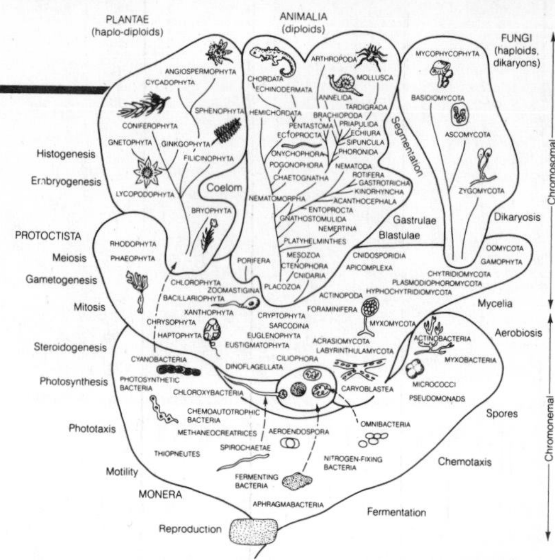

A phylogeny of life on Earth based on the Whittaker five-kingdom system and the symbiotic theory of the origin of eukaryotic cells. —***Five Kingdoms***

The Flamingo's Smile
Stephen Jay Gould
1985; 476 pp.

$17.95 postpaid from:
W. W. Norton
500 Fifth Avenue
New York, NY 10110
or Whole Earth Access

The Flamingo's Smile

The most ingratiating of all evolution writers has to be Stephen Jay Gould, whose monthly column in ***Natural History*** *(see p. 27) has been a beacon of scientific essay style for some ten years now. The cash crop of those columns is a sequence of books, all still worthily in print —* ***Ever Since Darwin, The Panda's Thumb, Hen's Teeth and Horse's Toes,*** *and the new one still available only in hardcover,* ***The Flamingo's Smile.*** *This book is particularly thrilling since we get to watch Gould's major scientific contribution, the idea of "punctuated equilibrium" (evolution by spurts), dealing with the emerging evidence of periodic mass extinctions, which apparently deal a whole different kind of articulation to the text of time (sort of like paragraph breaks, come to think of it; think I'll take one now . . .).*

The appeal of Gould is also his application. He finds illustrations of evolutionary themes absolutely everywhere — in comics (the infantilization of Mickey Mouse's face), in baseball batting averages (the extremes narrow with time), in Alfred Kinsey (his landmark sex research followed landmark wasp research). The reader acquires an evolutionary eye constantly rewarded because one theory fits all. —*Stewart Brand*

Nehemiah Grew's flamingo, 1681. The illustration accompanying the first important proposal that flamingos feed by moving their upper jaw up and down against their lower. Look at this figure upside down as well.

•

But another overarching, yet often forgotten, evolutionary principle usually intervenes and prevents any optimal match between organism and immediate environment — the curious, tortuous, constraining pathways of history. Organisms are not putty before a molding environment or billiard balls before the pool cue of natural selection. Their inherited forms and behaviors constrain and push back; they cannot be quickly transformed to new optimality every time the environment alters.

Darwin and the Beagle
Alan Moorehead
1969; 224 pp.

$10.95
($11.95 postpaid) from:
Viking-Penguin Books
299 Murray Hill Pkwy.
East Rutherford,
NJ 07073
or Whole Earth Access

Darwin and the Beagle

The story of Darwin's five-year circumnavigation, his revelation on the shores of Chile and confirmation on the isles of Galapagos. The story of how humans always fret about life as timeless-design vs. life as fluid-forming. From here, it is one easy step to Darwin's ***Illustrated Origin of Species.*** —*Peter Warshall*

Illustrated Origin of Species: Charles Darwin, 1979; 240 pp. **$12.95** postpaid from Hill and Wang, Inc., 19 Union Square West, New York, NY 10003.

•

The fame of the Galapagos was founded upon one thing: they were infinitely strange, unlike any other islands in the world. No one who went there ever forgot them. For the *Beagle* this was just another port of call in a very long voyage, but for Darwin it was much more than that, for it was here, in the most unexpected way — just as a man might have a sudden inspiration while he is travelling in a car or a train — that he began to form a coherent view of the evolution of life on this planet.

• The best college text on all aspects of evolution, especially genetics. **Evolutionary Biology:** Eli C. Minkoff, 1983; 627 pp. **$35.95** postpaid from Addison-Wesley Publishing Co., 1 Jacob Way, Reading, MA 01867.

• An interesting analysis of current problems in evolution. **The Problems of Evolution:** Mark Ridley, 1985; 160 pp. **$8.95** postpaid from Oxford University Press, 16-00 Pollitt Drive, Fair Lawn, NJ 07410.

Raw material for the atmosphere. Mayon volcano in the Philippines spews gasses into the atmosphere. Volcanic gasses are the major source of carbon, nitrogen, and sulfur for the atmosphere over geologic time. —*Ecology*

"ECOLOGY" HAS COME TO MEAN just about anything. Doom-gloom to the end-of-the-worlders. Mystical harmony to the religio-eco-freaks. Grants to the college crowd. The word comes from Greek: "Oikos" and "Logos." "Oikos" means house, or dwelling-place. "Logos" primarily means discourse, or "word, thought or speech." To the early Greeks, "logos" was the moving and regulating principle in things (associated with fire-energy), as well as the part of human nature that was able to see this ordering energy at work.

Ecology, at its root and origin, means domestic chatter; talking about where-you-live; feeling out the household rules; remaining open and perceptive to the moving and regulating principle of your watershed and/or planet home.

—Peter Warshall

Why Big Fierce Animals Are Rare

Ecology is having a kind of personality crisis at the moment . . . feeling bewildered . . . searching for new harmonies amid the raucousness of Nature's wild ways. It is a healthy time. Some even question if there is really a "system" in ecosystem. Life is certainly viewed as more complex than simple parallel, melodic lines — like a Bach canon — of foxes and rabbits.

— Ecologists must face the new metaphors of music: Nature as a 16-track multi-mix; African polyrhythms; raga modes or natural dissonance. New, less deterministic harmonies of community ecology await human expression. The new music will give great weight to the invisible, for example, special types of plant biotechnology like C3, C4 and CAM metabolism; to a karmic biogeochemistry of each community's soils and to the ability of some bacteria and pigeons to orient to their community by magnetism.

Until then, Colinvaux's **Why Big Fierce Animals Are Rare** *is the only literate book to confront fashionable math and information theory with naturalist news.*

—Peter Warshall

•

Why should large animals, particularly large hunting animals, always be so amazingly rare? . . . It took nearly twenty years for the corporate body of science to come up with the answer to the question . . . by thinking of food and bodies as calories rather than as flesh.

The ultimate furnace of life is the sun, streaming down calories of heat with never-fainting ray. On every usable scrap of the earth's surface a plant is staked out to catch the light. In those green transducers we call leaves, the plants synthesize fuel. Animals eat those plants, but they do not get all the plant tissue, as we know because the earth is carpeted brown with rotting debris that has not been part of an animal's dinner. Nor can the animals ever get the fuel the plants have already burned. So there cannot be as much animal flesh on the earth as there is plant flesh.

This would be true even if all animals were vegetarian. But they are not. For flesh eaters, the largest possible supply of food calories they can obtain is a fraction of the bodies of their plant-eating prey. If one is higher still on the food chain, an eater of a flesh-eater's flesh, one has yet a smaller fraction to support even bigger and fiercer bodies. Which is why large fierce animals are so astonishingly (or pleasingly) rare.

The grand pattern of life was clearly and directly a consequence of the second law of thermodynamics. We can now understand why there are not fiercer dragons on the earth than there are; it is because the energy supply will not stretch to the support of super-dragons. Great white sharks or killer whales in the sea, and lions and tigers on the land, are apparently the most formidable animals the contemporary earth can support.

Why Big Fierce Animals Are Rare
Paul Colinvaux
1978; 256 pp.
$7.95
($8.95 postpaid) from:
Princeton University Press
3175 Princeton Pike
Lawrenceville, NJ 08540
or Whole Earth Access

Ecology
Paul Colinvaux
1986; 725 pp.
$32.95 postpaid from:
John Wiley & Sons
Order Department
1 Wiley Drive
Somerset, NJ 08873
or Whole Earth Access

Ecology

The science of ecology has suffered from success. It can mean many things in the popular mind and seems to have emerged all at once as a full blown discipline around 1970. One of the best things this college text does is take pains to trace the evolution of ecology as a branch of science and explain the significant changes it has undergone since the early 70s. Colinvaux writes clearly and is sparing with the jargon and math unless absolutely necessary. He even offers several routes through his book for short-course browsers.

—Richard Nilsen

•

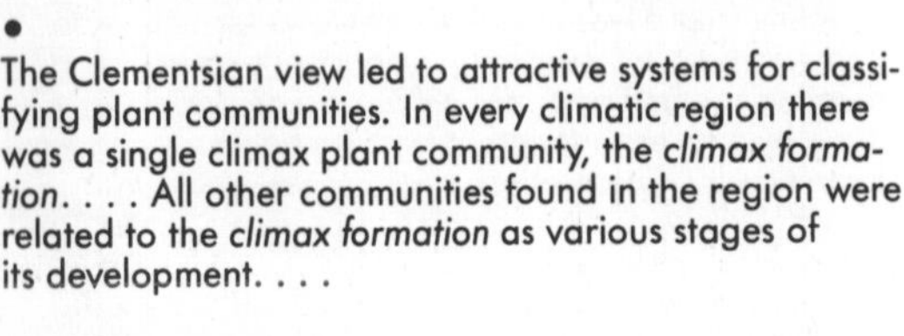

The Clementsian view led to attractive systems for classifying plant communities. In every climatic region there was a single climax plant community, the *climax formation*. . . . All other communities found in the region were related to the *climax formation* as various stages of its development. . . .

Essential to this point of view is the idea that a community is a *superorganism*, an entity of many species that has *emergent properties* of its own. Realizing that his *superorganism* drew some of its properties from animals as well as plants, Clements coined the word *biome* to replace the earlier *climax formation* for his ultimate community unit. . . .

Clements' work is still important because it lies at the root of many of the political or social movements that take their names from ecology in the present day. Whenever activists accuse their political or exploiter adversaries of "ecocide" they invoke Clements' teachings. They borrow from him the idea that the ecosystem of the climax is an organism, saying that therefore it can be killed.

The modern view is that succession is an inevitable consequence of the coexistence of plants with different strategies . . . Plants, like all products of natural selection, are individualists. This essential truth was argued strongly even in Clements' day, most notably by Gleason. But the final triumph of Gleason's *individualistic hypothesis of succession* came only with the concept of species strategies in the 1960s.

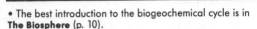

► **The vegetation at the edge of a pond in temperate latitudes. In the water can be seen floating leaves of water plants that are rooted in the bottom mud. In the wet mud at the edge is a line of reeds, and behind them bushes and small trees that grow in damp places. Well away from the pond, on drier ground, are trees of the local woods. This observation gave rise to the hypothesis that these successive kinds of vegetation were succeeding each other in time, as the pond filled with sediment and the encircling bands of vegetation constricted towards the center.**

• The best introduction to the biogeochemical cycle is in **The Biosphere** (p. 10).
• See also **Environmental Conservation** (p. 45).

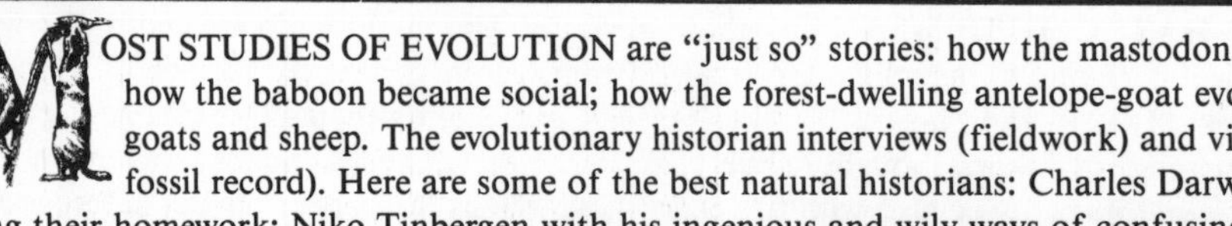

MOST STUDIES OF EVOLUTION are "just so" stories: how the mastodon got to South America; how the baboon became social; how the forest-dwelling antelope-goat evolved into all today's goats and sheep. The evolutionary historian interviews (fieldwork) and visits the archives (the fossil record). Here are some of the best natural historians: Charles Darwin and Konrad Lorenz doing their homework; Niko Tinbergen with his ingenious and wily ways of confusing and then revealing the lives of animals by outdoor experiments; George Schaller, the tireless note-taker of lions, tigers, and takins; and George Gaylord Simpson who trudges through geological time with careful steps and an eye to the present. —Peter Warshall

Curious Naturalists
Niko Tinbergen
1958, 1974; 269 pp.
$12.45
postpaid from:
University of Massachusetts Press
P. O. Box 429
Amherst, MA 01004.
or Whole Earth Access

Curious Naturalists

The best outdoor experiments on camouflage, finding "home," searching images for food, recognizing your own nest, and scaring your neighbors. —Peter Warshall

A field test on the 'visual cliff' — the chick is just turning away from the transparent half of the platform.

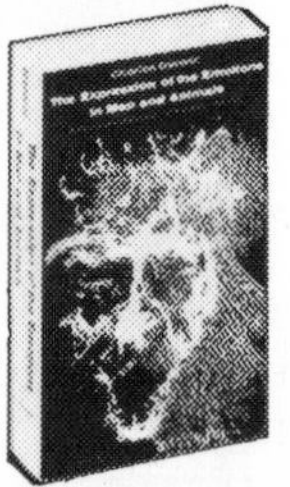

The Expression of The Emotions in Man and Animals
Charles Darwin
1873, 1965; 372 pp.
$9
postpaid from:
University of Chicago Press
11030 South Langley,
Chicago, IL 60628.
or Whole Earth Access

The Expression of The Emotions in Man and Animals

Are we less joyful than gorillas? Less fearful than baboons? Does each species have its own repertoire of emotional possibilities? Do some (the dolphins) express emotions we have no name for? Darwin started it. His followers prefer "aggression" to "anger;" "submission" to "affection." They copped out. —Peter Warshall

As the sensation of disgust primarily arises in connection with the act of eating or tasting, it is natural that its expression should consist chiefly in movements round the mouth. But as disgust also causes annoyance, it is generally accompanied by a frown, and often by gestures as if to push away or to guard oneself against the offensive object.

Splendid Isolation

The Whole Earth picture of changing animal forms and moving tectonic plates in South America. —Peter Warshall

◀ **Restoration of the typical astrapothere, genus *Astrapotherium*, from the early Miocene.**

Splendid Isolation: George Gaylord Simpson, 1980; 266 pp. **$10.45** postpaid from Yale University Press, 92A Yale Station, New Haven, CT 06520 (or Whole Earth Access).

Mountain Monarchs • The Serengeti Lion

Schaller's quest for the origin of sheep and goats and his quest to understand how lion society handles predation. Short-term, intense studies consider evolutionary heritage as well as present-day ecology. —Peter Warshall

Mountain Monarchs: George B. Schaller, 1977; 425 pp. **$12.50** postpaid.

The Serengeti Lion: George B. Schaller, 1972, 1976; 472 pp. **$12.95** postpaid. Both from University of Chicago Press, 11030 South Langley Avenue, Chicago, IL 60628 (or Whole Earth Access).

King Solomon's Ring
Konrad Z. Lorenz
1952; 202 pp.
$7.45
postpaid from:
Harper and Row,
2350 Virginia Avenue
Hagerstown, MD 21740.
or Whole Earth Access

King Solomon's Ring

The classic by the father of modern thoughts on animal behavior. —Peter Warshall

•

My friend Dr. Kramer had the following experience with these birds: he earned a bad reputation among the crow population in the neighborhood of his house, by repeatedly exposing himself to view with a tame crow on his shoulder. In contrast to my jackdaws who never resented it if one of their number perched on my person, these crows evidently regarded the tame crow sitting on my friend's shoulder as being "carried by an enemy," though it perched there of its own free will. After a short time, my friend was known to all crows far and wide, and was pursued over long distances by his scolding assailants, whether or not he was accompanied by his tame bird. Even in different clothing he was recognized by the crows. These observations show vividly that corvines make a sharp distinction between hunters and "harmless" people: Even without his gun, a man who has once or twice been seen with a dead crow in his hands will be recognized and not so easily forgotten.

• The clearest, action-packed version of our recent emergence.
Human Evolution: Roger Lewin, 1984; 104 pp. **$16.45** postpaid from W. H. Freeman, 4419 West 1980 South, Salt Lake City, UT 84104 (or Whole Earth Access).

• The most complete, textbooky textbook.
Animal Behavior: John Alcock, 1984; 596 pp. **$32.25** postpaid from Sinauer Associates, Inc., North Main Street, Sunderland, MA 01375 (or Whole Earth Access).

Vortex streets.

Patterns in Nature

This is a book in which, with a bunch of photographs, some clear uncomplicated text and an occasional number, you are plunged into nature's mysteries. I suspect that the route to the frontier need never be more complicated than this, but there are so few guides who can show you the way.

I wish the book were five times as long as it is because reading it is such a pleasure. There are eight chapters:

1. *Space and Size*
2. *Basic Patterns*
3. *All Things Flow*
4. *Spirals, Meanders and Explosives*
5. *Models of Branching*
6. *Trees*
7. *Soap Bubbles*
8. *Packing and Cracking*

—Steve Baer

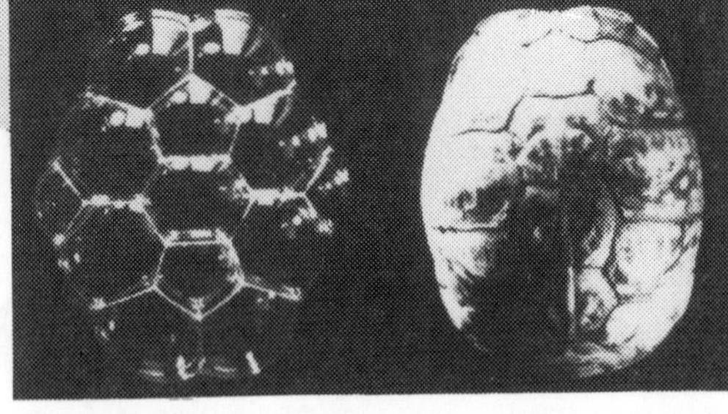

•

Shrinkage of surfaces allows us to understand the dramatic coincidence of form: why the shell of the box turtle looks like a regular cluster of bubbles. We know that the films between the bubbles minimize their area so as to join one another at 120°. The same holds for the lines between the plates of the shell. New cells grow along those lines and gravitate outward to join the edges of the plates. Consequently, as the plates increase in size, the lines between them keep to a minimum.

Patterns in Nature
Peter S. Stevens
1974; 240 pp.

$18.95
($20.45 postpaid) from:
Little, Brown & Co.
Attn.: Order Dept.
200 West Street
Waltham, MA 02254
or Whole Earth Access

Form, Function and Design

This book is wonderful. Here is a man trying to tell the truth about design and about our lives and civilization. I never heard of him. When I read his book I can't understand why not. *—Steve Baer*

There really is no better introduction to all that is admirable in design. Baer had to remind me of the book: I had forgotten how much I owe to it. It is full of the kind of lore and wisdom that you immediately take for your own.
—Stewart Brand

•

In design, the shortest distance between two points is not the straight line, but the slalom.

Slaloms are curves of natural acceleration and deceleration that represent trajectories *constantly controlled by man.*

A ballistic missile obeying only initial thrust and gravity will describe an orbit mathematically perfect of the conic section family. But as soon as man sits at the controls, he will make his own orbit, his *slalom.*

The Ganges Shark (Platypodon gangeticus)

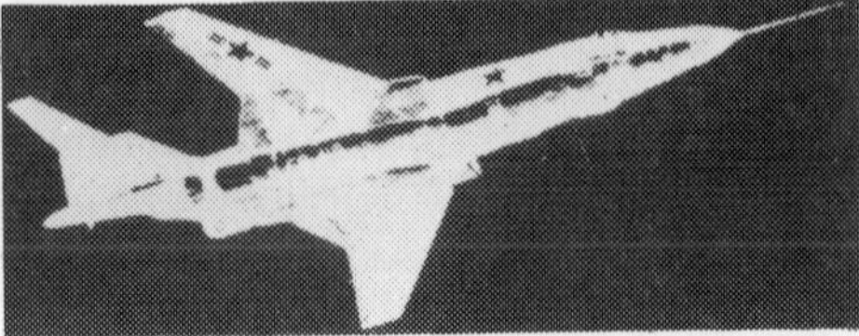

McDonnell Voodoo F-101A (1954)

Curves described by a man in movement — a car, a bicycle — on a flat surface, are two dimension slaloms, or curves of the second order that may be approximately analyzed in quadratic equations.

Form, Function and Design
Paul Jacques Grillo
1960; 238 pp.

$8.50
($9.50 postpaid) from:
Dover Publications
31 East 2nd Street
Mineola, NY 11501
or Whole Earth Access

On Growth and Form

A paradigm classic. Everyone dealing with growth of form in any manner can use the book. We've seen worn copies on the shelves of artists, inventors, engineers, computer systems designers, biologists. *—Stewart Brand*

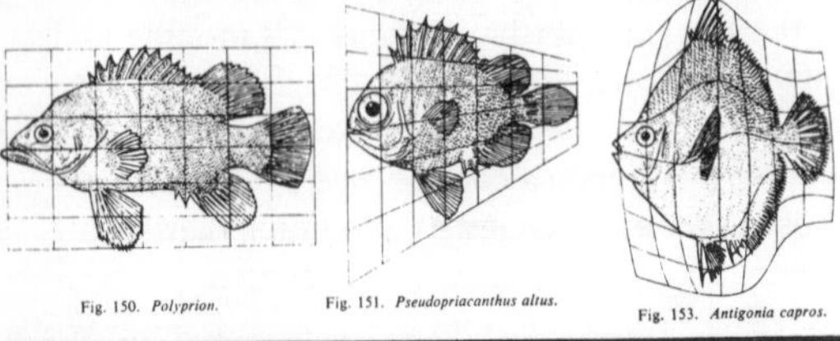

Fig. 150. *Polyprion.* Fig. 151. *Pseudopriacanthus altus.* Fig. 153. *Antigonia capros.*

•

For the harmony of the world is made manifest in Form and Number, and the heart and soul and all the poetry of Natural Philosophy are embodied in the concept of mathematical beauty. . . . Moreover, the perfection of mathematical beauty is such that whatsoever is most beautiful and regular is also found to be most useful and excellent.

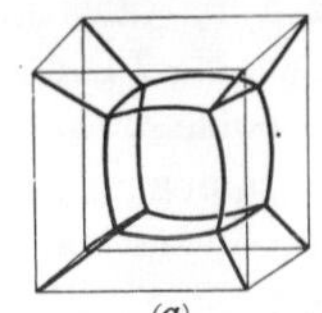

(a) (b)

Fig. 64. (a) Bubble suspended within a cubical cage; (b) *Lithocubus geometricus* Hkl.

• A somewhat technical, super-illustrated treatise on how bigness and smallness help and hinder living.
On Size and Life: Thomas A. McMahon and John Tyler Bonner, 1983; 255 pp. **$31.45** postpaid from W. H. Freeman & Co., 4419 West 1980 South, Salt Lake City, UT 84104 (or Whole Earth Access).

• A loving description of how animals find the materials and construct and live in their homes.
Animal Architecture: Karl Von Frisch, OUT OF PRINT.

On Growth and Form
D'Arcy Wentworth Thompson
(Edited by John Tyler Bonner)
1917, 1961; 346 pp.

$18.95 postpaid from:
Cambridge University Press
510 North Avenue
New Rochelle, NY 10801
or Whole Earth Access

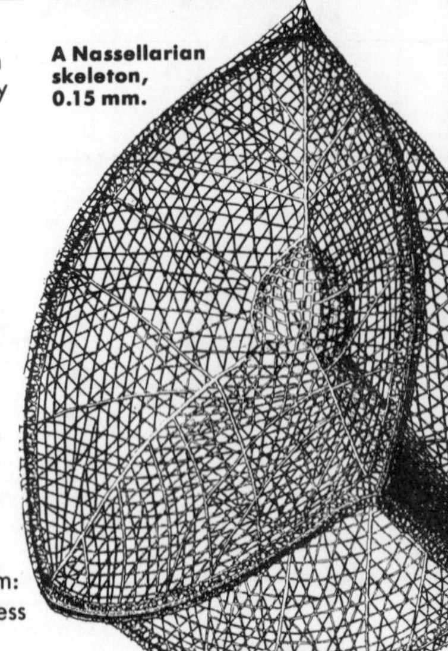

A Nassellarian skeleton, 0.15 mm.

"Although the river and the hill-side do not resemble each other at first sight, they are only extreme members of a continuous series, and when this is appreciated, one may fairly extend the "river" all over the basin and up to its very divides. Ordinarily treated, the river is like the veins of a leaf; broadly viewed, it is like the entire leaf."
—W.M. Davis (1899)

STREAMING WISDOM:

Watershed Consciousness in the 20th Century

By Peter Warshall

Stratification scheme for valley bottomland units.

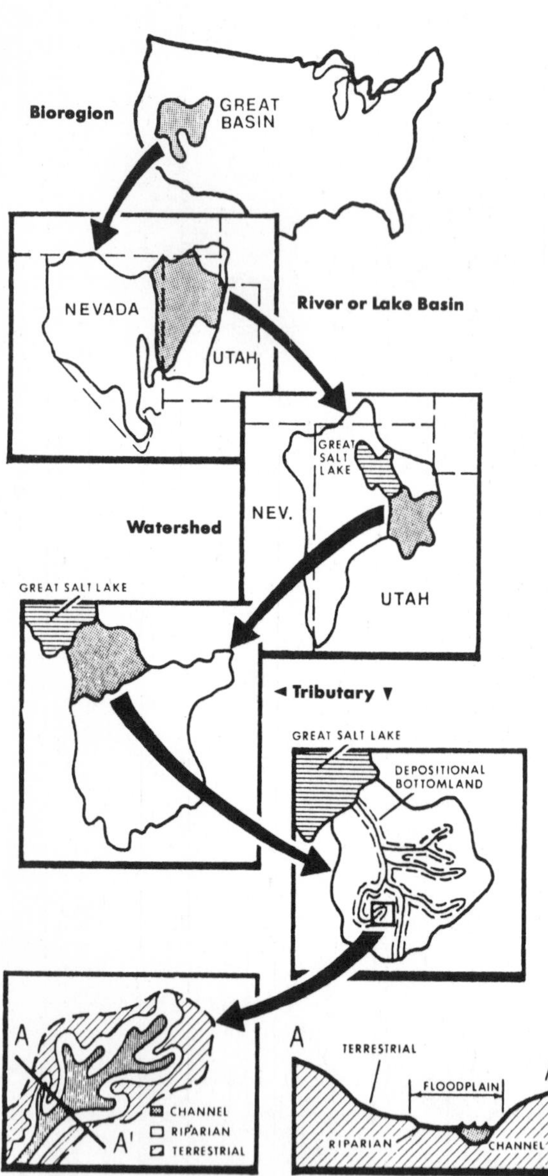

IN OUR TOWNS AND CITIES, two of the essential sources of life — water to drink and soil to grow food — remain hidden from our eyes. The hills and valleys are coated with asphalt, ancient streams are buried beneath housing, and soil is filler between gas, water and electric piping. Watershed consciousness is, in part, an invitation to peel off (not discard) the layer of industrial and technological activity that hides us from the water and soils of our communities. It is an invitation to reveal *where* you live and *how* your body's plumbing and, in many ways, community heart, are connected to Nature's pathways.

A watershed is a gatherer — a living place that draws the sun and the rain together. Its surface of soils, rocks, and plantlife acts as a "commons" for this intermingling of sun and water. Physically, a watershed takes many shapes. It is drawn emblematically in the shape of a teardrop or a cupped leaf or a garden trowel to depict the oblong dish-shape of the valley with its elevated hillslopes which gather runoff toward a central stream. But most watersheds do not faithfully copy the emblematic drawings. Uplifting or faulting or downwarping or layering give them a beautiful individuality. Human influences may distort or, as in city watersheds and strip-mining, completely destroy the original lay of the land. The bedrock texture of each watershed — its granite or shale, sand or limestone — holds (in a sense, cherishes) each watershed's fragile skin of soil. After the sun/water gathering has been accomplished, the watershed lets go: its unused water heading downstream or sky-up; its unabsorbed energy turning to heat or reflecting back through the atmosphere. This seasonal and daily passage of solar fire, water's flow, and the earth's metabolic breathing is as unique, in each watershed, as each human on the planet.

For humans, the watershed (and its big cousin, the river basin) is a hydraulic commons — an aquatic contract that has no escape clause. From the forested headwaters to the agricultural midstream valleys to the commercial and industrial centers at the river's mouth, good and bad news travels by way of water. Did my toilet flushing give downstream swimmers a gastrointestinal disease? Did the headwaters clearcut kill the salmon industry at the river's mouth? Did my city's need for water drain off a river and close upriver farmland that fed me fresh vegetables? Did a toxic waste dump leak into the groundwater table and poison people in the next county? Watershed consciousness is, in part, a promotional campaign to advertise the mutual concerns and needs that bind upstream and downstream, instream and offstream peoples together.

This journey is right out your window — among the hills and valleys that surround you. It is the first excursion of thought into the place you live. It is not inner geography — the continuing attempt to feel better by mapping the mysterious meanderings of our hearts and minds — nor is it whole Earth geography — the struggle to gain perspective of our place on the planet. It focuses on where your water comes from when you turn on the faucet; where it goes when you flush; what soils produce your food; who shares your water supply, including the fish and other nonhuman creatures. The watershed way is a middle way, singing a local song, somewhere close by, between Mind and Planet.

From *Landforms of the United States* by Erwin Raisz.

NO ONE HAS EVER TALLIED the types of watersheds in North America. There are probably about 75 basic "species." Here's access to the nitty-gritty of *your* watershed . . . its drainage pattern and density; its bedrock and soils; its channels and floodplains; its slopes and orientation to the sun. The best "dictionary" is *Terrain Analysis* which can also direct you to the best maps — U.S. Geological Survey topographics — and low-altitude photos.

To find maps, start with an "outdoors" store or look up "Photographers — Aerial" in the closest town or city's Yellow Pages. You can call the County and ask if they have a map room (especially if you need property boundaries). Many local and all university libraries have map rooms. If you're near the State capitol, it's easy. They usually have a staff cartographer. If still stuck, the USGS is the friendliest and easiest big government office to work with.

—Peter Warshall

Terrain Analysis

Probably too expensive for the average citizen. Go to the library. Xerox your watershed. Covers remote sensing; landforms and interpreting aerial photographs; landforms and development issues (highway, septic tank, groundwater, etc.); access to maps and photos; case studies . . . salt of the Earth. —Peter Warshall

•

The upper slopes of volcanic cones are visually sensitive, owing to their elevated position above the lowlands. Construction of roads on these slopes requires cuts which potentially could have a high visual impact. Many cinder cones and volcanic structures are regionally significant in size and scale and provide a regional identity, for example, Mt. Shasta in California or Mt. Fujiyama in Japan. ▶

Topography
Cinder cones

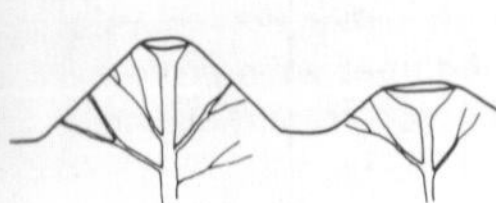

Rounded cinder cones are clear indicators of recent volcanic activity. Both mature and old dissected cones have some or all of the internal structure exposed, including the volcanic neck and radiating dikes.

Drainage
Radial

As the formation is dissected over time, a radial drainage pattern is developed around the circular volcanic cone. The texture of the pattern is dependent upon the climatic zone; the finest textures are found in arid climates. Many tributaries along the slopes appear parallel.

A typical profile of basaltic residual soil.

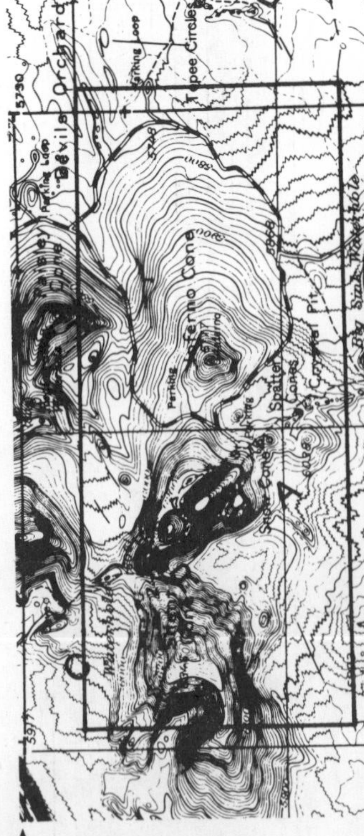

▲ **U.S. Geological Survey Map: Craters of the Moon National Monument.**

◀ **Young volcanic forms in Craters of the Moon National Monument, Butte County, Idaho.**

The Agricultural Stabilization Conservation Service (ASCS)

The ASCS has black-and-white photos for many seasons, with scales as large as 1″=400′. It's a branch of the Department of Agriculture with local offices in almost every county. (If you have no ASCS office near you, then contact your local State Forester or your County Extension Agent.) Request a photo by sending a map of the area (with the specific part you want clearly outlined) or the exact latitude and longitude. Ask for the scale you'd prefer or just the largest scale available. —Peter Warshall

ASCS Aerial Maps: 10″ x 10″ **$3**; 24″ x 24″ **$12**; 38″ x 38″ **$25** (all prices postpaid). Information **free** from ASCS Aerial Photography Division Field Office, 2222 West 2300 South/ P. O. Box 30010, Salt Lake City, UT 84130.

• What good are maps if you can't correlate them with the land you see in front of you? The skills you need are in **Land Navigation Handbook** (p. 272).

• For compasses, see "Camping Supplies" (p. 274).

USGS Topographic Maps and Low-Altitude Aerial Photographs

THE basic maps. Contour-lined for elevations, they come in two basic scales (one inch equals 2,000 feet, and one inch equals about one mile).

For maps by mail, write to the USGS in Denver. They'll also send you a list of USGS regional offices. —Peter Warshall

USGS Topographic Maps and Low-Altitude Aerial Photographs: information **free** from Map Distribution/U.S. Geological Survey, P. O. Box 25286, Federal Center Building 41, Denver, CO 80225.

Raisz Landform Maps

Erwin Raisz was perhaps the last great artist-cartographer. He invented little images of all the Earth's landforms and then drew delicate lines with an understanding eye and a hand for utmost clarity.

To place your watershed within the large context of its river basin, upstream and downstream neighbors, or bioregion, these maps are as fertile loam. —Peter Warshall

Terrain Analysis
Douglas S. Way
1978; 438 pp.
$48.95 postpaid from:
Van Nostrand Reinhold Co.
7625 Empire Drive
Florence, KY 41042

Raisz Landform Maps
Information **free** with SASE from:
Raisz Landform Maps
130 Charles Street
Boston, MA 02114

Craters of the Moon, at the top of the page, is in the Snake River watershed. The North Platte, flowing off the page to the right, joins the Missouri River.

WHERE ARE THE EARTH DOCTORS? Healing land requires diagnosing the problems correctly, spotting the symptoms of dis-ease, organizing the recovery, and watching carefully to ensure against relapse. —Peter Warshall

The Earth Manual
Malcolm Margolin
1975; 237 pp.
$8.95 postpaid from:
Heyday Books
P.O. Box 9145
Berkeley, CA 94709
or Whole Earth Access

The Earth Manual

Just like the man says:

"Between well-trimmed suburban lawns and the vast regions of mountain wilderness, there are millions of patches of land that are semi-wild. They may be wood lots, small forests, parks, a farm's 'back forty,' or even an unattended corner of a big back yard — land touched by civilization but far from conquered. This book is about how to take care of such land: how to stop its erosion, heal its scars, cure its injured trees, increase its wildlife, restock it with shrubs and wild flowers, and otherwise work with (rather than against) the wildness of the land."

A book of gentle advice and easily-absorbed wisdom. Great bibliography. —Peter Warshall

•

If your problem is bank erosion, there are several steps you might take.

First of all, stop all physical injuries to the banks. In particular, stop grazing animals (cows, horses and sheep) from breaking down the banks to get to the water. You may have to fence off parts of the stream and, if necessary, even build a watering trough away from the stream's edge.

Next, you can build deflectors. Deflectors are basically piles of stone placed upstream from an eroding bank to absorb the force of the water.

Rock deflector.

—Stream Conservation Handbook

Restoring Our Wetlands and Rivers • The Stream Conservation Handbook

*The Massachusetts Audubon Society's Water Resources publications are practical and philosophical introductions to protecting, preserving, and restoring streams. One of the many pamphlets from Audubon (**Wetlands and Floodplains on Paper**) explains how to use maps to save wetlands better than anything else we've seen. Write them for their "Water Resources Information" form. **The Stream Conservation Handbook** remains the best education for anglers wishing to take action against stream degradation. —Peter Warshall*

◄ A Vibert Box with five hundred brown-trout eggs incubating beneath the gravel of a spring creek in Oklahoma.

Salmonid eggs will not pass through ovular slots, but slot shape permits water circulation and frees young fry easily. Slot also prevents most predators from reaching incubating eggs.

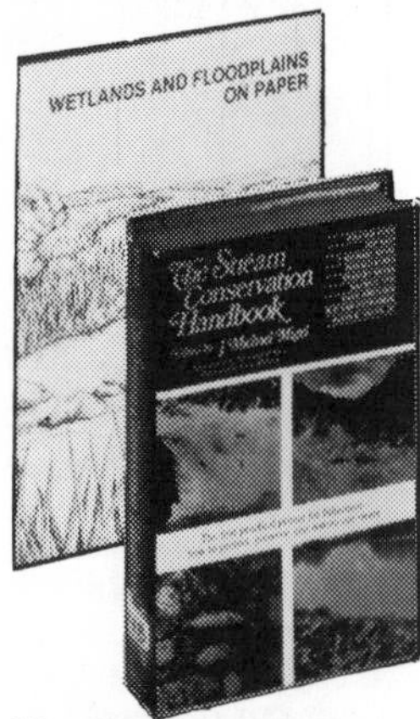

Massachusetts Audubon Society Water Resources Publications
Information **free** from:
Massachusetts Audubon Society
Public Information Office
Lincoln, MA 01773

The Stream Conservation Handbook
J. Michael Migel, Editor
OUT OF PRINT
Crown Publishers

Restoring the Earth

Breezy, thumbnail sketches of humans who spearheaded land and water restoration projects. Not a how-to-do-it book, but more like a rousing cheer, for the compassionate and caring U.S. citizens who are trying to do good for the Earth and its children. Stories include: cleaning a river and lake, reclaiming prairies, planting redwoods, and restoring strip-mined land. —Peter Warshall

•

Dominie plunged into the literature on lake restoration to find a treatment method. He discovered that a still experimental process involving the addition of aluminum in the form of alum (aluminum sulfate) to eutrophic waters had been used with apparent success on a few small lakes in the early seventies, but the largest of these were only a tenth the size of Annabessacook. Restoration of a 1,400-acre lake was "beyond the scope of existing technology," as one district staffer put it. Not only were those lakes small, but they were highly alkaline Midwestern lakes, unlike Annabessacook. Alum tends to acidify water. This was not a problem in the alkaline lakes, but it could be a serious problem in the waters of Lake Annabessacook.

•

How can more lakes be restored and protected? Each troubled lake needs to be individually assessed, and solutions have to be designed for each situation. Without the necessary funds, this is, of course, unlikely to happen. Controlling nonpoint source pollution is usually the most difficult lake problem to solve. To have a good chance of success, all activities in a watershed affecting its lakes and other natural resources need to be evaluated and vigilantly monitored.

Restoring The Earth
John J. Berger
1985; 241 pp.
$18.95
($19.95 postpaid) from:
Random House
Order Dept.
400 Hahn Road
Westminster, MD 21157

or
Whole Earth Access

• The watershed healing networker and giver of advice; all committed should read. **Restoration and Management Notes:** Bill Jordan, Editor. **$11**/year (2 issues) from University of Wisconsin — Madison Press, 114 North Murray Street, Madison, WI 53715.

• The best overall text. **Recovery and Restoration of Damaged Ecosystems:** John Cairns Jr. and Kenneth L. Dickson, Editors. 1977; 531 pp. **$25** ($26.50 postpaid) from University Press of Virginia, P.O. Box 3608, University Station, Charlottesville, VA 22903.

• The best technical text. **Bioengineering for Land Reclamation and Conservation:** Hugo Schiechtl. 1980; 404 pp. **$30** ($32 postpaid) from University of Nebraska Press, 901 North 17th Street, Lincoln, NE 68588.

Looking northeast up Barnard glacier, near the head of Chitina River, Alaska. —*Geology Illustrated*

Geology Illustrated

An artist of aerial photography, Shelton uses some 400 of his finest photos to illuminate a discussion of the whole-earth system. Not a traditional textbook, but a fascinating exploration of the problems posed by asking, "How did that come about?" Worth buying for the photos and book design alone, but you'll probably find yourself becoming interested in geology regardless of your original intentions. A masterpiece. —Larry McCombs

The Restless Earth

The new theory of the Earth accounts for earthquakes, volcanoes, mountain-building, and the formation of minerals in one comprehensive process: Movement of the plates of our planet's outermost shell. Nigel Calder is the best teller of the tale — though slightly out of date. Richly illustrated. —Peter Warshall

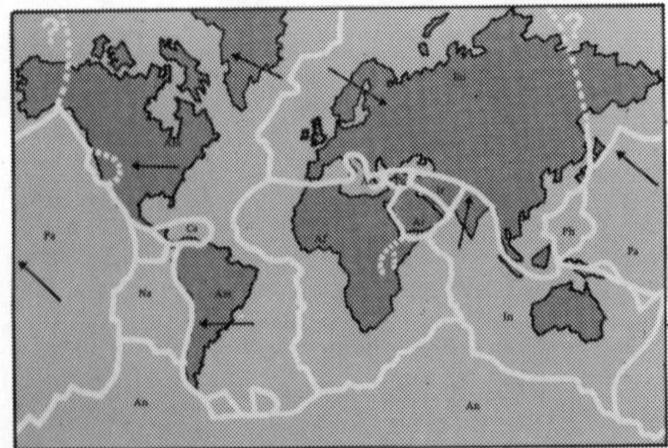

Map reveals the "plates" into which the shell of the planet is at present broken. They are moving in different directions, carrying the continents on their backs. The plates are rigid; major geological events are mostly confined to the boundaries between the plates.

Geology Illustrated
John S. Shelton
1966; 434 pp.
$29.95
($31.45 postpaid) from:
W.H. Freeman and Company
4419 West 1980 South
Salt Lake City, UT 84104
or Whole Earth Access

The Restless Earth
Nigel Calder
1972; 151 pp.
$9.95
($10.95 postpaid) from:
Viking Penguin Books
299 Murray Hill Pkwy.
East Rutherford, NJ 07073
or Whole Earth Access

Roadside Geology • Rocks and Minerals

The ***Roadside Geology Series*** *is one of the best for car nomadics. Coordinated with highway mileage markers, each book transforms endless roadcuts into millions of years of history. Each book has an introduction and vocabulary list. Turn off the radio and have your side-kick keep rock scouting.*

For roadside stops, the best field guide to examining rocks is ***Rocks and Minerals****, with an easy key and clear photos of rocks. —Peter Warshall*

Roadside Geology Series*
$9.95 - $13.95
postpaid from:
Mountain Press
P.O. Box 2399
Missoula, MT 59806
or Whole Earth Access

**Currently Available:* Northern California, Oregon, Washington, Colorado, Arizona, Virginia, Texas, Yellowstone, New York and Montana.
Soon to be released: Alaska, British Columbia, Georgia, Nevada, New Hampshire, New Mexico and Utah.

▲ Chromite bands in weathered gabbro (left), nodular chromite (center), hypersthene gabbro (right). —*Rocks and Minerals*

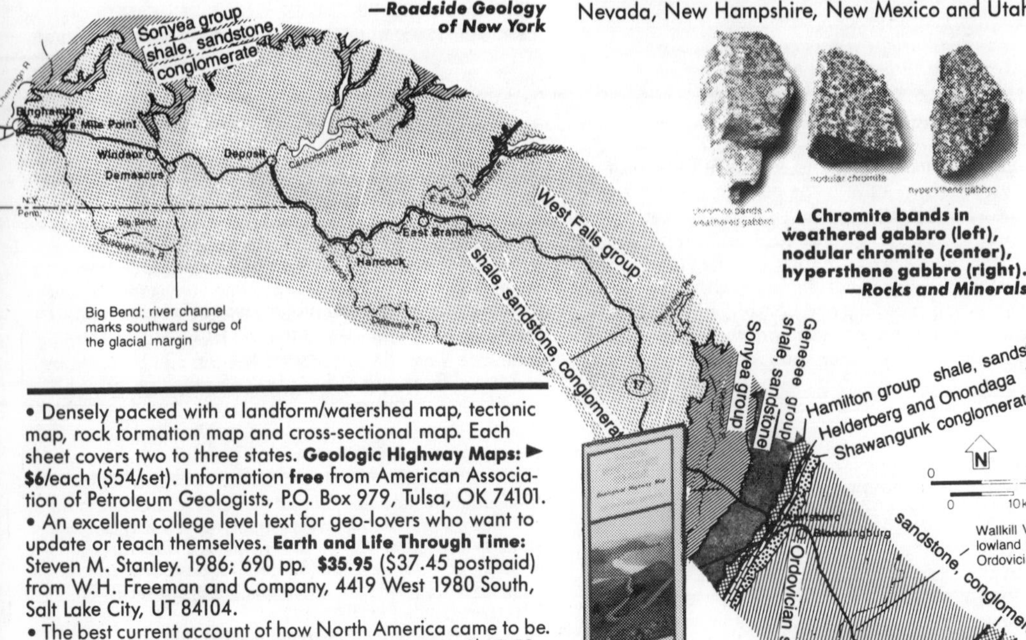

—Roadside Geology of New York

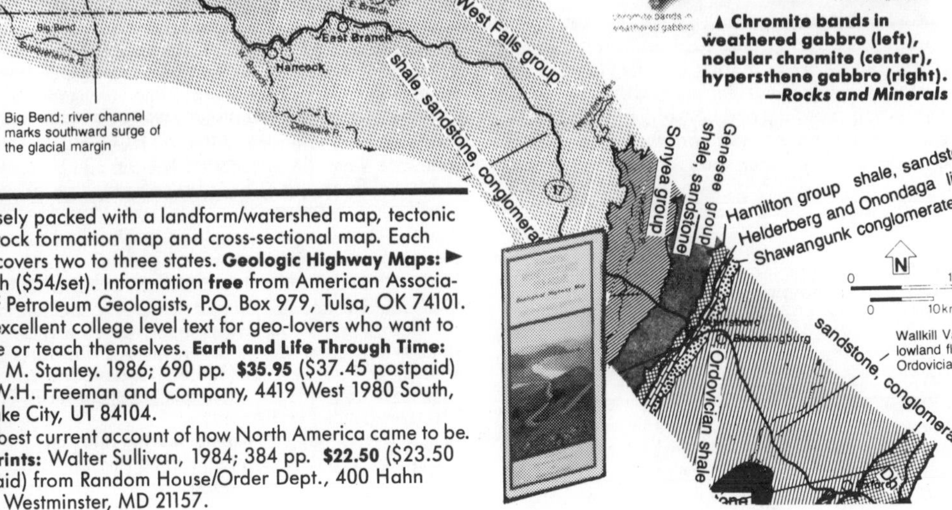

• Densely packed with a landform/watershed map, tectonic map, rock formation map and cross-sectional map. Each sheet covers two to three states. **Geologic Highway Maps:** ▶ **$6**/each ($54/set). Information **free** from American Association of Petroleum Geologists, P.O. Box 979, Tulsa, OK 74101.
• An excellent college level text for geo-lovers who want to update or teach themselves. **Earth and Life Through Time:** Steven M. Stanley. 1986; 690 pp. **$35.95** ($37.45 postpaid) from W.H. Freeman and Company, 4419 West 1980 South, Salt Lake City, UT 84104.
• The best current account of how North America came to be. **Landprints:** Walter Sullivan, 1984; 384 pp. **$22.50** ($23.50 postpaid) from Random House/Order Dept., 400 Hahn Road, Westminster, MD 21157.

Rocks and Minerals
Pat Bell and David Wright
1985; 192 pp.
$8.95 postpaid from:
Macmillan Publishing Co.
Order Dept.
Front and Brown Streets
Riverside, NJ 08075
or Whole Earth Access

▲ **In the open sea mighty vortices can arise in which the whole dynamic force of the suction centre becomes visible.**

Sensitive Chaos

The ways that flowing forms our heart, cyclones, rivers and bird flight. How we flowed as embryos and our bones still spiral and loop with the markings of past eddy movements. Here is spiritual guidance in the greatest book of Jungian-Taoist history. —Peter Warshall

Schocken Books has received numerous requests to reprint this classic book, they tell us. Look for a new edition sometime in 1987 or '88. Until then, go to the library. —Jeanne Carstensen

•

Together earth, plant world and atmosphere form a *single* great organism, in which water streams like living blood.

•

The activity of thinking is essentially an expression of flowing movement. Only when thinking dwells on a particular content, a particular form, does it order itself accordingly and create an idea. Every idea — like every organic form — arises in a process of flow, until the movement congeals into a form. Therefore we speak of a capacity to think fluently when someone is skillfully able to carry out this creation of form in thought, harmoniously coordinating the stream of thoughts and progressing from one idea to another without digression — without creating ''whirlpools.''

◄**When water flows through an opening into still water, the vortices form a rhythmical pattern.**

Sensitive Chaos
(The Creation of Flowing Forms in Water and Air)
Theodor Schwenk
OUT OF PRINT
Schocken Books, Inc.

Tao Te Ching
Lao Tzu/Gia-Fu Feng and Jane English, Translators
1972; 160 pp.
$10.95
($11.95 postpaid) from:
Random House / Vintage Books
Order Department
400 Hahn Road
Westminster, MD 21157
or Whole Earth Access

Tao Teh King
Lao Tzu
Archie Bahm, Translator
1958; 126 pp.
$4.95
($6.95 postpaid) from:
The Ungar Publishing Co.
370 Lexington Avenue
New York, NY 10017
or Whole Earth Access

Tao Te Ching

Taoists watched water; opened their hearts and minds to water's teachings; took water as an ally in understanding. Their aqueous attitude washed out preconceived notions of religious righteousness; dissolved rigid ways of viewing the universe; liquefied frozen ambitions, social convictions, ideals and hopes. The elegance of Taoism was taking humans from their everydayness but not to grace, being and nothingness, or samsara — simply to water, the liquid center of nature.

*The **Tao Te Ching** has many translators. Archie Bahm's is more fortune cookie than others. Orville Schell, who reads Chinese, recommends Gia-Fu Feng's translation. —Peter Warshall*

•

Nothing is weaker than water;

Yet, for attacking what is hard and tough,

Nothing surpasses it, nothing equals it.

The principle, that what is weak overcomes what is strong,

And what is yielding conquers what is resistant,

Is known to everyone.

Yet few men utilize it profitably in practice.

But the intelligent man knows that:

He who willingly takes the blame for disgrace to his community is considered a responsible person,

And he who submissively accepts responsibility for the evils in his community naturally will be given enough authority for dealing with them.

These principles, no matter how paradoxical, are sound.

—*Tao Teh King*

Future Water

If ever there was a need for circles, it is in sewage treatment. For centuries, we have taken our rivers, run them through our homes, added our fertile fecal nutrient, then run our sewage into rivers or the sea. This downhill, linear mind has been destructive to our land, waters and mental wholeness. This is a very important book written by two men who have dedicated a good part of their lives to looping city ''wastes'' back to farm productivity. For those interested in farms, cities, water, land, private vs. public sector politics, water and sewage bills, visions for a future structured with institutions that benefit humans . . . read it. —Peter Warshall

Future Water: John R. Sheaffer and Leonard A. Stevens, 1983; 269 pp. **$14.95** ($16.45 postpaid) from Wilmor, 6 Henderson Drive, West Caldwell, NJ 07006 (or Whole Earth Access).

•

The wastewater streams of our troubled cities contain tons and tons of potential resources, or raw materials. This valuable cargo is generally dumped, in whole or in part, into waterways and lakes where it reduces water quality, damages essential aquatic life and diminishes recreational opportunities. If these raw materials were reclaimed through circular systems and used in the production sector of the nation's economy, it would result in new sources of goods and services, and the current costs of conventional sewage disposal would be eliminated. From these reclaimed materials we can have fertilizer for growing food and fiber, methane to generate electricity and other energy sources, as well as clean water safe to reuse. Finally these investments in resources that would otherwise be thrown away can produce new revenues, which are badly needed to restore today's deteriorating water and wastewater systems. The job can be done by traditional financing of private ventures — perhaps organized as a form of public utility — to do for profit what the clean water laws of the 1970s failed to do through government construction grants.

• See what we mean by a great textbook. Academic in the best sense, with a deep reverence for water's ways.
Water in Environmental Planning: Thomas Dunn and Luna Leopold, 1978; 818 pp. **$47.95** ($49.45 postpaid) from W. H. Freeman & Co., 4419 W. 1980 South, Salt Lake City, UT 84104 (or Whole Earth Access).

• See also ''Household Water'' (pp. 138-139) and ''Watershed Care'' (p. 34).

SOIL IS THE STAGE from which all things — good, beautiful, vicious, creative, dull, outrageous and evil — emerge. A teaspoon of living earth contains five million bacteria, twenty million fungi, one million protozoa, and two hundred thousand algae. Amoebas slide over sand grains hunting bacteria. Bacteria swim through micro-rivers scarfing nutrients. Viruses attack bacteria. Nematode worms, like soil hyenas, devour almost anything. There are about 9,500 kinds of soil in the United States and no one has ever tried to create sanctuaries for any of them.

There is no single great book on soils; below we review the best of what's available. —Peter Warshall

◄ **Root system of a corn plant growing in deep open soil. Roots of crops such as alfalfa or of trees probably penetrate even further.**

The Nature and Properties of Soils
Nyle C. Brady
1984; 750 pp.
ISBN 0-02-313340-6
$27.50
postpaid from:
Whole Earth Access
(or order through your local bookstore)

The Nature and Properties of Soils

A college text on soil science. The writing is clear, there is a glossary of terms, and the section headings make it easy to find the information you want quickly. More facts than most people need, but well worth consulting on specific subjects. —Richard Nilsen

•

Of the six major factors affecting the growth of plants, only light is not supplied by soils. The soil supplies water, air, and mechanical support for plant roots as well as heat to enhance chemical reactions. It also supplies seventeen plant nutrients that are essential for plant growth. These nutrients are slowly released from unavailable forms in the solid framework of minerals and organic matter to exchangeable cations associated with soil colloids and finally to readily available ions in the soil solution. The ability of soils to provide these ions in a proper balance determines their primary value to humankind.

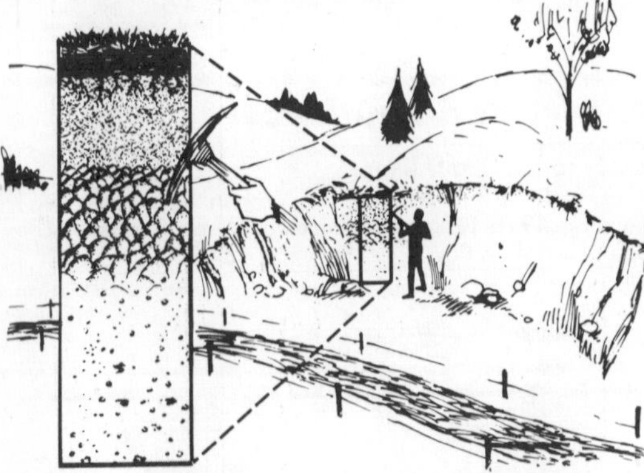

The closeup emphasizes soil layering and the distinctive character of the *soil profile*. The surface layer is darker in color because of its higher organic matter content. One of the subsurface horizons (point of pick) is characterized by a distinctive structure. The existence of layers such as those shown is used to help differentiate one soil from another.

• The best out-of-print book on soils, **The World of Soil** by Sir E. John Russell, should be available in most libraries and might be reprinted.

• For soils and civilization, gardening, forestry, and renewal, see the "Land Use" section (pp. 60-85).

Soil Conservation Society of America

*Over one million acres of prime farmland disappear in urban development each year. In the Great Plains and the Pacific Northwest, 85 percent of the farms lose five tons of their topsoil yearly. The Soil Conservation Society of America provides a meeting ground for all the specialized interests who are interested in preserving the ultimate strength of this nation: its soil. They publish a technical but, for my interests, totally absorbing magazine — **The Journal of Soil and Water Conservation.** It's a mature group, organized in 1945. —Peter Warshall*

Journal of Soil and Water Conservation
Max Schnepf, Editor
$25/year
(6 issues) from:
Soil Conservation Society of America
7515 NE Ankeny
Ankeny, IA 50021

Local Soils

Every citizen should be able to say: "I live on a sandy-loam that is about ten feet deep and covers half my community." Soil Conservation Maps are step one but are not detailed enough for some projects (like house-to-house septic tank assessment or gardening problems). Scales vary from one inch equals 1,320 feet to one inch equals one mile. Maps are available (for free, usually) from your local Soil Conservation Service (see telephone book) or write to the SCS in Washington, DC. —Peter Warshall

Soil Conservation Maps
Information **free** from:
Soil Conservation Service
Department of Agriculture
P. O. Box 2890
Washington, DC 20013

World Soils

This introduction to the soils of the world is complete with a brief course in soil science (pedology). A knowledge of what kind of soils are where, and why they are there, is critical for geographers, land use planners, and food-raisers. —JB

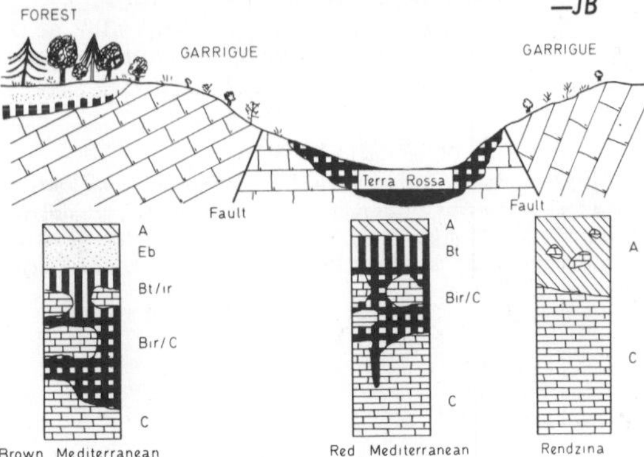

World Soils
E. M. Bridges
1978; 128 pp.
$11.95 postpaid from:
Cambridge University Press
510 North Avenue
New Rochelle, NY 10801
or Whole Earth Access

◄ **Mediterranean soils and relationship to landscape.**

Biology of Plants

Biology of Plants
Peter H. Raven,
Ray F. Evert, Helena Curtis
1986; 775 pp.
$39.95
($42.20 postpaid) from:
Worth Publishers, Inc.
33 Irving Place
New York, NY 10003
or Whole Earth Access

Peter Raven is the Godfather of American botany. This is his sequoian text. Though the prose tastes of leaf-litter, the information sparkles like a virgin tropical jungle at dawn. Everything you want to know and more, beautifully illustrated. —*Peter Warshall*

•

Comparing life on land with that in the sea, we find that only about 16 percent of animal species and perhaps 4.5 percent of the species of photosynthesizing organisms (plants and algae) are marine, even though the sea occupies about 71 percent of the earth's surface. The relative scarcity of marine species appears to be a reflection of the much less sharply defined habitats in the sea. Yet, more major groups are found in the sea than on land, probably because they evolved there. Only a few have been able to send successful colonists onto the land, but several of these — notably the insects and the flowering plants — have attained a truly spectacular level of diversity.

Hugo de Vries, standing next to *Amorphophallus titanium*, a member of the same family as the calla lily. The plant, a native of the Sumatran jungles, has one of the most massive inflorescences of any of the angiosperms. This picture was taken in the arboretum of the Agricultural College at Wageningen, Holland, in 1932.

How to Identify Plants

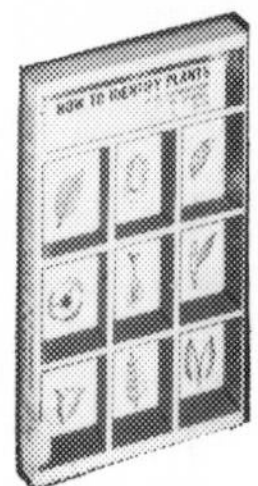

How to Identify Plants
H. D. Harrington
and L. W. Durrell
1957; 203 pp.
$7.95
($10.70 postpaid) from:
Harper and Row
2350 Virginia Avenue
Hagerstown, MD 21740
or Whole Earth Access

There is no easy road into plant architecture. Ovaries are superior or inferior; flower parts can be imbricate or valvate; surfaces can be scurfy, scabrous, comose, viscid, glaucous or otherwise. If you want to make the leap into botanical terms and use the more technical floras, then this book is the key to MONSTER VOCABULARY. Lists all the best technical floras by area. —*Peter Warshall*

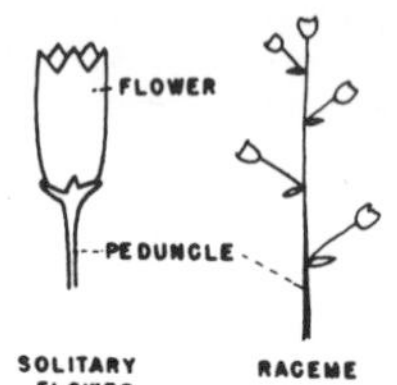

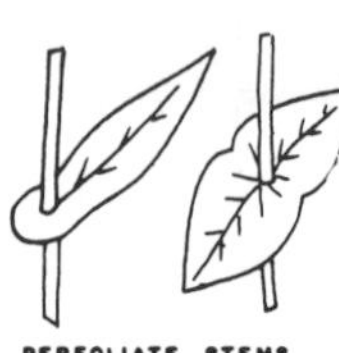

PERFOLIATE STEMS

Eastern Flowers

Arranged by shape and color. Over 1300 species with many line drawings.

A Field Guide to Wildflowers: Northeastern/Northcentral North America (Peterson Field Guide Number 17): Roger Tory Peterson and Margaret McKenny, 1968; 420 pp. **$10.95** ($11.95 postpaid) from Houghton Mifflin Co., Mail Order Dept., Wayside Road, Burlington, MA 01803.

By plant family. Best informed. Best color photos.

Common Wildflowers of the Northeastern United States: The New York Botanical Garden, 1980; 318 pp. **$12.95** ($14.95 postpaid) from Barron's Educational Series, 113 Crossways Park Drive, Woodbury, NY 11797.

Great car book. Arranged by color and season of peak bloom with color photos.

Roadside Plants and Flowers (A Traveler's Guide to the Midwest and Great Lakes Area): Marian S. Edsall, 1985; 143 pp. **$12.95** postpaid from University of Wisconsin Press, 114 North Murray Street, Madison, WI 53715.

—*Peter Warshall*

Western Flowers

Best overall guide. Arranged by shape and color plus fine photos and ID tips.

Audubon Society Field Guide to North American Wildflowers (Western Region): Richard Spellenberg, 1979; 862 pp. **$13.50** ($14.50 postpaid) from Random House/Order Dept., 400 Hahn Road, Westminster, MD 21157.

Arranged by color with some photos and excellent line drawings. Best nontechnical guides.

California Spring Wildflowers (From the Base of the Sierra Nevada and Southern Mountains to the Sea): Philip A. Munz, 1961; 122 pp. **$8.95** ($10.45 postpaid).

California Mountain Wildflowers: Philip A. Munz, 1963; 122 pp. **$7.95** ($9.45 postpaid).

Shore Wildflowers (Of California, Oregon and Washington): Philip A. Munz, 1965; 122 pp. **$5.95** ($7.45 postpaid).

All from University of California Press, 2120 Berkeley Way, Berkeley, CA 94720 (or Whole Earth Access).

Line drawings by simplified taxonomy. Titles include . . .

Pacific Coast Berry Finder, Pacific Coast Fern Finder, Redwood Region Flower Finder, Winter Tree Finder, and **Sierra Flower Finder**. Nature Study Guild "Finder" Series: **$1.50** each; complete list **free** from Nature Study Guild, Box 972, Berkeley, CA 94701.

Desert chicory —*Audubon*

Desert and Southwest

Totally corny! Totally thorny!

What Kinda Cactus Izzat? (Who's Who in the Desert): Reg Manning, 1941; 107 pp. **$3.95** postpaid from Reganson Cartoon Books, P.O. Box 5242, Phoenix, AZ 85010 (or Whole Earth Access).

A series arranged by elevation and flower color. Titles include

100 Desert Wildflowers, 100 Roadside Flowers of the Desert Uplands, Flowers of the Southwest Mesas, and **Trees and Shrubs of the Southwest Uplands.** Publications list **free** from Southwest Parks and Monuments Association, P.O. Box 1562, Glove, AZ 85501 (or Whole Earth Access).

For Mojave and lower Colorado an excellent guide arranged by color.

California Desert Wildflowers: Philip A. Munz, 1962; 122 pp. **$5.95** ($7.45 postpaid) from University of California Press, 2120 Berkeley Way, Berkeley, CA 94720 (or Whole Earth Access).

Knowing Your Trees

The encyclopedia of trees in America, with descriptions and illustrations. There are photos of leaves, seed pods, bark, and the natural range of each type of tree. Lovingly presented, in print for 50 years. —Lloyd Kahn
[Suggested by Rodger Reid]

Thick leathery leaves are light green, smooth and shiny. Small acorns occur singly or in pairs on stout hairy stems.

The mature Tanoak attains a usual height of from 50 to 75 feet, with a diameter of from one to two feet.

Knowing Your Trees
G.H. Collingwood and Warren D. Brush,
Revised and Edited by Devereux Butcher
1984; 389 pp.
$9.50
($10 postpaid) from:
The American Forestry Association
1319 18th Street, NW
Washington, DC 20036
or Whole Earth Access

The Great Forest

A history of our virgin forests and the ever-recurring conservation-preservation-industrial dialogue of America. A dialogue still fought bitterly though the acreage is vastly shrunk. I cannot recommend a book more passionately to those citizens in love with the scattered remains of our Great Forest. —Peter Warshall

The Great Forest
Richard G. Lillard
1947, 1973; 399 pp.
$49.50 postpaid from:
Da Capo Press, Inc.
233 Spring Street
New York, NY 10013
or Whole Earth Access

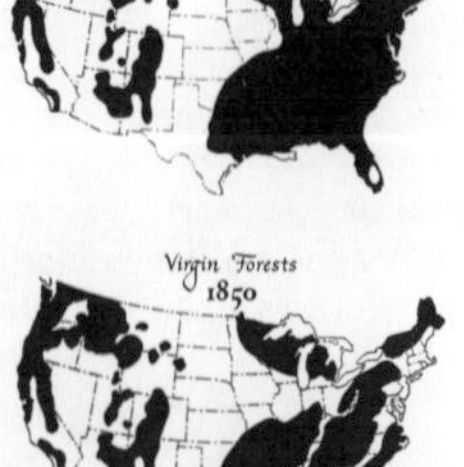

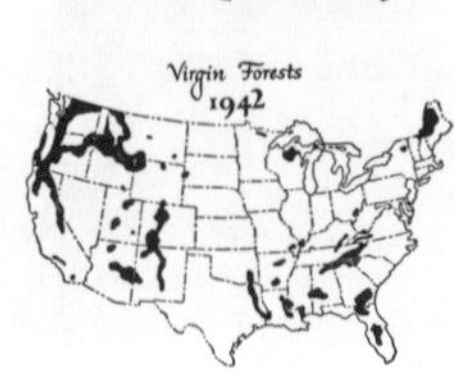

•
In 1882 Professor Charles S. Sargent, Harvard botanist, urged stringent state laws to protect forests in the Great Forest area, and outright Federal ownership and management in the Far West. He said:

> The American people must learn several economic lessons before the future of their forests can be considered secure. They must learn that a forest, whatever its extent and resources, can be exhausted in a surprisingly short space of time . . . that browsing animals and fires render the reproduction of the forest impossible; that the forest is essential to the protection of rivers; that it does not influence rain-fall, and that it is useless to plant trees beyond the region where trees are produced naturally.

With such arguments the nation fumbled toward its first major socialistic experiment since the Constitution created the United States Post Office.

Trees of North America

*The guide to travel with. Surpasses Peterson and Audubon for ease, drawings, and distribution maps. Keep in your glove compartment. For bare twig and dry leaf ID, the **Winter Tree Finder** (p. 38) is great fun.* —Peter Warshall

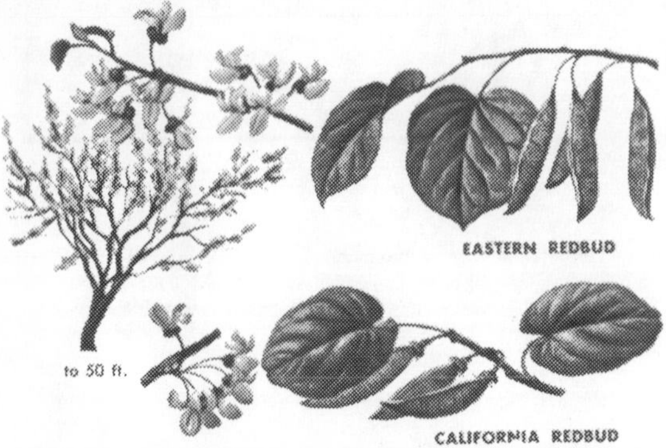

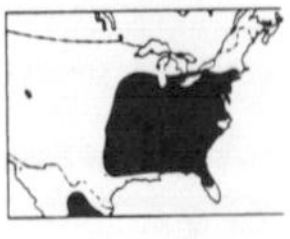

EASTERN REDBUD (*Cercis canadensis*) leaves are deciduous, broadly ovate to heart-shaped, 3 to 5 inches wide, with a pointed tip and smooth margins. Turn yellow in fall. Flowers pinkish to lavender, 0.5 of an inch long, in loose clusters of 4 to 8; appear before leaves. Pinkish, flattened pods, 2.5 to 3.5 inches long, have several seeds about 0.3 of an inch long. Bark reddish brown, scaly. Usually small, occasionally to 50 feet, with a broad, rounded crown.

CALIFORNIA REDBUD (*Cercis occidentalis*) leaves are round or notched at apex, 2 to 4 inches broad, with a heart-shaped base and smooth margins. Lavender flowers, 0.5 of an inch long, appear before leaves. Pods are dull red, 1.5 to 3 inches long and 0.5 to 0.8 of an inch wide. Though usually a shrub, California Redbud is sometimes a small tree, to 20 feet tall.

Trees of North America
C. Frank Brockman
1979; 280 pp.
$7.95
($8.95 postpaid) from:
Western Publishing Co.
P. O. Box 700
Racine, WI 53401
or Whole Earth Access

• Also see "Trees" (p. 62), "Orchards" (p. 63), "Landscaping" (p. 73), and "Livable Cities" (p. 113).

Fire in America

This book concerns fire, ecology, and mankind, and the history they have made together in North America. Nobody has ever written on the totality of this subject before, and while this dense volume may easily qualify as more than you ever wanted to know about fire regimes, fire-fighting techniques, and the history and politics of the U.S. Forest Service, it is a fascinating story and well told. And if anybody gives out awards for the best dust jacket photo, this book gets my vote. —Richard Nilsen

Fire in America
Stephen J. Pyne
1982; 654 pp.
$40
postpaid from:
Princeton University Press
3175 Princeton Pike
Lawrenceville, NJ 08648
or Whole Earth Access

Animals Without Backbones
Ralph Buchsbaum
1938; 1976; 392 pp.
$14 postpaid from:
University of Chicago Press
11030 South Langley
Chicago, IL 60628
or Whole Earth Access

Animals Without Backbones

The spineless wonders! —*Peter Warshall*

•

In terms of number of living species, 97 per cent consists of animals without backbones. We are all aware of the difference between these two groups of animals when we indulge in fish and lobster dinners. In the fish the exterior is relatively soft and inviting, but the interior presents numerous hard bones. In the lobster, on the contrary, the exterior consists of a formidable hard covering, but within this initial handicap is a soft edible interior. A similar situation exists in the oyster, lying soft and defenseless within its hard outer shell. The lobster and the oyster are but samples of a tremendous array of animals which lack internal bones and which are, from their lack of the vertebral column in particular, called *invertebrates.*

The giant squids are the largest of all invertebrates.

A jellyfish swims by alternately relaxing the bell, forcibly expelling the water from its concavity and so pushing the animal in the direction opposite to that in which the water is expelled.

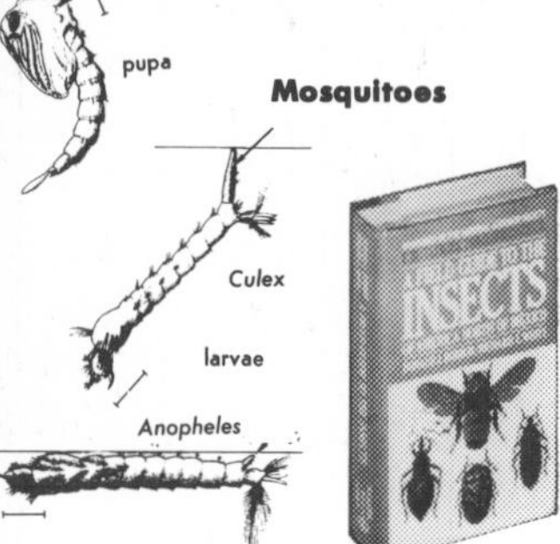

A Field Guide to the Insects
(of America North of Mexico)
Donald J. Borror and Richard E. White
1970; 404 pp.
$11.70
($12.70 postpaid) from:
Houghton Mifflin Co.
Wayside Road
Burlington, MA 01803
or Whole Earth Access

A Field Guide to the Insects

They may not make millions or drive BMWs, but the insects of the planet win top honors for biological success. Ninety thousand species inhabit North America: lice, earwigs, stoneflies, springtails, butterflies, beetles, thrips and bugs. This guide covers 579 of the insect families and has at least one illustration for each. Amazing! I have rarely found the exact moth or water scorpion but always came close enough to feel good. —*Peter Warshall*

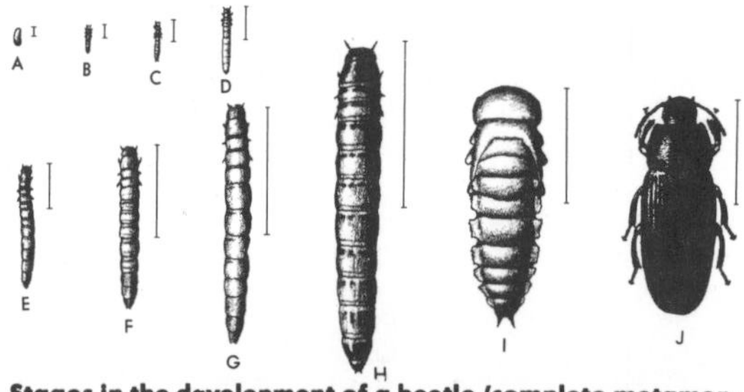

Stages in the development of a beetle (complete metamorphosis). A, egg; B-H, larval instars; I, pupa; J, adult.

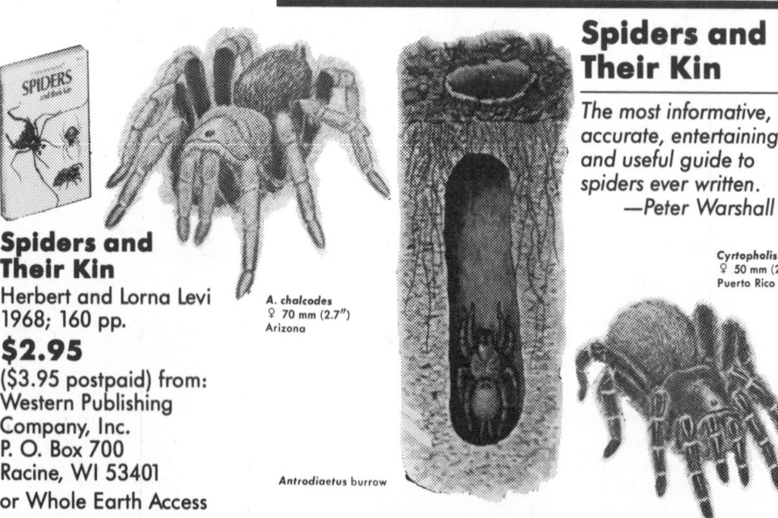

A. chalcodes
♀ 70 mm (2.7")
Arizona

Antrodiaetus burrow

Cyrtopholis sp.
♀ 50 mm (2")
Puerto Rico

Spiders and Their Kin
Herbert and Lorna Levi
1968; 160 pp.
$2.95
($3.95 postpaid) from:
Western Publishing Company, Inc.
P. O. Box 700
Racine, WI 53401
or Whole Earth Access

Spiders and Their Kin

The most informative, accurate, entertaining and useful guide to spiders ever written. —*Peter Warshall*

The Flutter-Bys Be Butterflies

Voyeurs of evolutionary eroticism! Uninspired artists! Urbanites seeking a sense of fragile, angelic loveliness! Buddhists confused about mysterious transformations! Here are the guides to North America's scaley-winged psychedelic nymphs . . . none better or easier to use. —*Peter Warshall*

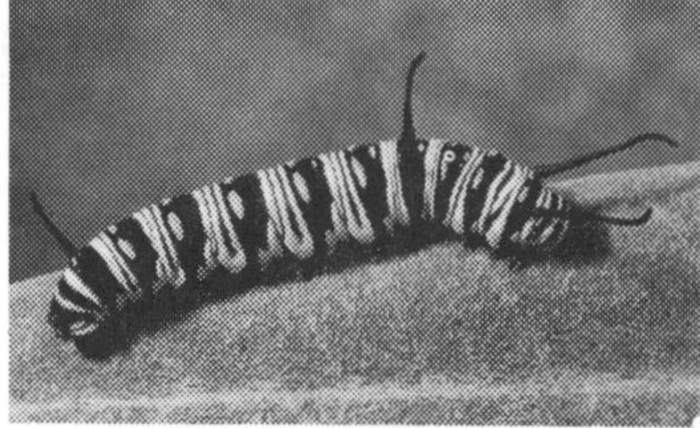
Queen caterpillar, 2''. —*Field Guide*

•

As a boy I sought Black Swallowtails on farmhouse lilacs, but frequented my neighbors' butterfly bushes for Painted Ladies. Add a patch of annuals — sweet William, zinnias, and marigolds for starters, and some phlox and aster — and you have a basic butterfly garden good from April through August. That's not all there is to butterfly gardening, but it is a start. —*Handbook*

A mating pair of Painted Crescents takes flight. The larger, stronger female carries. —*Handbook*

The Audubon Society Handbook for Butterfly Watchers: Robert M. Pyle, 1984; 274 pp. **$17.95** postpaid from Macmillan Publishing Co./Order Dept., Front and Brown Streets, Riverside, NJ 08075.
The Audubon Society Field Guide to North American Butterflies: Robert M. Pyle, 1981; 916 pp. **$13.50** ($14.50 postpaid) from Random House Inc., 400 Hahn Road, Westminster, MD 21157.
(Both books are available from Whole Earth Access.)

Yellow Bullhead, 18".

Banded Gecko

Field Guide to North American Fishes, Whales and Dolphins

Had it up to the gills with yuppie frenzy? Drop a line, cast, troll, scuba . . . go fishing with this fine guide . . . you might net a Freckled Madtom, see a Pancake Batfish, Blue Tang, Tautog or, with reverence, angle the Cutthroat.

—Peter Warshall

57 Yellow Bullhead
(*Ictalurus natalis*)

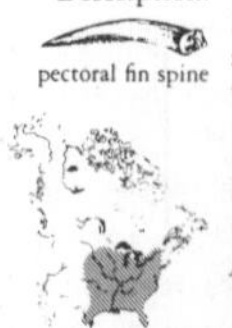

Description: To 18" (46 cm); 3 lbs (1.4 kg). Robust, heavy; back dark olive-brown; sides yellow-brown, *not mottled;* belly yellowish; fins dusky to olive. Head thick, long, rounded above; eyes small; mouth terminal; 4 pairs of barbels, *pair on chin yellow to white.* Serrations on rear edge of pectoral fin spine; *24–27 anal fin rays, base long, about equal to head length;* adipose fin present; caudal fin truncate to rounded.

pectoral fin spine

Habitat: Pools and backwaters of sluggish streams, ponds, and lakes; sometimes in slow riffles; usually in areas with heavy vegetation.

Range: SE. Ontario; central E. United States; widely introduced outside native range.

Comments: The Yellow Bullhead is a good sport and food fish. It is active at night, searching out food along the bottom by relying on its barbels and sense of smell.

Field Guides to Reptiles and Amphibians

West: Stebbins' guide is a combination of love, intelligence, and good writing. A model guide covering areas west of the Rockies. If you find something weird, it's probably a real discovery. East: Conant is older, less beautiful, but equally useful for areas east of the Rockies. —Peter Warshall

•

Geckos: Family Gekkonidae
A large family of tropical and subtropical lizards found on all continents and widespread on oceanic islands. Most are nocturnal and therefore limited in distribution by low night temperatures. Geckos communicate by chirping and squeaking. The name is based on the sound made by an oriental species. They are excellent climbers. They crawl with ease on walls and ceilings and are often found in houses and public buildings in the tropics.
—Western

A Field Guide to Western Reptiles and Amphibians: Robert C. Stebbins, 1985; 279 pp. **$10.45** ($11.45 postpaid).

A Field Guide to Reptiles and Amphibians of Eastern and Central North America: Roger Conant, 1975; 429 pp. **$11.45** ($12.45 postpaid). Both from: Houghton Mifflin Co./Mail Order Dept., Wayside Road, Burlington, MA 01803 (or Whole Earth Access).

A bullfrog, like other amphibians, is slippery. Encircle its waist with your fingers so it won't kick itself free. Any large or medium-sized frogs may be held in the same way, but small frogs are best grasped by the hind legs. —*Eastern*

The Audubon Society Field Guide to North American Fishes, Whales & Dolphins
H. T. Boschung Jr., et al
1983; 850 pp.
$13
($14 postpaid) from:
Random House
400 Hahn Road
Westminster, MD 21157
or Whole Earth Access

► Pattern variation in Western Aquatic Garter Snake.

So Excellent a Fishe

***So Excellent a Fishe** radiates chelonian love. Its beautifully crafted prose conjures an eerie feel — of eras of time with clouds and waves and turtles bumping onto shorelines in syncopated arrivals. Inside this intimacy one can almost believe that as long as this book remains in print turtles will survive in the sea.* —Peter Warshall

•

The green turtle was an important factor in the colonization of the Americas. It was herbivorous, abundant, and edible — even when prepared by cooks not aware that it can be made a gourmet's dish. . . . A green turtle was as big as a heifer, easy to catch, and easy to keep alive on its back in a space no greater than itself. It was an ideal food resource, and it went into the cooking pots of the salt-water peasantry and tureens of the flagships alike. . . . In England the green turtle came to be known as the London Alderman's Turtle, because an Alderman's Banquet was considered grossly incomplete if it failed to begin with clear green turtle soup.

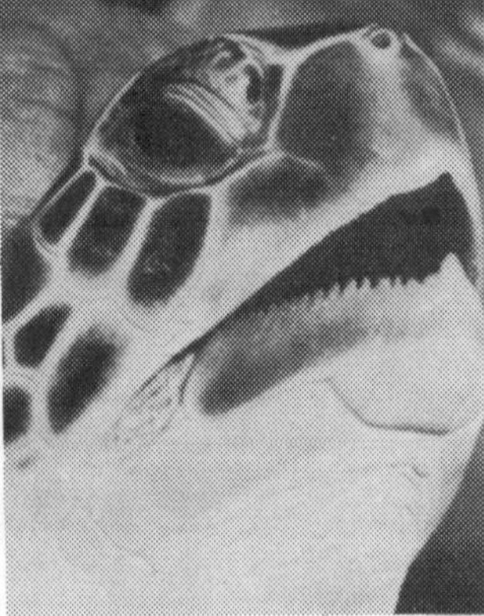

Young green turtle, showing serrated lower jaw characteristic of Chelonia and probably associated with the grazing habit.

So Excellent a Fishe
(The Classic Study of the Lives of Sea Turtles)
Archie Carr
1967; 280 pp.
$15.95
postpaid from:
Macmillan Publishing Co.
Front and Brown Streets
Riverside, NJ 08075
or Whole Earth Access

The Book of Sharks

As a novice scuba diver, living on a coast called "the White Shark Attack Capital of the World," I've been on the lookout for a good, unbiased source of information about these impressive creatures. Ellis has managed to cut through our "Jaws"-inspired hysteria without minimizing the real danger that does exist: sharks have been the oceans' top predators for over 300 million years; they are very good at their job. —David Burnor

The Book of Sharks
Richard Ellis
1983; 256 pp.
$14.95
(15.95 postpaid) from:
Harcourt Brace Jovanovich
1250 6th Ave., 4th Floor
San Diego, CA 92101
or Whole Earth Access

The reconstructed jaws of *Carcharodon megalodon.* ►

• See also "Fishing" (p. 251) and "Evolution" (p. 30).

• For more on aqueous environments turn to "Inland Waters" (p. 44) and "Coastal Edge" (p. 45).

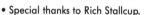

Field Guide to the Birds of North America
National Geographic Society
1983; 464 pp.
$13.95
($17.30 postpaid) from:
National Geographic Society
Washington, D.C. 20036

A Field Guide to the Birds East of the Rockies
Roger Tory Peterson
1980; 384 pp.
$11.95
($12.95 postpaid) from:
Houghton Mifflin Co.
Mail Order Dept.
Wayside Road
Burlington, MA 01803
or Whole Earth Access

Audubon Encyclopedia of North American Birds
John K. Terres
1980; 1,280 pp.
$75.50
postpaid from:
Random House
Order Dept.
400 Hahn Road
Westminster, MD 21157
or Whole Earth Access

Field Guide to the Birds of North America • A Field Guide to the Birds East of the Rockies

After much comparison and birder chit-chat, I accept the **National Geographic Field Guide to the Birds of North America** *as the best on the market. Without writing a book about bird books, here are the essentials:*

In the eastern region, beginners should use the familiar **Field Guide to the Birds East of the Rockies** *by Roger T. Peterson (although it has its own problems). The* **Geographic** *guide is too jargony, too full of casual or vagrant species which unnecessarily distract the novice. And it lacks good comparison pages (for fall warblers, for instance). In the western region, the* **Geographic** *leads the V-flight. It has some good pictures of western races found in no other guide and is excellent on western gulls. For experienced birders who will try to identify everything — including the vagrants, the shearwaters, and the immatures — the* **Geographic** *guide replaces the Golden Guide* **Birds**, *by Herbert S. Zim and Ira N. Gabrielson (another standard), as well as* **Peterson**.

The **Geographic** *book is not available through commercial booksellers and must be purchased from National Geographic or at select nature stores like your local Audubon education center.* —*Peter Warshall*
[Suggested by Captain Walker]

•

Pileated Woodpecker *Dryocopus pileatus*
. . . Pileated is the largest woodpecker commonly seen. Female's red cap is less extensive than in male. Juvenile plumage, held briefly, resembles adult but is paler overall. Call is a loud, rising and falling *wuck-a-wuck-a-wuck-a*, similar to Flicker. Generally uncommon and localized throughout much of its range; prefers dense, mature forest; but also seems to be adapting to human encroachment. . . . Listen for its slow, resounding hammering; look for the long rectangular or oval holes it excavates. Carpenter ants in fallen trees and stumps are its major food.
—*National Geographic*

Dawn Songs

No field guide or record can substitute for being out there and in tune with our avian cousins. But, like the guides, records (especially by region or bird family) can help. For those who know, a bird heard is a bird seen.

Free catalog. Best access to records coordinated with field guides and other birdomania.

Cornell University Laboratory of Ornithology: catalog **free** from 159 Sapsucker Woods Road, Ithaca, NY 14850.

Most records have minuscule cuts. These don't. Long choruses of frogs and operatic birds.

Droll Yankees: catalog **free** from Mill Road, Foster, RI 02825
Ara Records: catalog **free** from P. O. Box 12347, Gainesville, FL 32604.

Brown Pelican fishing.
—***Watching Birds***

More Than Names

Nature is much more than knowing names of birds. Nature has its own theater of voices, gestures, rages, intimacies, and power. Too many times, a birder will see a bird, check it off and ask: "What's next?"

"Next" is learning the vocabulary, lifestyle and concerns of each creature by patiently paying attention. Stoke's **Guide to Bird Behavior** *shows 25 common birds (mostly eastern), their territory, courtship, songs, seasonal movements, nests, and plumages. A true pleasure for those who feed birds.* **Watching Birds** *fields the gap between "sport-birding" and heavy ornithological texts. Concise summaries of giant notions help you see more richly.* **The Audubon Society Encyclopedia of North American Birds** *is the avian Brittanica, answering the questions that pop up outdoors. Expensively the best.* —*Peter Warshall*

A Guide to Bird Behavior: Donald W. Stokes, 1979; 336 pp. **$8.95** ($9.95 postpaid) from Little, Brown and Company, 200 West Street, Waltham, MA 02154 (or Whole Earth Access).
Watching Birds: Roger F. Pasquier, 1977; 301 pp. **$9.70** ($10.70 postpaid) from Houghton Mifflin Company/Mail Order Dept., Wayside Road, Burlington, MA 01803 (or Whole Earth Access).

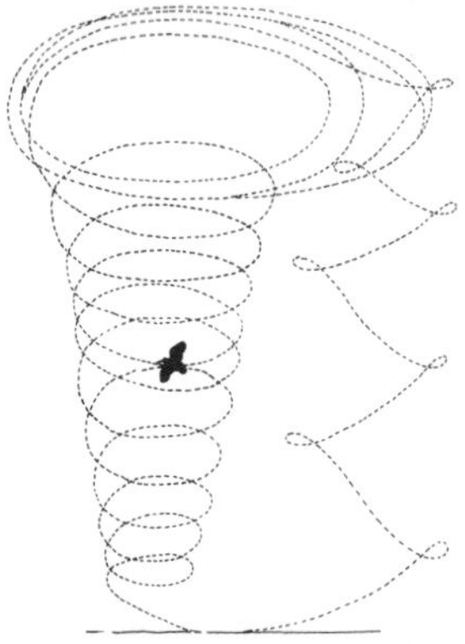

•
The woodcock begins his courtship flight by leaping from the ground and ascending in a widening spiral to about 300 feet, where he circles while singing and then begins his descent, zigzagging like a falling leaf.
—*Audubon*

◄ Distraction display: a killdeer's simulation of a broken wing draws an intruder away from its nest.
—*Audubon*

• Special thanks to Rich Stallcup.

• Best overview of all the families of birds. Covers the planet.
Families of Birds: Oliver L. Austin, Jr., 1985; 200 pp. **$7.95** ($8.95 postpaid) from Western Publishing Co., P. O. Box 700, Racine, WI 53401.

• See also **Evolutionary Biology** (p. 28).

• See page 44 for endangered members of the backboned elite of the Animal Kingdom.

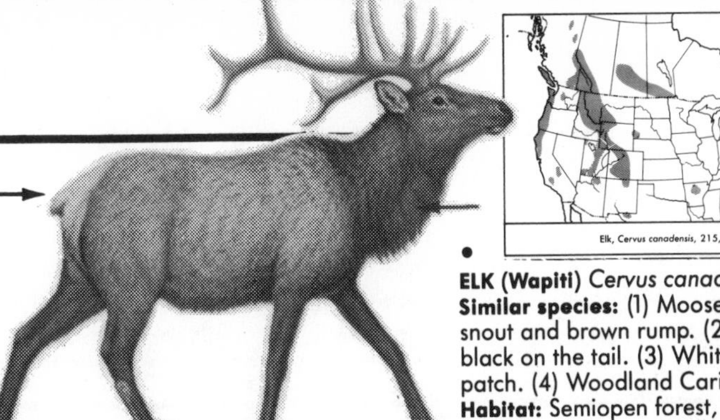

Elk, Cervus canadensis, 215, **Pl. 22**

•

ELK (Wapiti) *Cervus canadensis*
Similar species: (1) Moose has a large overhanging snout and brown rump. (2) Mule Deer is smaller and has black on the tail. (3) Whitetail Deer is smaller; no rump patch. (4) Woodland Caribou has whitish neck.
Habitat: Semiopen forest, mt. meadows (in summer), foothills, plains, and valleys. —*Mammals*

The Peterson Guides

The best guides to our tit-sucking, warm-blooded, hairy compatriots in North America belong to the Peterson Series. ***Animal Tracks*** *is the best-written Peterson Guide . . . good ol' backwoods detail . . . chewed branch, yesterday's scat, a chickaree's scolding, a javelina's stench. Since most mammals like the night, it is the signs that best inform. Murie includes bird, snake, and insect signs you'll find while tracking mammals.*

Although the drawings are mediocre in ***A Field Guide to the Mammals*** *(at least, the color plate reproductions), this is the best general guide to all of North America. I found difficulties with the subdivisions and descriptions of the Rocky Mountain chipmunks but, by using the annotated bibliography, you can get the needed details. Great section on skulls and many footprint diagrams.*

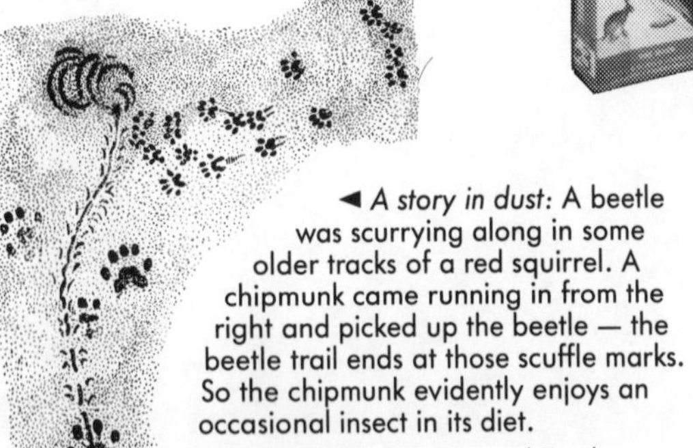

◄ *A story in dust:* A beetle was scurrying along in some older tracks of a red squirrel. A chipmunk came running in from the right and picked up the beetle — the beetle trail ends at those scuffle marks. So the chipmunk evidently enjoys an occasional insect in its diet.

—*A Field Guide to Animal Tracks*

For Mexico, use Aldo Starker Leopold's ***Wildlife of Mexico*** *(1959; $29.65 from University of California Press, 2223 Fulton Street, Berkeley, CA 94720).* —*Peter Warshall*

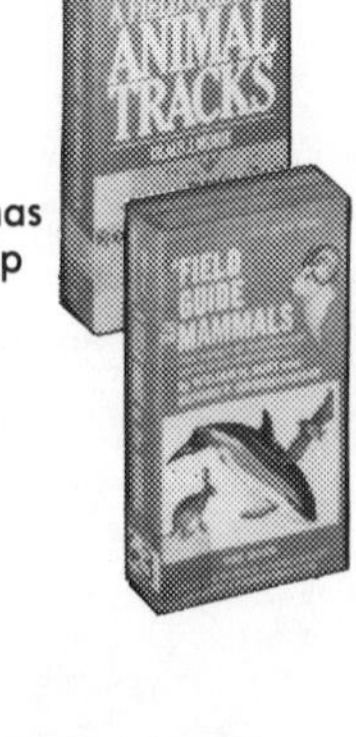

A Field Guide to Animal Tracks
Olaus J. Murie
1974; 376 pp.

A Field Guide to the Mammals
William H. Burt and Richard P. Grossenheider
1976; 289 pp.

$10.45 each
($11.45 postpaid) from:
Houghton Mifflin Co.
Mail Order Dept.
Wayside Road
Burlington, MA 01803
or Whole Earth Access

Whales and Dolphins

You will probably never see 99 percent of the cetaceans described here. The few you will see probably will be in oceanaria. Strangely, it doesn't seem to matter. Just knowing that all that incredible variety of mammalian life is happening heals a loneliness — Melville's marine melancholia of the arid seas. Not since Mark Twain personally funded Scammon's 1870s expedition has such a fine book of cetacean portraits and scholarship appeared.
—*Peter Warshall*

•

At sea, blue whales may be confused with fin whales and sei whales. Adult blue whales should be easy to distinguish by size alone from immature finbacks and from sei whales of any age. Fin whales are an even gray on the back and white on the ventrum, with asymmetrical head coloration; the right lower lip is white, the left gray. Also, they tend to have a sharper, more V-shaped head, and a comparatively prominent dorsal fin. Dead fin whales can be distinguished from blue whales by the gray to white appearance of much of their baleen, in contrast to the solid black baleen of the blue whale.

▲ Puget Sound is killer-whale country; sometimes these animals are seen in the shadow of Seattle's skyline. —*Whales and Dolphins*

The Sierra Club Handbook of Whales and Dolphins
Stephen Leatherwood and Randall R. Reeves
1984; 302 pp.

$12.95
($15.45 postpaid) from:
Sierra Club Bookstore
730 Polk Street
San Francisco, CA 94109
or Whole Earth Access

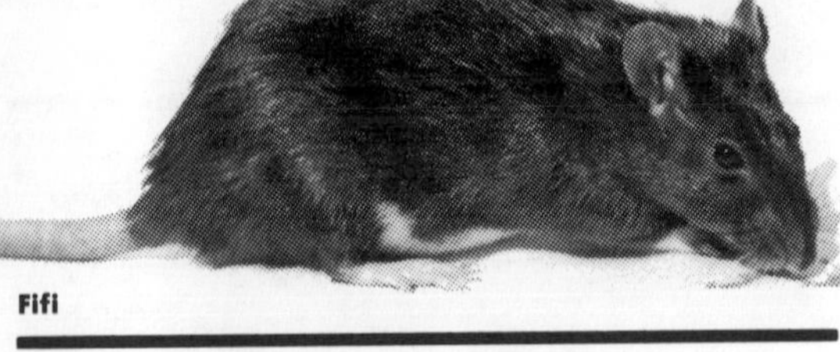

Fifi

Mammalian Celebration

It is amazingly easy to fall in love with a mammal, even Fifi, the pet rat here at Whole Earth. But few are the mammal lovers who can put passion in their prose. ***Never Cry Wolf*** *by Farley Mowat and* ***King of the Grizzlies*** *by Ernest Thompson Seton grab the task by the short hairs and hold on with aplomb.* ***Ring of Bright Water*** *by Gavin Maxwell (of sea otters),* ***Mice All Over*** *by Peter Crowcroft, and* ***Rats*** *by Martin Hart are three favorites on the "little guys." Less fun, but intriguing, are* ***In the Shadow of Man*** *by Jane Goodall (chimps) and* ***The Blue Whale*** *by George Small.*

There's currently no literate book on the Order of Mammals in print. Francois Bourliere's ***The Natural History of Mammals*** *and Time-Life's* ***Mammals*** *are both delightful surveys. The two-volume encyclopedia* ***Walker's Mammals of the World*** *has every living and extinct mammal (with photos of the living). It's technical, comprehensive, and especially for fanatic mammal patriots like myself.*
—*Peter Warshall*

• Many of the books mentioned here are out of print but irresistably good. Get 'em from your library.

Walker's Mammals of the World: Ronald M. Nowak and John L. Paradiso, 1983; 1,362 pp. (2 volumes). **$65** ($66.50 postpaid) from Johns Hopkins University Press, 701 West 40th Street/Suite 275, Baltimore, MD 21211 (or Whole Earth Access).

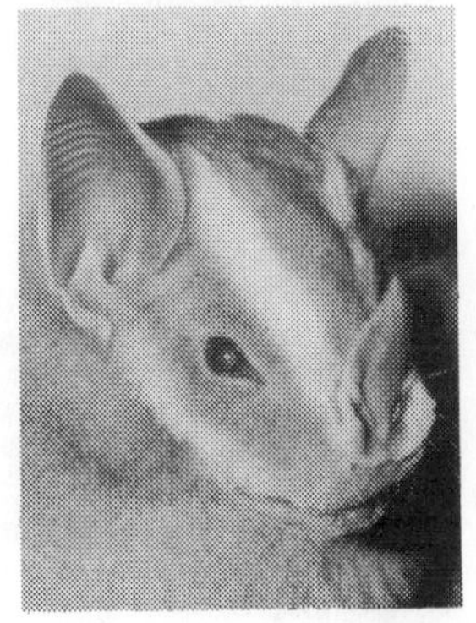

Great stripe-faced bat (*Vampyrodes major*). —*Walker's Mammals of the World*

During the Great Dying of the Dinosaurs one species vanished every 10,000 years. Species are now vanishing somewhere between 40 and 400 times faster. By the year 2000, perhaps one million species will have become extinct because of human influences on the planet. Compared to the Great Dying, this is the Holocaust.

There is perhaps no more noble or righteous employment on the planet than saving a living species (or its habitat). Try it. It's a world of smuggling, tears, beauty, petty bureaucracy, mockery, vigilance, money, and unbending vision.

—Peter Warshall

Furbish's Lousewort
—Wildflowers

The only recently known wild population of black-footed ferrets was discovered in 1981 at the base of the Carter Mountains, near Meeteetse, Wyoming. For four years, scientists trapped, tagged, and tracked the wild ferrets to ascertain their numbers and to learn about their behavior.
—Animal Kingdom

•

Because the Furbish lousewort has a funny-sounding name,/It was ripe for making ridicule, and that's a sort of shame./For there is a disappearing world, and man has played his role/In taking little parts away from what was once the whole./We can get along without them; we may not feel their lack/But extinction means that something's gone, and never coming back./So, here's to you, little lousewort, and here's to your rebirth./And may you somehow multiply, refurbishing the earth.

—Where Have all the Wildflowers Gone?

Where Have All the Wildflowers Gone?: Robert H. Mohlenbrock, 1983; 239 pp. **$15.34** postpaid from Macmillan Publishing Co./Order Dept., Front and Brown Streets, Riverside, NJ 08075 (or Whole Earth Access).

Vanishing Fishes of North America: Dr. R. Dana Ono, Dr. James D. Williams and Anne Wagner, 1983; 257 pp. **$29.95** ($31.95 postpaid) from Stone Wall Press, 1241 30th Street NW, Washington, DC 20007 (or Whole Earth Access).

Going, Going, Gone . . .

Where Have All the Wildflowers Gone? *and* ***Vanishing Fishes of North America*** *are extremely well-written, entertaining surveys of two groups of living beings that need allies. For specific species (bats, cycads, manatees, desert bighorns, salmon, peregrines, et al.), see the "Conservation" section in the index of the* ***Encyclopedia of Associations*** *(p. 309), where you'll find Defenders of Wildlife, the organization that keeps a report card on Congress and the administration's support for endangered species' salvation. In 1985 they received "D+."* ***Animal Kingdom*** *is the most thoughtful magazine on protecting wildlife in the Third World and the importance of zoos in keeping critters from oblivion.* *—Peter Warshall*

Unarmored threespine stickleback. ***—Vanishing Fishes***

Defenders of Wildlife: membership **$20**/year (includes 6 issues of **Defenders** magazine) from Defenders of Wildlife, 1244 19th Street NW, Washington, DC 20036. Information on individual species is available to members on request.

Animal Kingdom: Eugene Walter, Editor. **$9.95**/year (6 issues) from Animal Kingdom Magazine, New York Zoological Park, Bronx, NY 10460.

Our Magnificent Wildlife

An OUTSTANDING book, as we've come to expect from Reader's Digest. Not just a picture book, every page has some clearly presented new understanding, along with abundant encouragement for the reader to do something about it. The whole back end of the volume concerns making wildlife habitats in your backyard, photographing animals, and working with conservation organizations. This is the only book I've seen that tells preservation success stories.

Three cheers. *—Stewart Brand*

Our Magnificent Wildlife
The Reader's Digest Editors
1975; 352 pp.
$19.95
($21.64 postpaid) from:
Reader's Digest
Attn.: Order Entry
Pleasantville, NY 10570
or Whole Earth Access

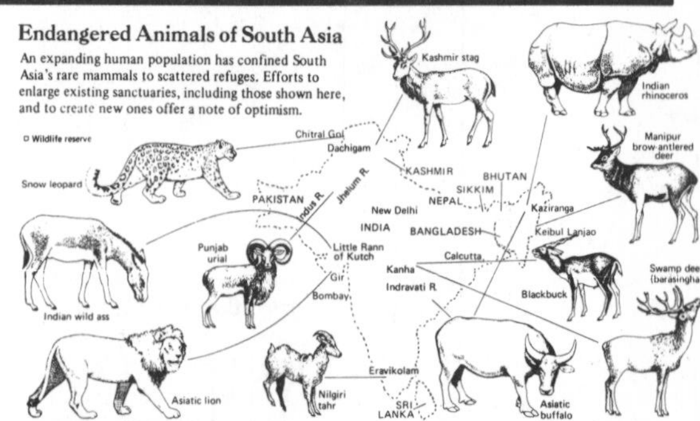

•

The overpowering impression of South Asia is people. More than 1,000 human beings per square mile are crowded into the Ganges Basin. The only hope for the survival of wildlife is in sanctuaries. But many existing sanctuaries contain villages, virtually all permit livestock grazing, some extract timber, and poaching is common. A comprehensive system of sanctuaries must be established in this generation, or the remaining lands will be swamped by the human tide.

• The most thorough account of how we've accelerated the extinction of species.

Extinction: Paul and Anne Ehrlich, 1981; 384 pp. **$4.95** ($5.95 postpaid) from Random House, Inc., 400 Hahn Road, Westminster, MD 21157 (or Whole Earth Access).

• The utilitarian argument: why extinctions hurt us and business.

A Wealth of Wild Species: Norman Myers, 1983; 300 pp. **$14.50** ($17 postpaid) from Westview Press, 5500 Central Avenue, Boulder, CO 80301 (or Whole Earth Access).

◄ **"An empty food bowl in Asia is not easily filled by wheat grown in the American Middle West."**

Environmental Conservation

This is the single most important text reviewed in this catalog — as true in Nairobi as in Anchorage — where I've heard young people talk of ***Environmental Conservation*** *with inspired hope that maybe, just maybe, the Earth could be a less aggravating, doomful, destructed place to be. Dasmann writes with a gentle, quiet passion always entwining the human, natural and spiritual worlds. Like all great teachers, his explanations are simple but not simplified. No fact about soils, food, water, industrialization, biomes, wildlife or thermal power remains unlinked. Each is connected by a deep understanding of the human needs to eat, be sheltered, and to feel themselves a part of a humane community. There is perhaps no other textbook that has survived as long (revised over 25 years) and spread so far into the school systems of the industrialized as well as Third World nations. Michelet said: "Education, Government, Religion. . . . These are the same word." Dasmann's text says it for the planet.* —*Peter Warshall*

•

Throughout the world, in prairie, steppe, pampas, and veld, ranges are still being damaged and deserts are encroaching on formerly useful land. The more productive ranges with high carrying capacities usually receive adequate care, but the more arid and marginal rangelands are frequently exploited with little apparent concern for the future. Abuse of rangelands carries not only the consequences of lowered carrying capacity and a diminished economic return from the land but affects all other natural resources as well. In some areas a valuable wildlife resource is destroyed to make room for livestock; the range is then damaged so that it is no longer suited for either wildlife or livestock. Such damaged areas are a source of erosion and disruption of watersheds, which can, in turn, affect still wider areas than those originally damaged.

Environmental Conservation
Raymond F. Dasmann
5th edition 1984; 486 pp.
$26.45
postpaid from:
John Wiley and Sons
1 Wiley Drive
Somerset, NJ 08873
or Whole Earth Access

A Sand County Almanac

The most important book on ethics ever written on American soil . . . honest, clear, graceful, superbly crafted . . . . It begins: "There are some who can live without wild things, and some who cannot. These essays are the delights and dilemmas of one who cannot." For Leopold, like Thoreau, human nature and nature's nature are inseparable natures and anything worth saying must be born from both. So ***The Almanac*** *exposes, reflects on, and strays into "values" that humans might cherish but it never strays too far from wildness, that teacher of many minds. In short, this is the bible of "oikos-logos" — the governing principle of our communal home — "ecology."*
—*Peter Warshall*

•

Thinking Like a Mountain

A deep chesty bawl echoes from rimrock to rimrock, rolls down the mountain, and fades into the far blackness of the night. It is an outburst of wild defiant sorrow, and of contempt for all the adversities of the world.

Every living thing (and perhaps many a dead one as well) pays heed to that call. To the deer it is a reminder of the way of all flesh, to the pine a forecast of midnight scuffles and of blood upon the snow, to the coyote a promise of gleanings to come, to the cowman a threat of red ink at the bank, to the hunter a challenge of fang against bullet. Yet behind these obvious and immediate hopes and fears there lies a deeper meaning, known only to the mountain itself. Only the mountain has lived long enough to listen objectively to the howl of a wolf.

•

The Ethical Sequence

This extension of ethics, so far studied only by philosophers, is actually a process in ecological evolution. Its sequences may be described in ecological as well as in philosophical terms. An ethic, ecologically, is a limitation on freedom of action in the struggle for existence. An ethic, philosophically, is a differentiation of social from anti-social conduct. These are two definitions of one thing. The thing has its origin in the tendency of interdependent individuals or groups to evolve modes of co-operation. The ecologist calls these symbioses. Politics and economics are advanced symbioses in which the original free-for-all competition has been replaced, in part, by co-operative mechanisms with an ethical content.

The complexity of co-operative mechanisms has increased with population density, and the efficiency of tools. It was simpler, for example, to define the anti-social uses of sticks and stones in the days of the mastodons than of bullets and billboards in the age of motors.

A Sand County Almanac
Aldo Leopold
1949; 226 pp.
$7.95
postpaid from:
Oxford University Press
16-00 Pollitt Drive
Fair Lawn, NJ 07410
or Whole Earth Access

• Tracking the smugglers and wildlife trade.
TRAFFIC (U.S.A.): Lynne Hardie Lehman, Editor. Membership **$10**/year (includes 4 issues) from World Wildlife Fund, 1255 23rd Street NW, Washington, DC 20037.

• See also **Audubon** Magazine (p. 27), **Earth First!** (p. 87), and the Sierra Club (p. 87).

Environmental Conservation Journal

The contributors cover the biosphere. And surprisingly, even when they are fairly technical, the articles are readily understandable — perhaps because the science involved is human scale. This magazine qualifies as the single journal most thoroughly in support of planetary diversity.

Read the subtitle ("the international Journal devoted to maintaining global viability through exposing and countering environmental deterioration resulting from human population-pressure and unwise technology"). Find it in the library. —*Stewart Brand*

Environmental Conservation Journal
Nicholas Polunin, Editor
190 Swiss Francs/year
(4 issues) from:
Environmental Conservation
Elsevier Sequoia S.A.
P. O. Box 851
1001 Lausanne 1
Switzerland

North American BIOREGIONS

by Peter Warshall

NEARCTIC REALM

1. Sitkan
2. Oregonian
3. Yukon Taiga
4. Canadian Taiga
5. Eastern Forest
6. Austroriparian
7. Californian
8. Sonoran
9. Chihuahuan
10. Tamaulipan
11. Great Basin
12. Aleutian Islands
13. Alaskan Tundra
14. Canadian Tundra
15. Arctic Archipelago
16. Greenland Tundra
17. Arctic Desert and Icecap
18. Grasslands
19. Rocky Mountains
20. Sierra-Cascade
21. Madrean-Cordilleran
22. Great Lakes

The BioRegional Quiz

1. **When you turn on your faucet, where does the water come from? (Can you trace it back to local storm systems?)**
2. **When you flush the toilet, where does the water go? (not just the treatment plant, but the final river or lake).**
3. **What soil series are you standing on?**
4. **How long is the growing season?**
5. **What are the major geological events that shaped your bioregion (faults, uplifts, downwarps, volcanics, sea floods, etc)? Does your community give them special attention . . . are they sacred, blessed, protected?**
6. **How did the original inhabitants eat, clothe, and shelter themselves? How did they celebrate the seasonal changes in times before you?**
7. **How many days until the moon is full?**
8. **From where you are sitting, point north.**
9. **What other bioregions of the planet have the most similar climate, culture, and analogous plants and animals? In other words, who are your Gaian cousins?**
10. **Name the major plant/animal associations that thrive in your bioregion. Name five resident and migratory birds; five grasses; five trees; five mammals and reptiles or amphibians. Which are native?**
11. **Name the plant or animal that is the "barometer" of environmental health for your bioregion? How's it doing? endangered? threatened? thriving? Has it become a symbol or totem of local power for your community?**
12. **Name the bioregions that grew each item of food on your dinner plate. Could you eat more locally? Support nearby farms?**
13. **Where does your garbage go?**
14. **What heavenly events most influence life in your bioregion? (Fire? lightning? hail? tornadoes? fog? blizzards? drought? permafrost? chubascos? spring thaw?)**

BIOREGIONALISM IS A recent revisioning of North America. It passionately opposes the homogenization and pasteurization of regional culture and natural landscape. Bioregionalists despise the you-could-be-anywhere motel room, Muzak, fast food, and highway strip as both gross and harsh on the human spirit. They encourage our uprooted, super-mobile citizenry to stop and look and feel the *bios* — the life of the natural and human world immediately surrounding them — a life, so to speak, that needs to be walked and talked to be loved.

Bioregionalism places great emphasis on time-depth. Its vision of the future is solidly enmeshed in a respect for the "ancient ones" — the long-term residents — be they rocks, bristlecone pine, creeks, kachinas, zithers, or gumbo. It celebrates a more personal and organic sense of beauty. Gifts, homes, poetry, pottery and painting connect directly to local materials — crafted by human hands — not the quick-and-easy purchase of prefabricated doodads from I. Magnin or the Seven-Eleven. In this sense, it is a quest to radically decentralized notions of beauty and values . . . from the Commodity Big Boys and National Television to homey, grassroots pride in local stuff. Self-reliance, even for entertainment.

Bioregionalism is also a knee-jerk kick to the recent hammering of American democracy. Who can feel part of America when their senator represents five million citizens and the Congress is packed with 50 percent lawyers? Today's democracy is a long way from Jacksonian times when a Senator might be the voice of 10,000 voters and Davy Crockett could actually make it to Congress. In other words, "representative democracy" is getting stretched thin. There is a yearning for more "direct democracy" — the New England town meeting or the tribal council — in which individual action has more weight. Imagine, come November, Americans going to the polling booth and voting directly on how their tax money should be divvied up: how much to military, to welfare, to preserve open spaces, to fight toxics and water pollution, to fund retirement, health, education and welfare. Could direct democracy really be any worse than electing a lawyer beholden to special interest groups to go to Washington to bargain with other lawyers?

Bioregionalism (*bios*, life; *regere*, rule or govern) is, in part, a desire to establish a more direct democracy by encompassing a larger sense of community in a more ecological sense of space: by the eco-culture, for the eco-culture, and of the land and waters. It is still embryonic, defining its shape and goals. But both a stronger voice for all minorities, including nonhuman creatures, and a switch from alientated voters to citizens who feel rewarded and happy participating in governing (self-determination) are two strong currents in the bioregionalist river.

The next 13 pages introduce North American bioregionalism with the broadest brushstrokes. In fact, too broad. But, space restrictions limit us to the "spirit" rather than the details of bioregionalism. For instance, the deserts are more properly five deserts; the broadleaf forests more properly seven or eight forest types; all the mountain zones are a patchwork of complex ecological inter-fingerings. You will have to refine each sense of bioregion by overlaying your own sense of cultural and biological boundaries with regional topographic wonders like the Ozarks or Great Lakes or Snake River Plateau. We emphasize the regional bards — the poets, novelists, historians, musicians — to help celebrate each region's *joie de vivre*. Simultaneously, bioregionalism continues to resist the Hostess Twinkie syndrome and to pray for the preservation of the continent's natural integrity. From song, spirit; from spirit, muscle; muscle, the common earth. ■

This introduction owes a lot to Jim Dodge's much more extensive intro in the special bioregional issue of the CoEvolution Quarterly *(No. 32, 1981), edited by Peter Berg and Stephanie Mills. Thanks to them and Kelly Kindscher; Destiny, M.D.; Joe Browder; Diana Hadley; Tony Burgess; Rosey Woolridge; Joanne Kyger; and Jim Katz.*

Harp seal pup.
—Mammals of the American North

FROM POLAR BEAR TO caribou, the far north is a land of wanderers. Sometimes seal, after fishing, wander onto ice floes and meet wandering bears. The frozen Arctic, at times like these, is hardly connected to the land. But a bit south of the permanent ice and snow, where maybe eight inches of soil thaw each year, the first lichens and mosses, then sedges and grasses beneficiently feed the caribou. This is the tundra. It always has permafrost, and when it freezes to the surface or gets covered in snow, the caribou head inland and south to the first scraggy trees (the taiga) and, in extreme years, to the thick forests (the boreal forest of spruce and hemlock). As they travel, the wolves go with them. When they reach their southern limit, they encounter their first close relative, the moose. Today, meat-eating remains; snow mobiles replace sleds; and oil drilling and cash replace starvation. TV, storytelling, and carving still fill the long night. —Peter Warshall

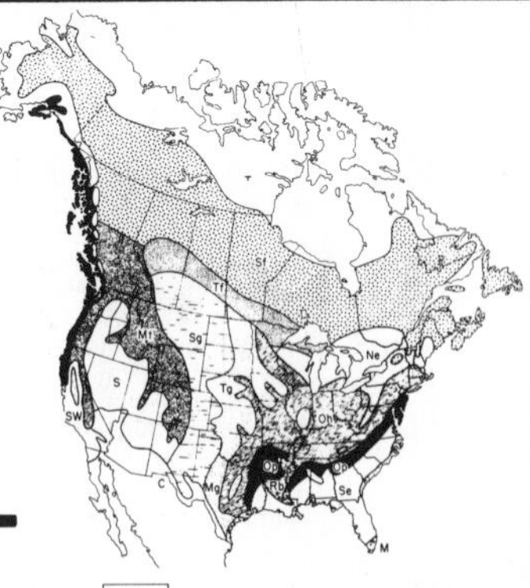

T Tundra
Sf Spruce-fir forest

James Ruben, bringing back meat from Brock River. *—Inuit*

•

The spring silence is broken by pistol reports of cracking on the river, and then the sound of breaking branches and the whining pop of a falling tree as the careening blocks of ice gouge the riverbanks. A related but far eerier phenomenon occurs in the coastal ice. Suddenly in the middle of winter and without warning a huge piece of sea ice surges hundreds of feet inland, like something alive. The Eskimo call it *ivu*. The silent arrival of caribou in an otherwise empty landscape is another example. The long wait at a seal hole for prey to surface. Waiting for a lead to close. The Eskimo have a word for this kind of long waiting, prepared for a sudden event; *quinuituq*. Deep patience. *—Arctic Dreams*

Arctic Dreams

Arctic Dreams *is the first lyric, philosophical reflection on the far north and its history of human visions. It is a quest for essences in a frozen, beautiful land.* ***Inuit*** *solidifies tundra/seashore dreams into images of the everyday life of the Inuit people. Honest as hard ice. Between tundra, taiga, and boreal forest, the celebration of bioregions becomes more jovial. Farley Mowatt knows it best; his* ***Never Cry Wolf*** *and* ***People of the Deer*** *are the best bedtime boreal travel.* ***Coming Into the Country*** *by John McPhee is a journalistic musing on the new Alaska with drop-out trappers and boreal borracho. Robert Service's poetry and Jack London's* ***Call of the Wild*** *are the classics. —Peter Warshall*

Arctic Dreams: Barry Lopez, 1986; 464 pp. **$22.95** postpaid from Macmillan Publishing Co./Order Dept., Front and Brown Streets, Riverside, NJ 08075 (or Whole Earth Access).
[Suggested by Wendell Berry]

Inuit: Ulli Steltzer, 1982; 216 pp. **$22.50** postpaid from University of Chicago Press, 11030 South Langley Avenue, Chicago, IL 60628 (or Whole Earth Access).

Never Cry Wolf: Farley Mowat, 1973; 164 pp. **$2.95** ($4.45 postpaid).

People of the Deer: Farley Mowat, 1975; 287 pp. **$3.50** ($5 postpaid).

Call of the Wild: Jack London, 1903; 101 pp. **$2.25** ($3.75 postpaid).

Coming Into the Country: John McPhee, 1977; 417 pp. **$4.95** ($6.45 postpaid).

All from Bantam Books, 414 East Golf Road, Des Plaines, IL 60016 (or Whole Earth Access).

Natural History

Audubon's ***Eastern Forests*** *(see p. 50) is the best introductory field guide to the forests of the far north. Volumes five and six (Arctic, Subarctic) of the Smithsonian series* ***Handbook of North American Indians*** *(see p. 56) present the most encyclopedic and complete bioregional understanding. One hundred and fifty species are covered in* ***Mammals of the American North****, a coffee-table-size book of beautiful color photography and writing that emphasizes human interconnectedness with animals in this harsh environment. —Peter Warshall*

Mammals of the American North: Adrian Forsyth, 1985; 351 pp. **$29.95** ($30.95 postpaid) from Firefly Books Ltd., 3520 Pharmacy Avenue, Unit 1-C, Scarborough, Ontario, Canada M1W 2T8 (or Whole Earth Access).

◄

Making a sledge at Pelly Bay. Driftwood was rare so wooden sledges were not common. Runners were made from frozen fish wrapped in sealskin with caribou antler pieces tied as crossbars with sealskin lines. A sludge of pulverized moss and water was then put on the underside of the runner in a thick coat, frozen, coated with ice, and rubbed with wet polar bear fur to produce a hard, resistant coat of ice that allowed the sledge to run smoothly. *—Handbook of North American Indians*

Wooden maps. (Left) Representation of the coast between Kangersuttuassiaq and Sieralik; (Center) Islands off the coastline shown on the map at left; (Right) Representation of the peninsulas between Kangersuttuassiaq and Sermiligaaq. Carved by Kunit from Umiivik. Length of left 14.2 cm; rest same scale.
—Handbook of North American Indians

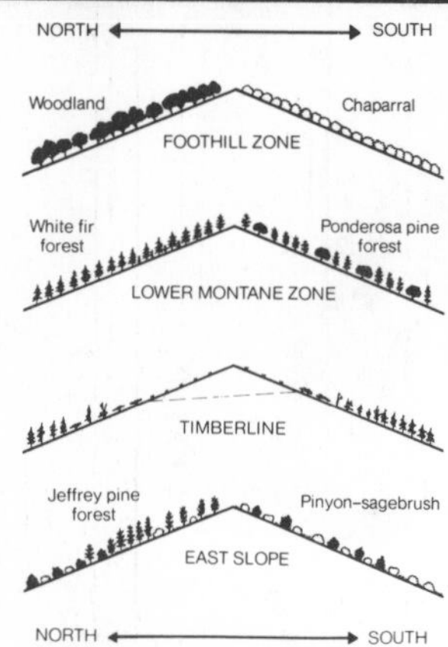

Vegetational differences between comparable north- and south-facing slopes in the Sierra Nevada.
—The Sierra Nevada

Western White Pine **Shasta Fir** **Sugar Pine** ***—Cascades and Olympics*** **California Ground Squirrel**

IT IS DIFFICULT to encapsulate this immense bioregional province, which includes the northwest coastal (Oregonian) rain forest; the Sierra, Cascade, and Siskiyou Mountains; and a ribbon of oak-chaparral woodlands in the semi-arid regions below the needle-leaf forests. The cone-shaped pines, spruce, and firs shade the forest floor, filter the light, and scent the air. The water ouzels, mountain thrushes, tree squirrels, and warblers speak the chit-chat of these forest homes. In the higher elevations, a short growing season and the rise and fall of the snowline frame the rhythm of the year.

These western forests harbor the last significant virgin forests of the United States. They are pressured in a manner that John Muir could only faintly envision — bioregional battles rage over gold and ores, timber, and more recently, recreational access and use.

—Peter Warshall

Natural History

Stephen Whitney has the monopoly on good introductory books: ***The Sierra Nevada*** *is a superb introduction to complex zonation and ecology.* ***A Field Guide to the Cascades and Olympics*** *is a good bioregional overview, giving a feel for the similarities that all forest dwellers experience. (It includes a good bibliography for going deeper.) And* ***Western Forests*** *broadly sweeps through all the forests of this region.* *—Peter Warshall*

The Sierra Nevada
Stephen Whitney
1979; 526 pp.

$10.95
($13.45 postpaid) from:
Sierra Club Bookstore
730 Polk Street
San Francisco, CA 94109
or Whole Earth Access

A Field Guide to the Cascades and Olympics
Stephen Whitney
1983; 288 pp.

$14.95 postpaid from:
The Mountaineers Books
306 Second Avenue West
Seattle, WA 98119
or Whole Earth Access

Western Forests
Stephen Whitney
1985; 672 pp.

$14.95
($15.95 postpaid) from:
Random House
Order Dept.
400 Hahn Road
Westminster, MD 21157
or Whole Earth Access

Cross section of the white fir forest, showing the layered understory characteristic of many stands.
—The Sierra Nevada

◄ **Shasta Fern *(Polystichum mohroides)*. Fronds evergreen, 2-divided, relatively soft, 4″-20″ long; pinniae overlapping, with pinnules lobed or toothed but never prickly or spiny; stipe straw colored, somewhat sticky or with fine hairs, scaly only toward base. Sori gen only on mid and upper pinnae, the indusia shieldlike. Rocky slopes, oft on serpentine, mont-subalp, Wenatchee Mtns. Cal Cas. s to S Amer.**
—Cascades and Olympics

fertile pinna

Pinyon-juniper woodlands.
—Western Forests

◄ (Far left) Forest conifers receive plenty of light simply by reaching above lesser plants. The pronounced tapering of the crowns of firs, hemlocks, spruces, and other trees not only aids in the shedding of snow but also permits light to penetrate to the lower branches, where flattened sprays are arranged in overlapping whorls around the central trunk. (Left) Among conifers growing in open situations, those found in areas of little snow rarely show the classic Christmas-tree shape. For example, the Digger Pine of California's oak woodland has an open, rounded crown not unlike that of a deciduous hardwood. The same is true of pinyons, junipers, and various pines and cypresses occurring in open, droughty woodlands.—*Western Forests*

•

Across western North America, from the Rocky Mountains to the Pacific Ocean, successive mountain ranges and intervening lowlands form a deeply corrugated landscape characterized by extremes of elevation, climate, and vegetation. Trending north and south, the mountains intercept moist air masses as they move eastward from the Pacific Ocean. This not only increases the moisture on the slopes, but also reduces the precipitation that hits the lowlands and other ranges located downwind. As a result, the cool, moist mountainous areas of western North America stand as climatic islands in a region that is generally characterized by drought. The Rocky Mountains, the Sierra Nevada, the Cascade Range, and most other high ranges in the region bear conifer forests on their flanks, while most of the valley and basins that lie between them are largely covered by grasslands or desert scrub.
—Western Forests

• In the grand tradition of American literary anthropology, Malcolm Margolin imaginatively reconstructs the bygone days of Northern California Indians. Such a book could be made for every region in the U.S., on the continent, on Earth. Without such *felt* history, respect is impossible.
The Ohlone Way (Indian Life in the San Francisco & Monterey Bay Areas): Malcolm Margolin, 1978; 182 pp.
$6.95 postpaid from Heyday Books, P. O. Box 9145, Berkeley, CA 94709.

East
Shrubs, grasses
Grassland, some oak
Oak and coniferous forest
Coniferous forest
Alpine plants
Sierra Nevada
Great Valley
Lithosols
Clayey subsoil
Gray-Brown Podzols
Noncalcic Brown Soils and Red and Yellow Podzols
Saline soils
Planosols

—Natural Regions of the United States and Canada

▲ **Raymond Dasmann's *Environmental Conservation* (see p. 45).**

Clearing Winter Storm, Yosemite National Park. ►
—Ansel Adams

Cultural Celebration

Tossed around by mountain uplifting and glaciation, pushed further and further from the benign influence of the sea, the northern needle-leaf forests diversified into a rich, highly mixed and complex series of ecological zones. Along the northern coasts, the redwoods, rain, fog, and soggy, mossy earth created North America's most luxuriant temperate rain forest and its teller of tales, Ken Kesey. Inland and further south, the montane Sierras and oak woodlands are drier and have rooted an equally spare and bare rock poet, Gary Snyder. Still further south, the original mountain bard, John Muir, paced the grass-lined valleys to the Sierran timberline spewing forth elegant prose. Almost half-way across the continent, the Rockies, North America's tectonic backbone, cornucopia of plains and Colorado River soils as well as desert irrigation, have no singular voice . . . perhaps because of their sheer immensity and height. Ansel Adams and Edward S. Curtis are their singers in photographic imagery.

***A Lady's Life in the Rocky Mountains** (written in 1873) by Isabella Bird and **One Day At Teton Marsh** by Sally Carrighar celebrate nature and pioneer life. Lew Welch (**Ring of Bone**) and Jaime DeAngulo (**The Jaime DeAngulo Reader**) are two bards of the transition between forest and woodlands, bioregion and city. Both write of coastal and Sierran landscapes.* —*Peter Warshall*

Water-Ouzel Diving and Feeding

•

During the golden days of Indian summer, after most of the snow has been melted, and the mountain streams have become feeble, — a succession of silent pools, linked together by shallow transparent currents and strips of silvery lacework, — then the song of the Ouzel is at its lowest ebb. But as soon as the winter clouds have bloomed, and the mountain treasuries are once more replenished with snow, the voices of the streams and ouzels increase in strength and richness until the flood season of early summer. Then the torrents chant their noblest anthems, and then is the flood-time of our songster's melody.

—*The Mountains of California*

•

You have not stepped out onto the bank of the Wakonda Auga but into some misty other-world dream . . . Yawning, walking thigh-deep through the ground-mist toward the house, you wonder vaguely if you are still asleep and at the same time not asleep, still dreaming and at the same time not dreaming. Couldn't it be? This swathed and muffled ground is like a sleep; this furry silence is like dream silence. The air is so still. The foxes aren't barking in the woods. The crows aren't calling. You can see no ducks flying the river. You cannot hear the usual morning breeze fingering the buckthorn leaves. It is very still. Except for that soft, delicious, wet hissing . . .

—*Sometimes a Great Notion*

•

A very pretty mare, hobbled, was feeding; a collie dog barked at us, and among the scrub, not far from the track, there was a rude, black log cabin, as rough as it could be to be a shelter at all, with smoke coming out of the roof and window. . . . The mud roof was covered with lynx, beaver, and other furs laid out to dry, beaver paws were pinned out on the logs, a part of the carcass of a deer hung at one end of the cabin, a skinned beaver lay in front of a heap of peltry just within the door, and antlers of deer, old horseshoes, and offal of many animals lay about the den.

—*A Lady's Life in the Rocky Mountains*

•

Pine Tree Tops
in the blue night
frost haze, the sky glows
with the moon
pine tree tops
bend snow-blue, fade
into sky, frost, starlight.
the creak of boots.
rabbit tracks, deer tracks,
what do we know.

—*Turtle Island*

View in the Sierra Forest
—The Mountains of California

A Lady's Life in the Rocky Mountains: Isabella Bird, 1960; 256 pp. **$4.95** ($6.45 postpaid) from Harper and Row, Keystone Industrial Park, Scranton, PA 18512.

One Day at Teton Marsh: Sally Carrighar, 1979; 239 pp. **$4.25** ($5.75 postpaid) from University of Nebraska Press, 901 N. 17th Street, Lincoln, NE 68588.

Ring of Bone: Lew Welch, 1960; 224 pp. **$6** from Subterranean Co., P. O. Box 10233, Eugene, OR 97440.

The Jaime De Angulo Reader: Jaime De Angulo, 1979; 254 pp. **$8.95** ($9.45 postpaid) from Turtle Island Foundation, 2845 Buena Vista Way, Berkeley, CA 94708.

Each of these books is available from Whole Earth Access.

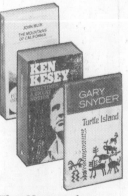

The Mountains of California
John Muir
1894, 1985; 264 pp.
$5.95
($6.95 postpaid) from:
Viking Penguin Books
299 Murray Hill Pkwy.
East Rutherford,
NJ 07073
or Whole Earth Access

Turtle Island
Gary Snyder
1974; 114 pp.
$4.95
($5.95 postpaid) from:
New Directions
80 8th Avenue
New York, NY 10011
or Whole Earth Access

Sometimes a Great Notion
Ken Kesey
1963; 628 pp.
$7.95
($8.95 postpaid) from:
Viking Penguin Press
299 Murray Hill Pkwy.
East Rutherford,
NJ 07073
or Whole Earth Access

Gulf Coast — Tennessee R. — Ohio R. — Straits of Mackinac

Marsh grass | Tall grass | Mixed pine and oak | Chestnut, chestnut oak, yellow poplar | Oak, hickory | Birch, beech, maple, hemlock | Pine | Spruce, fir | Spruce, lichens | Lichens

Southern pine forest | Central hardwood forest | Northern hardwood forest | Northern pine forest | Spruce-fir forest | Taiga | Tundra

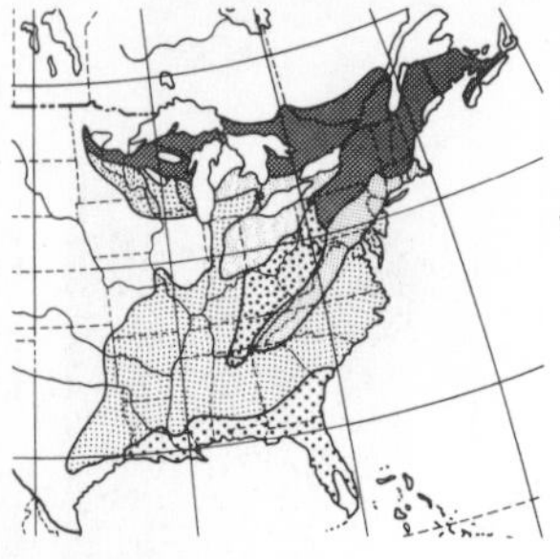

IN WINTER, the leafless open forest, grey and dormant. In spring, pale green leafing and explosive flowering. In summer, through the five-layered canopy, a random spot of forest floor sunlight galvanizes the eye. In fall, colors peak red, orange, yellow on a scale of ten. Oak, maple, beech or basswood are always present. The life/death/rebirth cycles are so dramatic that these forests have always magnetized poets, philosophers, and writers who exploit seasonal metaphor endlessly.

To me, the flowering dogwood establishes the sense of place. —Peter Warshall

Natural History

For a general pretty-photos field guide with a broadbrush overview of the leaf-shedding, cold-resistant forests, read ***Audubon's Eastern Forests.*** *For black-and-white drawings and photos but greater ecological intimacy, the more local Sierra Club guides to Southern New England and the Piedmont are a pleasure.* ***The North Woods*** *— transition between boreal and deciduous forest — is the land Hemingway cherished, harboring the East's last great wolf sanctuary. This guide is a must for citizens of Michigan, Wisconsin and Minnesota. The almost instantaneous conversion of southeastern forests into fields of cotton and tobacco has left the South with few naturalists and no detailed field guides. —Peter Warshall*

Shagbark hickory, *Carya ovata*, in winter. The characteristic shape and bark texture of many trees make them as recognizable in winter as in summer. *—Southern New England*

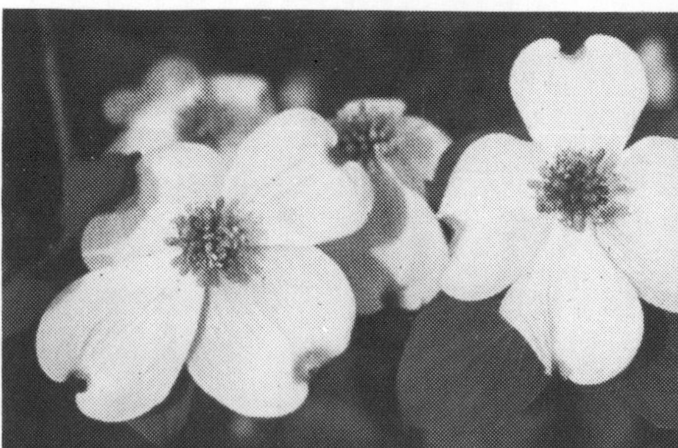

•

Flowering Dogwood is one of the most beautiful eastern North American trees with showy early spring flowers, red fruit, and scarlet autumn foliage. The hard wood is extremely shock-resistant and useful for making weaving-shuttles. It is also made into spools, small pulleys, mallet heads, and jeweler's blocks. Indians used the aromatic bark and roots as a remedy for malaria and extracted a red dye from the roots.
—Eastern Forests

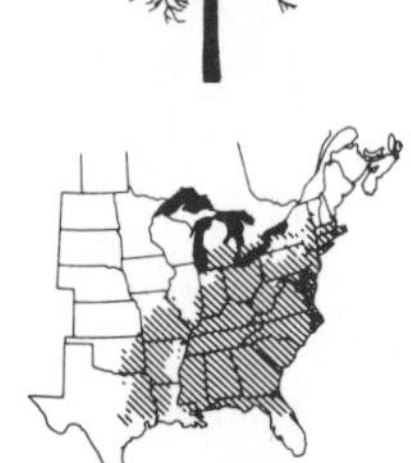

Wood Thrush *—Eastern Forests*

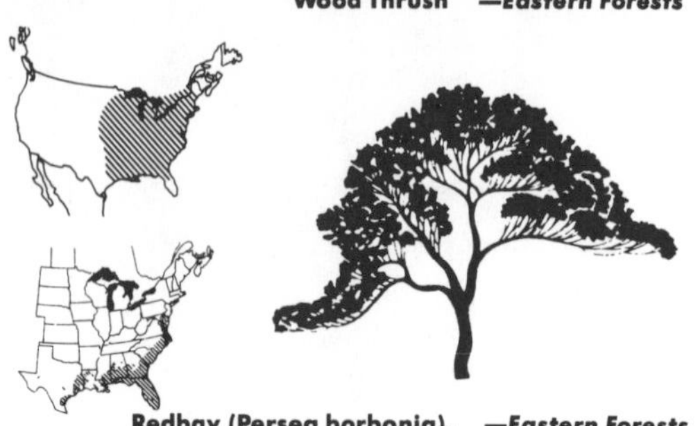

Redbay (*Persea borbonia*). *—Eastern Forests*

Eastern Forests: Ann & Myron Sutton, 1985; 638 pp. **$14.95** ($15.95 postpaid) from Random House, Order Dept., 400 Hahn Road, Westminster, MD 21157 (or Whole Earth Access).

The North Woods (of Michigan, Wisconsin, Minnesota): Glenda Daniel, Jerry Sullivan, 1981; 408 pp. **$10.95** ($13.45 postpaid).

The Piedmont: Michael A. Godfrey, 1980; 499 pp. **$9.95** ($12.45 postpaid).

Southern New England: Neil Jorgensen, 1978; 417 pp. **$12.95** ($15.45 postpaid).

All from: Sierra Club Bookstore, 730 Polk Street, San Francisco, CA 94109 (or Whole Earth Access).

Cultural Celebration: South

The South was completely different. The eco-culture of pine woods and hickory-beech, slavery, and hillbilly Caribe-French and Elizabethan roots graced the United States with its most popular bioregional music: the blues, bluegrass, country western, cajun zydeco, cross-over rock. (See pp. 342-343 for mail order music sources.) Perhaps because poetry is so close to music, the South generated fewer poets. Because of the intensity of the slave-based economy, human drama has overridden concern for the land; there is no more fertile ground for a poetic prose of humanized landscape. Joel Chandler Harris (Uncle Remus), William Faulkner, Tennessee Williams, Flannery O'Connor, and Carson McCullers are some of the greats. The preeminent voice of the culture in agriculture is Wendell Berry (see also p. 61), the South's main bioregional bard. —Peter Warshall

•

They stopped at The Tower for barbecued sandwiches. The Tower was a part stucco and part wood filling station and dance hall set in a clearing outside of Timothy. A fat man named Red Sammy Butts ran it and there were signs stuck here and there on the building and for miles up and down the highway saying, TRY RED SAMMY'S

Pictured Rocks National Lakeshore near Munising, Michigan.
—The North Woods

Cultural Celebration: North

Virgin forest is nearly impossible to find; the forests of the northeast have been settled longest, and with settlement has come a strong voice of love. "I have travelled a good deal in Concord . . ." is Thoreau's famous line and it had many followers. Here God and Nature became inextricably tangled. In second growth forest, the Mind remained pioneer: Ralph Waldo Emerson, Henry Wadsworth Longfellow, Emily Dickinson, Charles Olson, William Carlos Williams, Robert Creeley, Robert Frost. It's a bioregion of beautifully crafted poetry and very moral prose (e.g. Hawthorne, Melville). Thoreau's ***Journals*** *(also see* ***Walden****, p. 184) — part of the great quest to give transcendental truth to each act of Nature — contain the most loving attention to seasonal change ever recorded in North America. Ernest Hemingway's* ***The Nick Adams Stories*** *tells of Nick growing up in the north woods of Michigan with prose as direct and simple as a single white pine in winter snow.* —*Peter Warshall*

•

They came from the hot sun of the slashings into the shade of the great trees. The slashings had run up to the top of a ridge and over and then the forest began. They were walking on the brown forest floor now and it was springy and cool under their feet. There was no underbrush and the trunks of the trees rose sixty feet high before there were any branches. It was cool in the shade of the trees and high up in them Nick could hear the breeze that was rising. No sun came through as they walked and Nick knew there would be no sun through the high top branches until nearly noon. His sister put her hand in his and walked close to him.

"I'm not scared, Nickie. But it makes me feel very strange."

"Me, too," Nick said. "Always."

"I never was in woods like these."

"This is all the virgin timber left around here."

"Do we go through it very long?"

"Quite a way."

"I'd be afraid if I were alone."

"It makes me feel strange. But I'm not afraid."

"I said that first."

"I know. Maybe we say it because we are afraid."

"No. I'm not afraid because I'm with you. But I know I'd be afraid alone. Did you ever come here with anyone else?"

"No. Only by myself."

"And you weren't afraid?"

"No. But I always feel strange. Like the way I ought to feel in church."

—*The Nick Adams Stories*

•

Those sparrows, too, are thoughts I have. They come and go; they flit by quickly on their migrations, uttering only a faint *chip*, I know not whither or why exactly. One will not rest upon its twig for me to scrutinize it. The whole copse will be alive with my rambling thoughts, bewildering me by their very multitude, but they will be all gone directly without leaving me a feather. My loftiest thought is somewhat like an eagle that suddenly comes into the field of view, suggesting great things and thrilling the beholder, as if it were bound hitherward with a message for me; but it comes no nearer, but circles and soars away, growing dimmer, disappointing me, till it is lost behind a cliff or a cloud.

•

This is one of those ambrosial, white, ever-memorable fogs presaging fair weather. It produces the most picturesque and grandest effects as it rises, and travels hither and thither, enveloping and concealing trees and forests and hills. It is lifted up now into quite a little white mountain over Fair Haven Bay, and, even on its skirts, only the tops of the highest pines are seen above it, and all adown the river it has an uneven outline like a rugged mountain ridge; in one place some rainbow tints, and far, far in the south horizon, near the further verge of the sea (over Saxonville?) it is heaved up into great waves, as if there were breakers there. In the meanwhile the wood thrush and the jay and the robin sing around me here, and birds are heard singing from the midst of the fog. And in one short hour this sea will all evaporate and the sun be reflected from farm windows on its green bottom.

—*The Journal of Henry D. Thoreau*

The Nick Adams Stories: Ernest Hemingway. 1927, 1972; 268 pp. **$7.95** postpaid from Macmillan Publishing Co./Order Dept., Front and Brown Streets, Riverside, NJ 08075 (or Whole Earth Access).

The Journal of Henry D. Thoreau (14 volumes, bound as 2 volumes): Bradford Torrey and F. H. Allen. 1906; 1,804 pp. **$40** each ($41 each postpaid) from Dover Publications, Inc., 31 E. 2nd Street, Mineola, NY 11501 (or Whole Earth Access).

Selected Journals of Henry David Thoreau: Bode and Carl, 1967. **$3.95** ($5.45 postpaid) from New American Library, 120 Woodbine Street, Bergenfield, NJ 07621 (or Whole Earth Access).

Howlin' Wolf — from Down Home Records (p. 348).

FAMOUS BARBECUE. NONE LIKE FAMOUS RED SAMMY'S! RED SAM! THE FAT BOY WITH THE HAPPY LAUGH. A VETERAN! RED SAMMY'S YOUR MAN!

—*A Good Man Is Hard to Find*

•

Red Sam came in and told his wife to quit lounging on the counter and hurry up with these people's order. His khaki trousers reached just to his hip bones and his stomach hung over them like a sack of meal swaying under his shirt. He came over and sat down at a table nearby and let out a combination sigh and yodel. "You can't win," he said. "You can't win," and he wiped his sweating red face off with a gray handkerchief. "These days you don't know who to trust," he said. "Ain't that the truth?" —*A Good Man Is Hard to Find*

•

from "The Clearing"

February. A cloudy day/ foretelling spring by its warmth/ though snow will follow./ You are at work in the worn field/ returning now to thought./ The sorrel mare eager/ to the burden, you are dragging/ cut brush to the pile,/ moving in ancestral motions/ of axe-stroke, bending to log chain and trace, speaking/ immemorial bidding and praise/ to the mare's fine ears./ And you pause to rest/ in the quiet day while the mare's/ sweated flanks steam./ You stand in a clearing whose cost/ you know in tendon and bone./ A kingfisher utters/ his harsh cry, rising/ from the leafless river./ Again, again, the old/ is newly come.

—*Collected Poems*

◄ Nine-banded armadillo.
—Eastern Forests

A Good Man Is Hard to Find (and Other Stories): Flannery O'Connor, 1953, 1977; 251 pp. **$4.95** ($5.95 postpaid) from Harcourt Brace Jovanovitch, 1250 6th Avenue, 4th Floor, San Diego, CA 92101 (or Whole Earth Access).

Collected Poems (1957-1982): Wendell Berry, 1984; 268 pp. **$16.50** ($18 postpaid) from North Point Press, 850 Talbot Avenue, Berkeley, CA 94706 (or Whole Earth Access).

Mixed-prairie Valentine Refuge, Nebraska. —Grassla

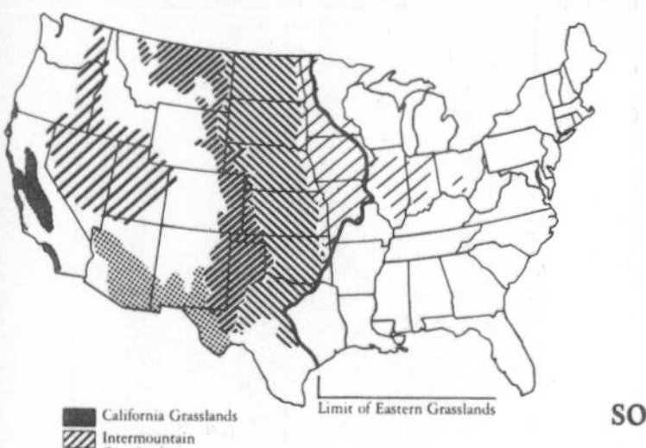

DIVIDED EAST TO West into the tall- and shortgrass prairies, the temperate grasslands have been the most productive and heavily used of all North America's soils. Deep in the Great Prairie earth grew the "totemic" grasses of the bioregion: bluestem, needle, and grama grasses. Here the pronghorn, prairie wolf and buffalo migrated. Badgers, prairie dogs, and prairie chicken were most at home. Fear struck in the north as ground blizzards; in the midriff as hail; and in the south as tornadoes. Fast moving fires blew everywhere. This is an inland bioregion with the heavens both battling and nurturing the earth. It is an earth in which roots go deep. It is where the dust bowl sat the longest and with most weight. It is the source of more human nutrition than any other area in North America. Corn, wheat, and soybeans replace the native grasses.

—Peter Warshall

Natural History

For an overview of the continent's grasslands — California, intermountain, desert, tallgrass, mixed, and shortgrass — get Audubon's ***Grasslands****. Donald Worster's* ***Dust Bowl*** *chronicles the 1930s devastation of the great plains with respect and awe for the region and condemnation of the ecological values taught by the capitalist ethos.* ***Sacred Cows at the Public Trough*** *by Denzel and Nancy Ferguson bitterly reveals how livestock ruined the public's open range.*

—Peter Warshall

Grasslands: Lauren Brown, 1985; 606 pp. **$14.95** ($15.95 postpaid) from Random House/Order Dept., 400 Hahn Road, Westminster, MD 21157 (or Whole Earth Access).

Dust Bowl: Donald Worster, 1979; 277 pp. **$9.95** postpaid from Oxford University Press, 16-00 Pollitt Drive, Fairlawn, NJ 07410 (or Whole Earth Access).

Sacred Cows At The Public Trough: Denzel and Nancy Ferguson, 1983; 250 pp. **$8.95** ($9.95 postpaid) from Maverick Publications, Drawer 5007, Bend, OR 97708 (or Whole Earth Access).

Spur-throated Grasshopper. —Grasslands

A black blizzard advancing over Prowers County, Colorado, 1937. It came from the north and lasted almost three hours. —Dust Bowl

Cultural Celebration

The land went so fast. The plains Indians had hardly created a new horse culture and the strongest spiritual vision quest in North America when the buffalo disappeared and the Indian people were scattered like the wolves. Singers of the grassland sing of the past. John Madson's ***Where the Sky Began*** *traces the prairie's bioregional history with rooted humor and obvious love. Willa Cather, tough romantic of sod and soil, is the first-rate bard of the plains. John C. Ewer's* ***The Horse in Blackfoot Culture*** *and Mari Sandoz's* ***Crazy Horse, The Strange Man of the Oglalas*** *document the great flowering of plains Indian culture.*

—Peter Warshall

Where the Sky Began: John Madson, 1982; 321 pp. **$8.95** ($11.45 postpaid) from Sierra Club Bookstore, 730 Polk Street, San Francisco, CA 94109 (or Whole Earth Access).

My Antonia: Willa Cather, 1973; 371 pp. **$5.70** ($6.40 postpaid) from Houghton Mifflin Company/Mail Order Dept., Wayside Road, Burlington, MA 01803 (or Whole Earth Access).

The Horse in Blackfoot Indian Culture: John C. Ewers, 1980; 374 pp. **$16.50** ($18.25 postpaid) from Smithsonian Institution Press/Customer Service, P. O. Box 4866, Hampden Station, Baltimore, MD 21211 (or Whole Earth Access).

Crazy Horse, The Strange Man of the Oglalas: Mari Sandoz, 1942; 413 pp. **$5.95** ($7.45 postpaid) from University of Nebraska Press, 901 North 17th Street, 318 Nebraska Hall, Lincoln, NE 68588-0520 (or Whole Earth Access).

•

July came on with that breathless, brilliant heat which makes the plains of Kansas and Nebraska the best corn country in the world. It seemed as if we could hear the corn growing in the night; under the stars one caught a faint crackling in the dewy, heavy-odoured cornfields where the feathered stalks stood so juicy and green. If all the great plain from the Missouri to the Rocky Mountains had been under glass, and the heat regulated by a thermometer, it could not have been better for the yellow tassels that were ripening and fertilizing the silk day by day . . . The burning sun of those few weeks, with occasional rains at night, secured the corn. After the milky ears were once formed, we had little to fear from dry weather.

—My Antonia

•

Some farmers still speak of native grass as "horse hay" with the inference that it's not respectable cattle feed. They forget that their grandfathers who fed cattle a simple fattening ration of clean water, salt, yellow corn, and prairie hay found that individual gains were seldom less than three pounds per day. We've come a long way since then. Now, with protein supplements, chopped clovers and bromes, mixed commercial feeds and expensive minerals and supplements, gains often range from 1½ to 2½ pounds per day. Maybe, as dad used to say, we've been educated beyond our intelligence.

—Where the Sky Began

A bison grazing on June grass at Yellowstone National Park, Wyoming. —Grasslands

• The best introduction to the life of John Wesley Powell. **Beyond the Hundredth Meridian:** Wallace Stegner, 1982; 458 pp. **$12.50** ($14 postpaid) from University of Nebraska Press, 901 North 17th Street, 318 Nebraska Hall, Lincoln, NE 68588 (or Whole Earth Access).

• Ecology of the Southwest — in depth. **Biotic Communities of the American Southwest:** David E. Brown, Editor. 1982; 342 pp. **$13.95** postpaid from Boyce Thompson Southwestern Arboretum, P. O. Box AB, Superior, AZ 85273 (or Whole Earth Access).

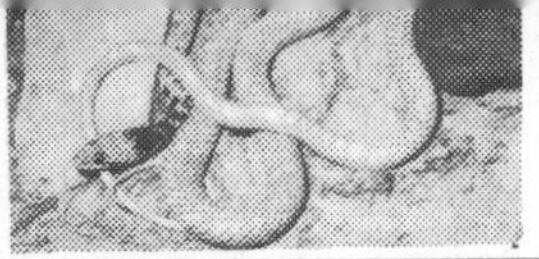

Common Kingsnake, Ground Snake, Coachwhip
—*Deserts*

THIS IS A BIOREGION defined by its lacks: no blizzards, no fog, no tornadoes, no regular rainfall. What it's got is solar heat. The light is intense. The rare clouds become instantly sacred. Rain is loved like nowhere else. The visual arts flourish: Pueblo pottery, Navajo weaving, outdoor ritual, Georgia O'Keefe. A common pride in survival connects humans, sidewinders, road runners and cacti. This is the most diverse cultural region (not counting cities). Native peoples still speak their languages and practice their blessings. A regional sense of spirit has been slowly fused together from Native American, Spanish, and Anglo-European influences. Mormons, followers of a religion native to the U.S., flex much moral and financial muscle. Sunbelt cities eat up the desert and suck the once lush rivers dry. It was all foretold by Hopi prophets and John Wesley Powell and fueled by a web of powerlines; there is no turning back.

—Peter Warshall

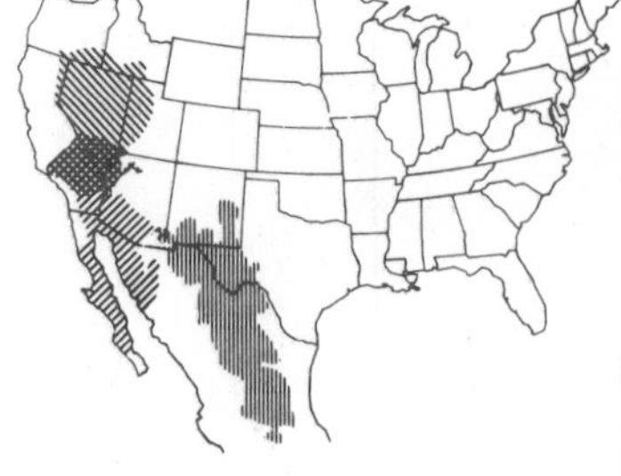

Black-on-white pitcher dating 1100-1200 from San Cosmos, Apache Co., Ariz.
—Handbook of North American Indians, Vol. 9 (see p. 56).

Celebration: Natural and Cultural

Audubon's ***Deserts*** *is a broad natural history of the four major North American deserts: the cold Great Basin, the lush Sonoran, the winter-rain Mojave, and the summer-rain Chihuahuan. Van Dyke's* ***The Desert*** *is the most painterly prose and (still) the best on the Sonoran. The strongest celebration comes from the residents: Simon Ortiz of Acoma is the poet; Native Americans no longer have to depend on anglo interpretations, thanks to Larry Evers' editing of* ***The South Corner of Time;*** *Rudolpho Anaya's* ***Bless Me, Ultima*** *places desert powers in the heart of a great bruja. Norman Mailer confronts Great Basin Mormonism in* ***The Executioner's song.***

—Peter Warshall

Deserts: James A. MacMahon, 1985; 638 pp. **$14.95** ($15.95) postpaid) from Random House/Order Dept., 400 Hahn Road, Westminster, MD 21157 (or Whole Earth Access).

The Desert: John C. Van Dyke, 1980; 272 pp. **$3.45** ($4.95 postpaid) from Gibbs M. Smith, P. O. Box 667, Layton, UT 84041 (or Whole Earth Access).

The South Corner of Time: Larry Evers, 1981; 240 pp. **$17.50** ($18.50 postpaid) from University of Arizona Press, 1615 Speedway, Tucson, AZ 85719 (or Whole Earth Access).

Bless Me, Ultima: Rudolfo A. Anaya, 1972; 249 pp. **$12** ($13 postpaid) from Tonatiuh-Quinto Sol International, Inc., P. O. Box 9275, Berkeley, CA 94709 (or Whole Earth Access).

The Executioner's Song: Norman Mailer, 1979; 1200 pp. **$25** ($26 postpaid) from Little, Brown and Company/Attn.: Order Dept., 200 West Street, Waltham, MA 02254 (or Whole Earth Access).

Georgia O'Keefe: Georgia O'Keefe, 1976, 216 pp. **$29.95** ($31.45 postpaid) from Viking/Penguin, 299 Murray Hill Parkway, East Rutherford, NJ 07073 (or Whole Earth Access).

A Good Journey: Simon Ortiz, 1984; 165 pp. **$8.95** ($9.95 postpaid) from University of Arizona Press, 1615 Speedway, Tucson, AZ 85719 (or Whole Earth Access).

Races for the sun. Run on a prescribed east-west course, the races were organized by the war chief, town chief, and ***xumpa,*** **as part of a series of related ceremonial events. Photograph by Charles F. Lummis, Apr. 19, 1896.**
—Handbook of North American Indians, Vol. 9 (see p. 56).

From the Faraway Nearby, 1937. Oil on canvas, 36 x 40.
—Georgia O'Keefe

•

The dust-particle in itself is sufficient to account for the warmth of coloring in the desert air — sufficient in itself to produce the pink, yellow, and lilac hazes. And yet I am tempted to suggest some other causes. It is not easy to prove that a reflection may be thrown upward upon the air by the yellow face of the desert beneath it — a reflection similar to that produced by a fire upon a night sky — yet I believe there is something of the desert's air-coloring derived from that source. Nor is it easy to prove that a reflection is cast by blue, pink, and yellow skies, upon the lower air-strata, yet certain effects shown in the mirage (the water illusion, for instance, which seems only the reflection of the sky from heated air) seem to suggest it. And if we put together other casual observations they will make argument toward the same goal. For instance, the common blue haze that we may see any day in the mountains, is always deepest in the early morning when the blue sky over it is deepest. At noon when the sky turns gray-blue the haze turns gray-blue also. The yellow haze of the desert is seen at its best when there is a yellow sunset, and the pink haze when there is a red sunset, indicating that at least the sky has some part in coloring by reflection the lower layers of desert air.

Whatever the cause, there can be no doubt about the effect. The desert air is practically colored air.

—The Desert

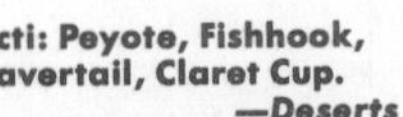

Cacti: Peyote, Fishhook, Beavertail, Claret Cup.
—Deserts

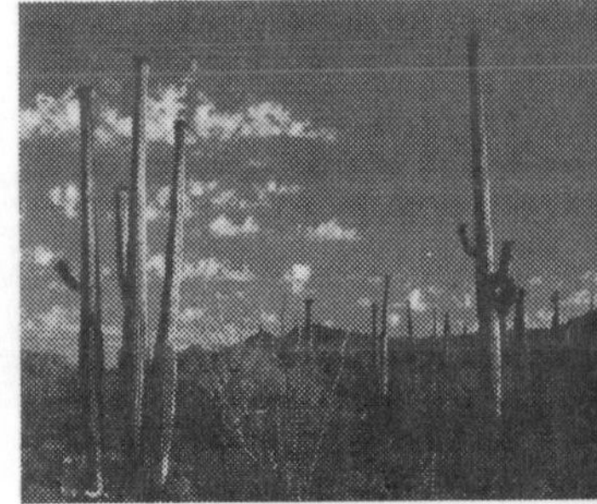

Upper bajada, Sonoran
—Deserts

Drainage areas.

Pacific
Great Basin/Desert and Montane
Plains/Prairie Potholes
Northeast/Midwest
Southeast/Southern Florida

EACH BIOREGION has its own: cienaga, tanque, branch, creek, swamp, marsh, bog, glade, slough, swale, wallow, bottoms, bayou, oxbow, pool, pond, brook, run, kill. Wetlands define bioregion personality, create the intimacy with the local lore and the local pacing of nature. Sources and springs used to be held in the highest regard . . . a few hot springs still remain associated with healing and a few springs have been given a second lease on life by the bottled water business. But water is so precious to commodity production (irrigated crops, cattle forage, land-filling and channelization for real estate, cooling power plants, etc.) that wetlands are our number one endangered ecological and cultural region. In the United States, there are fewer free-flowing rivers of any length than living condors. Riverlife, duck hunting, trout fishing, swimming, boating . . . many of the areas Americans use for escape are disappearing, just as the desire for open water floods our hearts. —Peter Warshall

A Fluent Celebration

*Audubon's **Wetlands** is the best of Audubon survey guides written by one of the finest ecologists to immerse himself in the subject. Appropriately, there is no one fluvial bard, but many . . . each pouring forth the mysterious solution of water and words. Here are words from some of my favorites.* —*Peter Warshall*

Round River: Luna B. Leopold, 1953; 173 pp. **$3.95** postpaid from Oxford University Press, 16-00 Pollitt Drive, Fair Lawn, NJ 07410 (or Whole Earth Access).

Life on the Mississippi: Mark Twain, 1961; 384 pp. **$1.95** ($2.95 postpaid) from New American Library, 120 Woodbine Street, Bergenfield, NJ 07621 (or Whole Earth Access).

A River Runs Through It: Norman McLean, 1976; 217 pp. **$7.95** postpaid from University of Chicago, 11030 South Langley, Chicago, IL 60628 (or Whole Earth Access).

Wetlands: William A. Niering, 1985; 638 pp. **$14.95** ($15.95 postpaid) from Random House/Order Dept., 400 Hahn Road, Westminster, MD 21157 (or Whole Earth Access).

Painted turtle (*Chrysemys picta*), length 4" - 9-7/8". —***Wetlands***

He who hears the rippling of rivers in these degenerate days will not utterly despair. —Thoreau

•

Carl also caught two huge pike, one on a barbless spoon and the other on a pork rind. Each took forty minutes to land — they were so heavy that the light rod acted exactly as if it were trying to lift a railroad tie.

Both pike had scars, and the smaller one a healed nick in his back. Both were the same length but the first one was deeper and heavier. It is impossible to squeeze in the gill covers on these huge fish — they can be lifted only by getting the fingers behind the gills. Even then one's hand would not reach around a much bigger one. Weighed them by using Starker's bow on a paddle, giving the scales three times the leverage of the fish, and multiplying the scale reading by three. Thus we stayed within the capacity of the scales. —*Round River*

•

Wetlands evoke powerful emotions. To some they are dark, mysterious, forbidding places, to be avoided at all costs. . . . Perhaps one of the most memorable descriptions of a wetland occurs in Sir Arthur Conan Doyle's *"The Hound of the Baskervilles,"* in which he describes the Great Grimpen Mire, where the villain meets his horrible fate:

Rank weeds and lush, slimy water plants send an odour of decay and a heavy miasmatic vapor into our faces, while a false step plunged us more than once thigh-deep into the dark, quivering mire, which shook for yards in soft undulations around our feet.

This is surely a masterful description of a bog, one of North America's most fascinating wetlands. —*Wetlands*

Marsh with common tule, Gray Lodge Refuge, Butte County, California. —***Wetlands***

•

When I returned to the pilothouse St. Louis was gone and I was lost. Here was a piece of river which was all down in my book, but I could make neither head nor tail of it; you understand, it was turned around. I had seen it when coming upstream, but I had never faced about to see how it looked when it was behind me. My heart broke again, for it was plain that I had got to learn this troublesome river *both ways.* —*Life on the Mississippi*

Beaverhead River near Dillon, Montana. —***Wetlands.***

•

"In the part I was reading it says the Word was in the beginning and that's right. I used to think that water was first, but if you listen carefully you will hear that the words are underneath the water."

"That's because you are a preacher first and then a fisherman," I told him.

"No," my father said, "you are not listening carefully. The water runs over the words . . ."

A river, though, has so many things to say that it is hard to know what it says to each of us . . . . Eventually, all things merge into one, and a river runs through it. The river was cut by the world's great flood and runs over rocks from the basement of time. On some of the rocks are timeless raindrops. Under the rocks are the words, and some of the words are theirs.

I am haunted by waters. —*A River Runs Through It*

• To help save rivers contact these two groups.

American Rivers Conservation Council: information **free** from 322 4th Street NE, Washington, DC 20002.

Friends of the River: information **free** from Building C., Ft. Mason Center, San Francisco, CA 94123.

• A pro-development but excellent basic river reference with river by river bibliography.

Rolling Rivers: Richard Bartlet, 1984; 298 pp. **$29.95** postpaid from McGraw-Hill, Order Dept., Princeton Road, Hightstown, NJ 08520.

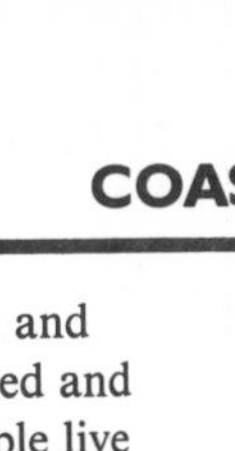

ROCKS, sand dunes, bays, marshes, and protected wharves . . . all lapped and slapped by the seas. More people live on coastal edges than anywhere else on the planet. —Peter Warshall

Waves crashing on the shores of Acadia National Park, Maine. —*The North Atlantic Coast*

Natural History

Once again, Audubon has put out the best overview of a diverse region. ***Pacific Coast*** *covers seashells, mammals, fish, seaweed, algae, invertebrates, and birds: it suffers, however, from nonseasonal bird plumages and unuseable views of whales. For a closer look I like this more detailed local guide:* ***Seashore Life of the Northern Pacific Coast.***

The Atlantic coast equivalent to the above Audubon guide is Peterson's ***A Field Guide to the Atlantic Seashore.*** *For home reading and car travel, Sierra Club's* ***The North Atlantic Coast*** *(Cape Cod to Newfoundland) and* ***The Middle Atlantic Coast*** *(Cape Hatteras to Cape Cod) serve as introductory ecology textbooks and great location guides for seeing the action. —Peter Warshall*

Pacific Coast: Bayard H. and Evelyn McConnaughey, 1985; 633 pp. **$14.95** ($15.95 postpaid) from Random House, Order Dept., 400 Hahn Rd., Westminster, MD 21157 (or Whole Earth Access).

Seashore Life of the Northern Pacific Coast: Eugene N. Kozloff, 1973, 1983; 370 pp. **$19.95** ($21.45 postpaid) from University of Washington Press, P. O. Box 50096, Seattle, WA 98145 (or Whole Earth Access).

Field Guide to the Atlantic Seashore: Kenneth L. Gosner, 1978; 329 pp. **$11.70** ($12.20 postpaid) from Houghton Mifflin Co., Mail Order Dept., Wayside Road, Burlington, MA 01803 (or Whole Earth Access).

The North Atlantic Coast: Michael and Deborah Berrill, 1981; 464 pp. **$10.95** ($13.45 postpaid) from Sierra Club Bookstore, 730 Polk Street, San Francisco, CA 94109 (or Whole Earth Access).

The Middle Atlantic Coast: Bill Perry, 1985; 470 pp. **$12.95** ($15.45 postpaid) from Sierra Club Bookstore, 730 Polk Street, San Francisco, CA 94109 (or Whole Earth Access).

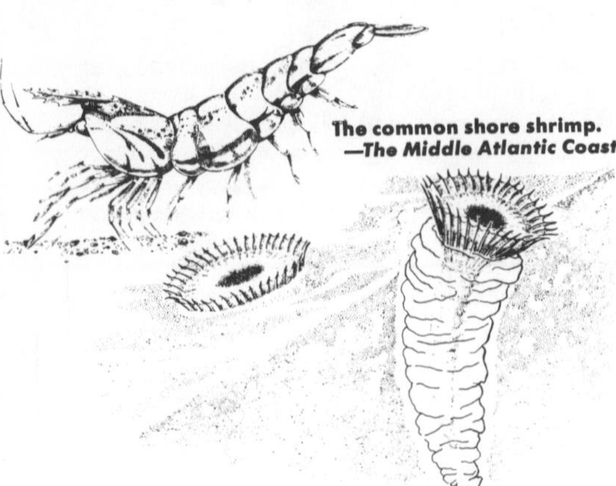

The common shore shrimp. —*The Middle Atlantic Coast*

The fan worm *Myxicola infundibulum* burrows in soft substrates. Its body is pink and composed of 60 segments, each with bristles and hooks. —*The North Atlantic Coast*

• The best access to coastline protection and news.
The Underwater Naturalist: D. W. Bennett, Editor. **$20**/year (4 issues) from The American Littoral Society, Highlands, NJ 07732 (or Whole Earth Access).

• Exquisite color photographs of life in the intertidal zone with clear text on the underlying ecological processes at work.
The Intertidal Wilderness: Anne Wertheim, 1984; 156 pp. **$14.95** ($17.45 postpaid) from Sierra Club Bookstore, 730 Polk Street, San Francisco, CA 94109 (or Whole Earth Access).

Cultural Celebration

Rachel Carson — the woman who first traced the path of DDT from the sea to the soul, awakening the world to toxic karmic feedback — loved the tangled ways of Nature. She wrote a much imitated, never quite reproduced naturalist prose in which language and knowledge meld like foam, waves, and the patterns of a sandy beach. ***The Edge of the Sea*** *is this bioregion's bible.*

North America's grandest Atlantic and Pacific coast bays have their seaward scribes. John Steinbeck's ***The Log from the Sea of Cortez*** *is his journey with primo coastal naturalist Ed Ricketts. It is one of his finest, widening works, as happens at the sea's edge. Chesapeake Bay is a clamshell: top lid is William Warner's* ***Beautiful Swimmers*** *on crabs, men and estuaries; the bottom lid is* ***Life in the Chesapeake Bay,*** *the single best field guide available. —Peter Warshall*

The Edge of the Sea: Rachel Carson, 1955; 276 pp. **$9.70** ($11.20 postpaid) from Houghton Mifflin Co., Mail Order Dept., Wayside Rd., Burlington, MA 01803 (or Whole Earth Access).

The Log from the Sea of Cortez: John Steinbeck, 1951; 336 pp. **$4.95** ($5.95 postpaid) from Viking/Penguin Books, 299 Murray Hill Pkwy., East Rutherford, NJ 07073 (or Whole Earth Access).

Beautiful Swimmers: William W. Warner, 1976; 304 pp. **$6.95** ($7.95 postpaid) from Viking/Penguin Books, 299 Murray Hill Pkwy., East Rutherford, NJ 07073 (or Whole Earth Access).

Life in the Chesapeake Bay: Alice J. Lippson and Robert L. Lippman, 1984; 229 pp. **$12.95** ($14.95 postpaid) from Johns Hopkins University Press, 701 40th Street, Suite 275, Baltimore, MD 21211 (or Whole Earth Access).

•

Compared to the oceans, the Chesapeake Bay is very shallow, the average depth of the main stem being less than 30 feet and the average depth of the entire system, including all tidewater tributaries, only 20 feet. . . . The vast expanses of relatively shallow water in the Bay support a wide variety of bottom life that thrives at depths of less than 20 feet. The Chesapeake's world-famous oyster and soft-shelled clam harvests are attributable to the amount of suitable shallow-water habitat present in the Bay. —*Life in the Chesapeake Bay*

•

Indeed, as one watches the little animals, definite words describing them are likely to grow hazy and less definite, and as species merges into species, the whole idea of definite independent species begins to waver, and a scale-like concept of animal variations comes to take its place. The whole taxonomic method in biology is clumsy and unwieldy, shot through with the jokes of naturalists and the egos of men who wished to have animals named after them. —*The Log from the Sea of Cortez*

Immense ice sheets still covered the region as recently as 10,000 years ago. Rivers of ice flowed down from the coastal mountains and merged, becoming a continuous ice sheet from Puget Sound to the Alaska Peninsula. In the Puget Sound region, the ice attained thicknesses of more than a mile; since the sea level was then some 200 to 300 feet lower than it is now, the ocean met this ice sheet well out on what is now the continental shelf. The retreat of the ice sheets opened up vast areas of new and still evolving coastal habitats from Alaska to Washington. —*Pacific Coast*

Common Black-fingered Mud Crab —*Life in the Chesapeake Bay*

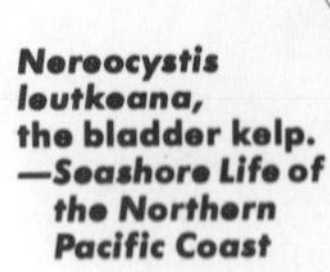

Nereocystis leutkeana,* the bladder kelp. —*Seashore Life of the Northern Pacific Coast

The Sacred

I love this book. I read it like Jews and Christians read the Bible or Asian peoples read Confucius or Buddhists their sutras. Life may be complex, but the religious principles of traditional native peoples are simple, straightforward and clear. **The Sacred** *quietly, carefully and somewhat bookishly lays out the everyday morality of Native Americans before the whiteman. This book is the growing bridge between modern Euro-American society and the strength, beauty and vitality of North America's earliest inhabitants.* —*Peter Warshall*

This book was prepared for use by young Native Americans and largely put together by Native Americans. It's a spiritual field guide for North America. —*Stewart Brand*

•

To us a clown is somebody sacred, funny, powerful, ridiculous, holy, shameful, visionary. He is all this and then some more. Fooling around, a clown is really performing a spiritual ceremony. He has a power. It comes from the thunder-beings, not the animals or the earth. In our Indian belief, a clown has more power than the atom bomb. This power could blow off the dome of the Capitol. I have told you that I once worked as a rodeo clown. This was almost like doing spiritual work. Being a clown, for me, came close to being a medicine man. It was in the same nature. (Lame Deer, 1972:236)

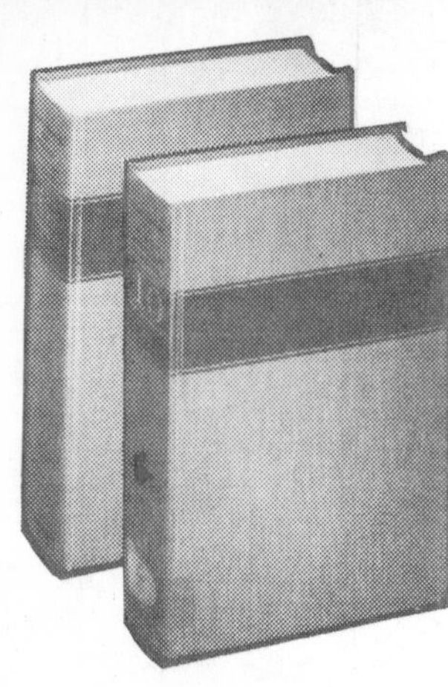

Handbooks of North American Indians

Reconstruction of ► Tolowa dwelling house. Exterior viewed from front, interior from rear. —*Vol. 8: California*

These volumes are the most straightforward history ever written on the peoples inhabiting North America before Anglo-European arrival. They are honest tracings of what happened to each tribal group — be it extinction; exodus from their homelands; fusion with Anglo-Europeans or another tribe; or decreased or increased tribal sovereignty and power. There are superb essays of the peoples known (even to the Indians) only from artifacts and diggings. Each volume features an "eco-cultural" area with excellent essays on local problems . . . snow or heat, grizzlies or witchcraft, food shortages or war. In short, these volumes will be our basic North American Indian references for all time. If you have even the slightest interest in the human, ecological, and spiritual history of the place you live in, you will devour your regional volume. Six published. Fourteen to go. Great prices and photos. —*Peter Warshall*

As usual, peerless work. —*Stewart Brand*

Ishi hunted to live, used each hock and hair of the animal he killed, and lived in proximity to, and knowledge of, all animal life. —*Ishi In Two Worlds*

Ishi In Two Worlds

One August day in 1911 the last wild Indian in America, near gone with starvation, the rest of his tribe dead, walked into a northern California town. Adopted by the brilliant anthropologist, Alfred Kroeber, he lived his remaining years in a California museum. This book by Kroeber's wife reconstructs Ishi's wild years in the Deer Creek area and tells with affection of his civilized years in San Francisco. For millions of readers, Ishi is our emotional link to native America. —*Stewart Brand*

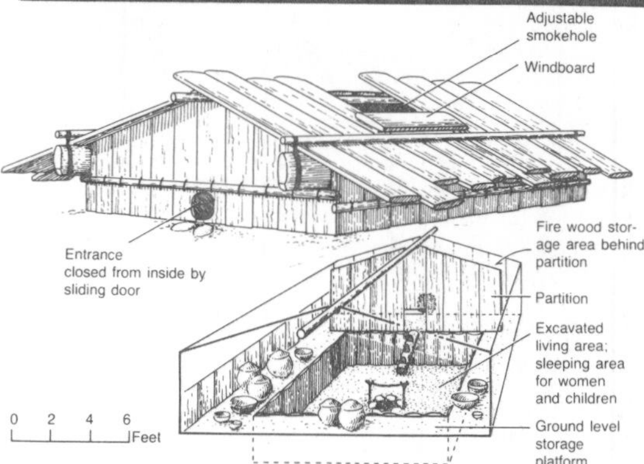

Handbooks of North American Indians:
Vol. 5 (Arctic): 1984; 829 pp. **$30.50.**
Vol. 6 (Subarctic): 1981; 837 pp. **$26.50.**
Vol. 8 (California): 1978; 800 pp. **$26.50.**
Vol. 9 (Southwest): 1979; 701 pp. **$24.50.**
Vol. 11 (Great Basin): 1986; 868 pp. **$28.50.**
Vol. 15 (Northeast): 1978; 924 pp. **$28.50.**

All postpaid from Smithsonian Institution Press, P. O. Box 4866/Hampden Station, Baltimore, MD 21211 (or Whole Earth Access).

Black Elk Speaks

The Pueblo tribes don't go in for visionary solitary mystical whizbangs. (Of all of them only Taos is into peyote very much.) The plains tribes are something else however. Their lives turned on their visions — solo manhood transports, dreams, name visions, sun dance ordeals, battle ecstasy, doctoring sessions . . . and later, ghost dance and peyote. This book is the power vision of one Oglala Sioux — and the extraordinary man it made. Black Elk's account, besides affording unusual insight into Sioux life and historical figures such as Crazy Horse, demonstrates the manner of recognizing a serious vision and being responsible for it, and the burden, joy and power of doing that. —*Stewart Brand*

•

Then I was standing on the highest mountain of them all, and round about beneath me was the whole hoop of the world. And while I stood there I saw more than I can tell and I understood more than I saw; for I was seeing in a sacred manner the shapes of all things in the spirit, and the shape of all shapes as they must live together like one being. And I saw that the sacred hoop of my people was one of many hoops that made one circle, wide as daylight and as starlight, and in the center grew one mighty flowering tree to shelter all the children of one mother and one father. And I saw that it was holy.

Black Elk said the mountain he stood upon in his vision was Harney Peak, in the Black Hills. "But anywhere is the center of the world," he added.

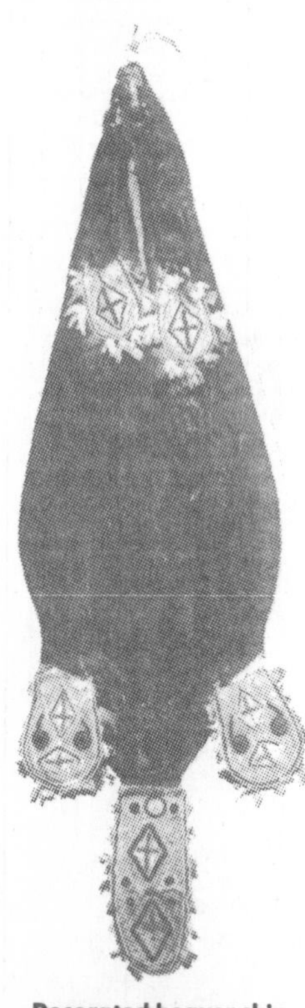

Decorated beaver skin. —*Vol. 15: Northeast*

• For young and old alike, **Man in Nature** (p. 387) provides the best introduction to pre-Columbian North America.

• A rip-roaring, controversial study of Celtic and Semitic migrations to pre-Columbian North America.
America B.C.: Barry Fell, 1976; 312 pp. **$9.95** postpaid from Simon & Schuster, Mail Order Sales, 200 Old Tappan Road, Old Tappan, NJ 07675 (or Whole Earth Access).

REINHABITATION means learning to live-in-place in an area that has been disrupted and injured through past exploitation. It involves becoming native to a place through becoming aware of the particular ecological relationships that operate within and around it. It means understanding activities and evolving social behavior that will enrich the life of that place, restore its life-supporting systems, and establish an ecologically and socially sustainable pattern of existence within it. Simply stated it involves becoming fully alive in and with a place. It involves applying for membership in a biotic community and ceasing to be its exploiter. —Peter Berg, *Reinhabiting a Separate Country*

The Sacred
(Ways of Knowledge, Sources of Life)
Peggy Beck and A. L. Waters
1977; 369 pp.
$14.40
($15.90 postpaid) from:
Navajo Community College Press
Navajo Community College
Tsaile RPO, AZ 86556
or Whole Earth Access

Ishi in Two Worlds
Theodora Kroeber
1961; 262 pp.
$8.95
($10.45 postpaid) from:
University of California Press
2120 Berkeley Way
Berkeley, CA 94720
or Whole Earth Access

Black Elk Speaks
John G. Neihardt
1932, 1959; 238 pp.
$3.95
postpaid from:
Pocket Books
Simon & Schuster
200 Old Tappan Road
Old Tappan, NJ 07675
or Whole Earth Access

Bioregional Magazines

Bioregional magazines serve ecological, rather than political boundaries. They are magnifying glass local. If you're lucky enough to have one roosting where you live, read it for insight into what's unique about the culture and politics of your particular biological region. These publications tend to alter your notion of where you live from, "I live in this county" to "I live in this watershed." The following survey covers only a few of a growing number. Seek one out near you —Jeanne Carstensen

Katuah

From the southern Appalachian Mountains (North and South Carolina, Georgia, Tennessee, and Virginia). Folksy and informative articles on Native American traditions and American pioneer know-how as important parts of the ongoing health of the region.

Marnie Muller, David Wheeler, et al., Editors. **$10**/year (4 issues) from Katuah, P. O. Box 873, Cullowhee, NC 28723.

High Country News

Intelligent and unique economic, political and bureaucratic reporting for the Rocky Mountains, Great Basin, and Colorado Plateau.

Betsy Marston, Editor. **$28**/year (22 issues) from High Country News, Box 1090, Paonia, CO 81428.

Raise the Stakes

Excels at integrating urban life and bioregional perspective. ***Raise the Stakes*** *comes from San Francisco (at the mouth of the great northern and central California watershed) and generally has the best reviews of regional art, music, and food. It's also THE place to get bioregional news from around North America and Europe.*

Robert Watts, Editor. **$15**/year (3 issues) from Planet Drum Foundation, P. O. Box 31251, San Francisco, CA 94131.

Ridge Review

Satisfying, in-depth explorations of one northern California coastal topic per issue, e.g., the wine industry, health, off-shore oil, the marijuana industry, local rivers. Nicely produced. One of the best.

Jim Tarbell, Judy Tarbell, Lucie Marshall, Editors. **$7**/year (4 issues) from Ridge Review, P. O. Box 90, Mendocino, CA 95460.

Siskiyou Country

Life in the Klamath-Siskiyou Mountains of California and Oregon revolves largely around the health of the timber industry and the health of the forests — which work against each other. This conflict is covered well, along with regional culture — a bit heavy on Native American rituals.

Pedro Tama, Editor. **$10**/year (6 issues) from The Siskiyou Regional-Education Project, P. O. Box 989, Cave Junction, OR 97523.

Akwesasne Notes

The largest and most thorough American Indian newspaper, ***Akwesasne Notes*** *is the best way to follow the ongoing Indian struggles over their sacred homelands. News from first peoples on other continents, as well.*

Dog George, Editor. **$10**/year (6 issues) from Mohawk Nation, P. O. Box 196, Rooseveltown, NY 13683-0196.

Planet Drum Foundation

The originators of ***Reinhabiting a Separate Country*** *and of the term "reinhabitation." A membership with Planet Drum gets you three issues of their newsletter,* ***Raise the Stakes*** *(above), access to the names and whereabouts of bioregional groups in North America, and a yearly Bundle. Each Bundle is a selection of context-shifting maps, poems, artwork and essays on such subjects as the Hudson Estuary or the Rocky Mountains. Exploratory thinking and publishing.* —Stewart Brand

•

Something is happening along the Hudson. Individuals, families and communities are rediscovering native and traditional life styles unique to the Hudson Estuary. At the same time, they are working toward a low energy future. By weaving together local heritage and long term sustainability, reinhabitants are shaping a new identity for themselves: A human culture that acts to preserve the health of the wider life community; felt personal responsibility as the keeper of this culture.
—Hudson Estuary Bundle

Planet Drum Foundation: membership **$15**/year; information **free** with SASE.

Hudson Estuary Bundle: $10.50 postpaid.

Backbone — The Rockies: $4 postpaid.

All from Planet Drum Foundation, P. O. Box 31251, San Francisco, CA 94131.

• Three good texts for budding bioregionalists

The Ecology of North America: Victor E. Shelford. OUT OF PRINT.

Natural Vegetation of North America: John L. Vankat, 1979; 261 pp. **$23.95** postpaid from John Wiley and Sons/Order Dept., 1 Wiley Drive, Somerset, NJ 08873.

Natural Regions of the United States and Canada: Charles B. Hunt, 1974; 725 pp. **$31.95** ($33.45 postpaid) from W. H. Freeman, 4419 W. 1980 South, Salt Lake City, UT 84104.

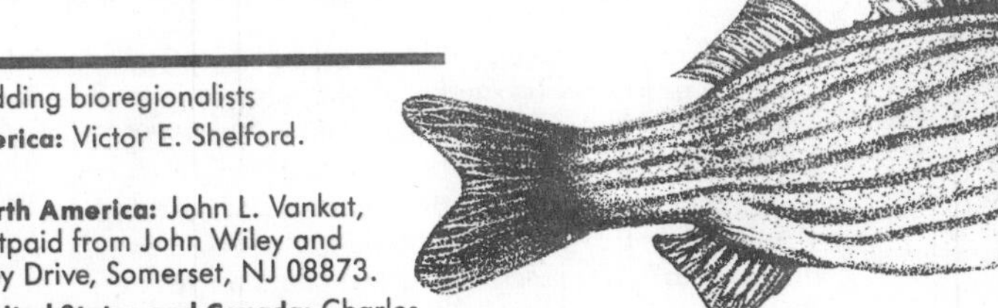

THE TROPICAL HUMID FORESTS, aka "rainforests," form a somber, green girdle around the equator. Shrouded in clouds, known for their steamy heat, they may support as many as one hundred species of trees in a single acre. Here is access to the fastest disappearing bioregion of the planet. For sheer enjoyment and a solid introduction, read the extravagantly illustrated *Jungles.* For the most affectionate portrayal of peoples evolved into rainforest life, read *The Forest People,* a study of the BaMbuti Pygmies of the Congo; it is and will remain a classic of anthropology. For a contemporary view, literate and concerned, Catherine Caufield's *In the Rainforest* reports on the destruction. For action, contact the *Rainforest Action Network* which has a monthly news alert about what you can do to help.

—Peter Warshall

Jungles
Edward S. Ayensu
1980; 208 pp.
$35
($37.90 postpaid) from:
Crown Publishers
34 Englehard Avenue
Avenel, NJ 07001
or Whole Earth Access

The Forest People
Colin Turnbull
1961; 295 pp.
$9.95 postpaid from:
Simon and Schuster
Mail Order Sales
200 Old Tappan Road
Old Tappan, NJ 07675
or Whole Earth Access

In the Rainforest
Catherine Caufield
1985; 304 pp.
$16.95
($17.95 postpaid) from:
Random House
Order Dept.
400 Hahn Road
Westminster, MD 21157
or Whole Earth Access

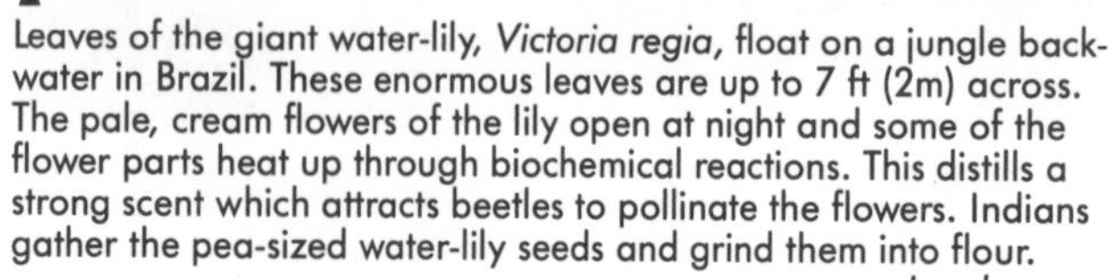

▲ Leaves of the giant water-lily, *Victoria regia*, float on a jungle backwater in Brazil. These enormous leaves are up to 7 ft (2m) across. The pale, cream flowers of the lily open at night and some of the flower parts heat up through biochemical reactions. This distills a strong scent which attracts beetles to pollinate the flowers. Indians gather the pea-sized water-lily seeds and grind them into flour.

—*Jungles*

Camayura people of South Amazonia, dancing. —*Jungles*

•

Whereas the other tribes are relatively recent arrivals, the Pygmies have been in the forest for many thousands of years. It is their world, and in return for their affection and trust it supplies them with all their needs. They do not have to cut the forest down to build plantations, for they know how to hunt the game of the region and gather the wild fruits that grow in abundance there, though hidden to outsiders. They know how to distinguish the innocent-looking *itaba* vine from the many others it resembles so closely, and they know how to follow it until it leads them to a cache of nutritious, sweet-tasting roots. They know the tiny sounds that tell where the bees have hidden their honey; they recognize the kind of weather that brings a multitude of different kinds of mushrooms springing to the surface; and they know what kinds of wood and leaves often disguise this food. The exact moment when termites swarm, at which they must be caught to provide an important delicacy, is a mystery to any but the people of the forest. They know the secret language that is denied all outsiders and without which life in the forest is an impossiblity.

—*The Forest People*

•

Between 40 and 50 percent of all types of living things — as many as five million species of plants, animals, and insects — live in tropical rainforests, though they cover less than 2 percent of the globe. . . .

A typical four-square-mile patch of rainforest, according to a report by the U.S. National Academy of Sciences, contains up to 1,500 species of flowering plants, as many as 750 species of tree, 125 species of mammal, 400 species of bird, 100 of reptile, 60 of amphibian, and 150 of butterfly, though some sites have more. Insects in tropical rainforests are so abundant and so little known that it is difficult to establish an average density. The same report cites a recent estimate that 2.5 acres might contain 42,000 species. Ten square feet of leaf litter, when analyzed, turned up 50 species of ant alone.

—*In the Rainforest*

•

Tropical rainforests are being destroyed faster than any other natural community. A United Nations study from 1976 offers the most optimistic assessment of forest loss. It found that, of the 2.4 billion acres of rainforest left in the world, 14 million are completely and permanently destroyed each year. That is almost 30 acres every minute of every day. In 1980 the U.S. National Academy of Sciences announced an even worse figure. It said that over 50 million acres of rainforest — an area the size of England, Scotland, and Wales — are destroyed or seriously degraded each year. The most comprehensive study to date, published in 1981 by the Food and Agriculture Organization of the United Nations, says that at present rates almost one fifth of the world's remaining tropical rainforest will be completely destroyed or severely degraded by the end of the century.

—*In the Rainforest*

Rainforest Action Network: Membership **$25**/year, $15 low-income (includes 12 issues of **Rainforest Action Network Alert**); from Rainforest Action Network, 466 Green Street, Suite 300, San Francisco, CA 94133.

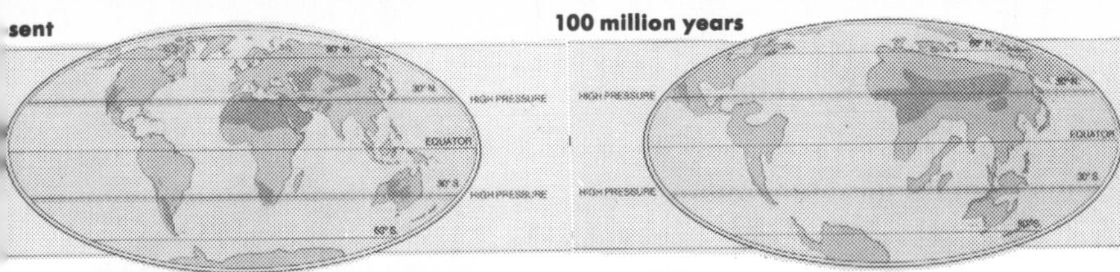

Arid Lands • The Mountain People

In the lands with little rain, erratic rain, and/or excessive heat, a unique eco-culture evolved in nonhuman and human species. ***Arid Lands*** *is a coffee table book but well researched with Time-Life photographic beauty. It ends with a peculiar optimism about turning the deserts green.*

On the other hand, 70 nations now confront expanding aridity. Never before has a combination of poor land management, misplaced foreign aid, self-serving local politics, and weather so dramatically led to starvation as in the recent drought in Ethiopia. ***The Mountain People*** *describes what happens during famine better than any book I know. The fabric rips and we see the Ik (a tribal people of northern Kenya) possessed by a dark humor and seemingly cruel betrayal of even their closest kin.*

The best pamphlet on desertification is ***Spreading Deserts — The Hand of Man*** *by Erik Eckholm and Lester Brown (Worldwatch Paper #13;* *see p. 92**). —Peter Warshall*

▲
An Australian frog creates a moist world of its own for protection from the desert's aridity. The frog lies dormant in its burrow most of the year, sheathed in a layer of skin that retains body moisture, and reemerges only during infrequent rains. —*Arid Lands*

▲
A comparison of present continental configurations with those predicted for 100 million years in the future shows a markedly different arrangement of land under the subtropical belts of high pressure (shaded bands). With far more land in the vicinity of lat. 30ºN., the Northern Hemisphere will have a colder, drier climate and more extensive deserts. Conversely, less land and more water in the Southern Hemisphere will contribute to a warmer, wetter climate and fewer deserts. —*Arid Lands*

Blind Logwara . . . when he tried to reach a dead hyena for a share of the putrid meat, his fellow Ik trampled him underfoot. He thought it quite funny. —The Mountain People

•
The problem of desertification is not Africa's alone. Each year immense clouds of hot dust rise over the Sahara and drift westward across the Atlantic. In 1982 a cloud more than 1,000 miles long reached Florida, dumping massive quantities of dust into the atmosphere along the way and raising air-pollution levels precipitously before it finally dissipated.

The United States in fact did not need a plume of Saharan sand to remind it of its own problems with advancing aridity. In the American West alone, 500 million tons of topsoil wash away into streams and rivers each year. —*Arid Lands*

Arid Lands
Jake Page
1984; 176 pp.
$14.95
($15.95 postpaid) from:
Silver Burdett Co.
Attn.: Order Processing
250 James Street / CN 1918
Morristown, NJ 07960
or Whole Earth Access

The Mountain People
Colin M. Turnbull
1972; 309 pp.
$9.95 postpaid from:
Simon and Schuster
Mail Order Sales
200 Old Tappan Road
Old Tappan, NJ 07675
or Whole Earth Access

The Future of the Oceans

This book is full of wonderful facts. It is the first to present and analyze the United Nations Convention on the Law of the Sea . . . perhaps the first global government of Third World and industrialized nations. It is well written with an extremely sophisticated sense of the marine resources, marine ecology, and marine-based economy of our largest bioregion: the vast ocean filled with fish, aquatic plants, mineral nodules, and petroleum power.
—Peter Warshall

•
Only four species of aquatic plants have been fully domesticated: the red algae *Porphyra* and *Eucheuma* and the brown algae *Laminaria* and *Undaria*. The main producer countries are China (*Laminaria*), Japan (*Porphyra* and *Undaria*), and the Philippines (*Eucheuma*).

Full domestication of aquatic plants passes through three stages: (1) prudent management of natural stocks (e.g., regulating the harvest seasons and harvest techniques); (2) manipulation of the environment (e.g., improving substratum and fertilization and regulating temperature and light); and (3) control of the reproductive process, artificial propagation of seeds and spores, and selective breeding of the plant.

Approximately two million wet tons of seaweed are harvested annually from cultivated and wild sources. The potential for further production is without limit.

•
Japan employs eight thousand undersea coal miners who produce about ten million tons of coal from the oceans per year. The mines are too far away from shore to make tunneling from shore practical, so the Japanese built artificial islands from which to drive their shafts into the seabed.

In the 1970s, the German oceanographic ship *Valdivia* explored off the coast of Mozambique and discovered heavy sands at a depth of between twenty and 500 meters. These sands contain about 50 million tons of recoverable ilmenite, 1.5 million tons of rutile, and 4 million tons of zircon, all of which add up to ten times the present annual production of the industrialized world.

The Future of the Oceans
(A Report to the Club of Rome)
Elisabeth Mann Borgese
1986; 139 pp.
$12.95 (Canadian)
($13.95 postpaid) from:
Harvest House Ltd. Publishers
Sales & Distribution Services
314 Judson Street
Toronto, Ontario,
Canada M8Z 4X7
or Whole Earth Access

• **Desertification of the United States**, by David Sheridan (U.S. Government Printing Office), is out of print but crucial to understanding U.S. problems.

• For more on oceans, see the World Ocean Floor Panorama Map and **Times Atlas of the Oceans** (p. 14).

• The Rachael Carson classic on oceans:
The Sea Around Us: 1950; 221 pp.; **$4.95** ($5.95 postpaid) from New American Library, 120 Woodbine Street, Bergenfield, NJ 07621.

THE ENDLESS BALANCING ACTS of civilization get played out on the land. Here starvation, there economic collapse from oversupply. Here urban claustrophobia, there rural loneliness. Human life dangles on a few threads — sunshine, rainfall and topsoil. From these come plants, and the kind of relationship we have with green things defines who we are.

—Richard Nilsen

Soil and Civilization
Edward Hyams
1976; 312 pp.
$14.95
($16.45 postpaid) from:
State Mutual Books
521 Fifth Avenue
New York, NY 10017
or Whole Earth Access

Soil and Civilization

Edward Hyams writes the first and best "watershed history" of ancient and present civilizations. Rather than focusing on the genius of Pericles or the naval talents of Themistocles, he focuses on the ultimate, long-term strength of Greece or any nation: its soil. He elegantly chronicles, for instance, how oak forest cutting led to topsoil erosion creating a subsoil economy (olives and vineyards) which made Athens dependent on naval trade to get topsoil crops (wheat). Includes the Euphrates and America's dustbowl. If one book on history should be read by everyone, I would choose **Soil and Civilization.**

—Peter Warshall

•

The Egyptians were not obliged to discover manuring before settling, not obliged to advance from soil/parasitism to soil-making in order to found cities. The Nile replaced every year what the Egyptians took out of it.

Many advantages of the Egyptian and of Mesopotamian environment have been put forward to explain the precocious rise of their urban civilizations, while the peoples of other regions were still held back in the simpler ways of Neolithic culture. But the attribute of the Nile valley, which it shared with the Euphrates-Tigris delta, and which assured to the Egyptian and Mesopotamian peoples their long lead in the progress towards civilization, was surely the one which enabled them to settle down and exploit the soils of their countries as soon as they had learnt to till them, and without having to find a way of re-making the soil every year.

Soil Erosion
Sandra S. Batie
1983; 136 pp.
$8.50
($10.50 postpaid) from:
The Conservation Foundation
1255 23rd Street NW
Suite 200
Washington, DC 20037
or Whole Earth Access

Soil Erosion

No moralizing. No righteous insinuations that farmers or corporations are out to starve future generations by mining the nation's soils. Instead, the political nitty-gritty: how terribly difficult it is to harmonize cash-flow problems (farm debt, land prices, fluctuating markets, federal subsidies, equipment purchases) and soil conservation practices. Learn how "targeting" erosion-control funds to the worst situations can slip into pork-barrel funding; how cross-compliance policies (e.g., the feds insure crops against weather disasters in exchange for farmers' following good erosion-control guidelines) lose control in times of high crop demand; how punishing farmers for sloppy land use practices has never worked; how incentives for farmers who rent must be different from those for farmers who own.

This book competently fills a vacant niche, the niche of America's most important politics — saving its topsoil.

—Peter Warshall

•

Erosion not only robs farmland of its fertility, it also seriously pollutes the nation's waterways. . . . Ironically, most Americans believe our soil erosion problem was resolved during the 1930s when severe droughts and dust storms swept across the prairies and midwestern soil accumulated on windowsills of the Capitol in Washington, D.C. . . . If Americans do not take seriously the accumulating evidence about the extent and consequences of erosion, the country's agricultural future may be undermined, perhaps not this decade or next, but sometime early in the twenty-first century.

•

Erosion is a natural process. When lands are covered by vegetation, the rate of erosion is slow, approximately 1 inch every 100 to 250 years, and is offset by the creation of new soil. But on lands devoid of vegetation . . . erosion rates increase by magnitudes.

Sediment pollution from the drainage area of the Loosahatchie River entering the Mississippi River 1 mile north of Memphis, Tennessee, April 1968.

Ecology of Compost
Daniel L. Dindal
1976; 12 pp.
25 cents postpaid from:
State University of New York, College of Environmental Science and Forestry
Syracuse, NY 13210

Ecology of Compost

Backyard composting, brief and simple. Whether you have a window box or a whole farm, the principle is the same — take care of your soil and your soil will take care of you. Soils need to be fed just like people.

—Richard Nilsen

ARRANGEMENT OF LAYERS FOR COMPOSTING

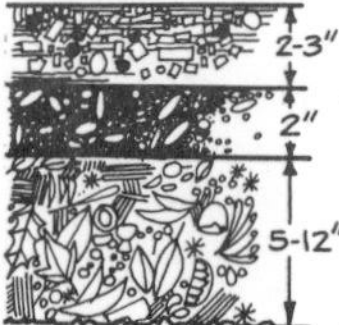

• Some soils need fertilizer or minerals before they'll grow crops. A soil test kit can tell you if your soil needs help. This kit includes a **Soil Handbook.**
LaMotte Model EL Garden Guide Kit: Information **free** from LaMotte Chemical Products Co., P. O. Box 329, Chestertown, MD 21620

• See also "earthworms," p. 82.

The Unsettling of America

Our land is more undone by our agriculture than by any other mischief. Farmer, poet, essayist Wendell Berry speaks to the matter with plain speech — it rasps the brain, leaves a memory of the thought. Don't say it is no longer possible to do our farming right. Berry is.
—Stewart Brand

•

We need wilderness as a standard of civilization and as a cultural model. Only by preserving areas where nature's processes are undisturbed can we preserve an accurate sense of the impact of civilization upon its natural sources. Only if we know how the land *was* can we tell how it *is.*

•

A part of the health of a farm is the farmer's wish to remain there. His long-term good intention toward the place is signified by the presence of trees. A family is married to a farm more by their planting and protecting of trees than by their memories or their knowledge, for the trees stand for their fidelity and kindness to what they do not know. The most revealing sign of the ill health of industrial agriculture — its greed, its short-term ambitions — is its inclination to see trees as obstructions and to strip the land bare of them.

The Unsettling of America
Wendell Berry
1986; 240 pp.
$7.95
($10.45 postpaid) from:
Sierra Club Bookstore
730 Polk Street
San Francisco, CA 94109
or Whole Earth Access

The One-Straw Revolution

By changing one of the grasses in his rice fields to another variety, Fukuoka started a process that brought his part of the ecosystem into a natural balance. On his farm he gets yields comparable to traditional farms' but without plowing; he lets nature do the work. He simply plants and harvests — pretty revolutionary. The book describes his method. *—Rosemary Menninger*

•

Make your way carefully through these fields. Dragonflies and moths fly up in a flurry. Honeybees buzz from blossom to blossom. Part the leaves and you will see insects, spiders, frogs, lizards and many other small animals bustling about in the cool shade. Moles and earthworms burrow beneath the surface.

This is a balanced rice field ecosystem. Insect and plant communities maintain a stable relationship here. It is not uncommon for a plant disease to sweep through this area, leaving the crops in these fields unaffected.

And now look over at the neighbor's field for a moment. The weeds have all been wiped out by herbicides and cultivation. The soil animals and insects have been exterminated by poison. The soil has been burned clean of organic matter and microorganisms by chemical fertilizers. In the summer you see farmers at work in the fields, wearing gas masks and long rubber gloves. These rice fields, which have been farmed continuously for over 1,500 years, have now been laid waste by the exploitive farming practices of a single generation.

"And yet these fields have not been plowed for twenty-five years."

The One-Straw Revolution
Masanobu Fukuoka
1978; 181 pp.
$9.95 postpaid from:
Rodale Press
33 East Minor Street
Emmaus, PA 18049
or Whole Earth Access

Meeting the Expectations of the Land

The title of this collection of essays about sustainable agriculture conveys an apt reversal. A line from Robert Frost might help: "The land was ours before we were the land's." The ideas here are visionary in that they look both forward and backward in time, but lest you think the book advocates a retreat to agricultural animism, it is worth emphasizing that these ideas are also very practical. You won't find them in use on most American farms today because there the emphasis has been on productivity and profits.

Profits? Even if your news from the farm comes only from the TV, you know you can forget about "profits" in farming. And productivity? Sure, that's there, but it is the same kind you find in a coal mine. When the coal is gone you shut it down and move on. When the topsoil is gone, or the soil is salted out from irrigation, where do you go?

You go to a kind of agriculture that can sustain; not only the land, but also the life on it and in it, as well as the people who work it and those who depend on them for food. This book is full of clues to how that kind of agriculture will work, by people like Gene Logsdon, John Todd and Gary Snyder. *—Richard Nilsen*

•

I once asked an Amish farmer who had only twenty-six acres why he didn't acquire a bit more land. He looked around at his ten fine cows, his sons hoeing the corn with him, his spring water running continuously by gravity through house and barn, his few fat hogs, his sturdy buildings, his good wife heaping the table with food, his fine flock of hens, his plot of tobacco and acre of strawberries, his handmade hickory chairs (which he sold for all the extra cash he really needed), and he said, "Well, I'm just not smart enough to farm any more than this well." I have a hunch no one could.

Meeting the Expectations of the Land
Wes Jackson,
Wendell Berry
and Bruce Colman
1985; 272 pp.
$12.50
($14 postpaid) from:
North Point Press
850 Talbot Avenue
Berkeley, CA 94706
or Whole Earth Access

Seaweed in Agriculture and Horticulture

Unlike most fertilizers, seaweed is a renewable resource. Either sprayed on the leaves of plants (foliar feeding) or added to the soil, it can often be a single solution to many soil deficiencies — including trace elements. This British book has all the details. *—Richard Nilsen*

Seaweed in Agriculture and Horticulture
W. A. Stephenson
1974; 241 pp.
$7 ($9 postpaid) from:
The Rateavers
9049 Covina Street
San Diego, CA 92126
or Whole Earth Access

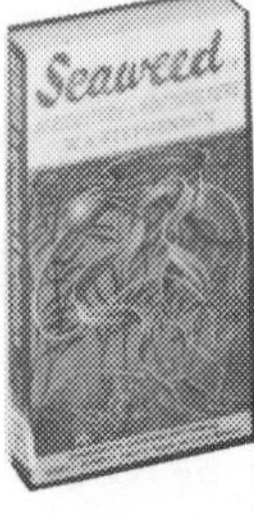

- See also **New Roots for Agriculture,** p. 85.
- *The* classic on the domestication of plants, by a damned interesting man. Bless him, he annotates his bibliography.

Plants, Man and Life: Edgar Anderson, 1952; 251 pp.
$3.95 ($5.45 postpaid) from University of California Press, 2120 Berkeley Way, Berkeley, CA 94720.
Or Whole Earth Access

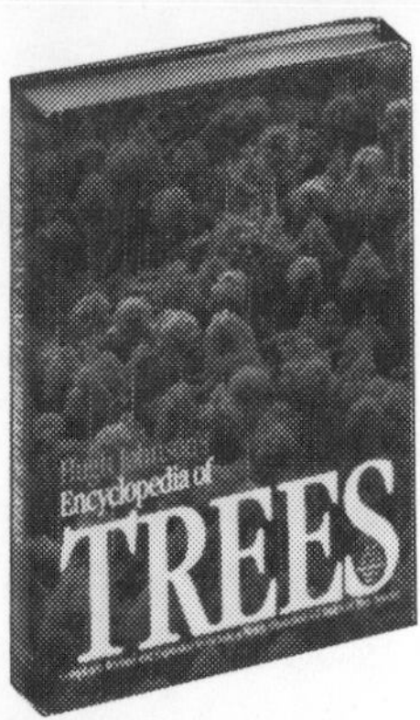

Hugh Johnson's Encyclopedia of Trees
Hugh Johnson
1984; 336 pp.
$17.98
($19.73 postpaid) from:
W. H. Smith, Publishers
80 Distribution Blvd.
Edison, NJ 08818
or Whole Earth Access

Woodland Ecology
(Environmental Forestry for the Small Owner)
Leon S. Minckler
1980; 241 pp.
$11.95
($13.45 postpaid) from:
Syracuse University Press
1600 Jamesville Avenue
Syracuse, NY 13244-5160
or Whole Earth Access

Permaculture Institute of North America
Membership **$25**/year (includes a subscription to *The Permaculture Activist*) from:
PINA
6488 Maxwelton Road
Clinton, WA 98236

Friends of the Trees 1986 Yearbook
Michael Pilarski, Editor
1986; 80 pp.
$4.60 postpaid from:
Friends of the Trees Society
P. O. Box 1466
Chelan, WA 98816

Hugh Johnson's Encyclopedia of Trees

If the quest is for one volume on trees, this is the choice. Ace popularizer Hugh Johnson is a great organizer with a wonderfully personal writing style. Well captioned color photographs are included and there are 65 pages of A-Z tree species encyclopedia as well. A bargain of a book. —Richard Nilsen

◄ **The New Zealand Kahikatea or 'white pine', *Podocarpus dacrydioiaes*, grows in swampy ground in both North and South Islands. Captain Cook measured a specimen with a clean bole to 90 feet.**

Woodland Ecology

Seventy-three percent of the forest land in the eastern United States is held by private, nonindustrial owners, according to the author. He considers the eastern hardwood forest types and explains very basic woodland ecology and discusses the options a small owner has in deciding how to maintain and use his woods. The book includes an extensive appendix of references, well annotated, and a section on growing and using wood for fuel.
—Richard Nilsen

A Planter's Guide to the Urban Forest

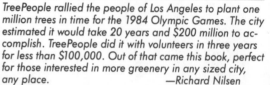

TreePeople rallied the people of Los Angeles to plant one million trees in time for the 1984 Olympic Games. The city estimated it would take 20 years and $200 million to accomplish. TreePeople did it with volunteers in three years for less than $100,000. Out of that came this book, perfect for those interested in more greenery in any sized city, any place. —Richard Nilsen

A Planter's Guide to the Urban Forest
TreePeople
1983; 96 pp.
$10
($11.50 postpaid) from:
TreePeople
12601 Mulholland Drive
Beverly Hills, CA
90210-9990
or Whole Earth Access

Permaculture Institute of North America

Permaculture Institute of North America (PINA) is expanding on the work begun in Australia by Bill Mollison. It was he who coined the term permaculture, a contraction of 'permanent agriculture,' for a kind of ecosystem design that recognizes that sustainable land use is only possible within the context of sustainable and humane culture. Whether in a backyard or an entire watershed the goal is the same: to produce food and energy in ways that mimic the conserving stability and resiliency of natural ecosystems. There is a great emphasis on tree crops here, but fundamentally permaculture is asking many of the same basic design questions being raised at The Land Institute (see p. 85). Membership includes a subscription to their newsletter, ***The Permaculture Activist.***
—Richard Nilsen

Friends of the Trees 1986 Yearbook

The ***Friends of the Trees Yearbook*** *is a rich source of information about planting trees and saving forests. A perennial seed exchange is included. The* ***Yearbook*** *is an excellent way to follow the news and the players in the international alternative forestry and sustainable agriculture movements, since most of the groups either advertise here or are reviewed. —Richard Nilsen*

•

Land Spandrel: a space between buildings, improvements, and pavement that occurs, sometimes by accident, or oversight, because of the structure of urban land use rather than by design.

Examples:

- railroad rights-of-way that are currently not being used to their fullest potential
- vacant lots
- land that abuts freeways, cloverleaves, and ramps
- abandoned alleys
- public school frontages or school yards
- areas adjacent to flood control channels
- side yards adjacent to public or private buildings
- steep slopes between roads or lots
- corner or triangular spaces in parking lots or areas between slots that are not used for parking
- areas under transmission lines in utility rights-of-way
- shopping malls or public plazas

• For more on trees in cities, see **The Granite Garden** (p. 73).
• For more on innovative systems of sustainable agriculture, see **New Roots for Agriculture** and The Land Institute (p. 85).
• See also "Trees" (p. 39), "Western Forests" (pp. 48-49), and "Eastern Forests" (pp. 50-51).

Miller Nurseries winter hardy Sweet Black Kristin cherry.

Nurseries

Chestnut Hill Nursery: *Home of the Dunstan Hybrid Chestnut, highly resistant to the bark fungus that wiped out the American Chestnut early this century. Chestnuts used to be the dominant species of the eastern hardwood forest, and their comeback is underway here.*
Catalog **free** from Rural Route 1, Box 341, Alachua, FL 32615.

Lawson's Nursery: *Owner James Lawson describes his business as "just a hobby that has gotten a little out of hand." He specializes in over one hundred old variety apples on dwarfing rootstocks.*
Catalog **free** from Route 1, Box 294, Bau Ground, GA 30107.

Miller Nurseries: *Family owned operation offering fruits, nuts, berries, and some ornamental trees. Strong on winter-hardy varieties, especially grapes.*
Catalog **free** from 5060 West Lake Road, Canandaigua, NY 14424.

New York State Fruit Testing Cooperative Association: *This cooperative exists primarily to evaluate and introduce new varieties of fruit, but they also sell some older apple varieties. Geared to serve commercial growers, but membership is open to all. Reasonable prices, even for individual trees.*
Catalog **$5** from Geneva, NY 14456.

Stark Bros.' Nurseries and Orchards: *One of the oldest and largest fruit nurseries in the country. They also sell nut, shade and ornamental trees and shrubs.*
Catalog **free** from P. O. Box 2281F, Louisana, MO 63353-0010.

Southmeadow Fruit Gardens: *Two hundred thirty-nine (!) rare and old apple varieties; also pears, peaches, apricots, plums, cherries, berries, and grapes. The catalog is a treasure-house of varietal information.*
Catalog **$8;** price list **free;** both from Lakeside, MI 49116.

—Richard Nilsen

North American Fruit Explorers (NAFEX)

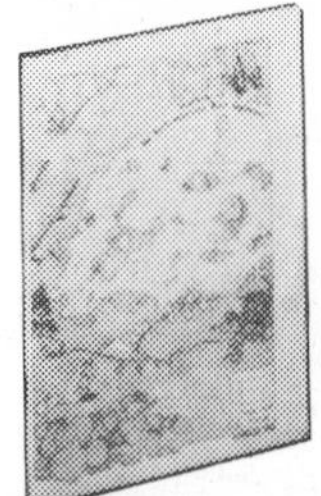

NAFEX
Membership **$6**/year
(includes quarterly *Pomona*) from:
POMONA / North American Fruit Explorers
10 South 055 Madison St.
Hinsdale, IL 60521

These folks are backyard orchardists, many with a lifetime of experience to share on everything having to do with fruit orchards. Their quarterly, **Pomona**, *exchanges member information that is priceless. They exchange plant materials, have a lending library, and stay together by refusing to argue over the finer points of organic vs. nonorganic orcharding. This policy of sunny noncontroversy is occasionally disrupted by a delightful downpour of disagreement, but there is no scientific snobbery. Anyone with some experience is urged to share it and they will let it stand on its own merit.*

—Peter Beckstrand

•

As the result of genetic research performed in Germany in the 1920's . . . we now have a new soft fruit worthy of trial here in America, the Josta.

The Jostaberry plant is the result of a cross between black currant and gooseberry. It is far more vigorous than all existing varieties of either of its parents. . . .

The taste of the Jostaberry is unique. The berries unite the refreshing acidity and the fine aroma of the gooseberry with the distinctly tasteable aroma of the black currant. . . . The berries are very suitable for jam and juice. They also freeze very well and can be stored for a long time without any loss of quality.

Ecological Fruit Production in the North

Ecological Fruit Production in the North
Bart Hall-Beyer and Jean Richard
1983; 270 pp.
$11.50
($12.75 postpaid) from:
Bart Hall-Beyer
R. R. 3
Scottstown, Quebec
J0B 3B0 Canada
or Whole Earth Access

Do you live so high up or so far north that every time you look something up in a gardening book you're right off the edge of the charts? If you are trying to raise fruit, this book should rank as a minor miracle. It is a self-published gem by two fruit farmers from Quebec who define "the North" as what's above a line running from New York City through St. Louis to Santa Fe, and then up the spine of the Rockies and over to Vancouver. In addition, author Jean Richard explains a method of restorative pruning for mature trees that he learned as a kid in Switzerland in the 1930s. It apparently works wonders on old standard apple trees and is about as different as you can get from the open-center pruning most books describe.

—Richard Nilsen

•

In temperate and boreal climates the ultimate factor controlling a plant's suitability is whether or not it will survive the winters. *Is it hardy?* . . . Far too many northerners, on both sides of the border, have planted trees which having come from milder climate are simply not suitable for their area. . . . Furthermore, it is an infrequent but regular occurrence to have an extraordinarily cold winter which rigorously eliminates all the trees which are marginally hardy in an area. In northeastern North America, the winters of 1904, 1917, 1934, and 1981 were especially cold, and fit into this category of "Test Winters" — winters that test the real hardiness of a tree. In the Northeast, trees which have survived one or more of these onslaughts can be assumed to be fully hardy.

Pruning

Pruning
Michael MacCaskey and Robert L. Stebbins
1983; 160 pp.
$9.95
($11.90 postpaid) from:
HPBooks
P. O. Box 5367
Tucson, AZ 85703
or Whole Earth Access

This book neatly combines what you need to do with why it needs doing. Since beginners often equate pruning with vegetative barbarism, these explanations are most helpful. Fruit trees are covered as well as grapes, berries, roses, hedges, and other ornamentals.

—Richard Nilsen

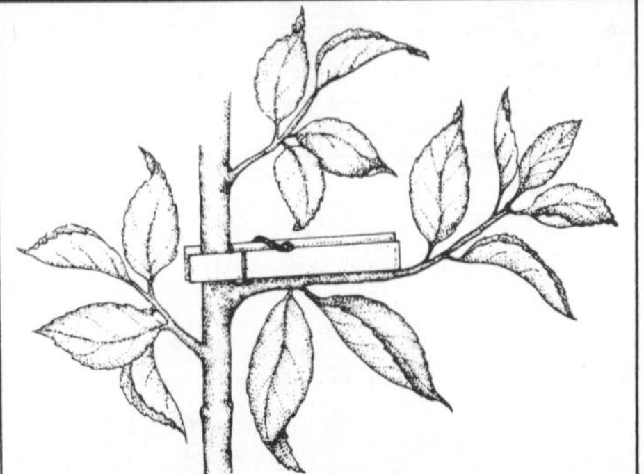

One of the easiest ways to train young trees to develop wider crotches is to use spring-type clothespins. Install clothespins when shoots are 6 to 8 inches long and still flexible.

• For more on selecting fruit trees see **Designing and Maintaining Your Edible Landscape Naturally.** (p. 69).

• For cultivating fruit trees see one of two regional HP books: **Fruits, Berries & Nuts for the Midwest and East** or **Western Fruit, Berries and Nuts** (p. 69).

• For buying fruit trees, see also Peaceful Valley Farm Supply (p. 85).

—Johnny's Selected Seeds

SEEDS are envelopes made for traveling, and seed catalogs aid and organize the process. Regional seed companies are worthy of support because their locally adapted varieties will often do best in your garden. The handful of catalogs reviewed on this page are included because they offer either a good selection for one climatic region, a very comprehensive selection, or exotic or unique varieties. —Richard Nilsen

Seed Catalog Directories

Keeping up with the fast-changing seed business is easier with a list of the players. Here are three good ones; two additional sources are cross-referenced at the bottom of this page.

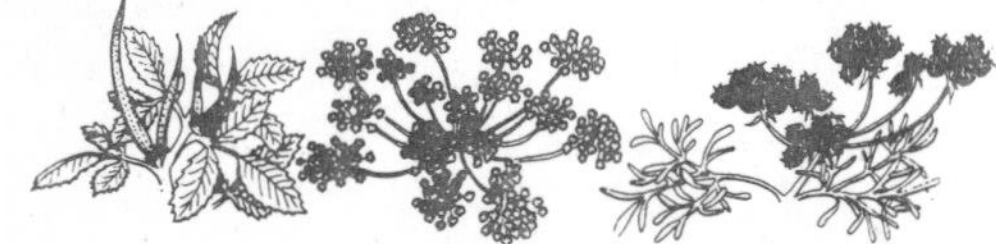
—Johnny's Selected Seeds

Sources of Native Seeds and Plants

$3 from Soil Conservation Society of America, 7515 Northeast Ankeny Road, Ankeny, IA 50021.

Over 270 sources of wildflower, native grass, tree and shrub seed are in this 35-page pamphlet, as well as sources for native plant material and nursery stock.

Directory of Seed and Nursery Catalogs

$3 from National Gardening Association, 180 Flynn Avenue, Burlington, VT 05401.

Close to 400 U.S. and Canadian mail order sources are included in this 14-page pamphlet. Updated annually.

Seed, Bulb, and Nursery Supplies

Free (with 40-cent SASE) from Rodale's Organic Gardening Reader Service/ attn. Seed List, 33 East Minor Street, Emmaus, PA 18049.

This 11-page list of U.S. and Canadian sources is updated annually.

Seed Catalogs

Abundant Life Seed Foundation

P. O. Box 772, Port Townsend, WA 98368.

Nonprofit source of vegetable, native, and endangered seed for the Pacific Northwest. Catalog ***free.***

Bountiful Gardens Ecology Action

5798 Ridgewood Road, Willits, CA 95490.

Organically grown heirloom vegetable seed; also herb, flower, and cover-crop seed. Catalog ***free.***

Butterbrooke Farm

78 Barry Road, Oxford, CT 06483.

This co-op has the cheapest prices for a basic selection of vegetable seed of anybody — 35 cents per packet. Catalog ***free.***

Good Seed

Box 702, Tonasket, WA 98855.

Open-pollinated vegetable seed, plus herb, flower, and cover-crop seed, all selected for the intermountain region east of the Cascades and west of the Rockies. Catalog ***$1.***

High Altitude Gardens

P. O. Box 4238, Ketchum, ID 83340.

Short-season vegetable and herb varieties for the western mountains. Their seed testing and production are done from 5,000 to 7,000 foot elevation. Catalog ***$2.***

Johnny's Selected Seeds

299 Foss Hill Road, Albion, ME 04910.

Well-designed catalog of vegetable seed adapted ideally for a cool 145-day-average frost-free season. Good germination and cultural directions, also recipes. Catalog ***free.***

Larner Seeds

P. O. Box 407, Bolinas, CA 94924.

Native plant seed of both California and New England, wildflower mixes and native grasses; much of it rarely collected. Catalog ***$.50.***

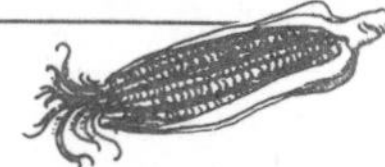

Le Marche Seeds International

P. O. Box 566, Dixon, CA 95620.

Best source for baby vegetable varieties used in nouvelle cuisine restaurants. What's new (to American gardeners) is here. Catalog ***$.50.***

Nicols Garden Nursery

1190 N. Pacific Highway, Albany, OR 97321.

Herb seed and plants, vegetable seed (large selection), some flower seed, plus beer- and winemaking supplies and dried herbs and spices. Catalog ***free.***

Park Seed Company

382 Cokesbury Road, Greenwood, SC 29647.

Full-color catalog of flower and vegetable seed from old and respected seed houses. See also two books they publish (p. 67). Catalog ***free.***

Plants of the Southwest

1812 2nd Street, Santa Fe, NM 87501.

Vegetable, flower, shrub and tree seed; also native grass and wildflower mixes. From and for the high southwest American deserts. Catalog ***$1.***

Redwood City Seed Company

P. O. Box 361, Redwood City, CA 94064.

Heirloom open-pollinated vegetable seed. Also herbs, tree seed, and books. Tiny print and dense with information. Catalog ***$1.***

Southern Exposure Seed Exchange

P. O. Box 158, North Garden, VA 22959.

Regional source for heirloom vegetable varieties adapted to the mid-Atlantic region. Good cultural instructions. Catalog ***$2.***

Stock Seed Farms

RR 1/Box 112, Murdock, NE 68407.

Native American prairie grasses and perennial and annual wildflower seed. Preserving and duplicating the tall grass prairie. Price list ***free.***

Stokes Seeds

P. O. Box 548, Buffalo, NY 14240.

Bulk vegetable and flower seed for commercial growers. Huge selections, and they also sell small packets of seed to home gardeners. Catalog ***free.***

Thompson & Morgan

P. O. Box 1308, Jackson, NJ 08527.

Full-color catalog of an enormous selection of flower seed, plus vegetables. American branch of one of the oldest British seed houses. Catalog ***free.***

Vesey's Seeds Ltd.

York, Prince Edward Island, Canada C0A 1P0.

Vegetable and flower seed adapted to the short-season requirements of Canada's Maritime Provinces and New England. Catalog ***free.***

A World Seed Service

J. L. Hudson, Seedsman; P. O. Box 1058, Redwood City, CA 94064.

Rare seed from all over the world. As much an encyclopedia as a source of seeds, this catalog has tiny print and is a botanical gold mine. Catalog ***$1.***

—Richard Nilsen

• See **Gardening By Mail** (p. 71) for more than 1,200 nursery and seed company listings in the U.S. and Canada.
• Other sources: herb seeds (p. 66); fruit trees (p. 63); ornamental plants and bulbs (p. 67).

SAVING VEGETABLE SEEDS has taken on new meaning for some — saving unique varieties from extinction. The seeds can be heirlooms passed down by tribe or family. They can be commercial strains lost as seed houses disappear due to mergers and attrition. Since close to half of the roughly 6,000 vegetable seed varieties for sale in the U.S. are available from only *one* source, this is an alarming problem as smaller companies disappear. The response is mostly amateur and the benefits can be very practical, for these endangered varieties are often the best suited of any to the needs of home gardeners.

—Richard Nilsen

The Garden Seed Inventory • Seed Savers Exchange

*The **Inventory** is a piece of cataloging heroics: an alphabetical listing of each and every variety of nonhybrid vegetable seed for sale by seed houses in the U.S. and Canada. That's 5,785 varieties from 239 wholesale and retail seed companies. So if you're a gardener used to buying your favorite chili pepper seed from the same source for years — only this year it's NOT THERE — you look that variety up and find out who sells it. If you're a northern gardener faced with a short growing season, you scan the column that lists days to maturity for each variety of a kind of vegetable, and come up with whatever is quickest and best for your situation.*

•

Moon & Stars Watermelon
Once nearly extinct, the legendary Moon & Stars watermelon is now being offered by about two dozen Members of the Seed Savers Exchange. After nearly a four-year search, it was finally located on a farm near Macon, Missouri. Several of the rare fruits are displayed here by Kent Whealy, Director of Seed Savers.

Moon & Stars is dark green and resembles Black Diamond, except for bright yellow spots which range from pea- to silver-dollar size. It is an incredibly beautiful garden plant.

—*Garden Seed Inventory*

Variety Name — Range of Maturities — Source Codes

ROUMANIAN HOT 065-075 AN BA 84 HE NI P2 RM SI 83 84 GE V2
BLOCKY 4 X 2.5" MED-WALLED FRUITS, TAPERS TO BLUNT POINT, YELLOW > RED, MED-HOT,
UPRIGHT 14" PLANTS, BEARS UNTIL FROST, FOR HOME OR PROCESSING (ROUMANIAN WAX).

Synonym

—Garden Seed Inventory

Seed Savers Exchange is the kind of good-works nonprofit outfit that people ought to leave money to in their wills. Run on a shoestring by Kent Whealy, it is the place where gardeners raising unique or endangered vegetables swap seeds. Many of the varieties have been passed down within families for generations. Here seeds are passed from the old to the young via the mailman. If you raise vegetables, consider joining in and adopting a variety or two.

—*Richard Nilsen*

•

CORN/POP *Zea mays*

Bear Paw: CA SO Z — HAS — early, adapted to short growing season of Pacific Northwest, distinctive flattened tips of ears resembling bears' paws, from Forest Shomer; *Butter Boy:* IL PL E — HAS — med-size kernel, great taste, plant falls over easily, didn't pollinate well in 1985, bugs ate tassel; *Butter Flavored:* IA MA L — HAS — 085 days, 3-4 ears per 6' stalk, large cream-colored seed; OH SI T — L.Q. — 090-100 days, creamy-white 5-6" ears, 5-6' stalks withstood high winds & drought, fat kernels pop big & tasty, O.S. 83 MI FE J who got it from PA farmer, in his family 100+ years.

—*Seed Savers Exchange*

The Garden Seed Inventory
Kent Whealy, Editor
1985; 448 pp.
$12.50 postpaid

Seed Savers Exchange
Yearbook
$12/year (2 issues)
information **free** with SASE

Both from:
Seed Savers Exchange
P. O. Box 70
Decorah, IA 52101
or Whole Earth Access

Growing and Saving Vegetable Seeds

This is a book for beginners with a completely self-descriptive title.

—*Richard Nilsen*

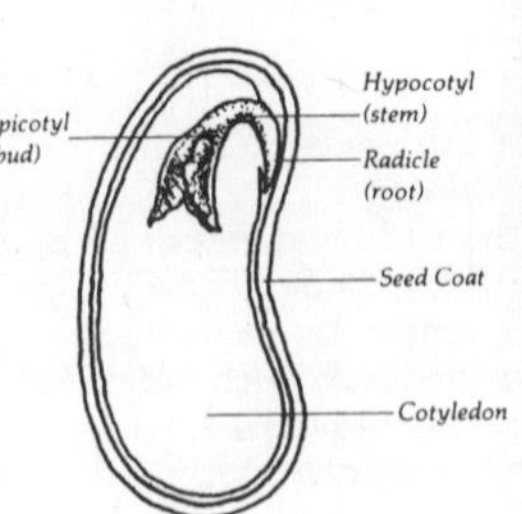

A seed and its many parts.

Growing and Saving Vegetable Seeds
Marc Rogers
1978; 140 pp.
$7.95
($9.95 postpaid) from:
Garden Way Publishing/
Storey Communications
Schoolhouse Road
Pownal, VT 05261
or Whole Earth Access

The late-bolting spinach plants should be saved for seed.

Native Seeds/SEARCH

Native Seeds/SEARCH is a nonprofit rescue mission for the food plants of native peoples in southwestern North America. The turf extends roughly north/south from Durango, Colorado, to Durango, Mexico, and west/east from Las Vegas, Nevada, to Las Vegas, New Mexico. The ethnobotany involved in searching out the survivors is as remarkable as the fact that so many varieties (over 230 for sale in the catalog) are still clinging to mostly marginal existences. For those interested in the work there is a newsletter, ***The Seedhead News****.* —*Richard Nilsen*

Native Seeds/SEARCH: membership **$10**/year (includes quarterly **Seedhead News** and 10% discount on seeds and publications); information **free**. 3950 West New York Drive, Tucson, AZ 85745.

Biotechnology and Genetic Diversity

Genes are Earth's most important resource. Genetic diversity is a prerequisite for abundant food and it is the ultimate reason for having confidence there will be food tomorrow and the day after.

That this is news to most people makes this an important book. Strategically designed for maximum impact, it is aimed at news writers and contains plain English, a good glossary, and an uncanny ability to demystify.

—*Richard Nilsen*

Biotechnology and Genetic Diversity
Steven C. Witt
1985; 145 pp.
$12.50
($14 postpaid) from:
California Agricultural Lands Project
227 Clayton Street
San Francisco, CA 94117
or Whole Earth Access

Herbal Bounty
Steven Foster
1984; 200 pp.
$11.95
($13.45 postpaid) from:
Peregrin Smith Books
P. O. Box 667
Layton, UT 84041
or Whole Earth Access

Herbal Bounty

Long on information and short on hype, this book details how to grow, dry and use, 124 herbs. This is an excellent choice for beginners, and since the author has spent time in his library and in his garden, it is also a book that will not offend a botanist. —*Richard Nilsen*

A place of solitude created within an enclosed garden space dates to Roman times. Herbal borders leading to the peaceful space can be in waves of soft textures and subtle coloration.

•

The family, genus, species, and subgroups of species serve as the most useful reference points for herb gardeners.

The family can be likened to a broad group of motorized vehicles known as automobiles. There are several genera in the family automobile including Chevrolets, Fords, Cadillacs, and Toyotas. In the genus Toyota, indigenous to Japan and naturalized throughout North America, is the species *corolla*. Thus for a specific organism in our hypothetical automobile family we have the binomial *Toyota corolla*.

•

Herbs should be dried in the shade. Direct sunlight will cause leaves to turn dark brown or black. . . . Rapid evaporation of the essential oil or changes in its chemical constituents may occur if an herb is dried at temperatures exceeding 90°F. If heat is forced too quickly over the outer cells of a leaf, those cells may harden before they can be replaced by moisture from the leaf's inner tissue, thereby sealing moisture in the leaf and causing it to mold in storage. Air temperature should be kept relatively low at first (80° to 85°F.) then increased when the plant material is almost dry.

A blueberry rake works well for harvesting camomile blossoms.

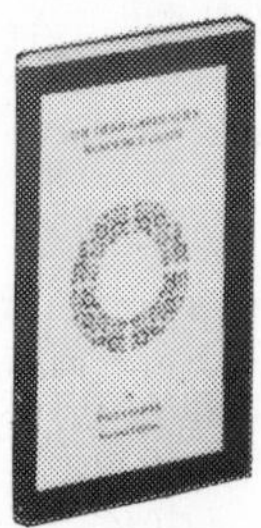

The Herb Gardener's Resource Guide
Paula Oliver
1985; 82 pp.
$7.95 postpaid from:
Northwind Farm
Route 2, Box 246
Shevlin, MN 56676
or Whole Earth Access

The Herb Gardener's Resource Guide

Praise be to catalogers, those diligent people who take cardboard boxes full of envelopes, brochures, and addresses and transform them into neatly alphabetized booklets. Paula Oliver is such a person, and her **Resource Guide** *contains over 500 entries, from nurseries and seed houses to botanicals and florist supplies. And for each listing the details are nicely tended to (wholesale/retail, mail orders, visitors, foreign orders). For anyone interested in herbs, I'd call it essential.* —*Richard Nilsen*
[Suggested by Portia Meares]

•

Borchelt Herb Gardens: 474 Carriage Shop Rd., East Falmouth, MA 02536. (617) 548-4571.
Seeds only. They offer more than 100 varieties of herb seeds. All are organically grown and hand-collected to insure viability and increase germination percentage. Detailed instruction sheet provided with each order. The seed list is quite informative and is available for a business-size SASE. Retail mail order only.

•

The Herb Quarterly: P. O. Box 275, Newfane, VT 05345. (802) 365-4392. A beautifully designed quarterly magazine for herb fanciers. HQ covers cultivation, cooking, herbal legend and lore, historical pieces, garden design, plant profiles, herb crafting, as well as offering excellent recipes and book reviews. Sample copy is $5. Brochure is free on request. Foreign subscribers welcome, but must add $2.50 to domestic rate. This elegant publication will be of interest to herb gardeners everywhere!

•

Well-Sweep Herb Farm: 317 Mt. Bethel Rd., Port Murray, NJ 07865. (201) 852-5390.
Plants, seeds, everlastings, wreaths, potpourri, books, and herbal gift items. One of the largest herb collections in the country, they offer 20 basils, 26 lavenders, 30 rosemaries, and 58 different thymes! Of special interest: violets from both Korea and Australia. A large display garden is open to visitors and they offer group garden tours by appointment. In addition, they offer lectures on herb gardening and everlastings during the fall and winter months. They host an annual spring and fall open house featuring crafts demonstrations, displays, tours, refreshments, etc. Retail sales, domestic only, by mail and from the farm. Catalog is $1 on request.

Wormwood/P (*Artemisia absinthium*): Intensely bitter leaves were an important ingredient in absinthe, vermouth, and other liqueurs. Has great reputation for stimulating the appetite and improving digestion. One of the oldest known remedies for worms. Seeds 90¢, Plant $2.50. —***Richters***

Herb Suppliers

Folklore Herb Company/Sanctuary Seeds: Catalog **free** from 2388 West 4th Avenue, Vancouver, B.C., V6K 1P1, Canada. *Folklore sells bulk spices and botanical herbs, also teas, oils, food items, and books. Sanctuary sells culinary and medicinal herb seeds as well as nonhybrid vegetable seed.*

Meadowbrook Herb Garden: Catalog **$2.** Plant and Seed List **$1** from Rt. 138, Wyoming, RI 02898. *Culinary herbs, teas, cosmetics, and books.*

Richters: Catalog **$2** from P. O. Box 26, Goodwood, Ontario, L0C 1A0, Canada. *An extensive selection of herbs, alpine and wildflowers, and dye plants. Plants sold in Canada only; seeds sold everywhere.*

Taylor's Herb Gardens: Catalog **$1** from 1535 Lone Oak Rd., Vista, CA 92083. *Herbs for cooking, smelling and healing sold as plants and seed. Good selection includes scented geraniums. They sell both wholesale and retail.* —*Richard Nilsen*

• Also see Drugs: Plant Power (p. 220).

• Also see **Indoor Marijuana Horticulture** and **Sinsemilla Tips** (p. 75).

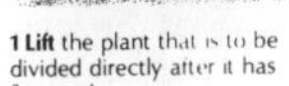

1 Lift the plant that is to be divided directly after it has flowered.

2 Shake off as much soil as possible.

3 Wash the crown and its roots in a bucket, or hose it clean.

4 Shorten all tall stems above the ground to minimize water loss.

5 Break off a piece with at least one good "eye" from the edge of the crown.

6 Divide any intractable pieces with an old carving knife or similar blade.

7 Make a hole and replant the new clump at once. Firm the soil and label.

8 Water very thoroughly, using a watering can with a spray attachment.

Herbaceous plants with fibrous crowns (e.g. Aster, Chrysanthemum, Geranium, Hemerocallis, Lupine, Rudbeckia).

Plant Propagation

__Plant Propagation__ clearly presents the tricks of the trade that make the difference between success and frustration. It is my basic reference for "how to" horticultural questions. Straightforward, nontechnical text and very helpful illustrations dispel the mystique surrounding plant propagation. Each procedure occupies facing pages. This allows the spiral-bound paperback to be folded and placed inside its see-through, plastic envelope so it may be used in the field without damage.

I qualify my praise with a caution against the book's excessive recommendations of fungicide use. Many commercial growers face serious problems with resistant strains of fungi that have developed from just such practices. A concerted sanitation program and observation schedule are better strategies for many reasons besides being ultimately more effective. Otherwise, this is the best practical guide to plant propagation available.
—Edward Goodell

Plant Propagation
Philip McMillan Browse
1979; 96 pp.
$9.95 postpaid from:
Simon & Schuster
Mail Order Sales
200 Old Tappan Road
Old Tappan, NJ 07675
or Whole Earth Access

Park's Success With Seeds • Park's Success With Bulbs

These two books from the venerable George W. Park Seed Company of South Carolina are handy when propagating. To a normal encyclopedic format of each species with a color picture of the fruit or bloom has been added a second color picture showing how each plant looks when small. __Success With Bulbs__ has photos of the bulbs themselves, so if the gladioluses get mixed up with the ranunculuses they can be identified and sorted. __Success With Seeds__ has photos of each plant just after it has put out its first true leaves, thus ending all confusion between what is a baby plant and what is a baby weed. With each set of photos comes a description of what each plant looks like, what it is used for, where it can be grown, and how it is propagated. *—Richard Nilsen*

Crocus species and hybrids: *Iridaceae*, Mediterranean Europe and Africa, Near East. ►

•

Culture: Crocus do best in cool areas. Plant 2-4 inches deep and 4 inches apart in a well-drained soil of low fertility, in full sun or very light shade. . . . Spring blooming crocus may also be forced in pots. Set 5-6 to a 5 inch pot, using a well-drained medium and covering the corms 1 inch deep. Pre-cool in the cold frame for about 6 weeks, then bring indoors and grow in a sunny situation with a night temperature of about 50°F.

Note: One species of fall-blooming crocus, C. *sativus*, is now, and was in the past even more so, of commercial importance as the source of saffron. Derived from the dried stigmas, saffron is used to dye and flavor foods, and in olden times for medicinal purposes.

—Success With Bulbs

Phaseolus vulgaris (Green Bean) *Leguminosae*, native to tropical America.

◄

Germination: Sow outdoors 1½-2" deep where plants are to grow after all danger of frost has passed. Sow bush varieties 2-3" apart in rows 18-24" apart and pole varieties 6-8" apart in rows 36" apart. Innoculate with a nitrogen fixing bacteria prior to sowing. Germination takes 6-10 days. Seeds may also be started indoors in individual pots 3 weeks before planting outside, maintaining a temperature within the medium of 70° during germination. Plant bush varieties successively every 2 weeks until 2 months before frost for a continuous crop.

—Success With Seeds

Park's Success With Seeds
Ann Reilly
1978; 364 pp.
$12.95
($13.95 postpaid)

Park's Success With Bulbs
Alfred F. Scheider
1981; 173 pp.
$9.95
($10.95 postpaid)
Both from:
George W. Park Seed Co.
P. O. Box 31
Greenwood, SC
29647-0001
or Whole Earth Access

• Also see pp. 230-231.

• Park's also has an herb book.
Park's Success With Herbs: Gertrude B. Foster and Rosemary F. Louden, 1980; 192 pp. **$9.95** ($10.95 postpaid) from George W. Park Seed Co., P. O. Box 31, Greenwood, SC 29647-0001 (or Whole Earth Access).

White Flower Farm • Wayside Gardens

Two excellent sources of ornamental plants. Wayside Gardens has a larger selection (including flowering trees) and White Flower Farm calls its catalog "The Garden Book" because it includes very chatty and detailed cultural information on the plant varieties that are sold. Both catalogs are worth having. *—Richard Nilsen*

The Garden Book: Catalog **$5** from White Flower Farm, Litchfield, CT 06759-0050.
Wayside Gardens: Catalog **free** from Wayside Gardens, Hodges, SC 29695-0001.

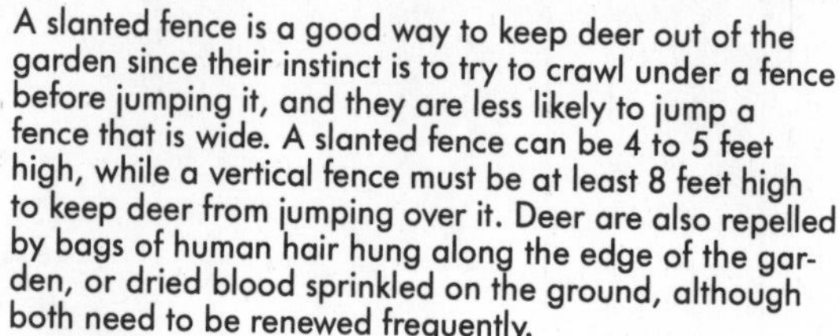

A slanted fence is a good way to keep deer out of the garden since their instinct is to try to crawl under a fence before jumping it, and they are less likely to jump a fence that is wide. A slanted fence can be 4 to 5 feet high, while a vertical fence must be at least 8 feet high to keep deer from jumping over it. Deer are also repelled by bags of human hair hung along the edge of the garden, or dried blood sprinkled on the ground, although both need to be renewed frequently.

Gardening
National Gardening Assoc.
1986; 431 pp.
$19.95
($22.45 postpaid) from:
The National Gardening Assoc.
180 Flynn Ave.
Burlington, VT 05401
or Whole Earth Access

Gardening

Every vegetable has a cultural requirement or two that practiced gardeners know. Lettuce wants shade, moisture, and a thick mulch in summer. Bell peppers like it hot. Tomatoes are either determinate or indeterminate, and you can't really call yourself a tomato grower unless you know the difference. The non-profit National Gardening Association has distilled, from its 250,000 members, knowledge about most of the important requirements of America's favorite vegetables and fruits, and laid out superbly detailed instructions for growing them in this big, beautiful book. —Jeff Cox

A soil thermometer can indicate precisely the optimum time to set out peppers. The soil 4 inches below the surface of the planting bed should measure 65° F or higher at 8 a.m. If set out too early, peppers will produce poorly all season.

Garden Way's Joy of Gardening
Dick Raymond
1983; 365 pp.
$17.95
($19.95 postpaid) from:
Garden Way Publishing
Storey Communications
Schoolhouse Road
Pownal, VT 05261
or Whole Earth Access

Garden Way's Joy of Gardening

When I first thumbed thru this fat, glossy paperback it looked a little strange, or at least unorthodox. The traditional garden-book format of dense pages and crowded layout was missing, all the illustrations were in color, there was white space to relieve the eye, and it was so slick I wondered if maybe it was a sales brochure for Toyotas and the cabbages were just there for background. Not to mention the huge, dramatic headings that introduced sections, like "My 12-point system for fewer and fewer weeds each year" or "Celery — How I grow this challenging vegetable."

Was it a garden book or another self-improvement plan?

I settled down for a more serious look and before long I was getting hooked on all kinds of stuff, like composting with alfalfa meal, "tunnel growing" — wire reinforced plastic formed into tunnels to make instant hot houses — and Raymond's weed theory, which states that weed seeds sprout only in the top quarter inch of soil, so shallow cultivating zaps them but deep tilling just churns more up to the surface. Along the way I found a thorough grounding in garden basics with well-illustrated details on growing just about any veggie you've got desires for, from the traditionals like corn and tomatoes to the experiments that the seed catalogs induce in all of us, experiments that generally flop. There's basic truths along with new insights and tips, and bygawd if he can grow peanuts and okra in Vermont then I'm going to try them again. So what if it looks like a Toyota sales brochure? Raymond has been working the soil for 40 years and his natural wisdoms are nice to have. —Dick Fugett

•

All my wide row crops planted from seed (except peas and beans) must be thinned out when they're quite small — about 1/4 to 1/2 inch high. This is true for most methods of planting, but I consider it essential with wide rows because the plants are so numerous.

When the plants are 1/4 to 1/2 inch high, I drag the rake across the width of the row so that the teeth dig into the soil only about 1/4 to 1/2 inch. The teeth in an iron garden rake catch just enough seedlings, and pull them from the row.

•

I've found alfalfa meal to be about the cheapest, quickest-acting activator for a compost pile. If you can't find any at your garden or feed store, look in the supermarket for "Litter Green," a kitty litter product that's 100 percent alfalfa meal.

Every time I add new material to the compost pile, I dust it thoroughly with alfalfa meal and moisten the pile a little. Alfalfa meal is an excellent source of nitrogen and protein. It is made from alfalfa hay and is usually 14 to 16 percent protein.

How to Grow More Vegetables
John Jeavons
1982; 159 pp.
$8.95
($9.95 postpaid) from:
Ten Speed Press
P. O. Box 7123
Berkeley, CA 94707
or Whole Earth Access

How to Grow More Vegetables

John Jeavons did not invent the biodynamic/French intensive method of gardening, but he clearly qualifies as its chief popularizer, and this book boils the technique down to its simplest terms. It is organic gardening using hand labor, raised beds, close spacing between plants to eliminate weeds and conserve soil moisture, and heavy feeding and composting. It can produce very large yields in very small spaces, and is therefore applicable to many diverse situations. —Richard Nilsen

•

A good growing bed will be 4 to 12 inches higher than the original surface of the soil. A good soil contains 50% air space. (In fact, adequate air is one of the missing ingredients in most soil preparation processes.) The increased air space allows for an increase in the diffusion of oxygen (which the roots and microbes depend on) into the soil, and the diffusion of carbon dioxide (which the leaves depend on) out of the soil. This increased "breathing" ability of a double-dug bed is a key to improved plant health.

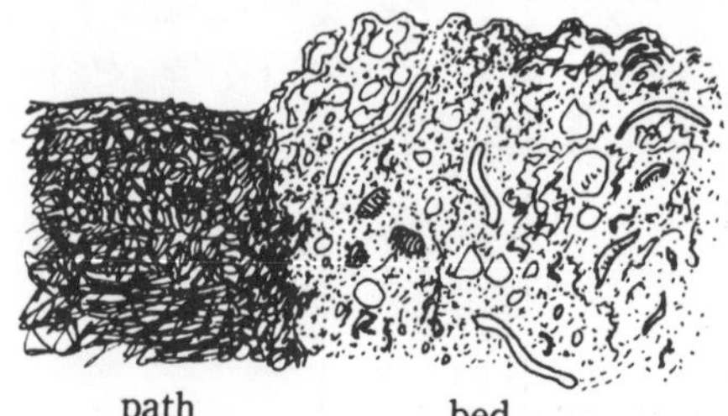

Soil in path is subject to compaction; soil in bed remains loose.

• To ensure proper garden sun, use the Solar Card (p. 132).

• If you garden where seasons are short and winters are cold.

The Harrowsmith Northern Gardener: Jennifer Bennett, Editor, 1982; 216 pp. **$19.95** ($21.45 postpaid) from Firefly Books, 3520 Pharmacy Avenue/Unit 1-C, Scarborough, Ontario, Canada, M1W 2T8.

This colorful patio planting combines red and green chard, red-leaved lettuce, and a miniature 'Garden Prince' almond with ornamentals. It exhibits two important rules of edible landscaping: put the salad vegetables as close to the kitchen as possible, and start very small.

When planting a grafted tree, face the bowed area of the graft into the wind.

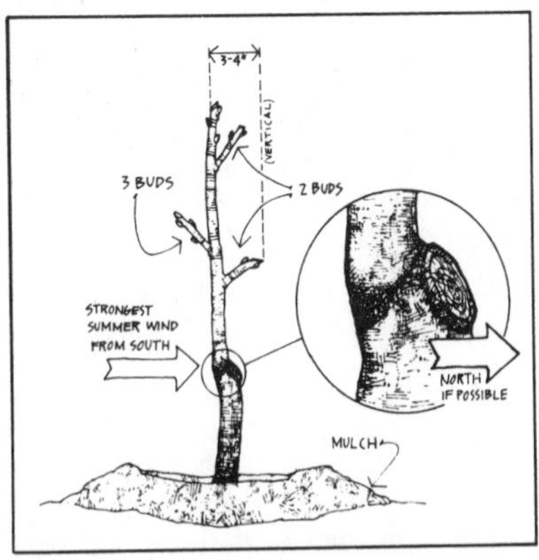

Designing and Maintaining Your Edible Landscape Naturally
Robert Kourik
1986; 400 pp.
$16.95
($18.95 postpaid) from:
The Edible Landscape Book Project
P. O. Box 1841
Santa Rosa, CA 95402
or Whole Earth Access

Designing and Maintaining Your Edible Landscape Naturally

Edible landscaping is a new term for an old idea. It is a reaction to the lawns and shrubs that make many suburban yards look so boring. Its goal is to integrate food plants into the landscape: specifically to liberate fruits and vegetables from rectangular prisons often hidden out at the back of the lot. Bring those salad herbs up and put them right outside the kitchen door where they will be tended and used. And put the peaches (dwarf) under a south-facing eave of the roof where they can enjoy maximum frost protection and warmth.

What used to be common sense was lost when people stopped growing any of their own food and ran out of time even to be in their gardens, let alone work them. That is changing, and these books suggest that vegetable gardening can also be aesthetic.

Robert Kourik has produced a classic homemade book in the best sense of the term. His mind works referentially and fortunately by publishing his own book he didn't have to meet up with a linear-minded editor eager to streamline his work. The book is massive, detailed, and totally indexed. It is full of charts and graphs that allow the kind of comparing and decision-making that landscape designing is all about. There is extensive information on selecting fruit tree varieties and appropriate rootstocks.

Best of all, he is not dogmatic. If there are two schools of thought, say till versus no-till gardening, he will explain the advantages and disadvantages of each in different situations. Like all gardening books, this one is written with a sense of place in mind (northern California), but Kourik is aware that your garden, right down to its microclimates, is unique. —Richard Nilsen

•

The amount of effort needed to sustain a landscape or garden is, perhaps, the single most important design consideration. Planting happens quickly, at the peak of the gardener's enthusiasm. Maintenance usually ends up being crammed into busy, everyday life.

•

Another way to understand the sunlight patterns and the microclimates of your yard is simply to grow vegetables. Instead of designing a landscape just after moving into your new home, wait and observe the yard through a complete cycle of seasons. For at least a year, grow edibles in a number of spots that seem to have beneficial sunlight and climate. You will probably get a very good feel for the nuances of sunshine patterns, frost pockets, windy spots, wet soils, rocky soils, and other important information before designing your edible landscape. The placement of your first edibles may turn out to be ill-advised or just right.

HPBooks
$9.90-$11.90
each, postpaid
HP booklist **free** from:
HPBooks
P. O. Box 5367
Tucson, AZ 85703
or Whole Earth Access

HPBooks

Trying to keep a young orange tree alive during a string of 20-degree nights and serious bug attacks had me looking for help, and when I asked my main nurseryman what to do, he reached back into the compact library behind the counter and pulled out his central citrus authority. It looked to me like another of the ORTHO series so I was anticipating a once-over-lightly approach, but instead there was a complete and thorough reference. The book was put out by HP Publishing in Arizona and was a most readable and informative volume, and led to my discovery of the wide range of their other gardening books.

The ORTHO similarity is genetic, for both operations were directly influenced by the Sunset garden book series that began in the '50s. But HP tried harder and surpassed the competition. Their books have more pages, more information, more color photos, and a middle-of-the-road approach to the chemical vs. organic philosophy. Currently 22 different gardening titles are offered. —Dick Fugett

HP titles include: Home Landscaping in the Northeast and Midwest; Southern Home Landscaping; Western Home Landscaping; Plants for Dry Climates; How to Grow Fruit, Berries & Nuts in the Midwest and East; Western Fruit, Berries & Nuts; Vegetables; Perennials; Bulbs; Annuals; Trees & Shrubs; Citrus.

Country Wisdom Bulletins
32 pp.
$1.95 ($3.95 postpaid)
List of titles **free**; all from:
Garden Way Publishing
Storey Communications
Schoolhouse Road
Pownal, VT 05261
or Whole Earth Access

Country Wisdom Bulletins

Garden Way Publishing has an ever-expanding series of 32-page booklets that are worth knowing about. There are nearly a hundred of them now, mostly on specific aspects of gardening, cooking, and householding. Sample titles include "What Every Gardener Should Know About Earthworms," "Grow the Best Tomatoes," "Curing Smoky Fireplaces," and "Attracting Birds." They are great for people who like their information short and sweet, for kids, for teaching situations, and for nosing around a subject that's new to you. —Richard Nilsen

•

Earthworms form an interconnected web of channels which allow rain water to penetrate quickly throughout the topsoil layer.

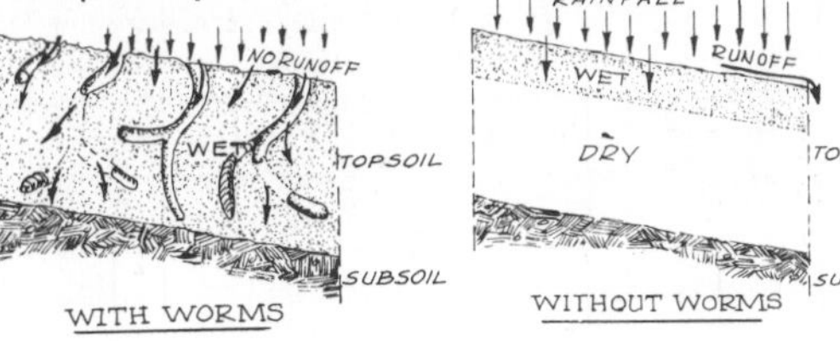

Reader's Digest Illustrated Guide to Gardening
Carroll C. Calkins, Editor
1978; 672 pp.
$22.98
($25.17 postpaid) from:
Reader's Digest
Attn.: Order Entry
Pleasantville, NY 10570
or Whole Earth Access

Reader's Digest Illustrated Guide to Gardening

Reader's Digest has trained its vast resources on gardening and produced an impressive book. The illustrations alone involved the work of 44 different artists. With captions providing step by step directions, they are frequently all that is needed for numerous how-to garden chores. And the oblong shape of the book keeps it flat and open while your hands are busy. The text explains more details than most people would have time for in a lifetime of gardening. My one reservation is the heavy reliance placed on synthetic pesticides and weedkillers — watch out here, or they will have you out there spraying everything from methoxychlor to paraquat. —Richard Nilsen

In very early spring, before leaves appear, cut back old branches to 2–6 ft. high.

A lilac (*Syringa*) will eventually become scraggly, its flowers sparse and discolored. Suckers will arise from the rootstock and will sap its energy. Prune in winter to renew it.

Remove all suckers below ground level with a pruning saw or the sharp edge of a spade.

Sunset New Western Garden Book
Editors of Sunset Books and Sunset Magazine, 1979; 512 pp.
$14.95
($16.70 postpaid) from:
Sunset Books / Lane Publishing Co.
80 Willow Road
Menlo Park, CA 94025-3691
or Whole Earth Access

Sunset New Western Garden Book

This continues to be the essential book for gardeners in the 11 western states. The 344-page "Western Plant Encyclopedia" illustrates each entry and keys it to 24 very specific climate zones. By acknowledging and incorporating the amazing diversity of western climates, Sunset has created a book that gets used. —Richard Nilsen

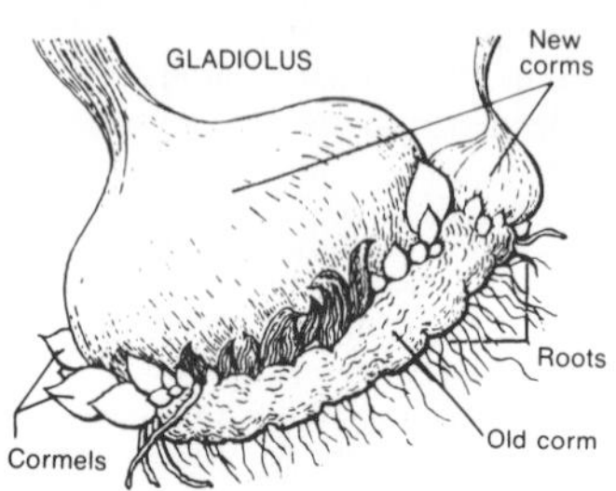

CORMEL. *While one to several big new corms are forming, smaller ones (cormels) are also being produced from the axillary buds on top of the old corm. The cormels will take two to three years to bloom, while larger corms will blossom the following year.*

Erythrina caffra

•
Plants with low fuel volume: No plant will stop a fire, but homeowners can lower the risk by removing highly combustible brush from around the home, introducing low-growing plants with potentially high water content and low fuel volume, irrigating new plantings as needed, and grooming to prevent build-up of potential fuel.

•
E. caffra (E. constantiana). Kaffirboom Coral Tree. Briefly deciduous tree. Zones 21-24. Native to South Africa. Grows 24-40 ft. high, spreads to 40-60 ft. wide. Drops leaves in January; then angular bare branches produce big clusters of deep red orange, tubular flowers that drip honey. In March or earlier, flowers give way to fresh, light green, often dense foliage. Magnificent shade tree in summer. Wicked thorns disappear as wood matures.

My Garden Companion
Jamie Jobb
1977; 352 pp.
$4.95 postpaid from:
MacMillan Publishing Co.
Order Department
Front and Brown Streets
Riverside, NJ 08075
or Whole Earth Access

My Garden Companion

This is a children's gardening book with heart and humor that's full of projects that nurture curiosity and educate effortlessly. Read it to the little ones, give it to a seventh grader, and get it for yourself if you are new to gardening and leery of introductory books that "talk down." This one won't. —Richard Nilsen

1. Recently planted seed begins to germinate.

2. Taproot emerges and begins its backbend.

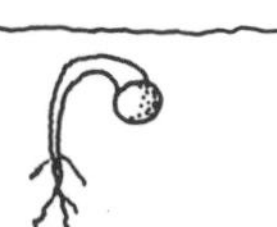
3. Taproot arches to create tension.

4. Seed springs to life!

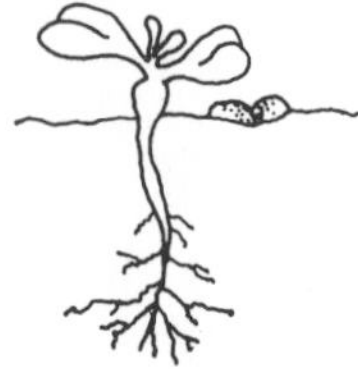
5. First leaves (cotyledons) open to meet sunlight.

•
The Phantom Underground High Jumper
To properly root themselves, many seeds need to do some underground gymnastics when they sprout and become seedlings. The seed's taproot must bend into a big arch before the seed can find energy to break out of the soil.

It's easy to see this happen. Find a clear plastic container and punch a hole in the bottom for drainage. Fill the container with soil. Wrap black paper around the outside of the container. Black paper keeps out light that would confuse the roots about where "up" is.

Plant radish seeds near the walls of the container. Water them and wait a day. The next day remove the paper every four or five hours to watch for progress of roots. Do this every day for a week. Be sure to replace the paper around the container after you've looked.

• Gardening tools and supplies are on pp. 78-79.
• Also see **Biology of Plants** (p. 38).

Root-bound plants fill the pots so tightly with roots that adequate water absorption by the soil cannot occur.

Living with Plants

This botany professor has taken all of the how-to's printed in current gardening books and woven them together with threads of why. It's an incredibly complete and clear botanical textbook on gardening, landscaping, and houseplants. —Rosemary Menninger

•

Overwatering: Plants are much less obvious about having been overwatered than about being underwatered. Oversaturation usually occurs in pots without drainage holes or when water is allowed to accumulate in the saucer beneath the pot. The results are slow, insidious, and usually fatal.

The roots begin to suffer from lack of oxygen as the excessive water forces the air out of the soil and occupies all of the pores between soil particles. This lack of oxygen leads to metabolic breakdown similar to salt poisoning. Root hairs die and decay begins. The decomposition process uses the little remaining soil oxygen and produces excessive carbon dioxide, thereby increasing respiration failure by the roots, and more root tissues die.

Living with Plants
Donna N. Schumann
1980; 325 pp.
$14.95
($15.95 postpaid) from:
Mad River Press
141 Carter Lane
Eureka, CA 95501
or Whole Earth Access

Simon and Schuster's Complete Guide to Plants and Flowers

A flower gardener's encyclopedia, a seed catalogue's companion, and a visual delight. Five hundred half-page color photos with graphic cultivation tips for common varieties of flowers, cactus, houseplants, and other ornamentals. —Rosemary Menninger

281 **BELLADONNA LILY**
Amaryllis belladonna:

Summer Autumn Winter Spring

Family: Amaryllidaceae. Named after the shepherd, Amaryllis, in classical poetry.
Place of origin: South Africa.
Description: a monotypic genus, the species a showy, late-flowering bulb. Leaves strap-shaped, channelled, appearing in winter or early spring. Flowers large, funnel-shaped, 6 parted, rose-red or paler, sweet-scented, on stout 18–30 in. (45–75 cm) stems, before the foliage in autumn.
Flowering time: early autumn.
Use: in temperate climates, against sunny walls or as pot plants; in climates with mild winters, in small flower beds or borders.
Propagation: by division of the bulbs at the base of the mother plant.
Environment and light: full sun.
Type of soil: plant bulbs 6–9 in. (15–23 cm) deep. Equal parts good fibrous loam, leaf-mould and sand.
Soil moisture: water quite sparingly, only as required.
Remarks: hardy. Cover with 1–2 in. (2–5 cm) soil. Reasonably hardy zones 5–8. Cover 9 in. (22 cm) of soil and give plenty of sun and shelter.

⑨

58 **WHITE SAILS**
Spathiphyllum wallisii:

Gardening by Mail

Take one reference librarian with green thumbs, add one Kaypro computer and two years of work and — lucky for us — comes this amazing book. More than 2,000 mail order sources are ingeniously listed. Separate alphabetical lists of seed companies and nurseries are followed by a plant index, so that if you are looking for, say, Siberian Iris, you go to that heading and there are all the sources that sell them. Then comes a geographical index of the same sources, providing traveling gardeners with a ready-made tour guide. This same detailed attention is also given to garden supply companies, societies, libraries, magazines, and even one hundred gardening books. —Richard Nilsen

I 8 SOCIETIES

Cyclamen Society
c/o Dr. David V. Bent
9 Tudor Dr.
Otford, Kent, England TN14 SQP
(09592) 2322
Cyclamen Journal (2)

Cymbidium Society of America
Mrs. Richard L. Johnston
6881 Wheeler Avenue
Westminster, CA 92683
(714) 894-5421
The Orchid Advocate (6)

The Daffodil Society (UK)
Ivor Fox
44 Wargrave Rd., Twyford
Reading, Berks, England

The Delphinium Society
Mrs. Shirley E. Bassett
Takakkaw, Ice House Wood
Oxted, Surrey, England RH8 9DW
Delphinium Year Book

Desert Plant Society of Vancouver
2941 Parker Street
Vancouver, BC, Canada V5K 2T9
(604) 255-0606

Epiphyllum Society of America
Betty Berg
P. O. Box 1395
Monrovia, CA 91016
(805) 259-4637
ESA Bulletin (6)

Farallones Institute
15290 Coleman Valley Rd.
Occidental, CA 95465
(707) 874-3060

Friends of the Farm
Hopewell Farms
Rt. 1, Box 32
Dalton City, IL 61925
(217) 864-2679

Gardening by Mail
Barbara J. Barton
1986; 265 pp.
$16
($18.50 postpaid) from:
Tusker Press
P. O. Box 597004
San Francisco, CA 94159
or Whole Earth Access

Brooklyn Botanic Garden

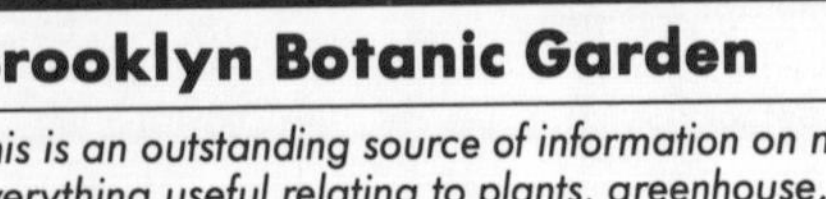

This is an outstanding source of information on nearly everything useful relating to plants, greenhouse, vines, bonsai, pruning, the lot. And a fine periodical, ***Plants and Gardens****.* —Stewart Brand

Miniature rose 'Over the Rainbow' has velvety red petals with striking yellow reverse. The flowers are fragrant and long-lasting. —Gardening Under Lights

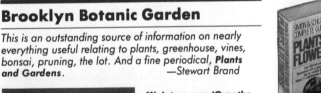

Plants and Gardens: Barbara Pesch, Editor. **$15**/year (4 issues; includes membership in Brooklyn Botanic Garden) from Brooklyn Botanic Garden, 1000 Washington Avenue, Brooklyn, NY 11225.

Simon and Schuster's Complete Guide to Plants and Flowers
Frances Perry, Editor
1974; 522 pp.
$10.95 postpaid from:
Simon & Schuster
Mail Order Sales
200 Old Tappan
Old Tappan, NJ 07675
or Whole Earth Access

Color In Your Garden
Penelope Hobhouse
1985; 239 pp.
$34
($35.50 postpaid) from:
Little, Brown & Company
Attn.: Order Dept.
200 West Street
Waltham, MA 02254
or Whole Earth Access

Color In Your Garden

Have you ever watched somebody do something they were really good at and then asked them to explain how they did it? Words often fail. Arranging color in a garden is like that because it involves positioning plants both in space and in time, through changes of bloom and season. Penelope Hobhouse succeeds at sharing years of gardening experience and at explaining the whys of her very refined sense of what goes with what. She begins with a color wheel and basic theory and moves on to chapters with titles like "Clear Yellows," "Pinks and Mauves," and "Hot Colors." Each chapter has a plant catalog arranged by season. The color photography is exceptional. —*Richard Nilsen*

►
The low tones of the deep purple lupin flowers (center) are echoed in the foliage of purple-leaved sage (lower left) in a wall border. Although contrast in lightness and darkness between the lupins and the pale pink papery-textured petals of the oriental poppy (left center) is extreme, nevertheless they both share characteristic redness, which remains distinguishable to the eye in the palest tints of pink, the darkest almost black reds, and the low smoky tones of textured foliage. Here we see two separate garden pictures. Sculptured gray leaves of artichoke (top right) (*Cynara scolymus* 'Glauca') prevent the dark lupins from seeming dull by enriching their color; at the same time the silver-gray leaves help to make the pale pink of the poppy flowers more brilliant, thus increasing the effects of contrast with lupin and sage.

Right Plant, Right Place
Nicola Ferguson
1984; 292 pp.
$14.95 postpaid from:
Simon and Schuster
Mail Order Sales
200 Old Tappan Road
Old Tappan, NJ 07675
or Whole Earth Access

Right Plant, Right Place

This is a very diligent book of lists, 27 in all, with categories that are either types of garden plants ("Plants with aromatic leaves"), or locations in the garden where they are to grow ("Plants suitable for crevices in paving"). Plants in each list are divided into sections running from sun tolerant to shade tolerant, and within each section they are presented in order of decreasing height. There is also extensive cross-indexing between the lists, and each of the more than 1500 plants has its own 2½-inch-square color photograph.

The lady who did all this lives in Scotland and says in her introduction that she got into this when she acquired a garden needing an overhaul and couldn't find a book like this to help her. I don't think I'd like to do her grocery shopping, but she has produced an extremely useful book. The American editor is Fred McGourty, who has spent 15 years editing the "Handbook" series for the Brooklyn Botanic Gardens. —*Richard Nilsen*

The Complete Shade Gardener

Shade seems a function of modern urban life. Scarce land is expensive, and architects who get to cram square interior feet onto tiny lots often have little time or inclination to consider what that does to the space outside. This author has the additional consideration of climate, since he gardens in Seattle, Washington. He says it got so bad one drippy August that toadstools sprouted on the carpet in his car. He takes all of these sufficient reasons not to garden and turns them into a wonderfully opinionated, and even humorous, display of all that shady sites can offer. —*Richard Nilsen*

•
Aesculus Hippocastanum (Common Horse Chestnut). Heavy shade, invasive roots. The fallen leaves cake together in a slippery mass. And yet, I know of a perfectly successful shade garden composed of a small maple, rhododendrons, and woodland perennials in new soil beneath an old Horse Chestnut. The lesson here is an extendable one: almost any "bad" tree can be pressed into service as a shade garden canopy *if* you plant in fresh soil and provide sufficient moisture.

The Complete Shade Gardener
George Schenk
1984; 278 pp.
$14.95
($15.95 postpaid) from:
Houghton Mifflin Co.
Mail Order Dept.
Wayside Road
Burlington, MA 01803
or Whole Earth Access

V. Sackville-West's Garden Book

I am reading this book for the fourth time in two years.

V. Sackville-West wrote a weekly gardening article for the London **Observer** *for fourteen years and built up a tremendous following in England because of her great knowledge of plants and flowers, her unusual capacity for combining utter romance and hard practical advice, and her great wit, intelligence, and independence.*

Color was the basis of the organization of her garden, with trees down to groundcovers in bloom in the same color range at the same time. She kept refining combinations, groupings of textures, shapes, and sizes.

The Garden Book *is written in twelve chapters, one for each month, and is a great book for learning, for sheer entertainment, and for endless inspiration in your own garden. You may have trouble finding some of the plants she talks about, but you will never have to worry about ending up with any oversized fluorescent geraniums!* —*Virginia Baker*

V. Sackville-West's Garden Book
Philippa Nicolson, Editor
1968; 250 pp.
$9.95 postpaid from:
Macmillan Publishing Co.
Order Department
Front and Brown Streets
Riverside, NJ 08075
or Whole Earth Access

Dutch woonerf, a residential street with special traffic regulations where cars share the street with people and gardens.

The Granite Garden

Very much in the tradition of Jane Jacobs, Ian McHarg, and Christopher Alexander, this author examines the role of nature in cities. The critique here is easy pickings, because cities, whether severely planned or done laissez-faire, almost always end up wrong. The value of this book is in its balance between problems and solutions. Spirn quickly makes it apparent that healthy, workable answers to the dilemma of urban designs are not scarce commodities — techniques abound. What is lacking is economic and political will, and enough of a sense of tradition to allow for perseverance. —Richard Nilsen

•

The Dutch have developed a new type of street, the "woonerf," that enhances the social role of the residential street. The woonerf ("residential yard" in Dutch) is a precinct with its own traffic rules: children and adults have precedence over cars and they use the entire roadway; cars must drive at a walking pace (about ten miles per hour). In the woonerf, distinctions between street and sidewalk are eliminated, and the resulting street space is shared by cars and pedestrians. The woonerf originated in Delft, where conventional streets were transformed by repaving them to eliminate curbs, by introducing obstacles like mounds, raised planters, and trees which forced drivers to wind their way around them, and by consolidating parking. The Dutch have created 800 woonerven in 200 cities and there is a long waiting list for future conversions.

The Granite Garden
Anne Whiston Spirn
1984; 334 pp.
$11.95 postpaid from:
Basic Books
10 East 53rd Street
New York, NY 10022
or Whole Earth Access

Nature's Design

If you are intent on landscaping without professional assistance, this is a great book to own. The emphasis here on using native plants can make sense for today's gardens, since natives are both low maintenance and drought tolerant. The plants are divided into 12 ecological regions covering the continental U.S.

Smyser is a landscape architect and she manages to be both straightforward and patient with her explanations. The coverage of all the steps that go into making a landscape plan is especially well done. Additional sections cover plant selection, construction techniques, planting, and maintenance. —Richard Nilsen

The grade around a tree can be lowered only if the roots of the tree are protected. This is done by maintaining the grade within the circumference of the drip line. Using lime, mark the drip line on the ground. Do the grading, but don't cut within the drip line. When the excavation is completed, build a retaining wall around the tree at the drip line.

Nature's Design
Carol A. Smyser
1982; 390 pp.
$22.95 postpaid from:
Rodale Press
33 East Minor Street
Emmaus, PA 18049
or Whole Earth Access

The House of Boughs

This book describes practically everything that has ever been put into a garden that is not a plant. From ancient Egypt, Persia, and China, through Europe, Japan, and into the contemporary American backyard, a common theme emerges: a garden is an attempt to construct an earthly paradise. —Richard Nilsen

***Tree houses:* A tree house may be anything from a few boards nailed together by ambitious children after reading *Swiss Family Robinson* to a guest house designed by an architect. They have been called *arbors, bowers, crow's-nests, roosting places, tree seats,* and *tree rooms.* The common factor is that all are made above ground level and in or around a tree.**

The House of Boughs
Elizabeth Wilkinson and Marjorie Henderson, Editors
1985; 226 pp.
$35
($36 postpaid) from:
Viking-Penguin Books
299 Murray Hill Pkwy.
East Rutherford, NJ 07073
or Whole Earth Access

• See also "Livable Cities" (pp. 112-113).

• Intelligent planting can help architecture be more energy efficient. See **Climatic Design** (p. 131).

The Food and Heat Producing Solar Greenhouse
Bill Yanda and Rick Fisher
1980; 208 pp.
$8
($9.75 postpaid) from:
John Muir Publications
P. O. Box 613
Santa Fe, NM 87501
or Whole Earth Access

The Food and Heat Producing Solar Greenhouse

In the ten years this book has been available, it has become the one where you look first. For good reason too — somebody or other has actually done what's shown, and there's a lot shown. More than shown, really, because there's also lots of how and why too. And a good bibliography with comment. And good photographs of proven details. And step-by-step instruction on both building and operating. In fact, the book is a marvel. Lots of love in it.
—JB

•

Since the first edition of this book, the Solar Room has proven itself to be one of the best buys in "BTUs for the buck." Literally millions of American homes could save heating dollars immediately by the installation of a Solar Room. . . .

Here is Steve Kenin's explanation of his product: "The Solar Room is a device that turns the southern side of a home into a solar heater. Made of a special plastic, a Solar Room can supply 35 to 65% of home space heating needs. With heat storage and insulation options, its heating capacity is greatly increased. The Solar Room is available in kit form and is designed to be an exterior room, seven feet wide and as long as space permits; 20, 30 or 40 feet. The longer the Solar Room, the more heat is collected.

The Solar Room.

The Bountiful Solar Greenhouse
Shane Smith
1982; 221 pp.
$8
($9.75 postpaid) from:
John Muir Publications
P. O. Box 613
Santa Fe, NM 87504
or Whole Earth Access

The Bountiful Solar Greenhouse

Books on designing and building solar greenhouses abound, but the scarce commodity until now has been an explanation of how to keep the plants inside them healthy and productive. Shane Smith helped start and has run the first large-scale solar greenhouse in America (Cheyenne, Wyoming's Community Solar Greenhouse, 5,000 square feet and 100 percent passively solar-heated). He has a wealth of experience and a knack for straightforward explanation. Consider a major niche well filled.
—Richard Nilsen

•

Plants use so much of the CO_2 in the air that in sealed environments like a greenhouse, the level of CO_2 may be depleted from 300 PPM to 100 PPM by noon. This can easily slow plant growth by 60 percent — not a pleasant thought. This phenomenon occurs only in winter greenhouses where there is no outside ventilation and the structure is sealed to the outside. CO_2 depletion is also less in greenhouses with soils high in organic matter, due to the billions of microbes breathing in that rich, black, pulsing-with-life, humus-laden soil.

I recommend use of an organic mulch to bring CO_2 levels to at least 1000 PPM — if not more. This enhanced level will help compensate for lower light and lower temperatures. It would be hard to find any other single low-cost thing you could do to make such a difference in food yield.

As the watermelons begin to develop on the vines, they will need support. The fruits can get so heavy they will rip the whole vine off the trellis. When a fruit is about tennis-ball size, slip it into an old nylon stocking and tie it securely to the trellis.

The Mushroom Cultivator
Paul Stamets
and J. S. Chilton
1983; 415 pp.
$25 postpaid from:
Homestead Book Co.
6101 22nd Avenue NW
Seattle, WA 98107
or Whole Earth Access

The Mushroom Cultivator

This is simply the best single manual ever published about each phase of home mushroom cultivation. Other books cover some of the more essential aspects of mushroom growing, like compost preparation, growing room construction, and maintenance of environmental conditions for optimum yield, but **The Mushroom Cultivator** *takes you further, into a deeper understanding of mushroom life. It includes a full course on the intricacies of "kitchen microbiology," essential for isolating and maintaining your own strains of mushroom cultures and for turning them into spawn — the "seed" for your mushroom garden. You'll appreciate the chapters on common microbial "weeds" and insect pests, and how to deal with them. Unlike many other writers on the subject, the authors are down on insecticides and fungicides.*

Whether you want to grow agaricus, the common grocery-store mushroom, or exotica like shiitake, psilocybe, or the oyster mushroom, either as a weekend hobbyist or a small-business farmer, this is the manual you want.
—Ted Schultz

Wild strain of Agaricus brunnescens fruiting in bag of cased compost.

•

In general, too much fresh air is preferable to insufficient air supply. However, fresh air displaces the existing room air which is then exhausted from the room. Unless this fresh air is preconditioned to meet the requirements of the species, one will be constantly disrupting the growing environment and thereby overworking the heating and humidification systems. For this reason the air circulation system should be designed to recirculate the room air. This is accomplished by a mixing box with an adjustable damper that proportions fresh and circulated air. In this regard CO_2-tolerant species give the grower a distinct advantage in maintaining the correct environment because they need less fresh air for growth.

Success with House Plants

The heart of this book is its most useful part — an A-Z guide to 600 house plants. Color illustrations accompany suggestions of varieties and instructions on care and propagation. Since this book was published some safer and less toxic remedies for house plant pests have come on the market (you can find out about them on p. 80). Otherwise this is a very comprehensive and useful book.
—Richard Nilsen

•

The genus *Begonia* includes more than 2,000 species and hybrids, and they are as varied in appearance and habit as these numbers suggest. . . . Begonias range in size from tiny, ground-hugging creepers to stout-stemmed specimens 8-10 feet tall.

Because the genus is so large, it is generally divided into groups based on the differing storage organs or root structures of these plants. Some have fibrous roots (as most plants do). A second group consists of species in which roots grow down from a thick creeping rhizome. A third group includes tuberous species that have a fleshy, swollen storage organ at the base of the stem.

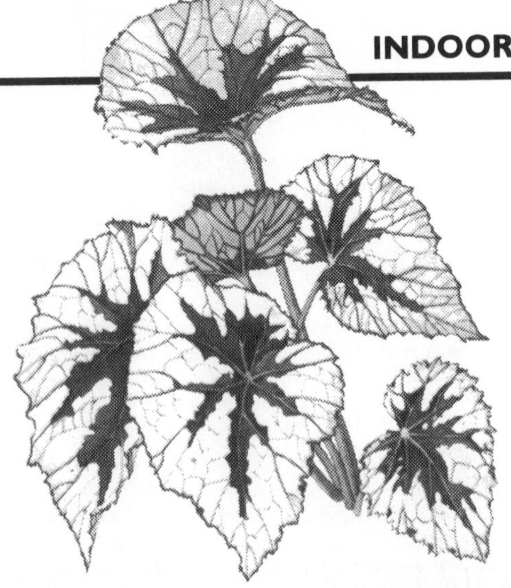

Success with House Plants
Anthony Huxley, Editor
1979; 480 pp.
$21.99
($23.93 postpaid) from:
Reader's Digest
Attn.: Order Entry
Pleasantville, NY 10570
or Whole Earth Access

Sinsemilla Tips • Indoor Marijuana Horticulture

*Smoking and then growing marijuana once introduced a generation of Americans to gardening. There is still only one state (Alaska) where it is legal to grow and possess marijuana for personal consumption. Between drug law enforcement and the neighbor kid down the block, growers today are becoming experts at high-tech indoor cultivation. High-intensity discharge lights, hydroponic cultivation and even computer-controlled indoor environments are all available. Companies selling this equipment advertise in **Sinsemilla Tips**, which covers political news and the latest in cultivation techniques. **Indoor Marijuana Horticulture** is the best introduction to the wonderful world of electricity that makes total indoor growing possible — fans, lights, timers, moisture meters, and CO_2 enrichment systems.*

Commercial marijuana growing tends to be armed, dangerous, and locked in a symbiotic bear-hug with government. There but for the police would go the price and market share to the likes of Philip Morris, R. J. Reynolds, and individual growers. There but for the illegal growers would go the need for an entire paramilitary bureaucracy fighting a war it can never win. Meanwhile the Fourth Amendment continues to get whittled away at, and nobody gets the tax revenues from a multibillion-dollar industry.
—Richard Nilsen
*[**Sinsemilla Tips** suggested by Charles Kelly]*

•

Technological breakthroughs and scientific research have shed bright light on indoor horticulture, by producing the *1000 watt metal halide and 1000 watt High Pressure (HP) sodium, High Intensity Discharge (HID) lamps.* Now, a reasonably priced artificial light source, providing the color spectrum and intensity necessary for marijuana growth, is on the market. With the HID lamps, a gardener may totally control the indoor environment. Together, these two types of HID lamps provide sufficient intensity, of the proper colors in the spectrum, to grow incredibly potent marijuana.

•

CAUTION: A HOT HID MAY EXPLODE IF TOUCHED BY A SINGLE DROP OF COLD WATER. BE VERY CAREFUL AND MAKE SURE TO MOVE THE HID OUT OF THE WAY WHEN SERVICING GARDEN.
—Indoor Marijuana Horticulture

Sinsemilla Tips
Tom Alexander, Editor
$20/year
(4 issues) from:
Sinsemilla Tips
P. O. Box 2046
Corvallis, OR 97339

Indoor Marijuana Horticulture
Jorge Cervantes
1984; 288 pp.
$14.95
($17.95 postpaid) from:
Jorge Cervantes
Indoor Garden Store
P.O. Box 02009
Portland, OR 97202
or Whole Earth Access

• See also "Drugs: Plant Power" (p. 220).

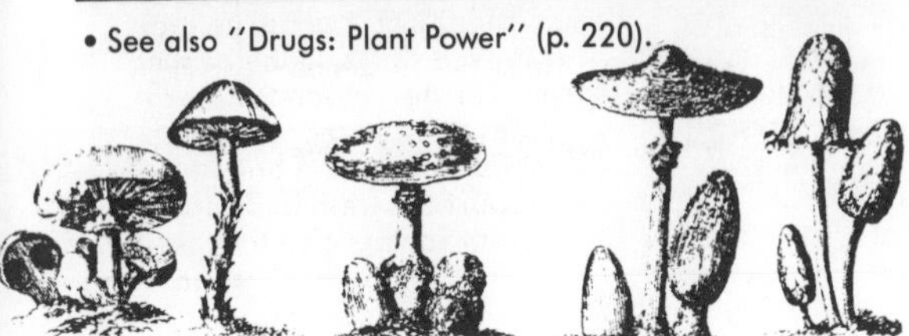

Mushroompeople

*Mushroompeople is the best place for a grower and mushroom lover to begin. Mushroompeople are super-competent and have a computer help line for their customers. They specialize in shiitake, sell specialized strains for greenhouses or outdoors and give mushroom tours to Japan. Costs are lower than equipment described in **The Mushroom Cultivator**. The catalog has all the best books for mushroom growing, hunting in the wild, feasting and cooking.*
—Peter Warshall

Shiitake mushrooms. ►

Mushroompeople
Catalog
$2 from:
Mushroompeople
P. O. Box 158
Inverness, CA 94937

Gardening Magazines

Harrowsmith *from Canada established itself early on as the best of the new magazines dealing with country living. Beautifully designed and intelligently written, it has now spawned an American edition. Both cover cold-climate gardening, plus architecture, cooking, and environmental politics.*

HortIdeas *is a monthly newsletter gleaned from reading mostly technical bulletins at an agricultural library — in this case the University of Kentucky's. Articles are capsulized for easy digestion and referenced for further investigation. It's an extremely fertile source of new gardening ideas.*

Horticulture *is a venerable general-interest gardening magazine; it is occasionally a bit stodgy but has consistently good color photography. Because it is aimed at an affluent audience it is an excellent place to keep up with what's new via the advertisements.*

The National Gardening Association (see next page) has a rapidly changing and improving house organ called **National Gardening.** *Backyard vegetable gardening is the subject, and readers furnish a good supply of new ideas and techniques. In a healthy attempt to live up to its name, there is steady coverage of solutions to problems caused by regional climates.*

Rodale's Organic Gardening *has watched the mainstream creep ever closer to its once-isolated position, so much so that the family name was just recently added to the masthead. Keeping backyard fruits and vegetables healthy without synthetic chemicals is the main idea, but like* **Horticulture** *— or any magazine with a long and successful career — the trick is to keep the contents fresh and interesting. The solution here includes branching into ornamental horticulture and an ongoing discussion of sustainable or regenerative gardening and economics. —Richard Nilsen*

Harrowsmith (Canadian Edition): Wayne Grady, Editor. **$19** /year ($15 in Canada); 6 issues; from Harrowsmith, 7 Queen Victoria Road, Camden East, Ontario, Canada KOK IJO. (U.S. Edition): James M. Lawrence, Editor. **$18**/year (6 issues) from Harrowsmith, The Creamery, Charlotte, VT 05445.

HortIdeas: Gregory and Patricia Y. Williams, Editors. **$10** /year (12 issues) from HortIdeas, Route 1, Box 302, Gravel Switch, KY 40328.

Horticulture: Thomas Cooper, Editor; **$18**/year (12 issues) from Horticulture, P. O. Box 2595, Boulder, CO 80322.

National Gardening: Ruth Page, Editor; **$18**/year (includes membership; 12 issues) from The National Gardening Association, 180 Flynn Avenue, Burlington, VT 05401.

Rodale's Organic Gardening: Robert Rodale, Editor; **$12.97** /year (12 issues) from Rodale Press, 33 East Minor Street, Emmaus, PA 18049

◄

A few years ago, Sibella Kraus was a chef at Alice Waters' well-known Berkeley restaurant, Chez Panisse. Kraus knew first-hand how difficult it was to find reliable sources of lovingly tended organic vegetables, and in 1983, she launched the Farm-Restaurant Project, to see if a link could be established between Bay Area restaurants looking for high-quality seasonal produce and growers willing to provide it.

The project was a huge success. Soon Kraus, working through Greenleaf Produce Co. of San Francisco, became the first food broker specifically for the fabled restaurants of the new cuisine. "When people start knowing who's growing great food or wine, people start caring about that hillside, that valley, that watershed where it's grown. Knowing where your food comes from enhances an ecological consciousness. You see that farmland should be treated like a resource, not a commodity."

—*Rodale's Organic Gardening*

Sweet Potatoes. —***Horticulture***

•

For growers experimenting with ways to keep deer, rabbits, and other plant eaters out of the garden, *HortIdeas* reader Virginia Henrichs suggests Goodart's (Star Route, Box 427, Milam, TX 75959) as a supplier of fox, coyote, and bobcat urine. Goodart's sells equipment for fur trappers, who use urine to lure *their* prey. —*HortIdeas*

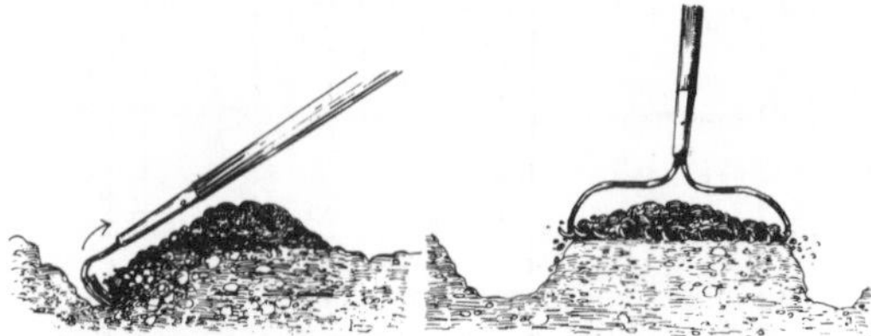

Raised beds the easy way. —***National Gardening***

•

Researchers at Cairo University in Egypt report that adding sugar (presumably sucrose, table sugar) to *Bacillus thuringiensis* biological insecticide can increase its effectiveness in killing insect pests. Larvae of the spiny bollworm, *Earias insulana*, were used in the experiments, but the researchers suggest that sugar *added as a feeding stimulant* to *B.t.* might aid its effectiveness in controlling other lepidopterous pests as well. —*HortIdeas*

The latest in protective covers are "spun-bonded" blankets. So lightweight that they can rest directly on the plants, they protect against frost and warm the soil.
—***Harrowsmith***

• A listing of 50 gardening magazines, society journals, and newsletters available by subscription can be found in **Gardening by Mail** (p. 71).

• The Brooklyn Botanical Gardens **Handbook** series (also on p. 71) is a valuable gardening periodical resource.

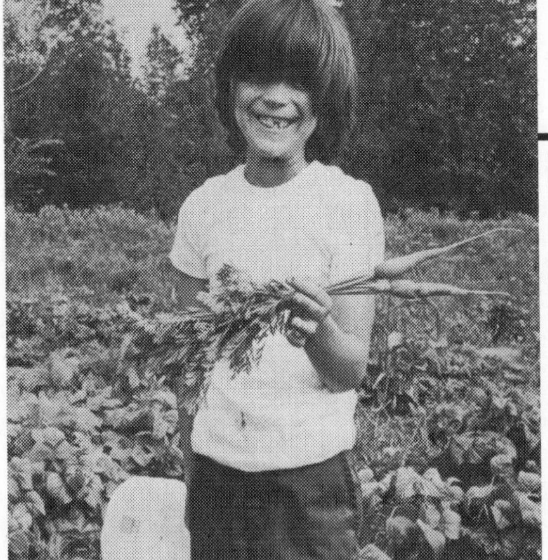

The Youth Gardening Book

Everyone knows that kids and gardens are a natural match-up, right? Wrong. I found out the first time I tried. Somehow gardens didn't have as much pizzaz as video games and all the other diversions. It became a challenge that I'm still working on. I wish I'd had this book at the beginning to help out: it covers everything from motivation to garden design and is especially strong in stressing the fun of gardens with 25 pages of experiments, tests and special activities. Whether your garden partner is your own child or a horde of school kids you'll find it a genuine ally. —Dick Fugett

•

Don't impose your expectations on the gardeners. Kids don't care too much about total yields. The experience of growing a radish is as important as the end product. A single radish is cherished by the child if she grew it herself. —*The Youth Gardening Book*

The Community Garden Book

This is like a yearbook on the current status of community gardening in the U.S. Many of the major programs are featured along with an overview of what's been learned about preventing vandalism, setting up irrigation and composting systems, fundraising, and more. A neighborhood group could start a garden with this. —Rosemary Menninger

•

A group that is high on enthusiasm, but low on budget, can make ends meet through creative scrounging. The items below are being used today in gardens across the country:

Item	*Possible Uses*
Used tires	Planting containers, fencing, swings
Plastic gallon jugs	Scoops, watering cans, hot caps
Metal bed frames and springs	Trellises, gates
Carpet scraps	Mulching, weather-stripping in cold frames
Old window screens	Food dryers
Gym lockers	Tool storage

• See also **My Garden Companion** (p. 70).

• A realistic but inspiring look at community gardening in New York City.
Struggle for Space: Tom Fox, Ian Koeppel, and Susan Kellam, 1985; 165 pp. **$15** ($16.50 postpaid) from Neighborhood Open Space Coalition, 72 Reade Street, New York, NY 10007 (or Whole Earth Access).

American Community Gardening Association

*The American Community Gardening Association and its publication, the **Journal of Community Gardening**, are in the business of promoting the practice of community gardening nationwide.*

Most of the people who got the Association rolling actually manage or operate community agriculture projects in major cities. They know firsthand how a community garden can transform the mood of a neighborhood, change lives for the better and instill pride in the residents. —Shane Smith

•

Most organizations have a small core of dependable, but vastly overworked volunteers who have assumed many responsibilities. This core group usually remains small due to a winnowing out of volunteers who lack staying power and a pervasive belief that it is more effective and efficient to do it yourself. Teaching new volunteers can be time consuming and frustrating but the rewards can be profound and long term. Give others the chance to share greater responsibility and to experience the inner workings of your organization. Make this a top priority.

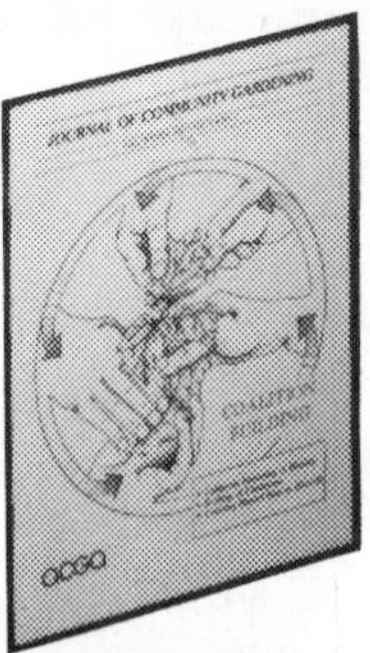

American Community Gardening Association
Membership **$15**/year
Information **free**

Journal of Community Gardening
Karen Bess, Editor
Free with ACGA membership (4 issues) All from:
American Community Gardening Association
P. O. Box 93147,
Milwaukee, WI 53202

The National Gardening Association

*The NGA began in 1972 by sponsoring community gardens in Burlington, Vermont. Today it is a 250,000-member national nonprofit organization with many useful and even unique publications. (See their book **Gardening** on page 68.) Although they rode to popularity on the high food prices of the 1970s, the NGA has always understood that gardening is more than vegetables. It is therapeutic, and when done by a community it is political. In addition to publishing a magazine (opposite page) and the two books on this page, they also offer a catalog of enabling hand tools for handicapped gardeners, a booklet on employee gardens for businesses, and a book on gardening for people in prison. Write them for a publications list and specific information.* —Richard Nilsen

The National Gardening Association
Publications catalog

free from:
The National Gardening Association
180 Flynn Avenue
Burlington, VT 05401

Some community gardening fanatics proved the point that almost anything can be used for gardening!
—The Community Gardening Book

The Community Garden Book
Larry Sommers
1984; 121 pp.
$8.95
($10.95 postpaid)

The Youth Gardening Book
Lynn Ocone
1983; 145 pp.
$8.95
($10.95 postpaid)
Both from:
Gardens for All/ The National Association for Gardening
180 Flynn Avenue
Burlington, VT 05401
or Whole Earth Access

Gardener's Supply Company

Catalog **free** from:
Gardener's Supply Company
128 Intervale Road
Burlington, VT 05401

Green River Tools

Catalog **free** from:
Green River Tools
5 Cotton Mill Hill
P. O. Box 1919
Brattleboro, VT 05301

Smith & Hawken

Catalog **free** from:
Smith & Hawken
25 Corte Madera
Mill Valley, CA 94941

Gardener's Supply Co.
• Green River Tools
• Smith & Hawken

All three of these mail order companies stress quality and useful innovation. Quality because it takes less material and energy to build one tool well than many tools cheaply. Cheap garden tools tend to break either themselves or your back and end up being expensive choices in the long run. The search for innovation and quality often leads abroad; many of the tools come from Europe and Japan. With rare exceptions, American manufacturers have abdicated the quality garden tool market.

Gardener's Supply Co. grew out of Gardens for All in Vermont (now known as the National Gardening Association — see page 76). The catalog is aimed squarely at home vegetable gardeners, and in addition to tools features home canning equipment and organic pest controls.

Green River Tools is the unique one of the three catalogs, and its top-of-the-line selections make it the most expensive on some items. It matches high quality with high idealism — for example, they do not sell teak gardening benches, currently a staple item in many catalogs. Instead you are politely advised that teak benches contribute to the destruction of endangered tropical rainforests and are offered American-made versions in white cedar or red oak. Green River is also strong on Dutch hand tools and features the revolutionary Ladbrooke soil block makers for propagating seedlings.

Smith & Hawken introduced American gardeners to the Bulldog line of English forks and spades, tools so well made they are likely to end up as items in wills. The catalog is aimed primarily at suburban horticulturists and also offers a fine selection of Japanese garden and flower arranging tools.

For such highly selective catalogs the amount of duplication among this trio is small; I suggest browsing through each of them. —*Richard Nilsen*

•

These unique season extenders perform an important double function — they protect young plants from the cold by night and shield them from excess heat by day. How they work is fascinating. During the day, the water absorbs heat, moderating temperatures inside the tepee. As the water cools down by night, it releases its heat slowly (as much as 900,000 calories of heat!). Even if the water begins to freeze, it releases more and more heat for better protection. *Wall O' Water* protects plants from temperatures as low as 10°F!
—*Gardeners Supply*

Dr. Hans Loehrl, a protege of Konrad Lorenz and retired head of the Bird Observatory of Radolfszell, West Germany, spent 30 years testing and improving the birdhouses shown here.
—Green River Tools

Garden Fork, 40" with FD handle, $42.40

Spading fork. Overall length 42". $35.80

Garden Fork, 44" with YD handle, $37.50

Garden Fork, 64" with straight handle, $42.40

The Gardening Fork (on right) has English-style, square shaped tines while the Spading Fork (on left) has broader, flatter tines recommended for heavier soil.
—Smith & Hawken

•

Weeder (hori hori). I first saw this tool strapped to a farmer's waist and thought it was a knife. Upon inspection, it turned out to be a knife-shaped weeder. This is a true grubber, a tool that can remove any rooted weed in the ground. It pulls, pierces, cuts and pries. Not a bad item for a camping trip either. Comes with case with belt loop. Weight: 10½ oz. Blade length: 6½"
#2700 $9.80 —*Smith & Hawken*

Hori hori
—Smith & Hawken

•

A Guide to Entrance Hole Sizes:

Use the guide below to select the right opening size for the bird species you want to attract:

1" — House Wren (a highly desirable species).

1¼" — Chickadee, Carolina Wren, Bewick's Wren, Tufted Titmouse, Nuthatch, Downy Woodpecker.

1½" — Tree Swallow, Bluebird.

2" — House Finch, Starling, larger Woodpeckers.

2½" — Purple Martin, Crested Flycatcher, Flicker.

•The **Necessary Catalogue of Biological Farm and Garden Supplies** provides access to a wide range of tools, books, and supplies for biological or organic agriculture. Included are pest and disease controls, foliar nutrients, seed and composting inoculants, and soil amendments.

Catalog **$2** from Necessary Trading Company, 640 Main Street, New Castle, VA 24127.

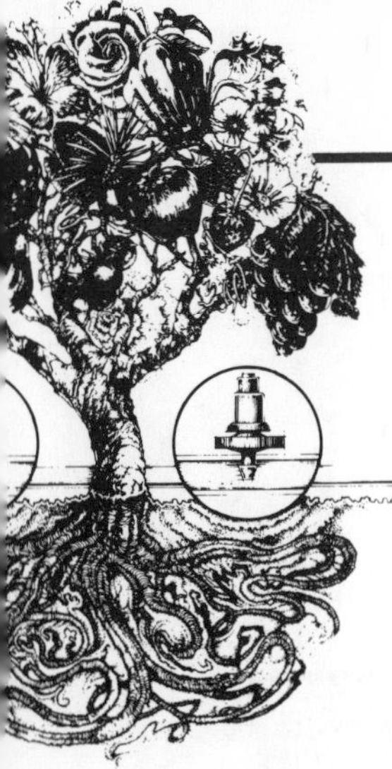

Drip Irrigation

Anything that saves a person time and money is bound to be popular; drip irrigation does both. Plastic tubing delivers water to each plant in a slow, steady drip. Timers can further control how often you irrigate. The small army of drip irrigation manufacturers and products can be confusing. A solution is to shop at a store where you know and trust the salespeople. Or shop by mail order with the Urban Farmer. They specialize in drip irrigation and carefully select what they sell from more than 40 manufacturers. Their catalog lists components and also explains the basics of design and installation.
—Richard Nilsen

•

Landscaping
While drip irrigation was designed with commercial agriculture in mind, many have discovered that the advantages of this type of irrigation apply equally to landscaping and ornamental applications. Accurate amounts of water can be applied to the root zone of each plant. Weed problems are reduced, water is kept off windows and sidewalks and individual plants receive the type of watering they need to flourish.

•

Advantages
A drip system gives healthy, fast-growing plants, and is very efficient in its use of water. Little is lost to evaporation, and walkways and areas between rows remain dry. This also reduces weed growth, and makes cultivation possible during and immediately after an irrigation cycle. Drip irrigation allows a large area to be watered from a small water source, since it uses water more slowly than other methods. The biggest savings for most home gardeners is time: they can now garden more ambitiously, and with an automatic system, travel and admire the gardens of the world.

Urban Farmer Store
Catalog **$1** from:
Urban Farmer Store
2121 Taraval Street
San Francisco, CA 94116

Troy-Bilt Tillers
$729-$1,679
Information **free**
Garden Way Carts
$95.50-$177.50
Information **free**
Both from:
Garden Way Manufacturing Co.
102nd Street & 9th Avenue
Troy, NY 12180

Troy-Bilt Tillers • Garden Way Carts

Troy-Bilt tillers have a personality of their own — they're built solid as a Russian dump truck for starters, besides coming with a well-written 200-page manual covering everything from tilling techniques to tune-ups and transmission tinkering. For good measure, the factory service department has a toll-free 800 number. When I've had to use it there has always been a competent and courteous response.

Troy-Bilt tillers range from three-and-a-half to eight horsepower, and the larger models now have a power take-off which allows use of accessories — generator, log splitter, and shredder. Tiller prices go from $729 to $1,679, and there's a unique pricing system in which hefty discounts are available in off season.

Troy-Bilt tillers are made by Garden Way Manufacturing Co., well known for their Garden Way carts. I've had mine for years and have lugged everything from bags of concrete to a full-sized refrigerator in it. Their success has spawned other big-wheeled carts — each of the catalogs on these pages carries a version. You won't go wrong with a Garden Way cart, but you might save money by checking out the competition.
—Dick Fugett

The 6 HP H-60, our all-time most popular model.

Mainline Rotary Tillers

Market gardeners, landscapers, or anyone who makes a living with a tiller will want to know about Mainline. This American company sells two kinds of high-quality Italian tillers made by S.E.P. and Goldoni. Thirty-three models are offered, ranging in horsepower from 5.7 to 18 and in price from $1,200 to $5,000. Some of the larger sizes are available in diesel. A key feature provides great versatility: the tiller comes off, revealing the power take-off spline; the handles and controls pivot 180 degrees so the power take-off is pointed forward, and attachments hook on. They include rotary lawn mowers, sickle-bar mowers, snow throwers, sprayer pumps, and log splitters. *—Richard Nilsen*

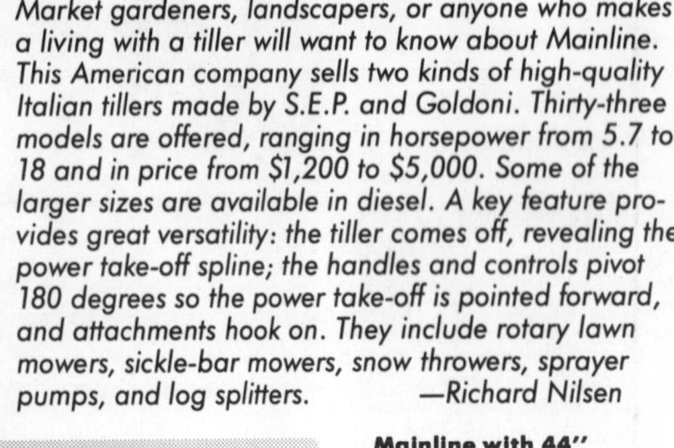

Mainline with 44" sicklebar attachment.

Mainline Rotary Tillers
$1,200-$5,000
(33 models)
Information **free** from:
Mainline North America
P. O. Box 348
London, OH 43140

• See also Peaceful Valley Farm Supply (p. 85).

• If you need to pump, haul, or store water in order to garden, Domestic Growers Supply has a catalog full of tools and supplies.
Domestic Growers Supply: catalog **$1** from Domestic Growers Supply, P. O. Box 809, Cave Junction, OR 97523.

Rodale's Color Handbook of Garden Insects
Anna Carr
1979; 241 pp.
$12.95 postpaid from:
Rodale Press
33 East Minor Street
Emmaus, PA 18049
or Whole Earth Access

Rodale's Color Handbook of Garden Insects

More than 300 pests and beneficial insects leap from these pages in close-up color photographs. While your own worst enemy may not appear (because the insect world is far more varied than a single book can cover), a similar species is probably listed — along with organic controls, geographic range and life cycle data.
—Rosemary Menninger

►

Range: throughout North America.

Description: Green with a light stripe; several hairs on each segment; ¾ inch long. *Adult:* Brownish yellow moth with gray and brown marking; ¾-inch wingspan. *Eggs: Laid in clusters on the leaves.*

Life Cycle: Two to four generations. Pupae overwinter in the soil.

Host Plants: Bean, beet, corn, pea, strawberry.

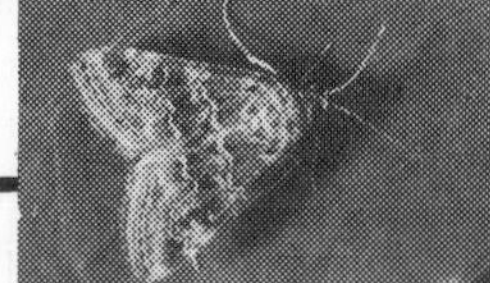

Adult

Larva

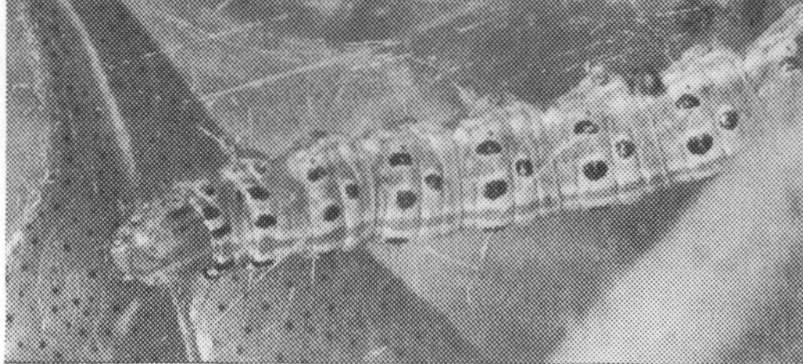

Larvae

Caterpillar: Garden Webworm (Achyra rantalis)

Feeding Habits: Larvae spin light webs and feed within, dropping to the ground when disturbed.

Insect Predators: Various trichogramma wasps.

Natural Controls: Use *Bacillus thuringiensis* or pyrethrum for intolerable infestations.

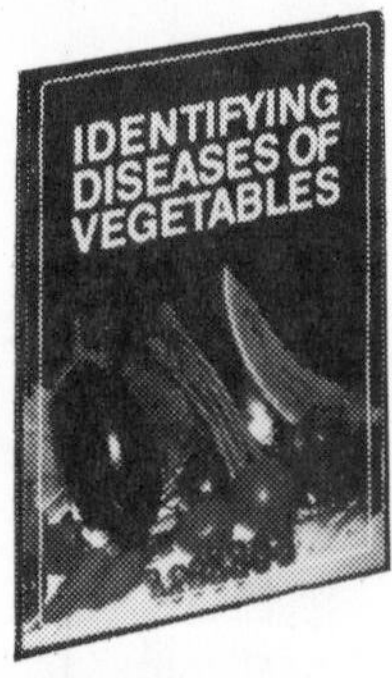

Identifying Diseases of Vegetables
A. A. MacNab, A.F. Sherf, and S.K. Springer
1983; 62 pp.
$8 postpaid from:
Agricultural Publications Department
The Pennsylvania State University
Agriculture Administration Building
University Park, PA 16802
or Whole Earth Access

Identifying Diseases of Vegetables

This book gives brief and nontechnical descriptions of the major diseases of common garden vegetables and illustrates each one with a high-quality color photograph. It does not prescribe cures of any kind, although from the explanations of environmental conditions that some diseases prefer — such as cool, wet weather or poorly drained soils — you may get clues as to what went wrong in your case. If this book needed a subtitle it would be "Keeping Ahead of the Fungi." *—Richard Nilsen*

Tobacco Mosaic of tomato.

•

Viruses and herbicides often cause leaf deformation that is most severe on new growth. Tobacco mosaic, cucumber mosaic, and 2,4-D are three common causes of these symptoms.

Tobacco Mosaic is caused by a virus that affects tomatoes, eggplants, peppers, and related plants. Symptoms on tomato foliage include light- and dark-green mottling with curling and slight malformation of leaflets. Sometimes green fruit are mottled. Affected plants may be stunted. The virus is very persistent and infectious, and can be spread by merely brushing against plants. The virus is not spread by aphids.

Insecticidal Soap

Soaps are made of fatty acids from plants and animals. There are hundreds of these fatty acids, and while most will get dirt off your hands, a select few will also kill insect pests yet not harm people, beneficial insects, or the plants themselves. Safer Agro-Chem has built an innovative line of products around these special soaps — the one for use against fruit and vegetable pests is safe to use right up to the day of harvest. Others kill moss and algae, powdery mildew, and fleas on pets. *—Richard Nilsen*

Insecticidal Soap
Information **free** from:
Safer's Inc.
P. O. Box 649
Jamul, CA 92035
or at your local
garden supply store.

Natural Pest Controls

Don't insects ever get sick? Yes, if they eat the right bacteria. Scientists have discovered naturally occurring microbial insecticides for many garden pests like tomato worms and grasshoppers, and even one for mosquitoes and black flies. And since they are specific as to what they infect, they do not harm fish, honeybees, chickens that eat grasshoppers, your ripe tomatoes, or you. Reuter Labs sells 18 of these products under the brand name "Attack." If you can't find them at your garden store then write the company. *—Richard Nilsen*

Reuter "Attack" Natural Pest Controls

Catalog **free** from:
Reuter Laboratories
8450 Natural Way
Manassas Park, VA 22111

• See Gardener's Supply Co. catalog (p. 78) for more pest control products.

• For more on pesticide reform, see "Biohazards" (p. 107).

Introduction to Integrated Pest Management

Integrated pest management (IPM) has come into its own in the last 15 years as the shortcomings of reliance on synthetic chemical pesticides have become glaringly apparent — the bugs become immune to the sprays, which are oil based and expensive; natural checks and balances get wiped out, groundwater becomes contaminated, birds die, and people eat foods laced with carcinogens. This is an easy reading introduction to a system based on looking at pests in their total environmental setting via careful monitoring in the field and use of computer-built predictive mathematical models of insect behavior. Compared to using only chemical pesticides, IPM is gentle on the earth and frequently cheaper. —Richard Nilsen

•

Grape growers in California have learned that blackberry bushes have their beneficial aspects, especially in the control of an important insect pest — the grape leafhopper. Insecticides have often failed to provide effective control of the leafhopper, or their use has aggravated other pest problems such as spider mites. Entomologists had known that a tiny natural enemy, the parasitic wasp *Anagrus epos*, which lays its eggs in the eggs of the grape leafhopper, kept the pest under control in some vineyards — but not in others. Nobody knew why.

The riddle was solved when it was realized that the wasp spent its winters parasitizing a different insect on a different plant host. Since the leaves fall off grapevines in the winter and the grape leafhopper retreats to the edge of the vineyard and becomes inactive, the nonhibernating parasitic wasp has no shelter, food, or means of survival in this environment. Nearby blackberry bushes, however, keep their leaves during winter and host their own leafhopper species all year round. Thus, the weedy blackberry patches were providing a winter home for this important natural enemy of the key grape pest.

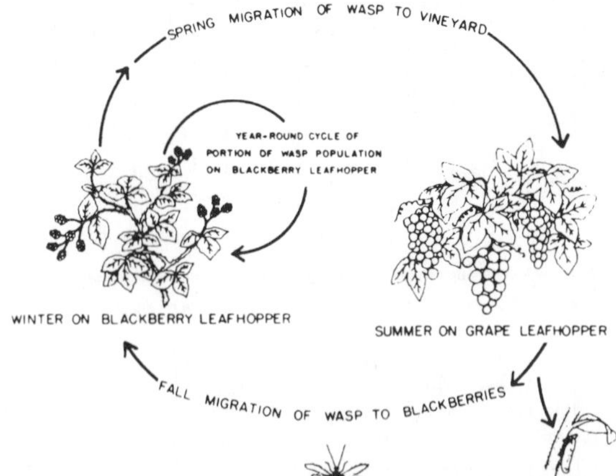

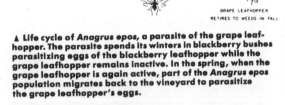

▲ Life cycle of *Anagrus epos*, a parasite of the grape leafhopper. The parasite spends its winters in blackberry bushes parasitizing eggs of the blackberry leafhopper while the grape leafhopper remains inactive. In the spring, when the grape leafhopper is again active, part of the *Anagrus epos* population migrates back to the vineyard to parasitize the grape leafhopper's eggs.

Introduction to Integrated Pest Management
Mary Louise Flint and Robert van den Bosch
1981; 240 pp.
$19.95 postpaid from:
Plenum Press
233 Spring Street
New York, NY 10013
or Whole Earth Access

Common Sense Pest Control Quarterly • The IPM Practitioner

*Integrated pest management isn't just for farmers and gardeners. It works on cockroaches, rats and clothes moths too. Plenty of techniques are known, and getting them to people who can use them are what these two newsletters are all about. The **Quarterly** is for a general audience and the subscription price includes one written consultation about a pest problem you may have of your own. Reprints of programs for safe and economical control of an amazing variety of pests are also sold — everything from mosquitos and head lice to poison ivy and lawn pests. The **Practitioner** is read by professional pest managers who serve the growing market of people demanding safe alternatives to chemical poisons.* —Richard Nilsen

•

For many years following the Second World War . . . sheep were commonly dipped with dieldrin and related materials to protect them from skin parasites such as blow flies. Dieldrin has a natural affinity for wool, chemically bonding to the fiber. The result was moth protection that lasted the life of any woolen garment. . . . Because of food-chain contamination, many pesticides such as dieldrin and its relatives have been banned. . . . The result has been the recurrence of fabric-eating insects as major residential problems.

—Common Sense Pest Control Quarterly

•

Clothes moths and other pests that damage fabrics sometimes make their homes in the abandoned nests of birds, rodents, bats, bees or wasps and in the carcasses of dead animals. These sources of moths need to be found and removed. Trapping, rather than poisoning, should be used to eliminate rodents. Poisoned rats or mice are too likely to die in inaccessible places in the walls of the dwelling, and these carcasses can feed fabric pests as well as flesh flies, which may then become pests within the house. —*Common Sense*

•

Chickens were used successfully as biological controls against grasshoppers in the Siskiyou National Forest in Oregon, where forest officials, rather than applying insecticide against an unusually large hatch of grasshoppers, fenced in a five-acre area containing valuable tree seedlings and stocked it with 175 chickens. At the start of the project, 200 to 600 grasshoppers per square yard were counted, but within a short time, the chickens had so reduced the grasshopper population that chicken feed had to be purchased. —*IPM Practitioner*

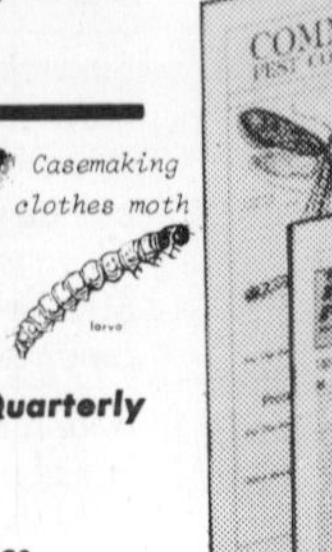

Common Sense Pest Control Quarterly
William Olkowski, Editor
$30/year (4 issues)
The IPM Practitioner
William Olkowski, Editor
$25/year (10 issues)
Publications catalog **$1**
All from:
BIRC (Bio-Integral Resource Center)
P. O. Box 7414
Berkeley, CA 94707

• Pesticide Hotline 800-858-7378.
This 24-hour seven days/week free phone line is operated by the U.S. Environmental Protection Agency and Texas Tech University in Lubbock. Everything from first aid for acute poisoning to advice about garden pests.

Rincon-Vitova Insectaries

Mail-order bugs that eat bugs. They're called beneficial insects, and ladybugs are best known. Also for sale here are bugs to control aphids, greenhouse whiteflies, and even a parasite to attack common flies that breed in livestock manure. —Richard Nilsen

Rincon-Vitova Insectaries
Catalog **free** from:
Rincon-Vitova Insectaries
P. O. Box 95
Oak View, CA 93022

Drone

Queen

Worker

—*The Hive and The Honey Bee*

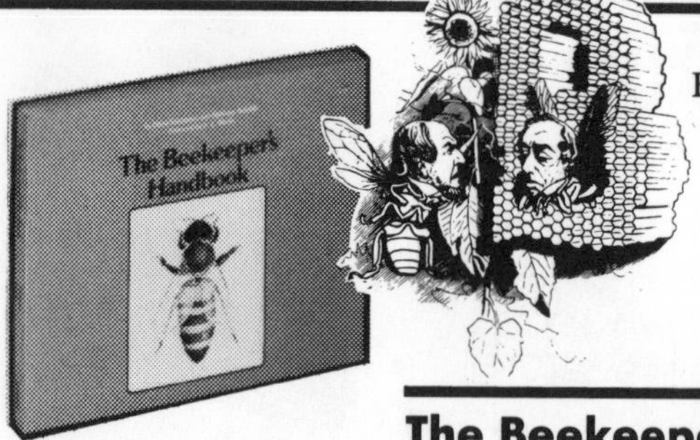

EES DON'T NEED MUCH ROOM. You can keep them in a back yard, on a city rooftop, or in your neighbor's empty lot. I've put mine in all three places over the years. I offer bees my clean and sturdy shelters more for the joy of having their fascination nearby than for the several gallons of honey a year they pay me as rent. They don't bark, or need milking twice a day, either. —Kevin Kelly

Capturing a swarm of bees can bring genuine adventure into your life, making it unnecessary to watch TV that day. —Dick Fugett

The Beekeeper's Handbook
Diana Sammataro and Alphonse Avitabile
1986; 150 pp.
$14.95
postpaid from:
Macmillan
Order Dept.
Front and Brown Streets
Riverside, NJ 08075
or Whole Earth Access

The Beekeeper's Handbook

Here's a book I wish had been around when I started working bees. ***The Beekeeper's Handbook*** *is a well-illustrated introduction covering most of the basics, from site location and equipment to the installation of package bees to basic management techniques. It's the best beginner's book I've seen, and most readable, so I won't quibble about small stuff like the authors' hang-up on mandatory chemotherapy.*

With this book and some equipment you'll be on your way. If you're beginning, you'd do well to find a local beekeeper and thus benefit from someone else's experience. More fun is to make contact with two local beekeepers. You'll soon discover that they disagree with each other half the time — that beekeeping is an art, not a science. With this understanding, you'll move forward with a more flexible mind. —Dick Fugett

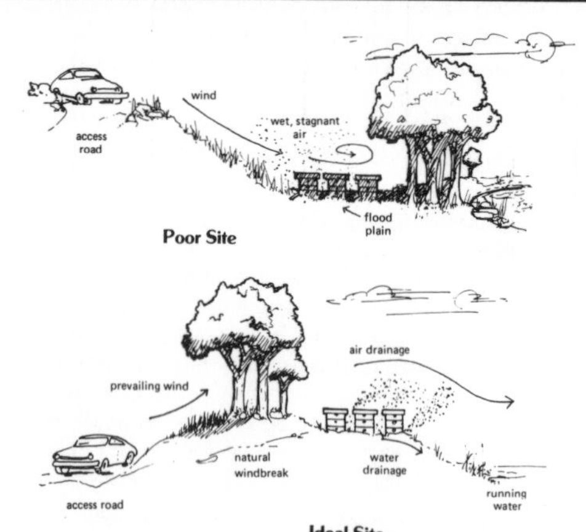

The Hive and the Honey Bee
Dadant and Sons, Editors
4th edition 1975; 740 pp.
$14.80
($17.30 postpaid) from:
Dadant & Sons, Inc.
51 South 2nd Street
Hamilton, IL 62341
or Whole Earth Access

The Hive and the Honey Bee

Since the major technical breakthroughs in beekeeping — movable frames, wax foundations, and the honey extractor — were all made over 100 years ago, beekeepers today can devote their efforts to improving technique rather than trying to keep up with state-of-the-art equipment advances. So when it comes to bee books, it follows that the old can be as useful as the new, and sometimes more so.

Hive *is still going strong after 40 years, now in a 7th printing of a 4th edition which was in fact inspired by a book published in 1853. It's passed the test of time — if any single volume could be said to present the topic, this would be it.* —Dick Fugett

•

The first consideration in choosing the location of an apiary is whether or not there are sufficient sources of nectar and pollen near. Bear in mind that honey bees obtain most of their nectar and pollen within a half-mile radius, but can gather at distances of 1 to 2 miles, depending on the ruggedness of the country and to some extent on the prevailing winds. Even in the heart of large cities, there are often sufficient sources of nectar and pollen to provide for a limited number of colonies, and even to produce surplus honey. A city lawn, a back yard, a flat roof, a pasture on a farm, a grove of trees — all will be satisfactory locations as the occasion demands.

Gleanings in Bee Culture

GIBC *has been published monthly for 113 years and appears to be permanent. It has current info on everything of interest to the hobbyist — from techniques, research and disease to books and equipment.* —Dick Fugett

•

Can you describe the taste and aroma of your honey or honey from your state or region? Our language lacks unique words to convey an accurate sensation of taste. A few years ago Arthur Strang and I attempted to begin a description of some of the mid-Atlantic region honey sources. Here are some honey sources for you to ponder and perhaps confirm for yourself:

Water White Alfalfa Blossom Honey: Very sweet, smooth, faintly fruity flavor with a pleasing sugary bouquet.
Basswood Honey: Sweet, slightly astringent flavor with a pleasing blossomy flavor.
Amber Blackberry Blossom Honey: Sweet, smooth, rich, roasted nut-like flavor with pleasing fruity bouquet.
Dark Buckwheat Honey: Sweet, smooth, nut-like flavor with a satisfactory fruity, nutty bouquet.
Extra Light Amber Sweet Clover: Very sweet, smooth, taint of cinnamon-like flavor with a pleasing sugary bouquet.
Extra Light Amber Lima Bean Honey: Moderately sweet, slightly tart flavor with satisfactory weak blossom bouquet.

Gleanings in Bee Culture
John Root, Editor
$11.20/year
(12 issues) from:
A. I. Root Company
P. O. Box 706
Medina, OH 44256

Mail Order Bees

Since bee supply stores are few and far between, mail order becomes a necessity. Each of the following dealers will send a free catalog on request. —Dick Fugett

Walter T. Kelley Company, Clarkson, KY 42726.
Dadant Bee Supplies, Dadant & Sons, Inc., Hamilton, IL 62341.
Root Bee Supplies. A. I. Root Co., P. O. Box 706, Medina, OH 44256.

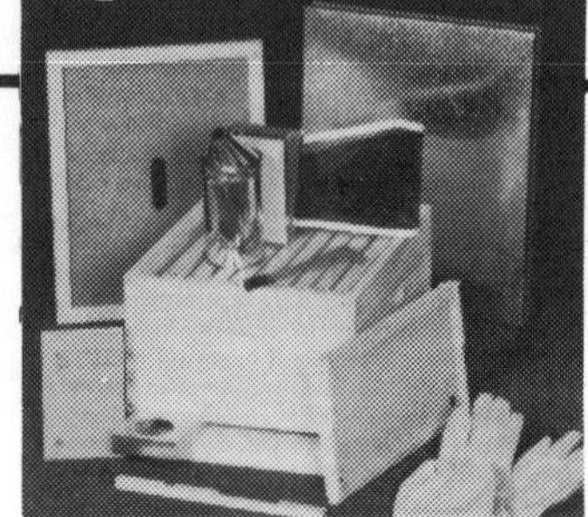
—*Dadant's*

Unit #1, the "Honey-of-a-Hobby" kit, contains everything necessary for the beginner to start that first colony of bees except the bees themselves. This complete beekeeping kit contains: one standard beehive with a unique reversible entrance reducer, 10 frames, 10 sheets of Dadant's Duragilt Foundation, protective bee veil, all-purpose hive tool, bee smoker to calm the bees, sting-resistant gloves, entrance feeder, "First Lessons in Beekeeping" book and assembly instructions. Additional equipment, necessary as the colony grows, is available in Units #2 and #3. Unassembled. $89.90

The Freshwater Aquaculture Book

This book deals with just about anything that moves in fresh water and is big enough to bite — fish species plus frogs, crayfish, shrimp, and clams. Normally, to get the kind of comprehensive information this book contains you would have to go to several books, and most of them would be aimed at the fellow who wants to know how to go about raising 30 acres of catfish in ponds. But as with agriculture so with aquaculture: a small pond provides "the best combination of productivity and manageability."
—Richard Nilsen

"Will-o-the-Wisp" bug light fish feeder installed on a farm pond in Wisconsin. Nocturnal flying insects are attracted to the UV light tube, sucked in by an impeller fan and blown down through the chute at the back of the unit and into the water.

The Freshwater Aquaculture Book
William McLarney
1984; 583 pp.
$40
($41 postpaid) from:
Hartley & Marks, Inc.
P. O. Box 147
Point Roberts, WA 98281
or Whole Earth Access

Raising Small Meat Aminals

If your average country vet doesn't know too much about sick rabbits and chickens, that's because he spends most of his time doctoring horses and cattle. Dr. Giammattei helps fill the void with this excellent book. There are 39 pages of diagnostic keys for various animal diseases, plus instructions on how to doctor your own flocks. Details on nutrition, housing, breeding, management, and butchering are equally well presented. —Richard Nilsen

•

Analysis of Savings on Home-Grown Small Meat Animals

Type of animal	1.	2.	3.
Chicken broiler	$ .45	$ .55	18.4
Turkey roaster	.56	.61	8.2
Cornish game hen	.70	.89	19.2
Rabbit fryer	.75	1.60	53.0
Squab	1.00	2.35	57.5

1. Approx. cost of home production per lb. of dressed carcass
2. Approx. retail price per lb. of dressed carcass
3. Savings on home-grown carcasses (%)

Raising Small Meat Animals
Victor M. Giammattei, D.V.M.
1976; 433 pp.
$19.95
postpaid from:
Interstate Printers and Publishers
19 North Jackson Street
P. O. Box 50
Danville, IL 61843-0050
or Whole Earth Access

Garden Way Livestock Books

Garden Way is the best single source for introductory books on raising back-yard animals. The size of your back yard determines which critter(s). A book each on poultry, rabbits, ducks, turkeys, goats, sheep, pigs, and cattle. —Richard Nilsen

Raising Poultry the Modern Way: Leonard S. Mercia, 1975; 220 pp. **$8.95** ($10.95 postpaid).
Raising Rabbits the Modern Way: Bob Bennett, 1975; 158 pp. **$7.95** ($9.95 postpaid).
Publications list **free**. All from Garden Way Publishing/Storey Communications, Schoolhouse Road, Pownal, VT 05261 (or Whole Earth Access).

Stromberg's Chicks & Pets Unlimited

For non-killed protein nothing beats milk and eggs. For ordinary chickens go to local sources. For particular chickens, fancy ones, and geese, ducks, pigeons, turkeys, peacocks — plus everything to house and care for them — Stromberg's.

Stromberg's Chicks & Pets Unlimited
Catalog
$1 from:
Stromberg's Chicks & Pets
Pine River, MN 56474

KHAKI CAMPBELLS
15 Ducklings $27.95 15 Eggs $16.95

WHITE CRESTED DUCKS $50.00 Pair
15 Ducklings $45.00 15 Eggs $16.95

• Medicines, equipment, grooming supplies and accessories for horses, cats, dogs and rabbits. Good prices. Wholesale Veterinary Supply: Catalog **free** from P. O. Box 2256, Rockford, IL 61131.

• Also see "Pets" (pp. 144-145).

Murray McMurray Hatchery

Many kinds of chicks both plain and fancy, great service, a catalog that's an education in itself, and good prices. They also respond quickly to questions — we got an individual reply to ours in less than a week.
—Daryl Ann Kyle

Murray McMurray Hatchery
Catalog **free** from:
Murray McMurray
P. O. Box 458
Webster City, IA 50595

Barred Rocks.

Earthworm Buyer's Guide • Worms Eat My Garbage

Down here at the bottom, underneath all this livestock by-product, are the earthworms, happily turning waste into compost. Get some and they'll do it for you.

***Worms Eat My Garbage** tells how to keep worms in a box to transform your kitchen organic garbage into humus.*
—Richard Nilsen

Earthworm Buyer's Guide 1986-87 (A Directory of Earthworm Hatcheries in the U.S.A. and Canada): Robert F. Shields, 1986; 64 pp. **$3** ($4 postpaid) from Shields Publications, P. O. Box 669, Eagle River, WI 54521 (or Whole Earth Access).

Worms Eat My Garbage: Mary Appelhof, 1982; 100 pp. **$7.95** postpaid from Flower Press, 10332 Shaver Road, Kalamazoo, MI 49002 (or Whole Earth Access).

The five phases of the jump showing the correct position of the horse and rider at each phase.
—The Manual of Horsemanship

The Whole Horse Catalog

As a newcomer to the equestrian scene, I found this book particularly helpful. It covers everything but the riding: selecting a horse, choosing a stable, horse health, tack, apparel, events, and organizations. In the **Whole Earth Catalog** *genre, it's an excellent resource book for books, magazines, and all sorts of products for both English and Western riders.* —*Patricia Phelan*

The Whole Horse Catalog
Steven D. Price, Editor
1985; 287 pp.
$12.95 postpaid from:
Simon & Schuster
Mail Order Sales
200 Old Tappan Road
Old Tappan, NJ 07675
or Whole Earth Access

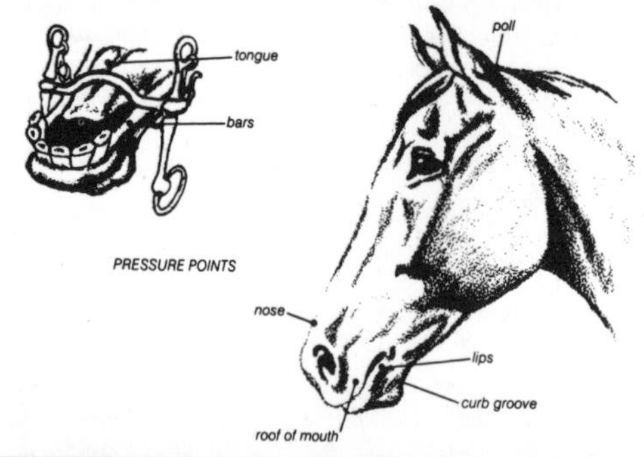

The Manual of Horsemanship

This is the classic book of English riding — on the flat and jumping fences. The first third of the book is devoted to riding skills (equitation). The rest is "horsemastership" — the care of the horse and the equipment involved. The text and illustrations are good for young or novice riders. —*Pamela Cowtan*

The Manual of Horsemanship
Marabel Hadfield, Editor
1983; 320 pp.
$10.95
($12.45 postpaid) from:
Barron's Educational Series
113 Crossways Park Drive
Woodbury, NY 11797
or Whole Earth Access

Supplies

King's Saddlery: *The best catalog for the working cowboy and all Western riders. They manufacture ropes and saddles and have a large selection of bits.*
Catalog **free** from King's Saddlery, 184 North Main, Sheridan, WY 82801.

Miller's: *This classy catalog offers tack and accoutrements for those riders of English persuasion. Lots of handsome apparel.*
Catalog **$2** from Miller's, 235 Murray Hill Parkway, East Rutherford, NJ 07073

Libertyville Saddle Shop: *Such an overwhelming selection of everything for all sorts of riding that it's difficult to order unless you already know what you want.*
Catalog **$3** from Libertyville Saddle Shop, P. O. Box M, Libertyville, IL 60048.
—*Patricia Phelan and Pamela Cowtan*

Elan II by Tress. Elegant hunt cap with a flexible peak. Covered in French velvet with a handsome, welted edge. Black only. American sizes 6½-7½. No. 0225 $49.95
—Miller's

▼
King's Saddlery's wall of bits, located in the front store.

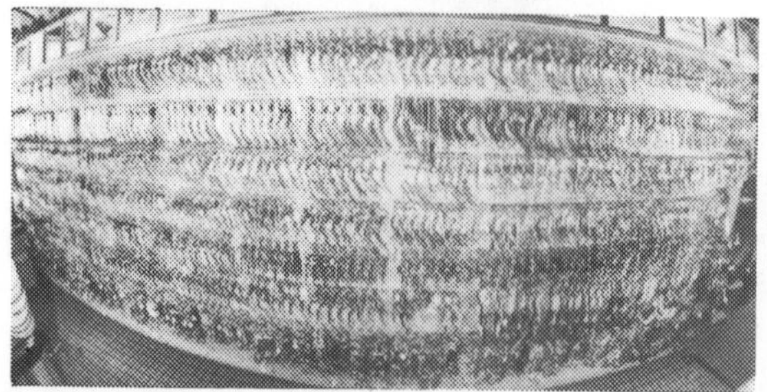

The Western Horseman

This is the horse magazine of the American Cowboy, probably second only to **Reader's Digest** *in subscriptions in ranchland. Includes a little of everything from rodeo fashions and twelve-year-old horsegirls looking for pen-pals, to new product evaluations and general coverage of all important national horse shows. It is quarter horse biased because the cattle industry is too, but every October it prints a special "All Breeds Issue" in which access information is published for all the various registries in this country. If you own a pleasure horse, here is your mag. If you plan on getting a horse when you get the rest of your shit together, you can do some nice picture-shopping while you wait. If you are scared of horses but like boots and hats, here is your mail-order marketplace.* —*J. D. Smith*

Western Horseman
Randy Witte, Editor
$15/year
(12 issues) from:
Western Horseman, Inc.
P. O. Box 7980
Colorado Springs, CO 80933

There are occasions when you need to tie a plastic or canvas tarp over a haystack to protect it from the weather, but you find that the grommets are missing or in the wrong places. You can still tie it down securely.

Practical Horseman

For those who ride English. There's lots about proper form, the hunt, and other activities associated with East Coast equitation. —*Patricia Phelan and Pamela Cowtan*

Practical Horseman
Pamela Goold, Editor
$19.95/year
(12 issues) from:
Practical Horseman
Subscription Service Dept.
P. O. Box 927
Farmingdale, NY 11737-0927

• And then there are the big ones, the ones that do real work, the ones that can take the place of machinery. Find out how this part of the horse world is doing.
The Draft Horse Journal: Morris Telleen, Editor. **$14**/year (4 issues) from The Draft Horse Journal, P. O. Box 670, Waverly, IA 50677.

The Farming Game

Farms and farmers have been disappearing in large numbers in America since the 1950s. ***The Farming Game*** *explains the arithmetic that has greased this economic slide, and also suggests strategies for people interested in surviving this trend and farming in the 1980s. Bryan Jones has a style reminiscent of Will Rogers — an ear for ironic humor, political savvy, and a simmering contempt for bureaucratic institutions (big banks, government, universities). His lectures on profit and advice on diversification are the perfect antidote for romantic agrarian notions. This is a book that any beginner will need and anyone with experience will nod at knowingly.*
—Richard Nilsen

•

"Hell, Ed, who ya tryin' to kid? You'd be the first dumb bastard plantin' corn if it was worth ten cents a bushel. Ya got the habit bad as anyone I know. The few birds you ain't killed yet start chirpin' in the spring, an' you'll wax that tractor a coupla times, fire 'er up, an' go plant corn. It ain't your fault. It's just like heroin, or overeatin', or any other kind of bad habit, is what it is."

Peaceful Valley Farm Supply

If for some absurd reason I had to do all my agricultural shopping with just one catalog, Peaceful Valley Farm Supply would be the one. With it I could buy a BSC tiller, Speedling Transplant Flats or beneficial insects for pest control. Or Fawn fescue grass seed (by the pound or the sack), earthworm castings or a bristlecone pine tree. More than 475 varieties of plants are for sale in the current catalog, including the Floyd Zaiger line of genetically dwarfing fruit and nut trees. The emphasis is on ecologically sound products and the service is friendly.
—Richard Nilsen

Peaceful Valley Farm Supply
Catalog **$2** from:

Peaceful Valley Farm Supply
11173 Peaceful Valley Road
Nevada City, CA 95959

JIFFY PEAT STRIPS

Same materials as Jiffy-Pots but molded into strips for easy handling and inserting into trays. Separate easily for planting.

2¼" square pots. 12 pots per strip.
Pack of 3 strips (36 pots): $2.35 (1#)
Case of 200 strips (2400 pots): $75.00 (26#)
1¼" square pots. 12 pots per strip.
Case pf 400 strips (4800 pots): $71.65 (22#)
1¾" square pots . 12 pots per strip.
Case of 300 strips (3600 pots): $79.50 (25#)

• This magazine is "dedicated to putting people, profit and biological permanence back into farming by giving farmers the information they need to take charge of their farms and their futures." It is run by a non-profit organization and is the best single source for economically sound alternative techniques for commercial farmers.
The New Farm: George DeVault, Editor; **$15**/year (7 issues) from Regenerative Agriculture Association, 222 Main Street, Emmaus, PA 18049.

New Roots for Agriculture • The Land Institute

New Roots for Agriculture *takes conventional agricultural wisdom and stands it on its head. The problem is not organic versus chemical methods, but rather the plow versus sod: plow and your soil will erode; leave the earth's vegetative skin undisturbed and the soil stays in place.*

By way of illustration, Wes Jackson begins by describing a rainy Sunday drive through the Mennonite country of south-central Kansas. These are among the best ecological farmers in business — land stewardship is even a basic tenet of their religion — yet the streams run black with soil from their freshly seeded fields. It's an image that percolates through the rest of the book, because if these are our "best" farmers, then how much mud is in everybody else's streams?

Jackson's solution is to imitate nature, and in this his method resembles Fukuoka's (see ***The One-Straw Revolution****, p. 61). Instead of raising annuals and churning up the soil every year, plant perennials and let the plant roots hold the soil where it belongs. Instead of monocultures like wheat, plant polycultures that mimic the native prairie flora. With perennial polycultures the trick is to get the yield high enough to make this method feasible.*

Will it work? Nobody knows, because most all the research so far has gone toward perfecting annual crops. At the Land Institute outside Salina, Kansas, Jackson and his wife Dana and staff are busy testing perennial native grasses. Follow their developments through ***The Land Report.*** *From their tiny test plots may come grains for the future. For now,* ***New Roots for Agriculture*** *is an eloquent and disturbing book.* *—Richard Nilsen*

•

I think we must acknowlege that humans can be expected to be wicked and stupid for a long time to come. And though there is no reason the land should not be punishing our evil and error, there is also no reason why the land should be the principal loser as it has been since till agriculture began. The task before us, therefore, is to build an agriculture that is resilient to human folly, an agriculture that rewards wisdom and patience, an agriculture in which the land remains resilient but not silent during those excursions toward some dangerous unknown, dangerous because we have become too enamored with our own cleverness and enterprise.
—New Roots for Agriculture

New Roots for Agriculture
Wes Jackson
1980; 151 pp.
$6.95
($8.45 postpaid) from:
University of Nebraska Press
901 North 17th Street
Lincoln, NE 68588-0520
or Whole Earth Access

The Land Report
Dana Jackson, Editor
$5/year (3 issues) from:
The Land Institute
Route 3
Salina, KS 67401

The Farming Game
Bryan Jones
1982; 221 pp.
$16.95
($18.45 postpaid) from:
University of Nebraska Press
901 North 17th Street
Lincoln, NE 68588-0520
or Whole Earth Access

agAccess

A slim, quarterly catalog of books and software doesn't seem like a big deal at first, but this is an almost unbelievably useful service, long needed. The agAccess folks offer to sell "every agricultural book in print," and to find you a reference on virtually any agricultural subject. The catalog consists of expert reviews of various publications and computer software programs useful to farmers. Though accenting the organic and generally eco-righteous, the service covers all sorts of cultivation — even turf for golf courses. It's run by nice people too.
—JB

•

Gaining Ground: The Renewal of America's Small Farms (by J. Tevere MacFadyen, 1984):

The author lets the farmers explain the myriad issues that face small farmers working toward economic viability. This book is about people as well as agricultural issues, and it provides a charming and thorough forum for both. Good reading for anyone interested in the small farm vs. agribusiness debate. 242 pages, hardcover. $16.95.

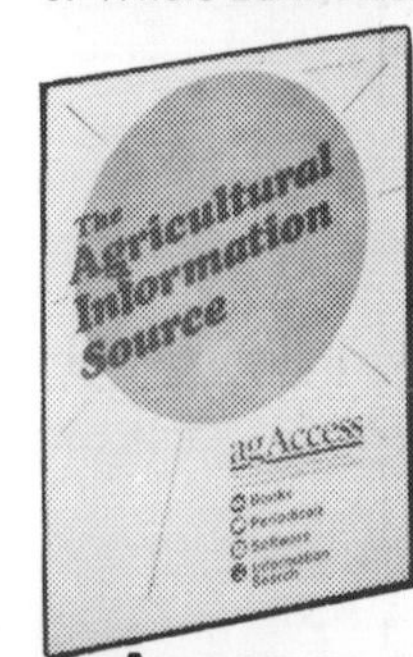

agAccess
David Katz, Editor
$8.50/year
(6 issues) from:
agAccess
615 Merchant Street
Vacaville, CA 95688

Land-Saving Action
Russell L. Brenneman and Sarah M. Bates, Editors
1984; 262 pp.

$34.95
($37.45 postpaid) from:
Island Press
Star Route 1, Box 38
Covelo, CA 95428
or Whole Earth Access

STATE NATURAL HERITAGE INVENTORIES

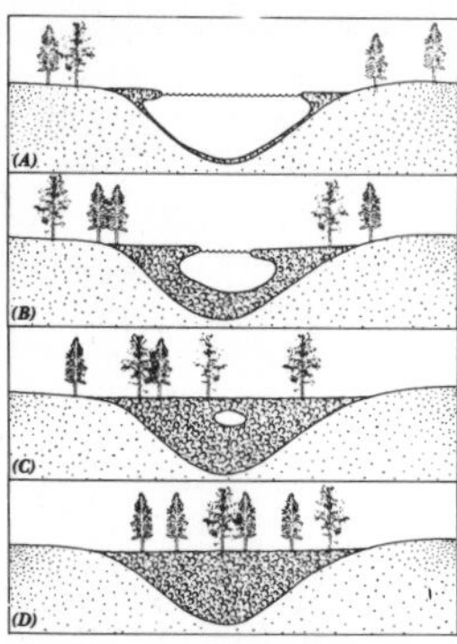

A bog lake succession. A floating mat vegetation advances out over the water surface in a small lake in a cool, humid climate [A]. As the mat advances farther and the lake ages [B] and [C], scarcely decomposed organic matter (peat) accumulates in the lake basin, until after some thousands of years, the lake will be converted to forest [D].
—Building an Ark

Building an Ark
Phillip M. Hoose
1981; 221 pp.

$12
($14.50 postpaid) from:
Island Press
Star Route 1, Box 38
Covelo, CA 95428
or Whole Earth Access

BE IT NEIGHBORHOOD OR NATION, the ideal community remains elusive. What turns out to be most important after spiritual matters are attended to is political and economic permission (some call it acceptance). You have to be resolute, clever, and lucky to make any advance; community is always work-in-progress.

—J. Baldwin

Land-Saving Action

The last decade has seen a tremendous expansion of private-sector preservation of open space lands. This book, with chapters by 29 experts, embodies the experience that ten years has produced, and will serve as a bible for anyone who loves a piece of land enough to want to find out how to save it.

—Richard Nilsen

•

Most land trusts are actually not trusts at all in the legal sense, but are nonstock corporations organized for charitable purposes. A genuine trust is usually established by an individual transferring property to a trustee and is administered under conditions stated in a trust document. In contrast, the corporate form used by land trusts allows much greater flexibility in involving interested individuals, obtaining contributions, and managing holdings.

Preservation Organizations

The Nature Conservancy

The Nature Conservancy is responsible for preserving over two million acres of land, as well as innumerable rare and endangered plants and animals. For my money, they manage their purchases with the best network of volunteer and professional land stewards. Recently, The Nature Conservancy has gone international because many of the birds we protect here winter south of the border. "To save them here, they must be saved there as well." A fringe benefit of joining is a 4-color, top-notch quarterly.

—Peter Warshall

The Nature Conservancy News: Sue Dodge, Editor. **$10**/year (6 issues) from 1800 North Kent Street, Arlington, VA 22209.

Land Trust Exchange

Most land preservation groups tend to be small, volunteer, community oriented, and with very specific tasks in mind. Land Trust Exchange serves as a national clearinghouse for all of them. Their ***National Directory*** *lists more than 500 groups by state. You can also find out if a group exists where you live and learn about other written material they distribute by writing them.*

—Richard Nilsen

National Directory of Local and Regional Land Conservation Organizations: $12 postpaid from Land Trust Exchange, P. O. Box 364, Bar Harbor, ME 04609.

The Trust for Public Land

TPL does not hold land permanently and it is not a membership organization. Instead it buys threatened land and then resells it to public agencies for open space. It is designed to represent the public interest in the "here today, gone tomorrow" world of real estate transactions. Open space is where you find or create it, and for TPL this includes inner city lots. Three hundred thousand more spacious acres have been transferred nationwide.

—Richard Nilsen

The Trust for Public Land: Information **free** from The Trust for Public Land, 82 Second Street, San Francisco, CA 94105.

Ducks Unlimited

This 560,000-member organization has been responsible for the preservation of more waterbird breeding grounds (especially marshlands) than any government or other group. Working internationally (ducks haven't learned about Canadian, U.S., and Mexican boundaries), Ducks Unlimited restores, manages, and purchases wetlands throughout North American waterfowl flyways.

—Peter Warshall

Ducks Unlimited: Membership **$20**/year from 1 Waterfowl Way, Long Grove, IL 60047.

Izaak Walton League of America

An old conservation group with a distinct midwestern twang. Rooted morality. Never upstarts. They are hard, persevering workers who maintain, protect, and restore soil, forests, water and air. A wholesome 50,000 members. Publishes ***Outdoor America*** *and has an endowment fund to purchase unique natural areas.*

—Peter Warshall

Izaak Walton League of America: Membership **$20**/year from 1701 North Fort Myer Drive, Suite 1100, Arlington, VA 22209.

Building an Ark

The nuts and bolts of wildlife preservation, by an exemplary land saver for The Nature Conservancy. The techniques of property are used to make sufficiently cherished land no longer be property in the buy and sell sense.

—Stewart Brand

•

A right of first refusal is an option, not an obligation. You don't *have* to buy the property when it becomes available. Thus for a nominal fee you have purchased:

1. The right to know that the owner of an important tract is considering an action that could jeopardize the natural features you wish to protect.

2. Thirty days or so to negotiate with the owner before he can sell.

3. Usually, the ability to talk to the person who made the offer, to discern his attitude toward protection, and thus the ability to gauge how he would manage it if you let him go ahead and buy the property.

4. The ability to make an offer.

•

Dedication is the strongest protection tool discussed in this book, increasing protection offered even through fee acquisition in two ways. First, a county clerk cannot lawfully record articles of dedication unless they contain terms protecting the land against modification or encroachment. Secondly, all nature preserves acts contain clear language protecting dedicated properties against condemnation or conversion.

Hella Hammid

"A man who has a vision is not able to use the power of it until he has performed the vision on Earth for the people to see . . ." —Black Elk

MANY HAVE VISIONS. More blab on. Few do anything until the pesticide planes fly overhead or the robins arrive no more. Here is the spectrum of environmental warriors — all effective and necesssary in different ways — all inspired by the hope that maybe, just maybe, our grandchildren will find a few spots of ancient, untouched planet to hear the sound of creeks, alone and with peaceful minds.

—Peter Warshall

Riparian corridor on The Nature Conservancy's 1,500-acre Kern River Preserve in California. The endangered yellow-billed cuckoo breeds here, and 200 other bird species have been sighted. This is one of the last intact remnants of riverside woodland in the state.

EARTH FIRST!
No Compromise in the Defense of Mother Earth!

Environmental Groups

Earth First!

Out on the front lines of eco-defense is Earth First!. "No compromise in the defense of Mother Earth!" Direct action against the machinery (not people) and eco-theatre is their modus operandi. Because many environmental groups have become top-heavy with managerial salaries and glossy promotions, Earth First! attracts more youth and makes more efficient use of limited funds.
—Peter Warshall

Earth First! (The Radical Environmental Journal): Dave Foreman, Editor, **$15**/year (8 issues) from Earth First!, P. O. Box 5871, Tucson, AZ 85703.

Sierra Club

The Sierra Club has many parts which provide different services. They have integrated their politics with the Big Boys so well that sometimes I think the leadership loses touch. This occurred, for instance when the Sierra Club supported a huge water project in California (the Peripheral Canal) which its membership overwhelmingly hated and its defense fund was essentially trying to halt. The Sierra Club is also the "hated" symbol for those who feel environmentalists are commie extremists. Caught in all these cross-currents, they can use more input and support from their membership. The voice of John Muir needs a 1980s broadcast system. *—Peter Warshall*

Sierra Club: Membership **$29**/year (includes 6 issues of **Sierra** Magazine) from Sierra Club: 730 Polk Street, San Francisco, CA 94109.

• Environment defenders can augment their political effectiveness by applying the strategies and tactics shown on pp. 104-105.

• For a novel approach to affordable housing in cities, see the Institute for Community Economics and their **Community Land Trust Handbook** (p. 110).

National Audubon Society

The strength of Audubon since 1905 has been its naturalist backbone. More than any other environmental organization, its members actually know the animals and plants they try to conserve. Not only that, they seem to love their knowledge with early naturalist enthusiasm. The educational aspects of Audubon are truly admirable. Their politics vary locally and, if you contribute, it's good to earmark your contribution for a particular purpose, especially for specific sanctuaries. *—Peter Warshall*

National Audubon Society: Membership **$30**/year (includes 6 issues of **Audubon** Magazine) from National Audubon Society, Membership Data Center, P. O. Box 2666, Boulder, CO 80322.

The Conservation Foundation

Runs an eco-mediation "Dispute Resolution Program" to bypass lawyers, courts, and the big bucks (see mention of their book on next page). *—Peter Warshall*

Lobbying Groups

In groups like the Environmental Defense Fund, National Resources Defense Council and Sierra Club Legal Defense Fund (not the same as Sierra Club) hardnosed lawyers keep Congress and the courts from slouching and swallowing even more eco-destruction, pollution, and poisoning of the planet. *—Peter Warshall*

Environmental Defense Fund: Membership **$20**/year (includes 6 issues of **EDF Letter**) from EDF, 1616 P Street NW, Washington, DC 20036.

Natural Resources Defense Council: Membership **$10**/year (includes subscription to **Amicus Journal** and **Newsline Newsletter**) from NRDC, 122 E. 42nd Street, New York, NY 10168.

Sierra Club Legal Defense Fund: Information **free** from 2044 Fillmore Street, San Francisco, CA 94115.

Ansel Adams

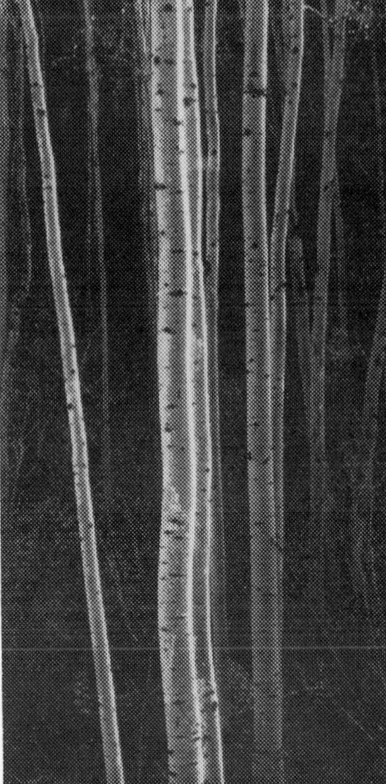

Aspens

The Environmental Impact Statement Process
Neil Orloff
1978; 242 pp.
$7.50
($9.50 postpaid) from:
Information Resources Press
1700 N. Moore St.
Suite 700
Arlington, VA 22209

Environmental Impact Assessment
Patrick H. Heffernan and Ruth Corwin, Editors
1975; 277 pp.
$13.50
($15.14 postpaid) from:
Freeman, Cooper & Co.
1736 Stockton Street
San Francisco, CA 94133

Environmental Impact Assessment • The Environmental Impact Statement Process

The Environmental Impact Statement (EIS) is one of the most remarkable examples of participatory democracy alive in the United States. It's perhaps the most viable political tool in this catalog and has brought together scientists, citizens, corporate executives, congressmen, and lawyers in an unprecedented manner, forcing humans to consider the consequences of their acts.

Unfortunately, the EIS has stopped few projects, and it's currently under attack by the Reagan administration. But it has slowed a percentage, with the benefit of reducing environmental damage and, at times, development costs. It gives Americans a say in projects that they subsidize with their taxes and must live with long after the developer goes home. These two books are still the best introduction. —Peter Warshall

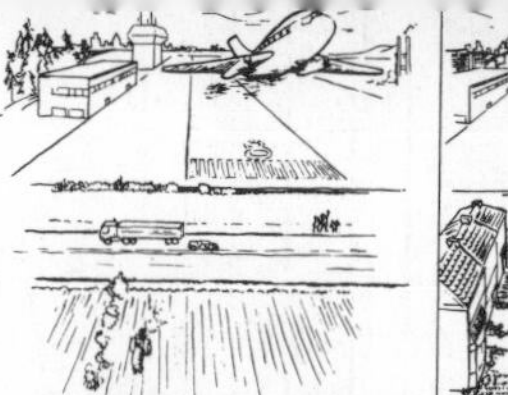

Whether a project "significantly" affects the environment depends partly on the kind of envirnoment in which the project is to be located.
—The Environmental Impact Statement Process

•

54. Does the table of contents list at least the following seven elements required by CEQA, as distinct sections? (Section 15085(b))

(a) The environmental impact of the proposed action
(b) Any adverse environmental effects which cannot be avoided if the proposal is implemented
(c) Mitigation measures proposed to minimize the impact
(d) Alternatives to the proposed action
(e) The relationship between local short-term uses of man's environment and the maintenance and enhancement of long-term productivity
(f) Any irreversible environmental changes which would be caused by the proposed action should it be implemented
(g) The growth-inducing impact of the proposed action

—Environmental Impact Assessment

Ecodefense

Inspired by Ed Abbey's ***The Monkey Wrench Gang,*** ***Ecodefense*** *sports proven techniques of tree spiking, road spiking, disabling heavy equipment, fence cutting, trap clearing, lock jamming, billboard trashing, and sundry skills of propaganda, camouflage, sneaking around, escape and evasion, and the like. Fascinating stuff; best not to skim and try, but really study before trying — for two good reasons. One is that monkeywrenching mostly takes place in country where retribution is not only in the courts but also by direct action: you get the living shit beat out of you. The second is that monkeywrenching the wrong target is grotesquely counterproductive; you have not only to be right every single time, but conspicuously right, or you're just another random vandal making everyone else feel sick about being alive. The book constantly warns about knowing your target cold before making a move, and if in doubt, don't.* —Stewart Brand

•

Tree-spiking is an extremely effective method of deterring timber sales, which deserves to be employed far more widely than heretofore. Mill operators are quite wary of accepting timber which has a likelihood of contamination with hidden metal objects — saws are expensive, and a "spiked" log can literally bring operations to a screeching halt, at least until a new blade can be put into service. The Forest Service is nervous enough about tree spiking that it has failed to publicize past incidents, for fear that the practice might spread.

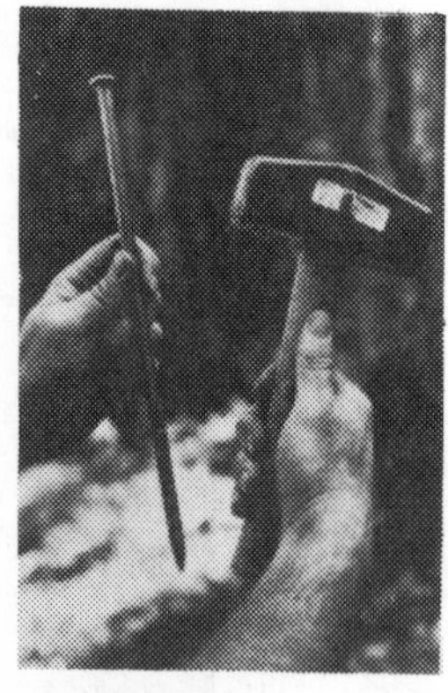

A bridge timber spike and single jack hammer for use with very large trees. Smaller spikes are fine for general use and can be driven in with a heavy standard hammer.

Ecodefense
Dave Foreman, Editor
1985; 197 pp.
$10
($11 postpaid) from:
Earth First!
P. O. Box 5871
Tucson, AZ 85703
or Whole Earth Access

Conservation Directory

From the publishers of ***Ranger Rick*** *(p. 386) comes a useful catalog of private and public organizations, governmental agencies, and officials (like Senators or department heads) concerned with natural resources, wildlife, and their management. Anyone trying to coordinate their activities (such as stream restoration for fish) with other groups or wanting to know all the conservation groups within their state or trying to contact the relevant Washington authority can use this catalog.*
—Peter Warshall

•

Kentucky Bass Chapter Federation:
(An organization of Bassmaster Chapters, affiliated with the Bass Anglers Sportsman Society, to fight pollution, assist state and national conservation agencies in their efforts and to teach the young people of our country good conservation practices. Dedicated to the realistic conservation of our water resources.)
President: Alex Thomasson, 333 Jesselin Dr., Lexington, KY 40503 (606, 278-4018/232-3795)

Conservation Directory 1986
Rue E. Gordon, Editor
1986; 302 pp.
$15
($17 postpaid) from:
The National Wildlife Federation
1412 Sixteenth Street NW
Washington, DC 20036
or Whole Earth Access

Ambio

Authoritative and glossy. This Sweden-based magazine is the voice of establishment international environmentalism. When I was working a couple of years ago on an article about genotoxins — the flood of new chemicals that cause cancer and gene damage — ***Ambio*** *was my most indispensable source of up-to-date information.*
—Stewart Brand

Ambio
Don Hinrichsen and Kai-Inge Hillerud, Editors
$32/year
(6 issues) from:
Pergamon Journal, Inc.
Maxwell House
Fairview Park
Elmsford, NY 10523

• A survey of a decade of eco-mediation with an interesting appendix of case studies. **Resolving Environmental Disputes:** Gail Bingham, 1985; 250 pp. **$17** postpaid from The Conservation Foundation, Dept. QQ, 1255 23rd Street NW, Washington, DC 20037.

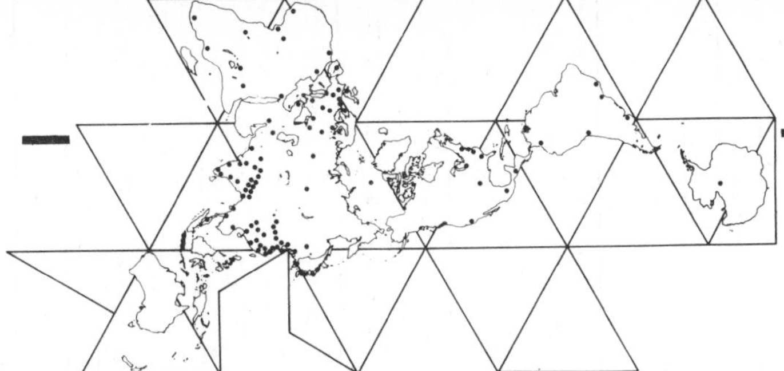

• = 45 million people = 1% of humanity —*The World Game*

GIMME SOME NUMBERS! And that's just what you get from these folks as they attempt to discover and understand the flow of energy and resources through society. They're doing our homework for us. —JB

The World Game
Membership **$25**/year
(includes newsletter)

Global Data Manager
(MS-DOS, CP/M)
$77 postpaid
All from:
The World Game
University City
Science Center
3508 Market Street #214
Philadelphia, PA 19104

The World Game

"To make the World work / for 100% of Humanity / in the shortest possible time / Through spontaneous cooperation / Without ecological offense / Or the disadvantage of anyone."

Buckminster Fuller initiated the World Game in 1969 as one means of accomplishing this worthy goal. The idea is that with enough data on world resources and their distribution (including accumulated technology and problem-solving skills), the world's citizens will do what's best for all. Fuller assumed that once it was obvious that there was enough of everything to go around, people would stop fighting wars and get to work making the world work — if not as a utopia at least not continuing the current suicidal path. World Game is still developing. Recent sessions use an enormous basketball-court-size map in order to more easily visualize various strategies as they are suggested by participants. A formidable software database called Global Data Manager allows individuals to play with the numbers on their PCs. Universities and the UN are beginning to pay attention to this attempt at manipulating global data. In many ways, it's a giant version of the other work shown on this page. There's hope for us yet. —JB

Rocky Mountain Institute
Publications list **free**
Newsletter (4 issues) **free**
both from:
RMI
P. O. Drawer 248
Old Snowmass, CO 81654

Rocky Mountain Institute (RMI)

Since its humble beginnings in 1982, RMI (Amory and Hunter Lovins, props.) has shown the way in energy and resource management research; I'll let them explain themselves:

"Because the problems of the world cannot be solved by piecemeal thinking, the interdisciplinary staff of 20 emphasizes synthesis. RMI has documented, for example, how least-cost energy strategies can inhibit nuclear proliferation, abate acid rain, save wild rivers, rescue troubled utilities, cut electric rates, forestall the CO_2 threat to global climate, make farms and industries more profitable, rebuild distressed local economies, and save enough money to pay off the National Debt by 2000."

Fact is that RMI has actually done much of the above, or at least made a good start. A host of corporations and governments have taken their advice to heart because it's based on the same information and methodology used by conventional analysts (who have not been paying attention). I recommend the RMI newsletter highly, though it makes many of us sound like lazy bums by comparison. The RMI record is both a marvel and an inspiration. —JB

•

A sample "supply curve" from Peter Butler's recent research shows that installing 1-gallon toilets, faucet aerators, and 2-gallon/minute showerheads *without charge* would cost Aspen, Colorado *minus* $5 million in 20-year present value, because the energy savings on hot water would more than pay for the whole program. The actual benefit would be bigger: the city wouldn't have to expand its water and wastewater systems.

Regeneration
Jeff Bercuvitz, Editor
$12/year
(4 issues)
Publications list **free**
both from:
The Regeneration Project
33 East Minor Street
Emmaus, PA 18049

The Regeneration Project

This project is based on a simple truth: if you import products, food, and energy into your area, you export money out of your local economy. Not good. Not efficient. Dumb, even. The Regeneration Project offers the analytic and organizing skills to counter such forces. The idea is to maximize conservation where possible, then minimize imports by making, repairing, or growing what you need locally, locally. The project is increasingly successful because it works — not surprising with the hand of Rodale involved. —JB

•

As the Project studied dozens of individual states, a startling pattern emerged.

Virtually every state — including many of our most agriculturally oriented states — "imported" a vast amount of the food they consumed. This not only placed their states in a vulnerable position; it also caused a dollar drain that weakened their overall economy.

•

The *Local Economy Inventory* serves to match local businesses with local suppliers in order to replace costly imports coming into a region. It comprehensively surveys all enterprises and institutions in a region. It covers both primary and secondary material inputs as well as waste products that may have potential economic value.

New Alchemy Institute

The Alkies have been working on sustainable technology and agriculture for about 15 years now and doing a good job of it too. Recent work includes a composting greenhouse and designs for eco-righteous housing that'll appeal to builder/developers as well as owners. They offer lots of classes, consulting services, and a host of publications. The quarterly newsletter always seethes with interesting action, much of it backed by strict scientific methodology — one reason NAI has been so successful. —JB

New Alchemy Quarterly
Kate Eldred, Editor
$35/year
(4 issues; membership)
Publications list **free**
both from:
New Alchemy Institute
237 Hatchville Road
East Falmouth, MA 02536

Inside the New Alchemy Arc bioshelter.

• See also "Biohazards" (p. 107), "Conservation" (p. 45), and land preservation groups (p. 86).
• See also Permaculture (p. 62) and **Sustainable Communities** (p. 113).
• See **The Ecologist** and **Audubon** (p. 27) for more on environmental politics.

Peace Corps
Information
free from:
Peace Corps
806 Connecticut Avenue
Room P-301
Washington, DC 20526

Appropriate Technology Microfiche Reference Library
Information **free**
Library in case
$695
fiche reader
$250-350
(postage and handling varies by destination)
Appropriate Technology Project
Volunteers in Asia, Inc.
P.O. Box 4543
Stanford, CA 94305

VITA News
Margaret Crouch, Editor
$15/year
(4 issues) from:
Volunteers in Technical Assistance
1815 North Lynn Street
Suite 200
Arlington, VA 22209

TRANET
Dan Behrman, Editor
$30/year
(4 issues) from:
TRANET
P.O. Box 567
Rangeley, ME 04970

IVAN ILLICH ONCE COMMENTED rather impolitely that righteously inclined Americans would do more good if they worked at local U.S.A. problems instead of imposing themselves on foreign hosts. (My own experience abroad agrees; I suspect a contribution of my air fare money would have done more good than I did.) Nonetheless, there are certainly places where spirited yet humble application of expertise can help. If you want to get into this line of work, the Peace Corps is probably your best bet, but there are many other possibilities — especially church groups. "Doing time" is one of the best ways to learn.
—J. Baldwin

Peace Corps

If the Peace Corps were ten percent as effective in saving the world as its ads imply, then the fact that 110,000 volunteers have now returned from overseas would indicate that world salvation was in the bag. However, Peace Corps ads are more effective than the Peace Corps itself. So despite the genuine and highly publicized successes of the rare "super volunteer" — the term we had in Ecuador for the one guy who beat the odds — the third world is more deeply mired in poverty, oppression, and debt than when JFK launched the organization in 1961.

Also, Peace Corps remains forever aligned with U.S. foreign policy, e.g., it has returned to Grenada, and is long gone from Nicaragua. So why join an outfit that marches to the same beat as the State Department and has no significant effect on lessening the woes of the underprivileged? Because the Peace Corps offers something that isn't emphasized in their ads, and definitely isn't available here at home — a close look at underdevelopment, or life at the bottom of the food chain. Understanding how the rest of the world lives can be a mind opener.

Should you take the gamble, realize that the charm of native life will disappear the first day you see the village you've been assigned to; but you'll still receive basic language training, an excellent salary (by your coworkers' standards), a month's vacation each year plus travel allowance, access to good medical care, and finally a $175 readjustment allowance for each month of service when you return home.

In other words, you'll experience the living conditions and poverty that the world's majority lives in, without having to really eat it. I know of no other organization that can offer such an opportunity, and anyone interested in languages, politics, and the human condition, or just serious travel (as opposed to tourism) should consider this option.

Don't plan on changing the world though, just yourself.
—Dick Fugett

Appropriate Technology Microfiche Reference Library

No less than 1000 of the best appropriate tech books and documents — about 140,000 pages — have been microfiched to fit into a small suitcase. A simple 120 AC, 240 AC, or 12-volt (vehicle battery) fiche reader accompanies this deluge of information. Instant library! Affordable, too; the price of all this is about five percent of the real books, not to mention the cost of shipping and storing them. More than 100 countries have partaken of this opportunity so far.

This powerful idea was hatched by Ken Darrow of VIA (Volunteers in Asia). He has a book coming out soon (but too late for our deadline) containing sharp reviews of all 1000 of the fiched books. Watch for the ***Appropriate Technology Sourcebook*** *in late '86. If you work overseas, you need this book and the library. Spread the word. —JB*

We put our appropriate technology library in a box...

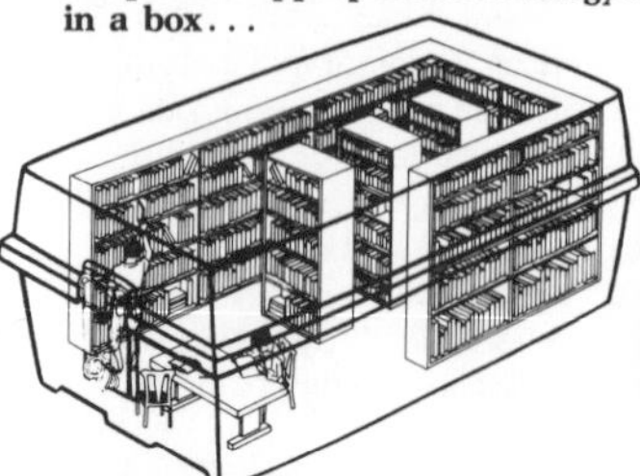

so you can put it on your desk!

ITDG

Stands for Intermediate Technology Development Group, founded by the late E. F. Schumacker of ***Small Is Beautiful*** *fame (p. 184). They've executed successful projects all over the world, and publish some of the more useful literature available on alternative technologies. —JB*

Intermediate Technology Development Group of North America, Inc: Information **free** from 777 United Nations Plaza, Suite 9A, New York, NY 10017.

VITA

For 25 years, Volunteers in Technical Assistance has been a reliable source of expert advice and an experienced stack of publications. You don't join VITA as you would the Peace Corps, for instance, but you can make your special knowledge available through them. Their record of action is inspiring; see for yourself in ***VITA News.*** *—JB*

VITA cooperated with another group to develop a method for making these stove fuel briquettes from agricultural residues such as stalks and straw.

TRANET

Networking and information exchange is the name of the game, and TRANET (from TRANsnational NETwork for appropriate/alternative technologies) has done it better and wider for ten years now. The quarterly newsletter has good reviews of pertinent books plus lots of news excerpts. Lively and effective despite a bit of '70s character, TRANET is the place to look first to see what's going on globally among people taking control of their own lives. —JB

•

Private bus systems cost half as much as public ones to move the same number of people in many Third World cities, the World Bank's transport adviser comments in *The Urban Edge* (World Bank, Room K 908, Washington, DC 20433, USA — free to developing countries, $25/year elsewhere). Private lines succeed in places like Hong Kong and Seoul while public systems run in the red (Sao Paulo's takes $90 million a year in subsidies). Newsletter also mentions paratransit innovations such as Manila's jeepneys and bus convoys in Sao Paulo that hope to move 21,000 passengers an hour.

Salvadoran voters being "helped" to the polls.

CovertAction Information Bulletin

The actions and covert actions of the intelligence agencies of the world affect us every day — usually in ways unknown to us. ***CovertAction Information Bulletin*** *has been keeping tabs on our own spies since 1978 and has earned a bucketfull of criticism from those same spies for its efforts.*

I look to ***CAIB*** *for information running counter to the received truths of our pundits and quiescent press corps.* ***CAIB*** *has its own axes to grind (of a largely leftist variety) but that doesn't lessen its fundamental value. If you want to begin discerning the difference between information and disinformation, between the aboveboard and the underhanded,* ***CAIB*** *is a good place to start.* —Jay Kinney

•

In the early 1970s, Gelli's goal in Italy was to destabilize the political system in such a way that the right wing, already under his direct control or influence, would acquire power with popular support. To bring this situation about, Gelli, in concert with other shady rightwing characters, organized the "Strategy of Tension." Terrorist acts, such as the bombing of the Rome-Munich express train in 1974, and the Bologne railway station bombing in 1980, were organized and carried out by the rightwing groups. The bombings were investigated by the intelligence agencies under Gelli's control, which placed responsibility for the bombings on leftwing terrorists.

The strategy of tension envisioned that numerous "leftwing" bombings and acts of terrorism would build popular support for extreme antiterrorist legislation in the name of national security. Antiterrorism laws would then allow Gelli's supporters in the military and intelligence agencies to target leftwing groups with few legal restrictions. (Sergei Antonov is now in an Italian jail under the authority of an Italian antiterrorist law which permits the imprisonment of suspected subversives and terrorists for up to five years without a trial.)

CovertAction Information Bulletin
Louis Wolf, Editor
$15/year
(4 issues)
from: CAIB
P.O. Box 50272
Washington, DC 20004
or Whole Earth Access

The Puzzle Palace

The Puzzle Palace *is a monumental reporting feat on the National Security Agency, the most secret government agency America has ever had. Organized in 1952 as a codemaking and codebreaking agency, the NSA has also tapped and translated foreign radio, scanned satellite signals, and burglarized offices. It's gathered intelligence on organized crime and Cuba (for President Kennedy), and Vietnam protesters and drug dealers (for Johnson and Nixon). It has tried to completely avoid public scrutiny and legal constraint; it's the kind of agency that can only exist in a government that feels it is at war. I got lost sometimes in the book's voluminous detail, but it's a necessary book and I'll forgive some denseness. It's our first glimpse of the police that Ivan Illich foresees for the electronic highways of the future. I'm grateful that James Bamford stuck with his topic and that Houghton Mifflin (the hardcover publisher) and Penguin fought what must have been considerable pressure to suppress it.* —Art Kleiner

•

Because of NSA's vacuum cleaner approach to intelligence collection — whereby it sucks into its system the maximum amount of telecommunications and then filters it through an enormous screen of "trigger words" — analysts end up reviewing telephone calls, telegrams, and telex messages to and from thousands of innocent persons having little or nothing to do with the actual focus of the effort. Thus if an organization is targeted, all its members' communications may be intercepted; if an individual is listed on a watch list, all communications to, from, or even mentioning that individual are scooped up. Captured in NSA's net were communications about a peace concert, a communication mentioning the wife of a U.S. senator, a correspondent's report from Southeast Asia to his magazine in New York, and a pro-Vietnam War activist's invitations to speakers for a rally.

The Puzzle Palace
James Bamford
1982, 1983; 655 pp.
$7.95
($8.95 postpaid) from:
Viking Penguin Books
299 Murray Hill Parkway
East Rutherford, NJ 07073
or Whole Earth Access

• Covert politics are the last straw to some folks; general avoidance of governmental interfence — anarchy — is one answer. The Loompanics catalog (p. 142) has some interesting reading on the subject.

Critique

What Richard Hofstadter characterized in 1965 as the "Paranoid Style" in American politics — the nativist notion that we are being manipulated and subverted by secret conspiracies — dates back to the earliest days of our country when a furor against supposed Illuminati skullduggery exploded in 1798. Since then, popular scapegoats for domestic ills have included Freemasons, Papists, immigrants, and more recently Communists. The penchant for fingering secret enemies is hardly exclusive to the U.S. — the Nazis rode to power in Germany by exploiting fears of Reds and Jews, after all — but it may be only in America that this world view has been able to bloom into its lushest, most mutant varieties.

Critique*, a small, handsomely typeset biannual subtitled "A Journal of Conspiracies and Metaphysics," is sort of a social* ***Organic Gardening*** *for those who cultivate this realm of suspicious imagination. Recent topics have included Hollow Earth theories, perpetual motion, Nazis and UFOs, the Bilderbergers, the secret Muslim Brotherhood, and of course the ever-popular Illuminati and Freemasons.*

What rescues ***Critique*** *from terminal crankiness and makes it potentially worth your attention is editor Bob Banner's even-handed objectivity. Throwing the journal's pages open to competing theories, scenarios, and musings, Banner favors none over any other.* ***Critique*** *provides a rare forum for hearing out accusations (wild and otherwise) that would probably just fester beneath the surface of the American psyche if left to their own devices.*

I can't claim total detachment regarding ***Critique*** *— it's printed a couple of my reviews — but I find it a generally delightful antidote to the myopic seriousness of most political fare. You may too.* —Jay Kinney

•

The techniques of psychotherapy, widely practiced and accepted as a means of curing psychological disorders, are also methods of controlling people. They can be used systematically to influence attitudes and behavior. Systematic desensitization is a method used to dissolve anxiety so that the patient (public) is no longer troubled by a specific fear, a fear of violence for example. A progressively more graphic depiction of violence in the movies and on television desensitizes the viewer, especially young people, to real-life violence. . . .

Thus, *The Day After* and *Special Bulletin* could leave many viewers so numbed by a sense of hopelessness and helplessness that they could succumb to deep apathy with regard to anything that has anything to do with the prospect of nuclear confrontation.

Critique
Bob Banner, Editor
$14/year
(2 issues) from:
Critique Foundation
P.O. Box 11451
Santa Rosa, CA 95406

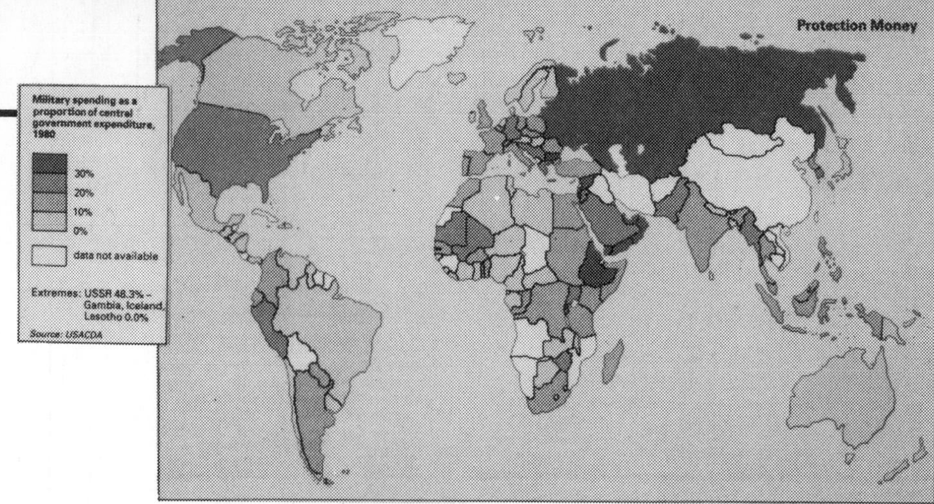

The New State of The World Atlas
Michael Kidron
and Ronald Segal
1984; 172 pp.
$10.95
postpaid from:
Simon & Schuster
Mail Order Sales
200 Old Tappan Road
Old Tappan, NJ 07675
or Whole Earth Access

The New State of the World Atlas

Put this next to the superb ***Times Atlas of World History*** *(p. 17) as by far the most provocative atlas of contemporary history. Understanding leaps to your eye when you survey a map such as "No. 26: A Sort of Survival," where arrows and numbers show the torrents of dislodged humans sluicing across continents and oceans (100,000 from Argentina to Spain since 1976? 130,000 from China to Hong Kong in 1979 alone?). Wonder what nations have political prisoners, the death penalty, or routine torture? — check map No. 25. Wonder where the gold is, the unemployment, the nuclear weapons, the nuclear reactors, the jobs, the separatist movements, education, the worst slums, the degrees of inflation, the degrees of population growth, the degrees of pollution?*

A fascinating hour here, and all the world news you see will begin to make sense.

(Note: Our black-and-white reproduction does no justice to the highly effective color coding in all the maps.)
—Stewart Brand

State of the World
Lester R. Brown, et al.
1986; 268 pp.
$8.95 postpaid

Worldwatch Papers
Subscription
$25/year
(Includes 5-8 papers and the year's edition of *State of the World*)
Back issues
$4 each postpaid
($3 each for 2-5 copies)
Both from:
Worldwatch Institute
1776 Massachusetts Avenue NW
Washington, DC 20036

Worldwatch Institute

This is the best single source for understanding the problems that face our planet. Worldwatch Institute examines the kinds of economic and environmental issues that politicians by their very nature have a tough time grappling with, and it suggests solutions in a politically even-handed and unhysterical way. Five to six papers on specific subjects are issued yearly and these become an annual book called ***State of the World.*** *—Richard Nilsen*

•

Tobacco causes more death and suffering among adults than any other toxic material in the environment. . . . The worldwide cost in lives now approaches 2.5 million per year, almost 5 percent of all deaths. Tobacco kills 13 times as many Americans as hard drugs do, and 8 times as many as automobile accidents. Passive smokers (those who must inhale the smoke of others' cigarettes) are perhaps three times likelier to die of lung cancer than they would be otherwise. *—State of the World*

Amnesty International

It's always a shock to learn that God is not interested in your pain. The best you can hope for is the help of other people.

The use of torture is steadily increasing worldwide. It is difficult to find out about and nearly impossible to check. So far the only deterrent is public opinion. That requires a respected international investigative organization. Amnesty International delivers.

Torture is a runaway phenomenon — far from preventing fanaticism, it increases fanaticism, which leads to more torture, and so forth. It will not cease until indeed it becomes as universally unthinkable as slavery. If we're going to have an intelligence and espionage establishment, let it work on this one.

*You can participate in Amnesty International with donations, letterwriting campaigns, and attention to their various publications. [****Amnesty Action****, sundry special reports, and their book* ***Torture in the Eighties****.]*
—Stewart Brand

Amnesty International
Membership **$25**/year
(includes 6 issues of *Amnesty Action* newsletter)

Torture in the Eighties
1984; 263 pp.
$10.20 postpaid

Amnesty International Annual Report
$10.20 postpaid
Publications list **free**
All from:
Amnesty International USA
322 8th Avenue
New York, NY 10001

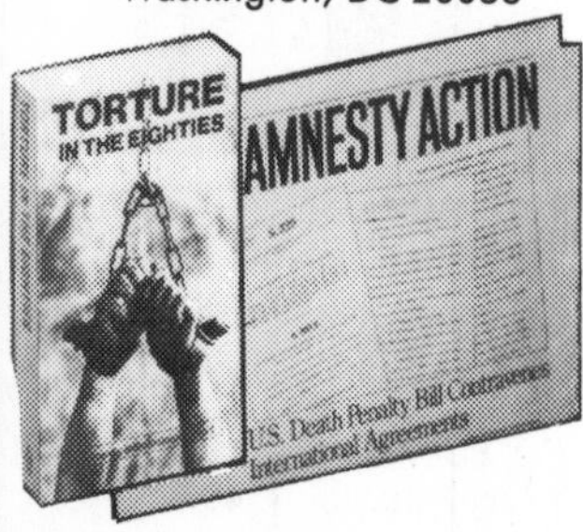

•

Paraguay:

A state of siege has been renewed in Paraguay as a matter of routine every three months for the past 29 years, although since 1978 it has been limited to the Central Department. In Amnesty International's view the state of siege, combined with the wide powers of the police and the inability of the judiciary to achieve independence from the executive, has facilitated the persistent torture and ill-treatment of political prisoners.

The government's failure to acknowledge arrests promptly and to give information regarding place of detention put prisoners at particular risk of torture during early stages of detention. Amnesty International has received frequent reports of prisoners tortured in unacknowledged detention for days or even weeks before being transferred to official detention and being allowed visits.

The methods of torture most commonly alleged to have been used were the following: *picana electrica* (electric cattle prod); *pileta*, where the victim's head is plunged into a tank of water, which is sometimes polluted with excrement, until a sense of asphyxiation is induced; beatings, particularly on soles of feet with truncheons; *cajones*, prolonged confinement in a box or other restricted place — positions used are: *feto*, in which the victim is forced to remain for hours at a time in foetal position; the *guardia*, where the victim is placed upright in a large box with holes to enable him or her to breathe; *secadera*, in which the victim is wrapped in a plastic sheet and placed in a metal cylinder; and *murcielago*, suspending the victim by the ankles. *—Torture in the Eighties*

(IZVESTIYA, Dec. 23)

Christmas tree for Western Europe.

Pravda • Pravda Pulse

I can imagine few things less inviting than reading **Pravda**, *the official newspaper of the Communist Party of the Soviet union, over breakfast each morning. However, if you are looking for the official Soviet version of the news (and for interminable transcripts of Party Congress speeches), this is the place. Curiously enough, if you are looking for unexpected insights into Russian culture,* **Pravda** *is also worth checking out. You're likely to discover that prime-time TV fare in Moscow consists of I. Smoktunovsky reading verses from Pushkin! Since the English-language edition of* **Pravda** *has been turning up on some newsstands lately, you may be able to locate a recent copy nearby.*

As an alternative glimpse into the official news, Florida-based **Pravda Pulse** *provides a bi-weekly eight to ten page newsletter condensing and excerpting the previous month's articles.* **Pravda Pulse** *also reprints news items from Tass and Soviet radio, as well as the satirical cartoons of* **Krokodil**, *the Russian humor magazine.*

*—Jay Kinney [***Pravda** *suggested by Brian Siano]*

•

Managers caught distorting results quite often explain their "slyness" like this: "Well, sure, I may have added something, but then I worked it out." As they say, just a white lie. It must be firmly declared that the law does not recognize a single valid reason that would justify deceiving the State. The so-called "objective" difficulties with the delivery of materials and completed articles are also used as arguments of justification. Upon checking they quite often turn out to be the result of partners going easy on one another, inabilities, and at times a lack of desire to use legal means to influence violators of State discipline. . . .

A criminal case brought against several workers of the Rostov Province Trade Administration can be cited as a serious warning. Former administration head K. Budnitsky found "like-minded" individuals within the RSFSR Trade Ministry, and for a bribe obtained favorable apportionments of transport, technological equipment, supplementary funds for textiles, clothes and shoes, and corrections of commodity circulation plans. Those taking bribes, as well as those doling them out, will be held criminally responsible.

—Pravda

Contra troops, slow to learn low-intensity methods.
—Report on the Americas

• For a contrasting view, see **The Wall Street Journal** (p. 312).
• World politics are better understood when science news is considered as a primary force. See pp. 26-27.

NACLA Report on the Americas • MERIP Middle East Report

Latin America and the Middle East: two hotspots, one near, one far. Their usual coverage in the media is as running sores of strife and woe. These two magazines take a different tack, attempting to describe the regions with depth and sympathy. The North American Congress on Latin America and the Middle East Research and Information Project are nonprofit research groups whose forte is political and economic analysis. NACLA's reports tend to be journalistic looks at the effect of U.S. foreign policy south of the border, while MERIP's have a somewhat stiffer academic stamp. Both have moved beyond the "Third Worldism" of the 60s New Left to a more considered approach where the complexities of real world politics are given their due. I recommend both for unexpected insights.

—Jay Kinney

•

In the marketplace in Omdurman, a large bazaar city across the Nile from Khartoum, there is a special section of the market totally controlled and regulated by women. They are often economically autonomous, and they extend this autonomy into the domestic sphere (unlike the market women of Kumasi in Ghana). They are able to do this through the collective power they have built within their various kin networks as an extension of their workplace. Also, many of them live within walking distance of the market and are at their workplace most of the day, turning the work site into a temporary residence replete with a social network. The interface of kin, residential and occupational networks gives the collectivity of the women's market the potential for mobilization. . . .

Behavior encouraged in the *zaar* gives women a rare chance for uninhibited entertainment and drama. At the *zaar* ceremonies I attended, the protagonists entered states of trance and the possessed exhibited bawdy or lewd behavior not acceptable in Sudanese society. These are often occasions for transvestism and sexual role-switching, with male homosexuals often acting as functionaries, and women playing male roles and being erotic toward other women. Those possessed by their spirits may also insult the males of their family and wear outlandish costumes. But the benefits are even more profound:

> There is ample evidence that women actively use this network to form friendship and patron-client relationships, to promote economic transactions, and to offer and gain services. Moreover, once established, the network tends to extend well beyond the actual activities of the cult itself. The reciprocity principle is quite strongly institutionalized in the Northern Sudan.

—MERIP Middle East Report

•

Before engaging the enemy in the Third World, the advocates of low-intensity conflict must convince the Pentagon bureaucracy, civilian officials and other government agencies of their case. They must win over key decision-makers — both political and military — in the security establishments of their foreign allies. And, increasingly, they must complement this internal debate and diplomacy with a full-scale effort to rally the U.S. public behind the policy.

Low-intensity conflict is also radical, however, in the comprehensiveness of its approach. It draws on a wide-ranging study of the different elements of conflict, few of which are strictly military. Researchers at think tanks and universities attempt to analyze and mimic the politico-military structures of revolutionary movements; others study the "backwards" tactics of guerrilla warfare, which invert traditional military rules of engagement, or delve into anthropology and social psychology; others still, like Britain's Brig. Gen. Frank Kitson, dwell on the British and French colonial experiences, and propose sophisticated police states as the means for preventing insurgencies.

—NACLA Report on the Americas

Pravda
$630/year
(356 issues) from:
Associate Publishers, Inc.
2233 University Avenue
Suite 225
St. Paul, MN 55114

Pravda Pulse
Timothy Sinnott, Editor
$64.20/year
(26 issues) from:
News Pulse, Inc.
Drawer 4323
Fort Pierce, FL 33448

NACLA Report on the Americas
George Black, Editor
$20/year
(6 issues) from:
NACLA
151 West 19th Street
9th Floor
New York, NY 10011

MERIP Middle East Report
Joe Stork, Editor
$18/year
(6 issues) from:
MERIP
475 Riverside Drive
New York, NY 10115

Whole Earth Security: A Geopolitics of Peace
(Worldwatch Paper 55)
Daniel Deudney
1983; 93 pp.
$4 postpaid from:
Worldwatch Institute
1776 Massachusetts Avenue NW
Washington, DC 20036

The Evolution of Cooperation
Robert Axelrod
1984; 241 pp.
$6.95 postpaid from:
Basic Books, Inc.
10 East 53rd Street
New York, NY 10022
or Whole Earth Access

Gandhi on Non-Violence
Thomas Merton, Editor
1965; 82 pp.
$4 postpaid from:
W. W. Norton
500 Fifth Avenue
New York, NY 10110
or Whole Earth Access

•

Merely to refuse military service is not enough. . . . This is [to act] after all the time for combating evil is practically gone.

Whole Earth Security: A Geopolitics of Peace

Ninety-three pages. The most original analysis of the nuclear impasse in print, leading to the most realistic and hopeful policy. The new terrain of battle contains the transformation of impasse into sight.

A masterpiece. —*Stewart Brand*

•

With the advent of planetary warmaking, security strategy has been based on the militarization of the commons — the ocean depths, the atmosphere and orbital space. With the enclosure of the planet by warmaking systems, security itself has become indivisible, a commons in its own right. Common security has ceased being utopian and unnecessary and become both possible and necessary.

•

The arms control process has stimulated weapons innovation by encouraging the search for new "bargaining chips" to be traded off at the next round of negotiations. Less able to express itself with quantitative growth, the military turned with renewed vigor to qualitative growth and to areas of weapons technology beyond the existing restraining treaties. Superpower arms control to date is like treating an infection with just enough antibiotics to make the grosser symptoms disappear, soothing the patient's worries, but driving the remaining, now strengthened contagions into more vital, less accessible organs.

•

The next several hundred, if not thousands, of years of human history could be decisively shaped in little more than an hour. The time span of decision making has become shorter at the point of inception and longer at the point of consequence. Only by dismantling the technical apparatus of planetary holocaust can the scale of consequence be brought into line with the responsibility.

The Evolution of Cooperation

The "Prisoner's Dilemma" is a situation where two individuals can choose to cooperate with each other or not cooperate (defect). If they both cooperate they each get three points. If they both defect they each get one point. If one cooperates and one defects, the cooperator gets zero and the defector gets five. Axelrod uses this non-zero-sum game to explain the arms race, international relations and the interaction of regulatory agencies with those they regulate.

First the good news: in a population of individuals interested in their own welfare, where no central authority exists, it pays to cooperate. Cooperative rules "won" over noncooperative ones in simulated iterations.

Now the bad: in the same situations it also pays to be provokable (to defect in retaliation). Rules that were totally cooperative without retaliation did not win.

There is little value for complexity here. The best strategy is simple enough to be readily recognized by another player. No strategy is a winning strategy by itself. It can only be judged by its interaction with other strategies.
—Judith Brophy

The universe in a grain of sand. The grain is a mathematical/sociological paradox, much studied, called "Prisoner's Dilemma." The universe is the one we might survive into if these lessons are believed and applied. Scholarly tour-de-force. —*Stewart Brand*

•

The foundation of cooperation is not really trust, but the durability of the relationship. . . . Whether the players trust each other or not is less important in the long run than whether the conditions are ripe for them to build a stable pattern of cooperation with each other.

Gandhi on Non-Violence

You might as well go straight to the fountainhead and listen to the piercing words of the humblest servant of nonviolence, Mahatma Gandhi. No one else's example in modern times has so radically shifted so many people's lives (mine included) as this "half-naked" saint. The late Thomas Merton, a Christian monk with his own inspiring life of nonviolence, selected the few statements Gandhi wrote down of his experiment in truth for this slim volume. As Gandhi said, "Nonviolence cannot be preached. It has to be practiced." —*Kevin Kelly*

Reading Gandhi's words is scary. They will start something in your mind and break down barriers of "that's impossible" and then you don't know what your life will do. New British officials in old India were told, "Stay away from Gandhi. He'll get you." Don't speak to him personally, were the instructions, don't listen to him speak from a crowd. Because he said "always ally yourself with the part of your enemy that knows what is right" and he knew how to do it. He also knew that what is right is inherently possible, and he'll make you think that, too.
—Anne Herbert

•

To me it is a self-evident truth that if freedom is to be shared equally by all — even physically the weakest, the lame and the halt — they must be able to contribute an equal share in its defense. How that can be possible when reliance is placed on armaments, my plebian mind fails to understand. I therefore swear and shall continue to swear by non-violence, i.e., by *satyagraha*, or soul force. In it physical incapacity is no handicap, and even a frail woman or a child can pit herself or himself on equal terms against a giant armed with the most powerful weapons.

•

Non-Violence in Great Nations?
If they can shed the fear of destruction, if they disarm themselves, they will automatically help the rest to regain their sanity. But then these great powers will have to give up their imperialistic ambitions and their exploitation of the so-called uncivilized or semi-civilized nations of the earth and revise their mode of life. It means a complete revolution.

•

I do not appreciate any underground activity. Millions cannot go underground. Millions need not.

•

We have all — rulers and ruled — been living so long in a stifling, unnatural atmosphere that we might well feel in the beginning that we have lost the lungs for breathing the invigorating ozone of freedom.

•

Under no circumstances can India and England give non-violent resistance a reasonable chance while they are both maintaining full military efficiency.

•

Non-violent opposition:

1) It implies not wishing ill.
2) It includes total refusal to cooperate with or participate in activities of the unjust group, even to eating food that comes from them.
3) It is of no avail to those without living faith in the God of love and love for all mankind.
4) He who practices it must be ready to sacrifice everything except his honor.
5) It must pervade *everything* and not be applied merely to isolated acts.

38. Martyred Earth

As fighting forces become more technically sophisticated they damage each other relatively less and nature relatively more.

Indochina: the US attack and the environment

The War Atlas

The current placement and strength of armies and weapon systems; the fruits of wars already waged; the flow of the arms trade — all these rather dry yet scary statistics are here converted into handsome, multicolored maps which effortlessly make the obscure clear. If, like me, you've been questioning whether we really need yet another dozen or two books examining the arms race and nuclear dilemma to the point of utter redundancy, you'll probably find **The War Atlas** *conveys most of the same information in a much more interesting form.*
—Jay Kinney

The War Atlas
Michael Kidron
and Dan Smith
1983; 120 pp.
$9.95 postpaid from:
Simon & Schuster
Mail Order Sales
200 Old Tappan Road
Old Tappan, NJ 07675
or Whole Earth Access

How to Make War

Did you ever wonder what would really happen if our navy and the Russian navy went to war? Or perhaps you would like to know just how much a war would cost (monetarily). Whatever your interest, if it concerns the implements, components, and probabilities of war, James F. Dunnigan has covered it in **How to Make War.** *I couldn't put this book down. It makes the defense budget debates much more transparent and infuriating.* —Hal Ham

•

Most men do not enter combat thinking they will be killed or injured. In warfare during this century, the odds of serving in the infantry during combat and being uninjured have been less than one in three. If potential recruits knew their chances, it would be much more difficult to get anyone into the infantry.

Indeed, given a choice, many would volunteer for any other branch of the armed forces to avoid the infantry. Most other branches are no more dangerous than civilian life. Even the armor and artillery branches offer a better-than-even chance of seeing a war's end uninjured.

•

The cost of fighting a war today will be substantially higher than for peacetime operations. This is largely due to the high cost of ammunition. Currently a ton of conventional ammunition costs about $7000. A ton of missile munitions costs over half a million dollars. Some improved conventional munitions (ICM) cost ten times more than standard shells and bombs. The high cost of the more expensive munitions represents two things. One is the greater developmental cost. Second, their greater complexity requires much more labor during manufacturing. Under wartime conditions, economies of scale could reduce their cost by five or more times. Still, the price of an average ton of munitions could still be $22,000 or more.

•

Drones and remotely piloted vehicles (RPV's) are pilotless aircraft. A drone flies a preprogrammed course, sometimes with onboard navigation equipment to correct any flight deviations. An RPV is controlled from the ground. With electronic warfare becoming ever more intense, the advantages of the drones over RPVs have increased. An RPV's link with its ground controller can be jammed. A drone is impervious to such jamming.

The rationale for such aircraft is simple; you don't lose a pilot if a drone is shot down. . . . However, there is a major problem. One man's technological breakthrough is another man's threat. Drones threaten to take away pilot jobs. Few people in the air forces will come right out and say this. But halfhearted enthusiasm for drones can be traced back to pilots' unease over their becoming too effective. This is ironic, as the air forces themselves had to fight similar prejudice in their early years.

How to Make War
James F. Dunnigan
1982; 442 pp.
$8.95
($10.45 postpaid) from:
William Morrow
Publishing Co.
6 Henderson Drive
West Caldwell, NJ 07006
or Whole Earth Access

Soldier of Fortune

Repulsive, ghoulish, brutal, sickening. That's war. And that's often the response to this notorious magazine that serves as a clubhouse for self-avowed mercenaries and gung-ho warriors. The talk is of guns and guns and bigger weapons, strategies, and heroics. Us against them. But war is really the enemy we should be fighting. Know thy enemy, portrayed unflinchingly in these pages.
—Kevin Kelly

•

Terrorism Training . . .
The opening of Iran's new "College of Information and Security" was approved 19 January by Iranian officials in a high-level Tehran meeting. . . . A class of 250 will begin training in April, various SOF sources report, who say instruction will prepare students for careers in Iranian intelligence — and terrorism. . . . Fifty and possibly more students will come from Kuwait, Saudi Arabia and Bahrain, sources told the magazine.

•

There's little doubt the Warsaw Pact powers will be our opponent should another major conflict occur, and our entire defense doctrine is based upon that premise. How can we best prepare our troops for that possibility? Simple. Create our own pseudo-Soviet adversary, train him with Soviet doctrine, arm and equip him with Soviet gear, and pit him against our own regular Army forces.

Charging an enemy ambush. It may be your first, last, and only chance for survival.

Soldier of Fortune
Robert K. Brown, Editor
$23.95/year
(12 issues) from:
Soldier of Fortune
P. O. Box 348
Mount Morris, IL 61054

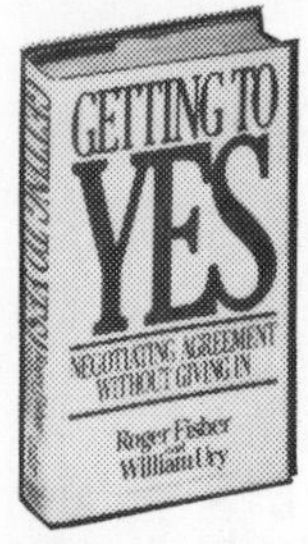

Getting to Yes
Roger Fisher and William Ury
1981; 163 pp.
$11.95
($12.95 postpaid) from:
Houghton Mifflin Co.
Attn.: Mail Order
Wayside Road
Burlington, MA 01803
or Whole Earth Access

THESE DAYS many people try to avoid our formal court system as they might avoid a rabid skunk. The hopelessness of resolving any dispute through civil litigation has spawned a considerable industry dedicated to solving disputes in other ways. Mediation is a principal alternative. Disputing parties arrive at their own solution with the help of a mediator who has no power to impose a decision but is skilled in helping the parties do so. The adversary system encourages people to overstate their claims and often results in bitter lying contests, decreasing the likelihood the disputants will ever have a constructive relationship. But for mediation to succeed, both parties must agree that their most important concerns have been dealt with; they end in a win-win, rather than a win-lose, posture.

Today there are over 200 community-based groups formed to mediate disputes (for a list, contact the National Association for Community Justice, 149 9th St., San Francisco, CA 94103). Some deal with landlord-tenant disputes, others with domestic problems, and many such as the truly creative Community Board Program in San Francisco, focus on the sorts of corrosive neighborhood disputes that have never been handled by the formal court system because there was no profit in doing so. —Jake Warner

Getting to Yes

This book on negotiation comes as a great personal relief to me and may well to you. I've always avoided situations that involved bargaining because of all the dishonesty that seemed to be required. When I was forced, by life, to bargain anyway, I usually did poorly, which reinforced my reluctance. All that is now cured by this modest 163 pages of exceptional insight and clarity.

The point is to negotiate on principle, not pressure — on mutual search for mutually discernible objectivity, patiently and firmly putting aside every other gambit. The book is a landmark, already a bible for international negotiators but just as useful for deciding which movie to see tonight or which school to send the family scion to.

***Getting to Yes** is a model in every way of ideal how-to writing.* —*Stewart Brand*

•

A good case can be made for changing Woodrow Wilson's appealing slogan "Open covenants openly arrived at" to "Open covenants privately arrived at." No matter how many people are involved in a negotiation, important decisions are typically made when no more than two people are in the room.

•

A variation on the procedure of "one cuts, the other chooses" is for the parties to negotiate what they think is a fair arrangement before they go on to decide their respective roles in it. In a divorce negotiation, for example, before deciding which parent will get custody of the children, the parents might agree on the visiting rights of the other parent. This gives both an incentive to agree on visitation rights each will think fair.

•

A good negotiator rarely makes an important decision on the spot. The psychological pressure to be nice and to give in is too great. A little time and distance help separate the people from the problem. A good negotiator comes to the table with a credible reason in his pocket for leaving when he wants. Such a reason should not indicate passivity or inability to make a decision.

The Community Conflict Resolution Training Manual
Judith Lynch, Editor
$25 from:
Community Board Programs, Inc.
149 Ninth Street
San Francisco, CA 94103

The Community Conflict Resolution Training Manual

There are hundreds of mediation groups in the U.S. Some specialize in a narrow type of dispute. Others are the quasi-official arms of juvenile or domestic relations courts. (California and several other states require court-sponsored mediation of all contested child custody lawsuits.) Perhaps the group with the broadest vision of the full range of disputes is the Community Board Program, founded and directed by Roy Shonholtz. Headquartered in San Francisco, this organization has helped start similar groups in two dozen other communities. They offer topnotch training sessions (run periodically at different locations around the country), designed for both community people and professionals. (For information call 415/ 552-1250.) These folks also publish a number of newsletters, manuals, and videotapes. —*Jake Warner*

•

More Effective Listening Techniques
- Stop Talking: You can't listen while you are talking.
- Empathize: Try to put yourself in the other's place so you can understand what he is trying to communicate and why it matters to him.
- Ask Questions: When you don't understand, when you need more explanation, when you want to show that you are listening, ask. But don't ask questions to embarrass or show up the speaker.
- Be Patient: Don't rush people; give them time to say what they have to say.

•

People in Conflict Will Use the Panel Process When:
- The benefits of resolving their dispute through conciliation are apparent.
- They believe that they can resolve their conflicts by using the Panel process.
- They are convinced that their conflict should be resolved, and that neighborhood conciliation is their best alternative.
- They realize that the program will respond to their dispute quickly and at no cost.

The Mediation Process
Christopher W. Moore
1986; 348 pp.
$24.95
($26.95 postpaid) from:
Jossey-Bass Publishers
433 California Street
San Francisco, CA 94104
or Whole Earth Access

The Mediation Process

This is the best and most accessible general text in the field. I particularly like it because there is relatively little material on the general wonders of mediation, but lots of specifics on how mediation sessions should be conducted. Although Moore probably overdoes it a bit when he divides a typical mediation into twelve stages (a half dozen would surely serve as well), I found it a real learning experience to follow him through each. —*Jake Warner*

• There are dozens of local mediation-oriented newsletters popping up, but this is the best.
Mediation Quarterly: John Allen Lemmon, Editor. **$25**/year (4 issues) from Jossey-Bass, Inc., 433 California St., San Francisco, CA 94104.

BOOKS BY AND ABOUT gay men and lesbians no longer hide their covers. They range from the personal through the political, touching on history, culture, legal rights, parenting, and literature. Gay and lesbian writing (their worlds do not always overlap) explores community and its ramifications, using specifics of culture to propose universals of human experience. —Aaron Shurin

Christianity, Social Tolerance and Homosexuality

Boswell nails down history with scrupulous scholarship, using a wide variety of source materials to explore the problematic relationship between the Christian church and homosexuality. Changing, evolving attitudes towards sexuality, from the pre-Christian era through the middle ages, portray homosexuality as a natural expression caught in a social crisis. The introduction and appendices are invaluable historical documents. —Aaron Shurin

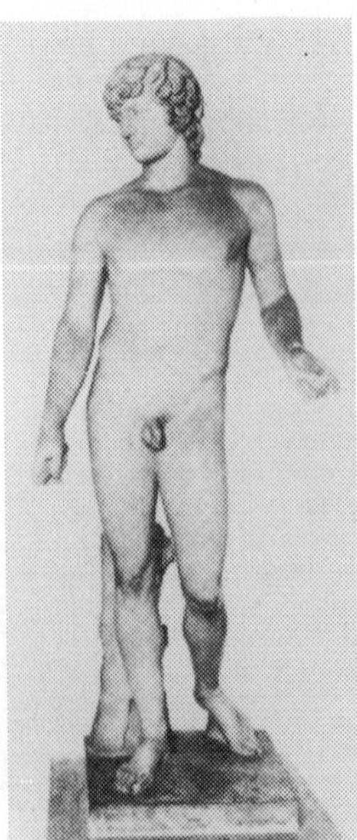

Christianity, Social Tolerance and Homosexuality
John Boswell
1980; 424 pp.
$12.95
postpaid from:
University of Chicago Press
11030 South Langley Ave.
Chicago, IL 60628
or Whole Earth Access

•

Antinous. Roman, second century A.D. (?). One of the best of many surviving statues of the young man from Bithynia loved by the Emperor Hadrian. Antinous was drowned in the Nile in 130 A.D., and the grief-stricken emperor honored his memory by founding cities, establishing games, and erecting statues in his name throughout the empire. *(Courtesy of Museo archeologico nazionale, Naples).*

Another Mother Tongue

Poet Judy Grahn traces gay cultural history from the legends and vocabulary of gay life, bringing new meaning and cohesiveness to same-sex experience. Dykes and Faggots (she celebrates these words, revealing their etymology and power) have served as shamans in various cultures throughout history — including our own. They flame; they burn; they change themselves and the world. —Jeanne Carstensen

•

That's literally what *dike* means — balance, the path. The name of the goddess Dike of Greece, who was old Gaia's granddaughter, meant "the way, the path." And her social function was natural balance, the keeping of the balance of forces. With her two sisters Eunomia ("Order") and Eirene ("Peace"), she was present at the birth of Hermes. The three sisters were known as the Hours and were worshipped in conjunction with Demeter as a foursome, mostly by women.

Another Mother Tongue
Judy Grahn
1984; 324 pp.
$9.95
($11.95 postpaid) from:
Beacon Press
25 Beacon Street
Boston, MA 02108
or Whole Earth Access

A Legal Guide for Lesbian and Gay Couples

Anyone who's entered into a business with a friend without signing a contract knows what pressure that can put on a personal relationship. This book approaches lesbian/gay relationships with the same concerns — how to deal with money, time, and parental issues before they become problems. And its information on financial agreements, wills, and child custody and support is as useful for unmarried straight couples as it is for gays.

Included are case histories, sample contracts, and established legal precedents (including, for example, what precedents the Marvin vs. Marvin case established). But the book is especially valuable for its simple language and tone of loving concern — it is about how to keep it together. —Annette Jarvie

•

The legal position of lesbian and gay students has changed dramatically — and for the better — in the past decade. One striking example is the court order which required that a gay high school senior be allowed to attend his school's senior prom with his male date. The rights of students to speak, form organizations, and sponsor activities, all explictly lesbian- and gay-oriented, have been firmly established by the courts.

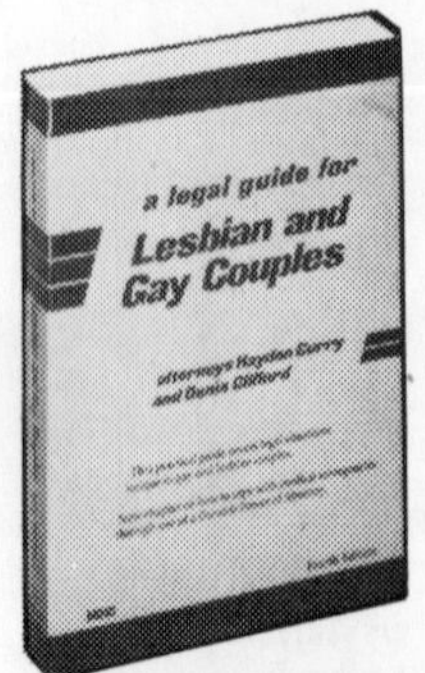

A Legal Guide for Lesbian and Gay Couples
(4th Edition)
Hayden Curry and Denis Clifford
1986; 257 pp.
$17.95
($19.45 postpaid) from:
Nolo Press
950 Parker Street
Berkeley, CA 94710
or Whole Earth Access

Jack the Modernist

Robert Gluck's post-modern prose is all a reader could ask for: wryly self-conscious, full of careening rhythms and inventive formal approaches, love-laden, psychologically probing, and politically smart. Gluck writes about sex with the unabashedness of Genet and the perceptiveness of Proust. Always before him is the integration of eroticism and the social issues that feed it. —Aaron Shurin

• The best weekly coverage of gay and lesbian current events. Politically progressive.
Gay Community News: G. Gottlieb, S. Poggi and L. Hayes, Editors. **$29**/year (50 issues) from GCN, 167 Tremont Street, Boston, MA 02111.

• Political and cultural reporting with colorful features and interviews.
The Advocate: Lenny Giteck, Editor. **$39.97**/year (26 issues) from The Advocate, P. O. Box 4371, Los Angeles, CA 90078.

The Lesbian Path

This anthology draws on the work of over thirty of America's finest lesbian writers, including Judy Grahn, Susan Griffin, Audre Lorde, and Jane Rule. The stories offer a range of always-true tales, exploding the boundaries of traditional autobiography, and proposing a view of lesbianism as more than a sexual or political fact: it's a way of being in the world. —Aaron Shurin

The Lesbian Path
Margaret Cruikshank
1985; 219 pp.
$8.95
($9.95 postpaid) from:
Subterranean Co.
Box 10233
Eugene, OR 97440
or Whole Earth Access

Jack the Modernist
Robert Gluck
1985; 166 pp.
$7.95
($9.20 postpaid) from:
Gay Presses of New York
Box 29
Village Station, NY 10014
or Whole Earth Access

FEMINISM QUESTIONS THE USE of difference to legitimate hierarchy, an arrangement that Starhawk terms "power over." The idea that there's no justification for using woman as "the nigger of the world" (Yoko Ono) remains fundamental to the whole cause. For most of the women (and some of the men) who absorb that truth, feminism is a life-changing, irreversible experience: hard to practice day to day, harder not to.

So feminism is a way of being that's still uphill, not quite a campaign that can be won. Thus it should come as no surprise that the founding mothers of contemporary feminism are still hard at it, pushing the understanding forward. Three of them — Steinem, Friedan, and Morgan — have lately produced books. Although their books are by no means of a mind, taken together they provide a good introduction to mature mainstream feminist thought. The mainstream is plenty radical as far as it goes, and it goes to the boundary of the human species.

But for profounder consciousness alteration, something that takes in the whole planet, and the problem of hierarchy itself, read Starhawk.

"What's new in feminism," I hope, will be the imminent demise of the monkey-see, monkey-do Kirkpatrick/Thatcher/Gandhi syndrome. Watching what becomes of women who make it in the patriarchy could finally persuade us that all power really does corrupt.

Heresies and other ephemera are recommended as charts and visits to emergent feminist culture, the islands for us to swim to. It could be a new world, and certainly a better refuge. And in spite of all the difficulty, this much is certain: there's no turning the clock back and there'll be no end of trying. —Stephanie Mills

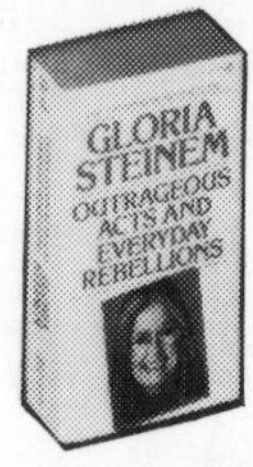

Outrageous Acts and Everyday Rebellions
Gloria Steinem
1985; 420 pp.
$4.50
($5.50 postpaid) from:
New American Library
120 Woodbine Street
Bergenfield, NJ 07621
or Whole Earth Access

Outrageous Acts and Everyday Rebellions

This collection, which is Steinem's first book — she's been too busy as an organizer and journalist for the last twenty years to write one before now — is a better place than most to begin to learn what feminism is today.

Gloria Steinem may be one of the finer human beings around, a noble exponent of an epochal cause. Start with her courage: in surviving, without self-pity, an arduous childhood (see "Ruth's Song"), and the slings and arrows aimed at her as America's Best-Known Feminist ("Introduction"). Add to that her unyielding insistence on justice for all, her constant awareness of the contributions and concerns of women and men of color, and her attention to the economic inequity between the dominant minority and the diverse majority. Then there's her intelligence and discernment (evident in "Erotica vs. Pornography"); a generous compassion (which notes the tender, bitter commonalities among women as different as Alice Walker, Pat Nixon, and Linda Lovelace); and a devastating wit ("If Men Could Menstruate"), and you've got yourself a true champion, one who humbly disavows any exceptionality.

Isn't that just like a woman? Read her.
—Stephanie Mills

•

Men who want children must at least find women willing to bear them. That seems little enough to ask. And governments that want increased rates of population growth must resort to such humane measures as lowering infant mortality rates, improving health care during pregnancy, distributing the work of child rearing through child care and equal parenthood, and lengthening the productive lives of older people.

Obviously, this ultimate bargaining power on the part of women is exactly what male supremacists fear most. That's why their authoritarian impulse is so clearly against any sexuality not directed toward family-style procreation (that is, against extramarital sex, homosexuality and lesbianism, as well as contraception and abortion). This understanding helped feminists to understand why the adversaries of such apparently contradictory concerns as contraception and homosexuality are almost always the same. It also helped us to stand up publicly on the side of any consenting, freely chosen sexuality as a rightful form of human expression.

Sisterhood Is Global
Robin Morgan, Editor
1984; 838 pp.
$12.95
postpaid from:
Doubleday and Company
Direct Mail Order
501 Franklin Avenue
Garden City, NY 11530
or Whole Earth Access

Sisterhood is Global

This book is almost overpowering. A formidable (838 pp.) anthology cum almanac, it presents articles on the conditions of women's lives and their movements as understood by contributors from seventy different countries. The contributors employ a variety of genres — from rather dry sociological prose, to colloquial accounts of organizing experiences, to impassioned pleas for support of revolutionary movements, to folktales, to bitterly funny political nonsatire.

All these are prefaced by entries sketching the demography, government, economy, "gynography," "herstory," and mythography of the countries represented. What emerges is a picture of ubiquitous injustice being met by widespread awakening and activism. Robin Morgan's powerful introduction brilliantly focuses on the implications of global feminism, a vision of startling possibility.
—Stephanie Mills

•

How many women know it is now possible for a women's group or *an individual woman* to register a human rights violation complaint (which can include battery, rape, job discrimination, deleterious "cultural" practices, etc.) directly by confidential or standard letter to the Secretariat of the Commission on the Status of Women (in care of the Women's Unit, United Nations Center, Vienna, Austria) — and that every complaint requires a formal investigation by the Commission, requiring in turn a response from the national government involved?

We must — and can — demystify the channels to power, in order to travel them.

Connexions
Connexions Collective, Editors.
$12/year
(4 issues) from:
Connexions
4228 Telegraph Avenue
Oakland, CA 94609

Connexions

A quarterly magazine covering the same unwieldy beat as ***Sisterhood is Global, Connexions*** *gathers reports from women around the world on one theme (e.g. Media: Getting to Women or Women and Militarism) for each issue. The diverse voices and concerns of women from both industrial and nonindustrial countries convey the real challenge of an international women's movement — creating not just common theory, but understanding that spans continents. The best place to begin without having to buy a plane ticket.* *—Jeanne Carstensen*

Dreaming the Dark

Starhawk is a witch, and ***Dreaming the Dark*** *is a thoughtful exposition of paganism — the timeless and eternally new "old religion," witchcraft, which was the religious practice of men and women before god was extricated from immanence, unsurprisingly becoming a patriarch in the process. The politics of male sky-god religion parallel the politics of female oppression, which is why it is no coincidence that a lot of good churchmen once tortured hundreds of wise women (and men) to death in order to confirm spirituality as the franchise of a masculine elite. In spite of all that, magic never died.* ***Dreaming the Dark*** *is convincing propaganda against hierarchy of any sort, religious or temporal, and for high anarchy. It's also a straightforward introduction to the philosophy and practice of magic.*

Starhawk's magic is a spiritual path, a tried-and-true method of nonegocentric self-realization and community building; a practice of awakening and acknowledging the divine power immanent within each of us, that awakening not mediated by hierarchy, that power not apart from human beings.

Starhawk synthesizes insights from psychology, sociology, history, and religion, and in her appendix on the witch-burning times of the "Renaissance" achieves brilliance without resort to detailing the horrors of that era. ***Dreaming the Dark*** *is the most effective argument I've seen that the personal is the political. Hence it points to the way of integrity. On that way, we must dream, not deny, the dark in life, the dark in us, and hallow the earthly, lifegiving powers of sex and gender. If we continue to alienate and project those parts of our being, they will turn on us and we will perish, shattered.*

The how of dreaming the dark is simple, interesting, and valuable. During her ten years in a coven, and through her work as a therapist and political activist, Starhawk has developed an organic sense of group and individual psychodynamics. She stresses our mortal need for community, offering what others might term a systems theory or family therapy approach to social change. She relates her understanding in good instruction on fostering the life and work of any group, sharing her experiences in therapy, in the craft, and in jail for her protest, with unstinting self-honesty. Persons of all genders, religions, and politics interested in healing self or planet would do well to avail themselves of this extraordinary text. —*Stephanie Mills*

[Suggested by Evy Gershon]

•

We must demand that our politics serve our sexuality. Too often, we have asked sexuality to serve politics instead. Ironically, the same movements that have criticized sexual repression and bourgeois morality have themselves too often tried to mold their sexual feeling to serve the current political theory. This tradition includes nineteenth century revolutionary ascetism, the New Left's demand that women practice free love (meaning sex without involvement), the fear of lesbianism in the early women's movement, and the mandatory separatist line taken by some in the later women's movement. Too many generations have asked: What do my politics tell me I should feel? The better question is: What do I, at my root, at my core, desire?

Dreaming the Dark
(Magic, Sex and Politics)
Starhawk
1982; 242 pp.

$9.95
($11.95 postpaid) from:
Beacon Press
25 Beacon Street
Boston, MA 02108
or Whole Earth Access

The Second Stage

The Second Stage *continues the obdurately fair appraisal of the relationship between the sexes begun twenty years ago in* ***The Feminine Mystique****. Fair in that Betty Friedan doesn't let women off the hook. She foresees a positive synthesis emerging from the women's movement and proclaims that it is not for women only. So she doesn't exempt men from the opportunity to change, either.*

There's a lot to quibble with in Friedan — she's straight, she has odd blind spots around lesbianism, race, culture, and ecology, and she extrapolates from the present in a rather linear way. She is, however, aware of the extent to which the megainstitutions like the State and Capitalism have gone haywire, and that makes for a fairly meaningful larger context.

Attitudes aside, though, the valuable thing about Friedan is that she exerts herself and derives her conclusions and prescriptions from reality: she reports research on the positive psychological (and physical!) consequences of feminism; she discusses surveys in which women recount their experience and opinions of their changing working and parenting arrangements. In addition to recounting other peoples' discoveries, Friedan has traveled widely and observantly and made some of her own. Her account of what's going on at West Point now that women are being admitted is an arresting example.

The Second Stage*, if not a completely visionary book, is an essential one. It is both forward-looking and cautionary. Assessing the moment and the future, Friedan points out that the improved access to opportunity enjoyed by today's career women (many of whom disclaim feminism) was hard-won by feminists a decade ago, and is now jeopardized by reactionaries. It never hurts to be reminded that eternal vigilance is the price of liberty.*

—*Stephanie Mills*

•

Do they really want to force women to have more children? Do they really want to outlaw abortion? Or do they want to keep pushing it as a diversionary issue, twisting and manipulating the agonizing conflicts people can't help facing now, about the costs and problems of having children, and their own values of life — diverting the rage away from those who profiteer from inflation, with sexual, "moral" red herrings? But the power of their campaign, and the rage they are able to divert against those who speak openly and honestly about the choices all must make now, comes, at least in part, from the pain and the deep insult to their human core that people may be truly experiencing as they are manipulated deeper and deeper into the depersonalizing material rat race, losing control of their lives. The very rhetoric of the first stage "pro-abortion" campaign exacerbated or played into that rage.

The Second Stage
Betty Friedan
1981; 346 pp.

$8.95
postpaid from:
Simon & Schuster
Mail Order Sales
200 Old Tappan
Old Tappan, NJ 07675
or Whole Earth Access

Heresies

Produced by a collective, each issue of ***Heresies*** *is a special: Feminism and Ecology, Third World Women, Women Working Together, and Sexuality have been among their subjects. Some of the material is a grind — theoretical, rhetorical stuff on feminism as a subject. Some of it is revelatory, especially that dealing with feminism as a practice or perspective. Everything they publish has consequence, and the art they include is striking — images that hit home.*

There are scores of excellent feminist magazines, from stately small-press literary journals to scholarly quarterlies to outraged tabloids to the rangier, avant-garde offering of ***Heresies****. Its inclusion here as the sole representative of all that rich cultural activity is not to anoint it as the best of the lot (although it is very good), but to advance a personal favorite as exemplary of a whole realm of riches. I suggest you prowl for a personal favorite, too.*

—*Stephanie Mills*

Heresies
Heresies Collective, Editors

$15/2 years
(4 issues) from:
Heresies
P. O. Box 1306
Canal Street Station
New York, NY 10013

IVIDING THE POLITICAL REALM up into Left and Right is a legacy of the French Revolution and, like the guillotine, not always applicable to the modern world. Nevertheless, until someone comes up with a better set of pigeonholes, we are stuck with the Left/Right metaphor, and most activities and actors in the political realm end up falling on one side of the fence or the other.

The conceit of this two-page spread is that the following selection of magazines serves as a rough introduction to the spectrum of the Left and Right. This is similar to trying to boil the world's cuisines down into a half-dozen fast food restaurants. It's both an interesting exercise and an impossible task, and should be read with no illusions about its completeness.

—Jay Kinney

—*The Progressive*

Liberal/Progressive

The Nation and *The Progressive* are the two best general magazines on the American Left. They are also two of the oldest national magazines — of any political stance — still being published. (*The Nation* was founded in 1865 and *The Progressive* in 1909.) Long considered "liberal," both magazines have responded to the languishing disintegration of liberalism by broadening their purview to include democratic socialism as a serious option.

As a weekly, *The Nation* provides timely commentary on late-breaking news. Alexander Cockburn's slash-and-burn Press criticism column is particularly provocative. *The Progressive's* forte on the other hand is longer analytical articles presented with striking black-and-white graphics.

Socialist/Communist

One notch to the left is *In These Times,* the "independent socialist newspaper" published weekly in Chicago. *ITT* distinguishes itself from the preceding publications through its emphasis on hard news and its overt stumping for socialism. The writing in *ITT* is intelligent, nonsectarian and nonrhetorical, and includes good coverage of popular culture. If a good case for socialism can be made in the late '80s, it'll likely be in *In These Times.*

Though the *Guardian's* subtitle, "the independent radical newsweekly," sounds similar to *ITT*'s, the *Guardian* is a distinctly different entity. Progressive in the '50s, New Left in the '60s, Marxist-Leninist in the '70s, the *Guardian* has tended to reflect the changing tilt of left activists from era to era. These days, the *Guardian* has cut back on the rhetoric, undergone a much-needed graphic redesign, and tempered its penchant for revolutionary dogmatism. If pinned down under duress, the *Guardian* would probably still call itself communist, though the word doesn't surface often in its pages.

—*Guardian*

Anarchist/Anti-Civilization

Even farther to the left we run into the anarchists who may not like Capitalism but hate governments even more. *Open Road* is the most accessible, regularly published anarchist paper in North America. Since its inception several years ago, *Open Road* has reported on a variety of anti-authoritarian activities ranging from anti-nuke demos to Native American struggles to bombings by alleged revolutionaries.
With "terrorism" so much in the news, *OR* is one of the few publications that prints communiques from leftists undertaking armed actions.

On the far-left fringes of the far left is the *Fifth Estate.* Starting out in Detroit as one of the seminal underground papers of the '60s, *FE* evolved into a unique radical publication defying any easy label. Suspicious of any 'ism', despairing of the bitter fruits of industrial civilization, and with grave misgivings about the role of words and numbers themselves in warping human consciousness, *FE* publishes brilliant, if wordy(!), critiques of nearly everything.

The Nation
Richard Lingeman, Editor
$45/year
(47 issues) from:
The Nation
P. O. Box 1953
Marion, OH 43305

The Progressive
Erwin Knoll, Editor
$16.97/year
(12 issues) from:
The Progressive
409 East Main Street
Madison, WI 53703

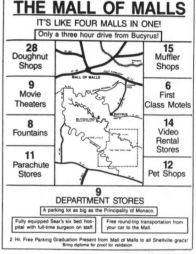

Compliments
THE MALL OF MALLS
IT'S LIKE FOUR MALLS IN ONE!
Only a three hour drive from Bucyrus!
28 Doughnut Shops
15 Muffler Shops
9 Movie Theaters
6 First Class Motels
8 Fountains
14 Video Rental Stores
11 Parachute Stores
12 Pet Shops
MALL OF MALLS
BUCYRUS
9 DEPARTMENT STORES
A parking lot as big as the Principality of Monaco.
Fully equipped Sear's six bed hospital with full-time surgeon on staff.
Free round-trip transportation from your car to the Mall.
2 Hr. Free Parking Graduation Present from Mall of Malls to all Shellville grads! Bring diploma for proof for validation.

—*The Fifth Estate*

• For another look at political extremes, check "Covert Action" (p. 91).
• Supplies for anarchists may be found in the Loompanics catalog (p. 143).

In These Times
James Weinstein, Editor
$34.95/year
(41 issues) from:
In These Times
1300 West Belmont Ave.
Chicago, IL 60657

The Guardian
William A. Ryan, Editor
$27.50/year
(47 issues) from:
The Institute
for Independent
Social Journalism, Inc.
33 West 17th Street
New York, NY 10011

Open Road
2 hours' pay/year
(4 issues) or $50 (sustainer)
from:
The Open Road
Collective
P. O. Box 6135, Station G
Vancouver, BC
Canada V6R 4G5

The Fifth Estate
$5/year
(4 issues) from:
The Fifth Estate
Cooperative
P. O. Box 02548
Detroit, MI 48202

Conservative

Suspected of being moribund only ten years ago, conservatism and the GOP have experienced a wave of popularity during the '80s that has left the Left gasping for air. As indicative of this phenomenon, the following two publications spent much of the '70s as wistful outsiders, but have increased in influence and prestige in recent years.

Human Events, "the National Conservative Weekly," is touted as one of Ronald Reagan's favorite publications and is a good place to go to gain insight into the perspective he represents. With conservatives in power the tabloid gives particular attention to Capitol affairs, though national and international news and issues are also covered.

The American Spectator spent the '70s handcrafting its mix of snide humor, biting opinions, and copious book reviews in Bloomington, Indiana. In recent years it has moved to Arlington, Virginia, as its editor, R. Emmett Tyrrell, Jr., has risen from obscurity to become a nationally syndicated columnist. With a format roughly similar to the *New York Review of Books, The American Spectator* delivers a wholly conservative assemblage of wit, bile, and criticism.

Reason
Robert W. Poole, Jr.,
Editor
$24/year
(11 issues) from:
Reason
P. O. Box 27977
San Diego, CA 92128

Laissez Faire Books
Catalog **free** from:
Laissez Faire Books
532 Broadway, 7th Floor
New York, NY 10012

Libertarian

Libertarians prefer to consider their philosophy of minimal government and maximum liberty as being beyond both Left and Right. However, what distinguishes most contemporary libertarians from the anarchists on the left is the libertarians' enthusiasm for nonregulated "free enterprise" economics. With that in mind, *Reason* magazine in California and Laissez Faire Books in New York can be arguably included with others on the Right.

A lot of libertarian publications have come and gone in the last decade, but *Reason* (subtitled "Free Minds and Free Markets") has stuck it out. Some good investigative reporting, a selection of columns (including one on investments), and both slick paper and slick design make this a very readable magazine.

Laissez Faire Books is a modest bookstore in lower Manhattan with a sizeable mail-order business. It claims to have the "world's largest selection of books on Liberty" which is probably an accurate claim if you define Liberty as synonomous with libertarian politics, the Austrian school of ("free market") economics, and Ayn Rand's Objectivism.

The White Patriot Party strives to make activism compatible with family life. Many members are family members. —*Spotlight*

Far Right

Finally, the *Spotlight,* published by the Liberty Lobby, is the best place to get a handle on the surge in support of the far right in middle America. By turns populist, anti-Zionist (its critics say anti-semitic), isolationist, and anti-communist, the *Spotlight* claims a bigger paid circulation than any other publication on these pages. Photo features on paramilitary groups like the White Patriots Party rub elbows with articles on embattled doctors touting alternative cancer cures and investigative pieces on organized crime. It's an explosive mix you should be aware of.

—Jay Kinney

—American Spectator

Human Events
Thomas S. Winter
and Allan Ryskind, Editors
$25/year
(52 issues) from:
Human Events
422 1st Street SE
Washington, DC 20003

The American Spectator
R. Emmett Tyrrell, Jr.,
Editor
$21 /year
(12 issues) from:
The American Spectator
P. O. Box 10448
Arlington, VA 22210

The Spotlight
Vincent J. Ryan, Editor
$15/year
(51 issues) from:
The Spotlight
300 Independence Ave. SE
Washington, DC 20003

Rules for Radicals
Saul Alinsky
1971; 224 pp.
$3.95
($4.95 postpaid) from:
Random House
Order Dept.
400 Hahn Road
Westminster, MD 21157
or Whole Earth Access

Rules for Radicals

Toward a science of revolution. Much radical literature is aimed at fighting. This book is aimed, by an expert, at winning. —*Stewart Brand*

•

Always remember the first rule of power tactics: *Power is not only what you have but what the enemy thinks you have.*

The second rule is: *Never go outside the experience of your people.* When an action or tactic is outside the experience of the people, the result is confusion, fear, and retreat. It also means a collapse of communication, as we have noted.

The third rule is: *Wherever possible go outside of the experience of the enemy.* Here you want to cause confusion, fear, and retreat . . .

The fourth rule is: *Make the enemy live up to their own book of rules.* You can kill them with this, for they can no more obey their own rules than the Christian church can live up to Christianity.

The fourth rule carries within it the fifth rule: *Ridicule is man's most potent weapon.* It is almost impossible to counterattack ridicule. Also it infuriates the opposition, who then react to your advantage.

The sixth rule is: *A good tactic is one that your people enjoy.* If your people are not having a ball doing it, there is something very wrong with the tactic.

The seventh rule: *A tactic that drags on too long becomes a drag . . .*

The eighth rule: *Keep the pressure on,* with different tactics and actions, and utilize all events of the period for your purpose.

The ninth rule: *The threat is usually more terrifying than the thing itself.*

The tenth rule: *The major premise for tactics is the development of operations that will maintain a constant pressure upon the opposition.*

Round up your committee supporters in time for the vo

Lobbying on a Shoestring
Judith C. Meredith
and Linda Myer
1982; 160 pp.
$6.95
($8 postpaid) from:
Massachusetts Poverty Law Center
69 Canal Street
Boston, MA 02114
or Whole Earth Access

Lobbying on a Shoestring

Nuts-and-bolts advice for lobbying your state legislature. This well-organized step-by-step run-through is especially geared to the Massachusetts legislature, but much of its advice is applicable to most any state government. Reproductions of typical documents and irreverent cartoons relieve the text and help make it a pleasure to read. —*Jay Kinney*

•

Of the thousands of bills introduced in each legislative session, only a handful address *public issues.* Is your bill one of these?

Your bill is a public issue if almost everyone (1) has heard of it, (2) knows it's being debated in the legislature, (3) has an opinion on it, and (4) knows who the players are on each side.

•

About ninety percent of the bills in the legislature address *nonpublic issues.*

•

Don't assume that bigger is always better in the game of passing legislation. Working on big public issues appears glamorous, but these fights are often the hardest to win because the opposition mobilizes so forcefully against them. (The old law of Newtonian physics: To every action there is an equal and opposite reaction.) Often it's easier to succeed in lobbying for bills addressing nonpublic issues. If you keep quiet, these bills may arouse no opposition and will pass unnoticed.

National Center for Policy Alternatives (NCPA)

Formerly known as the Conference on Alternative State and Local Policies, this public policy think-tank and resource center was established in 1977 to provide innovative policy ideas for state, city, county and town governments. The organization produces reports and legislative proposals on farmland preservation, energy conservation, pension fund investment, economic development and more. It also schedules regular national seminars and publishes a quarterly newsletter, ***Ways and Means.*** —*Tim Redmond*

NCPA
Publications list **free**
Ways and Means
Scott Johnson, Editor
$15/year:
(4 issues) both from:
NCPA
2000 Florida Avenue NW
Washington, DC 20009

The Almanac of American Politics

Who did what, where, when. For each state and congressional district a recent political history; for every Senator and Representative, a profile, ratings by political interest groups (who their friends and enemies are) and their voting records on key issues; and federal funds spent in each district. Know your representatives in Congress. —*Diana Barich*

The Almanac of American Politics 1986
Michael Barone and
Grant Ujifusa
1985; 1593 pp.
$28.95
($30.95 postpaid) from:
National Journal
1730 M Street NW
Washington, DC 20036
or Whole Earth Access

Elected 1982; b. Nov. 11, 1940, Brooklyn, NY; home, Greenbrae; Brooklyn Col., B.A. 1962; Jewish; married (Stewart).

Career Stockbroker, researcher, 1962–65; Journalist, *Pacific Sun*, 1972–74; District aide to U.S. Rep. John Burton, 1974–76; Marin Cnty. Bd. of Sprvsrs., 1976–82, Pres., 1980–81.

Offices 315 CHOB 20515, 202-225-5161. Also 450 Golden Gate Ave., San Francisco 94102, 415-556-1333; 823 Marin, Rm. 8, Vallejo 94590, 707-552-0720; and 901 Irwin St., San Rafael 94901, 415-457-7272.

Committees *Budget* (17th of 20). Task Forces: Defense and International Affairs; Income Security; State and Local Government. *Government Operations* (14th of 23 D). Subcommittees: Environment, Energy, and Natural Resources; Intergovernmental Relations and Human Resources. *Select Committee on Children, Youth, and Families* (8th of 15 D). Task Force: Crisis Intervention.

National Journal Ratings

1984	*Economic*	*Social*	*Foreign*
Liberal	86%	84%	84%
Conservative	0%	0%	13%

Key Votes

1) Cap Tax Cut	FOR	5) OK School Pray	AGN	9) Cancel MX Missile	FOR
2) Extend SS Benefit	FOR	6) Limit Abortions	AGN	10) Halt Aid to Contras	FOR
3) Estab Dom Content	FOR	7) Approve ERA	FOR	11) Incr Aid to El Sal	AGN
4) Bar Imm Amnesty	AGN	8) Pass Imm Reform	AGN	12) Supp Nuclear Freeze	FOR

League of Women Voters

This volunteer organization has come to stand for citizen participation in responsible and responsive government. Its nonpartisan stance allows the League to concentrate on researching the facts about candidates and issues and getting them out to voters. For local to national issues, their publications catalog is a useful first stop in the search for answers. —Richard Nilsen

•

Simplified Parliamentary Procedure. Robert's Rules of Order condensed and simplified in an easy-to-understand pamphlet. Newly revised. 1979, 12 pp. 75¢.

•

Letting the Sunshine In: Freedom of Information and Open Meetings. Provisions of the federal laws: how citizens can take advantage of them. 1977, 4 pp. 65¢.

•

Know Your Community. Guide to help citizens and organizations interested in change take a good look at the existing structure and functions of their local government. 1972, 48 pp., $1.75.

•

The Nuclear Waste Primer. New edition. Contains basic information on sources and types of radioactive waste. Outlines past and present government waste management programs and describes future policy options and opportunities for citizen participation in the decision process. 1985, 90 pp., $5.95.

League of Women Voters

Catalog **free** from:
League of Women Voters of the United States
Publication Sales
1730 M Street NW
Tenth Floor
Washington, DC 20036

How to Lobby Congress

Abundant, detailed savvy on effective use of Washington, DC. Affecting national policy is not impossible, merely difficult. —Stewart Brand

•

The Press Aide also edits the Congressman's newsletter to his constituents. This so-called newsletter is thinly disguised political propaganda designed to inform the electorate on the Member's activities in Washington. It is usually a four-to eight-page pamphlet; until recently, it has always been written in the first person singular and the Congressman has been characteristically egotistical about his accomplishments on behalf of his constituency. Usually, these newsletters will consider half a dozen issues and will often have pictures of the Congressman meeting with various groups. An extremely effective way to promote your issue is to have a feature article on it included in a Congressman's newsletter. It's free, it reaches over fifty thousand people by first-class mail and it's the closest thing to a free lunch you'll find in Washington.

How to Lobby Congress
Donald deKieffer
1981; 241 pp.
$8.95
($10.45 postpaid) from:
Dodd, Mead and Co.
P. O. Box 141000
Nashville, TN 37214
or Whole Earth Access

Center for Innovative Diplomacy (CID)

Omnipresent: the nuclear threat, and the feeling that there's nothing to be done about it. Given the unresponsiveness of national politicians to disarmament proposals, that feeling is mostly right. The occasional nuclear free zones just don't make me feel that safe.

Stubborn CID believes that local governments should act in international affairs; citizen participation in "municipal state departments" would empower localities to challenge national politicians. CID's newsletter and frequent special reports hash out the vision and strategy. They also have a manual, ***Having International Affairs Your Way****, on how to be a citizen diplomat. Here's one route to making changes for the long haul.* —Jeanne Carstensen

•

According to the Logan Act, no U.S. citizen may "directly or indirectly" correspond with or meet with "any foreign government . . . with intent to influence the measures or conduct of any foreign government . . . in relation to any disputes or controversies with the United States." Any citizen who violates these rules awaits up to three years in jail and a five thousand dollar fine.

•

The Logan Act remains a living testament to our government's resistance to citizen diplomacy and, indeed, all democratic participation in foreign policy. So long as the act exists, it is a potential snakepit that someday can — and will — be used against citizen diplomats. If citizen diplomacy is to become a regular tool for American foreign policy, we should prepare to jettison the Logan Act once and for all.

• For tracking current alternative political theories and tactics, and for glimpsing the shape of future politics — both national and international — try this newsletter.
New Options: Mike Satin, Editor, **$25**/year, (12 issues) from: New Options Incorporated, P. O. Box 19324, Washington, DC 20036.

Center for Innovative Diplomacy
Membership
$25/year:
(includes quarterly *CID Report*)
Information **free** with SASE
Having International Affairs Your Way
$4 postpaid
All from:
CID
17931 F Skypark Circle
Irvine, CA 92714

Information U.S.A.

This mammoth directory is dedicated to "all federal bureaucrats" and makes the point that 710,000 members of this much maligned profession are actually information specialists. The premise at the heart of the book is simple: "somewhere in the federal government there is a free source of information on almost any topic you can think of." A book that opens doors and gives the name, address, phone number and price list behind each one. —Richard Nilsen

•

Consumer Product Safety Commission

Publications

Up to 10 copies of the following publications are available free by writing to the U.S. Consumer Product Safety Commission, Washington, DC 20207:

Children's Sleepwear (Fact Sheet No. 96)
Holiday Safety No. 7T (teacher's guide on decorations, toys and other gifts)
CPSC Publications List
Wake Up! Smoke Detectors (available also in Spanish)
Wood and Coal Burning Stoves (Fact Sheet No. 92)
Hair Dryers and Stylers (Fact Sheet No. 35)
Urea Formaldehyde Foam Insulation — Information Packet
Hot Tips for Hot Shots on Skateboarding Safety (illustrated brochure)

•

Environmental Protection Agency

Data Experts

The following experts can be contacted directly concerning the topics under their responsibility.

Bottled Water, Home Purifiers/Frank Bell/202-382-3037
Acid Precipitation/Mike Maxwell/919-541-3091
Asbestos in Buildings/William Cain/202-684-7881
Groundwater Protection/Jack Kelley/405-332-8800
Integrated Pest Management/Darwin Wright/202-426-2407
Watershed Management/Lee Mulkey/404-546-3581
Fishkills/Ed Biernacki/202-382-7008

Information U.S.A.
Matthew Lesko
1986; 1253 pp.
$22.95
($24.45 postpaid) from:
Viking Penguin Books
299 Murray Hill Pkwy.
East Rutherford, NJ 07073
or Whole Earth Access

LIKE IT OR NOT, if you're involved in local politics you will have to deal with the press. Whether you want publicity or need secrecy, at some point the newspapers and broadcast media will become a factor in your plans.

In any community with a population of more than about 500 people situated within a half-day's drive of a modern metropolis, newspapers and TV will be the dominant means of political communication. In most moderate-to-large towns and cities, events that are not reported in the local papers (or on the local TV news) might as well not have happened — at least as far as most of the population is concerned.

If you're working in any sort of community politics, read the local newspapers, watch the local TV news, listen to the radio talk shows. The media may be lousy, but that's how most people in town learn about their community — and if nothing else, you need to know what they're being told. Learn the names and follow the records of all the local officials. Chances are no matter what your cause, a few are potential allies.

I can't stress this last point enough. A lot of my friends can talk for hours about "green politics" and "bio-regional perspectives," but they don't know the name of their city council members. They can identify every warring faction in Chad (and which superpower supports each one), but they don't know where their garbage goes. I don't care what you think about electoral politics or mass media — they are part of your community right now, like it or not, and you need to learn how they work.

—Tim Redmond

How Can I Help?
Ram Dass
and Paul Gorman
1985; 243 pp.
$5.95
($6.95 postpaid) from:
Random House
Order Dept.
400 Hahn Road
Westminster, MD 21157
or Whole Earth Access

How Can I Help?

Ram Dass and Paul Gorman approach charitable service as a liberation from the prison of self and separateness, and as a solution to the inarticulate loneliness we feel when we lack a connection to others. The anecdotes are the best part here, and the reader wants more of them. Between people's stories, the authors narrate simple psychology directed to the helping professions.
—Sallie Tisdale

•

There's one thing I've learned in twenty-five years or so of political organizing: People don't like to be "should" upon. They'd rather discover than be told.

•

The basic social institution is the individual human heart. It is the source of the energy from which all social action derives its power and purpose. The more we honor the integrity of that source, the more chance our actions have of reaching and stirring others.

Women Winning
Barbara M. Trafton
1984; 164 pp.
$9.95
($11.20 postpaid) from:
Kampmann & Company
9 East 40th Street
New York, NY 10016
or Whole Earth Access

Women Winning

The advent of women as candidates for elected offices in America began in earnest in the 1970s. This book conveys the excitement of a new group reaching out for elected political power and also includes strategic and organizational advice that candidates of either sex will find valuable. The author is a Democratic Party committeewoman and a seasoned veteran of six years in the Maine state legislature.
—Richard Nilsen

•

Over the past decade most women candidates have underemphasized the planning stage of campaigning. . . . You can develop a solid strategy at the outset if you follow these fundamental principles:

1. Know your message.
2. Know the issues.
3. Know the voters.
4. Know the limits of your resources.

•

Once you've determined what your message will be, your brochures, newspaper interviews, radio spots, balloons, door hangers, and all your other campaign materials should be designed to deliver your message to the voters.

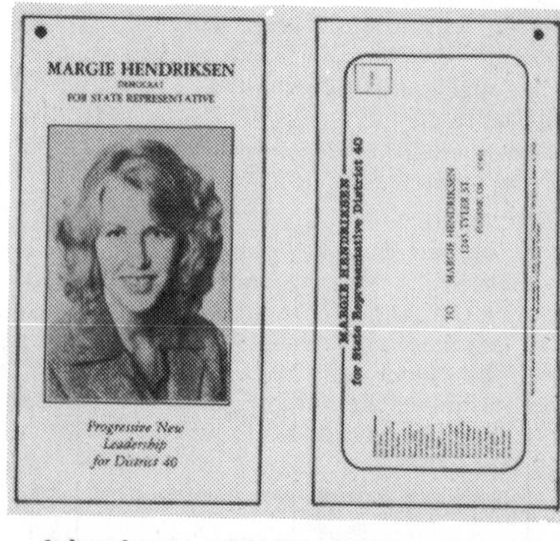

A door hanger with detachable return card.

How to Make Meetings Work
Michael Doyle and
David Straus
1976; 301 pp.
$3.95
($4.70 postpaid) from:
Berkley Publishing Group
390 Murray Hill Parkway
East Rutherford, NJ 07073
or Whole Earth Access

How to Make Meetings Work

It always amazes me how a group of otherwise pleasant people can go collectively insane as soon as they get in a meeting together. Anyone who suffers through the wrangling and frustration of poorly run meetings will find this book very useful. I particularly like its emphasis on achieving consensus, a worthy goal that lots of people talk about without knowing much of how it can be achieved.
—Linda Williams

►
A clearly legible record of the key ideas of the meeting taped to the walls is called a group memory.

•

The very presence of the group memory has many beneficial effects. It provides a physical focus for the group. Rather than sitting in a closed circle around a conference table, channeling their energies toward each other, the members sit in a semicircle and automatically focus their energies on the problem as represented by the group memory. This simple change can make a tremendous difference.

One of my favorite stories about local politics goes back to the late 1970s, when Abbie Hoffman was living under an assumed name in a small town on the St. Lawrence River in upstate New York. The way Abbie tells it, he read in the newspaper one day that the Army Corps of Engineers had plans to blast a new shipping channel right through the section of the river that ran by his home. The project would involve dynamiting several small islands and opening an environmentally sensitive stretch of waterway to major shipping.

Hoffman decided to risk blowing his cover and start fighting the plan. For weeks, he went around and knocked on his neighbors' doors and urged them to write letters opposing the project to the Corps and to their legislators. But time after time, the working-class river folk declined to get involved. "They kept telling me," Hoffman explained, "that there was nothing they could do — that nobody paid any attention to them. All they knew was that winter was coming and they needed firewood. All they cared about was their damn chainsaws."

Suddenly an idea came. Hoffman put on a tie, took $20 cash down to the local newspaper and placed a classified ad that read: "FREE CHAINSAWS. The Army Corps of Engineers has unexpectedly amassed a surplus supply of 200 19-inch chainsaws in top condition, and will give them free to the first 200 citizens who send a suitable self-addressed shipping carton with a request letter and postage, to the Army Corps of Engineers, Syracuse, NY."

Within a week, the Corps office was flooded with hundreds of large shipping crates and letters requesting "surplus chain saws." Nobody could figure out who had placed the ad, or why, but the event attracted national media attention. It was also a sensation in Hoffman's tiny community — everywhere people were talking about it.

That week, Hoffman repeated his doorknocking rounds. But this time, he had a different message. "What do you mean, nobody pays attention to you?" he asked. "What about those chainsaws? Look at the fuss you can make just by writing a few letters." That, of course, was the beginning of a potent citizens' group "Save the River" — and the beginning of the end for the Corps channel widening plans.

There's a lesson there for everyone: nothing brings a community to life like a tangible demonstration of its own latent power.

—Tim Redmond

The Reporter's Handbook
Investigative Reporters and Editors, Inc.
1983; 504 pp.
$16.95
($18.20 postpaid) from:
St. Martin's Press
Cash Sales Dept.
175 Fifth Avenue
New York, NY 10010
or Whole Earth Access

The Reporter's Handbook

Most good reporting starts when a reporter smells that something's wrong. But you don't have to be a professional reporter to follow your nose. Anyone can help stop a local abuse by tracking down the facts, but it often means an extended hunt down a trail of paper and interviews. This manual for following that trail is an encyclopedic directory in itself, listing dozens of documents, agencies, and reports that you might never hear about any other way. Put together by a group of experienced investigative journalists, it's one of the few college textbooks that's fun to read. —*Art Kleiner*

•

You're methodically researching your project on the ridiculously expensive monorail the county wants to build at the new zoo when your editor starts flailing his arms and hollering at you. The police desk has an update on a bust at a disco last night. It turns out they found in the back room 10 bales of marijuana, 20 kilos of cocaine and 100,000 Quaaludes. A Colombian citizen was among those arrested.

The cops are cooperating with the Drug Enforcement Administration, not with you. They're giving out nothing beyond the arrest sheets.

There are a hundred unanswered questions: Who owns the disco? What else does this person own — land, buildings, cars, boats, airplanes? What's the disco owner's economic background? Has the owner ever been accused of a crime? Does the owner use corporations to hide behind? Is there a limited partnership involved? Who are its investors? How much did they invest? Who's in business with this person?

Public records will answer every one of those questions for you in a few hours.

The Whole World Is Watching
Todd Gitlin
1980; 327 pp.
$9.95
($11.45 postpaid) from:
University of California Press
2120 Berkeley Way
Berkeley, CA 94720
or Whole Earth Access

The Whole World is Watching

Todd Gitlin is probably the country's second-best observer (after Abbie Hoffman) of how media manipulates, shapes, defines, and creates popular political movements — and how those movements can turn the relationship around. Nobody involved with politics at any level should be without this book. —*Tim Redmond*

•

An opposition movement is caught in a fundamental and inescapable dilemma. If it stands outside the dominant realm of discourse, it is liable to be consigned to marginality and political irrelevance; its issues are domesticated, its deeper challenge to the social order sealed off, trivialized, and contained. If, on the other hand, it plays by conventional political rules in order to acquire an image of credibility — if, that is, its leaders are well-mannered, its actions well-ordered, and its slogans specific and "reasonable" — it is liable to be assimilated into the hegemonic political world view; it comes to be identified with narrow (if important) reform issues, and its oppositional edge is blunted. This is the condition of movements in all the institutions of liberal capitalism; one major site of the difficulty lies within the mass media.

A look at the other photos UPI sent out that day to its subscribers, including the *Times*, throws the *Times'* choice into especially sharp relief. I retrieved the five other April 17 photos from UPI's archives. Two show a mass of antiwar pickets carrying signs bearing readable slogans . . . ; one shows a large mass at the antiwar rally at the Washington Monument; and the other two give an accurate sense of the degree to which the antiwar people outnumbered the counterdemonstrators. All five were, in formal terms, printable; the pictures of the picketers with their signs were elegantly composed, with high contrast and good formal balance. But the effect of the photo the *Times* chose was visually to equate the antiwar and right-wing demonstrations, and to give the impression — since the photographed segment of the two picket lines were identical in length — that they were equally large.

15,000 White House Pickets Denounce Vietnam

From the *New York Times*, Sunday, April 18, 1965, page 1.

Waste to Wealth

Waste to Wealth
Jon Huls and
Neil Seldman
1985; 109 pp.
$35
($36.50 postpaid) from:
ILSR
2425 18th Street NW
Washington, DC 20009

This is the most exciting of many publications from the Institute for Local Self-Reliance (p. 108). Taxpayers pay $10 billion a year for waste disposal — not counting the costs of cleaning up leaky landfills. ***Waste to Wealth*** *defends the 100 percent pollution-free alternative of finding ways to re-use garbage. Ground-up old tires (crumb rubber) become rubber products once again; recycled scrap plastic becomes virgin plastic for another loop of consumer use; discarded industrial oils fuel homes.*
—Peter Warshall

•

Scrap Tire Collection and Transfer

Tires are usually collected for a fee by junk dealers, recappers, and municipal waste collectors and then disposed at the local landfill. Recycling offers savings from disposal costs, but the crumb rubber manufacturing plant (CRMP) must take into account the cost of collection which is a major expense. While any variety of collection schemes can exist, it is probably best to (1) allow generators to collect and tip their scrap rubber at a set cost per tire at the CRMP or (2) levy a larger charge to pay for collection costs. For purposes of calculation, we will assume a charge for tipping at the CRMP; and that the CRMP does not have any collection equipment. Further, local market conditions will determine the charge per accepted tire.

Garbage Reincarnation

Garbage Reincarnation
Sonoma County Community Recycling Center
1982; 49 pp.
$5.95
postpaid from:
Sonoma County Community Recycling Center
P. O. Box 1375
Santa Rosa, CA 95402

This classroom manual on garbage recycling is the gem at the bottom of the trash heap and like all great "activity" books for kids, a book every adult will learn tons from. The authors are champions of human energy over the false application of high technology.
—Peter Warshall

•

Making a small scale replica of a *sanitary landfill* will give you a better understanding of what a *sanitary landfill* is and how it's made. You will experience some of the problems that must be dealt with by *landfill* operators when you see *subsidence* taking place and *leachate* being created right in your own *mini landfill*.

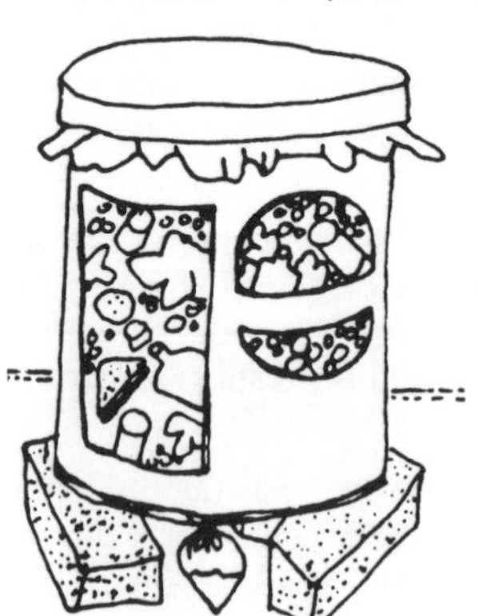

Profit from Pollution Prevention

Profit from Pollution Prevention
Monica E. Campbell
and William M. Glenn
1982; 404 pp.
$25
($26 postpaid) from:
Firefly Books
3520 Pharmacy Avenue
Unit 1-C
Scarborough, Ontario,
Canada M1W 2T8

Bucky Fuller said for years that pollution is just good stuff in the wrong place at the wrong time. This Canadian book offers hard evidence that not only can many pollutants be controlled but that the control can produce income. Experience has proven over and over that without economic incentive, polluters won't do much. Turns out that even with economic incentive, they won't be much inclined to do much until convinced. This book examines a host of common industrial polluting materials and practices. Alleviation tactics are discussed. For many nasties, successful case studies are presented. If you need to deal with a polluter, this book should be included in your homework.
—JB

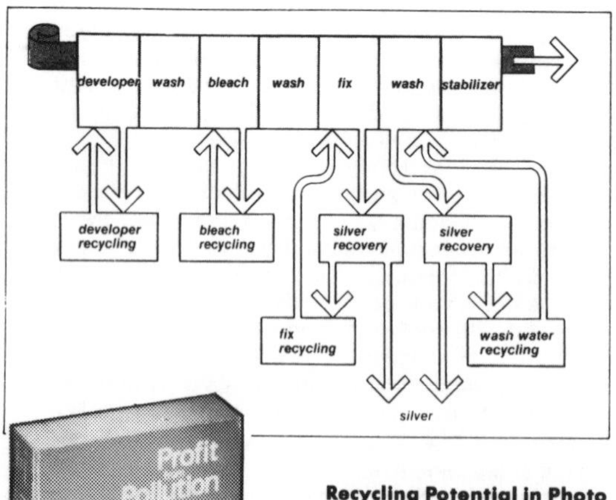

Recycling Potential in Photo Processing. Commercially available recycling equipment exists that makes it possible to re-use spent developer, bleach, bleach-fix and fix process solutions. Equipment is also available to recover the dilute amounts of silver present in the washwater after the fix bath.

High-Grade Magazines

BioCycle *is close to my feces-fertilizer-farm-food-feces revolving vision. It features my favorite Compost Guru, Clarence Golueke. I once thought their bumper sticker should read: "Have You Hugged Your Humus Today?" Herein, the creators of America's long-term wealth.*

Resource Recycling *focuses more on heavy metal; if they could, the editors would probably mine old landfills. For the moment, the magazine works closely with industrial producers exploring ways for the consumer and companies to both profit by reuse and waste reduction.*
—Peter Warshall

BioCycle: Jerome Goldstein, Editor. **$43**/year (10 issues) from BioCycle, Box 351, Emmaus, PA 18049.

Resource Recyling: Jerry Powell, Editor. **$20**/year (7 issues) from Resource Recycling Magazine, P. O. Box 10540, Portland, OR 97210.

To Burn or Not to Burn

Modern incineration plants require a guaranteed volume of garbage, squeezing competitive recycling operations out of the market. They also produce toxic gases and a residue ash which must often be buried in hazardous waste landfills. The ILSR (see above) and the Environmental Defense Fund (see p. 87) are the groups most informed. EDF's ***To Burn or Not to Burn*** *does a thorough and instructive cost-benefit comparison of garbage burning and recycling for New York City.* *—David Finacom*

To Burn or Not to Burn: Dan Kirshner, Adam C. Stern, 1985; 101 pp. **$20** postpaid from Environmental Defense Fund, 444 Park Avenue South, New York, NY 10016.

• A computer network for recyclers.

RecycleNet: Modem (609) 641-9418; 300 Baud, 8 data bits, 1 stop bit, no parity; Factsheet **$1** from Association of New Jersey Recyclers, P. O. Box 625, Abescon, NJ 08201.

• **Worldwatch Papers**, number 23, 36, and 56 (p. 92) give the global overview.

Love Canal

Lois Gibbs describes herself — "before Love Canal" — as a typical "dumb housewife," preoccupied with raising her children, keeping a tidy house, and pursuing her hobbies. In December 1977, three months after her son started kindergarten, he developed epilepsy and a lowered white blood count. Soon afterward, she read in the local paper that her son's school had been built on an abandoned chemical dump, where Hooker Chemical and Plastics Corporation had dumped over 43 million pounds of toxic industrial wastes before selling the site to the school board for one dollar. Mrs. Gibbs' battle to transfer her son to another school grew into all-out war against local, state, and federal governments, resulting in national publicity and — finally — a federal order to relocate some one thousand families whose homes had become deathtraps. The Love Canal battle alerted the nation to the hazards of thousands of toxic time bombs hidden across the country by negligent, unscrupulous industries.
—Carol Van Strum

•

Be careful you don't step in any goop." We showed him some of the holes. He got a sinus headache from the walk across the canal. He said he felt it immediately. As we went across the canal, we found one of those black holes that is so deep that you can't get a stick to the bottom of it. You pull the stick out and see black gunk its entire length.

We showed him the barrel that was coming to the surface right near Debbie Cerrillo's swimming pool and the hole with the black gunk in her yard. Pete Bulka lived next door to Debbie. Pete had been complaining to the City of Niagra Falls for a long time, but nothing was ever done. Pete explained how his sump pump had to be replaced every few months because it corroded. The county health commissioner wanted to cap everyone's sump pump because they were pumping chemicals from the canal into the storm sewers and then into the Niagra River. He acted as if it were the citizens' fault that they were pumping poison into the river, that it was better that it just stayed in people's basements.

Love Canal
Lois Marie Gibbs
as told to Murray Levine
1982; 174 pp.
$6.95
($8.45 postpaid) from:
Grove Press
Order Dept.
196 West Houston Street
New York, NY 10014
or Whole Earth Access

Hazardous Waste in America

The compendium of information about the particular components of the 80 billion pounds of hazardous waste materials generated annually by American industries — 350 pounds per year for each inhabitant of the U.S. The book includes a directory of 8000 toxic dumps located in all 50 states; a field guide to locating undisclosed waste sites; a selection of case studies of toxic dumps and their tragic human toll; an excellent "citizen's legal guide to hazardous wastes"; and an intelligent, emphatic discussion of the political, legal, practical, and philosophical solutions to a toxic nightmare that is all too real.
—Carol Van Strum

The cream of the crap, so to speak. —Peter Warshall

•

Some wastes are effectively *immortal;* their toxic qualities are intrinsic to their elemental structure. The heavy metals are in this category, and, in a different sense, so is asbestos, whose toxicity is a function of its physical structure, which, for practical purposes, is indestructible. Some radioactive wastes, particularly uranium and plutonium, retain their radioactive properties for so long that we should also view them as immortal.

A second group of wastes is *semi-mortal.* Destruction or degradation occurs in the environment, but very slowly. Chlorinated hydrocarbons, especially complex ones, are *semi-mortal* in natural environments, but can be destroyed in high-temperature incinerators.

A third group of toxics is very short-lived or *mortal,* including acids and bases and other strongly reactive materials like cyanides, which are rapidly destroyed or neutralized in the environment.

Citizen's Clearinghouse for Hazardous Waste

Founded by Lois "Love Canal" Gibbs. Assists grassroots struggles about waste dumps. "Organize" is their battle cry and they're the best. ***Everyone's Backyard*** *is their quarterly. CCHW's* ***Action Bulletin*** *covers the nation. Good reviews and access. A wonderful spirit of hope and rightful action exudes from their clamoring. Just what tons of toxic goop requires. —Peter Warshall*

Citizen's Clearinghouse for Hazardous Waste: Membership **$15**/year (includes 4 issues of **Everyone's Backyard** and periodic **Action Bulletins**) from Citizens Clearinghouse for Hazardous Waste, P. O. Box 926, Arlington, VA 22216.

Biohazards: Concerned Groups

Federation of Homemakers, Inc. *The homemaker bloodhounds that sniff out poisonous hanky-panky in foods, drugs, and cosmetics. To protect their families they police the FDA. The group where Ralph Nader seeks advice.*

Membership **$10**/year (includes 4 issues of their newsletter) from Federation of Homemakers, Inc., P. O. Box 5571, Arlington, VA 22205.

Environmental Action. *The national political lobby that created Earth Day. Coordinated efforts on the Clean Air Act, Clean Water Act, Occupational and Safety Act, Toxic Substances Control Act, etc. Best magazine.*

Membership **$20**/year (includes 6 issues of **Environmental Action**) from Environmental Action, 1525 New Hampshire Avenue NW, Washington, DC 20036.

National Coalition Against the Misuse of Pesticides (NCAMP). *Be it insecticide, herbicide, rodenticide, or fungicide, NCAMP has the long and short of it. A broad-spectrum coalition (farmers, churches, labor, health, homemakers and politicos) who stress less damaging alternatives like Integrated Pest Management* *(see p. 81).* ***Pesticides and You*** *is their most potent newsletter.*

Membership **$10**/year (includes 5 issues of **Pesticides and You**) from NCAMP, 530 Seventh Street SE, Washington, DC 20003.

Society for Occupational and Environmental Health. *The academic neutral forum has conferences with papers like "Sperm Count Suppression in Lead-Exposed Men" and "Spontaneous Abortion and Type of Work." Mainly for higher income brackets, but their knowledge is a powerful aid to all workers who contract an occupational disease.*

Membership **$50**/year (includes 6 issues of **The Archives of Environmental Health Journal** and 4 issues of the SOEH **Letter**) from Society for Occupational and Environmental Health, 2021 K Street NW, Suite 305, Washington, DC 20006.

Northwest Coalition for Alternatives to Pesticides (NCAP). *More action. NCAP takes the broadest political overview of pesticides on the planet. Their muckraking is a bit too anxious to get me bloody scared, but they're here to inform and help and they do it well. Publishes* ***Journal of Pesticide Reform*** *and great info on herbicide spraying in forests.*

Membership **$12**/year (includes 4 issues of **Journal of Pesticide Reform**) from Northwest Coalition for Alternatives to Pesticides, P. O. Box 1393, Eugene, OR 97440.
—Peter Warshall

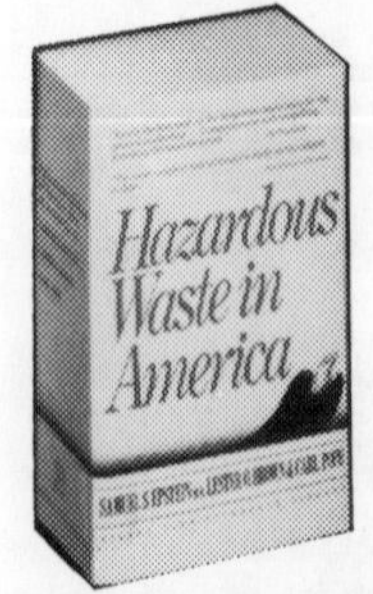

Hazardous Waste in America
Samuel S. Epstein, M.D.,
Lester O. Brown, Carl Pope
1982; 593 pp.
$12.95
($15.45 postpaid) from:
Sierra Club Books
730 Polk Street
San Francisco, CA 94109
or Whole Earth Access

LURKING FOR YEARS
IN CORPORATE
BOARDROOMS,
IT HAD TO
COME OUT...
IN YOUR
BILLS!!
RATE
$HOCK
PRODUCED AND DIRECTED BY RED E. KILOWATT
STARRING JOE & JANE CONSUMER
NOW PLAYING AT A UTILITY NEAR YOU!
RATED
PSCG
PSC GUIDANCE SUGGESTED

—Environmental Action

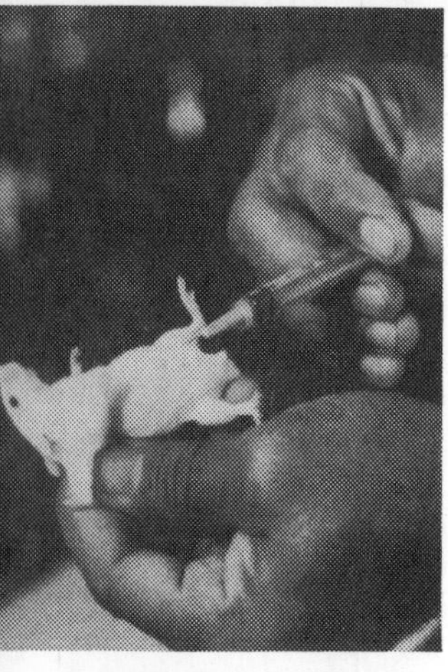

Remarkably curious, intelligent, sensitive and gentle — both to humans and to one another, rodents feel as much pain and fear as any dog or guinea pig. Their friends are few however, and no laws protect them from abuse.
—PETA

OUR GROWING UNDERSTANDING of evolution has eroded much of the artificial separation between "human" and "animal," making it increasingly difficult to ignore the suffering of nonhumans bent to human purpose in agribusiness "animal factories" and biomedical research labs. Today the moral philosophers of our nation's universities regularly debate the animal rights question in an abundance of books and journals devoted to the topic, while less patient activists break into animal experimentation labs to free the victims and publicize their abusive treatment.

Opinions may vary on where to draw the line in considering the needs and rights of nonhuman animals, but the growing number of animal rights activists agree that we must extend some degree of compassion to our fellow inhabitants of planet Earth.
—Ted Schultz

Animal Liberation

This powerful and meticulously reasoned book is credited with sparking the recent animal rights movement in America. Not simply a documentation of ill treatment, it is also a skillfully presented case for animal protection.

All of the chemical products we use, from cosmetics to oven cleaner, are tested on living animals. Death for these animals comes after days, weeks, or even months of pain. Factory farms are equally bad; millions of calves, chickens, and other animals spend their lives in tiny cages just larger than their bodies. The factory farms and laboratory horrors Singer exposed ten years ago remain prevalent.

Copies of ***Animal Liberation*** *are being left inside laboratories — not on the bookshelves, but in empty cages, replacing animals liberated by raiders in the night.*
—Bradley Miller

•

The core of this book is the claim that to discriminate against beings solely on account of their species is a form of prejudice, immoral and indefensible in the same way that discrimination on the basis of race is immoral and indefensible. . . .

Animal Liberation
Peter Singer
1975; 297 pp.
$4.95
($5.95 postpaid) from:
Avon Books
P. O. Box 767
Dresden, TN 38225
or Whole Earth Access

The Animals' Agenda

The Animals' Agenda *is a must for anyone interested in keeping up to date on animal rights. Independent of any particular animal organization, the magazine freely explores the issues and controversies behind the headlines, and offers a unique and open forum for participation to all parties concerned.* *—Bradley Miller*

•

Karen, 38, a health care worker in a large eastern city, is one of the members of the Animal Liberation Front who broke into the Head Injury Clinical Research Center at the University of Pennsylvania in May 1984. In the most widely-publicized break-in of its kind, the ALF stole more than 60 hours of videotapes of experiments and initiated an exhaustive campaign that led ultimately to the Center's closing.

The Animals' Agenda
Jim Mason, Editor
$18/year
(10 issues) from:
Animals' Agenda
P. O. Box 5234
Westport, CT 06881

Faroese men load headless pilot whales onto truck for distribution around the islands. Sea Shepherd Conservation Society is working to prevent such slaughter.

Here's where the action is:

People for the Ethical Treatment of Animals (PETA):

The vanguard of the animal rights movement. These gutsy and articulate activists have made the name PETA synonymous with "landmark victory." In five short years this group has developed a track record which puts most older and wealthier organizations to shame. Saving laboratory animals has been their focus. PETA is directly responsible for halting numerous government-funded animal experiments. *—Bradley Miller*

People for the Ethical Treatment of Animals: membership **$20** (includes quarterly newsletter; information **free** from PETA, P. O. Box 42516, Washington, DC 20015.

Humane Farming Association (HFA)

Expanding the boundaries of animal protection, HFA is spearheading a campaign against the intense confinement and brutal treatment of farm animals.
—Bradley Miller

Humane Farming Association: membership **$10** (includes quarterly newsletter); information **free** from 1550 California Street/Suite 6, San Francisco, CA 94109.

The Fund for Animals

If someone is threatening to make dog food out of wild horses in Nevada . . . call the Fund for Animals.
—Bradley Miller

The Fund for Animals: membership **$15** (includes quarterly newsletter); information **free** from 200 West 57th Street, New York, NY 10019.

International Primate Protection League (IPPL)

The murder of IPPL advisor Diane Fossey is but one tragic example of the risks primate protectors face. Harassed by lawsuits from chimpanzee dealers and threats of violence from black market smugglers, IPPL continues its valiant struggle to protect the Earth's primate species. They also run a sanctuary for primates rescued from abusive institutions. *—Bradley Miller*

International Primate Protection League: membership **$10** (includes quarterly newsletter); information **free** from IPPL, P. O. Box 766, Summerville, SC 29484.

Buddhists Concerned for Animals

If you hang around Buddhists all day, by and by you hear yourself making an interesting pair of statements:

"Sentient beings are numberless."

"I vow to save them." *—Stewart Brand*

Buddhists Concerned for Animals: membership **$10** (includes quarterly newsletter); information **free** from 300 Page Street, San Francisco, CA 94102.

This community is Stelle, Illinois. A closer look at Stelle reveals that it is very different from a typical suburban community. It was started in 1973 by Richard Kieninger — a man who rejects traditional religion and says that he was directed to build his city by invisible "Brotherhoods" in preparation for a doomsday in the year 2,000 that would destroy 90 percent of humanity.

Communities

These days communes are not what they used to be. To find out what they are becoming, read this journal, which has been around as long as the oldest ongoing commune has. —Kevin Kelly

•

The benefits of collective economies have included not only economic security within the group and insurance in the labor of one's brothers and sisters against illness, injury and old age. They have been full employment, work lightened by comradery, rotation in jobs to avoid boredom and to learn new skills, and involvement with technology on a human scale.

•

The Illusion of Utopia
Two thousand years of experimentation have proven communal societies ineffective in the attempt to realize a general utopia. From the Jewish Essene monastic community on the shore of the Dead Sea a century and a half before Christ to the Chinese People's Communes which were abandoned in 1982, both voluntary and involuntary communitarianism have been frustrating routes to utopia.

•

Twin Oaks permits the accumulation of labor credits by individual members. This means that I can work 55 hours one week, say, instead of the required 48, and bank the extra 7 until I want to use them for vacation. I can take my vacation either here on the farm or elsewhere. In either case the vacation time I've earned by working "over quota" is in addition to the 2½ weeks the community gives every member each year outright. The average Twin Oaker by these means takes 7 weeks of vacation per year.

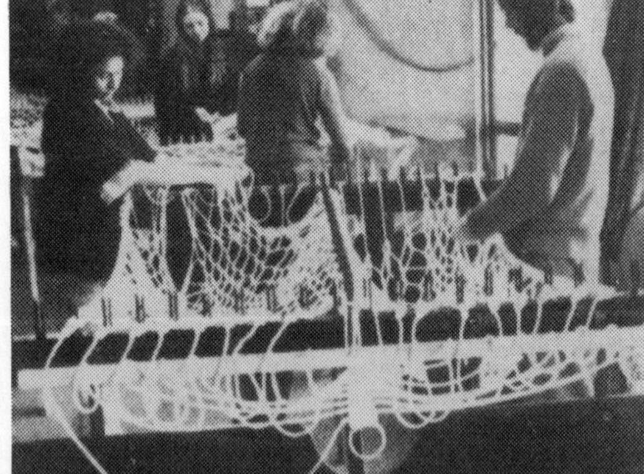

Making hammocks at Twin Oaks.

Communities
Charles Betterton, Editor
$12/yr. (4 issues)
from:
Communities
Journal of Cooperation
105 Sun Street
Stelle, IL 60919

Community Referral Service

A) Communities seeking new members publish their circumstances in this complete directory. B) Potential members seeking to join an established commune can shop for a suitable one. C) Those searching for other commune-bent individuals connect up. Friendly service. —Kevin Kelly

The New Age Community Guidebook
Bobbi Corcoran, Editor
1985; 112 pp.
$8 postpaid from:
Community
Referral Service
P. O. Box 2672
Eugene, OR 97402

Builders of the Dawn

This comprehensive gathering of interviews, guidelines, and analyses proves that experience more than theory is designing the current evolution of American communes. Pass through this accumulated advice first if you are headed for an intentional community. Dwell here if you intended to manage one. —Kevin Kelly

•

Another problem is the astounding amount of bureaucracy needed at Twin Oaks to operate its labor credit system fairly. Its government is more centralized than it needs to be, according to some members. "If you want something here," member Martha commented, "there are a million committees to go through."

•

Some comparisons: '60s Communes/'80s Communities

1960s

- Freedom and "doing your own thing" most important value; "laying a trip" on someone is a cardinal sin
- Few rules, restrictions, or expectations; largely unstructured; "work only if you feel like it"; spontaneity highly valued
- Mainly alternative lifestyle and values — drugs, rock and roll, "free sex"
- Non-exclusive; usually anyone with same lifestyle can join
- Visitors not always requested to contribute money or labor; no formal guest programs
- Return to a romanticized rural past; rejection of technology; few communication links with society
- Return to innocence of childhood; rejection of responsibility

1980s

- Cooperation with others and "the good of the whole" important; everyone needs to contribute his/her share; erratic behavior less acceptable
- Agreed-upon rules and expectations; fairly structured work and financial requirements
- Variation in lifestyle in different communities — ranging from alternative to middle-class professional
- More restrictive about membership — must be harmonious with group and committed to group's purpose
- Visitors usually requested to contribute money and/or labor; more structured guest programs
- Closeness to nature highly valued, but appropriate technology also welcomed; more communication links with society (telephone, TV, radio, some computers)
- Generally more mature and reponsible adult attitudes; valuing some balance of playfulness, although sometimes too serious

Builders of the Dawn
Corrine McLaughlin and Gordon Davidson
1985; 372 pp.
$12.95
($14.70 postpaid) from:
Stillpoint Publishing
P. O. Box 640
Meetinghouse Road
Walpole, NH 03608
or Whole Earth Access

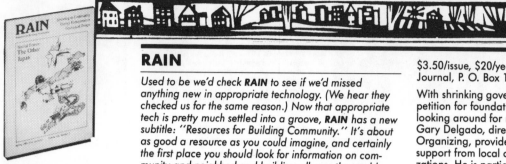

RAIN
F. Lansing Scott, Editor
$18/year
(4 issues) from:
RAIN
1135 SE Salmon
Portland, OR 97214

RAIN

*Used to be we'd check **RAIN** to see if we'd missed anything new in appropriate technology. (We hear they checked us for the same reason.) Now that appropriate tech is pretty much settled into a groove, **RAIN** has a new subtitle: "Resources for Building Community." It's about as good a resource as you could imagine, and certainly the first place you should look for information on community and neighborhood building all over the world. The new staff carries on the **RAIN** tradition of accurate, proven information presented with erudite commentary.* —JB

"Raising Money from Churches," by Gary Delgado, *Grassroots Fundraising Journal*, February 1986, $3.50/issue, $20/year from: Grassroots Fundraising Journal, P. O. Box 14754, San Francisco, CA 94114

With shrinking government resources and intense competition for foundation dollars, many nonprofits are looking around for new sources of support. In this article Gary Delgado, director of the Center for Third World Organizing, provides a basic introduction to securing support from local churches and national church organizations. He is particularly effective in spelling out what you need to know and do at each stage in the process. The article also provides access information on related publications and some national church funding resources. This seven-page article is the best guide I have seen for community groups exploring church support for the first time.

Institute for Community Economics
Information **free**

Community Land Trust Handbook
1982; 224 pp.
$6
($7.05 postpaid)
Both from:
ICE
151 Montague City Road
Greenfield, MA 01301
or Whole Earth Access

Institute for Community Economics (ICE)

*ICE helps local groups form community land trusts. In Dallas, Texas, 11 neighborhood groups have banded together to buy up vacant urban lots. Houses scheduled for demolition are moved onto the lots. The land trust owns the lots; individuals own the houses and lease the land. This keeps the land off of the speculative real estate market so that the only increases in price are from inflation or improvements to the houses. Result: affordable housing for low-income people. The **Handbook** explains how to do it in your neighborhood.* —Richard Nilsen

•

To most people, *private* is a very attractive word. It is strongly associated with the privacy and security of the home. However, much private land in America is not owned by people who live on it. Most land today is concentrated in the hands of a relatively small part of the population (75 percent of the privately held land in America is owned by 5 percent of the private landholders). And absentee ownership is increasingly common.

Grading Old Houses

As mentioned in Chapter 8, the Cedar Riverside PAC, with the help of a local contractor, developed a system for grading the condition of old houses. It was used to determine which houses were worth rehabilitating, and serves as a starting point for more specific redevelopment planning. The point system used in the evaluation sheet was designed specifically for the Cedar Riverside situation and may need to be modified for other localities.

	GRADING Good	Fair	Poor
A. STRUCTURAL			
1. Foundation	20	10	0
2. Windows	15	10	0
3. Siding	10	7	4
4. Roof/soffets	10	7	2
B. MECHANICAL			
1. Heating	10	7	2
2. Electrical	10	7	7
3. Plumbing	10	7	2
C. DESIGN/INTERIOR CONDITION			
1. Floor plan	7	6	5
2. Ingress/egress	7	6	5
3. Wall surfaces	10	7	2
D. SITE	7	6	5

Range:

Poor	*34 to 75*	Fair+	*90 to 95*
Fair−	*76 to 82*	Good−	*96 to 100*
Fair	*83 to 89*	Good	*101 to 106*
		Good+	*107 to 116*

Going Co-op

*If my group of 14 aspiring homeowners had read this book before we purchased the seven-unit apartment building we turned into a co-op a few years back, we would have saved a lot of time and energy. **Going Co-op** is a solid, readable, nuts-and-bolts introduction to creating your own housing cooperative: selecting and financing the building; working out the legalities; keeping things democratic; and setting group policies, for example, the crucial issue of buying in and selling out. It includes a sample set of co-op bylaws (very important) and a sample occupancy agreement (even more important). I just wish the coauthors had placed more emphasis on the fact that even the best of contracts don't hold co-ops together — friendships do.* —Michael Castleman

•

A co-op is assessed property taxes as a single building. In many cities this means co-ops pay lower taxes than condominiums, because condominium units are assessed individually.

Co-op members may also be eligible for the personal income tax deductions enjoyed by other homeowners. They are allowed to take their share of the deductions for the co-op's mortgage interest and property taxes. For many co-op members, this may mean a net reduction of 10 to 30 percent of their monthly housing costs.

Sample Co-op Income Statement

ALWAYS COOPERATIVE
Statement of Income and Expenses
For the Year Ended December 31, 1982

Income	
Gross potential carrying charges	$80,735
Less: Vacancies	1,948
Net carrying charges	$78,787
Parking	2,065
Interest	491
Laundry	412
Other income	300
Total income	$82,055

Expenses	
Gas	$ 2,249
Electricity	5,499
Water	798
Payroll	371
Repair and maintenance	2,510
Supplies	767
Depreciation	29,160
Real estate tax	16,625
Interest expense	18,269
Insurance	8,012
Management fee	4,850
Administrative expense	275
Total expense	$89,415
Net Income (Loss)	($ 7,360)

Going Co-op
William Couglan, Jr. and Monte Franke
1983; 249 pp.
$9.95
($11.45 postpaid) from:
Harper and Row
2350 Virginia Avenue
Hagerstown, MD 21740
or Whole Earth Access

Institute for Local Self-Reliance (ILSR)

ILSR's goal: self-reliant urban communities that can generate income from within rather than suck from the resource tits of rural communities. They've established a good reputation in waste-recycling (see p. 106) and they're active in other areas as well. —Peter Warshall

Institute for Local Self-Reliance
Membership **$35**/year
Publications list **free**

Both from:
ILSR
2425 18th St. NW
Washington, DC 20009

• A monthly listing of community jobs and internships. **Community Jobs:** David Guttchen, Editor. $12/year (12 issues) from 1319 18th Street NW, Washington, DC 20036.

• The whole fleamarket schtick, plus a directory of where they are. **Flea Market America:** Cree McCree, 1983; 180 pp. **$8.50** postpaid from W. W. Norton, 500 Fifth Avenue, New York, NY 10110.

• For information on conservation land trusts, see p. 86.

• See p. 89 for more on self-reliance.

Downtown Thermopolis, Wyoming, contains a wealth of historic structures such as the Klink Block that can be renovated to ensure many more years of useful life.
—Small Town

The Small Community

People could probably have very interesting times, lifetimes, even, following the precepts laid out in this good old (vintage 1942) book. There are definite ways and means of developing community, it says — certain things are known, and there are rules to play by.

Author Arthur Morgan wrote forthrightly, with a (now) rare sense of assurance about his values. Indeed, his elegant sense of honor seems quite out of place amid the pragmatisms, corruptions, and complications of our time. But his straightforward aspiration to human greatness, democratic practice, fine culture, and high ideals, coupled with the belief that these aspirations can best be fulfilled in the small community, makes resoundingly good sense.

Because the creation of that context is of such great importance, Morgan provides a spare but definitive guidebook. He covers a lot of ground, talking about the appropriate scale of communities, economic self-reliance, skills banks, the importance and liabilities of regional planning, and provision for the community welfare, among many other topics. The only problem is that it all adds up to working in groups, which might tear us away from our VCRs and other toys. —Stephanie Mills

I would call this book a recipe for civilization.
—Kevin Kelly

•

Selfishness nearly always is organized in the community. Unless unselfishness and public interest also can be organized, they can have little chance.

•

Where community life is dissolved and the only remaining sense of social identity is with vast societies, such as great nations, serious-minded young people who wish to be socially effective often measure their small powers against national or world movements, and develop a feeling of frustration and futility. On the other hand, where they are members of small communities they have opportunities to deal with problems within their grasp. They can be realists and can be effective within the community, and so can have a feeling of validity denied them when their primary relations are to vast social aggregations.

•

Young people look about them, half-consciously wondering what kind of world it is into which they are born. If they see favoritism and political manipulation, with the best people of the community timidly unwilling to expose themselves by vigorous political activity, the young people of the community will have learned their lesson. Their school textbooks may discuss civic righteousness, but they will know that is only make-believe. The realities are before their eyes. They will be convinced that they live in a world of arbitrariness, favoritism, and special interests, and that they must be like the world they are in. On the other hand, whenever young people see integrity and a businesslike attitude in business management, they are likely to decide that the world they live in is like that, and they will act accordingly.

The Small Community
Arthur E. Morgan
1984; 313 pp.
$10
($11 postpaid) from:
Community Service, Inc.
P. O. Box 243
Yellow Springs, OH 45387
or Whole Earth Access

Small Town

A little magazine bound to be useful to any community large enough to have a town hall. It's about character, controlled growth, and planning. —Stewart Brand

•

One proposal, funded with a grant through the Wyoming Main Street Program, provided a 50% match for design costs incurred by merchants engaged in restorations. This approach gave merchants enough incentive to hire professional assistance, but simultaneously committed them to complete the project. Since the merchants paid 50% of the design costs, little public outcry occurred concerning the use of grant funds.

Small Town
Kenneth Munsell, Editor
$30/year
(6 issues) from:
Small Towns Institute
P. O. Box 517
Ellensburg, WA 98926

The Barter Network Handbook

Another one of those slightly fusty do-gooder manuals, but the subject is one that, like open-air farmers' markets and (sometimes) recycling centers, can do a lot to connect a community. Sometimes you barter goods, but mostly people barter services; either way, you leave the IRS out of it. Village economics in an urban world, self-rewarding.
—Stewart Brand

•

Tom Glynn, assistant to the commissioner of the IRS, has conceded that many of the informal barter arrangements that take place between friends and neighbors carry no tax liability, since they fall into the category of "favors." . . . The IRS has ruled that members of barter "clubs," who receive credits valued at $1 each for services they perform, must report them as income when they are received, even though they may not make use of them until a later time. Credits possessing no monetary or "time-spent" income, however, have not been covered by any IRS rulings to date.

The Barter Network Handbook
David Tobin and Henry Ware
1983; 69 pp.
$5.95
($9.45 postpaid) from:
Volunteer Readership
1111 North 19th Street
Arlington, VA 22209
or Whole Earth Access

PLANNERS SEEM TO BE getting better at tempering idealism — not by selling out, but by developing environmentally and socially effective designs that can attract financiers. Don't lose hope yet! —J. Baldwin

How the Other Half Builds

How The Other Half Builds
Witold Rybczynski et al.
1984; 89 pp.

$6.00
($8.00 Canadian)
postpaid from:
Center for
Minimum Cost Housing
3550 University Street
Montreal, Quebec
H3A 2A7, Canada
or Whole Earth Access

"Existing informal sector housing, often termed slums, represents a solution rather than a problem." This is a radical concept to many theoretical low-income housing planners, but not to its author, Witold Rybczynski; he's well-known for puncturing the ineffectual arguments of self-righteous do-gooders. The basic premise is simple: In order to determine what to plan as housing for the poor, find out what they need; to find out what they need, go see what they've done without the aid of planners. You'd think this would go without saying, but planners often are blinded by class differences and elitist educations. This paper should help, and not just in less-developed areas of the world. The idea that the people can handle a lot of their own needs should be a major premise of any democratic society.

This paper is the first of a series. The second part should be available as you read this. —*JB*

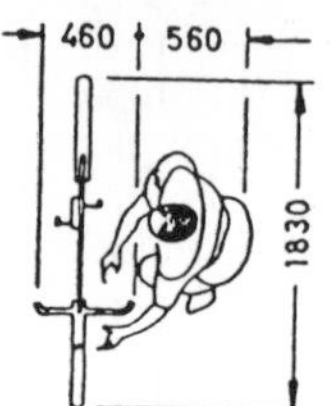

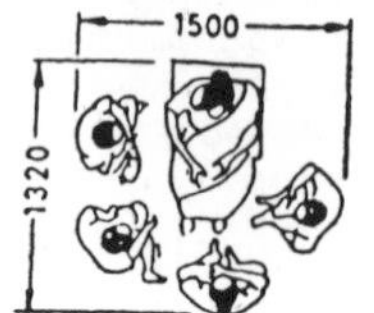

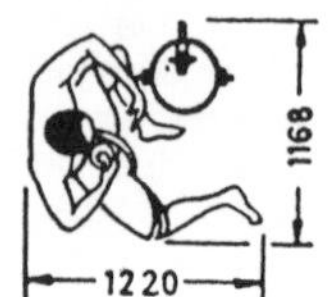

Recommended dimensions of spaces for human activity.

•

The priorities of the slum-dweller are frequently not those of the municipal authorities. Space takes precedence over permanence. A porch may be built before a bathroom; a work place may be more important than a private bedroom. The apparent inversion of values is especially evident in the public spaces. Whereas planned sites and services projects usually incorporate rudimentary, minimal circulation spaces, the public areas of slums are characterized by richness and diversity.

Historic Preservation • Preservation News

National Trust For Historic Preservation
Membership

$15
(includes subscriptions to *Historic Preservation* and *Preservation News*) from:
National Trust for
Historic Preservation
1785 Massachusetts
Avenue NW
Washington, DC 20036

It may be ironic, but the best hope for preserving wonderful old buildings — conservation — is innovation. Imaginative new uses for the aging structures plus creative methods of finance are what it takes. Confrontation and emotional hassling don't usually work. The sophisticated techniques of preservation are discussed, in color, in the bimonthly ***Historic Preservation*** *magazine. News from the front lines arrives in the monthly* ***Preservation News****. Both come with a membership in the lively National Trust for Historic Preservation.* —*JB*

•

The effect of letting the real estate market do as it pleases is to be far less conservative in the long run. What, in the final analysis, do conservatives really wish to conserve? At a time in which there is no real social contract so far as building is concerned, no real community of values in the urban environment, the laissez-faire city is not likely to be the civilized city. It is more likely to be the overbuilt city, the tense, dark, harsh city, the city whose lack of grace should be far more threatening to the values of a true conservative.

Displacement

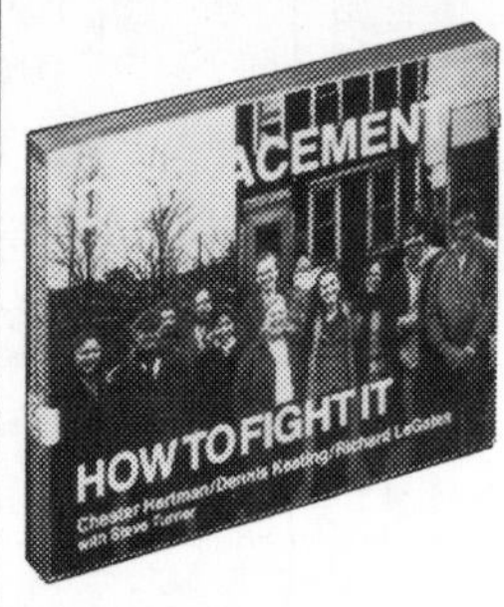

Displacement
Chester Hartman,
Dennis Keating, and
Richard LeGates
1982; 224 pp.

$10 postpaid from:
National Housing
Law Project
2150 Shattuck Ave.
No. 300
Berkeley, CA 94704

One of Atlantic City's proposed casinos purchased an entire block for their project. A lone resident refused to sell, even after an offer of over $1 million, plus lifetime free residence in the new hotel. After she turned the offer down, construction went ahead around her.

Few experiences provoke as much frustration, outrage, and even grief as being forced to move. It's distressingly common — 2.5 million U.S. residents are displaced from their homes and neighborhoods each year. It's happened to me and many people I know. Written by a nationwide team of community lawyers and organizers, ***Displacement*** *describes all the methods by which you could be thrown out of your house — evictions, condo conversions, rent hikes, arson, and mortgage foreclosures just for starters — and the (mostly) legal methods for fighting back. (Sometimes the government eventually learns it's cheaper to give illegal squatters their occupied houses than to keep them empty.) Individuals about to lose their homes should look here, but the book is really about building and maintaining neighborhoods. It will instruct you in the legal hassling which is unfortunately necessary to keep a neighborhood intact.* —*Art Kleiner*

•

In places with no or weak laws regulating condo conversions, negotiating with the converter is an important tactic. Concessions won this way are nothing to be sneezed at. They might include lowering the sales price for all units, paying moving costs and relocation bonuses, extending time for tenants to move, or even reserving some units for low- and moderate-income tenants.

Negotiating for concessions is actually another term for squeezing the converter's profits. It's possible — even though many of the concessions listed above are quite costly to the developer — since speed is one of the important factors in the most lucrative forms of conversion. The converter's objective is to sell all the units in a building as quickly as possible and move on, tying up borrowed capital as briefly as possible. So substantial concessions often will be made simply to avoid delays.

• Two founders of the New Alchemy Institute (p. 89) make some interesting urban proposals based on the Institute's work. **Bioshelters, Ocean Arks, City Farming** (Ecology as the Basis of Design): Nancy Jack Todd and John Todd, 1984; 210 pp. **$10.95** ($13.45 postpaid) from Sierra Club Bookstore, 730 Polk Street, San Francisco, CA 94109 (or Whole Earth Access).

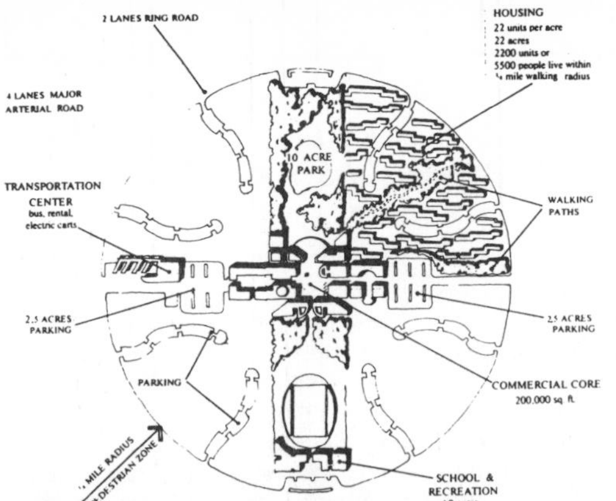

Sustainable Communities

"Sustainability implies that the use of energy and materials in an urban area be in balance with what the region can supply continuously through natural processes such as photosynthesis, biological decomposition and the biochemical processes that support life. The immediate implications of this principle are a vastly reduced energy budget for cities, and a smaller, more compact urban pattern interspersed with productive areas to collect energy, grow crops for food, fiber and energy, and recycle wastes."

How this concept is to be implemented is what this book is about. It isn't just talk; there are case studies and lots of eminently practical ideas here, complete with the economics. The call to action is backed philosophically by seven essays from authors such as Paul Hawken and John Todd. Solid and timely, the book is a recipe for what we can and probably must do. —JB

The Village Center proposal is a direct descendant of the "neighborhood school planning" dogma which dominated surburban planning a generation ago. Then, the key concept was to locate neighborhoods around a half mile walking radius of the elementary school. Today, education and other key consumer services may form the core for new pedestrian oriented energy efficient communities.

Sustainable Communities
Sim Van der Ryn
and Peter Calthorpe
1986; 238 pp.
$25
($29.50 postpaid) from:
Sierra Club Bookstore
730 Polk Street
San Francisco, CA 94109
or Whole Earth Access

Livable Cities

All over the U.S.A., deteriorating neighborhoods and even entire towns are being revitalized. And not necessarily by displacing the people living there either. How is this being done? By people getting together! Lots of successful war stories and the winning tactics and strategies are presented here with a voice in keeping with the subject: positive, tough, competent, and experienced. Good hopeful reading for people who want to get control of their neighborhood's destiny. This is all easily read, too — a pleasure! —JB

•

Community activists should also *beware of constructive alternatives*. Sometimes, the enemy, seeing he is about to be defeated, tries to turn the tables on you and says, "All right, if you're so smart, tell us what to do." Be careful how you handle this situation. It's not your role to tell the sanitation department how to pick up the garbage; all you care about is that they pick it up regularly. Don't fall into the trap of trying to do the enemy's job. Let the enemy solve his own problems. Concentrate instead on making sure he meets your demands.

•

The only foolproof way to prevent families from being displaced is to have them own their homes, either individually or through a neighborhood corporation. There are a number of ways this can be done. All the methods described previously in this book to help families obtain low-cost home improvement loans and mortgages — rehabilitation financing schemes, revolving loan funds, homesteading programs, sweat equity, low-down-payment mortgages, rebate programs, and so on — serve to keep the original residents in their homes at prices they can afford.

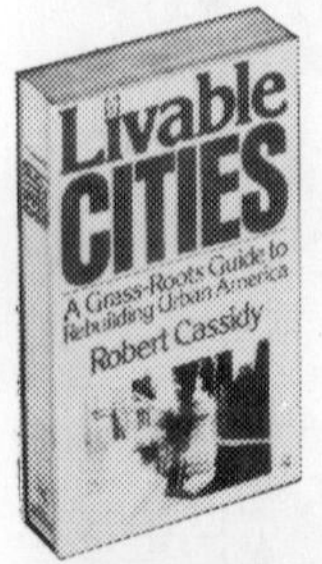

Livable Cities
Robert Cassidy
1980; 340 pp.
$8.95
($10.95 postpaid) from:
Henry Holt & Co.
521 5th Avenue, 12th floor
New York, NY 10175
or Whole Earth Access

Livable Streets

We all know that "we gotta do something about all these cars," but what's to be done? This book is divided into two parts: the first is an exhaustive (so to speak) study of the effects of traffic on the denizens of 21 San Francisco streets; part two chronicles the history of an attempt to change traffic patterns in Berkeley for the better. That politically tumultuous move is compared to a similar effort in England. Theory meets reality in both cases. Interesting, instructive, and fortunately easy to read. Highly recommended for car-haters. —JB

•

What happens on the street where there is little or no traffic was studied by Zerner in a number of cul-de-sacs in San Francisco. Such is the power of the automobile on our thinking that these streets are called "dead end" streets, when of all the streets in the city they are the most alive with children. They come from all over the neighborhood to those rare, protected places. In fact, they are so rare that a street like Shotwell becomes overloaded with children.

Before and after drawings showing the transformation of a conventional street into a woonerf ["residential yard," where traffic rules afford the pedestrian priority].

Livable Streets
Donald Appleyard
1981; 364 pp.
$14.95
($16.45 postpaid) from:
University of California Press
2120 Berkeley Way
Berkeley, CA 94720
or Whole Earth Access

• See **Architecture Without Architects** (p. 115) and **A Pattern Language** (p. 117).
• See also "Alternative Technology" (pp. 89-90).

• This seminal study remains one of the most accurately honest looks at the wonders and terrors of city living.
The Death and Life of Great American Cities: Jane Jacobs, 1961; 458 pp. **$4.95** ($5.95 postpaid) from Random House/Order Dept., 400 Hahn Road, Westminster, MD 21157 (or Whole Earth Access).

HOUSEHOLD: Where you come home to, what you come home to, who you come home to. A place you can call your own, if you work at it. —JB

Redesigning the American Dream

Redesigning the American Dream
Dolores Hayden
1984; 270 pp.
$17.95
postpaid from:
W. W. Norton
500 5th Avenue
New York, NY 10110
or Whole Earth Access

Do you dream of living in a single-family home? You might find this eloquent argument against the idea provocative. Architect Dolores Hayden shows that the traditional home is often inappropriate for the rising number of single-parent families, families with more than one adult wage earner, and the elderly. Much better would be further development of the housing we already have by means of "mother-in-law" apartments and cleverly refurbished neighborhoods. The role (some would say plight) of women is discussed with unusual sensitivity — rare in books addressing planning — with women's needs incorporated centrally into every proposed design. I found the level of research to be deeper than other books on the subject, and mercifully free of simplistic analysis. Easy to read too; no academic poopadoodle at all. —JB
[Suggested by Stephanie Mills]

•

San Diego estimated overall costs to the city of one new detached suburban house at $13,500 and began billing this infrastructure charge to startled developers. Fairfield, California, estimated that total tax revenues from new housing development would cover half the cost of police services and nothing more.

Most of the towns and cities of the United States simply cannot afford this kind of new development: not the infrastructure cost, or the service cost, or the energy cost.

•

Access to the public domain is especially difficult for older women. After age sixty-five, many women reap the results of a lifetime of low earnings, limited mobility, and self-sacrifice. In a study of 82,000 widows in Chicago, Helena Lopata found that over half of them did not go to public places, and over a fifth did not even go visiting. While 82 percent were not in a position to offer transportation to others, 45 percent had no one, of any age, to rely on for transportation.

The Plan of St. Gall in Brief

The Plan of St. Gall in Brief
Lorna Price
1982; 104 pp.
$30
($31.50 postpaid) from:
University of California Press
2120 Berkeley Way
Berkeley, CA 94720
or Whole Earth Access

One of the most thrilling publications in years, the three-volume ***Plan of St. Gall*** *also had a thrilling price — $450. (It's now out of print, and it's worth over $1,000!) This condensed version leaves a surprising amount of the thrill intact. The richness of the color, the wealth of models, drawings, diagrams, and maps, leads you into the heart of deeply civilized intelligence circa 800 A.D. St. Gall is the smartest intentional community (monastery in this case) ever designed.* —Stewart Brand

•

Proximity to the gardens was a boon for both birds and their keepers — garden clippings might provide the chickens and geese with additional food, while in the beds and orchard manure from the pens could quickly be distributed, enhancing sanitation.

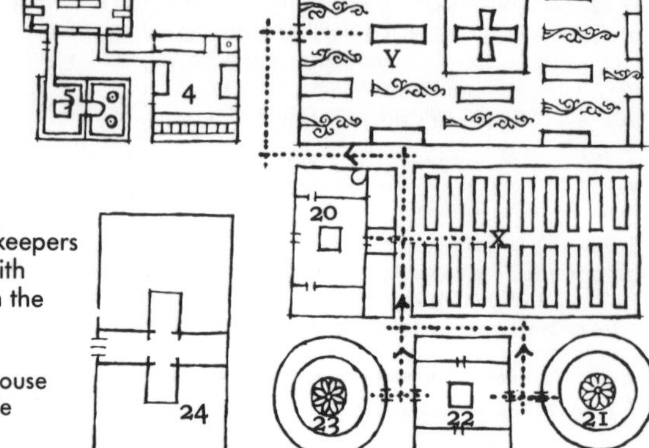

Dormitory, **3**; Privy **4**; Laundry **5**; Gardener's House **20**; Goosehouse **21**; Fowlkeepers' House **22**; Henhouse **23**; Granary **24**; Vegetable Garden **X**; Cemetery & Orchard **Y**.

Paolo Soleri and the Arcosanti Project

Arcosanti is the name of the first "arcology," a compact city that will someday shelter 5,000 people, their art, and their work. Arcosanti will temper its own climate and make its own energy. Huge built-in greenhouses will grow the food and heat the entire complex in winter. The work goes slowly — in 15 years only about three percent of the project has been completed, but what's there is wonderful to see. It's been built mostly by volunteers who have paid to work with master architect Soleri. Workers I've talked to agree that the experience was worth it, though not without controversy.

The Cosanti Foundation also supports itself by giving workshops on a variety of related subjects, publishing books by and about Mr. Soleri (the drawings are terrific) and by casting bells in bronze and stoneware. Visitors are welcome.

I consider Arcosanti to be an affair of the spirit; it's good to know that people are putting their time and effort into attempts of this sort. Beats complaining about the state of the world any time. —JB

◄ **A bevy of Solari bells.**

Arcosanti under construction near Prescott, AZ.

Arcosanti
Information on educational programs, bells, and Soleri books **free** from:
Cosanti Foundation
6433 Doubletree Road
Scottsdale, AZ 85253

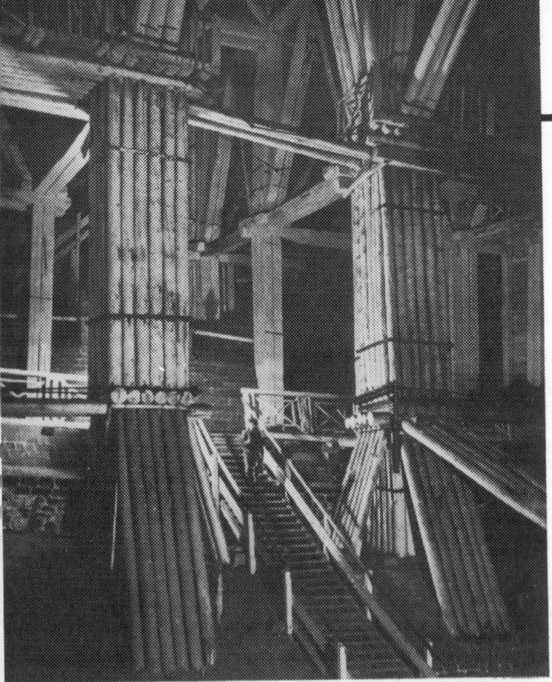

Architecture Without Architects • The Prodigious Builders

These books utterly changed my basic ideas of shelter and building. The variety, ingenuity, art, and wit of folks building without restrictions or architectural training can be both inspiring and shocking to a citizen of a major industrialized nation. ***Architecture Without Architects*** *is now out of print (dumb!) but it remains the best and most provocative collection of its kind — worth seeking out at your library or bookstore. It's mainly photographs.*

Mr. Rudofsky adds erudite commentary to photographs in ***The Prodigious Builders,*** *based on his many years of observing vernacular architecture. His ideas make most modern architecture proposals seem limp or effete.* —*JB*

•

This interior, reminiscent of Piranesi's fantasies, consists of shorings in the eleventh-century salt mine of Wieliczka in Poland. This underground labyrinth extends over sixty miles and reaches a depth of 980 feet. The seven levels, one below the other, are connected by flights of steps.
—*Architecture Without Architects*

Architecture Without Architects
Bernard Rudofsky
OUT OF PRINT
Doubleday

The Prodigious Builders
Bernard Rudofsky
OUT OF PRINT
Harcourt Brace Jovanovich

Commonsense Architecture

Hundreds of expert sketches with captions show us how clever folks can be designing their buildings. No text, and it's not missed. Many of the ideas, all taken from real construction, are so smart that you wonder what all the talk these days is concerning energy efficiency and other problems that seem to have been well solved centuries ago. Embarrassing and humbling and a real mind-stirrer. —*JB*

CHANNELING THE WIND

DEVICES THAT COOL HOUSES BY DIRECTING THE WIND INSIDE HAVE BEEN USED FOR CENTURIES.

EGYPTIAN HOUSE WITH WIND SCOOPS
MIDDLE KINGDOM

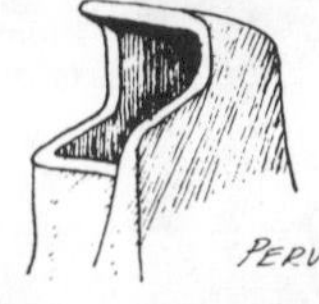

PERUVIAN WIND SCOOP
(PRE - A.D. 700)

SHADING THE OPENINGS

IN A WARM CLIMATE IT IS IMPORTANT TO DESIGN OPENINGS THAT ADMIT THE COOLING WINDS BUT NOT THE HEAT OF THE SUN. ONE WAY TO DO THIS IS TO RECESS THE WINDOW OR DOOR SO THAT THE DEPTH OF THE WALL SHADES MUCH OF TH OPENING.

DOORWAY, AFGHANISTAN

HORIZONTALLY HINGED SHUTTERS DOUBLE AS SHADES.
KAVALLA, GREECE

Commonsense Architecture
(A Cross-Cultural Survey of Practical Design Principles)
John S. Taylor
1983; 160 pp.
$5.95
postpaid from:
W. W. Norton
Order Dept.
500 5th Avenue
New York, NY 10110
or Whole Earth Access

The Jersey Devil Design/Build Book

Football house. ►

Architects usually "have it built," preferring to act only as designers. (Well, maybe they don't prefer to act only as designers, but that's how things usually go.) The Jersey Devil crew contracts and builds their own designs, thus maintaining complete and doubtless scary control of their creations. No excuses. Result: highly unusual buildings with a sassy spirit not often seen. Nice book too. —*JB*

•

Our first thought is, "How do you build it?" I'd like to think all architects do that. My father taught me never design something you can't build. I may have to learn how to build it, but I'm sure I can build it before it's finished.

The Jersey Devil Design/Build Book
Michael J. Crosbie
1985; 96 pp.
$19.95
($21.45 postpaid) from:
Gibbs M. Smith, Inc.
P. O. Box 667
Layton, UT 84041
or Whole Earth Access

• See "Livable Cities" (pp. 112-113).

• For another view of designing with nature look at **The Granite Garden** (p. 73).

Traditional Islamic Craft in Moroccan Architecture

The good news that Andre Paccard conveys in these books is that the masterful artisans of Islamic architecture and design are alive and well, producing exquisite work of a quality we might associate only with earlier centuries. Paccard was able to obtain permission to photograph many Moroccan buildings (palaces in particular) that are normally closed to visitors or the camera, and the splendid results are shown, in color, on over 1,000 pages. Paccard was also privy to the traditionally secret craft techniques passed down orally from master to apprentice, and some of these are presented here in text, diagrams, and photos. —*Jay Kinney*

•

In a famous *hadith*, Al Bukhari said: *On the day of Resurrection, the most terrible of punishments shall be meted out to the painter who has imitated beings created by God, for God shall say to him: "Now endow these creatures with life."*

Thus we find in pictures figures whose necks have a black line drawn through them, to show that they could not possibly be alive, or others with shapes so monstrous and tormented that they could not possibly be resurrected.

These problems were such that Moslem thought became oriented toward the geometric. It became little by little the major art form of Islam, for the infinite lines reflect the indivisibility of God, the basis of the Moslem faith, and the complexity of the pattern conforms to the idea of the atomic structure of the universe.

On the work site of the Royal Palace of Marrakesh: tile-setting, in reverse, a motif surrounding a twenty-four-pointed star.

Meknes: Royal Palace. **Two little inside doors surmounted by a tympanum.**

Traditional Islamic Craft in Moroccan Architecture
Andre Paccard
(Two volumes)
1980; 508 pp., 582 pp.
$250 postpaid from:
Editions Atelier 74
5 East 57th Street, 16th floor
New York, NY 10022

Finland: Living Design

Elegant is a word not often used to describe design in our country, but in Finland it's hard to avoid: Finnish designers seem incapable of producing anything tacky. Perhaps more than in any other country, designers and architects combine the ultra-modern with traditional materials, color, and light. The resulting aesthetic has a subtle beauty that stands as an antidote to sleaze. So does this well-crafted book. —*JB*

The Kukkapuro house sits in a forested community fifteen minutes outside Helsinki. The fine-lined window grid and bright exterior panels contrast crisply with blanketing snow and call to mind the color composition of a Mondrian painting.

Warm welcomes are given by a host of doorways with pleasing proportions.

Finland: Living Design
Elizabeth Gaynor
1984; 250 pp.
$35.00
($37.00 postpaid) from:
Rizzoli International Publications, Inc.
597 Fifth Avenue
New York, NY 10017
or Whole Earth Access

Japanese Homes and Their Surroundings

One of the most wonderful books in print. In 1877 the American, Morse — curator of the Peabody Museum in Salem, Massachusetts and an early solar inventor — traveled to Japan, fell in love with the culture, and opened the West to it (Fenollosa and Ezra Pound followed his lead). Lovingly perceived, understood, and illustrated, the detailed genius of Japanese home life comes across intact. —*Stewart Brand*

Fig. 268. — Stone Foot-bridge.

Japanese Homes and Their Surroundings
Edward S. Morse
1972; 372 pp.
$6.50
($7.50 postpaid) from:
Charles E. Tuttle Co., Inc.
28 South Main Street
Rutland, VT 05701-0410
or Whole Earth Access

• A more detailed study of Japanese architecture can be found in this intimate, sensitively illustrated book.
The Japanese House: Heinrich Engel, 1964; 495 pp. **$66** postpaid from Charles E. Tuttle Company, Inc., 28 South Main Street, Rutland, VT 05701-0410.

◄ The Mexicali project.

A Pattern Language

This project is overwhelmingly ambitious — to establish a language for talking about what people really need from buildings and communities, drawing from many epochs and cultures but focusing on our own. The genius of Alexander et al. is that they simply ignore the stylistic fad-mongering that passes for architectural thought, and get on with sensible, useful, highly distilled wisdom about what works and what doesn't. They're not shy about laying down rules of thumb (''Balconies and porches which are less than six feet deep are hardly ever used'') — often with research citations to back them up, and charming, pointed illustrations.

The most important book in architecture and planning for many decades, a landmark whose clarity and humanity give hope that our private and public spaces can yet be made gracefully habitable. —Ernest Callenbach

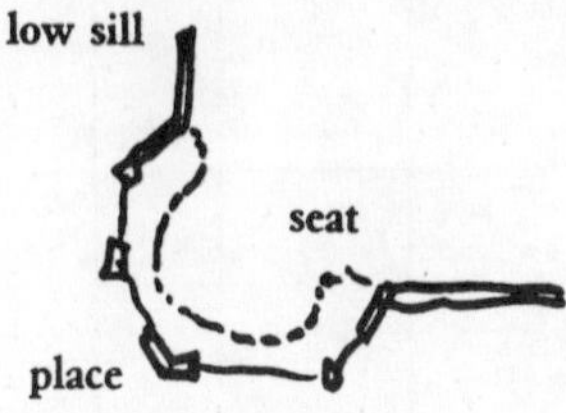

•

In principle, any window with a reasonably pleasant view can be a window place, provided that it is taken seriously as a space, a volume, not merely treated as a hole in the wall. Any room that people use often should have a window place. And window places should even be considered for waiting rooms or as special places along the length of hallways.

•

Look how beautiful the workspace in our main picture is. Nearly the whole counter is lined with windows. The work surface is bathed in light, and there is a sense of spaciousness all around. There is a view out, an air of calm.

The Production of Houses

This records the successful completion of a housing project done according to architect Christopher Alexander's unorthodox theories. The project was set in Mexico, mostly to avoid American building codes which conspire to keep design and construction in the hands of architects and builders. Alexander requires that the end users of a building can and must participate in its construction from start to finish — not merely in an advisory capacity. If necessary, the project is guided by a ''master builder'' (in this case Alexander) who acts as coordinator, inspiration, and source of critical information.

I find this book inspiring, essentially ''right,'' and certainly one to read before building anything. My only qualm is that the ideas are offered as THE way to build — an extreme claim. But this may be the only way to effectively emphasize a position that is, regrettably, seen by many people as radical. Too bad. In this case, ''radical'' is just good sense. —JB

•

In the Mexicali project, it was, above all, a very human thing that happened on the site. For in the end, the reality of the process — quite apart from the principles of the architect-builder, and the house cluster, and cost accounting, and all that — is what people dealt with day by day, and what now remains in everyone's memory even after the construction has stopped.

The night watchman walking by the window at sunrise on his way home, the dusty sun already beginning to bake our rooms . . . The men who deliver the sand and gravel coming by every couple of days, the great piles of gravel slipping out of the truck; writing a bill; giving them a check every week . . . Driving across town to buy electrical supplies; waiting in the supply house with the electricians, drinking cool water; loading the tubing and fittings into the truck.

The Linz Cafe

Christopher Alexander's books, especially **A Pattern Language**, *ask for demonstration of the ideas presented. The enlightened sponsors of a design exposition offered him a chance to show his stuff in the summer of 1980. He responded with a deceptively simple and subtle cafe. This modest book shares that same spirit with quiet, lucid explanations of what he was trying to achieve, and photographs for those unlucky enough to be unable to stop in for a beer. Judging by this book only (I have not seen the cafe), I'd say the cafe has that charm one finds now and then in a building designed by somebody who has not been messed up by an education in architecture. The designer's love and regard for the people who will use the building shows. It's appalling that this is considered unusual or difficult to achieve, but we live in strange times.* —JB

•

In order to get each detail to work just right, within the framework of these rough visions, it was of course necessary to work each detail out, very exactly, by trial and error, using full scale mockups to get size and shape and proportion just exactly right. For example, in the case of the alcoves, I spent several hours in the office, playing with chairs, tables, and pieces of plywood, until I had the dimensions of the alcove exactly right. I knew I had it right when it felt so comfortable that everyone in the office clustered round, sat in the simulated alcove drinking brandy, and refused to leave.

A Pattern Language
(Towns, Buildings, Construction)
Christopher Alexander, Sara Ishikawa, and Murray Silverstein
1977; 1,169 pp.
$47.50 postpaid

The Production of Houses
Christopher Alexander (with Howard Davis, Julio Martinez, and Don Corner)
1985; 383 pp.
$39.95 postpaid

The Linz Cafe
Christopher Alexander
1982; 94 pp.
$25 postpaid

All from:
Oxford University Press
16-00 Pollitt Drive
Fair Lawn, NJ 07410
or Whole Earth Access

▲ The Linz Cafe.

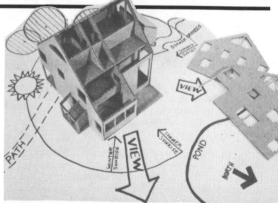

Right Where You Live

House buyers or renters are the intended readership of this book, but it serves equally well as a primer for house designers and remodelers. Good features and bad are examined in an easygoing conversational style that makes the information easily readable even to kids — a nice way to get them into the process. For practice, try testing your present digs against the criteria presented here. (You might want to move.) The kitchen chapter is especially good. Note that this is just the basics; you'll have to supply the imagination. —JB

•

A flow diagram is used to program the design of most commercial kitchens. It is an assembly line that works straight through from delivery of food, to preparation and serving, back to washing and storing dishes. Not only is it not triangular, it is obvious that it is another path, a *footpath!* When cooking is seen as a journey through all the operations of food assembly, it becomes apparent we can deal with it in a businesslike manner.

STORAGE: BOWLS AND PANS BELOW, REPEATABLES ABOVE
FR. REF. SINK RANGE
DELIVERY COLD STOR. COLD PREP. HOT PREP. ASSEMBLY SERVICE
STORE WASH RETURN
PANTRY OVEN DISH STORAGE D.W. SINK

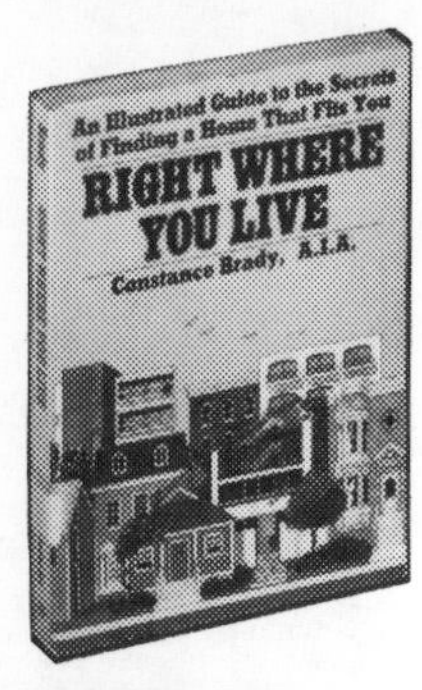

Right Where You Live
Constance Brady, A.I.A.
1979; 188 pp.
$9.95
($10.84 postpaid) from:
Conarc
P. O. Box 339
Bethel Island, CA 94511
or Whole Earth Access

House

Like the needle of the acupuncturist, this book is accurately, painfully, exquisitely right. On the surface it chronicles the building of a home from conception to move-in. But what it's really about is the subtle class struggles that go on between people who are "professionals" and those "in the professions" — in this case the owners are a lawyer and a Ph.D educator confronting equally educated carpenters. Ego trips abound. Misunderstandings worthy of a tempestuous-yet-loving marriage illuminate the scene with snarls, huffs, laughs, and compromises. Just like real life. —JB

•

"Actually, I wanted it August first," says Jonathan. "But I guess that's impossible. Why four months?"

"Our labor is four and a half months of solid time," Jim repeats. "And there are a couple of vacations in there."

"Why a couple of vacations in there?" says Jonathan, tilting his head. "The farmers I know, the builders I know, take their vacations in the winter."

"Okay," says Jim. He's raised his chin. He purses his lips now and stares at the wall to Jonathan's right.

"Hey, it's none of my business. But it affects *me*."

"If you've got money," says Jim, turning back to Jonathan, whose face still bears the tan he got on his late-winter vacation in Florida, "you take time off in the winter. If you don't have money, you take time off in the summer."

House
Tracy Kidder
1985; 341 pp.
$17.95
($18.95 postpaid) from:
Houghton Mifflin Co.
Attn.: Mail Order Dept.
Wayside Road
Burlington, MA 01803
or Whole Earth Access

Designing Houses

Though not billed as such, ***Designing Houses*** *is a thing-maker's dream book! Even if designing and building your own "big house" is not within your current reach, you cannot help being caught up in the enthusiasm generated within. Modelmaking is stressed throughout, starting with the setting up of your own "architect's office," obtaining the instruments and tools of the trade and quite an ample course on cardboard construction. Best of all are the drawings: neat, simple, funky, their inevitable influence on your own sketches makes this handsome volume underpriced . . . now where did I lay my X-acto . . .*
—Joe Eddy Brown

I agree with Joe Eddy Brown that this is an exceptionally fine book. My only reservation is that the presentation subtly tends to keep you traditional, which for many will do just fine anyway. —JB

VIEW
PATH
VIEW
WINTER SUNRISE
SUMMER SUNRISE
POND
NORTH

The model is placed on a large piece of white paper and the site is sketched at an appropriate size so that views, sun, shade, and breezes can be checked.

Designing Houses
Les Walker
and Jeff Milstein
1976; 153 pp.
$9.95
($12.40 postpaid) from:
The Overlook Press
RR 1, Box 496
Woodstock, NY 12498
or Whole Earth Access

Design Works Kits

Design Works offers a series of kits to help you visualize your ideas before taking action. The Architect's Drawing Kit consists of grids drawn in perspective. You tape these under tracing paper, then draw your heart's desire to scale in three dimensions, just as real architects do. (Many of them use grids just like these.) It's easier than you think. Interior Design Kits are available too; one each for kitchen and bath, home furniture, office furniture, and architectural components such as windows and doors. You don't draw these. Instead, you cut out little perspective pictures of the items and stick them on a slick perspective-chart sheet. They don't stick permanently, so you can try different configurations by shuffling them around. Design Works also sells a House Building Kit containing everything you need to make models as described in ***Designing Houses*** *(above). The kits even include scale people.*

I consider all these kits a boon, but remember that this sort of thing tends to channel your ideas toward the interests of the kits' author, or at least toward what's easy to model, e.g. you'd be unlikely to come up with designs like those of the Jersey Devil design group (p. 115). Watch it.
—JB

Design Works Kits
Daniel K. Reif
$13.95-$17.95
postpaid;
brochure **free**
All from:
Design Works, Inc.
11 Hitching Post Road
Amherst, MA 01002
or Whole Earth Access

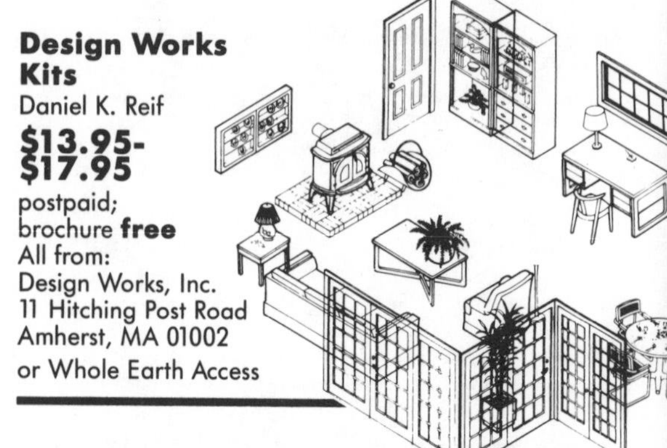

• For peace of mind in earthquake country, you should design or retrofit your place using the information detailed here.
Peace of Mind in Earthquake Country: Peter Yanev, 1974; 304 pp.; **$8.95** ($10.45 postpaid) from Chronicle Books, One Hallidie Plaza, Suite 806, San Francisco, CA 94102.

Drafting

When I first got this book, I kept mumbling "Arrgh . . . I wish I'd had this book last year," or some such remark born of unhappy memories of a past disaster. Mr. Syvanen has a good knack for explaining things you don't see explained elsewhere. Your beginnership is assumed. —JB

I HAVE DONE A LOT OF FREEHAND TRACING ON A WINDOW.

WHEN IN A ROOM THAT FEELS GOOD AND COMFORTABLE, TRY TO FIGURE WHY. IS IT THE CEILING HEIGHT, LENGTH TO WIDTH RATIO OF THE ROOM, WINDOW SIZES AND SPACES? MEASURE ALL THE CONTRIBUTING FACTORS. HOW FAR IS YOUR HAND FROM THE CEILING WHEN RAISED? COUNT FLOOR TILES AND HERE IS A GOOD TIME TO USE YOUR HAND SPAN. TILES ARE EITHER 9" OR 12". TAKE NOTES ABOUT THINGS THAT DON'T PLEASE YOU TOO; WE LEARN FROM GOOD AND BAD.

ALWAYS TWIRL THE PENCIL WITH THE FINGERS WHEN DRAWING HORIZONTAL AND VERTICAL LINES. THIS WILL KEEP THE WEAR EVEN ON THE POINT AND THE LINE WILL BE A CONSISTENT THICKNESS. IT TAKES A LITTLE GETTING USED TO, BUT IS A MUST.

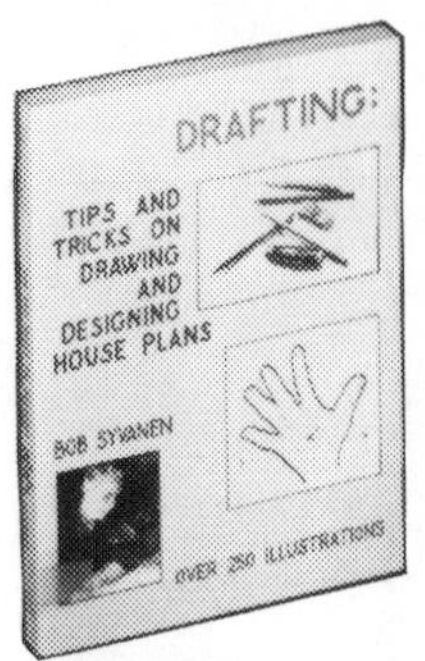

Drafting
Bob Syvanen
1982; 111 pp.
$7.95
($9.45 postpaid) from:
East Woods Press
429 East Blvd.
Charlotte, NC 28203
or Whole Earth Access

Structures

Guess who stayed up all night reading a structure book? That's extreme behavior even for a technotwit! What fascinates me about this book is the way it illuminates a traditionally difficult subject. Most other books challenge the reader not so much with the task of understanding the subject matter, as with comprehending the writing. No problem here; this must be one of the all-time great examples of clear presentation combined with an interest-holding writing style. (What good are clear explanations if you fall out of your chair with boredom?) Such matters as stress, strain, Young's Modulus, cantilevers, shear, and torsion are discussed as theory nicely tied to real-life examples. Simple illustrations and competent photographs reinforce the often witty text. The Secrets Are Revealed. Now if Mr. Gordon would only write on elementary physics and chemistry. In these days when an exclusive knowledge of technology can be used to exploit a populace, such books as this one have a particular importance. I recommend it highly both as a means of understanding the structures around you and as an example of how good a technical book can be. —JB

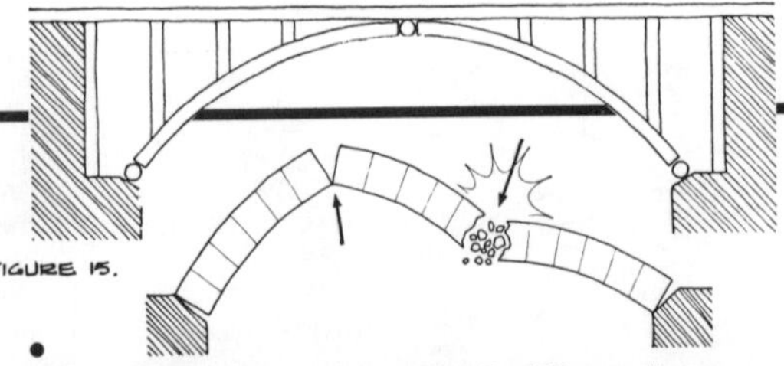
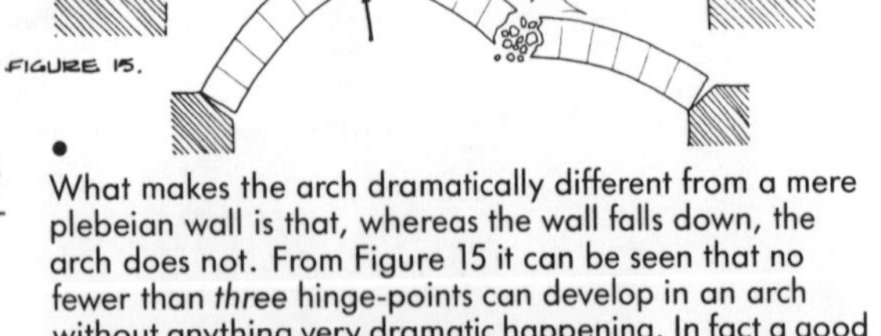

FIGURE 15.

•

What makes the arch dramatically different from a mere plebeian wall is that, whereas the wall falls down, the arch does not. From Figure 15 it can be seen that no fewer than *three* hinge-points can develop in an arch without anything very dramatic happening. In fact a good many modern arch bridges are deliberately built with three hinged joints so as to allow for thermal expansion.

If we really want the bridge to fall down then we shall need *four* hinge-points so that the arch can become in effect a three-linked chain or 'mechanism' which is now at liberty to fold itself up and collapse.

All this means that arches are extraordinarily stable and are not unduly sensitive to the movements of their foundations. If there is any appreciable movement in the foundation a wall will probably collapse; arches do not much mind, and some sort of distortion is quite common.

Structures
J. E. Gordon
1978; 395 pp.
$10.95
postpaid from:
Da Capo Press, Inc.
233 Spring Street
New York, NY 10013
or Whole Earth Access

The Owner-Builder and the Code

Whether you're a complier or defier, you're going to have to deal with the building code sooner or later. Well, the code isn't correct . . . there are hundreds. Worse, the interpretation of whatever codes apply to you is up to your inspector, who may not be friendly for a variety of reasons, including political. With the exception of obvious safety regulations, inspectors and codes generally work against innovation, art, good sense, and the democratic process. This book presents some horror stories and some field-proven tactics for getting the inspector to see things your way. The examples are from a largely bygone era of California "funkadelic" building, but the principles certainly apply to the present. Did you know that the sheriff can force you to leave your new home if the bedroom isn't the right size? —JB

•

O. C. Helton, a third-generation log cabin builder, attempted to get a permit to build a log house for himself, his wife, and five children. When he realized that the required architect's drawings and engineer's stamp would cost him more than $1,000, he decided to go ahead

without the permit. The county issued a stop-work-order and charged Helton with building without a permit. O. C. fought the charge claiming that the requirements for a building permit were, in his case, unreasonable. A jury of five men and a woman eventually found him innocent. "If you don't get this government slowed down and back to the people," he later said, "by the time my children want to build their home, they'll be surrounded by rules."

•

Building departments must consider the expense of bringing offenders to court and the effect that confrontation will have on its bureaucratic routine. In cases where the proposed construction will not comply with the codes, it is generally advisable for the home builder to take the initiative to build first and face possible legal repercussions later.

The Owner-Builder and the Code
Ken Kern, Ted Kogan, and Rob Thallon
1976; 173 pp.
$5
($6.50 postpaid) from:
Owner-Builder Publications
Box 817
North Fork, CA 93643
or Whole Earth Access

• If you want a look at the enormous variety of hardware available to a builder, look at a **Sweet's File** at your library or an architectural firm. **Sweet's** doesn't show everything, but it's close. But bear in mind that **Sweet's** shows the lowest acceptable quality stuff, too — the goods that facilitate a low bid. This leads to the uncomplimentary phrase "Sweet's File Architecture." Watch it.

◄ Work space is organized according to the various functions taking place in each annex: woodworking, metalworking, and automotive repair. A large, unobstructed paved area in the center of the workshop, partially indoors and partially outdoors, is used as a work space in which to build sizable projects or to repair bulky equipment. This area, located at the intersection of the other activity areas, provides the worker with convenient access to all tools and resources of the shop.
—*Ken Kern's Homestead Workshop*

Ken Kern ►

The Owner Built Home
Ken Kern
1975; 374 pp.
$8.95
($10.45 postpaid)

Ken Kern's Homestead Workshop
Barbara and Ken Kern
1981; 166 pp.
$9.95
($11.45 postpaid)

Also available:
The Earth Sheltered Owner-Built Home, The Owner-Built Pole Frame House, The Work Book, Ken Kern's Masonry Stove, The Owner-Built Homestead, The Owner-Builder and The Code, Stone Masonry, Fireplaces, Local Materials.
Send S.A.S.E. for information and price list.
All from:
Owner-Builder Publications
Box 817
North Fork, CA 93643
or Whole Earth Access

The Owner Built Home

Ken Kern's first book has been around just about as long as the original **Whole Earth Catalog,** *and is written in a similar spirit. Ken seemed unwilling to take anyone's word for anything. He liked to think for himself, working against government meddling in his life, challenging conventional wisdom. This book is full of wise decisions and clever details. Philosophy is mixed with experience — both getting richer with time. My guess is that thousands of interesting people have been encouraged to act by Ken's books, lectures, and workshops. He practiced what he preached more than anyone I've ever met (except perhaps for monks). Ironically, he was killed in February of this year when a partially completed experimental structure collapsed during a violent storm.*

At the time of his death, he was at work on **The Owner Built Home Revisited,** *which he intended to self-publish. His wife and co-conspirator, Barbara, is in the process of finishing the work. Meantime you can partake of his wisdom and spirit by reading from this list. I reckon his work won't go out of date for a long time.* —JB

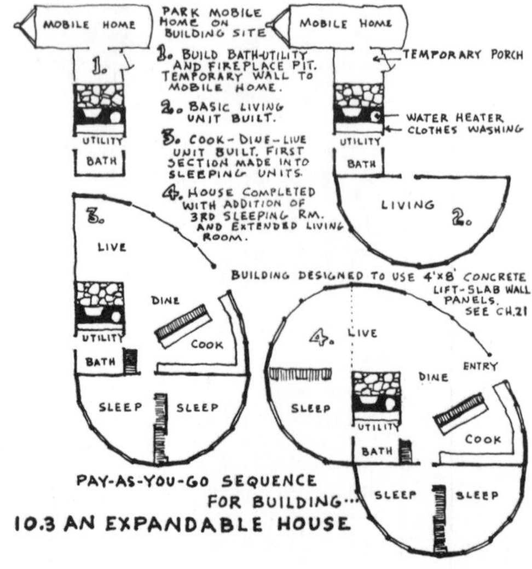

Ken Kern's Homestead Workshop

Well . . . Ken's shop is so different from mine, yet I gotta agree with just about everything he's showing in this uniquely personal book. He and his wife Barbara cover the entire shop bit — from construction of the actual structure to the use of the tools. Hand tools. Nonelectric hand tools, especially. They end the book with a case history of how they invented, made, and refined an all-purpose cart as an example of how their shop and themselves interact so well. It isn't often I say "I wish I'd written that," but I'm saying it now. This book is certainly the most informative and proper-attitude-inducing I've ever seen, and it should be very helpful to anyone ready to do a shop. —JB

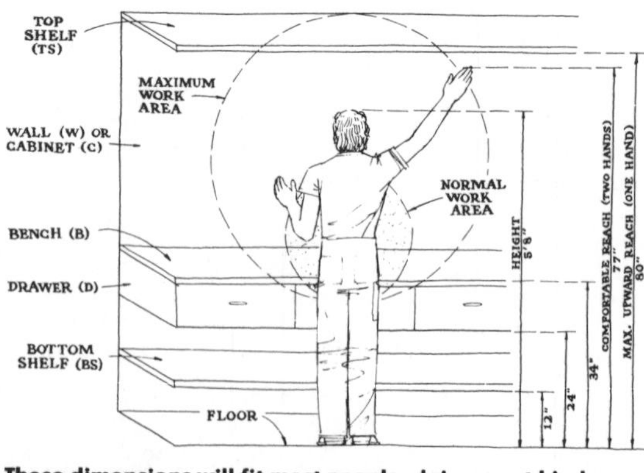

These dimensions will fit most people, doing most kinds of shop work.

• Something you might keep in mind: Many banks will not loan money for an owner-built home unless it's a kit. In fact, the Owner Builder Center (above) recommends using a kit.

• Log houses also come as kits. See **The Log Home Guide for Builders and Buyers** (p. 126).

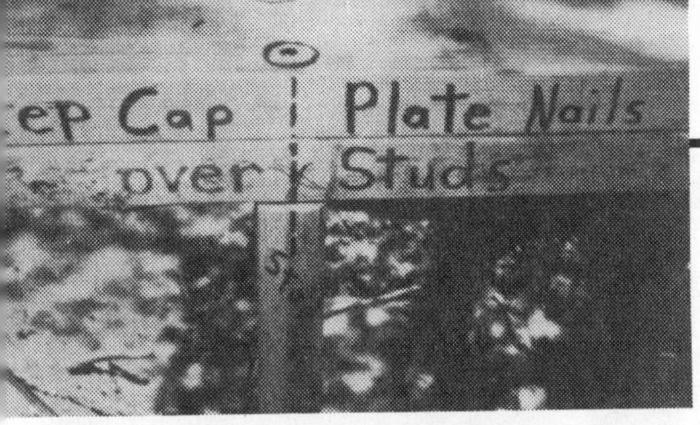

◄
Nail on the Cap Plates

Margin of Error: Exactly flush with top plate.

Most Common Mistakes: Bowed stock; nails not over studs; falling off the wall; splinters in your rear end.

Use good, straight stock for these plates. Secure the 2 plates together with two 16d CC sinkers over each stud. By placing the nails over the studs, they will never be in the way of drill bits when you have to drill holes for plumbing and electricity later. Be sure that the edges are flush with the edges of the top plate, and that the cap plates fit tightly to make a strong interlocking joint.
—*Building Your Own House*

The Owner Builder Center

Some of the best news in years is the success of the Owner Builder Center in Berkeley, California. It's one of the first, and certainly the biggest of such enterprises — they've taught more than 10,000 people how to build or remodel their own place while saving up to 40 percent. The "OBC" has also spawned about 20 other centers and doubtless inspired many more. They are strongly nonsexist.

What the OBC staff has learned from all that teaching has been gathered into a series of books. Begin your homework with **Before You Build**. *Everything you need to know is explained in chronological order. Equally important, the author wisely insists you be realistic about your desires, needs, competence, attitude, time and finances. The psychological effects of the project — often ignored until too late — are discussed in experienced detail. This book is by far the best of its kind.*

Next step is **Building Your Own House**. *Watching many students make the same mistakes over and over has led the author to accent the tricky parts. In addition to the expected instruction, he answers the questions he knows you will ask: "How accurate do I have to be here?" "What will the inspector want to see, and when?" "What if a board has a curve in it?" The book gets the foundation in and frame up. Later books will guide you to move-in day. The information is complete, jargon-free, well illustrated, and liberally festooned with sample worksheets, schedules and checklists. Really good.*

OBC also puts out a newsletter, **The Owner Builder**. *You'll find schedules of classes, descriptions of new projects (such as an owner builder condo), friendly consulting services and suppliers, and articles on a variety of suitable subjects.*

Owner-building is certainly going to grow as families get priced out of the market. I'm glad that OBC has given the movement such a great start. —JB

•

Trees are a wonderful asset to a site both for beauty and shade, but they are alive and therefore, like all of us, vulnerable to change.

•

The distance materials have to be carried may seem like a small matter, but it can tremendously influence the building process. If supply trucks cannot get close to the site, all of the materials will have to be carried in, which adds hours to each work week. Few people really understand the amount of time, energy, and persistence it takes to build a house unless they have already built one. If materials have to be carried in to the building site, it does not mean that the project is not feasible, only be sure that you understand that you are adding another element of time and labor to an already immense task.

•

Even though knowing the depths of the neighbors' wells is of value, do not place too much weight on this information. A friend dug a well in North Carolina 130 feet deep and the church across the road had to go down 450 feet. Information about others' wells is most valuable in ascertaining if your area has problems with locating water at reasonable depths. —*Before You Build*

Using a come-a-long to plumb a wall.

Before You Build
(A Preconstruction Guide)
Robert Roskind
1983; 197 pp.
$8.95
($9.95 postpaid)

Building Your Own House
Robert Roskind
1984; 435 pp.
$17.95
($18.95 postpaid)

both from:
Ten Speed Press
P. O. Box 7123
Berkeley, CA 94707
or Whole Earth Access

The Owner Builder
Pat Bradley, Editor
$4/year
(4 issues) from:
Owner Builder Center
1516 5th Street
Berkeley, CA 94710

The Complete Guide to Factory-Made Houses

If you buy a factory-made house, you won't be doing anything unusual; about 50 percent of new housing is now made somewhere other than where it ends up. We're talking kits — panelized, precut and modular: log houses, domes, mobile homes (that hardly ever hit the road again once they're delivered), and factory-made rooms such as kitchens and bathrooms. We are no longer talking cheap junk — factory-made homes are often better made than on-site building because quality control is easier. Statistics show that many, if not most, owner-built homes are kits. This book gives you the advantages and disadvantages of the various options, buying tips, and a list of manufacturers. Worth a look. —JB

•

Here are a few tips when you inspect a used mobile home for sale. Take along a rubber ball and place it in the center of the kitchen and bathroom floors. If it rolls to a corner, the mobile may need leveling, or the chassis may be sagging which could lead to painful plumbing problems. Also take a small light lamp to check all wall sockets. Test *all* appliances, including the smoke detectors. Don't worry that the dealer may think you're too cautious. Look at it this way: he'll know that he's not dealing with an amateur!

Recent factory-made homes are a far cry from "prefabs" of ill repute. Acorn Structures Inc. of Massachusetts makes this one.

The Complete Guide to Factory-Made Houses
A. M. Watkins
1984; 184 pp.
$8.95
($10.95 postpaid) from:
Caroline House, Inc.
5S 250 Frontenac Road
Naperville, IL 60540
or Whole Earth Access

• Before you get too far with your house design, better check **Reducing Home Building Costs with OVE**, [Optimum Value Engineered] **Design and Construction.** For manual, send **$7** to NAHB Research Foundation, 627 Southlawn Lane, Rockville, MD 20850.

Fine Homebuilding
John Lively, Editor
$22/year
(7 issues) from:
The Taunton Press
P. O. Box 355
Newtown, CT 06470

Fine Homebuilding

Fine is the word for this attractively produced magazine. The articles are about building, as you'd expect, and are unusually complete. They're aimed at anyone who is interested in building, but the attitude of professionalism together with a proper spirit is what makes the magazine different. Whether the subject is modern or (more likely) traditional, you'll find an emphasis on excellence, quality, and refinement lacking in other publications. A pleasure! The same folks also publish **Fine Woodworking** *(p. 168) and* **Threads** *(p. 177) — equally good.* —JB

• *Victorian extravagance.* Designers and builders of Victorian homes had more fun with porches than anybody before or since. The time was right, since materials and tools were available to do intricate work, and the homes' inhabitants were still interested in spending time between the sidewalk and the house, engaging the members of the neighborhood. This house in Cape May, N.J.

Practical Homeowner
(Formerly *New Shelter*)
John Viehman, Editor
$10.97/year
(9 issues) from:
Rodale's Practical Homeowner
33 East Minor Street
Emmaus, PA 18099-0017

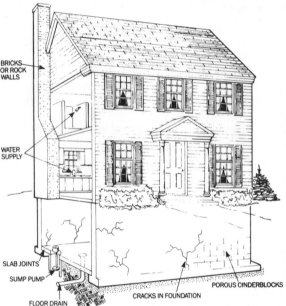

Practical Homeowner

A particularly good article on the hazards of radon in the home (January '86 issue) is typical of the sort of well-researched news you'll find in this magazine. You'll also find "road tests" of household hardware done by Rodale's product testing lab, lots of do-it-yourself, and new product news. I find every issue has something I hadn't heard about. —JB

Practical Homeowner *is aimed at an audience that has ambition but little practical experience.* **Fine Homebuilding** *is geared more towards people who already know the difference between a rip and a crosscut saw, and it has better paper, sumptuous photography, and a finer attention to graphic detail. I'm reading and using both of them.* —Richard Nilsen

BRICKS OR ROCK WALLS
WATER SUPPLY
SLAB JOINTS
SUMP PUMP
FLOOR DRAIN
CRACKS IN FOUNDATION
POROUS CINDERBLOCKS

HOW RADON ENTERS YOUR HOUSE

Radon is a colorless, odorless, radioactive gas that rises to the surface from underground rock formations. Here are some ways it can get inside a house.

Carpentry
Bob Syvanen
1982; 100 pp.

Interior Finish
Bob Syvanen
1982; 126 pp.

Each
$7.95
($9.45 postpaid) from:
The East Woods Press
429 East Blvd.
Charlotte, NC 28203
or Whole Earth Access

Carpentry • Interior Finish

"How do I get outta this mess?" If you'd read this book first, you probably wouldn't be in a mess. If you're already in a mess, the answer is probably in here; tricks of the carpentry trade is what this book is about. It's a very useful addition to any general carpentry text. The 400 drawings by architect Malcolm Wells make things especially clear.

Interior Finish *has more tips and tricks of the trade for those inside jobs. Equally good.* —JB

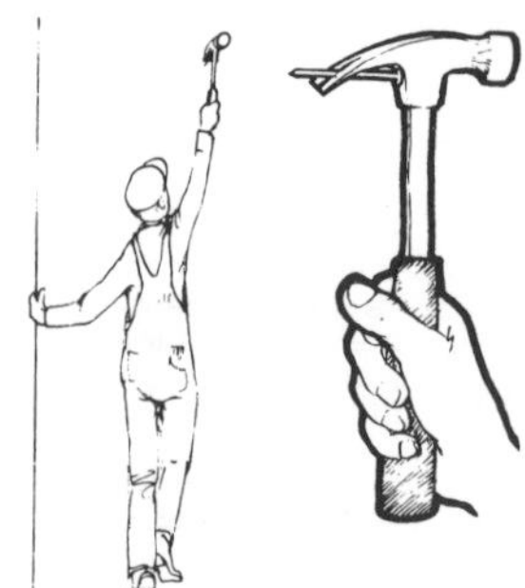

EVERY ONCE IN A WHILE THERE IS A TIME WHEN A NAIL MUST BE LOCATED TOO HIGH OR TOO FAR FROM THE WORK PLATFORM, TO BE REACHED WITH BOTH HANDS (ONE FOR HOLDING THE NAIL, ONE FOR THE HAMMER). IT CAN BE REACHED IF A NAIL IS TUCKED IN THE CLAWS OF THE HAMMER WITH THE NAIL HEAD AGAINST THE HAMMER NECK AND THE NAIL POINTING OUT. SOME HAMMERS ACCEPT A NAIL THIS WAY BETTER THAN OTHERS. WEDGE THE NAIL IN AND IT SHOULD STAY. THEN REACH UP AND START THE NAIL WITH A SWING. ONCE IT'S HELD FIRMLY BY THE WOOD, THE HAMMER IS REVERSED AND THE NAIL DRIVEN HOME.

—**Carpentry**

ADJUST PLYWOOD SHEETS BY JUMPING UP AND IN THE DIRECTION THE SHEET SHOULD GO. AS YOU LAND DRIVE FEET IN THE DIRECTION OF MOVEMENT. VARY INTENSITY OF MOVEMENT BY VARYING EFFORT. SMALL EFFORT LESS MOVEMENT

BIG EFFORT BIG MOVEMENT....

—**Carpentry**

• There are lots more tricks of the building trades shown under "Renovation" (p. 128) and "Repair" (p. 129).
• See also **The Moveable Nest** (p. 141).

Residential Carpentry

You can tell that this is a vocational-ed. textbook; it's utterly competent and utterly coldblooded. Has test questions at the ends of chapters too. The instructions are given as "procedures" (e.g. Procedure for Framing a Dormer) that are divided into steps detailed right down to which size nail to use. The nails themselves, and even the hammer, are explained in the introductory chapters. If you're smart enough to read, you're not likely to screw things up. I can see why the Owner-Builder Center recommends this book. —JB

[Suggested by Blair Abee]

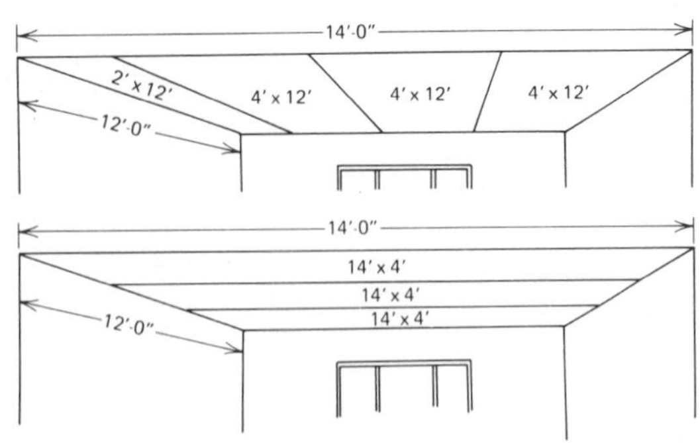

Residential Carpentry
Mortimer P. Reed
1980; 705 pp.
$17.95
($19.90 postpaid) from:
John Wiley & Sons
Order Dept.
1 Wiley Drive
Somerset, NJ 08873
or Whole Earth Access

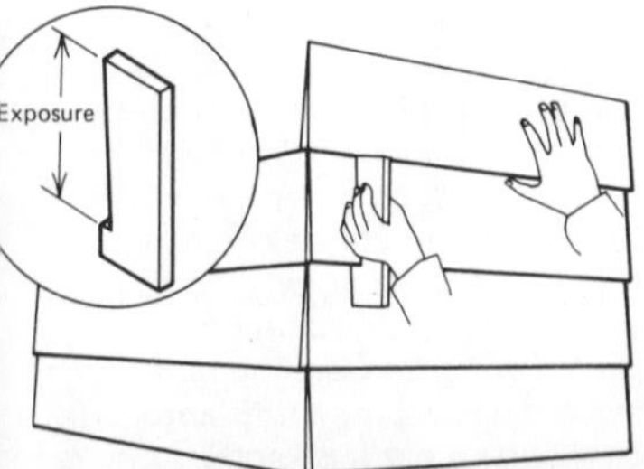

A spacer block notched to the correct exposure assures proper alignment of siding courses.

•

In order to determine the best direction to run ceiling panels, you may have to plan the layout both ways. Suppose that the room to be finished is a bedroom 12' wide and 14' long. If you use 3½ panels 12' long, you have 36' of joint to finish (top). If you use three 14' panels (above), you have only 28' of joint to finish. Obviously, the longer panels are better.

Do-It-Yourself Plumbing

There are many books that adequately handle this subject, but this one is special: in addition to being commendably clear on repairs, both graphically and in the text, it has a really fine section on designing your own plumbing system. I especially like the author's insistence on explaining the basic reasons underlying his instructions, as well as the building codes. That way you really learn something. This is another of the excellent Popular Science books. —JB

•

It has been found by means of a series of noxious tests that soil flows best in a pipe pitched at ¼ inch to the foot. A pitch greater than ½ inch to the foot causes the liquids to run off and leave the solids behind. In time the drain will plug up. Pipes pitched at less than ⅛ inch to the foot do not provide sufficient water velocity and the solids tend to settle and clog and there is insufficient scouring action.

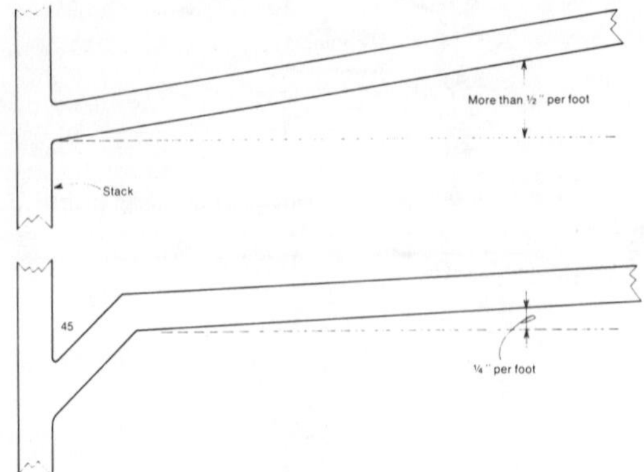

If you have to pitch any drainpipe more than ½ inch to the foot to reach a stack, run a section of the pipe at 45 or more degrees and the balance at ½ or ¼ inch to the foot.

• There's also good instruction in a variety of building skills on the previous two pages.
• More esoteric construction technique can be found on "Boat Building" (p. 288).

Do-It-Yourself Plumbing
Max Alth
1975; 310 pp.
$13.95
($16.69 postpaid) from:
Popular Science Books
P. O. Box 2018
Latham, NY 12111
or Whole Earth Access

Wiring Simplified

Not only is this book a most useful tool for the home electrician, it also has a hole punched all the way through it, for hanging over a nail. That is a kind of practicality that all American publishers should learn. Everything you'll need to wire your home yourself. —J. D. Smith

If the service head cannot be located higher than the insulators, provide drip loops. Splice at bottom of loop, and insulate. This keeps water from flowing into the cable.

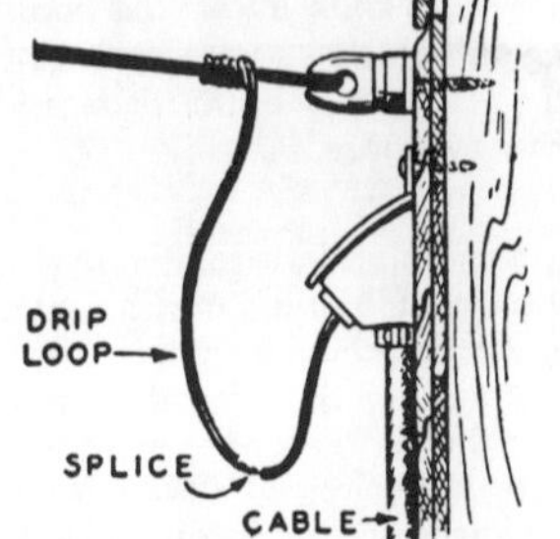

Wiring Simplified
H. P. Richter
and W. C. Schwan
34th Edition
1983; 160 pp.
$2.95
($4.45 postpaid) from:
Park Publishing, Inc.
1999 Shepard Road
St. Paul, MN 55116
or Whole Earth Access

Builders Booksource

Oh boy, a bookstore just for people who build things. The catalog is very comprehensive, covering every aspect of building with at least one good book, and usually with several — each with a review. The store carries many more titles than are in the catalog (lucky Bay Area residents can visit). If you have special needs, ask them for a reference. Bet they have it. —JB

•

Beyond the Kitchen: A Dreamer's Guide Cowan
The kitchen is one of the most commonly remodeled rooms in a house. Many childhood memories are often attached to the kitchen, and most people want this to be the room where they feel most at home. This book provides many ideas to help create the ideal kitchen, from country style to modern minimalism; from loft kitchens to media centers. Learn to consider often-neglected details such as lighting, cupboards and work surfaces, pantries and nooks, and much more. 1985. Running Press. 127 pp., over 150 color illus. $9.95 (pb).

Builders Booksource
Catalog **free** from:
Builders Booksource
1801 4th Street
Berkeley, CA 94710

Adobe

A very thorough book on many aspects of adobe construction. Mientras que descansas has adobes (while you're resting, make some adobes). —Lloyd Kahn

Well, making adobe isn't particularly restful, but sooner or later you have made enough to raise a house. This revised edition includes the modern with the ancient; energy efficiency and code-meeting along with the traditional techniques and aesthetic considerations. —JB

Adobe
(Build It Yourself)
Paul Graham McHenry, Jr.
1985; 158 pp.
$18.50
($19.85 postpaid) from:
University of Arizona Press
1615 East Speedway
Tucson, AZ 85719
or Whole Earth Access

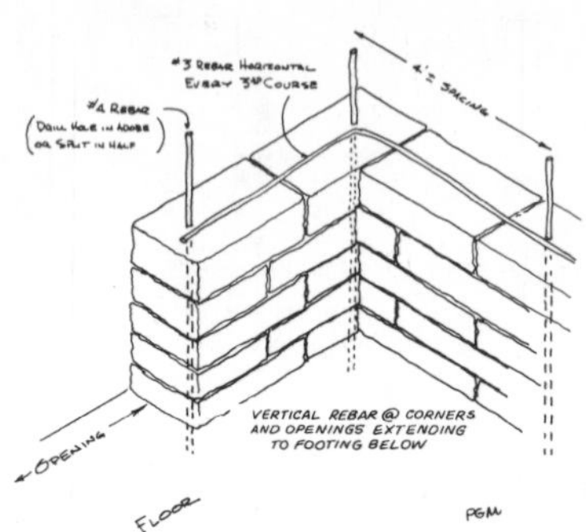

Earthquake treatment for adobe walls.

Adobe bricks being laid up in the wall. Ends and corners of wall (leads) are measured and leveled carefully, with bricks in between laid to the string stretched between leads.

Earth Sheltered Housing Design

Clearly not the last word, and just as clearly not the first, this second edition presents the state of the art in earth sheltered building technique. It's illustrated with a wonderfully varied collection of real, lived-in houses with examples from virtually all feasible climates. Critics have been claiming that earth sheltering has no future, but you'd never know it from this book. As experience has been gathered — sometimes painfully — the advantages and efficiencies of earth sheltered houses are becoming harder to ignore. —JB

•

The main objective in building below grade was to preserve the low profile of the beachfront property from the street side. Approaching from this side, one can see the ocean over the dunelike forms of the house. A small penetration in the center for the entrance is the only indication of a structure below. Viewed from the beach side, the dune forms appear larger but still blend unobtrusively with the landscape of the coast. Two oval-shaped openings are the only man-made forms visible from the beach. (William Morgan, Architect)

Earth Sheltered Housing Design
John Carmody
and Raymond Sterling
1985; 350 pp.
$17.50
postpaid from:
Van Nostrand Reinhold Co.
7625 Empire Drive
Florence, KY 41042-0668
or Whole Earth Access

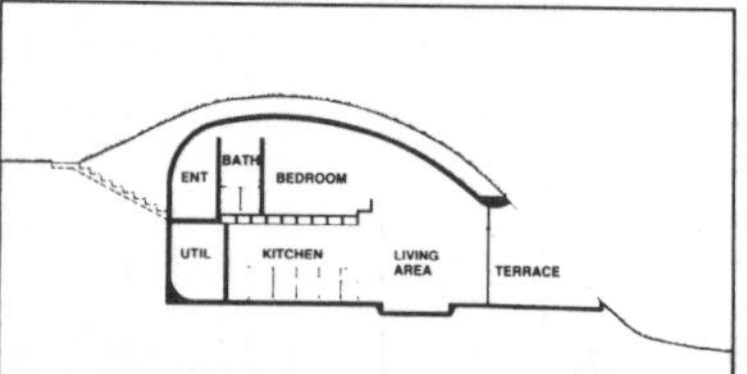

Dune house.

▲ Dune house, looking out.

◄ Clarke-Allison house, River Falls, Wisconsin.

Passive Annual Heat Storage

Insulate the Earth? Uh huh. Sure. At first that's what this book seems to be saying, and it sounds outrageous. It's against everything we've been taught. But it works. Until now, earth sheltered housing has had to be carefully waterproofed and insulated to protect against dampness. The alleged benefits of using the surrounding earth as a heat source in winter and a heat absorber in summer can't work if the house is insulated against the earth surrounding it. But what if the surrounding earth is kept dry and is itself insulated? This book is a complete exposition of that radical idea. The few places built using this concept have worked, absorbing and storing summer heat for use in winter, just as the designers hoped. This may be the break earth sheltered housing has needed. —JB

Passive Annual Heat Storage
John Hait and the Rocky Mountain Research Center
1983; 152 pp.
$14.95
postpaid from:
Rocky Mountain Research Center
P. O. Box 4694
Missoula, MT 59806
or Whole Earth Access

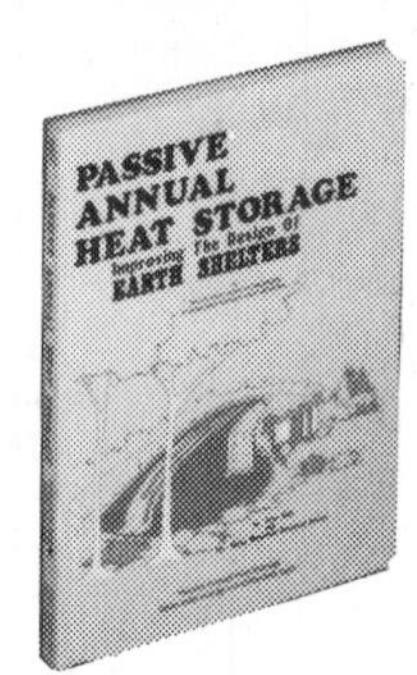

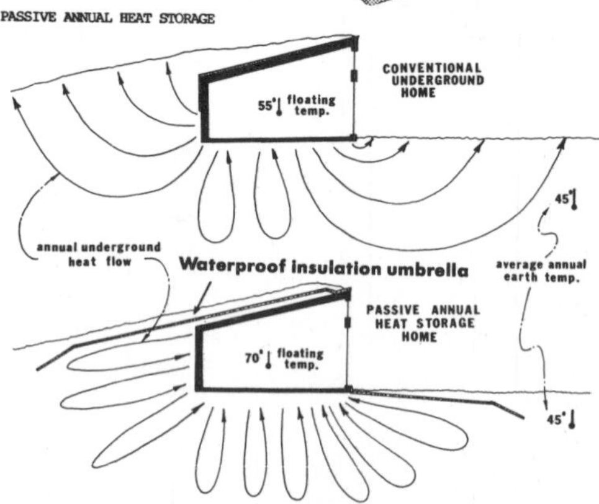

The "floating temperature" of a building is the basic average temperature an earth sheltered home will maintain if left unheated and without sunshine for a couple of weeks or so.

• You'd never guess from the title that this book is about baking adobe houses into permanent ceramic structures. An inspiring story, worth reading for the spirit involved. **Racing Alone:** Nadar Khalili, 1983; 241 pp. **$14.95** ($16.45 postpaid) from Harper & Row, 2350 Virginia Avenue, Hagerstown, MD 21740 (or Whole Earth Access).

▲ A simple and quickly erected silo. Costs can be considerably reduced in comparison with concrete or steel silos of equal capacity, and erection can be effected in the shortest possible time. This is of great importance during sudden accumulations of valuable bulk goods, when losses in storage must be kept to a minimum.

Tensile Structures

Tensile structures (air buildings are included in this category) are one of the most economical and daring ways of covering a space with minimum material. As materials and techniques improve, ambitious projects are becoming more common; the main airport terminal at Jeddah, Saudi Arabia, for instance, is a "tent" several thousand feet long. Closer to home, we are beginning to see tensile-structure shopping malls, greenhouses, and warehouses. There's talk of hotels and dormitories.

This book is a tantalizing visual introduction with lots of photos of models and real buildings. The theory chapters are for engineers who are not intimidated by calculations, but you don't need the intricate math to try your ideas in model form. —JB

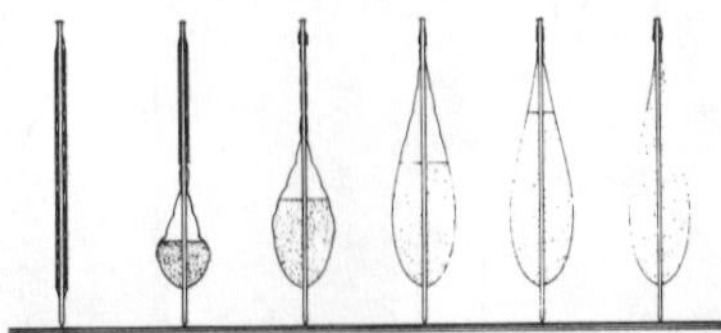

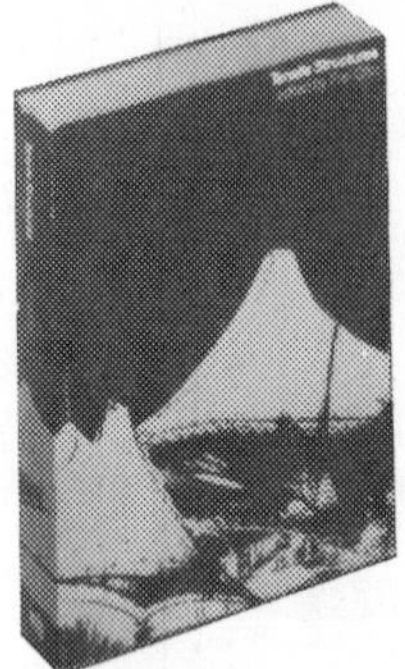

Tensile Structures
Frei Otto, Editor
1973; 491 pp.
$19.95
($21.45 postpaid) from:
MIT Press
28 Carleton Street
Cambridge, MA 02142
or Whole Earth Access

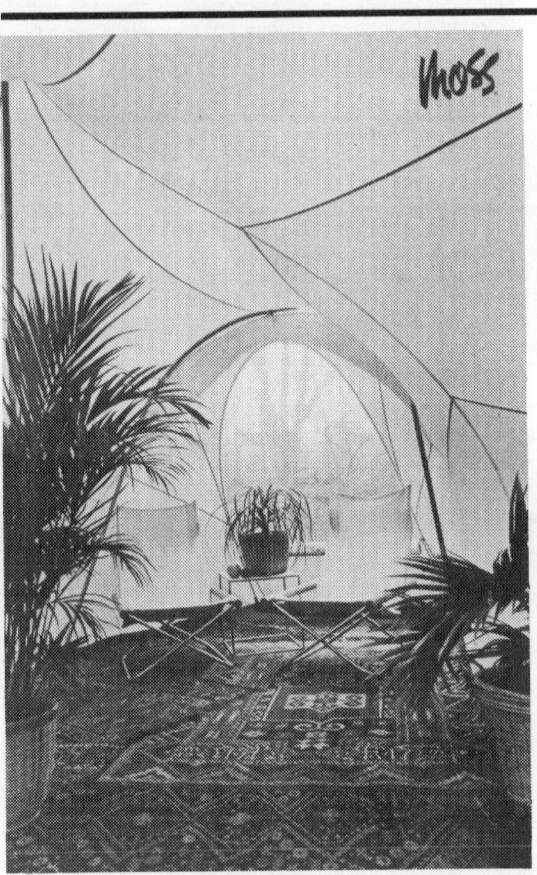

Interior of Moss OP 350 tent.

• And then there are tipis. Often misunderstood and misused by Anglos, a real tipi can be a joy to live in. The best book has been best for a long time now.
The Indian Tipi (Its History, Construction, and Use): Reginald and Gladys Laubin, 1977; 350 pp. **$21.95** ($23.45 postpaid) from Harper & Row, 2350 Virginia Avenue, Hagerstown, MD 21740.

Moss Fabric Structures

The same Moss that makes the especially fine camping tents *(p. 274)* *also makes larger structures for shelter and exhibit purposes. I know of at least one code-meeting home that's a group of Moss's larger, double-walled structures. It's nice; I may live in one myself soon. Bill Moss advocates his designs as an answer to the ridiculous costs of conventional building. It's an idea that might just work.* —JB

Moss Fabric Structures
Information **free** from:
Moss Exhibits
Box 309
Camden, ME 04843

The Yurt Foundation

In the '70s, yurts earned respect for being simple, cheap, and charming. A hippie image gained at the same time seems a disadvantage now, but that hasn't stopped progress — they're now highly developed permanent structures. These folks are the experts on this side of the pond. They sell plans for models up to 54 feet in diameter and three stories high. Nice people to work with, too. —JB

The Yurt Foundation
Yurt plans
$10-$30
Information **free**;
both from:
The Yurt Foundation
Bucks Harbor, ME 04618

Building the Alaska Log Home

Why should an Alaska log home be any different? Maybe it's the fierce individualism that seems to permeate anything that has to do with Alaska — folks go there to do things their way. Maybe it's the irrefutable climate — you have to be right or you freeze. The homes shown here, in enticing color, are masterpieces of the logsmith's art. No funky miner's cabins for these folks. The book isn't funky either; it's surprisingly slick and includes lots of Alaska bush-living lore mixed in with the competent instruction. Yet the author carefully avoids the usual log home fantasy hype. He makes it sound like the hard work it most assuredly is. —JB

Building the Alaska Log Home
Tom Walker
1984; 178 pp.
$19.95
($20.95 postpaid) from:
Alaska Northwest Publishing Company
130 2nd Avenue South
Edmonds, WA 98020
or Whole Earth Access

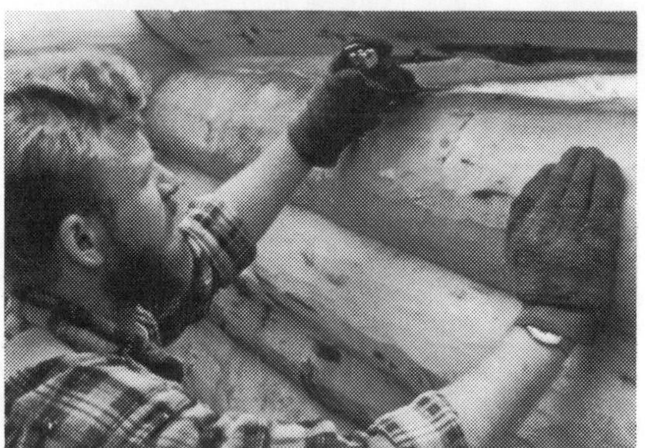

Expertly scribed logs are a tight fit both visually and structurally. They stay tight as logs shrink over time.

◄ The whole idea of scribe-fitting is to match the upper log to the shape of the lower log. The scribe, one with a double level attachment, becomes an important, almost indispensable tool here. With it, the logsmith transfers the shape and contour of the bottom log onto the upper log. Thus, the quality of the scribe has a great deal to do with the efficiency and speed with which this work can be done. In essence, we are making a log-long notch, with the top log being notched to fit not only at the corners, but to the entire length of the log below. The log obviously cannot be hewn any better than it is marked.

Timber Frame Construction

If you live where big wood is available, timber frame construction (also called post-and-beam) offers an interesting alternative to the usual 2x4 stick building. Done right, timber frame buildings are charming, strong, and not necessarily more expensive than more common construction. The weight of the parts, as well as tradition, makes a congenial crew a necessity, which can be fun. This handsome and experienced book will get you started. It covers the whole bit from history to how to hold the chisels. The complete procedure for making a simple garden shed is presented as a practice project — a fine idea. —JB

Timber Frame Construction
Jack Sobon and Roger Schroeder
1984; 204 pp.
$12.95
($14.95 postpaid) from:
Garden Way Publishing
Storey Communications
Pownal, VT 05261
or Whole Earth Access

•

Have your timbers center-cut. This not only makes the timber stronger, but it also makes knots less of a problem. Why? Knots, since they are branches, start from the middle of a tree. Therefore, they will not go from one side of the tree to the other. A timber taken from a quartered tree could conceivably have a knot entirely through it. And knots can fall out, thus weakening the timber.

Temporary braces are applied to the bent to stabilize it. The opposite wall bent, lying in the foreground, is next. The remainder or the timbers are carefully stacked according to their placement in the frame.

Practical Pole Building Construction

Why hang a house up in the air on a bunch of poles? The biggest advantage of this building method is adaptability to otherwise unbuildable sites. Hillsides, unstable soils, and flood plains are no problem. In most cases, poles are much cheaper than a normal foundation, and since the poles, instead of the walls, carry the structural loads, dramatic open plans can be accommodated. This book tells you how to do it, including calculations. —JB

Practical Pole Building Construction
Leigh Seddon
1985; 183 pp.
$9.95
($11.20 postpaid) from:
Williamson Publishing Company
P. O. Box 185
Charlotte, VT 05445
or Whole Earth Access

• A magazine devoted to (guess what) log building. The winter issue is a massive directory of logsmiths and kits. **Log Home Guide For Builders & Buyers:** Doris L. Muir, Editor; **$18**/year (5 issues) from Muir Publishing Co., Ltd., P. O. Box 1150, Plattsburgh, NY 12901.

• Ken Kern has a pole building book. See p. 120.

Chainsaw Savvy

How to tame, train, and feed a chainsaw, done in enough detail to keep you safe yet efficient. First you cut the tree down. Then you cut it up. —JB

[Suggested by Peter Ladd]

Having removed a 90-degree pie, Tilton pauses to compare the face with the intended direction of fall. This is the time to spruce-up the face cuts if they're not precise. If you've held the tobacco in your lower lip, it's also the time to spit — first lifting the face screen.

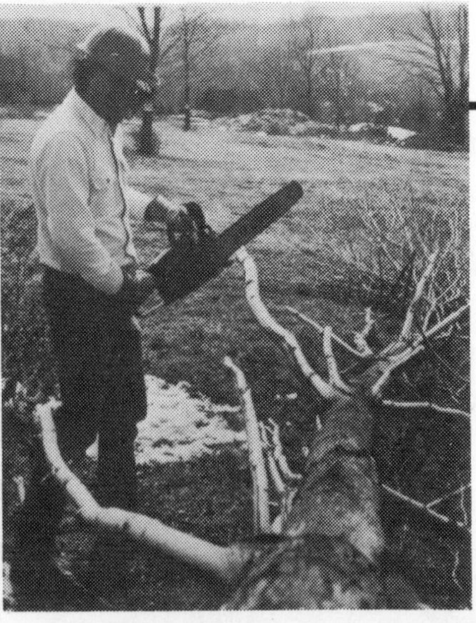

▲ Firewood cutters often mistakenly cut off whole limbs near the trunk and then chase around after them on the ground — letting the chain torment the dirt a bit. With hundreds of chain cutters passing any one point on the bar per second, it takes only a fraction of a second to thoroughly dull a chain. It's better to trim limbs back with loppers or bowsaws until they are stable enough not to chatter under a chainsaw. Then saw stove lengths right back to the trunk.

Chainsaw Savvy
(A Complete Guide)
Neil Soderstrom
1982; 144 pp.

$10.95
($12.45 postpaid) from:
Morgan & Morgan
145 Palisades Street
Dobbs Ferry, NY 10522
or Whole Earth Access

Chainsaw Lumbermaking

It takes nerves of steel and good ear protectors, but it's otherwise entirely feasible to turn trees into boards with a chainsaw. This book escorts you through the entire process, commencing with tree selection. The critical and delicate business of sharpening chains for lumbermaking purposes is covered in practiced detail, as are plans for constructing your own lumbermaking device. Exceptionally well illustrated. —JB

•

Bolting on the mill — the standard Mark III Alaskan Mill clamps onto the chainsaw bar. This design lets you use the same bar for both crosscutting and milling by simply clamping on the mill, but to replace a dull chain with a sharp one, you have to remove the entire mill unit. So I use a separate bar or another saw for crosscutting and modify my mill so that it bolts onto the milling bar. This lets me change chains while the mill remains mounted.

If you use one saw engine both for felling and lumbermaking, you will now need to remove the felling bar and crosscut chain. . . . Chain often gets tangled into what seems like a hopeless mess when it is moved around. To roll the kinks out, hold the chain in both hands. Starting with the most serious kink, roll the chain as shown. Pull the two loops into the final loop, and you're ready to mount the chain on the bar.

Chainsaw Lumbermaking
Will Malloff
1982; 212 pp.

$23.95
postpaid from:
The Taunton Press
63 South Main Street
Newtown, CT 06470
or Whole Earth Access

One of the simplest forms of chainsaw lumbermaking is straight slabbing. The boards are left unedged and are easily stacked and stickered for air-drying. The yield is a full assortment of flat-grain and edge-grain cuts.

• Timber framers get together for a chat in this newsletter. The ads are instructive too.
The Joiners' Quarterly: Steve Chapell, Editor; **$5**/year (4 issues) from Fox Maple Press, Snowville Road, West Brownfield, ME 04010.

• Alan Mackie, master Canadian log builder, has many books.
Log House Publishing Company, Ltd: Information **free** from Log House Publishing Company, Ltd., R.R. 1, Pender Island, B.C., Canada V0N 2M0.

Bailey's

Saws, accessories, calk boots, sharpeners, safety equipment, and everything else loggers need, at a discount. They're nice people, too. —JB

Bailey's
Catalog

$2 from:
Bailey's
P. O. Box 550
Laytonville, CA
95454

Log debarker takes minutes to install on most models of chainsaws. Cuts debarking time by two thirds.

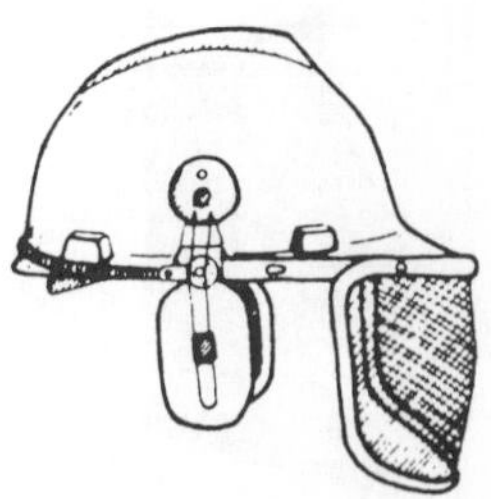

V-Guard cap with flip-up eye & ear protection.

Renovation

Renovation
Michael Litchfield
1982; 571 pp.
$34.95
postpaid from:
John Wiley & Sons, Inc.
1 Wiley Drive
Somerset, NJ 08873
or Whole Earth Access

If I owned a hardware store or ran the local lumberyard, I'd buy a desk copy of this book for do-it-yourself customers to paw through. The ones who should have done some homework before they walked in can here learn the names of the things they need. Those with questions about the best way to do something will find the explanation of methods well-integrated in text, line illustration, and photographs. Both groups will return to the sales desk informed and encouraged.

In an age when people write books on subjects they have scarcely mastered, and publishers back them, what makes **Renovation** *shine is experience and teamwork. The illustrator used to be a contractor. The photographer had previously remodeled a loft and wasn't afraid to lug her camera into grungy buildings. The author renovated three houses and had a hand in the beginnings of* **Fine Homebuilding** *magazine (p. 000). What was supposed to be a year-long project ended up taking four, and several copy editors got burned out along the way, but the result is a book that probably won't have any serious competition for years to come. —Richard Nilsen*

•

◄ Plywood, used as a flitch plate between two joists or, as shown here, as "sisters," is very rigid when used on edge. It is most effective when glued and screwed to the tired joist or joists.

The Davenport house interior, before and after.

The Old-House Journal

A Marvin Round Top under construction.

Fix up an old house and "you will have made a home while cherishing a piece of history — all without destroying the beauty of your old house or compromising the unique story it has to tell. Rather, you will have enriched that story and made it part of your own." So say the editors of this monthly that is obviously as much a labor of love as the restorations they champion. Articles are likely to deal with such matters as authentic architectural styling details, restoration of windows, and rewiring. The tone is do-it-yourself, and generally inspiring. A lively letters department lets readers trade information easily. The ads are probably worth the price of the subscription.

Since 1976, **Old-House Journal** *has printed compendiums of each year's editorial content. The* **Restoration Manuals** *are available individually or in sets at great savings.*

The real goodie from these folks is the massive **OHJ Buyer's Guide Catalog***. It lists hard-to-find sources of materials, ornaments, recycled house parts, columns, staircases, tin ceilings, fixtures, and all the other stuff you'll need to make your place right. —JB*

The Old-House Journal: Patricia Poore, Editor; **$18**/year (10 issues). **The OHJ Yearbook (1985): $18** postpaid. **The 1980s Set: $69** postpaid. **The 1986 Buyer's Guide Catalog: $10.95** postpaid to **OHJ** subscribers; **$13.95** postpaid to nonsubscribers. All from: The Old-House Journal, 69A 7th Avenue, Brooklyn, NY 11217.

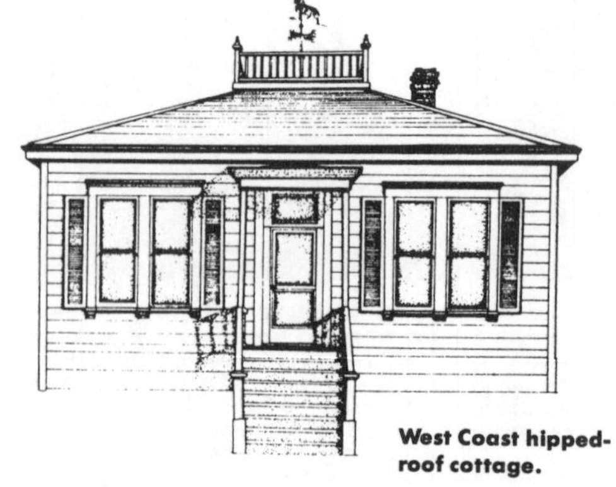

West Coast hipped-roof cottage.

• The Renovator's Supply has a tasty selection of old-house hardware such as knobs, lamps, and escutcheons. Catalog **free** from Renovator's Supply, Inc., Renovator's Old Mill, Millers Falls, MA 01349.

Ortho's Home Improvement Encyclopedia

"Hm . . . bet we could fix up this hovel with a little work. Wonder if we could handle the job ourselves?" With this weighty tome in your grasp, you probably can, assuming you have conquered initial fears and are thus able to start, and even that'll be easier because of the color pictures of the results you may expect. It's so comprehensive that the table of contents takes up the entire back cover in fine print; if what you need isn't there, you probably don't need to know it. It covers house and grounds, adding and repairing. —JB

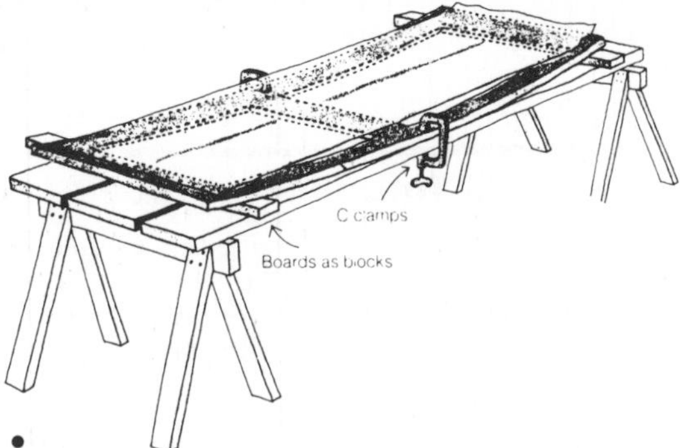

•

To stretch the screen:
Bend the door frame slightly by placing sticks under each end of the door and clamping the middle down to the sawhorse planks. Staple the top of the screen in place, release the tension slowly, then staple both sides. Do not staple the center rail until last. Trim the excess screen with a sharp knife and replace the molding.

Ortho's Home Improvement Encyclopedia
Karin Shakery, Editor
1985; 512 pp.
$24.95
($25.95 postpaid) from:
Ortho Books
575 Market Street
San Francisco, CA 94105
or Whole Earth Access

Reader's Digest Fix-It-Yourself Manual

Say what you will about ***Reader's Digest*** *magazine, you're going to have to admit they do a great manual. With this at your side, you can undertake the repair of just about anything found in a typical household. If you don't know about tools or how things work, the book tells you what you need to know — and without any trace of chauvinism. The range of subjects covered is huge, everything from tightening the rungs in the kitchen stool to whipping that rusty Coleman stove back into shape. The Dreaded Oversimplification only appears briefly in the auto section. A superior book in every way, especially in clarity. Cheaper than a repair person's house call too.* —JB

Hidden screws and trick connections

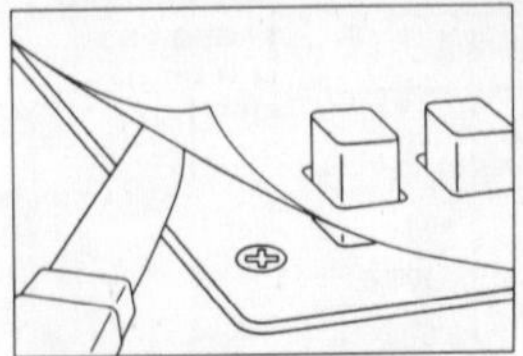

Screws are often concealed under decorative metal facings. Press facing with finger to locate screws, then pry facing up with knife. Work carefully to minimize creasing. Use strong contact cement to reglue.

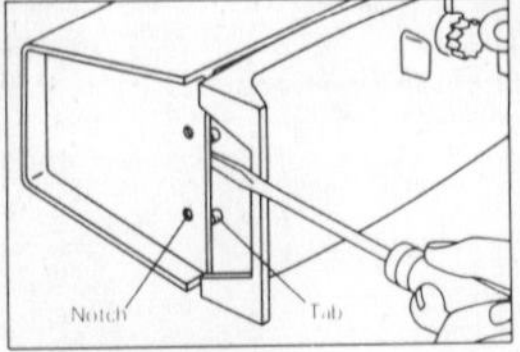

Natural springiness permits plastic parts to be connected by simple tab and notch arrangements. Illustration shows housing of can opener. Posts on one half of housing are being pried from holes in other half.

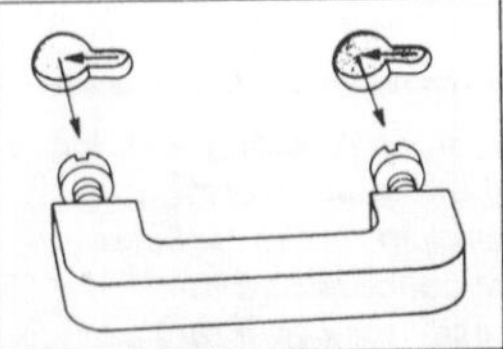

To separate parts held together by keyhole and bolt method, slide one part horizontally with respect to the other, then pull the two apart. Sharp rap may help if parts are stuck. Bolts are adjustable for tighter fit.

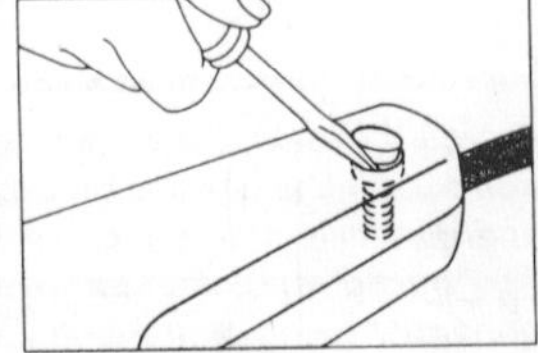

Plastic plug in housing of appliance is almost sure to have assembly screw beneath it. Pry plug out with strong, sharp instrument. Some marring of finish is inevitable no matter how carefully you work.

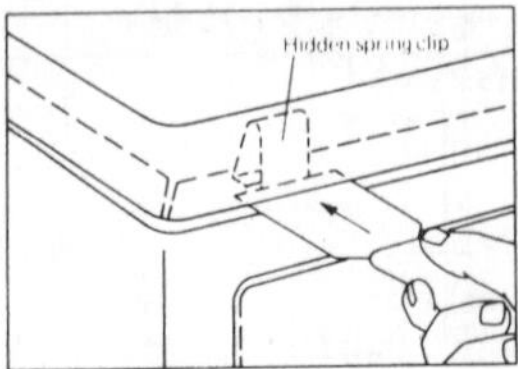

Top of clothes dryer may be held by hidden spring clips. To release top, insert putty knife under it, push knife against clip, and pull up on top. Pair of clips 2 in from each end are usually used.

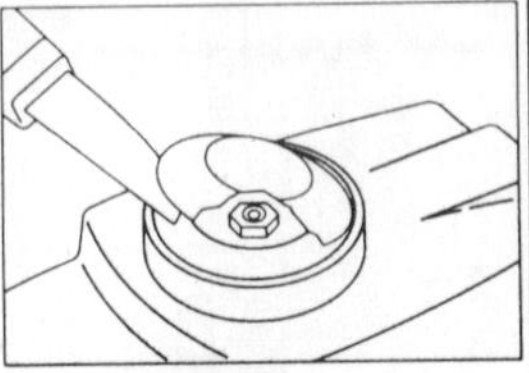

Metal cap must be pried off to reach both main assembly nut and thermostat adjustment screw of this fryer control. Nut can be removed with hollow shank nut driver. Adjustment screw is in center of control shaft.

Reader's Digest Fix-It-Yourself Manual
1978; 480 pp.
$19.98
($21.92 postpaid) from:
Reader's Digest
Attn.: Order Entry
Pleasantville, NY 10570
or Whole Earth Access

The Straight Poop

This charming home-published book takes a chatty personal approach rather than a scary authoritarian one, but it's professional nevertheless. A special section dubbed "The Dirty Dozen" will get you through most emergencies without calling a plumber. Other repairs are discussed with unusual realism, especially concerning the yukkiness likely to be encountered. (Things are rarely as neat as other books would have you believe.) A boon: old-style plumbing such as Victorian commodes that sound like dragon burps are addressed with an expertise I've never seen anywhere else. —JB

•

If your wet sag or drip from the ceiling is below a tub or shower, discovering whether you have a pressure leak or a gravity leak can sometimes be quite exasperating. At least 70 percent of these complaints that I look at end up being a gravity leak. . . .

If you can remove the shower head from the shower arm and find exposed pipe threads, then go to the hardware store and purchase a ½ inch *female pipe by male hose adapter.* Thread it onto the shower arm and then thread a garden hose onto the adaptor. Now run the hose out a convenient window or door and then turn the shower on full (hot and cold) and let it run for a good ten minutes or more.

With the water going out the hose and not the tub drain, if you do not have any more leakage, then you can assume that you do have a drain related gravity leak.

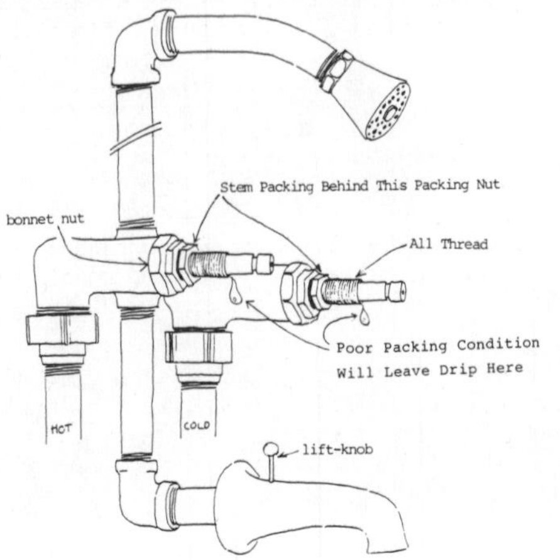

The Straight Poop
Peter A. Hemp
1986; 176 pp.
$8.95
($9.95 postpaid) from:
Ten Speed Press
P. O. Box 7123
Berkeley, CA 94707
or Whole Earth Access

• Learn to paint your house, in great detail, from . . .
How To Paint Your House: Kirk Harbeck, 1982; 52 pp.; **$6.95** ($7.95 postpaid) from McDaniel House Publishing, P. O. Box 13265, Portland, OR 97213 (or Whole Earth Access).

• Find out about indoor pollution from this book.
Indoor Air Quality and Human Health: Isaac Turiel, 1985; 173 pp. **$24.95** postpaid from Stanford University Press, Stanford, CA 94305 (or Whole Earth Access).

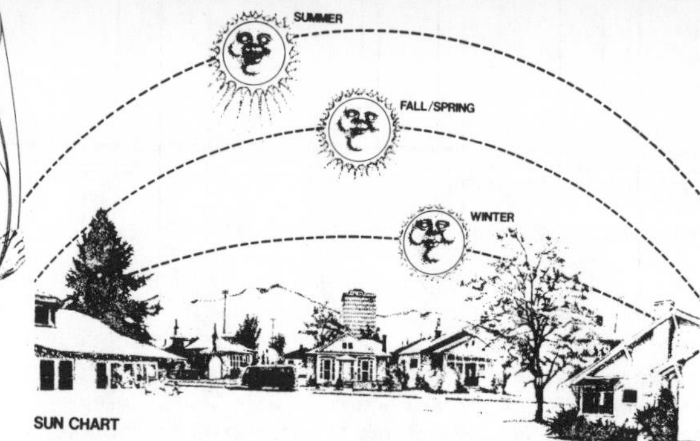

Using the sun chart to visualize solar obstructions.

The Passive Solar Energy Book

Despite advanced age in a fast-changing field, Mazria's book remains the single best guide to passive solar house design. Its basic information on solar energy, orientation, and the arrangement of rooms is current. Organization, illustration, assemblage of tools, and use of patterns (based on Christopher Alexander's **A Pattern Language** *— see p. 117) are first-rate.*

Use the book with confidence but consider these warnings: Mazria works in the sunny Southwest and shows a slight bias towards that climate. The book recommends far too much south glass per square foot of floor area given today's tight, well-insulated houses.

High-performance glazings threaten to replace movable insulation but weren't around in 1979 and aren't mentioned here. And, finally, you won't find discussion of such current issues as radiant floors, vapor barriers, back-up heating systems, phase-change materials, and the anomalous heat leaks that can rob insulation of its value.

The professional edition adds several hundred pages of useful climate data and performance calculations for fine-tuning designs. —*David Godolphin*

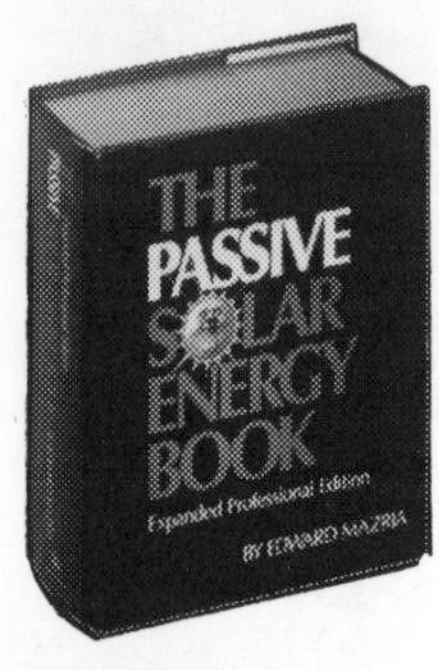

The Passive Solar Energy Book
Edward Mazria
1979; 687 pp.
$29.95 postpaid from:
Rodale Press
33 East Minor Street
Emmaus, PA 18049
or Whole Earth Access

Solar Home Design

This compendium of 12 articles from **Solar Age** *magazine (now called* **Progressive Builder***) covers conservation (the first step in any solar job), sizing the south-facing glass, window and appliance choices, thermal mass, and the basic passive solar house configurations. Understandable graphs, charts, and construction details are plentiful.*
—*David Godolphin*

Degree Days per year	Average January Temp. °F	Percent Floor Area Allowed in Glass	
		Average House*	Well Insulated House**
4000	40	11	6
5000	30	13	6
6000	25	13	7
7000	20	14	7

Most homes contain enough mass in the conventional building materials and have enough heat losses during the day to support a significant area of passive solar aperture. This table gives the approximate direct gain aperture that can be accommodated by conventional and well-insulated houses. The levels are known as the overheating points. The penalty for using more aperture area than is shown here is some degree of overheating — unless additional mass is built into the house.

*equals approximately R-11 walls, R-19 ceiling, double-glazed windows
**equals approximately R-25 walls, R-38 ceiling, triple-glazed windows

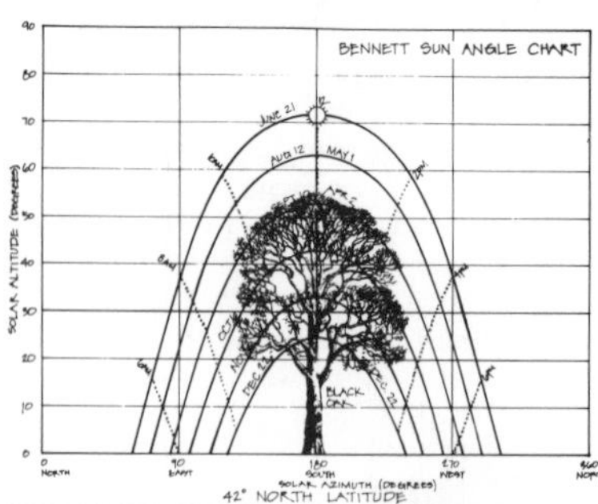

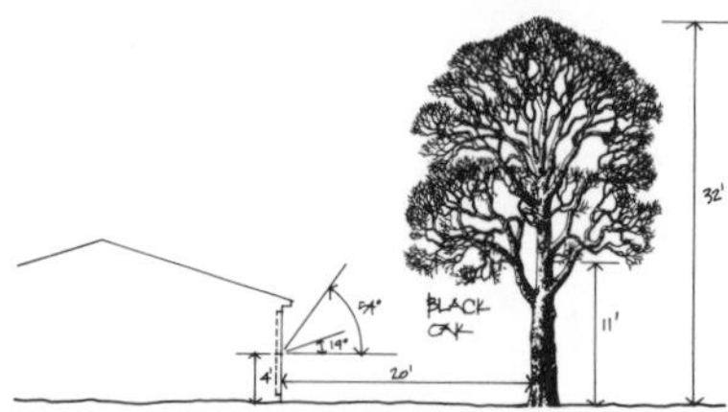

Tree shading can be visually determined by plotting the tree location and shape on a sun angle chart.

Solar Home Design
(Selections from Recent Issues of Solar Age Magazine)
1983; 38 pp.
$3.95 postpaid from:
Solar Vision, Inc.
7 Church Hill
Harrisville, NH 03450
or Whole Earth Access

Progressive Builder

This newcomer used to be a department of that most excellent of solar architecture magazines, **Solar Age***. Now the department has grown and taken over —* **Solar Age** *is no more, and* **Progressive Builder** *takes its place.*

► ***Asking a lot:*** **In the Wintergreen house, the owner and designer sought an "all-solar, affordable, small two-bedroom home." Large glazing areas and ample water storage make 100 percent solar heating possible in relatively cloudy Maine.**

As you'd expect, the accent has changed along with the name. Still lots of solar stuff, but the main interest is in energy-efficient, cost-efficient building methods. **Solar Age** *built a reputation for honest criticism and for generally being on the ball. Doesn't look as if that's changed a bit. It's still where I learn what's new.* —*JB*

Progressive Builder Magazine
William D'Alessandro, Editor
$28/year
(12 issues) from:
Progressive Builder
P. O. Box 470
Peterborough, NH 03458-0470

• This rousing history of solar architecture shows that most "modern solar innovations" have been around a long time. It's instructive and humbling to see our heritage.
A Golden Thread (2500 Years of Solar Architecture and Technology): Ken Butti and John Perlin, 1980; 304 pp. **$9.95** ($11.20 postpaid) from Kampmann & Company, 9 East 40th Street, New York, NY 10016 (or Whole Earth Access).

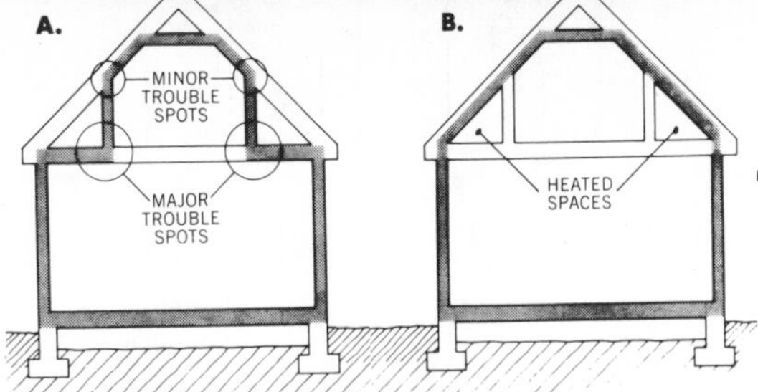

Two possible thermal envelope boundary configurations. A. Insulated knee-walls. This configuration is difficult to insulate and seal at the "trouble spots." B. Insulated roof. This is the preferred configuration, even though it encloses more heated space, because the insulation system is less likely to have defects.

The Superinsulated Home Book

If you want a house that uses very little energy, you should probably make it superinsulated and relatively airtight. Amply illustrated and very current, this book covers the principles and practice that apply to every square foot of a low-energy house, from the tapered foundation insulation to the continuous ridge vent. On the way it thoroughly treats key subjects like the air/vapor barrier, ventilation systems, and energy efficient appliances.

Just as ***The Passive Solar Energy Book*** *ignores superinsulation, this one doesn't know what to make of solar. The reading is slow going in parts, but it's worth it; the authors have done their homework heroically. All the information is there.* —David Godolphin

The Superinsulated Home Book
J. D. Ned Nisson and Gautam Dutt
1985; 316 pp.
$19.95 postpaid from:
John Wiley & Sons, Inc.
Attn.: Order Dept.
1 Wiley Drive
Somerset, NJ 08873
or Whole Earth Access

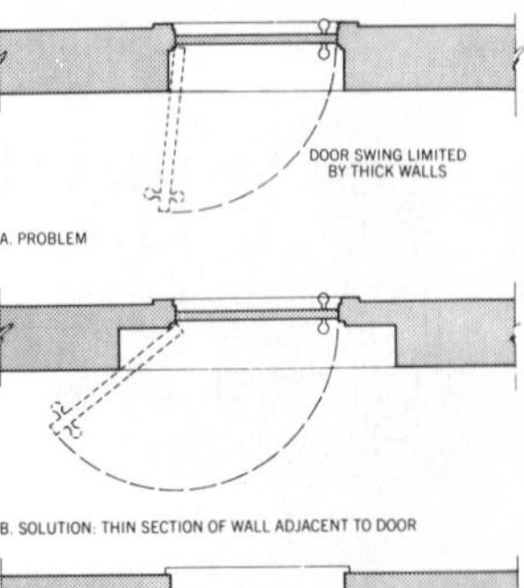

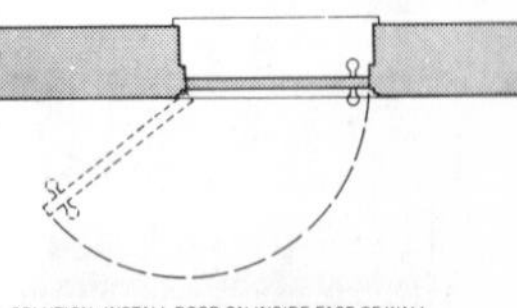

Problem of inadequate door swing with thick walls.

Climatic Design

Climatic Design *is attaining nearly biblical status among energy-conscious designers and architects. It's valuable as a reliable and comprehensive reference to the layperson as well, but it's not bedtime reading.*

Much of the book is organized as a series of specific maxims, replete with text and drawings, that form parts of broad bioclimatic strategies such as "promote earth cooling" and "minimize infiltration." Some of the theory is abstruse and hard to use, but the bulk of the book is excellent background for those thinking about a new house in the broadest terms: site, orientation, and rough floor plans. —David Godolphin

Comparison of different types of weatherstripping for doors and windows. These are listed in order of estimated overall durability.

KEY: E—Excellent; VG—Very Good; G—Good; F—Fair; P—Poor

TYPE	MATERIAL	Estimated Overall Durability	Effective Uses (1)	Suitable for Non-uniform gaps	Visibility When Installed
FLAT METAL STRIP	Brass or bronze	E	C/A	No	Very low
	Aluminum	VG to E	C/A	No	Very low
TUBULAR GASKET	Vinyl or rubber, foam-filled	VG	C/A	Yes	High
	Vinyl or rubber, hollow	VG	C/A	Yes	High
REINFORCED GASKET	Aluminium and vinyl	VG	C/A	Yes	High
REINFORCED FELT	Wool felt and aluminum	G	C	No	High
	Nonwool felt and aluminum	F to G	C	No	High
NONREINFORCED FELT	Wool	G	C	No	(2)
	Other	F to G	C	No	(2)
RIGID STRIP	Aluminum and vinyl	G	C	Yes	Low (3)
	Wood and foam	F	C	Yes	Low
FOAM STRIP	Neoprene or rubber	F	C	Yes	(2)
	Vinyl	F	C	Yes	(2)
	Polyurethane	P to F	C	Yes	(2)

(1) C—Where material will be subject to compression
A—Where material will be subject to abrasion
(2) Low if under sash or inside doorjamb. High if used along window frame or against door stop.
(3) On aluminum door, its primary use.

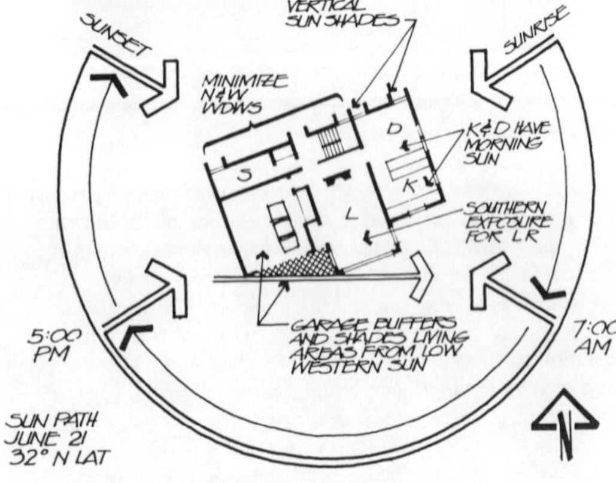

◄ A house can be made more energy efficient simply by designing the plan so that the order of rooms in which the normal daily sequence of activities occurs "follows" the path of the sun.

Suggested room orientations

	N	NE	E	SE	S	SW	W	NW
Bedroom*	•	•	•	•	•			
Bath*	•	•	•	•	•	•	•	•
Kitchen			•	•	•			
Dining			•	•	•	•		
Living				•	•			
Family				•	•	•		
Utility / Laundry*	•	•						•
Workshop*	•	•						•
Storage*	•						•	•
Garage*	•					•	•	•
Sun porch				•	•	•		
Outdoor space*			•	•	•	•		

*The most suitable location of those indicated will depend on local climate — whether largely too hot or too cold, direction of winter winds and summer breezes, etc.

Climatic Design
Donald Watson, FAIA and Kenneth Labs
1983; 280 pp.
$37.50 postpaid from:
Order Services,
McGraw-Hill Book Co.
Manchester Road,
Manchester, MO 63011
or Whole Earth Access

Solar Software: SUNPAS/SUNOP, F-CHART 5.2

Solar calculations can be a maddening time consumer, particularly when you're trying to ascertain the effects of small design changes. A computer can help; it only takes one a few seconds to try your ideas. Solarsoft draws rave reviews from all over the solar field for its smooth, quick, and versatile programs. Best is the Macintosh version of SUNPAS, a program that calculates the energy performance of 94 passive solar house designs. It also generates an energy performance file that its companion SUNOP program uses to analyze the economics of building options. You can even figure in local construction costs, fuel prices, and inflation. You get the results as graphs and tables.

Despite a few well-documented faults, F-CHART is the premier program for analyzing active solar collector systems. It tells you how much heat you'll get from air or liquid collectors used for space heating, domestic hot water, or swimming pool heating. Not all F-CHART programs are easy to use; early versions were notoriously crude. Solarsoft has put its stamp of grace on this one. —David Godolphin

SUNPAS/SUNOP, F-CHART 5.2
$189 each
Information **free** from:
Solarsoft
1406 Burlingame Avenue
Burlingame, CA 94010

• Deservedly famous, it's back (too late to feature here), better than ever with the latest information for solar builders and designers.
The New Solar Home Book: Bruce Anderson and Michael Riordan, 1986; 320 pp. **$16.95** ($18.95 postpaid) from Brick House Publishing Co., 3 Main Street, Andover, MA 01810 (or Whole Earth Access).

Solar Catalog
$3 from:
Solar Components Co.
P. O. Box 237
Manchester, NH 03105

GREENHOUSE SHADE

This strong vinyl coated, polyester fabric admits only 37% of the available light — just right for reduced summer heat with a pleasant light level for solar greenhouses, sunspaces and passive solar homes.

Solar Catalog

This juicy catalog features a good selection of hardware needed for solar heating. It's where you order products made of Sun-Lite® — the best fiberglass-reinforced plastic glazing. It can be had in rolls, or in prefabricated panels ready to install. The roll stock can be used to make solar heated water tanks for thermal storage and aquaculture. It works well for greenhouses. Note that this catalog, like most others, doesn't criticize or otherwise comment on suitability of items shown. It pays to read up on prospective purchases, and to discuss them with folks who have some experience. —JB

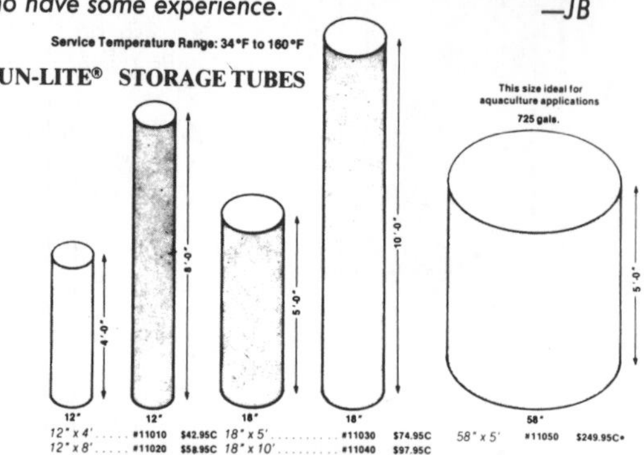

Solar-H-Foil
Black Chrome Absorber
For High Efficiency Systems

Selective surface absorbers are made of copper strip and foil continuously electroplated with black chrome for its excellent absorptive properties. They can be used directly as an absorber. When used instead of paint, less collector square footage is required due to higher efficiencies; resulting in cost savings. Absorbers can be brazed or soldered without damaging the black chrome coating. Widths of 24" make this product ideal for placement between rafters. Textured pattern provides improved heat transfer due to 18% more surface area than flat metal. Absorptivity = .95, emissivity = .11, .005" thick.

Black Chrome Absorber	**10' length**	**#05600**	**$59.95P**
	25' length	**#05610**	**$139.95P**
	50' length	**#05620**	**$250.00P**

Wood Stove Absorber Fins

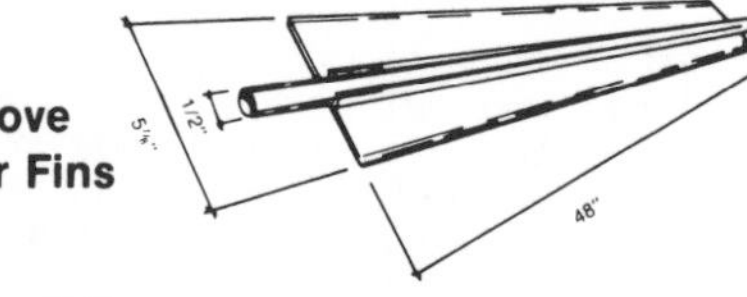

Reduce Hot Water Costs Now!

These 6" x 4' Aluminum Fins easily snap on to ½" I.D. copper pipe. Allows homeowner to place fins behind a woodstove to inexpensively preheat domestic hot water. Dozens of uses. Fins may be painted black or coated with a selective surface such as our catalog #06100.

Absorber Fins **#05300** **$5.95 C**

Solar Card
$14.95
postpaid from:
Design Works, Inc.
11 Hitching Post Road
Amherst, MA 01002

Zomeworks
Information
free from:
Zomeworks Corp.
P. O. Box 25805
Albuquerque, NM 87125

Zomeworks

In a business rife with doubtful quality and broken promises, Zomeworks has attained a reputation for reliable products. Their formula for success: Clever, simple products that perform like the advertisements say they will. Founder Steve Baer has a knack for whipping things down to essentials, and the products show that. No government largesse has been involved either; perhaps that's one reason for the lean, no-nonsense designs. Look at their catalog for a lesson in clarity. —JB

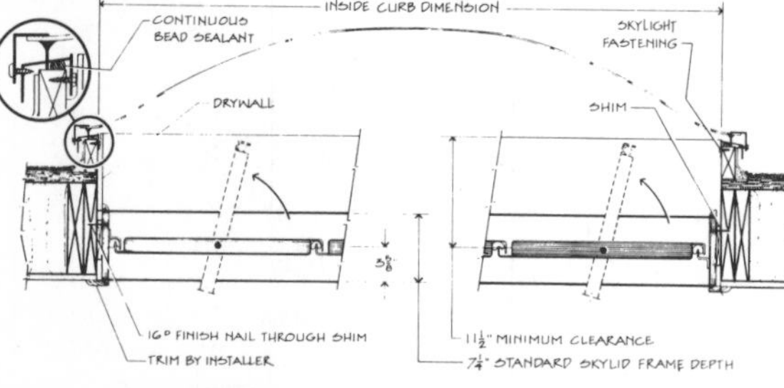

•

SKYLID® self-operating insulating louvers are sets of panels that open beneath a skylight to allow the sun to enter during the day and close to seal against heat loss at night. They are self-operating: The sun controls their responsive weight shifting system. SKYLIDS® are available for maximum direct gain and sunlighting or for indirect gain and daylighting. A manual override allows the louvers to be held in a closed or partially closed position to prevent overheating or to control light levels.

SUMMER

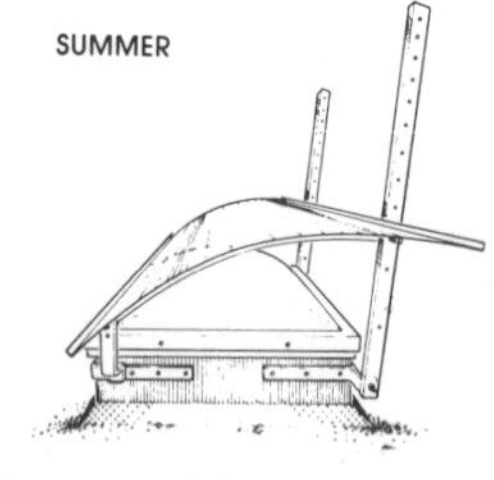

WINTER

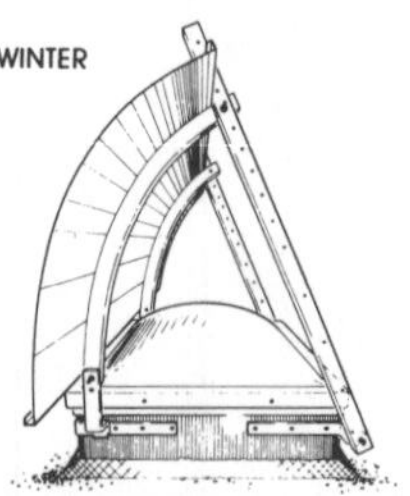

•

The Sunbender® Reflector/Shade is designed to fit any well built, sturdy curb mount skylight. During the heating season, it reflects from 100,000 to 200,000 extra Btu's per square foot of skylight into the building below. In the lowered summer position, it shades the skylight and greatly reduces heat gain, while still allowing light to enter.

Solar Card

Is the neighbor's tree gonna shade your solar hot water heater in February? Will your proposed garden get enough sun for tomatoes? You can find out easily by viewing your surroundings through the lines printed on a Solar Card. It's a bit awkward to use but it's cheap and it works. Tell them your city and state when ordering. —JB
[Suggested by David Godolphin]

The Spec Guide

Like a showroom without sales pressure, this guide lists more than one thousand energy related products and their specifications. You'll find side-by-side comparison of such things as hot water heating systems, collectors, controls, instruments, thermal storage hardware, and wind energy sets. You won't find judgment though; that's up to you. Note that performance claims are the manufacturer's. If the Guide's price seems high, think of what it would take you in time and postage to round up all this stuff. Be grateful. —JB

•

HEAT MIRROR™
55, 77, 88
Product Description:

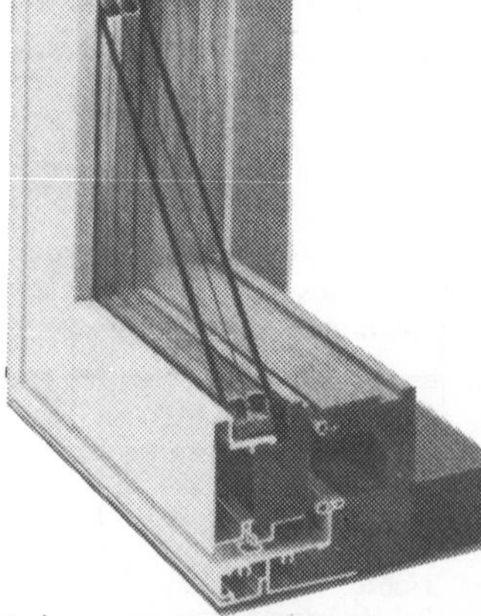

Heat Mirror™ transparent window insulation is factory mounted in the air space of a sealed, double pane unit by leading window manufacturers throughout the world. It dramatically increases the insulating properties of the window by reflecting the long-wave infrared energy ('heat') and transmitting solar energy.
Heat Mirror equipped windows reject most of the damaging ultra-violet energy, transmit light without color distortion, and have R-values from 4 to 4.3.

The Spec Guide
(8th Edition)
$49.50
from:
Spec Guide
P. O. Box 470
Peterborough, NH
03458-0470

—Practical Photovoltaics

—RVer's Guide to Solar Battery Charging

PHOTOVOLTAIC (PV) PANELS make electricity when the sun shines on them. They do it quietly, simply, reliably (at last!), and if not cheaply, at least for less money than last year. They're already competitive with all other nonutility sources of electricity. The price has been steadily dropping, if you take inflation into consideration, and will drop further as production rises, which it is. Watch a billion dollar industry being born, folks — PV is coming on line fast. —J. Baldwin

Photovoltaics (PV)

***Practical Photovoltaics** presents the theory and practice of photovoltaics in a nontechnical manner; read it and you'll have good reason to claim you know what you're doing. There are complete instructions for assembling your own panels from individual cells (which are often available at a discount) — a great way to save money.*

***The New Solar Electric Home** is an update of one of our favorite PV books. The new version concentrates on the design of complete household PV systems, especially the equipment that "inverts" the low voltage DC power into the 110-volt AC power you and your appliances are used to. (The author recommends the Heart Interface, a device available from most of the suppliers shown on this page.) Recent developments make photovoltaic homes truly practical for the first time.*

***RVers' Guide to Solar Battery Charging** is a finely detailed guide to installing PV systems in your motorhome, trailer, boat, or cabin. I've lived PV-powered for six years now and can vouch that this book is what you need to know. Wish I'd had it in 1980.* —JB

•

The Sun Frost refrigerator/freezer, very popular with homeowners, has now been discovered by RVers because of innovations which achieve exceptionally low power consumption. The Sun Frost is superinsulated with 3-4 inches of polyurethane foam. A top-mounted, hermetically sealed compressor runs cool and prevents heat from entering the cabinet. A high level of efficiency is developed in a "low differential" evaporator coil. . . . Its superinsulation allows 24-hour shut-off without spoilage.

Technically, this unit could run on the output of only two standard PV panels; however, this would not allow any reserve for bad weather. We allow three panels full output just for refrigeration.

—*RVers' Guide to Solar Battery Charging*

A cell can be permanently damaged if a large reverse voltage is applied to the electrodes. There is one circumstance under which this reverse voltage condition can occur: when one cell is shaded while the rest of the cells in a series string are in sunlight. The current through the string immediately stops, and the sum of all the open-circuit voltages of all the other cells shows up across the shaded cell. The resistance heating effect of the current can make a cell hot enough to melt the solder connections.

—*Practical Photovoltaics*

Installing a photovoltaic module.

Practical Photovoltaics
Richard J. Komp
1984; 196 pp.
$16.95
($18.45 postpaid)

The New Solar Electric Home
Joel Davidson
1986; 220 pp.
$14.95
($16.45 postpaid)

RVers' Guide to Solar Battery Charging
Noel and Barbara Kirkby
1986; 200 pp.
$11.95
($13.45 postpaid)
All from:
AATEC Publications
P. O. Box 7119
Ann Arbor, MI 48107
or Whole Earth Access

Photovoltaic Suppliers

There are now many competent suppliers of trustable equipment. These are a few that I or friends have found to be pleasant to work with. Prices vary; you should shop around.

Independent Power Company. Now one of many Photocomm dealers, they hawk their wares in this comprehensive and educational catalog. They offer complete packaged systems for residential power and water pumping, among other things.

Wm. Lamb • Solar Electric Specialties. Send Wm. Lamb a letter outlining your needs anywhere in the world, and they'll make recommendations based on their free engineering service. No catalog, but they'll supply what they recommend.

Solar Electric Specialties offers a similar service.

*Solar Electric Systems. Specializes in PV for recreational vehicles. Prices are good. They wrote a book too: **RVer's Guide to Solar Battery Charging** (above).*

WindLight Workshop. One of the most experienced supplier/experimenters. Windy Dankoff offers this annotated catalog of PV electricity, making and using hardware.

Talmage Energy Systems. One of the first Eastern suppliers. Has lots of experience with New England weather conditions. —JB

Independent Power Company: Catalog **$5.95** from Catalog and Mail Order Center, P. O. Box 649, No. San Juan, CA 95960

Wm. Lamb Corp.: Information **free** from Wm. Lamb Corp., 10615 Chandler Blvd., North Hollywood, CA 91601

Solar Electric Specialities Co.: Information **free** from Solar Electric Specialties Co., P. O. Box 537, Willits, CA 95490

Solar Electric Systems: Catalog **free** from Solar Electric Systems, P. O. Box 1562, Cave Creek, AZ 85331

WindLight Workshop: Catalog **$4** from WindLight Workshop, P. O. Box 548, Santa Cruz, NM 87567

Talmage Energy Systems: Catalog **$3** from Talmage Energy Systems, P. O. Box 497A, Beachwood Road, Kennebunkport, ME 04046

• Fredson's RV Supply (p. 271) and the marine supply catalogs (p. 289) stock many devices that run on 12-volt DC — just what you need in a simple photovoltaic electric setup.

The PV Network News

This quarterly newsletter continues to serve as a clearinghouse for PV knowhow developed by folks using photovoltaics in their daily lives. The product reviews and field-proven tips are often way ahead of more formal publications not so intimately involved with reality. A feature, "Solar Works," is an up-to-date bibliography and source list — itself worth the price of the subscription. —JB

The PV Network News
A.D. Paul Wilkins, Editor
$15/year,
includes membership
(4 issues) from:
The PV Network News
Route 2, P. O. Box 274
Santa Fe, NM 87505

WOOD HEAT WENT from hick to chic in the '70s, when energy prices inspired many folks to turn from fossil fuels. But the drawbacks soon became apparent: there is a lot of work involved, some fire danger, and ecological problems. While it is true that wood heat saves fossil fuel, and the total energy obtained from wood heat approximates the total output of nuclear power plants, it is also true that wood burning results in pollution. Oregon has led the way with a tough state law that mandates clean-burning designs, thus beginning a strong trend.

Noted wood fuel expert Jay Shelton (see below) recently assured me that properly designed stoves with catalytic converters work well, pollute little, are durable, and reduce the amount of wood used. He wouldn't recommend any particular brand, and neither will we; there are too many variables. (I do recommend you look at *Consumer Reports* magazine, October '85, p. 150, for a controlled test of several brands.) And remember, please, that if you aren't replacing the trees you burn you are contributing to deforestation, a scourge that has brought down more than one civilization. —JB

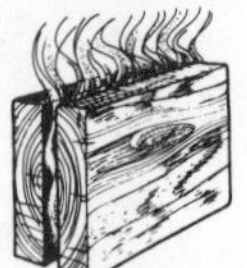

When too close together, not enough air can get in; the fire smoulders and goes out.

With appropriate spacing, there is enough air and mutual heating to sustain good combustion.

When too far apart, too much heat is lost to sustain pyrolysis, and the fire goes out. —*Solid Fuels Encyclopedia*

Solid Fuels Encyclopedia

Solid Fuels Encyclopedia
Jay W. Shelton
1983; 268 pp.
$12.95
($14.95 postpaid) from:
Garden Way Publishing
Schoolhouse Road
Pownal, VT 05261
or Whole Earth Access

The name Jay Shelton is often heard when wood heat is being discussed. His research has developed a trustworthy body of information on wood and coal burning for household heating. This book covers every aspect of the subject: stoves, fireplaces, chimneys, furnaces, air circulation, safety, and proper operation. It's done in plain language with excellent illustrations. —JB

•

A pair of gloves kept near the stove can be useful. Some stoves have door handles and air-inlet controls that are too hot to touch with a bare hand. Gloves are especially important for handling burning wood in an emergency. Should a burning log roll out of a fireplace stove with its doors open, or a hot coal get beyond the floor protector during ash removal, or should the last log in a new fuel load have to be removed because it would not go in far enough to permit closing the door, or should the hot cooking-hole cover be dislodged from its hole by a back-puff, or . . . A good pair of gloves could save the day.

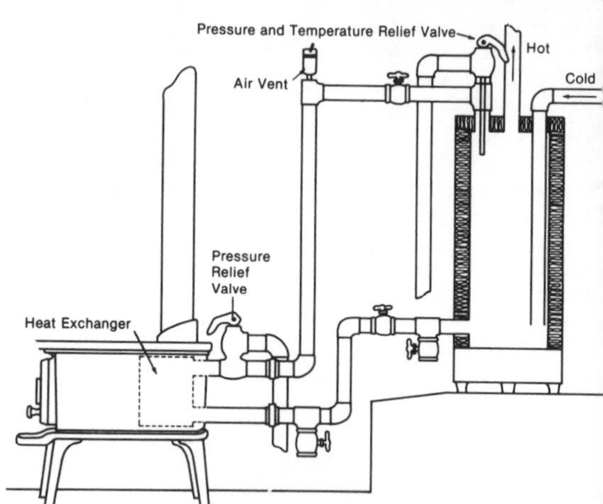

An installed water-heating heat exchanger in a stove. The size of the plumbing is exaggerated.

Wood Heat Safety

Wood Heat Safety
Jay W. Shelton
1979; 165 pp.
$9.95
($11.95 postpaid) from:
Garden Way Publishing
Schoolhouse Road
Pownal, VT 05261
or Whole Earth Access

Fire inspectors, code writers, and insurance companies are all getting tougher about standards for wood heating appliances. They have good reason too; the statistics show the sad results of inexpert or careless wood heating practices. This book probably has your exact situation and what to do about it, illustrated and discussed down to the last tiny detail. Particular attention is given to problems found in older houses, a subject not often dealt with in other books. Of course, the information you'll need for a new place is there, too, equally detailed. The calm and competent presentation is mercifully free of horror stories and especially easy to use. —JB

•

My personal preference, not considering cost or convenience of installation in an existing house, is an interior masonry chimney with all its walls exposed to the living spaces. By trying to avoid smoldering fires I manage to avoid much creosote buildup, and the exposed masonry contributes considerable heat. However I have installed some prefabricated metal chimneys in my homes because of the ease of installation.

Best (least creosote)
Intermediate
Worst

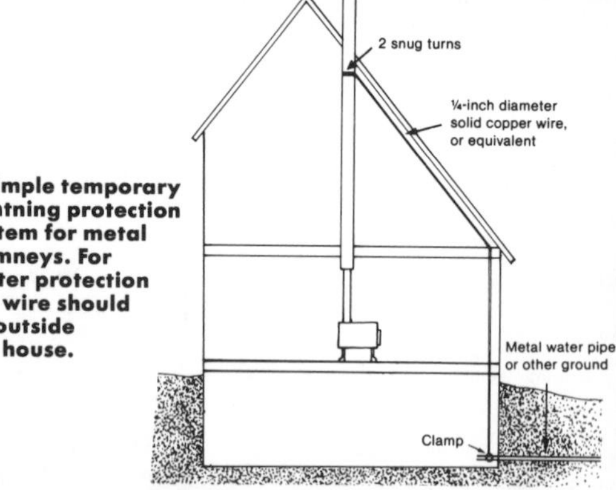

A simple temporary lightning protection system for metal chimneys. For better protection the wire should be outside the house.

Shelton Research, Inc.

Jay Shelton's own lab publishes results of their research, in pamphlet form, usually well before it appears elsewhere. For a list of current hot topics, send a S.A.S.E. to Shelton Research, Inc., P. O. Box 5235, Santa Fe, NM 87502. —JB

• Wood cookstoves can be bought at Lehman's Hardware and Appliances (p. 143).
• Woodcutting needs are well served at Bailey's (p. 127).
• The best splitting wedge is the one sold by Brookstone (p. 159).
• For chainsaw technique, see p. 127.

rushing clean the entire stove inside — including cooking ‑lates and all removable parts.

‑e Your Own Chimney Sweep

‑ew enterprises are so ripe for disaster as sweeping ‑he creosote and the potential fire hazard thereof out ‑f your chimney. This clearly written book tells you how ‑o do it right, and appears to be realistic about the ‑ifficulties. —JB

•

‑reosote is undesirable, not only because it is fuel for ‑himney fires, but for several other reasons. It decreases ‑he effective flue diameter of the stack. This reduction is ‑nost dramatic in smaller stacks. For example, a six-inch ‑ipe with a one-half-inch buildup of creosote loses 30 ‑ercent of its area.

Drying Wood with the Sun

Remember those government "Energy Grants" a few years back? Not all turned out to produce worthy designs, but these well-proven solar firewood dryer plans are fine. Several basically similar ideas are presented in easily understood drawings accompanied by the expected explanations and materials lists. The rig will work just about anywhere, greatly speeding the drying process of any wood, or whatever else you put in there. Vegetables, even. Looks good to me. Be sure and pay attention to their warning not to attach the dryer to your house; the damp heat and wood-loving insects could damage it. —JB

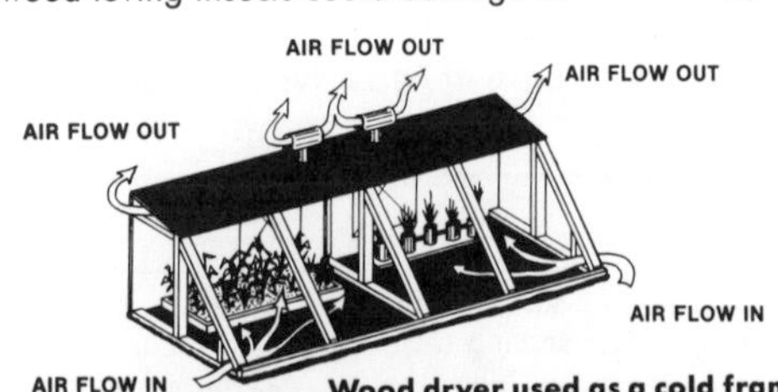

Wood dryer used as a cold frame.

Be Your Own Chimney Sweep
Christopher Curtis
and Donald Post
1979; 101 pp.
$5.95
OUT OF PRINT
(Whole Earth Access has limited supply)
Garden Way Publishing

‑he August West System

‑leed a job? If there's no tough competition nearby, you ‑ould get into the chimney sweeping business. This outfit ‑vill outfit you, teach you the trade, and help you set up ‑he business. Their reputation as professionals will rub off ‑n you, allaying customer fears. Alas, you'll have to do ‑our own chimney free. —JB

‑nformation kit **free** from August West Systems, Inc., ‑. O. Box 658, Worcester, MA 01601.

‑How To Get Parts Cast For Your Antique Stove

‑This booklet tells you how to get or make the parts you ‑need to keep that old beast cookin'. They have other old-stove information too. Send S.A.S.E. for list. —JB

‑How To Get Parts Cast For Your Antique Stove
Clifford Boram
1982; 52 pp.
$5
postpaid from:
Autonomy House Publications
417 North Main Street
Monticello, IN 47960
or Whole Earth Access

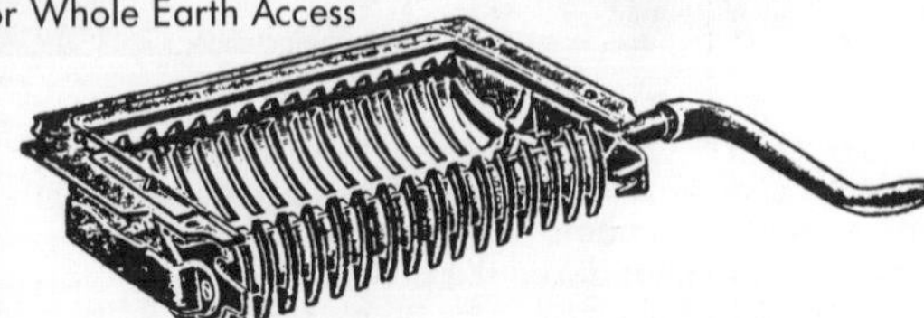

This grate is duplex in that it is composed of two bars and in that it has two positions — one for coal and one for wood. Most other grates are intended for one fuel only.

• Check **Ken Kern's Masonry Stove** (p. 120).

• If you burn 'em, you should plant 'em or at least buy from a managed woodlot or forest. Check "Trees" (p. 62).

Finnish Fireplace Construction Manual 1984

Nice books extolling the virtues of massive masonry woodstoves head you in the right direction, but don't lead you by the hand past the potential disasters. Building one of these monsters is tricky business — you must allow for expansion, and must not build pockets that could trap explosive or noxious gases. This book, by an acknowledged master of the art, is a minutely detailed, illustrated and genuine manual. It really does get down to the tiniest moves, and that's hard to do when one is psychologically involved with tons of material. I expect this manual will have the desired effect: lots of Finnish fireplaces will now be built, and they'll be good ones. —JB

•

Once the burn is completed, dampers in the chimney flue are shut and the entire mass radiates heat for the next 12-24 hours. While the gas flow in the heater moves in a downdraft past the heat exchange surface of the heater, room air outside the heater moves in an updraft pattern along the vertical faces of the heater setting up a circulating flow of warmed air in the living space. It is from the opposing flows of warming heater gases and warmed room air that the name contraflow heater is derived.

•

Mortar
Modern cement mortars are not appropriate for masonry heater inner core construction and are never used in Europe. Traditionally, European masonry heaters have always been constructed with clay-based mortars. The mortar we have found is a high quality, clay-based mortar called Uunilaasti, made in Finland. With care, we find it possible to build our standard heater in such a way that only a single bag of the special mortar, at an approximate cost of $30, is required. For those working with the mortar for the first time we recommend that they buy two in order not to run out at some critical point and have to delay work while waiting for supply.

Modern double brick construction with ceramic tile facade.

Drying Wood With the Sun
N.C.A.T.
1983; 24 pp.
$5 postpaid from:
National Center for Appropriate Technology
P. O. Box 3838
Butte, MT 59702
or Whole Earth Access

Finnish Fireplace Construction Manual 1984
Albert A. Barden, III
1984; 65 pp.
$17
postpaid from:
Maine Wood Heat Co.
RFD 1, Box 640
Norridgewock, ME 04957
or Whole Earth Access

WHEN WHOLE EARTH publications started in 1968, there was much glib talk of "free energy" from the sun, wind, and methane digesters. Some folks (not us) even thought that this free energy would by itself cause extensive political decentralization, a naive, or at least premature, view. But we *have* learned a few things:

Funky hardware gives funky results, regardless of the righteousness of the maker. Reliable hardware is harder to produce and costs more than one would hope. Reduction of demand (conservation) is not very exciting but is the cheapest energy strategy and certainly is step one. Household-size methane digesters don't work. We were right about one thing: There is nothing alternative about solar energy. 'Twas ever thus.

But the decade has produced some reliable knowledge and hardware — much of it from the minds and hands of experimenters. We now know that superinsulated houses are the most economical way to go, whether passively solar heated or otherwise; and photovoltaics are the simplest, most economical way to make electricity on-site if you live where there's sun. Sounds easy. It wasn't. More later. Keep working.

—J. Baldwin

ASE
Larry Stoiaken, Editor
$48/year
(10 issues) from:
Alternative Sources of Energy
107 South Central Avenue
Milaca, MN 56353

ASE

__ASE__ (Alternative Sources of Energy) started long ago as a funky publication serving experimenters and has matured along with the technology it serves. No more homemade windmill articles; sad but realistic. Instead we read the industry news and latest developments in commercially available hardware, all slickly presented as befits the serious business at hand. Each issue concentrates on a specific subject such as cogeneration or wind power. __ASE__ is one of the best ways to keep up with ASE. —JB

◄ **The City of Dixon [California] recently dedicated this 20kW. photovoltaic energy system on top of the roof of their City Hall.**

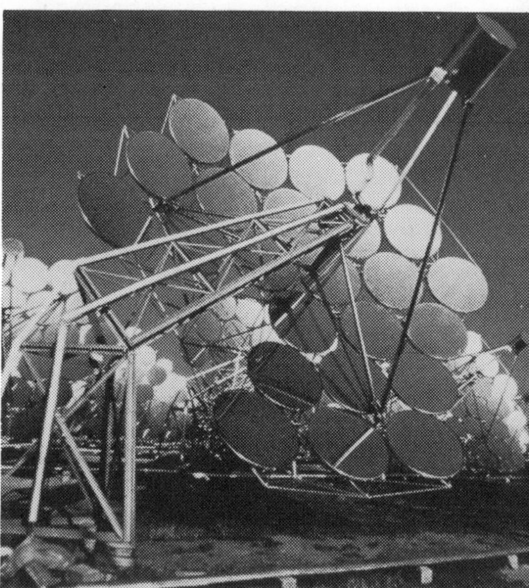

The mylar film reflectors [above], which were the product of five years and $15 million of research and development, can be seen in this photo. According to LaJet, the low-cost concentrators reduced the per-watt installation cost of a solar power plant by some 80 percent.

NATAS
Information **free** from:
NATAS
U.S. Department of Energy
P. O. Box 2525
Butte, MT 59702

NATAS

The National Appropriate Technology Assistance Service is associated with NCAT, but does business in a different way: when you need technical advice on energy matters, you call their 800 number. You will be connected with an expert who will get you the best information available. Right then. Call 1-800-428-2525 (1-800-428-1718 in Montana) 9am-6pm Central Time on weekdays. They'll take on anything from a homeowner's simple solar water heater dilemma to municipal energy policy. In this case, our gummint is doing something right. —JB

NCAT
Publications Catalog
free from:
NCAT
P. O. Box 3838
Butte, MT 59702

NCAT

"En-Cat" (National Center for Appropriate Technology) publishes the findings of their research as inexpensive booklets (most less than $5). The subject matter is aimed at ordinary folks who wish to know more about subjects common to the appropriate tech field: solar water heaters, composting toilets, biogas, weatherizing a mobile home . . . lots more. Their publications tend to summarize the baffling amount of information available elsewhere — a very useful service. —JB

• See "Rocky Mountain Institute" (p. 89).

• Here's a rousing story of a hard-fought victory over obtuse power company policy. Inspiring and true. **Dynamos and Virgins** (Forcing the Future on the Nation's Utilities): David Roe, 1984; 288 pp. **$18.95** ($19.95 postpaid) from: Random House, Order Dept., 400 Hahn Road, Westminster, MD 21157.

By late 1984, small, innovative firms had installed almost 8,500 turbines throughout California, producing enough electricity for 70,000 modern homes. By the end of 1985, the state Energy Commission predicts developers will have built over 1,000 megawatts of wind capacity, the equivalent of a large nuclear reactor.

Solar Lobby
Membership
$20/year
(includes bimonthly newsletter and special reports)
Booklets **$4** each
Center for Renewable Resources
Publications list **free**
Both from:
CRR
1001 Connecticut Ave. NW
Suite 638
Washington, DC 20036

Solar Lobby and the Center for Renewable Resources

The Solar Lobby is in there hammering away at legislators who still think there's no energy problem. Denis Hayes, an old hand at this, is at the helm. The Center for Renewable Resources is the educational arm of the outfit. They publish attractive booklets full of disquieting facts and figures on current energy topics, particularly useful for teachers. All well done and effective. —JB

•

Congress claims to be worried about the trade deficit, and has begun erecting barriers to protect us against myriad imports. But it steadfastly ignores the one that really counts. Foreign oil is the largest item, by far, in our negative balance of trade. Oil caused a net drain of $51 billion dollars last year — nearly half of our $123 billion trade deficit. . . .

•

Nuclear power, which provides less than 2 percent of the nation's delivered energy and for which there have been no new orders since 1978, receives 34 percent of all federal energy subsidies.

Common Sense Wind Energy

Read about commercial scale wind energy in **ASE** *magazine. Read up on residential scale wind energy in this remarkably clear, mercifully brief roundup of the basics. In contrast to most other wind power books, this one is realistic — a very essential ingredient for success in this oft overhyped field.* —JB

Common Sense Wind Energy
California Office of Appropriate Technology
1983; 83 pp.
$8.95
($10.95 postpaid) from:
Brick House Publishing Co.
3 Main Street
Andover, MA 01810
or Whole Earth Access

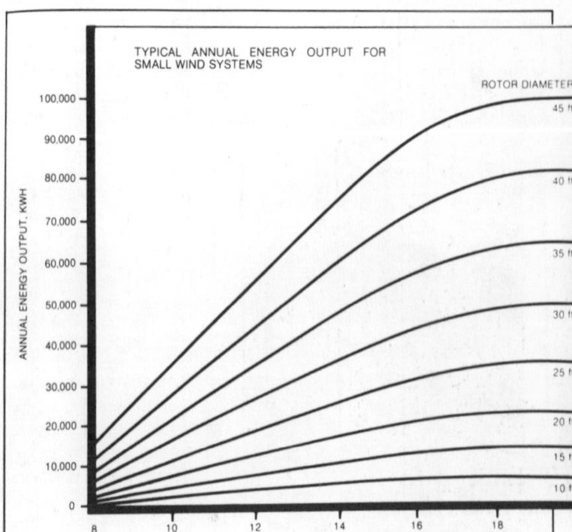

The Residential Hydro Power Book

You can put that nearby stream to work making electricity, maybe. Individual experimenters have been messing around for years with small hydro generator sets that are well within most budgets. As is common with such enterprises, a body of reliable information together with acceptable hardware has slowly developed — everything learned the hard way. Here's the first good book on the subject. It's informal, subjective, and real: what has worked so far and what hasn't. What isn't known reliably yet is admitted and discussed as far as is possible. (That's called honesty.) Alas, our lawsuit-happy society has necessitated the censoring of certain procedures known to work but at some risk. Too bad. Nonetheless, you'll learn enough to set up a working system from dam to end use. A list of suppliers makes the book commendably useful and complete. —JB

•

Virtually every DC hydro system manufacturer in the world contributed information and first hand accounts of good (and bad) system installations. So read this book, then go with confidence to install your own hydro system. As you start your turbine for the first time, you too, can feel the quiet satisfaction of true energy independence.

•

At the turbine, install a gate valve, union, and pressure gauge. Don't install a fast-closing valve like a ball valve or butterfly valve. You could accidentally close it too fast, causing the moving water in the pipe to slam suddenly into the valve. This slamming action can cause enormous pressures, rupturing pipes or valves.

The Residential Hydro Power Book
Keith Ritter, P.E.
1986; 150 pp.
$10 postpaid from:
Homestead Engineering
32801 Highway 36
Bridgeville, CA 95526
or Whole Earth Access

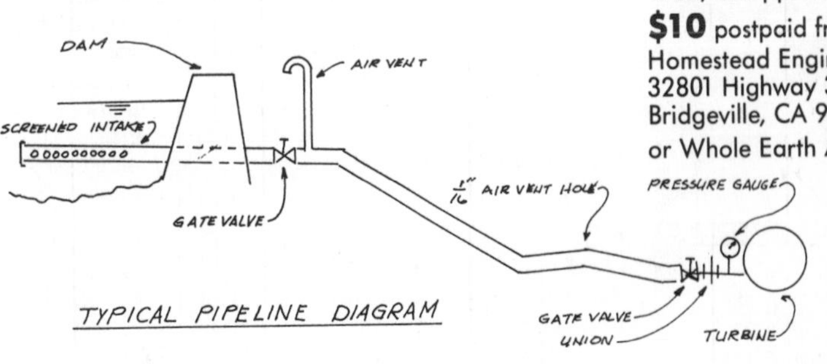

TYPICAL PIPELINE DIAGRAM

• Buying lights or devices that feed upon electricity? Better read **Saving Energy and Money with Home Appliances.** Which ones to buy are listed in **The Most Energy-Efficient Appliances.** It's updated semiannually.

Saving Energy and Money with Home Appliances: Steven Nadel and Howard Geller, 1985; 34 pp. **$2** postpaid.

The Most Energy-Efficient Appliances: American Council for an Energy-Efficient Economy, 1986; 18 pp. **$2** postpaid.

Both from ACEEE, 100 Connecticut Avenue NW, Washington, DC 20036.

The Official Captain Hydro Water Conservation Workbook
1982; 39 pp.
Available to teachers and school districts
Information **free** from:
East Bay Municipal Utility District
P. O. Box 24055
Oakland, CA 94623

WATER CONSERVATION HAS entered the mainstream. It is as common as small cars. Utilities now understand: Citizens would rather cut use by half than pay for bonds and new taxes to double supply. River lovers have been an effective lobby: Save water at home; you save trout streams in the hills. Even the tortoise-like plumbing industry has accepted low-flush toilets as the sound of the future. This is a success story. But don't forget to insist that your plumbing supply store sell water-saving shower heads. And flow reducers and toilets (should be less than 2 gallons per flush). Don't forget to vote against unnecessary bonds when conservation can do the job. Hats off to water savers. Relish it next time you swim or fish or float downstream. There is no longer any single book in print that sums up home water conservation. *Captain Hydro* is to teach the kids. *We All Live Downstream* (best equipment access) and *Septic Tank Practices* (see next page) both have good chapters on water saving. —Peter Warshall

Planning for an Individual Water System

The book you want will depend on the volume of water you need (enough for washing dishes or for fire protection), the possible source (well, pond, or roof collector), the quality of the water (potable or possibly polluted), the conveyance mechanism (electricity or gravity feed) and trade-offs between how much money you have and how much time you can spend operating and maintaining your water supply (hand pumps, backwash filter or automatic chlorinator). ***Planning*** *is the best, no-fooling-around American-style do-it-yourself manual. The best for electric pumps and wiring your water supply system. Gorgeously illustrated with lots of great safety tips.*
—Peter Warshall

•

Methods of roof washing for cistern water. (a) Hand-operated diversion valve used to waste first rainfall. After roof is washed, the valve is changed so water will enter the cistern. (b) Automatic roofwash. The first rainfall flows into the drum. After the drum is filled, the remaining water flows into the cistern. During a period without rainfall, water dripping from the opening in the waste line empties the drum.

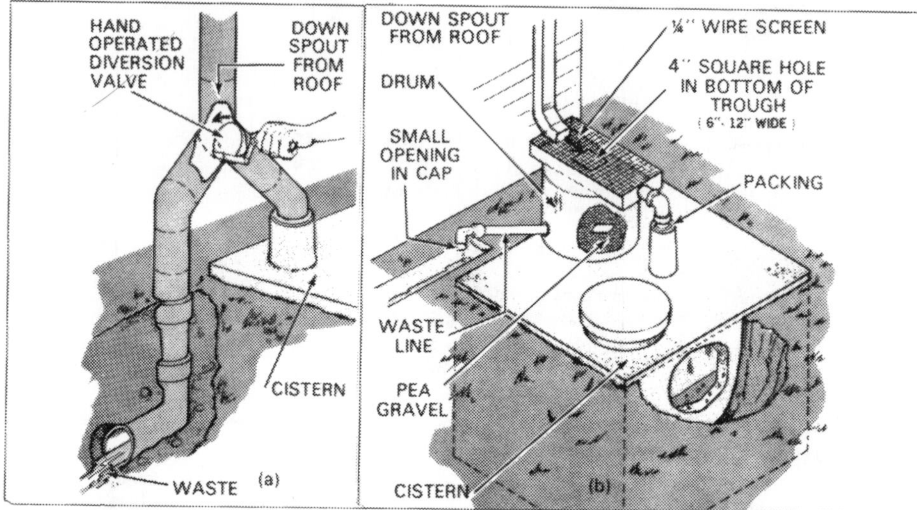

Planning for an Individual Water System
A.A.V.I.M.
1982; 160 pp.
$12
($14 postpaid) from:
American Association for Vocational Instructional Materials
120 Driftmier Engineering Center
Athens, GA 30602
or Whole Earth Access

Troubled Water

"Till taught by pain, man knows not water's worth." —Byron
The question I have been most asked by readers is: "Is my water safe?" The news in this book is not easily swallowed: plastic pipes leach carcinogens into drinking water; the Clean Water Act has not been effective; in-house water treatment like activated carbon helps but far from ensures clean water; bottled water may be just as polluted as tap water.

The quick-flowing prose, muckraking style, and good advice make this the best access to household water safety and aquatic politics. In general, if we forget cost, distillers and reverse osmosis filters are better than activated charcoal (AC). Under-the-sink AC is better than tap-installed. Don't ever use powdered AC filters (only granulated or solid block). All filters need attentive maintenance. Replace or clean 25 percent earlier than manufacturer's claims. *—Peter Warshall*

•

Quick fixes: Here are a few short-term measures for reducing the concentrations of pollutants in your water. They are simple, but limited in the protection they provide.

• Let your water run at full force for two or three minutes first thing in the morning. This will clear out relatively high levels of lead, cadmium, and copper that may have built up in the water sitting overnight in the pipes.

• You can eliminate bacteria and some organic chemicals from your water by boiling it at least 20 minutes. Experiments conducted by the EPA have shown that boiling removes only *volatile* organic chemicals — or those that evaporate easily. The chemicals escape into the air, so try not to breathe the air directly over the boiling water. Boiling is time-consuming and energy intensive and may concentrate the nonvolatile organics, heavy metals, and nitrates left behind in the water.

• Whipping your water in an electric blender can remove some volatile chemicals. You should blend the water for about 15 minutes, with the top off.

Troubled Water
Jonathan King
1985; 235 pp.
$8.95 postpaid from:
Rodale Press
33 East Minor Street
Emmaus, PA 18049
or Whole Earth Access

• For water conservation programs, see "RMI" (p. 89).
• For more about water pollution you should check "Biohazards" (p. 107).
• You can save lots of garden or farm water by using drip irrigation. See the "Urban Farmer" (p. 79).

We All Live Downstream

From the karst (limestone) watersheds of Eureka Springs comes the most radical support for waterless toilets. Plagued by underground pollution, The Water Center has produced the only in-print book surveying dry toilets — from commercial varieties to home-grown; from incolets to moulder (cold, slow compost) varieties. I would like more about dry toilet headaches: flies, shock loading, maintenance, installation, quality of final compost. But there is no better access.

***Downstream** also surveys greywater systems and community water politics, knowing full well that water connects and our feces are but fine fertilizers for future food. An impressive, populist production.*
—Peter Warshall

•

Ultra-One/G-Eljer: Concept: Uses one gallon of water to flush without any additional systems. Permanently installed reservoir meters one gallon of water from the tank to the bowl and maintains a high static head of water. *Requirements:* Standard plumbing. Fast, easy installation. *Operation:* Same as conventional toilet. *Models:* Contemporary look; fashion colors. *Cost:* Same as any top-of-the-line conventional two-piece toilet. *Available:* From any Eljer dealer or plumbing supply store.

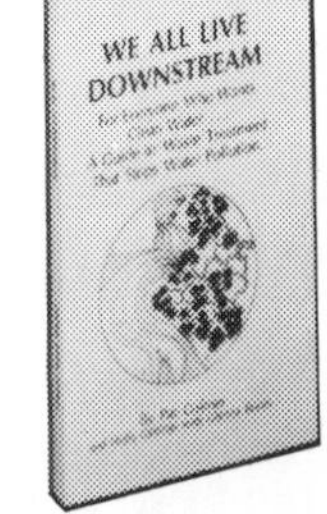

We All Live Downstream
Pat Costner with Glenna Booth and Holly Gettings
1986; 92 pp.
$6
($7.50 postpaid) from:
The Water Center
P. O. Box 548
Eureka Springs, AR 72632
or Whole Earth Access

Septic Tank Practices

A modest title for a book that clearly lays out aspects of various types of on-site sewage treatment and their relationship to soil, water use, construction, maintenance, and politics. Written by a brilliant biologist who has integrated theory with a practical hands-on approach.
—Sim VanDerRyn

This book is wonderful — outrageous and authoritative simultaneously. *—SB*

•

The septic-tank system actually has two distinct sections: the septic tank itself and the drainfield. The tank is a box that eliminates at least half the excrement by allowing time for solids to settle and be eaten by microbes. The wastewater then passes into a hole in the ground. The hole can be of almost any shape and depth. The most common shape is a linear trench usually between three and six feet deep. This trench design is called the drainfield (or leachfield, filterfield, absorption bed, disposal or subirrigation field). The wastewater from the septic tank receives further treatment in the drainfield. The soil absorbs viruses, strains out bacteria, filters large wastes, and chemically renovates them into nutrients that can be used by plants. Treatment is reliable for the lifespan of the drainfield.

•

Finally, the Big Sewer works against American freedom of choice. If a sewer runs by your house, you *must* hook up to it and pay the costs. In other words, you are not allowed to keep your home-site system, with all its advantages — even if it's working beautifully. This loss of option is killing the old American sense of self-reliance and responsibility. Undoubtedly, some backwoods Benjamin Franklin, unimpressed by the language of city-educated sewage experts, will soon stand up and say, "I won't." It will be a fine American court battle.

Septic Tank Practices
Peter Warshall
1979; 177 pp.
$4.95
($6.95 postpaid)
Only from:
Whole Earth Access

• For recycling urban wastes to the farms, see **Future Water** (p. 36). Other water concerns are discussed on p. 34. For Third World- style privies and waste disposal, read **Excreta Disposal for Rural Areas and Small Communities:** E. G. Wagner and J. N. Lanoi, 1958; 187 pp. **$14** ($15.25 postpaid) from WHO Publications, 49 Sheridan Avenue, Albany, NY 12210. For recycling household garbage, see p. 106. For plumbing see p. 129.

Raising Water

Electric pump sets (as, for instance, from Sears) aren't the only way to move water uphill. You can pump water with the sun, utilizing photovoltaic panels and matching pumps available from any of the suppliers on p. 133. Then there's the old standby, the hand pump. They're available from Baker. Some models can mate with windmills, such as the traditional models from Heller-Aller and Dempster. If you want to raise water from a moving stream, a ram will do the job, incessantly (and noisily), without any power source other than the stream itself. They're available from Rife. A silent but more expensive water-powered water pump will lift efficiently from a flow as little as one quart a minute, from High Lifter. *—Peter Warshall*

Dempster Industries: catalog **free** from Box 848, Beatrice, NE 68310.
Heller-Aller Co.: information **$1.50** from Corner — Perry and Oakwood, Napoleon, OH 43545.
Baker Manufacturing: catalog **free** from Evansville, WI 53536.
Rife Hydraulic Engines: catalog **$2** from Box 790, Norristown, PA 19404.
High Lifter Water Systems: information **free** from P. O. Box 397, Willits, CA 95490.

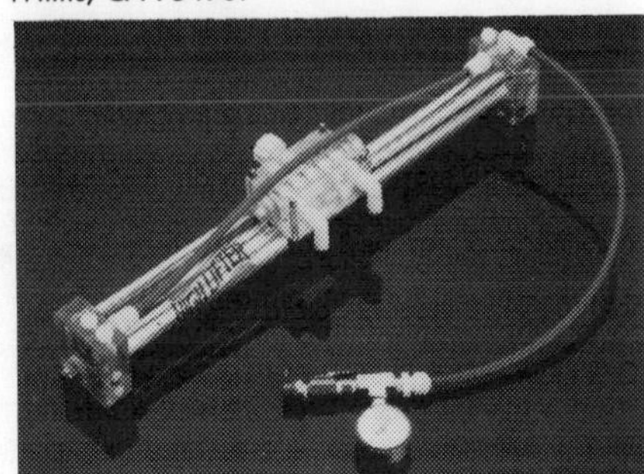

High Lifter water-powered water pump.

Hand Lift Pump Stands** are recommended for shallow well installations. This Hand Lift Pump comes with an angle iron brace, multi-position cap and siphon spout.* ***—Baker

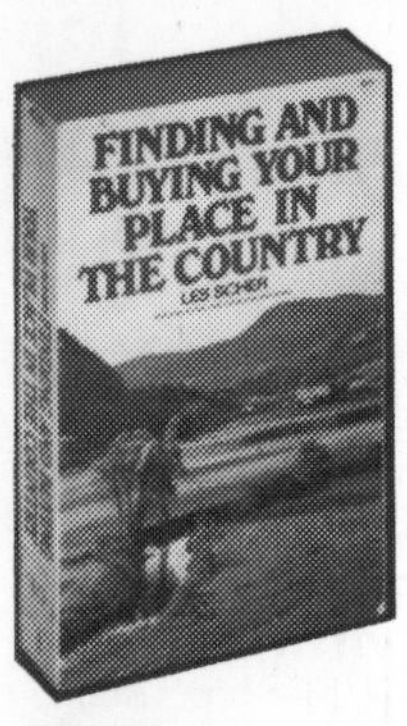

Finding and Buying Your Place in the Country
Les Scher
1974; 393 pp.
OUT OF PRINT
Macmillan Publishing co.

Clear evidence that a good builder did this new development: the trees, a pleasantly curved street, and a variety of house designs. This is part of Strathmore at Stony Brook, New York, development by Levitt & Sons, Inc.
—How to Avoid the 10 Biggest Home-Buying Traps

Finding and Buying Your Place in the Country

I'm glad somebody wrote this book and did it so thoroughly. Scher is a lawyer who manages to wade with you through the waters of easements, zoning, taxes, contracts, deeds of trust, mortgages, and escrow without muddying them up. Also advice on evaluating property — soil, water, structures, and on bargaining strategies. If you study this book, there's no excuse for being "taken."
—Richard Nilsen

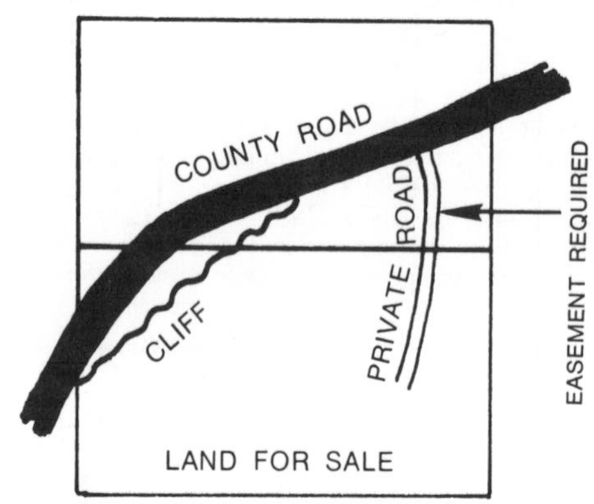

"The land has frontage on county road"
You will frequently see the above phrase in real estate advertisements. Don't make the assumption that road frontage necessarily means direct road access. The side of the property that borders the county road might be a cliff or a ravine. In such cases, entrance must be gained by crossing a neighbor's land. The illustration shows road frontage with easement access required.

How to Avoid the 10 Biggest Home-Buying Traps

Here they are folks, and history shows that people like yourselves blow it over and over again on these not-necessarily-obvious matters: the house with too high a price; the unforeseen expenses; the tight mortgage; the gyp builder; the no-design house; the garbled floor plan; the old-house lemon; the marginal house (where everything about it just gets by); the energy guzzler; the gimmick house. The author shows how subtle the traps can be and gives a great lesson in avoiding them. The book ends with a handy checklist, an antidote to naivete. *—JB*

•

It's also important to check on the local zoning rules, assuming you don't want to see those lovely woods across the street invaded by bulldozers someday to make way for a new shopping center or chemical factory. Your best protection is an area that is strictly zoned chiefly for residential use, permitting little or no other kind of development. If there are commercial and industrial zones nearby, watch out.

•

There is so much marginal quality because nearly everything that goes into a house — the flooring, wall products, roofing, siding, heating, wiring, paint, and virtually every other product — can be had in more than one grade or in some cases more than one weight or thickness. . . . The lowest-grade economy materials are used widely in house construction to keep down costs. They are designed to meet certain *minimum* standards. What's more, marginal quality is not limited to low-priced houses. It's also prevalent to a degree in many high-priced houses including luxury houses.

How to Avoid the 10 Biggest Home-Buying Traps
A. M. Watkins
1984; 180 pp.
$8.95
($10.95 postpaid) from:
Caroline House
5S 250 Frontenac Road
Naperville, IL 60540
or Whole Earth Access

How to Inspect a House

Hopes and lies get put to the test when a prepurchase house inspection is performed. You can have it done for you, but best is to have at the task yourself; that way you'll learn more about the place. This manual shows you how to check all the things that must be right if you are to live without regret. Termites! Rot! There's a lot to it, but there's also a lot to a 30-year mortgage. The book is a handy guide to keeping an eye on the house after you buy it, too. *—JB*

•

V Cracks: While inspecting the foundation, check the corners, which are the weak areas. Without sufficient steel in the concrete, the corners could break. Steel helps make the foundation act as one firm unit. The illustration shows two cracks in a level perimeter foundation. These are V cracks, wider at the top than the bottom. Undoubtedly the corner of the whole structure has settled. You might find hairline cracks anywhere. I wouldn't worry about them. It's the V cracks that give cause for alarm.

•

Another thing to inspect, without getting on a ladder, is the end of downspouts. If you see a lot of mineral crystals, it's a good sign that the roof is old and worn.

How to Inspect a House
George Hoffman
1985; 186 pp.
$8.95 postpaid from:
Addison-Wesley Publishing Co.
1 Jacob Way
Reading, MA 01867
or Whole Earth Access

• You can get a look at what's available in other parts of the country (as well as your own) in this illustrated catalog. **Strout Realty:** Catalog **$2** from P. O. Box 4528, Springfield, MO 65808.

• See also **Right Where You Live**, p. 118.

PAINT TRICK:
To make a room visually larger, paint baseboards the same color as the floor. If your baseboards are narrow, or non-existent, paint them in. Best tool for this is a paint edger.

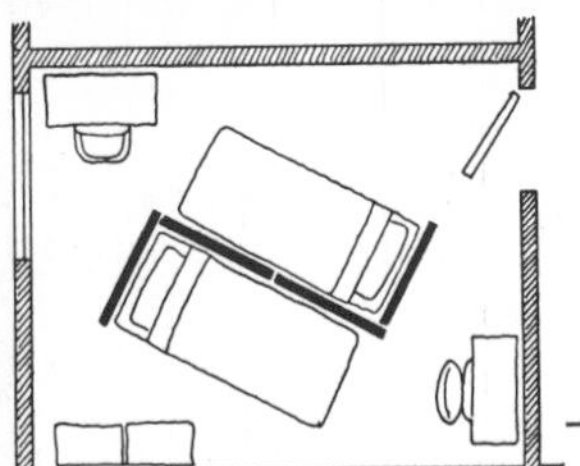

•
Removing walls may be a no-no. But who's to say we can't *add* some. Hollow-core doors are light-weight, stable, and inexpensive — *quite* inexpensive if you find your way to the lumberyard's damaged-door department. Doors become partitions, strictly speaking, rather than walls, because they're only 6'8'' tall. But this is enough for visual privacy, as in a bedroom shared by two kids. Illustration 1 shows four doors bracketed together as a free-standing unit that separates two beds.

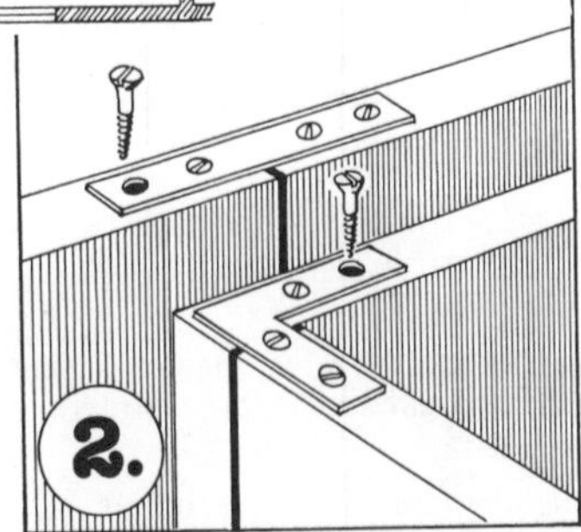

Doors are fastened, top and bottom, with metal ''corner irons'' and wood screws (Illustration 2).

The Moveable Nest

One of our favorites in past **Whole Earth Catalog***s, this book is an inspiring array of ideas for making a rented place into your own personal home — without losing the damage deposit. The suggestions are imaginative, and the instructions are the most lucid I've ever seen for anything. The whole thing is done in a friendly, non-chauvinist, encouraging manner that should lure even the most chickenhearted novice into action. Give a copy to someone you like.* —*JB*

The Moveable Nest
Tom Schneider
1984; 191 pp.
$8.95
($9.95 postpaid) from:
Ten Speed Press
P. O. Box 7123
Berkeley, CA 94707
or Whole Earth Access

•
For hanging really heavy objects on masonry:
The way these hangers work is a bit like the trick my dad used for getting a brad to go into concrete. He formed a collar of support for the nail with the tight grip of his fingers. This kept the nail from bending. In a similar way, the solid plastic surrounding the nails in these fasteners provides a collar of support that directs all the force of the hammer blows straight to each steel point. This, plus the extreme sharpness of the points, allows penetration of hard surfaces without the nails bending or the wall cracking.

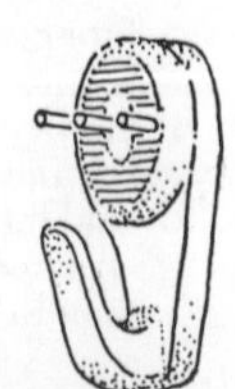

"Bulldog Hardwall Picture Hanger"
Available in 1" and 1/2" sizes.

High-Tech

Jim and Penny Hull, of Culver City, California, designed the Toobline furniture system using fiber tubes, but Sonotubes can be used to make similar beds.

• If you crave to get fancier than the schemes shown in **The Moveable Nest**, better read **Interior Carpentry** (p. 122) before starting.

I have no doubt that if I were acquisitive I would be equipping my life with high-tech house gear and decor. The stuff is sturdy, highly practical, often cheap, and — except for right now — outside of fashionability. The fashion is understandable — the clarity of the high-tech approach is often quite beautiful. But I think sewer manhole covers and military architecture are beautiful and Regency furniture is strictly for unfrequented museums.

This well-made book lavishly covers the range of high-tech possibilities, with a generous, if unannotated, directory of suppliers — over 2000! —*Stewart Brand*

◄
The Sonotube is manufactured by Sonoco Products Company, which has distributors listed in the Yellow Pages under Concrete Construction Forms and Accessories.

***Good Mixer.* Large cement trough on wheels that can be turned to face the light holds a mini-jungle in Ward Bennett's Long Island house.**

High-Tech
Joan Kron and
Suzanne Slesin
1978; 286 pp.
$29.95
($32.55 postpaid) from:
Crown Publishers
34 Englehard Avenue
Avenel, NJ 07001
or Whole Earth Access

►
Ash canoe seat with caned back and seat folds for easy storage, from L. L. Bean.

Amish Society
John A. Hostetler
1980; 414 pp.
$9.95
($11.45 postpaid) from:
John Hopkins
University Press
701 West 40th Street
Suite 275
Baltimore, MD 21211
or Whole Earth Access

The Simple Life
David E. Shi
1985; 332 pp.
$8.95
postpaid from:
Oxford University Press
16-00 Pollitt Drive
Fair Lawn, NJ 07410
or Whole Earth Access

The Vermont Country Store
Catalog **free** from:
The Vermont
Country Store
Mail Order Office
P. O. Box 3000
Manchester Center
VT 05255

Lehman's
Catalog
$2 from:
Lehman Hardware and
Appliances, Inc.
P. O. Box 41
4779 Kidron Road
Kidron, OH 44636

Cumberland General Store
Catalog
$3.75 from:
Cumberland
General Store
Route 3
Crossville, TN 38555

Amish Society

The Amish are a religious community that originated in Europe during the Reformation and is now concentrated in Ohio, Pennsylvania, and Indiana. They are one of the most resilient subcultures in America and also some of our best farmers. Sociologists keep waiting for them to die out or otherwise homogenize into the goo of the American melting pot, but this they refuse to do.

This definitive study, by an Amishman turned college professor, is a fascinating history and provides a detailed look inside the Amish character. Their way of life, which from the outside may look hard or dull or quaint or boring, turns out to be a model for the necessary values embodied in the concepts of community and local politics.
—Richard Nilsen

•

Amish communities are not relics of a bygone era. Rather, they are demonstrations of a different form of modernity.

•

The Amish people maintain a human rather than an organizational scale in their daily lives. They resisted the large, consolidated school and the proposition that big schools (or farms) were better than small ones. A bureaucracy that places pupils together within narrow age limits and emphasizes science and technology to the exclusion of sharing values and personal responsibility is not tolerated. The Amish appreciate thinking that makes the world, and their own lives, intelligible to them. When human groups and units of work become too large for them, a sense of estrangement sets in. When this happens the world becomes unintelligible to them and they cease participating in what is meaningless.

The traditional barn-raising, a form of economic sharing in times of need, symbolizes the concern Amish members have for one another's welfare.

The Simple Life

Those of us who would like to see the simple life become a norm in this great land of ours may find this a distressing book. Since Colonial times, numerous ideologies of and attempts at simple living have flamed briefly, only to be overwhelmed by the indomitable spirit of materialism and privatism that seems far more native to the American character than material simplicity. Nevertheless, plain living is an idea that can't be conquered, and in chronicling its history Shi relates a considerable sweep of this nation's history and higher yearnings.
—Stephanie Mills

•

Essentially, it seems, the much-ballyhooed "frugality phenomenon" of the 1970s was limited to middle- and upper-middle-class activists. Students, professors, environmentalists, consumer advocates, and idealists of various kinds were its most prominent and serious participants, and the predictions of a massive shift to simpler ways of living among the larger public were overstated.

•

The weaknesses seem clear. Proponents of the simple life have frequently been overly nostalgic about the quality of life in olden times, narrowly anti-urban in outlook, and too disdainful of the benefits of prosperity and technology. . . .

The radical critics of capitalism and promoters of spartan rusticity among the advocates of the simple life would be well advised to acknowledge that material progress and urban life can frequently be compatible with spiritual, moral, or intellectual concerns. As Lewis Mumford, one of the sanest of all the simplifiers, stressed in *The Conduct of Life:* "It is not enough to say, as Rousseau once did, that one has only to reverse all the current practices to be right . . . If our new philosophy is well-grounded we shall not merely react against the 'air-conditioned nightmare' of our present culture; we shall also carry into the future many elements of quality that this culture actually embraces."

Country Store Catalogs

Like the Amish community it serves, Lehman's is gentle, bucolic, and competent. Not a trace of tourist-fake-nostalgia in the farm-kitchen gear: gas refrigerators, wood cookstoves, and 50-gallon iron "cannibal" cauldrons. You can still get real Flexible Flyer sleds here! Cumberland General Store has similar country stuff, plus a wonderful selection of horse drawn buggies and wagons. The Vermont Country Store specializes in old-style cotton clothes and household goodies. They still make 'em like they used to. *—JB*

THE ENTERPRISE MONARCH. The most beautiful coal and wood range we have had in our 30 year history! —*Lehman's*

• See "Local Dependency," p. 111.

• A sympathetic look at living low on the hog.
Voluntary Simplicity: Duane Elgin, 1981; 312 pp. **$6.95** ($8.45 postpaid) from William Morrow Publishing Co., 6 Henderson Drive, West Caldwell, NJ 07006 (or Whole Earth Access).

(D) **COMBAT GLASS FRAMES.** Non-reflective neoprene self-adjusting frames specially designed to fit Army M17 Gas Mask, Tanker Helmets and other protective head equipment. Use for athletic or utility purposes. Accepts your prescription or sunglass lenses. Black.
B05-1290 . . . . **$24.95**

Extreme Cold Weather Mask. Includes 2 nose-mouth covers, a full face mask that is padded and lined with 100% cotton and a throat bib. One size fits all. $13.95

U.S. Cavalry

These folks stock a variety of genuine, not-surplus, military and law enforcement equipment. You probably won't be interested in official United States Army dress uniforms, but the field uniforms, packs, and boots may be just what you want if you're looking for brute function to government specs. —JB

One of the more fascinating catalogs you can get. It's designed for people in, around, and after the tanks part of the U.S. Army — a bizarre mix of wonderful military boots and clothing, grotesque military memorbilia and decorations, kid's stuff, and oddments findable nowhere else. —Stewart Brand

U.S. Cavalry
Catalog
$3 from:
U.S. Cavalry
1375 North Wilson Road
Radcliff, KY 40160

Loompanics Unlimited
Information **free** from:
Loompanics Unlimited
P. O. Box 1197
Port Townsend, WA 98368

A long time ago when we were the first to revive and make popular the old-time calico cloth, Mrs. Orton had an old-fashioned Vermont apron her grandmother had given her. This we used as a pattern and began making these sensible aprons. We're still doing it today because it remains stylish. With full calico ties in back, this apron, ruffled at bottom, will fit most women. They're made for us in Vermont homes by Vermont seamstresses - not a factory product. *COLORS:* Yellow (YEL), Blue (BLU), Green (GRN), (RED), Pink (PNK) and Lavender (LAV). (Please state *first and second choice* when you order.) *SIZES:* REG (8-12) or LG (14-18). **No.704 Calico Apron $18.95.** Ship. wt. 1 lb.

—The Vermont Country Store

Loompanics Unlimited

"We are the lunatic fringe of the libertarian movement," announces the introduction to this extraordinary catalog. You better believe it. Here are books that are very definitely not at your local library or bookstore. (Indeed, in Canada, many of them are illegal.) How to develop a fake ID; how to make explosives in your kitchen; lockpicking (by Eddie the Wire); Ninja; tax avoidance; privacy; survival. Ah yes, survival. Yours. Paranoid, you say? Don't you worry just a little about what you'd do if the economy collapsed or if The Bomb dropped? There are so many ways of looking at "survival" that I'll just let you decide for yourself which of the survival books offered here are for you. Hell, Loompanics couldn't be TOO lunatic — they stock the ***Whole Earth Catalog*** *. . .* —JB

VONU means invulnerability to coercion

VONU
The Search for Personal Freedom
By Rayo
Edited by Jon Fisher

Vonu means "invulnerability to coercion." The legendary Rayo was a Vonu pioneer. His writings are well worth reading for every libertarian and freedom seeker. Mostly, his works appeared in obscure underground periodicals, such as *Libertarian Connection, Vonulife,* and *Innovator.* Now Jon Fisher has collected together the best of Rayo's articles in one easily-accessible volume.

This is hard-core material, differentiating between "liberty" (rights and loopholes granted by government) and "freedom" (*vonu*, or invulnerability to coercion), Rayo discusses such things as how to develop liberty at a profit, libertarian strategy, movementism vs. self-liberation, the possibility of living as a nomad, and much more. Far from being an armchair theorist, Rayo actually lived his ideas, and many of the articles tell of his life in a van, and as a squatter in National Forests — "out of sight and out of mind of those unwilling to let live."

VONU is an excellent example of the type of thinking necessary to break free and live your own life. It is for those willing to go to lengths to be rid of Big Brother and other oppressors. Highly recommended.

1983, 5½ x 8½, 112 pp, illustrated, soft cover.
VONU: $5.95
(ORDER NUMBER 17025)

SI Outdoor Food and Equipment

A good place to get military and other long-term-storage rations. They have lots of other survival gear too. —JB

SI Outdoor Food and Equipment
Catalog
$1 from:
SI
P.O. Box 3796
Gardena, CA 90247

Cumberland's General Purpose Buggy. Model H1 with top. With rubber tires. 7041 .. $3025.00
—Cumberland General Store

Shown
With Drop Axle

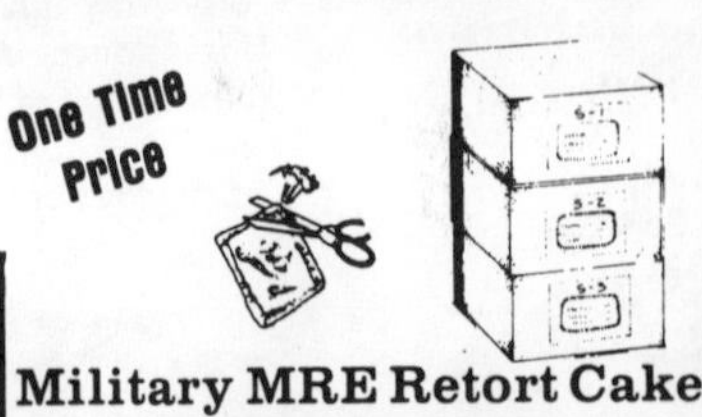

Military MRE Retort Cakes
THREE CASE SPECIAL

We find we have 300 cases more cakes than we want to stock at this time. These are all 1985 MRE cakes and come packed 72 individual cakes to a case. We are offering three cases (216 cakes) of these cakes at the price you would expect to pay for two cases. You get a case each of Pineapple Nut, Maple Nut and Cherry Nut. But this offer is good only for the first 100 orders. So if you want some of these excellent cakes for camping, scouts, hunting, lunch treats or for storage you should order early. Sold in stores for about $140 a case and on special in our Newsletters for $64 a case.
#R580
3 Case Cake Special $ 125.00 + 30.00 S&H
Limit 6 Cases

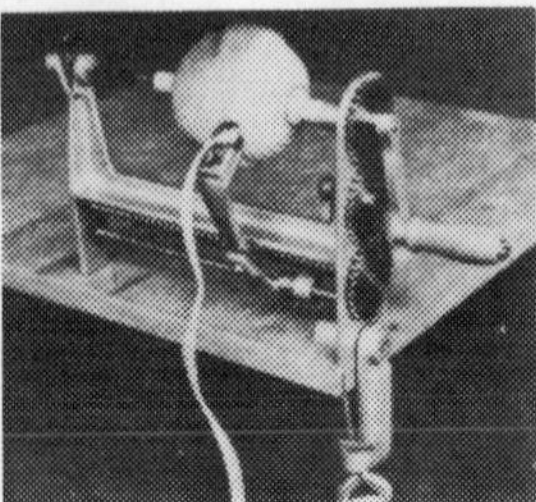

Oranges, lemons, pears, apples, most other firm, round fruits and vegetables up to 3 1/2" long. No spike to pierce fruit. Spindle is quickly and easily locked for varying lengths. Doesn't require resetting to start new peeling cycle. 5¾" H x 8" L. Clamps to any surface up to 1⅞" thick. $39.75 Postpaid.
—Lehman's

THE ORIGINAL "STEERABLE" SLED
FLEXIBLE FLYER EAGLE

The same fine tradition of quality and craftsmanship that made Flexible Flyer the best sled on the market in 1889 makes it the best sled on the market today! For five generations, Flexible Flyers have been made from the highest quality hardwoods and toughest tempered steel. The heavy chrome bumper and built-to-take-it construction held together by tough steel rivets and screws (not staples and glue) make it the "king of the hill".

And being the world's first "steerable" sled the Flexible Flyer remains a classic example of American ingenuity — and far safer than uncontrollable "straight runner" sleds.

No. F748-2	48" long overall	$42.00 Postpaid
No. F754-2	54" long overall	$49.50 Postpaid
No. F760-2	60" long overall	$56.00 Postpaid

(Don't confuse the real "Flexible Flyer" we sell with the cheaper-made "Flexible Flyer III" sold in discount stores. This is the original — King of the Hill since 1889.

FLEXIBLE FLYER

• *Same high quality since 1889.*
• *Sizes up to 5 feet long.*
• *Incomparable speed and handling.*

—Lehman's

• See also "Food by Mail" (p. 249), "Political Tactics" (pp. 102-103) and Brigade Quartermaster (p. 274).

How to Be Your Dog's Best Friend

This is an exceptional book not only on training, but also on canine behavior. I was surprised to discover the breadth and depth of understanding and knowledge shown by the authors. This is not a religious book, except in the devotedness shared by the monks with their dogs. With this system the dogs are with their handlers nearly 24 hours a day, even during the monks' lengthy periods of silence, with which the dogs must cooperate. One of the most amazing photographs in the book (to me) was of the monks at a meal, with all their dogs lying down silently, in the dining room, with no friction among the dogs.

This book covers basic obedience training, but more importantly it attempts to teach you how to develop a real closeness with your dog. It does not shrink from the unpleasant aspects of training either — correcting deep-seated problems. The Brothers are famous for de-tuning or de-training attack dogs "gone bad," which is no simple task.

—*Jill Bryson*
Aeroglen Irish Wolfhounds

How to Be Your Dog's Best Friend
The Monks of New Skete
1978; 202 pp.

$15.45
($16.95 postpaid) from:
Little Brown & Co,
Attn.: Order Dept.
200 West Street
Waltham, MA 02254
or Whole Earth Access

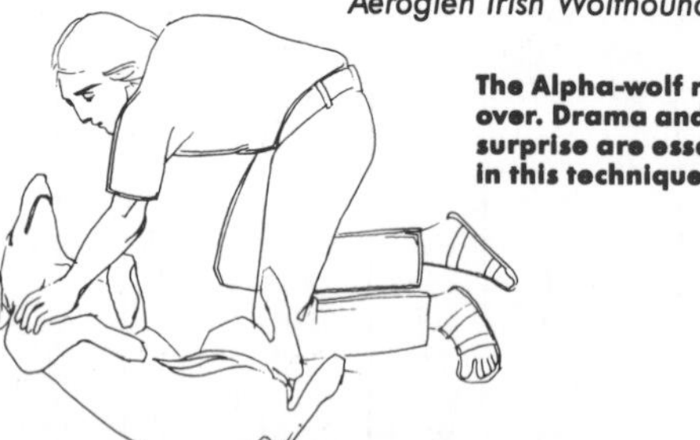

The Alpha-wolf roll-over. Drama and surprise are essential in this technique.

Chronic forgers can be halted by passing the leash behind you and leaning back into it as you come to a dead stop.

•

One of the biggest obstacles to healthy pet-owner relationships is pet loneliness. Dog owners, busy with their own activities, may never suspect that their friend suffers from isolation. A case in point: Sassy, an Airedale terrier, spent the hours between eight and five at home, alone. . . . After a week's observation, we noticed that Sassy reponded well to four- or five-hour periods of isolation, entertaining herself with toys, napping, and looking out windows. She was not tense or anxious, but became so after six or seven hours. We were able to observe the dog through a one-way window. While her owners had complained of Sassy's lack of pizazz and spirit, on our turf she was exuberant and playful.

Dog Owner's Home Veterinary Handbook
Delbert G. Carlson and James M. Giffin
1980; 364 pp.

$16.95
postpaid from:
Howell Book House
230 Park Avenue
New York, NY 10169
or Whole Earth Access

House Rabbit Handbook

Rabbits make great pets. This book introduces you to 20 pet rabbits and their owners, revealing personalities, offering advice, and exposing humor and bad habits. Having a pet rabbit requires a certain degree of bunny-proofing, for instance, or your furniture could end up in shreds. Harriman, who has lived with rabbits, shares a sensible, realistic knowledge that will enable you to appreciate the difficulties and joys of owning an urban rabbit.

—*Beverly Lowe*

•

If you want to add a pet without the complications of mating or fighting, a good choice is a companion of another species. There are a number of combinations that work well, but the most common mix is a rabbit with a cat. You can raise them together or introduce a youngster later. It doesn't matter which comes first. You can give a kitten to a fully grown rabbit or a baby bunny to a fully grown cat. Obviously, this last choice would take more caution and would be impossible if your cat hunts larger game than mice.

House Rabbit Handbook
Marinell Harriman
1985; 108 pp.

$5.95
postpaid from:
Drollery Press
1615 Encinal Avenue
Alameda, CA 94501
or Whole Earth Access

Dog Owner's Home Veterinary Handbook

Comprehensive and comprehensible, this is a first rate extension of the medical self-care literature. Instead of anguished uncertainty about what's wrong with your friend, you get confident diagnosis and prompt treatment. Lotta tricks of the trade in here, too.

—*Stewart Brand*

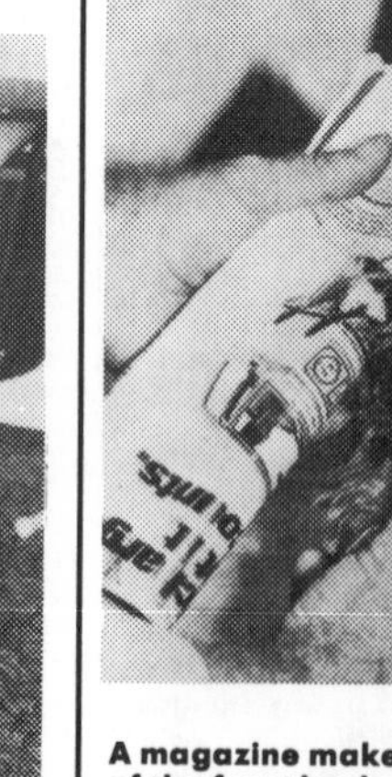

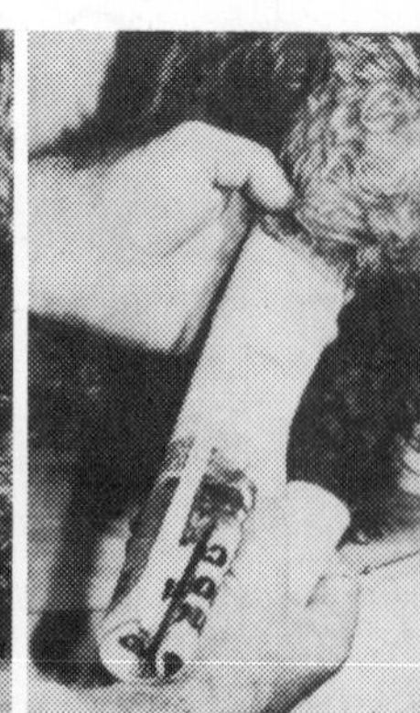

A magazine makes a good temporary splint for fractures of the front leg below the elbow.

• See **Raising Rabbits the Modern Way** and Wholesale Veterinary Supply, p. 83.

• See also Safer's Insecticidal Soap (p. 80) and **Common Sense Pest Control Quarterly** (p. 81).

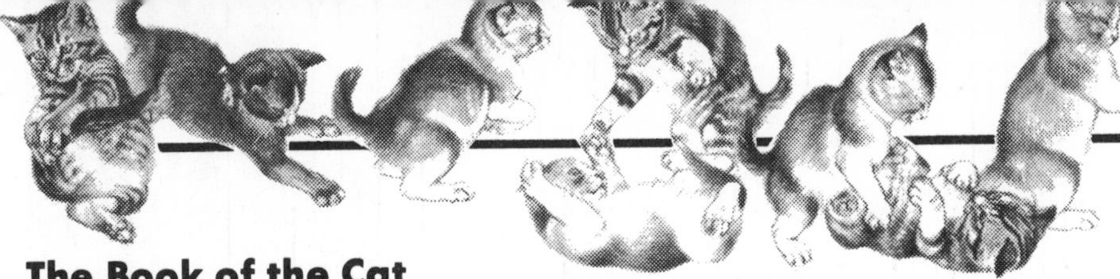

The Book of the Cat

Whether you own four blue ribbon Abyssinians or a freebie street orphan (as I do), this book answers every possible question about cats. It is graphically a joy to look at, with abundant images of kitties in all their charismatic postures. The chapter on breeds is particularly impressive; sophisticated charts clearly indicate how, for example, Siamese genotypes are combined to produce twenty different varieties of point colors. There are superb illustrations and diagrams describing feline anatomy, behavior patterns (including hunting, dreaming, mating, grooming), and health (diet, geriatrics, first aid). Instead of immediately urging you to "see your vet" should your puss have a problem, this book thoroughly examines common and uncommon disorders, outlines care and remedy procedures, and offers a section on choosing and using a vet. No pet store or cat lover should be without this excellent book. —Rosanne Kramer

Swinging a drowned cat drains water from its lungs and is such a safe and good way to stimulate breathing that many vets advise its use as a routine method of artificial respiration. Hold the hind legs of the cat – one leg in each hand – above and around the hock (ankle), with the cat's belly facing towards you. Stand with your legs apart. Swing the cat forward and then, with a slight jerk at the end of the upward swing, bring the cat down and between your straddled legs. Swing it back to the front of you again, ending each swing with the cat horizontal. Repeat about six times before trying other methods. It is surprising how much space is needed to 'swing a cat'!

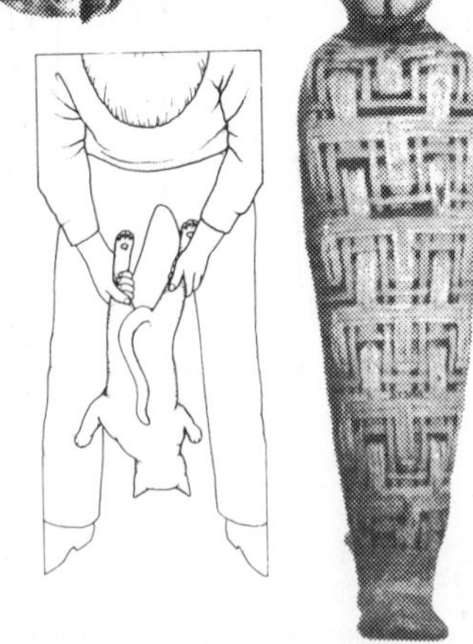

► **Cat Mummy 2000 BC, dedicated to Goddess Pasht, from whom we get the name Pussy.**

The Book of the Cat
Michael Wright and Sally Walters, Editors
1981; 256 pp.
$15.95
postpaid from:
Simon & Schuster
Mail Order Sales
200 Old Tappan Road
Old Tappan, NJ 07675
or Whole Earth Access

Caring for Your Pet Bird

Pet birds are not ornamentation. They're companions. Which means you need to know how to maintain their health, recognize problems, and develop a rapport. It means caring. Whether you bought your bird from the pet store or found it injured by the roadside, Axelson will help you keep it chipper. —Cindy Craig

•

Ripe fruits and vegetables should not consist of more than 25% of the bird's total diet, and everything should be thoroughly washed to remove all traces of insecticide. Here is a good rule of thumb: any fruit, vegetable or green that you can eat, your bird can also eat, quite safely.

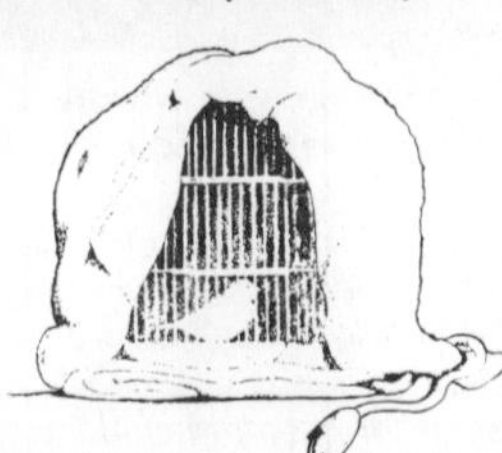

▲ **In an emergency, keep the bird warm.**

◄ **Initially, you may have to wear protective gloves when training your bird.**

Supplies

The best resource for pet supplies is your local retailer. Establishing rapport with them is your quickest reference for information on new and quality supplies. They can probably special order for you, too. Several companies offer pet supplies by mail and phone. AVP is strictly for cats and dogs; Animal City includes products for birds, fish, hamsters and gerbils as well. Both supply everything from books and brushes to shampoos and vaccines and some nonchemical alternatives to flea control. —Beverly Lowe

Animal City: Catalog **free** from P. O. Box 1076, La Mesa, CA 92041-9984.

Animal Veterinary Products: Catalog **free** from AVP for cats and dogs, P. O. Box 1267, Galesburg, IL 61401.

The Natural Cat

Sensitive, interesting, natural, well written. A great reference book. —Susan Erkel Ryan

To comb the inner thigh, slip the stroking hand under the outside foot and gently lift it up. DON'T LIFT TOO HIGH because your cat must balance on three legs.

The Natural Cat
(A Holistic Guide for Finicky Owners)
Anitra Frazier and Norma Eckroate
1983; 216 pp.
$9.95
($11.20 postpaid) from:
Kampmann & Co.
90 East 40th Street
New York, NY 10016
or Whole Earth Access

The Care of Exotic Birds

A commonsense and informative booklet that touches on the ethical considerations of owning an exotic bird. If, after reading this, you still decide to get one, this booklet will tell you how to take care of it. —Beverly Lowe

The Care of Exotic Birds: Roberta Lee, 50 pp. **$2** postpaid from San Francisco SPCA Education Department, 2500 16th Street, San Francisco, CA 94103

•

For every parrot that makes it into a pet shop, many others have died — estimates run as high as 10 for each one that survives. It is probably even higher for illegal birds. Considering all a bird goes through before it reaches someone's home and how many others died along the way, why do people still buy parrots? Dr. Donald Bruning, curator of birds at the Bronx Zoo, N.Y., thinks that, "if people knew, most of them wouldn't want parrots as pets."

Caring for Your Pet Bird
Dr. R. Dean Axelson
1981; 168 pp.
$6.95
($8.45 postpaid) from:
Sterling Publishing Co.
2 Park Avenue
New York, NY 10016
or Whole Earth Access

Chi Pants

Chi pants are amazingly comfortable. What makes Chi pants different is that they have a gusset, a panel of fabric that goes across the crotch instead of a seam going up and down the crotch.

This makes a couple of differences. For people like me who sit a long time it means the seam doesn't ride tight on your genitals and hurt. For active people, it means you can do things like squatting and karate kicking with no danger of ripping out your pants. For everyone it means a lot more looseness around the loins.

For me Chi pants make the same kind of difference my first pair of running shoes did — a whole new category of comfort. The kind I have look like jeans — the design difference doesn't show. Nondenim styles are available.

The shorts are supposed to be especially good for guys because the gusset cradles your balls so they don't hang out. —Anne Herbert

Wear-Guard®
LADIES JUMPSUITS
Get the jump on the day. Made specially for women requiring comfort, style and durability. Breathable, lightweight and long lasting Dacron® polyester/cotton, is acid resistant and reinforced throughout. The accent is on style with trim, neat fitting elasticized waist. Six strong pockets, 2 way zipper. No ironing needed, machine wash, tumble dry. No shrinkage. Made in USA.
Sizes: S (6-8), M (10-12), L (14-16), XL (18-20)

LONG SLEEVE		SHORT SLEEVE	
Style 375NV	Navy	Style 372NV	Navy
Style 375RD	Red	Style 372RD	Red
Style 375TN	Tan	Style 372TN	Tan
~~$32.99~~		~~$31.99~~	
Our Price $27.99		Our Price $26.99	

Wear-Guard Work Clothes

You need a shop apron? Coveralls with Chester or Vince embroidered on the pocket in script? Industrial rainwear? Postman's shoes? Here's where a lot of such items come from. —JB

Gohn Brothers

Gohn Brothers supplies chiefly the stricter Mennonite orders and the various orders of the Amish Mennonite people all over the country. Since the Amish have managed communal living successfully for about 350 years, I figure at least some of their practices must be valid. Their clothing in particular is comfortable, durable and of low price. I can recommend from experience their broadfall work pants (no fly: broad button flap like lederhosen in front), overshirts (plain jacket with two roomy pockets on the inside) and overcoats (heavy dark wool, with cape). Many hard-to-find practical items listed, as well as a broad selection of rather plain yard goods. Service is fast and courteous. —Peter R. Hoover

No. 868 MEN'S FLEECE LINED UNION SUITS ..... **$16.98 ea.**
50% polyester, 50% cotton. Long sleeve, ankle length. Sizes 38 to 48.

MEN'S LONG SLEEVE UNION SUITS. Natural colors . **$12.98 ea.**
No. C821 Winter weight. Sizes 34 to 48. 100% cotton.

No. 822 MEN'S RED UNION SUITS. 100% cotton .... **$14.98 ea.**
Long sleeve, ankle length. Sizes 34 to 48.

David Morgan

This unusual catalog is hard to pin down: it carries the traditional English waxed cotton rainwear (Britton brand), Welsh woolens, Pacific Northwest Indian style jewelry (I have some; it's nice), Australian Akubra hats, and kangaroo hide bullwhips. A strange combination. I've had good service from these people. —JB

Richmond Jacket: The traditional belted English fishing and shooting jacket. It is made from heavyweight waxed cotton, with a pure cotton lining and nylon drip strip. It has a double storm fly over the zipper, and three storm-flapped outer pockets. Inside there are two large nylon-lined pockets and a zippered wallet pocket. The corduroy collar has a throat flap for greater protection. The underarm ventilation eyelets are caged to prevent rain from trickling in when your arms are raised. No. 7302 Richmond Jacket: $155.00. No. 7303 Richmond Lined Overtrousers: $70.00.

Filson Outdoor Clothes

Extra long mackinaw cruiser for the tall man. Sleeves 1½" longer — body 1½" longer. Colors: red/black, forest green.

Cars are tinny, silverware is stainless steel, and fiberboard boxes are palmed off as houses. Contemporary economics seem designed to diminish standards of excellence. Even the durability and construction of clothing has deteriorated: Levi's will not stand four months of normal work; "Can't-bust-ems" have disappeared, and except for Ben Davis' polyester gorillas, there's hardly a tough, trim line of clothing available at all, especially in natural fibers.

Hardly, but the C. C. Filson Co. of Seattle is an exceptional line of clothing and outerwear for loggers, game wardens and outdoor workers. Filson is to work clothes what White is to workboots (p. 275). Their all-wool shipcords will survive four or five Levi's. Filson canvas or "tin" pants and coats are waterproof and extremely resistant to wear.

The top of the line is the Filson "Cruiser," an all-wool, water-repellent coat with nine pockets, in a rich forest green. It is tough enough for the woods but elegant enough for town — warm as a toaster and handsome as a Douglas Fir.

The company responds promptly to requests for their free catalog. —Peter Coyote

• For cotton clothing, see Hanna Anderson (p. 357).

• Deva, a cottage industry, sells mail order clothes crafted of fine natural fibers that allow the body to move freely. Beautiful fabrics and colors. Wonderful clothes. Catalog **$1** (includes fabric swatches) from Box FF, Burkittsville, MD 21718.

Chi Pants
$20-$40 (approx)
Catalog **free** from:
Chi Pants
P. O. Box 7400
Santa Cruz, CA 95061

Wear-Guard Work Clothes
Catalog **free** from:
Wear-Guard Work Clothes
P. O. Box 400
Hingham, MA 02043

Gohn Brothers
Catalog **free** from:
Gohn Brothers
Box 111
Middlebury, IN 46540.

Filson Outdoor Clothes
Catalog **free** from:
C. C. Filson Co.
P. O. Box 34020
Seattle, WA 98124

David Morgan
Catalog **free** from:
David Morgan
P. O. Box 70190
Seattle, WA 98107

New Fashion Japan

A Kimono: three kinds of fabric sewn together, two rectangles overlapping, a simple covering of the human form. Then she lifts her arms. An open square appears under each — windows into another dimension. Japanese design has always taken paradox into its folds, combining blue cotton fabric with ornate embroidery, or many different fabrics into a basic work garment: simple yet complex.

The designers in this exquisite book of photography and brief quotes on Japanese fashion speak like fashion monks — with deep understanding and respect for their thousands of years of fashion heritage. For them, fashion isn't something you put on in the morning; it's you and it's your culture. Worldviews are built into fashion design.

—Jerri Linn and Jeanne Carstensen

•

"Clothes must be comfortable, enhance one's beauty, be chic, express one's personality, and so on. But most importantly clothes should be something to improve human beings." —Shinji Fujiwara, Writer

"Traditional Japanese clothes have 'water nature.' The kimono adjusts itself to your body whether you have a fat stomach or are skinny. The same size clothing fits everyone by adjusting the cloth that wraps around your waist." —Katsuhiro Serizawa, Kyoto Zen Center Press Representative

New Fashion Japan
Leonard Koren
1984; 176 pp.
$24.95
($27.45 postpaid) from:
Kodansha International
Mail Order Department
P. O. Box 1531
Hagerstown, MD 21741
or Whole Earth Access

Klader!

Fun, fun, fun! Everything in this colorful book of fashion draws from the imagination. Try designing and making clothing for yourself that you've never seen before. Design your own image. Some pattern instructions are included to get you started on transferring your ideas into cloth — you'll need some knowledge of sewing. But **Klader!** *won't dissuade you from trying anything.*

—Jerri Linn

Personal ties are hard to find — but easy to make.

• A newsletter of support, inspiration, and resources for vintage clothing enthusiasts.
Vintage Clothing Newsletter: Terry McCormick, Editor. **$10**/year (12 issues) from P. O. Box 1422, Corvallis, OR 97339.

• See "Sewing," pp. 182-183.

Folkwear Patterns

Evolution of man-made design, as in nature, seeks elegant and effective solutions. Ethnic clothing with its strict parameters of comfort and economy gives us samples of simple, elegant beauty. Folkwear, Inc., with a broad and exciting selection of clothing patterns based on traditional folk garments, provides the home sewer an opportunity to create beautiful, comfortable, individual, and long lasting garments. Over 65 patterns are currently available — from Afghani nomad dresses to Japanese field garments to Victorian shirts and Edwardian underthings. Eight new patterns are introduced every year. The patterns, carefully derived from folk garments, are simple and easily made, with clear instructions and, where appropriate, detailed descriptions of finishing touches such as traditional embroidery designs.

—Rafael Diaz-Guerrero

Sporty Forties' Dress
This flattering shirtwaist dress buttons to a below-the-knee hem. The bodice pleats from the shoulder seams and into the waistband. Clean simple lines make this an ideal daytime dress. *—Misses' 6-16.*

AFGHANI NOMAD DRESS

Klader!
Nina Ericson
1983; 175 pp.
$17.95
($19.20 postpaid) from:
Lark Books
50 College Street
Asheville, NC 28801
or Whole Earth Access

Folkwear Patterns
$4 - $8 (approx.)
Catalog **$1** from:
Folkwear Patterns
P. O. Box 3798
San Rafael, CA 94912

The American Historical Supply Catalogue

Good old stuff, some of it great old stuff from all manner of mail order suppliers. Nineteenth-century furniture, clothing, kitchenware, building fixtures, clocks, stoves, tools, food, books, musical instruments, nautical instruments, toys, bathroom items, and even tours. A nice selection sumptuously illustrated. God what a relief from the like of The Sharper Image and other purveyors of ephemeral high-tech glitz. —*Stewart Brand*

The American Historical Supply Catalogue
Alan Wellikoff
1984; 240 pp.
$16.95
($17.95 postpaid) from:
Schocken Books
62 Cooper Square
New York, NY 10003
or Whole Earth Access

1884 MILK BOTTLES

"Your customers will be willing to pay more for milk if delivered in sealed bottles," advised the Sears-Roebuck catalogue of 1908. Jenifer House's milk bottles are reproductions of those used by the "Thatcher Dairy" in 1884 and have the desired airtight seals. That the bottles are embossed "Absolutely Pure Milk" should not limit your imagination in putting them to use at home.

Price: set of three, $28.95, ppd. (add $1 west of the Mississippi). Specify clear, cobalt, pink, or amethyst glass.

Gift catalog available.

JENIFER HOUSE

New Marlboro Stage
Great Barrington, MA 01230
Tel. 413/528–1500

•
Clawfoot Bathtubs. Sunrise Specialty of Berkeley, California, offers clawfoot bathtubs of the type commonly used in the late 1800s. These are not reproductions but salvaged antiques, restored and refitted with new brass fixtures and oak rims. Sunrise Specialty uses the Chicago Faucet Company's taps exclusively. These have been continuously manufactured by that company since the nineteenth century and are the best available. Clawfoot tubs are obtainable in the Berkeley store or by special order.

The 2nd Underground Shopper • The Wholesale by Mail Catalog Update 1986

*These catalogs ain't much to look at, but they sure are a lot to send for. There's little duplication between these rivals, and I'd say they are about equal as Pied Pipers of the Pocketbook. The variety is more than we have room to list here. Some of the items in our **Catalog** came from these catalogs of catalogs.* —*JB*

The Wholesale by Mail Catalog Update 1986
The Print Project
1986; 364 pp.
$3.95
($5.45 postpaid) from:
St. Martin's Press
Cash Sales
175 5th Avenue
New York, NY 10010
or Whole Earth Access

The 2nd Underground Shopper
Sue Goldstein
1985; 470 pp.
$7.95
($8.95 postpaid) from:
Andrews, McMeel & Parker, Inc.
4900 Main Street
Kansas City, MO 64112
or Whole Earth Access

•
The King Size Company
24 Forest St.
Brockton, MA 02402
(800) 343-9678
(617) 580-0500: MA residents
MC, V, AE

The kingpin of King Size, James Kelley, stands tall when he professes his motto: "A 6'8" man should not have to pay a penalty for being tall." They try to position their prices within 10 percent of what a 5'8" man would pay for the same clothing. They also have clothing to outfit large men (pants sized from 44 to 60; shirts from 17 to 22). They have their own label as well as *Jockey, Haggar, Botany 500, Palm Beach, Hush Puppies,* and *London Fog.* Shipping via UPS costs 10 % of the order up to $3.75 maximum; there's an unconditional guarantee. Their free catalog comes out 10 times a year; January and June are sale issues. —*The 2nd Underground Shopper*

•
Paradise Products
P. O. Box 568
El Cerrito, CA 94530
(415) 524-8300
CK, MC, V

We thought Paradise Products consisted of apples, fig leaves, and serpents until we looked through their catalog and discovered nothing was lost. They've got party goods for 23 international and nine seasonal themes with tempting discounts of 25% on an assortment of favors, posters, crepe paper, hats, banners, flags, and masks (in their Party Host line). Say "Aloha!" to Hawaiian orchids and packets of beach sand or "How!" to an Indian peace pipe. You can even save a fortune, cookie, on fortune cookies for your next Chinese party. Finding the proper decorations to set the mood for a fifties or sixties party is no problem when you flip through this company's 72-page catalog. There's a $30 minimum order — if you order less than this amount enclose $3 as a service charge. All items are guaranteed to be as represented in the catalog with shipments guaranteed to arrive on time (not fashionably late) for the party and in perfect condition or they'll cheerfully refund your money. Catalog $2. —*The 2nd Underground Shopper*

•
Sultan's Delight Inc.; P. O. Box 253; Staten Island, NY 10314-0253 (718) 720-1557/Cat.: free (1 & 7)/Save: to 50%/Pay: C, MO, MC, V Sells: Middle Eastern foods, gifts/Mail Order only.

Comment: Middle Eastern food specialities are sold here at excellent prices — to 50% below comparable goods in gourmet food stores. Est. in 1980.

Sample Goods: Near East and Sahadi products; canned tahini, cous cous, tabouleh, fig and quince jams, stuffed grapevine leaves, bulghur, semolina, green wheat, orzo, fava beans, Turkish figs, pickled okra, stuffed eggplant, olives, herbs and spices, jumbo pistachios and other nuts, roasted chick peas, halvah, Turkish delight, marzipan paste, olive oil, Turkish coffee, fruit leather, filo, feta cheese, Syrian breads, etc. Cookbooks for Greek, Lebanese, Syrian, and Middle Eastern cuisine offered, and gifts, belly-dancing clothing, musical instruments, cookware, and related items.

Special Factors: PQ by phone or letter with SASE; min. order $5. —*Wholesale by Mail Catalog*

GATOR GRIP™ HANDSAVER

new versatile Gator-Grip HandSaver provides a comfortable, safe, efficient way of handling awkward objects and saves trapped fingers and cut hands.

FOB FL

Model Number	Lifting Capacity	Pulling Capacity	Jaw Capacity	Weight	Price 1-11	Price 12+
GGH-1	200 lbs.	340 lbs.	⅝''	1½ lbs.	$25.00	$22.00

Abbeon Cal. Inc., 123 Gray Ave., Santa Barbara, Ca. 93101 Phone (805) 963-7545

Abbeon

If you can get through this big, fat, 700-page catalog without reaching for the order blank, you are made of very stern stuff indeed. A mind-boggling array of goodies that spans from the electronic lab to the homestead. Run by a self-confessed ''garrulous old man,'' the outfit reeks of integrity. Service on my smallish order was very good. The price of the catalog is refundable with your first order. —Gerald E. Meyers

This is one of the most eclectic assortments I've ever seen. Scalpels; clocks; wheels (make your own wagon); lab, graphic, optical, and measuring supplies; you-name-it, etc., plus a few, are all in there. This is a great example of a catalog that can give you ideas you might not have gotten otherwise. One of my favorites. —JB

Abbeon: Catalog **$4.50** from Abbeon Cal. Inc., 123 Gray Avenue, Santa Barbara, CA 93101.

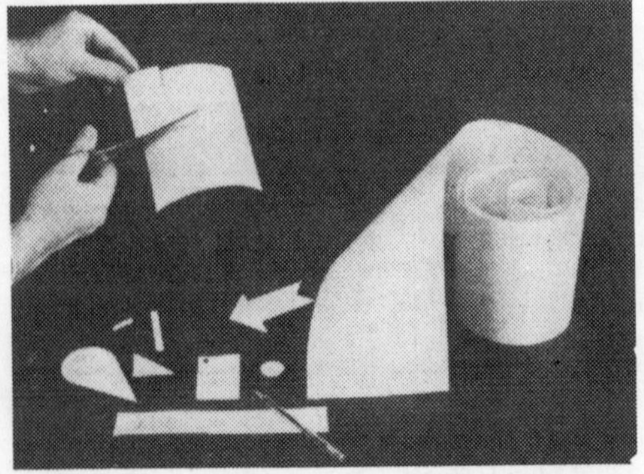

•

Spunbonded Plyoletin is practically indestructible. Use it indoors, outdoors — even under water. Cuts easily with scissors. Type, write or draw on it — has the look and feel of paper. Sticks to virtually all materials — wood, glass, metals, plastics. Cut labels of any shape and use them on laboratory glassware or anywhere else you need durability. Perfect for all outdoor applications — swimming pools, garden tools, autos, motorcycles, pipe labeling, etc. A great material for repairing broken book bindings. Hi-tack adhesive grabs securely — doesn't slide or get brittle.

Lefthander's Catalog

A modest selection here of household gadgets and tools designed for southpaws, including a few for the ambidextrous. —Kevin Kelly

Lefthander's Catalog: $1.50 from Lefthander International, P. O. Box 8249, Topeka, KS 66608.

•

Traditional Can and Bottle Opener. It's back to the basics with this tried-and-true, long-wearing can opener. Fashioned of stainless steel, this can opener will serve you well. The handles and turnkey are constructed for left hand use. The upper handle doubles as a bottle opener, too. *316*. *$5.00*

Lightweight Steam/Dry Iron sports a Silverstone® finish on the soleplate which insures smooth handling: adjustable cord allows convenient lefthanded use — all for a very special price. Includes one year manufacturer warranty. *350*. *$34.50*

The Nature Company

Lots of good quality stuff that encourages an interest and appreciation of nature: telescopes, toys, maps, T-shirts, all manner of eco-chic doodads, plus a nifty selection of books. I Christmas shop here a lot, if I can get in the door of the store. —JB

The Nature Company: Catalog **free** from The Nature Company, P. O. Box 2310, Berkeley, CA 94702.

The Irresistible Bearhug Backpack! **With its arms and legs anchoring adjustable front straps, our synthetic fur bear will happily tote along the day's lunch in its 12'' x 12'' zip-up pouch. His head turns to face straight ahead, or sideways to catch the passing scene. 16'' x 12''** ***#5318*** **$39.95.**

Archie McPhee & Company

This is where you get those pink plastic flamingos and other bizarreties. —JB

Archie McPhee & Company: Catalog **free** from: Archie McPhee & Company, P. O. Box 30852, Seattle, WA 98103.

8092. TEETH TONGS. Top quality, lifesize false teeth choppers (red gums, white teeth) attached to 7'' metal tongs. Many uses! We have heard that a present of one of these to your dentist could result in free gold crowns. $2.95 each. Dental Convention Special: 5 for $10.50. Each in clean, hygienically sealed bag.

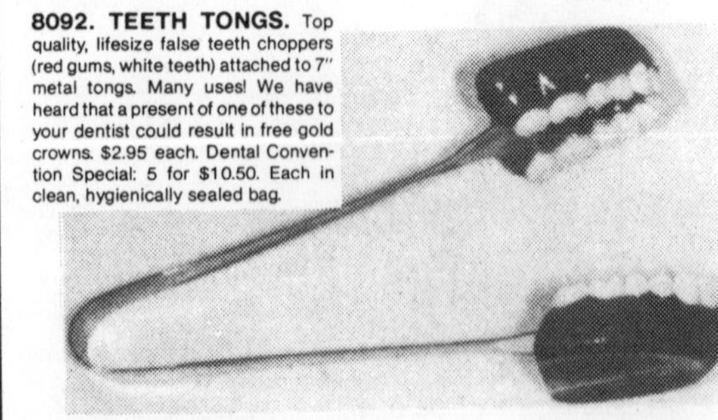

Amazing Reprints

This catalog offers 300 booklets of reprinted how-to information that first appeared in 1910-1948. Some are useful: ***Human-Powered Tools & Machinery****. Some are a trifle strange: plans for a tiny real airplane, the Santos-Dumont ''Demoiselle'' of 1910. All are interesting. A bit o' the past is still with us.* —JB

Amazing Reprints: Catalog **$2** from S & S Press, P. O. Box 5931, Austin, TX 78763.

—Amazing Reprints

A. Brill's Bible of Building Plans

Amuse your cows with a 43-whistle circus calliope? Join a carnival as a knife thrower or 'shake-em-up' ride owner?

What A.K. Brill sells is methods of making fantasy less improbable. His ***Bible*** *is part book, part catalog. The catalog offers for sale all the plans and info required to entirely recreate the midway of a sleazy county fair: scary rides, fair games of skill, and curious concessions.*

The building plans he sells are uncommon. They convey the old builder's art of scrounging up the parts needed from what's lying around. It's kind of like hunkering down with the old builder and hearing: ''Now you can build this out of a surplus gear box or this way out of an old truck differential . . .'' A typical twenty-buck building plan might be twenty dittoed legal size pages. Ten pages of single-spaced monologue, the rest sketches, plans and drawings. You learn the cheapest ways of building it in Muncie or Micronesia.

On top of some 200 building plans there are offered for sale tricks of the trade — the Magic Horseshoe (No. 719, $5) actually enables anyone to letter large signs easily. —Alan Kalker

A. Brill's Bible of Building Plans: Catalog **$2** from A. B. Enterprizes, P. O. Box 856, Peoria, IL 61601.

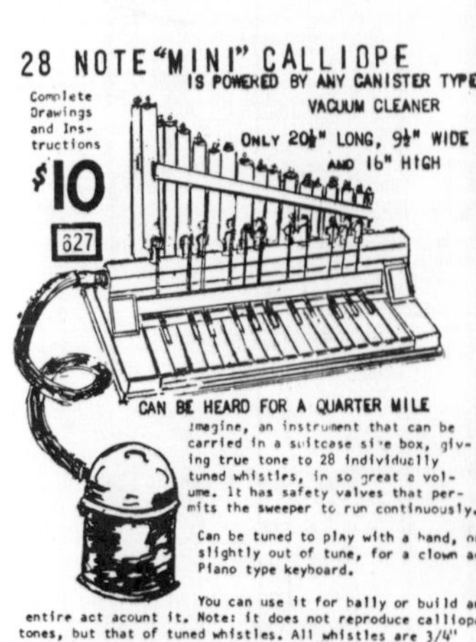

28 NOTE "MINI" CALLIOPE
IS POWERED BY ANY CANISTER TYPE VACUUM CLEANER
Complete Drawings and Instructions
$10
627
ONLY 20½" LONG, 9½" WIDE AND 16" HIGH
CAN BE HEARD FOR A QUARTER MILE
Imagine, an instrument that can be carried in a suitcase size box, giving true tone to 28 individually tuned whistles, in so great a volume. It has safety valves that permits the sweeper to run continuously.
Can be tuned to play with a hand, or slightly out of tune, for a clown act. Piano type keyboard.
You can use it for bally or build an entire act acount it. Note: it does not reproduce calliope tones, but that of tuned whistles. All whistles are 3/4" diameter tubing of varying length. Requires considerable lathe work, but not expert machining. Uses auto fittings and street "L", and very little welding.
A.B. Enterprizes BOX 875, PEORIA, ILLINOIS 61601 U.S.A.
74

Consumer Reports
John R. Dorfman, Editor
$16/year
(11 issues plus the *Buying Guide issue*)

Consumer Reports Buying Guide
Consumer Union Staff, Editors (Annual)
$5.95 postpaid
Both from:
Consumer Reports
P. O. Box 2886
Boulder, CO 80322

Consumers Union News Digest
Edited by staff of Consumer Reports
$48/year
(24 issues) from:
Consumers Union
256 Washington Street
Mount Vernon, NY 10553

***Consumer Reports Buying Guide** is also available from Whole Earth Access.*

Consumer Reports

No advertisements sully the pages of **Consumer Reports;** *consequently no bias sullies their tests and analyses of consumer goods and services. CU (as they refer to themselves) best gathers information that's outright impossible to gather yourself, such as the opinions of 250,000 auto owners as to which cars are most reliable and which are awful. CU is less convincing when being more subjective about such matters as the taste of tomato soup, but somewhere in each report is what you want and need to know. CU sums up the year's work in their annual* **Buying Guide Issue** *printed (so typically) in pocket size so you can take it shopping with you. It's free with a subscription. Twice each month* **Consumers Union News Digest** *brings you the latest consumer information as it breaks. Peerless.*
—JB

•

Plymouth Voyager
Passenger van: $9659;
SE, $9938;
LE, $10,681.
Cost factors: car, 0.89; options, 0.85.
Destination charge: $465

The Voyager and Dodge Caravan are twins.

On the road. The optional 2.6-liter 4 started and ran well. The automatic transmission shifted smoothly; however, when it was cold, it occasionally delayed shifts into high gear. This front-wheel-drive van handled much like a typical passenger car in normal driving, but was sluggish and vague in emergency maneuvers. The front brakes locked a bit too soon, extending stopping distances.

Comfort and convenience. Exceptionally comfortable front seats and driving position. Passenger's seat is not adjustable. Fairly comfortable second seat for two. Fairly comfortable third seat for two or three. Moderate noise level. The Voyager rode more like a car than a truck. The ride was pleasant on good roads, but rough on back roads. The ride improved when the van carried its maximum load. Excellent climate-control system. Very good controls and displays.

Major options. 2.6-liter 4, $335. Automatic transmission, $502. Air-conditioning, $799. Seven-passenger seating package, $368.

Fuel economy. Mpg with 2.6-liter engine and automatic transmission: city, 14; expressway, 30. Gallons used in 15,000 miles, 725. Cruising range with optional 20-gallon tank, 470 miles.

Bumpers. Dented. Structural damage in rear. Repair estimates: front, $516; rear, $566.

Predicted reliability. Average.

Last full report. January 1986.

Buyer's Market

The hand of Ralph Nader, consumer advocate extraordinaire, guides this skinny newsletter. But the information is distilled and highly useful as it ranges over the nuances, outrages, lowdown, and inside dope on the subject selected for concentration in each issue. Typical subjects: banking, autos, food, complaints. The information is topped with a short bibliography. Useful and current. *—JB*

•

Most people rely on recommendations from their friends when finding a dentist. This may be good for openers, but also get advice from someone who is an expert or works closely with those who are. Several sources include:

The faculty of a University's School of Dentistry. Many of those associated with dental schools are among the best dentists and they usually know other top-notch practitioners. Ask for the name of a faculty member with a practice in a convenient location.

A dental specialist who tends to be interested in preventive dental care and saving teeth. Try calling an orthodontist, periodontist or endodontist. An orthodontist is an expert at straightening teeth, the periodontist an expert on gum diseases and an endodontist specializes in treatment of diseases of the pulp of the tooth (including root canal work). These specialists are good sources of information because they need good sound teeth to work on; they are especially on guard against general practitioner dentists whose poor work means their patients will have unsound teeth.

Buyer's Market
Luke W. Cole, Editor
$10/year
(10 issues) from:
Buyer's Market
P. O. Box 19367
Washington, DC 20036

Satisfaction Guaranteed

Ever feel like you've been had? How to prevent that sorry state and what to do if it's too late is the subject of this breezy book. Tactics are laid out move by move, but you'll have to supply the chutzpah. If you're willing to do that, you have reason to expect a happy ending. The author's expertise is wider than seems possible for one lifetime, but apparently he's successfully dealt with doctors, lawyers, mechanics, brokers, realtors and mail order companies. I'd hate to be on his wrong side; his motto must be "reasonable but deadly." *—JB*

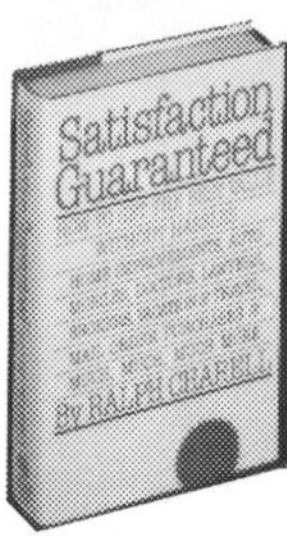

Satisfaction Guaranteed
Ralph Charell
1985; 253 pp.
$14.95
postpaid from:
Simon & Schuster
Mail Order Sales
200 Old Tappan Road
Old Tappan, NJ 07675
or Whole Earth Access

•

When Big picks up the call, never rub it in by saying "I thought the secretary said you weren't in." The idea is for Big to want to help you but not to bludgeon him or her and thus induce resistance or, equally unproductive, have him/her give you apparent agreement followed by nonperformance.

•

The test was taken and the results duly printed out, at a cost to my friend of about $200. The doctor then discussed the results and cautioned my friend to avoid the foods and substances to which he had been "found" allergic.
"How can I avoid things like household dust? It's everywhere. What about a cure?"
The doctor was not optimistic.
"How accurate is this test?" my friend belatedly asked.
"About 50 percent."
"I wish I had known that I could have gotten equally valid 'information' by tossing a coin before I took the test."

• Stand up for your rights! The whole complex mess of consumer protection laws is presented here along with operating instructions — dully but fully.
The Consumer Protection Manual: Andrew Eiler, 1984; 658 pp. **$29.95** postpaid from Facts On File Publications, 460 Park Avenue South, New York, NY 10016 (or Whole Earth Access).

The Burglar Alarm Book

Yipe! In some parts of the country the chances of having your house burglarized this year are one in ten or even worse. Your best defense is a cohesive neighborhood full of people you know. Next best is some appropriate hardware correctly installed. How to choose the hardware is what this book is about. Everything is explained in lay language with lots of tips for proper false-alarm-free installation, but mostly on principle — the nitty gritty isn't there. If you're not handy with tools, you'll need ***Home Security.***
—JB

•

Microwave detectors: Microwave detectors use high frequency radio waves to detect intrusion. A transceiver sends and receives radio waves while the detector monitors the reflected energy. An alarm is initiated when the waves sent out have been distorted by someone or something moving in the protected area.

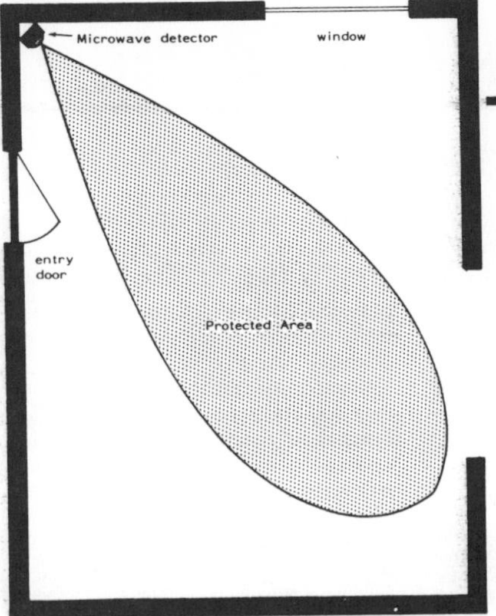

Typical microwave detector pattern (view from above).

The Burglar Alarm Book
Doug Kirkpatrick
1983; 128 pp.
$9.95
($11.45 postpaid) from:
Baker Publishing
P. O. Box 8322
Van Nuys, CA 91409
or Whole Earth Access

Home Security

You won't find much electronic wizardry here, but you will find clear writing and brilliantly done illustrations showing how to install security equipment. The book covers the installation of lights, door and window locks, grilles, safes, alarms, and all the detailing that goes with them. The chapter on fishing wires through walls is the best I've ever seen on this tricky procedure. Fire safety, fencing, and a good discussion of accident-proofing your place completes the book. It's all done in that well-turned-out Time-Life manner.
—JB

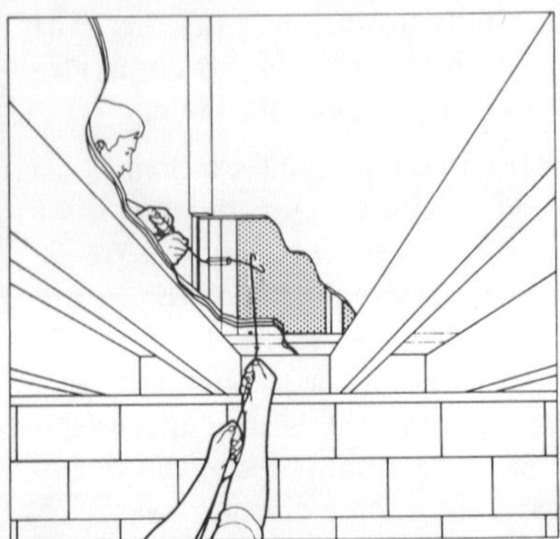

◄ **Fishing wires through a wall.**

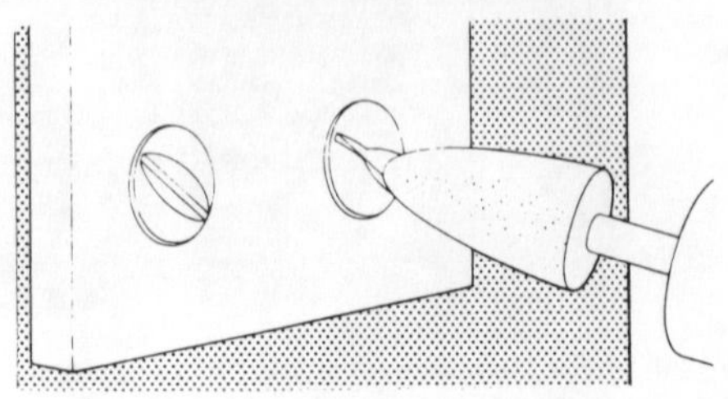

***Putting in screws for keeps.* A nonretractable screw (top) has a special head, making the screw impossible to remove without destroying the screw or framing. Before tightening such screws, be certain that the lock you are fastening is positioned correctly. If nonretractable screws are not readily available, use the tip of a conical grinder in an electric drill to erase the screw slot (above). Grind only along the sides of the slot; excessive grinding can weaken the screw.**

Home Security
Editors of Time-Life Books
1979; 136 pp.
$10.95
($13.78 postpaid) from:
Time-Life Books
541 North Fairbanks Court
Chicago, IL 60611
or Whole Earth Access

Mountain West Security Catalog and Reference Manual

This fascinating catalog is where you find the hardware to use with the instructions in the two books above. The selection is comprehensive, sophisticated (though not CIA level), and useful. Educational too; each item's purpose is explained briefly.
—JB

Mountain West Security Catalog and Reference Manual
Catalog **free** from:
Mountain West
P. O. Box 10780
Phoenix, AZ 85064

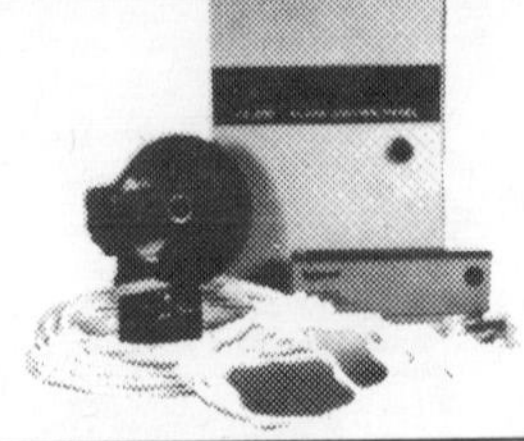

Alarm Package Includes:
1 72A56-003 Burglar Control Panel (see pg. 17)
1 72B9-002A Plug-In Transformer (see pg. 56)
100′ 72B14-115 General Purpose Wire (see pg. 61)
1 72C1-011 Momentary Remote Control Keyswitch (see pg. 62)
4 72M18-005 Hi-Rel Magnetic Contacts (see pg. 22)
1 72H5-001 Single Channel Siren (see pg. 43)
1 72A56-001 Musical Pre-Alert (see pg. 42)
1 72G2-005 Rechargeable Standby Battery (see pg. 55)
5 72MW-040 Window Decals (see pg. 89)
5 72MW-041 Standard Decals (see pg. 89)

Suggested Accessories:
72D10-101, -102, -202, 72A11-076A Extra Keyed Remote Control (see pg. 21)
72D14-025 Extra Digital Remote Control (see pg. 20)
72A14-031 Strobe Light (see pg. 45)
72R16-002 Infrared Motion Detector (see pg. 29)
72RK-101 Window Foiling Kit (see pg. 10)
72RK-102 GlassGard Kit (see pg. 27)
72RK-351 Tape Dialer Subsystem (see pg. 9)
72RK-350 Panic Button Subsystem (see pg. 9)
Additional Detectors, pp. 10-11

Using Passive Infrared With Pets

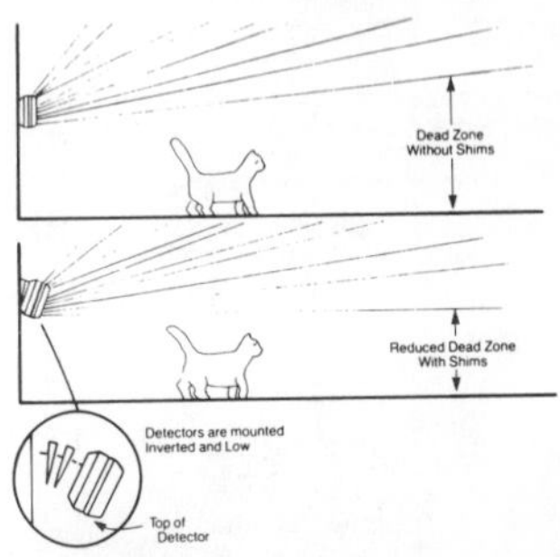

The easiest way to avoid the areas of animal movement is to mount the detector inverted and low to the ground. The detector must be mounted high enough so that it will not view animal motion, and low enough as to minimize the area below the detector where an intruder could crawl about. Be sure there are no tables, chairs, etc. which the pet could jump up on and enter the area of coverage. Some PIRs come with shims, or wedges, that can angle the coverage a little closer to the floor.

• Wanna read up on a product or service? This index tells you all the magazine articles that have appeared on the subject this year.
Consumers Index: C. Edward Wall, Editor. **$79.50**/year (4 issues) from P. O. Box 1808, Ann Arbor, MI 48106.

ONE HIGHLY EVOLVED TOOLBOX

by J. Baldwin

It took about 35 years for our toolbox to evolve into this portable shop. An hour of diddling opens the truck into an efficient 200-square-foot workspace containing (in addition to about a ton of hand tools) a drill press, band saw, table saw, radial-arm saw, air compressor, grinder, generator, and another ton of supplies. *Note: suppliers mentioned in text and captions are described on following pages.*

▲ SLOTTED ANGLE is a good building material where strength and compact size requirements make wood inappropriate, as in these workbenches. It comes in several sizes and weights, bolts together easily, and can be reused. Three good brands are DEXION, AIM, and BAY. (Look in the Yellow Pages of a largish city under "Rack" or "Slotted Angle.")

◄ STEEL CABINETS make a good home for tools and also work well for art supplies, sewing accessories, and medical equipment — anything that'll benefit from orderly, lockable storage. We upholster the drawer bottoms with carpet.

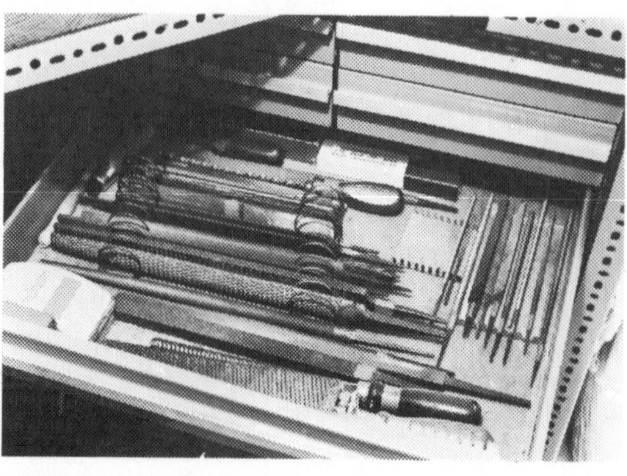

▲This is our abrader department. Old chair springs keep the files from filing each other. Sears makes exceptionally nice cabinets which often go on sale. We got ours freight damaged (ask!) for half price, then fixed them with a bit of sheet metal-fu.

THIS TOOLBOX WAS BORN inauspiciously in 1949 as a few rusty screwdrivers and a battered adjustable wrench living in a demoted Buster Brown lunch bucket. These days it takes form as a two-and-a-half-ton walk-in van that unfolds into a neighborhood workshop wherever it parks. It's set up so anyone can use it with minimal instruction; no point letting a ton of tools sleep most of the time. The tools are a diverse lot chosen for versatility, quality, and the ability to work well together. They *enable* you, literally, to do just about anything short of precision machining.

Folks have used this tool set to build hardwood furniture, boats, bicycles, solar collectors, and even whole houses. We've mass-produced 300 looms and thousands of parts for geodesic domes. Innumerable repairs have been made to plumbing, appliances, and vehicles. Best of all, the shop encourages invention. It was intentionally designed to be a three-dimensional sketchpad — a place to make the first physical manifestation of an idea. (That's something inventors should do themselves in order to maintain control as their ideas develop, just as artists do their own painting.) It's a teaching shop too. Hundreds of people have learned to extend their bare-hands abilities by means of these tools and a bit of friendly advice. Women have been especially welcomed, both as instructors and students.

Having lots of shop users has turned out to be the best defense against vandalism and theft. In 20 years we've lost less than $200 in tools and damage despite living in vulnerable locations. Tool loss is also controlled by marking everything with an obvious blue stripe and an antitheft ID number, and by having a specific home for each tool just like libraries do for books. We've found that tool drawers work better

◄ DELTA RADIAL DRILL PRESS is the most versatile available at a home shop price. The head tilts at any angle, and the arm not only rotates 360⁰ around the vertical post, it also slides in and out. This permits drilling objects too big for the drill table — even things sitting on the floor. Though not rigid enough for machine shop use, it does just fine for anything less demanding. Ours has served flawlessly for 20 years. (See Yellow Pages under "Tools — Electric." May also be called Rockwell.)

▲ CROSS VISE permits accurate location of work, left-right and front-rear, making it easy to put holes where you want them. Smooth feed allows light milling operations such as slotting. Even this crude model greatly enhances the usefulness of any drill press. (Bowden Wholesale, less than $30.)

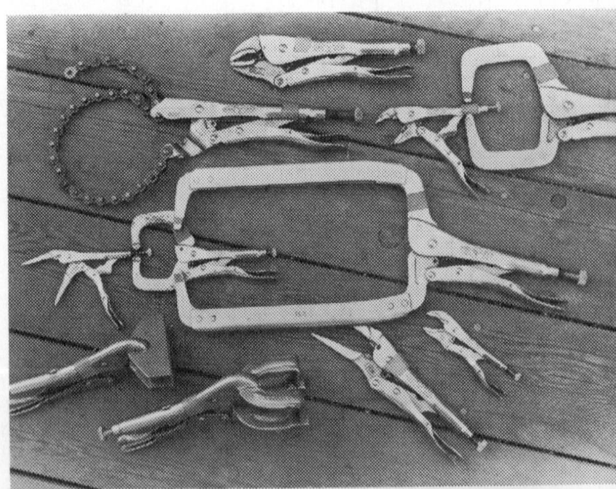

VISE-GRIPS come in many shapes and ► sizes, all with the squeeze force adjustable between delicate and prodigious. They lock, increasing the number of hands you have for other work. Buy only the genuine Vise-Grip brand — fakes fail fast. (U.S. General.)

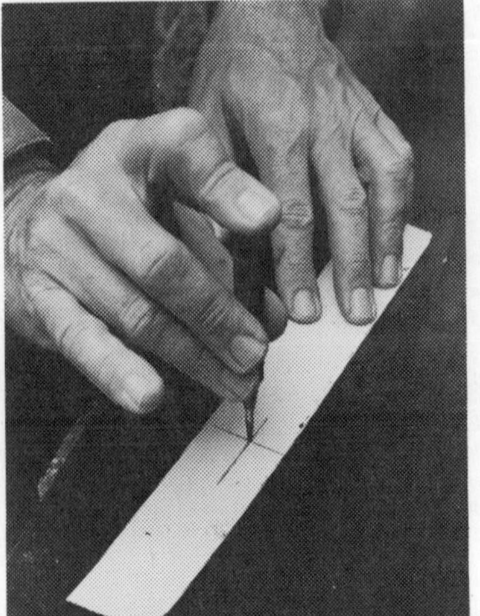

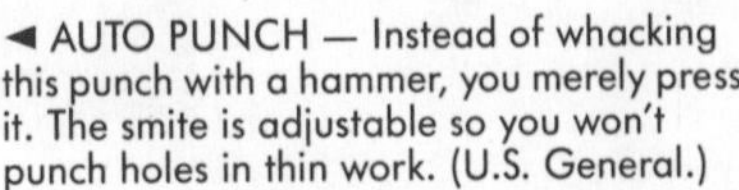

◄ AUTO PUNCH — Instead of whacking this punch with a hammer, you merely press it. The smite is adjustable so you won't punch holes in thin work. (U.S. General.)

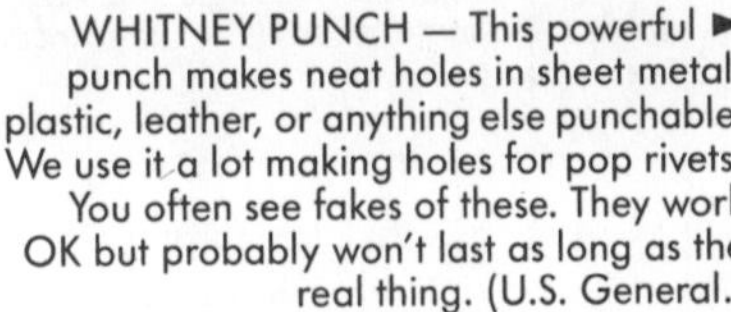

WHITNEY PUNCH — This powerful ► punch makes neat holes in sheet metal, plastic, leather, or anything else punchable. We use it a lot making holes for pop rivets. You often see fakes of these. They work OK but probably won't last as long as the real thing. (U.S. General.)

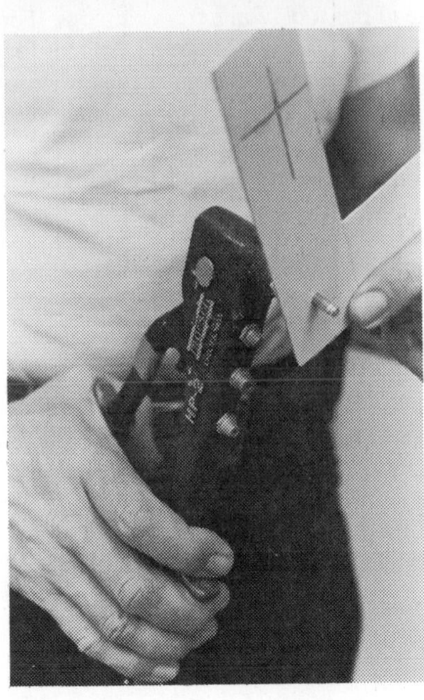

◄ POP RIVETS are great for attaching thin stuff to thin stuff. They work on car bodies, leather, plastic, and Masonite and are installed from one side — no need to have access to the back. Buy a rivet gun with longish handles; you'll need the leverage unless you're Godzilla. (Sears #9HT74747 is particularly handy.)

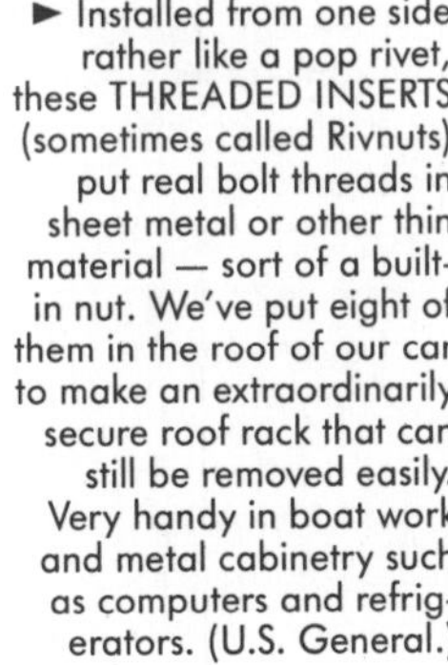

► Installed from one side rather like a pop rivet, these THREADED INSERTS (sometimes called Rivnuts) put real bolt threads in sheet metal or other thin material — sort of a built-in nut. We've put eight of them in the roof of our car to make an extraordinarily secure roof rack that can still be removed easily. Very handy in boat work and metal cabinetry such as computers and refrigerators. (U.S. General.)

◄ LEVEL LEGS make it safe and easy to use a ladder on uneven ground or even on stairs. Once you've tried them, no ladder feels right without 'em. (U.S. General.)

▲ LEVELS are the only way to get things, uh, level. *Pro* has 360⁰ scale with pointer accurate to half a degree. It's great for roof angles, and especially for aiming solar equipment. *Line level* hooks on string — handy for rough estimates over stringable distances. *Bull's eye* levels in all directions at once. (All from U.S. General.)

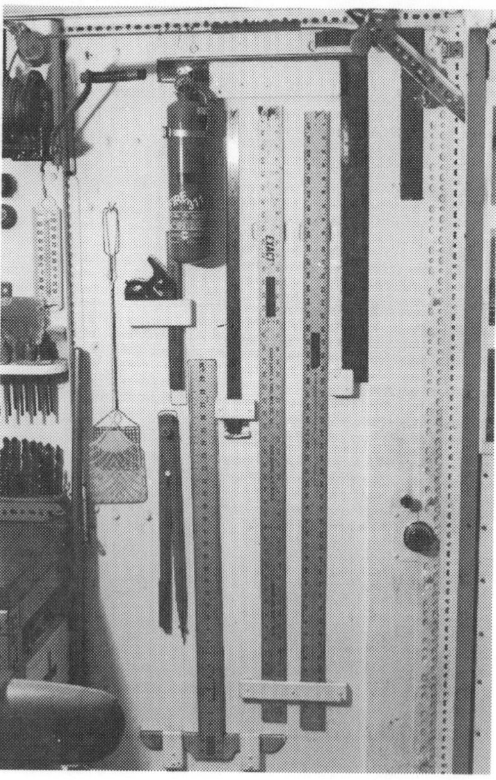

▲ FOUR-FOOT RULERS will save you lots of time and grief when working with 4x8' sheets, especially now that you can't trust plywood to be square. The best rulers have etched numbers that won't rub off. (At your local hardware or art supply store.)

◄ OFFSET CUTTERS keep your hands away from the all-too-sharp edge of the metal while allowing very tight turns. Design won't wrinkle thin metal. Comes in lefts and rights — you need both. (U.S. General.)

than hanging tools over silhouettes on the wall because there isn't enough wall space and because we're constantly adding new tools as our interests change.

Our tools are sorted by function rather than by name. Whackers, twisters, nabbers, and hole-makers live with their functional kindred. Just seeing them there together can give you an insight into how to do something more easily. Their drawers are color-coded so that go-phers can easily be sent to the right place: "The punch is in the green drawer."

Our tools range in quality from Taiwanese (for infrequent use, such as a plastic pipe cutter) to Teutonic or industrial (for tools we often beat up, such as electric drills). Stay away from the 99-cent bargain table: most tools need better steel than you'll find there. Fake ViseGrips, for instance, wilt the first time out; no-name screwdrivers are like noodles. On the other hand, we've picked up many of our tools at garage sales and flea markets. Take a Sears tool catalog with you for reference to new-tool prices. That's one way to ensure that the bargain is a bargain.

Most of our bought-new hand tools come from Sears. Quality is respectable, though you should inspect each item for workmanship these days. Sears' Craftsman brand warranty is peerless: if something breaks, they give you a new one. They recently replaced my broken 30-year-old wrench without a murmur.

Electric hand tools are another matter. For once-in-a-while household use, cheap ones will do . . . for a while. They wear out quickly and won't stand up to tough jobs. For hard work, try the medium-priced Japanese models from Makita, Ryobi, and Hitachi. They've gained a deservedly good reputation at the expense of U.S. manufacturers who made the same mistake that Detroit did with cars: waiting too long to update designs and improve quality. For heavy-duty professional tools, we've had the best luck with Bosch and Milwaukee. Ours are still going strong after 16 years of severe abuse. We recommend that any electric tool you buy be "double insulated" (marked ▢), a feature that greatly reduces shock hazard.

Some of our tools come from catalogs. (For our favorites, see pp. 158-159.) We wait for sales that can be 40 percent off list price, but you should always check for local sales before sending away for anything. Check local stores for demonstrators and freight-damaged merchandise too. What's a few scratches? Don't be too shy to ask the salesperson about it. As this toolbox has evolved, we've hardly ever paid list price for anything except for items needed immediately.

We don't own any cordless tools. They're certainly handy if you work where there's no power supply or where a cord would be in the way or dangerous, but the batteries apparently don't like infrequent use. That's what they'd get in our shop, so we'll wait until the need arises. As always.

Tools aren't all there is to a good shop. To speed the work, we stock about 600 sizes and types of fasteners, neatly arrayed. And

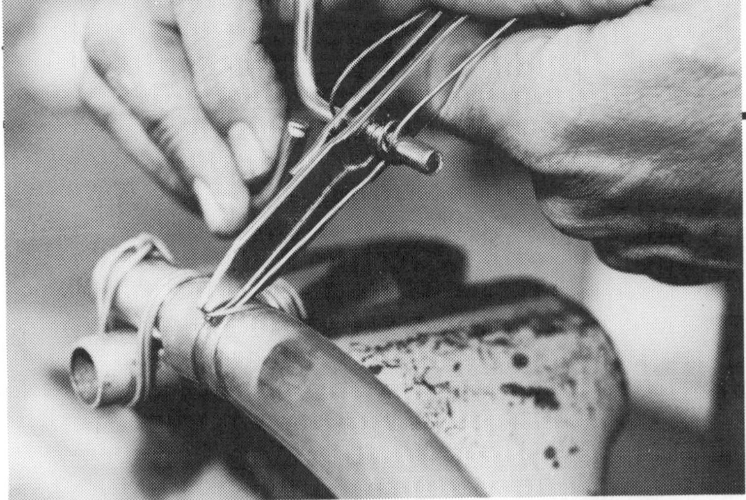

◄ HAYWIRE KLAMPER is a disconcertingly simple tool that mercilessly tightens a 14- to 16-gauge wire into a hose clamp affair. What is clamped needn't be round; diameter is limited by how much wire you have. Use it for bundling, making trellises, clamping for welds, for emergency ''baling wire'' repairs, etc. The clamping force is surprisingly strong. ($8.35 postpaid from Woodbern Manufacturing, P. O. Box 353, Libby, MT 59923.)

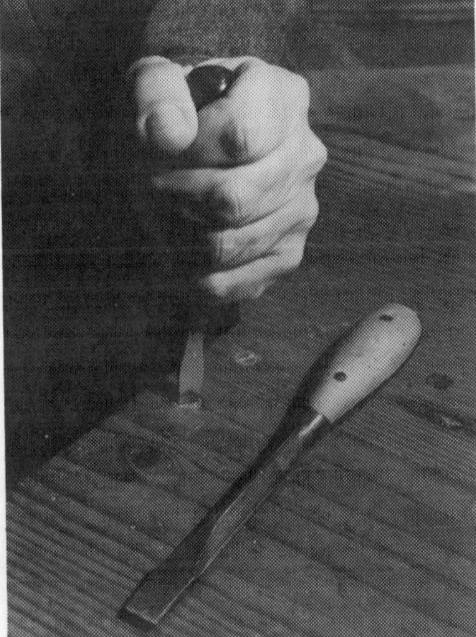

◄ FAT SCREWDRIVERS — Big handle, heavy blade, and compact size make this Sears #41586 our favorite. Square shanks on large screwdrivers permit helping the twist with a wrench. Big driver is from Garrett Wade.

► NAIL YANKER grabs the head or broken-off shank of the nail when you slam down the built-in slide hammer. Then you rock the tool back, and out pops the nail — leaving a reusable board. Wear heavy gloves when using this thing, as the pounding will soon bruise your unprotected hand. (U.S. General.)

◄ ESTWING HAND SLEDGE is forged from one handsome piece of steel. The handle won't break, and the head won't fly off even in dry weather. The grip is textured, squishy nylon. Comes in three weights, all great for confident, enthusiastic pounding. (At your local hardware.)

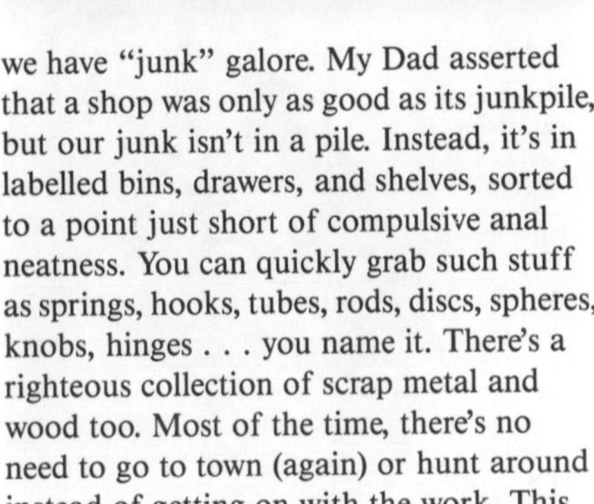

we have "junk" galore. My Dad asserted that a shop was only as good as its junkpile, but our junk isn't in a pile. Instead, it's in labelled bins, drawers, and shelves, sorted to a point just short of compulsive anal neatness. You can quickly grab such stuff as springs, hooks, tubes, rods, discs, spheres, knobs, hinges . . . you name it. There's a righteous collection of scrap metal and wood too. Most of the time, there's no need to go to town (again) or hunt around instead of getting on with the work. This makes it easier to get things done, and so things GET done.

That's the whole idea: making it easy to work makes it easy to try new concepts, to prove them in an irrefutable way. You can actually *change* things out there! Maybe not in a big way, but at a scale you can comprehend. Instead of technology taking over, *you* are in control — at least locally, and perhaps universally if the idea works well for lots of people. That's subversive tech. It can be fun. It's always satisfying. Work up your toolbox and give it a try. ■

▲ IMPACT DRIVERS work like those auto-repair air wrenches, except in this case, *you* supply the impact. This tool is often the only way to loosen rusted screws and bolts. Wear goggles while using. Comes with screwdriver bits. You can also use air wrench sockets. (Sears.) ■

A BASIC HOUSEHOLD TOOLBOX

You'll need these for hanging pictures, fixing the bike, tightening the faucet or the cupboard door hinge, making a shelf. Add more tools as demand arises. Sears' quality is fine. Watch for sales. —JB

Hammer: 16-ounce, curved claw (pulls nails best), non-wood handle.

Crosscut saw: name brand.

Hacksaw with blades: a simple one is fine.

Adjustable "crescent" wrench: 8'', name brand.

Socket wrench set: cheapo (less than $10), no-name, lots of pieces.

Vise-Grips (real): 6'', with wire cutter feature.

Four-way screwdriver: Two sizes of flat blade and two sizes of Phillips blade in one handle.

Rasp: four-way (''shoe'' type), one side flat, one side half-round, fine and coarse teeth on each.

Electrician's pliers ("side cutters"): I like ''needle-nose'' best.

Tape measure: 10' ; 1'' wide so it'll stand up.

Drill: hand crank or electric. If electric, get a ⅜'', variable-speed, double-insulated model. Start with ⅛'', 3/16'', ¼'', 5/16'', and ⅜'' bits of ''HSS'' (high-speed steel). Good for drilling metal, wood and plastic.

Duct tape: tapes most anything that doesn't have to withstand direct sunlight.

WD-40: to unstick stuck mechanisms and lubricate 'em so they won't stick again. Prevents rust too, for a while.

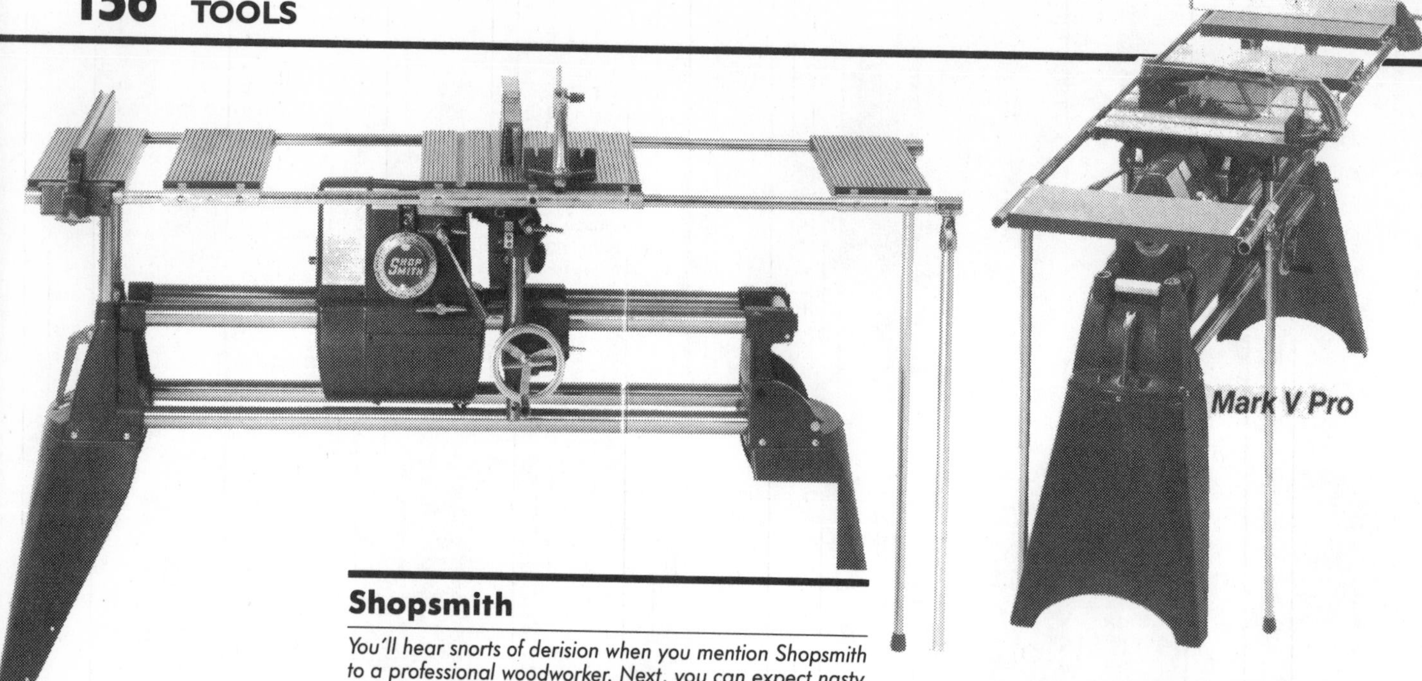

Shopsmith

You'll hear snorts of derision when you mention Shopsmith to a professional woodworker. Next, you can expect nasty comments pertaining to jack-of-all-trades-master-of-none, lightweight, and so forth. While it is true that this machine is not well suited for work with heavy structural lumber, it'll easily handle most anything a home craftsperson will ask it to do. It is at one time (with a bit of fiddling) a drill press, lathe, table saw, sander, and boring machine. With attachments it can do more, but it won't take up more space. And that's the great advantage of the Shopsmith: it's not an awful lot bigger than an ironing board. You can have a home shop in an apartment, condo, mobile home, boat, or anywhere else a whole roomful of power tools won't fit. Unlike imported imitations, Shopsmith is backed by a solid dealer network and what amounts to a cult of users. Local classified ads often have them used at substantial savings. —JB

Shopsmith
$1500 (approx.)
Information **free** from:
Shopsmith, Inc.
6640 Poe Avenue
Dayton, OH 45414

Cutawl

This relatively unknown tool can be found in virtually every display and exhibit shop. It's used to make the layers of those architectural landscape contour models, to cut out fancy lettering, and to make slick prototypes of displays that will later be cut out on production machinery.

The thing is a sort of sabersaw combined with a woodpecker. It cuts with a tiny chisel or sawblade, leaving a flawless machined edge. The steering is so accurate that it is feasible to cut lacework out of Masonite, Formica, thin metal, or any other thin, cuttable sheet material. It's unique; no other tool can match its capabilities. I've used one a lot. Used ones can sometimes be found at less cost. —JB

Cutawl
$550 (approx.)
Information **free** from:
Blackstone Industries
Route 6
Bethel, CT 06801

Ryobi 10'' Planer

At last, a thickness planer that can be carried to the job site by one worker — it only weighs 58 pounds. It'll handle wood up to five inches thick and ten inches wide, taking off an eighth of an inch at a time under suitable conditions. The price is right too: less than $400, on sale. —JB

Ryobi Planer
About
$400 (on sale)
Information **free** from:
Ryobi America Corp.
1158 Tower Lane
Bensenville, IL 60106

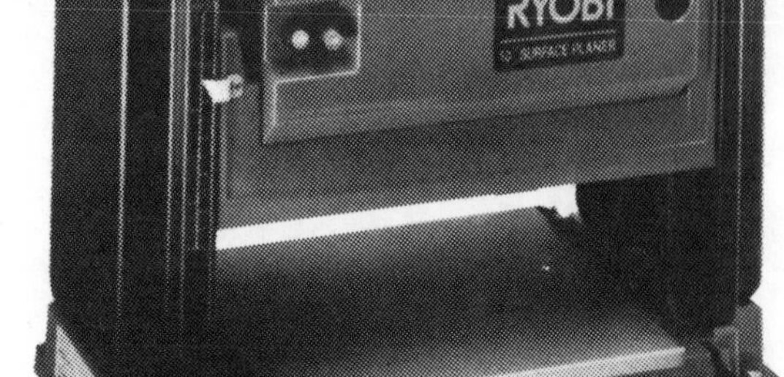

• Whole Earth Access (p. 245) has good tool selection and prices.

• Every shop should have a first aid kit. See our recommendations on p. 214.

Gerstner Tool Chests

If you enjoy reading this ***Catalog*** *you are probably the kind of person who is seized by an irresistible urge to open all those beautifully fitted little drawers in antique cabinets. You can satisfy the urge in your home thanks to H. Gerstner & Sons, Inc.*

They make superb wood cases that will hold small interesting things of almost any size and shape: machinist's chests, medical instrument cases, boxes for artists, photographers, dental hygienists, and so on, ad infinitum. The thing that sets Gerstner apart from their competitors is their concern with quality. You can buy a box from them that will stand with perfect aplomb on your Chippendale end table. Their cases are made of polished quartersawed oak, American black walnut, or can be covered with black leather or vinyl. Prices range from $260 to $405, and one look will convince you that their products are a rare bargain in an injection-molded age. Their service is personal and quick; illustrated literature is available. You can get factory seconds at reduced prices (less 20%) too.
—Morton Grosser

Gerstner Chests
$260-$405
Information **free** from:
H. Gerstner & Sons
P. O. Box 517
Dayton, OH 45402

•
STYLE 82: *Our largest, most popular chest.*
☐ Lockable front lid ☐ 4'' deep top compartment
☐ Lockable handbook compartment ☐ 3 wooden dividers
☐ 2 fluted trays ☐ accommodates 24'' scale

Pyramid Foundry Sets

The ability to make castings adds great potential to a workshop or art studio, yet few people get into it. The techniques aren't difficult, but they are unfamiliar. Pyramid makes it easy to understand and do; their kits set you up with supplies, equipment, and instruction. I've seen the sets used for boat restoration, machine repair, and making antique auto parts. The projects were successful, though there was certainly some time spent learning the hard way. Even that wasn't too bad; you can recast your boo-boos. The sets can handle aluminum, bronze, grey iron, and jewelry metals. *—JB*

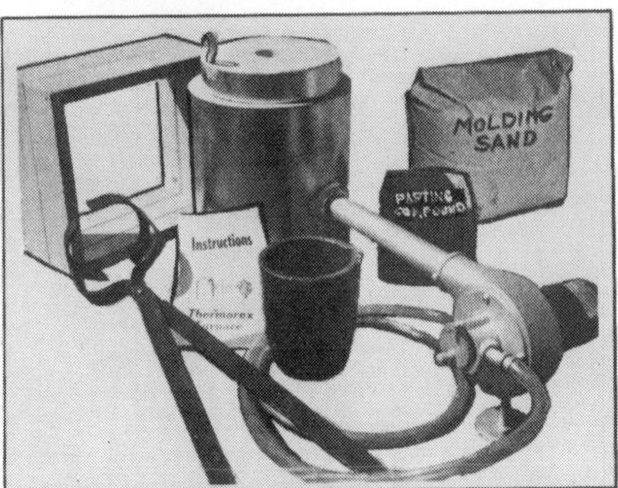

Pyramid
Foundry Sets
$250-$450 (approx.)
Information **free** from:
Pyramid Products Co.
3736 South 7th Avenue
Phoenix, AZ 85041

Fox Maple Tools

Where do you get wooden-boat-building tools? Here. They have stuff for timber framing too — all good quality.
—JB

Fox Maple
Joiners Supply
Catalog **free** from:
Fox Maple Joiners Supply
P. O. Box 445-M
231 Congress Street
Portland, ME 04112

Greenlee Short Unispur Power Bit

The best bit we know of for quickly removing wood in mortising operations, in which its short length is a real benefit. Three milled flats on shank ensure no slipping in electric drill chuck. The 2" bit is one of the most frequently used timber framing tools. You should save enough time in one day to pay for this bit! Single spur with lead screw, 6½" overall.

GN1021	GN1022	GN1023	GN1024
1⅜"	1½"	1¾"	2"
$33.72	$37.22	$46.55	$52.50

GN1025 2½" Regularly $72.33 **Sale Price $59.93**

Irwin Auger Handle

Where electric power is inconvenient, unavailable, or unsafe, and for holes beyond the capacity of your electric drill, the old-fashioned auger handle is the way to go. Affords much more leverage than a bit brace. Accepts all conventional taper square shanks, hex shanks, and nut augers. Ash handle with heavy steel clamps.

IR1094 Auger Handle $13.15

Irwin Barefoot Power Ship Auger

An extra-heavy, strong bit which excels at boring straight and true holes in heavy timbers. The screw points found on most other bits will often follow splits or even the grain of the wood. These will not, and will produce the most accurate deep holes. Of tool steel, hardened and tempered their full length, with polished edges. 5/16" hex shanks on ⅜" and ½" bits, 7/16" hex shanks on larger bits – will not slip in drill chuck. May also be used in auger handle. 12" twist, 17" overall.

IR1011	IR1012	IR1013	IR1014	IR1015
⅜"	½"	⅝"	¾"	1"
$15.95	$15.95	$17.59	$20.09	$23.39

U.S. General

U.S. General
Catalog
$2 from:
U.S. General
100 Commercial Street
Plainview, NY 11803

U.S. General

As far as I know, this is the only large-inventory mail-order hardware store left, which is too bad. Also too bad is that this catalog is a lot thinner than it used to be — much less variety. The lack of variety will reduce the apparent demand for less familiar but nonetheless very useful tools, leading their makers to discontinue production. Too bad again. You should note that not everything shown is of top quality, but U.S. General usually doesn't hide that — they grade the selections "Homeowner's," "Mechanic's," and "Industrial." Prices and service are decent. —JB

4-pc. File Pack has it all!

A Nicholson file for every purpose. One 8" mill bastard, one 6" round bastard, one 6" slim taper, one 8" flat and half-round shoe-rasp. Plastic pouch.

32474—4-pc. File Pack **$13.95**

Also Available Separately

105015—8" Shoe Rasp .... **(A) $5.90**
105023—6" Slim Taper .... **(B) 2.70**
105056—6" Round Bastard .... **(C) 3.45**
105064—8" Mill Bastard .... **(D) 3.25**

1/2" Heavy-duty Air Wrench... the fastest way to remove nuts, bolts

Ideal for overall automotive service, body repairs, farm and light truck work. Permits single-handed operation for direction change. Reversible with positive-action trigger for fine speed control. Long-lasting ball bearing construction. For bolts up to 9/16". Ultimate torque at 90 PSI is 275 ft. lbs. Requires 3½ SCFM @ 90 PSI, 3/8" min. hose. 1/4" air inlet. Length 7⅜". Wt. 5 lbs. Mfr. Model 734.

102608—Air Wrench **$49.80**

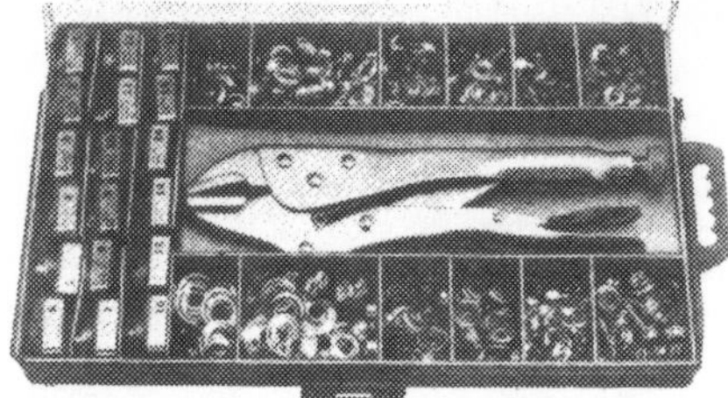

Easily install snaps, eyelets, grommets and rivets . . . everything is in this Complete Kit

THE kit for making or repairing car or boat covers, tarpaulins, lawn furniture, toys, tents, belts, handbags—almost any item that uses snaps, grommets, rivets or eyelets. 479-pc. kit includes heavy-duty adjustable locking pliers, 44 button snaps, 66 eyelets, 190 rivets (sizes: 3/16, 5/32, 1/8"), 160 grommets and washers (sizes: 1/4 and 5/16"), and 18 fastening adapters for installing the hardware. Compartmented case with complete instructions. Imported.

121137—Snap Kit **$21.95**

Soft-face Dead-blow Hammers will not spark, mar or rebound

Named "The Power Hitters," these are the hammers you can count on to protect the job as well as the workman. Ideal for engine, transmission, body work, glass and muffler installation, wheel and tire service. Dead-blow head contains metal shot to absorb the bounce; steel rod in handle. Head length for both models 4¼".

Item No.	Type	Face Dia.	Overall Length	Hammer Weight	Price
24703	Standard	2"	12¾"	2 lbs.	**$20.95**
24711	Slimline	1¼"	10½"	1⅓ lbs.	**16.95**

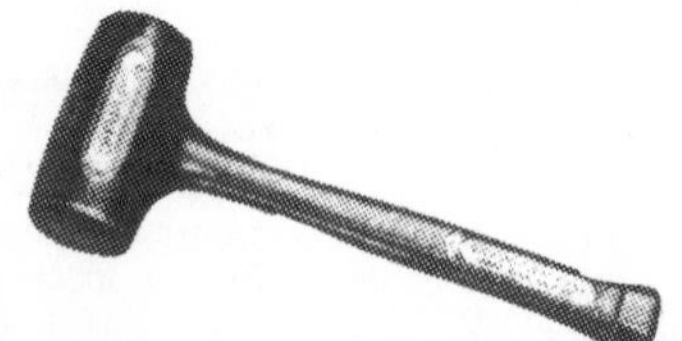

Save on drycleaning bills—this low cost coverall protects your clothes while doing dirty jobs around the house, in the yard or garage. Keep one in the car for changing tires and other roadside emergencies. Ultra-strong Tyvek is tough, durable and tear-resistant, yet is machine washable so you can use it over again. Comfortable and lightweight with easy-on full-length zipper. One size fits all.

127175—Coveralls **$5.90**

Protective Coveralls made of tough tear-resistant Dupont Tyvek® material

Sears Power and Hand Tools

Catalog **free** from:
Sears, Roebuck and Co.
Dept. 609
Sears Tower
Chicago, IL 60607
or check your phone book under Sears.

Sears Power and Hand Tools

Sears is the place to look for wrenches, steel cabinets, and reasonably priced power tools. Quality is fine. Warranty is honored without argument (if you're honorable). They have lots of other stuff too, at average prices. But their sales . . . (ah, their sales) are often remarkable. Decide what you want, and wait to pounce. Patience can save you 40 percent or more. Large stores often have freight-damaged and reconditioned goods too. Ask a clerk. Many of Sears' tools are national bestsellers. —JB

Our finest flush-cutting Saw has quick-release blade feature with self-adjusting tension. Cuts in 6 positions; incl. blade. Can be used as a jab saw. Aluminum and steel frame with enclosed handle. $17.99

(Above) Add-on chest atop maintenance cart with optional sliding work surface and cantilever tray (with flip-out compartmented sub-trays), flanked by vertical-storage side box and folding side shelf with socket holder. Grand total: about $468.44 (plus tax).

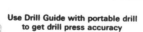

Get accurate, straight cuts whether you rip, crosscut, miter or bevel with this CRAFTSMAN 8-in. Bench-top Aluminum Table Saw

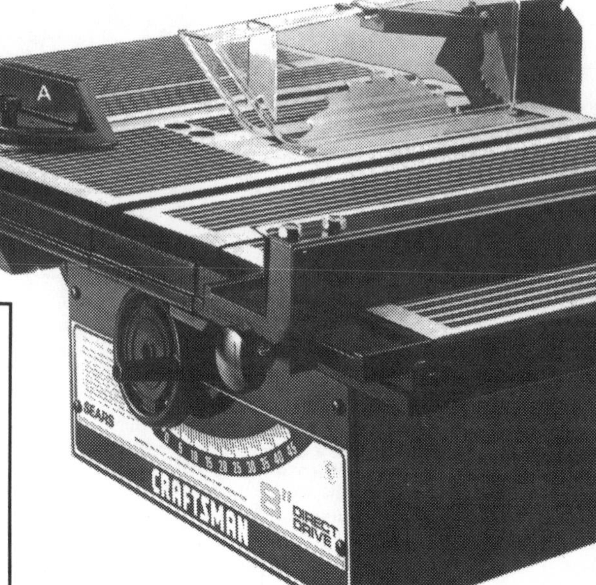

Use Drill Guide with portable drill to get drill press accuracy

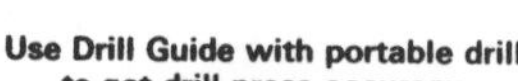

Helps you make perfect holes when drilling at 90° to surface, or up to 45° left or right. Lets you install locks, chamfer, do center drilling or doweling. Base holds round stock for center drilling. Angles marked on base in 5° increments. Angle lock knobs help provide accuracy. Guide rods. Adjustable depth control. For ¼, ⅜-in. electric drills. Drill, chuck, bit are not incl. Wt. 2 lbs. 1 oz.
9 HT 11233 .... $17.99

Brookstone

Ah me, Brookstone has become gentrified. But that hasn't reduced the quality or selection of interesting tools, many of which are available only here. Prices tend to be high, service good, and the warranty impeccable: if you don't like it, send it back. My experience with Brookstone has been uniformly pleasant. —JB

Brookstone
(Hard-to-find tools)
Catalog **free** from:
Brookstone Company
127 Vose Farm Road
Peterborough, NH 03458

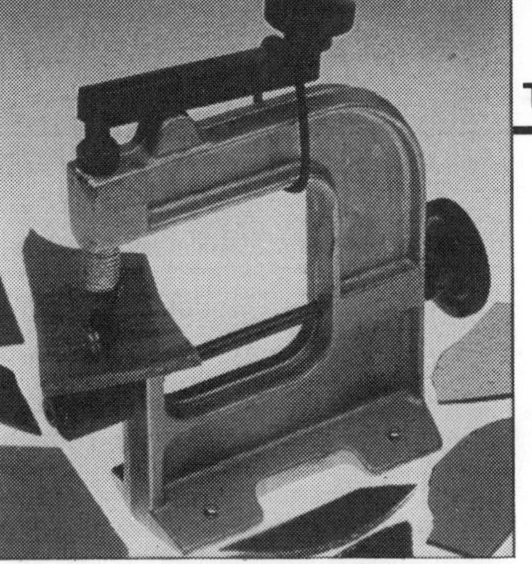

Cut All Types Of Glass With Remarkable Control

The unique design of this bench-mounted glass-cutter gives you remarkably sensitive control over all sorts of intricate work—even the difficult inside curves required in shaping individual pieces of stained glass. The hand-wheel on the side turns a rubber drive wheel for closely-regulated and careful feeding, and you maintain full control over the speed of the cutting. By adjusting the arm at top, you can change the angle of the tungsten carbide cutting wheel. Another important feature is that you can set the cutting wheel precisely to the thickness of the glass you're cutting: the spring-loaded arm keeps the pressure constant, which is essential in getting perfect results. The frame is made of cast aluminum in an I-beam configuration for strength. There are 4 holes in the base for stable, permanent bench mounting. Six space cutting wheels are stored in the cutter turret for extra convenience.

W-10790 Sure-score glass cutter **$59.95**

Magnetic Heater Warms Pipes, Engines, Locks

Heat radiators, transmissions, pumps, livestock troughs, drains and tanks from freezing and damage. This heater is fitted with a powerful magnet that holds it onto any ferrous metal surface. Attach it to the oil pan of an engine to make cold weather starting easier. There's a built-in thermostatic control to conserve energy. The 4[illegible]-ft. long power cord has a 3-wire plug and the heater operates on 115-120 volts, uses only 150 watts. The handle makes it easy to place and remove. It measures 4" long x 2[illegible]" wide x 4[illegible]" deep.

W-10273 Magnetic handy heater **$24.95**

Jensen

Tools for precision assembly and repair of electronics and other high-tech equipment. Jensen is famous for stunning assortments of best-quality tools packed in classy attache cases. Prestige is involved here, with prices to match. Fortunately, quality is here too. —JB

Jensen
Catalog **free** from:
Jensen Tool Incorporated
7815 South 46th Street
Phoenix, AZ 85044-5399

JTK-76™ Computer Systems Maintenance Kit

Jensen's JTK-76 contains a complete selection of tools for in-the-field troubleshooting, service and repair of CPU's, desktop computers, high speed printers and word processors. It features long-bladed screwdrivers plus a 7" extension blade for use with the selection of nutdrivers and hexdriver blades to assure easy access to hard-to-reach repair areas. In addition there are complete sets of combination wrenches and socket wrenches, measuring tools, pliers and cutters, soldering equipment and more. (See complete tool listing). The tools are contained in a deep injection molded attaché case with two removable pallets and ample space in the bottom of the case for additional tools and equipment. Inside Dimensions: 17¾ x 12¾ x 6½". Offered with optional test meters.

Cat. No.	JTK-76 Kit	Each 1-2	3-9†
H-76L	Kit In Case	$349	$314
H54B225	Tool Case Only	99	89
For Kit With Meter Add to Above Kit Prices			
H317B021	Fluke 8021B DMM (p.48)	$159	$149
H317B777	Fluke 77 DMM (p.48)	129	121
H56B200	Triplett 310 VOM (p.52)	60	56

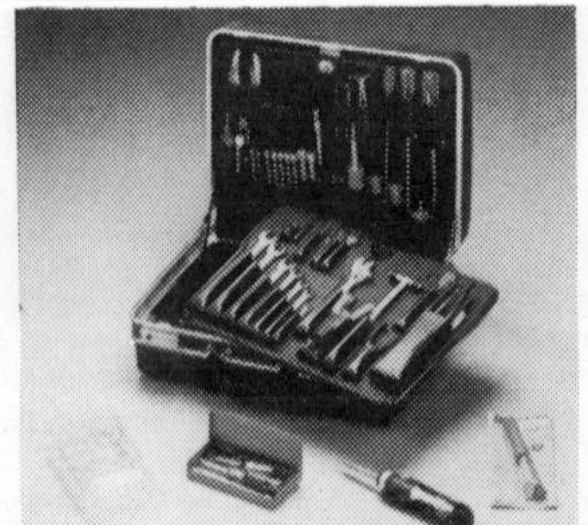

Eastwood

This catalog is an inspiring assortment of auto body restoration tools, many of which you've probably not seen before. By inspiring, I mean that the tools are so well described that even metalworking illiterati can understand enough to see potential uses beyond the automotive. A good bibliography of instruction books accompanies the tools and materials. I heartily recommend this catalog as the beginning of an education, particularly if all you know is wood. —JB

Eastwood
Catalog **free** from:
The Eastwood Company
147 Pennsylvania Ave.
P. O. Box 296
Malvern, PA 19355

A Rust Remover That Really Works

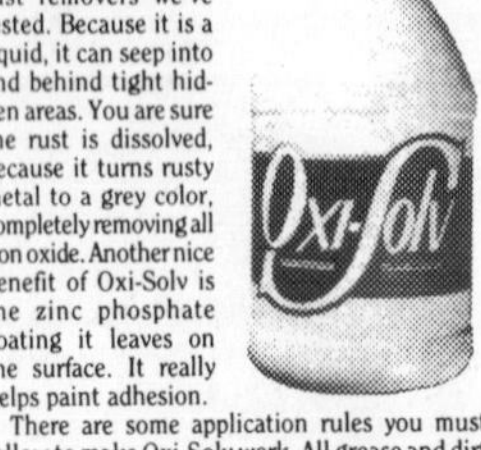

This product is the best of the many chemical rust removers we've tested. Because it is a liquid, it can seep into and behind tight hidden areas. You are sure the rust is dissolved, because it turns rusty metal to a grey color, completely removing all iron oxide. Another nice benefit of Oxi-Solv is the zinc phosphate coating it leaves on the surface. It really helps paint adhesion.

There are some application rules you must follow to make Oxi-Solv work. All grease and dirt must be removed from the part. Temperature is really critical; all parts must be between 60°F and 90°F. The actual application depends on the part. Large parts can be sprayed (old Windex bottles work great) or brushed. A sponge helps to keep an area wet for a long time. For smaller items use a bucket to soak the part. A paint brush dipped in Oxi-Solv can help agitate the surface for good penetration. A door with severe internal rust at the bottom might take soaking for 1-2 hours. The trick is to keep the parts wet with Oxi-Solv long enough to let it dissolve the rust. See the chart below.

Oxi-Solv is not a primer and you should prime-coat the surface before painting. It can be painted over without rinsing. Some customers rinse with warm water, but it's not necessary. You can reuse it without it losing its rust removal strength. Another plus is that it's safe — non-toxic, non-caustic, and non-flammable. It really works and is pleasant to use.

3430 Rust Remover
16 oz. container **$8.95**
3432 Rust Remover
1 gal. container **$24.95**
3436 Rust Remover 5 gal. pail **$99.00**

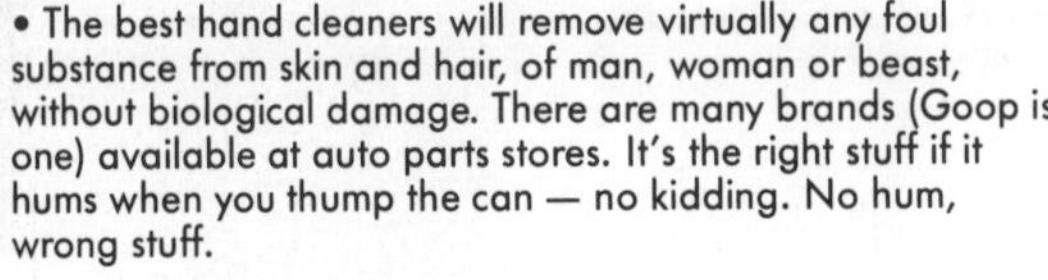

• The best hand cleaners will remove virtually any foul substance from skin and hair, of man, woman or beast, without biological damage. There are many brands (Goop is one) available at auto parts stores. It's the right stuff if it hums when you thump the can — no kidding. No hum, wrong stuff.

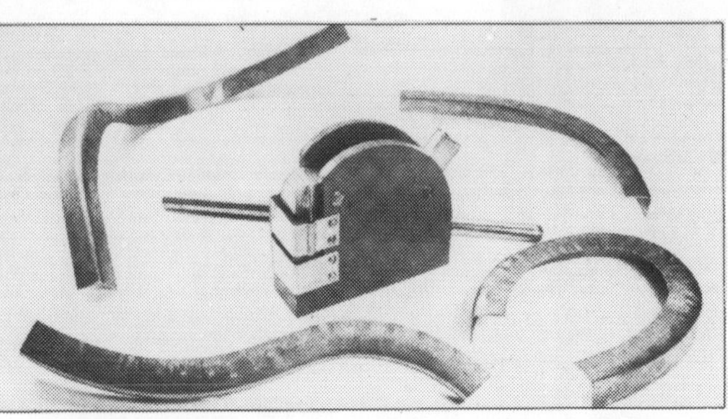

Our Shrinker & Stretchers Make Unbelievable Curves

These exceptional metal formers are great for making smooth radius bends in sheet metal without cutting, heating, or hammering the material. Reproduce wheel wells, dog legs, windshield openings, just about anything with a curved edge. On our initial test, we made a replacement part to go around the trunk opening on a '38 Buick in about 10 minutes, and it was a complex angle! Mount them on your workbench or in a vise and use the shrinker to contract metal to make inside curves, and use the stretcher to expand the metal for outside curves. Use them both for complex curves, you can even make circles as small as a 3" radius. The hand operated press gives a 45-to-1 leverage to move the hardened alloy steel jaws. Works metal up to 18 gauge mild steel, 20 gauge stainless and 16 gauge aluminum in widths of two inches. Parts above are 2" wide, 18 gauge mild steel that were formed to a 90° angle on a metal brake. They were then inserted into the shrinker or stretcher jaws to form the curved shapes. Each unit comes completely assembled ready to use.

7730 Shrinker & Stretcher Set ... **$249.00**

Moving Heavy Things
Jan Adkins
1980; 48 pp.
$6.95
($8.45 postpaid) from:
Houghton Mifflin Co.
Attn.: Order Processing
Wayside Road
Burlington, MA 01803
or Whole Earth Access

RENTING TOOLS by J. Baldwin

Rented tools let you do the job yourself instead of hiring someone whose only attribute may be possession of a tool you don't own or don't care to own. Renting is also a good way to try out several brands of something expensive before you buy. A surprising variety of tools can be rented these days. You should shop around; I have found very different prices, policies, and selection at competing rent-its. One thing is common to all though: a damage deposit. Be sure and bring some cash.

Check the tool for proper operation before leaving the store. Write down any defects on the rental agreement form or you may lose your damage deposit later. Machines that endure lots of abuse should be checked with extra care. If one machine is in better shape than another, you can reserve "the good one" ahead of time by talking up the friendliest clerk. Get the clerk's name for future use, and be generous with your thanks if all goes well. Sometimes you can arrange to take a tool home the night before at no extra charge.

Ask for tips on tool use; the instructions (make sure they are supplied) may not tell all. Floor sanders, for instance, rarely come with hints for preventing the dreaded and expensive WHAP-flup-flup-flup of sandpaper ripped on an exposed nailhead. (Meticulously pound them in before starting the sander.) Machines that eat material may run up a supply bill that exceeds the rental fee. The clerk should be able to give an estimate.

Get a time estimate too, allowing extra for adventures in learning. You should also allow for time lost to breakdowns of abuseable equipment such as ditchdiggers. The rent-it won't charge you for time lost due to breakdowns that aren't your fault, but they won't pay you for your lost Saturday either.

When renting, a flexible attitude is appropriate. That, with a bit of luck, should get the job done for less money while increasing your independence. That's a pretty good deal these days. ■

Moving Heavy Things

I remember once watching in wonder as a lone man carried a full-size upright piano up a flight of stairs! How did he do it? This marvelous little primer brings to us mere mortals the secrets of manipulating weighty objects — without damaging them or us. Not only are the secrets well explained and illustrated (with Mr. Adkins' nifty drawings), the proper spirit is attended. The book encourages independence. Every household should have one. —JB

ANGLES

<°	tension	pull-out
90°	.5	0
80°	.51	.10
70°	.53	.18
60°	.58	.29
45°	.71	.50
30°	1.00	.87
25°	1.18	1.07
20°	1.46	1.37
15°	1.93	1.86
10°	2.88	2.83
5°	5.74	5.72

Multiply the weight of your load by the factors beside the angle of your cable droop to get the tension in your cable and the pull-out force.

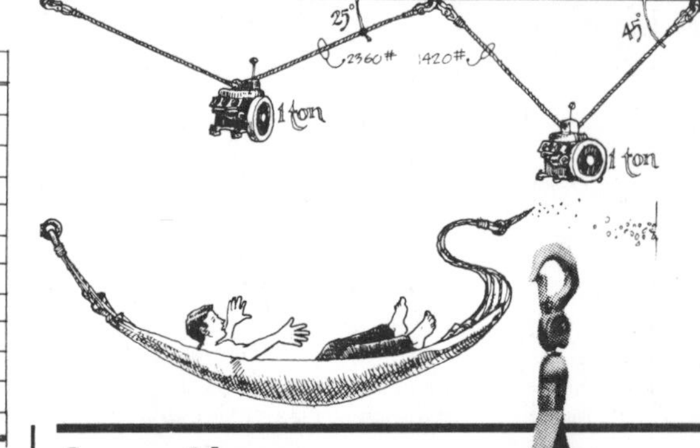

Handyman Jack
$45-$75
Information **free** from:
Harrah Manufacturing Co.
46 West Spring Street
Bloomfield, IN 47424

Handyman Jack

Basically the Handyman Jack is a super-heavy-duty bumper jack, but it bears no resemblance to the inadequate things that Detroit supplies with their inadequate automobiles. It weighs 29 pounds, has a capacity of three and one-half tons, and a lift of three feet.

I've used mine for lifting my truck, stretching shrunken plastic water pipe, and a number of odd lifting and spreading jobs, and wouldn't part with it for anything.

Warning: Beware of the handle, or EAT TEETH.
—Douglas Canning

I recently used mine for lifting an entire barn corner back to level after a flood, pulling fence posts out of the ground, and manipulating a downed tree. You can get a permanent sheath for the jack so it can ride theft-resistantly in your pickup. This thing is old-time American know-how at its best. —JB

Come-Along Hoist/Winch/Puller

You can put a half-ton of moxie on anything and lift or drag it 12 feet. If you'll settle for six feet, the capacity grows to a full ton. Load is released a notch at a time without danger of running amok. I've used mine for fence stretching, car unstucking (you can even drag 'em sideways), aligning house framing, lifting engines from vehicles, river rescue work, and hoisting things to the rooftops. I've had good luck with Maasdam brand ($25 or so), from Burden's. —JB

• Lifting, prying, dragging, pushing, and pulling are all explained scientifically in **Conceptual Physics** (p. 388).

Jerryco

This imaginative and often zany catalog describes a melange of surplus from both military and civilian enterprises obsoleted or gone wrong or sometimes merely overdone. I've found that the offerings can stimulate my design process. I've also bought things just for the hell of it. Service has been exceptionally pleasant, honest, and fast. Highly recommended. By the way, Jerryco is sort of the bargain basement of Edmund's Scientific (p. 389), with whom they are associated. —JB

PERISCOPE HEADS
Real, second world war periscope heads. But before you leap for the phone, these are the mirror type, not the prism type. Each metal mounted mirror has flat glass protected entrance and exit faces 1"x 5". They were meant to fit onto rectangular bodies, one at either end. By looking in the bottom, one sees out the top, thereby reducing the chances of widowing your your young bride. More interesting today for short people at the back of sidewalk parades. Or to take a peek at the high shelf you're about to reach onto. Or for secret inspections from a snow fort or tree house. You'll need to make your own body, which can be solid or skeletal depending on the environment. The heads, however, will be authentic.
J-3270-2 Pair of Periscope Hds. **$3.50**

GRUNGY FIRESTARTERS
Double convex lenses about 2" in diameter with a focal length of about 3-1/2". Used by boy scouts the world around as firestarters - - not workable on cloudy days or at night. These lenses may have small chips and may have a light haze that won't clean off. The latter is oxidation from getting wet in paper cartons, some of which may have to be scraped or soaked off by you, the aware buyer. Dandy for scouting projects, artworks, or playing with lenses.
J-1582-1 Sample firestarter **$1.00**
J-1582-10 (10) firestarters **6.00**
J-1582-100 (100) firestarters **40.00**

GIANT Z–I–P–P–E–R
Please, no wise ones about how to make an elephant fly. This is serious business. We have these 41" white Robin zippers.
Laying flat they are 1" side to side. The metal zipper itself is 3/16". The zipper is stopped at both ends, so it would be of limited value on the front of your fur coat. Great for slip covers, and for sofa cushions. How about turning loose kids or/and artists. Imagine a wall hanging made of zippers sewn side by side with a different "surprise" behind each one? Or, make your own folios that zip all around for carrying art work, pictures, big lunches and the like. These are long zippers.
J-1805-3 Three Zippers **$1.50** **J-1805-50** Box of (50) **$15.00**

Jerryco
Catalog
50¢ from:
Jerryco, Inc.
601 Linden Place
Evanston, IL 60202

Burden's

There's not much "war surplus" around these days, so old-time stores like Burden's have concentrated on hydraulic and pneumatic components, electronic parts, industrial leftovers, and discounted tools. As with all surplus outlets, you are at an advantage if you have some experience with this sort of merchandise; there are few explanations beyond the specifications. Imaginative use of a catalog like this can lead to unexpected new capabilities; indiscriminate use can lead to an overstuffed garage. —JB

Burden's Surplus Center
Catalog **free** from:
Burden's Surplus Center
P. O. Box 82209
Lincoln, NE 68501

Cab Heater
$49.99
F.O.B. Lincoln
Shpg. 10 lbs.
11-1/2" x 8-1/4" x 8-1/4"

- **ITEM 28-1028** - - Brand new, made by RED DOT. For use on campers, truck cabs, busses, etc. to provide extra heating. Beige finish with grillwork to protect exchange fins.
- Two speed fan operates on 12-VDC. Provides 230-CFM airflow on high speed. Maximum output, 2300-BTU's per hour. Motor draws 3.3-amps. Water connections are 1/2" NPT.

ITEM 28-1028
Cab Heater Illustration Showing Rear View

Fountain Pump
FOR DISPLAY FOUNTAINS
AIR CONDITIONERS
ROCK GARDEN POOLS
AQUARIUM CIRCULATION
$12.95 F.O.B. Lincoln

- **ITEM 2-948** - - New surplus. Excellent for fountain display pump Also useful as circulating pump for evaporative air conditioners, etc. Delivers 1-GPM at 2 ft. height above pump. Shaded pole 115-VAC motor. 2 discharge ports for 3/8" I.D. tubing. Size 4-1/4" x 2-3/4" x 2-3/4". Shpg. wt. 2 lbs.

115-VAC

"Build-Your-Own" Hydraulic Log Splitter Components
(3) (3)
(2) (1) (2) (1)
ITEM 1956-CP — **$118.95** F.O.B. Lincoln
ITEM 1956-TE — **$119.50** F.O.B. Lincoln

- Essential components for log splitter builders. 3-component sets consist of (1) butt block, (2) sliding block, (3) splitting wedge. **ITEM 1956-CP** for use with clevis end cylinders; **ITEM 19-56-TE** for cross tube cylinders with 1-1/2" diam. piston rod.

2-Ton Pickup Truck Box Hoist with Electric-Hydraulic Power Pak

- Heavy duty, electric/hydraulic unit designed for operation on 1/2-ton pickups with standard 8-foot boxes. Will dump loads up to 2-tons less than 40-seconds, 45-degree dumping angle.
- Easy and simple to install. Will not alter the profile height of truck body to any appreciable degree. Supplied with the ENERGY EMC-16 Remote Control Power Pak (same as our Item 9-038) which is especially designed for the SF-2 pickup hoist. Power Pak includes electric-hydraulic pump, dash push-botton, wiring and mounting bracket.

BRAND NEW

ENERGY MODEL SF-2
Designed for 1/2-Ton Pick-ups With Standard 8 ft. Boxes

- **SPECIAL NOTE: Hoist is not designed for use with pickup that has gas tank attached to the box. Not recommended for use on '69 and '70 Chev. or GMC 1/2-ton pickups.**

Hoist SPECIFICATIONS	Power Pak
• Load capacity 4000-lbs. at 2000-PSI	• Operates on 12-VDC
• Single-acting type	• Pressures to 2000-PSI
• Cylinder bore/stroke 3-1/2" x 8-11/16"	• Volume 1.1-GPM
• Chrome plated rod	• Outlet 1/4" NPT
• Dump angle 45°	• Built-in relief valve, ball check, control valve
• Lift time 37-seconds	• Reservoir cap. 1/2 gal.
• Shpg. wt. 180-lbs.	• Shpg. wt. complete with Power-Pak, 230 lbs.

ENERGY MODEL EMC-16 POWER PAK
(COMPLETE OUTFIT)
HOIST ONLY
ITEM
$4
ITEM 3-924

Mail-Order Discount Tools and Supplies

If you keep firmly in mind that you get what you pay for, stores such as these can be a good place to shop. Typically, a few name-brand items are featured at attractive prices. If there is no brand name, and the price seems unbelievable, then be sure your needs don't require top quality. I don't say that last with a sneer either — there are many times when top quality is silly: the wrenches you keep in the trunk of your car, for instance. (Mine came from Harbor Freight.) The companies listed here are two of many and are shown as examples only. I've had adequate service from both. —JB

Harbor Freight Salvage: catalog **free**; 3491 Mission Oaks Blvd., Camarillo, CA 93010.

Bowden Wholesale Co.: catalog **free**; 111 First Street NE, Cullman, AL 35055.

7 PC. NUT DRIVER SET

- Sizes 3/16", 1/4", 5/16", 11/32", 3/8", 7/16", 1/2"
- Overall length 6-3/4"
- Hardened steel 6 pt. sockets
- Chrome plated mirror polished
- Color coded plastic handles
- In heavy duty plastic tool wrap

Lot No. 944-2
$1.75

—Harbor Freight

K-1005
52 PC. SOCKET SET 1/4, 3/8, 1/2 DRIVE SAE & MM
INCH & METRIC SIZES IN ONE BOX
Set consists of: 1½" Drive 10" Ratchet Handle. 1⅜" Drive 8" Ratchet Handle. 1⅜" Drive 3" Extension Bar. 1¼"x⅜" Adapter. 1⅜"x13/16" Spark Plug Socket (12 Pt.). 1⅜"x⅞" Spark Plug Socket (6 Pt.). 1¼" Drive 8" Spinner Handle. 1 Spin Disc 1-Metal Carrying Case.
S.A.E. INCH SIZE SOCKETS
12—1/4" Drive 6 Pt. Sockets: 5/32, 3/16, 7/32, 1/4, 9/32, 5/16, 11/32, 3/8, 13/32, 7/16, 15/32, 1/2
3—1/4" Drive 8 Pt. Sockets: 1/4, 5/16, 3/8
3—3/8" Drive 6 Pt. Sockets: 9/16, 11/16, 3/4
10—1/2" Drive 6 Pt. Sockets: 3/8, 7/16, 1/2, 9/16, 5/8, 11/16, 3/4, 25/32, 13/6, 7/8
METRIC SIZE SOCKETS
12—1/4" Drive 6 Pt. Sockets: 4mm, 4.5mm, 5mm, 5.5mm, 6mm, 7mm, 8mm, 9mm, 10mm, 11mm, 12mm, 13mm
3—3/8" Drive 6 Pt. Sockets: 14mm, 16mm, 17mm

$8.50
—Bowden

Why Gov't Surplus is Cheap

This is irrelevant, but good: friend of a friend in San Diego bought a big steel cabinet-machine at a government surplus place ($50). Took it home and tried all the knobs and switches; nothing worked. Pried open the back and saw some connectors out of their sockets. Plugged them in. Tried a switch. Machine whined and began to clang — loud. Tried more switches. It wouldn't shut off. After ten minutes, a siren started — deafening. Tried all the knobs and switches. Wouldn't stop wailing. He got scared and ran out. His house blew up. It was a U.S. Navy self-destruct bomb designed to destroy captain's cabin and all papers, in case of capture. —Will Baker

The WEST SYSTEM

The Gougeon Brothers on Boat Construction
(Wood and WEST SYSTEM Materials)
1985; 297 pp.
$24.50 postpaid;

WEST SYSTEM Product Catalog
free;

WEST SYSTEM Technical Manual
31 pp.
$2 postpaid

All from:
Gougeon Brothers, Inc.
P. O. Box X-908
Bay City, MI 48707

This system is a well-worked-out method of "cold molding" wood into complex shapes that would otherwise be difficult to accomplish. The completed item is a laminate of thin wood strips or sheets, and epoxy resin; it's light, strong, and not subject to the bane of conventionally used wood: rot. If you like, the work can be finished "bright" (natural) bringing out the beauty of the wood, but purists insist that the WEST SYSTEM is mostly plastic. In truth, the end result is a bit of both plastic and wood — the best of both. A more valid criticism is that the epoxy is dangerously toxic to work with. No two ways about it, you must be careful. Proper procedures are well developed in this literature, and seem to work OK if followed with discipline.

*To me, the most interesting aspect of cold molding is that it need not be used only for boats. I've seen car bodies, aircraft, windmill blades, furniture (**Fine Woodworking** March/April '86 [p. 74] has a detailed article on cold*

*molding a wonderful cradle), and even parts of houses. The technique is easy to learn and not awfully expensive. Basics are nicely laid out in the booklet, **The WEST SYSTEM Technical Manual**. A hardbound book, **The Gougeon Brothers On Boat Construction**, is the latest collection of the brothers' experience and that of others using the WEST SYSTEM. Proper detailing of joints and other structural matters is well developed now, and herewith presented in a way that is easily understood and adaptable to other ends. The WEST SYSTEM catalog makes the necessary materials and accoutrements available.*

I can vouch that it all works. —JB

100 — MENDING/EVALUATION KIT — Complete compact case is ideal to have for emergencies. Contains — 2.5 lbs. 105 resin, .5 lb. 205 hardener, 4 oz. solvent cleaner, 20' graphite fibers, 1 bag 403, 1 bag 406, 1 bag 409, 6 mixing pots, mixing sticks, applicator brushes, 1 squeegee, 1 syringe, 2 pr. gloves, mini-pumps, 5 oz. tube skin cleanser, 1 yd. 6" glass tape.
ship. wt. – 8 lbs. kit

Plywood panels spread out to designed angle
Tighten loose wires by pushing down on the center here
or
Tighten by further twisting here

Tightening wires at keel joint. —The Gougeon Brothers on Boat Construction

Livos Organic Wood Finishes

Livos Organic Wood Finishes
Catalog **free** from:
Livos
614 Agua Fria Street
Santa Fe, NM 87501

Wood finishing is one of those places where nasty chemicals and nice people tend to meet intimately. If this has bothered you, a choice is now available. These finishes have no petroleum distillates, lead, or other carcinogenically suspicious substances — they're entirely brewed from plantstuffs. They don't evaporate or otherwise get into your environment even through direct contact. Sounds good to me, though I have not tried any (yet). Obviously it's a fine idea. German-made. —JB

VINDO-ENAMEL PAINT #4000

TECHNICAL INFORMATION:
SURFACE HARDENING, protecting and water resisting capacities.
APPLICATION is similar to common paints. VINDO can be applied by brush, spraying and in some cases by dipping. For spraying purposes VINDO can be thinned up to 30% with LIVOS-Natural Citrus Thinner #7222. For highest quality finish, sanding between coats and steel wooling is recommended. Sanding should only be undertaken when paint is completely dried.
TEN COLORS, derived from earth pigments with the exception of green and blue, being derived from non-toxic minerals. A large variety of pastel or medium dense colors can be obtained by mixing VINDO White #4091 with LIVOS Earthen and Mineral Stain Pastes or for larger quantities with any of the other colors of VINDO.
COMPONENTS are a concoction of weather resistant plant resins and dryable plant oils as binders, titan white from recycle process finely dispersed in above binders, earten and mineral pigments, lead free natural dryers and evaporative dryable plant oils as thinners. No chemical additives such as stabilizers, preservatives or mineral spirits.
COVERAGE approximately 100 square feet / Liter.
DRYING TIME can vary from 8 to 24 hours, depending on percentage of mixture with thinner #7222, climate, materials used and method of application. LIVOS research has improved the formula for faster drying capacity, however, the drying time is longer than that of common products.

* VINDO has been approved to be saliva and perspiration proof according to the West German Industrial Norm DIN 53160.

Devcon

Devcon
Catalog and nearest dealer location
free from:
Devcon Corporation
30 Endicott Street
Danvers, MA 01923
or check your local industrial supply dealer.

One way to conserve energy and resources is to fix things that break rather than throwing them away. The Devcon Corporation makes a wide variety of products that can solve some very nasty repair problems as well as increasing the life of various hardware. Typical are Plastic Steel and Plastic Aluminum. A far cry from their sissy hardware store counterparts, they are super strong and you can (for instance) repair engine blocks. Devcon makes a paint called "Z" that actually outperforms hot dip galvanizing (Milspec, no less). Devcon Rubber repairs split rubber boots better than anything else I've seen. They make a wear-resistant self-lubricating epoxy compound that can be used to make long-wearing bearing surfaces in wood. (It can also be used to build up worn shafts.) The list goes on. I've used all this stuff and find it to be at least as good as Devcon says. Not many companies are worthy these days. This one is. You'll probably have to get their products from an industrial supply house. The catalog is available there too. —JB

Floor Patch
☐ Silica-filled epoxy for patching and resurfacing small areas of damaged floors, walks.
☐ Consistency and workability of concrete.
☐ Compression strength three times that of concrete.
☐ Bonds to new and old concrete, brick, wood and masonry.
☐ Color additive is supplied to achieve color of concrete.

Plastic Steel putty for pipe repair.

• See **Canoecraft** (p. 283) and **Wood Finishing** (p. 165).

• If it's good enough for chapped cow teats, think of how nice it'd be for chapped hands (and cheeks).
Bag Balm: **$3.80** (10 ounces), information **free** from Dairy Association Co., Inc., Lyndonville, VT 05851.

3½'' cast, flush campaign chest handle (full size).

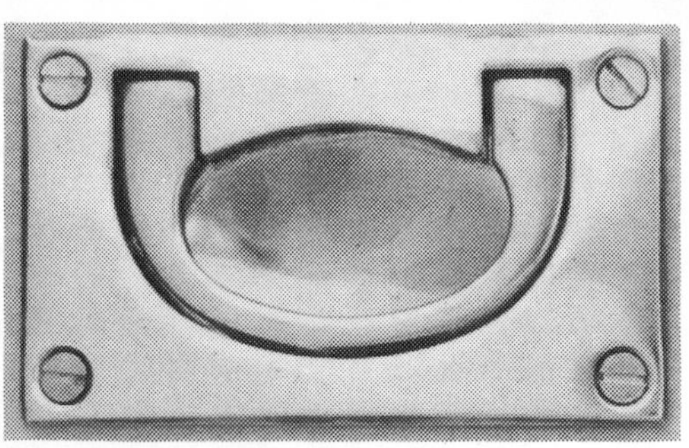

2½'' cast, flush campaign chest handle (full size).

Classic Hardware

Being primarily a ''design-as-you-go'' craftsperson, I got particularly excited about this hardware catalog from Garrett Wade. The color photographs of their British- and North American-made hardware are reproduced in full scale. That means I can cut out the pictures, place them on my piece of furniture, or whatever, and see exactly what I'll be getting — no surprises! —Stephen Seitz

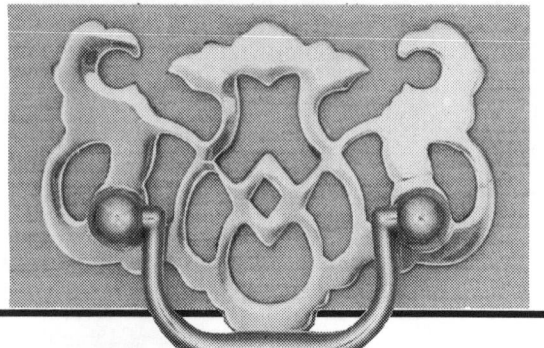

Classic Hardware
Catalog **free** from:
Garrett Wade
161 Avenue of the Americas
New York, NY 10013
(In Canada)
Lee Valley Tools Ltd.
2680 Queensnew Drive
Ottawa, Ontario K2B 8J9

C&H Buyer's Guide

In a way, this could be considered a shop ''furniture'' catalog; they carry racks, bins, shelving, office stuff, material handling equipment, safety items, and (oops) pneumatic tools. Much of the stock could be used in hi-tech household interiors too — a bit of thought will doubtless suggest uses that the makers never dreamed of. Distribution is nationwide. $15 minimum order. —JB

4-Tier Spin-A-Bin

For Work Bench, Counter Top

Rotating sections bring all parts into reach! Each tray rotates on ball bearings. Heavy-welded steel construction with easy working revolving mechanism. Includes 20 dividers. Measures 12½" in diameter, 18¼" high Color: green. Wt. 12 lbs.
IN STOCK—FOB GA, NJ, NV, TX, WI.
52-185/6A—Net each **$37.63**
Each (4+) **$35.75**
52-186/4A—Dividers. Net each..... **90¢**
GALVANIZED FINISH:
52-205/2A—Net each **$39.40**
Each (4+) **$37.42**
52-206/0A—Dividers. Net Each... **$1.10**

C&H Buyer's Guide
Catalog **free** from:
C&H Distributors
P. O. Box 04499
Milwaukee, WI 53204

12", 18" & 24½" Polyethylene Bins

Leakproof, greaseproof molded polyethylene plastic bins fit 12", 18" and 24½" shelves. Front handle makes gripping easy; notched back suspends bin on the lip of the shelf above while parts are removed. Bins nest for storage. **Sold only in carton quantities shown. Priced per each. Specify color:** 09 yellow, 18 blue. **IN STOCK—FOB GA, NJ, NV, TX, WI.**

Stock No.	Outside WxDxH	Quantity	Ctn. Wt.	Net Ea.	Ea. (3+ ctn.)
44-021/4AAL	4-1/2" x 12" x 4"	36/ctn.	15 lbs.	$1.03	$ .99
44-022/2AAL	6-1/2" x 12" x 4"	30/ctn.	15 lbs.	1.24	1.19
44-020/6AAL	8-1/4" x 12" x 4"	20/ctn.	16 lbs.	1.53	1.48
44-023/0AAL	4-1/2" x 18" x 4"	20/ctn.	12 lbs.	1.47	1.42
44-024/8AAL	6-7/16" x 18" x 4"	20/ctn.	15 lbs.	1.80	1.74
44-038/8AAL	8-1/4" x 18" x 4"	20/ctn.	20 lbs.	2.28	2.19
44-044/6AAL	6-5/8" x 24-1/2" x 4"	16/ctn.	24 lbs.	3.20	3.05
44-025/5AAL	Inner 2-1/8 x 3-3/8 x 3"	100/ctn.	7½ lbs.	.28	.25
44-026/3AAL	Inner 5-1/2 x 3-1/2 x 3"	40/ctn.	7 lbs.	.50	.48

• See ''House Renovation'' (p. 128) and ''Living Spaces'' (p. 141).

• For more general supplies, see the Abbeon catalog (p. 148).

Allen Specialty Hardware

Several people have asked me to build video cabinets with ''Lazy Susan'' bases so the TV monitor can be turned toward the viewer. The design problem is how to provide enough clearance to turn a television set without building a cabinet the size of a small outbuilding. One solution is an extension slide with a built-in swivel. This allows the TV to slide out of the cabinet before it is turned, reducing the amount of clearance required (some counterbalancing is usually needed). These extension slides and many other hard-to-find items (concealed hinges, folding leg devices, etc.) are available from this unpretentious catalog. —Stephen Seitz

Concealed, self-closing hinge.

Allen Specialty Hardware
Catalog and Handbook
$1 from:
Allen Specialty Hardware
332 West Bruceton Road
Pittsburgh, PA 15236

Knock-Down Fittings (K-D Hardware)

Knock-down fittings are often used by professional cabinet makers ot construct cabinets whcih must be shipped in a compact form and assembled wher tools may be limited. The two types of K-D hardware presented here use a simple Allen wrench for assembly, although each works on a different principa

Type 1 - Order inserts and mating bolts separately

On the ''minifix 15'' knock down fitting, a completely novel design principle has been implemented for connecting furniture parts: the so-called ''centricsphere principle'' in which the connecting bolt head, designed as a hemisphere, locks positively in the casing, designed as spherical pan. This technical innovation guarantees that the connecting bolt is guided centrically when tightened in any position.

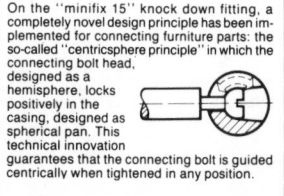

INSERT - Totally hidden when installed. Finish is natural metal. An Allen wrench and cover caps are free with each order. (Metric note: 16mm 5/8 in., 19mm ¾ in., 25.4mm = 1 in.)

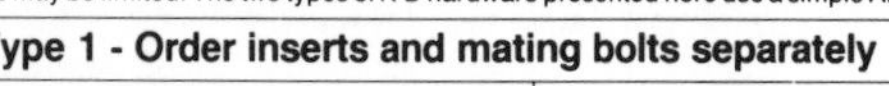

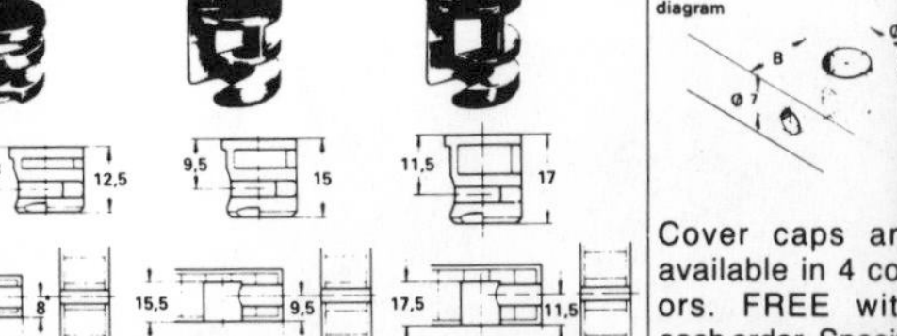

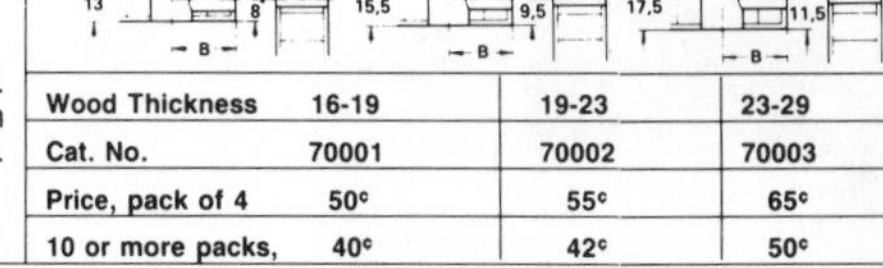

Wood Thickness	16-19	19-23	23-29
Cat. No.	70001	70002	70003
Price, pack of 4	50¢	55¢	65¢
10 or more packs,	40¢	42¢	50¢

Drilling diagram

Cover caps ar available in 4 co ors. FREE wit each order. Specif color-pine, brow black or white Brown will be sent not specified o order.

BREAKING THE WHOLESALE BARRIER

by J. Baldwin

So ya wanna buy it wholesale? Of course! That's what a retailer does before adding the typical 40 percent to the price tag. If the services and handy-but-high-rent location of the retailer mean little to you, the galling markup can be avoided at your local wholesaler. The problem is getting accepted there; the wholesaler is definitely not interested in small-order, walk-in trade. On the other hand, anyone with stuff for sale wants to sell it. With this in mind, here are some effective ways of penetrating the wholesale barrier.

The best and straightest way is to obtain a business license and the "resale" or "tax" number that goes with it. Wholesalers assume that anyone with a resale number is a professional and is likely to be a good customer. If you are involved in a major project, the money saved may make up for the hassle and expense of becoming a business. You can also attempt to fake it by printing up your own business letterhead.

A variation on this theme is to find someone with a resale number and borrow it. Architects, designers, contractors and job shops usually have a number. Though it costs them nothing to have you use it, etiquette requires that you offer to pay for the paperwork. (Remember them at Christmastime too.) You should not bother folks with small orders or other deals that are barely worth the trouble.

You might also try approaching contractors who are in the process of ordering materials for a job. Adding your order to theirs will increase the volume and thus the discount for everyone involved. This works easily and well for building materials. Again, a suitable gratuity such as a sixpack or a bottle of Cutty Sark may be in order, particularly if you want to continue the relationship.

It is also possible to break the wholesale barrier legitimately with a big order. If you need $5,000 worth of electrical supplies, not only should you directly approach a wholesaler, you should shop around for the best deal. The barrier is mainly there to protect the retail network set up to sell small quantities. Your retailer may even give a worthy discount for a big order. You might be pleasantly surprised.

If all else fails, you can attempt to brazen it out by walking in (appropriately disguised) and making an order at the counter. By the time the order is taken from stock and the paperwork is made out, the resistance is less and the wholesaler might just accept your cash. You should have done your homework: know the terminology, model numbers, types, sizes, and everything else that a pro should know. ► *To be treated like a pro, you have to act like one.* ◄ This will only work if the order is for a respectable amount, say $100 or so. If you get away with it, be sure and get the clerk's name so you can call in future orders. Be friendly. Do not abuse the privilege with small orders for low-cost items.

The wholesale barrier is part of a sort of game. You win some and lose some. Give it a try. If you're successful, you'll save money and, perhaps more satisfying, boost your self-image as an actor. Good luck! ■

Grainger's

Grainger's
Catalog **free** from:
W. W. Grainger, Inc.
5959 West Howard Street
Chicago, IL 60648
or check your local phone book.

Here's some incentive for breaking the wholesale barrier. Grainger's fat catalog features tools and shop equipment at good prices, but is most famous for motors, fans, compressors, pumps, and other stuff commonly found under "industrial supplies" in the Yellow Pages. I've had very good service from Grainger's, as both a legitimate and an illegitimate customer. They're easy to find with 188 stores across the U.S.A. (see their catalog for locations nationwide). —JB

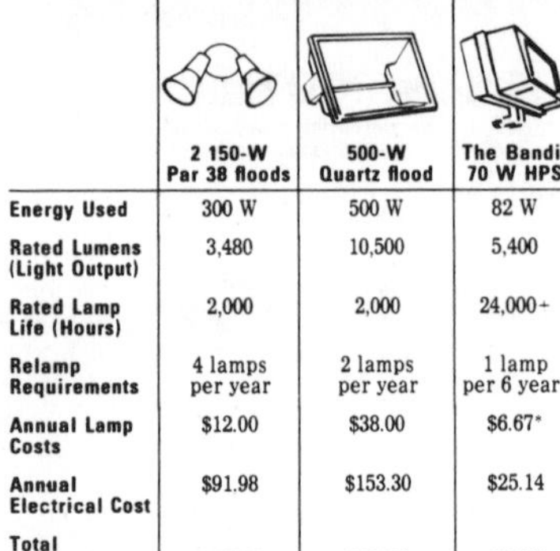

THE BANDIT vs TRADITIONAL FIXTURES

	2 150-W Par 38 floods	500-W Quartz flood	The Bandit 70 W HPS
Energy Used	300 W	500 W	82 W
Rated Lumens (Light Output)	3,480	10,500	5,400
Rated Lamp Life (Hours)	2,000	2,000	24,000+
Relamp Requirements	4 lamps per year	2 lamps per year	1 lamp per 6 years
Annual Lamp Costs	$12.00	$38.00	$6.67*
Annual Electrical Cost	$91.98	$153.30	$25.14
Total Annual Cost	$103.98	$191.30	$31.81

Bandit mini-floodlight.

Dayton
E19455 35886 No. 4C596 Nos. 4C548, 4C549 4C653, 4C827 No. 4C550 Fan Guard

For ventilation and spot cooling where space is limited. Widely used in computers, copy machines, office equipment, industrial control equipment, audio/visual equipment, vending machines, telephone equipment, light projectors, TV cameras and a wide variety of other electrical equipment. Fans are ruggedly constructed with rigid, one-piece, die cast zinc venturi frame which eliminates warping and provides proper grounding while acting as a heat sink. Molded, glass-filled polycarbonate fan blades are dynamically balanced. Impedance protected motor is permanently lubricated, shaded pole, unit bearing type with micro-polished shaft, designed for years of continuous duty. Bearings are sleeve type of porous bronze construction. Fans are all position mount. Air flow reversible by turning fan end-over-end. All models will accept cord set No. 4C552 listed below except model 4C596 which has 22-ga. 12" long leads. All models are 60/50 Hz, UL Component Recognized, file No. E19455, and CSA Certified: No. 35886. Maximum ambient temperature 120°F (48.9°C). Black finish.

CFM*	Volts	RPM	Watts	Amps	SIL dB†	Dimensions H	W	D	Mt. Hole OC	Stock No.	List	Each	Shpg. Wt.
27	115	2800	9	0.11	25	3⅛"	3⅛"	1½"	2 13/16"	**4C596**	$29.75	**$17.80**	1.1
55	115	1800	11	0.14	18	4 11/16	4 11/16	1½	4⅛	**4C548**	29.75	**17.80**	1.9
70	115	2200	16	0.19	28	4 11/16	4 11/16	1½	4⅛	**4C827**	26.55	**17.69**	2.0
100	115	3000	15	0.20	38	4 11/16	4 11/16	1½	4⅛	**4C549**	27.90	**16.70**	2.0
100	230	3000	19	0.14	38	4 11/16	4 11/16	1½	4⅛	**4C653**	28.65	**17.15**	1.9
110	115	3000	19	0.29	39	4 11/16	4 11/16	1½	4⅛	**4C550**	34.15	**20.45**	1.6

(*) In free air, on 60 Hz power. (†) SIL = Speech Interference Level, in decibels. This figure represents an average of the sound pressure levels in the 500, 1000 and 2000 Hz octave bands.

The Razor Edge Book of Sharpening

"How do you sharpen this?" No myth or mystery to that question after reading this book. Using his method the first time, I obtained an edge on my Swiss Army knife that would, as Juranitch promised, "shave the hair off the back of my dry arm." Equally amazing, the edges are durable.

His company (Razor Edge Systems) designs, manufactures, and sells sharpening equipment — everything from hand held hones and sharpening guides up to the sharpening machines in meat packing plants. —J. D. Adams, M.D.

•

Notice how the cutting edge is sitting up in the breeze, while the rounded section of side CD is where actual contact is. So many are frustrated because their single bevel blade seems sharp, yet won't cut. It could even shave easily, but if the cutting edge isn't the contact point on the material to be cut, you are going nowhere.

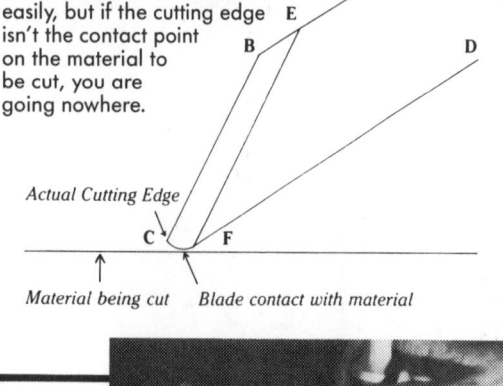

A
E
B
D
Actual Cutting Edge
C
F
Material being cut
Blade contact with material

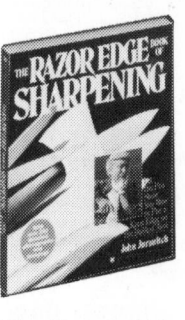

The Razor Edge Book of Sharpening
John Juranitch
1985; 145 pp.
$12.50* ($14.50 postpaid);
Razor Edge Systems
Brochure **free**
Both from:
Razor Edge Systems, Inc.
P. O. Box 150
Ely, MN 55731
*or Whole Earth Access

Wood Finisher's Handbook

Few do-it-yourself enterprises are as redolent of potential disaster as applying that final finish to wood. Even the more obedient among us — those who read the instructions on the can — often come to grief, gnashing in despair as our paintbrushes with their cargoes take on a life of their own quite out of control. How do those creeps in **Fine Woodworking** *do it? They know what's in this book, is how.*

I like the way the author answers your questions just before you ask. I also like the range of techniques shown — everything from "lost art" procedures to the latest in chemical wonders. The book is easier to read than many of its genre, so our last excuse for imperfect finishing is gone. —JB

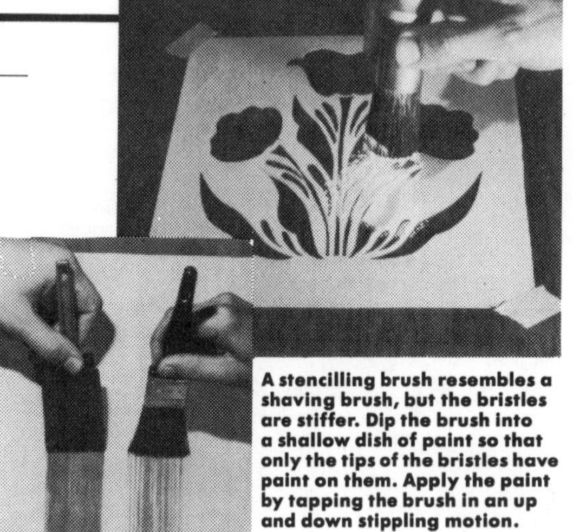

Foam brushes are very good for applying stain. In this comparison between a foam brush and an inexpensive nylon brush, notice that the foam brush carries more stain and leaves a smooth application of stain without brush marks.

A stencilling brush resembles a shaving brush, but the bristles are stiffer. Dip the brush into a shallow dish of paint so that only the tips of the bristles have paint on them. Apply the paint by tapping the brush in an up and down stippling motion.

Wood Finisher's Handbook
Sam Allen
1984; 160 pp.
$9.95 ($11.45 postpaid) from:
Sterling Publishing
2 Park Avenue
New York, NY 10016
or Whole Earth Access

Welder's Handbook

Think of welding as metal glue; lots of interesting possibilities appear when you can stick pieces of metal together in a trustworthy manner. Welding isn't all that difficult, either. Best bet is an evening welding class at your local high school. Next best, or as a brushup, is this book. It's just the basics — all you need for most work. The examples are mostly automotive, but the principles hold true whether you're repairing a farm tractor, welding up a driveway gate, or fixing the kids' swing set. Don't forget that you'll need to practice a bit; books aren't everything. —JB
[Suggested by Dick Fugett]

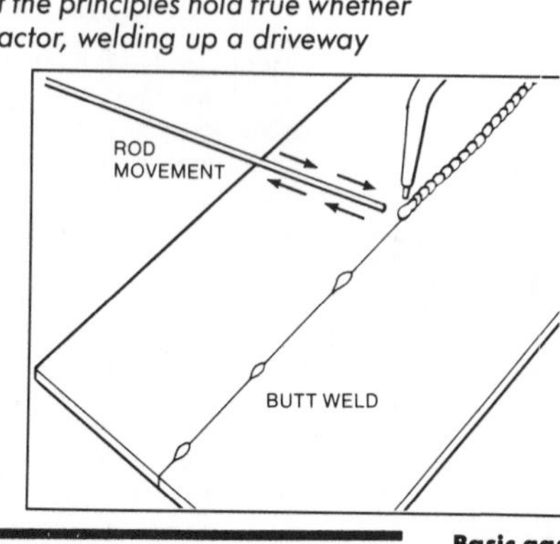

Sheet metal needs plenty of tacks — about every 1 in. — to reduce warpage. Tack welds are melted into weld bead as final bead is made.

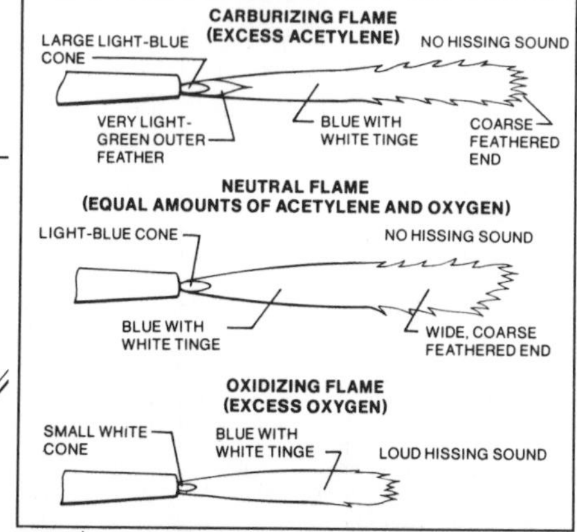

Basic gas-welding flames: Each has distinctive shape, color and sound. Neutral flame is the most used.

Welder's Handbook
Richard Finch
and Tom Monroe
1985; 160 pp.
$12.95 ($14.90 postpaid) from:
HP Books
P. O. Box 5367
Tucson, AZ 85703
or Whole Earth Access

• See "Livos Organic Polish" (p. 000).

• I always carry a tiny 10-foot tape measure in my watch pocket. That way I can measure any interesting design detail I come across. Get Stanley Model MYT 10 at any hardware store.

Stationary Power Tool Techniques

Wow! Not just a how-to, but a remarkably comprehensive collection of methods of getting your power tools to do everything but sit up and beg. The author has a good reputation, and it's easy to see why: the only way he could possibly have accumulated all these tricks is by working with the tools many thousands of hours. He's especially good on jigs and fixtures that expand the tools' capabilities. And here I thought I knew all there was to know . . . —JB

◄ **Fly cutter is used here for a double cut to create a wooden ring. Be careful at breakthrough for the ring will be free in the hole.**

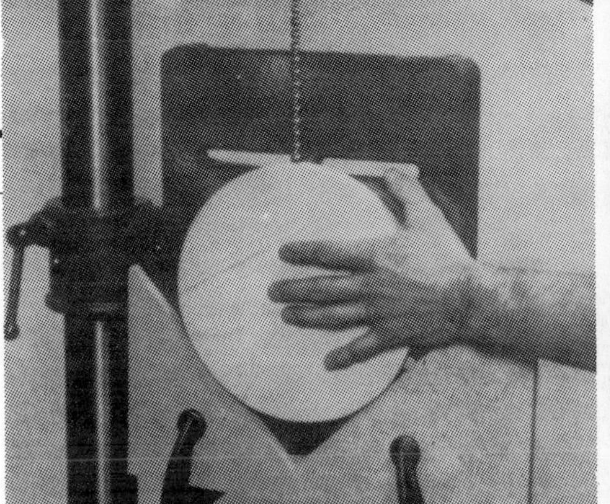

Edge holes in circular pieces can be drilled this way. The clamped V-block supports and positions the work. The center of the "V" and the point of the bit must be on the same line.

The Complete Book of Stationary Power Tool Techniques
R. J. De Cristoforo
1985; 388 pp.
$31.95
($35.19 postpaid) from:
Popular Science Books
P. O. Box 2018
Latham, NY 12111
or Whole Earth Access

Tools and How to Use Them

The best guide to the range of tools a householder or homesteader might need to know and use. There are 1500 drawings of common items as well as forgotten tools. Descriptions include the alternative generic names the tools have been known by, usage, sizes, and care of the tool. The section on brushes alone is worth the price of the book. Even though I trained as an apprentice house painter, not until Jackson and Day's book did I hear of a washing down brush, a mottler, a flogger, a softener, a pencil overgrainer, or a fitch. —Paul Hawken
[Suggested by Lloyd Kahn]

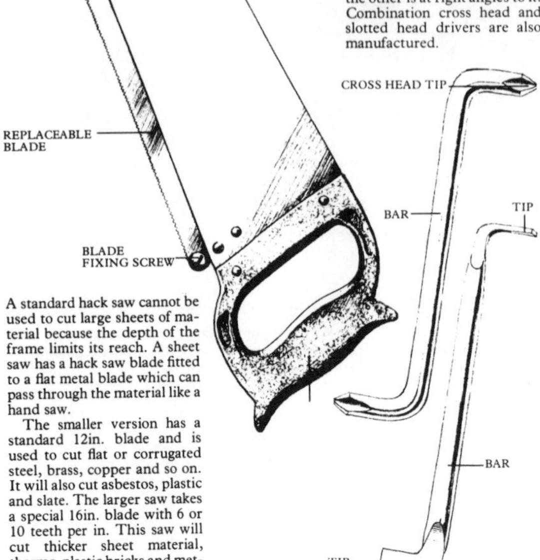

A standard hack saw cannot be used to cut large sheets of material because the depth of the frame limits its reach. A sheet saw has a hack saw blade fitted to a flat metal blade which can pass through the material like a hand saw.

The smaller version has a standard 12in. blade and is used to cut flat or corrugated steel, brass, copper and so on. It will also cut asbestos, plastic and slate. The larger saw takes a special 16in. blade with 6 or 10 teeth per in. This saw will cut thicker sheet material, thermo-plastic bricks and metal covered plywood.

The offset driver is used where there is insufficient room to use a conventional screwdriver. It is also good for applying extra torque to a stubborn screw.

The driver is simply a steel bar, either hexagonal or round in section, with the ends bent at right angles and ground to form a screwdriver tip. It is double ended and can be used for cross head or slotted head screws. In the latter case one tip is in line with the bar while the other is at right angles to it. Combination cross head and slotted head drivers are also manufactured.

Tools and How to Use Them
Albert Jackson
and David Day
1978; 352 pp.
$11.95
($12.95 postpaid) from:
Random House
400 Hahn Road
Westminster, MD 21157
or Whole Earth Access

Shop Tactics

This is a truly useful book for those who make things or would like to be able to make things. After years of being a professional thing-maker I find much I didn't know here. It's a good reference, in case you need to solder something but have forgotten how, for instance. Best of all, the book is written in an encouraging, friendly way so that the Mysteries of the Shop are revealed about as much as they can be short of lousing up some material practicing. Virtually all common shop practices are shown, explained, and illustrated. Many of the basic principles involved in various shop tactics are explained so that you learn in depth. My only regrets arise from a basic philosophy the author holds: "Overbuild everything." This is how a lot of American waste gets generated, as that attitude tends to discourage sharp thought. Bill Abler wants you to make things as easily as he does. With this book and a few brains, you probably can. —JB

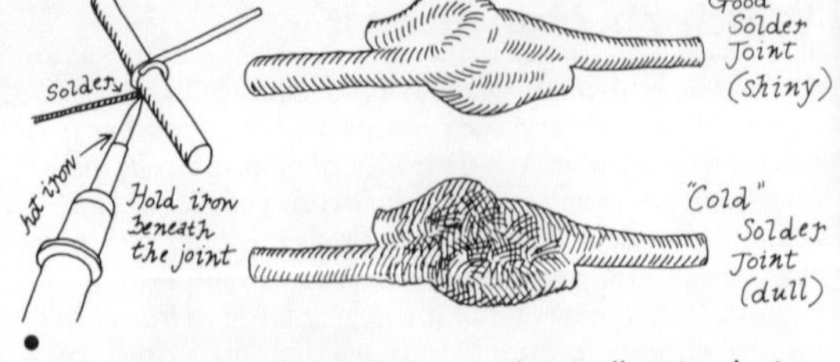

•

Hold the hot iron *beneath* the mechanically joined wires, pressing it firmly against the joint, and press the solder between the wires and the iron. The object of these procedures is to heat the wires as quickly as possible. The advantage of this is that the shorter the time that the wires are hot, the less time the heat will have to be conducted along them and ruin electrical components, and the less time the metal will have to oxidize. As the solder begins to melt it will conduct heat to the wires and further increase the speed of their heating. The solder will flow by capillarity into the narrow crack between the joined pieces of wire. *After* the solder has flowed you may want to touch the solder to the top of the wire joint to add a bit of solder there. Usually this is not necessary.

Shop Tactics
William Abler
1976; 117 pp.
$3.95
($4.95 postpaid) from:
Running Press
125 South 22nd Street
Philadelphia, PA 19103
or Whole Earth Access

• More technique can be found in **WoodenBoat** magazine (p. 289); see also pp. 122-123.

• The young 'uns can get into the act too. See **Woodworking With Kids** (p. 367).

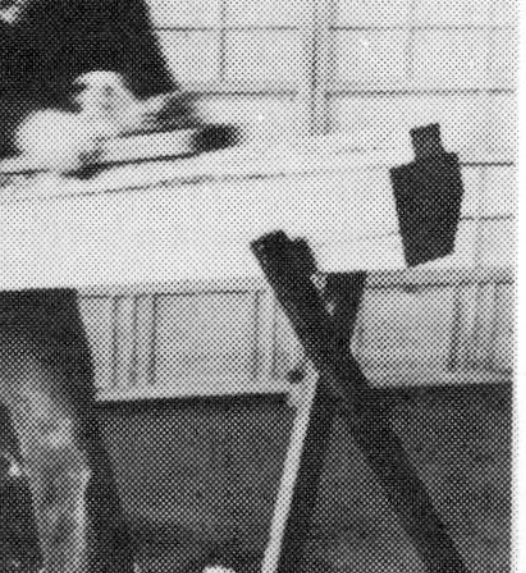

Shokunin [artisans] plane long materials using a pull stroke down an angled planing beam. Speed, a small blade angle, and holding the blade on a skew to the wood help the plane leave a smooth, highly polished surface.

Japanese Woodworking Tools

The Western love for things Japanese includes woodworking tools and attendant mystique. I've heard it said that the finest Japanese tools are beyond the skill of Western craftsmen to use properly. Part of the problem is that it is relatively easy to put a chisel in a box and ship it across the ocean, but much more difficult to transport knowledge of the handling, care and lore that are part of any tool.

The author of this book has a nice blend of Eastern tradition and Western savvy. The trade he learned in Japan was making sliding doors, but for the past 25 years he has worked and taught in America. The book is full of his own line drawings, good photographs of him using the tools, and a loving attention to detail. —Richard Nilsen

•

For any type of Japanese tool, there are about three levels of quality: the low level (inexpensive tools of low quality), the middle level (reasonably priced tools that are well forged), and the high level (extremely expensive tools of the highest quality). . . . Most *shokunin* [craftsmen] depended on middle-level blades forged by common blacksmiths.

. . . Almost any kind of woodworking at the time [of my apprenticeship] depended on these middle-level tools.

Today, however, many sophisticated, small power tools are common in society. Naturally, *shokunin* use them, and to some extent they have taken over the job of the middle-level tools, leaving society the very cheap or the very expensive tools. In addition, many of the middle-level tools that are being produced are made to look like high-level tools — dramatic signs are put on plane blades, saw handles are wrapped with cane in a *samurai*-sword pattern and fake temper marks are put on sawblades.

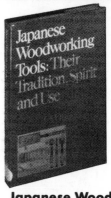

Japanese Woodworking Tools
(Their Tradition, Spirit and Use)
Toshio Odate
1984; 189 pp.
$23.95
postpaid from:
Taunton Press
Box 355
Newtown, CT 06470
or Whole Earth Access

Woodline: The Japan Woodworker

For exquisite woodworking with exquisite tools, you can do no better than Japanese techniques and implements, the products of centuries of carefulness. Woodline has some of the best such tools available in America, many of them far finer than our skills can make use of yet. It's an interesting experience to be shamed by a tool.
—Stewart Brand

•

KUGIHIKI NOKO GIRI (NAIL CUTTING SAW)
Kugihiki Noko Giri are used to trim wooden nails and plugs flush with the surface of the work. The blade is quite thin and flexible, so that in use, it can be bent with a portion of the blade held flat against the work surface. The teeth have a very minimal set making it possible to cut the nail or plug flush without scratching the surface of the work.

Overall length: 19¾″ Length of blade: 7⅜″
# of teeth/inch: 22
Price $51.95

Adjustable chamfer plane (Mentori Ganna); Tadao brand.

• See "Japanese Architecture" (p. 116).

• The correct use of Japanese tools is best learned from a teacher. Woodline (above) has classes or can connect you with some. Write for information.

The Japan Woodworker
Catalog
$1.50 from:
Woodline:
The Japan Woodworker
1731 Clement Avenue
Alameda, CA 94501

Kugihiki noko giri.

Masterpiece Tools

"Tools-as-jewelry" is what we've called the ultra-high-quality offerings of such companies as Garrett Wade and Woodcraft Supply (p. 169). Their tools can be used of course, it's just that they are so beautiful it seems a shame to mess them up. In any case, they are an expression of the character of both their makers and users. At Masterpiece Tools they take this all a step further: Tools-as-Art. Lest you think I exaggerate, check page 22 of their gracious catalog: 210mm Tama Hagane Sword Steel Ryoba, "Promise of the Future" by Miyana Tetsunosuke. $14,400. That's fourteen thousand, four hundred dollars.

The catalog takes lots of space to explain what's going on to those of us who know no better. It tells of the master saw maker and how he works and why the tools are so incredibly perfect. I confess that I'd never thought of tools in this way. I also confess that this is the most extreme example. There are plenty of tools here in the several-hundred-dollar range — planes, chisels, Bonsai instruments, and sharpening stones. There are also many that are eminently affordable by ordinary workers who will appreciate and use the extraordinary quality and traditional forms. Even if such things aren't going to tempt you into uncontrollable buying, you might enjoy the catalog; it's truly an education in itself. —JB

Masterpiece Tools
Catalog
$5 from:
Mahogany Masterpieces
RFD 1, Wing Road
Suncook, NH 03275

210mm Tama Hagane Sword Steel Ryoba ▲

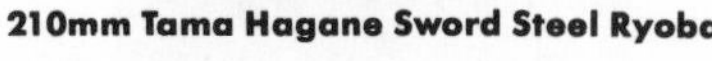

6x6mm double-forked mortise chisel. ▼

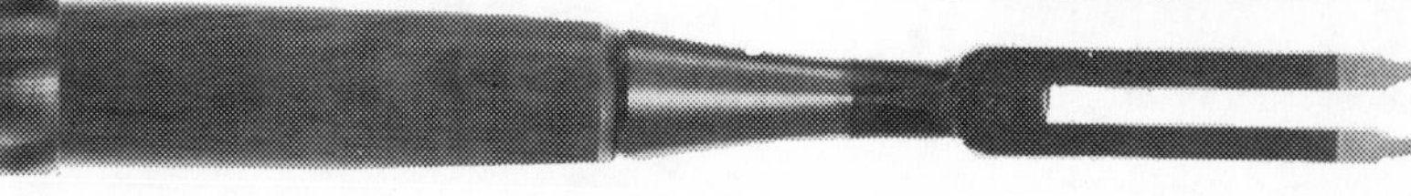

▲ **Designed and built by Gregg Fleishman, the chairs are made of 5/8" plywood routed into flexible loops. With few parts and no fasteners, the chairs disassemble and store flat.**

Fine Woodworking

The impeccable production of this magazine reflects the same spirit and imaginative classy workmanship as the work it shows. Articles are much more detailed than you'd find in a less specialized magazine, yet are written in nontechnical language, and illustrated as if the reader was a beginner. There is no trace whatever of artzy-craftzy.

And we mustn't forget the advertisements. A good mag attracts quality advertisers. In this case, the ads are an invitation to fiscal madness. They're nicely produced too, tending to show the latest innovations just as the editorial content of the magazine does. Perhaps the editors should put out a Fine Magazine-Making magazine. (They do put out others equally good, however: **Fine Homebuilding** *[p. 122] and* **Threads** *[p. 177].)* —JB

The wood between the ridges of the flame is removed with a sharp fluter or 5mm gouge (left).

If wood begins to tear out, reverse the cutting direction by moving your hands (right) rather than wasting time by walking around the bench.

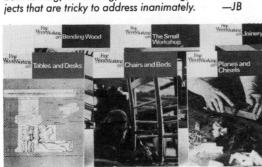

Fine Woodworking On . . .

Bending wood, chairs and beds, planes and chisels, woodworking machines . . . and a bunch of other subjects. The series is made up of articles (about 30 in each book) from the past ten years of **Fine Woodworking** *magazine, and that means good writing, good illustrations, and lots of different voices and opinions. These books give me a feeling of being a student with lots of teachers.* —JB

Fine Woodworking Techniques

Another series from the pages of **Fine Woodworking**, *this time exclusively concerned with the technical articles they've published in past issues. By pros, for pros or those about to be.* —JB

Fine Woodworking Video Workshops

Stuff one of these in your Beta or VHS and see how it's done. Certainly the wave of a how-to future, these video cassettes lead you by the hand through such subjects as bowl turning, dovetailing, wood finishing, and other subjects that are tricky to address inanimately. —JB

Fine Woodworking
Paul Bertorelli, Editor
$18/year
(6 issues)

Fine Woodworking On . . .
(12-book series)
$6.95
each, postpaid;
information **free**

Fine Woodworking Techniques
(7-book series)
$17.95
each, postpaid;
information **free**

Fine Woodworking Video Workshop
$49.95-$59.95
information **free**

All from:
The Taunton Press
63 South Main Street
Box 355
Newtown, CT 06470

B
A
Pencil notch
Slide.
Move nail to other end and reverse board to complete curve.

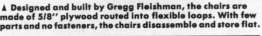

•

Drawing large shallow curves:
When I was a boatbuilder we used this shallow-curve drawing method to set out the deck beams of yachts. The trick works for drawing any such curve with a known rise and run.

You'll need two nails and a "spile board." Cut the spile board as wide as the curve's rise and taper the board on one end with the length of the taper equal to the curve's run. Notch the board at the location shown to catch a pencil point.

Drive one nail at point A and another at point B. With a pencil in the notch and the spile board positioned as shown in the sketch, slide the board toward the nail at A to draw the curve. Nail A can be removed and driven in the other end to complete the curve. In our situation the method was used to make a template from which all the shorter beams and carlings could be marked.
—*Ernie Ives, Sproughton, Ipswich, Eng.*

• One of the great classics in a new edition.
The Complete Woodworker: Bernard E. Jones, Editor, 1980; 408 pp. **$8.95** ($10.45 postpaid) from Ten Speed Press, P. O. Box 7123, Berkeley, CA 94707 (or Whole Earth Access).

Garrett Wade

This catalog of super-quality woodworker's tools comprises irresistible studio color portraits of each tool, backed by a brief discussion of the tools' merits and uses so you can be sure you need one. Or all — they really are hard to resist when presented in this way. Garrett Wade also distributes the high-precision Swiss INCA power tools and the Swedish all-purpose professional woodworking machines made by LUNA. A well-stocked book selection tells you how to use all these things. Hide my checkbook!
—JB

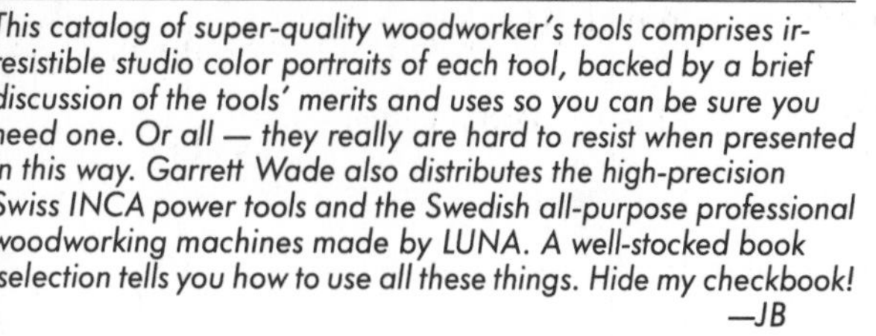

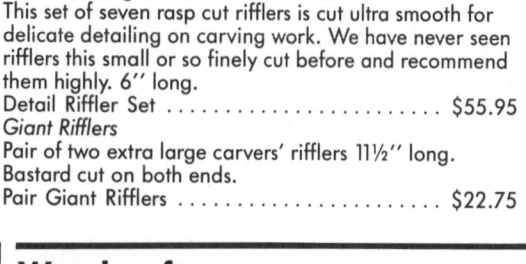

Inca radial-arm saw: $495.

Garrett Wade
Woodworking Tools
Catalog
$3 from:
Garrett Wade Company
161 Avenue of
the Americas
New York, NY 10013
In Canada:
Lee Valley Tools Ltd.
2680 Queensnew Drive
Ottawa, Ontario K2B 8J9

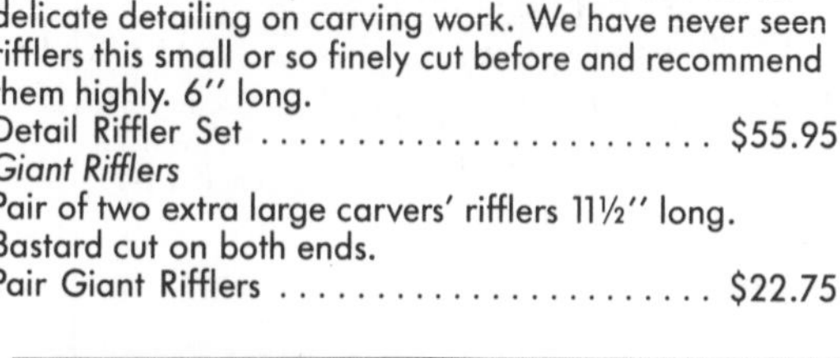

◄
Ultra Fine Detailing Rifflers Are Terrific for Delicate Work
This set of seven rasp cut rifflers is cut ultra smooth for delicate detailing on carving work. We have never seen rifflers this small or so finely cut before and recommend them highly. 6'' long.
Detail Riffler Set $55.95
Giant Rifflers
Pair of two extra large carvers' rifflers 11½'' long. Bastard cut on both ends.
Pair Giant Rifflers $22.75

►
Handy Knife Sets For Chip Carving And Whittling
It's surprising how much easier it is to do the work you want with the right tools. These very attractive, splendid knives are for chip carving or whittling. Conveniently shaped and comfortable to use. Fine German steel will give years of satisfying use. Polished White Beech handles. Overall length about 6''. . . .
$4.50 each; 5-knife set $22.50; 10-knife set $45.

Woodcraft

A rival of Garrett Wade, Woodcraft has similar but not identical goods, often cheaper but with less selection. When I need something, I shop both catalogs. —JB

Right Arm Clamp was developed by a woodworker who needed an extra hand in the shop. The multi-purpose shape is so versatile that it can take the place of a "C" clamp, bench vise, miter clamp, framing vise and many others, offering you hundreds of uses. Virtually eliminates the need for confusing and unstable multiple-clamp setups. Cast aluminum with steel pivot pins and threads. Clamping capacity 1⅝" and 2" depending on setup.
08R22-DH **NEW** **$14.95 ppd.**

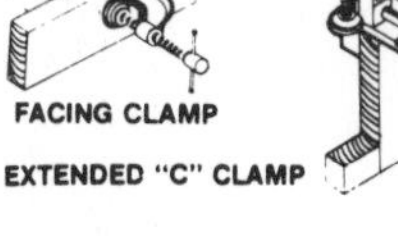

Woodcraft
Catalog
$3 from:
Woodcraft
41 Atlantic Avenue
Box 4000
Woburn, MA 01888

•
Combination Drill Has Jacobs Chuck To Hold Bits Firmly
A double pinion drill that operates smoothly. It has two features not normally found in this type of drill. Firstly, it can be used as a hand drill or a breast drill. (The parts are interchangeable.) More importantly it has a Jacobs chuck which holds bits much more tightly than an unkeyed chuck. 5/16'' chuck capacity. Overall length of 14''. Made in Sheffield.
Combo. Drill $29.90

• Some folks think the ultimate woodworking is the fancy, load-bearing structure of wooden boats (pp. 288-289).

Constantine's

Wood: Bubinga, Padouk, Zebrawood, Purpleheart, Prima Vera . . . In chunks for lathe turning or furniture making or carving. In thin slices for veneering and marquetry. And all the tools, glues, and instruction books too. —JB

Constantine's
Catalog **$1** from:
Albert Constantine
and Son, Inc.
2050 Eastchester Road
Bronx, NY 10461

50 LARGE BEAUTIFUL SAMPLES OF EXOTIC WOODS
YOU CAN EXPAND YOUR KNOWLEDGE OF THE RARE WOODS OF THE WORLD WITH OUR SET OF 50 LARGE, BEAUTIFUL SAMPLES OF EXOTIC WOODS and the HARDWOODS SELECTORAMA

Constantine brings you this truly fabulous collection of the world's most colorful and exciting woods —50 veneer samples, 4 x 9", attractively boxed. An accompanying list identifies each with the common and botanical name and country of origin. With these samples, you can actually feel and enjoy the distinctive texture, the interesting grain and the rich color of each wood, and quickly recognize some of the woods used in furniture today. They are also useful in enriching small craftwork, making small inlays, or for testing various finishes before applying the finish to your favorite project. Schools find them invaluable as a visual source of learning. Start enjoying this wonderful Treasure Chest of Woods today.
No. 53S50 **$8.95**

To add to your knowledge and enjoyment of the set of samples the FINE HARDWOODS SELECTORAMA, published by the Fine Hardwoods Association, is a handsomely illustrated book showing over 174 species of woods in their natural color. It is a guide to the selection and use of the world's most popular woods and gives essential facts concerning the more important commercially available species of hardwoods and some softwoods used in the manufacture of furniture. 57 pages.
No. FHS57 **$10.00**

Combination sample set and book offer
No. CO58 **$18.25**

Country Blacksmithing

Country Blacksmithing
Charles McRaven.
1981; 191 pp.
$9.95
($11.45 postpaid) from:
Harper & Row
2350 Virginia Avenue
Hagerstown, MD 21740
or Whole Earth Access

Here's a good how-to book by a good how-to writer. Charles McRaven is an accomplished blacksmith, and here he shows you all you need to know about the basics of blacksmithing; enough to get you started cheaply and working on your own. McRaven has built four smithies, each on separate homesteads he has set up by himself. With this experience to back him up, he shows in **Country Blacksmithing** *how to make a forge from a brake drum and tools from scrap metal, and how to hammer hot iron into many useful things: nails, knives, hinges, hardware, household items, fireplace tools and fixtures, a trailer hitch, chains and hooks for logging. There's a chapter on horseshoeing and one called "Income from Your Forge" with sound advice for smiths who wish to sell their wares as craftsmen. This may not be the be-all and end-all book of blacksmithing, but for teaching a skill which depends so much on just plain experience, it's a helpful start, more helpful than most.* —John Warde

•

I have heard several veteran blacksmiths reply to the question of what exactly they do, in this way:

"Well, you get a piece of iron hot, then you hit it with a hammer." And that's what it's all about. Iron and steel are malleable when red hot, and hammering lets the smith shape them by degrees to his purposes.

◂ This drawknife was made of medium-carbon shaft steel, heated and quenched only. The relatively low carbon content kept it from becoming brittle and produced a tool of toughness with just this one-step process.

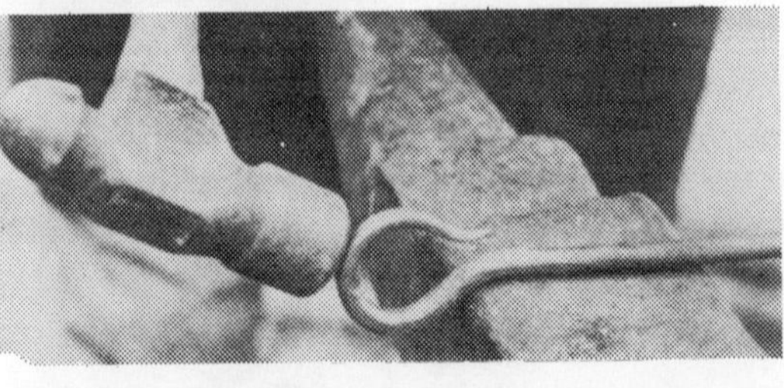

If a reversed tip is desired on the loop handle, it's put in last, then the loop is trued up.

The Making of Tools

The Making of Tools
Alexander G. Weygers
1973; 93 pp.
$11.95
postpaid from:
Simon and Schuster
200 Old Tappan Road
Old Tappan, NJ 07675
or Whole Earth Access

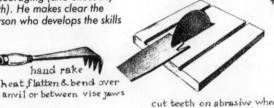

Blacksmithing can be a lot more than making horseshoes and barn door hinges. Mr. Weygers' beautiful book shows techniques of making your own tools by the clever use of scrap metal. His attitude is encouraging (and unusually nonchauvinistic for a blacksmith). He makes clear the many paths that open to a person who develops the skills of a blacksmith. His lucid drawings and obvious love of his work draw you in; you want to try it. The book itself is a model of how good books can get if properly nurtured. —JB

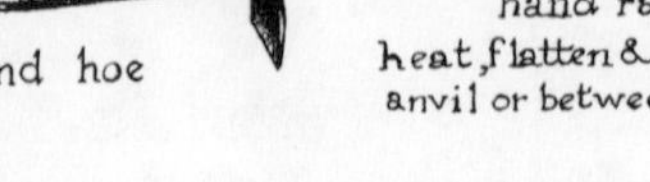
hand hoe
hand rake
heat, flatten & bend over anvil or between vise jaws

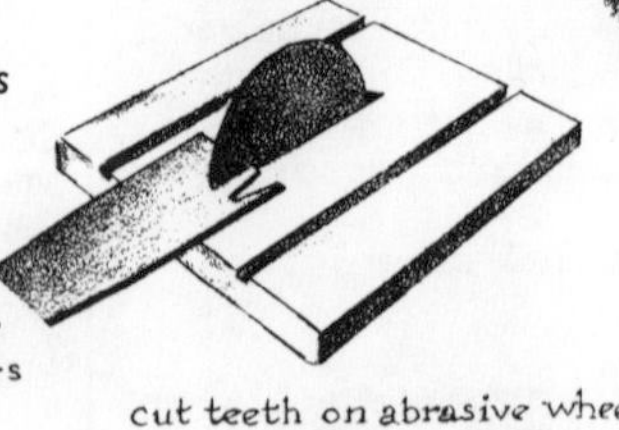
cut teeth on abrasive wheel
before or after bending

Lindsay's Technical Books

Lindsay's Technical Books
Catalog
$1 from:
Lindsay Publications, Inc.
P. O. Box 12
Bradley, IL 60915-0012

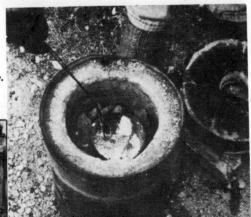

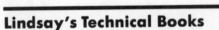

Arcane wouldn't be too strong a word to describe the contents of this wide-view catalog. It's well stocked with how-to-make and how-to-use books — mostly concerned with shop tools and procedures. Many of the books are old classics, and some are references to technologies long gone but still interesting, such as steam engines. There are also books on Nikola Tesla, embalming, perpetual motion, casting, and steam-powered airplanes. Everything shown is reviewed so you get some idea of what it is. Interesting, useful, and fun. —JB

•

Building machine tools takes hours and hours, but building the charcoal foundry is far simpler, and loads of fun. You can make castings for any purpose. Anyone can build a furnace, and almost everyone will become hooked on melting metal once they try it.

The "Charcoal Foundry" is a small book with a big price tag, but it's worth every penny, and then some. Every page is loaded with practical how-to useful advice. This 1983 revised edition contains many, many drawings and many excellent photographs that will show you step-by-step how to build a foundry.

Highest recommendation! Top rate! Get a copy. 5½x8½ paperback, 80 pages Cat no. 163 $6.95

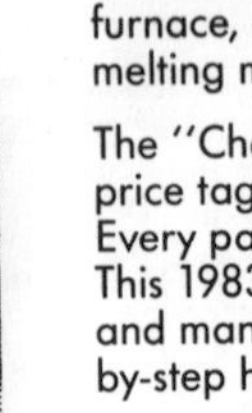

Charcoal foundry.

"Build a Precision Milling Machine!"

• The Artist-Blacksmith's Association of North America gives you their pithy newsletter with a membership.
The Anvil's Ring: Robert Owings, Editor. **$25**/year (4 issues) from ABANA, P. O. Box 303, Cedarburg, WI 53012.
[Suggested by John Matzke]

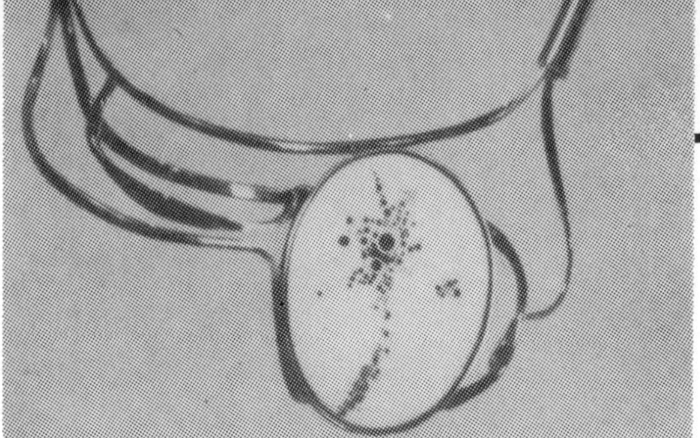

JOHN E. SATTERFIELD, U.S.A. Silver necklace with ▲ ivory plaque into which *pique point* silver wire and tubing has been inserted through holes made completely through the ground (when one-sided patterns are created) or partly through (when two-sided patterns are the aim). Tubes are flared slightly to fix them in place. In addition, epoxy resin mixed with a catalyst and color in powdered form is forced into some holes with a flexible knife. After setting, the entire surface is sanded with 400 or 600 grit wet/dry sandpaper. The process is repeated for another color. The colors used here are red and black. Plastic, nylon, Teflon, Delrin, or wood could also be used as a ground for pique work.

Jewelry Concepts and Technology

"My stars!" is what my grandmother would say when confronted with the need for superlatives but unable to think of any that would fit. That's what she'd say about this work. Total, comprehensive, magnificent, fascinating — your choice. Quite literally, Mr. Untracht has looked at every style, technique, form, and material (even plastic) used in jewelrymaking in just about every culture, past and present. History, symbolic meaning (something most jewelers seem to ignore), heretofore-secret methods are all shown in minute detail along with tables of metal characteristics. There's seemingly no end to it, and it's all presented in a way that makes it hard to quit reading even when your thing isn't jewelry. In short, the book itself is a work of art. And obviously a work of love as well. Reading along I've also been struck by how few of us moderns really get into something, in depth, all the way. I'm amazed that one person could know all this. Physically, the book is well done too. Everything illustrated and diagrammed. All it lacks is wheels and a towbar to haul its massive bulk around. —JB

Jewelry Concepts and Technology
Oppi Untracht
1982; 864 pp.
$65
postpaid from:
Doubleday and Company
501 Franklin Avenue
Garden City, NY 11530

◄ *A miniature snarling iron.*
This self-made tool is used to bulge small hollow forms, such as tubing, outward from within. Tap the shaft just above the clamped tang end with a small hammer held in the left hand. With each blow of the hammer, the end inserted in the tube vibrates, the ball kicks upward, each time making a bump appear on the tube wall. By watching the position where the bumps appear, and moving the tube accordingly, the bulging can be controlled. The effect of this tool's action is exactly as if a repousse punch had been used on the open work.

The Complete Metalsmith

*Let's say you're a jewelrymaker and you can't figure out a way to make a hidden hinge for a box. So you write your uncle, the master goldsmith. He sits down, gets very stoned, and sends you a beautifully descriptive letter, complete with imaginative little drawings, written in a tight, clear hand. Now imagine a whole book on jewelry-making done in this very personal, friendly, and accessible way, and you have **The Complete Metalsmith**. The title to the contrary, this book won't tell you much about black-smithing, titanium, or stainless steel, but it will tell you a lot about goldsmithing, and in a marvelous way. Tim McCreight's style is light and humorous, as well as technically knowledgeable. The book is visually and factually stimulating enough that I reread it a second time as soon as I finished it once, to try and take more of it in. The illustrations are clear, to the point, and homey. The quotes by everyone from Voltaire to W. C. Fields add a bit of far-flung perspective. And I appreciate the safety alert symbols scattered throughout, used when describing a tool or technique that has a hazard potential. A gem of a handmade book.* —David Clarkson

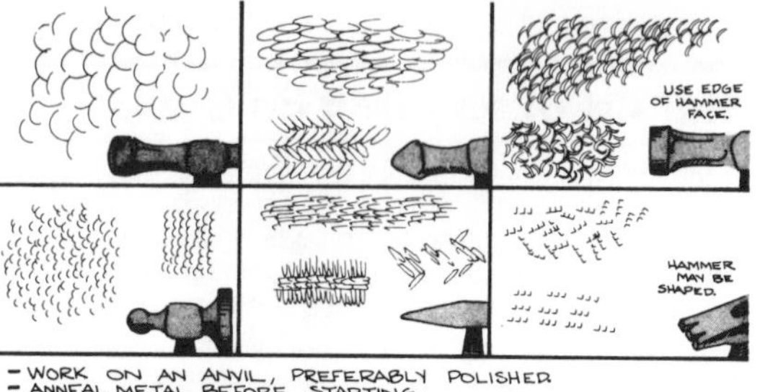

- WORK ON AN ANVIL, PREFERABLY POLISHED
- ANNEAL METAL BEFORE STARTING.
- USE STOCK THICK ENOUGH TO ABSORB BLOW.
- HOLD HANDLE WHERE IT IS COMFORTABLE. A LOWER GRIP INCREASES POWER.
- YOU MAY ALSO CREATE A RICH SURFACE BY HAMMERING THE METAL ONTO A TEXTURE, LIKE RUSTED STEEL OR CONCRETE.

The Complete Metalsmith
Tim McCreight
1984; 150 pp.
$10.95
postpaid from:
Davis Publications
Printers Building
Worcester, MA 01608
or Whole Earth Access

Dixon Precision Tools and Equipment • Allcraft

Here are two good sources for jewelrymaking equipage. Quality is high, with prices to match. Many of the tools are suitable for fine work other than jewelry. Both of these catalogs are full of tools I'll bet you didn't know existed. Yum. —JB

Busch Burs

Busch burs are made of tungsten vanadium steel unless otherwise noted, have 3/32" diameter shanks, and are approximately 1-3/4" long. They are used primarily with the straight handpieces of flexible shaft machines. The wide variety of shapes and sizes offered is intended to fill the complete needs of jewelers, diesinkers, and other craftsmen with requirements for high quality precision burs. Busch Burs packed six to a plastic box.

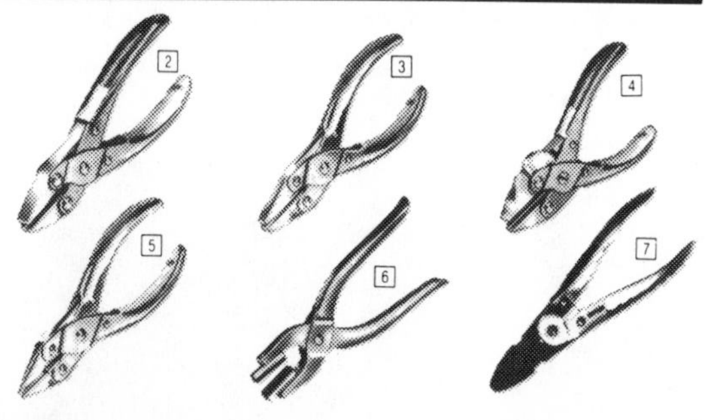

Combination Pliers [#4] — Flat nose pliers with serrated ▲ jaws and "V" slot, combined with a wire cutter.
No. 46.514-1 — Overall length 5". Shipping weight 5 oz.
No. 46.516-1 — Overall length 5½". Shipping weight 6 oz.
—Dixon

Dixon Precision Tools and Equipment
Catalog
$5 from:
William Dixon, Inc.
750 Washington Avenue
Carlstadt, NJ 07072

Allcraft
Catalog
$3 from:
Allcraft Tool & Supply Company, Inc.
100 Frank Road
Hicksville, NY 11801

The return of Halley's Comet —*Professional Stained Glass Magazine*

Stained Glass Primer
Peter Mollica
(Vol. 1) 1971; 87 pp.
$3.95
($4.95 postpaid)

Stained Glass Primer
Peter Mollica
(Vol. 2) 1977; 207 pp.
$4.95
($5.95 postpaid)
both from:
Mollica
Stained Glass Press
10033 Broadway Terrace
Oakland, CA 94611
or Whole Earth Access

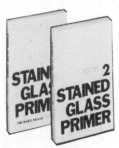

ONE OF THE MOST magical moments I experience is what happens in taking a just-completed stained glass window off the workbench and holding it up to the sunlight. The window transforms before my eyes from a cold grouping of pieces of glass into an entity that is almost alive.

There are exciting things happening in glass these days which will shatter any limiting beliefs you may have about this material. For clarity's sake, glass can be broken into three main subject categories: cold glass (includes working with stained glass, sandblasting, etching, etc.), warm glass (includes lampworking and techniques such as fusing, slumping, painting glass between 1100 degrees F and 1650 degrees F in a kiln), and hot glass (working with molten glass — employing a furnace at temperatures usually over 2000 degrees F).
—David Jouris

Stained Glass Primer 1 and 2

Peter Mollica has put together an excellent pair of books on stained glass. It was from them that I learned the basics when I first began. Volume one teaches the fundamentals of the craft by going step-by-step through the making of a leaded glass window, and using the copper-foil technique. The straightforward instructions are accompanied every step of the way by helpful black-and-white photos. Volume two introduces more advanced techniques including the use of easels, painting on glass, firing in a kiln, and how to reinforce and install a window. An annotated bibliography of books on glass completes this solid introduction to the craft. —*David Jouris*

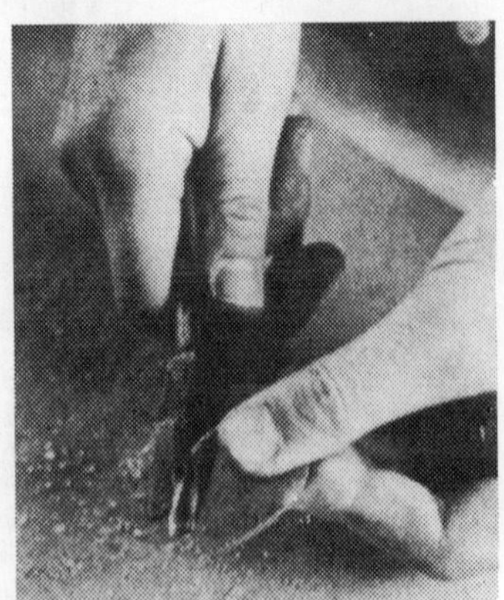

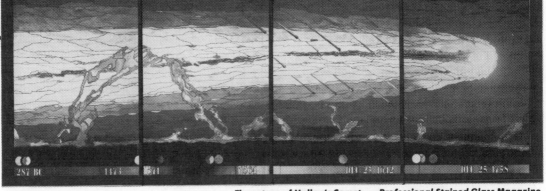

► The action used in grozing is difficult to describe, but it is closest to chewing at the side of your mouth with your back teeth. . . . Using the edge of the jaws, grasp firmly the chip of glass to be grozed away and turning your wrist outward as you close the jaws "chew" or "groze" away the unwanted chip.

The Art of Painting on Glass

A marvelous book on vitreous painting by a man who clearly loves his craft. Albinas Elskus gives a personal and comprehensive discourse on paints and how to mix them and explains the necessary tools and equipment a beginner would need. Most of the book is devoted to the techniques involved in painting on glass, including designing, tracing, matting, staining, enameling, etching, and firing. Full of wonderful photographs and drawings. —*David Jouris*

The Art of Painting on Glass
Albinas Elskus
1980; 147 pp.
$12.95
postpaid from:
Macmillan Publishing Co.
Order Dept.
Front and Brown Streets
Riverside, NJ 08075
or Whole Earth Access

•

(Below, left to right) blender's badger hairs are pressed to the glass as the blending begins.

To assure shading, the pressure on the hairs is released toward the edge of the glass.

Sample of a shaded matt.

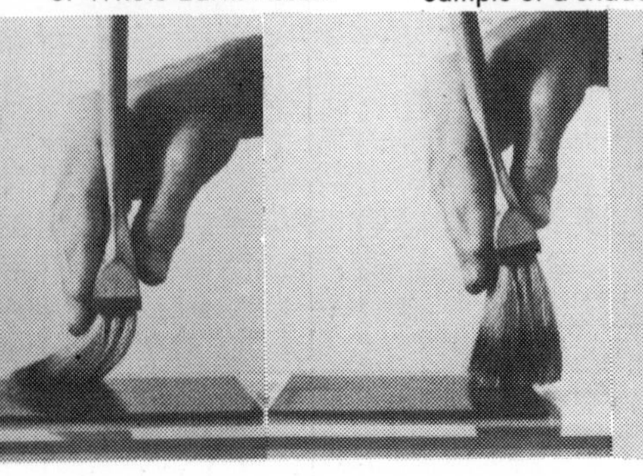

Glassworking Periodicals

Professional Stained Glass

Features articles on stained glass technique, equipment evaluations, and designing. The December issue is devoted to a nationwide listing of suppliers in all areas of glass work. —*David Jouris*

Professional Stained Glass: Albert Lewis, Editor. **$15**/year (10 issues) from 270 Lafayette Street, Room 701, New York, NY 10012.

•

Designer Lawrence Korgan and artist John Forbes created *The Return of Halley's Comet* [above], a panorama of glass twenty feet in length. The work consists of four art glass window panels, each five feet wide by seven feet tall.

• A fat, fascinating catalog of glassworking supplies and tools can be had **free** from Whittemore-Durgin Glass Co., P. O. Box 2065, Hanover, MA 02339.

• Craft researcher and reviewer David Jouris runs his own postcard, photography, and graphics business and is a self-described dabbler in anything involving the use of the hands. Also see his craft page in the "Livelihood" section (p. 198).

Glass Fusing

Here is a beautifully designed manual on the basics of warm glass. It's loaded with clearly written technical information on kilns, tools, supplies, firing, fusing, annealing, sagging, slumping, molding, and finishing. And there's an extended appendix which includes a helpful "glassery" for definitions of glassworking terms and a list of suppliers. This book also has some of the best illustrations I've seen — with hundreds of color photos. It is practically impossible to look at this work and not be inspired to try it yourself. Wow!
—*David Jouris*

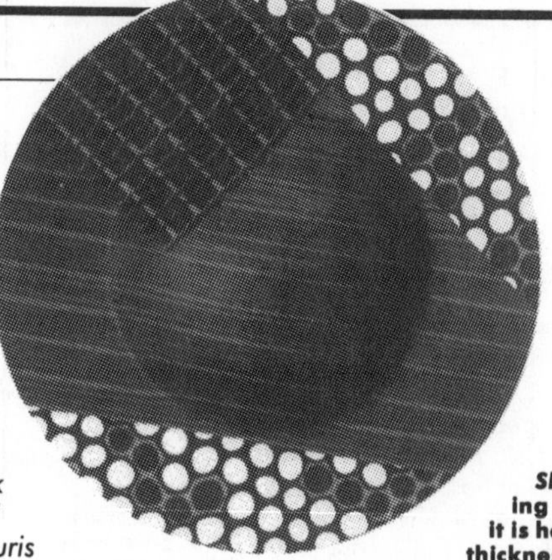

Klaus Moje made this bowl by fusing 1/8" x 3/8" glass strips together, then "slumping" them into shape.

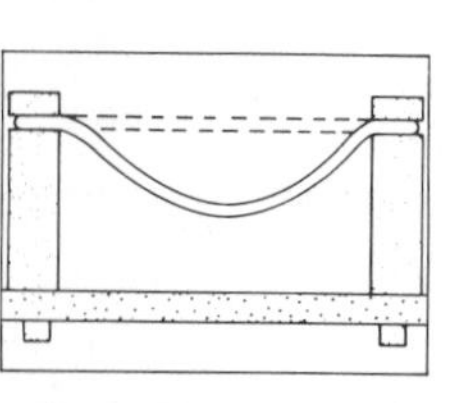

***Slumping* is the downward sinking of glass by its own weight as it is heated, while retaining uniform thickness.**

Glass Fusing
Boyce Lundstrom
and Daniel Schwoerer
1983; 137 pp.
$19.95
($21.45 postpaid) from:
Vitreous Publications, Inc.
Camp Colton
Colton, OR 97017

Glassblowing: A Search for Form

Glassblowing *is out of print but well worth looking for at the library or used book shops, as there is a dearth of well-written, inspiring books on this subject. Littleton begins by discussing the nature of glass and its history, but devotes most of the book to a personal account of his techniques and what he has learned during his years of work with hot glass.*
—*David Jouris*

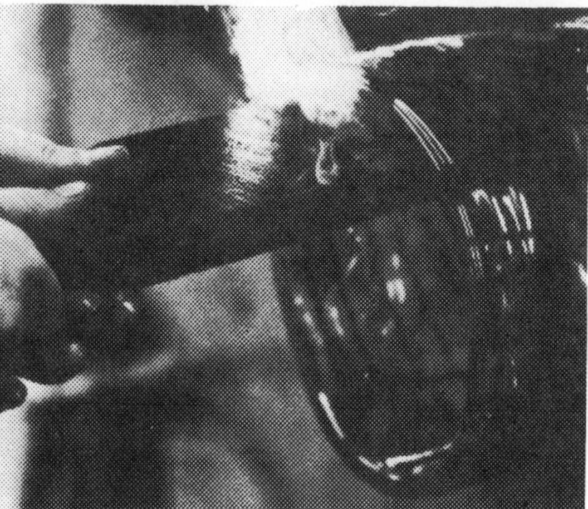

A wet wooden paddle is used to develop bowl from thick blown glass bottle shape.

When the artist lifts his blowpipe, he must be prepared to intervene with all his aptitude, training, form-sense, as well as physical and mental energy. Everything he knows converges all at once on this curious scene reenacted millions of times in human history: a man breathing his desire into the molten glass.

Glassblowing
Harvey K. Littleton
OUT OF PRINT
Van Nostrand Reinhold Co.

Glass Art Society Journal

The Glass Art Society puts out this handsome journal each year after their annual conference. New techniques, controversy, and classy photographs of recent work abound.
—*David Jouris*

Glass Art Society Journal: Christine Robbins, Editor. **$17**/year (annual) from Glass Art Society, P.O. Box 1364, Corning, NY 14830.

New Work

This quarterly tabloid magazine includes articles, portfolios, news, reviews; plus listings of classes, seminars, fairs, exhibitions and positions open. Published by people who are actively involved in glass work. —*David Jouris*

New Work: Karen S. Chambers, Editor. **$12** (4 issues) from New York Experimental Glass Workshop, Inc., 142 Mulberry Street, New York, NY 10013.

Neues Glas

This German/English magazine is as sleek and glittery as a gallery showcase — which it sort of is. The work shown is a good representation of the cutting edge of glass artistry.
—*JB*

Neues Glas/New Glass: $32.50/year (4 issues) from Neues Glas, Verlagsanstalt Handwerk GmbH/Postfach 8120, D4000 Dusseldorf 1, West Germany.

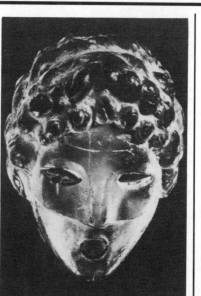

▲ **Henri Navarre, "Masque de Fontaine," for the "Ile de France." Collection of the Musee de Chartres.** —***Glass Arts Journal***

Where to Learn the Glass Arts

Year-round school offering classes, workshops, and demonstrations in all areas of glass work. Facilities available for rent to independent glass artists.
N.Y. Experimental Glass Workshop: Catalog **free** from 142 Mulberry Street, New York, NY 10013.

A summer school with classes in all areas of glass work, featuring many of the best glass workers around.
Pilchuck School: Catalog **free** from 107 South Main Street/#324, Seattle, WA 98104.

A summer school for basic and advanced fusing work.
Camp Colton Glass Program: Catalog **free** from Camp Colton, Colton, OR 97017.

A spring and fall workshop series covering both cold and warm glass, featuring well-known glass workers.
Fenton and Gaines Glass Studio: Catalog **free** from 4001 San Leandro Street/No. 8, Oakland, CA 94601.
—*David Jouris*

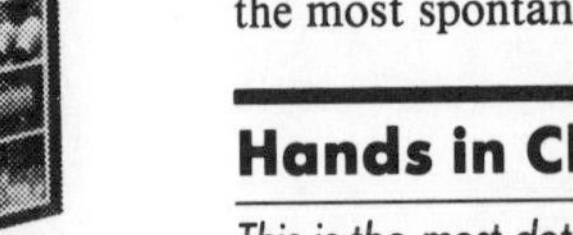

I T'S NO COINCIDENCE THAT CLAY has been in use constantly for at least 9,000 years; what other material can be shaped to almost any form, kept workable (moist) as long as necessary, dried, and then fired until it achieves a rock-hard permanence? Its immediacy makes it one of the most spontaneous of media. —Mary Law

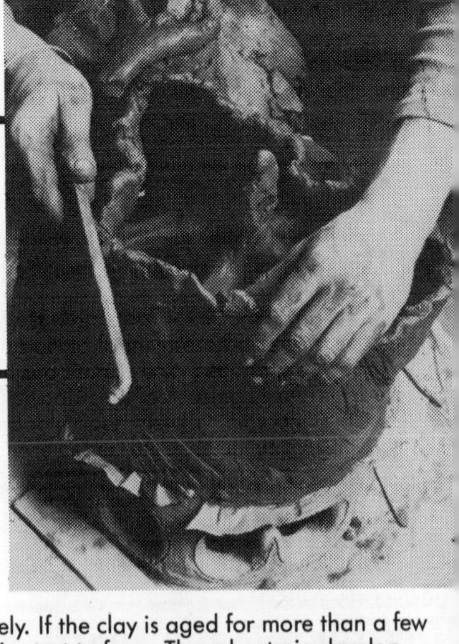

Hands working in moist clay have shaped it into sculpture or pottery for thousands of years.

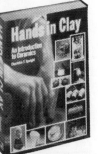

Hands in Clay

This is the most detailed of the general texts that I know. Almost half the book is about historical ceramics, showing the enormous variety of ways clay has been used over the centuries, with lots of good pictures of ancient pots and diagrams of methods and tools used. The second half focuses on your hands in clay, explaining various methods (handbuilding, making sculpture, working on the wheel and casting, surface treatments), glazing, and firing. Glaze chemistry is explained in the Appendix, with a good example of glaze calculation, too. —*Mary Law*

•

Clay, like bread, is improved by the action of bacteria. It needs to be left alone for a period of aging after it has been mixed, allowing the water to permeate the particles completely. If the clay is aged for more than a few days, bacteria start to form. These bacteria develop acids and gels and secrete enzymes that help break the clay into smaller particles, increasing its plasticity. Two weeks will probably ripen the clay, although most potters say the longer the better. Legends tell us that ancient Chinese potters prepared clay to be put aside for use by their sons and grandsons.

Hands In Clay
Charlotte F. Speight
1983; 348 pp.
$17.95
($19.95 postpaid) from:
Mayfield Publishing
285 Hamilton Avenue
Palo Alto, CA 94301
or Whole Earth Access

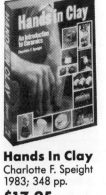

The Ceramic Spectrum

My absolute favorite on glazes and materials testing. Every time I open it I want to run out to my studio and mix some test glazes. —*Mary Law*

Ulla Viotti (Sweden). Detail of relief. White stoneware, painted with cobalt oxide, which is then rubbed off with steel wool. Once-fired in electric oxidation at cone 9.

The Ceramic Spectrum
Robin Hopper
1984; 223 pp.
$40
($42.25 postpaid) from:
Chilton Book Co.
Cash Sales Dept.
Chilton Way
Radnor, PA 19089
or Whole Earth Access

The Kiln Book

The best book on kilns and kiln building that I've seen. It's well designed, clear, and the information is easy to find when you need it. —*Mary Law*

The Kiln Book
Frederick L. Olsen
2nd Edition 1983; 291 pp.
$24.95
($27.20 postpaid) from:
Chilton Book Co.
Cash Sales Dept.
Chilton Way
Radnor, PA 19089
or Whole Earth Access

Bottle kiln, Segra Pottery, Breda, Spain.

Studio Potter • Ceramics Monthly

*Written by potters for potters, **Studio Potter** is packed with information about how potters think and operate. They sponsor a program to help people sponsor apprenticeships.*

***Ceramics Monthly** has lots of pictures of recent work, latest technique, profiles of noted potters, and a listing of upcoming exhibitions. Each April issue features an exhaustive list of summer classes.* —*Mary Law*

Studio Potter
Gerry Williams, Editor
$15/year
(2 issues) from:
Studio Potter
P. O. Box 65
Goffstown, NH 03045

Ceramics Monthly
William Hunt, Editor
$18/year
(10 issues) from:
Ceramics Monthly
P. O. Box 12448
Columbus, OH 43212

Stoking at the side ports widely varies ash deposits.
—*Ceramics Monthly*

• There are many ceramic supply houses. A.R.T. is one of our favorites. Catalog **$2** from A.R.T. Studio Clay Co., 1555 Louis Avenue, Elk Grove Village, IL 60007.

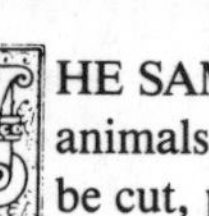

HE SAME QUALITIES OF TOUGHNESS and flexibility which make it *the* covering for many animals make leather a great covering for everything from shoes to books to furniture. Leather can be cut, punched, sewn, riveted, laced, braided, glued, laminated, dyed, bleached, painted, carved, stamped, burned, tooled, stretched, and molded — giving it an incredible span of possibilities.

—David Jouris

Leathercrafting • Modern Leather Design

Both of these books offer a good, basic introduction to leathercraft. They cover the tools and materials needed and explain the techniques for working with them. Donald Willcox communicates a love of the craft. He's inspiring and goes into enough depth to be interesting; however, the line illustrations provide little helpful instruction and the black-and-white photos of leather goods are difficult to see clearly. Raymond Cherry's text is a bit simple, but he does provide good step-by-step instructions (aided by helpful photos), and details 34 projects which put his instructions to use. —*David Jouris*

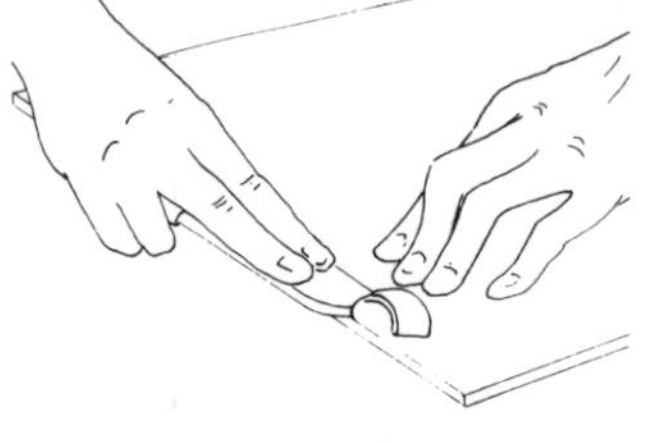

Position of the arm and hand while skiving. —*Modern Leather Design*

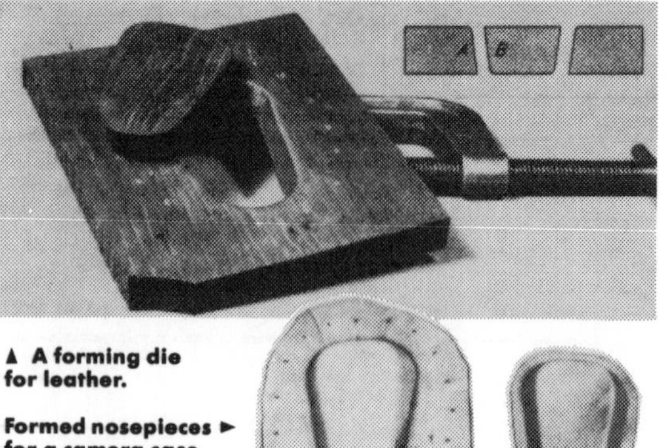

▲ A forming die for leather.

Formed nosepieces ► for a camera case. —*Leathercrafting*

•

What is Skiving?
Skiving is the process of reducing the thickness of leather, of actually slicing away negative leather from the original thickness. Skiving is a functional procedure rather than a decorative embellishment. . . .

While reducing thickness, the process of skiving also makes leather more flexible. Skiving is therefore used whenever you run up against any thickness problem in folding, creasing, flexing, or edge turning.

—*Modern Leather Design*

Leathercrafting
Raymond Cherry
1979; 118 pp.
$10.65
($11.15 postpaid) from:
Glencoe Publishing Co.
Order Dept.
Front and Brown Streets
Riverside, NJ 08075
or Whole Earth Access

Modern Leather Design
Donald Willcox
1969; 160 pp.
$12.95
($15.15 postpaid) from:
Watson-Guptill Publishers
P. O. Box 2013
Lakewood, NJ 08701
or Whole Earth Access

My World of Bibliophile Binding

The first quarter of this book is a description of the author's craft technique. The remaining 150 pages are devoted to color photographs of the beautiful work she has produced. A lovely, inspiring book in both its form and content. —*David Jouris*

Wonderful, beautiful, gorgeous! —*Susan Erkel Ryan*

My World of Bibliophile Binding
Kerstin Tini Miura
1984; 216 pp.
$125
($126.50 postpaid) from:
University of California Press
2120 Berkeley Way
Berkeley, CA 94720

Thousand Cranes by Yasunari Kawabata.

• For information on teachers, contact the Guild of Bookbinders (information **free** from 521 5th Avenue, New York, NY 10175) and/or Handbookbinders of California (information **free** from P. O. Box 3216, San Francisco, CA 94119).

Tandy Leather

Mail order and over 380 retail outlets nationwide. Has tools, leather, hardware and books. Tandy's big advantage is that it affords the beginner the opportunity to select leather in person. It's not that there'll be fewer mistakes if you buy leather in person, but the mistakes will be your mistakes. —*David Jouris*

Tandy Leather
Catalog
$1 from:
Tandy Leather
Dept. WEC
P. O. Box 2934
Fort Worth, TX 76113

The Practical Guide to Craft Bookbinding

A well designed book intended for the novice. It provides a good foundation in the craft with inviting clarity. I was immediately drawn to the fine illustrations, which I find of great help in understanding unfamiliar procedures. The last section of the book has step-by-step procedures for a number of different styles of binding.

—*David Jouris*

•

The flat-backed book opens well but is intended only as a temporary binding. The 'backed' book, on the other hand, although it has a restricted opening, has a considerably longer life. ▼

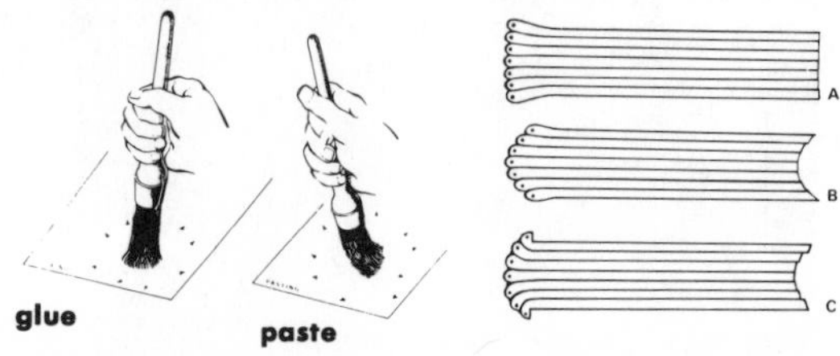

Glue is applied with a stabbing action and paste is applied with a brushing action.

The Practical Guide to Craft Bookbinding
Arthur W. Johnson
1985; 96 pp.
$9.95
postpaid from:
W. W. Norton
500 5th Avenue
New York, NY 10110
or Whole Earth Access

▲ Adding twined lengths of some materials requires laying the new length behind one spoke and cutting the old end off so it is hidden behind a different spoke. —*Basketry Today*

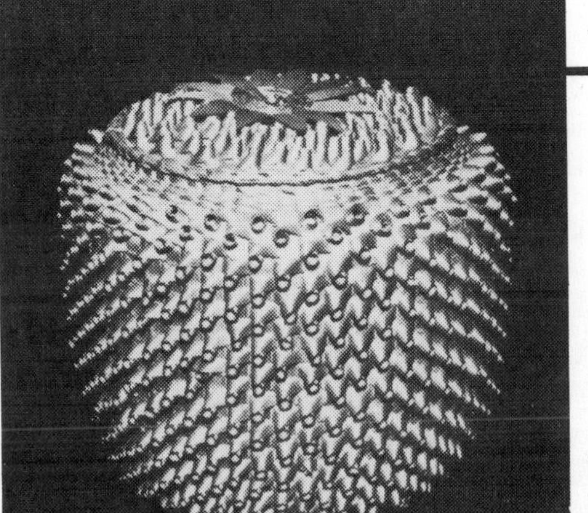

Plaited basket of the Winnebago Indians with curls around the surface and on the cover. —*Basketry Today*

A KAMPUCHEAN FRIEND, Meng Sovan, once made several small bamboo baskets for me to take home to my family. They were lovingly crafted — clearly a special gift. I thanked my friend for his kindness, and asked how I could carry them unharmed for the duration of my travels. "No problem," he said. He sat down and made me a nice big basket to carry them in.

—David Jouris

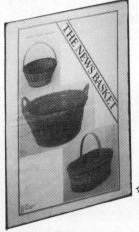

Basketry Today with Materials from Nature

An inspiring introduction to basketry, with chapters on gathering and dyeing natural materials, weaving, plaiting, twining, coiling, pine needle baskets, and nontraditional free-style forms. Clear, well-made photos and drawings explain the steps in making the different basket styles.

—David Jouris [Suggested by Shereen LaPlantz]

Basketry Today
Donna Z. Meilach
and Dee Menagh
1979; 200 pp.
$8.95
($11.55 postpaid) from:
Crown Publishers
34 Englehard Avenue
Avenel, NJ 07001
or Whole Earth Access

The Nature of Basketry

This book will cure your narrow mind about baskets. The range of human basketry is awesome, ingenious, gorgeous. You can't beat it, but you can join it. —Stewart Brand

The Nature of Basketry
Ed Rossbach
1986; 192 pp.
$14.95
($15.95 postpaid) from:
Schiffer Publishing
P. O. Box E
Exton, PA 19341
or Whole Earth Access

Bamboo basket, Japan. The elements are in a complex organization which combines plaiting, twining, and wickerwork.

The News Basket

A newspaper rich in enthusiasm for basketry, oriented toward serious professional work. Full of information on what's happening in basketry and where. —David Jouris

The News Basket
Shereen LaPlantz,
Editor
$10/year
(6 issues) from:
LaPlantz Studios
899 Bayside Cutoff
Bayside, CA 95524

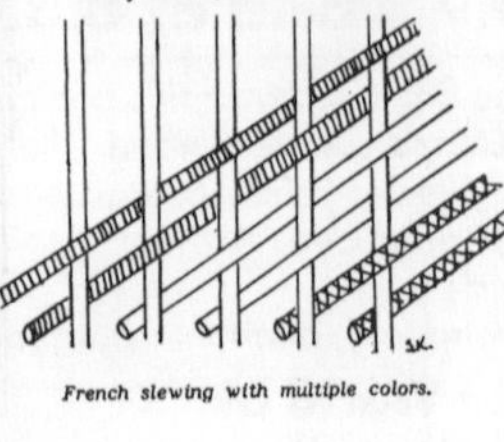

French slewing with multiple colors.

Basketry Suppliers

The Caning Shop: Catalog **$1** from 926 Gilman, Berkeley, CA 94710. *A reputation for taking a personal interest in customers and giving interesting classes. Carries basketry and caning supplies, tools, and books.*

Tint & Splint Basketry: Catalog **free** with SASE from 29529 Ford Rd., Garden City, MI 48135. *Full line of basketry supplies, tools, books. Known for really good colored reed. Reputed to have best wholesale rates. Offers classes and workshops.*

H. H. Perkins: Catalog **free** from P. O. Box A.C., Amity Station, Woodbridge, CT 06525. *Nice folks to deal with, and in the business for over 70 years. Tools, supplies, and books.*

Linda Snow Fibers: Catalog **free** from 3209 Doctors Lake Drive, Orange Park, FL 32073. *Said to be very helpful and a good source for hard-to-find materials. Free brochure with SASE — for list of supplies, tools, & books.*

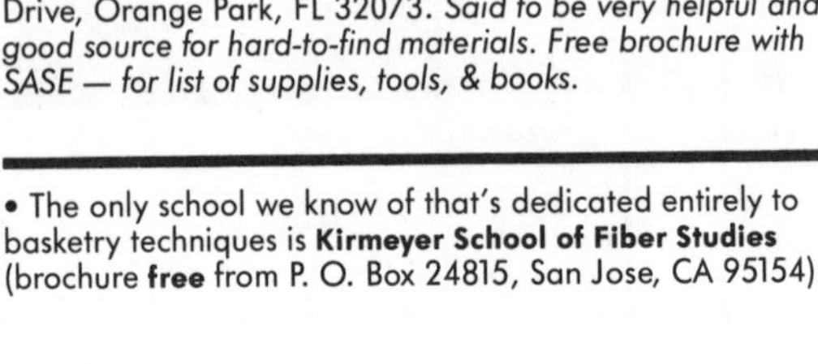

• The only school we know of that's dedicated entirely to basketry techniques is **Kirmeyer School of Fiber Studies** (brochure **free** from P. O. Box 24815, San Jose, CA 95154).

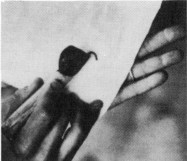

—Threads

◄ **Nek Chand's fantasy garden, at the Capital Children's Museum in Washington, D.C., is a magical, charmed place, a world not our own. . . . The cloth people begin as metal skeletons. They are wrapped, like mummies, with long pieces of cloth pieced together from smaller fragments. When a body is full, it is tautly covered with large patchworked cloth. Then it is dressed in cast-off clothing.**

Threads

The publishers of **Fine Woodworking** *(p. 168) and* **Fine Homebuilding** *(p. 122) have come out with another beautiful magazine,* **Threads***. With a style and look all its own,* **Threads** *is not just another pretty face. It is filled with interesting, well-written articles that cover the gamut of the fiber arts field. It has articles about and by leading textile artists as well as pieces on freestyle embroidery, Gobelins-style tapestry, weft twining, hand-quilting, knitting, dyeing, felting, sewing hand-wovens, and on and on. My particular interests are in embroidery and weaving, but I find that every time an issue of* **Threads** *arrives, I read it cover to cover. The piece de resistance is the back cover, which is like a great dessert after a wonderful meal.*
—Susan Erkel Ryan [Suggested by many]

Using the Indonesian method of laying fabric against the open palm of the hand to apply wax with a tjanting tool.

Threads
John Kelsey, Editor
$16/year
(6 issues) from
The Taunton Press
Subscription Dept.
P.O. Box 355
Newton, CT 06470

Fiberarts

A copy of **Fiberarts** *will fill you in on the latest shows, classes, and events in the field. They run lots of color pictures of fiberwork, making the magazine a good source for inspiration.*
—Marilyn Green

Fiberarts
Kate Mathews-Pulleyn, Editor
$18/year
(6 issues) from
Fiberarts
50 College Street
Asheville, NC 28801

***At Play,* black-on-white silk screen print by Harwood Steiger. His printed fabrics are produced entirely by hand, from mixing dyes and cutting stencils to the actual printing.**

"Garden Wall II," 48 in. x 46 in. cotton, was Elizabeth Gurrier's last white-on-white quilt to be exhibited. She has since moved on to color, hand painting before she quilts.

• Marilyn Green, who helped assemble these pages (and introduced us to weaver Rhoda London), is a librarian, crafter, craft collector, mail-order aficionado, and writer.

► ***Beast of Burden,* from the Dog Table series, 1985; fabric over welded steel frame, glass; 20 x 26 x 36 inches. "I consciously wanted to change my work because it was reminding me of how-to kits in 'Woman's Day' magazine," fabric sculptress Lynn DiNino remarked wryly about her recent transition from purely "soft" pieces to works which include steel, wood, and wire, as well as fabric.**

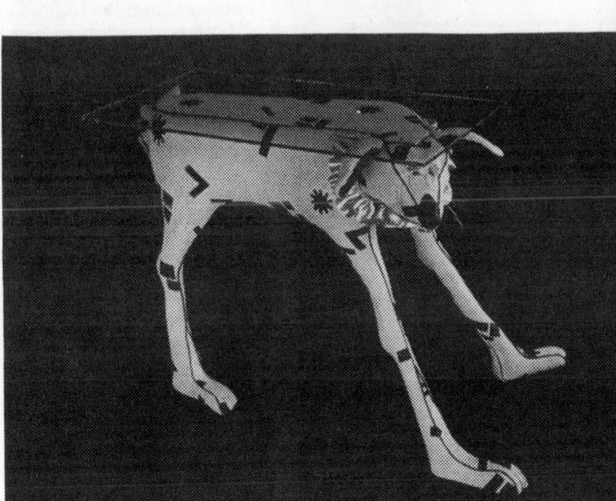

The Key to Weaving
Mary E. Black
1980; 698 pp.
$35 postpaid from:
Macmillan Publishing Co.
Order Dept.
Front and Brown Streets
Riverside, NJ 08075
or Whole Earth Access

The Key to Weaving

Written by a master weaver, this comprehensive book covers looms, weave structures (with instructions for dozens of new patterns), tapestry techniques, color, and an in-depth chapter on fibers. If you can only have one book on weaving, this is it. —Rhoda London

Warp: Linen, homespun, coarse, single-ply
Weft: Same

Warp: Cotton, Egyptian, 30/3

•

TYPE Balanced Weaves
PATTERN Plain Weave

These samples show textures achieved through the use of various kinds and sizes of threads.

Warp: Carpet Warp
Weft: Same

4-harness Reverse Twill Threads, reed, sley, tie-up same as for sample 1

TREADLE		TREADLE		TREADLE		TREADLE	
3 light 1 dark 4 light 2 dark 1 light 3 dark 2 light 4 dark	twice	2 light 3 dark 1 light 2 dark 4 light 1 dark 3 light 4 dark	twice	3 light 1 dark 4 light 2 dark 1 light 3 dark 2 light 4 dark	once	2 light 3 dark 1 light 2 dark 4 light 1 dark 3 light 4 dark	once

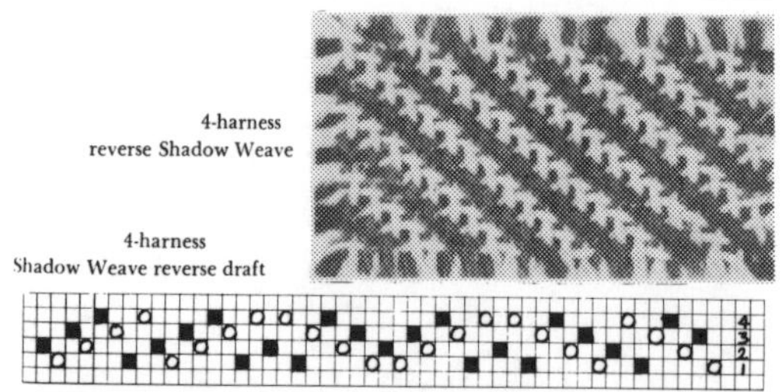

4-harness reverse Shadow Weave

4-harness Shadow Weave reverse draft

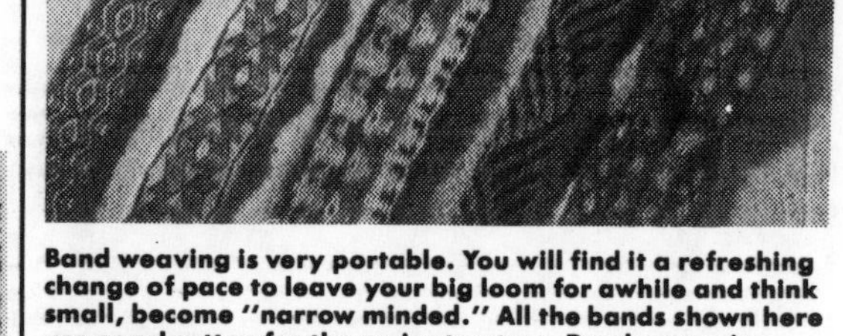

Band weaving is very portable. You will find it a refreshing change of pace to leave your big loom for awhile and think small, become "narrow minded." All the bands shown here use pearl cotton for the main structure. Pearl cotton is strong and smooth, primary requirements for easy shedding in a warp-faced band woven under considerable tension.

Handwoven
Jane Patrick, Editor
$18/year
(5 issues) from:
Interweave Press
306 North Washington Ave.
Loveland, CO 80537

Handwoven

The best weaving journal, with specific focus in each issue on a particular area of weaving — Early American, tapestry, etc. An "instructions supplement" shows you how to make the items shown in the feature articles. —Diana Sloat

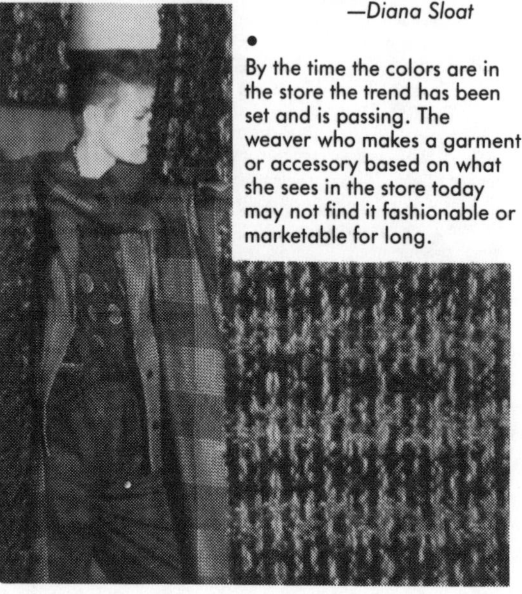

•

By the time the colors are in the store the trend has been set and is passing. The weaver who makes a garment or accessory based on what she sees in the store today may not find it fashionable or marketable for long.

Specialized Weaving Books

Clearly-drawn patterns of basic clothing designs: tunics, skirts, scarfs, blouses, vests, capes. Truly handwoven clothing made easy.

Fashions from the Loom: Betty J. Beard, 1980; 96 pp. **$10** ($11.50 postpaid) from Interweave Press, 306 North Washington Avenue, Loveland, CO 80537.

The most comprehensive book ever on weaving an authentic Navajo rug.

Working With the Wool (How to Weave a Navajo Rug): Noel Bennett and Tiana Bighorse, 1983; 105 pp. **$8.95** ($10.70 postpaid) from Northland Press, P. O. Box N, Flagstaff, AZ 86002.

Each of these books is available from Whole Earth Access.

Ikat-dyed silk makes an especially dramatic fabric for a Monk's robe, equally suitable for a man or woman.
—Fashions from the Loom

The total rug book.

Techniques of Rug Weaving: Peter Collingwood, 1969; 480 pp. **$35** ($37 postpaid) from Watson-Guptill Publishers, P. O. Box 2013, Lakewood, NJ 08701.

Everything you ever wanted to know about warping a loom.

Warping All By Yourself: Cay Garrett, 1974; 159 pp. **$6** ($7.50 postpaid) from Interweave Press, 306 North Washington Avenue, Loveland, CO 80537.

Traditional patterns with tie-up, threading, and treadling drafts.

A Handweaver's Pattern Book: Marguerite Porter Davison, 1977; 217 pp. **$20** ($22.50 postpaid) from John Spencer, Inc., 8th and Sproul Streets, Box 10, Chester, PA 19016. —Rhoda London

• Many people have recommended this as the best book on knitting.
Mary Thomas's Knitting book: Mary Thomas, 1972; 269 pp. **$3.95** ($4.95 postpaid) from Dover Publications, 31 East 2nd Street, Mineola, NY 11501 (or Whole Earth Access).

• Innovative and colorful knitting technique.
Glorious Knits: Kaffe Fassett, 1985; 160 pp. **$22.50** ($25.10 postpaid) from Crown Publishers, 34 Englehard Avenue, Avenel, NJ 07001 (or Whole Earth Access).

The Weaving, Spinning, and Dyeing Book

For the beginning weaver, this is a meaty, provocative, well-formatted introduction to a variety of weaving techniques — card, inkle, backstrap, Navajo — all covered well enough to get you started and keep you inspired with endless project ideas. Its sections on buying a floor loom, synthetic acid dyeing, and suppliers are superb. —*Diana Sloat*

•

A short-cut method for tie-dying that I use is to put part of the skein into the dyepot and let the other part hang over the edge of the pot (have it supported in some way so the heat or fire does no damage). After that is dyed, turn the skein around so that a new section hangs in the dye liquor.

Actually, some of these yarns, when woven or knitted are quite hideous, unless a deliberate design is planned, so I would experiment in a small way, if I were you.

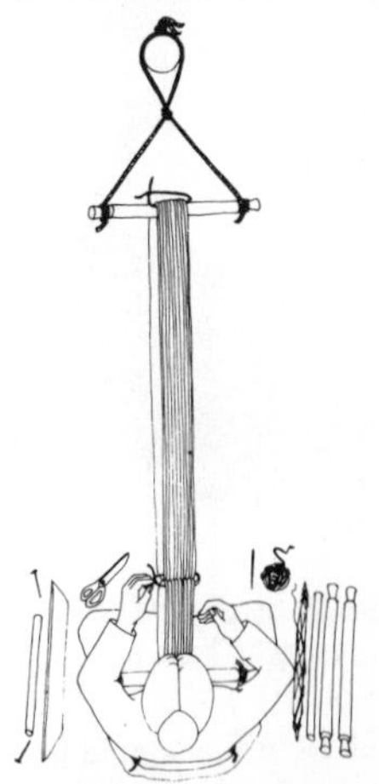

Stretching the warp of a backstrap loom.

The Weaving, Spinning, and Dyeing Book
Rachel Brown
1978; 366 p.
$18.95
($19.95 postpaid) from:
Random House
Order Dept.
400 Hahn Road
Westminster, MD 21157
or Whole Earth Access

Spinning and Weaving with Wool

How to card and spin, illustrated with excellent photographs. There are specifications and sources (some obsolete) for a wide variety of spinning wheels. Best of all, there are plans for building your own rough but inexpensive hand carder, drum carder, hand-cranked table spinning wheel, counterbalanced loom (well-designed), warping reel, and umbrella swift. —*Diana Sloat*

Modern spinning wheel designs don't look like Granny's but work on the same principle.

▼ Held in one hand, the new fiber supply and the last of the unspun fibers are feathered together in a perfect joining, which will be undetectable and as strong as the rest of the yarn skein.

•

Another possibility for a homemade spinning device is one in which you use a bicycle wheel for the drive wheel. Although it is shown here with a double belt propelling a flyer and bobbin, it is even simpler to make if it turns a spindle because it then needs only a single belt. With flyer and double belt, keep in mind that the spinning fork (with hooks for yarn guides) is fixed to the spindle shaft and that the bobbin must turn freely on that shaft. The bobbin pulley groove must be smaller than the flyer pulley grooves. About a 2:1 pulley ratio is good for medium-size yarn and about a 1.5:1 ratio for finer yarn.

Spinning and Weaving with Wool
Paula Simmons
1977; 221 pp.
$13.95
($15.45 postpaid) from:
Pacific Search Press
222 Dexter Avenue North
Seattle, WA 98109
or Whole Earth Access

• An exquisite book on historical and contemporary dyed fabrics.
The Dyer's Art: Jack L. Larsen and Alfred Buhler, 1977, **$50** postpaid from Van Nostrand Reinhold Co., 7625 Empire Drive, Florence, KY 41042.

Synthetic Dyes for Natural Fibers

An easy, step-by-step book for dyeing, explaining dye procedures with tables and formulas for using Cibacron, Procion, and acid dyes. Good coverage of color theory, color mixing, and the chemistry of fiber and dye. Supplier list and glossary of terms. Easy to read and follow. It's the most exciting book I've seen for the serious fiber artist. —*Rhoda London*

Synthetic Dyes for Natural Fibers
Linda Knutson
1986; 170 pp.
$12
($13.50 postpaid) from:
Interweave Press
306 North Washington Ave.
Loveland, CO 80537
or Whole Earth Access

Soft Sculpture
Carolyn V. Hall
1981; 112 pp.
$16.95 postpaid from:
Davis Publications
50 Portland St.
Worcester, MA 01608
or Whole Earth Access

Soft Sculpture

A book to help you turn your wildest fabric fantasies into sculpture that won't come apart at the seams. A soft sculpture can be anything from a silk cactus to a velvet dog to a life-size corduroy drum set. Who needs clothes anyway?
—Jeanne Carstensen [Suggested by Rhoda London]

▲

Wings by Rosalie Sherman. 112″ wide, 27″ tall, 9″ thick. Nylon fabric stretched with grommets, snaps, and D-rings on a carved cherry wood frame create this fantasy equipment "relic of another culture, familiar as in dreams."

Self-Portrait by Lynn DiNino. 5′8″ tall, 18″ wide, 10″ thick. "It's creepy to have a life-sized stuffed figure of yourself sitting in your living room, but it makes a great burglar deterrent!"

Reader's Digest Complete Guide to Needlework
Virginia Colton, Editor
1979; 504 pp.
$19.98
($21.92 postpaid) from:
Reader's Digest
Attn.: Order Entry
Pleasantville, NY 10570
or Whole Earth Access

The Reader's Digest Complete Guide to Needlework

The title of this book should be changed to **The Reader's Digest GOOD Guide to Needlework.** *Though it is not complete, the skills are covered with an excellence I've come to expect from Reader's Digest how-to books. Tools, basic techniques, and instructions are covered thoroughly, with sample projects. Recommended jumping-off point for a beginning needle worker.*
—Evelyn Eldridge-Diaz

Fern stitches: Start at upper left and work all rows down the canvas.

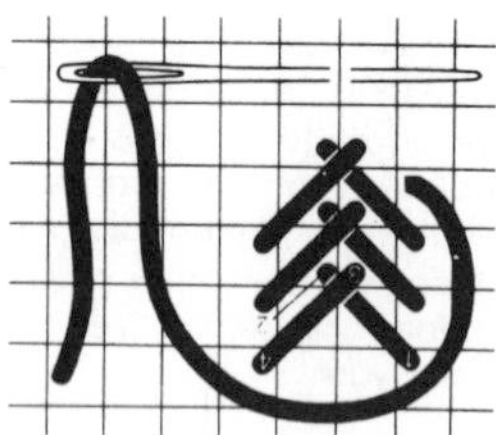

If left-handed, turn canvas, start in lower right corner and work all rows up the canvas.

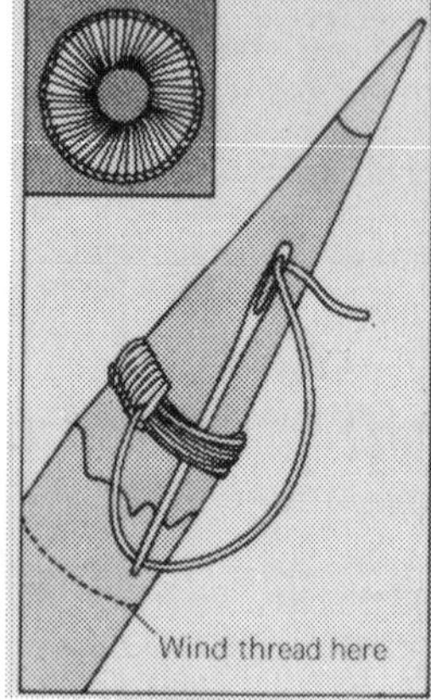

●

Rings: These are made separately, then sewed onto the work wherever desired. Wind thread around a pencil 15 times, then buttonhole over all of the strands. (The buttonholing is easier if you push the threads up toward the pencil point.) When ring is complete, remove from pencil, flatten, and sew in place.

Inspiration for Embroidery
Constance Howard
1985; 240 pp.
$15.50
($16.50 postpaid) from:
Charles T. Branford Co.
P. O. Box 41
Newton Center, MA 02159
or Whole Earth Access

Inspiration for Embroidery

If I were to choose one book from all the fiber art books, it would be **Inspiration for Embroidery.** *I always pick it up between projects and it never fails to get me working again.*
—Marilyn Green

A hedgehog worked in various metal threads and padded gold kid.

• The latest books in textiles, fiber arts, needle arts, costumes, and related subjects are listed (some with expert reviews) in **The Textile Booklist**: Kaaren Buffington and Kay Sennot Hofweber, Editors, **$12.50/year** (4 issues) from Textile Booklist, P. O. Box 4392, Arcata, CA 95521.

Angora baby bunny from Deaton Farms.

The Fiberworks Source Book

Keep a firm grip on your Visa card when you delve into this succulent catalog — the variety alone will make you greedy. You'll find goodies such as rubber stamps (for use with permanent fabric color), the addresses of professional associations and schools, and every sort of stuff to use for knitting, weaving, spinning, papermaking, basketry, and just about everything else that can possibly be construed as fiber. —*JB [Suggested by Marilyn Green]*

•

Cerulean Blue, Ltd., P. O. Box 21168, Seattle, WA 98111, Telephone (206) 625-9647: Cerulean Blue is probably the most popular supplier for textile and fiber artists. And it's really no wonder — they have the most comprehensive catalog of fiber supplies available anywhere. An in-depth educational catalog is $3.25 — includes health and safety tips, periodic "Blue-News" updates with new products, price changes, gallery information, etc.

•

Deaton Farms' Angora, 9095 Paddock Road, Eaton, OH 45320, Telephone (513) 456-5630. Manufacturer; Mail Order; Established in 1981. Diane Deaton, of Deaton Farms' Angora, raises angora rabbits for the special fibers that they provide. She has white angora rabbit wool available. She also is interested in doing custom spinning, as well as teaching workshops on the angora rabbit.

Send $3.00 for Diane's basic catalog and angora sample.

(By the way, this is no ordinary catalog. It contains extensive information on angora rabbit wool, angora fiber chemistry, spinning angora wool, dyeing the wool, designing angora yarns, and instructions for a French angora beret. Well worth $3.00!)

•

Straw Into Gold, 3006 San Pablo Avenue, Berkeley, CA 94702. Telephone (415) 548-5241. Mail Order, Retail Shop; V/MC; Established in 1971. Straw Into Gold carries many materials for basketmaking; fiber rush, Fiber Flex, reed, raffia, untreated pigtail raffia, and seagrass in various sizes. Send a SASE for a current catalog and price list.

The Fiberworks Source Book
Bobbi A. McRae
1985; 223 pp.
$9.95
($11.45 postpaid) from:
Betterway Publications
P. O. Box 469
White Hall, VA 22987
or Whole Earth Access

Universal Yarn Finder

An invaluable source for choosing the right yarn for each project. One thousand four hundred yarns (fingering, sport, heavy worsted or four-ply, bulky, and specialty) are listed in tabbed sections, with description, specifications, cleaning instructions, and how much of the yarn you'd need to knit a crewneck sweater. You can use the book to determine if the yarn you have at home will work for the project you've planned. Included are mail-order addresses.
—*Marilyn Green*

Class A Light Weight Fingering 3-ply worsted smooth classic
Class A Light Weight Fingering Number 5 perle' cotton
Class A Light Weight Fingering 2-Ply worsted smooth classic nylon and wool
Class A Light Weight Fingering 3-Ply worsted smooth classic heather blend
Class A Light Weight Fingering 3-Ply worsted smooth classic wool
Class B Medium Weight Sport Metallic combination

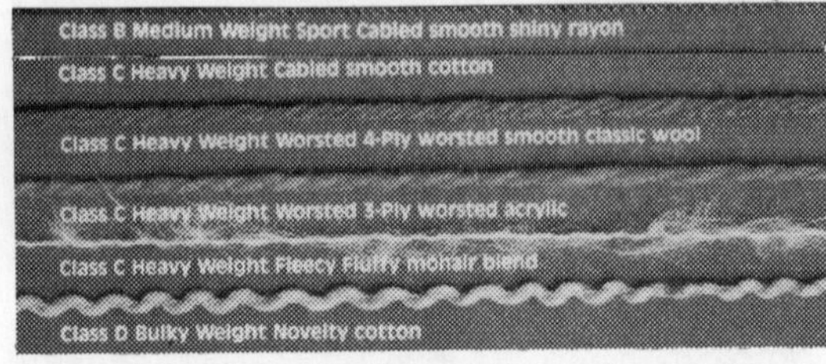

Universal Yarn Finder
Maggie Righetti
1983; 100 pp.
$9.95
($11.95 postpaid) from
Maggie Righetti Designs
P. O. Box 49707
Atlanta, GA 30359

A Silk Worker's Notebook

Once a precious, handmade book fit for museums (silk fabric samples throughout), this loving treatise about the character of silk has been issued as an affordable trade paperback (no samples, alas). It's about the practical techniques of using silk, in all its varieties, and how silk's unusual origins shape the personality of its fabrics. It's by hands passionately intimate with this queen of fibers.
—*Kevin Kelly*

Rayon and some other synthetics weaken when wet — silk does not.

Good: fiber length 2" or more, singles or plied, with slubs or thick-thin

singles, medium twist

Other silk yarns can be used for warp if they are sized or handled carefully.

•

Lye Test: A hot lye solution will dissolve all animal fibers in 10 to 15 minutes. White silk will dissolve very quickly, some wild silks may take longer. Wool will also dissolve quickly, but the cellulose/synthetic fibers will remain, more or less unchanged, although some swell and most turn yellow.

►

Direct spinning from opened-out cocoons, using a light-weight drop spindle. The right hand pulls out a long draw, releases the yarn to let the twist run up, then begins the next draw from the point where the twist stopped. The illustration shows the hands at the beginning of the draw. By the end of the draw the hands are about two feet apart.

•

The sound of silk tearing:

A hundred trees rent by a storm in a moment — gone!

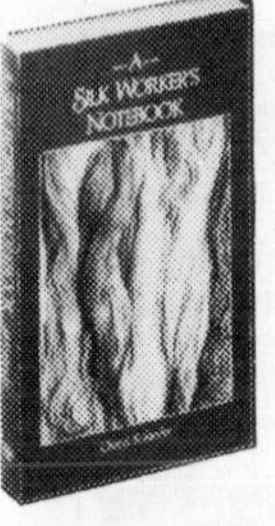

A Silk Worker's Notebook
Cheryl Kolander
1985; 155 pp.
$12
($13.50 postpaid) from:
Interweave Press
306 N. Washington Ave.
Loveland, CO 80537
or Whole Earth Access

I F YOU WERE as picky about the clothes you buy as the ones you make, you'd be naked most of the time.
—*Sew Sane*

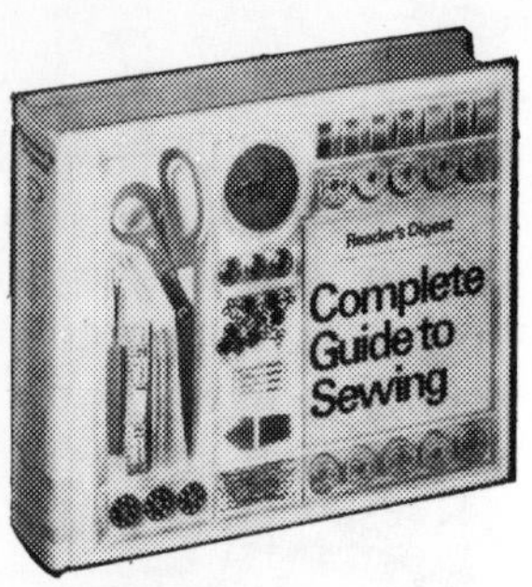

Reader's Digest Complete Guide to Sewing
1976; 528 pp.
$19.98
($21.92 postpaid) from:
Reader's Digest
Attn.: Order Entry
Pleasantville, NY 10570
or Whole Earth Access

Reader's Digest Complete Guide to Sewing

Easily the one book I would recommend for any home sewer, whether beginner or accomplished old-timer. Tools, methods, and techniques are covered with thorough and easy-to-follow instructions and every option and variation imaginable. The sewing machine section, compiled with the aid of Singer, is a comprehensive overview of electric sewing machines: how to use, maintain, and understand them. Sections on special techniques for men's and children's clothing, and sewing for the home, are included.
—Evelyn Eldridge-Diaz

Still the best. —JB

Making garments easy to put on and take off

Elasticized pull-on pants and skirts can be managed by even young toddlers (sewing is easy, too). If garment front and back are different, mark back with ribbon or tape.

Large buttons are a great incentive for do-it-yourself dressing, because they don't take much dexterity and are easy for little fingers to grasp. Sew buttons very securely.

A zipper with a large pull is best for first attempts at zipping up. Buy a decorative zipper with a fancy pull, or add a ring to any type. Install zipper in garment front.

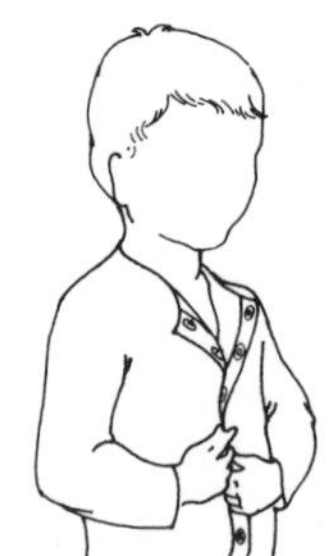
No-sew snaps are the easiest type for small fingers to cope with, and they have good holding power. Use single snaps for spot closings and snap tape for longer plackets.

Power Sewing
Sandra Betzina
1985; 255 pp.
$20
postpaid from:
Power Sewing
P. O. Box 2702
San Francisco, CA 94126

Power Sewing

How to make things fit without having a fit. Unfortunately, the illustrations are crudely printed, but the information is sophisticated, easy to use, and hard to find elsewhere.
—JB

Know Your Fabrics

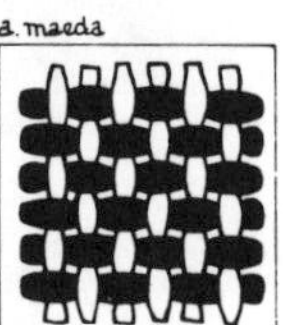

PLAIN WEAVE

TWILL WEAVE

SINGLE KNIT

The small woman has the same problem as the large woman — patterns do not come in her size. . . .

Although some patterns do come in size 6, they are few and available only by special order. Since a size 8 is readily available, let us learn how to convert a size 8 to a size 6 or 4.

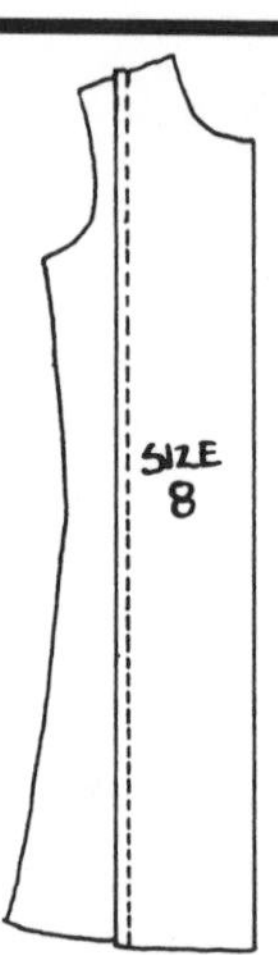

① CONVERT TO SIZE 6. FOLD OUT 1/2" FROM FRONT AND BACK.

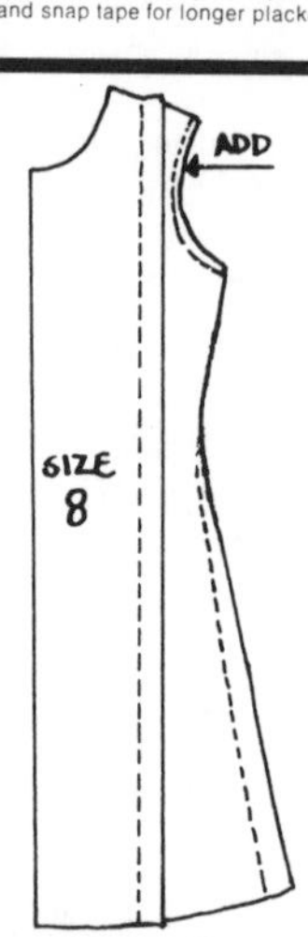

② CONVERT TO SIZE 4. FOLD OUT 1". IF NEEDED, ADD TO HIPS AND WAIST.

Sew Sane
Gale Grigg Hazen
1985; 63 pp.
$12.95
($14.70 postpaid) from:
Sewing Place
P. O. Box 4762
San Jose, CA 95150

Sew Sane

Sewing machines occasionally take on a recalcitrant character that will drive you batty if you let 'em get away with it. This book unmasks the "gremmies" that cause puckers, missed stitches, and all those maddening stigmata of the amateur sewer. It's written for the totally unmechanical mind. —JB

•

Do not use polyester thread on silk, because it is four to seven times stronger than silk. If you do, you will wear a garment that looks as if it were sewn with band saws. In fact, when working on thin fabrics, remember that you are hardly going to play basketball in them. The seams don't have to be as strong as those in jeans.

•

After you've tried everything you know, including reading your manual and rethreading the machine, you may need to take it into the shop if it in fact isn't working.

Kindly do not strip it before taking it in. Don't take off the needle, don't remove the thread. Leave all the knobs in the positions they were in when the problem occurred. Do not remove the bobbin or its casing, and do not clean anything. Some people are embarrassed by taking in a dirty machine, but if you remove all the evidence, chances are the repair persons can't solve the mystery.

• I've learned as much about sewing from this color newspaper as I have from working with my sewing machine and reading sewing manuals. —Marilyn Green

Sew News: Linda Jones, Editor. **$13.95**/year (12 issues) from P. O. Box 3137, Harlan, IA 51593.

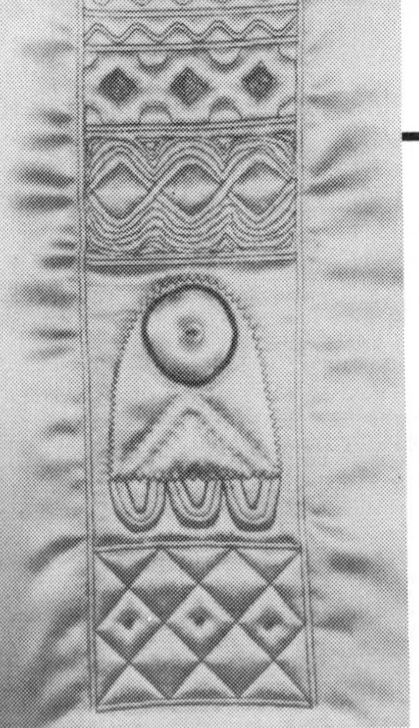

A sampler of machine-quilting techniques: (from the top) twin-needle quilting — serpentine stitch, free-machine quilting, mock trapunto, satin stitch circle, zigzag quilting, button tying by machine, invisible thread quilting with zig-zag stitch, Italian cording, straight stitch quilting with presser foot — diamond grid, decorative-stitch tying.

The Complete Book of Machine Quilting

Most books on quilting don't go into much (if any) detail on quilting with a sewing machine. ***The Complete Book of Machine Quilting*** *makes up for what the other books have skipped. This book has everything — including a very clear and complete explanation of how a sewing machine does what it does, and instructions for projects and cautions/directions for working with unusual materials on the sewing machine. The discussion of finishing the edges of a quilt is the best I have seen. In a section entitled "How NOT to Machine Quilt a Sheet," the Fannings follow someone else's instructions and the project doesn't work. They explain what's going wrong as they work on it so the same won't happen to us. The book is clever, comprehensive and useful. It's a good buy for traditional quilters as well as for the busy person who wants to make a quilt in one day.* —Marilyn Green

The Complete Book of Machine Quilting
Robbie Fanning
and Tony Fanning
1980; 334 pp.
$16.95
($19.45 postpaid) from:
Chilton Book Company
Cash Sales Dept.
Chilton Way
Radnor, PA 19089
or Whole Earth Access

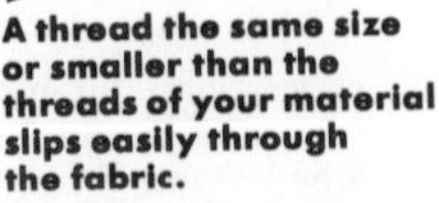

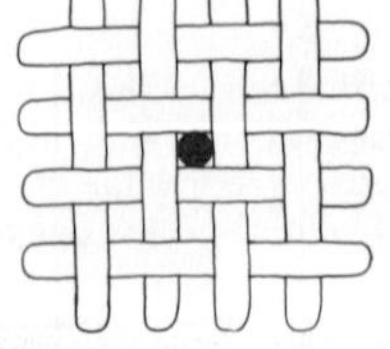

► **A thread the same size or smaller than the threads of your material slips easily through the fabric.**

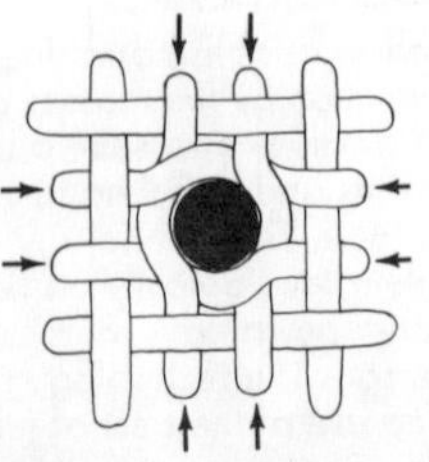

► **A thread too big for your material pushes the fibers apart and puckers your fabric. This shows up often in piecing quilts of lightweight cotton with too-heavy thread.**

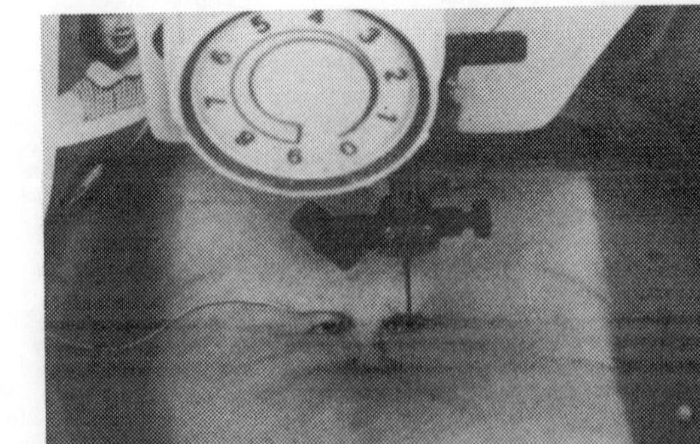

Cut-up nylons can be free-machine quilted and used for faces on dolls, ornaments, and even quilts. If you can't draw, use school pictures, advertisements, and the like for guidance, or trace them.

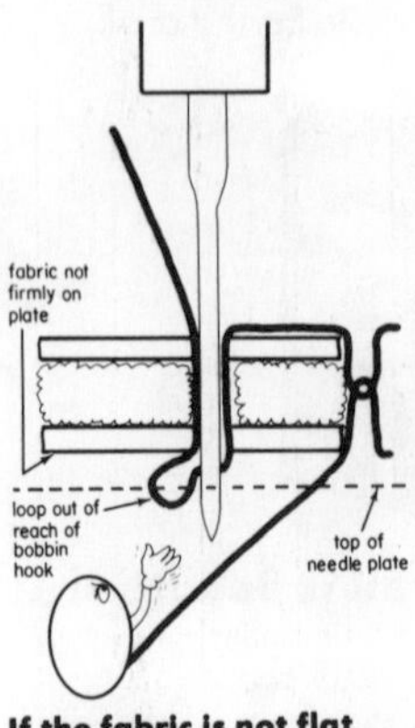

If the fabric is not flat against the needle plate, the loop lifts out of reach of the bobbin and a stitch is skipped. —*Machine Quilting*

Sewing Supplies

These mail order companies provide a sewing shop in your mailbox. Sewing Emporium carries a complete line of sewing machines and attachments. Clotilde has unusual, clever sewing notions, and offers videotapes teaching you how to sew. Newark Dressmaker Supply is like an old general store; they carry the basics including some fabrics and even "doll ingredients" (heads and other body parts). —Marilyn Green

Newark Dressmaker Supply: Catalog **free** from P. O. Box 2448, Dept. WE, Lehigh Valley, PA 18001.

Clotilde Inc.: Catalog **$1** from 237 SW 28th Street, Fort Lauderdale, FL 33315.

Sewing Emporium: Catalog **$1.50** from 1087 3rd Avenue, Chula Vista, CA 92010.

Patchwork Patterns

Once you've gotten hooked on patchwork, you'll find Beyer's book a fascinating discovery. The appeal of the book is her innovative system for drafting geometric patchwork patterns. She uses paperfolding and makes drafting seem easy even to math klutzes like me. Her methods could be used for any craft requiring a geometric design — not just for quiltmaking. Beyer's quilts are breathtaking in their use of color and intricate technical perfection. Now you can do it, too. —Marilyn Green

Joseph's Coat

Nelson's Victory

Jacob's Ladder

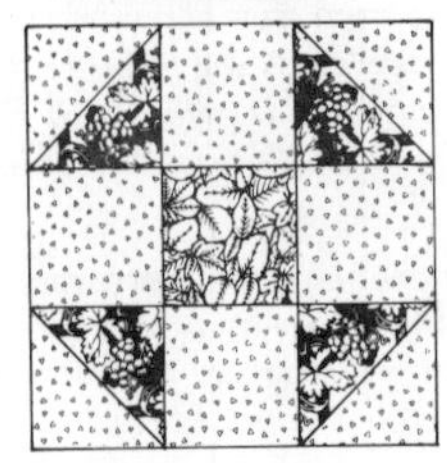

Shoo-fly

Patchwork Patterns
Jinny Beyer
1979; 200 pp.
$15.95
($17.45 postpaid) from:
EPM Publications
P. O. Box 490
McLean, VA 22101
or Whole Earth Access

• See also "Clothing" (pp. 146-147).

• Clothkits is a British firm specializing in kits silkscreen-printed on high-quality fabrics. Cutting lines are marked; notions are included.
Clothkits: Catalog **$2** from Charing Cross Kits, Box 798, Meredith, NH 03253.

THE BIOLOGICAL PARALLEL of "livelihood" is niche — the position by which an organism, or a community of organisms, supports itself. Livelihood is about managing the position of survival, about doing useful work. All the talk about money on the following pages is meant to impart the lesson that money, like sunlight, is free, but that managing, storing, and passing money on costs something. Those who handle this efficiently flourish in their main purpose. Another way of saying that is: Livelihood success, whether of an individual or nation, depends on ignoring the pursuit of wealth, and paying horrific attention to the mighty details of money's pattern. These tools are for that. —Kevin Kelly

Walden
Henry David Thoreau
1854; 255 pp.
$1.95
($2.95 postpaid) from:
New American Library
120 Woodbine Street
Bergenfield, NJ 07621
or Whole Earth Access

Walden

The prime document of America's 3rd Revolution, now in progress. This edition is the one, I believe, that Thoreau would have bought. —*Steward Brand*

•

I see young men, my townsmen, whose misfortune it is to have inherited farms, houses, barns, cattle, and farming tools; for these are more easily acquired than got rid of.

•

Near the end of March, 1845, I borrowed an axe and went down to the woods by Walden Pond, nearest to where I intended to build my house, and began to cut down some tall, arrowy white pines, still in their youth, for timber. It is difficult to begin without borrowing, but perhaps it is the most generous course thus to permit your fellow-men to have an interest in your enterprise. The owner of the axe, as he released his hold on it, said that it was the apple of his eye; but I returned it sharper than I received it.

•

For more than five years I maintained myself thus solely by the labor of my hands, and I found that, by working about six weeks in a year, I could meet all the expenses of living. The whole of my winters, as well as most of my summers, I had free and clear for study. I have thoroughly tried school-keeping, and found that my expenses were in proportion, or rather out of proportion, to my income, for I was obliged to dress and train, not to say think and believe, accordingly, and I lost my time into the bargain. As I did not teach for the good of my fellow-men, but simply for a livelihood, this was a failure.

•

I learned this, at least, by my experiment: that if one advances confidently in the direction of his dreams, and endeavors to live the life which he has imagined, he will meet with a success unexpected in common hours.

Small is Beautiful
E.F. Schumacher
1975; 305 pp.
$4.95
($6.45 postpaid) from:
Harper and Row
2350 Virginia Avenue
Hagerstown, MD 21740
or Whole Earth Access

Small is Beautiful

I doubt if Americans have been so influenced by printed eloquence since Thomas Paine's **Common Sense** *helped focus our founding independence. Schumacher is fighting a similar oppression, only this time we colonized ourselves, as he reveals by sub-titling his book "Economics as if People Mattered."*

The wonder of Schumacher's work is his eminent practicality, based on his years with the British Coal Board.

With good sense and a mature spirituality, Schumacher comes on like John Henry against the mega-machine, sure that he will win, and he is. —*Stewart Brand*

•

As Gandhi said, the poor of the world cannot be helped by mass production, only by production by the masses. The system of *mass production*, based on sophisticated, highly capital-intensive, high energy-input dependent, and human labour-saving technology, presupposes that you are already rich, for a great deal of capital investment is needed to establish one single workplace. The system of *production by the masses* mobilises the priceless resources which are possessed by all human beings, their clever brains and skilful hands, *and supports them with first-class tools*. The technology of *mass production* is inherently violent, ecologically damaging, self-defeating in terms of non-renewable resources, and stultifying for the human person. The technology of *production by the masses*, making use of the best of modern knowledge and experience, is conducive to decentralisation, compatible with the laws of ecology, gentle in its use of scarce resources, and designed to serve the human person instead of making him the servant of machines. I have named it *intermediate technology* to signify that it is vastly superior to the primitive technology of bygone ages but at the same time much simpler, cheaper, and freer than the supertechnology of the rich. One can also call it self-help technology, or democratic or people's technology — a technology to which everybody can gain admittance and which is not reserved to those already rich and powerful.

The Zero-Sum Society
Lester C. Thurow
1980; 230 pp.
$5.95
($6.95 postpaid) from:
Penguin Books
299 Murray Hill Parkway
East Rutherford, NJ 07073

or Whole Earth Access

The Zero-Sum Society

"Zero-Sum" is a crack at the no-free-lunch dilemma America finds itself in after three decades of tumultuous prosperity. Whatever we do, whatever we want, whomever we listen to economically, there are real and unavoidable trade-offs. But rather than simply analyzing the downside, Thurow provides a long and articulate series of proposals to get us off dead center. He points out that it's not for the lack of solutions that we stand aside from true economic change — it's due to the fact that few of us will tolerate the possibility of redistributing our nation's wealth. Read Thurow for lack of cant and for richness and originality of thought. —*Paul Hawken*

•

The problem with zero-sum games is that the essence of problem solving is loss allocation. But this is precisely what our political process is least capable of doing. When there are economic gains to be allocated, our political process can allocate them. When there are large economic losses to be allocated, our political process is paralyzed. And with political paralysis comes economic paralysis.

•

Since economic gains are relatively easy to allocate, the basic problem comes down to one of allocating economic losses. Whose income "ought" to go down?

Historically we have used economic growth to avoid having to make this judgment. If we just have more growth, we can have more good jobs for everyone, and we won't have to worry about taking jobs away from whites and giving them to blacks. If we just have more economic growth, we won't have to worry about government collecting taxes in the Northeast and spending them in the Southwest. More is obviously better than less, and economic growth has been seen as the social lubricant that can keep different groups working together.

•

As they say in Colorado, a conservationist is a person who built his mountain cabin last year, while a developer is someone who wants to build his mountain cabin this year.

The Next Economy

Economic civilization is going around a corner the like of which it's never seen before. This is the only guidebook so far. Customers and citizens and adaptive businesses are leading the way. Governments and major corporations are following. Where we come out is better. The now waning Mass Economy amassed fabulous wealth. The emerging Information Economy may not be so opulent, but it presents greater opportunity for wholeness and happiness.

Because Hawken is a businessman — the only economist who is (Smith and Hawken tools, p. 78) — his writing has a street savvy you find nowhere else (except Peter Drucker). His economics is rooted in the individual. It speaks clearly to individual understanding and gives good counsel for individual behavior — "how to invest your life" — which in turn benefits the commonweal as well as the individual. —Stewart Brand

•

Thus the amount of energy embodied in products has become a large component of our costs. This has become especially evident as the price of oil has gone up. What has not been so evident is the effect the cost of energy has on the level of information contained within our goods and services. Since using more energy, whether directly or indirectly, makes goods more expensive and therefore less available, we will have to use less energy to produce the same or better goods if we are to maintain our standard of living. To do this, the amount of information per unit of production must increase correspondingly. Remember that we are defining *information* here as design, utility, and durability or, to put it another way, the application of the knowledge of how to best make or accomplish something. The manufacturer must seek ways to make his product a better product, using fewer resources as well as less energy and work. Doing this means finding a better material, redesigning the product, or employing new manufacturing techniques. It may mean using computers to process information, monitor the flow of work, or design components. It may mean using robots to do repetitive mechanical tasks. It may mean changing the way the product is distributed. Whatever methods of improvement are chosen, the goal is the same: to produce more using less. The critical difference between now and twenty years ago is that the manufacturer can no longer just use more energy to increase productivity. It's too expensive. Instead, the manufacturer has to become smarter at what he does.

► The *Wall Street Journal* showed two different energy forecasts. The first was the Exxon/Shell/CIA model used in the mid-to-late seventies that projected inelastic energy demand clashing with limited supply, a forecast that would result in soaring energy prices (top). The second model was a simple supply-and-demand curve, in which the rising price of a commodity lowers demand while simultaneously drawing forth more supplies (bottom).

The *Journal* cited an editorial printed five years earlier that said the free market would solve the energy problem if left to its own workings. And so it has.

EXXON / SHELL / CIA FORECAST

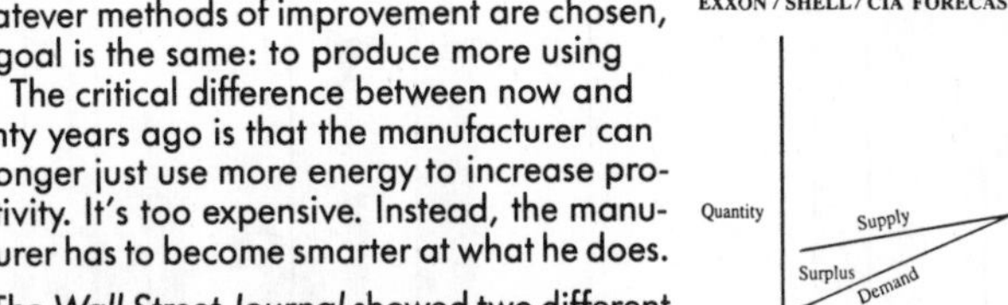

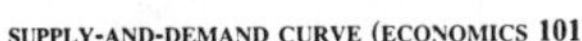
SUPPLY-AND-DEMAND CURVE (ECONOMICS 101)

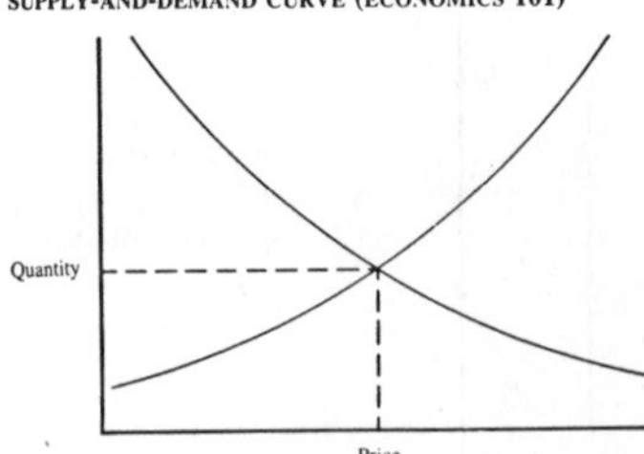

•

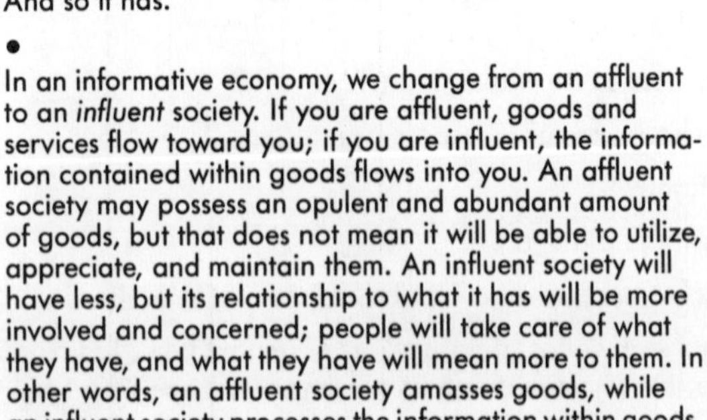
In an informative economy, we change from an affluent to an *influent* society. If you are affluent, goods and services flow toward you; if you are influent, the information contained within goods flows into you. An affluent society may possess an opulent and abundant amount of goods, but that does not mean it will be able to utilize, appreciate, and maintain them. An influent society will have less, but its relationship to what it has will be more involved and concerned; people will take care of what they have, and what they have will mean more to them. In other words, an affluent society amasses goods, while an influent society processes the information within goods.

•

The informative economy requires more intelligence from everyone — management, labor, consumers, governments. Those who do not become learners again, regardless or age or rank, will find themselves at an increasing disadvanatage as the informative economy takes root.

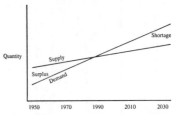

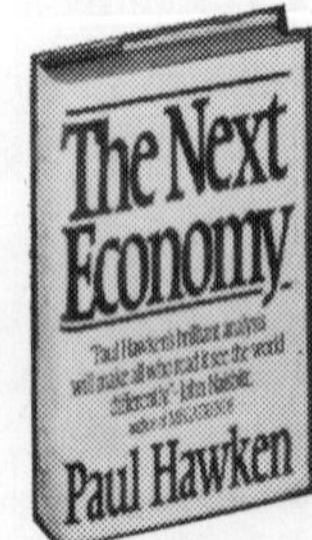

The Next Economy
Paul Hawken
1983; 215 pp.
$14.50
($16.50 postpaid) from:
Henry Holt and Co.
521 5th Avenue,
12th Floor
New York, NY 10175
or Whole Earth Access

Innovation and Entrepreneurship

According to long-term business cycles reliable in the past, the economy should be bleak right now. It's not. What appears to be taking up the slack is an entrepreneurial zest and ferment unlike any in history, and it's being built into the society. The old-time master of management, Peter Drucker, has written his handbook of entrepreneurial "practice and principles." There's a lot of such books these days. He blows them away. —Stewart Brand

•

Three hundred years of technology came to an end after World War II. During those three centuries the model for technology was a mechanical one: the events that go on inside a star such as the sun. This period began when an otherwise almost unknown French physicist, Denis Papin, envisaged the steam engine around 1680. They ended when we replicated in the nuclear explosion the events inside a star. For these three centuries advance in technology meant — as it does in mechanical processes — more speed, higher temperatures, higher pressures. Since the end of Word War II, however, the model of technology has become the biological process, the events inside an organism. And in an organism, processes are not organized around energy in the physicist's meaning of the term. They are organized around information.

•

Entrepreneurship rests on a theory of economy and society. The theory sees change as normal and indeed as healthy. And it sees the major task in society — and especially in the economy — as doing something different rather than doing better what is already being done. This is basically what Say, two hundred years ago, meant when he coined the term *entrepreneur*. It was intended as a manifesto and as a declaration of dissent: the entrepreneur upsets and disorganizes. As Joseph Schumpeter formulated it, his task is "creative destruction."

•

Specifically, systematic innovation means monitoring *seven sources* for innovative opportunity.

- *The unexpected* — the unexpected success, the unexpected failure;
- *The incongruity* — between reality as it actually is and reality as it is assumed to be or as it "ought to be";
- *Innovation based on process need;*
- *Changes in industry structure or market structure* that catch everyone unawares;
- *Demographics* (population changes);
- *Changes in perception, mood, and meaning;*
- *New knowledge,* both scientific and nonscientific.

• Easily the most astute seer in business is Peter Drucker. This is his classic.
Managing in Turbulent Times: Peter F. Drucker, 1980; 239 pp. **$6.95** ($8.45 postpaid) from Harper and Row, 2350 Virginia Avenue, Hagerstown, MD 21740 (or Whole Earth Access).

• Also see Drucker's **The Effective Executive** (p. 193).

Innovation and Entrepreneurship
Peter F. Drucker
1985; 277 pp.
$19.45
($20.95 postpaid) from:
Harper and Row
2350 Virginia Avenue
Hagerstown, MD 21740
or Whole Earth Access

The Four Illusions of Money

and the non-money truths they hide

by
Michael Phillips, Salli Rasberry, and Andorra Freeman

Condensed from Honest Business *(p. 192).*

WHY DO PEOPLE WORK AT JOBS they don't like? Why do they say their goal in life is to "make a lot of money?"

"A lot of money will let me be free to do what I want."

"People with a lot of money command more respect from others."

"I need more money for my family."

"Money is necessary for security in old age."

These statements are illusions — inaccurate perceptions of the world we live in.

Nearly all high school students seek "a lot of money" as a lifetime goal. Less than 5 percent of them will become wealthy. The remaining 95 percent will shape their lives around these inappropriate values.

"A lot of money will let me be free to do what I want."

You can feel this way when you work at a job you dislike, or when you desperately want to buy some object, experience, or service. Instead, deal with these feelings directly and positively. Write down your specific goals — the things you need (experiences, knowledge, skills, talents) to shape the kind of person you want to be. Make sure your list doesn't include money itself.

You may find from your list that having a lot of money will help you achieve goals a little sooner. But that effect is not worth the time spent, nor vigor and joy lost, earning money. Most accomplishments require, instead of money, that you actively pursue them and *learn* in the process. If you want to travel the world, join the crew of a sailing ship. Later you'll be useful as a sailor and have the necessary great stories about hitting sharks on the nose in the Bahamas.

Check your list again and see how many possessions are listed there. The possessions unrelated to your livelihood are often amassed to help you feel better about yourself. Many of them can be borrowed from friends who are willing to share — everything from a ski condominium in Snowmass to an Aston-Martin race car. Or consider renting pieces of equipment you are unable to locate among your friends. Find and restore "discards," or trade your existing possessions or skills to a friend or neighbor in exchange for something you want.

In examining your values it's helpful to talk to someone who is wise. The goal of amassing money is traditionally called "greed" and regardless of your motives (freedom, charity, etc.), the results will not be what you hope for. Instead, the teachers of tradition tell us to become good at the things we want to do. In that lies our freedom.

"People with a lot of money command more respect from others."

We often believe that the owners of the big cars and houses can do much more than we can. If indeed they can, then it probably isn't their money. It's other qualities such as knowledge, experience, and friends.

It helps to make a list of the qualities that lead others to respect us — qualities we want our children or friends to have. Do words such as loyal, honest, and generous occur on your list? Each of these qualities has to do with how we conduct our daily lives, not how much money we have.

Now list the people you love. See if they're ranked in order of wealth. There is probably no relationship. Money isn't a reason for friendship or respect.

"I need more money for my family."

When someone works at a job that they find unpleasant, monotonous, stressful, or frustrating, and say they do it for their family, they're talking nonsense.

Stop and ask your family what they want. Would your children rather have a Winnebago camper or would they rather have time to spend with you and go on a camping trip with ordinary sleeping bags and tents? Give your family the choice between those possessions and the time and peace of mind you divert from them to earn the possessions.

Look at a picture of two houses — a glamorous mansion, and a modest home with a bicycle near the front door. Which one has a happier family? Most people would say "I can't tell," because we know in our hearts money and possessions have nothing to do with happiness.

"Money is necessary for security in old age."

Michael is blessed with a father who is a living contradiction of this. When he was 65, his father retired from teaching anthropology and social sciences with a modest pension and Social Security income of $300 a month. He sold his home and belongings, bought a van in England, and drove East with his wife (Michael's parents were divorced 15 years earlier). He got teaching jobs along the way and stopped anywhere he found interesting.

They ended up in Malaysia where they bought part of an island near Singapore for $2,000. They now live with a sandy beach, coconut trees, fresh fish, and lots of friends, for less than $100 a month. They save their money for numerous trips to all parts of the world and the U.S. Surprisingly, they see many of their old friends regularly; everyone wants to visit their tropical paradise for a vacation.

In the seven years since Michael's father retired he hasn't touched his savings. How about health care? One of his closest friends is chief of a nearby first-class research hospital. Friendship is better than money.

People who are happy in their old age have the same qualities as Michael's father: being friendly and flexible. Money makes no difference. With friends, especially ones of all ages, you can solve problems that other people can't handle. Friends also provide vitality, emotional support, and new friends — especially valuable after age 75 when one out of ten old friends dies each year.

Flexibility is essential as your body becomes less reliable. We all know old people who say, "I can't sleep in that bed, it's too soft," and "I don't like to be around those kinds of people." With that attitude, who wants to be around *them?*

Michael's mother has lived on her own for 20 years — always gregarious and flexible. Even past seventy, she's involved in city politics, art-related projects, and the ACLU. When she visits Michael, his friends insist on spending time with her. She travels regularly, often invited on global trips for her company and knowledge. You don't hear her complaining about discomfort or how terrible the world is today.

How do you prepare for old age and uncertainty? By being the kind of person other people want to be around. Competent, helpful, flexible, curious, generous, and experienced in dealing with the world.

The moral

If you have friends and make an effort to be an interesting person, money is irrelevant. However, if you are a loner, rather selfish, with narrow interests, then making a lot of money may be your only way to make it through life. ■

What Color Is Your Parachute?

In a domain positively viscous with lame books, this perennially best-selling guide to job-seeking has no competition. It is updated annually (that's impressive), it is cheery for a reader who could probably use some cheer, and it has sound, detailed advice for an all-important task that is well-served with a bit of skill. —Stewart Brand

•

Just because the opportunities for higher level jobs or careers are harder to uncover, the higher you aim the fewer people you will have to compete with — for that job. In fact, if you uncover a need which your skills can help solve, that organization may well create a brand new job for you. This means you will be competing with no one, since you will be the sole applicant.

•

If you come in to the employer's office, having done your homework first — knowing a *lot* about yourself, and knowing *a lot* about this organization, any employer *that you would want to work for, anyway* — will be impressed. You will stand out from other job-hunters or career-changers, *as one who is better at solving problems* than the others. Because, obviously, you went about solving *this* problem — the job-hunt — in such a thorough and professional way.

•

The importance of sending a thank you letter to *everyone* is one of the most essential steps in the entire job-hunt. *Yet it is the most overlooked step in the entire process.* We know of one woman who was told she was hired because she was the *only* interviewee, out of 39, who sent a thank you letter after the interview.

That's right, the thank you letter may actually get you the job. *You cannot afford to think of this as simply an optional exercise. It is critical to your getting hired.*

•

You can't decide what you want from a job until you're clear on what you want from life.

What Color Is Your Parachute?
Richard Nelson Bolles
1986; 397 pp.
$8.95
($9.95 postpaid) from:
Ten Speed Press
P. O. Box 7123
Berkeley, CA 94707
or Whole Earth Access

You must identify the persons who have the power to hire you and show them how your skills can help them with their problems.

The Damn Good Resume Guide

This useful book advocates a short, precisely tailored resume as the best aid in a job search. Yana Parker developed her resume models based on her own years working for a state employment office, her more recent experiences running a resume service, and extensive feedback from employers. It's all summed up here in 60 highly readable pages which include 14 sample resumes illustrating how different individuals with varied skills put their best feet forward.

At least one person I know got her present job by using this book. Recommended. —*Jay Kinney*

•

a) *Quantify* — Tell HOW MANY, HOW OFTEN, describe tangible products and results.

Examples: "supervised 10 people," "produced 24 consecutive issues of a 16-page newsletter," "sold a million dollars of real estate the first year as an agent."

b) *Create* Pictures in the reader's mind — Quantifying is one way (you can SEE the 10 people above, and the 16-page newsletter and the million dollars). Being very explicit is another; avoid vagueness. Generalizations do NOT create mental pictures and so they don't "register" with the reader.

The Damn Good Resume Guide
Yana Parker
1983; 60 pp.
$4.95
($5.95 postpaid) from:
Ten Speed Press
P. O. Box 7123
Berkeley, CA 94707
or Whole Earth Access

Two Approaches To Writing Your Resume

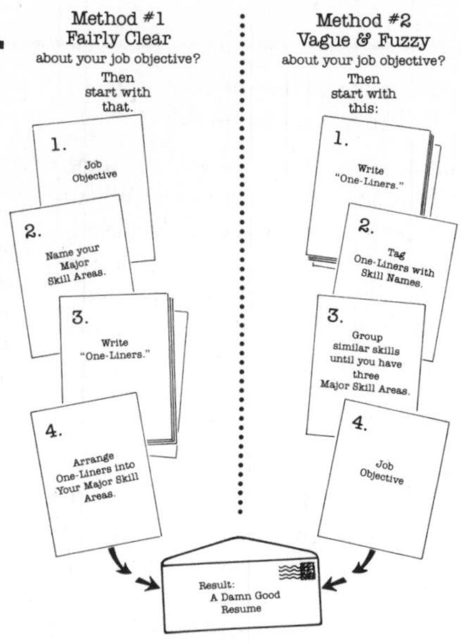

•

"CAN'T I JUST SKIP THE JOB OBJECTIVE? I DON'T WANT TO LIMIT MYSELF."

NO!

Clearly stating your Objective serves to FOCUS you, not to box you in. It's critically important to KNOW WHAT YOUR OBJECTIVE IS, as explicitly as possible, and to state it, and then to have everything else on your resume directly related to it. THAT'S what makes it a DAMN GOOD RESUME.

The American Almanac of Jobs and Salaries

An amazingly complete and comprehensive survey of what people do for work here in America and what they get paid for it. Useful if you want to find out what is ahead of you in your job, or if you are surveying different professions, or if you just want to learn something about the social fabric as it applies to power, prestige, and money in the workplace. —*Bruce E. Coughran*

•

In towns and cities, both large and small, from coast to coast, starting salaries for teachers are usually between $12,000 and $14,000, with maximums after twenty years (with an M.A.) hovering between $24,000 and $27,000. Exceptions to these figures can usually be found (especially for high maximums) in large cities such as Los Angeles, Chicago, Philadelphia, and Washington, D.C., where local wage rates are high and where teaching conditions are often horrendous. Still, even in these areas a teacher rarely earns over $30,000.

The American Almanac of Jobs and Salaries
John W. Wright
1984; 779 pp.
$12.95
($13.95 postpaid) from:
Avon Books
P. O. Box 767
Dresden, TN 38225
or Whole Earth Access

The Rights of Employees

Surprise: American employees don't have many rights. This book from the American Civil Liberties Union explains the murkiness of labor law in a relatively clear question-and-answer format. It includes discrimination, occupational safety, privacy on the job, sexual harassment, pensions, overtime, and unions. If you earn wages, you probably need it — even if you don't realize why until after you read it. —*Art Kleiner*

The Rights of Employees
Wayne Outten
and Noah Kinigstein
1983; 369 pp.
$3.95
($4.95 postpaid) from:
American Civil Liberties Union — Books
1400 20th Street NW
Room 119
Washington, DC 20036
or Whole Earth Access

The 100 Best Companies To Work For In America

This is the best book on management for operating managers. It has one clear lesson. Among these 100 companies, of all sizes and in a wide range of businesses, there are at least 50 different management styles. They all lead to profitability and satisfied employees. It's a great antidote for fads that continually sweep management theory, and it's reassuring for the innovative manager who wants to try something new. —*Michael Phillips*

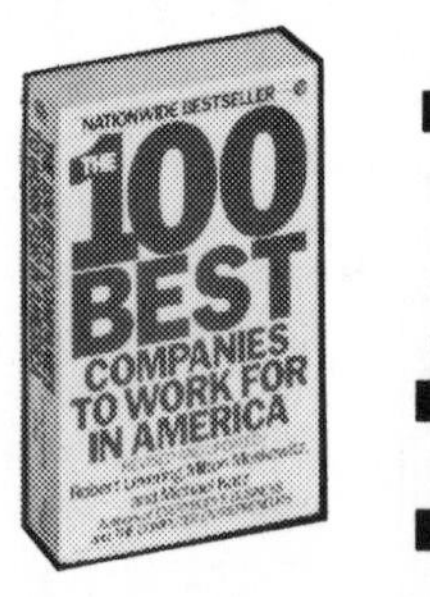

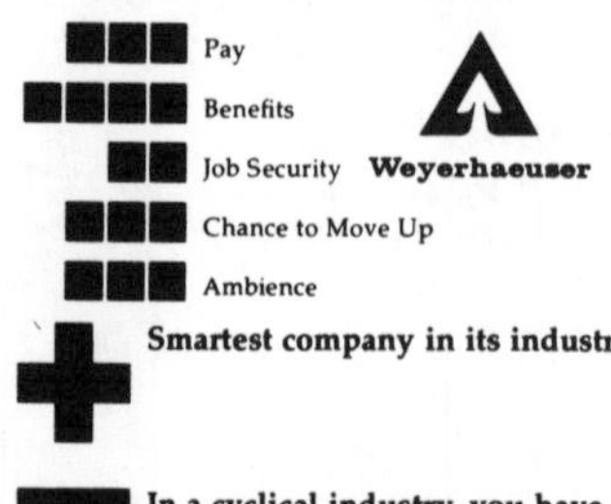

•

Weyerhaeuser Company

This is the class act in the timber industry. If you wanted to work in wood products, which can range anywhere from planting and taking care of trees to cutting them down and then processing them into salable products of all kinds (logs, lumber, plywood, shipping cartons, newsprint, disposable diapers), then Weyerhaeuser would have to be the company to look at first. It's one of the biggest, fattest cats in its industry but has a well-developed sense of responsibility to go with that size, so much so that an *Audubon* magazine article on the company was once titled "Best of the S.O.B.'s."

The 100 Best Companies To Work For In America
Robert Levering,
Milton Moskowitz
and Michael Katz
1985; 396 pp.
$8.95
($10.45 postpaid) from:
New American Library
120 Woodbine Street
Bergenfield, NJ 07621
or Whole Earth Access

Hewlett Packard
MEDAL OF DEFIANCE
CHARLES H. HOUSE

Awarded in recognition of extraordinary contempt and defiance beyond the normal call of engineering duty.

In total defiance of adverse market studies and surveys concluding the existence of a worldwide market of no more than 50 total large screen electrostatic displays, Charles H. House, using all means available — principally pen, tongue, and airplane to extol an unrecognized technical contribution, planted the seeds for a new market resulting in the shipment of 17,769 large screen displays to date.

1 April 1982

Intrapreneuring

This book is aimed at the corporation that wants to keep its entrepreneurs happy and creative, and at those entrepreneurs who need strategy for being effective within a corporation. Both sides of the coin are explored with many examples of people who developed significant new products within the confines of corporate life.
—*Michael Phillips*

•

In the beginning no one else understands the intrapreneur's ideas well enough to make them work. As a result, others say it can't work. Intrapreneurs thus find themselves crossing organizational boundaries to do what are officially other people's jobs.

When intrapreneur Art Fry, the inventor of Post-it Notes (those now familiar yellow pads with the gently adhesive backs), was told by the marketing division his idea wasn't wanted by customers, he did his own market research. When manufacturing told him Post-it Notes were impossible to make, he worked out the production technology himself. No problem, no matter how far from his supposed area of expertise as a lab person, fell outside his responsibility, because Art was an intrapreneur.

•

In almost every corporation, there exist large numbers of hard-boiled characters who no longer believe the platitudes that emanate from the corporate staff. They know the system backward and forward and know how to acquire what they need to get the job done, regardless of what the official system dictates. Whether he knows it or not, the CEO has turned large chunks of the corporation's assets over to these people and their informal network of swapping favors and equipment. All he can do under the current system is hope the corporation has chosen the right people.

Intrapreneuring
Gifford Pinchot III
1985; 368 pp.
$19.45
($20.95 postpaid) from:
Harper and Row
2350 Virginia Ave.
Hagerstown, MD 21740
or Whole Earth Access

Further Up the Organization

This book has an amazing amount of truth, some of it pretty radical truth, about how to run an enterprise.
—*Stewart Brand*

•

When you're off on a business trip or a vacation, pretend you're a customer. Telephone some part of your organization and ask for help. You'll run into some real horror shows. Don't blow up and ask for name, rank, and serial number — you're trying to correct, not punish. If it happens on a call to the Dubuque office, just suggest to the manager (through channels, dummy) that he make a few test calls himself.

Then try calling yourself up and see what indignities you've built into your own defenses.

•

A lesson very few have learned: If you want to approach the head of XYZ Corporation, call him cold. Tell him who you are and why you want to talk to him. A direct and uncomplicated relationship will follow.

The common mistake is to look for a mutual friend — or a friend's friend on his board, in his bank or investment bank or law firm — to introduce you. This starts all sorts of vibrations and usually results in a half-assed prologue by the intermediary, who is apt to grind both edges of his own ax.

•

Freedom from a secretary

For years I had the standard executive equipment — a secretary. Most of them are very good. Then I used the Man from Mars approach. Then I didn't have a secretary. Here's my analysis:

TRIPS

Before: One of my close associates had a great secretary. Whenever he called in from out of town to get or leave messages, she was "away from her desk." And when he came back, she would have all the mail and memos and appointments spread out so he couldn't find his desk for two days.

After: When I called in, the telephone operators had my messages. The mailroom also had a rubber stamp: "I'm away. Please handle this in your own style and don't tell me what you did. Thanks. R.C.T." They'd open the mail, stamp it, route it appropriately. When I got back — clean desk.

Further Up The Organization
Robert Townsend
1984; 254 pp.
$15.95
($16.95 postpaid) from:
Random House
Order Dept.
400 Hahn Road
Westminster, MD 21157
or Whole Earth Access

Games Mother Never Taught You

Corporations are modelled after the military and women must understand this model to function in any large business. Betty Harragan explains the jargon and system of the corporate world. Why didn't we have this book fifteen years ago? It would have saved me and my women business colleagues from reinventing the wheel. Read it now, and you'll have the opportunity to invent a new game or at least succeed at the old one. —*Anne Kent Rush*

•

While you're at your salary research, if you discover that a man who held your job previously got paid more than you or that a man doing substantially the same work as you (never mind his title, the job functions are the key) is getting paid more, don't go home in fury and frustration. Pick up the phone book, look under U.S. Government, Department of Labor, Wage and Hours Division. Call up and ask about the simple process to file an Equal Pay Complaint. No one will ever find out because this agency, which enforces the Equal Pay Act, operates in secrecy and confidentiality.

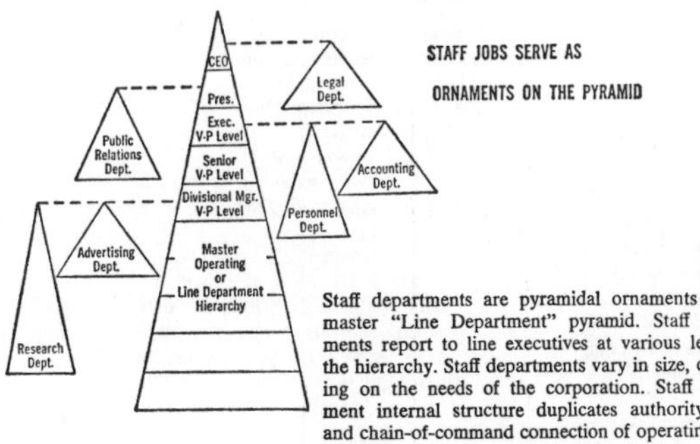

Staff departments are pyramidal ornaments to the master "Line Department" pyramid. Staff departments report to line executives at various levels of the hierarchy. Staff departments vary in size, depending on the needs of the corporation. Staff department internal structure duplicates authority levels and chain-of-command connection of operating pyramid except that the top job is head of department instead of corporate chief executive.

Games Mother Never Taught You
Betty Lehan Harragan
1977; 400 pp.
$4.95
($5.95 postpaid) from:
Warner Books
P. O. Box 690
New York, NY 10019
or Whole Earth Access

• Who makes what and what is made by whom. Astoundingly complete! At your library.
Thomas Register of American Manufacturers: Annual; 21 volumes, 33,664 pp. **$210** postpaid from Thomas Register/Sales Division, 250 West 34th Street, New York, NY 10109 (or Whole Earth Access).

The Grass Roots Fundraising Book • Grassroots Fundraising Journal

Joan Flanagan tells how to put some power in your organization's purse, without worrying about strings that may be attached to government or foundation grants. The book methodically outlines the planning process for fundraising events of all sizes, from a neighborhood book sale to a $50-a-plate dinner, and it offers suggestions for year-round fundraising like membership dues or setting your group up in business. As treasurer of an organization struggling to meet a $55,000-a-year budget, I referred to Flanagan's book for both inspiration and nuts-and-bolts advice. —Nancy E. Dunn

The journal follows in the book's footsteps — giving concrete examples of experience and always relating it back to the basic issues: Your supporters are the best source of funds, and they need to know what you're doing and that you have a role for them that is interesting and useful. Details to carry this out range from good mailing-list maintenance to imaginative events and persistence. —Michael Phillips

The Grass Roots Fundraising Book
Joan Flanagan
1982; 219 pp.
$11.95
($13.95 postpaid) from:
Contemporary Books
180 N. Michigan Avenue
Chicago, IL 60601
or Whole Earth Access

Grassroots Fundraising Journal
Kim Klein and
Lisa Honig, Editors
$20/year
(6 issues) from:
Grassroots Fundraising Journal
P. O. Box 14754
San Francisco, CA 94114

•

Grass roots fundraising can be a magnet to bring in new members. People are naturally more eager to join a group of people they have met at a party or pot luck dinner. After they have had a chance to meet the folks they will feel more comfortable at a business meeting or an action. Everyone feels shy in a new group and afraid of being different from the old members. The more controversial your program is, the more timid potential members may be about joining unless they know a current member. The hoopla and fun of fundraising events give the new people a chance to learn who you really are in the most pleasant surroundings.

•

Always consider which fundraising events will be most economical in terms of the volunteers' time. It is much easier and quicker to ask for one $100 donation than it is to sell twenty $5 dance tickets or four hundred raffle chances for a quarter each. The time of your skilled members is your most valuable asset — don't waste it. . . It takes thorough research to calculate what will be the highest amount you can get from each giver, and it take real courage to ask for it. Boldness pays off. The more money you can get from each meeting, the more time you will have left to prepare your testimony for the city housing committee. —*Grass Roots Fundraising Book*

•

Make your income and expenses public information. Prin your budget, and your list of donors in your newsletter, and have a financial report at your office available to anyone who wants to see it. (Don't worry about being swamped with requests — people generally figure if you are willing to be public, you have nothing to hide.)

•

If you're looking for a profitable and fun way to raise money, staging your own (legal) kidnapping may be the answer. In this "kidnapping" you put one or more people, one at a time, in a "cage," holding them there for "ransom."

Your "victims" should be well known and respected people with a good sense of humor who will cheerfully go along with your plans. For a church fundraiser, the pastor and his wife are good choices, or a church council member, a deacon, the associate pastor, etc. (For other groups, choose a city council member, TV personality, local music celebrity — the list is endless.) —*Grassroots Fundraising Journal*

The Foundation Directory • National Directory of Corporate Charity

The most effective way to get grant money is to be Highly Visible. —Stewart Brand

The method that works for 95 percent of all successful grant applications is to apply to an appropriate agency every year for three years. Why three years? They don't trust you until they know you're established. These two reference books will tell you how to find the right agencies for your project. —Michael Phillips

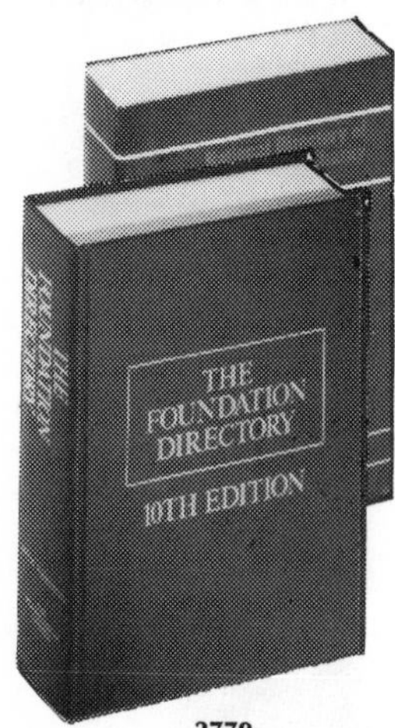

The Foundation Directory
Loren Renz
1985; 885 pp.
$65
($67 postpaid)

National Directory of Corporate Charity
Sam Sternberg
1984; 500 pp.
$80
($82 postpaid)
Both from:
Foundation Center
79 Fifth Avenue
New York, NY 10003

2779
New-Land Foundation, Inc., The
200 Park Ave., Suite 3014
New York 10166 (212) 867-5500

Incorporated in 1941 in New York.
Donor(s): Joseph Buttinger, Muriel M. Buttinger.†
Financial data: (yr. ended 12/31/82): Assets, $9,698,366 (M); gifts received, $42,246; expenditures, $1,063,733, including $899,169 for 123 grants (high: $50,000; low: $500).
Purpose and activities: Broad purposes; grants for civil rights, mental health, environmental preservation, arms control and disarmament, cultural programs, minority and medical education, and social services.
Types of support awarded: General purposes, annual campaigns, seed money, research.
Limitations: No grants to individuals; no loans.
Publications: Application guidelines.
Application information:
Initial approach: Proposal
Copies of proposal: 2
Board meeting date(s): Spring and fall
Final notification: 2 weeks after board meeting
Write: Robert Wolf, President
Officers and Directors: Robert Wolf, President; Renee G. Schwartz, Secretary-Treasurer; Constance Harvey, Hal Harvey, Joan Harvey, Anna Frank Loeb, Albert Solnit.
Number of staff: None.
Employer Identification Number: 136086562

—***Foundation Directory***

How to Read a Financial Report

This is not an accounting book. It is a hard-nosed and clear analysis of what accounting information can tell you about your business, or any business. This understanding is vital when considering your needs for a loan or new capital, when selling a business or buying one, or when trying to cope with business problems. This is the best book on this subject, and the only book aimed at intelligent people with no academic accounting background. —Michael Phillips

How to Read a Financial Report
John A. Tracy
1983; 161 pp.
$9.95 postpaid from:
John Wiley & Sons
Order Department
1 Wiley Drive
Somerset, NJ 08873
or Whole Earth Access

•

Behind all the numbers is a simple, vital concept you must never lose sight of — *cash flow.* Business is run by keeping money moving. Financial statements report *where the money came from, where it's invested for the time being,* and, most important, *how often it has turned over.*

$ O YOU WANNA START your own small business? A half-million people do just that every year, and a hefty majority of those people go bankrupt within a year. Why? For businesses started by novices, the Number One reason is probably lack of foresight. The people just don't think their ideas through very well. They don't do any "market research," which is just a fancy term or "look before you leap."

t's a real shame, too, because a few nights reading with these few well-chosen books would save a lot of hese failed businesses.

—Bernard Kamoroff

Small-Time Operator
Bernard Kamoroff
1986; 190 pp.
$9.95
($10.95 postpaid) from:
Bell Springs Publishing Co.
P. O. Box 640
Laytonville, CA 95454
or Whole Earth Access

Small-Time Operator

Small-Time Operator *is most of the financial record-keeping information you need for a small business, plus one year's worth of ledger forms with excellent instructions on how to use them, along with good advice on key issues (such as when the IRS is likely to consider someone your employee).*

The author lives the advice in the book. You can order a copy directly from him in Laytonville. He will package and ship it to you after he feeds the chickens and tends the garden. —*Michael Phillips*

•

The most important lesson to learn, I feel, is that you can start out easily and simply. You don't have to make the Big Plunge, selling everything you own and going into debt. Start slowly, try it out and learn as you go. You'll get there.

•

I've known a lot of people in business — some who made it, some who didn't. And while nobody has a guaranteed secret for success in business, I believe that there are a few basic characteristics that you've got to have or be willing to develop if you're going to start a business, *any* business.

The first and most important characteristic, I feel, is a clear head and the ability to organize your mind and your life. The "absent-minded professor" may be a genius, but he will never keep a business together. In running a small business, you are going to have to deal with many different people, keep schedules, meet deadlines, organize paperwork, pay bills, and the list goes on. It's all part of every business. So if balancing your checkbook is too much for you, or you just burned up your car engine because you forgot the oil, maybe you're not cut out for business. The work in a small business is rarely complicated, but it has to be done and done on time. Remember, this is going to be *your* business. It's all up to you.

•

The best definition of an entrepreneur is someone who spends 16 hours a day working for himself so that he doesn't have to work 8 hours a day for someone else. —Mark Stevens, "Profit Secrets For Small Business"

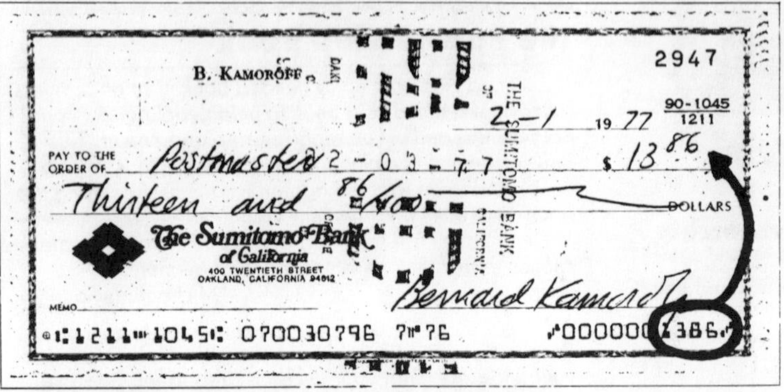

Another possible error if your bank account won't balance: compare the amount of the check to the computer-punched amount in the bottom right-hand corner of the cancelled check. They should be the same.

Starting on a Shoestring

I've known for a long time that starting a business with little or no money is not only possible, it happens all the time. I started two businesses that way; and many of my tax clients are small businesses whose start-up capital borders on zero. This book spells out how it's done better than any other I've seen, and is equally useful for people who have a lot of money to start with. Business success really has little to do with how much money you do or don't have; it has more to do with common sense.
—*Bernard Kamoroff*

•

You can start a business with one-tenth the capital normally required (or even no cash at all), but in return you must work ten times as hard to make it succeed.

•

So the message is clear. If you don't have the experience in the type business you have in mind, then don't try to open it just yet. Defer it until you can obtain valuable "hands-on" experience as an employee. You may have to moonlight to pick up the experience or sacrifice some income for a few months but it will be a much smaller loss than what you will sustain by operating a business you know nothing about.

•

Most people think money is the number one priority in selecting a business. Put it on the bottom of your list. The psychic rewards — enjoyment — head the list. When you enjoy your business, the success and money are bound to follow, but it never quite works in reverse. And if you happen to make serious money in a business you don't enjoy, I'll guarantee you'd make twice the money in a business — any business — that does get your adrenalin flowing.

•

MBA students at Suffolk University Business School surveyed start-ups to determine the relationship of rent and equipment costs to profits and success. The most successful businesses had the lowest rent and capital equipment costs. The study went further: 92 percent of the businesses examined could have started on an appreciably less expensive scale, with no anticipated drop in sales but with a healthy jump in profits. The big spenders were everywhere. With a tighter purse string they would now have a fatter purse.

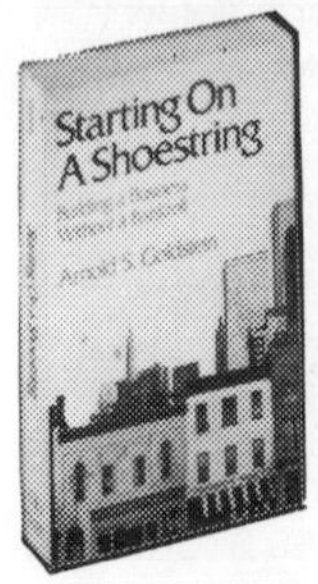

Starting On A Shoestring
Arnold S. Goldstein
1984; 286 pp.
$12.95
($13.95 postpaid) from:
John Wiley & Sons
Order Department
1 Wiley Drive
Somerset, NJ 08873
or Whole Earth Access

Honest Business
Michael Phillips and Salli Rasberry
1981; 209 pp.

$6
($7 postpaid) from:
Random House
Order Dept.
400 Hahn Road
Westminster, MD 21157
or Whole Earth Access

Honest Business

Innovative and practical are not contradictory, merely seldom met with together. The reason this book is full of small business advice which is both innovative and practical is that it is primarily reporting — anecdotal material from the Briarpatch, an entrepreneurial network in the San Francisco Bay area with a wealth of gentle success behind it. Michael Phillips has been in the thick of it since the beginning in the early 70s. Here is the full body of what he has learned and has been teaching.

—Stewart Brand

***Honest Business** is unique in its combination of simple truths and business moxie.*

—Bernard Kamoroff

•

What are the things we can learn about our businesses from studying the books? Two good things are: what days off you can take, and when you can take a vacation.

Sherry had bought Skin Zone, a small bath and scents business, which she had previously managed for a period of six months. Now that she was the owner she had to work seven days a week to cover the costs of the loan she had gotten to buy the business. After a few months of working seven days a week she looked pretty bad and couldn't shake off her constant cold. With just a tiny amount of surplus cash, how could she afford to take even one day off?

We took a look at her daily sales record and found that Sunday sales were generally quite low, with most of the transactions in the mid-afternoon. Instead of keeping the store open seven hours on Sunday, Sherry decided to open it from 1:00 to 4:00 and hire a friend, who agreed to work for $3 an hour during those times. We knew from the books that even if she lost all of her Sunday business it would not significantly affect the net income.

The Green Gulch Greengrocer in San Francisco was started by the Zen Center, primarily as a way of helping the neighborhood, secondarily as a source of income.

The result: Sherry regained her health, which helped to improve the overall business climate, and the Sunday sales remained about the same.

•

The opportunities for fun in business are endless. They are the natural consequence of running an honest business.

The Partnership Book
Denis Clifford and Ralph Warner
1984; 221 pp.

$17.95
($19.45 postpaid) from:
Nolo Press
950 Parker Street
Berkeley, CA 94710
or Whole Earth Access

The Partnership Book

The second most commonly needed book in small business (after bookkeeping) is a book to help people understand partnerships and set up a partnership agreement. This book is perfect, complete, wise, and miraculous. If potential partners can write an agreement themselves using this book, they have a 70 percent greater chance of succeeding than if they use a lawyer, and a 300 percent greater chance than if they have no written agreement.

—Michael Phillips

•

Partnership agreements are simply contracts that express your understanding, your decisions, regarding how you want your business relationship to work. There is a body of law — primarily the Uniform Partnership Act (the U.P.A.) — which establishes most basic legal rules applicable to partnerships, such as the date a partnership commences. However, almost all these rules can be varied — if you decide to do so — by an express statement in the partnership agreement. As we proceed, we discuss not only what the standard rules are, but how you can alter them if you wish.

Who would have thought we'd be naturals in the chicken biz?

•

Subjects often covered in partnership agreements:
• Name of the partnership (and names of individual partners);
• Term of the partnership (indefinite, or for a set, limited time); and date started;
• Purpose of the partnership; the type of business to be conducted;
• Personal business goals of the partners and partnership;
• Cash and property contributed to start the business;
• What happens if more cash is needed;
• Skills to be contributed (hours to be worked, work duties of partners, management roles, possible other business activities, etc.);
• Distribution of profits;
• Losses (how divided);
• Salaries, guarantees, or drawing accounts;
• Disputes (rule by majority voting, provision for arbitration or mediation, etc.);
• Sale, assignment, etc. of a partnership interest;
• Admission of new partners;
• Expulsion of a partner;
• Continuing business if a partner withdraws, dies, becomes disabled, or retires;
• Determining value of a departing partner's interest, provisions for payment of that interest;
• Dissolution, winding up, and termination.

Franchise Investigation and Contract Negotiation
Harry Gross and Robert S. Levy
1985; 48 pp.

$3.95
($4.95 postpaid) from:
Pilot Books
103 Cooper Street
Babylon, NY 11702

Franchise Investigation and Contract Negotiation

Personally, I would discourage anybody from buying a franchise business. You pay someone else money — sometimes a large sum of money — to use their business name, to do business according to their rules, and to sell what they tell you to sell. After a while you begin to wonder whether you are starting a business or paying a whole lot of money to be ordered around. Obviously, franchises are profitable; there are more McDonalds than there are slugs after a spring rain. But franchises can be trouble, too, especially if you hook up with an unsound or unstable company. You will need quality professional help.

This is an important little book on the subject. If its 40-some pages don't scare you away from franchises, probably nothing will. Don't do anything until you read it.

—Bernard Kamoroff

"We have to get far away from the workshop where we can play and forget the business," says Chris Caswell. He and his wife, Teresa, build and sell Celtic harps.

10 Tips For Beginning Couples

Janet and Dick Strombeck, owners of Sun Designs in Delafield, Wisconsin, say the following tips are helpful for couples who are just breaking into business together:

1. Be honest with yourself about your egos, emotions, capabilities and motivation. Discuss feelings with your partner. You cannot shortcut on these things.

2. Have 100 percent faith in each other.

3. Understand that all people have individual needs. Be prepared to bite your tongue and overlook unimportant gaffs in the relationship. It may be your day tomorrow. Keep your eyes on the major goals and overall performance.

4. Make a list of what you will be giving up personally (time, money, social life, etc.) and make a conscious decision.

5. If you have children at home, talk to them. Tell them what you want to do and why, and how it will affect them.

6. Evaluate personal finances. Can you afford this? Are you willing to sell equity in a pinch?

7. Is your health good enough to stand the work load?

8. Prepare for a commitment of time, thoughts and finances.

9. Decide you will have quality in whatever you do and make employees understand this.

10. Believe in yourself and your spouse. Be patient. Train yourselves to be positive in overcoming adversity. Take a day at a time and it will soon develop into a habi and a way of life.

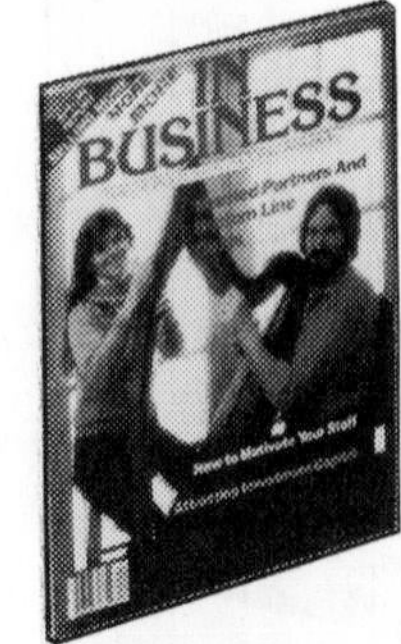

In Business
Jerome Goldstein, Editor
$18/year
(6 issues) from:
The JG Press
P. O. Box 323
Emmaus, PA 18049

In Business

The most essential magazine a small business can get is the main trade journal for that particular type of business. Inquire of other business owners, or consult ***The Small Business Sourcebook*** *(p. 197) for the best one.*

The most helpful general business magazine I've found for the small-time operator is ***In Business****, a friendly, low-key bimonthly. It runs feature articles about unusual success stories: it recently featured a family-run dairy, a short-line railroad, and a backwoods bed and breakfast. The magazine has regular how-to advice on advertising, marketing, and the like. For my own taste, I find* ***In Business*** *a bit too tame, reluctant to be blunt or controversial (a problem you won't, by the way, likely find in a trade journal). But it is valuable; I subscribe to it.*
—Bernard Kamoroff

•

No deductions for front lawn:
Generally, decorations, furnishings, and maintenance of business premises can be written off (or depreciated) as business expenses. When the business is conducted in the taxpayer's home, however, the rules change. Deductions are allowed for business use of the taxpayer's residence only if they are allocable to a portion of the home used exclusively and regularly as the principal place of a trade or business, or to meet clients and customers in the course of a business.

The taxpayer, a professional landscape architect, worked out of his home and had his office there. In the yard, on display to customers who visited, was his own landscaping, on which he incurred significant expense. Had the landscaping been on different, nonresidential premises, some deduction for the planting and upkeep would have been likely. However, the IRS noted that the taxpayer's home office and his yard were separate portions of his residence: the exclusive use attributable to the one did not carry over to the other.

The Effective Executive
Peter F. Drucker
1967; 192 pp.
$6.95
($8.45 postpaid) from:
Harper and Row
2350 Virginia Avenue
Hagerstown, MD 21740
or Whole Earth Access

The Effective Executive

Wherever there's a bunch of people doing something, somebody is bearing executive relation to the group, usually badly, therefore unhappily for everyone, and nothing much is going on besides frustration. But some leaders are good, and with them a lot happens and everybody feels good. This book takes a deep look into how "good" executives behave in common. The generalizations that emerge are useful to anybody with responsibility, from the honcho of a commune to the Pope.
—Stewart Brand

•

The people who get nothing done often work a great deal harder. In the first place, they underestimate the time for any one task. They always expect that everything will go right. Yet, as every executive knows, nothing ever goes right. The unexpected always happens — the unexpected is indeed the only thing one can confidently expect. And almost never is it a pleasant surprise. Effective executives therefore allow a fair margin of time beyond what is actually needed. In the second place, the typical (that is, the more or less ineffectual) executive tries to hurry — and that only puts him further behind. Effective executives do not race. They set an easy pace but keep going steadily. Finally, the typical executive tries to do several things at once. Therefore, he never has the minimum time quantum for any of the tasks in his program. If any one of them runs into trouble, his entire program collapses.

•

Alfred P. Sloan is reported to have said at a meeting of one of his top committees: "Gentlemen, I take it we are all in complete agreement on the decision here." Everyone around the table nodded assent. "Then," continued Mr. Sloan, "I propose we postpone further discussion of this matter until our next meeting to give ourselves time to develop disagreement and perhaps gain some understanding of what the decision is all about."

•

When you borrow money is also important in what interest rates you pay. You should try to borrow when rates are low. This involves proper planning so that you are not caught needing money "right now," in which case you have to pay whatever the loan costs at that time.

Successful Small Business Management
David Seigel and Harold Goldman
1982; 346 pp.
$17.50 postpaid from:
Fairchild Books & Visuals
Book Division
7 East 12th Street
New York, NY 10003
or Whole Earth Access

Successful Small Business Management

It's a fact that certain types of people are likely to succeed in a business while others in that same business will fail. It has a lot to do with the owner's personality, ambition, temperament, and other "human" traits.

This excellent book identifies and discusses these human traits in a logical and well-organized manner. It covers pre-start-up, getting started, different types of businesses, pricing, selling, advertising, and even accounting from the personal perspective of the business owner.

The authors emphasize that you need to understand the common-sense basics of operating a business (which they explain well), but that you also need to offer a quality product or service, and that you need to treat your customers honestly and with respect.
—Bernard Kamoroff

Marketing Without Advertising

Marketing Without Advertising
Michael Phillips and Salli Rasberry
1986; 200 pp.
$14
($15.50 postpaid) from:
Nolo Press
950 Parker Street
Berkeley, CA 94710
or Whole Earth Access

The first two chapters of this startling book argue convincingly, and with documented proof, that almost all advertising is totally ineffective and an utter waste of money; and that most business owners, including top executives of large corporations, have been successfully duped into believing advertising is both necessary and productive in spite of obvious evidence to the contrary. The evidence presented — the at-times hilarious ads themselves, the statistics, the quotes from advertising executives, the ***Wall Street Journal*** *articles — will actually make you laugh, or if you're a buyer of advertising, maybe make you cry. Next time you see or hear an advertisement, think about it a minute. Would you buy what they're trying to sell you? When was the last time an ad convinced you to buy anything? If you run a business, how successful have your ads been? Read the beginning of this book, and I guarantee you'll have an entirely new perspective on advertising.*

The rest of the book, the bulk of the writing, explains clearly and in detail how you can promote your business without advertising, primarily by encouraging personal recommendations. The ideas are useful and well presented, of value to any business. But it's those first two chapters. . . . —Bernard Kamoroff

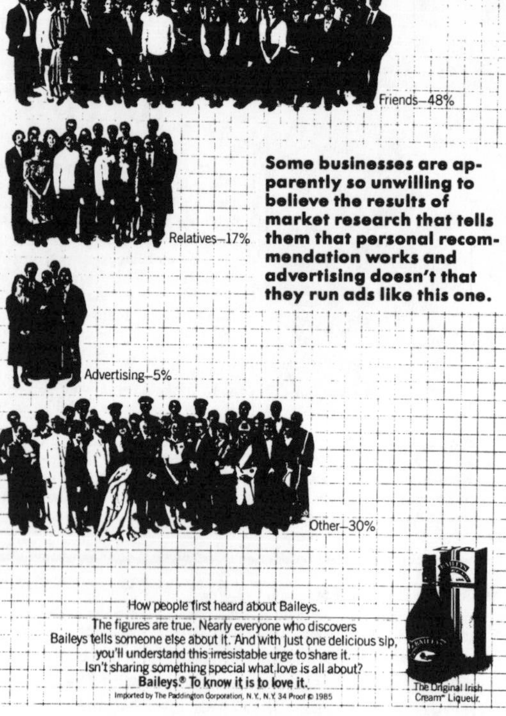

Friends–48%
Relatives–17%
Advertising–5%
Other–30%
How people first heard about Baileys.
The figures are true. Nearly everyone who discovers Baileys tells someone else about it. And with just one delicious sip, you'll understand this irresistable urge to share it.
Isn't sharing something special what love is all about?
Baileys.® To know it is to love it.
Imported by The Paddington Corporation, N.Y., N.Y. 34 Proof © 1985
The Original Irish Cream™ Liqueur.

Some businesses are apparently so unwilling to believe the results of market research that tells them that personal recommendation works and advertising doesn't that they run ads like this one.

Guerrilla Marketing

Guerrilla Marketing
Jay Conrad Levinson
1985; 226 pp.
$7.95
($9.45 postpaid) from:
Houghton Mifflin Co.
Mail Order Dept.
Wayside Road
Burlington, MA 01803
or Whole Earth Access

It's a rare business that will survive without successful, ongoing marketing. Marketing means promotion, and ***Guerrilla Marketing*** *offers up a couple dozen creative, inexpensive promotion ideas. I'm still not sure what "guerrilla" means except that it is a good example of what's in the book: the title is a marketing device itself — it catches your eye, makes you a little curious about it, costs nothing. The bulk of the book deals with advertising, which I view with great skepticism since reading* ***Marketing Without Advertising*** *(above). But I personally got several good ideas from the book, a couple of very good ideas, and one business-saving idea. What more could you want for nine dollars?* —Bernard Kamoroff
[Suggested by Bill Huckabee]

•

A business card can double as a brochure, a circular, a wallet-sized advertisement. The cost to produce such a card is not much more than one pays for a standard card. . . . A business card can be more than a mere listing of one's name, address, and phone number; it can be an advertising medium. . . .

That is what guerrilla marketing is all about.

•

It is possible to generate word-of-mouth advertising. There are several ways to accomplish this. The first, of course, is to be so good at what you do, or to offer products that are so obviously wonderful, that your customers will want to pass on the good word about you. Another way to get the ball rolling is to give brochures or circulars to your customers. This reminds them why they patronized you in the first place and spurs word-of-mouth endorsements. A third way to obtain positive recommendations is literally to ask for them. Tell your customers: "If you're really satisfied with my service (or products), I'd sure appreciate it if you'd tell your friends." Finally, you can *bribe* your customers. Tell them, "If I get any customers who mention your name, I'll send you a free gift (or give you a ten percent discount next time you're in)." Which of these methods should you employ? As a guerrilla, you should use *all* of them.

•

George then distributed his circulars by several methods: He mailed 1000; he placed 1000 on auto windshields (he had a high school student do some of this for him); he distributed 1000 more at a home show in his area; he handed out 1000 more at a local flea market; and he held on to 1000 to give to satisfied customers to pass on to their friends and neighbors. Being bright as a penny when it comes to saving money, the enterprising George also asked each of his customers where they had heard of him. When they said, "I saw your flier," George asked where they got it. This way, he learned which of the five methods of circular distribution were most effective.

Now that's guerrilla marketing. Not expensive whatsoever. But very effective.

P.R.

P.R.
Michelle Cauble
1977; 22 pp.
$1.50
($3.50 postpaid) from:
Do It Now Foundation
Institute for Chemical Survival
P.O. Box 5115
Phoenix, AZ 85010

What people haven't heard about they can't take action about. Uncommunicated issues DON'T EXIST. For local promotion on the quick and dirty and cheap, here's a quick, dirty, and cheap pamphlet of how-to. —Stewart Brand

This was written for community organizations but the tricks work for community businesses as well. —Kevin Kelly

•

In the beginning at least, one person, preferably with previous experience in media relations, should be the MAIN MEDIA CONTACT, rather than different people contacting the media on different occasions. This allows a personal relationship to develop, rather than haphazard or impersonal — "just another group trying to get publicity" — relations.

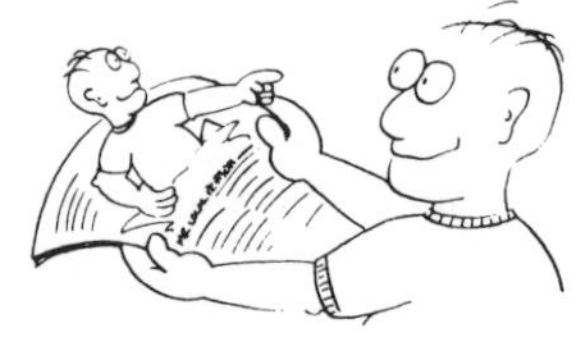

Always remember, "the sexiest item for local press is a local name." That rule holds with one minor qualification: the more you can relate the local name to the issue, the better. Mr. & Mrs. Middle America want desperately to be reassured that people THEY know, people who live in THEIR town, actively support your issue.

Office Supplies

Good cheap office gear — cardboard filing drawers, inexpensive business forms, address labels, and discounted prices on tape, pens, etc. We used to use Quill. They are fast, and easy to work with. Now we use Reliable because their prices are often a tad cheaper. Nicely serving all one-person-one-computer businesses is NEBS, supplier of every conceivable kind of tractor-fed stationery and microcomputer need (daisy wheels, ribbons, disks and so on). All three provide excellent quick service and allow you to order by phone, toll free.
—Kevin Kelly

"Nebs continuous, pressure sensitive mailing labels save addressing time."

SAVE 60%
QUILL® TYPING ELEMENTS
FOR IBM SELECTRIC II and III
SALE PRICE
9.88 each
Save off IBM's list on a variety of elements. Sold on pg. 24.

—Quill

Delivered Free!
$49.95
With minimum Freight Plan Order
Reliable
EASY ADJUST
POSTURE CHAIR

—The Reliable Corp.

Payroll Check: in blue, green or tan tint. (500)$41.95 (250)$31.50
—Nebs

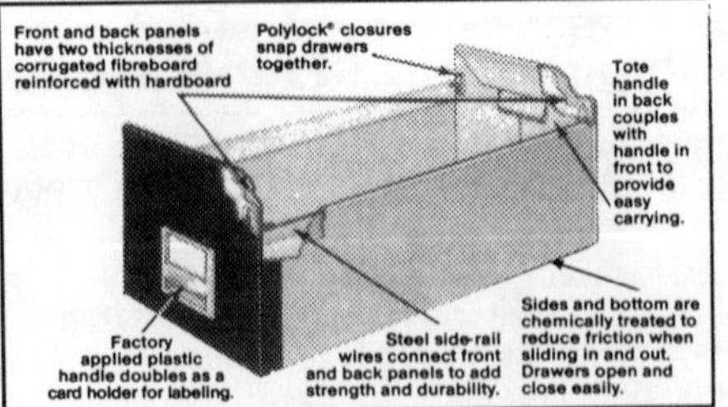
Front and back panels have two thicknesses of corrugated fibreboard reinforced with hardboard
Polylock® closures snap drawers together.
Tote handle in back couples with handle in front to provide easy carrying.
Factory applied plastic handle doubles as a card holder for labeling.
Steel side-rail wires connect front and back panels to add strength and durability.
Sides and bottom are chemically treated to reduce friction when sliding in and out. Drawers open and close easily.

—The Reliable Corp.

NEBS
Computer Forms
NEBS
Business Forms
Catalogs **free** from:
NEBS
500 Main Street
Groton, MA 01471

The Reliable Corp.
Catalog **free** from:
The Reliable Corporation
1001 West Van Buren St.
Chicago, IL 60607

Quill
Catalog **free** from:
Quill
P. O. Box 4700
Lincolnshire, IL 60197-4700

ECONOMY DISPENSER
3.49 each
For easy application!

—Quill

Small Business Software

What software do you need for a small business computer? (See pp. 352-353 for hardware recommendations.) Any good spreadsheet program. Spreadsheets are living ledger pages. You use them to design relationships between all the numbers that represent the money flowing through your hands. Because they instantly play out the ramifications when you change your estimates, spreadsheets allow you to plan more effectively. On an IBM PC, we like SuperCalc 4 ($495) the most; on a Mac, Excel ($395). Any old spreadsheet can be used as a low-cost accounting program with the computer edition of ***Small-Time Operator.***
—Art Kleiner

A more sophisticated system can be set up using prepackaged accounting programs. Two that run on the IBM PC and compatibles which we recommend are:

One Write Plus ($295). It extends the "one-write," or "safeguard," check-writing system into the world of microcomputers. This is the checkbook-style accounting. The computer handles the debits and credits, prepares those pesky financial reports, and writes the checks. It makes the setting up and operation of a general ledger accounting system so easy it's almost fun.

But there's a price: since this isn't a true double-entry system, entry errors are harder to catch. The cash and distribution report printouts need to be carefully audited to catch keying-in errors.
—Howard Dyer

Dac Easy ($70). An inexpensive system with everything most businesses need (but stay away unless you have a confident understanding of double-entry accounting).

Moving your accounting from book ledgers over to a computer ledger can take from 6 to 18 months if all goes smoothly. This is because you must move only one ledger or function at a time, and run it for several accounting periods while still keeping your books manually in case something goes wrong.
—Claude Whitmyer

Manual one-write system. At the same time you write out a check, the same information is duplicated by carbon paper in a ledger book. This elementary system is duplicated by computer.

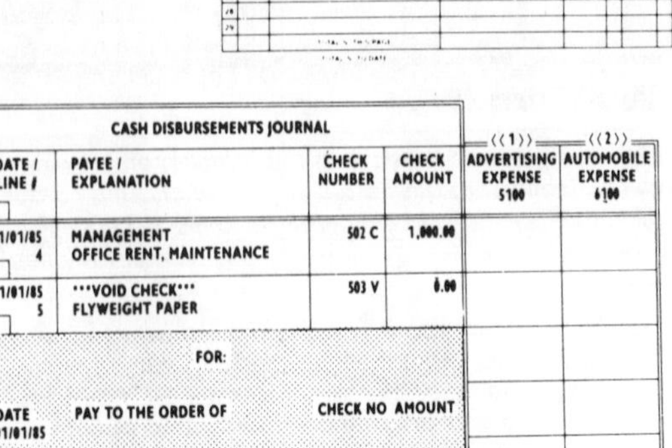

CASH DISBURSEMENTS JOURNAL

DATE / LINE #	PAYEE / EXPLANATION	CHECK NUMBER	CHECK AMOUNT	((1)) ADVERTISING EXPENSE 5100	((2)) AUTOMOBILE EXPENSE 6100
01/01/85 4	MANAGEMENT OFFICE RENT, MAINTENANCE	502 C	1,000.00		
01/01/85 5	***VOID CHECK*** FLYWEIGHT PAPER	503 V	0.00		

FOR:

DATE 01/01/85 PAY TO THE ORDER OF CHECK NO AMOUNT

Enter the check date, press F3 to edit or void a check, or press F10 to end

We all make mistakes. It's possible to record a manual check incorrectly, so *One-Write Plus* allows you to change the check description and distribution account, that is, all the check information contained on the Cash Disbursements Journal. Computer checks, already printed, cannot be easily changed. The only information you can change in a computer check is that information which does not appear on the printed check, namely, "Explanation of check" and "Distribution account." If you need to change the date, check amount, payee, or check number on a computer check you must void that check and print another.

One Write Plus: $295 from Great American Software, Inc., P. O. Box 910, Amherst, NH 03031.

SuperCalc 4: $495 from Computer Associates, 2195 Fortune Drive, San Jose, CA 95131.

Excel: $395 from Microsoft, P. O. Box 97107, Redmond, WA 98073-9717.

Dac Easy: $70 from 800-Software, 940 Dwight Way, Berkeley, CA 94710.

Small Time Operator, (Computer Edition), Bernard Kamoroff and Emile Krause, 1984; 190 pp., **$11.95.** ($12.95 postpaid) from Bell Springs Publishing Co. P. O. Box 640, Laytonville, CA 95454.

How to Start and Operate A Mail-Order Business

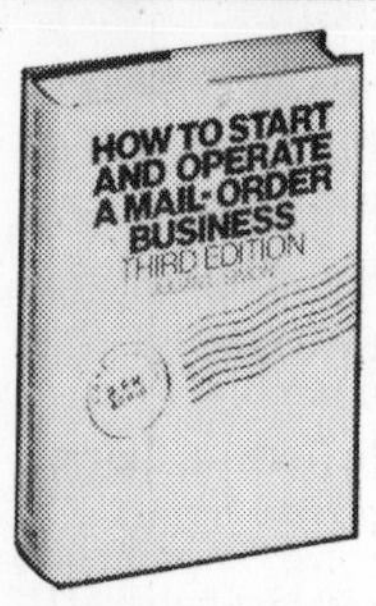

How to Start and Operate a Mail-Order Business
Julian L. Simon
1981; 553 pp.
$32.95
($34.27 postpaid) from:
McGraw-Hill
Order Dept.
Princeton Road
Hightstown, NJ 08520
or Whole Earth Access

If you want to start a mail order business, don't do anything until you read this 553-page book. It's been selling steadily for years. It is a thorough, in-depth study of mail order. It is, in my opinion, the best book on the subject, period.
—Bernard Kamoroff

I started a successful (still growing) mail order business using this book as my text. It's the wisest investment of $30 a mail order hopeful could make. —Kevin Kelly

•

Most mail-order businesses that are successful for a long time sell a product that the customer buys again and again: cigars, uniforms, office supplies, etc. Invariably, they "lose money" on the first order from the ad, but they make their profit on the second or tenth sale to the customer.

A BUSINESS OF YOUR O
REPAIR HYDRAULIC JACK
Earn while you learn at home. Millions
Jacks in gas stations, trucking firms, et
need servicing. We show you HOW. Sta
spare time in your basement or garag
Big opportunity for mechanics.
Write for folder No. V5 & free bonus off
HYDRAULIC JACK REPAIR MANUAL CO.,
G.P.O. BOX 3 • STATEN ISLAND, N.Y.

Examples of successful repeat-order businesses.

The strength and weakness of a repeat-line mail-order business is that it requires more capital and more courage to get started. It takes more time and money before you can tell whether or not you're going to make a success. You can't cut your losses as quickly in a repeat-line business as you can with one-shot items.

The Secrets of Consulting

The Secrets of Consulting
Gerald M. Weinberg
1985; 228 pp.
$25
($26.50 postpaid) from:
Dorset House Publishing
353 West 12th Street
New York, NY 10014
or Whole Earth Access

If Machiavelli were alive today, he would be a consultant. This is the book he'd write. —Art Kleiner

•

In order for a consultant to get credit, the client would have to admit there had been a solution. To admit there was a solution, the client would have to admit there was a problem, which is unthinkable. As a result, the only consultants who get invited back are those who never seem to accomplish anything.

If they don't like your work, don't take their money.
—The Sixth Law of Pricing

Freelance Foodcrafting

Covers every possible way to make money from food except starting a restaurant. —Kevin Kelly

Freelance Foodcrafting
Janet Shown
1983; 172 pp.
$9.95
($10.95 postpaid) from:
Liberty Publishing Co.
50 Scott Adam Road
Cockeysville, MD 21030
or Whole Earth Access

•

Profits from pushcart vending largely depend on the nature of your product and the location of your cart, as well as the season of the year. An average day's sales in Boulder, Colorado, in 1982 ran about $150, with a good day bringing in over $300 for some. With low overhead and minimal supply costs, most of that is profit, but pushcart vending will never make you rich. If you're planning on making your primary income from pushcart vending, you'll probably need to place several carts around town.

We Own It

Nitty-gritty how-to for starting and running employee-owned (collective) businesses — plus purchasing co-ops (like food co-ops) and cooperatives to market your wares together. —Art Kleiner

•

Naturally, we occasionally ponder the reasons for our success thus far, given the high mortality rate of small businesses and especially businesses in new industries where the markets are small and difficult to penetrate. The main factors seem to be these:

1. Hard work;
2. Moderate pay (about $800 per month till now);
3. Careful husbanding of capital (we've learned to get by with low inventory and used trucks);
4. Friendly investors;
5. Satisfied customers (of course we worked hard to satisfy them);
6. The idealism that got us into the business in the first place;
7. The togetherness that comes from shared ownership, equal pay, collective decision-making, and mutual concern for everyone's growth and job satisfaction.

We Own It
Peter Jan Honigsberg,
Bernard Kamoroff,
Jim Beatty
1982; 165 pp.
$9
($10 postpaid) from:
Bell Springs Publishing
P. O. Box 640
Laytonville, CA 95454
or Whole Earth Access

Word Processing Profits at Home

Word Processing Profits at Home
Peggy Glenn
1984; 213 pp.
$14.95
($15.95 postpaid) from:
Aames-Allen Publishing Co.
1106 Main Street
Huntington Beach, CA 92648
or Whole Earth Access

You can do what typists do faster with a word processor. This book tells you how to make a business out of it — from your home or nearby office. —Jeanne Carstensen

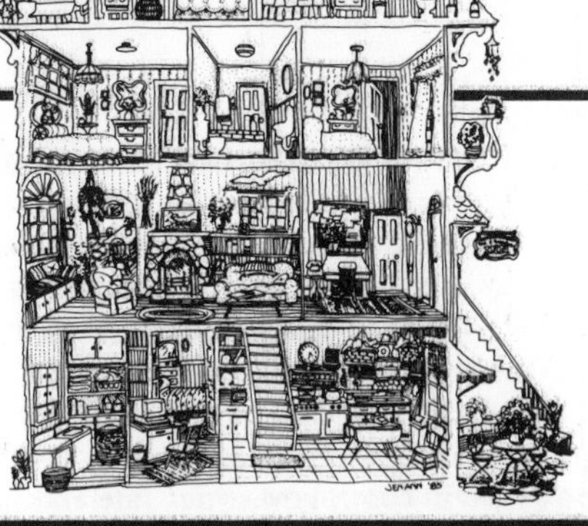

So . . . You Want To Be an Innkeeper
Mary E. Davies, Pat Hardy, JoAnn M. Bell
Susan Brown
1985; 218 pp.
$10.95
postpaid from:
Scribner's Book Company,
Order Dept.,
Front and Brown Streets,
Riverside, NJ 08075
or Whole Earth Access

So . . . You Want to Be an Innkeeper

I have owned and operated a bed and breakfast inn for nearly three years now. I wish this book would have been available when I started. Fortunately, my inn has accomplished all the suggestions and tips listed in the book, but not without a lot of trial and error. This book is by far the best on the market. —Hugh Daniels

•

The longer an inn is in business, the more likely the innkeepers will hire staff, take vacations, and even move off the premises. This is important for the innkeepers, but guests often don't like it; they tend to want to see the owner.

How to Open Your Own Shop or Gallery

A good, detailed book on retail business, with step-by-step examples. The advice is based on experience; the motives are very American. —Michael Phillips

How to Open Your Own Shop or Gallery
Leta W. Clark
1980; 229 pp.
$5.95
($6.95 postpaid) from:
Viking Penguin Books
299 Murray Hill Pkwy
East Rutherford, NJ 07073
or Whole Earth Access

•

Set foot in Tiffany's and you know by subtle inference that you will spend Money. Stroll into Woolworth's and you know you'll spend a lot less. The messages you get from the decor are carefully planned out; nothing happens by accident.

•

In a very real sense, personal service is the main thing a small shop has to offer. True, you might be making much of your own inventory and carefully hand-picking the rest to offer your customers a merchandise mix the likes of which they've never seen. But the retailing giants who are your competitors are offering the same customers a gigantic selection of wares, often with vast price cuts and revolving credit plans, layaway arrangements, and periodic clearaways. As long as you compete against them with the magic of personal service, you'll stand to win every time.

• I know of no other single source with so much small business information. Check your library.
The Small Business Sourcebook: 1986; 1000 pp. **$150** postpaid from Gale Research Co., Book Tower, Detroit, MI 48226.

Starting a Small Restaurant

A tough hands-on guide for people who think their own cooking is great and that they should do it in their own restaurant. —Michael Phillips

•

Restaurant is theater. If you view your dining room operation with this perspective, you will work from the right starting point. From the moment the customers first make contact with the players — whether this is on the telephone, in person, or even by letter — the tone of the response they get is essential to their dining pleasure. As in theater, both the voice and the body must convey your message. The message a small restaurant gives is friendship, calm and graceful service, and artfully prepared food of the highest quality. The mood and demeanor of the dining room staff bespeaks this message in the subtlest ways.

Starting a Small Restaurant
Daniel Miller
1983; 224 pp.
$9.95
($11.95 postpaid) from:
The Harvard Common Press
535 Albany Street
Boston, MA 02118
or Whole Earth Access

You're Gonna Love It!

How to be effective at selling while remaining a (mostly) decent human being. —Art Kleiner
[Suggested by John Ward]

You're Gonna Love It!
Chuck Lewis
1985; 190 pp
$7.95
($8.95 postpaid) from:
Ten Speed Press
P. O. Box 7123,
Berkeley, CA 94707
or Whole Earth Access

•

The secret to a decent transaction is one simple question. Did everyone involved walk away from it smiling?

Landlording

The advice is clear, concise, and based on experience in Berkeley, California — a tough area. —Michael Phillips

Landlording
Leigh Robinson
1986; 352 pp.
$17.95
($19.95 postpaid) from:
Express Publications
P. O. Box 1639,
El Cerrito, CA 94530-4639
or Whole Earth Access

Making Money Making Music
James Dearing
1982; 305 pp.
$12.95
($14.95 postpaid) from:
Writer's Digest Books
9933 Alliance Road
Cincinnati, OH 45242
or Whole Earth Access

How to Make and Sell Your Own Record
Diane Sward Rapaport
1984; 183 pp.
$12.95
($15 postpaid) from:
The Headlands Press
P. O. Box N
Jerome, AZ 86331
or Whole Earth Access

Making Music
George Martin, Editor
1983; 352 pp.
$10.95
($12.45 postpaid) from:
William Morrow Publishing Co.
6 Henderson Drive
West Caldwell, NJ 07006
or Whole Earth Access

THE MAINSTREAM MUSIC INDUSTRY is a modern-day Siren of dreams of wealth and fame. The rocky shores that will tear your musical vessel apart are the accountants, lawyers, and marketing directors who run the business and make their decisions based on market research. Today's Golden Fleece is the lowest common denominator of musical taste. Happily, you can keep your own dreams and make music by putting the music first and muzzling the desire for mass acclaim. These books will help you retain control over your fate and spread your music. You can be your own Orpheus. —Jonathan E.

The New Miss Alice Stone Ladies Society Orchestra (Harmony Club Records).

Making Money Making Music

While you wait for that big break, don't forget that you can still earn a decent living as a musician working locally. This book details a multitude of ways you can turn your talent into cash from performance gigs, teaching, studio work, renting your equipment, and selling your songs. It also deals with other musicianly concerns such as who drives the van, how to manage drink, drugs, and smoky barrooms, and how to avoid being ripped off by shady business characters. The chapters on how to organize and run a band show how to deal with the personalities (you're going to have to do a lot of that), the finances, and the logistics. If you want to reach for the stars, this book will help you build a solid launch pad.
—Jonathan E.

•

Any price you're quoted is the *least* that person or organization can afford. Here's what one nightclub owner told me: "My auditor keeps me posted on how I'm doing, and how much I can afford. If she tells me I can afford $6,000 a month for entertainment, I'll only budget about $4,500, and plow the other $1,500 back into the business." If your band is making $1,200 a week, chances are good that your employer can pay you $1,400-$1,600 without needing to draw more customers. That's the amount he budgeted for you, but you didn't negotiate for it! You accepted his first offer, the $1,200.

•

Is it really an audition? This is an infamous employer excuse for getting good entertainment cheap. Exhaust all options before agreeing to a free audition: Has she heard the tape? Can she come out to see the act perform somewhere else? Go ahead and pay their expense money to come see you perform at a job. This is cheaper than the whole group driving, setting up, playing, tearing down, and not getting paid.

How to Make and Sell Your Own Record

Still the indispensable guide for those who wish to go vinyl on their own behalf. Gets in the groove of the independent recording business and stays there from early planning of promotion right through to tax returns. The work sheets will help you stay in the financial groove, as well. There's an appendix on cassette-only releases, a discussion of new technologies such as CD, and a bit on foreign licensing. Read it before you book your studio time.
—Jonathan E.

•

Selling in stores: Placing your record for sale in record stores should be one of your main sales goals. Once you have persuaded an audience that your record is worth buying, it will be important that stores in the area carry it. . . . You will probably find that the most receptive stores are the small, individually owned ones, especially those specializing in particular kinds of music, such as jazz, bluegrass, or reggae. The owners of these stores are often sympathetic to individual business efforts, which in many ways resemble their own. Like independent labels, they are attempting to provide customers with records they might not find in the larger chain stores.

•

We chose to do an EP in accordance with our budget ($2000, which ended up $2500 plus) — not wishing to have such an important step to us result in only a two-song single, but not being able to afford an LP. Also, the record was an experiment to see whether our established audience would come through for record sales, as well as the already proven aspect of ticket sales. Fortunately, we found success.

Making Music

All too often the sound of music is lost in the labyrinth of the music industry where bank notes are as important as musical notes (I'm being charitable). ***Making Music*** *strikes a balance between the business and the music by acting as a guide to how the industry is structured and operates and to how music is actually made. Through interviews and articles by 65 industry insiders (with names most music fans will recognize) these successful individuals let you in on their secrets in a way that manages to integrate art and commerce, throwing light on both.*
—Jonathan E.

Home Studio: an area about the size of a garage can be ► turned into a workable studio in a short space of time. Judicious use of screens can reduce spillage, and the same area can be used as both a studio and control room.

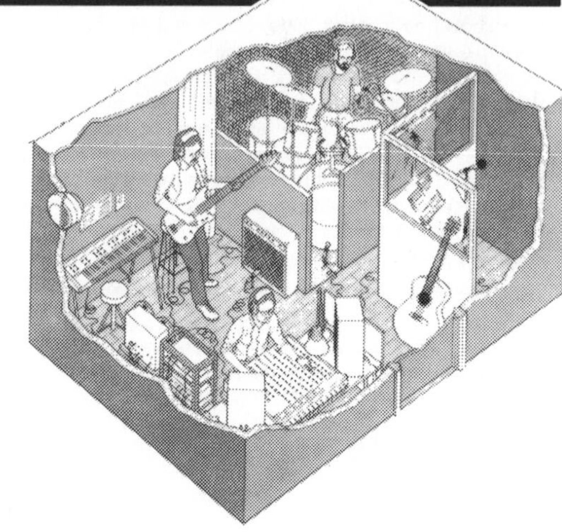

MONEY IS NOT CONTRADICTORY to craftwork. Your main inspiration for starting a business may have been your love of your craft rather than money, but to succeed with your crafts business you'll need to make both well. Once you do, it will seem like the best of all possible worlds — doing what you love and getting paid for it. —David Jouris

Goodfellow Catalogs of Wonderful Things

These are mail order catalogs of crafts available directly from craftspeople from all over the country, giving each one a page to explain a bit about who they are and what they do, as well as showing photos of the crafts they make. (For information on how to be listed write to the Goodfellow Catalog Press, P. O. Box 4520, Berkeley, CA 94704.) —*David Jouris*

Tempting! —*JB*

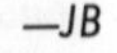

Car comb by Ellen Halloran. Approx. 3" end to end. In nickel silver, $17.50 each. In sterling silver, $36 each. —*Gifts Under $50*

▲

Our carousel figures of classical design are made from Brazilian Honduras mahogany or poplar. Each animal is singly handcarved and engineered using traditional stack lamination and joint work. Both natural and colored finishes are applied. —*The Goodfellow Catalog of Wonderful Things for Home & Office*

**Goodfellow Catalog of Wonderful Things for the Home and Office*
**Goodfellow Catalog of Wonderful Things — Gifts Under $50*
**Goodfellow Catalog of Wonderful Things to Wear & Wear & Wear*
**Goodfellow Catalog of Wonderful Things for Kids of All Ages*

Goodfellow Catalogs of Wonderful Things*
Christopher Weills, Editor-in-Chief
1984; 200-300 pp.
$14.95 each
($17.20 postpaid) from:
Chilton Book Co.
Cash Sales Dept.
Chilton Way
Radnor, PA 19089
or Whole Earth Access

The Crafts Business Encyclopedia

Its big advantage over the other crafts business guides is that entries are organized in convenient dictionary form. It's a good general reference guide which will either tell you what you want to know about the crafts business or, if not, where to find out. —*Marilyn Green*

•

You may want to ask yourself (and the gallery owner) a few other questions: do you have any say in the manner in which your work is displayed, or what is shown near yours; what happens if you and the gallery owner don't see eye to eye; how are you protected if the gallery goes bankrupt; does the gallery have the right to put your work out on loan; does the gallery's sales contract with its customer include a clause that gives you a share in any increased value if the work is later resold by the customer at a higher price; does the gallery want your work exclusively or can you sell to and through anyone; when and how does the gallery pay you, and what kind of records does it keep?

•

Another situation arises in which craftspeople may not even consider that they are cutting the price. This happens when you take a booth at a craft show and sell your work at prices below those that are charged by nearby retail stores which stock your craft objects. Undermining the retailer's established price for your work when you are, in effect, in direct competition with him, is ill advised. You're in town for only a few days. The retail store (you hope) will sell your work all year long and reorder from you in the future.

•

Price is another factor. The higher the price, the greater the public's perception of quality (and vice versa). The story is told of a supermarket which installed carpeting. The public stayed away in droves. Carpeting was associated in the public's mind with high priced stores. Not a single price had been changed in the supermarket, but the image had changed.

Crafts Business Encyclopedia
Michael Scott
1977; 286 pp.
$5.95
($6.64 postpaid) from:
Harcourt Brace Jovanovitch
1250 6th Avenue, 4th floor
San Diego, CA 92101
or Whole Earth Access

Health Hazards Manual for Artists

Who would expect to be poisoned by sawing a red cedar board? (The sawdust causes severe asthma.) Back when we didn't know any better such things were common, and many folks, including nonartists, are still needlessly hurt. No excuse though — this book briefly discusses known hazards by specific art or craft. There's an especially good chapter on protecting children. Wintergreen-flavored library paste isn't mentioned. I suppose if it were toxic we'd have lost an entire generation. —*JB*

•

In many instances, powders can be mixed in a simple, enclosed glove box as shown. The box can be made of cardboard and sealed inside with shellac or a similar sealant to make it easier to clean. The purpose of the glove box is to prevent dust from escaping.

Enclosure for mixing powders.

Heath Hazards Manual for Artists
Michael McCann, Ph.d.
1985; 100 pp.
$7.95
($8.95 postpaid) from:
Foundation for the Community of Artists
280 Broadway, Suite 412
New York, NY 10007
or Whole Earth Access

• This elegant magazine comes with membership in the American Craft Council.
American Craft: Louis Morgan, Editor; **$39.50**/year (6 issues) from American Craft Council, Membership Dept., 401 Park Avenue South, New York, NY 10016.

• Keep up with crafts business news in **The Crafts Report:** Michael Scott, Editor; **$16.75**/year (11 issues) from The Crafts Report Publishing Co., Inc., 700 Orange Street, Wilmington, DE 19801.

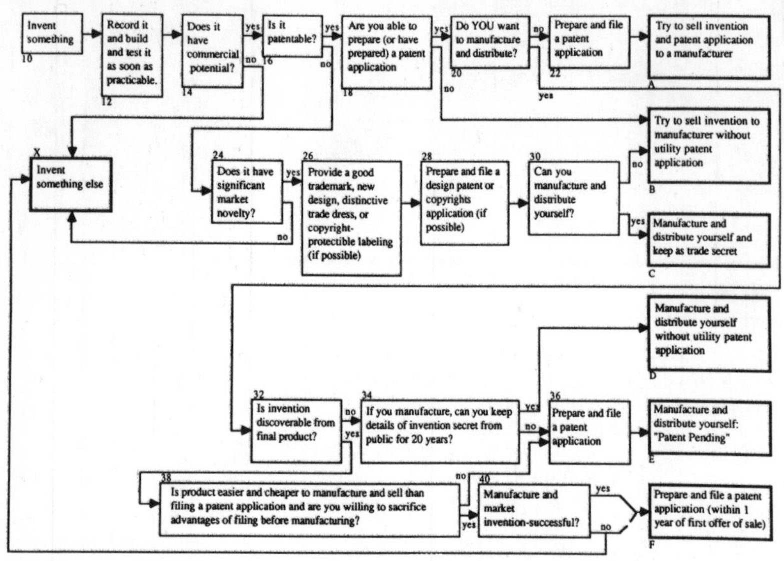

◄ **Invention decision chart.**

WHEN ASKED, "OF WHAT USE is your latest invention?" Benjamin Franklin replied, "Of what use is a newborn baby?"

Patent It Yourself

Other patent-it-yourself books seem like mere abstracts compared to this detailed gem of a book. Every step of the patent process is presented in order, complete with official forms to practice upon. The language is free of legalese except where readers are trained to sling a bit of it themselves for effect. The book is especially helpful in making tough tactical decisions, such as whether or not to patent at all. The copyright process is covered too. —JB

Patent It Yourself
David Pressman
1985; 421 pp.
$24.95
($26.45 postpaid) from:
Nolo Press
950 Parker Street
Berkeley, CA 94710
or Whole Earth Access

A Handbook for Inventors
Calvin D. MacCracken
1983; 211 pp.
$18.95 postpaid from:
Macmillan Publishing Co.
Order Department
Front and Brown Streets
Riverside, NJ 08075
or Whole Earth Access

A Handbook for Inventors

So you have an idea. What next? For 90 percent of the folks with a good idea for a product, what's next is failure — usually attributable to ineptitude. (I can vouch from sad experience that the sharks are many.) This savvy book is a useful guide for those who dare to bring their brainchild to the market. In contrast to many other books of this type, the author avoids rah-rah success stories that don't tell you what the protagonists really did. He concentrates on the strategies and tactics necessary for dealing with the realities of business. His advice is just what you need to hear, and it's presented in a friendly manner that's easy to assimilate. That's important, because when you're in somebody's office and have to make a decision on your feet, you won't be able to consult a manual — you'll have to have your moves right there in the top of your mind. —JB

•

Generally, the people involved in certification are fair and honest citizens trying to protect the public. However, as most have been burned before by products they'd accepted that subsequently created hazards, they tend to be extremely cautious; therefore you may have to devote a great deal of time to educating them before they'll move. This is a cost for which most innovators and entrepreneurs never budget properly, and many a new product has not bridged this last hurdle.

•

In selecting a licensee, it is often wise to pick a company that would like to get into your product's general field but is not yet involved in it. When I had invented a blanket that worked by circulating warm water in tubes the size of wires, I made the mistake of licensing it to Fieldcrest Mills, who were number one in electric blankets, selling over 2 million blankets a year. They told me their electric blanket business wasn't as profitable as they would like it to be and that the more even comfort of the "water blanket" would bring a higher price and give them something new over the competition.

Unfortunately, the water blanket's biggest selling point was that electric blankets cause fires and that a large number of people are afraid of having electric wires covering them at night. Fieldcrest would never say that for fear of hurting their major business.

•

Licensing professionals like Robert Goldscheider of the International Licensing Network, Ltd., in New York City go to great lengths to find a potential licensee whose business will benefit in every way from the license and who will make it part of the company's long-range planning. Here is Goldscheider's plan as he gave it to me in a recent interview:

1. Search out a licensee in terms of its ability to sell, not to engineer or to manufacture. (For example, stick to those that advertise heavily.)
2. Avoid internal conflicts of interest. (For example, if your product is a plastic chain, avoid chain manufacturers and find plastics marketers.)
3. Get through to a decision maker. (Call the president's office at 9 a.m., and someone will put you in touch with the person who can give the project the presidential seal of approval.)
4. Prepare a licensing memo of seven or eight pages containing:
   - The history of the innovation
   - Background on the inventors (their qualifications)
   - A rundown of the market and economics of the invention
   - The package of intellectual property (patent, trademark, lawyer's opinion and reputation, etc.)
   - What deal you want (for example, a three-month option for $20,000 with right to renew at the same fee, with half of option fees credited against final license down payment.
5. Try to connect your invention to a scholarly article.
6. Find out what is a must for the licensee's side, and agree to it only after many concessions on their part.
7. Make yourself look successful. (Pay attention to shoes, fingernails, clothes.)
8. Rehearse negotiations, getting someone to play the role of prospective licensee.
9. Offer five days free consulting (to give the licensee time to get the reaction of his key thinkers).
10. Use *your* license form for discussion, not theirs.

•

Probably the best bet is the trade show, exhibit, convention, or whatever it is called in your field. . . . Pick out a booth exhibiting a similar or related product or component and ask to talk to an engineer. Tell him you're working on a product to do a certain thing. Don't say "inventing," because that word arouses legal concern and suspicion. Ask what technical matters he'd be worried about, and had he ever heard of anyone developing, writing about, making, or selling such a product.

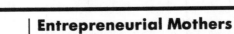

WHY ONE-PERSON BUSINESSES?

The one-person business is the most rapidly growing form of new business in the U.S. They have the potential for great efficiency. We are consultants for hundreds of such clients, and find that five well-run one-person businesses can produce more for the same amount of money as one business with eight employees — and they can do the same amount of work for two-thirds the cost (as long as real overhead costs are calculated for the employees). Every one-person businessperson should have two books: *How to Get Control of Your Time and Your Life* (p. 225) and *Small-Time Operator* (p. 191).

—Claude Whitmyer and Michael Phillips

Working From Home
Paul and Sarah Edwards
1985; 420 pp.
$11.95
($13.20 postpaid) from:
St. Martin's Press
Cash Sales
175 Fifth Avenue
New York, NY 10010
or Whole Earth Access

Working From Home

Best of the books we've seen on this subject, but there's not enough detail. For instance, the authors mention health insurance, a major knot to untangle, but don't really point you toward sources. But the table of contents lists almost everything that you need to think about if you are going to work from home. —Art Kleiner

•

Tips for Keeping Your Home and Work Separate:
1. Clearly define your workspace.
2. Set definite work hours.
3. Have a way to signal that you're working; for example, keeping the office door closed or putting up a Do Not Disturb sign.
4. Learn how to firmly, but nicely, say, "No, I'm working now."
5. Use a separate business telephone line and an answering machine or answering service.
6. Soundproof your office.
7. Dress in a certain way when you're working.
8. Keep work materials, paper, and equipment in your office space.
9. Have a door or other barrier to your office. Close it while you're working and after you've finished working.

Sideline Business

A newsletter for moonlighters and for people who have jobs but are thinking about starting their own businesses. It's a good place to keep up on IRS rulings likely to affect you. —Claude Whitmyer

Sideline Business: Jerome Goldstein, Editor. **$30**/year (12 issues) from Sideline Business Newsletter, Box 323, Emmaus, PA 18049.

Entrepreneurial Mothers

A rare book in that it skillfully combines "you can do it" inspiration with common sense. Mothers looking to start a business have more considerations and obstacles to deal with (kids, family, lack of encouragement) and these issues permeate the text. But anyone starting a home business — woman or man — will benefit from the well-chosen advice. —Bernard Kamoroff

The book also offers what amounts to a course in bargaining techniques — some of the best advice I've seen. —JB

•

Creative buying: Get together with other entrepreneurial mothers and buy in bulk or make a pitch to a wholesaler who normally deals only in large quantities. Place ads in your local newspaper if you think area residents might have the supplies you need. "Call me. I want to buy your backyard produce," was the ad placed by the enterprising owner of a California crepe and salad house.

•

There is a vast difference between a mate who is a sounding board and one who is actually involved in your venture. You may make mistakes, but they will be your mistakes, and you will learn from them. Make sure he knows that you welcome his support and advice but that you make the decisions. Your business is not his success; it is your success. *You* are his success.

Sometimes couples do go into business together. When it works, it can become the basis of a mutually satisfying relationship.

Entrepreneurial Mothers
Phyllis Gillis
1984; 374 pp.
$9.95 postpaid from:
Macmillan Publishing Co.
Order Dept.
Front and Brown Streets
Riverside, NJ 08075
or Whole Earth Access

Home Office

Brought to you by Time, Inc., this magazine is ***Time*** *magazine slick, well researched, and a must for the millions of Americans working, or soon to be working, in offices in their home* —Kevin Kelly

•

Independent typists often advertise at stationery stores or copy centers, leaving loose-leaf notebooks with samples of their work and a list of machines they're familiar with. Unlike the big services, they probably won't provide pickup and delivery. But independent typists, who usually charge by the hour, will be cheaper. And by using them you'll be giving a boost to people who, like you, are working out of their homes.

•

Nutrition: For people who work just around the corner from a well-stocked refrigerator, nibbling all day is a strong temptation — and an easy way to procrastinate. To avoid this double threat, establish regular mealtimes and try hard to avoid snacking. Most people find it easiest to stay trim by eating the three balanced meals a day that almost every doctor and mother recommend.

—Home Office

Home Office
Barbara Thompson Howell, Editor
$3/issue from:
Time Inc.
c/o Home Office
Time and Life Building
Rockefeller Center
New York, NY 10020

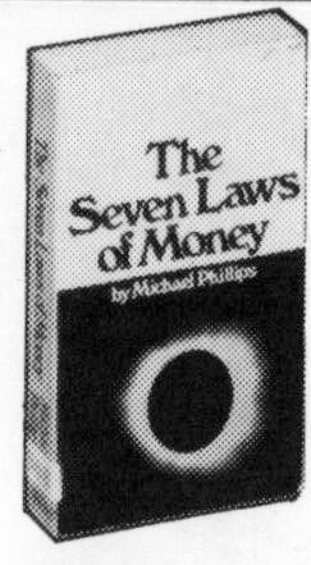

The Seven Laws of Money
Michael Phillips
1974; 194 pp.
$5
($6 postpaid) from:
Random House
Order Dept.
400 Hahn Road
Westminster, MD 21157
or Whole Earth Access

The Seven Laws of Money

The great hippie money book. Written in 1973 (and full of Whole Earth lore from that time), it taught a lot of people about how to live with money without letting it take over their lives. The advice still resonates.
—Art Kleiner

This wise and original book has made a lot of people cheeky enough to try stuff, and it's helped them get away with it.
—Stewart Brand

•

Not too long ago a group came to me and wanted to buy a gigantic piece of land. It was a group oriented around an Eastern religion and they naturally wanted to raise money for the gigantic piece of land. I said "You don't want money, you want supporters. You can go out and look for supporters and in the process ask for money, but don't forget what you're really after. Supporters." They did this. They contacted countless people, always asking for a small amount of money but in the process realizing that the commitment of a small amount of money was a commitment of support. And, of course, it was the support that built the institution and helped it grow. The institution is still growing. If this religious group had gotten a grant in the beginning it probably would have blown their whole future. Where would their supporters and friends and energy have come from, especially when the grants and funds began to run out in two or three years?

•

The First Law: Do it! Money Will Come When You Are Doing the Right Thing.

The Second Law: Money Has its Own Rules: Records, Budgets, Saving, Borrowing.

The Third Law: Money is a Dream: A Fantasy As Alluring As the Pied Piper.

The Fourth Law: Money is a Nightmare: In Jail, Robbery, Fears of Poverty.

The Fifth Law: You Can Never Really Give Money Away.

The Sixth Law: You Can Never Really Receive Money As A Gift.

The Seventh Law: There Are Worlds Without Money.

•

When you're asleep and dreaming, that's a world without money.

Sylvia Porter's New Money Book for the 80s
1979; 1305 pp.
$10.95
($11.95 postpaid) from:
Avon Books
P. O. Box 767
Dresden, TN 38225
or Whole Earth Access

Sylvia Porter's New Money Book for the 80s

Sylvia Porter is not kidding. This is about money, not so much how to make it, but how to keep, save, and judiciously spend it. There is advice and information on every purchasing decision, and it is usually good advice.
—Paul Hawken

•

The key to a good system of money management lies in spreading your big expenses and your savings so that each month bears a share of them. When you put aside $20 every month to meet a $240 yearly insurance premium, for instance, you will not risk spending that insurance money on an unnecessary luxury. . . . Include in your savings total an emergency fund equal to at least two months' income, to cover you should you be hit by big unforeseen expenses such as illness, unexpected home repairs, moving expenses. Note: the emergency part of your savings fund should be kept in a readily accessible ("liquid") form — for instance, a savings account.

As a starter, earmark 5 per cent of your total monthly income for savings, and boost the percentage from there if you can swing it.

•

I do not find the modern attitudes toward debt any cause for alarm. I see nothing wrong with paying money to use "someone else's money." I approve of "planned debt," which really is a kind of thrift. And, to an important degree, payments on an installment loan are merely replacing many old-time cash payments — like the money Americans used to dole out to the iceman or the cash we paid to the corner laundry.

•

If you are paying higher than standard rates for your life insurance because of medical considerations, and if your health has improved since your policy was issued, call your insurance agent, tell him you want your policies reviewed, and then apply to your insurance company for a reduction or elimination of the extra-risk premiums. Even if your health hasn't improved, you might be able to get a lower risk rating.

Managing Your Money
Version 2.0. Copy-protected. For IBM PC Family (128K)/PC jr (256K) and compatibles.
Street price
$120; List
$200 from:
MECA
285 Riverside Avenue
Westport, CT 06880.

Managing Your Money

No other computer program is so utterly useful, so well-designed, so well written (not the code, but the words on the screen), so humorous, so easy, so exploitative of what a computer does best.

It's a life-brightener, a marriage-saver. Money, as they say, matters. Most of us can keep up with the checkbook, but investments, tax stuff, loans, and insurance seem to inhabit worlds of their own, from which come a steady supply of bad surprises.

This program eliminates all that. All those "chapters" in the program, in your life, keep track of each other and keep a steady summary of their overall effect on your financial health.

For the first time I not only know what's going on, I relish my monthly session with the program, when the actuals take on the imagineds (the budget), and I come out ahead or behind in the computer game of life. This is a unique program in that it speaks to you in a personal voice, that of financial author Andrew Tobias (see **The Only Investment Guide You'll Ever Need***, next page).*
—Stewart Brand

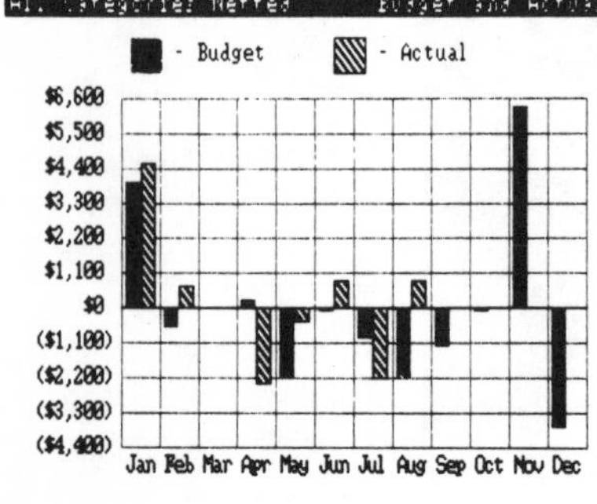

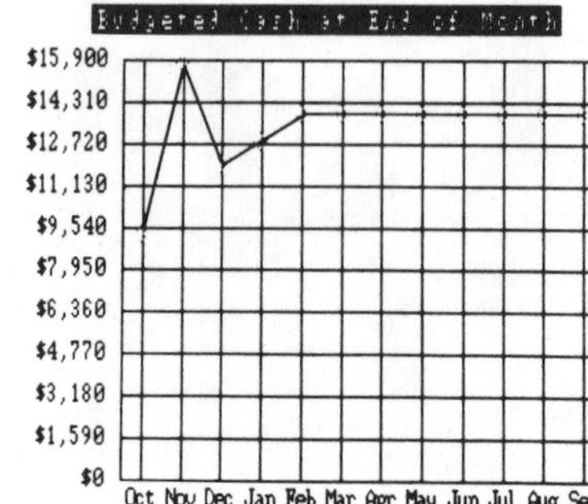

◄ **Printouts of the reviewer's bottom line for 1984 — all income versus all expenses, with reality (through August) compared to budget, followed by my predicted cash situation for the coming months.**

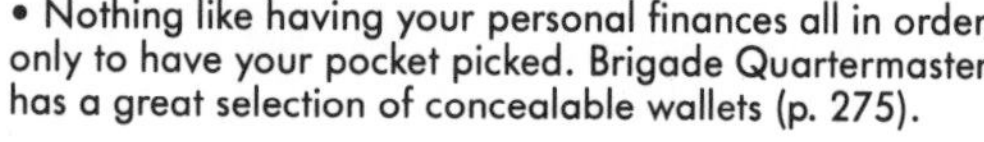

• Nothing like having your personal finances all in order, only to have your pocket picked. Brigade Quartermaster has a great selection of concealable wallets (p. 275).

The Only Investment Guide You'll Ever Need

There are a lot of problems with personal investing that don't meet the greedy eye but can clutter up your life. Andrew Tobias cuts through all of that. This book is a brisk, cheery compendium of highly sophisticated common sense. The most efficient way to make money, he reminds right at the start, is not to spend it. As for investing itself, he preaches a bare-bones, conservative line — discount brokers, no-load mutual funds, a healthy IRA account, and very little action. He's got good detailed tricks and tips (save money in your children's names and it'll mount tax free), but the basic strategy is simple, slow, wise — freeing. —Stewart Brand

•

Simple insulation may be the best "investment" you can make, returning as much as 35% or more, tax-free, in annual savings on heating and cooling. Why put $1,500 into the stock of some utility and earn $150 in annual taxable dividends if you can put the same money into insulation and save $150 tax-free on your utility bill? (Check also the federal and state tax credits that may be available to encourage such energy-saving investment.)

•

OK. You have some money in a savings bank; you have set up an Individual Retirement Account — and a Keogh Plan, if possible — and are contributing to them at the maximum rate allowed; you have equity in a home, if you want it; you've tied up $1,000 in bulk purchases of tunafish and shaving cream; you have lowered your auto and homeowner's insurance premiums by increasing your deductibles; you have adequate term life insurance; you've paid off all your 18% installment loans; there is a little solar water heater sitting on your roof above your well-insulated attic; and you own enough IBM (or some other solid common, or even preferred, stock) to take full advantage of the $100 ($200) dividend tax exclusion. In short, you have done all the things that scream to be done. You have made the easy decisions.

Now what?

There are three compelling reasons to invest a portion of your funds in stocks.

1. *Over the long run — and it may be very long — stocks should outperform bonds. . . .*

2. *Unlike bonds, stocks offer at least the potential of keeping up with inflation. . . .*

3. *If all goes well, stocks can act as a tax shelter.*

Catalyst

Resources for giving away or investing your money to good end. ***Catalyst*** *is three good newsletters in one, devoted to three purposes: 1. helping socially-conscious investors; 2. helping progressive organizations and businesses that need loans or investors; 3. linking 1 and 2.* —Art Kleiner

•

What is a fair return?

One of the first lessons I learned in business school was that for every risk there should be a corresponding rate of return. The greater the risk, the higher the return. Thus, one expects to earn more in the stock market than in a money market fund because of the higher risk.

This formula is somewhat modified for alternative investing. Here, the investor is sometimes willing to accept a lower return to advance the social goals of the project. Call this a "social subsidy." The amount of this subsidy is a personal decision of each socially conscious investor. Generally, if your return on a loan is more than 3% below what a similar traditional investment would pay, your "subsidy" is bordering on a charitable gift.

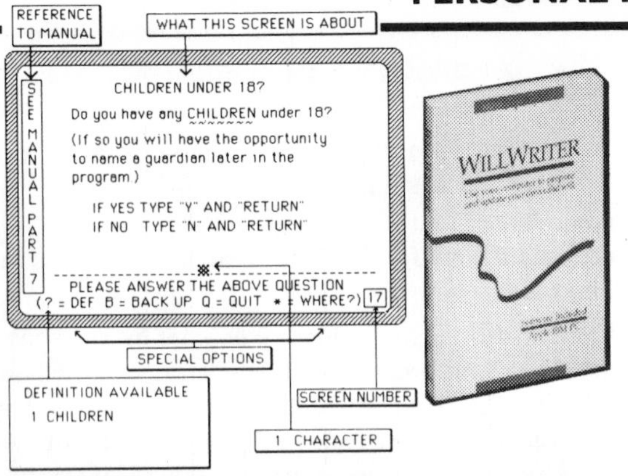
REFERENCE TO MANUAL
WHAT THIS SCREEN IS ABOUT
SEE MANUAL PART 7
CHILDREN UNDER 18?
Do you have any CHILDREN under 18?
(If so you will have the opportunity to name a guardian later in the program.)
IF YES TYPE "Y" AND "RETURN"
IF NO TYPE "N" AND "RETURN"
PLEASE ANSWER THE ABOVE QUESTION
(? = DEF B = BACK UP Q = QUIT * = WHERE?) 17
SPECIAL OPTIONS
DEFINITION AVAILABLE
1 CHILDREN
SCREEN NUMBER
1 CHARACTER
WILLWRITER

WillWriter

A fertile hybrid that I expect to see more of: can-do software that lives inside a how-to book. In this case, the book itself is one of the better ones on preparing your own will. The will-making procedures have been made precisely methodical in order to please the vaguely dumb logic of the computer. At the same time, the software (slow and somewhat crude) has an articulate book to introduce and speak for it. It's quick enough to think differently depending on what state you say you live in. The combination makes it quite painless to write or update a will. —Kevin Kelly

PC/TAXCUT

This tax prep/planner software is a great aid, if not a total replacement for your accountant. It does not advise, but it does everything else. If you need to refer to past years (for income averaging or credits) it directs you to the exact line of your old returns. The program is a pleasure to work with. You can succeed at even complex tax returns on your own, or take a printout with you to your tax appointment to greatly streamline the procedure. —Andrea and Daniel Sharp

PC/TAXCUT calculates income, deductions, credits, taxes, and payments; considers all the interrelationships; assesses the different methods of calculating taxes; determines which is most beneficial; then shows you the result. It prints virtually every one of the commonly used tax forms on everyday computer paper — except the 1040 long form which the IRS requires on their preprinted form. Five 1040 computer forms are supplied free with the program.

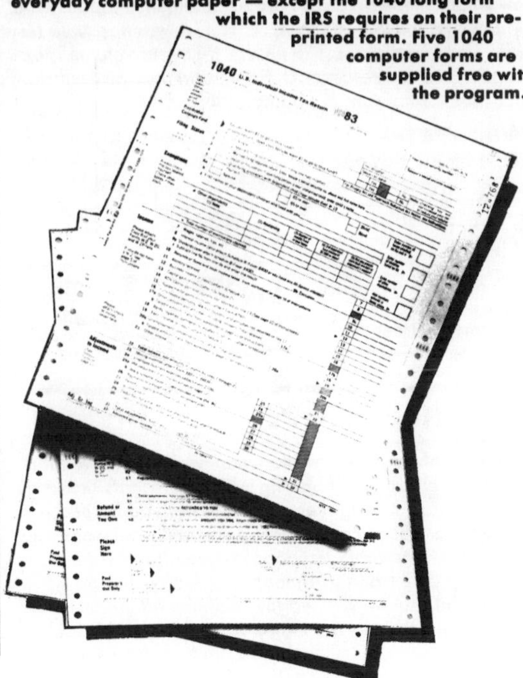

WillWriter
(with software for IBM PC or Apple II)
1985; 170 pp.
$39.95
($41.95 postpaid) from:
Nolo Press
950 Parker Street
Berkeley, CA 94710
or Whole Earth Access

The Only Investment Guide You'll Ever Need
Andrew Tobias

The Only Investment Guide You'll Ever Need
Andrew Tobias
1983; 180 pp.
$3.95
($5.45 postpaid) from:
Bantam Books
414 East Golf Road
Des Plaines, IL 60016
or Whole Earth Access

PC/TAXCUT
1986 Version. Copy-protected. IBM PC/XT/AT and compatibles (128K).
Street price
$150
List
$195 from:
Best Programs
5134 Leesburg Pike
Alexandria, VA 22302

SOCIAL CHANGE
GUIDE TO INVESTING IN SOCIAL CHANGE

Catalyst: Investing in Social Change
Susan Meeker-Lowry, Editor
$30/year
(6 issues) from:
Catalyst Newsletters
P. O. Box 363
Worcester, VT 05682

In most states it is possible to have someone from the sheriff or marshal's office sent to the business of a person who owes you money to collect it from the cash on hand. . . . A deputy goes to the business one time and picks up all the money in the till. The fee for this service normally varies from $15-$50.

SUPPOSEDLY, LAWYERS HATE and fear self-help law books because they encroach on our sacred turf. But as a lawyer myself, I think self-help law books are a wonderful idea.

Why? Think of a toothbrush. Think of dental floss. Does your dentist scoff at them? Imagine what your teeth would look like to the dentist if you never brushed or flossed. That is typically how a lawyer finds the legal affairs of a client who has never practiced simple legal self-care. With awareness and thoughtful action, you can avoid major legal disasters that can be as costly and as painful as a root canal.

Caution: Just as you would not attempt to wire your child's braces, you should be wary of initiating or defending your own lawsuit. These legal self-care books will help you determine when to have a professional by your side. Even if you do hire an attorney after reading legal self-care books, you will be better off — you will have avoided legal mistakes that can cost pain, time, and money. —Donna Hall

Everybody's Guide to Small Claims Court

This is a superb book, flawless! No small business should be without it. If you like to sue other people and businesses, then you'll also find it helpful.
—*Michael Phillips*

•

Litigation should be a last, not a first, resort. Suing is not as bad as a shooting, but neither is it as much fun as a good back rub. Rarely does anyone have a high time in court. In addition to being time consuming and emotionally draining, lawsuits tend to polarize disagreements into win-all or lose-all propositions in which face-saving (and pocketbook saving) compromise is difficult.

This doesn't mean that I don't think you should pursue your case to court if necessary. What I am suggesting is this: before you file your case, ask yourself whether you have done everything reasonably possible (and then a little more) to try to settle the case.

•

There are three great advantages of Small Claims Court. First, you get to prepare and present your own case without having to pay a lawyer more than your claim is worth. . . .

The second great advantage . . . is simplicity. The gobbledygook of complicated legal forms and language is kept to a minimum. To start your case, you need only fill out a few lines on a simple form (e.g., "Honest Al's Used Chariots owed me $1,000 because the 1977 Chevette they sold me in supposedly 'excellent condition' died less than a mile from the car lot." When you get to court, you can talk to the judge without a whole lot of "res ipsa loquiturs" and "pendente lites." If you have documents or witnesses, you may present them for what they are worth, with no requirement that you comply with the thousand years' accumulation of fusty, musty procedures, habits and so-called rules of evidence of which the legal profession is so proud.

Third, and perhaps most important, Small Claims Court doesn't take long.

•

Here is a one-sentence definition. If, as a result of another person's conduct, your property is injured and that person didn't act with reasonable care in the circumstances, you have a case based on his or her negligence. It's as simple — or complex — as that.

Everybody's Guide to Small Claims Court
Ralph Warner
1985; 263 pp.
$10.95
($12.45 postpaid) from:
Nolo Press
950 Parker Street
Berkeley, CA 94710
or Whole Earth Access

Nolo Press

Nolo has been producing high quality self-help law books since 1971 and has set the standard for understandable and comprehensive volumes. They are to law what Chilton's (p. 269) are to automotive repair. All of Nolo's books are updated as the law changes. As their newsletter, ***Nolo News****, remarks, out of date equals dangerous! To ensure that your volume is up to date they print a number you can call in each book, and they give substantial discounts to individuals who want to update older editions.* —*Donna Hall*

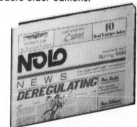

Nolo Press
Publications list **free:**

Nolo News
$7/year
(4 issues)

Both from:
Nolo Press
950 Parker Street
Berkeley, CA 94710

At a convention of biological scientists one researcher remarks to another, "Did you know that in our lab we have switched from white mice to lawyers for our experiments?"

"Really?" the other replied, "Why did you switch?"

"Well, for two reasons. First we found that lawyers are far more plentiful, and second, the lab assistants don't get so attached to them."

ACLU Handbooks

As Andrew Fluegelman wrote when we first reviewed this series 15 years ago, "Knowing what your rights are won't keep you from having them violated, but you'll stand a much better chance of protecting yourself when someone tries." These essential handbooks, published by the American Civil Liberties Union, are, deplorably, going out of print; but we still heartily recommend the ones remaining. Also, see **The Rights of Employees** *(p. 188).*
—*Art Kleiner*

ACLU
Handbook Price List
free from:
ACLU - Books
1400 20th Street NW
Room 119
Washington, DC 20036

• A good way to follow developments in legal reform.

Americans for Legal Reform: Richard Hebert, Editor; **$15**/year (4 issues) including membership, from HALT — An Organization of Americans for Legal Reform, 1319 F Street N.W., Suite 300, Washington, DC 20004.

Legal Research

This is the simplest, most comprehensive book I have found on legal research. It tells you everything except how to find the county law library. Take it there with you. Research skills come in handy whenever you have a problem that involves finding out about a particular law — problems ranging from fighting a ticket to figuring out how to get the neighborhood bird lover to refrain from feeding pigeons on top of your new car. —Donna Hall

•

In the Land of the Law judges are master. Thus, to properly interpret a statute you usually need to know how courts have previously interpreted one or more of the specialized words and phrases (i.e., jargon) it contains. One tool to help you do this is **Words and Phrases** (*West Publishing Co.*), a multi-volume set of one-sentence interpretations of common words and phrases that have been pulled from cases and organized alphabetically according to words and phrases that are commonly found in statutory and case law. In essence, this publication allows you to find out whether courts have interpreted or used any particular word or phrase you are interested in, and if so, how.

– 488 –
(68CA3d835)
→ v148CaR379
v582P2d970
Minn
271NW448

•

After you review the appropriate background resources, you will want to proceed to the law itself. Other things being equal, you should hunt for statutory law first, as represented in the next box. Why do we direct you first to statutory law instead of case law? Because in most instances the law starts with legislative or administrative enactments and ends with court decisions that interpret them. It therefore usually makes sense to deal with the statutory material first and the cases second.

LEGAL RESEARCH

Legal Research
Steven Elias
1986; 262 pp.
$14.95
($16.45 postpaid) from:
Nolo Press
950 Parker Street
Berkeley, CA 94710
or Whole Earth Access

Media Law

Whenever you write you are exposing yourself to lawsuits and possible jail sentences. Galvin's book helps writers do their job without legal troubles. —Donna Hall

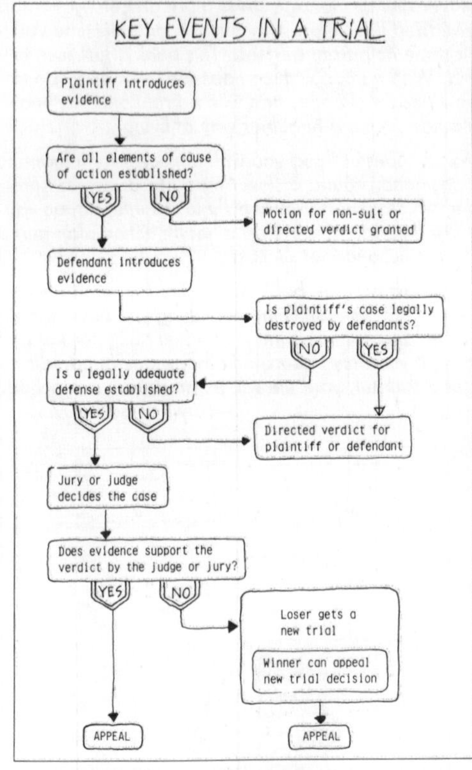
KEY EVENTS IN A TRIAL
Plaintiff introduces evidence
Are all elements of cause of action established?
YES
NO
Motion for non-suit or directed verdict granted
Defendant introduces evidence
Is plaintiff's case legally destroyed by defendants?
NO
YES
Is a legally adequate defense established?
YES
NO
Directed verdict for plaintiff or defendant
Jury or judge decides the case
Does evidence support the verdict by the judge or jury?
YES
NO
Loser gets a new trial
Winner can appeal new trial decision
APPEAL
APPEAL

•

Avoiding Misappropriation Claims:
Here are some do's and don'ts you may find helpful when dealing with another person's name or likeness:

- Photos and descriptions of people in public places are protected as long as used in a "news" or "feature" context.
- Photos and descriptions of public people (those who routinely trade commercially on their own name or likeness) used for advertising or other commercial purposes are not protected and may well give rise to a successful lawsuit.
- If you are in doubt as to whether you are infringing on another's commercial privacy, arrange for his or her consent.

•

Novelists' Note: If any character in a story is based, even loosely, on a real person, you will be wise to change enough facts so that the connection is not apparent. Further, it is wise to take reasonable care to be sure that you have not accidentally used the names of real people. For example, if you write a mystery story in which a New York police inspector is cast in unfavorable light, you would do well to check to be sure that there is not a real inspector with the same name. This is even more necessary if you are writing about a singer or performer who lives by exploiting the value of her name.

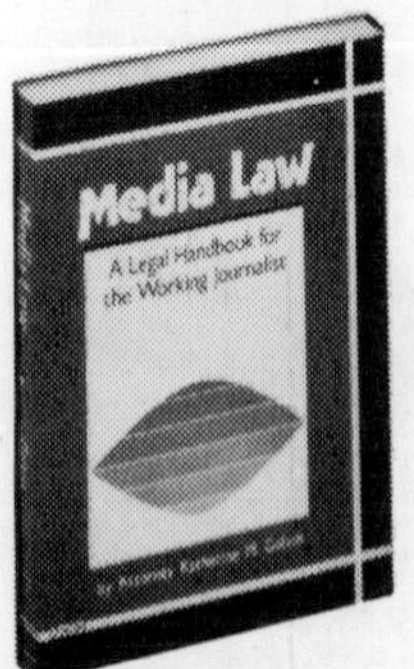
Media Law
A Legal Handbook for the Working Journalist

Media Law
Katherine M. Galvin
1984; 224 pp.
$14.95
($16.45 postpaid) from:
Nolo Press
950 Parker Street
Berkeley, CA 94710
or Whole Earth Access

• This book will help eliminate the nervousness you feel while engaging self-care law by pointing out some of the absurdities of the legal animal. 29 reasons, all of them true.
29 Reasons Not to Go to Law School: Ralph Warner and Toni Ihara, 1982; 140 pp. **$6.95** ($7.95 postpaid) from Nolo Press, 950 Parker Street, Berkeley, CA 94710 (or Whole Earth Access).

Redress for Success

In order to know "how-to-do-it" you sometimes have to know what has gone before. I have never read a more complete overview of the current state of the legal rights of women. Complete and completely fascinating reading. If you're a woman you need this book. —Donna Hall

•

People who defend themselves against property crimes tend to be exonerated, if not commended, by the legal system and by juries (if it gets that far). Women who defend themselves against rape may face more difficulties. Judges, who no doubt thought they were being adorable, have been quoted calling rape "assault with a friendly weapon" and "assault with failure to please" (Har-har). It is usually accepted that burglars and muggers pose a real threat, and have not dropped over to get subway directions, but sometimes women are treated as if they solicited, desired, or enjoyed the attentions of rapists and would-be rapists.

REDRESS FOR SUCCESS
USING THE LAW TO ENFORCE YOUR RIGHTS AS A WOMAN
DANA SHILLING

Redress for Success
Dana Shilling
1985; 325 pp.
$8.95
($9.95 postpaid) from:
Viking Penguin Books
299 Murray Hill Pkwy.
East Rutherford, NJ
07073
or Whole Earth Access

"Be careful about reading health books. You may die of a misprint."
—Mark Twain

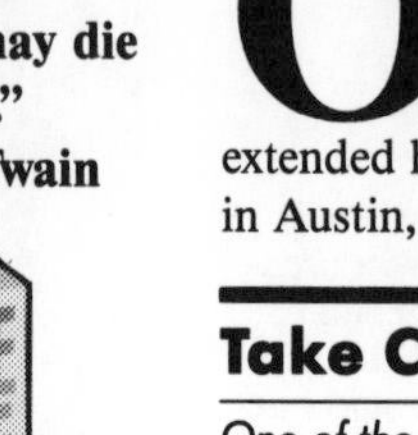

OUR PRINCIPAL REVIEWER of things medical is Tom Ferguson, M.D. He founded *Medical Self-Care* magazine ten years ago when such ideas were considered radical. These days, he's extended his practice to include Self-Care Productions, based in Austin, Texas. Watch for a book from him soon. —JB

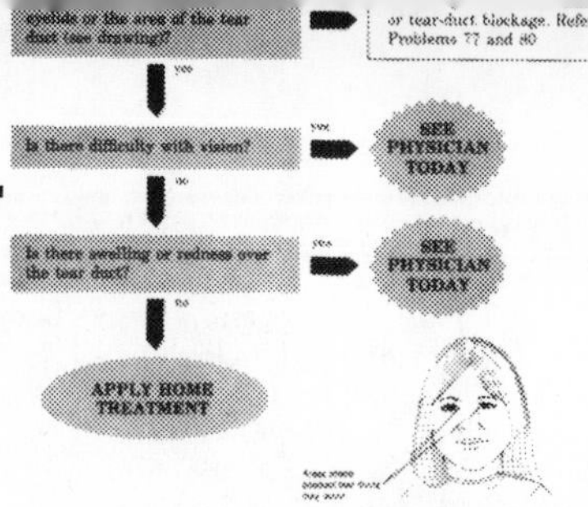

—Take Care of Yourself

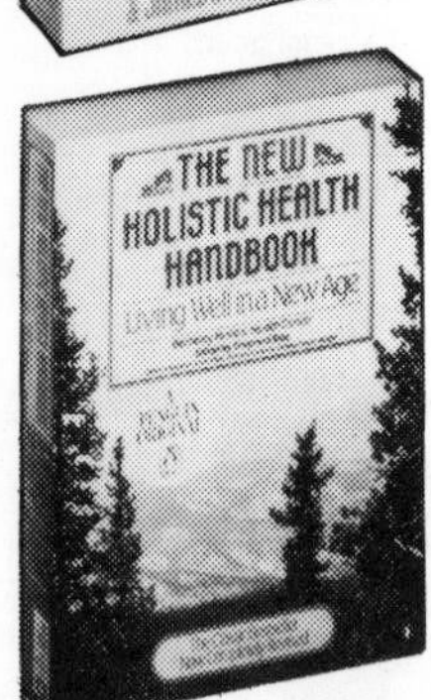

Take Care of Yourself

One of the most useful tools to come out of the new paramedic training programs is the clinical algorithm — big, detailed flow charts, one for each of the common medical complaints (such as sore throat, dizziness, low back pain) that might bring a person to a medical clinic. They tell you the key questions to ask to decide whether the person needs to see the doctor NOW, needs to see the doctor sometime soon, or if home remedies are indicated.

The heart of this book is the 94 most commonly used clinical algorithms, presented in full-page size with nice graphics. There are additional chapters on skills for the medical consumer such as how to find a physician.
—Tom Ferguson, M.D.

Take Care of Yourself
Donald M. Vickery, M.D.
James F. Fries, M.D.
1986; 401 pp.
$14.38
($15.32 postpaid) from:
Addison-Wesley Publishing Co.
1 Jacob Way
Reading, MA 01867
or Whole Earth Access

•

Stye: Apply warm, moist compresses for ten to fifteen minutes at least three times a day. As with all abscesses, the objective is to drain the abscess. The compresses help the abscess to "point," which means that the tissue over the abscess becomes quite thin and the pus in the abscess is very close to the surface. After an abscess points, it often will drain spontaneously.

The New Holistic Health Handbook

For some of us around this office, the very word holistic is usually taken as sufficient cause for rejecting a book as airheaded. Fortunately, this ***Handbook*** *gets right to work presenting a comprehensive overview of the alternatives to conventional medical practice. Homeopathy, Rolfing, healing with sound, biofeedback, herbs, yoga, acupuncture, and Native American methods are all here. So are a whole bunch of ideas you've probably never heard of even if you live in California. You'll have heard of many of the presenters though; Ph.D.s and M.D.s abound (including Tom Ferguson, M.D.). The information is solid and informative, enthusiastic but not annoyingly proselytizing. This is probably the best place to learn about alternative ways of healing.* *—JB*

The New Holistic Health Handbook
Edited by Shepherd Bliss
1985; 429 pp
$14.95
($15.95 postpaid) from:
Viking Penguin
299 Murray Hill Pkwy.
East Rutherford, NJ 07073
or Whole Earth Access

•

"What would you recommend for my asthma?" the woman behind the counter asked. "I'll ask my colleagues at the Berkeley Holistic Health Center," I answered. So I approached our acupuncturist. "Do you treat asthma?" His response: "No, but I do treat people who have asthma." This distinction between treating the whole person and treating the disease helps define holistic health.

•

Why Does Reflexology Work?
Reflexology refers primarily to reflex points on the feet and hands, but there are many other usable reflex points throughout the body.

There are several theories on how reflexology works. Some say that each of the 72,000 nerve endings on each foot connects to a different body area; in massaging those nerve endings, we send a stimulation to a corresponding body area. Others say that we are activating energy points along meridian lines as in acupressure.

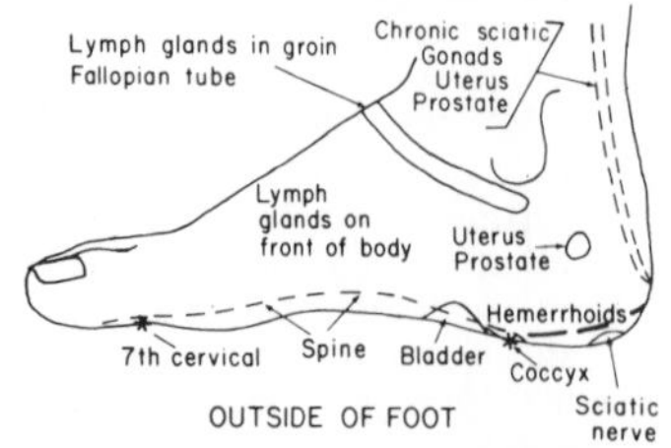

Pathways: A Success Guide for a Healthy Life

Suppose you want to start an exercise program or eat a healthier diet or manage stress more gracefully. Perhaps you've tried this before on your own and this time you want some help from a friend. This book is just such a friend. With humor, with compassion, with understanding of how people change, and with a firm hand this book can guide you to a healthier way of living.

Pathways *doesn't flood you with unnecessary information. It is designed around a clever map-like device, a pathfinder, which guides you directly to the information you need and helps you develop a health action plan to maximize your chances of success.*

For the most part the book is realistic. It doesn't assume that promoting health is the only thing you have to do in your life, and it doesn't make you feel guilty for not being a saint. If you only absorb and follow one-hundredth of its good counsel, your life will be measurably enriched.
—David S. Sobel, M.D.

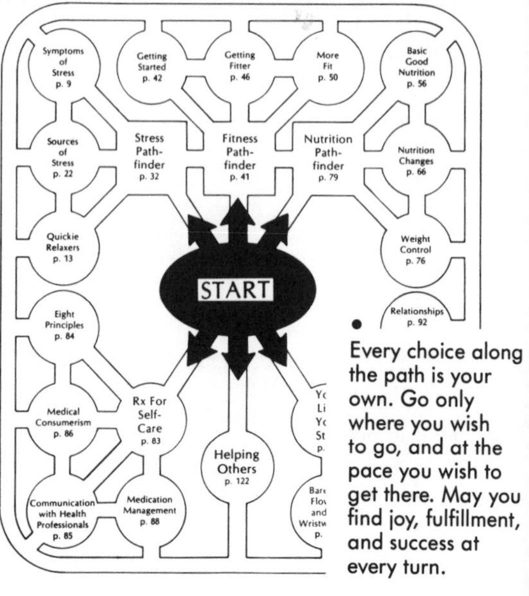

•

Every choice along the path is your own. Go only where you wish to go, and at the pace you wish to get there. May you find joy, fulfillment, and success at every turn.

Pathways
Donald W. Kemper,
James Giuffre and
Gene Drabinski
1985; 144 pp.
$10
($11.25 postpaid) from:
Healthwise
P. O. Box 1989
Boise, ID 83701
or Whole Earth Access

Medical Self-Care

As you might guess, this magazine encourages wellness — staying healthy — as the primary self-care. Articles are current, authoritative, and mercifully free of fearmongering, hype, and fad. (Some of the ads aren't quite as picky about that, though.) The issue I have here on my desk has a thorough article on something I recently needed to know: Are those new Urgent Care Centers often found in shopping malls any good, or are they "Docs-In-A-Box" and "Medical McDonald's?" (The article says they're mostly OK and half the price of an emergency room. That turned out to be the case.) Useful stuff. The book reviews are particularly good. —JB

Medical Self-Care
Michael Castleman, Editor
$15/year
(6 issues) from:
Medical Self-Care
P.O. Box 1000
Point Reyes, CA 94956

The Medical Self-Care Catalog

A catalog of self-help medical tools put together by ***Medical Self-Care*** *publisher Carole Pisarczyk. The catalog carries all kinds of handy gadgets to help you stay in shape and deal with health problems on your own — you can order your own black bag of medical tools, the ultimate back support cushion for your car, a heating pad that supplies moist heat, an otoscope for examining your kid's ears, a doctor-quality bathroom scale, a child's stethoscope, a vaginal speculum, an ovulation thermometer, a super-duper first aid kit, a chinning bar that slips into any door frame, and, as they say, much, much more.* —Tom Ferguson, M.D.

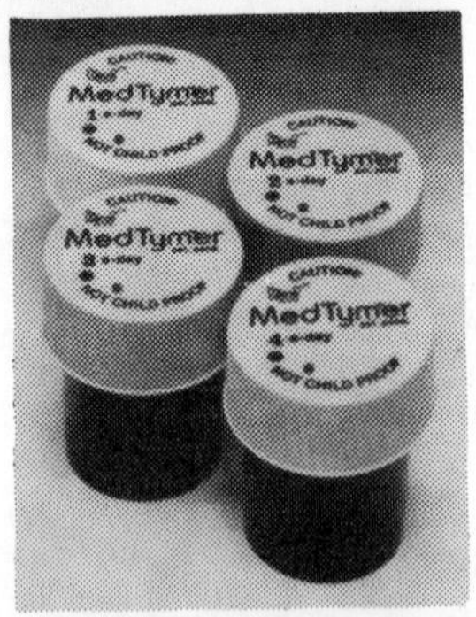

The Medical Self-Care Catalog
Catalog **free** from:
The Medical
Self-Care Catalog
P.O. Box 999
Point Reyes, CA 94956

•

MEDTYMER. Clinical studies show that more than half of people on regular medication do not take their medicines on schedule. MedTymer is a unique electronic cap that replaces the standard cap on most pill bottles. When it's time to take your medication, MedTymer flashes a light and sounds a reminder. The reminder beeper is automatically silenced when the cap is removed, and advanced to the next dose time when the cap is replaced. Available in four different color-coded versions consistent with your prescription schedule, the MedTymer makes it virtually impossible to forget to take medications on time. Please specify 1 a-day, 2 a-day, 3 a-day, 4 a-day.
No. 2007 $16.95 ($1.50)

Earscope Notoco, $21.00.
A low-cost way to check the condition of ears, especially useful for small children with recurring ear infections. It throws a strong beam of light into the ear canal and helps you determine when you or your child needs to see a physician. Made of tough plastic. Comes with instruction booklet and batteries. Small animal model also available.

Sears Home Health Care Catalog

Done in the usual Sears manner, this "Specialog" offers a good selection of the hardware and gadgetry more commonly needed for taking care of the sick and disabled at home. Has the usual Sears sale price specials, too. —JB

Sears Home Health Care
Catalog **free** from:
Sears Roebuck and Co.
Dept. 139
925 South Homan Avenue
Chicago, IL 60607

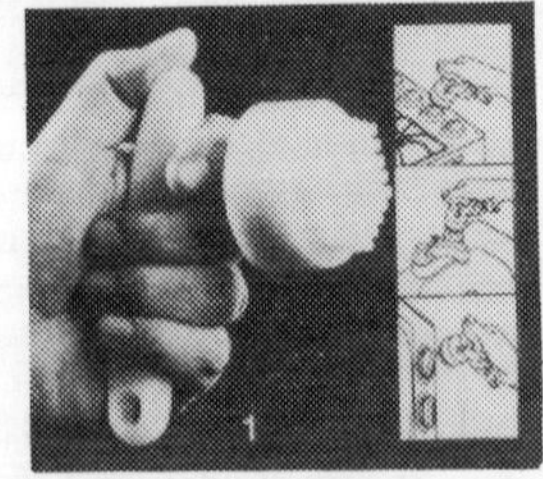

•

(Above) Turning Knob Operator (TKO)™ is ideal for those with weak or arthritic hands. It provides leverage to operate most rotating handles, knobs and controls. Its unique surface of 61 pegs grasps an irregular shaped knob such as those found on many stoves, television sets and water faucets. So the knob turns on or off as you twist the TKO™. Constructed of lightweight nylon, the TKO™ is durable enough to turn the most stubborn knobs. The handle is comfortable to hold and designed for a palm or finger grip. Use in right or left hand. Handle has hole at end for hanging, so your TKO™ is always near.
8 AH 1371 — Shpg. wt. 4 oz $9.99

• You can rent most of the equipment needed for medical self-care at home. The rules are much the same as for tool rental. (p. 160)

Planetree Health Resource Center

Planetree started as a layperson's medical library. (If you think that's nothing special, try getting useful health or specific disease information at your local library.) Now with more than two thousand volumes, it's a model for similar efforts in other cities. This year, Planetree opened a Model Hospital Unit in Presbyterian Medical Center in San Francisco. A ward has been transformed into a friendly place where patients can interact with their families, recreating in the lounge, cooperating in treatment, and even preparing healthy meals themselves. Instant success!

Planetree also offers a catalog of useful self-care hardware and books, bibliographies of readings on specific diseases, in-depth research packets on the disease of your choice, a selection of video tapes, and supporting memberships which include the newsletter ***Planetalk*** *and discounts on other offerings. Their booklet,* ***How to Start a People's Medical Library*** *($4.45 postpaid), should help spread the Planetree seeds.* —JB

Planetree
Membership
$15/year
(includes subscription to ***Planetalk*** newsletter)
Catalog **free**
both from:
Planetree Health
Resource Center
2040 Webster Street
San Francisco, CA 94115

Managing Incontinence by Cheryle B. Gartley, ed. Ottawa, IL: Jameson Books, 1985. $12.95 hardcover.

Loss of bladder control is a problem that nobody talks about, but is so socially unacceptable that many people remain prisoners in their own homes in fear of having an "accident" in public. With over 10,000,000 Americans of all ages suffering from incontinence, there is finally a book which confronts the problem and provides hope. The contributing editors are physicians, psychologists, and nurses who give clear explanations of urinary system function, coping mechanisms, products and devices, surgical remedies, and sexual guidance. A compassionate, much needed book.

A Guide to Physical Examination

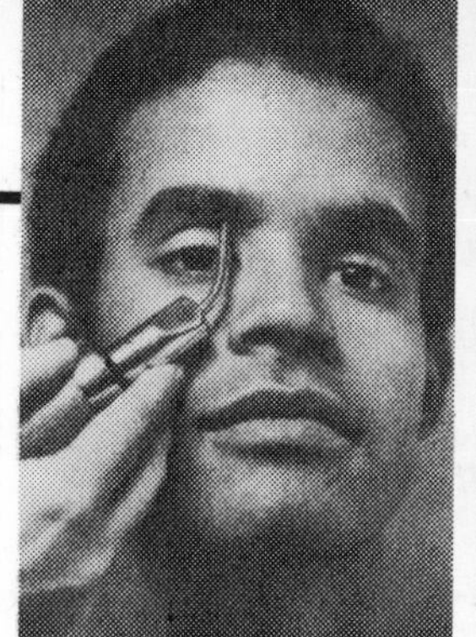

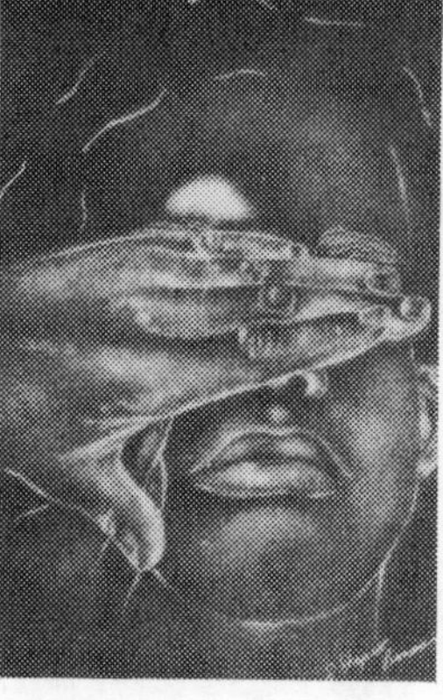

Although transillumination is not part of a routine examination, it is often helpful when sinus tenderness or other symptoms suggest sinusitis. The room should be thoroughly darkened. Using a strong, narrow light source, place the light snugly deep under each brow, close to the nose. Shield the light with your hand. Look for a dim red glow as light is transmittted through the air-filled frontal sinus to the forehead. Absence of glow on one or both sides suggests a thickened mucosa or secretions in the frontal sinus, but it may also result from developmental absence of one or both sinuses.

Lange's ***Current Medical Diagnosis and Treatment*** *(below) is an excellent reference, but it must be used in conjunction with a carefully taken medical history and careful physical examination. It's necesssary to know what you're treating. When you have the patient's signs and symptoms in hand, then you go to Lange or any of the numerous other texts.*

May I please recommend ***A Guide to Physical Examination****? This excellent book is the central core for most courses in physical diagnosis. It is in a large, well-illustrated format with an excellent discussion of the art of interviewing patients so that they give the story. Each system of the body is arranged by chapter, techniques for examination are outlined without jargon, and abnormal findings are noted in red in the margin.*

It is interesting to note that while M.D. training may spend one to two weeks covering the material outlined in Bates' book, physician assistants' training devotes four to five months on the same . . . .

This book will be useful to anyone interested in any aspect of the health sciences — imagine studying mechanics without an idea of where to find the car's motor!

—John Benecki, P.A.

A Guide to Physical Examination
(Third Edition)
Barbara Bates, M.D.
1983; 561 pp.
$35.95
($37.45 postpaid) from:
Harper and Row
2350 Virginia Avenue
Hagerstown, MD 21740
or Whole Earth Access

Current Medical Diagnosis & Treatment

This is probably the single most useful medical reference book you can own. With it you can do two things: you can begin to understand your illness or injury, and — more important perhaps — you can decide whether your doctor understands it. Is your doctor current? Has she (he) diagnosed and treated your condition according to the latest medical research? Here's where you find out.

Being the book doctors use, it's dense and comprehensive, and takes a little work from the lay reader. It's absolutely worth the effort. It's updated every year and offers not just diagnosis of almost every known medical malady from dandruff through toenail atrophy but also prognosis (how long it'll last), standard treatment, and short bibliographies for further research. It's the most used book at Planetree Health Resource Center *(p. 207)**.*

(Keep in mind, though, that **CMD** *is a standard reference, very much rooted in AMA-style medicine. Hence you'll find recommended such therapies as shock treatment and tranquilizers).* *—Joe Kane [Suggested by Planetree]*

•

Sinus Infection
Acute:
- History of acute upper respiratory infection, dental infection, or nasal allergy.
- Pain, tenderness, redness, swelling over the involved sinus.
- Nasal congestion and purulent nasal discharge.
- Clouding of sinuses on x-ray or transillumination.
- Fever, chills, malaise, headache.
- Teeth hurt or feel "long" (maxillary sinusitis), or swelling occurs near the nasal canthus of the eye (ethmoid sinusitis).

General Considerations
Acute sinus infection usually follows an acute upper respiratory infection, swimming or diving, dental abscess or extractions, or nasal allergies, or occurs as an exacerbation of a chronic sinus infection.

Clinical Findings
Symptoms and Signs:
Acute sinusitis — The symptoms resemble those of acute rhinitis but are more severe. There is headache and facial pain, tenderness and swelling with nasal obstruction, and a purulent nasal and postnasal discharge, sometimes causing sore throat and cough. The headache typically is worse during the day and subsides in the evening. Acute maxillary sinusitis may cause pain in the teeth and a feeling of "long teeth." Acute ethmoiditis causes headache between and behind the eyes, and eye motion increases the pain. Tenderness medially in the roof of the orbit occurs with frontal sinusitis. Fever and systemic symptoms vary with the severity of the infection.

Treatment
Acute Sinusitis: Place the patient at bed rest and give sedatives, analgesics, a light diet, and fluids. Oral nasal decongestants (eg. phenylpropanolamine, 25-50 mg 3 times daily) and systemic antibiotics frequently produce prompt resolution of the infection. Ampicillin or erythromycin, 1-2 g/d, is most commonly used. Other antibiotics may be used as determined by culture and sensitivity testing.

Local heat, topical nasal decongestants (eg 0.25% phenylephrine), and gentle spot suctioning of the nasal discharge are helpful.

The sinuses must not be manipulated during the acute infection. Antrum irrigation is of value after the acute inflammation has subsided. Acute frontal sinusitis is treated medically and conservatively; cannulation is rarely warranted. Trephining of the sinus floor may occasionally be indicated in acute fulminating infections. Acute ethmoid infections respond to medical management; if external fluctuation develops, incision and drainage are indicated.

Prognosis
Acute infections usually respond to medical management and irrigation.

Current Medical Diagnosis & Treatment
Marcus A. Krupp,
Milton J. Chatton, and
Lawrence M. Tierney, Jr.,
Editors
1986; 1,166 pp.
$29.50
($32.50 postpaid) from:
Lange Medical Publications
Drawer L
Los Altos, CA 94023
or Whole Earth Access

Worker's Trust

When the Whole Earth crew decided to have health-insurance, we looked for a company that had low prices, good coverage (including nontraditional care), and company attitudes that were similar to ours. Worker's Trust is all of these. It's owned and controlled by members, and invests its money in socially responsible enterprises. They only insure workers in democratically run organizations like their own. Our experience with them has been good. My experience with them has been good; they promptly paid my recent claim with no crap at all.

—JB [Suggested by David Cohn]

Worker's Trust
Information **free** from
Worker's Trust
P.O. Box 11618
Eugene, OR 97440

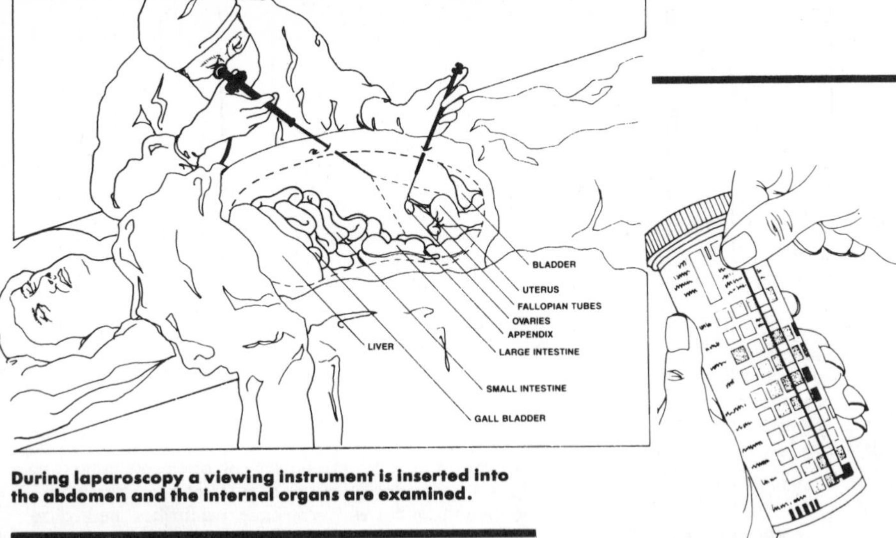

During laparoscopy a viewing instrument is inserted into the abdomen and the internal organs are examined.

***Home Urinalysis.* After dipping the reagent strip into a urine specimen, the color change of the reagent pads on the strip is compared with the standard color blocks on the reagent strip container. (Available from Medical Self-Care Catalog, p. 207).**

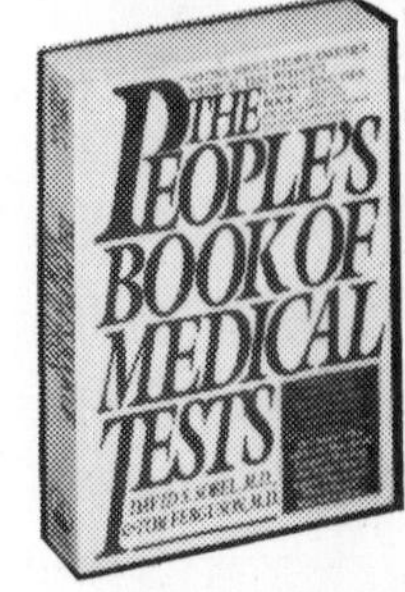

The People's Book of Medical Tests

It's your choice: a possible disease or a dangerous diagnostic test — either of which may be detrimental to your health. Before slipping into a hospital gown, I'm going to consult this book. It tallies up the recognized risks of common medical tests (pain, expenses, and complications). It'll also give the honest details of each procedure, its preparation, and the normal range of results so I can ask the doctor intelligent questions afterwards. It could help me avoid an unnecessary operation or medication, and for that I'll give it my kiss of eternal gratitude.

Coauthored by Tom Ferguson, M.D., one quarter of this book addresses medical tests that can be done at home and evaluates them in the same careful manner.

—Kevin Kelly

•

The first and most important question should be whether you really need the test at all. Before agreeing to any test you should ask your doctor, "What will we do if the test results are abnormal?" and "what will we do if the results are normal?" If the answer to both questions is the same, you probably do not need the test.

The People's Book of Medical Tests
David S. Sobel, M.D. and Tom Ferguson, M.D.
1985; 510 pp.
$12.95
($14.40 postpaid) from:
Summit Books
1230 Avenue of the Americas
New York, NY 10020
or Whole Earth Access

The People's Medical Society

Doctors have the American Medical Association to look after their interests. Hospitals have the American Hospital Association. Now health consumers have the People's Medical Society (PMS).

PMS now has more than 70,000 active members. The group was established in response to the "growing cost and depersonalization of medical care, and the monopolistic excesses of the medical profession." In addition to pro-consumer lobbying on health issues, PMS provides a newsletter and other publications to help its members: avoid unnecessary medical care; save money on the care they do need; obtain access to the medical information they need; become experts on the health issues which concern them; join together with other local consumers to provide support and to encourage reform of local medical institutions; evaluate local doctors. (The PMS national office circulates visit evaluation forms, tabulates the results, and publishes consumer satisfaction ratings of all doctors evaluated.)

A sample newsletter, list of publications, and membership information is available on request. Health workers are invited to send for a copy of the PMS Code of Practice. Names of providers who have subscribed to the Code are made available to PMS members. —Tom Ferguson, M.D.

The People's Medical Society
Charles B. Inlander, President
Membership
$15/year
(includes bimonthly newsletter)
Information **free** from:
The People's Medical Society
14 East Minor Street
Emmaus, PA 18049

Complete Home Medical Guide

This has become my favorite medical encyclopedia. Virtually anything you need to know about medicine at home is in here. I now rely mainly on two books: ***Harrison's Principles of Internal Medicine*** *(the classic text used in most medical schools) and this one, which is written for the lay person. For a book written by an Ivy League med school, it is surprisingly supportive of pediatrics for parents and other medical self-care. Four stars.*

—Michael Castleman (editor of Medical Self-Care)

•

Start in the middle years to expand interests and horizons. The greater the number of interests, the larger the circle of potential friends and acquaintances, the greater the opportunity for new learning, the less the chance of becoming bored. Recent studies show that variety of interests may be even more important than family history of longevity as a predictor of life expectancy.

•

People who travel to areas where there is endemic infection or who contract intestinal infections from contaminated food may develop fever, diarrhea, and intestinal cramps. Many of these appear to be viruses that are self-limited and can be treated symptomatically with a low-fiber diet and such anti-diarrheal medications as kaolin and pectin (Kaeopectate), or bismuth (Pepto-Bismol).

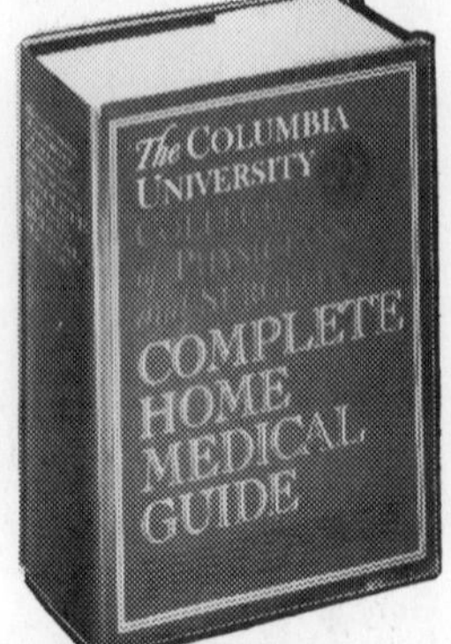

The Columbia University Complete Home Medical Guide
1985; 911 pp.
$39.95
($41.95 postpaid) from:
Crown Publishers
34 Englehard Avenue
Avenel, NJ 07001
or Whole Earth Access

National Self-Help Clearinghouse (NSHC)

If you have a pressing social or health concern, there's probably a corresponding self-help group. There are now an estimated 500,000 groups in the U.S. alone — with 20 million members.

NSHC is a clearinghouse for all U.S. (and many international) self-help organizations. If you want to find an arthritis support group in San Jose or the chapter of Parents Without Partners nearest to Goshen, Indiana, they're the ones to ask. They publish a newsletter and a journal ***(Social Policy)*** *and can provide information on current self-help research, advice on starting your own group, and addresses for the twenty-odd regional self-help clearinghouses that have sprung up around the U.S. within recent years.* *—Tom Ferguson, M.D.*

National Self-Help Clearinghouse
Information **free** (with SASE) from:
NSHC
33 West 42nd Street
New York, NY 10036

Social Policy
Frank Reissman and Alan Gartner, Editors
$20/year
(4 issues) from
Social Policy
33 West 42nd Street
New York, NY 10036

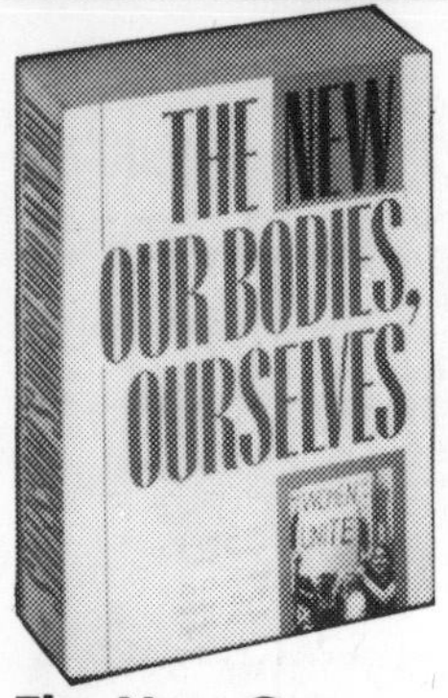

The New Our Bodies, Ourselves
The Boston Women's Health Book Collective
1984; 647 pp.
$14.95 postpaid from:
Simon & Schuster
Mail Order Sales
200 Old Tappan Road
Old Tappan, NJ 07675
or Whole Earth Access

The New Our Bodies, Ourselves

Breathe deeply of this wonderful book. It expands our notions of what it means to be women and stay healthy in our minds, our relationships, our workplaces, and our bodies. Like a perceptive friend, it nurtures and challenges us to take control of our own well-being.

***The New Our Bodies, Ourselves** is itself a model of health; it has the strength of its original convictions and the flexibility to adapt to changes that bear on those convictions. This 1984 edition is two-thirds revised with new chapters on alternative medical care, alcohol and drugs, environmental and occupational health, and new reproductive technologies. I hope this rare book continues to adapt and expand for at least a few more decades.*

A Spanish language edition is available directly from the Boston Women's Health Book Collective.

—Jeanne Carstensen
[Suggested by Tom Ferguson, M.D.]

Nuestros Cuerpos, Nuestras Vidas: (Our Bodies, Ourselves) 1979; 383 pp. **$5.00** ($6 postpaid) from The Boston Women's Health Book Collective, Spanish Edition, P. O. Box 192, West Somerville, MA 02144.

•

In expanding the concept of prevention even further, we risk defining more and more aspects of life in terms of health and illness — that is, according to a medical model. We may end up seeing exercise, eating, meditation, fresh air, dance, for example — all pleasures in their own right — simply as measures of our potential health or nonhealth. In this way, ironically, we further medicalize our lives.

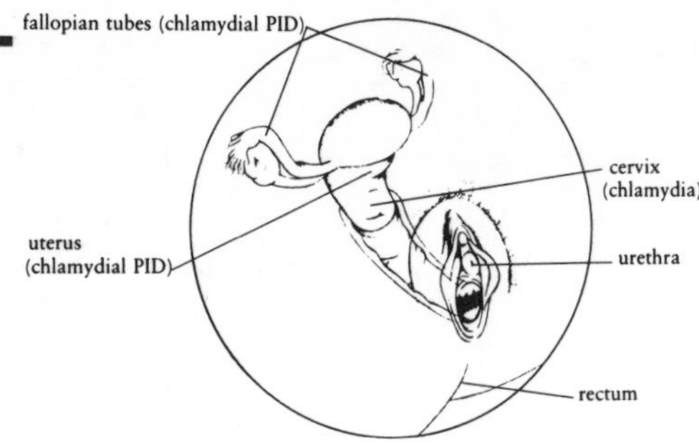

CHLAMYDIA AND UREAPLASMA
Chlamydia can also be transmitted to the eyes via the hands.

•

Chlamydia

Until recently, the bacterium *Chlamydia trachomatis* was thought to affect only men, causing half of the cases of male nongonococcal urethritis (NGU), while women were silent "carriers." Now we know that chlamydia can cause very serious problems for women, including urethral infection, cervicitis (inflammation of the cervix), PID and infertility as well as dangerous complications during pregnancy and birth.

My Body, My Health
Felicia Stewart, M.D., Felicia Guest, Gary Stewart, M.D., Robert Hatcher, M.D.
1981; 564 pp.
$11.95
($13.45 postpaid) from:
Bantam Books
414 East Golf Road
Des Plaines, IL 60016
or Whole Earth Access

My Body, My Health

Written by several people long-respected in gynecology and family planning circles, its concise yet surprisingly thorough chapters cover the gamut of women's most frequently encountered health concerns: pregnancy, birth control, abortion, surviving a pelvic exam, common infections, menstrual problems, abnormal pap smears, breast self-exam, breast lumps, cancer, sexual problems, menopause, surgery, etc.

The sections on teenage sexuality, vaginal hygiene, recognition of early signs of pregnancy, facing surgery, and special help in choosing a method of birth control are sensitively written and cover topics not easily found elsewhere.

This is a fine piece of work — our first lay gynecology textbook. I'd like to see a copy in every library, every women's clinic, and every gynecologist's waiting room.

—Carol Berry, R.N., N.P.
[Suggested by Tom Ferguson, M.D.]

*This more medically detailed guide belongs on the shelf next to **The New Our Bodies, Our Selves**. Look for a completely revised edition in 1987, probably from Bantam.*

—Jeanne Carstensen

•

I've examined my breasts each and every month for at least ten years, and I still have to *make* myself do it every time! I always do it *in the morning of a weekday*; so I know I can call my doctor *immediately* if I find anything. I don't think I could do it at night.

—Woman, 33

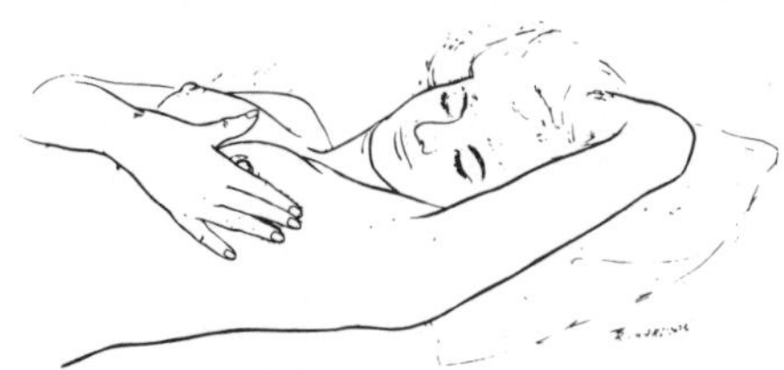

Use the flat part of your fingertips to feel each area of the breast. Repeat your exam in a standing or sitting position.

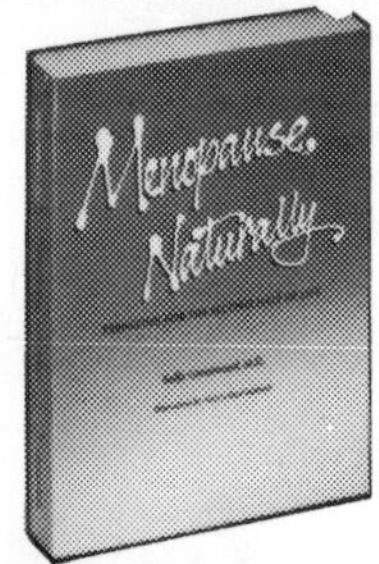

Menopause, Naturally
Sadja Greenwood, M.D.
1984; 201 pp.
$10
($11.25 postpaid) from:
Volcano Press
330 Ellis Street, Dept. W
San Francisco, CA 94102
or Whole Earth Access

Menopause, Naturally

A guide for women entering the frightening territory of their 40s and 50s. This new phase of life inevitably brings up deep feelings — mostly negative. Most younger women believe that menopause means depression, irritability, unhappiness, and sexual decline. Greenwood gently explains that it means none of these things. She puts a sisterly arm around the worried reader and tells her the facts: hot flashes — a mildly uncomfortable sign of hormonal changes, something like a midlife case of pimples; emotional upsets — no more common than in younger women; the end of sex — no way!

She goes on to explain in appropriate detail the two primary medical concerns of most midlife women — preventing osteoporosis and considering estrogen replacement therapy.

Like most women, I spent the first half of my life responding to the needs of others. One of the good things about the period ahead is that the world now makes fewer demands on me, leaving me free to pursue my own agenda, to find out who I really am. Greenwood's warm, sensible guide makes this seem an exciting challenge indeed.

—Neshama Franklin

•

In Western culture, with its strong emphasis on female youth and beauty, the menopause is seen as a time of decline and loss of status for women. . . . Among many non-Western groups, the older woman enjoys increased status in the family and greater freedom in society at large. Menopause and the cessation of childbearing become positive events in a woman's life, and physical symptoms are given less attention.

• **Menopause Naturally** author Sadja Greenwood, M.D., updates her book in this annual newsletter.
PMZ Newsletter: Sadja Greenwood, Editor. **Free** with SASE from Volcano Press, 330-WEC Ellis Street, San Francisco, CA 94102.

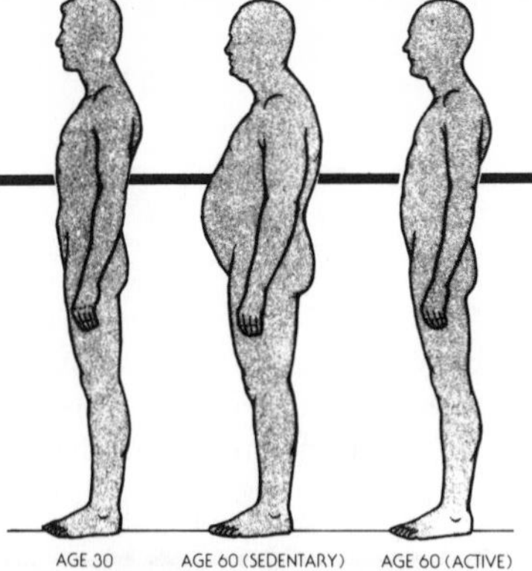

How A Man Ages

This is a fast, breezy overview of the aging process in men — what happens to you independent of illness. There's a lot on how to stay in shape, and there is frank discussion of attempts (such as face-lifts) to hold off the appearance of the inevitable. You could say it's a book on how the healthy man ages. —Michael Castleman

As I wend my way towards old-fartdom, I find this book to be horrifyingly, encouragingly, true. —JB

•

Cardiac ouput (volume of blood pumped per minute) is what you get when you multiply the stroke volume (the amount of blood pumped with each beat) by the heart rate (number of beats per minute). Since heart rates at maximum exercise levels decline with age, you might expect that cardiac output during vigorous exercise would also fall. Not so. Research now shows that, contrary to previous expectations, one's so-called end-diastolic filling volume increases as one ages. This means that during vigorous exercise the heart fills with more blood between beats, making more blood available to be pumped with the next beat. Again, this is a kind of compensatory gesture that the body seems to make to keep things running smoothly over time.

A man who early on gets the habit of regular, vigorous exercise is likely at 60 to have much the same body shape as he had at 30. His shoulders will be narrower and he will have lost upper body mass, but he will have avoided that all-too-common result of age, overeating, and inactivity — potbelly.

Age and Memory

After about age 50, the slight loss of memory that typically afflicts a healthy man is more a matter of faulty retrieval than of lost information. If an old man and a young man each try to memorize a list of words and are then given clues to each of the words, the older man recalls them as well as the younger man. But without clues, the old man has a tougher time remembering what was on the list:

Age 20: 14 of 24 words recalled
Age 30: 13 words recalled
Age 40: 11 words recalled
Age 50: 10 words recalled
Age 60: 9 words recalled
Age 70: 7 words recalled

However, new tests show that older people can greatly improve their memory function when they are taught to use mnemonic devices.

How A Man Ages
Curtis Pesmen
1984; 226 pp.
$7.95
($8.95 postpaid) from:
Random House
Order Dept.
400 Hahn Road
Westminster, MD 21157
or Whole Earth Access

The Seasons of a Man's Life

This book was the original inspiration for the popular book ***Passages****. Interviews with a small group of men at various stages of their lives show a fascinating thing: personal and emotional growth doesn't stop when you become an "adult." This idea isn't new, but this book was the first to show the processes involved. Its revelations have stood up over time despite the lack of depth in the sample chosen for study.* —Michael Castleman

•

Men rarely have mentors after about 40. A man may have valued relationships with family, friends, counselors and co-workers, but the mentor relationship in its developed form is rare. It is surrendered, with other things, as part of Becoming One's Own Man. One result is a greater ability and interest in being a mentor to others.

•

He needs to separate himself from the striving ego and the external pressures, so that he can better hear the voices from within.

To the extent that a man succeeds in this task during middle adulthood, the Self acquires an importance for him roughly equal to that of the external world. He can draw more upon his inner resources and is thus less dependent on external stimulation. He enjoys solitude more, since he has internal company when other persons are absent. He places less value on possessions, rewards and social approval. He lives more in the present and gains more satisfaction from the process of living — from being rather than doing and having. More in touch with his own feelings, he can be more esthetic, sensual, aware.

• Heart problems or the fear of "dying in the saddle" needn't ruin your sex life, this book says.
Sound Sex and the Aging Heart: Lee D. Scheingold and Nathaniel N. Wagner, 1974; 168 pp. **$19.95** postpaid from Human Sciences Press, Order Dept., 72 5th Avenue, New York, NY 10011.

• See also **Circumcision** (p. 237).

Men's Reproductive Health

This comprehensive book is by far the best on the subject. It's written by experts for an audience of health professionals, but it's easily understood by nonmedical readers willing to work at it. Covers common problems such as prostate, AIDS, sexually transmitted diseases (STDs), and urology. —Michael Castleman

•

Benign prostatic hypertrophy, or BPH, is the most common cause of bladder outlet obstruction in males over the age of 50. Autopsy studies have shown that 50-60 percent of men over the age of 50 have significant enlargement of the prostate gland, and this prevalence increases with age. The bladder outlet obstruction is characterized by urinary hesitancy, diminished force and caliber of the stream, and post-void dribbling, as well as urinary frequency and nocturia, that is, getting up at night to urinate. . . .

The only currently available treatment for BPH is prostatectomy. In the future, perhaps, pharmacological therapy to diminish the size of the obstructing gland may be available. . . .

Prostatectomy should not produce organic erectile impotence; however, psychogenic impotence may follow any genitourinary surgery.

Drug-induced Sexual Dysfunction and Gynecomastia in Males

Drug	Decreased Desire	Decreased Erectile Ability	Decreased Ejaculatory Ability	Gynecomastia	Decreased Sperm Quality
Hormones					
Progestins	common	24–70%	occurs	occurs	common
Estrogens	common	common	occurs	common	common
Corticosteroids	none	none	none	none	occurs
Antiandrogens	common	common	none	common	common
Androgens	occurs[3]	occurs	none	occurs	common
Sedative-Hypnotics					
Diazepam (Valium®)	none	none	occurs	occurs	none
Chlordiazepoxide (Librium®)	none	none	occurs	none	none
Barbiturates (secobarbital, pentobarbital, etc.)	increase or decrease[4]	common	occurs	none	none
Methaqualone (Quāālude®)	increase or decrease[4]	common	occurs	none	none
Ethyl Alcohol	increase or decrease[4]	common	occurs	occurs	occurs
Stimulants					
Amphetamine and analogs	increase	occurs	occurs	occurs	none
Cocaine	increase	occurs	occurs	none	none
Opiates					
Heroin	60%	39%	70%	none	occurs
Methadone (Dolophine®)	6–38%	6–50%	5–88%	none	common

The Seasons of a Man's Life
Daniel Levinson
1978; 363 pp.
$9.95
($10.95 postpaid) from:
Random House
Order Dept.
400 Hahn Road
Westminster, MD 21157
or Whole Earth Access

Men's Reproductive Health
Janice Swanson and Katherine Forrest
1984; 398 pp.
$27.95
($29.95 postpaid) from:
Springer Publishing Co.
536 Broadway
New York NY 10012
or Whole Earth Access

A Handbook for the Disabled
Suzanne Lunt
1984; 276 pp.
$9.95
postpaid from:
MacMillan Publishing Co.
Order Dept.
Front and Brown Streets
Riverside, NJ 08075
or Whole Earth Access

THE BEST SOURCE OF INFORMATION on any particular disability is someone who has had that disability for a few years.

Occupational therapists are another good source, but don't let the "experts" make decisions for you. Ask questions. Beware of rumors of medical or engineering wonders and never buy anything unless you've used it, preferably at home. When dealing with agencies, firmly tell them what you want. Don't let doctors, salespeople, or the U.S. government intimidate you. —Mark O'Brien

A Handbook for the Disabled

A comprehensive guide to devices (store-bought and homemade) and agencies for paralyzed and temporarily bedridden people. Lunt thoroughly researched this book and has included manufacturers' addresses. This is the only book I've seen that discusses both equipment and agencies. My only qualm is that she calls disabled people "patients," an inappropriate word for people who are not living in a hospital. —Mark O'Brien

Reading this book made me realize how many unsung heroes are working in their basements, inventing new problem-solvers for the disabled. —Sallie Tisdale

•

Automatic fork: 8½ inches; handles, when squeezed, cause metal plate to slide down and push food off tines. (About $4, American Foundation for the Blind.)

Side-cutter fork: Adds moderate cutting ability to edge of fork; will not injure mouth; cuts most foods, but not all meats. (About $10, Help Yourself Aids.)

•

Some tips from a disabled driver:

To lock and unlock passenger door from driver's seat: Keep a length of wood 24½'' long and 1'' wide, notched at the end.

To hold lid of trunk open on windy days: Keep another stick 50'' long and 1¼'' wide in the trunk.

To pull things forward that have slid to back of trunk: Keep a cane in the trunk and use the curved end to pull things forward.

To support your right arm while driving: Pad a small wooden box by gluing sheet foam to it. Place it on the seat at your right side.

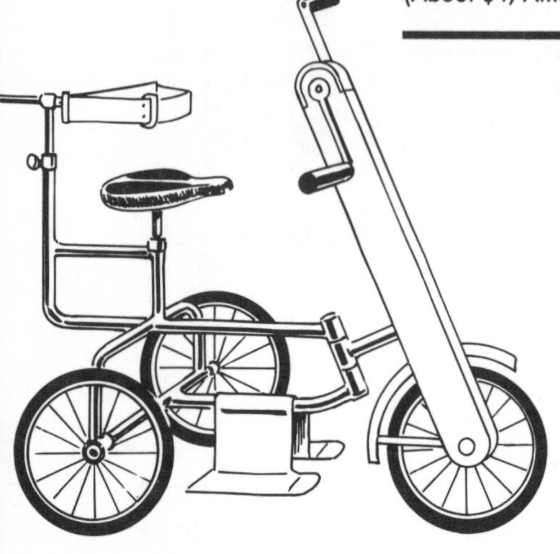

Hand-propelled tricycles are popular with children between four and ten years of age. Most can be ridden in braces and have a range of foot and back rests. —*The Wheelchair Child*

The Wheelchair Child

I wish my parents could have had a book like this when I became disabled in the '50s. Russell, who has a disabled child, speaks from experience and she's had all the experiences that come with raising a kid who uses a wheelchair. In direct language, she offers advice on the education, clothing, recreation, and socialization that disabled children need. Russell is British, so about half of her practical advice applies only to people in the U.K. Her advice on dealing with problems like sibling jealousy, parent burnout, and sexuality is universally applicable. —Mark O'Brien

•

Many handicapped girls are convinced that they will never get pregnant, and are woefully ignorant of the symptoms of pregnancy if it should happen. Some parents might contend that the subject was better left alone, because of embarrassment and because of the relaxation of restrictions on abortion facilities. But this attitude ignores the fact that many handicapped girls will desperately want a child of their own. Childbearing will prove their normality and identity as a woman — a healthy child will to some extent diminish their own feeling of disability and will also be seen as a source of love and attention. Needless to say, agreement to an abortion will be very difficult and filled with emotional problems in a case of this kind.

Hugh in action on a grade 5.12 climb.

The Wheelchair Child
Philippa Russell
1985; 262 pp.
$9.95
postpaid from:
Prentice-Hall Press
Mail Order Sales
200 Old Tappan Road
Old Tappan, NJ 07675
or Whole Earth Access

Other Product Sources

A computer databank listing all commercially available items for disabled people, ABLEDATA includes everything — clothing, wheelchairs, speech synthesizers. It can be searched by computer or you can make voice requests.

Products For People With Vision Problems is a fascinating catalog that features a wide-range of useful products for blind and vision-impaired people. —Mark O'Brien

ABLEDATA: Information **free** from NARIC, 4407 Eighth Street NW, Washington, D.C. 20017; 1/800/34-NARIC (TDD and voice).

Products for People with Vision Problems: Catalog **free** from American Foundation for the Blind/Customer Service Division, 15 W. 16th Street, New York, NY 10011.

• Sports from a wheelchair and all sorts of chairs built with racing bicycle technology are what this lively magazine is about. The March/April '86 issue has a survey of available chairs.

Sports and Spokes: Nancy Crase, Editor. **$8**/year (6 issues) from Sports and Spokes, 5201 North 19th Avenue, Phoenix, AZ 85015-9986.

The Cripple Liberation Front Marching Band Blues

Not a how-to book so much as a what-it's-like book that describes the author's experience with polio, hospitals, rehabilitation, and his efforts to live independently. There is a great deal of pain in this book, the pain inherent in the sudden onset of disability. Tough, realistic, and decidedly unsentimental, it is also often tender, wise, and hilarious in its account of disability. Honest to the bone, it is the best written book on how it feels to be disabled.
—Mark O'Brien

•

He was brave, that Roosevelt. O Lordy he was brave. He must have known that he would never be whole, but he was brave. A clear-cut nothing-from-the-waist-down case, and yet he forced himself to walk. With steel and fire, he forced his arms to take him across the room, across the lawn, down the steps. He knew, some part of him knew he would never be walking at the head of the Labor Day parade again, but he kept on pouring his will into what was left of his muscles, trying to walk that walk again. He put on his twenty-pound steel braces, and sweating and puffing, demanded of his body that it produce steps for him. There were none there; yet he created them from somewhere. From his burning will he created whole steps where there should have been none.

The Cripple Liberation Front Marching Band Blues
Lorenzo Wilson Milam
1984; 220 pp.
$9.95
($11.45 postpaid) from:
Mho & Mho Works
P. O. Box 33135
San Diego, CA 92103
or Whole Earth Access

The Disability Rag

*The **Rag** conveys the opinions and the politics of disabled people with vigor and clarity. It deals with the nitty-gritty of disability — attendants, accessible buses, and employing a reader. The **Rag** also addresses the fear and anger disabled people feel about living in a world that sees us in stereotypical terms. This is a tough, scrappy, honest magazine, without advertising.* *—Mark O'Brien*

•

A counselor's phone rings. The nurse at a local hospital maternity unit wants to put her in touch with the parents of a new baby. A difficult birth has caused neurological distress for the child; she might have cerebral palsy.

When the parents arrive at her office, the counselor meets them at the door and leads them to comfortable chairs. She lays her crutches beneath her chair and scoots back into her chair in short, pushed bursts of movement. The parents, startled, are obviously ill at ease.

After forced introductions and stiff, nervous chatter, the counselor, to jolt the parents into confronting their own negative feelings, bluntly asks, "You weren't expecting a cripple for a counselor, were you?"

The Disability Rag
Mary Johnson, Editor
$9/year
(6 issues) from:
The Disability Rag
P. O. Box 145
Louisville, KY 40201

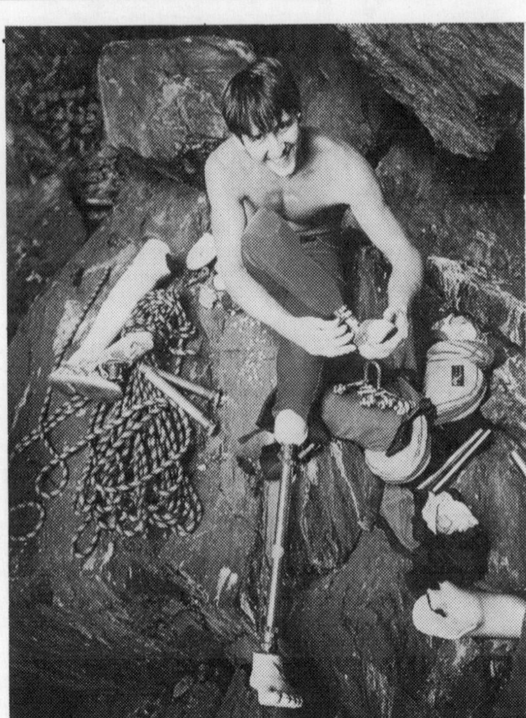

Hugh Herr's legs were amputated as a result of frostbite suffered during an ice climbing accident. Now he climbs using a selection of prosthetic legs and feet.
—Climbing Magazine **(see p. 276).**

• See National Gardening Association (p. 77) for tools for disabled gardeners.

Resources for Independent Living
by Mark O'Brien

Access to the World

Tells disabled people everything they need to know about travel.

Access to the World (A Travel Guide for the Handicapped): Louise Weiss, 1983; 221 pp. **$14.95** postpaid from Facts on File, Inc., 460 Park Avenue South, New York, NY 10016 (or Whole Earth Access).

Design for Independent Living

Through photos and interviews, this book shows that disabled people can live well outside of hospitals and institutions.

Design for Independent Living: Raymond Lischez and Barbara Winslow, 1981; 208 pp. **$9.95** ($11.45 postpaid) from University of California Press, 2120 Berkeley Way, Berkeley, CA 94720 (or Whole Earth Access).

World Institute on Disability

A place to find out about independent living centers near you, either in North America or abroad.

World Institute on Disability: information **free** from 1720 Oregon Street/Suite 4, Berkeley, CA 94703.

Disability Rights Education and Defense Fund

I was almost kept out of graduate school once because I was disabled. DREDF helped me realize I had a case. A lobbying and litigation group, they are the first place to go if you think you may be a victim of discrimination.

Disability Rights Education and Defense Fund: information **free** from 2212 6th Street, Berkeley, CA 94710.

—Design for Independent Living

◄ The Heimlich maneuver. (A) As quickly as the victim signals distress, the rescuer grasps him from behind. (B) The rescuer's fist should be pressed into the upper abdomen at the spot marked by the cross. (C) Correct position of rescuer when patient is found lying face up. Note the placement of the hand, which permits a quick upward thrust.

Emergency Medical Guide

Emergency Medical Guide
John Henderson, M. D.
1978; 681 pp.
$7.95 postpaid from:
McGraw Hill
Order Dept.
Princeton Road
Hightstown, NJ 08520
or Whole Earth Access

No special knowledge or skill is required to use this up-to-date first aid guide, though one might wish for a less academic tone of voice. "Emergency" doesn't just mean accident, either — there are instructions for treating acute illness and delivering a baby away from medical assistance. An anatomy lesson is included to help you understand what's going on, and there is a good bit of emergency prevention advice. Everybody should have this sort of knowledge available, preferably in their head. —JB

•

Pavement can get surprisingly hot (up to 172° F or more) even on relatively cool days, and black asphalt surfaces get much hotter than white concrete surfaces since they absorb more and reflect less heat. A person lying unconscious, unable to move, on such a surface can sustain severe burns on exposed areas of the body in a relatively short period of time.

Mountaineering First Aid • Medicine For Mountaineering

Mountaineering First Aid
Martha J. Lentz, Ph.D., R.N., et al.
1985; 112 pp.
$4.95 postpaid

Medicine For Mountaineering
James A. Wilkerson, M.D., Editor
1985; 438 pp.
$10.95 postpaid
Both from:
Mountaineer Books
306 Second Avenue West
Seattle, WA 98119
or Whole Earth Access

First aid books tell you what to do 'til the doctor comes. But what if the doctor isn't coming? ***Mountaineering First Aid*** *is a brief, light booklet outlining seven steps (including basic first aid) that will help "stabilize the situation." The steps are intended to help you organize and keep psychologically cool under trying circumstances. First aid is only part of it; you must insure the safety of the other members of the party and get everyone back to safety. Good stuff to know for anyone who ventures beyond the parking lot.*

Medicine for Mountaineering *is a much more detailed discussion of the same principles and situations. It, too, accents the psychology involved in boondock emergencies — a critical aspect that is only now being recognized.* —JB

•

Seven steps for first aid response:
Step 1. Take charge of the situation
Step 2. Approach the victim safely
Step 3. Perform emergency rescue and urgent first aid
Step 4. Protect the victim
Step 5. Check for other injuries
Step 6. Plan what to do
Step 7. Carry out the plan

—*Mountaineering First Aid*

•

Normal reactions to stress: Reactions to stress may be immediate or delayed. Immediate reactions among rescuers at the accident site — which are normal — include anxiety and apprehension, doubts about their abilities, or hopelessness and despair, which are often mixed with denial or "splitting." Some rescuers experience cognitive difficulties, forgetting where they put things and finding decisions hard to make. "Rescuers in all types of incidents report nausea, a pounding sensation in their hearts, muscle tremors, cramps, profuse sweating, chills, headaches, and muffled hearing."

—*Medicine for Mountaineering*

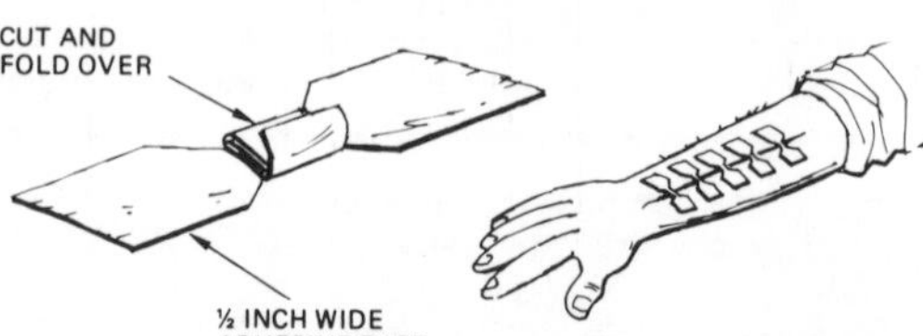

—Mountaineering First Aid

•

Fingers: Dislocations of the fingers, which occur most commonly at the second joint, may be corrected quite easily immediately after the dislocation by pulling on the injured digit. The injured finger can then be splinted effectively by taping it to an adjacent uninjured finger. Dislocations of the thumb are usually accompanied by a fracture of the bone at the base of the thumb. Such injuries are seldom stable when corrected by manipulation alone and are best treated in the field by total immobilization.

—*Medicine For Mountaineering*

A Sigh of Relief

A Sigh of Relief
Martin J. Green
1984; 264 pp.
$12.95
($14.45 postpaid) from:
Bantam Books
414 East Golf Road
Des Plaines, IL 60016
or Whole Earth Access

This is an ultra-simple first aid handbook for childhood emergencies. Some would say too simple, but it'll get things started and may greatly decrease unnecessary worry. The large format and bold index make it easy to find what you need fast. Just the thing for babysitters. —JB

•

Electric shock: *Important: do not touch the child directly while he remains in contact with the current.* Stand on something dry — a blanket, rubber mat, newspapers, etc. — and push away the child or the source of the shock with a dry board or pole. ▼

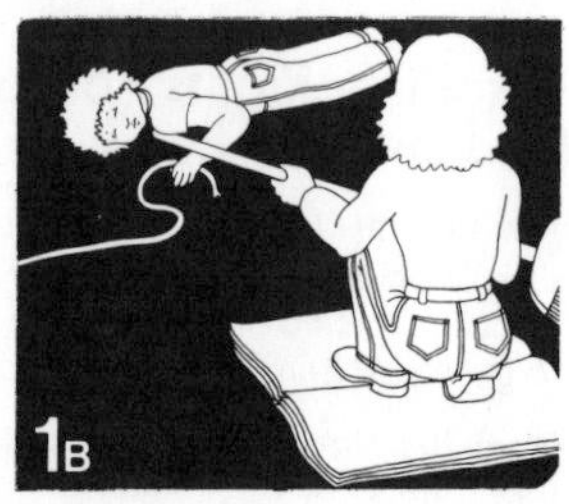

First Aid Kits

Two extra nice first aid kits: one for timber workers from Bailey's (p. 127) and the one you see in fancy foreign cars (packed in a handy pillow), from Mecial Self-Care Catalog (p. 207). —JB

• The best book for Third World medical situations. (Also available in Spanish, Portuguese, and Khmer.)
Where There Is No Doctor: David Werner, 1977; 403 pp. **$8** postpaid from The Hesperian Foundation, P. O. Box 1692, Palo Alto, CA 94302 (or Whole Earth Access).

Where There Is No Dentist

This is a manual for those with no knowledge of dentistry but who nonetheless have been appointed by the fates to do some. The book is thorough, cautious, and illustrated well enough to upset the squeamish. If you expect to work in less-developed countries or other bush situations, you might need to know all this. The same outfit also publishes **Where There Is No Doctor** (p. 214). —JB

◄ In India and Guatemala, health workers use a foot treadle to power a drill, the same way they operate a sewing machine. This kind of drill is slower than a compressed-air drill, and the grinding produces a lot of heat, so one must take care not to let the tooth get so hot that it kills the nerves. Still, this is one of the simplest and cheapest ways to place a permanent filling.

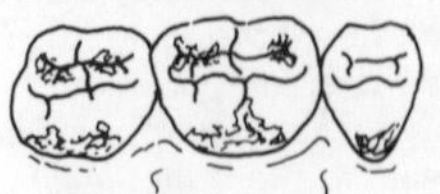

If you do not fill a cavity, it grows bigger. It also grows deeper.

When decay touches the nerve inside, the tooth aches, even when you try to sleep.

How to Save Your Teeth

It takes implacable discipline to keep those choppers chipper, but it can be done. This book explains how to do it (in case your dentist hasn't) and explains most of the other dental procedures you're likely to encounter in this mortal coil. —JB

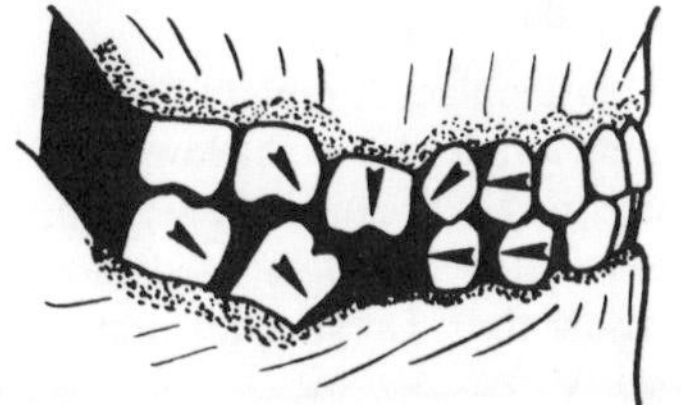

Seven teeth are affected by the loss or removal of one tooth.

•

Shifting and Tilting

Basically, what happens when you lose a tooth, particularly a rear tooth, is that the opposing tooth moves toward the space. This is particularly true of the missing lower first molar. The upper tooth drops into the space. Teeth next to the space lean in to try to fill it. There are actually seven teeth affected by the loss of the lower first molar.

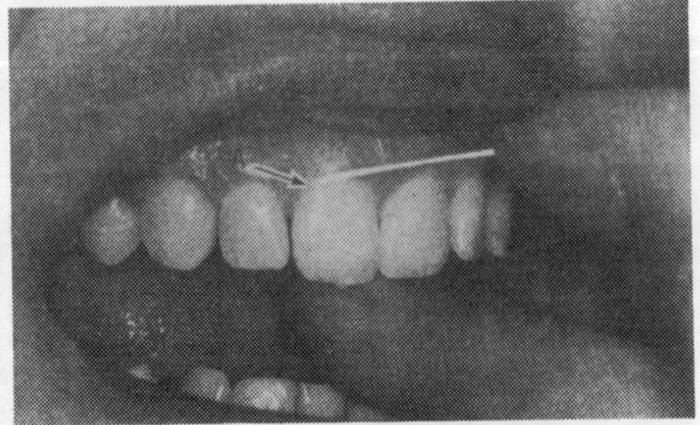

Flossing the upper teeth — note floss under gum.

How to Save Your Teeth
Howard B. Marshall
1980; 334 pp.
$5.95
($6.95 postpaid) from:
Viking/Penguin Books
299 Murray Hill Pkwy.
East Rutherford, NJ 07073
or Whole Earth Access

Where There Is No Dentist
Murray Dickson
1983; 195 pp.
$4.50 postpaid from:
The Hesperian Foundation
P. O. Box 1692
Palo Alto, CA 94302
or Whole Earth Access

Dental Emergency Kit

Worst Fears Confirmed Department: — you're about halfway down the Colorado River on that long-dreamed-of (and expensive) ten-day raft trip and a filling falls out, leaving you in attention-demanding pain. The butterfly bandages and iodine in the first aid kit aren't going to help save the day, but this dental emergency kit likely will; it has everything you need to take care of most unexpected tooth terrors. A booklet tells you what to do. —JB

• This inexpensive publication from the American Dental Association shows you how to care for the family fangs. **Guide to Dental Health:** Lucy Maloney, Editor. Annual; 64 pp. **$2.50** postpaid from American Dental Association, Subscription Dept. CG-29, 211 East Chicago Avenue, Chicago, IL 60611.

Dental Oral Care
$21 (with mirrored box)
$13 (with plain box)

Information **free** from:
Medical Self-Care Catalog
P. O. Box 999
Point Reyes, CA 94956
or Whole Earth Access

The Astrodent

I have one of those mouths that requires twice-a-year visits to the dentist for cleaning, each session featuring fountains of blood, much character-building pain, and stern lectures threatening doom to my gums if I don't shape up and start flossing every half hour or so. I cringe and pretend to agree and show up six months later with four pounds of plaque in my head. That was before Astrodent.

I still go every six months for cleaning, but it's a far more civilized experience now. The only difference is that instead of brushing my teeth in the morning I now have at them with the two tip on the gum-tooth machine. The pointy tip massages gums, all along the edges and into the crannies between teeth. The cupped tip takes a tiny dollop of toothpaste or powder and expertly polishes the teeth, also massaging gums on the way. That's it. Every couple months I need a new AA battery. Big improvement. —Stewart Brand

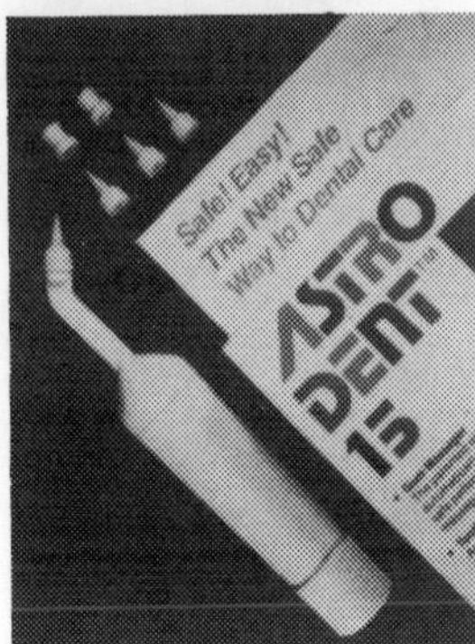

The Astrodent
$17.50
postpaid from:
Planetree
2040 Webster Street
San Francisco, CA 94115
or Whole Earth Access
(For more on Planetree see p. 207.)

Sourcebook for Older Americans
Joseph L. Matthews, with Dorothy Matthews Berman
1984; 274 pp.
$12.95
($14.45 postpaid) from:
Nolo Press
950 Parker Street
Berkeley, CA 94710
or Whole Earth Access

The Senior Citizen Handbook
Marjorie Stokell and Bonnie Kennedy
1985; 260 pp.
$9.95
postpaid from
Prentice-Hall Press
Mail Order Sales
200 Old Tappan Road
Old Tappan, NJ 07675
or Whole Earth Access

Elderhostel
Catalog **free** from
Elderhostel
80 Boylston Street
Suite 400
Boston, MA 02116

IF WE CAN LET GO OF THE TRITE IMAGE the words evoke, "senior citizen" is actually a lovely and respectful appellation. Alex Comfort wrote, " 'Old' people are people who have lived a certain number of years, and *that is all.*" I appreciate the sentiment, but that isn't quite all: old people are people who have had more experience, learned more, seen and felt and, perhaps, understood more than young people. A long life deserves to be capped with the honorific "senior" — may we all achieve it some day.

The marketplace is rapidly filling with advice on how to "be" old. Many of these books repeat each other, dipping into topics in shallow, even patronizing ways. Older people don't really need different nutrition or exercises merely because of age; common sense holds true at all times. But as we age we do run into a number of pragmatic challenges: Medicare, pensions, nursing homes, more frequent chronic illnesses, longer stretches of leisure time. Do your research, but take only your own advice. —Sallie Tisdale

Sourcebook for Older Americans

It is unfortunate that the government's provision of basic financial support for older people requires 250-plus pages to explain, but it does. Given the almost incomprehensible nature of the current Social Security and Medicare system, anyone using it is best equipped with a tour guide. This book, while failing to make a complex system exactly simple, explains it in far simpler and more patient language than you will ever hear on the phone — that is, if you ever get off hold. —*Sallie Tisdale*

•

If you think some of the rules and regulations we've gone over so far are a little confusing, you haven't seen anything yet! For sheer dizziness, those that follow take the cake. They are best dealt with slowly; read them over several times. If they still seem confusing to you, you are not alone. When you apply for disability benefits, the best way to cut through all these rules is simply to ask the eligibility worker: "When will I actually receive my first check?"

•

Before Medicare pays anything under Part B medical insurance, you have to pay the first $75 of covered medical bills each year. This is called your deductible. Although Medicare is supposed to keep track of how much of your deductible you have paid in a given year, it's a good idea for you to keep track, too, so you can make sure you've been given accurate credit. Unfortunately, many people have found that the Medicare accounting practices of the private companies that administer the program are not all they should be.

The Senior Citizen Handbook

Written by two retired teachers who have sped up with age, this encyclopedic book touches on many subjects of particular interest to seniors. You'll find good information (including current addresses and bibliographies) on such disparate matters as pets, spots before your eyes, credit discrimination, swindlers, taxes, and senior citizen discounts. The authors talk as peers, never down, although I could wish for more detail on certain medical points. —*Sallie Tisdale*

•

Golden Age Passport

Off to visit the national parks this summer? The national government has a bargain for you. If you are over sixty-two, stop at a Forest Service office or the first national park, monument, or federally owned recreation center you come to and get your free Golden Age Passport, good from here to eternity.

The Golden Age Passport will admit you and any family or friends in your vehicle to any or all national parks, monuments, and recreation areas *and* give you a 50 percent discount on fees charged for federal facilities and services such as camping, boat launching, and parking. (Don't expect it at privately owned concessions, however.)

Elderhostel

Elderhostel offers an international program of classes and seminars for people over 60. (Spouses under 60 and companions over 50 are welcome too.) You can study aborigine culture in Australia, barns of Vermont, dance, religion . . . it's an impressive and ever-changing list. The prices are low and may include travel fare, room and board. Scholarships are available. The catalog is exuberant, and the people involved seem to share that feeling. We hear 100 percent good news about Elderhostel, both from "students" and leaders. —*JB*

•

Bermuda Biological Station

The Bermuda Biological Station is situated on the water's edge in 15 acres of well-kept tropical park, at the eastern end of Bermuda, a crescent-shaped chain of islands settled by the British in 1609 and located approximately 700 miles from the eastern United States. The nearby town of St. George is rich in history and contains many fine examples of traditional Bermudian architecture. Participants will be housed in rooms in the main building and in cottages and apartments around the grounds. Access to the main building, dining hall, and lecture hall involves a single lengthy flight of stairs. In winter, daytime temperatures average in the mid 60s, with evenings about 10° cooler. Calm sunny periods alternate with brisk bouts of windy weather. By late April daytime temperatures rise to the low 70s. As is typical of many Bermudian homes, common areas in the main hotel buidling and in cottages contain space heaters, but bedrooms are unheated. All programs begin at 4:00 pm Thursday and end at 10:00 am the following Wednesday. The cost does not include transportation to and from Bermuda.

Program Charge $345. $100 deposit required.

Feb 27 - Mar 5 #10011-0227
Bermuda's Delicate Balance — People and the Environment
Bermuda's Historical and Architectural Heritage

• There's a national organization of old (and young) people working for social change related to issues affecting the elderly.
Grey Panther Network: Information **free** (with SASE) from 311 South Juniper Street/Suite 601, Philadelphia, PA 19107.

• Aging needn't decrease the old libido.
Love, Sex and Aging: Edward M. Brecher and the editors of Consumer Reports Books, 1984; 441 pp. **$19.45** ($20.45 postpaid) from Little, Brown & Co., 200 West Street, Waltham, MA 02254.

Anatomy of an Illness

*Peerless reading for the hospital bed. Norman Cousins, longtime editor of **Saturday Review**, acquired a second fame a few years ago with an article in the prestigious **New England Journal of Medicine** chronicling his self-inflicted recovery from a crippling and supposedly irreversible ailment (his spine was disintegrating).*

With the aid of his unusual doctor Cousins got the hell out of the hospital, took full responsibility for his own treatment, and began trying stuff — massive vitamin C, massive cheerfulness (the famous home-showing of Marx Brothers and Candid Camera films).

The miracle of cure plus Cousins' intellectual and lively presentation have made this one of the most influential medical documents ever. Patients read it and act differently. So do doctors. So do hospitals. —*Stewart Brand*

•

I had a fast-growing conviction that a hospital is no place for a person who is seriously ill. The surprising lack of respect for basic sanitation; the rapidity with which staphylococci and other pathogenic organisms can run through an entire hospital; the extensive and sometimes promiscuous use of X-ray equipment; the seemingly indiscriminate administration of tranquilizers and powerful painkillers, sometimes more for the convenience of hospital staff in managing patients than for therapeutic needs; and the regularity with which hospital routine takes precedence over the rest requirements of the patient (slumber, when it comes for an ill person, is an uncommon blessing and is not to be wantonly interrupted) — all these and other practices seemed to me to be critical shortcomings of the modern hospital.

•

I made the joyous discovery that ten minutes of genuine belly laughter had an anesthetic effect and would give me at least two hours of pain-free sleep. When the pain-killing effect of the laughter wore off, we would switch on the motion-picture projector again, and, not infrequently, it would lead to another pain-free sleep interval. Sometimes, the nurse read to me out of a trove of humor books. Especially useful were E. B. and Katharine White's *Subtreasury of American Humor* and Max Eastman's *The Enjoyment of Laughter.*

Anatomy of an Illness
Norman Cousins
1979; 173 pp.
$5.95
($7.45 postpaid) from:
Bantam Books
W. W. Norton and Co.
414 East Golf Road
Des Plains, IL 60016
or Whole Earth Access

Take This Book to the Hospital With You

*When hurt, maybe dying, who doesn't tend to kowtow to someone who offers to make everything OK again? The illness of modern medicine is that it abuses this time of natural deference. It has forgotten that the patient is part of the cure. **Take This Book** stridently urges all bodies to restore their roles in the healing wards. Take this book to the hospital with you and you'll make yourself a better patient, your doctor a better doctor, and your hospital a better place to get well.* —*Kevin Kelly*

•

Don't allow yourself to be admitted on a nonemergency basis on a Friday afternoon or evening. You will just languish, expensively and in no particular comfort, until Monday. Most of the labs that would be performing your diagnostic workup don't do those things on weekends. Wait until Monday; better yet, Tuesday, some experts say. By Tuesday, the hospital is back in gear after the weekend, and the end-of-the-week blahs haven't hit yet.

•

Rosenberg discovered that doctors, many of whom haven't the foggiest idea of what things cost, end up unwittingly socking it to their patients. For example, a doctor treating a pneumonia caused by gram-negative bacteria might go for the new, state-of-the-art antibiotic, cefoperazone. A ten-day treatment would cost the ill consumer $1,510. But if the doctor went with the equally effective antibiotic gentamicin instead, the same job would be done at half the price.

It's just that doctors don't know this. They need to learn, and your questions can help them do that. Ask if there is a less expensive viable alternative to drugs when a doctor prescribes them. You could save a bundle.

•

In 1983-84, Atlanta-based Equifax Services, Inc. conducted a 41-state audit of 3,850 hospital bills and found errors in 98.1 percent of them. Not just little errors, either. The average reduction, after the overcharges were eliminated and the bills retallied, was a whopping $1,254.

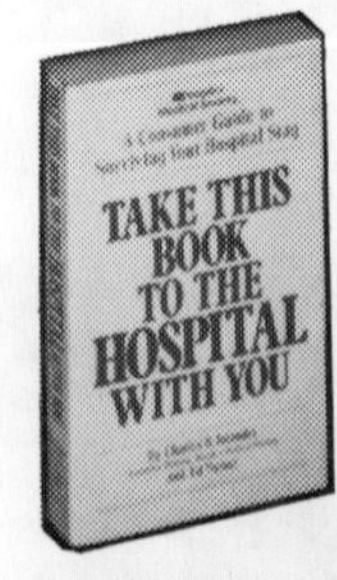

Take This Book to the Hospital With You
Charles B. Inlander
1985; 221 pp.
$9.95 postpaid from:
Rodale Press
33 East Minor Street
Emmaus, PA 18049
or Whole Earth Access

The Home Alternative to Hospitals and Nursing Homes

A hospital isn't a good place to get well; intuition tells you that, and statistics agree. But caring for someone at home ain't easy — how does a person go about doing that? This book will get you started with the basics: fitting the patient into your schedule, setting up the home for the job, and dealing with professional assistance. And of course there are instructions for the hard work of actual care: bedpans, bathing, bedsores, diet, pills, and all the other things that most people would rather not think about except that now they have to. For most folks, the effort will be worth it both physically and financially. —*JB*

•

Home-Care Basic #8: Cast Care That's Foolproof
Physicians apply plaster casts to keep particular body parts in proper position. Casts are placed on arms, ankles, legs, and larger body areas such as hips or abdomen. They are even applied to broken bones after some surgeries.

If skin under cast itches *do not* stick anything inside cast to scratch — especially if there are stitches. Watch children to make sure they do not stick foreign objects inside casts. Tip: tap on the cast over the itching. Use a blunt instrument. Or you can blow air inside with a bulb syringe.

NO-PRESSURE BOX

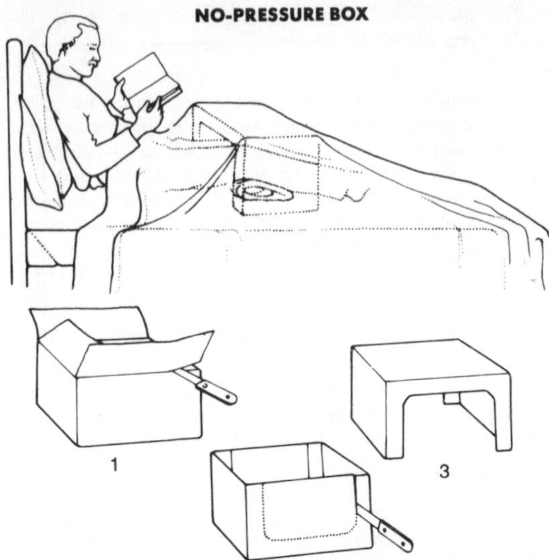

No-pressure box: this device lifts blankets and sheets off the patient. Get a medium-size cardboard box and cut in the shape of a table. Place under bed covers.

The Home Alternative to Hospitals and Nursing Homes
Mara B. Covell
1983; 339 pp.
$15.95 postpaid from:
Macmillan Publishing Co.
Order Dept.
Front and Brown Streets
Riverside, NJ 08075
or Whole Earth Access

ospice is an attitude, not a place or process. It refers to the approach of comfort rather than cure, involvement of the patient and his or her family in all aspects of care, and especially, the meeting of *every* need the patient expresses, whenever possible. Hospice is the way we used to take care of our elderly and ill fellows, without thinking. A positive step backward. —Sallie Tisdale

Dying at Home With Hospice
Deborah Chase
1986; 204 pp.
$15.95
postpaid from:
C.V. Mosby
11830 Westline
Industrial Drive
St. Louis, MO 63146
or Whole Earth Access

Dying at Home with Hospice

This prosaic overview of hospice care is aimed at families and potential recipients. The book includes an interesting history of care for the dying, basic physical care, and problems unique to dying children. It isn't just about home care; in-hospital and independent hospices are also discussed. There's a list of hospices, too.
—*Sallie Tisdale*

•

The heart of the hospice idea is to do away with the terrible alienation that the dying feel because of the regimentation and narrow-mindedness of the medical profession. One dying patient said to a hospice doctor, "Nobody wants to look at me." Hospice does not look away from death; it faces the unpleasant truth with compassion and love.

•

One woman who applied to a hospice for care was a 70-year-old cancer patient from a large family. She told the interviewer that she was certain her family would want to take care of her; but the interviewer thought it odd that the patient had come in alone. When he called in the patient's husband, son, and daughter-in-law, the interviewer got a different perspective on the patient's personality. All her life she had been a perfectionist and a complainer. . . . Not surprisingly, the family wanted nothing to do with her care.

Hospice: Complete Care for the Terminally Ill
(2nd Edition)
Jack M. Zimmerman, M.D.
1986; 311 pp.
$29.50
postpaid from:
Urban and Schwarzenberg
7 East Redwood Street
Baltimore, MD 21202

Hospice: Complete Care for the Terminally Ill

The physical experience of dying has long been ignored by writers of medical texts. At last, an accurate, easy-to-read textbook on dying and hospice care, useful for physicians, nurses, and support workers. Covers physical, psychological, spiritual, and ethical issues with an aggressively liberal perspective. —*Sallie Tisdale*

•

For those dying patients who have pain, it must be controlled before other symptoms can be handled effectively. Almost all patients with advanced malignancy fear both uncontrollable pain and the possibility of being so mentally obtunded from pain relief that they are rendered subhuman. They must be assured from the beginning, and shown thereafter, that it is possible to be kept pain free and alert throughout much of their terminal illness.

•

Using all that morphine, aren't patients knocked out and don't they become addicted?

Addiction is not a problem with the terminally ill. To begin with, the course of most patients is of such a nature that addiction is irrelevant.

Do you permit connubial visits?

Yes. In our program, however, this has rarely been a consideration because most patients who are well enough to be sexually active are not on the inpatient unit. For those few exceptions our hospice staff has discreetly demonstrated its imagination, ingenuity, and compassion in arranging connubial visits.

Gramp
Mark Jury and Dan Jury
OUT OF PRINT
Viking Penguin Books

Gramp

A remarkable, difficult book. With starkly beautiful photographs and almost painfully frank narrative, **Gramp** *tells the story of a respected, popular man as he declines into senility and finally dies. His loving family cares for him to the last day, shunning all manner of 'help' aimed at masking or prolonging Gramp's condition.*

It is a rare and honest story which shows us pictures of an old man naked in a bare room and, later, the same man newly dead; such images are imbued with a palpable affection. A unique and enlightening book.
—*Sallie Tisdale*

•

"My first impression of Gramp was that he smiled a lot and was outgoing and friendly. When I came around more he would tease me and he was affectionate. He talked out of context, but he didn't do anything strange and at that time I didn't notice his senility. I heard stories about how he was, but I felt that maybe he was just playing and doing things to tease Nan, because he would turn around and wink and chuckle."

•

Gramp was as bewildered as anyone at the turn of events. At each recurring accident, he'd react with a startled grunt. During the umpteenth trip to the bathroom (we'd quit counting when he hit nine before noon) Dee said, "Oh no, Gramp, you didn't go in your pants again, did you?"

"No," replied Gramp, "that other guy did."

•

Finally, Gramp slipped into what we guessed was a coma. Dr. Kline came to the house and examined him, finding that his heart and lungs were still functioning all right — which prompted the doctor to comment that the term used to describe a person who was being kept alive by tubes was "a heart and lung case." Family opinion was resolute: if Gramp had stoically endured his tongue cracking and the roof of his mouth flaking off from lack of liquid, no way were we going to sneak nourishment into him now.

• Executors and executrixes need to know everything in this thorough book. **The Executor's Manual:** Charles K. Plotnick and Stephen R. Leimberg, 1986; 462 pp. **$17.50** postpaid from Doubleday and Company/Direct Mail Order, 501 Franklin Avenue, Garden City, NJ 11530.

Who Dies?

No Grim Reaper and no sappy platitudes lurk in these pages. The gentle, powerful philosophy is based on love and awareness in the best Buddhist sense. It's about being.

There are few books in this catalog that have been recommended by so many of our readers. Perhaps that's because **Who Dies?** *is such a good recipe for living.*
—JB [Suggested and tested by Peter Rabbit]

•

The old who live in their body are bent under the strain. The old who live in their hearts are aglow.

•

Many we have worked with who were not in pain had less of a tendency to investigate, had less motivation to examine and begin to let go of their suffering. Because things weren't "so bad after all," they imagined they could somehow hide from death in the same way they had hidden from life.

•

When you let go of control of the universe, when you let go of everything, only the truth remains. And like a roshi you start responding from the moment. Your actions come out of the present. There is no force. Your boat is empty. The currents move you to the left, "Ahhh, the left." They move you to the right, "Ahh, the right." But you never feel as though you are to the left or to the right, you only feel that you are here now, in the present. Open to all the possibilities and opportunities of the moment. Fully present. Able to respond, not out of personal desire, but out of a sense of the appropriateness of things. You respond from the flow itself, or perhaps better stated, the flow responds to itself. No separation anywhere. Nowhere to go. Nothing to do. No one to be.

Who Dies?
Stephen Levine
1982; 317 pp.
$9.95
postpaid from:
Doubleday and Company
Direct Mail Order
501 Franklin Avenue
Garden City, NY 11530
or Whole Earth Access

Recovering From the Loss of a Child

Who would argue that there is a worse experience than the sudden loss of a child? It would be a moot argument; for those who have been through it, nothing can compare. Katherine Donnelly begins with the premise that, contrary to our social myths, bereaved parents desperately want to talk about their pain. Silence is their worst enemy. Here she tells, beginning with the death, the stories of many families who have lived this nightmare. She follows them, with sensitive descriptions, to that far-off land of recovery. *—Sallie Tisdale*

•

What you are saying in prolonged grief is: 'My world has ended.' That is the message parents are sending if they go on and on with their grief. The surviving child wonders, 'Don't I mean anything to you?' Many times parents tend to idealize the dead child, and for that reason siblings often feel the child who died was the favorite.

•

Judith says that in surviving, you can't do everything as you once did. "Everyone has a thing they can't do — like going to the cemetery, or back to a favorite spot of your child's, or to a supermarket where your child may have shopped with you, or to any place that stirs painful memories. Although you will go forward in many areas, there are also many areas in which you cannot go back."

Recovering from the Loss of a Child
Katherine F. Donnelly
1982; 226 pp.
$13.94
postpaid from:
Macmillan Publishing Co.
Order Dept.
Front and Brown Streets
Riverside, NJ 08075
or Whole Earth Access

A Manual of Death Education and Simple Burial

All the details you need to know about simple funeral arrangements and other practical aspects of dealing with death are in this famous book. *—Sallie Tisdale*

Dealing Creatively with Death (A Manual of Death Education and Simple Burial): Ernest Morgan, 1984; 156 pp. **$6.50** postpaid from The Celo Press, 1901 Hannah Branch Road, Burnsville, NC 28714.

• Make your own coffin with these plans.
St. Francis Center: information **free**; plans **$3.25** postpaid from 2201 P Street NW, Washington, DC 20037.

On Death and Dying

On Death and Dying *establishes a psychological fact that most people close to a dying person already know, even if they can't admit it: one tends to turn away. Even from husbands, even from wives, even from one's own children. Dying people are casualties of life. Their dying, especially if it is a long, drawn-out affair, is a reminder of how vulnerable we all are, and that's something most people want to forget.*

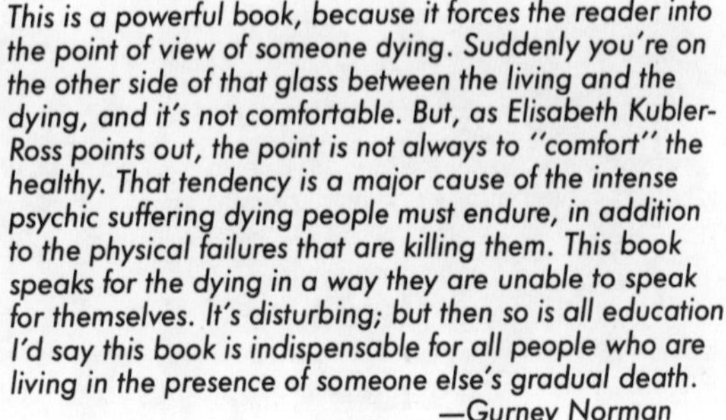

This is a powerful book, because it forces the reader into the point of view of someone dying. Suddenly you're on the other side of that glass between the living and the dying, and it's not comfortable. But, as Elisabeth Kubler-Ross points out, the point is not always to "comfort" the healthy. That tendency is a major cause of the intense psychic suffering dying people must endure, in addition to the physical failures that are killing them. This book speaks for the dying in a way they are unable to speak for themselves. It's disturbing; but then so is all education. I'd say this book is indispensable for all people who are living in the presence of someone else's gradual death.
—Gurney Norman

What Rachel Carson's ***Silent Spring*** *did for pesticides, this book did for the subject of death. Unlike Carson's book, it hasn't dated a line, although the author maybe has.*
—Stewart Brand

•

While the surgeons believed that another surgical procedure could possibly prolong her life, the husband pleaded with them to do everything in their power to "turn the clock back." It was unacceptable to him to lose his wife. He could not comprehend that she did not have the need to be with him any longer. Her need to detach herself, to make dying easier, was interpreted by him as a rejection which was beyond his comprehension. There was no one there to explain to him that this was a natural process, a progress indeed, a sign perhaps that a dying person has found his peace and is preparing himself to face it alone.

•

First Stage: Denial and Isolation
Second Stage: Anger
Third Stage: Bargaining
Fourth Stage: Depression
Fifth Stage: Acceptance

•

When we asked our patients how they had been told, we learned that all the patients knew about their terminal illness anyway, whether they were explicitly told or not, but depended greatly on the physician to present the news in an acceptable manner.

On Death and Dying
Elisabeth Kubler-Ross, M.D.
1969; 289 pp.
$4.95
postpaid from:
Macmillan Publishing Co.
Order Dept.
Front and Brown Streets
Riverside, NJ 08075
or Whole Earth Access

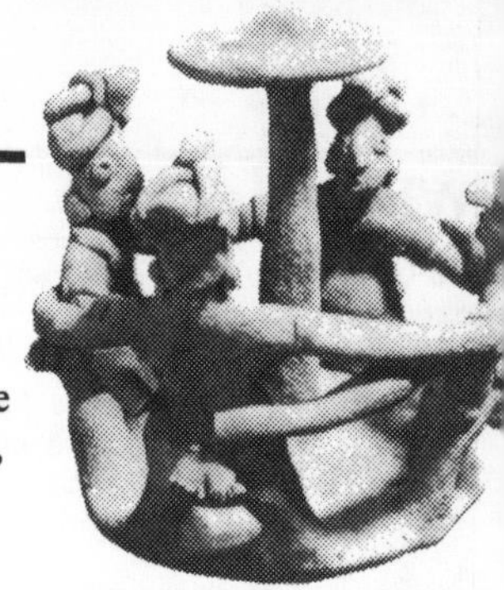

PLANTS, OF COURSE, are subject to as much moralizing as anything else. They provide our essential power — the energy to live, the medicines to be cured of diseases, the materials for clothes and shelter, and the relief from ordinary, everyday experience. In preparing this page, we were shocked by how many books on all aspects of plant power had disappeared. It felt like modern humans wished to hide, and in some sense, deny the massive vegetative influences in their lives. So, with respect and rebelliousness, this page has mostly out-of-print books. Hopefully, the carrots and the ayahuasca understand.

—Peter Warshall

Plants of the Gods • Medicines from the Earth

Plants of the Gods
Richard Evans Schultes
and Albert Hofmann
OUT OF PRINT
McGraw-Hill Book Co.

Medicines from the Earth
William A.R. Thomson, M.D., Editor
Revised by Richard Evans Schultes
1978; 179 pp.
$12.95
($15.95 postpaid) from:
Harper and Row
2350 Virginia Avenue
Hagerstown, MD 21740
or Whole Earth Access

Richard Evans Schultes has been the nexus of almost everything interesting and supportive concerned with economic and cultural uses of plants. ***Plants of the Gods*** *gives precise and illuminating portraits of the many peoples of the Earth who pay homage and gain insights with the aid of psychedelic plants: an exquisite, thoroughly scholarly book.* ***Medicines from the Earth*** *has 250 of the plants most used for complaints and ailments. Cross-referenced by plant, illness, preparation (teas, compresses, etc.); best season to collect; and by chemical constituents discovered by pharmacologists. It's the best modern "herbal."* —Peter Warshall

•

A faded Romanesque fresco in the late thirteenth-century Plaincourault Chapel depicts the Biblical temptation scene in the Garden of Eden. The Tree of Knowledge, entwined by a serpent, bears an uncanny resemblance to the *Amanita muscaria* mushroom. There has been considerable controversy concerning this fresco. Some feel that the figure represents the Fly Agaric. —*Plants of the Gods*

•

Dated somewhere between 200 B.C. and A.D. 100, the beautiful ceramic artifact from Colima, Mexico (above) shows celebrants dancing around a mushroom effigy. From this artifact and the relative size and position of the fungus, it would appear that the mushroom represents something akin to the World Tree, the *axis mundi*. The mushroom, with its peaked cap, could well be *Psilocybe mexicana* or a close relative of this species.

—*Plants of the Gods*

•

It has been estimated that fewer than 10 percent of the world's flora has even been superficially examined from a chemical and pharmacological point of view. Thus, the potential for new medicinal agents has hardly been tapped. —*Medicines from the Earth*

►

Some evidence, although weak and indirect, suggests that the Cree Indians of northwestern Canada may occasionally chew the root-stalk of Sweet Flag for hallucinogenic effects. In large doses, it induces visual hallucinations and has other effects similar to those of LSD.

—*Plants of the Gods*

◄ Achillea Millefolium
Yarrow, Milfoil
—Medicines from the Earth

•

YARROW
Contains: Essential oil with cineole and chamazulene, bitter principle achillein, tannin.
Effect: Antiseptic, antispasmodic, expectorant, stimulates secretion of gastric and intestinal glands, choleretic, regulates kidney function, astringent, inhibits inflammation.

Gather whole stalk or blossom when blooming (June-September), free from thick pieces of stem. Dry in shade, not over 40°C. —*Medicines from the Earth*

Wizard of the Upper Amazon

Plunged into the middle of a jungle foodweb, only visions, plant narcotics, hunting skills, and an incredible intimacy with the natural world sustain Cordova-Rios. In no other book have I felt the mixing of human and animal and dream worlds to be so clear and direct. This book is far superior to anything Castaneda (*p. 384*) *has attempted. The Huni Kui have pleasant and important communal visions much more astounding and connected-to-life than the individualistic "fearful" visions of Castaneda. This is one of the best books I have encountered while reviewing for* ***Whole Earth.*** —Peter Warshall

Wizard of the Upper Amazon
F. Bruce Lamb
Houghton Mifflin Co.
$9.95
($10.95 postpaid) from:
North Atlantic Books
2320 Blake Street
Berkeley, CA 94704
or Whole Earth Access

•

I was still kept on a strict diet, and it turned out that this was to be a period of intensive training for me. Once every eight days I would have a session of visions with the chief. These included examination of plants and their various uses both as food and as medicine, as well as further study of the animals. During the time between sessions I was taken often to the forest on both day and night trips with small groups of hunters. On these excursions I found to my delight that the intensified sense of perception and increased awareness of my surroundings originating in the sessions with the chief stayed with me. In the forest my companions would point out origins of sound and smell and continually test my progress in becoming completely one with the forest environment.

The People's Pharmacy • The Essential Guide to Prescription Drugs

The Graedons' three volumes are the books on drugs for the general reader. Written by a pharmacologist who knows his stuff and shoots from the hip, **The People's Pharmacy** *series helped create the current medical consumer revolution and remains the most personable and readable assemblage of self-care information, opinions, and recommendations on prescription and over-the-counter drugs currently available.*

But while the Graedons provide an excellent overview and hit all the high points, they do not deal with every detail of every drug. You may want a drug encyclopedia as a backup. My favorite is **The Essential Guide to Prescription Drugs,** *one of the most detailed and easily the most usable of the breed. It contains in-depth listings of the 200+ most frequently prescribed drugs, complete with mode of action, side effects, contraindications, time required for benefit, recommended follow-up exams, interactions with other drugs, and — especially hard to find — use during pregnancy and breastfeeding. No opinions or recommendations here, just the facts.*

—*Tom Ferguson, M.D.*

•

Most people think that FDA approval is drugdom's version of the Good Housekeeping Seal of Approval. But it isn't that simple.

Let's suppose, for a moment, that the Consumer Product Safety Commission tested one thousand toasters of a certain manufacturer. While nine hundred of them worked fine, the other one hundred caused a variety of problems ranging from minor cases of burned toast to life-threatening electrical shocks. There would be righteous indignation and no Seal of Approval for such a bread burner. Yet drugs are often approved with a 10 percent incidence of adverse effects, and in some cases the numbers go much higher. Even death (which we can think of as the ultimate adverse effect) is a risk that the FDA considers acceptable for a surprisingly large number of drugs.

—*The People's Pharmacy*

•

Minoxidil, a potent vasodilator used orally in the treatment of hypertension, appears to have "dramatic" hair-growing properties when applied topically to some patients with male pattern baldness or *alopecia areata*, Dr. Vera Price said at the annual meeting of the American Academy of Dermatology.

Although the search for a treatment of male pattern baldness has been rivaled in duration and intensity only by that for the Holy Grail, Dr. Price strongly urged physicians to refrain from the temptation of using minoxidil on their bald patients until after Upjohn's controlled clinical trials are completed within the next year. . . .

Not waiting for FDA approval is Cambridge Chemists, a drugstore on New York City's East Side. Pharmacists there make a liquid version of minoxidil for patients of about 20 area physicians, including Dr. Reed. The pharmacy crushes prescription tablets of Loniten (the form in which Upjohn sells the drug for severe high blood pressure), mixes them with an alcohol-based solution and sells them a one-month supply of two ounces for about $75.

—*The New People's Pharmacy*

CODEINE

Common Synonyms ("Street Names"): Painkiller, pain reliever, robo, schoolboy, syrup

Drug Class: Analgesic, Mild (Narcotic)

Prescription Required: Yes (Controlled Drug, U.S. Schedule II)*

Available for Purchase by Generic Name: Yes

Available Dosage Forms and Strengths
Tablets — 15 mg., 30 mg., 60 mg.
Syrup — 10 mg. per ml.
Injection — 15 mg., 30 mg., 60 mg. per ml.

Tablet May Be Crushed or Capsule Opened for Administration: Yes

How This Drug Works
Intended Therapeutic Effect(s)
Relief of moderate pain.
Control of coughing.
Location of Drug Action(s)
Those areas of the brain and spinal cord involved in the perception of pain.
Those areas of the brain and spinal cord involved in the cough reflex.

INFORM YOUR PHYSICIAN BEFORE TAKING THIS DRUG IF
—you are taking sedatives, other analgesics, sleep-inducing drugs, tranquilizers, antidepressants, or narcotic drugs of any kind.
—you have impaired liver or kidney function.
—you have underactive thyroid function.
—you plan to have surgery under general anesthesia in the near future.

Time Required for Apparent Benefit
Usually 15 to 30 minutes when taken orally.

Possible Side-Effects *(natural, expected, and unavoidable drug actions)*
Drowsiness, lightheadedness, constipation.

Possible Adverse Effects *(unusual, unexpected, and infrequent reactions)*

IF ANY OF THE FOLLOWING DEVELOP, DISCONTINUE DRUG AND NOTIFY YOUR PHYSICIAN AS SOON AS POSSIBLE

Mild Adverse Effects
Allergic Reactions: Skin rashes, hives, itching.
Other Reactions
Nausea, vomiting.
Dizziness, sensation of drunkenness.
Serious Adverse Effects
None reported.

Advisability of Use During Pregnancy
Pregnancy Category: C (tentative). See Pregnancy Code inside back cover.
Animal reproduction studies in hamsters reveal significant birth defects due to this drug.
Information from studies in pregnant women indicates no significant increase in defects in 2522 exposures to this drug.
It is advisable to avoid use of this drug during first 3 months.
Ask physician for guidance.

Habit-Forming Potential
This drug can produce psychological and physical dependence (see Glossary) when used in large doses for an extended period of time.

Effects of Overdosage
With Moderate Overdose: Marked drowsiness, nausea, vomiting, restlessness, agitation.
With Large Overdose: Stupor progressing to deep sleep, convulsions, cold and clammy skin, slow and shallow breathing.

Possible Effects of Extended Use
Psychological and physical dependence.

While Taking This Drug, Observe the Following
Foods: No restrictions.
Beverages: No restrictions.
Alcohol: Use with extreme caution until combined effects have been determined. Codeine can intensify the intoxicating effects of alcohol, and alcohol can intensify the depressant effects of codeine on brain function, breathing, and circulation.
Tobacco Smoking: No interactions expected.
Marijuana Smoking
Occasional (once or twice weekly): Mild and transient increase in drowsiness and relief of pain.
Daily: Significant increase in drowsiness, relief of pain, and impairment of mental and physical performance.
Other Drugs
Codeine may *increase* the effects of
• all sedatives, analgesics, sleep-inducing drugs, tranquilizers, antidepressants, and other narcotic drugs.
Driving a Vehicle, Operating Machinery, Engaging in Hazardous Activities: This drug can impair mental alertness, judgment, reaction time, and physical coordination. Avoid hazardous activities.
Aviation Note: The use of this drug *is a disqualification* for the piloting of aircraft. Consultation with a designated Aviation Medical Examiner is advised.

—**The Essential Guide to Prescription Drugs**

• There's an equally good Essential Guide to Nonprescription Drugs too. Watch for the new edition in 1987.
The Essential Guide to Nonprescription Drugs: David R. Zimmerman, 1987; 886 pp. **$27.50** hardcover, **$12.95** paperback from Harper and Row, 2350 Virginia Avenue, Hagerstown, MD 21740.

The Essential Guide to Prescription Drugs
James W. Long, M.D.
1985; 1,025 pp.
$10.95
($12.45 postpaid) from:
Harper and Row
2350 Virginia Avenue
Hagerstown, MD 21740
or Whole Earth Access

The People's Pharmacy #1
Joe and Teresa Graedon
1985; 386 pp.
$16.95
($18.45 postpaid) from:
St. Martin's Press
Cash Sales
175 Fifth Avenue
New York, NY 10010
or Whole Earth Access

The People's Pharmacy #2
Joe Graedon
1980; 000 pp.
$5.95
($6.95 postpaid) from:
Avon Books
P. O. Box 767
Dresden, TN 38225

The New People's Pharmacy #3
Joe and Teresa Graedon
1985; 427 pp.
$8.95
($10.45 postpaid) from:
Bantam Books
414 East Golf Road
Des Plaines, IL 60016

20 Questions
Are You An Alcoholic? *

To answer this question, ask yourself the following questions and answer them as honestly as you can.

1. **Do you lose time from work due to drinking?**
2. **Is drinking making your home life unhappy?**
3. **Do you drink because you are shy with other people?**
4. **Is drinking affecting your reputation?**
5. **Have you ever felt remorse after drinking?**
6. **Have you gotten into financial difficulties as a result of drinking?**
7. **Do you turn to lower companions and an inferior environment when drinking?**
8. **Does your drinking make you careless of your family's welfare?**
9. **Has your ambition decreased since drinking?**
10. **Do you crave a drink at a definite time daily?**
11. **Do you want a drink the next morning?**
12. **Does drinking cause you to have difficulty in sleeping?**
13. **Has your efficiency decreased since drinking?**
14. **Is drinking jeopardizing your job or business?**
15. **Do you drink to escape from worries or troubles?**
16. **Do you drink alone?**
17. **Have you ever had a complete loss of memory as a result of drinking?**
18. **Has your physician ever treated you for drinking?**
19. **Do you drink to build up your self-confidence?**
20. **Have you ever been to a hospital or institution on account of drinking?**

ABOUT FIVE YEARS BEFORE I made it to AA, I answered 14 of those questions yes. Because I didn't relate drinking to the damage that was already underway, I decided the test must be bullshit. Denial, they tell me, is characteristic of alcoholics.

I had a great life. I didn't enjoy it much. I had *reasons* to drink. (Only alcoholics need reasons to drink, they tell me.) I drank because everyone else did. I drank because I was sensitive.

I was depressed, hung over, and incapacitated a lot. (Not surprising, considering that alcohol is a depressant, and toxic.) After another couple of years of prodigious daily drinking, I began to think that I might have a drinking problem after all.

LIFE *without* alcohol had become inconceivable, but I sure wished I could drink less. I rarely intended to get drunk, but I generally did, and expended a lot of energy on trying to seem sober. After a few more years of this miserable futility, I figured I was a moral failure, unable to stop hurting those I cared for — and myself — so badly; and, by no coincidence, unable to control my drinking. Things had got hopeless enough for me to admit my alcoholism. It was obvious that I couldn't quit drinking by myself, and obvious that if I continued to drink my health, my psyche and my life were guaranteed to deteriorate until I died.

For some reason, Ann Landers' good advice probably, I believed that Alcoholics Anonymous was how to quit drinking. (Most cities of any size list AA in their telephone directories, and AA's General Service Office, Box 459, Grand Central Station, New York, NY 10163, will help alcoholics in remoter places by mail.) So I called Alcoholics Anonymous, and found that there was a meeting in my neighborhood that night. I went.

That was six years ago. With the help of AA, I haven't taken a drink since. Because I consider my sobriety to be a daily reprieve from a deadly progression, I go to as many AA meetings as I can every week, and I just don't drink between meetings no matter what.

"Forever non-professional," AA is pure mutual aid. AA meetings are endlessly interesting and usually funny. Something very special comes out of our discussion of the homely business of facing life without booze.

IN this country, seven out of ten people drink. One out of ten is an alcoholic, just like me. We don't opt to be alcoholic any more than others opt to be colorblind. Alcoholism's the existential card we're dealt. We have to play it, one way or another. I tried drinking for fifteen years, and sobriety for six-and-some. I like sobriety better. If, like me, you passed that twenty questions test, I hope you'll save yourself a lot of time and trouble and find the help you need to deal with your drinking problem today.

The general idea is to choose life.

—A member of Alcoholics Anonymous

"Alcoholics Anonymous is a fellowship of men and women who share their experience, strength, and hope with each other that they may solve their common problem and help others to recover from alcoholism.

The only requirement for membership is a desire to stop drinking.

There are no dues or fees for AA membership; we are self-supporting through our own contributions.

AA is not allied with any sect, denomination, politics, organization or institution; does not wish to engage in any controversy; neither endorses nor opposes any cause. Our primary purpose is to stay sober and help other alcoholics to achieve sobriety."

If you have answered YES to any one of the questions, there is a definite warning that you may be an alcoholic.

If you have answered YES to any two, the chances are that you are an alcoholic.

If you have answered YES to three or more, you are definitely an alcoholic.

Check your telephone book for an AA listing. Or write:

AA World Services, Inc., P. O. Box 459, Grand Central Station, New York, NY 10163.

AA will send introductory pamphlets and a catalog and order form. All free.

Alcoholics Anonymous

Known to most AAs as the Big Book, ***Alcoholics Anonymous*** *is the Bible of the program. It explains briefly how AA came into being and how it works. It describes AA's program for living (and thriving) sober. It also contains accounts by 42 AAs of their alcoholism, from progressive drinking to hitting bottom to entering AA and on to recovery.*

Two other AA books — in ***Twelve Steps and Twelve Traditions****, "a co-founder of Alcoholics Anonymous tells how members recover and how the society functions."* ***Living Sober*** *has "some methods AA members have used for not drinking."* —*A member of Alcoholics Anonymous*

Alcoholics Anonymous
1976; 575 pp.
$5.65 postpaid;
Living Sober
1975; 87 pp.
$1.75 postpaid;
Twelve Steps and Twelve Traditions
1953; 192 pp.
$4 postpaid;
all from:
Alcoholics Anonymous
World Services, Inc.
P. O. Box 459
Grand Central Station
New York, NY 10163

•

We have three little mottoes which are apropos. Here they are:

First Things First
Live and Let Live
Easy Does it —*Alcoholics Anonymous*

Kicking It

This is a tough but supportive book, discussing the physiological and emotional dependency on cigarets. Through a series of habit-breaking techniques, the book teaches you how to conquer your addiction to smoking. Author David Geisinger also provides a thoughtful analysis of the sociology of smoking.
—*Rochelle Perrine Schmalz*

•

Wrap your cigarettes. By wrapping the pack of cigarettes in a piece of newspaper held on by a rubber band in such a way that a cigarette cannot be removed without taking off the band and unwrapping the paper, you will be raising your awareness and beginning to "de-robotize" yourself. . . .

If you are asked by anyone why you have your cigarettes wrapped, say something like, "It's part of a program I'm engaged in to stop smoking." Always remember to stay with the spirit of this program, which is to "go public" whenever it seems reasonable to do so. If people ask about the program, they deserve an honest answer; give them one.

* Rochelle Perrine Schmalz is director of PlaneTree Health Resource Center (p. 207).

• See **Don't Shoot the Dog** (p. 225).

Out of the Shadows

A few years ago we were asked to research sex addiction and found little information on the subject.* ***Out of the Shadows*** *addresses this issue in a frank, readable, and compassionate manner, and brings into the open the problem of compulsive sexual behavior.*

Author Patrick Carnes identifies three levels of sexual addiction and discusses the importance of family relationships in the development of the recovery from this compulsive behavior.

By using the 12 Steps program of Alcoholics Anonymous, Carnes gives hope and understanding to the 6-10 percent of us who suffer from this kind of addiction.
—*Rochelle Perrine Schmalz*

•

When a child's exploration of sexuality goes beyond discovery to routine self-comforting because of the lack of human care, there is potential for addiction. Sex becomes confused with comforting and nurturing. Moreover, the assumption is made that everyone else feels and acts the same. Therefore, to feel secure means to be sexual.

Consequently, the child's relationships with people have the potential of being replaced with an addictive relationship with sexuality. Addiction is a relationship — a pathological relationship in which sexual obsession replaces people. And it can start very early. The final core belief of the addict emerges clearly: *Sex is my most important need.*

Out of the Shadows
Patrick Carnes, Ph.D
1983; 173 pp.
$8.95
($10.45 postpaid) from:
CompCare Publications
2415 Annapolis Lane
Minneapolis, MN 55441

The Coke Book

A reliable reference book on what cocaine is, its uses and abuses, its effects on mind and body, and how the drug can profoundly affect your life.

The authors don't preach, but they do provide straightforward information that allows you to make your own decisions about cocaine. —*Rochelle Perrine Schmalz*

•

The coca plant — *Erythroxylum coca* — is indigenous to the eastern Andes mountains of South America, where today it is most commonly cultivated at elevations between 500 and 1,500 meters.

The plant is thought to have emerged long before the first human — or humanlike creature — walked the earth. The fourteen alkaloids in its leaves — cocaine is but one of these — probably evolved as chemical defenses to ward off animals anticipating a good meal of fresh greenery. Coca remains today relatively free of insect pests, and grazing animals seldom bother the plants.

•

Euphoria: The most sought-after (and talked about) response to coke. At low doses (anywhere from one to seven "lines" if snorted, depending on the drug's purity) it has been described as rapture, exhilaration, joy, giddiness, and an intense "rush." At continued high doses (four to nine "lines" depending on purity), agitation and nervous excitability are often reported, sometimes, with chronic abuse, leading to delirium.

The Coke Book
Lawrence D. Chilnick
1984; 233 pp.
$3.50
($5 postpaid) from:
Berkeley Publishing Group
G. P. Putnam's Sons
200 Madison Avenue
New York, NY 10016
or Whole Earth Access

Kicking It
David L. Geisinger
1980; 160 pp.
$2.50
($3.50 postpaid) from:
New American Library
120 Woodbine Street
Bergenfield, NJ 07621
or Whole Earth Access

Narcotics Anonymous

Based on the ***12 Steps and 12 Traditions*** *of Alcoholics Anonymous, NA serves the needs of addicts who have decided to quit using drugs. Like AA, NA is not affiliated with other organizations. They welcome anyone with an honest desire to quit using drugs, "regardless of age, race, color, creed, religion or lack of religion." Approximately 6,200 NA groups currently meet in the U.S.*
—*Jeanne Carstensen*

Narcotics Anonymous
information **free** from:
World Service Office, Inc.
Narcotics Anonymous
16155 Wyandotte Street
Van Nuys, CA 91406

REAL SUICIDE NOTES:

Single female, age 21

My dearest Andrew,
It seems as if I have been spending all my life apologizing to you for things that happened whether they were my fault or not.

I am enclosing your pin because I want you to think of what you took from me every time you see it.

I don't want you to think I would kill myself over you because you're not worth any emotion at all. It is what you cost me that hurts and nothing can replace it.

Married female, age 38

I can't bear the pain any longer. I'm tired, discouraged and unhappy.

Married male, age 52

Dear Joan,
For 23 years we lived happy together. Our married life was ideal, until two years ago when I witnessed Kristy die in the hospital something snapped in me. You remember when I returned from the hospital I broke down. That was the beginning of my illness. Since then my condition was getting progressively worse, I could neither work nor think logically. You have been thru "Hell" with me since then. Only you and I know how much you have lived thru. I feel that I will not improve and can't keep on causing you and the children so much misery. I loved you and was very proud of you. I loved the children dearly and could not see them suffer so much on account of me.

Dear Children:
Please forgive me.

Love, Frank

ABOUT 30,000 PEOPLE kill themselves in the United States every year. An estimated ten to forty times that number try to kill themselves but don't die — either because they don't really want to die, or because they don't know how.

Suicide attempters go through ordeals on top of the ordeals that made them want to die in the first place. When I was researching a long article about suicide in 1982 (reprinted in *"News That Stayed News"*), I heard about a woman who jumped from a high building and hit a parked car several stories below, but didn't die. Instead she was wheeled, conscious, to the local emergency room. She spent the next year in bed, her still-suicidal mind the only functioning part of her body.

People who swallow chemicals endure inner burns, stomach pumping, brain damage (from drowning in their own vomit) or unpredictable side effects. People who shoot themselves miss surprisingly often and cripple themselves. People who slash their wrists often end up with bruised wrists or damaged nerves. Many suicide attempters have no permanent physical damage; but they all go through some psychiatric "hold" process, which can last anywhere from an hour to 14 days.

I've talked to a number of emergency room personnel about suicides; they agree that the most common reason they see is frustrated anger or just wanting to be noticed by a particular person. "My husband says he's too busy to take me out to dinner," one woman told the emergency room staff at our local hospital. "But for this he makes time."

If someone you know is thinking of suicide, or you think they are, and you don't want them to die, tell them. "Please call me or call suicide prevention before you try anything because I care about you and I don't want to see you die." Don't argue with them about why life is worth living; you can't win that one in rational argument. Tell them how you and other people will feel when they're gone. If there are mental health services you trust in your neighborhood, suggest them.

If you are scared that you may commit suicide, and you don't want to, there may be more options than you realize. Even if, like me, you distrust mental health services, it's worth calling Suicide Prevention — where anonymous volunteers who have undergone rigorous, compassionate training will talk with you about your problems and possible alternatives to suicide. They're listed under that name in the phone book white pages, or call the American Association of Suicidology at (303) 692-0985. —Art Kleiner

Let Me Die Before I Wake

The Hemlock group counsels people who face terminal illness and would rather die quickly and painlessly first. Their book describes several case histories and techniques. Personally, I believe most people facing painful death would be better served by other options — hospice care, home care, or pain relief centers. However, Hemlock's book and newsletter can guide the people who need it toward a prepared, graceful exit — that doesn't emotionally wound the people left behind. Reading about voluntary euthanasia makes suicide seem less like a romantic escape and more like a tedious chore. —Art Kleiner

•

It's an obvious point — but one often overlooked for whatever reasons — that people who have decided to die alone because illness has made their life unbearable must decide to act before becoming absolutely dependent on others. It is necessary to decide in advance on the method and secure the means, and then act when there is no risk of interference. The means must therefore be fairly fast-acting and, as our stories have indicated, with drugs this is not always so. (Of course, if a person has decided to use a gun, these difficulties do not arise. But I have probably talked to more people intending voluntary euthanasia than most and have yet to meet one who plans their eventual death by shooting. A very few have decided on the car exhaust method.)

—Let Me Die Before I Wake

Let Me Die Before I Wake
Derek Humphry
1984; 132 pp.
$6 ($8 postpaid) from:
Hemlock Society
P. O. Box 66218
Los Angeles, CA 90066
or Whole Earth Access

The Hemlock Society
Membership **$20**/year
(Includes Hemlock Quarterly Newsletter)
Information **free**
(address at left)

After Suicide

How to recover from the devastating fact that someone you love has committed a suicide at you. This book has what you might not expect from a series called Christian Care Books: lots of insight, some solid taboo-busting, no rejection of nonChristians and hardly any preaching. —Art Kleiner

After Suicide
John H. Hewett
1980; 119 pp.
$7.95
($8.95 postpaid) from:
The Westminster Press
925 Chestnut
Philadelphia, PA 19107

•

You are going to feel a constant temptation to take a short backward look. Take a long one instead. People have been purposely taking their lives for thousands of years. Suicide shows up in all kinds of societies and throughout every historical epoch. It is as ancient as humanity itself. It occurred among the ancient Hebrews. The Greeks and Romans also were plagued with the problem of self-destruction. They held a hard-line position opposing it, except for the Stoics and Epicureans, who adopted a softer approach. The early Christian church was forced to take stern measures to deal with the epidemic of suicides that took place. So many believers were eager to gain heavenly glory that martyrdoms became commonplace. Augustine, and later Thomas Aquinas, labeled suicide a mortal sin equivalent to murder. With a few exceptions, they gave the church's sanction to the civil laws against the act.

Don't Shoot the Dog!

There are two kinds of training. One is the sort I used to do for the infantry — intense imparting of information and skills. An activity far worthier and more interesting than it's given credit for. But even worthier (and more uncredited) than that is the second kind of training — the shaping of behavior. This new book looks like the very best on the subject — a full-scale mind-changer.

It is customary to apologize whenever saying something favorable about behavior modification and the insights of B.F. Skinner. I now hasten to fail to do that. We all strive to modify the behavior of everyone around us (including ourselves) all the time, usually with monumental ineptitude. Learning to do it well is a service to all. Now that both I and my wife have read Karen Pryor's book we're busily training each other, some of it overt, some covert.

In the course of becoming a renowned dolphin trainer Karen Pryor learned that positive reinforcement (the only kind useable with dolphins, who can't be reached with leashes, bridles, fists, or yells) is even more potent than prior scientific work had suggested. A daughter of novelist Philip Wylie, she is also a fine writer. —*Stewart Brand*

•

There are eight methods of getting rid of a behavior. Only eight. The eight methods are:

- *Method 1:* "Shoot the animal." (This definitely works. You will never have to deal with that particular behavior in that particular subject again.)
- *Method 2:* Punishment. (Everybody's favorite, in spite of the fact that it almost never really works.)
- *Method 3:* Negative reinforcement.
- *Method 4:* Extinction; letting the behavior go away by itself.
- *Method 5:* Train an incompatible behavior. (This method is especially useful for athletes and pet owners.)
- *Method 6:* Put the behavior on cue. (Then you never give the cue. This is the porpoise trainer's most elegant method of getting rid of unwanted behavior.)
- *Method 7:* "Shape the absence;" reinforce anything and everything that is *not* the undesired behavior. (A kindly way to turn disagreeable relatives into agreeable relatives.)
- *Method 8:* Change the motivation. (This is the fundamental and most kindly method of all.)

Don't Shoot the Dog!
Karen Pryor
1984; 187 pp.
$3.95
($5.45 postpaid) from:
Bantam Books
414 East Golf Road
Des Plaines, IL 60016
or Whole Earth Access

How to Get Control of Your Time and Your Life

Almost a parody of the self-help genre, this glib book nevertheless can shake your bad time-management habits and start better ones. I've used it and wasn't sorry. Last time I saw author Alan Lakein he was headed for an indefinite vacation at Big Sur — proving something, I would say. —*Stewart Brand*

•

The 80/20 rule suggets that in a list of ten items, doing two of them will yield most (80 percent) of the value. Find these two, label them A, get them done. Leave most of the other eight undone, because the value you'll get from them will be significantly less than that of the two highest-value items.

These examples, drawn from everyday life, should enable you to feel more comfortable about concentrating on high-value tasks, even at the cost of ignoring many lower-value tasks:

- 80 percent of sales come from 20 percent of customers
- 80 percent of production is in 20 percent of the product line
- 80 percent of sick leave is taken by 20 percent of employees
- 80 percent of file usage is in 20 percent of files
- 80 percent of dinners repeat 20 percent of recipes

How to Get Control of Your Time and Your Life
Alan Lakein
1973; 160 pp.
$2.95
($3.95 postpaid) from:
New American Library
120 Woodbine Street
Bergenfield, NJ 07621
or Whole Earth Access

The Relaxation & Stress Reduction Workbook

Stress, a universal fact of existence, differs in degree and kind from one person to another. The three basic sources of stress — your environment, your body, your thoughts — require different responses. This book offers a wealth of tools for reducing stress and increasing relaxation. It's mainly instruction with a minimum of theory. An excellent resource for creating a relaxation program that suits you. —*Corinne Hawkins*

•

Insight: It is important to recognize that there are three levels of insight necessary to change:

1. Knowledge that you have a problem, and awareness of some of the events that may have caused the problem.

2. Seeing clearly that the irrational ideas which you acquired early in life are creating the emotional climate you live in now, and that consciously or unconsciously you work fairly hard to perpetuate them.

3. The strong belief that after discovering these two insights, you will still find no way of eliminating the problem other than steadily, persistently and vigorously working to change your irrational ideas.

Without a commitment to this last insight, it will be very difficult to alter your habitual emotional responses. . . .

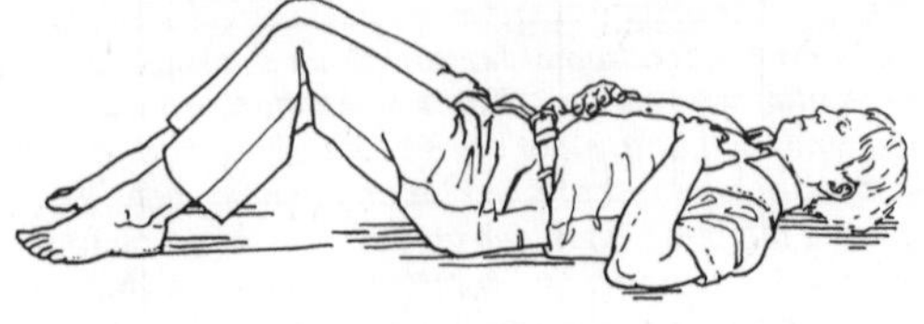

•

Breathing Awareness
1. Lie down on a rug or blanket on the floor in a "dead body" pose — your legs straight, slightly apart, your toes pointed comfortably outwards, your arms at your sides, not touching your body, your palms up, and your eyes closed.
2. Bring your attention to your breathing, and place your hand on the spot that seems to rise and fall the most as you inhale and exhale. Note that if this spot is in your chest, you are not making good use of the lower part of your lungs. People who are nervous tend to breathe many short, shallow breaths in their upper chest. . . .

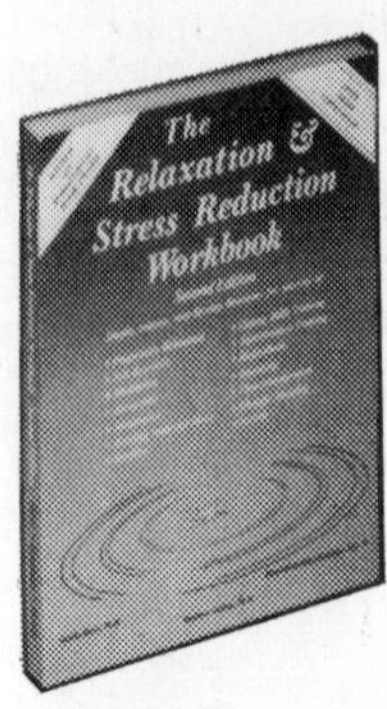

The Relaxation & Stress Reduction Workbook
Matthew McKay, Martha Davis, Elizabeth Robbins
1982 (2nd ed.); 208 pp.
$12.50
($13.75 postpaid) from:
New Harbinger Publications
2200 Adeline, Suite 305
Oakland, CA 94607
or Whole Earth Access

• The way you live can kill you before your time, but it's not too late to change. Here's how.
Treating Type A Behavior — And Your Heart: Meyer Friedman and Diane Ulmer, 1984; 308 pp. **$3.95** ($4.95 postpaid) from Random House/Order Dept., 400 Hahn Road, Westminster, MD 21157.

SELF-HELP AND HOW-TO BOOKS all have one thing in common: They all help you achieve some kind of result — fixing a car, buying a computer, building a house, or losing weight. Psychology, on the other hand, is about process — the process of being human. A psychological perspective can help you achieve just about any other end, but it is not an end in itself.
—Michael Robertson

Psychology self-help books have to be read at the right time. The psychological insight one person gains from a book leaves other people cold. They've already "been there" or they're not "ready" for it yet.
—Corinne Hawkins

Here are some guides that may help you find a good therapist.

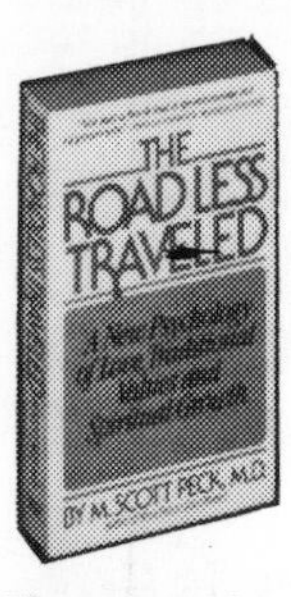

The Road Less Traveled
M. Scott Peck, M.D.
1978; 316 pp.
$9.95 postpaid from:
Simon & Schuster
Mail Order Sales
200 Old Tappan Road
Old Tappan, NJ 07675
or Whole Earth Access

The Road Less Traveled

A psychological (not pop-psychological) guide to modern living. The first 60 pages are practical descriptions of the type of discipline that is needed to face the problems of life. The remainder of the book deals with love, grace, and spiritual growth. It is simple enough to be used immediately, and also deep enough to work on for a lifetime.
—David Hawkins [Suggested by everyone]

•

Whenever a patient says, "It's ridiculous, but this silly thought keeps coming to my mind — it doesn't make any sense, but you've told me I have to say these things," I know that we have hit pay dirt, that the patient has just received an extremely valuable message from the unconscious, a message that will significantly illuminate his or her situation.

•

Falling in love is not an extension of one's limits or boundaries; it is a partial and temporary collapse of them. The extension of one's limits requires effort; falling in love is effortless. Lazy and undisciplined individuals are as likely to fall in love as energetic and dedicated ones. Once the precious moment of falling in love has passed and the boundaries have snapped back into place, the individual may be disillusioned, but is usually none the larger for the experience. When limits are extended or stretched, however, they tend to stay stretched. Real love is a permanently self-enlarging experience. Falling in love is not.

•

Ultimately, if they stay in therapy, all couples learn that a true acceptance of their own and each other's individuality and separateness is the only foundation upon which a mature marriage can be based and real love can grow.

•

Some even suggest that the path toward enlightenment or knowledge of the oneness of reality requires that we regress or make ourselves like infants. This can be a dangerously tempting doctrine for certain adolescents and young adults who are not prepared to assume adult responsibilities, which seem frightening and overwhelming and demanding beyond their capacities. "I do not have to go through all this," such a person may think. "I can give up trying to be an adult and retreat from adult demands into sainthood." Schizophrenia, however, rather than sainthood, is achieved by acting on this supposition.

•

How was it possible to play chess without wanting to win? I had never been comfortable doing things unenthusiastically. How could I conceivably play chess enthusiastically but not seriously? Yet somehow I had to change, for I knew that my enthusiasm, my competitiveness and my seriousness were part of a behavior pattern that was working and would continue to work toward alienating my children from me, and that if I were not able to modify this pattern, there would be other times of unnecessary tears and bitterness.

My depression is over now. I have given up part of my desire to win at games. That part of me is gone now. It died. It had to die. I killed it. I killed it with my desire to win at parenting. When I was a child my desire to win at games served me well. As a parent, I recognized that it got in my way. So it had to go. The times have changed. To move with them I had to give it up. I do not miss it. I thought I would, but I don't.

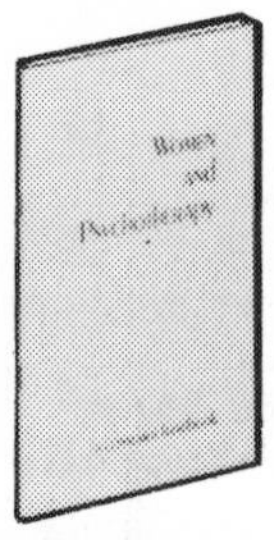

Women and Psychotherapy
1985; 32 pp.
$3.75
($5 postpaid) from:
Federation of Organizations for Professional Women
2437 15th Street NW #309
Washington, DC 20009

Women and Psychotherapy

This is the best consumer handbook for thinking about psychotherapy I've seen. There are chapters on sexism and feminist therapy that are specifically aimed at women, but the rest of it will be as useful to men. It answers the basic questions on deciding if you need therapy, the therapeutic "contract," guidelines for psychoactive drug use, and grievances.
—Corinne Hawkins

•

Sexism in therapist behavior falls into four general categories:
• promoting traditional sex roles;
• stereotyped expectations, such as believing that women possess certain "feminine" personality characteristics;
• sexist use of theoretical concepts, such as the view that it is in "women's nature" to want to be dominated by men;
• responding to women as sex objects, including seduction of female clients.

The Whole Self-Help Directory
Mental Health Association of San Francisco
1985; 186 pp.
$5 postpaid from:
Mental Health Association of San Francisco
2398 Pine Street
San Francisco, CA 94115

Whole Self-Help Directory

This fine local San Francisco Bay Area directory lists self-help groups — a low-cost, effective way of getting support and understanding about specific problems. Besides women's and men's support groups, it lists groups on Alzheimer's disease, Neurological Impairments, etc. It also has a section on starting your own group. Check your local Mental Health Association for their version. They're in the telephone book (white pages).
—Corinne Hawkins

• Eighty percent of the population feels shy in one situation or another. For some it's a minor nuisance, for others it's debilitating. This is the first and only self-help book to thoroughly cover the subject.
Shyness: Philip G. Zimbardo, 1984. **$3.95** ($4.70 postpaid) from Berkley Publishing Group, 390 Murray Hill Parkway, East Rutherford, NJ 07073 (or Whole Earth Access).

Do I Have To Give Up Me To Be Loved By You?

Traditional concepts of romantic commitment can no longer sustain relationships. The intimacy that we all seek breaks down in the face of competing demands and conflicting expectations. This book provides a new model, based on personal growth in a committed relationship, to fill the gap created by the collapse of old forms. They supply practical tools for understanding and communicating about the intense feelings that are often provoked by a long-term relationship or marriage. The last part of the book contains exercises that have proved to be valuable to many of the couples I've seen in therapy.
—*Michael Robertson*

•

It's hard to believe that we aren't wrong for actions that upset another; we've been told so many times that doing what we want is selfish. But when we do something for ourselves that unintentionally offends another's sensibilities and/or frightens him or her, have we done wrong? If you believe that you should never do something for yourself if it hurts someone you care for — that is, you should give yourself up if your mate is hurt by something you want to do — then whenever you meet your own needs, you'll feel guilty. You can't win. If you don't do what you want, you lose yourself, and if you *do* what you want, you'll feel guilty. You're caught in a classic Catch-22.

•

The choice is usually hard. Either we can be protected from feelings in an attempt to be safe or we can express feelings and be open to the joy and the pain they create. Since protecting from pain frustrates all intimate possibilities, the sharing of pain is the key to releasing us to Intimate Love.

•

Although a request may hope to change the other person, it is not an attempt to control if the partner is free to say "No" without disapproval, and free to say "Yes" without feeling a loss of integrity. Often a demand may *sound* like a request, as in "Honey, would you take out the garbage?" If the response "No, I'm busy right now" gets back a congenial "Okay," then the question has been a request. But if the retort is a sarcastic "Thanks a lot," or silent anger, then the question has been an attempt to control.

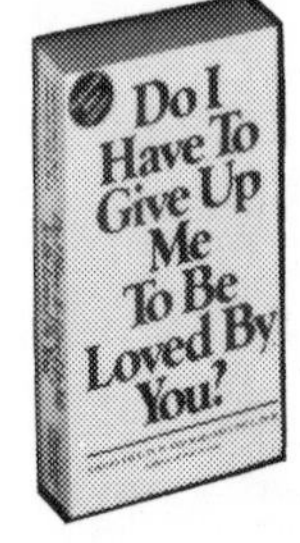

Do I Have To Give Up Me To Be Loved By You?
Jordan Paul, Ph.D., and Margaret Paul, Ph.D.
1983; 313 pp.
$9.95
($11.45 postpaid) from:
CompCare Publications
2415 Annapolis Lane
Minneapolis, MN 55441

Madness Network News

I've never gone crazy enough at the right time for somebody to grab my ass, lock me up, and pump me full of social drugs and electricity, so that I might be a milder member of modern American society. Thousands of folks are sleeping behind bars tonight because they got a little weird once too often, or let their mind shine through a little too strongly at the wrong time, or pushed a relative just a little too far.

***Madness Network News** and its **Reader** represent the collected efforts of a few folks to try "to put an end to the degrading and alienating practices of the psychiatric system." The publications are full of scary things, funny things, crazy things, revolutionary things, all having something to do with the overthrow of the mind control industry.*
—*J.D. Smith*

•

Lonely, hell! I feel crowded.

Sometimes Catatonia sits with me for hours. I do not speak to her. She does not speak to me. We communicate this way.
—*Paul Mariah, Madness Network News Reader*

Madness Network News Reader
Edited by Sherry Hirsch, Joe Kennedy Adams, Leonard Roy Frank, et al.
1974; 192 pp.
$5 postpaid

Madness Network News
Sue Doell and Anne Boldt, Editors
$14/year
(3 issues)
Both from:
Madness Network News
P. O. Box 884
Berkeley, CA 94701
or Whole Earth Access

•

Atwake we keep our dreams of sleep
because we see life's seems are cheap.
—*Marsha Lois Hunt, Madness Network News Reader*

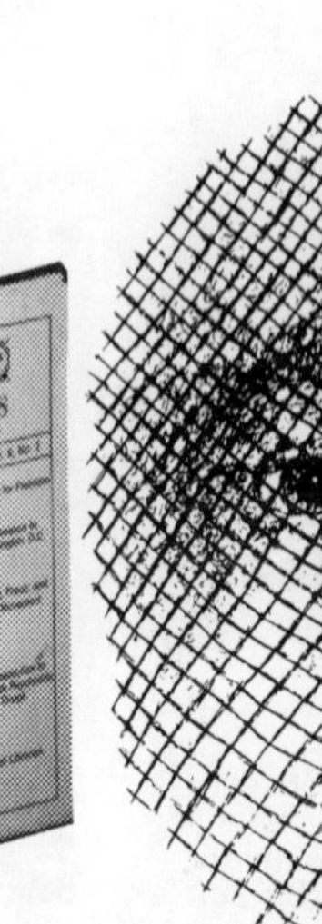

—Madness Network News Reader

Panic

The chapters "The Territory of Fear," "The Descent of Panic," and "Fears Abound" lead the reader through the escalation of anxiety from fear to phobia. The final chapter provides a useful self-assessment tool to help us decide if our fears are garden-variety or could benefit from professional help. Along the way, we are treated to a thorough explanation of both physiological and psychological mechanisms of anxiety. Stewart Agras balances his descriptions of the strengths and weaknesses of different treatment approaches. He talks about the short-term efficacy of drug treatment while noting that it doesn't address the belief system that maintains anxiety, resulting in possible drug dependency. —*Michael Robertson*

•

Fears conditioned by association tend to be short-lived. Most conditioned reflexes will weaken and disappear after a few exposures to the fear-provoking event, quite unlike the more persistent fear and avoidance behavior that we call a phobia. One important finding may, however, help to resolve this problem and explain how a conditioned fear response could persist and become a phobia. Avoidance of a feared situation blocks the normal process of unlearning the fear response.

Panic
Stewart Agras
1985; 151 pp.
$11.95
($13.45 postpaid) from:
W. H. Freeman & Co.
4419 West 1980 South
Salt Lake City, UT 84104
or Whole Earth Access

Staying Alive
Roger Walsh, M.D.
1984; 125 pp.
$7.95
($8.95 postpaid) from:
Random House
Order Dept.
400 Hahn Road
Westminster, MD 21157
or Whole Earth Access

Staying Alive

Arms race nuttiness is so obvious; why doesn't somebody do something about it? Dr. Walsh gives us a look at the psychology involved, and suggests what we may do as individuals. It's gonna be work, but it's not hopeless (I hope). The book is brief, sharp, and free of airhead cliches — a nonpolitical call to action starting with self-understanding.

"When I do not know who I am I serve you.

"When I know who I am I am you."

—JB

•

The more I reflected on our current crises, the more I recognized that they were all human-caused. To the extent they were human-caused, then to that extent their causes were to be sought in human behavior and in the psychological forces — the desires, defenses, phobias, and fantasies — that motivated that behavior. In other words, the roots of our dilemmas were largely psychological. The dilemmas themselves could therefore be seen as symptoms: global symptoms of our collective psychological disturbances.

•

It is important to recognize that doing things out of guilt or "shoulds" is counterproductive. Such motivation spawns anger, tension, and righteousness with which you will infect other people. This is hardly helpful since emotions such as these are part of the problem and our task is to reduce them.

That is why it is so important to learn a little-known secret about contribution and service: it is okay to have a good time. All too often we approach service with grim-faced determination and a hidden assumption that we are not really serious about it if we are not suffering. Yes, it is true the world is in bad shape, but creating more suffering in ourselves is hardly the way to relieve it.

Thou Shalt Not Be Aware
Alice Miller
1984; 331 pp.
$16.95
($18.45 postpaid) from:
Harper and Row
2350 Virginia Avenue
Hagerstown, MD 21740
or Whole Earth Access

The Right to Feel Bad

"Wazza matter? You look depressed." This upbeat book says that's natural, just as feeling joyful is natural. You're not sick. Things will be better (or feel better) later if you just hang in there. Drugs usually won't help and may hinder progress by masking the natural processes going on, processes that are essential to growth and healing. The book hit me dead center as no other on the subject has. My heart says, "yeah ... this is how it is." —JB

•

The lie of depression as illness is right there in the language. "I've got a cold," we say, or "I've got hepatitis." But we do not say — at any rate, not yet — "I've got a depression." Acknowledging it as a state of being, we say, "I am depressed."

•

Creation, after all, is based on emptiness, on the initial existence of nothingness.

One creates from emptiness and returns to it afterward in order to find the space for the next creation to grow. Depression becomes the nothingness in which "something" begins.

•

Both happiness and depression are fueled by the same source: the capacity to feel, to allow ourselves emotion, and to experience the full range of life. This is vitality. Far from being a waste of time, as so many people still insist, depression is as integral a part of human experience as is happiness.

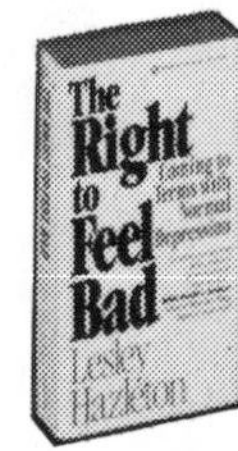

The Right to Feel Bad
Lesley Hazelton
1984; 263 pp.
$3.50
($4.50 postpaid) from:
Random House
Order Dept.
400 Hahn Road
Westminster, MD 21157
or Whole Earth Access

Thou Shalt Not Be Aware

This is a compelling, compassionate book about both childhood and psychoanalysis. Freudian psychology so pervades our thought and language that Alice Miller's corrections of its errors are necessary for our continued use of its concepts. For all of us who want to understand how childhood affected us, but particularly for those of us who were abused or are tempted to abuse, this is an essential book. It also gives all of us some ideas for thinking about how to prevent the violence and self-destruction that are the adult consequences of abusive and neglectful parenting. —Michael Robertson

•

But who is it actually who is so eager to see that society's norms are observed, who persecutes and crucifies those with the temerity to think differently — if not people who have had a "proper upbringing"? They are the ones who learned as children to accept the death of their souls and do not notice it until they are confronted with the vitality of their young or adolescent children. Then they must try to stamp out this vitality, so they will not be reminded of their own loss.

•

The consequences of sexual abuse, however, are not restricted to problems in one's sexual life; they impair the development of the self and of an autonomous personality. There are several reasons why this is so:

1. To have one's helplessness and total dependency taken advantage of by the person one loves, by one's mother or father, at a very early age soon produces *an interlinking of love and hate.*

2. Because anger toward the loved person cannot be expressed for fear of losing that person and therefore cannot be lived out, ambivalence, the interlinking of love and hate, remains *an important characteristic of later object relationships.* Many people, for instance, cannot even imagine that love is possible at all without suffering and sacrifice, without fear of being abused, without being hurt and humiliated.

The Evolving Self
Robert Kegan
1982; 318 pp.
$7.95
($9.45 postpaid) from:
Harvard University Press
79 Garden Street
Cambridge, MA 02138
or Whole Earth Access

The Evolving Self

Kegan sees our journey as a cyclical process of continuing growth and loss. He pinpoints the obstacles to growth and suggests how to overcome those obstacles, depending on the cycle of development in which they occur. The result is a very clear and readable book about how people can grow psychologically, written with a great deal of respect for the reader's individual integrity.
—Michael Robertson [Suggested by Jane Vinson]

•

I used to have two sets of clothes — one for my husband and one for my mother who visited often. Two sets of clothes, but none for me. Now *I* dress in *my* clothes. Some of them are like what my mother would like me to wear but that's a totally different thing.

How exhausting it's becoming holding all this together. And until recently I didn't even realize I was doing it.

Children of Alcoholism

I came from a teetotaling family but lots of my friends didn't. The kids with alcoholic parents often behaved in ways that I didn't understand (and they probably didn't either). This book makes it so clear what was going on, I wish I'd had it then. If you have alcoholic parents in your life (or are an alcoholic parent) you'll probably learn a lot here. —JB

Children of Alcoholism
Judith S. Seixas
and Geraldine Youcha
1985; 208 pp.

$14.95
($16.95 postpaid) from:
Crown Publishers
34 Englehard Avenue
Avenel, NJ 07001
or Whole Earth Access

•

There is so frequently a discrepancy between what they are told is happening and what is actually going on that children of alcoholics are not sure of what they see, what they hear, and what they feel. In other words, they don't believe their own perceptions.

•

Betty is one of those young women who won't trust anyone to be there to catch them if they trip. "I haven't told my husband about my miscarriage," she confides. "I don't want to upset him." By keeping quiet and choosing to suffer alone with the loss, she has effectively created a gap between herself and the person who should be sharing her sadness. Patterns of dishonesty and withholding information automatically destroy intimacy so that chances of true emotional closeness become slim.

Betty had learned early from her alcoholic mother that anger, joy, love, fear, and all other feelings had to go unacknowledged. So how was she going to talk openly to her husband?

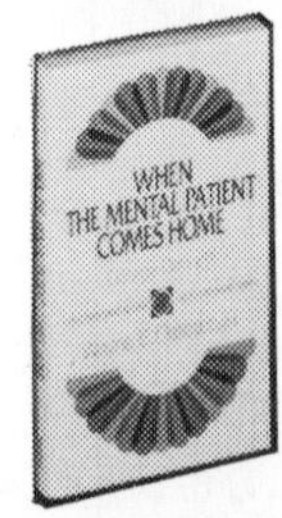

When the Mental Patient Comes Home

Dealing with a mental patient in my life has been like dealing with parts of myself that I'd just as soon avoid. Getting past the guilt and distaste turns out to be part love and part technique, like so many other skills. This nonpreachy, nonsectarian book has helped a lot. —Art Kleiner

•

Psychiatrists on active duty during the war learned that soldiers who "broke down" in combat should not be kept in recovery areas too long. Those who were returned rapidly to active duty did well. Those hospitalized for long periods tended toward further disintegration of personality and ability to function.

•

Family and friends often wish to protect recovering patients from the full range of human experience. They seek to insulate patients from sorrow, excitement, fear and even joy. They fear that "too much" weeping, thrill, fright, laughter, might cause the patient to regress.

Usually this is done out of love for the recovering patient. Patients experience this form of love differently. They experience it as being controlled.

When the Mental Patient Comes Home
George Bennett
1980; 118 pp.

$7.95
($8.95 postpaid) from:
The Westminster Press
925 Chestnut
Philadelphia, PA 19107
or Whole Earth Access

Advanced Techniques of Hypnosis and Therapy

Gradually the sciences of the human mind are achieving levels of abstraction and rigor appropriate to the discussion of mental processes. But Milton Erickson has been ahead of the field in this respect for forty years. This big book is a collection of his papers with some commentary by Jay Haley, and it is a most extraordinary collection. Erickson's method, whether of therapy or research, is the precise use of hypnosis. Under this investigation, the human mind turns out to be as precise in its evolutions and timing as a minuet. —Gregory Bateson

•

But utilizing hypnosis as a technique of deliberately and intentionally shifting to the patient his own burden of responsibility for therapeutic results and having him emphatically and repetitiously affirm and confirm in his own thought formulations and his own expressed verbalizations of his own desires, needs and intentions at the level of his own unconscious mentation, forces the therapeutic goals to become the patient's own goals, not those merely offered to them by the therapist he is visiting.

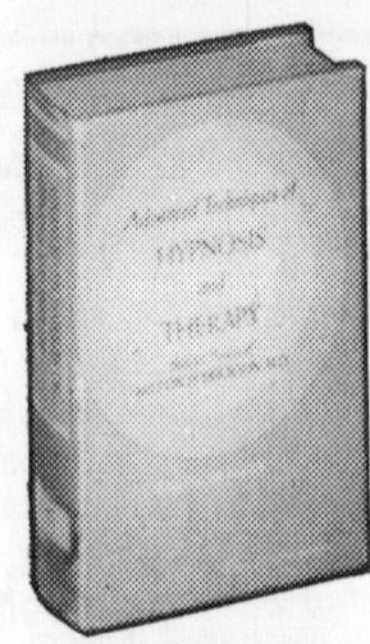

Advanced Techniques of Hypnosis and Therapy
(Selected Papers of Milton H. Erickson, M.D.)
Jay Haley, Editor
1967; 557 pp.

$74.50
($76.50 postpaid) from:
Grune & Stratton
Book Services Dept.
Orlando, FL 32887
or Whole Earth Access

The Love Tapes

The personal growth movement has spawned a booming industry in self-hypnosis tapes that promise to do everything from increase your bustline to clean up your karma from past lives. Outrageous claims notwithstanding, such cassettes can be powerful tools for helping to change old habits, and many are used in hospitals for stress management and to accelerate healing. Of the couple dozen brands I've sampled, ***The Love Tapes*** *provide the best combination of strategies in the most easily accessible format.*

Despite the name, the tapes are refreshingly neutral about pushing any particular ideological viewpoint. A wide range of topics, from health and relationships to business, feature messages consistently well-grounded in modern psychological theory. The sound quality is great, with music occasionally blended into the background as a pleasant male voice guides you through several levels of hypnotic induction. Beginning with a relaxing meditation which evokes pleasurable sensations, the suggestions increasingly address themselves to the source of the unwanted behavior and to reprogramming basic self-concepts, vividly imagining the desired end result.

For example, the weight-loss tape "Slim Image II" works on engendering a positive body image and releasing guilt, resentment, and blame, while also making such concrete suggestions as "Sweets taste too sugary to me," "I prefer nourishing foods," and "I eat only what I choose to eat, and only when I am relaxed." My personal favorite is "Developing Creativity," in which quotes from Einstein and Edison are combined with suggestions for merging right- and left-brain activities. Each tape ends with post-hypnotic suggestions of health, vigor, alertness, etc. When I listen to them before bed, no matter what the topic, I tend to sleep more soundly and to awaken fresher in the morning.

All subjects are also available in a subliminal format in which the same messages are masked beneath the sound of ocean waves. Though the jury is still out on the validity of subliminal programming, these can be played during any daily activity and at least serve as a reminder of the desired changes. Consistency of intention is probably the real key to change, and these are tapes I enjoy enough to listen to daily. —Rebecca Wilson

The Love Tapes
$11.98 - $13.98
Catalog **free** from:
Effective Learning Systems
5221 Edina
Industrial Blvd.
Edina, MN 55435

THREE RECENT TRENDS MAKE ACCESS to good information about sex more important than ever. First, the highly visible controversies about pornography and abortion (which have the effect, in my opinion, of obscuring useful personal information). Second, the rise of the VCR's popularity and the growing number of sexual videotapes. Third, the proliferation of sexually transmitted diseases (see p. 282). Here are the essentials, compiled from suggestions by Michael Castleman (author of *Sexual Solutions*), Joani Blank (Good Vibrations), Susie Bright (editor of *On Our Backs*), Stewart Brand, and myself.

—Art Kleiner

The Joy of Sex
Alex Comfort
1972; 253 pp.
$14.95
postpaid from:
Simon & Schuster
Mail Order Sales
200 Old Tappan
Old Tappan, NJ 07675
or Whole Earth Access

The Joy of Sex

If a book is judged on how profoundly it affects people's lives, and how many lives it reaches, this book is one of the all-time greats. You can't read it without trying some of the ideas in it, and those lead to others, and human relationships grow steadily warmer. In the writing, the content, and the illustrations, warmth is what the book is about. And imagination, and variety. Contact. Health.

—Stewart Brand

•

. . . The quickie is the equivalent of inspiration, and you should let it strike lightning fashion, any time and almost anywhere, from bed in the middle of the night to halfway up a spiral stair: anywhere that you're suddenly alone and the inspiration is bilateral. Not that one or other won't sometimes specifically ask, but the inspirational quickie is mutual, and half the fun is that the preliminary communication is wordless between real lovers. The rule is never to resist this linkup if it's at all possible — with quickness, wit and skill it usually is. This means proficiency in handling sitting, standing and other postures, and making love without undressing. The ideal quickie position, the nude matrimonial, will often be out. This may mean on a chair, against a tree, in a washroom. If you have to wait and can go straight home, it will keep up to half an hour. Longer than that and it's a new occasion. Around the house, try not to block, even if you *are* busy.

My Secret Garden • Forbidden Flowers • Men in Love

By female and male acclaim these are the horniest books in print. They are made of letters to Nancy Friday by innumerable women telling their sexual fantasies in vivid detail. They're liberating and a turn-on for women — completely defusing any lingering guilt about having such fantasies — and enlightening and a turn-on for men, dissolving what was long thought to be a major difference and barrier between the sexes (also tangentially educating males on how to be a sensitive and imaginative lover rather than a narrow-minded clod).

The second book, **Forbidden Flowers**, *is even more explicit since the women are responding to the excitement of* **My Secret Garden**. *A number of the correspondents announce gleefully that they are masturbating as they write. Nice books to read alone, or aloud with a good friend. —SB*

And now there's a third book, **Men In Love**. *It, too, is erotic as all getout, though somehow the men don't seem as imaginative as the women in the other books. —JB*

My Secret Garden: Nancy Friday, 1973; 336 pp.

Forbidden Flowers: Nancy Friday, 1975; 324 pp.

Each **$4.50** postpaid from Simon & Schuster/Mail Order Sales, 200 Old Tappan Road, Old Tappan, NJ 07675 (or Whole Earth Access).

Men In Love: Nancy Friday, 1980; 542 pp. **$4.95** ($5.70 postpaid) from Dell Books, P. O. Box 1000, Pinebrook, NJ 07058-1000 (or Whole Earth Access).

•

Okay, here goes . . . (I may have to go and masturbate before I can finish this, as my mind goes blank).

I have often thought it would be very yummy (and now that I think of it, very messy, too) if somebody would pee inside me (depends on who's washing the sheets). . . .

—*My Secret Garden*

•

I am now divorced but have a lover, and most times when we make love I imagine it is the penis of a large dog or horse that is entering me, or a dog licking me and hordes of dogs all screwing madly. This really turns me on. I don't know why this should be or why it is only dogs and horses. My lover knows about this and likes to talk about it, but he does not understand either. While we are making love he says, "Don't you wish I were a large Alsatian or that this was a stallion's penis between your legs?"

—*My Secret Garden*

•

I feel the smooth rush of power available to me whenever I ask for it, and as we reach the crest of a short hill, I accelerate just enough to raise both of us slightly from the seat. As my tight pants stretch across my crotch, I become aware of the engine's throbbing heat against it, as if I were riding a huge flying cock.

—*Forbidden Flowers*

Sexual Mail Order

In many places mail order is the only way to buy vibrators, lingerie, and sex toys. The companies here send catalogs discreetly (usually in plain envelopes) and don't release your name without permission. As Stephanie Mills once wrote, "If all the electric pleasuring devices available herein were plugged in simultaneously, both coasts would be browned out. So much the better."

—Art Kleiner and Joani Blank

Eve's Garden, 119 West 57th Street, New York, NY 10019; catalog **$2**. *A classy, comparatively mainstream source for lingerie and toys.*

As You Like It, P. O. Box 59077, Dept. W, San Francisco,

• First of its kind: a serious (but not boring) newsletter on sexuality written for the general public.

Sexual Well-Being: Diane Morrissette, Editor. **$36**/year (12 issues) from Sexual Health Resources, P. O. Box 60332, Palo Alto, CA 94306.

Self Love and Orgasm • For Yourself • For Each Other

*In **Self Love**, Dodson takes the reader on an autobiographical journey through her discovery and celebration of masturbation. It's filled with helpful and lucid information and spirited writing, illustrated with Dodson's fine and famous erotic drawings.*

***For Yourself** is an important women's source book. Masturbation and orgasmic potential are discussed. Specific exercises and pleasure-oriented "homework" are given to help the woman who has never had an orgasm or who is dissatisfied with her sexual responsiveness. **For Each Other**, also by Lonnie Barbach, is written for women about sexual intimacy with the men in their lives. Discusses orgasm, increasing sexual desire, communicating about sex, changing sexual patterns, and other similar concerns.*
—Susie Bright and Joani Blank

•

Effective stimulation can be anything that arouses you. If it doesn't arouse you, it is obviously not effective for you. Consequently, you may be very turned on by manual or oral stimulation before intercourse and feel very close to having an orgasm, but once intercourse starts, and the focus shifts to vaginal stimulation by the penis, you may experience a drop in the level of arousal. Although you may enjoy the physical and psychological experience of intercourse, you may not be able to reach orgasm. Again, this experience does not hold for all women, but a drop in excitement can occur because the kind of stimulation that was arousing you before intercourse was replaced by another kind when intercourse began.
—For Yourself

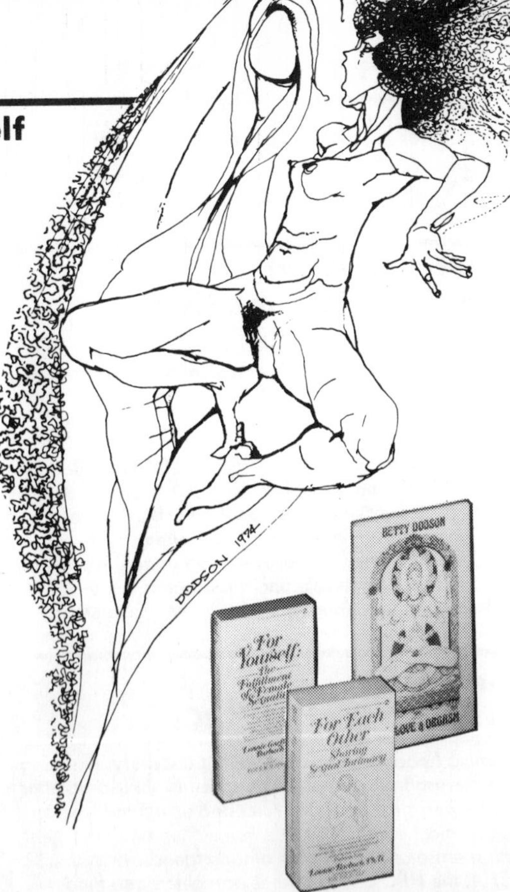

Self Love and Orgasm
Betty Dodson
1983; 80 pp.
$6 postpaid from:
Betty Dodson
P. O. Box 1933,
Murray Hill Station
New York, NY 10156
or Whole Earth Access

For Yourself
Lonnie Barbach
1975; 191 pp.
$3.50
($4.50 postpaid)

For Each Other
Lonnie Barbach
1984; 316 pp.
$4.50
($5.50 postpaid)
Both from:
New American Library
120 Woodbine Street
Bergenfield, NJ 07621
or Whole Earth Access

CA 94159; catalog **$3**. *Calm and professional, yet lighthearted catalog of carefully chosen "sensuous accessories" — toys, oils, feathers, vibrators, etc.*

A tasteless, odorless clear lubricant made of three simple and safe ingredients. With a water base and a pH near neutral (7.5), Probe does not alter the body's vaginal or anal environments. Another wonderful aspect of Probe is its tendency to produce laughter in the bedroom, or wherever you happen to use it. How? Place a drop or more on your hand. Press it against skin and slowly draw your hand away. Before your eyes will stretch a glistening strand of clear fluid—very reminiscent of other body secretions. With friction this lubricant will *eventually* become less moist.

Good Vibrations: 3492-A 22nd Street, San Francisco, CA 94110; catalog **$1** ($5 with a guidebook to vibrators). *Joani Blank's catalog describes vibrators in variety, with panache.*

Geisha: A soft figurine that swivels at the top and vibrates at the base. 8".

Beaver: The vibrator is inside the beaver which has amazing tongue action perfect for the clitoris. The figurine it stands by swivels slowly for vaginal stimulation. Black. Tan and Hot Pink. 8".

Turtle: Similar to the Beaver except that the insertable portion spirals up and down a little as it swivels and the part that tickles your clit is the curved tail of a turtle. 8"

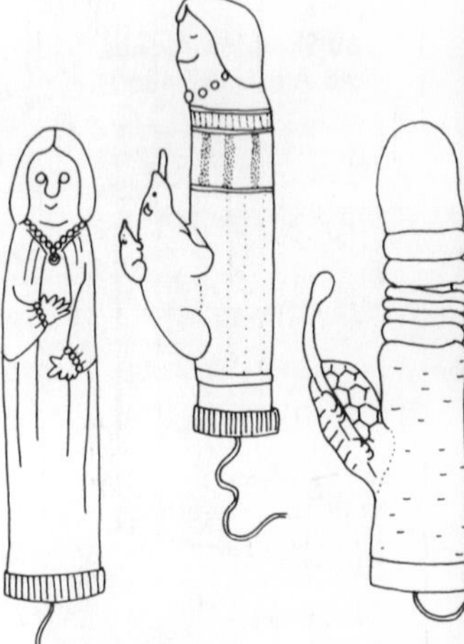

Sexual Solutions

Finally — a book written by a man for men, which says what we women have been trying to tell them lo these many years — it's not how long you make it, it's how you make it long. Castleman, a medical journalist, describes how to do it with humor, sensitivity, and thoroughness. He covers obstacles to problem-free lovemaking, ejaculation and erection problems, what turns women on and off, what to do if the woman you love gets raped, and how to develop or enhance your sensuality.

Once or twice I've had the pleasure of a lover who understood that sex wasn't a job to get done, but rather a game to play. The lover always laughed at my suggestion he give courses on lovemaking to other men. Well, Castleman's done it between the covers of his book. I pray for wide, wide distribution! —Carolyn Reuben, M.D.

•

A widely held notion about lovemaking is that it is divided into three distinct stages: foreplay, intercourse, and afterglow. The very word "foreplay" suggests that it happens before the "real thing." However, the idea that foreplay precedes actually "doing it" is an indirect cause of many men's sexual difficulties.

There are no such things as foreplay and afterglow. There is only *loveplay.*

•

Few men — and fewer women — understand that men also fake orgasm and for the same reasons. Nonejaculatory men may fake orgasm to avoid being considered abnormal, since "everyone knows" there's only one thing on a man's mind — getting his rocks off. Some men fake it to reassure their lovers about their sexual attractiveness. Some fake orgasm simply to get sex over with.

Sexual Solutions
Michael Castleman
1983; 288 pp.
$8.95 postpaid from:
Simon & Schuster
Mail Order Sales
200 Old Tappan
Old Tappan, NJ 07675
or Whole Earth Access

• Depression can make a mess of your love life, but it isn't forever. See **The Right To Feel Bad** (p. 227).

ex is still fun (see previous pages) but it's getting riskier, too. The epidemic of STDs has changed the very nature of our intimate lives. With ten million new cases of STDs annually, caution is a more common sexual milieu. The best cure is still prevention. Read on. —Jeanne Carstensen

American Social Health Association (ASHA)

A sexually transmitted disease information supermarket. Michael Castleman, editor of **Medical Self-Care** *(p. 207), called ASHA "THE place to find out about STDs." Free pamphlets are available on herpes, chlamydia, AIDS, pelvic inflammatory disease, and other forms of VD. Their VD National Hotline (800-227-8922; 800-982-5883 in California) can make local referrals to clinics and doctors, as well as answer questions about all STDs. They also put out a free quarterly newsletter, the* **Hotliner**, *with features like "Vaginitis: The Familiar Foe" and update reports on various STDs. The people and publications are uniformly knowledgable and friendly.* —*Jeanne Carstensen*

Sexually Transmitted Disease Pamphlets
free with SASE
Hotliner
Helen K. Shaw, Editor
free (4 issues)
both from:
ASHA
260 Sheridan Avenue
Palo Alto, CA 94360

The Herpes Resource Center (HRC)

Learning I had herpes was a painful discovery. Plugging into the resources of the HRC, especially their newsletter, **The Helper**, *provided sorely needed emotional support and medical information. It's well-written and intelligent, with a sense of humor; I felt among friends. Part of ASHA, the HRC also publishes pamphlets and funds research.* —*Cindy Craig*

•

All of our knowledge about herpes is useless unless couples are able to communicate. For many folks sex is somehow easier to do than to talk about. With herpes in the picture it may be even more difficult to discuss, but talking is essential. A partner who shares knowledge is a teammate. Talking about genital herpes may seem difficult if not down right impossible. Practicing with friends or in a support group can be invaluable. Getting clear on the facts about herpes and hearing about other people's successes and duds can give you practical knowledge and help you feel more confident and relaxed. Don't underestimate yourself or your partner. For most people and their partners, genital herpes is no big deal. If it is a problem for you, there's help available.

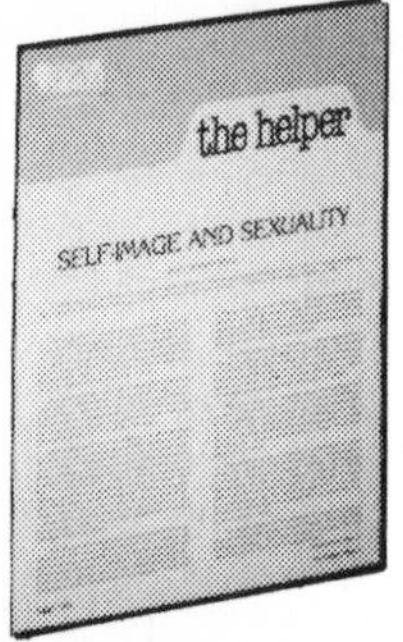

Herpes Information Pamphlets
free with SASE
The Helper
John A. Graves, Editor
$20/year (4 issues)
both from:
HRC
P. O. Box 100
Palo Alto, CA 94302

AIDS Alert

AIDS is here and we all have to learn about it. Undeniably. According to our medical consultants at Whole Earth there isn't a book yet that's accurate, up to date, and unbiased. The monthly newsletter **AIDS Alert** *will give you the news from inside the medical profession on AIDS research and treatment, plus talk on health care workers and AIDS. I learned more from reading the May 1986 issue than from months of news in the national media. It's a bit expensive; you might try the nearest university library.*

If you want to talk to a human being about AIDS, contact the San Francisco AIDS Foundation (800-863-2437 in northern California, 415-863-2437 nationwide) or the national AIDS Hotline (800-342-AIDS). The S.F. AIDS Foundation also sends out free information pamphlets on request. —*Jeanne Carstensen*
[Suggested by Michael Castleman]

AIDS Alert
Terri Thorton, Editor
$79/year
(12 issues) from:
American Health Consultants
67 Peach Tree Park Dr. NE
Atlanta, GA 30309

San Francisco AIDS Foundation
Information **free** from:
San Francisco
AIDS Foundation
333 Valencia Street
San Francisco, CA 94103

The Truth About Herpes

If you've got herpes, you've got questions. Whether you just got herpes or have had it a long time, this book can help alleviate that sense of unease that comes from not knowing. Stephen Sacks does an admirable job of not preaching, which means some questions ("should I tell my partner?") are left for you to decide. Recommended by the Herpes Resource Center. —*Cindy Craig*

•

If you engage in oral sex, specifically with your partner's mouth in contact with your genitals, then you might get genital herpes because your partner had an active cold sore, or fever blister or mouth sore (or no recognized symptoms at all), which happened to be caused by herpes. In fact, 50 to 80 percent of us may harbor the virus in the latent state and shed the virus in the mouth during recurrences of active infection. If you have oral sex at the right moment — genital herpes may result.

The Truth About Herpes
Stephen L. Sacks, M.D.
1986; 184 pp.
$10 postpaid from:
HRC
P. O. Box 100
Palo Alto, CA 94302

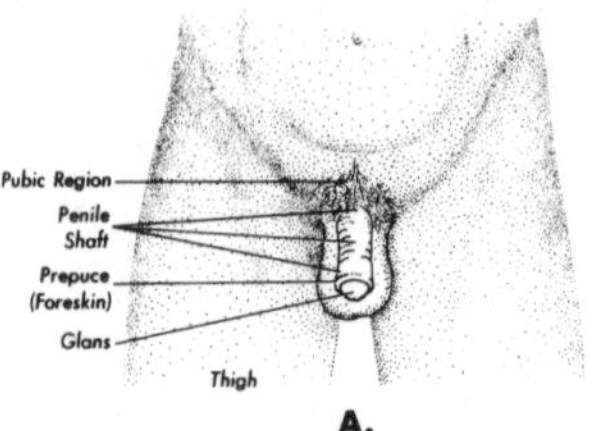

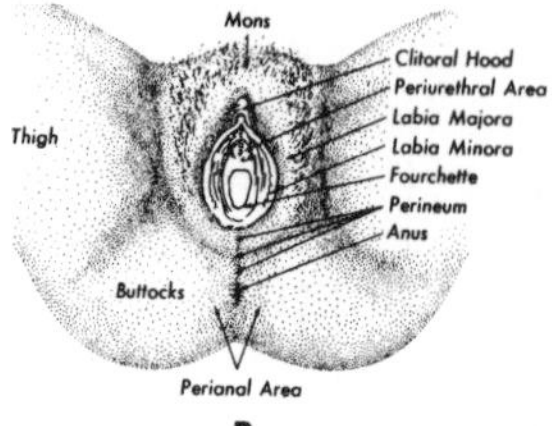

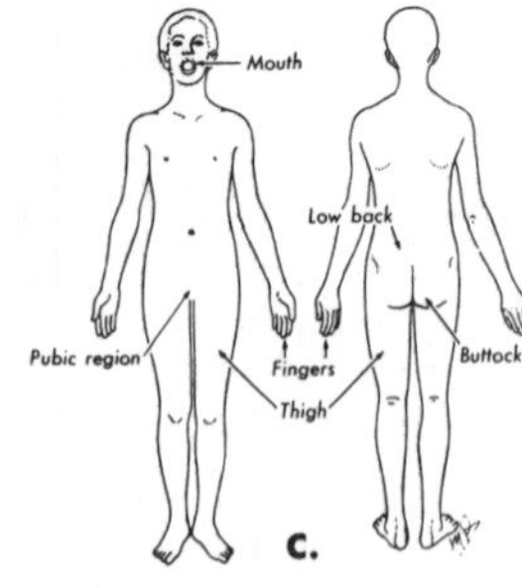

A. Commonly affected genital areas in recurrent genital herpes – male.
B. Commonly affected genital areas in recurrent genital herpes – female.
C. Commonly affected nongenital areas in "genital" herpes.

• See also "Women's Health/Men's Health" (pp. 210-211).

• You can make your own tentative diagnoses of most sexually transmitted diseases by referring to books on p. 208.

Contraceptive Technology

Current books on birth control are harder to find now that they're not the hot sellers they were during the 60s and 70s. Yet most of us, even baby boomers, continue to need birth control in the 80s. ***Contraceptive Technology*** *is written for physicians, but it's still the best, most current source of birth control information for the layperson. It contains almost anything you could ask about birth control use, safety and effectiveness. I count on the biennial editions to keep me posted on any new methods and to nourish my hope that a perfect "no risk, no mess" contraceptive will be discovered.* —Janna Katz

•

The following options are available to women and men in the United States:

- Abstinence from and alternatives to sexual intercourse
- Condoms
- Combined birth control Pills
- Progestin-only Pills or Mini-Pills
- Morning-after Pills or IUD insertion
- Inert IUD's
- IUD's that are medicated with copper
- IUD's that elaborate progesterone
- Diaphragms
- Cervical caps (an option in some communities)
- Spermicidal sponges and suppositories
- Contraceptive foam
- Natural family planning approaches
- Tubal ligation and hysterectomy
- Vasectomy
- Therapeutic abortion

•

The trend to lower doses — lesser is better — "small is beautiful"

Current combined Pills contain 1/25 to 1/4 the amount of progestin contained in our first Pills, and 1/5 to 1/2 the amount of estrogen. Some Pills, the progestin-only Pills or "Mini-Pills," contain no estrogen and less progestin than any of our current combined Pills. Three new technologies release a constant low dose of hormones: the progestin-elaborating IUD's, subcutaneous silastic capsules, and injectable preparations. Similarly, the vaginal ring reduces the steroid dosage, which leads to fewer complaints of nausea and headaches than are observed in oral contraceptives. IUD's have become slightly smaller, more delicate, more flexible. Abortions are being performed at earlier stages of gestation, and tubal ligations are being performed with less anesthesia and smaller incisions.

•

Unlike condoms or diaphragms, oral contraceptives (OC's) provide no physical barrier to the transmission of sexually transmitted diseases (STD's). OC's have, in fact, been linked by some to increasing STD rates by (1) causing abandonment of barrier methods and (2) leading to increased sexual activity. Clinicians caring for women using OC's should have a heightened index of suspicion for lower genital tract infections, especially if symptoms or signs of cervicitis are present.

Contraceptive Technology
Robert A. Hatcher, M.D., et al.
13th edition
1986-87; 310 pp.
$15.95
($17.70 postpaid) from:
Irvington Publishers
740 Broadway, Suite 905
New York, NY 10003
or Whole Earth Access

The New No-Pill, No-Risk Birth Control

At first glance, natural family planning sounds like my idea of the "perfect contraceptive": it's safe; completely natural, and nearly 100 percent effective. So why isn't everyone using it? Maybe because they haven't read Nona Aguilar's recently-updated book. To be sure, natural family planning isn't for everyone. For all the benefits described in this book, not everyone is ready for the required periods of sexual abstinence and meticulous charting of daily fertility signs. But for couples in search of an ideal birth control method, this guide has a lot to offer. There is excellent instruction on every aspect of the method, sensitive advice, resources, and a lot of encouragement. Interviews with couples using the method give real motivation and even show the positive side of abstinence. And for those of us not quite ready to relinquish our pills, IUD, or barrier method, the techniques of charting described in this book can give clues to our hidden fertility. —Janna Katz

•

The event of ovulation occurs during a very narrow time frame — twenty-four hours or less — and sperm cells survive less than five days in the woman's reproductive tract. When the sperm's estimated (maximum) survival time of five days is combined with the woman's single day of fertility, then there are six days out of every cycle that lovemaking can cause pregnancy. Six days — barely 20 percent of the average cycle — that's all!

When you are infertile, your finger can easily touch your cervix, which is low in the vagina. The os ("mouth") is also closed, and the cervix feels firm to the touch. As you enter your fertile phase, your cervix will rise progressively higher in the vagina and will also open and soften to your touch. Sometimes during the fertile time the cervix rises so high that it becomes impossible to reach. If you can't reach your cervix, you are fertile!

A HIGH, SOFT AND OPEN CERVIX

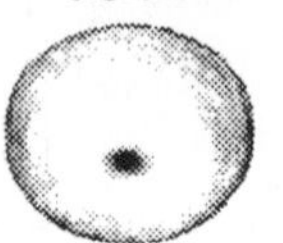
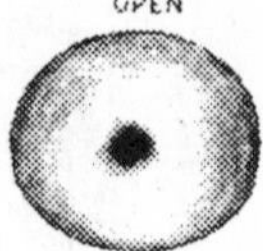

The Cervical Os

The top row shows the dimplelike appearance of your cervix if you have not delivered a child vaginally. The bottom row shows its slitlike appearance if you have had a vaginal delivery. The cervices on the extreme left indicate infertility because they are closed; those on the extreme right are open so indicate fertility.

The New No-Pill No-Risk Birth Control
Nona Aguilar
1986; 240 pp.
$9.95 postpaid from:
Macmillan Publishing Co.
Order Dept.
Front and Brown Streets
Riverside, NJ 08075
or Whole Earth Access

• **My Body, My Health** (p. 210) has 200 pages of excellent birth control information.

• Is it anti-life to be pro abortion rights? Author Kathleen McDonnell shows how public focus on that question is hindering understanding of abortion — especially of women's feelings about it. Outstanding book.
Not An Easy Choice: Kathleen McDonnell, 1984; 157 pp.
$8 ($9.50 postpaid) from South End Press, 116 Saint Botolph Street, Boston, MA 02115.

The Rubber Tree

Male and female contraceptives by mail. All kinds of condoms, sponges, and cream and jelly spermicides. —Kevin Kelly

The Rubber Tree
Catalog **free** from:
ZPG — Seattle
4426 Burke Avenue North
Seattle, WA 98103

How It Feels to be Adopted

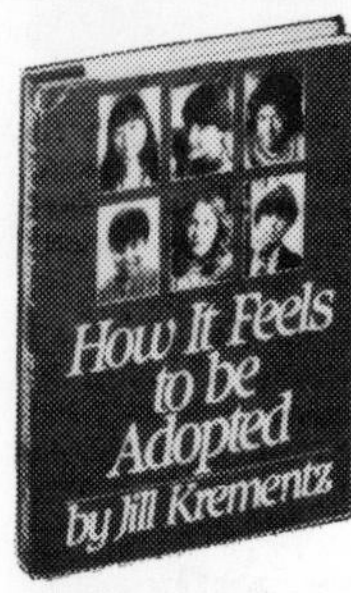

How It Feels to be Adopted
Jill Krementz
1982; 107 pp.
$12.95
($13.95 postpaid) from:
Random House
Order Dept.
400 Hahn Road
Westminster, MD 21157
or Whole Earth Access

Jill Krementz has created a wonderful book in this collection of revealing portraits of nineteen adopted children. Ranging from eight to sixteen years in age, the children talk candidly about their experiences and feelings. Some were adopted at birth, some first lived in foster homes, some have single parents, some are in transracial homes, and some have made the journey from other countries. This book offers prospective adoptive parents the valuable opportunity to look down the road and anticipate at least some of the feelings their child(ren) will encounter. An excellent book to give an adopted child who will discover that other adopted children share the same yearnings, fears and joys. The photographs of the children and their families tell stories of relationships touched with tenderness and pride. The images linger long afterward.
—David and Mary Lee Cole

•

I guess the hardest thing for me in the first year was when I had to go back to the agency for follow-up visits. I was always terrified that I would see my other mother there and she would want to take me home with her again. That's because when I was in foster care we had monthly visits — my mother and I — in the playroom at the agency.

Melinda, age 10, and her adoptive parents.

•

Sometimes I think about my first mother — like I wonder if she's lonely and if she's worked out all her problems. I hope she has a better life. It must be hard for her not to have her kids and it would be nice if the agency people told her what a happy life Lauren and I have now. Now that the adoption is final, I'd like to see her again. I still remember what she looks like — she has short brown hair and brown eyes and she looks just like me.

The Adoption Resource Book

The Adoption Resource Book
Lois Gilman
1984; 318 pp.
$7.95
($8.35 postpaid) from:
Harper and Row
2350 Virginia Avenue
Hagerstown, MD 21740
or Whole Earth Access

Written by a librarian and an adoptive parent, this is a thoroughly detailed introduction to the ''hows'' of adoption. Gilman explains how agencies work, how intercountry adoptions are arranged, how to find a child independently, and how to answer the inevitable questions from parents, friends, and your adopted child once you have adopted. She explains the requirements, procedures, and paperwork involved in the alternative methods of adopting, and illustrates each method with brief anecdotes. The book includes both an extensive annotated bibliography and a directory of agencies and services. Those looking for basic information will find it here, plus some perspective on how adoption has changed in the last fifteen years.
—David and Mary Lee Cole

•

If you legally adopted your child abroad, the adoption is valid. Still, most adoption authorities recommend as an additional safeguard that you readopt your child in the United States under the laws of your state. This will also give you readily available evidence of the validity of your child's adoption. Some states may not permit readoption, so check locally to see if this can be done.

If your child left his or her country of birth under a guardianship, not a final adoption, then you *must* adopt in the U.S.

•

Maternity leaves and adoption leaves are clearly treated differently by employers. The parent group FACE turned up some basic facts about leaves in a survey they conducted. FACE found that 95 percent of the employers surveyed had a policy allowing biological maternity leave, while only 39 percent had an adoption leave. Three-fourths of the employers provided paid maternity leaves, while less than a quarter offered paid adoption leaves. The rationale for offering paid leave for maternity and unpaid leave for adoption rested on the premise that pregnancy created a physical disability, while adoption did not. Most employers had health-insurance programs covering pregnancy expenses; only two employers provided adoption benefits.

The Adoption Triangle

The Adoption Triangle
Arthur D. Sorosky, M. D.,
Annette Baran, M. S. W.,
Reuben Pannor, M. S. W.
1984; 237 pp.
$9.95 postpaid from:
Doubleday & Co.
501 Franklin Avenue
Garden City, NY 11530
or Whole Earth Access

Written in something of an academic style, ***The Adoption Triangle*** *nevertheless provides important insights into the process of adoption and how it affects all those involved: the triangle of children, birth-parents, and adoptive parents. Unlike other books listed here, this one was written by professionals in the field of social work and adoption with the intention of affecting public policy and private practice. The author's advocacy of open adoption, radical at the time of the book's first edition in 1978, is now widely supported. Readers will continue to find the book useful for its exploration of the strong and complex emotions felt by everyone involved in adoption.*
—David and Mary Lee Cole

•

Taking a child from one set of parents and placing him/her with another set, who pretend that the child is born to them, disrupts a basic natural process.

•

Very few adoptees are provided with enough background information to incorporate into their developing ego and sense of identity. The adoptive parents are reluctant to impart known information, especially any of a negative nature, that might hurt the child. The adoptees in turn are often reluctant to ask genealogical questions because they sense their parents' insecurities in these areas. Information given to adoptive couples at the time of adoption is scanty and usually describes immature, confused, adolescent unwed mothers and fathers.

•

It is our conviction that adult adoptees should have access to their birth records, if they so desire, when they reach the age of eighteen. For those adoptees who are determined to find their birth parents, the information available in the original birth records may not be sufficient. In order to avoid situations where adoptees spend agonizing years and large sums of money tracking down trivial clues, we would support methods to facilitate the search. Regional or national registries where adoptees and birth parents could indicate their interest in reunion, for example, have been suggested. In addition, agencies could provide identifying information and reunion services upon request.

•

''In a way, I am very angry toward the law. The law still refers to me as a child when they refer to 'in the best interests of the child.' I resent that because in my opinion, I am twenty-one years old and I feel I am quite old enough, mature and responsible enough to be making my own decisions. I don't feel as if any decision concerning my life should be left up to a judge or to anyone else.''

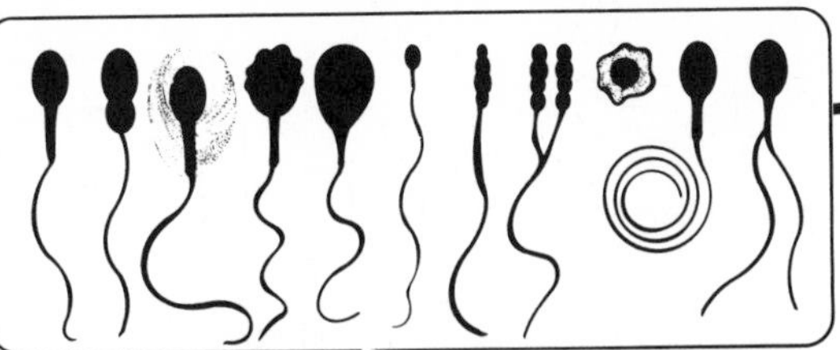

You Can Have a Baby

With an estimated one out of ten Americans suffering from infertility, chances are you know someone trying to get pregnant and failing month by month. Give them ***You Can Have a Baby*** *and they might name the kid after you! A great source of basic information about what infertility is and how to overcome it. In a factual, not frightening, way, it tells you when to seek medical help and what to expect at the office of your local infertility specialist.*

Surprisingly, a lot of infertility is caused by popular misconceptions about the best way to get pregnant. If this is your problem, the facts in this book will set you straight and let mother nature get back on course. If your problem is more serious, there are clear explanations to prepare you for different medical tests and treatments. As a complete guide, this book will be especially valuable to couples who are just starting to realize they need help conceiving.
—Janna Katz

Fifty percent of the time the problem is the male's. This covers male infertility nicely. *—Kevin Kelly*

•

Women who smoke have a 25 percent greater chance of aborting than nonsmokers. Chronic smoke inhalation prevents oxygen from getting from the lungs through the blood and to the baby. As a result, the fetus is deprived of oxygen during its critical growth phase.

•

The length of time a woman stays on the pill doesn't seem to affect the recovery of the hormonal axis. But erratic use does. A woman can take the pill indefinitely with little risk to her fertility if she uses it consistently, stopping only when she wants to get pregnant. When a woman initially takes the pill, the brain control center is shocked. Stopping and starting the pill repeatedly jerks the system on and off, until it loses its buoyancy. After such a series of shocks, treatment with fertility drugs can usually help the ovulatory system start up again.

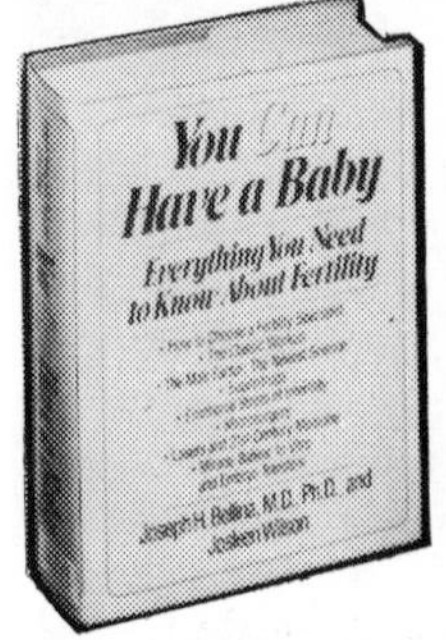

You Can Have a Baby
Joseph H. Bellina, M.D., Ph.D., and Josleen Wilson
1985; 427 pp.
$18.95
($21.55 postpaid) from:
Crown Publishers
34 Englehard Avenue
Avenel, NJ 07001
or Whole Earth Access

New Conceptions

Making babies by any method other than the usual way is the immense subject of this book. It is not surprising that when procreation is moved from the bedroom to the lab bench, confusion is born. This author does an admirable job in weaning the confusion away from the tools so you can decide if you want to use them. I came away from her compassionate reporting with the distinct sense that new-fangled conceptions are a long lever bending our culture profoundly. *—Kevin Kelly*

•

Other women enter into surrogate arrangements because they enjoy being pregnant. "Many say they would like to be pregnant their whole lives," states Parker. "They just don't want to rear children their whole lives." For example, nineteen-year-old Corinne Appleyard, who served as a surrogate for George and Sheila Syrowski, claims that she feels more energy when she's pregnant. Surrogate Elizabeth Kane once remarked, "I have babies so easily. They just pop out."

•

For the woman who can provide the uterus for a child but not the egg, one answer in the future will be an egg donation. Already the use of the procedure is being explored by scientists in Italy. They call it TDO, the transfer of donor oocytes (eggs). Through a laparoscopy they extract an egg from the ovary of a woman donor. They use another laparoscopy to place the donated egg in the lower part of the fallopian tube of the recipient. The woman who receives the egg can then have sex with her husband or be artificially inseminated with his sperm in the hope that the sperm will fertilize the egg in her body and the pregnancy will develop normally.

•

Dr. Cecil Jacobsen of George Washington University Medical School fertilized a chimpanzee egg *in vitro* with chimpanzee sperm, implanted it in the abdomen of a male chimpanzee, later delivering a healthy baby chimp through a Caesarean section. Australian researchers predict that the technique could be adapted to male humans, leaving open the possibility of surrogate fathers.

New Conceptions
Lori B. Andrews, J.D.
1984; 326 pp.
$14.95
($16.45 postpaid) from:
St. Martin's Press
Cash Sales
175 5th Avenue
New York, NY 10010
or Whole Earth Access

Test-Tube Women

Needles, tubes, and speculums are probing ever deeper into women's bodies, seeking a scientific understanding of the mystery of creation. ***Test-Tube Women*** *is a feminist map to this new and largely foreign world of motherhood in the age of in vitro fertilization, sex selection, amniocentesis, surrogate mothering, and other rapidly expanding reproductive technologies. In 35 essays, studies, and first-person accounts, the authors collectively argue that the new reproductive technologies are an extension of men's attempts to control women's bodies and, further, are biased toward white upper-class eugenics.*

This is important and insightful reading for anyone interested in how these technologies are changing our lives — which they are — even if you don't completely agree with the book's position. *—Jeanne Carstensen*

•

Why are they splitting the functions of motherhood into smaller parts? Does that reduce the power of the mother and her claim to the child? ('I only gave the egg. I am not the real mother.' 'I only loaned my uterus. I am not the real mother.' 'I only raised the child. I am not the real mother.')

•

The advantages that egg farming offers women within a patriarchial context must be seen in light of our losses. Through egg farming, women can be divided into two groups: egg donors and embryo recipients. In an entire society, all women could be engaged in reproduction, either as egg layers or egg hatchers. Both egg layers and egg hatchers would be controlled in terms of food, travel, work, and stress to ensure optimal conditions for the embryo. Women as egg layers are already in demand. I. D. Cooke announces the need for female ovum donors in the next decade. Women as egg layers and egg hatchers would be seen by patriarchy as the means to a vital commodity — eggs.

Test-Tube Women
Rita Arditti,
Renate Duelli Klein,
and Shelley Minden,
Editors
1984; 482 pp.
$9.95
($11.45 postpaid) from:
Methuen Inc.
29 West 35th Street
New York, NY 10001
or Whole Earth Access

• See also "Women's Politics" (p. 98).

• You can also gain some insights into fertility matters from the books shown on "Women's Health" (p. 210) and "Men's Health" (p. 211).

Labor and Delivery.

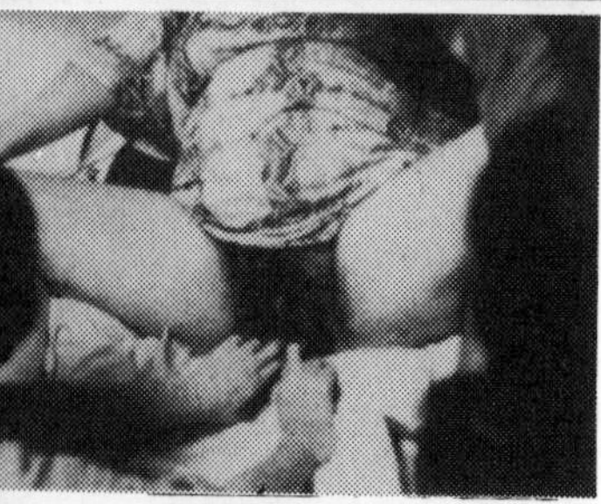
Stretching the perineum with olive oil.

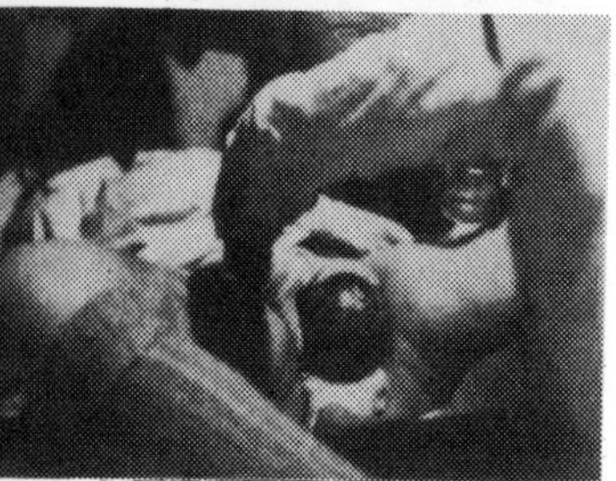
A nine-pound baby born without tearing.

Special Delivery

__Special Delivery__ affirms that birth is normal and that all births are different. It covers homebirth, hospital birth, and birth center birth, with information on the physical, emotional, and spiritual elements of birth; tools for handling labor, nutrition, and exercises; preparation for birth and labor; emergencies and complications; care of the newborn; and post-delivery care of the mother. This is an easy to read book, full of pictures, illustrations, and personal stories balanced by the advice and suggestions of the author who is a midwife, childbirth educator, mother, teacher, and founder and head of the national organization Informed Birth and Parenting.

—Peggy O'Mara McMahon

•

There are several things that your birth attendants can do to help you deliver without tearing. One is to apply hot compresses to your lower belly, vulva and perineum during the early part of second stage to keep the tissues supple and aid relaxation. Then once the head starts to be visible at the vaginal opening, your attendant or husband should begin to massage the perineum (the area between the vagina and anus) in between contractions. You can also massage the area yourself, both during pregnancy and during labor.

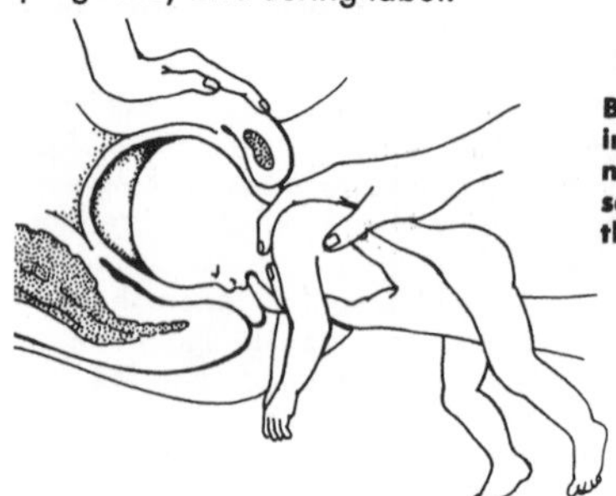
Breech birth: keeping head flexed, if necessary, by inserting a finger in the baby's mouth.

▲ Early labor: 2 cm dilation; 80 percent effaced.

Transition: 8 cm ► dilated; the mother should be at about a 45-degree angle; the hardest part of labor, but the shortest.

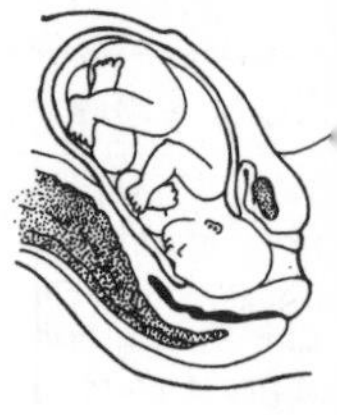
Descent: dilation is complete and ► the baby's head passes through the cervix and down the birth canal; the waters have usually broken; the head turns down.

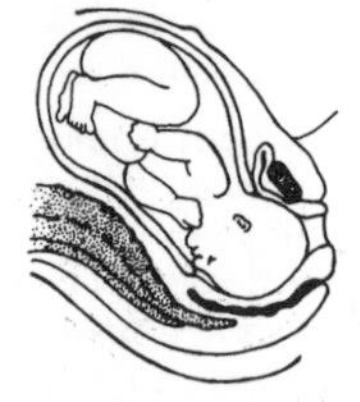
◄ Continued descent: with each contraction, the baby's head travels further down the birth canal; the rectum becomes compressed, causing strong pushing urges.

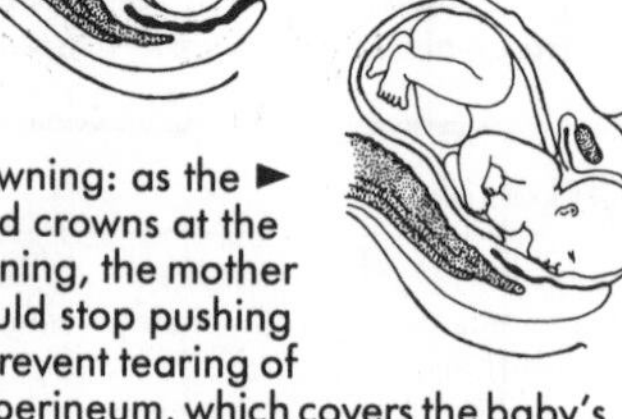
Crowning: as the ► head crowns at the opening, the mother should stop pushing to prevent tearing of the perineum, which covers the baby's face as it "sweeps the perineum."

Restitution: the head turns back toward the side and ▲ then the shoulders are born one at a time and the body slides out.

Special Delivery
Rahima Baldwin
1979; 169 pp.
$10.95
($11.95 postpaid) from:
Celestial Arts
P. O. Box 7327
Berkeley, CA 94707
or Whole Earth Access

The Tentative Pregnancy

Dramatic advances in medical technology now allow doctors to detect birth defects in a child before it is born. What effect does this have on pregnant women? This difficult subject is tackled by __The Tentative Pregnancy__. This is not an insensitive consumer guide. It is a deeply caring look at the powerful emotions and ethics of "amniocentesis," a test that determines whether an unborn baby is deformed. Until now the feelings of the expectant mother have been rarely heard on this subject. Anyone considering amniocentesis will want to hear what over 120 women said and felt about the procedure. The lessons of this book will become even more important as amniocentesis and other fetal tests become routine. *—Janna Katz*

•

New research is beginning to indicate that it is possible to discover chromosomal abnormalities in placental material which are not to be found in the fetus: That is, the cells of the placenta may develop with missing or with extra chromosomes while the fetus itself has normal chromosomes. Thus some women will abort a normal fetus because of an abnormal placenta.

A Good Birth, A Safe Birth
Diana Korte
and Roberta Scaer
1984; 336 pp.
$7.95
($9.45 postpaid) from:
Bantam Books
414 East Golf Road
Des Plaines, IL 60016
or Whole Earth Access

The Tentative Pregnancy
Barbara Katz Rothman
1986; 274 pp.
$6.95
($7.95 postpaid) from:
Viking Penguin Books
299 Murray Hill Pkwy.
East Rutherford, NJ 07073
or Whole Earth Access

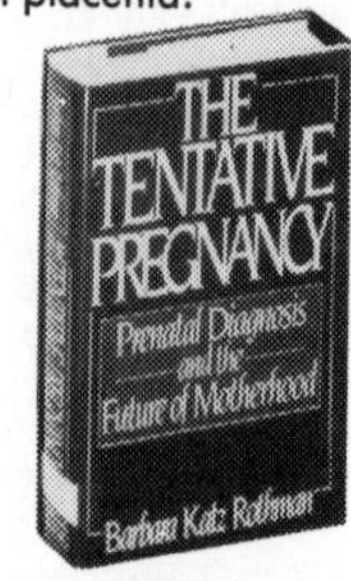

A Good Birth, A Safe Birth

__A Good Birth, A Safe Birth__ assumes that pregnant women must know their options before they can determine their birthing preferences; this book tells you your options by analyzing scientific data supporting the safety and normalcy of birth in various settings.

Based on interviews with 2000 women and the best of the childbirth books of the last few years, it's a consumer's guide for finding "Dr. Right," for avoiding unnecessary cesareans, for evaluating high-tech interventions, for choosing a pediatrician, for successfully breastfeeding, and for accepting the roller coaster emotions of new motherhood. Also included is an extensive list of resources and an impressive bibliography.

—Peggy O'Mara McMahon

•

One way of evaluating where to have your baby is to look at the likelihood of intervention for each place of birth. The fewer interventions there are the less risk there is to mother and baby. With fewer interventions there will be fewer problems as a result of intervention, fewer c-sections, and, we believe, a safer birth for the normal mother and baby. . . .

With less intervention, mother, baby, and father are more likely to have a strong attachment to each other, and this fragile new family will have the mutual loving start they need. The pleasure principle, the full expression of a woman's sensuality in birth, operates best with the least intervention. And finally, with less intervention, a woman feels more that she has "given birth" rather than that she has been "delivered." Her enhanced self-esteem from this achievement helps the woman in her new role as a mother.

THE CROWNING, by Judy Chicago; poster, 25" x 38" from JC/WIN, 1728 Bissonnet, Houston, TX 77005. $10 unsigned, $20 signed (plus $3.00 shipping).

The Whole Birth Catalog

*The title says it all — 300-plus pages about birth. A true panoply executed in the **Whole Earth Catalog** format, it's the best source for everything on the topic I have seen. This book is advocacy as well as education for alternative and innovative birthing options.* —*Andrea Sharp*

*Janet Isaacs Ashford also edits **Childbirth Alternatives Quarterly**, "the on-going **Whole Birth Catalog**," and maintains a list of updated addresses for the **Catalog**.*
—*Jeanne Carstensen*

NURTURING NEWS

First-Time Father

"Doing" Matthew

FATHERS

in the company of a child. As a father I am not expected to enjoy and participate in my FATHERHOOD to the same extent that mothers enjoy and participate in their MOTHERHOOD. So much for expectations!"

—from " 'Doing' Matthew" by Michael Robinson, ***Nurturing News***, June 1982.

•

Sherri Nance, with the help of other members of her organization, Premature, Inc., has written a desperately needed book and has done an excellent job of it. The book is the only one we know of that is specifically designed for the parent of a premature baby. Because it is written by other parents of prematures, the book focuses on exactly what a parent needs to know. In the first half of the book, Nance deals with the hospital experience after the birth of a premature child. She discusses some causes and effects of prematurity, and parents' role in the care of their baby. She gives detailed descriptions of the Neonatal Intensive Care Unit, its equipment, and staff — explaining everything briefly but clearly. She also provides a list of steps that can be taken to cope financially with the child's care. Nance recommends asking questions of the staff and giving the baby as much love and stimulation as possible (and/or permissable). In short, she tries to help parents feel as comfortable with the situation as possible through preparation and knowledge. The second half of the book focuses on parenting the premature infant. She discusses the reactions of friends and families and the emotional state of the parents, including their fears. A large portion is devoted to feeding the child, with information on breast pumping, care of the breast, and switching from bottle to breast when the baby comes home. She does include information on formulas and instances when formula use would be indicated.

Premature Babies (A Handbook for Parents): Sherri Nance, 1982; 322 pp., illus. **$15.95** from Arbor House Publishing Company, 235 E. 45th St., New York, NY 10017.

Childbirth Resources

To find out about childbirth classes, midwives, and birth options in your area, write to any or all of the following organizations:

Informed Birth and Parenting: catalog **free** from P. O. Box 3675, Ann Arbor, MI 48106

National Association of Parents and Professionals for Safe Alternatives in Childbirth: membership **$15**/year (includes **NAPSAC News Quarterly**); information **free**; all from NAPSAC International, P. O. Box 646, Marble Hill, MO 63764.

Birthworks: catalog **free** from Cesarean Prevention Movement, P. O. Box 152, Syracuse, NY 13210.

International Childbirth Education Association: catalog **free** from P. O. Box 20048, Minneapolis, MN 55420.
—*Peggy O'Mara McMahon*

Ixcuina, the Aztec goddess of childbirth.

The Whole Birth Catalog
Janet Isaacs Ashford, Editor
1983; 313 pp.
$12.95
($13.95 postpaid) from:
The Crossing Press
P. O. Box 640
Trumansburg, NY 14886
or Whole Earth Access

Whole Birth Catalog
Address Update $2
Childbirth Alternatives Quarterly
$15/year (4 issues)
Both from:
Janet Ashford
14230 Elva Avenue
Saratoga, CA 95070

Circumcision

It isn't often one has an option with surgery. Circumcision, often done routinely, is one of those times. My husband and I used this book to help make our decision (further complicated by our both being Jewish) not to circumcise if we had a son. All aspects of the question are fully covered, including a description of the operation and before and after diagrams. The decision to not circumcise is reversible, but circumcision is irrevocable.
—*Andrea Sharp*

•

According to many American physicians, the uncircumcised penis is a difficult organ to keep clean; in fact, so difficult that preventive surgery is urged for the sake of cleanliness. No other body organ is dealt with so summarily for supposed hygienic purposes. If the penis is actually such an unhygienic organ, then it should follow that about 75% of the world's male population, i.e., those who remain uncircumcised throughout life, must be paying a dreadful price in pain and disease as a result. There is no evidence that this is true. If the world's uncircumcised male population had severe foreskin problems, physicians in other countries would have adopted either newborn or adult circumcision practices. They have done neither.

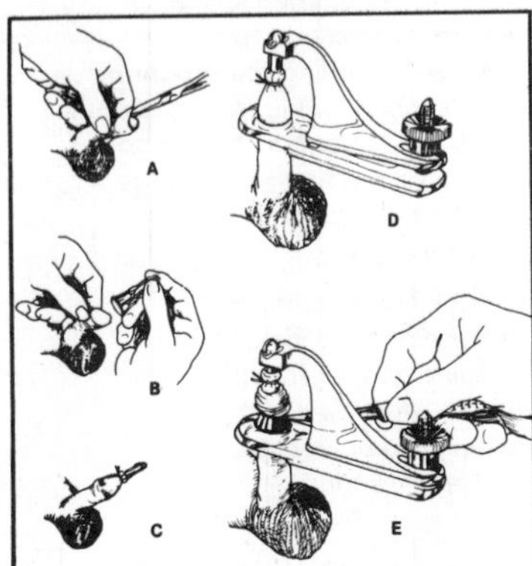

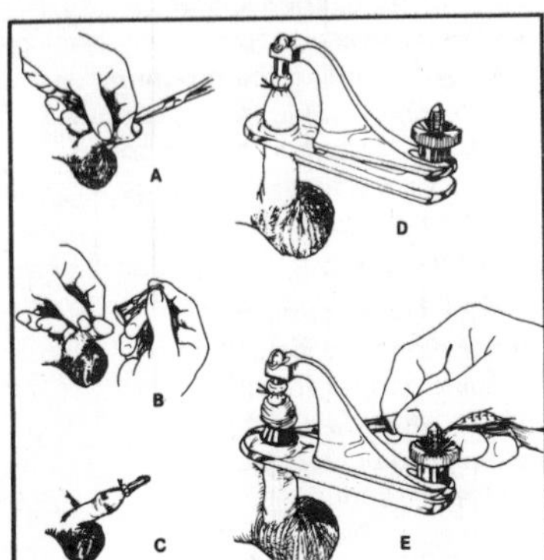

Diagrammatic Representation of Circumcision with the Gomco Clamp.

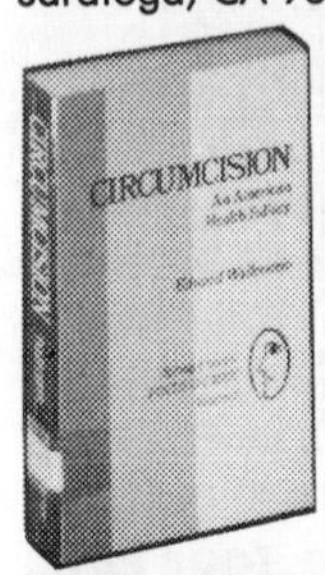

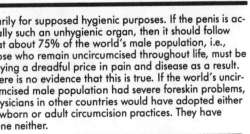

Circumcision
Edward Wallerstein
1980; 281 pp.
$16.95
($18.95 postpaid) from:
Springer Publishing Co.
536 Broadway
New York, NY 10012
or Whole Earth Access

• A hen sat on an orange, and it hatched!
This story is (1) Inconceivable
(2) Impregnable
(3) Unbearable

15 times each direction (page 31)

Stretching

30 seconds (page 56)
20 seconds each leg (page 33)

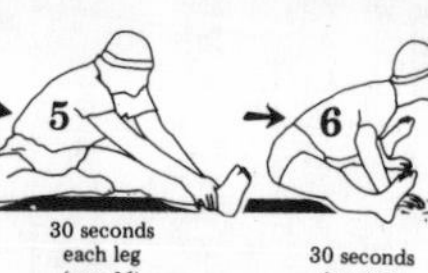

30 seconds each leg (page 36)
30 seconds (page 93)

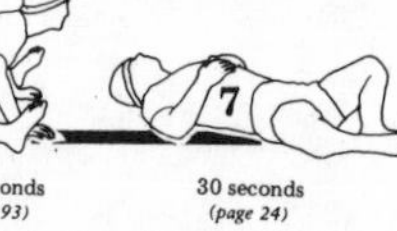

30 seconds (page 24)
3 times 5 seconds each (page 25)

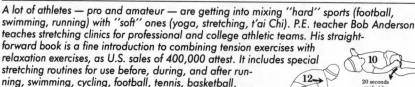

Before and After
Volleyball
Approximately 14 Minutes

A lot of athletes — pro and amateur — are getting into mixing "hard" sports (football, swimming, running) with "soft" ones (yoga, stretching, t'ai Chi). P.E. teacher Bob Anderson teaches stretching clinics for professional and college athletic teams. His straightforward book is a fine introduction to combining tension exercises with relaxation exercises, as U.S. sales of 400,000 attest. It includes special stretching routines for use before, during, and after running, swimming, cycling, football, tennis, basketball, etc. I've been doing his stretching routines before and after running. It makes quite a difference.
—Tom Ferguson, M.D.

1 — 25 seconds each leg (page 71)
14 — 20 seconds (page 40)
13 — 25 seconds each leg (page 48)
12 — 10 seconds each leg (page 47)
10 — 20 seconds each side (page 29)
9 — 30 seconds each side (page 24)
11 — 3 times 5 seconds each (page 28)

Stretching
Bob Anderson
1980; 192 pp.
$8.95
($10.45 postpaid) from:
Home Book Service
P. O. Box 650
Bolinas, CA 94924
or Whole Earth Access

The Aerobics Program for Total Well-Being

Kenneth Cooper, the George Washington of the fitness movement, has probably had more positive impact on the lives of more Americans than any other living physician. This is his introduction to aerobic exercise, and it is a good one indeed.

Exercises covered include walking, running, swimming, biking, exercise biking, basketball, tennis, raquetball, badminton, and nearly any other form of activity you can think of. Cooper evaluates them all in terms of "aerobics points" per hour, which you can use to estimate the aerobic value of virtually any athletic activity. Thus unlike most exercise programs, you can pick your favorite activity, or can mix and match several different kinds of exercise. Highly recommended for people who want to start exercising regularly, as well as for ex-exercisers coming back from a sedentary spell.
—Tom Ferguson, M.D.

•

For the purposes of illustrating the way to calculate your target heart rate, let's assume for the rest of this discussion that you are a 50-year-old man or woman.

Next, use the formula that we use for men: Predicted Maximum Heart Rate (PMHR) = 205 minus ½ your age. (For women use PMHR = 220 minus age.) For example, at 50 years of age, a man's predicted maximum heart rate would be 205 minus 25 = 180. For women, it would be 220 minus 50 = 170.

The third step is a rather simple calculation: Take 80 percent of 180, and you get 144 beats per minute. If your heart rate exceeds that figure for a minimum of 20 minutes, four times per week, then you will get an aerobic training effect. In fact, combinations of a heart rate of 130 for 30 minutes, or 150 for 10 minutes, four times a week, will in general give you the same results.

•

We are finding that the *timing* of aerobic exercise can provide an additional benefit in controlling stress. If you exercise at the *end of a high pressure day* — prior to the evening meal — aerobic activity can help to dissipate the stress you feel, relax you more, and even energize you so that you can continue to work or play much later into the evening than might be possible otherwise.

The Aerobics Program for Total Well-Being
Dr. Kenneth H. Cooper
1982; 320 pp.
$10.95
($12.45 postpaid) from:
Bantam Books
414 East Golf Road
Des Plaines, IL 60016
or Whole Earth Access

Listen to Your Pain

Every blessing has its price, and for the rewards of sport there are injuries. Whether you call them counterblessings, learning experiences, or just agony and frustration depends on your philosophical system. But when it gets down to physiology, all systems are similar, and so is our first question — what's wrong, and what can I do about it?

***Listen to Your Pain** explains basic body structure and general causes of injury. Where it excels is in the very practical, how-to-find-it sections. Each section has a label like "Chin-up Pain," "Tennis Elbow," or a generic "Outer Knee Pain, Slightly to the Front." After finding the problem, you're given an explanation, a do-it-yourself test to confirm the diagnosis, and finally treatments that range from ice and aspirin to a trip to the doctor.*

This book has become my primary reference for aches and pains and is especially valuable when deciding whether a complaint is an annoyance or serious.
—Dick Fugett
[Suggested by Lloyd Kahn]

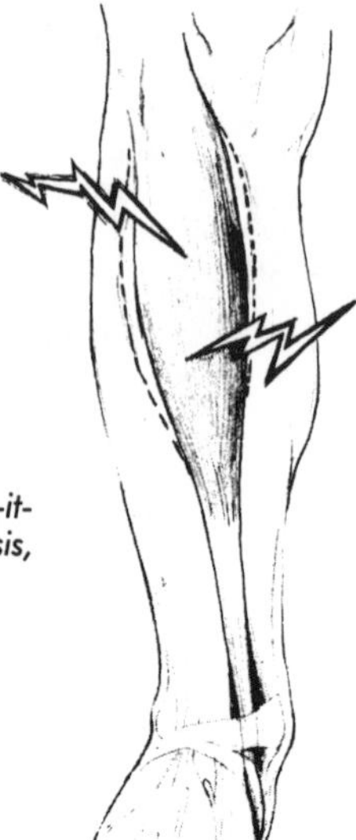
"Shin Splints"

•

You have a lot of trouble kicking people when you have this injury, and running up hills and jumping aren't fun either. This injury has been with us so long and is so common that it's acquired a totally nonsensical nickname, "shin splints."

•

Diagnostic Verification
Test 1. If your pain is in the front part of your shin and slightly to the outside, at least one of the following two tests should reproduce your discomfort. The first one is simple. Wearing shoes, raise your toes off the floor and balance on your heels. Be sure to hold onto something so you don't fall. After doing this for a moment, severely strained shins will begin to hurt.

•

Treatment Choice
Self-Treatment. Self-treatment is possible only when fatigue is the major factor in your strain. In these cases rest and ice treatment done along with Ankle Flexion, p. 266, are effective. During an ice treatment, exercise by flexing and pointing your foot thirty to fifty times every fifteen minutes. If possible you should stop all the activities that are causing you pain.

Listen to Your Pain
Ben E. Benjamin, Ph.D.
with Gale Borden, M.D.
1984; 340 pp.
$9.95
($10.95 postpaid) from:
Viking Penguin Books
299 Murray Hill Pkwy.
East Rutherford, NJ 07073
or Whole Earth Access

• If you want muscle to replace your fat, exercise aerobically, eat low-fat foods, and read this book.
Fit or Fat? Covert Bailey, 1978; 107 pp. **$5.95** ($6.95 postpaid) from Houghton Mifflin Co., Mail Order Dept., Wayside Road, Burlington, MA 01803 (or Whole Earth Access).

The most efficient way to run is to have your head, neck and shoulders erect, as at right. When you run leaning forward, as at left, you're always fighting gravity.

Galloway's Book on Running

Back in the dark ages of running — ten years ago — the only way to learn was by making your own mistakes and then attempting to figure out what had gone wrong. Sooner or later the dedicated runner experienced everything from tendonitis and failed knees to orthotics and the high cost of sports medicine. Those who were lucky are still running while those who were not are lame forever.

If books like this had been around there'd be more old runners running and fewer of us sitting around wishing we'd known then what we know now. Galloway, a former Olympic team member, covers everything from training and injuries to physiology and nutrition in an easy to read volume that is as relevant to a casual jogger as to an experienced marathoner. In addition, he has anecdotes from 25 years of running that give the book both a personal flavor and an inside look at what it's like at the top.
—Dick Fugett

•

Stride Length. Believe it or not, a longer stride will not lead to faster running. *Experienced competitive runners find that their stride length shortens as they run faster.* A key to faster running is stride frequency. If you increase the speed of your footfall and get a good strong pushoff you'll improve. Most runners I've worked with have too long a stride.

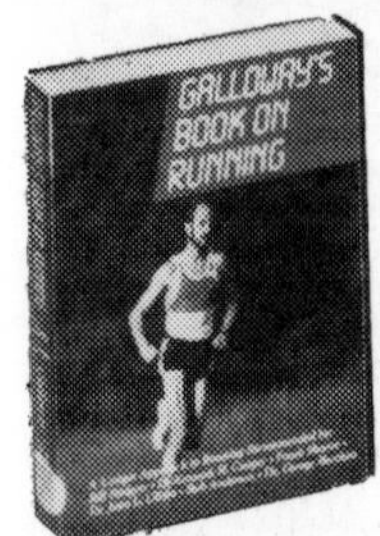

Galloway's Book On Running
Jeff Galloway
1984; 287 pp.
$8.95
($10.45 postpaid) from:
Home Book Service
P. O. Box 650
Bolinas, CA 94924
or Whole Earth Access

Getting Stronger

Until recently, the beginning weightlifter had only a few unenthused manuals to assist in training. But now Bill Pearl, a four-time Mr. Universe, has come out with a book for the beginner and intermediate. It not only introduces weightlifting but goes on to give specific programs for strength training in 19 sports. From running, swimming, and cycling to tennis, skiing, and soccer, there are specific routines designed to increase strength and improve performance.

The book gives a core group of all the basic lifts with illustrations and explanations, and for each sport there's a specific series of exercises selected from the core group. The routines were developed with some impressively qualified coaches, like Doc Councilman on swimming and John Howard on cycling, and the reader benefits from their wisdom. *—Dick Fugett*

•

Standing Inner Biceps Curl
Inner Biceps

- Hold dumbbells.
- Stand erect with feet 16'' apart.
- Keep back straight, head up, hips and legs locked.
- Start with dumbbells at arm's length, palms in, at sides of upper thighs.
- Curl dumbbells out and up, rotating wrists to turn palms up. Keep forearms in line with outer deltoids.
- Lower dumbbells to starting position using same path.
- Inhale up, exhale down.

• The best known running book, now nine years old. **The Complete Book of Running:** James F. Fixx, 1977; 314 pp. **$13.95** ($14.95 postpaid) from Random House, Order Dept., 400 Hahn Road, Westminster, MD 21157 (or Whole Earth Access).

Exercisewalking

Attention joggers: When your joints give out (and they will), keep in mind that walking (quickly) is surpassed only by swimming as a whole body workout. To earn as many aerobic points as you do running, you'll have to walk up hills or stairs, or carry weights, or spend more time moving. This book tells how. It's a lifelong exercise.
—Kevin Kelly

•

While it's true that the average walking speed of 2-3 mph per hour (60-90 steps per minute) is not sufficient to raise your heart rate into the training zone of 60-85 percent of maximum capacity, there are ways to overcome this. One way, of course, is to increase your pace (more than 3.5 mph). Others include walk climbing or stair climbing. But perhaps the most clever walk-to-work training routine is walking with a weight-loaded backpack.

Aerobic walking.

Runner's World • The Runner

Although the bloom has faded along with the publicity, the running boom produced a multitude of converts, from joggers sold on the physical and mental rewards to the hardcore runners who can't do without that race-day energy.

*Back in the boom days **Runner's World** was the only show in town, but over the years **The Runner** kept trying harder, and that vitality produced a wider-ranging magazine. **Runner's World**, recently purchased by Rodale Publications of **Organic Gardening** fame, keeps a tight focus on running. Take your choice.* *—Dick Fugett*

Runner's World: James C. McCullagh, Editor. **$19.95**/year (12 issues) from Rodale Press, 33 East Minor Street, Emmaus, PA 18049.

The Runner: Marc A. Bloom, Editor. **$16.97**/year (12 issues) from The Runner, P. O. Box 2730, Boulder, CO 80302.

Getting Stronger
Bill Pearl with
Gary Moran, Ph.D.
1986; 320 pp.
$12.95
($14.45 postpaid) from:
Home Book Service
P. O. Box 650
Bolinas, CA 94924
or Whole Earth Access

The Complete Book of Exercisewalking
Gary D. Yanker
1983; 266 pp.
$9.95
($11.95 postpaid) from:
Contemporary Books
180 North Michigan Ave.
Chicago, IL 60601
or Whole Earth Access

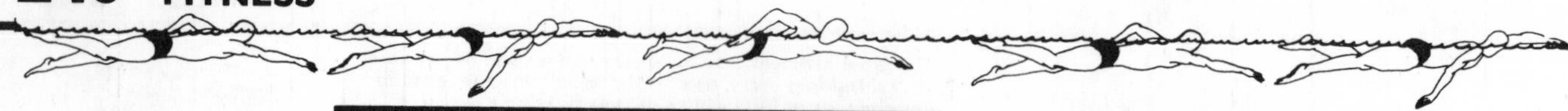

Swim for Fitness

The explanations of what to do in the water are brief and to the point, and the diagrams are excellent. Unless you are already an expert swimmer, this book will help you swim more efficiently. It's written by an avid competitive swimmer. —Richard Nilsen

◄

In freestyle, as in the other strokes, you move forward not by moving water backward, as is sometimes thought, but by pushing the arms and legs against the resistance offered by the water. . . .

If you can press your hand against water that is not moving, you can push yourself further forward than if you are in water that is already moving backward. . . . Make an elongated "S" pattern with your hands when you swim freestyle. This way your hand will avoid following a column of water that is moving from the moment you begin your pull backwards.

The hand zigzags back and forth so that it may constantly encounter still water, which will offer the greatest resistance. . . .

The arm is bent significantly throughout the major portion of the pull. The reason for this is that leverage is greatest with a bent arm.

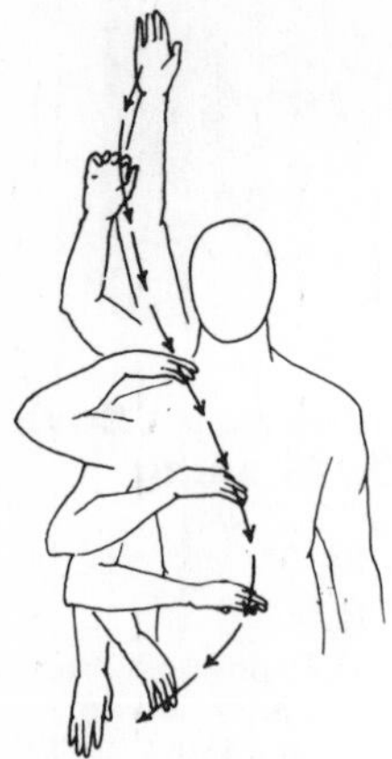

Underwater elongated "S" pull pattern.

Overtraining

Overtraining occurs when the body suffers failing adaptation to stress.

Stress must decrease in order for recovery to take place. Signs of overtraining are:

1. Insomnia.
2. Awakening hot and sweaty at night.
3. An increased basal heart rate.
4. Irritability and sudden anger.

Possible signs of overtraining:

1. A working heart rate which is reluctant to drop.
2. Sudden weight loss.
3. An increase in resting blood pressure.

The chance of heat exhaustion and injury because of overtraining is quite low in swimming.

►
Butterfly with breastroke

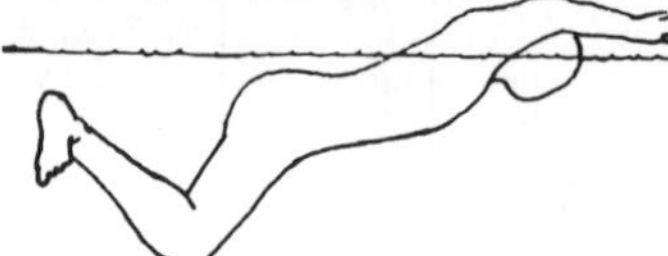

Timing of the arms and legs.

Swim for Fitness
Marianne Brems
1979; 173 pp.

$7.95
($9.45 postpaid) from:
Chronicle Books
One Hallidie Plaza
Suite 806
San Francisco, CA 94102
or Whole Earth Access

Fitness Video Cassettes

In most video parlors, the sports section ranges from All Star Wrestling to SuperBowl Highlites, but for those who'd rather participate than spectate, there are a few fitness tapes, beginning with the Jane Fonda workouts, and including how-to videos on golf, tennis, and baseball.

More specialized topics exist, but seldom as rentals. Boardsurfing, soccer, running, and yoga are among the newer issues, and are advertised in the magazines that cover each activity.

The more complex the skill, the more a visual demonstration can help. Take swimming, where technique not only makes all the difference, but is frustratingly hard to learn. **Swimming for Fitness**, *featuring ex-Olympian Donna de Varona, is a somewhat mistitled tape that's actually aimed at improving form. Beginning with arm pull for beginners and going through advanced butterfly techniques, there's enough to keep anyone studying for hours. The slow motion and underwater shots teach in a way that no book could.*

A different approach is taken by SyberVision. Their ski cassette, for example, shows the same skiers doing the same turns on the same hill, time after time. The theory is that this neural programming will translate into improved performance, and indeed I found that after watching for an hour, I was unconsciously weighting and unweighting as I mentally made turns.

I'd guess that this approach is most effective if seen immediately before skiing, whereas the swim cassette is something to be mulled over during many workouts. The whole field is new, so you pay your money and take your chances. Let me know what happens. —Dick Fugett

Swimming for Fitness Video

$53.95
postpaid from:
Swimming for Fitness
16 East 3rd Avenue
Suite 2-G
San Mateo, CA 94401

Neuromuscular Training Skiing Video

$93.45 postpaid
Catalog **free** from:
SyberVision
Fountain Square
6066 Civic Terrace Ave.
Newark, CA 94560

United States Masters Swimming

Swimming is the easiest way we earthlings can escape the relentless force of gravity. Because water is denser than flesh, the body floats. Moving through water uses all the muscles in the body and avoids continuous jarring contact with terra firma. That's why swimming is the single best physical therapy for injured bodies.

It is also an excellent form of lifetime exercise. As an organized activity it is called Masters Swimming. This international body has 20,000 U.S. members and offers competition within 5-year age brackets from the twenties clear into the eighties. Fully half of the members never compete and swim only for the exercise. Masters Swimming offers access to pools, instruction for improvement in stroke techniques, and camaraderie. —Richard Nilsen

U.S. Masters Swimming, Inc.
Information **free** from:
U.S. Masters Swimming
C/O Dorothy Donnelley
5 Piggott Lane
Avon, CT 06001

• For adult fitness and competitive swimmers, with specialized articles ("Chlorine, Asthma and Swimming") and nontechnical presentation.
Swim Magazine: Bob Hansen, Editor. **$12**/year (6 issues) from Swim, P. O. Box 2168, Simi Valley, CA 93062.

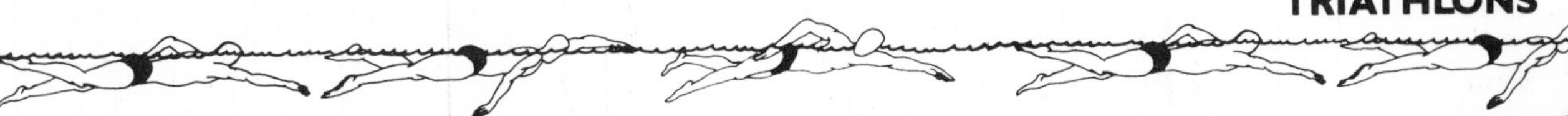

According to legend, the Ironman triathlon was conceived when a group of inebriated navy jocks stationed in Hawaii debated an Ultimate Physical Test, based on what was then available. There was the Waikiki 2.4 mile Rough Water Swim, the Around-Oahu 112 mile bike ride, and of course, the Honolulu Marathon.

"Harhar!" announced one inspired participant just before sliding under the table. "Let's do 'em all!" (Or at least that's my favorite interpretation of the event.) But unlike most beer-assisted schemes, this one actually materialized, and in 1978 15 entrants did their darndest, with 12 finishing. With only a little imagination, you can picture the blood, sweat, and toil. So could the TV executives, and before long the Ironman drama was on the tube, the world was watching, and a new sport was born.

It took off fast, for besides the challenge and reward of dealing with three sports, triathlons offer the benefits of cross-training, as well as fewer injuries than single sport intensity can produce.

The Ironman remains the showcase, but grassroots popularity is based on shorter, more humane events. A 1500-meter swim, 25-mile bike and 10-kilometer run would be typical, with a winning time around two hours. Often called a Tinman in deference to the founding event, these shorter races can also feature local variations like cross-country skiing and canoeing. What's common to all is the challenge, reward, and fun.
—Dick Fugett

Dave Scott's Triathlon Training
Dave Scott and Liz Barrett
1986; 224 pp.
$9.95
postpaid from:
Simon & Schuster
Mail Order Sales
200 Old Tappan Road
Old Tappan, NJ 07675

Cross-Training
Katherine Vaz
1984; 239 pp.
$9.95
($10.95 postpaid) from:
Avon Books
P. O. Box 767
Dresden, TN 38225
or Whole Earth Access

Cross-Training • Triathlon Training

If you're planning your premier triathlon, then look at **Cross-Training** *by Katherine Vaz. It will give you basic techniques, training schedules, and equipment needs without smothering you with details. Go do a triathlon and have fun before you decide to make life complex.*

But after you've tasted the high that comes from a three-sport immersion in physical and mental challenge, you may get serious in your efforts, as well as more advanced in your reading. For the most information, try Dave Scott's **Triathlon Training***. His coverage of each sport is as good as you'll find anywhere, as well as being quite readable. Besides the basics, he discusses everything from heat and altitude training to weights, stretching, and race psychology, besides having a quality chapter on nutrition.*

Scott's record of four Ironman victories speaks for itself, and he's produced a book to match it. —*Dick Fugett*

•

As a triathlete, you can save yourself a lot of wasted time and energy by learning how to swim properly from the start. Some of the information in this chapter might seem prohibitively technical to beginning swimmers, but don't let it scare you. When you get in the water and follow the instructions, you'll see for yourself that little details such as the way your wrist is flexed make a big difference in how efficiently you can swim.
—*Dave Scott's Triathlon Training*

•

It holds that an organism, muscle, or enzyme system stressed beyond its threshold will recover *slightly beyond that level* if allowed time to rebuild and repair itself. *Overload work* is what the phrase implies. You are stressing your body just beyond what it can handle (called *demand*), essentially breaking the systems down.

The systems will, however, rise to the occasion and reconstruct themselves to the level you insisted on *if allowed adequate rest time*. If this rest time is either too short or nonexistent, an added overload session on the same systems will only break them down further.
—*Cross Training*

In timing your swim to determine your optimal aerobic training pace, you will need a pace clock and a friend with a lap counter to keep track of the distance you have covered. Immediately after ceasing exercise, count your pulse for 10 seconds and compare with your target rate. By comparing your pulse rate with elapsed exercise time and target rate, you can judge the intensity of your workout. Two minutes later another check of your pulse should show considerable recovery — a 10-second count of less than 20 is desirable.
—Cross Training

Triathlete

There's no longer a struggle to decide which magazine to recommend — they just merged. The new hybrid is **Triathlete***, combining coverage of training tips with race results, personalities, and schedules. Even a single sport enthusiast would do well to browse through it, for there are good stories on technique for each sport. Beginning swimmers, for whom little exists, will find it especially beneficial.* —*Dick Fugett*

• For bicycle coverage, see pp. 264-267. For bicycle racing info try this magazine.
Winning: John Wilcockson, Editor. **$19.97**/year (12 issues) from Winning, 1127 Hamilton Street, Allentown, PA 18102.

Michael Garcia

Silviane Puntous

Richard Wells

Triathlete
Harald Johnson,
Editorial Director
$19.95/year
(12 issues) from:
Triathlete
1127 Hamilton Street
Allentown, PA 18102

Nutrition and Physical Degeneration
Weston A. Price, D.D.S.
1945, 1970; 526 pp.
$27.50
($29.50 postpaid) from:
Cancer Book House
Cancer Control Society
2043 North Berendo St.
Los Angeles, CA 90027

Nutrition and Physical Degeneration

Of all the books written on nutrition, I still find this the most interesting. Dr. Price was a practicing dentist who noticed the marked decline in his young patients' health and dental condition. In 1930, he began a 150,000-mile trek around the globe seeking out healthy primitive peoples whose teeth (and health) were excellent. In his book 14 tribal diets are completely examined, diets which give their people almost perfect dental and physical health. Wonderfully, each diet is radically different from the other. What is consistent is not the foods, their proportion or kind, but the fact that each of the diets is completely indigenous and totally derived from a direct relationship to the person's environment. The Gaels of the Outer Hebrides ate little but fish, oats, barley, and some seaweed. The Kikuyus of Africa ate primarily sweet potatoes, corn, beans, and bananas. While the Indians of the Pelly mountain country in northwest Canada ate almost solely wild animals.

In contrast to the racial stock that was eating indigenous foods, Price sought out a neighboring tribe or group that had been exposed to foods of western civilization, particularly refined foods such as flour, sugar, as well as canned foods and meats. The comparisons between the "control" and the newly civilized group invariably showed a rapid deterioration of teeth, malocclusion, a rise in infectious diseases, and even more startling, a rapid change in the skeletal and racial characteristics that are supposedly genetic. Flat-nosed Indians had aquiline noses within two generations, and sinus trouble as well. New Zealand Maori would not only find that their dental arches would narrow, but that their pelvic arches would contract causing pain, injury, and even death at childbirth. Again, Price found these changes within one generation of change in diet.

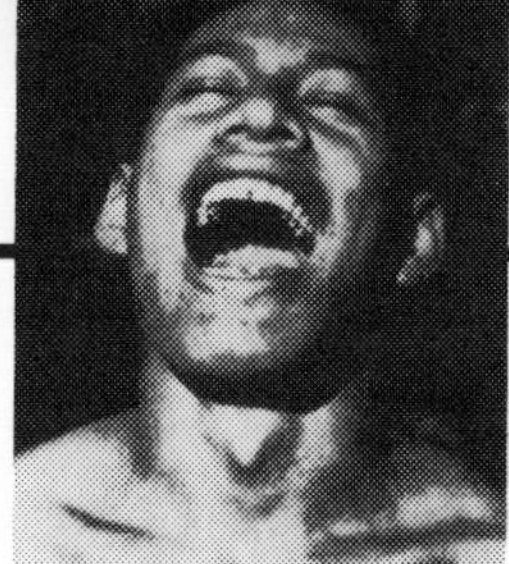

Polynesians are a beautiful race and physically sturdy. They have straight hair and their color is often that of a sun tanned European. They have perfect dental arches.

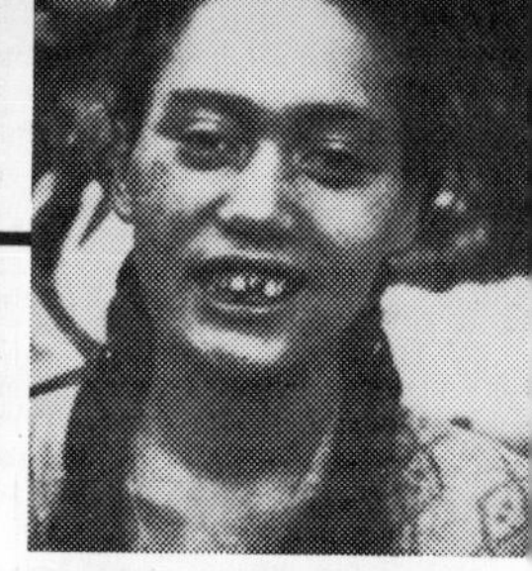

Wherever the native foods have been displaced by the imported foods, dental caries becomes rampant. (Above) a typical modernized Tahitian.

All of the foods grown and gathered by primitives were taken and analyzed. While diets differed widely, all were high in protein, vitamins, and minerals. Corresponding foods grown by primitives were in many cases 10-50 times as high in minerals as the similar foods in our own culture. Just as important was the observation that when primitive peoples reverted back to their original diets, their health improved, dental caries halted, and the physiology of their offspring resembled again their racial origins. He never found a healthy child that wasn't breast fed. No book written since has as effectively demonstrated the relationship between good health, nutrition, and the environment. —Paul Hawken

Prevention
Robert Rodale, Editor
$13.97/year
(12 issues) from:
Prevention
33 East Minor Street
Emmaus, PA 18049

Prevention

They put it so homely, have been at it so long (38 years), and have been right so often, that you can't ignore **Prevention** *when talking about nutrition and health, even though they seem to recycle the same stories over and over again. ("SELENIUM: A Critical Mineral"). You'll have to wade through a tide of vitamin supplement ads to get to the interesting news, but in recent years, as they explore new medical territory such as diet and the immune system, it's worth the trip.* —Kevin Kelly

•

Magnesium. Much of the Western world doesn't get enough magnesium, and the result could be a higher incidence of heart disease and hypertension. That's because many areas are served by a soft-water drinking supply, which lacks the magnesium content of hard water. Magnesium plays a part in keeping your heart muscle beating rhythmically.

People living in hard-water areas may bemoan the fact that their soap won't lather as readily. On the other hand, the incidence of heart-disease-related death is 10.1 percent lower there than in soft-water regions, according to the journal *Magnesium* (vol. 4, no.1).

•

We know that our minds can regulate our behavior. We almost always decide consciously how we want to act. But now there's a good possibility that we can also decide consciously how well an important part of our immune system is going to function.

Nutrition in Clinical Practice
Marion Nestle, Ph.D.
1985; 328 pp.
$16.95
($18.55 postpaid) from:
Jones Medical Publications
355 Los Cerros Drive
Greenbrae, CA 94904

Nutrition in Clinical Practice

All around, the most levelheaded scientific treatment of nutrition — a field rife with unbalanced theories. Cautious, yet open minded. A good clear summary for students. —Michael Lerner

•

Hair analysis
The idea that minerals are incorporated into growing hair in proportion to their levels in the body has led to the widespread use of high energy emission techniques to evaluate trace mineral status. The proportionality of dietary intake and hair concentration, however, has yet to be established for a single essential nutrient.

Nutrition Action

The Center for Science in the Public Interest (CSPI), a pro-consumer lobbying group, publishes some of the most useful consumer materials on the subject of food and nutrition. Ask them for a sample copy of their newsletter, **Nutrition Action**, *and their catalog of books and computer programs. My own personal favorite is their Nutrition Scoreboard ($3.95), a kitchen wall poster which lists "health scores" for dozens of different kinds of foods. This is the expert to consult when making out your shopping list. If you are committed to healthy eating, you should consider becoming a member of CSPI.*
—Tom Ferguson, MD

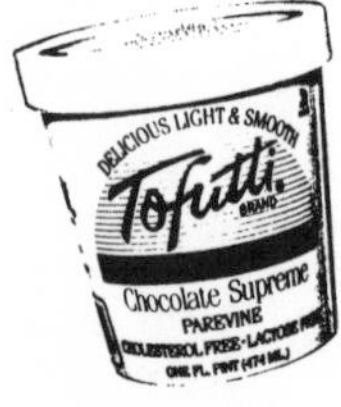

•

Despite Tofutti's oft-repeated claim to be a "tofu frozen dessert" and its maker Tofu Time's ads showing the product surrounded by chunks of tofu, Tofutti doesn't contain enough tofu to shake a chopstick at. The product contains less than 10 percent tofu, according to soyfood-industry insiders, and probably much, much less.

Nutrition Action Healthletter
Michael Jacobson, Editor
$20/year
(10 issues)
Catalog **free**
Both from:
Center for Science in the Public Interest
1501 16th Street NW
Washington, DC 20036

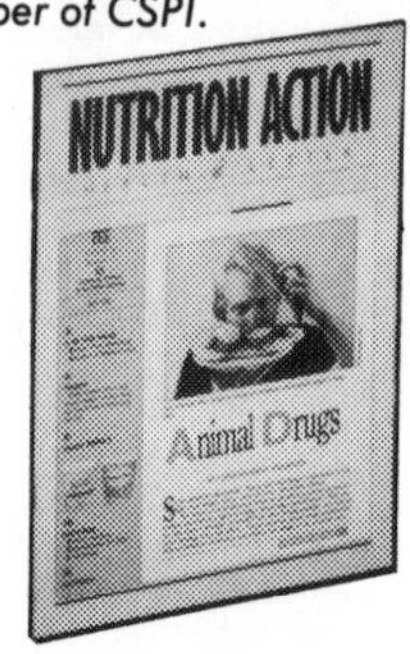

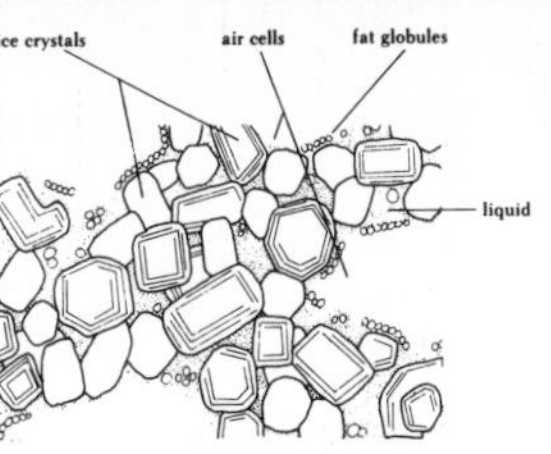

ıe structure of
e cream. It is
foam in which
ır bubbles are
rapped by freezing much, but not all, of the liquid phase.
oth sugar and milk solids are dissolved in the liquid.

Unlike the muscles of mammals or birds, fish muscle is arranged in layers of short fibers — the myotomes — which are separated by very thin sheets of delicate connective tissue — the myocommata.

On Food and Cooking

's an incredible task to write an encyclopedia, but Harold McGee carries it off. He has written a summary of what he world knows (well, what the West knows; he only had 684 pages) about the science of food. Each kind of food — plant and animal — is discussed, its history, and all the ways of cooking and brewing that we use. McGee makes complexities comprehensible: He uses technical terms and he explains them simply and lightly. He makes accessible the knowledge about food that our culture has gained in the last several millenia. Cooks cannot stop reading this book; they mutter, red-eyed, "Just one more page!" —*Birell Walsh*

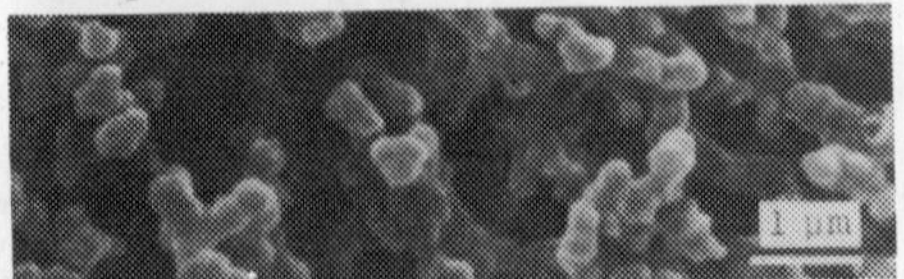

•

There is very little connective tissue in fish — about 3 percent of its weight, as opposed to 15 percent in land animals — and what there is is very fragile and easily converted into gelatin. The combination of sparse, weak connective tissue and short muscle bundles results in the tenderness of fish, and its troublesome tendency to fall apart altogether during cooking.

•

The landmark study of bread staling came as early as 1852, when the Frenchman Jean-Baptiste Boussingault, a pioneer in the study of nitrogen fixation (he demonstrated that certain plants increase the nitrogen content of soil and that soil alone — or, as we know today, certain soil bacteria — could do the same), showed that bread could be hermetically sealed to prevent it from losing water, and yet still go stale. He further established that staling could be reversed by reheating the bread to 140°F (60°C): the temperature, we now know, at which starch gelatinizes. Subsequent research has shown that the starch phase is indeed the culprit, though gluten is involved in a minor way.

◄

(Top) yogurt made from unheated milk. Casein micelles form large, coarse clusters when bacteria produce acids. (Bottom) yogurt made from milk preheated to 185°F (85°C). At this temperature, whey and casein proteins complex in such a way as to inhibit this clustering. The resulting yogurt has a finer, firmer texture.

On Food and Cooking
Harold McGee
1984; 684 pp.
$29.95
postpaid from:
Macmillan Publishing Co.
Order Dept.
Front and Brown Streets
Riverside, NJ 08075
or Whole Earth Access

Unmentionable Cuisine

This engrossing book of lore and recipes makes a great contribution to eco-cuisine which ain't of the vegetarian persuasion.

***Unmentionable Cuisine** gives the how and why of eating all the icky parts of conventional livestock, then goes on to suggest that eating surplus dogs, cats, starlings, and giant African snails could be a way for Americans to have protein while muddling towards frugality. I say Americans, because other cultures have been eating weird things for millenia, and with gusto. In fact, most of the recipes Calvin Schwabe presents are traditional, some of them dating way back into Europe's pagan past, when communicants drank real blood.*

Eaters of road kills, pet haters, eco-hunters, and truly serious cooks should find this book indispensible. It suggests savory ways to get your goat (or eel or porcupine), and how to do it sanitarily and in good taste. —*Stephanie Mills*

Properly prepared (this is critical) almost any critter, or part of it, is tasty. I had no trouble enjoying the dishes mentioned at right. You shouldn't either with the moral support of this book. —*Kevin Kelly*

•

Stir-Fried Dog (Nan tsao go zo)/China

Eviscerate and clean a puppy. Remove the hair by singeing in a rice-straw fire; continue this heat treatment until the skin is golden brown. Cut the meat into cubes and dry-fry them in a *wok*. Add oil, ginger, garlic, and dried, salted black beans to another *wok* and stir-fry for 10 minutes. Add the meat, soy sauce, green onions, and deep-fried bean curd. Stir momentarily.

•

Broiled Sparrows (Suzume yaki)/Japan

Broil birds slightly over charcoal; dip in a sauce of equal parts *shoyu*, sake, and *mirin*; return to the broiler. Repeat this alternate dipping and broiling several times. Split the bird open but keep in one piece, sprinkle with fresh-ground pepper, and serve.

•

Fried Grasshoppers (Jourad)/Arab Countries

Boil prepared locusts and then fry them in oil and butter. Or fry the prepared insects without boiling and serve in a little vinegar.

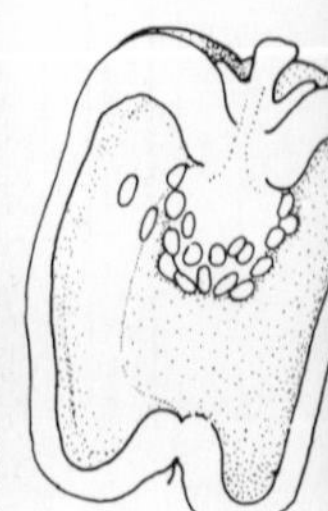

Unmentionable Cuisine
Calvin W. Schwabe
1979; 423 pp.
$20
($21.50 postpaid) from:
University Press of Virginia
P. O. Box 3608
University Station
Charlottesville, VA 22903
or Whole Earth Access

Nutritive Value of Foods

Since natural food does not come with a list of ingredients on the label, the Department of Agriculture has kindly prepared this authoritative analysis of common foods. If you're serious about nutrition, it's a buy. —*Stewart Brand*

Item No.	Foods, approximate measures, units, and weight (weight of edible portion only)			Water	Food energy	Protein	Fat	Fatty acids: Saturated	Fatty acids: Monounsaturated	Fatty acids: Polyunsaturated
			Grams	Percent	Calories	Grams	Grams	Grams	Grams	Grams
	Carrots:									
	Raw, without crowns and tips, scraped:									
784	Whole, 7-1/2 by 1-1/8 in, or strips, 2-1/2 to 3 in long	1 carrot or 18 strips--------	72	88	30	1	Tr	Tr	Tr	0.1
785	Grated------------------------	1 cup----------	110	88	45	1	Tr	Tr	Tr	0.1
	Cooked, sliced, drained:									
786	From raw---------------------	1 cup----------	156	87	70	2	Tr	0.1	Tr	0.1
787	From frozen------------------	1 cup----------	146	90	55	2	Tr	Tr	Tr	0.1

Nutritive Value of Foods
Susan E. Gebhardt and
Ruth H. Matthews
1985; 72 pp.
Stock #001-000-04457-5
$2.75
postpaid from:
Superintendent
of Documents
U.S. Government
Printing Office
Washington, DC 20402

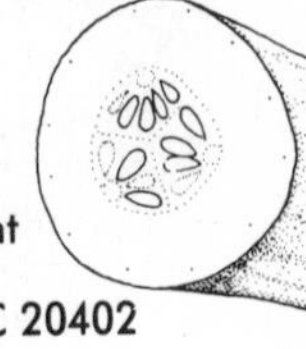

Joy of Cooking
Irma S. Rombauer and Marion Rombauer Becker
1931, 1979; 930 pp.
$16.95 postpaid from:
Macmillan Publishing Co.
Order Department
Front and Brown Streets
Riverside, NJ 08075
or Whole Earth Access

Joy of Cooking

You really need only one book in the kitchen. This book. Along with everything (!!) else, it is the only cookbook with two handy red ribbons to mark your place. Don't bother with the paperback editions. They will not survive kitchen duress. —*Stewart Brand*

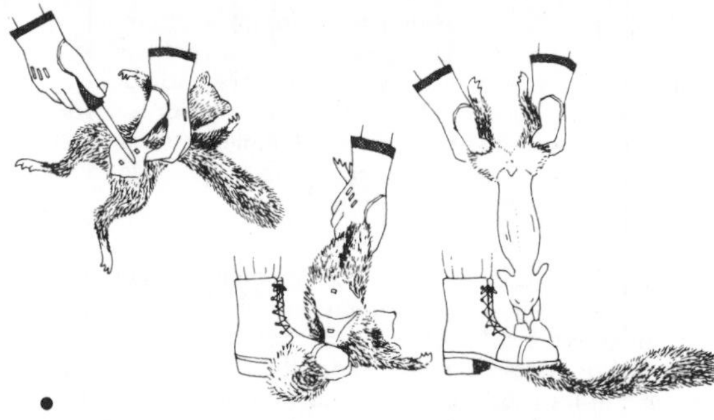

•

Gray squirrels are preferred to red squirrels, which are quite gamy in flavor. Stuff and roast squirrels as for Pigeons, 441, barding them, or as for Braised Chicken, 425, or use them in Brunswick Stew, 427. Season the gravy with Walnut Catsup, 848, and serve with Polenta, 201.

◄ The Romans used to say if they wanted something in a hurry, "Do it in less time than it takes to cook asparagus."

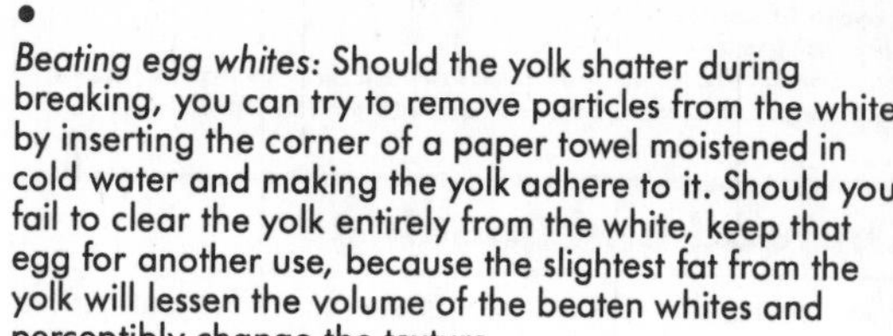

•

Beating egg whites: Should the yolk shatter during breaking, you can try to remove particles from the white by inserting the corner of a paper towel moistened in cold water and making the yolk adhere to it. Should you fail to clear the yolk entirely from the white, keep that egg for another use, because the slightest fat from the yolk will lessen the volume of the beaten whites and perceptibly change the texture.

•

Nothing is more important in frying than proper temperatures. As that wise old gourmet, Alexandre Dumas, so aptly put it, the food must be "surprised" by the hot fat, to give it the crusty, golden coating so characteristic and so desirable. The proper temperature in most instances is 365°, as easy to remember as the number of days in a year.

•

When adding seasoning, the greatest care must be used to enhance the natural or previously acquired flavor of the food at hand. The role of the seasoner is that of impresario, not actor: to bring out the best in his material, not to stifle it with florid, strident off-key delivery or to smother it with heavy trappings.

Easy Basics for Good Cooking
Sunset Editors
1982; 192 pp.
$9.95
($11.70 postpaid) from:
Lane Publishing Company
Attn.: Mail Order Dept.
80 Willow Road
Menlo Park, CA
94025-3691
or Whole Earth Access

Easy Basics for Good Cooking

***Joy of Cooking** and **Fannie Farmer** are my two favorite references for creating in the kitchen, but if I didn't already know what is so clearly taught in **Easy Basics**, they might easily be too advanced. The illustrations and instructions in this book are so clear and logical I would use them to teach a child.* —*Evelyn Eldridge-Diaz*

CREATING THE PERFECT MUFFIN

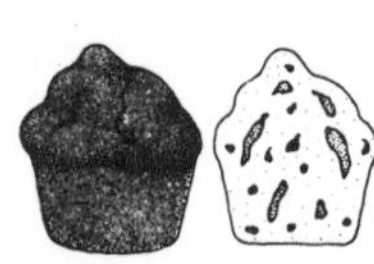

Overstirred muffins have peaked tops usually sloping to one side. When muffin is cut, inside texture shows tunnels—elongated air cells.

Well-made muffins have pebbly tops and a golden crust. When muffin is cut, inside texture shows even cell structure.

Banana Bread

- **3 large ripe bananas**
- **1 cup sugar**
- **1 egg**
- **4 tablespoons butter or margarine, melted and cooled**
- **1½ cups all-purpose flour**
- **1 teaspoon *each* salt and baking soda**

Preheat oven to 325°. Lightly grease a 9 by 5-inch loaf pan; set aside.

In a bowl, mash bananas; you should have 1 cup. Beat in sugar, then egg and butter. In another bowl, stir together flour, salt, and baking soda; add to banana mixture and stir just until all flour is moistened. Pour batter into prepared pan.

Bake for 55 to 60 minutes

◄ Making Stirred Custard: Stir constantly until custard coats a metal spoon — about 10 minutes. A finger drawn across spoon should leave a clean path, and consistency should be smooth and creamy. Cool immediately.

The New Laurel's Kitchen

*There are a lot of vegetarian cookbooks around. The big difference here, the one which makes this book superior, is that **The New Laurel's Kitchen** has a giant section on nutrition. There are complete descriptions of the different food components, analyses of foods, calorie-computation tables, and a good bibliography. You can cook a recipe from the front of the book, then refer to the back and see how much of which minerals, carbohydrates, etc., you gave your family that day. Tasty recipes, too.* —*Evelyn Eldridge-Diaz*

•

Raita

Raita is an Indian salad, refreshing and low in calories. Two or three spoonfuls makes an ample serving.

1½ cups yogurt
1 cup finely chopped raw vegetables
2 teaspoons finely minced fresh ginger
dash cayenne
dash curry powder

Stir vegetables into yogurt, choosing two or more of these: radishes, cucumber, green pepper, green onions, tomatoes, or beets. Season with cayenne, curry powder, and fresh ginger.

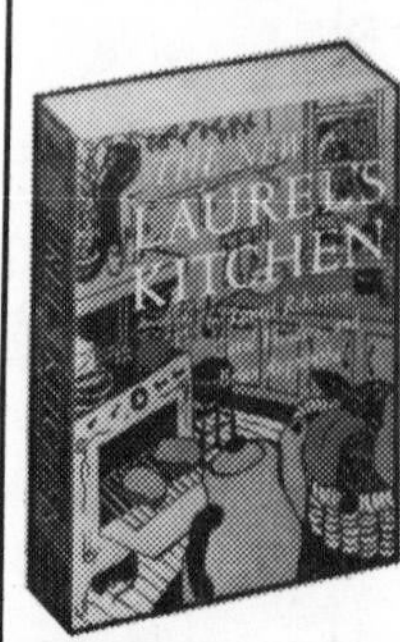

The New Laurel's Kitchen
Laurel Robertson, Carol Flinders, and Brian Ruppenthal
1986; 512 pp.

$15.95
($16.95 postpaid) from:
Ten Speed Press
P. O. Box 7123
Berkeley, CA 94707
or Whole Earth Access

Williams-Sonoma Catalog for Cooks

A comprehensive selection of the best cooking equipment, from ovenware and serving pieces and stoves to non-skid flooring. Many of their handsomest items they import directly. Like most good tools, these are pricey. They're worth it in the long run however, for the savings in anguish and scorched dishes.

Local comparison shopping for some of these things might save you a little money, but if you're outfitting a kitchen by mail, this is the place to begin.
—Stephanie Mills

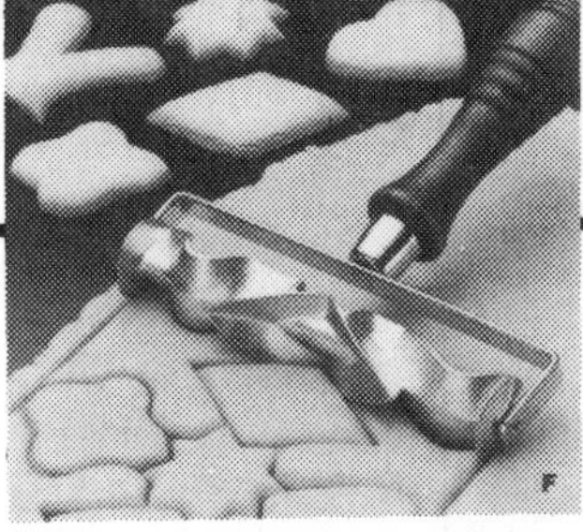

This ingeniously designed Cookie Roller from W. Germany cuts out five differently shaped cookies all at once with no waste of dough. You will find that your cookies have a far better texture as the dough is not over-handled. (Rolling and rerolling tend to toughen it.) Cast aluminum, 5" W. with 5" hardwood handle. Recipe included. #50-43992 $11.00

The Rolling Mincer, with its five sharp stainless steel circular blades and firm grip handle, makes short work of mincing parsley, onions, chives, shallots, etc. Pulls apart for easy cleaning. 6" L., from France. #50-41582 $10.50

Well designed Mix and Measure Batter Bowl of Pyrex® ovenproof glass has easy-to-read gradations in U.S. standard and metric amounts. Ideal for mixing and pouring all kinds of cake, muffin and pancake mixtures, and the "open" handle permits nesting into other bowls. Dishwasher safe. 2 qt. cap. #50-82388 $7.00

Williams-Sonoma
Catalog **free** from:
Williams-Sonoma
Mail Order Dept.
P. O. Box 7456
San Francisco, CA 94120-7456

Food Finds

There's one in every neck of the woods — a persistent local kitchen that continues to cook up the best food that good ingredients will allow. Because of notoriety or entrepreneurship, some of these finicky cooks sell their vittles by mail — mostly the kinds that ship well: like regional sauces, home-baked goods, cheeses, and preserves. What you'll get in your mailbox is premium food mindfully prepared in the "old-fashioned" way of small batches begun with fresh ingredients. The manna comes at premium prices (no free lunches) from family businesses with primarily rural addresses (there's a few monks, too). This catalog has their stories, addresses, and mail order prices.
—Kevin Kelly

Mail Order:
Eclipse Food Products Inc.
240 Bald Hill Road
Flavor Park
Warwick, RI 02886
401/739-3600

Marge Murray

Mrs. Murray, who lives on a 150-acre orchard in Duncan, Oklahoma, has been baking the cakes commercially for about nine years in the separate kitchen her husband built for her in the back of their home. Although she ships more than seven hundred cakes annually and has received national acclaim, she still bakes them one by one, weighing all ingredients to achieve consistency, creaming the sugar and shortening in a separate bowl, and folding in the beaten egg whites after the yolks.

Each cake weighs three pounds, serves at least ten generously, and costs $10.95 postpaid. Allow two weeks for delivery after receipt of order.

• Cooking on the trail is an art in itself. For recipes see p. 273. For equipment, check the catalogs on p. 274.

Food Finds
Allison Engel and Margaret Engel
1984; 224 pp.
$12.95
($14.45 postpaid) from:
Harper and Row
2350 Virginia Avenue
Hagerstown, MD 21740
or Whole Earth Access

Whole Earth Access

Wowee. A whole gamut of food preparation and other gear (building, stoves, energy stuff) at very low prices.
—Stewart Brand

Distantly related, Whole Earth Access has no financial tie to us. *See p. 3 for more information.*
—Kevin Kelly

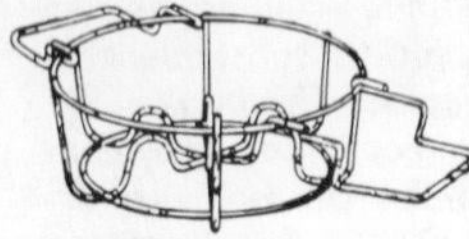

CANNING RACK
Sturdy welded construction with hanger handles, holds seven jars, either pint or quart. Diameter is 12", fits any pot 16 qt. or larger. Keeps jars apart so water can circulate freely & the jars won't hit each other.

JUICIT CITRUS JUICER ►
A very dependable & convenient electric citrus juicer, the Juicit has stood up to large-quantity catering use. Stainless steel strainer oscillates to strain the juice faster & allows some of the pulp to enter the juice. Juice pours easily from a spout straight into your glass. Makes as many glasses as you want. Strong motor is activated by hand pressure of the fruit on the ceramic reamer. Durable metal housing. Rinse juicing parts with water right away & it's easy to keep clean. Made by Procter-Silex. 125 watts.

Model	Sh. Wt.	List Price	Your Cost
White/Brown Juicit			
J101W	6 lbs.	30.00	**19.75**
Chrome Juicit			
J111C	6 lbs.	33.00	**23.57**

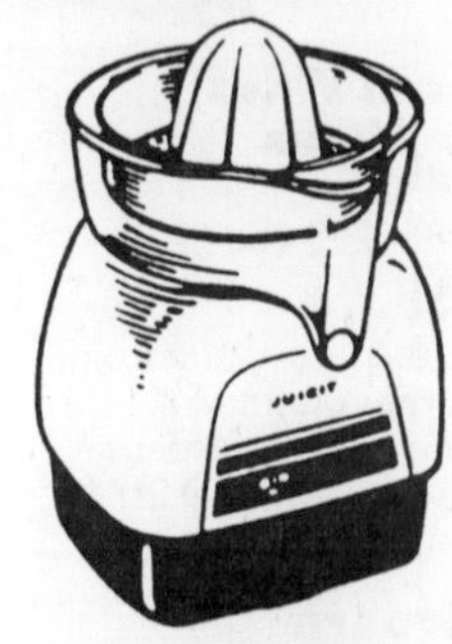

HENCKELS KNIVES
Utility:
General use plus boning & trimming hams, fowl, game, filleting fish.

C. 5" Durawood	31060-140	.5 lb.	$33.00	$23.10
6" Poly	31070-160	.5 lb.	$37.50	$26.25

Whole Earth Access Mail Order Catalog
Catalog **$7**
($5 deductible with $25 purchase)
from:
Whole Earth Access Co.
2950 Seventh Street
Berkeley, CA 94710

Jessica's Biscuit Cookbook Catalog

An excellent selection of cookbooks (over 1,000). These include: ethnic, international, and regional cookbooks; locally published cookbooks; vegetarian and other special diet cookbooks; food commentary and history; professional cooking texts and references; wine books; restaurant guides. If you use cookbooks, you'll love this catalog.
—Walt Noiseaux

Jessica's Biscuit Cookbook Catalog
Catalog **free** from:
Jessica's Biscuit
Box 301
Newtonville, MA 02160

Hop flowers.

WHERE A DECADE AGO there were perhaps four brewing conglomerates and a double handful of major wineries in New York and California, there are now over 50 microbreweries from coast to coast and commercial wineries in over 40 states. The making of fermented beverages is as old as culture itself and has roots on all continents in all latitudes, with adaptation for local ingredients and climate. Home beer- and winemaking can be a bioregional event at a gut level and a reward for all your senses.
—Don Ryan

The Complete Joy of Home Brewing
Charlie Papazian
1984; 331 pp.
$8.95
($9.95 postpaid) from:
Avon Books
P. O. Box 767
Dresden, TN 38225
or Whole Earth Access

The Complete Joy of Home Brewing

The joy comes through indeed in this very thorough book by the editor of **Zymurgy**, *and president of the American Homebrewers Association. The book's logic is quite clever: after an engaging history lesson the beginner is run through a simple recipe and instructions for making five gallons of beer of rewarding quality. There follow chapters of greater depth on processes and ingredients, then a cycle through a more demanding recipe where the brewer can use more complicated techniques and can exercise more choice over ingredients. That is followed by descriptions of the chemistry of malt, yeast, hops, and water, and of techniques and theory so that brewers can create their own recipes. Then a cycle through the process once again.*

There are 13 appendices, from a glossary to a treatise on siphoning, but no index. —*Don Ryan*

•

Miscellaneous Ingredients
Chocolate — The addition of bitter baker's chocolate or bittersweet nonmilk chocolate intrigues a growing number of homebrewers. There you are, brewing a batch of dark beer, and perhaps having a few in the process. And there it is just sitting there in the cupboard, staring you in the face . . . a 1 - 6-ounce chunk of chocolate. "I wonder . . .," you think, and before you know it, in it goes. Wallah, chocolate beer. And it doesn't turn out badly, in fact you brew one special batch once a year, to celebrate your impulse.

From Vines to Wines
Jeff Cox
1985; 253 pp.
$18.45
($20.45 postpaid) from:
Harper and Row
2350 Virginia Avenue
Hagerstown, MD 21740
or Whole Earth Access

Modern Winemaking
Philip Jackisch
1985; 289 pp.
$25
($26 postpaid) from:
Cornell University Press
124 Robert's Place
Ithaca, NY 14850
or Whole Earth Access

Modern Winemaking • From Vines to Wines

Modern Winemaking *fills the need for a book that anticipates the first-time winemaker's wish to evaluate deficiencies in their first bottling and to approach subsequent efforts with efficiency and sophistication. This book is neither dry nor pretentious. The author is the happy combination of a research chemist, commercial vintner and vineyardist, teacher, and engaging writer. The amateur winemaker could do no better except, perhaps for . . .*

From Vines to Wines. *This book is so satisfyingly inclusive it could almost have gone in the Whole Systems section of this catalog. Jeff Cox, an editor at* **Organic Gardening** *for about 15 years, may be the John McPhee of winemaking. He talks about wine by detailing the influences on it, then dissects those influences until he has described a huge circle of interrelatedness. The chapters on selecting the site for your vineyard are a pure, sweet ecology lesson. This book is a little thinner than Jackisch's — with greater scope — so it lacks a tiny bit of the depth, but it's soooo good. Get 'em both.* —*Don Ryan*

•

My wife, Marilyn, scrubs her legs and feet until they're squeaky clean. Then from the shower, making sure all soapy water is rinsed off her feet, into clean socks. These she strips off one by one as she steps into the vat of grapes. Given the size of our vats, the juice and pulp reach above her knee, and she treads in place until the grapes have been crushed and are all off the stems. The sight of her thighs dripping with grape juice never fails to quicken my pulse. This is not a bad time to put your Bo Diddley record on the turntable and pass around some wine that's good for gulping. —*From Vines to Wines*

Amateur Brewer • Zymurgy

*Erstwhile photojournalist Bill Owens (***Suburbia***), proprietor of Buffalo Bill's Brewery, has gotten together with editor Georgia Weathers of* **Home Fermenter's Digest** *to publish a new magazine under the name of Fred Eckhardt's* **Amateur Brewer**, *with Eckhardt as technical editor. This formidable team has come up with a new quarterly that is both stylish and competent, with many familiar brewer/writers as regular contributors, such as Bill Moore, author of the classy primer,* **Home Beermaking**.

Offering the new **AB** *strong competition is* **Zymurgy**, *the journal of the American Homebrewers Association. A slightly thicker magazine than* **AB**, **Zmurgy** *carries lots of political and convention news and seems, because of relative maturity, to be able to reach higher into the next level of professional beermaking for ideas on techniques and ingredients.* **Zymurgy** *also features stories by and about recognized brew experts, such as a recent profile of Byron Burch, author of the classic* **Quality Brewing** *(soon to be updated and vastly enlarged), who was the supplier of ingredients and recipes for my first beers of ten years ago.* —*Don Ryan*

Amateur Brewer: Bill Owens, Editor **$13.50**/year (4 issues) from Amateur Brewer, P. O. Box 713, Hayward, CA 94541.
Zymurgy: Charlie Papazian, Editor **$17**/year (5 issues) from American Homebrew Association, P. O. Box 287, Boulder, CO 80306-0287.

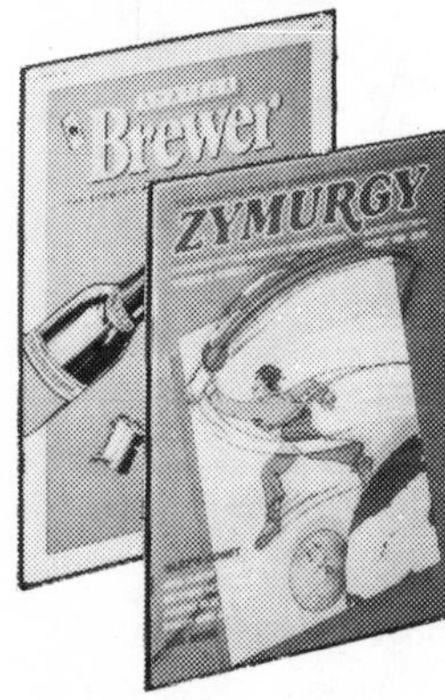

The Way to Make Wine From Fruit • The Way to Make Beer

Two video cassettes, taped in a home kitchen, show just how simple it can be to make fruit wine or beer at home, using pots, measuring cups, and strainers you probably already have. No specific recipes, you'll still need one of the books or magazines reviewed here. Rent one from your retailer or have your club buy the pair. —*Don Ryan*

The Way To Make Wine From Fruit; The Way To Make Beer: $39.95 each postpaid.
Information **free** from Great Fermentations, 87 Larkspur, San Rafael, CA 94901.

• Most mail order suppliers advertise in the magazines above. First check your local yellow pages. What you get in the mail ranges from simple price lists to informative newsletters. Here's a sample, all free:
Bacchus and Barleycorn: 6110 Johnson Drive, Mission, KS 66202.
Cape Cod Brewers: P. O. Box 1139, South Chatham, MA 02659.
The Cellar: P. O. Box 33525, Seattle, WA 98133.
Great Fermentations: 87 Larkspur, San Rafael, CA 94901.
William's Brewing: P. O. Box 2195, San Leandro, CA 94577.

Cheese molds give cheeses their traditional shapes. These molds are all made of durable polyethylene and are very easy to clean and sterilize. $4.95-$19.35
—New England Cheesemaking Supply Company

Cheesemaking

Cheesemaking, like home brewing, seems eminently suitable for amateurs. Both are really small-time bacteria farming. A knack for livestock, or something similar, might help because you raise and breed whole populations of little beasties, keeping them fed and sheltered in your kitchen.

The complete and almost sole source for amateur cheesemaking information and tools is New England Cheesemaking Supply Company. Their ***Cheesemakers' Journal*** *is an encouraging bimonthly with just the right mix of how-to tips, recipe swaps, and new improvements in the art.* ***Cheesemaking Made Easy*** *is the book to start with. Given an abundant supply of milk you can roll out hard, soft, salty, moldy, quick, or old cheeses. With well-aged confidence* ***Home Dairying*** *tells how to produce recognizable cheeses as well as their next of kin: cream, yogurt, and butter.* ***Goat Cheese*** *is the whole story on small-scale goat cheese brewing written by the Nuns of the Benedictine Monastery of Mount-Laurier, France. The necessary gear — tough plastic cheese molds, rennet paste, cultured bacteria — anything you need is stocked in the New England Cheesemaking Supply Company's catalog. —Kevin Kelly [Suggested by Walt Noiseux]*

•

Fresh curd consists primarily of casein and fat. If the proper conditions required for each variety of cheese are provided during the ripening process, these substances are changed and broken down into simple compounds which develop the taste, soften the texture and increase the digestibility of the cheese.

In this particular instance, the change occurs primarily from the outside of the cheese to the center and is induced by *Penicillium candidum*, a mold with white spores belonging to the Ascomycetes family in which the mycelia are septate. This mold or fungus grows wild in the Brie country of France. Particularly active and pure strains have been selected and are now supplied by laboratories that guarantee the quality of the strains.
—*Goat Cheese*

Packing feta cheese into a jar of salt water brine.
—Cheesemakers' Journal

—Goat Cheeses

•

Home-made butter, cream cheese, ice cream and many desserts are all possible when using the MINICREM 80 MANUAL CREAM SEPARATOR. It is a durable and compact, table-top model. It will handle the milk from a family cow or a small herd of goats. All parts in contact with the milk are of a special aluminum alloy, which is resistant to acid conditions and will never need retinning. $395.95
—*New England Cheesemaking Supply Company*

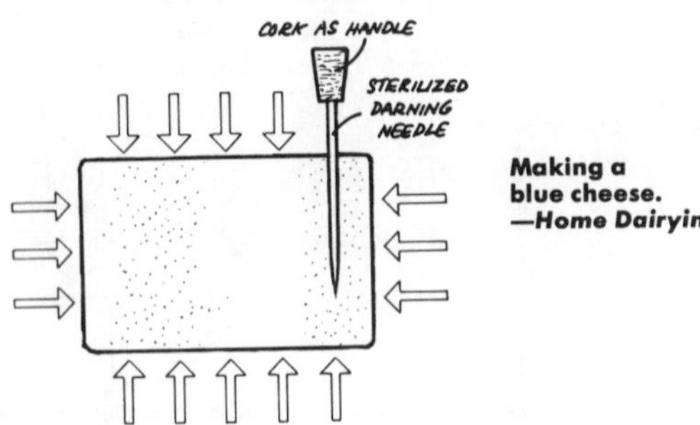

Making a blue cheese.
—Home Dairying

•

Blue Moulds. For the home cheesemaker perfectly good results can be obtained by using a piece of shop-bought blue cheese, breaking it up into small particles and mixing with water as a starter. Alternatively, small particles of the mould from a shop cheese can be sprinkled onto the curds at the salting stage. Once the cheese is shaped, the mould must have air in order to grow properly. The easiest way of ensuring this is to make holes in the cheese with a sterilized stainless steel needle; a kebab skewer easily available in most kitchen suppliers is ideal for this. . . .

White moulds. These develop on the outside of soft cheeses and the most famous are Brie and Camembert. Spores of *Penicillium camemberti* and *Penicillium candidum* are available and these are normally sprayed on to the cheeses when they are put out to ripen. . . .
—*Home Dairying*

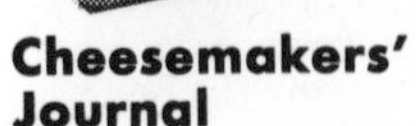

Cheesemakers' Journal
Robert Carroll, Editor
$10/year
(6 issues)

Cheesemaking Made Easy *
Ricki and Robert Carroll
1982; 143 pp.
$6.95
($8.45 postpaid)

Home Dairying *
Katie Thear
1983; 96 pp.
$8.95
($10.45 postpaid)

Goat Cheese *
The Mont-Laurier Benedictine Nuns
1983; 95 pp.
$6.95
($8.45 postpaid)

New England Cheesemaking Supply Company
Catalog
$1

All from:
New England Cheesemaking Supply Company
P. O. Box 85
Ashfield, MA 01330
* or Whole Earth Access

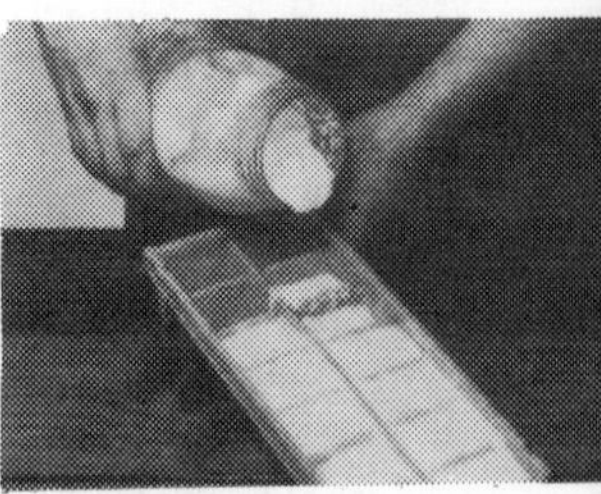

To store culture, freeze it in sterilized ice cube tray.
—Cheesemaking Made Easy

Putting Food By
Ruth Hertzberg,
Beatrice Vaughan
and Janet Greene
1984; 533 pp.
$7.95
($8.95 postpaid) from:
Viking Penguin Books
299 Murray Hill Pkwy.
East Rutherford, NJ 07073
or Whole Earth Access

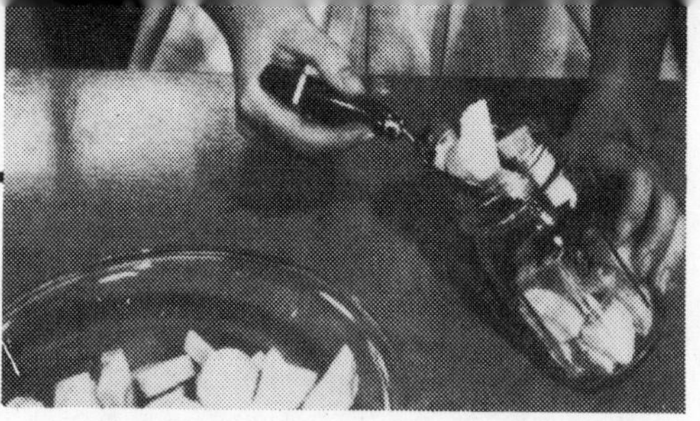

Pressure-processing will condense this raw pack of summer squash a great deal, even after its tamped down and given generous headroom.

Covered barrel root cellar for a mild climate.

Putting Food By

Even a tiny garden can grow more than one family can immediately use. ***Putting Food By*** *is 500 pages of readable instructions on drying, freezing, canning, smoking and root cellar storage. The book is laid out with frequent topic headings and charts, making it handy for quick reference. Freezing is by far the easiest method, and feasible for nearly every type of food, even eggs. Sun drying is ideal for fruit, except where it's humid; so there are instructions for making an indoor box dryer. With nearly two-thirds of every food dollar going to processing and marketing, it is easy to see that home processing saves money. This book, with suggestions on freezing TV dinners from leftovers and storing pre-cooked meals, even shows how it can save time.* —*Rosemary Menninger*

•

The beauty of root-cellaring is that it deals only with whole vegetables and fruits and there are no hidden dangers: If it doesn't work, we know by looking and touching and smelling that the stuff has spoiled, and we don't eat it.

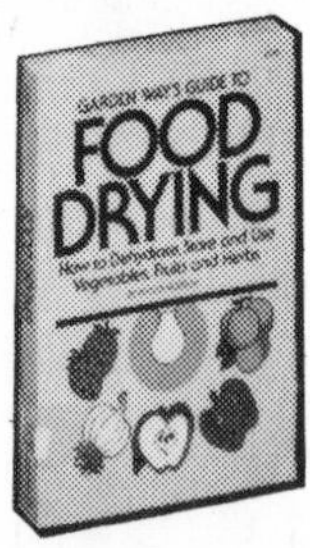

Garden Way's Guide to Food Drying
Phyllis Hobson
1980; 216 pp.
$7.95
($9.95 postpaid) from:
Garden Way Publishing
Storey Communications
Schoolhouse Road
Pownal, VT 05261
or Whole Earth Access

Garden Way's Guide to Food Drying

Drying is a good way to preserve food if canning and freezing are not viable options. Here is the best overview of preserving food in this fashion. A plan is included for building your own electric dehydrator. Detailed instructions are given for drying many fruits, vegetables, meats, dairy products, grains, herbs, and blossoms (for potpourris and herbal teas) by sun or oven. Included are storage techniques, recipes, and other uses for the drying equipment such as bread raising and yogurt making.
—*Evelyn Eldridge-Diaz*

•

Even if you don't plant a garden, you can still save money by drying foods at home. During the harvest season fruits and vegetables can be purchased cheaply by the bushel at the country markets and roadside stands.

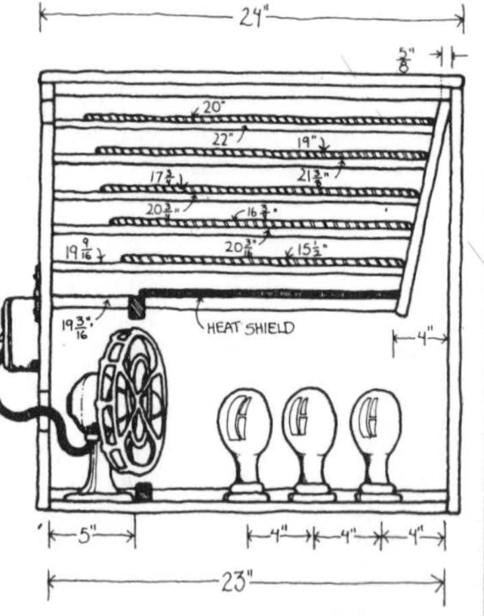

Dry It — You'll Like It

In addition to an excellent, somewhat funky little book, ***Dry It — You'll Like It!*** *a group called Living Foods offers a catalog of dehydrators and accessories, as well as a quarterly newsletter,* ***Drying Times.*** —*Dick Fugett*

Each tray will dry 4-6 lbs. of produce. This large capacity food dehydrator is handcrafted from the finest grade birch plywood.
—Living Foods Dehydrators

Dry It — You'll Like It
Gen MacManiman
1983; 75 pp.
$4.95
postpaid from:
MacManiman, Inc.
P. O. Box 546
Fall City, WA 98024
or Whole Earth Access

Drying Times
Barbara Beach-Moody, Editor
$6.50/year
(4 issues)

Living Foods Dehydrators
Catalog **$1**
both from:
Drying Times
P. O. Box 546
Fall City, WA 98024

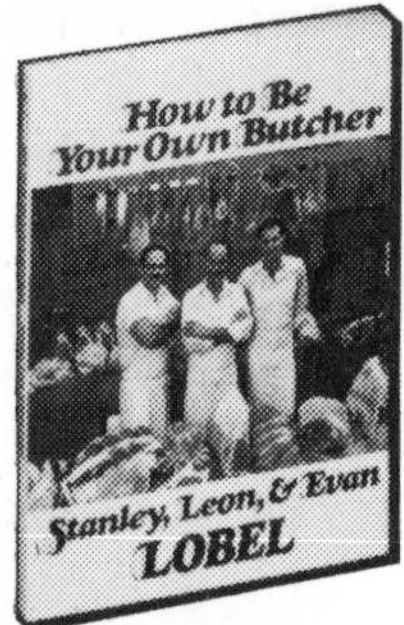

How to Be Your Own Butcher
Stanley, Leon,
and Evan Lobel
1983; 128 pp.
$8.95
($10.45 postpaid) from:
Putnam Publishing
Special Sales
200 Madison Avenue
New York, NY 10016
or Whole Earth Access

How to Be Your Own Butcher

A fact-packed book written by fourth- and fifth-generation professional butchers. Emphasizes independence, health, and saving money as reasons for learning home butchering. Describes the tools you'll need and how to choose and care for them. Tells how and where to obtain animals. Great advice on how to select animals, transport carcasses, butcher the beasties, and wrap and store the cuts of meat. Lamb, chicken, beef, veal, pork, game birds and variety meats are all covered in detail. Plenty of step-by-step illustrations to inspire confidence and guarantee success. For the price of a good steak, you really can become your own butcher. —*Mary Bowling*

•

If you are purchasing a section of beef, the outside fat should be milky-white and fresh-looking to the eye. Avoid meat with yellow or deep-yellow outside fat.

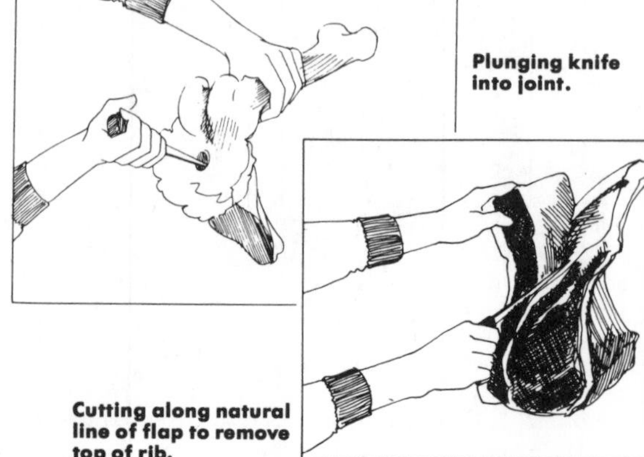

Plunging knife into joint.

Cutting along natural line of flap to remove top of rib.

THERE'S BEEN A world of change in co-ops and small distributors since we last gathered together this page in 1981. Small companies have gotten bigger; big companies have grown chillier. And a lot of companies have disappeared. Far fewer are willing to do mail order business with individuals or food-buying clubs. But those who have survived this financial winnowing are still friendly, cheerful, and know each other, and their customers, well.

—Sallie Tisdale

The Simpler Life Food Reserves

Specializes in emergency food programs ranging from six days to two years, including water storage capability of all sizes. Uses freeze-dried, pouch foods, and others. Offers an earthquake-preparedness kit complete with optional stove, cookbooks, menu plans. No minimum order.
—Sallie Tisdale

Catalog **free** from Arrowhead Mills, P. O. Box 2059, Hereford, TX 79045.

3-Month Variety Unit - 10 Cases

Cases	Food Items/Cans Per Case
1	Food Maxi-Pak/6(#10 cans)
below: #2½ cans	
1	Rice, Short Grain/6, Cracked Wheat Cereal/6
1	Bulghur-Soy Grits/6, Oat Flakes/6
1	Maple Nut Granola/12
1	Pasta Elbows, Whole Wheat/12
1	Pintos/3, Split Peas/3, Lentils/3, Mungs/3
1	Potatoes, F.D./6, Celery/3, Mushrooms/3
1	Carrots/6, Onions, F.D./3, Gr. Peppers/3
1	Apple Dices, Low Moisture/12
1	Protein Powder/2, Date Sugar/1, Milk, Non-instant, Non-fat/8, Vitamins/2 bottles

Starflower

Fourteen years as a worker-owned and operated business. Starflower distributes 1,650 products, including staples, groceries, almost 200 herbs, spices, and teas, and body care products. Strong focus on organic foods and foods native to the N.W. United States. Shipping throughout the U.S. Information guides available on every single product.
—Sallie Tisdale

Catalog **free** from Starflower, 885 McKinley St., Eugene, OR 97402.

QUONG HOP

90148 Marinated Tempeh Burgers (Vacuum packed) Organic soy tempeh (soybeans), herbs & spices, water, onion powder, garlic, salt.

90149 Savory Baked Tofu (Vacuum packed) Organic tofu (water, organic soybeans, nigari solidifier), and other natural ingredients including safflower oil, natural soy sauce, spices (cayenne, fennel, anise, ginger).
6 week shelf life. Cholesterol free. 22% protein.

90142 Nigari Tofu, Firm (Vacuum packed) Organic tofu (water, organic soybeans, nigari solidifier), and other natural ingredients including safflower oil, natural soy sauce.
6 week shelf life. Cholesterol free. 13% protein.

Walnut Acres

Baby Swiss Cheese

Walnut Acres is practically a village unto itself, with its own farm, bakery, mill, cannery, and a small processing plant for condiments and dressings. Most of the produce and grains grown at the farm are organic. Also specialty items like jams and small housewares. Will ship anywhere by UPS or common carrier with no minimum order.
—Sallie Tisdale

Catalog **free** from Walnut Acres, Penns Creek, PA 17862.

Ozark Cooperative Warehouse

A large, consumer-owned warehouse, doing about ¾ of its business with private food-buying clubs. Minimum order varies depending on location in its 8-state region of the mid-south. Over 1,000 products with an emphasis on organic products and small, local growers. Also staples, teas and coffees, and herbs. Happy to make referrals and answer questions, too.
—Sallie Tisdale

Catalog **$4.78** from Ozark Cooperative Warehouse, P. O. Box 30, Fayetteville, AR 72702.

Mountain Ark Trading Company

Lots of the staple macrobiotic foods — whole grains, sea vegetables, and soy products — plus other natural foods. The miso selection includes 28 varieties! You have no idea how plump, well-formed, and tasty brown rice can be until you've tried Chico San's Macrobiotic Quality Short Grain Brown Rice. Really, try some side by side with the typical food co-op variety. The catalog is beautiful and educational; mail order service is quick and accurate.
—Jeffrey Bonar

Catalog **$1** from Mountain Ark Trading Co., 120 South East Street, Fayetteville, AR 72701.

North Pacific Sea Vegetables - from the Mendocino Sea Vegetable Co.

Pacific Sea Palm - An undiscovered treasure, even for many people who eat sea vegetables already! Pacific sea palm is one of the most delicious sea vegetables anywhere in the world. Even those who have yet to develop a taste for sea vegetables will love this food. Sautéed or fried with onions and/or mushrooms, sea palm is a delight at any meal.
16535 1 oz. 2.95

—Mountain Ark Trading Company

Coffee Bean International

The owner, Jeff Ferguson, travels to Latin America several times a year and takes along an organic farm certifier annually, to guarantee the integrity of his line of organic coffees. He does all his own roasting and packs in vacuum bags. Also offers coffee from China, East Timor, and Jamaica; a large selection of black and green teas, including several exotics; herbs, spices, and candies. One hundred and fifty-seven varieties of coffee total. Guarantees same day roast and ship.
—Sallie Tisdale

Catalog **free** from Coffee Bean International, 2181 NW Nicolai, Portland, OR 97210

ASIAN COFFEES (from the Indian and South Pacific Oceans)

Celebes Kalossi	7.55
Indian Malabar	**4.50
Java Estate	5.05
Java Regular	4.25
New Guinea A	4.49
Sumatra Arabica/Mandheling	4.70
Sumatra CBI "Estate" Mand.	**5.85
Sumatra Blue Lingtong	5.25
Sumatra Boengie	4.55

Meat on the Table

If you're a carnivore, you either hire someone (in effect) to do your killing for you, or you do it yourself. Here's how to do it yourself — equipment, technique, procedures — all served up in a chatty personal way by a famous hunter of small game. —JB

Meat on the Table
Galen Geer
1985; 206 pp.
$14.95
($17.95 postpaid) from:
Paladin Press
P. O. Box 1307
Boulder, CO 80306
or Whole Earth Access

Handguns or Rifles	Excellent	Good	Fair	Poor	Remarks (shot size/
.22 Short			□		
.22 Long			□		
.22 Long Rifle	□				
.22 Magnum		□			
Centerfire			□		
Air Gun		□			
Shotguns					
10-gauge				□	
12-gauge	□				5 or 6 shot; 2½–3¼ drams
16-gauge	□				same
28-gauge		□			same
20-gauge		□			same
.410				□	
Archery		□			
Crossbow		□			
Slingshot				□	
Other	□□		□		□□ Trapping □ Blowgun

MARSH RABBIT
Description:
Length: 15-19 in.
Weight: 2½-3 lbs.
Coloration: *Body sides* and *front* and *back legs:* buff/brown.
***Back:* dark buff to brown. *Belly, chest,* and *rump:* buff. *Tail:* white under tail.**
***Underfur:* off-white to buff.**
Distribution: Florida, southern Georgia, and north along the coast to North Carolina.
Preferred habitat: Edge areas near lakes, streams, and swamps. Swims easily and is often found in water.
Table fare: Excellent.

Getting the Most From Your Game and Fish

Be it for dinner, trophy, or pelt, this friendly book shows you how to treat your kill. The tone is non-macho and respectful of the dead — a rarity in this sort of thing. The illustrations deserve special mention for effectiveness in showing the procedures, oogy parts and all. (Vegetarians may gain a few converts.) —JB

Having a Ball — Skinning!
(Works best on a muley or white-tailed deer.)

1. Pull, or work a knife, between hide & carcass.
2. Drop ball into pocket formed.
3. Hard ball (golf or a wooden one) is squeezed, pushed and rolled over the carcass, lifting and loosening the hide.

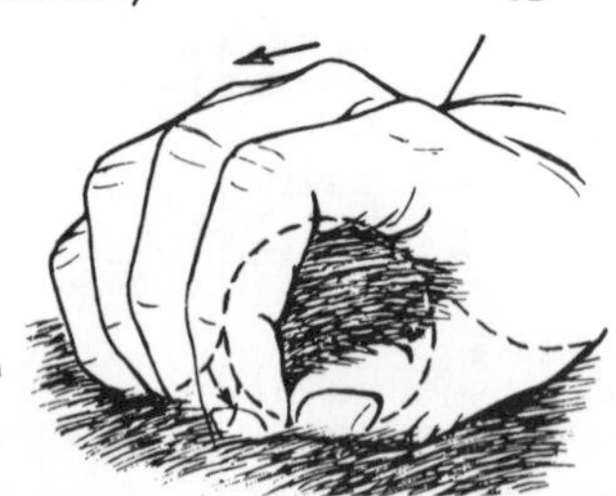

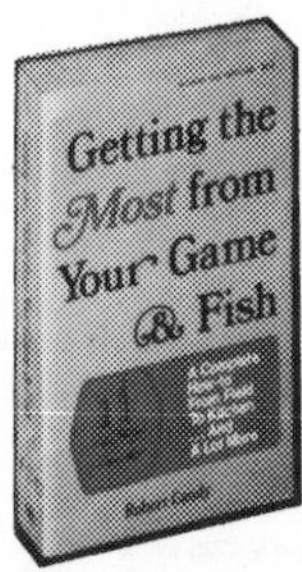

Getting the Most From Your Game and Fish
Robert Candy
1978; 278 pp.
$12.95
($14.95 postpaid) from:
Backcountry Publications
P. O. Box 175
Woodstock, VT 05091
or Whole Earth Access

Shooting

Just about everything you need to know about rifles, pistols, and shotguns is here — how to choose and how to use. There's a bit about black powder arms and archery, too. While a bit short of the cover's promise of "how to become an expert," the book is a good overview with less of the author's personal bias than in many other books; you're taught enough to make your own decisions. —JB

Shooting
Edward A. Matunas
1986; 438 pp.
$31.95
($34.95 postpaid) from:
Stackpole Books
P. O. Box 1831
Harrisburg, PA 17105

When feet are positioned correctly, a line drawn across the toes will point directly at the target. Also, your weight will be evenly distributed between both feet, turning your body into a stable bipod.

The Beginning Bowhunter

The difference between firearms and bow-and-arrow is a bit like the difference between a backhoe and a shovel; doing it by hand may be more work, but the direct contact leads to a more intimate knowledge of the business at hand. A bowhunter must truly understand the habits of the intended quarry (in this case deer) to get close enough to shoot. This book is a personal instruction, rather like having the author at your side as you learn. —JB

Try to get above some natural cover with your tree stand.

The Beginning Bowhunter
Tony Kinton
1985; 122 pp.
$9.95
($11.95 postpaid) from:
Stackpole Books
P. O. Box 1831
Harrisburg, PA 17105
or Whole Earth Access

Beeman Precision Airguns

Quiet, extraordinarily accurate, cheap to feed, and legal almost anywhere, modern adult airguns are a worthy substitute for common ".22" firearms. Beeman has been the leading source of airguns for a long time now, and this catalog/guide is a good example why. —JB

Beeman R1: World's highest velocity precision air rifle.

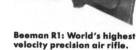

Beeman Precision Airguns
Catalog **free** from:
Beeman Precision Arms
47 Paul Drive
San Rafael, CA 94903

The forward rolling loop of the roll cast.

Fly-Fisherman's Primer

*The **Fly-Fisherman's Primer** is an excellent basic guide to the gentle art of fly fishing. All the most important topics are covered in the text, including equipment, knots, casting, presentation, insect life, nymphing and wading. A beginning fly fisherman could pick up this book, spend a few evenings with it, then head out to the river and do fairly well. (Of course, that depends on the river. A knowledgeable friend and a little experience help, too.)*

*The book also contains knowledge useful to more than advanced fly fishermen. Plenty of competent fly fishermen cannot tie a decent nail knot or distinguish a may fly from a caddis fly. The **Fly-Fisherman's Primer** will remedy this. Clear line drawings illustrate the various casting and fly tying techniques. Nice color plates of trout species and fly patterns, too.* —Danielle Toussaint

Brook Trout (Char)

Fly-Fisherman's Primer
Paul N. Fling and
Donald L. Puterbaugh
1985; 160 pp.
$8.95 postpaid from:
Sterling Publishing Co.
2 Park Avenue
New York, NY 10016
or Whole Earth Access

Trout

Above all, this is the one book to buy. It is a window on the entire subject for $125 — just about what a top river guide charges for the day. However, no guide will get you through the hard times — the long winter months of the off-season — the way this book will. If there is a college course on fly fishing somewhere, this is the text, for beginners and experts. Unlike a text, each chapter sparkles with fishing tales.

*The two volumes of **Trout**, in an attractive slip case, are divided into six separate books or subjects (1745 pages): The Evolution of Fly-Fishing; American Species of Trout and Grayling; Physiology, Habitat, and Behavior; The Tools of the Trade; Casting, Wading and Other Skills; Trout Strategies, Techniques, and Tactics. Color plates, drawings, and diagrams are all done by the author.*

Eighty-seven pages are devoted to a primer of modern fly casting. Few books convey fly casting well, because understanding it relies so much upon feel. This section comes as close to imparting feel as a book can. —Tom Macy

•

Stealth and cunning are the primary rules. Your approach must be muffled, and you cannot plunge through the stream-side willows and alders without alarming the fish. Your final presentation must be gentle, placing your fly softly in the current so the trout will not be frightened. Careful fishermen will most often approach from downstream on a small river, behind skittish trout, and usually conceal themselves behind willows and tree trunks and grass. It is valuable to watch the reaction of the fish, either taking the fly readily or refusing it. Such lessons are not easily learned on larger streams, where you seldom see the trout at close range.

•

There are moods when the cacophony and leg-wearying power of a big river become oppressive. Difficult wading and countless double hauls can erode both body and soul. Big water holds big trout, and there is a period in the maturing in the career of every fisherman when he is addicted to the pursuit of a trophy-size fish. Once you have that fever in your blood, it is a passion that drives you beyond good judgment.

Trout
Ernest Schwiebert
1978; 1745 pp.
$125 postpaid from:
E. P. Dutton
Two Park Avenue
New York, NY 10016
or Whole Earth Access

Dan Bailey's Fly Shop • Cabela's

Reading Dan Bailey's Fly Shop mail order catalog during the off-season is sweet torture for anglers of the fly fishing persuasion. The color photographs of fly patterns, rods, reels, fly boxes, and tying supplies can easily intoxicate fly fishermen caught in these painful winter doldrums.

Bailey's catalog not only offers a good selection of pre-tied dry flies, wet flies, nymphs, and streamers but all the necessary fly-tying accessories and supplies. The company doesn't charge for postage if you spend $50 or more, and a quick perusal of their catalog will convince most fly fishermen to adjust the balance in their checkbooks by at least that amount.

Cabela's doesn't have quite the variety of Bailey's, but the prices are generally lower. —Danielle Toussaint

Bailey's: catalog **free** from Dan Bailey's Fly Shop, P. O. Box 1019, Livingston, MT 59047.
Cabela's: catalog **free** from Cabela's, 812 13th Avenue, Sydney, NE 69160.

• This angling classic, originally published in 1654, is the first serious written work about fishing.

The Compleat Angler: Izaac Walton, 1654, 1985; 160 pp. **$4.95** ($5.95 postpaid) from Viking Penguin Books, 299 Murray Hill Parkway, East Rutherford, NJ 07073 (or Whole Earth Access).

The Compleat Angler's Catalog

*Would a golfer read 349 pages about golf equipment? Not likely. But serious fishermen read — and appreciate — Scott Roederer's **The Compleat Angler's Catalog**. As the author notes in the first chapter, "Perhaps nothing will ever be written that fully accounts for the fascination most fly fishermen feel for their sport. . . . Nowhere in the sport is that fascination so clearly evident than in the fly fisherman's love of his equipment."*

Every type of fly fishing equipment imaginable is critiqued in this catalog. Prices and company listings are also included. While the book is basically a buyer's guide, it also lists fly fishing and conservation organizations. —Danielle Toussaint

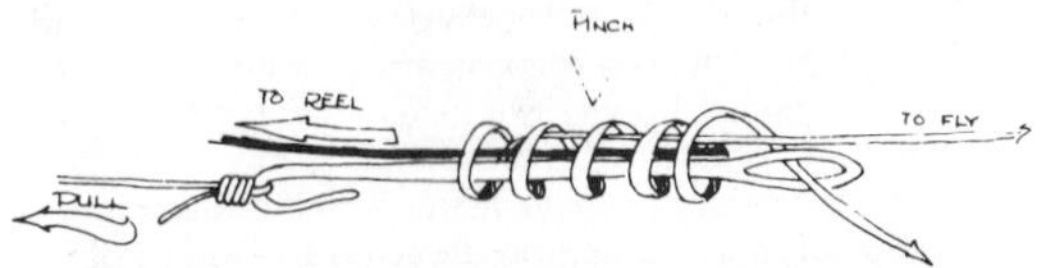

***Orvis Fly Threader.* A nifty device for getting that tippet through the hook's eye, even in darkness. $5.25-$5.50 Kau, Hun, Orv**

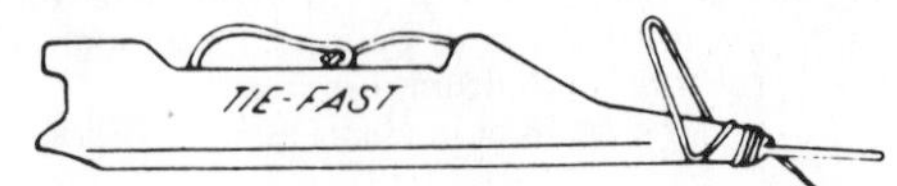

***Tie-Fast Knot Tyer.* For nail and blood knots. $2.95-$3 Kau, Fly, Pen**

The Compleat Angler's Catalog
$14.95 from:
Johnson Books
1880 South 57th Court
Boulder, CO 80301

Mushrooms of North America
Orson K. Miller, Jr.
1979; 368 pp.
$14.08
($15.58 postpaid) from:
New American Library
P. O. Box 999
Bergenfield, NJ 07621
or Whole Earth Access

The Mushroom Feast
Jane Grigson
1975, 1983; 305 pp.
$5.95
($6.95 postpaid) from:
Viking Penguin, Inc.
Order Department
299 Murray Hill Parkway
East Rutherford, NJ 07073
or Whole Earth Access

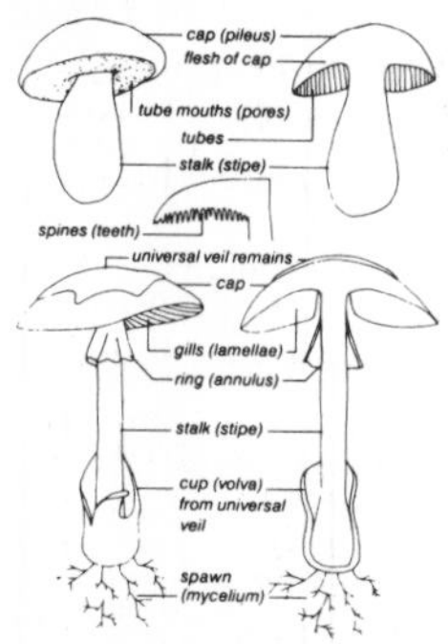

—Mushroom Hunter's Field Guide

MUSHROOMS ARE THEIR OWN KINGDOM . . . on the Earth and to the palate. They require a love, study, philosophy, and walking pace unique in life. There is no one book; you must buy a few. The best teachers are other mycophiles. Look up the word "mushroom" or "mycology" in the phone book and join a 'shroom society. If you can't find one, call, join, or write the North American Mycological Association.*

No mushroom can be identified easily. Poisoning is the expert's number one occupational hazard. But armed with a small vocabulary, perseverance, patience, and spore prints, you can stay alive and eat pretty well. To expand gourmet risks and further probe fungal secrets, you *must* immerse yourself in Latin. There's no escape.

The best overall guide with an illustrated glossary is Miller's *Mushrooms of North America.* In addition, you will want your regional, but more difficult, Alexander Smith guide. (The "southern" guide is really southeastern.) Your 'shroom society can acquaint you with even more local introductions.

—Peter Warshall

Mushrooms of North America

•
Pleurotus ostreatus: Edible, choice/Common. Fries [''Oyster Mushroom'']. Cap white to yellow-brown, moist, oyster-shell shape; stalk absent; flesh thick.

Single but usually in large overlapping clusters on branches, logs, and stumps of hardwoods and conifers in Sp., early S., F., and in the W.; widely distributed. I have found it commonly on aspens, willow, beech, and pines, but it occurs on many other trees.

The distinctive characteristics include white, oyster-shell-like caps, white to buff spores, and usually a sessile growth habit. A closely related species, *P. sapidus* (Schulzer) Kalch., has a dull white to brown cap, lilac-colored, narrow spores (2.5-3.5 microns wide), and often has an off-center, short stalk. *Pleurotus columbinus* Quel. apud Bres. is a name which was once used for the brown variant of *P. sapidus* and is not a separate species. A shiny black beetle will very frequently be found in numbers between the gills of both species; it lays eggs in the tissue of the cap where the grubs feed until they mature and reproduce the adult. Both *P. ostreatus* and *P. sapidus* are delicious edibles, so you are fortunate if you find this fungus before the beetles do. *—Mushrooms of North America*

Regional Guides

The Mushroom Hunter's Field Guide: Alexander H. Smith and Nancy S. Weber, 1980; 316 pp.; **$14.95** ($15.95 postpaid).

Field Guide to Western Mushrooms: Alexander H. Smith, 1975; 280 pp.; **$18.50** ($19.50 postpaid).

Field Guide to Southern Mushrooms: Nancy S. Weber and Alexander H. Smith, 1985; 280 pp.; **$16.50** ($17 postpaid). All from University of Michigan Press, 839 Greene Street, Ann Arbor, MI 48106 (or Whole Earth Access).

•
Cyclopeptide poisoning. The first symptoms of this type of poisoning appear from about ten to fourteen hours after the mushrooms were eaten, but they may be delayed as many as forty-eight hours. The symptoms include nausea, vomiting, and bloody diarrhea. Usually these symptoms abate, and the victim may feel so much better that he/she may even be discharged from the hospital. On the second to fourth day signs of liver, and sometimes kidney, failure appear. These are manifested by severe abdominal pain, jaundice, convulsions, coma, and sometimes death. Laboratory studies have shown that the toxin attacks the liver tissue within a few minutes of ingestion. This effect can be detected by studies of blood chemistry very soon after the mushroom is eaten, although the results of this attack may not be evident for a few days. This group of compounds is the cause of most fatal mushroom poisonings. At present there is no certain antidote for this type of poisoning, although with proper medical care most victims recover.

—The Mushroom Hunter's Field Guide

The Mushroom Feast

I had to choose one in a world of mouth-watering mushroom books. This is it . . . the apex of fungal finesse . . . vraiment francaise. *—Peter Warshall*

•
Cooking: Morels are usually split down the centre, or sliced, so that all sandy grit and earth can be washed from the intricate convolutions. Put a handful of salt into the washing water, in case there are any ants or other creatures lurking in the crevices. Can be fried, but are best cooked *a la creme*, or with poultry.

Croutes aux morilles
a la normande
Omelette a la provencale
Fish meuniere aux morilles
Ragout de laitances
aux morilles
Fillet of beef with morels
Ris de veau (d'agneau)
a la creme
Poulet aux morilles

Morel, Merkel, Sponge Mushroom (*Morchella esculenta* and *Morchella vulgaris*)

• If you don't want to hunt for gourmet mushrooms, you can grow them at home. See **The Mushroom Cultivator** and Mushroompeople (both on p. 75).

***North American Mycological Association:** membership **$15/year**, information **free** (with SASE) from North American Mycological Association, Attn.: Harry Knighton, 4245 Redinger Road, Portsmouth, OH 45667.

Ox-Eye Daisy and English Daisy (Aster or Composite Family). —*Edible Garden Weeds of Canada*

GARDENING IS STACKING THE DECK against Nature. Foraging wild edibles is a confrontation with Nature in all its glorious fickleness. Sometimes Miner's Lettuce just can't be found. Was it deer? A drought? Overharvested last year? A new drainage drying the soil? Insects? Foraging, like hunting, attunes the body, mind, and spirit to life cycles and seasonal change. It's still the most direct-connect to plant powers.

Foraging is a skill. How much can you harvest without subverting next year's supply? Is the fruit ripe enough? Is the root large enough? Is it endangered like American ginseng? Is it a poisonous look-alike?

—Peter Warshall

Field Guide to North American Edible Wild Plants

The best introduction: great photos, clear descriptions of each plant's favorite spot, range maps, seasonal coverage, harvesting advice, recipes, and a list of poisonous look-alikes for each plant. You'll love their elderberry blossoms deep fried in batter or their sassafrass jelly.

—*Peter Warshall*

•

Summer: Marsh mallow (also edible autumn, winter) Althaea officinalis Habitat: edges of brackish and salt marshes; introduced from Europe and now grows wild. *Identification: perennial herb* from 0.6—1.2m (2—4 ft) tall, from thick, large taproot; stems upright, often branched, stout, hairy . . . *Flowers: several in cluster at base of upper leaves in summer; each with 5 pink, spreading petals 2—3 cm (0.8—1.2 in) long. Fruit is dry, flattened disc, divided into 15—20 segments. Harvest:* leaves in early summer, flower buds in summer, and roots from late summer through winter. *Preparation:* whole plant contains mucilagelike material; roots are best source. Use young leaves in early summer as okra-like soup thickener or as potherb. Pickle flower buds. Boil thin sliced, peeled roots for 20 min in enough water to cover them. Strain off roots; for candy sweeten the liquid and boil until very thick. Beat and drop spoonfuls on waxed paper to cool. Roll pieces in confectioner's sugar. For vegetable, fry boiled root slices with butter and chopped onion until browned. Use water from boiling any parts of plant as substitute for egg white in meringue or chiffon pies. Also used for hand lotion and cough syrup. Use leaves for poultices for infected wounds. *Related edible species:* other Mallow family species, especially those of genus *Malva*. Eat *Malva* fruits raw or substitute roots for meringue. *Poisonous look-alikes:* none.

Field Guide to North American Edible Wild Plants
Thomas S. Elias
and Peter A. Dykeman
OUT OF PRINT
Van Nordstrand Books

Regional Guides: Western

***Edible Wild Plants of Canada** is the most elegant and informative series of books on wild edibles. If it had U.S. locations, it would have been my top choice. **Edible Native Plants of the Rocky Mountains** is the best on the Rockies and some more southern species.*

Edible Wild Plants of Canada: No. 1, Edible Garden Weeds of Canada (1978; 184 pp.); No. 2, Wild Coffee and Tea Substitutes of Canada (1979; 111 pp.); No. 3, Edible Wild Fruits and Nuts of Canada (1979; 212 pp.); No. 4, Wild Green Vegetables of Canada (1980; 179 pp.) **$12.95** each postpaid from University of Chicago Press, 11030 South Langley, Chicago, IL 60628 (or Whole Earth Access).

Edible Native Plants of the Rocky Mountains: H. D. Harrington, 1974; 292 pp. **$9.95** ($10.95 postpaid) from University of New Mexico Press, Albuquerque, NM 87131 (or Whole Earth Access).

►

How to Use: The use of the dried flowers of basswood and linden for making a hot beverage is quite well known in North America and famous in Europe. Similar to camomile tea, linden (basswood) tea is one of the most popular teas in France and other European countries. Promoting perspiration, it is commonly used as an alternative to aspirin in the treatment of colds. As it also soothes the nerves, aids digestion, and helps to provide good sleep, it is one of the favourite mild medicines, given even to small children.

—*Wild Coffee and Tea Substitutes of Canada*

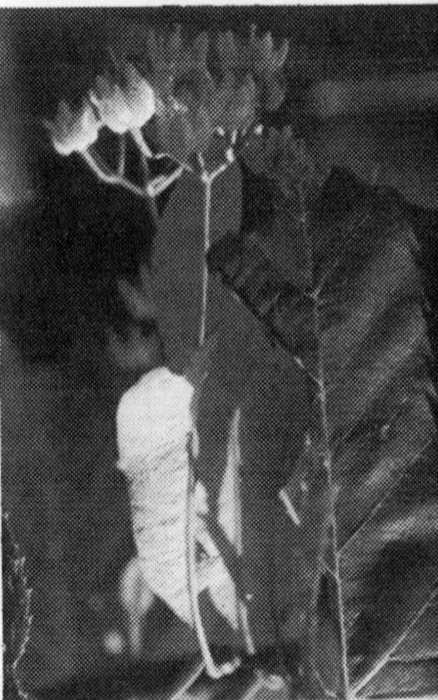

Basswood (Basswood Family). Other Names: American linden, lime, lime-tree, whitewood.

Regional Guides: Eastern

Peterson's has a cozy appendix — edibles are clustered by old fields, waste grounds, swamps, thickets, still water, and (like Japanese haiku) by season. Identification remains difficult. ***Roots** digs the deepest into specialty foraging: good drawings, botany, Indian uses, medicinal uses, harvesting, drying, and preparing of roots, tubers, corms, and rhizomes.* —*Peter Warshall*

Roots (An Underground Botany and Forager's Guide): Douglas B. Elliott, 1976; 128 pp. **$6.95** ($8.70 postpaid) from The Chatham Press, 6 North Water Street, Greenwich, CT 06830 (or Whole Earth Access).

A Field Guide to Edible Wild Plants (Eastern/Central North America): Lee Allen Peterson, 1977; 330 pp. **$10.95** ($11.96 postpaid) from Houghton Mifflin Company, Wayside Road, Burlington, MA 01803 (or Whole Earth Access).

•

Suggested Recipes: Mulberry Fudge

150 mL ripe mulberry juice	⅔ cup
500 mL sugar	2 cups
30mL butter	2 tbsp

Cook about 375 mL (1½ cups) of mulberries lightly, mash and drain through a fine sieve or jelly bag to obtain the juice. Mix juice together with sugar and butter and place over low heat until sugar is dissolved. Bring to a boil on medium heat and boil *without stirring* until soft-ball stage on a candy thermometer is reached (115°C or 240°F). *Warning:* Be careful not to eat the raw fruit until it is ripe. Unripe fruits and the milky sap in the leaves and stems of mulberries are toxic and can cause gastric upsets. The leaves and stems also may cause dermatitis if touched by susceptible individuals.

—*Edible Wild Fruits and Nuts of Canada*

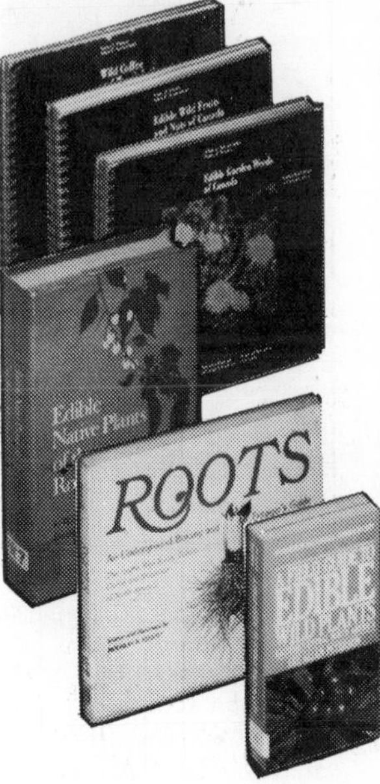

I CAN'T THINK OF ANYTHING more sure to change minds than traveling. Some advice about what to take: very little. Baggage is what you are supposed to leave behind. Take as little money as your wealth of time will let you afford. I've noticed that time-rich travelers come back more satisfied than money-rich travelers.

Ideal time to go: right now. Where: as far away as you can imagine (hardly costs any more these days). How to prepare: I start with old *National Geographics* at the library, and then go hire out the new guidebooks on the shelf. I tell EVERYONE I meet what I'm doing, save any addresses I collect, and then actually startle the hosts by showing up. I bring a small pocket album of pictures of my home and friends. I smile all the time. Everyone smiles back and then stares politely at my ignorance. Slowly they change my mind.

—Kevin Kelly

Lonely Planet Newsletter
Maureen Wheeler
$10/year
(4 issues); Catalog **free** both from:
Lonely Planet Publications
1555 D Park Avenue
Emeryville, CA 94608

Lonely Planet Newsletter

Inferior travel guides tend to dwell on architecture styles and the merits of larger hotels because these artifacts change slowly and information about them can be recycled with confidence. Not so with loose personal traveling. The former Tuesday open-air market is now on Friday. To keep alive and useful, the superior guidebooks published by Lonely Planet rely on mail from a legion of readers on the road to revamp each guide every other year.

One year, print information out. Next year, information floods in, revised by users/readers on site. Third year, information edited by staff goes out again. That's an uncommonly healthy respiration rate for a travel book. The result is a series of indispensable guides for remote and exotic places like Burma, Tibet, Papua New Guinea, Kashmir, Turkey, and Africa, to name a few.

In between breaths, Lonely Planet funnels the best hundred or so update letters mailed in by traveling readers into a quarterly newsletter. This is the place to check for the latest gossip on border crossings, the el-cheapo hotels of choice, and a feel for current prices in Asia, Africa or South America. The latest issues have been overflowing with red-hot advice from independent travelers in Tibet.

—KK

•

Tibet

There are plenty of other good restaurants in Lhasa, especially the Muslim places behind the mosque. Tibetan specialties are available everywhere in Lhasa — curd is 50 fen for half a kilo, sold in a glass jam pot. It's delicious, incredibly creamy, just consider the green pastures all over the country!

Tsampa (barley flour that you mix yourself with water, or if you are well-off, with butter-tea), tastes no worse than porridge. Most Tibetans live on it — it's hard to find it in restaurants.

Tchang is the local barley beer. At 10 fen a glass, you find it in open-air tents in the street.

Excellent donuts can be found in the CAAC street, a few metres north of the office.

Globe
Barbara Macanas, Editor
$14/year
(6 issues) from:
The Globetrotters Club
BCM/Roving
London, WC1N 3XX UK

Globe

The drifters of Europe in the '60s invented a contemporary form of education: extended world travel. At about $3000 per year, all adventures included, it is still the cheapest college there is. As a guide to what is offered, ***Globe****, the newsletter of the Globetrotters Club, is consistently the best tutor for long-term travel. Ramblers just back from around-the-world-tours file meaty debriefings on conditions and prices in, say, Timbucktu, or Norway.* ***Globe*** *prints them quickly before they decay. Unlike* ***Lonely Planet Newsletter*** *they also review books, supply a place to advertise for travel-mates, and cover tripping in Europe and the U.S. (exotic if you don't live here). With genuine club spirit, you can contact other members overseas for on-the-spot inquiries. Gather no moss (or ivy).*

—KK

•

Campmobile Around the World

Tom and Beverly Tarnow (California) have recently completed a four-year around the world trip covering 102 countries. They drove their campmobile through Europe, Africa, South America, North America, Australia (Asia by airplane). They say they are willing to offer supporting correspondence about overland experience with a VW campmobile through the less developed areas of South America and Africa: Algeria, Nigeria, Zaire, Kenya, South Africa.

TEL AVIV — Dead Sea.

New York Times Practical Traveler
Paul Grimes
1985; 412 pp.
$10.95
($11.95 postpaid) from:
Random House
Attn.: Order Dept.
400 Hahn Road
Westminster, MD 21157
or Whole Earth Access

Practical Traveler

When I have a travel question this is the expert I reach for. It's a reference collection by the only decent newspaper travel columnist in the country, Paul Grimes at the ***New York Times.*** *I use it when I want to find out how to charter a bus, or rent a car in Europe, or scare up some legitimate tricks for buying an around-the-world airline ticket. His conception of travel is admirably broad, and his facts well researched. To keep current you might check your local Sunday paper; his column is syndicated in many of them.*

—KK

•

A more common way to save money on domestic flights is to take advantage of what the trade calls flyover, point-beyond or hidden-city ticketing. For example, not long ago the normal one-way coach fare between San Francisco and Atlanta was $420 on nonstop flights of Delta or Eastern. But Delta was selling seats on the same flight to Tampa, Florida — a point beyond Atlanta — for $179. Thus, a San Franciscan bound for Atlanta could have saved $241 by buying a ticket to Tampa and simply leaving the plane at its first stop.

•

In the New York area, a forty-six-passenger bus equipped with a rest room will probably rent for $500 to $700 a day for transportation alone, depending on distance. Elsewhere the rates are probably cheaper.

•

Contrary to what seems to be popular opinion, American embassies and consulates are not travel agencies, law offices, Red Cross stations, banks, or hostels for the weary of foot and empty of pocket. Their staffs will not change hotel reservations, post bail, tend the sick, lend money, or provide sleeping bags to ease the discomfort of sleeping on their foyer floors. American travelers' expectations of what consuls can do can be extraordinarily high.

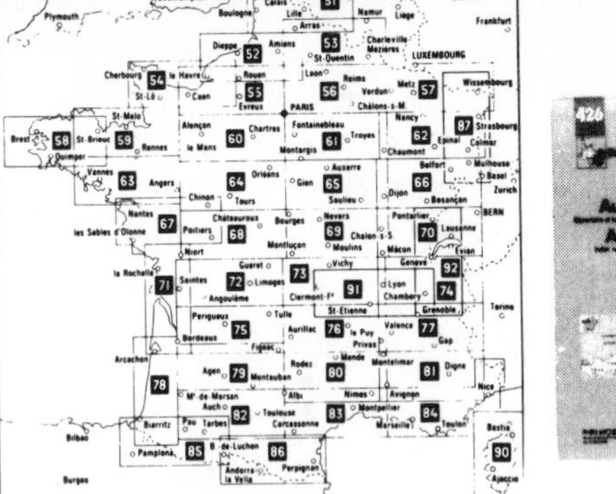

France: detailed maps $2.50 each. Order from Map Diagram by number (Lyon-Marseilles $3.95). —*Easy Going*

Easy Going • Nomadic Books

Two sources for hard-to-find travel guides to offbeat places in the world. Both stress budget travel, exploring on your own, and going by various modes — bicycle, foot, train.

***Easy Going** also offers a supplemental catalog of travel maps. Check with them for getting hold of maps of particularly obscure foreign locations.* —*Kevin Kelly*

•
Sanyo Rechargeable Shaver — Recharges on 110v and 220v. Small and lightweight. If fully charged, will perform for about 7/3-minute shaves. Comes with sideburn trimmer, cleaning brush and carrying case. Requires adapter plugs for foreign travel (see section on Converters & Adapters). $39.95

•
Holland — Is apparently the best place to buy a vehicle in Europe. Change of ownership is easy, and there are plenty for sale. An old VW van can still be had for $400; or $800 will get you a good one. —*Easy Going*

•
Galapagos — The Ecuadorian Navy offers the cheapest tours at U.S. $330 for an 11-day inclusive tour, five of the days at sea. Book these tours at its office, *Transnave*, Malecon 905, Guayaquil. If you prefer to travel independently, the cheapest way is to put your own food together and camp. Note that you're only allowed to camp in certain areas, and you must get permission first from the National Park Office. —*Nomadic Books*

Multinewspapers

Before leaving town on extended travel or moving to a new home, check out your destination by reading its local newspaper. Local newspapers fill in details like no other travel reading can, and you can get an idea of the most current prices for things from the ads. This service has great rates and a global selection. Their random selection service would be one way to spice up your mailbox. —*Bud Spurgeon*

Multinewspapers
Information **free** from:
Multinewspapers
Box DE
Dana Point, CA 92629

• One of the real ruiners of trips is dental trouble. There's a dental first aid kit that'll get you by on p. 215.

World Status Map

*It's always been unwise (though often possible) for international travelers to ignore political and economic difficulties in countries they visit; nowadays, increasingly volatile situations suggest that a little extra pretrip research may be in order. The **World Status Map** uses information from the State Department, World Health Organization, the National Center for Disease Control, and news services to produce a monthly report of travel advisories, warnings, war zones, and danger areas for travelers. Included along with a war-zone map is updated information on passport, visa, health, and other requirements around the world, which has never before been available from a single source.* —*Steve Cohen*

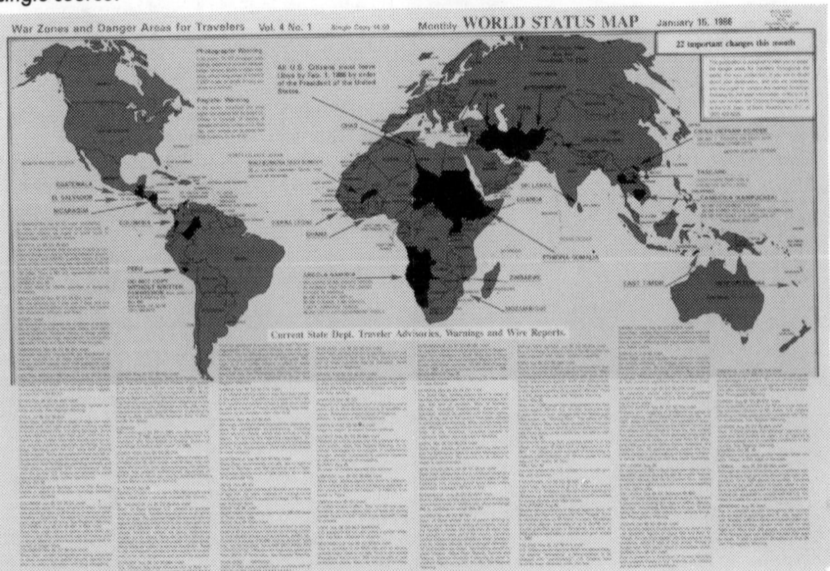

Easy Going Travel Source
Catalog **$2** from:
Easy Going
Travel Source
1400 Shattuck Avenue
Berkeley, CA 94709

Nomadic Books
Catalog **free** from:
Nomadic Books
201 NE 45th
Seattle, WA 98105

World Status Map
Earl May, Editor
Latest copy
$4.50 from:
World Status Map
Box 466
Merrifield, VA 22116

The Tropical Traveller

For lack of a better book on traveling in the tropics, I suggest this one. It's a little short on the effects of hot climate, equatorial terrain, and tropical disease, but it's long on the difficulties of zipping through materially poor societies, which, unfortunately, most tropical countries are these days. You get an honest picture of on-the-road life in an undeveloped country. —*KK*

•
Travellers should take an antiseptic cream. I would never travel without a tub of Savlon (which contains cetrimide). It is safe, soothing, cleansing, and non-greasy and is useful for a wide variety of skin ailments and sores, as well as the usual cuts and scratches. Even a sore anus, which is often caused by bad attacks of diarrhea, is soothed by this versatile cream. It is a good idea to take a few sachets of antiseptic wipes. You may have to cope with cuts (say on a bus trip in the Indian desert) when you can't find clean water.

'Travel with as little luggage as possible'

The Tropical Traveller
John Hatt
1985; 267 pp.
$2.95
(£ 3.30 postpaid)
from:
Pan Books, Ltd.
CS Department
P. O. Box 40
Basingstoke, Hants,
England

China
(A Travel Survival Kit)
Alan Samagalski
and Michael Buckley
1984; 819 pp.

$14.95
($15.95 postpaid) from:
Lonely Planet Publications
1555 D Park Avenue
Emeryville, CA 94608
or Whole Earth Access

China

Now that China's leaders have adopted a new "open door" policy towards the outside world, travel possibilities have loosened up in the People's Republic. Individuals can simply go to Hong Kong, pick up their own visas, and slip across the border. The main problem involved with this kind of solo travel has been that without a guide it is often difficult to find one's way around the country, since few people speak fluent English. Here's 800 pages of help for anyone who wants to know how to take buses, boats, and trains on their own, where to find inexpensive lodging, and how to get outside the deep ruts left by the juggernaut of tours now swamping China. The guide's two Australian authors have written a witty, up-to-date, and enormously informative guide for adventuresome people (like themselves) who want to travel about China and Tibet as the spirit moves them. —Orville Schell

•

It's worth hanging onto cheap room or dormitory hotel receipts — the fact that you've been allowed to stay cheaply at some other hotel will weigh in your favour at the next place you're trying to get cheap accommodation. Likewise, hang on to any Chinese-price tickets you happen to buy.

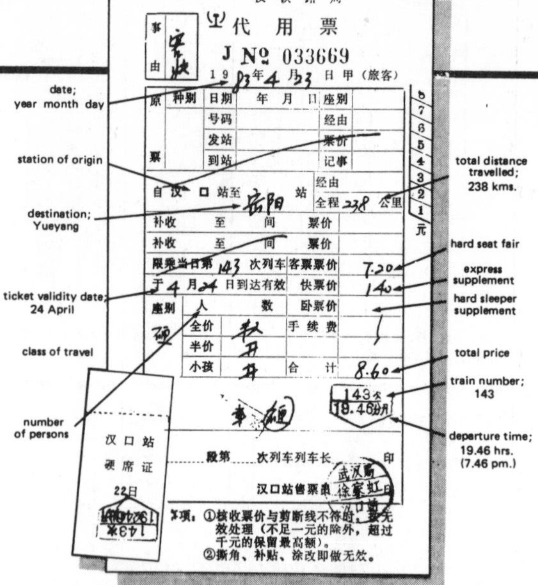

***Deciphering a train ticket:* This tourist-price rail ticket (above right) is for a hard seat on Train No. 143 from Wuhan to Yueyang. The train travels a total distance of 238 railway KM and the ticket is valid for two days. Total price is Y8.60, of which Y1.40 is the express train supplement. The triangular-bottomed stamp in the bottom right-hand corner of the ticket shows the train number and the time of departure.**

The 1986 South American Handbook
John Brooks, Editor
1986; 1325 pp.

$25.95
($30.95 postpaid) from:
Rand McNally Retail Store
23 East Madison Street
Chicago, IL 60602
or Whole Earth Access

The South American Handbook

This small, hardbound, fine print book is absolutely packed with information on South and Central America, the Caribbean, and Mexico. For each country there are maps, information on climate, geography, history, food, holidays, and best of all, city by city and town by town — how to get around, what to see, and where to stay and eat. Furthermore, the **Handbook** *isn't just for ricos. It includes listings for good 50¢ meals and two dollar a night hotels with hot water. For most of us, the "how to get around" information is most valuable: what bus lines to take (and which to avoid), which border crossings are easiest, what to expect on long train rides (pack food), and which little airlines go where.* —Lynn Meisch

•

Travel in Bogota, Colombia: Flag buses down; no stops to speak of. Bus fares are US$0.15, *busetas* charge US $0.30. Green buses saying TSS (i.e. unsubsidized) are more expensive. Urban buses are not good for sightseeing because if standing — as likely as not — you can't see out. Most scenic route, is 149 "Capilla — via La Calera," which starts on Cra 14 (Av. Caracas) with Calle 68 and goes up into the mountains to the east of the city. A metro is under consideration.

A Guide to Trekking in Nepal
Stephen Bezruchka
1985; 352 pp.

$10.95
postpaid from:
The Mountaineers
306 Second Avenue West
Seattle, WA 98119
or Whole Earth Access

A Guide to Trekking in Nepal

You can hike in the Himalayas on your own, without porters, without a tent, without carrying food, for less than $5 per day with this book as your only guide. Wearing dumpy running shoes, I used it to walk to the base camp of Mt. Everest and beyond to rarely visited valleys, without getting lost. —KK

Swings are set up around the festival of DasAAI.

Getting a haircut in Tatopani.

• The best guides to Africa.

Africa on a Shoestring: Geoff Crowther, 1983; 368 pp. **$14.95** ($15.95 postpaid) from Lonely Planet Publications, 1555 D Park Avenue, Emeryville, CA 94608 (or Whole Earth Access).

Backpacker's Africa: Hillary Bradt, 1983; 193 pp. **$11.95** ($13.95 postpaid) from Bradt Enterprises, 93 Harvey Street, Apt. 8, Cambridge, MA 02140.

South Pacific Handbook • Indonesia Handbook

A sumptuous feast of detail. On one page, a map of the routes of Fiji passenger ships; on another, the stamps of the Solomon Islands; on another, the cost of the hot dogs in Honiara. Essentials, bonuses: all here, all extraordinarily accurate and up-to-date. In American Samoa, where I live, **South Pacific Handbook** *has scooped even the most inventive island travelers. The best guidebook this road junkie has seen anywhere.*

Even more than for its accuracy or its graphics, I value this book for its ethics. On the first page, Stanley stresses that his is a book for the traveler, not the tourist. He decries the tourism that debases, distorts, and leeches upon the traditional island cultures. He lists in the book the basic facilities used by the people themselves. He urges open exchange between traveler and host: "You not only learn more and spend less but you actually become part of the country while you're there." I only wish more guides were as sensitive to the impact of their words.

There is a companion guide called the **Indonesia Handbook** *— worth checking into if you're headed that way.*
—Robert Brock

•

Mauke: There's a good beach on the E side at Arapaea landing, but the best beaches are on the S side of the island. Especially inviting is the beach at Anaokae, where a long stretch of clean white sand rings a green lagoon. This piece of paradise is flanked by rugged limestone cliffs, and backed by palm, pine, and pandanus. A short track leads down to the beach. No one lives on the S or E sides of Mauke, so these fine secluded beaches are ideal for those who want to be completely alone. There's good reef walking at low tide on the W side of Mauke.

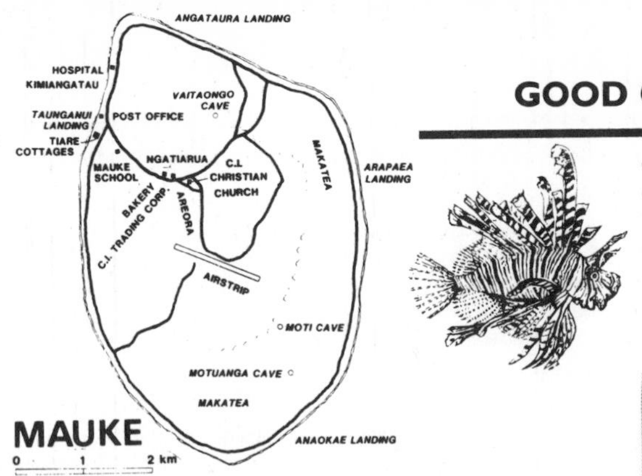

The zebra or lionfish (Pterois volitans) is among the most toxic in the Pacific. Its striking red coloration and long spines may be nature's warning.

South Pacific Handbook
David Stanley
1986; 578 pp.
$13.95
($15.20 postpaid)

Indonesia Handbook
Bill Dalton
1985; 602 pp.
$12.95
($14.20 postpaid)
Both from:
Moon Publications
P. O. Box 1696
Chico, CA 95927
or Whole Earth Access

Let's Go: Europe

Each summer a select band of Harvard students tramps Europe rewriting the next edition of this reliable classic. It's a two-decade-old tradition that requires them to completely revise and dazzlingly outdo the previous edition. Even if you are not intending to zoom around the entire continent, buy this rotund book and razor-blade out the sections you won't get to, keeping what you need. You'll still have the most economical guide to economical hotels and eating places in Europe you can get. Lively and accurate. They did their homework well. A-plus job.

The Harvard students have an expanding line of country-specific guides (Italy, Greece, etc.), equally dependable.
—KK [Suggested by Walt Noiseaux]

•

Finding a place to sleep in Segovia [Spain] is seldom a problem, even in August, since so many travelers mistakenly limit Segovia to a daytrip. The area surrounding Plaza Mayor has the highest concentration of places.

Albergue Juvenil, Paseo Conde de Sepulveda (tel. 42 00 27). An unofficial hostel. A great place to stay — quiet, uncrowded, close to town, few rules, and no lockout. 325ptas [about $2.50]. Open July-Aug.

Casa de Huespedes Velarde, Pl. de Guevara, 3 (tel. 43 16 99), near the Trinidad Church. Flowers on the windowsills and the cheapest in town — arrive early. Singles 500ptas [about $4.50], doubles 900ptas. Showers 125 ptas.

Let's Go
(The Budget Guide to Europe)
Harvard Student Agencies, Inc.
1986; 841 pp.
$10.95
($12.45 postpaid) from:
St. Martin's Press
175 5th Avenue
New York, NY 10010
or Whole Earth Access

The People's Guide to Mexico

The best 360° coverage of traveling and short term living in Mexico that's going. Reading the book is almost like being there and going through the problems, pleasures and wonders of dealing with a new environment, new people and new ways of doing things. But by golly every page, every step of the way you're learning something. Carl is candid, and leaves few, if any, questions unanswered in telling you how to handle just about everything: border crossing, driving in Mexico, public transportation, hitching, camping, indigenous living (living on the beach, building a hut, stove, digging a well, etc.) and scrounging for food, renting a house, legal hassles, communication services, car repairs, the language and customs, cantinas and whorehouses, buying things, and so forth. A fantastic book and well written. *—Al Perrin*

This book has probably compelled more people to visit Mexico than all the travel agents in the world combined. Although updated recently, you won't find the usual menu of prices, hotel names, and places to see; you'll need a different kind of guidebook for that. *—KK*

•

The Mexican custom of packing up the entire family for a Christmas or Easter vacation at the beach has created a large number of rental houses and apartments designed for groups. These are generally known as *bungalos* and *cabanas*. Because most are fully equipped, from linen to kitchen utensils, they can be ideal for the foreign tourist. This is especially true for people with children, who don't want to be cooped up with them in a hotel room or forced to rent two rooms to get a little privacy.

Building a palapa.

The People's Guide to Mexico
Carl Franz
1986; 624 pp.
$10.95
($12.70 postpaid) from:
John Muir Publications
P. O. Box 613
Santa Fe, NM 87504
or Whole Earth Access

• Before leaving on any trip you may want to read **Zen and the Art of Motorcycle Maintenance** (p. 385) just to get loosened up.

• For a real trip, cruise your VW bus through the Sahara. Here's how.
Sahara Handbook: Simon and Jan Glen, 1980; 316 pp. **$29.95** ($31.95 postpaid) from Bradt Enterprises, 93 Harvey Street, Apt. 8, Cambridge, MA 02140.

Earthwatch Research Expeditions

Want to participate in a real scientific expedition? You can by joining one sponsored by this group. Yeah, you have to pay instead of them paying you, but many agree that the money is well spent — you'll learn a lot (including how to do an expedition). Looks interesting! You have to be between 16 and 75 years old. —JB

•

Field conditions: Sturdy volunteers will dig in the cut and around the unexplained building, carefully brush skeletons clean, draw finds, and wash pottery. The team will live and eat in a Spartan 17th-century hall at the Repton School, a two-minute walk from the site (rooms for married couples are available). The school's staff will prepare all meals. The hard work this summer will pay off in tangible and potentially very exciting finds about early monastic, royal, and Viking life at Repton. *Related interests: European history, anatomy, pottery, mapmaking.*

"Frogs' legs?" Two volunteers sort through the herons' and egrets' typical menu.

Earthwatch Research Expeditions
Membership
$25/year
(includes 4 issues of Earthwatch Magazine)
Information **free** from:
Earthwatch
680 Mount Auburn Street
P. O. Box 403
Watertown, MA 02172

The Adventurous Traveler's Guide • Mountain Travel

An unusually wide range of trips and unusually inviting catalog distinguish Mountain Travel among the many new adventure-brokers. Their mouth-watering catalog has swelled into this fat informative book. You go on a couple of these organized trips and pretty soon you're organizing your own. —Stewart Brand

After a three-day visit to Lhasa, capital of Tibet, we drive for two days by truck to southeastern Tibet, arriving by road at Namche Barwa Base Camp at 9,000 feet.

A camel trek in the Flinders [Australia] is a leisurely experience — riding saddles are available every day. The weather is warm and sunny with cold, crisp nights. We sleep in "swags" at night (bed rolls on stretchers or mattresses).

What's nifty about this catalog is that the treks offered are possible — people are actually doing this now. Each trip is detailed day by day. There are maps of the routes, and suggestions for further reading. Dates of departure and prices, too. Going with Mountain Travel on one of these is a good way to get into an unfamiliar locale, and may be more pleasant than your own struggles. Bye. —JB

I study this thoroughly as I plan my own trips because I figure their leaders have scouted the area for the most interesting routes and if they can move a dozen desk-bound tourists with luggage along it, I can do it myself with a backpack. —KK

Adventurous Traveler's Guide
Leo Le Bon
1985; 174 pp.
$14.95 postpaid from:
Simon & Schuster
Mail Order Sales
200 Old Tappan
Old Tappan, NJ 07675
or Whole Earth Access

Mountain Travel
Abbreviated catalog
$2 from:
Mountain Travel
1398 Solano Avenue
Albany, CA 94706

A Connoisseur's Guide

Although I've never joined a hired adventure tour, I have many friends who've gone to some of my favorite exotic places that way, and they had nearly as good a time as I did. The adventures you can buy are quite sophisticated — very small groups, highly informed guides, experienced schedules, and lots of choices. To aid shopping among these choices, check out this paper database of 2,000 unusual trips led by pro guides. You select a journey by place, by mode (bicycle, canoe, hiking, etc.) and by the date it all happens. Say, for example, you dream of cruising in a four-wheel-drive through the Sahara in January. Well, you've got a couple of possibilities here. Hope they keep it updated. —KK

TRIP PROFILES — WILDLIFE SAFARIS 167

Company	GameTrackers International Inc.	InnerAsia	InnerAsia	InnerAsia
Mode of Transportation	4WD, Plane	Coach, 4WD	Coach, 4WD	4WD, On Foot, Canoe
Name of Trip	Okavango	Adventure in Paradise	In Search of Royal Bengal Tiger	Wilderness and Wildlife of Nepal
Location	Okavango Delta	Various Game Parks	Various Parks and Reserves	Royal Bardiya Wildlife Reserve
City State Country	Victoria Falls Zimbabwe	Colombo Sri Lanka	Delhi India	Kathmandu Nepal
Duration, Days Distance Elevation	5	16	19	19
Trip Month	J F M A M J J A S O N D	J F M A M J J A S O N D	J F M A M J J A S O N D	J F M A M J J A S O N D
Cost	P1328*	$1075	$2340	$1730
Degree of Difficulty	Open	Open	Open	Open
Baggage Carried By	Vehcile	Vehicle	Vehicle	Vehicle
Meals Lodging	Included Camp, Lodge	Some Included Hotel	Some Included Camp, Hotel, Lodge	Included Camp, Hotel, Lodge
Comments	*Botswana Pula - Physically Handicapped, Seniors, Dietary	Seniors, Dietary	Seniors, Dietary	Seniors, Dietary

• You can also see some world as a student. See "Learning Abroad" (p. 375).

• For good travel gear, see pp. 274-275.

A Connoisseur's Guide
Suzi Kobrin
1985; 325 pp.
$19.95
($21.95 postpaid) from:
ZappoDel Inc.
P. O. Box 1049
Del Mar, CA 92014
or Whole Earth Access

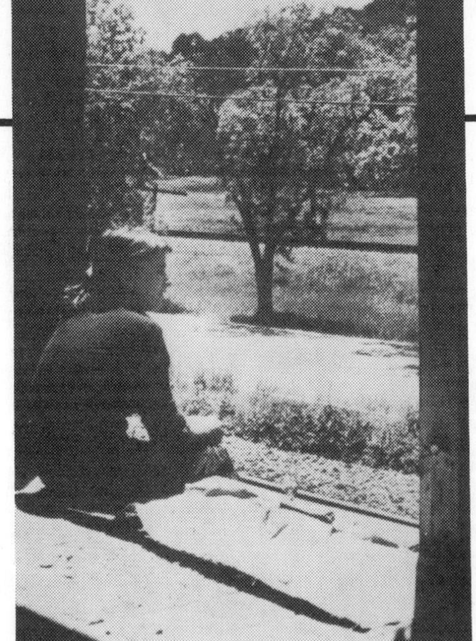

A fringe benefit of freighthopping: aesthetic enjoyment.

The Freighthopper's Manual for North America

Making a big comeback with college age. "Yeah Ma, I'll be home for Thanksgiving. Uh, no I don't know when I'll be getting in." Cheap travel, real adventures, often good company. Some lines and yards are still too hot, but many a railroad is operated largely by aging hippies these days, who will help you. A fine little book, all you need.
—Stewart Brand

•

When you're running on the ground you're in one frame of reference, and when you're in the boxcar you're in another. But when you're leaving one and not yet in the other — that's reality!

The Freighthopper's Manual for North America
Daniel Leen
1981; 95 pp.

$6.95
($7.95 postpaid) from:
Daniel Leen
P. O. Box 191
Seattle, WA 98111
or Whole Earth Access

Hitchhiking, the homilies

Use a sign. Have a map.

Look like who you want to pick you up.

Wait where it's easy for drivers to see you and stop.

Be of use to the driver, or at least no bother.

Don't take it personally when they don't pick you up. See it as their problem.

Stay on the curb, and off freeways. Don't rob or murder or rape anybody; it makes it hard for the rest of us.
—Stewart Brand

Hitch A Yacht

by Peter Moree, at Sea (Mediterranean)

I live aboard my steel 36-foot ketch and sailed around the world of late, hence my story: There's an easy way to hitch rides on yachts from ocean to ocean.

Every year about 700 yachts sail from Europe to the Caribbean and approximately 300 sail from the U.S. west coast to Tahiti, etc. Generally these yachts go away for a year but a small percentage continue around the world. About 60 to 80 yachts cross the Indian Ocean each year.

Yachts are almost always crewed by couples or men only and are short of crew for the longer passages. No experience is necessary, just taking turns in keeping lookout for big ships (call your skipper when in doubt).

I've sailed from Europe via Panama to such places as Easter Island, Tonga, Australia, Indonesia, Sri Lanka, Jakarta, Sudan, etc. To get to some places the *only* way is by private boat.

Yachts travel with the trade winds preferably and also in warm climates. This means they go *west.* Most land travelers go via Boeing 747 and go *east.* Here might be a conflict.

How to find yachts: Cruising yachts generally have the following characteristics (nice when you're looking around in Los Angeles): Foreign flags, windvane steering gear, generally sturdy appearance, laundry of the people who *live* on board hung out to dry.

Cost: Share food costs. This seems normal. I charged $50 a week for food and lodging and took care of all harbor dues, oil, propane, etc. Some people still think this is expensive. (Nobody realizes that with depreciation, insurance, maintenance, and operating expenses, my boat ends up costing $50 a day.)

The best way to approach a skipper is to state that you're not the seasick type (check this out) and have money to share food *and* money to travel home in case of emergency. Show your proof in traveler's checks. Generally be helpful with work, cooking, etc. on board. With a bit of luck, a good skipper will teach you the ropes as well as navigation. Go for a week's trial if the route and time permit.

Leave the boat at the appointed end of your joyride. The ship is also the skipper's home and, as you will experience, affords little privacy. Boating is the last freedom left, but hassles with official permits, paperwork, visas, etc. are getting worse, especially in the so-called "free world." Still, it is beautiful to share the experience. And we do need more ladies out here (adventurous types naturally). ■

Yacht hitching on the Leopard Normand III.

Vagabonding in the USA
Ed Buryn
1983; 424 pp.
$10.95
($12 postpaid) from:
Ed Buryn
P. O. Box 31123
San Francisco, CA 94131
or Whole Earth Access

The Hot Springs Gazette
Suzanne Hackett, Editor
$12/year (issued spasmodically) from:
The Hot Springs Gazette
P. O. Box 61
Burbank, CA 91503

The New Improved Good Book of Hot Springs
George W. Berry et al.
1984; 99 pp.
$4.95
($5.70 postpaid) from:
The Doodly-Squat Press
P. O. Box 480740
Los Angeles, CA 90048

Vagabonding in the USA

Without hyperbole, there is no country in the world better suited to vagabonding than the USA. We are, in a real sense, a nation of vagabonds, without roots. This book is a nonstop encyclopedia of vagabonding visions, methods and tips by a master gypsy. It's about finding a shower along the way, hopping small airplanes, travelling back roads, being free, and looking at America like you never lived here before (and if you haven't, this book is perfect for foreign visitors). It's about possibilities.

—*Kevin Kelly*

•

If you don't know you're going, you're there.

—*Anonymous*

•

The thesis of this book is that traveling on the loose and on the cheap is about the least boring way to spend your time. Not knowing where you're going, you pay more attention to where you are, wherever that is. This time it's the U.S.A., a place you'd better pay attention to.

•

Time Versus Money: We say that time is money, meaning both are valuable. Both are a form of power. Usually there is a reciprocal relationship between them; that is, abundance of money seems to go along with shortage of time, and abundance of time with shortage of money. Money is the wealth of the materialist, and works miracles in the realm of the physical. Time is the wealth of the pilgrim, and works miracles in all realms.

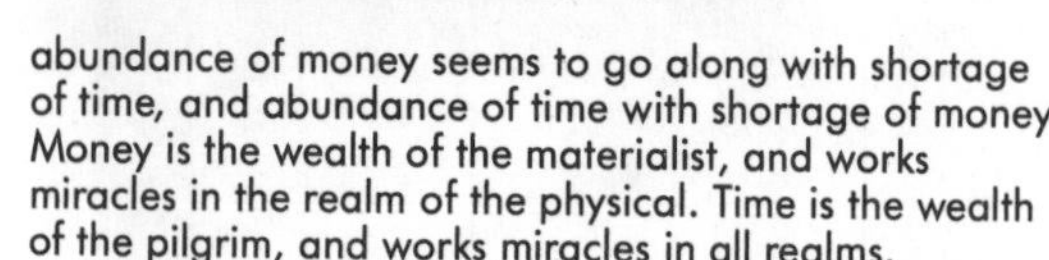

•

Stop and ask someone if they know of an inexpensive place to stay. The key to doing this successfully is in picking the right person to ask. If you're a student or young person, ask someone who looks like you. Frequently, another good person to ask is a policeman. Often he'll be familiar with the worst places, and can steer you away from those, at least. Ask him about bunking in the city jail for a night; this often works, especially in small towns. Cab drivers are also good sources.

•

Credit cards, the sure sign of being middle class, are more useful to vagabonds than anyone else. They may brand you as being bourgeois, but look at it this way: you probably are. Vagabonds sometimes sport an air of irresponsibility; they sometimes need to prove their respectability, or bail themselves out of a jam. For this, a credit card is a sure winner. Moreover, simply *owning* one doesn't cost you anything. No matter how I travel, I always bring at least one of the three major kinds of credit cards: oil-company card, bank card, and executive card.

Hot Springs Gazette • New Improved Good Book of Hot Springs

"Stalking the Wild Hot Springs" might be an appropriate subtitle for these funky periodic booklets. The game is to find out and get into one of the thousands of undeveloped wild hot springs that hide in yonder hinterlands (look for a plume of steam on the horizon). It's not as easy as it sounds and that makes for good adventure.

These booklets are directories to known hot spots, complete with reports from sundry hotspringers who have actually dipped in, on where the waters are, how to get there from your car, what the bottom is like, what the temperature is, is anybody around? There's also lots of questing stories and poolside yarns about stalking the Ultimate Wild Bath. Occasionally there are testimonies of soaks in extra-national hot springs, but in the main, access is to North American baths.

For rediscovering the many untamed hot springs not mentioned by other sources, you'll need ***The Good Book****, a geological listing of all known hot springs west of Kansas. The data was compiled by George Berry et al., and printed by the government. Not to be confused with an earlier, less comprehensive list by Gerald Ashley Waring, also printed by the government and warmly known as the Good Book, now out of print. Berry's list gives the map coordinates and topo map name where each spring is found (they are still remarkably arduous to locate). Many of the entries are merely boiling trickles. The editor of* ***Hot Springs Gazette*** *chattily comments on the bathable springs.*

—*Kevin Kelly*

Gila Monster

•

New Mexico:

Turkey Creek Hot Springs. 4 stars. Near the town of Gila. See map. Plan to do no work on the natural soaking pools; they're ready and waiting. The drive into the area will discourage most sightseers — 12 miles of dirt road. Don't try this trip in the late spring or early summer unless you are prepared to drown in the floodwaters of the Gila River. At any other time, preferably summer to late fall, park at the Gila River crossing and begin your 3.5 mile hike. Cross the river and head East to a private ranch, then North along Turkey Creek. Enjoy the 3 or 4 creek crossings, waterfall, and 12-foot deep pool in the creek. Rest thy weary bones, hiker!

—*The Hot Springs Gazette*

• See also **Walden** (p. 184) for lessons in thriftiness.

• Traveling across America ain't new. For a natural and human history along one popular highway see this book. **Adventures On and Off Interstate Eighty:** Eleanor Huggins and John Olmsted, **$12.95** ($14.45 postpaid) from William Kaufmann, Inc., 95 First Street, Los Altos, CA 94022.

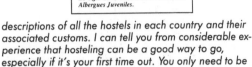

The logo of the French Youth Hostel Association./*Le sigle de la Féderation Française Unie des Auberges de Jeunesse.*/Das Zeichen des französischen Jugendherbergsverbandes./*La sigla de la Federación Francesa de Albergues Juveniles.*

International Youth Hostels

A membership in the American Youth Hostels lets you stay at more than 200 inexpensive hostels in the U.S. and something like 5,000 more around the world. You'll meet all sorts of other travellers, exchange lies, make alliances, and perhaps modify your plans after hearing of some more interesting option from someone who's just been there. The two international handbooks have some mediocre general tips on trip planning and travel, but their main use will be the comprehensive listing and descriptions of all the hostels in each country and their associated customs. I can tell you from considerable experience that hosteling can be a good way to go, especially if it's your first time out. You only need to be young at heart; all ages are welcome. —JB

International Youth Hostels: 1 year membership (valid in 62 countries); **$20** (Information **free**).
American Youth Hostels Handbook: 255 pages; **$5** ($7 postpaid); **free** with AYH membership.
International Youth Hostel Handbook: (Volume 1: Europe and Mediterranean) 1986; 325 pp.; (Volume 2: Africa, America, Asia, Australasia); 1986; 186 pp. **$6.95** each ($8.95 postpaid).

All from American Youth Hostels, Inc., P. O. Box 37613, Washington, DC 20013.

HIROSHIMA

Hiroshima
(3) (a) Hiroshima YH, 1–13–6, Ushita-shin-machi, Hiroshima-shi, 730. 104 Hiroshima Ushita-shin-machi 1-chome, 8 min ☎ 082–221–5343.
(13) (b) **J** Hiroshima Sakamachi YH, Ueda, Sakamachi, Hiroshima-shi-kōgai, 731–43. 25 Saka 30 min, Hiroshima Saka-ueda, 15 min ☎ 082–885–0700.
(15) (c) **J** Higashi Hiroshima YH, 3148 Hara, Happonmatsu-machi, Higashi Hiroshima-shi, 739–01. 27 Happonmatsu Nogyo-Shikenjo, 3 min ☎ 0824–29–0305.

—International Youth Hostel Handbook

International Home Exchanges

Swap houses for a real adventure. With the assistance of these services you exchange homes with someone living in (and somewhat tired of) your vacation destination. Your home then becomes their vacation place. This possibly unpredictable deal is made as fail-safe as possible by several directories chock-full of homes around the world with photos, specifications, and a little data about the owners. Two of the services (Home Exchange International and Global Home Exchange Service) do not publish directories — instead for a fee they pick a place to your specs, then arrange and guarantee the swap.

Either way, you not only get a place to stay but also instant, knowledgeable neighbors. To swap successfully I recommend early planning. —Kevin Kelly

•

No hotel tab at the end of your vacation is just one of the benefits of exchanging. You can cut down on restaurant costs by cooking your own meals, and you can frequently include a car in your exchange. "Exchangers" give each other helpful hints that only a native can give about where to go or not to go; where to shop and where to play. Friends and neighbors can sometimes be called upon as hosts. The worries about your vacant home being robbed, your plants or even your pets being properly cared for are greatly reduced. *—Intervac*

Global Home Exchange Service: information **free** from P. O. Box 2015, South Burlington, VT 05401-2015.

Travel Companion Exchange: information **free** from P. O. Box 833, Amityville, NY 11701.

Vacation Exchange Club: Two-volume directory **$16**, information **free** from 12006 111th Avenue, Unit 12, Youngtown, AZ 85363.

Intervac: $45/year with your home listed, **$60** without (3 issues), from International Home Exchange Service/Intervac U.S., P. O. Box 3975, San Francisco, CA 94119.

Home Exchange International: information **free** from 185 Park Row, Suite 14D, New York, NY 10038.

Interservice Home Exchange: $24/year with home listing; **$18**/year without. Information **free** from P. O. Box 87, Glen Echo, MD 20812.

►

Ireland: IRL027 R Dublin: Hilary Kelly, 2ad/f4,m12,10. Drogheda, Co.Louth. *—Intervac*

►

Germany: M, 7821 Grafenhausen, Gregor Nunier, Berlinersts, 36, 7809 Denzlingen (07666-5910) ret. government official. *—Intervac*

Ireland.

Germany.

International Workcamp Directory

For more than 60 years, since WWI ended, International Workcamps have provided a way for people to think globally and act locally. Last summer there were more than 2000 of these two four-week camps in Europe alone, not counting those in Russia, Turkey and Nicaragua. In fact, the catalog says they are the "only sizable medium of citizen exchange across the Iron Curtain." The camps run in the summer only and do good-works type projects — you'll exercise your muscles a lot. The rules are: you donate your labor, pay for your own travel, and you don't have to speak a foreign language. They take care of everything else.

—Richard Nilsen

•

Zbroslawice Riding Camp, Poland. 10 volunteers

Work on the student horseback riding center doing carpentry, cleaning and grooming the horses. Volunteers will be able to horseback ride daily. The camp is located in the Upper Silesia Region, near Tarnowskie Gory in the countryside.

•

Ecological camp, Finland. 15 - 17 volunteers

Karttula, near Kuopio. There is an ecological project started some years ago in Karttula municipality in the village of Syvanniemi. The authorities support experiments which try to use products of nature, for example, herbs and plants, honey, birch sap. The volunteers will build a structure to dry herbs and to gather different kinds of herbs. Some time will be used for cleaning and repairing the houses where the campers dwell.

International Workcamp Directory
Annual membership
$10/year
(includes current Directory); newsletter **free** from:
Volunteers For Peace
Tiffany Road
Belmont, VT 05730

• You'll need to get your youth hostel card in your own country before you travel overseas. You can renew it each year as you travel. You might also ask the U.S. passport office for a passport with extra pages on it (no extra cost) if you're headed out for a long trip. Carry a bunch of extra passport photos for visas, too.

Work Your Way Around the World

Work Your Way Around the World
Susan Griffith
1983; 292 pp.
$10.95
($12.95 postpaid) from:
Writers' Digest Books
9933 Alliance Road
Cincinnati, OH 45242
or Whole Earth Access

This book should help you find work overseas if what you have in mind is odd jobs or seasonal work. The lucrative gigs are landed in Europe and North America. There's little that can be predicted about more exotic corners like Africa and Asia, but what is known has been rounded up here. What you really want to know, of course, is how much you can make. This is nicely covered together with working conditions, seasons, and addresses when possible.

Usual employers that hire travelers are described in much detail — all you need to know about picking apples in Australia, for instance. Honest first-hand accounts by other workers who have survived overseas employment keep the Ultimate Romance strapped into reality. —KK

•

Apple-picking is notoriously unrewarding for the beginner. Claire Mansfield picked apples for one day in March near Myrtleford, Victoria, Australia. After working with a partner for six hours, three bins of apples had been filled. The piece rate was $7.50 for one bin. Neither room nor board was provided so they gave it up as hopeless though if they had stayed longer their speed could certainly have increased. . . .

Rob Kay did much better in the apple harvest around Donnybrook and Manjimup in Western Australia. By his seventh week of apple-picking (early May) he was able to fill 28 bins at $9 per bin, in 7 hard days of work. He stayed with the harvest for a full ten weeks and easily earned enough for his air fare to London. He doubled his speed between the first and last days, so his perseverance was rewarded.

International Employment Hotline

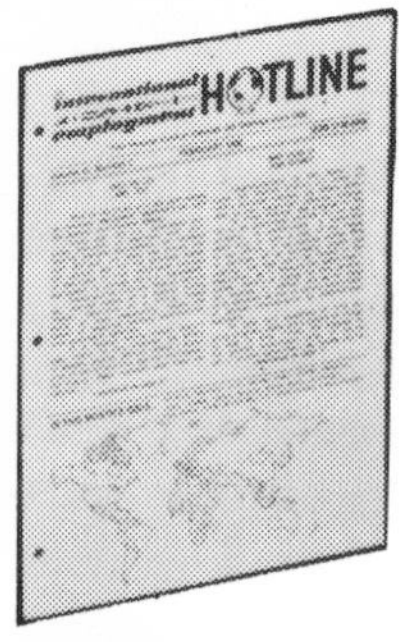
HOTLINE

International Employment Hotline
Will Cantrell, Editor
$26/year
(12 issues) from:
International Employment Hotline
P. O. Box 6170
McLean, VA 22106

There are two ways to work your way around the world. One is to travel until you meet a job you like, then stick with it until you're rich enough to breeze across the border to the next one. (See ***Work Your Way Around the World****.) The other, more sure, is to bank on a skill you have and sign yourself up before you leave. Inflexible employees picture overseas "assignments" as hardship; should you have an opposite view check out this newsletter — a monthly summary of international opportunities. It's an honest, up-to-date bulletin board of employers with specific needs for people or bunches of people. The jobs are real. You contact the potential boss yourself from the address and phone number printed in the newsletter. Any skill you have is needed somewhere, including the remarkable ability to speak English. Most overseas jobs of this type require you to stay two years. That's just enough time to stash away a comfortable pile of dough, exhaust the local pleasures, and be ready to move on.* —KK

•

EGYPT *Publications Director* — for divisions of the American University in Cairo Press, including AUC publications, AUC printshop, the University bookstore and duplicating center. Applicants should have broad management experience in publishing, good administrative abilities and an entrepreneurial spirit. The AUC, 866 United Nations Plaza Rm. 517, New York, NY 10017.

•

INDONESIA Specify the job title and job number, and send your resume to: Mr. Leo Michael, c/o Resources Management International, Inc., 2000 L Street NW, Suite 200, Washington, D.C. 20036.

Electrical Design Engineer — with BSCE and strong background in AC/DC control, circuits, materials and class, pertaining to petroleum industry installations. Experience in instrumentation control and design applicable to petroleum production and shipping operations is also required. Job #851216.

•

JAPAN *English Teacher* — to set up curriculum and teach conversational English to employees of leading hi-tech firm. Applicants must be state certified. Will be based in Japan for 2 year contract. Send resume to: Sumitomo Electric USA, Inc., 551 Madison Ave., New York, NY 10022.

How to Be an Importer and Pay for Your World Travel

Just what the title says. The whole story is in this readable and wise book. —KK

COMMERCIAL LETTER OF CREDIT

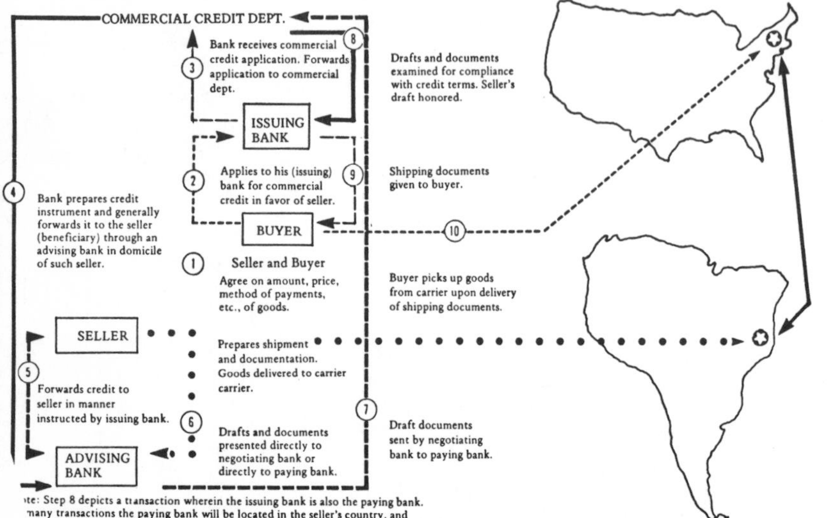
COMMERCIAL CREDIT DEPT.
8
3
Bank receives commercial credit application. Forwards application to commercial dept.
ISSUING BANK
Drafts and documents examined for compliance with credit terms. Seller's draft honored.
2
Applies to his (issuing) bank for commercial credit in favor of seller.
9
Shipping documents given to buyer.
4
Bank prepares credit instrument and generally forwards it to the seller (beneficiary) through an advising bank in domicile of such seller.
BUYER
10
1
Seller and Buyer
Agree on amount, price, method of payments, etc., of goods.
Buyer picks up goods from carrier upon delivery of shipping documents.
SELLER
Prepares shipment and documentation. Goods delivered to carrier carrier.
5
Forwards credit to seller in manner instructed by issuing bank.
6
Drafts and documents presented directly to negotiating bank or directly to paying bank.
7
Draft documents sent by negotiating bank to paying bank.
ADVISING BANK

ıte: Step 8 depicts a transaction wherein the issuing bank is also the paying bank. nany transactions the paying bank will be located in the seller's country, and r payment at that point, the draft and documents would be sent to the issuing bank designated in step 2.

•

Many small museums have shops attached to them with items for sale from all over the world. You may be able to interest them in some of your purchases. The people working there most frequently are easy to approach as they are often there in a volunteer capacity. We find such people often have a real interest in the store and its merchandise.

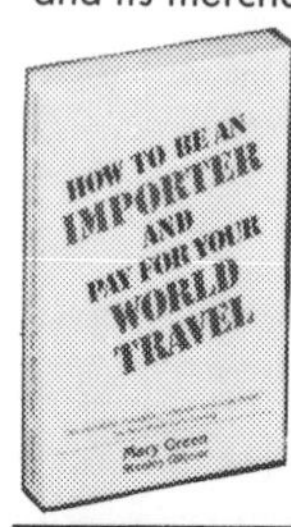
HOW TO BE AN
IMPORTER
AND
PAY FOR YOUR
WORLD
TRAVEL

How to Be an Importer and Pay for Your World Travel
Mary Green
and Stanley Gillmar
1979; 182 pp.
$6.95
($8.20 postpaid) from:
Celestial Arts
P. O. Box 7123
Berkeley, CA 94707
or Whole Earth Access

• Before getting into importing or any other business, you should do some reading selected from the small business books on pp. 191-193.

Today English plays a part in most tests. Parents start their children's language training early. Children's English *buysyibans* are scattered all over Taipei and pay English teachers quite well, as much as NT$400 (US $10) an hour, plus providing a Chinese teaching assistant to keep the kids in line.

Transitions Abroad

A guide to independent and educational travel that consists almost entirely of articles and travel tips sent in by its traveling readers. It's usually about 60 pages long, printed on newsprint. The format and the writing are generally unpolished, but the articles are interesting, informative, and very timely. There are lots of specific addresses to help the traveler find work, classes, or any number of other situations all over the world. A number of inexpensive charter flights and other groups providing cheap transportation also advertise regularly. ***Transitions'*** *articles are often about Africa, Asia, and a lot of the less-touristed parts of the world as well as Europe and the more popular tourist spots.* —*Steve Dunnington*

•

Studying Chinese in Taiwan
On Taiwan foreign students don't have to live in dorms, tuition is cheap and when money runs low one can drop out of class for a month or two without changing visa status. In addition, there are several schools to choose from. The only disadvantage is that the Chinese on Taiwan speak heavily accented Mandarin. Would you study Oxford English in *Joisy City*? . . .

Unquestionably, the best school on the island is the Inter-University Program for Chinese Studies in Taipei. The other Mandarin centers on the island fall short of the standards set by IUP. Shop around. Even after carefully choosing one of them, getting a teacher that suits one's needs is a bit like playing Russian roulette.

The problem may lie in the Chinese concept of education. The Chinese don't study, they *shou jyau-yu*, literally "receive learning." Foreign students often end up in a small room with an instructor who wants him to blindly recite from a book, hardly a method for developing active language skills. Students also complain that teachers give few corrections. If you find yourself in either situation ask for a new teacher.

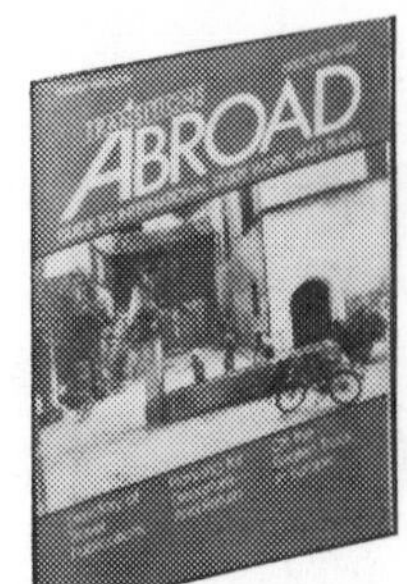

Transitions Abroad
Clayton A. Hubbs, Editor
$15/year
(6 issues) from:
Transitions Abroad
P. O. Box 344
Amherst, MA 01004

Living in the U.S.A.

An astonishing book. Though it's written for foreigners planning to travel or work in the U.S. — and serves that purpose splendidly — I would recommend it most strongly to Americans who are planning to travel elsewhere or are expecting to deal routinely with foreign visitors. Americans are very odd. Everybody else is expending considerable effort to treat us as if we were human beings. It is well to know the details of what they are putting up with and, by implication, what is normal for the rest of humanity. —*Stewart Brand*

•

INFORMALITY
Although American informality is well known, many interpret it as a lack of respect when they first encounter it, especially in the business world. The almost immediate use of first names, for example, jars on nerves long accustomed to deference or respect from men of lower rank.

Don't be surprised if Americans do not shake hands. They often just nod or smile instead. A casual "Hi" or "How are you doing?" or "Hello" often takes the place of a formal handshake, but it means the same thing. Nor will you find Americans circulating about a group in the office or at a party giving each one a personal farewell. Instead — again the different sense of timing and pace — they will just wave a cheery "good-by" or say something informal to the whole group such as "Well, see you tomorrow" or "So long everybody." Then they will disappear. No handshakes.

Often you will see men working at office desks in shirtsleeves, sometimes without their ties. They may lean far back in their chairs and even put their feet on the radiator or desk while they talk on the telephone. This also is not meant to be rude. Once we get out of the tense, hurried city streets, we are a loose-jointed, informal, relaxed people.

Our pace is total — either totally hurried, intense, work-absorbed, and competitive (in play as well as work), or else totally at ease, relaxed, "laid back" and informal, our manner breezy. We tend to swing between these extremes. This is the pendulum you need to understand if you are to understand America and its people.

Living in the U.S.A.
Alison R. Lanier
1981; 213 pp.
$8.95
($9.95 postpaid) from:
Intercultural Press
P. O. Box 768
Yarmouth, ME 04096
or Whole Earth Access

Culturgram

"Culturgrams are briefings to aid understanding of, feeling for, and communication with other people." They succeed admirably.

Each Culturgram contains much of the sort of information usually left out of guidebooks: how to act when invited into someone's home, how to avoid being unintentionally obnoxious or frightening.

The price is right: $1.25 postpaid, for each four-page, 8½ x 11 inch pamphlet. There are currently 90 Culturgrams available. Other publications to encourage international communications are also available. —*Walt Noiseux*

•

Japan
Visiting: Shoes should be removed before stepping from the enclosed porch *(genkan)* into a Japanese-style home. However, western-style buildings may be entered with shoes on. After removing the shoes, place them together pointing toward the outdoors. Slippers are usually worn inside Japanese-style homes and buildings but should be removed before one enters rooms with the immaculate straw mat floors *(tatami)*.

Japanese traditionally emphasize reserve and modesty. When offered something, one should express a slight hesitation to accept it. Guests should avoid excessive compliments on items of decor; otherwise the host may feel obligated to give the items as gifts. It is customary for guests to take a gift (usually fruit or cakes) to their host. Gifts are given and accepted with both hands and a slight bow. Deny all compliments graciously.

Eating: Eating while walking on the street exhibits poor taste. Snack foods are sold at street stands, but people stay at the stand until they are finished. . . .

Culturgram
1984 edition
$1.25 each (postpaid);
$5.75/package of 10
from:
Brigham Young University
KCIS Publications
280 HRCB
Provo, UT 84602

Modolo's Kronotech is built up from two shells of hot-cast carbon fiber reinforced by honeycomb composite. Domenico Modolo's design features hydraulic brakes, a built-in computer, and an estimated weight of 18.7 pounds. Believe it or not, production is in the works.
—*Bicycle Guide*

LONG STAGNATED by a tradition of being traditional, bicycle designers and makers have awakened at last. The results are encouraging: new ideas are being tried, excellent steeds can now be had for a reasonable price, and bikes in general have become more competent. About time. —JB

The All New Complete Book of Bicycling
Eugene A. Sloane
1980; 736 pp.
$12.95
postpaid from:
Simon and Schuster
Attn.: Mail Order Dept.
200 Old Tappan Road
Old Tappan, NJ 07675

The All New Complete Book of Bicycling

Well, it's not quite all new, but it is extensively updated from the previous (and good) editions. This isn't just a repair book — virtually everything likely to affect bike and rider is covered. It even gets into elementary frame straightening and painting. If you're going to have just one bike book around to help, this one is it. —JB

•

Various tests have been made pedaling with and without toe straps and toe clips. Most of the test results show that with toe clips and straps you increase pedalling efficiency about 40 percent. My own experience bears this out. But just because you have toe clips and straps, and even cleats on your shoes (which you must have to achieve this added efficiency) you are by no means guaranteed this improved efficiency. Clips and straps alone, even with cleats, will do little for you unless you learn to pedal correctly, so that you pull *up* with one foot as you press *down* with the other.

Bicycle Guide
Theodore Costantino, Editor
$10/year
(9 issues) from:
Bicycle Guide
P. O. Box 5325
Boulder, CO 80322

Bicycle Guide

It has a masthead that reads like a Who's Who of bicycling. It has articles covering a wide variety of bicycling matters — not just racing and body building. The writing has a personal tone to it. —JB
[Suggested by Eli Rubin]

•

The Browning Automatic Transmission will soon be available for mountain bikes. The firearms maker recently showed a triple chainwheel (28, 38, 48 tooth) version of their system. It uses multiple front chainwheels like a derailleur system, but instead of a derailleur shoving the chain sideways, the chainwheels hinge to divert it, much like a railroad switch. Since the system is constantly engaged, you are actually in two gears at one time when you shift, so the chain can carry a full load at all times. Our man John Schubert comments that the Browning shifts effortlessly even under heavy load. A two-speed BMX version is currently available, and the mountain bike version should be out in 1986. Contact Browning at 105 West 2950 South, Salt Lake City, Utah 84115 for more details.

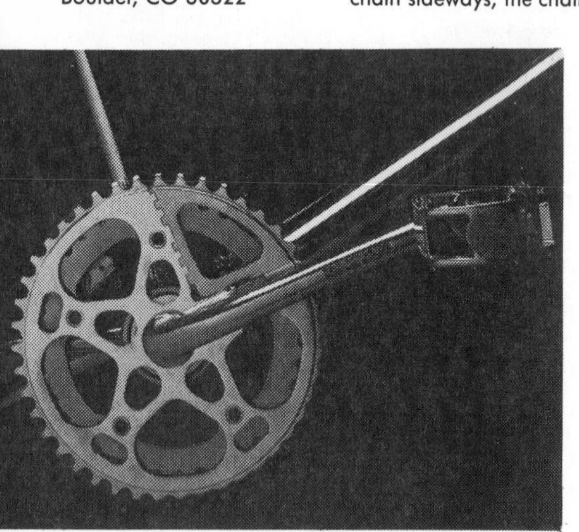

The Browning Automatic Transmission.

Bikes by Mail

The best place to buy a bicycle is at your local dealer where a good fit can be assured. But if you know what you want, buying by mail will likely save you money — sometimes lots. Here are three outfitters we've come to trust:

Bike Nashbar • Performance Bicycle Shop

Both these places stock an astounding variety of bicycles and associated gear, but not necessarily the same brands. I'd look at both catalogs. Our experience with their mail-order service has been good.

Bike Nashbar: Quarterly catalog **$2**; P. O. Box 290, Middletown, OH 44442.
Performance Bicycle Shop: Catalog **free**; 404 East Main Street, Carrboro, NC 27510.

Pt. Reyes Bikes

This store is right in the heart of where the Mountain Bike (All-Terrain Bicycle or ATB) was invented. Their expertise is the expertise of many of the innovators of the breed who still live and work in the area. They stock a wide selection, including some strange and wonderful items not found elsewhere. —JB

Pt. Reyes Bikes: Catalog **free**; P. O. Box 362, Pt. Reyes Station, CA 94956.

• The physical fitness part of bicycling, training for racing, and triathlons is covered on p. 241.

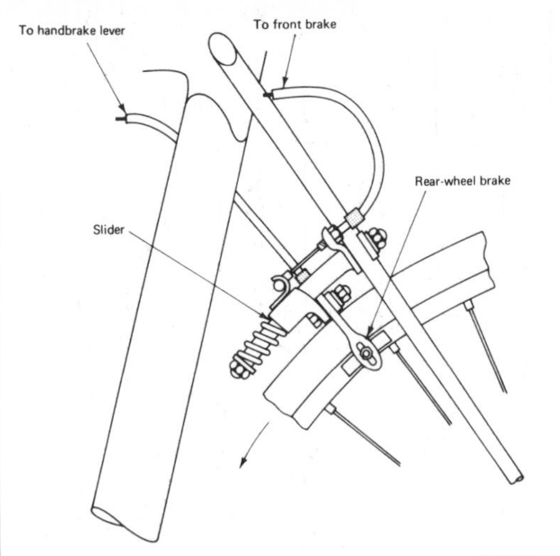

Calderazzo feedback brake system. When handbrake is operated, rear brake is carried forward on slider against spring, actuating front brake simultaneously. If bicycle starts to pitch forward, rear wheel is no longer rotated by road surface, and front brake is released.

Bicycling Science

For 12 years this book has been the best place to learn the engineering principles of bicycle design. The information is solidly backed by extensive lab and field testing, yet is presented in a jargon-free, easily understood manner. All aspects of the bicycle are covered, including the rider and bike/rider relationship (ergonomics). If you're considering the construction of a bike or HPV, or are just curious about your mount, this is lesson one. —JB

Bicycling Science
Frank Rowland Whitt and David Gordon Wilson
1982; 364 pp.
$9.95
($11.20 postpaid) from:
The MIT Press
Attn.: Ordering Dept.
28 Carleton Street
Cambridge, MA 02142
or Whole Earth Access

Human Power
David Gordon Wilson
$15/year
(4 issues) from:
International Human Powered Vehicle Association
P. O. Box 2068
Seal Beach, CA 90740

Human Power

People-as-engines is the underlying theme of this lively journal put out by the International Human Powered Vehicle Association. There is an air of pioneering about it all; the people involved are trying everything imaginable in the search for more efficient transportation. Controversy abounds. Innovation abounds. Hot-blooded spirit abounds. Just what you'd expect on a frontier. —JB

•

Prior to designing my first recumbent, I measured myself. (Married people, or those with steady "opposites" have an advantage in this process.) I then made a scale cutout of each portion of my body (head, torso, upper and lower leg, feet, upper and lower arm, and hands), with an overlap at each end. The parts were then fastened with straight pins at the pivot points. Then by drawing potential designs to the same scale (1-to-8 was the one I used), I could trace the outline of my body in various positions on the bike.

The first recumbent.

Bike Tech
Robert Rodale, Editor
$11.97/year
(4 issues) from:
Bike Tech
33 E. Minor Street
Emmaus, PA 18049

Bike Tech

Technical articles, innovation, and a vigorous reader response make this thin-but-lively magazine a good place to keep up with what's coming next. —JB

•

DuPont's New Twist in Composite Fibers: The DuPont Company, well-known to cyclists as the maker of Kevlar high-tensile fabrics and Nomex honeycomb, announced plans to become a full service supplier of *all* the components needed to produce fiber-composite structures. This includes adhesives, resins, yarns, woven fabrics, and design/testing services, according to Mike Bowman, director of DuPont's composites group. DuPont recently purchased the carbon-fiber production facilities of Exxon Enterprises (source of the ill-fated Graftek G1 bikes of the mid-'70s), and is now developing several low-cost Kevlar and carbon hybrids. If you are designing bicycle frames or other components that use structural composites, you should probably be in touch with DuPont. For a copy of DuPont's "Access Guide" to composite materials, or a subscription to the *KEVLAR UPDATE* newsletter, contact Jim Mondo, Recreation Products Group, DuPont Composites Venture, Center Road, Wilmington, DE 19898.

Sutherland's

If you have your bike shop do the work, you don't need Sutherland's. But they do. This is the only place where you can find out which parts will interchange with other brands, models, and years. Or what spoke length you need to build a particular wheel. Or how to deal with the innards of intricate mechanisms. Just what you need if you're working up an HPV or custom job. The book is a model of clarity. —JB

Sutherland's Handbook for Bicycle Mechanics
Howard Sutherland, et al.
1985; 275 pp.
$45
postpaid from:
Sutherland's Bicycle Shop
P. O. Box 9061
Berkeley, CA 94709

• If these folks don't have the bike tool you want, you probably don't need it.
The Third Hand Cycle Tools: Catalog **free** from The Third Hand, P. O. Box 212, Mt. Shasta, CA 96067.

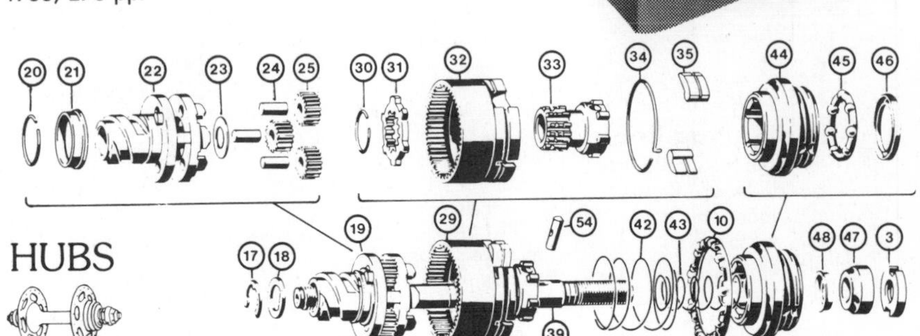

Bicycle Rider
Don Alexander, Editor
$15.98/year
(9 issues) from:
Bicycle Rider
29901 Agoura Road
Agoura, CA 91301

Bicycle Rider

At last, a magazine dedicated mostly to touring. The travel articles, redolent with irresistible color photographs, include adventures all over the world. Mountain bikes are featured as tourers too, taking their riders places where no ordinary bike, or even Jeep, could follow. Equipment tests avoid forked-tongue opinions despite all the fancy ads. The editors also manage to avoid that subtle snobbery that too much racing seems to engender. It's all friendly (to women and men equally), enticing and competent. No wonder their readership is approaching 100,000 after only one year of publication. —JB

Freewheeling
(Bicycling the Open Road)
Gary Ferguson
1984; 193 pp.
$8.95
postpaid from:
The Mountaineers — Books
306 Second Avenue W.
Seattle, WA 98119
or Whole Earth Access

Freewheeling

Touring on the open road is different from going to the supermarket. This book will get you started just fine, both with advice and encouragement. The advice covers what you'd expect — equipment, weather, safety, and where to stay at night. The encouragement is enhanced by the book's readability. There's not a trace of racing snobbery here. It's just what you need to know. —JB

•

No matter what the manufacturer may claim about his panniers, assume they will leak in the rain! Treating the seams of new panniers is of course recommended, but protection of your equipment from inclement weather should go much further.

To begin with, line each pannier with a *heavy-duty* garbage bag (the 13-gallon size will do nicely). It's not a bad idea to then load clothes and delicate equipment into separate smaller bags, just in case the large one should get torn.

•

Rain Factoring
There's a fairly simple technique the cyclist can employ to make a rough estimate of the influence that rain may have on a particular trip. The National Oceanic and Atmospheric Adminstration publishes a list of cities and their average number of days with precipitation for each month of the year. October in Seattle, for instance, has an average of 13 rain days, or nearly one-half of the month. If a cyclist is determined not to ride in the rain at all, he would have to allow at least three or four layover periods for every week of Seattle-area riding. October in San Francisco, on the other hand, averages five days of rain, or roughly one-sixth of the month. Here, you could reasonably hope to keep layover days down to one or two a week.

Bikecentennial

Born ten years ago, Bikecentennial has become a sponsor of organized bike tours, a lobbying force, and the best source of bicycle touring maps. It's the maps that are special; they're drawn with the biker in mind as they indicate the best routes through both country and urban tangle. —JB

Bikecentennial
Catalog **free** from: Bikecentennial
P. O. Box 8308, Missoula, MT 59807

Bikecentennial prints detailed maps for these routes ▶ as well as many more modest tours.

Anybody's Bike Book
Tom Cuthbertson
1984; 215 pp.
$6.95
($7.95 postpaid);

The Bike Bag Book
(A Manual for Emergency Roadside Bicycle Repair)
Tom Cuthbertson and Rick Morrall
1981; 129 pp.
$2.95
($3.95 postpaid)

Anybody's Bike Book • The Bike Bag Book

This friendly beginner's fix-it book remains the best of its kind for the average nonmechanic rider. It's like having a kindly uncle at your side urging you to be brave and clever. ***The Bike Bag Book*** *is a physically smaller version you can take with you on the road.* —JB

Both from:
Ten Speed Press
P. O. Box 7123
Berkeley, CA 94707
or Whole Earth Access

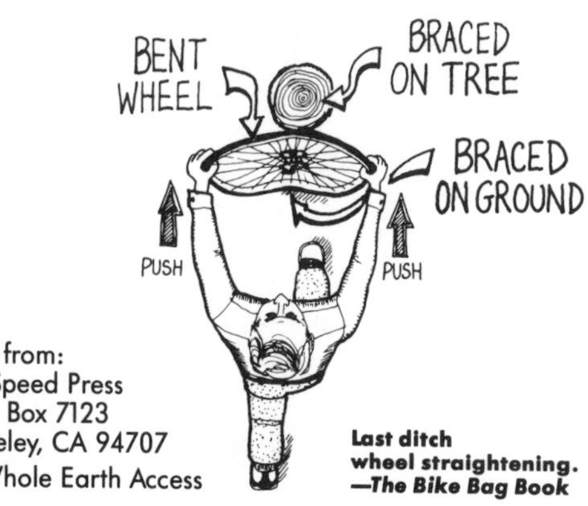

Last ditch wheel straightening. —*The Bike Bag Book*

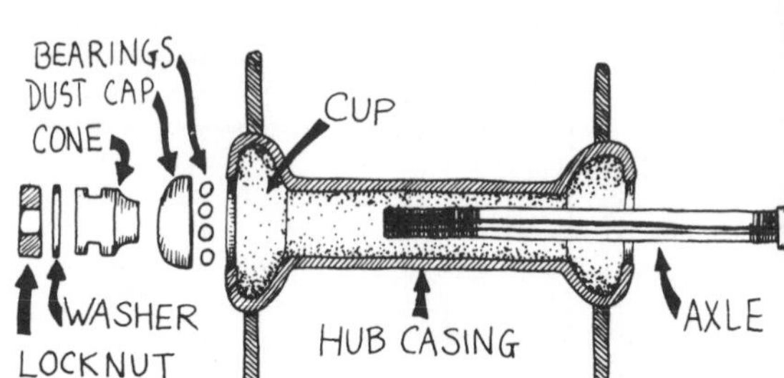

Hub, exploded view. —*Anybody's Bicycle Book*

• You can tow 100 pounds of kid or cargo in the Burley Lite bicycle trailer. Axle hitch makes it more stable than others. The catalog is free from Burley Design Cooperative, 4080 Stewart Road, Eugene, OR 97402.

• See Yakima Racks (p. 283).

• Bicycle safety is well attended in **Bicycle Forum:** John Williams, Editor. **$12**/year (4 issues) from Bicycle Forum, P. O. Box 8311, Missoula, MT 59807.

WHY? YOU MIGHT ASK. Two main reasons: they store compactly out of reach of thieves, and they can be with you under circumstances where a fullsize bike can't, such as on a bus or even an airplane. I've taken mine canoeing downriver and ridden it back to get the car. There is a remarkable variety of folders available. The trend is increasingly toward easier folding, good road manners, and cleverness.

—J. Baldwin

Moulton's windshield cuts air drag 20%. Low racks give stable ride with load.

Alex Moulton Bicycles

Probably the state of the art in bicycles, the AM utilizes a supple suspension to enhance roadholding and ride comfort. Small wheels permit a low center of gravity for stable load carrying, and combine with a clever take-apart feature to give compact storage. Models available for touring, racing and commuting. You have to ride one to believe how good it is. —JB

Alex Moulton Bicycles
$950-$1,900
Catalog **$1** from:
Alex Moulton Ltd.
Bradford on Avon
Wiltshire BA15 1AH
England

DaHon (about $200): folds smallest.

DaHon Bicycles
$150-$300
Information **free** from:
DaHon California, Inc.
17924 Star of India Lane
Carson, CA 90746

Berkeley Wheel Works

This store offers the biggest selection of folding bikes anywhere and will modify them to your taste in their machine shop if you so desire. These folks are experts on the subject. —JB

Folding Bikes
Catalog **$2** from Berkeley Wheelworks
1500 Park Avenue/C 104, Emeryville, CA 94608

Bickerton (about $350): lightest (mine has served well for 10 years —JB). ►

▼ **Airframe (about $500): most advanced.**

• See "Folding Boats" (p. 281).

Workman Cycles

Getcha Good Humor vending tricycle-with-cold-box here, folks! You can also find a wide range of other heavy-duty commercial trikes and bikes — most of the ones you see on the job come from here. This company has made 'em like they used to since 1898. —JB

Bridgestone (about $300): handiest per dollar.

Worksman Cycles

Catalog **$2** from:
Worksman Trading Corporation
94-15 100th Street
Ozone Park, NY 11416

CARS OF THE '80s

by J. Baldwin

LIKE IT OR NOT, most of us need a car. We rent, hire, borrow, ride in, or buy them — new and used. A used car can be a good deal. A thorough overhaul typically costs less than the *interest* on the payments of a new one. That goes for old, unfashionably fat jobs too. They can be had cheap, and will often cost less to own than new economy models.

If a new car is what you need, I recommend a front-wheel-drive machine whose characteristics have been deemed desirable by *Consumer Reports* (p. 150). If you need lots of room, one of the minivans is worth a look. Most are merely shrunken trucks, but the front-wheel-drive Dodge/Plymouth vanlet represents a new sort of vehicle. It behaves more like a car than a truck, gets decent gas mileage, and makes efficient use of its modest exterior dimensions. You can buy one as an empty one-passenger "tin bin" or in various gussied-up versions seating as many as eight. The success of this design has engendered competition that will appear soon, but you should give any new model at least a year for debugging before you buy.

Four-wheel drive is another interesting development, not in its usual heavy-duty boulder-crawling form, but as an accessory on an otherwise normal passenger car or station wagon. The 4x4 option gives a reassuring sure-footedness on slick roads, and a remarkable ability to hustle through snow and mud. My own car is one of these: a Toyota Tercel 4x4 wagon. In 60,000 miles of various driving conditions, it has proven to be competent, frugal, and reliable, though a trifle dull. It has plenty of excellent competition from Honda, Subaru, Dodge Colt Vista, Nissan Stanza, Audi, and VW, with more to come.

If you buy a small car, order a model with folding rear seats and a hatchback — that layout uses the limited space most efficiently. Get a light color; a white car will be about 35 degrees cooler than a black one on a hot day, and thus may make expensive air conditioning unnecessary. If low-cost transport is your goal, go for a simple base model. They're surprisingly good these days. In fact, most cars are significantly better in all respects than they have ever been. ■

Drive It 'Till It Drops
Joe Troise
1980; 117 pp.
$6.95
postpaid from:
and books
702 South Michigan Street
South Bend, IN 46618
or Whole Earth Access

Drive It 'Till It Drops

If bottom-line costs are your main concern, then an older model makes a lot of sense; keeping the oldie going can often save you thousands of dollars. This chatty book is full of good information that remains true in principle despite being a bit out-of-date with prices. —JB

•

When a schedule says to install a "new" something or other, that means new and not rebuilt. Some automotive components, like alternators and starters, can be rebuilt with a high degree of success, but others, such as carburetors and water pumps, are much more likely to last if they are installed as brand-new units. This is the voice of experience talking.

•

The year of your car is a very important consideration in deciding whether or not to restore it. As far as I'm concerned, the very best automobiles were manufactured between 1955 and around 1970, give or take a few years. Now when I say best, I mean *reliable* on a day to day basis. Cars made before 1955 are usually a little overweight, running on a feeble 6 volt electrical system, and powered by an inefficient flathead engine. While these characteristics are charming in some respects, they don't fit well in the world of the 1980's. Cars made after 1970 or so tend to be severely burdened with assembly defects, loss of quality control and very complex emissions controls. Many domestic cars built in the mid 1970's also enjoy eating rather large amounts of gasoline.

The Car Buyer's Art
Darrell Parrish
1985; 183 pp.
$7.95
postpaid from:
Book Express
P. O. Box 1249
Bellflower, CA 90706
or Whole Earth Access

The Car Buyer's Art

Would you be willing to work hard as an actor for $500 an hour? That's about what you'll "make," tax free, if you follow the advice given here the next time you buy a car or other high-ticket item. This is definitely not just another boring How-To-Buy-A-Car effort. It is no less than a military manual on assault of a dealership. The instructions are very explicit, right down to a minute-by-minute script in some cases. When we bought a car recently, we used most of the strategies given here and took it for about $2,000 less than anyone else we know, so we can vouch that the suggestions work. It's rare to see insider's information available in so useful a form and I recommend this book highly. It even has an exam at the back (with answers) so you can practice. —JB

•

Turnover in the car selling profession is high. Because of this, a young salesman is very likely to be a *new* salesman, which is exactly what you want. Here's why. Being new in the business, he will lack the hardened "take 'em to the cleaners at all cost" attitude of the more experienced veteran. Along the same lines, his persuasive skills will probably not be fully developed. And finally, remember, he is keenly aware that in order to remain employed he must sell cars. In order to accomplish this and gain an initial foothold in the profession, there's a good chance he'll work his heart out for you and settle for a sale "on the books" even if the commission is small.

Classic Motorbooks
Catalog
$2.95
postpaid from:
Classic Motorbooks
P. O. Box 1
Osceola, WI 54020

Classic Motorbooks

You need a reprint of the factory shop manual for '57 Chevy pickups? Or would you like to find some decent books on converting your vehicles to alcohol? Or how about a place which carries Bentley, Haynes, Clymer, Chilton, and Autobook workshop manuals for popular models? All of this, and a lot more you never thought about, is available from Classic Motorbooks. They claim to have the world's largest selection of automotive literature; if you don't believe it, take a look at their catalog. I've been doing business with Classic Motorbooks for quite a number of years now, and service has been excellent. —Jim Baker

• To buy or sell antique, vintage, or special-interest cars and parts, check:
Hemmings Motor News: Dave Brownell, Editor. **$16.75**/year (12 issues) from HMN Subscriptions, Box 100, Bennington, VT 05201.

• The best used car information.
Consumer Reports Guide to Used Cars: Consumer Reports Editors with Alex Markovich, 1986; 564 pp. **$6.95** ($9.10 postpaid) from Consumer Reports Books, 540 Barnum Avenue, Bridgeport, CT 06608 (or Whole Earth Access).

Chilton's Easy Car Care

Car maintenance is one place do-it-yourself really pays; taking care of your machine will probably take less time than it would take you to earn the mechanic's fee. You also get the job done at your convenience and at high quality. Assuming you know how. With this weighty tome at your side, you can confidently take on virtually all maintenance and minor repair of any common car or small truck. The book is written for the utterly naive: there are even illustrated instructions for pumping your own self-serve gas! The information is pretty general, but surprisingly detailed and useful because it's supported by simple explanations of how basic auto systems work. (There are specifics for a selection of common models, but for complex repairs you'll need a shop manual for your particular car.) A great book for beginners.
—JB

To replace a turn signal, stop light or back-up light bulb, push down on the bulb while turning it counterclockwise. When installing the new bulb, be sure the indexing lugs match the socket; the bulb will only fit one way.

TROUBLESHOOTING BASIC CHARGING SYSTEM PROBLEMS

There are many charging system problems you can fix yourself. This chart will show you which ones you can fix and which ones require professional service.

Problem	Is Caused by	What to Do
Noisy Alternator	• Loose mountings • Loose drive pulley • Worn bearings • Brush noise • Internal circuits shorted (High pitched whine)	• Tighten mounting bolts • Tighten pulley • Have bearings replaced • Have brushes cleaned/replaced • Have alternator replaced or overhauled
Squeal when starting engine or accelerating	• Glazed or loose belt	• Replace or adjust belt
Indicator light remains on or ammeter indicates discharge (engine running)	• Broken fan belt • Broken or disconnected wires • Internal alternator problems • Defective voltage regulator	• Install belt • Repair or connect wiring • Have alternator overhauled/replaced • Have voltage regulator replaced
Car light bulbs continually burn out—battery needs water continually	• Alternator/regulator overcharging	• Have voltage regulator/alternator overhauled or replaced
Car lights flare on acceleration	• Battery low • Internal alternator/regulator problems	• Charge or replace battery • Have alternator/regulator overhauled or replaced

Chilton's Easy Car Care
2nd Edition
1985; 567 pp.
$12.95
($15.20 postpaid) from:
Chilton Book Company
Customer Service Dept.
Radnor, PA 19089
or Whole Earth Access

John Muir Publications

In the classic **How To Keep Your Volkswagen Alive**, the late John Muir advised mechanically naive VW owners to "come to kindly terms with your ass, for it bears you." Unusually encouraging and free of jargon, this book has enabled countless fumblefingers to keep their Beetles buzzing. Lucky owners of Hondas and Rabbits can now partake of similar fare in more recent books by the same publisher. Would that all repair manuals were like these!
—JB

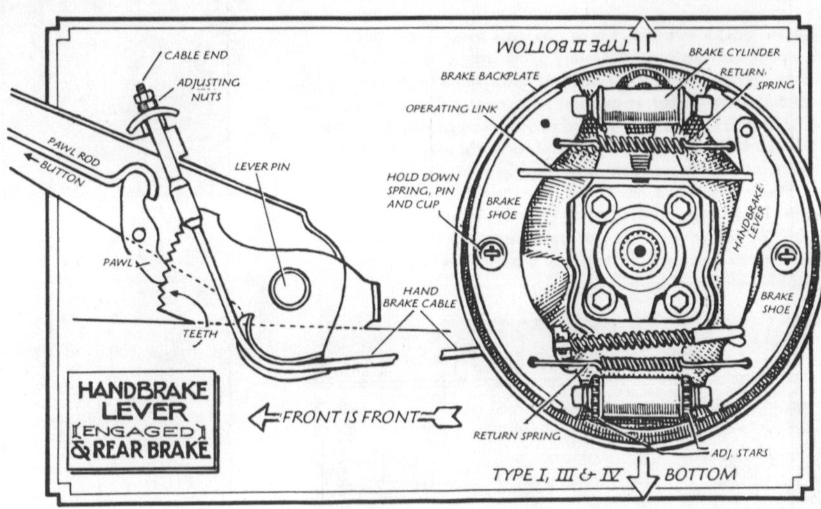

How To Keep Your Volkswagen Alive
John Muir
1986; 376 pp.

How To Keep Your Honda Alive
Fred Cisin and Jack Parvin
1986; 266 pp.

How To Keep Your VW Rabbit Alive
Richard Sealy
1986; 440 pp.

$14.95 each
($16.70 postpaid) from:
John Muir Publications
P. O. Box 613
Santa Fe, NM 87504
or Whole Earth Access

Highway Driving Schools

No, this isn't the usual statistically ineffective Driver's Ed. This is what you really need to know when things go awry on the road. Under the watchful eye of a race driver, you learn skid prevention and control, controlled stops from high speed, and just plain control. Classes are held on a track and on a very slick "skid pad" where ineptitude is not punished as you gyrate — there's nothing to hit. I credit my life to this sort of training received nearly a million miles ago. It's been better insurance than insurance. Give a course to one you love.

Here are three reputable schools. There may be others near you, usually at a race track. Classes cost about the same as a year's insurance.
—JB

Bertil Roos School of Motor Racing: catalog **free**; course **$595**. P. O. Box 221A, Blakeslee, PA 18610.
Bob Bondurant School of High Performance Driving: catalog **free**; courses **$295-$1,800**. c/o Sears Point International Raceway, Highways 37 & 121, , Sonoma, CA 95476.
Skip Barber Racing School: catalog **free**; courses **$400-$795**. Route 7, Canaan, CT 06018.

• Anything from rare old parts to the most bizarre frippery can be had from the catalog of J. C. Whitney & Co. (also known as Warshawsky).
Catalog **$2** from J. C. Whitney & Co., 1917-19 Archer Avenue, Chicago, IL 60680.

SCOOTERS are pretty slick these days. Fancy new designs are quiet, quick, and perhaps most important, chic. Electric starting, automatic transmissions, splash guards, and windshields make the modern scooter as easy to use as a car on smooth urban roads. Some scooters are fast enough to be freeway legal, though they really don't belong there or on roads rough enough to challenge the pudgy little tires. Think of the scooter as a small second car — in good weather.

Honda Scooters
$448-$2,498
Call 800/447-4700
for information on
your nearest dealer

THEY GET YOU THERE, sweatless, faster than a bicycle. They cost far less to own and run than a car, are more agile, and park easily. Part machine and part animal, even the less inspired designs give an invigorating feeling of oneness with the mechanism. They're *fun!*

Statistically, two-wheeled transport, whether powered or not, isn't encouragingly safe. But the statistics also show that most of the accidents happen to young, inexperienced riders during the first few months of ownership, and that the fault is usually rider error. Use good sense, resist challenging the laws of physics, wear your helmet, and don't ride when the roads are slick.

The machines on this page are shown only as examples of the breed; choosing and fitting a bike to your needs is a very personal thing. You should read a lot, talk to riders and dealers, and ride as many different brands as you can before buying.

—JB

Puch Mopeds
Catalog **free** from:
Puch Moped Catalog
640 Stanyan Street
San Francisco, CA 94117
or your nearest Puch dealer

MOPEDS are the cheapest to buy and cheapest to run. The pedals are useless — existing only as a means of dodging some states' licensing requirements. (Godzilla couldn't pedal one for more than five minutes at one mph.) Mopeds are too fast to mix safely with bicycles, and too slow to mix safely with auto traffic. They *are* fast enough, however, to trash you if things go wrong. Think of them as fast bicycles without the work.

MOTORCYCLES — believe it or not, this motorcycle has about the same size engine and price tag as the scooter shown above. Besides the obvious difference in ambience (which may work for or against your cause, depending), you'll find the motorcycle to be much more at home on the open road. The supple suspension, big wheels, powerful brakes, and brisk performance enable even this modest machine to easily keep up with auto traffic on all sorts of roads. There is a motorcycle to fit every proposed use and whim, if not budget. Plan on spending some time choosing one that fits you well, just as you would developing any intimate relationship. ▼

Honda Rebel
$1,298-$1,498
Information **free** from
any Honda dealer

• A good magazine for keeping up with motorcycling.
Cycle: Phil Schilling, Editor. **$13.95**/year (12 issues) from P. O. Box 2776, Boulder, CO 80302.

Home Is Where You Park It • Survival of the Snowbirds

Me, live in a trailer or RV? As my permanent home? Well, yes. Matter of fact, I've done just that for about 12 years now in a small Airstream trailer — the "Silver Turd." You can be a "boomer," following work as it becomes available. (That's pretty much what I've done.) Or you can be a "snowbird," following the good weather. Thousands of people (some say millions) are doing this right now. But there are problems: how do you license your vehicle year after year? What about banking, taxes, medical care, postal service, insurance, and legal matters? Where do you park? What about electricity, sewage, and water? All these things have been well worked out, through experience, by the author of these most useful books. My experience says they are right on the mark. Read both, you'll be glad you did. —JB

•

Every motor requires repairs from time to time. Since it is the motor that wears out first, the trailerist can trade his tow rig for a new one and still keep the same RV. The motor-home owner usually ends up buying an entire new rig. —*Home Is Where You Park It*

•

Nomadic children are exposed to a variety of cultural backgrounds. They learn that there are many different ways of doing things. As their views widen, they are more apt to become complete individuals. I believe that what nomadic children lose in social roots, they gain in the development of their inner resources. And because they are so often among strangers, they also learn to be independent. —*Home Is Where You Park It*

•

Since it is difficult to get credit cards once you become a transient, be sure to apply for the credit you want before you give up your permanent residence. Even if you've always been dead set against using credit, you may change your mind after you start full-timing. If you don't, you haven't lost anything; having credit cards does not mean you have to use them! —*Home Is Where You Park It*

•

All too often I hear someone complain, "I wish I could travel the way you do, but . . ." Then there follows a list of reasons that boil down to these two things: LACK OF COURAGE and LACK OF MONEY.

I can do nothing to give you courage for that must come from within. But I can assure you that "lack of money" is not a reason to give up your place at the feeding tray of life. Lack of money is an EXCUSE — but never a REASON for giving up on your travel dreams. —*Survival of the Snowbirds*

Home Is Where You Park It
Kay Peterson
1982; 199 pp.
$7.95
($8.95 postpaid)

Survival of the Snowbirds
Kay Peterson
1982; 222 pp.
$7.95
($8.95 postpaid)

Both from:
Roving Press Publications
Route 5, Box 310
Livingston, TX 77351
or Whole Earth Access

Fredson RV, Van, Truck & Boat Supplies

This fat catalog is full-to-bustin' with equipment and supplies that pertain to living in vehicles, boats, or any other minimal digs. There's lots of 12-volt stuff: appliances, lights, pumps, fans, and repair parts for them. There are propane refrigerators, RV toilets, tanks, vents, water heaters, stoves, aerials, awnings, jacks, mirrors, and just about anything else you can think of. It's the biggest assortment I've ever seen. Prices are good — far better than those of many RV stores that offer half the selection. —JB

Fredson RV Supply
Catalog
$3 (coupon enclosed) from:
Fredson RV Supply
815 North Harbor Blvd.
Santa Ana, CA 92703

Rinnai Instantaneous Water Heater

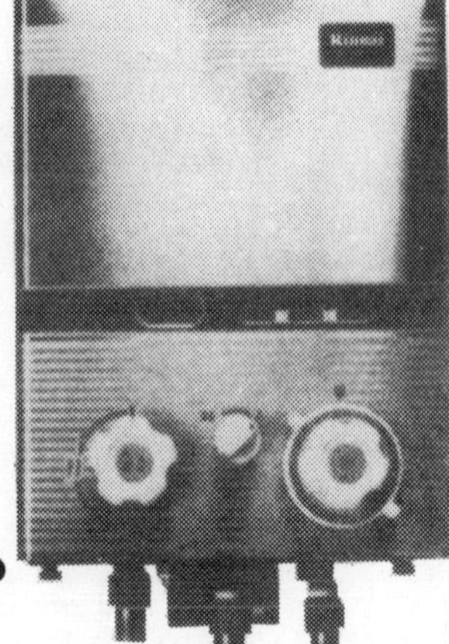

The Rinnai instantaneous hot water heater is ideal for recreational vehicles, residential, commercial and industrial applications. Easily installed as a central unit as well as at point-of-use to provide hot water in seconds, for as long as it is needed. Heater can be completely shut down when hot water is not needed, and quickly started up again using the fingertip controlled piezoelectric igniter. Designed for wall mounting to save valuable floor space and a variety of installation possibilities. Other features include: • By-pass mixing system for long life. • Stainless steel casing. • Pilot jet cleaning device for safe ignition every time. • Baffle.

SPECIFICATIONS: • Water pressure—high, 5.69 psi—low, 4.90 psi. • Overall dimensions—14" high x 11" wide x 9-1/4" deep. • Inlet connections—LPG, 3/8 flare 45° —NG, NPT 1/2—water NPT, 1/2. • Hot water outlet connection, NPT 1/2. • (GPM) capacity 50° rise, 1.2. • Gas consumption, BTU rating—40,000 maximum—24,400 minimum. • Net weight 14 pounds.

17-0519-00 REU-502 Instantaneous LPG Hot Water Heater

Woodall's Campground Directory

More than 600 pages of campsites — with maps, descriptions, and a brief description of what there is to do around there. Private campgrounds are rated by Woodall's staff, based on personal visits. Lots of other useful information is included, along with advertisements. A classic, as they say. I've found the information to be reasonably accurate — it's updated annually. Mexico and Canada are included. —JB

Woodall's Campground Directory
annual; 1,852 pp.
$12.95
($14.30 postpaid) from:
Woodall Publishing Co.
11 North Skokie Highway
Suite 205
Lake Bluff, IL 60044
or Whole Earth Access

Don Wright's Guide to Free Campgrounds USA

Six thousand of 'em no less, briefly described and located with reference to the nearest town. By states. Don't expect deluxe accommodations. Checking my own favorite locations, I find this listing to be trustable. —JB

Don Wright's Guide to Free Campgrounds
Don Wright
1986; 540 pp.
$12.95
($14.95 postpaid) from:
Lifestyle Publications
24396 Pleasant View Dr.
Elkhart, IN 46517
or Whole Earth Access

• "Escapees" is a club serving the needs of those who live on the road. Membership includes free parking at a number of sites, and a useful newspaper. The club also operates the S-K-P Mail & Message Service, which gives you an official address and phone — both with forwarding capability — for about a dollar a month.

Escapees: $35/year membership fee. Includes 6 newsletters, mail and message service, and other membership services. Escapees Club, Route 5, Box 310, Livingston, TX 77351.

The Complete Walker III

The Complete Walker III
Colin Fletcher
1984; 668 pp.
$11.95
($12.95 postpaid) from:
Random House
Order Dept.
400 Hahn Road
Westminster, MD 21157
or Whole Earth Access

This venerable book has been around just about as long as the **Whole Earth Catalogs**, *and like them, has been updated from time to time in order to keep current. The III version is a genuine revised edition; the editors claim it's 75 percent new. The latest in technotwitics are considered in detail after being subjected to Mr. Fletcher's traditional field testing. Material he has found worthy over the years remains intact, complete with a laconic humor sorely missing from most Deadly Serious Hiker writing. Usefulness is aided by a remarkable cross-referencing in the text that makes the overall logic of the author's trail philosophy seem irrefutable without being dogmatic. It's a good way to do a book of this sort; after 16 years, it's still the best around.* —JB

•

An Illinois reader has made a simple but interesting modification to the Sierra Club cup handle. "The extra bend," he writes, "affords a secure grip and counterbalance that I have not found in any other cup. If you fill the cup with liquid you will get the full impact of its practicality."

•

I had a 5-by-6-inch pocket sewn onto the front of my yoke of shoulder strap, roughly where the shirt pocket comes. Into it go notebook and map, and sunglasses when not in use. Pen, pencil and thermometer clip onto the rear, between pocket and strap, where they are very securely held — not, as they used to, in front, where removing map or notebook can flip them out unnoticed. I cannot imagine how I ever got along without such a pocket. Mine is made of ordinary blue-jean material, but anything stout will do.

•

The actual speed at which you walk is a personal and idiosyncratic matter. Settle for whatever seems to suit you best. It is really a question of finding out what you can keep up hour after hour in various kinds of terrain carrying various loads. Until you know your own limits, aim for a slow, rhythmic, almost effortless pace. You'll be surprised, I think, at the ground you cover. The miles will come to meet you. In time you'll learn that, generally speaking, the way to hurry is not to hurry but to keep going. To this end I have two walking speeds: slow and slower.

•

After years of doubt, two fundamental facts of belt design now seem to be generally, though still not universally, accepted. First, a fully encircling belt works better than sidestraps from the base of frame or bag. Second, the essential element in a fully effective encircling belt is a continuous, unbroken base of some semistiff material such as webbing.

Starting Small In the Wilderness

The grim possibility of having to drag a squalling brat down the trail to a rejected dinner and a soggy bed has kept many families from enjoying the beauties of wilderness adventure. Many unexpected problems can arise with the kiddies along, but with this long-needed book you'll likely be able to handle things OK. Common problems such as where to get child-size equipment and what to do about picky eaters are discussed with a convincing knowledge that can only have been gained from the field experience of what must have been hundreds of families. The book deals with bike, canoe, and ski trips too. The tone is encouraging. The quality is high in the expected Sierra Club manner. —JB

•

Getting children to enjoy carrying a loaded frame pack requires some parental ingenuity. Toting gear is work. Parents must somehow disguise or soften that fact for youngsters.

A good principle is to begin small, both with pack size and weight, and to start young children with some kind of soft, frameless pack (see Chapter 4, "Frameless Packs"). If youngsters carry something every time the family hikes, they will grow up thinking that pack toting is perfectly natural.

•

Occasionally you can find a trail that actually leads downhill to a choice location. Children delight in the ease of a descent. Getting them back up the trail again will be harder, but generally the lure of home provides good motivation.

Homemade sleeping sack and jacket for the very young child, infants through four-year-olds.

Starting Small in the Wilderness
(The Sierra Club Guide for Families)
Marilyn Doan
1979; 273 pp.
$6.95
($9.45 postpaid) from:
Sierra Club Bookstore
730 Polk Street
San Francisco, CA 94109
or Whole Earth Access

Land Navigation

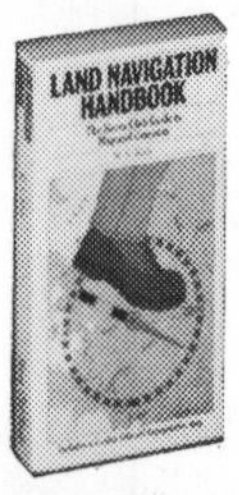

Land Navigation Handbook
(The Sierra Club Guide to Map and Compass)
W. S. Kals
1983; 230 pp.
$8.95
($11.45 postpaid) from:
Sierra Club Bookstore
730 Polk Street
San Francisco, CA 94109

We've run reviews of many "Where are we?" books over the years, but this one is easily the most clear and easy to use. Absolutely everything is explained in a way that does not subtly assume that you have a degree (so to speak) in advanced trigonometry. All those little symbols you see on maps are discussed, and after 25 years of trail experience I finally found out what those yellow square markers you see along trails are for. He even gets into navigation with an altimeter! And there's a good chapter on finding your way by the stars — even in the Southern Hemisphere in case you end up in New Zealand. All this stuff is presented in a commendably relaxed way that makes it easy to remember without the book. A sample topo map is included so you can try things in the safety of your own home. It'll be a long time before someone does this subject better. —JB

•

You can approach the peak from any direction and be certain to avoid the swamp as long as the peak bears less than 60° or more than 110° from you. You can see from this drawing that you'd pass South of the marsh when the bearing of the peak is less than 60°. You'd pass North of the swamp when the bearing is more than 110°.

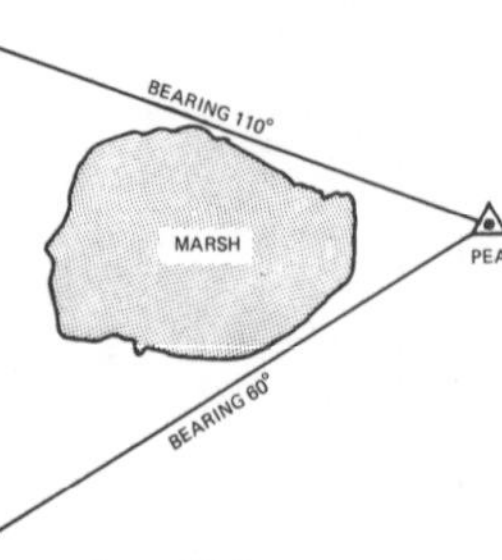

• Sometimes you can go farther, easier, using pack horses. Here's how.
Packin' In On Mules and Horses: Smoke Elser and Bill Brown, 1980; 158 pp. **$12.95** ($13.95 postpaid) from Mountain Press Publishers, Inc., P. O. Box 2399, Missoula, MT 59806.

• For compasses, see REI, p. 274.

The Well-Fed Backpacker

A big sack of Twinkies will get you through an easy weekend hike, assuming the weather is mild and the altitude low. Otherwise you're going to need real food. The trail food found in camp supply stores is expensive and may not be to everyone's taste. What to do? This nifty book abounds in tasty recipes made up from commonly available ingredients. There's a discussion of nutrition, advice on how to estimate how much to take with you, and a very useful chapter on the tricky business of winter cooking. I've used the book for many years. It works. —JB

•

Logan Bread
This makes a *huge* batch of sixty 2-inch squares, high in protein, vitamins, iron and calcium. Keeps weeks on the trail, longer in the refrigerator, indefinitely in the freezer.

4 pounds (14⅓ cups) whole wheat flour
1½ cups brown sugar
½ cup instant dry milk
1 teaspoon salt
2 teaspoons baking powder
1 teaspoon ground cinnamon
1 teaspoon ground nutmeg
1 cup chopped nuts
4 cups water
1¼ cups honey
1½ cups blackstrap molasses (much better nutritionally than regular molasses)
1¼ cups melted shortening
2 cups chopped dried fruit

Preheat oven to 300° F. To blended dry ingredients add water, then honey, molasses, shortening and fruit. Pour batter about an inch thick into greased pans and bake for 1 hour. Reduce oven to 200° F, leave door open slightly and continue to dry the bread for several hours. The drier it is, the longer it will keep.

Supermarket Backpacker

Choose recipes from this book.

Stock up on ingredients (by brand name) from local super.

Remix.

Repackage.

Eat well for cheap. —JB

*We lived on the Appalachian Trail using this method.
—Kevin Kelly*

•

Lipton's Mushroom Cup-O-Soup — To two cups boiling water add two pkgs. soup, ¾ cup instant rice, ½ tsp. rosemary, ½ small jar of chipped beef, ½ cup dried frozen peas. Simmer 7-10 minutes. Serves 2.

CHICKEN 'N DUMPLINGS

At home, combine:
1/2 cup cooked, cubed, dried chicken
2 tsp. dry onion flakes
1/2 tsp. each dry parsley and celery leaves
Dash of pepper
2 tsp. instant chicken bouillon
1/4 cup each dry carrot slices and dry peas

In another plastic bag, combine:
1 cup flour
2 tsp. baking powder
1/2 tsp. salt
1/3 cup dry milk

At camp: Rehydrate dry chicken and vegetable package. Add more water to cover about 1/2" and bring to a boil. Combine flour package with 1/2 cup water. Mix into a thick batter and drop by spoonfuls into boiling chicken mixture. Cover tightly, reduce heat and cook 20 minutes without raising the lid.

3-4 servings

To Betty Crocker Noodles Almondine mix, add:
Rehydrated chicken or tuna
Rehydrated pineapple slices, cubed
Rehydrated green pepper cubes
Rehydrated mushroom pieces
Rehydrated carrots, green beans, or peas

Supermarket Backpacker
Harriett Barker
1977; 194 pp.
$8.95
($10.95 postpaid) from:
Contemporary Books
180 N. Michigan Avenue
Chicago, IL 60601
or Whole Earth Access

The Well-Fed Backpacker
June Fleming
1985; 181 pp.
$6.95
($7.95 postpaid) from:
Random House
Order Dept.
400 Hahn Road
Westminster, MD 21157
or Whole Earth Access

Wilderness Search and Rescue

Walking through the woods hollering isn't the best way to find a lost kid. In fact, search turns out to be much more calculating than you might think. What to do when you find 'em can be even more complex. This professional's textbook presents the state of the art. It's a state that's changing too. I worked as an Arctic-based rescuer 25 years ago, and I note with some alarm that nearly all the techniques we used have been supplanted by much more sophistication. Much higher rate of success too. This process isn't hidden by the author either — he boldly gives examples of failures in order to show the sense behind currently approved procedures. Thankfully, detailed shots of flat climbers are minimized as is the other evidence of macho-hero stuff that one sees all too often in other books of this sort. You'll still need field training, of course, but this book is your homework. —JB

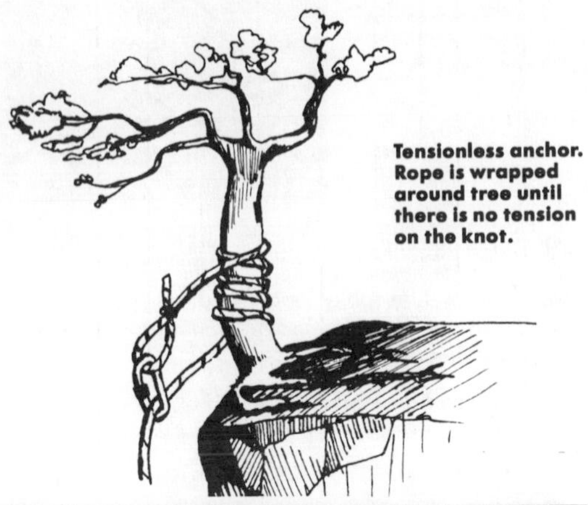
Tensionless anchor. Rope is wrapped around tree until there is no tension on the knot.

•

Amazingly, one trained search dog can patrol a tract in six hours that it would take 106 workers 370 man-hours to comb with the same probability of detection.

•

How low is the probability that the subject is still alive? The U.S. Coast Guard's data, for example, have shown that people have repeatedly survived far longer than was thought possible. A general rule of thumb for predicting survival is to multiply the time frame felt realistic for survival of a particular person in specific conditions times *three*.

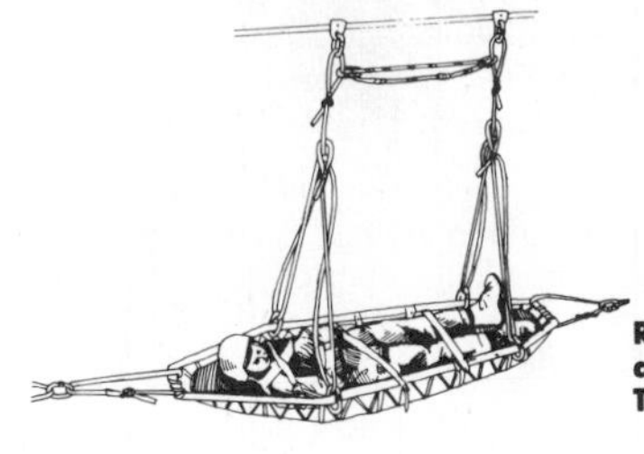
Rigging a litter for a Tyrolean. The haul rope may be attached to the lead pulley, helpful when the main Tyrolean rope is very slack.

Wilderness Search and Rescue
Tim J. Setnicka
1980; 637 pp.
$19.95
($21.45 postpaid) from:
Appalachian Mountain Club
5 Joy Street
Boston, MA 02108
or Whole Earth Access

• Reliance on an environmentally inimical automobile to get you to the wilderness is more than a little ironic. There's an alternative.
How to Get to the Wilderness Without a Car: Lee W. Cooper, 1985; 211 pp. **$9.95** ($10.95 postpaid) from Frosty Peak Books, P. O. Box 80584, Fairbanks, AK 99708-0584 (or Whole Earth Access).

HOW CAN YOU CHOOSE a parka, for instance, from an entirely excessive number of available models? You can't just ask, "What's the best parka?" You have to ask "best for my use" and be honest or you might end up with an expedition model suitable for your dream trip to Nepal instead of your shopping trip in Des Moines. The adage "you get what you pay for" doesn't apply unless you include stylishness — an increasingly important aspect of outdoor-wear marketing.

As usual, your best bet is to buy from a reputable dealer. We present a few of them here, but just a few — there are many more good ones. The ones on these pages are folks we've learned to trust through good personal experience with their wares and service.

—J. Baldwin

The North Face

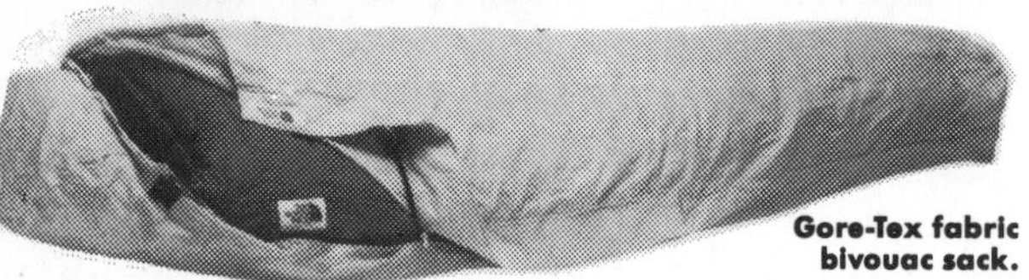

Gore-Tex fabric bivouac sack.

The North Face is one of the biggest outfitters now, and still one of the best. Their dramatic catalog goes beyond mere description by offering a short course in how to choose and care for equipment (not necessarily theirs). —JB

Catalog **free** from The North Face, 999 Harrison Street, Berkeley, CA 94710.

•

Use a Vapor Barrier Liner (VBL) and the Waterproof Bivouac Cover in conjunction with polypropylene underwear, a sleeping bag and an insulated pad and you've got a flexible, layered sleeping system designed to handle everything from extremely cold-weather camping to lightweight summit assaults. Field and lab tests show that this layered sleeping system boosts the thermal efficiency of the sleeping bag by 15 to 30 percent.

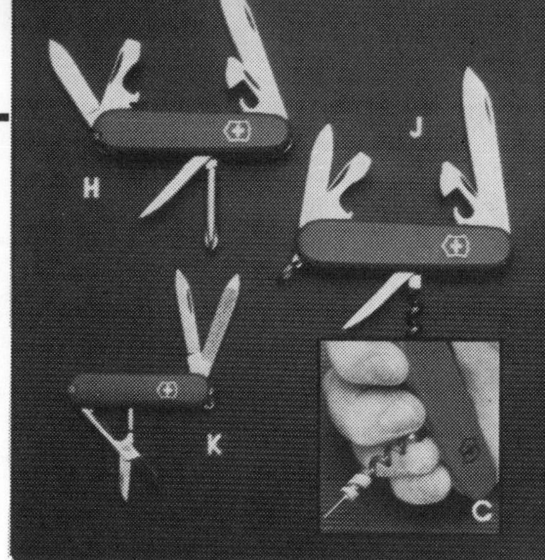

C **New!** The 1"-long **Accessory Screwdriver for Swiss Army Knives** fits inside the corkscrew of your knife. Perfect for tiny screws in sunglasses, etc.
Item #G403-031—Wt.: 0.25 oz. **$1.95**

—REI

REI

REI is the supermarket — their catalog is huge and includes many brands besides their own. There is little explanation; you have to know what you need. REI is a co-op offering members a dividend each December. —JB

REI: catalog **free** from Recreational Equipment, Inc., P. O. Box C-88126, Seattle, WA 98188.

Stephenson's Warmlite

*Engineer **Jack Stephenson's Warmlite** designs are radical, controversial, and widely copied (without credit). His catalog is a design treatise as radical as the equipment it shows. My Warmlite sleeping bag and tent have served me well for 16 years.* —JB

Stephenson model 5 sleeps 6 adults, weighs less than 5 lbs., rolls up to 15" x 8".

Catalog **$3** from Stephenson's Warmlite Equipment, R.F.D. 4 #145, Hook Road, Gilford, NH 03246.

Moss Tents

Moss Solet is just the thing for solo hiking and biking. 3 lb, 2 oz.

***Bill Moss's** tents have "inspired" nearly every other supplier of modern tents, but Bill's are still the best in every way. They feature subtle shapes and colors that seem as natural as the landscape around them. I regularly use two Moss models — both superb.* —JB

Catalog **free** from Moss Tents, P. O. Box 309, Camden, ME 04843.

L. L. Bean

L. L. Bean continues as a bastion of traditional New England trail equipage, mixed now with more modern stuff as they cater a bit to current tastes. Their reputation is deservedly impeccable; their store (open 24 hours) is a sight to behold if you can jam your way in. —JB

Catalog **free** from L. L. Bean, Inc., Freeport, ME 04033.

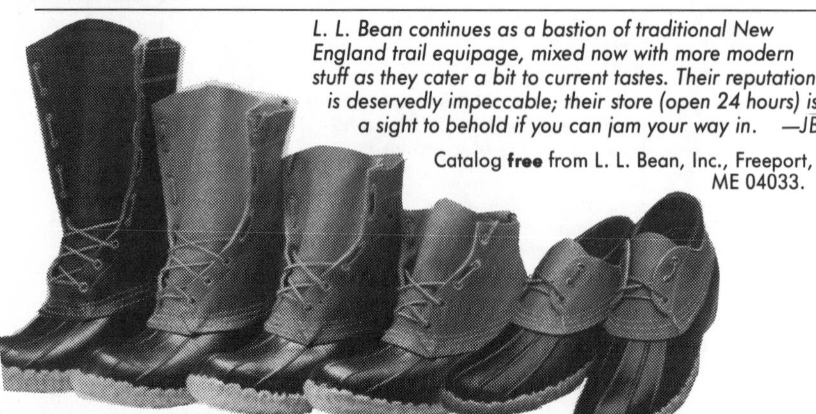

•

Bean's Maine Hunting Shoe
Uppers are of supple, long-wearing full-grain cowhide, organically treated in the tanning process to resist water. Will not stiffen with wetting and drying. Tan or Brown finish. Bottoms are made on a swing last of tough, ozone-resistant rubber compounded especially for us to provide longer wear. Cushioned innersole. Outersole of durable crepe is permanently vulcanized to the vamp and features Bean's famous Chain Tread. Made by us in Freeport, Maine.

• Lowe packs aren't the only good ones around, but their unique suspension, Torso Trac, makes the usually maddening strap adjustments easy — by eliminating them; Lowe's traveler packs retract their harness to become chic luggage. Nice.

Information **free** from Lowe Alpine Systems, P. O. Box 189, Lafayette, CO 80026.

Patagonia

irst with pile garments that are notably warm under wet onditions, Patagonia continues to show competitors the vay with their new Synchilla® pile that resists pilling and Capilene® polyester that doesn't hold body smells or ose its sweat-wicking ability. Add wild colors, snappy tyling, and good workmanship, and, uh, what are the lisadvantages? The only one I can see is that it's hard not o order one of each item. I regard Patagonia's corporate attitude as especially fine; their products are just what is claimed. —JB

Catalog **free** from Patagonia, P.O. Box 86, Ventura, CA 93002.

•

Synchilla® is a fine denier Dacron polyester from Dupont with a very soft hand that won't ever pill. It has unequaled stretch, but always recovers its shape to the millimeter. Because it absorbs so little water, it dries really fast and has great applications for activities around water.

Men's and Women's Synchilla® Jackets

CUSTOM BOOTS ARE LIKE having leather feet. No ready-made boots can compare, especially if your feet are of unusual contour. My boots are Limmers (see below). They're still in good shape after 16 years of trail abuse. My *feet* are still in good shape after 16 years of trail abuse, oo. Here are a few custom bootmakers we've learned to trust. The fit is guaranteed. No jogging shoe clones for *these* folks. —J. Baldwin

Boot pictured has
12" top and spring heel.

***White's Handmade Boots** come in a wide variety of styles sold off-the-shelf, but they'll custom-fit you for an extra fifty bucks. You see their work adorning the feet of loggers, linemen, farmers and the like. Heaviest of the heavy-duty, they might outlast your feet.* —JB

White's Handmade Boots: $160-$300. Information **free** from White's Boots, North 6116 Freya Street, Spokane, WA 99207.

Calked Loggers No. 75 Calk

8" top	10"	12"	14"	16"
$202.00	$212.00	$222.00	$240.00	$250.00
Standard	Standard	Standard	Special Height	Special Height

—White's

16-year-old Limmers.

***Peter Limmer & Sons** make both custom fit and handcrafted ready-mades. They're distinctive enough to be recognizable; I've had many folks come up (wearing Limmers) and say, "Hey, I see you got Limmers too!" I've yet to hear a complaint.* —JB

Limmer Custom-Made Hiking Boots: $160-$175. Information **free** from Peter Limmer & Sons Inc., P. O. Box 88, Intervale, NH 03845.

Oneida
1278
1278-C

***Russell** is where you get real moccasins and moccasin boots. They have a bunch of styles. They'll make 'em to fit, including your bunions. Tradition lives.* —JB
[Suggested by Sam Abrams]

Russell Moccasin Boots and Shoes: $65-$220. Information **free** from The W. C. Russell Moccasin Co., 285 SW Franklin, Berlin, WI 54923.

•

Russell Oneidas feature the only triple sole construction available on the market and are the only ones that are easily factory resoleable. The outer soles are cut from heavy bull-hide Sole Leather Bends especially tanned for superior wear and hand molded for a better fit. Only Russell gives you a moccasin with the fit and support of a shoe.

• Brigade Quartermasters have a military thrust to all they sell. The Ramboness may or may not be to your taste, but the goods are military tough and free of stylistic fripperies. Catalog **$3** from Brigade Quartermasters, Inc., P. O. Box 100002, Marietta, GA 30061.

***Randal Merrell Hiking Boots** are made by Mr. Merrell himself. The boot shell and lining are each made from one piece of leather with no foot-annoying ridges and seams. Elegant and expensive.* —JB

Merrell Boots: $340-$420. Information **free** from Randal I. Merrell, 3400 North 3500 West, Vernal, UT 84078.

Randal Merrell at work.

Ascent
Steve Roper and
Alan Steck
1984; 175 pp.
$25
($29.50 postpaid) from:
Sierra Club Bookstore
730 Polk Street
San Francisco, CA 94109
or Whole Earth Access

Ascent

It's hard to tell fact from fiction in this collection of unusual mountain tales, but then aesthetics have always been an important part of climbing. The seventeen stories and two photo essays are sufficiently intense and clear-eyed to satisfy both ascender and ass-ender.
—JB [Suggested by Dan Zimmerlin]

•

Metilkja suffered none of my neurotic ambivalence. He understood function much better than I. He knew that the doing was the important part and that the outcome would either reward or penalize our boldness. One acted out of strength without hesitation or consorting with hope. One suffered the consequences to the extent he was capable of influencing them. Everything else was either magic or religion. Metilkja threaded the rope through a carabiner and prepared to back off. The ends of the rope waved above us like tentacles, blown straight up into the night by the surging wind and illuminated by our headlamps. And again, for an instant, our eyes met. Then he was gone.

The ultimate refinement of "traditional" climbing: John Bachar free soloing a classic jamcrack on the second pitch of Outer Limits (Yosemite Valley). ►

Mountaineering
(Freedom of the Hills)
Ed Peters, Editor
1982; 550 pp.
$17 postpaid from:
The Mountaineers/Books
306 2nd Avenue West
Seattle, WA 98119
or Whole Earth Access

Mountaineering

By far the most sensitive and complete treatment of mountaineering available. Oriented around Pacific Northwest mountaineering, where trails often end miles before the peaks begin, it is particularly relevant to wilderness camping and travel. It is much more than a book on how to climb; it reflects several generations of a respectful relationship with mountains. If you move (or sit) where there are trees, rocks, snow and brush, it speaks to your terrain. *—Michael Templeton*

•

Good self-arrest form may be aesthetically satisfying, but, in practice, *instantaneous application may be absolutely critical*. A sloppy but fast arrest may be all that is needed to stop. Excessive concern for good form that results in a slower application may allow the climber to accelerate to a speed that even perfect form will not check. *The emphasis is on driving in the pick as hard and as quickly as possible.*

• Not nearly as comprehensive as **Mountaineering**, but much more detailed in the basic moves it depicts so well.
Learning to Rock Climb: Michael Loughman, 1981; 192 pp. **$10.95** ($13.45 postpaid) from Sierra Club Bookstore, 730 Polk Street, San Francisco, CA 94109

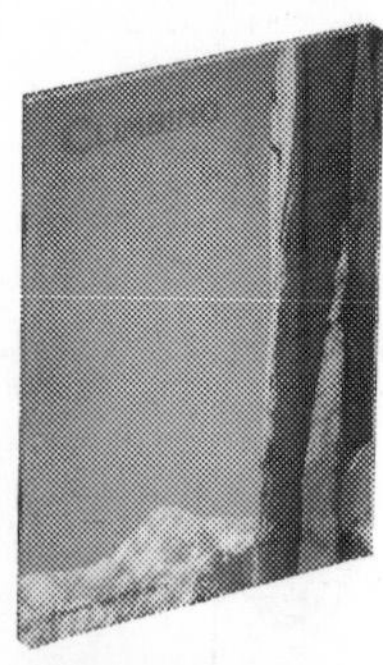

Climbing
Michael Kennedy, Editor
$15/year
(6 issues) from:
Climbing Magazine
P. O. Box E
Aspen, CO 81612

Climbing

Bloodboiling (and bloodcurdling) stories, rousing controversy, and lots of awesome photographs elicit Wows from nonclimbers and satisfied smirks from those who actually do such deeds. As is usual with this sort of magazine, the ads show the latest equipage more completely than many catalogs.
—JB [Suggested by Dan Zimmerlin]

John Long hanging around on Giant Rock, California. Photo: Bob Gaines.

• There are many excellent suppliers of mountaineering equipment. Three held in high regard are **International Mountain Equipment** (catalog **free** from Box 494, Main Street, North Conway, NH 03860); **Midwest Mountain Sports** (catalog **free** from P. O. Box 87, Worthington, OH 43085); and **Mountain Tools** (catalog **free** from P. O. Box 22788, Carmel, CA 93922.

• See "REI," p. 274.

Caving combines the sport of exploring caves with the science of speleology. Those who overcome claustrophobia and fear of the dark to master the skills of climbing, crawling, and finding one's way underground are well rewarded. Besides the sensual delight in rounded rock forms, in tiny hidden rooms and passage mazes far from the outside world, and in the discovery of secret places where few or no people have ever been before, cavers also find satisfaction in mapping caves and in learning about cave geology and biology.
—Richard A. Watson

Caving
Lane and Peggy Larson
1982; 311 pp.
$10.95
($13.45 postpaid) from:
Sierra Club Bookstore
730 Polk Street
San Francisco, CA 94109
or Whole Earth Access

Speleology

This is the only short introduction in English to the science of speleology. It shows that caving can be an intellectual activity of the highest rank. There are still many unsolved problems in cave science. —Richard A. Watson

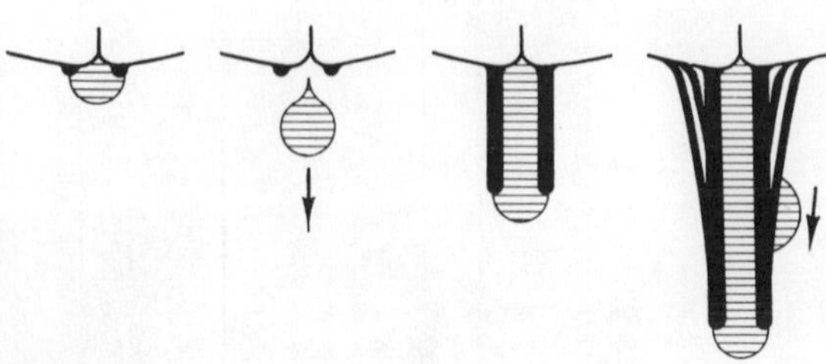

A stalactite begins growing as a small ring of calcite where the surface of a water drop intersects the ceiling of a cave. This ring grows into a tube, which often acquires a tapering shape when water flows down its outer surface.

National Speleological Society

You must be trained in safety techniques, and especially in conservation methods for the protection of caves, which are relatively rare on Earth and which contain endangered animal species and fragile rock formations. Anyone who wants to explore a cave should write for information to the only caving organization in the United States, The National Speleological Society, Cave Avenue, Huntsville, AL 35810. Information free; membership $22.50/year including the monthly ***NSS News*** *(available separately for $15) and their scientific journal,* ***NSS Bulletin****. NSS will get you in touch with cavers near you.*
—Richard A. Watson

Caving

A good general guide to caving. When you are experienced you may disagree with the Larsons on some points, but they do provide an unambiguous standard for beginners. —Richard A. Watson

Speleology
George W. Moore and
G. Nicholas Sullivan
1978; 150 pp.
$5.95
($6.95 postpaid) from:
Cave Books
756 Harvard Ave.
St. Louis, MO 63130
or Whole Earth Access

The Longest Cave

This is the dramatic story of several generations of cavers whose exciting and dangerous explorations in Kentucky's limestone labyrinths culminated in the big connection between the Flint Ridge cave system and Mammoth Cave, forming the longest cave in the world (144 miles plus). Here is the romance and adventure of big time caving, told by two of the participants. —Richard A. Watson

•

His chest stuck.

For a few moments, Roger allowed himself to enjoy the horrible fantasy of being stuck there until Tom and Richard returned, his lamp out of reach, slowly dimming and then going out. Blackness. And then what if they could not pull him out or push him through?

Actually, neither the lamp nor the bag was out of reach. Roger suddenly exhaled all his breath, pushed hard with his feet, and ground his way through the tightest part of the Chest Compressor.

Hands and knees crawl in shallow water.

The Longest Cave
Roger W. Brucker and
Richard A. Watson
1976; 316 pp.
$9.95 postpaid from:
Southern Illinois
University Press
P. O. Box 3697
Carbondale, IL 62901
or Whole Earth Access

• Cave books and maps may be had from Speleobooks, P. O. Box 333, Wilbraham, MA 01095.

Movin' On

(Equipment & Techniques for Winter Hikers)
Harry Roberts
1977; 135 pp.

$8.95

($9.95 postpaid) from:
Stone Wall Press, Inc.
1241 30th Street NW
Washington, D.C. 20007
or Whole Earth Access

Movin' On

When someone asks me to recommend a book on winter camping and hiking this is the one I tell 'em about. It's the one I use too. —JB

•

A winter stove is a gasoline stove. Accept that as gospel. Gasoline is a fluid that can be supercooled. Its freezing point is savagely low. If you're filling a stove on a -20°F day, that fuel is at -20°F. To spill it on your hands is to invite instant frostbite. *Don't handle gasoline on a cold day without hand protection.* Period. Don't even grab the container without hand protection.

•

If there's a "secret" to pitching a tent on snow, it's this — start with a firm platform. Truck around on your skis or your snowshoes, pack out the kitchen and the tent area and pack out a trail to the area you'll use as a latrine. Be meticulous; be thorough — which means, get to camp on time! . . . If you start with semi-fluff, you'll find that the heavier parts of your body settle very deeply indeed into the snow and the rest of you "floats." If you don't pack down the snow under your tent, you'll end up like a jackknife.

Cross-Country Skiing

This book accents technique and the learning thereof (kids are included too). The photographs are very fine; it must have been lots of work to get them all so clear. Most of the instruction is aimed at what backcountry skiers sometimes refer to as "slot-car" skiing — doing your thing on prepared tracks and on groomed slopes. Nothing wrong with that though. It's good to learn where there are fewer problems. That's where the racing action is too, another subject this book covers. —JB

Cross-Country Skiing

Ned Gillette
and John Dostal
1984; 234 pp.

$3.95

($5.45 postpaid) from:
Bantam Books
414 E. Golf Road
Des Plaines, IL 60016
or Whole Earth Access

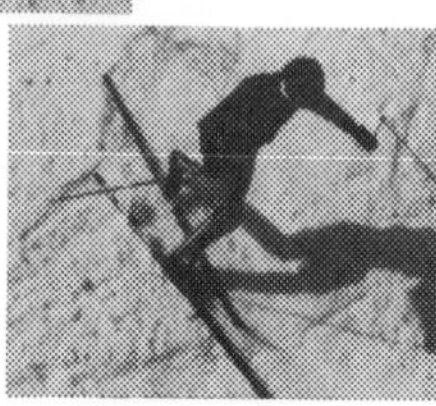

Stepping to initiate a turn.

Mountain Skiing

Another ski book. This one, however, concerns cross-country and Nordic skiing where the penalties tend to be more severe than on the groomed and patrolled slopes of Happy Valley. Back in the boonies you need to know more than you are likely to get from a few hours with a handsome instructor. Lots of quite exceptional photographs show what you should look like out there, including detailed recovery from mistakes. The accompanying advice is the most experienced I've seen — I wish I'd been able to read it before spending time in Uncle Sam's Ski Infantry. The point of view is state-of-the-art rather than traditional. The attitude is friendly, jargon-free, and competent. The effect is to encourage you to greater things. —JB

•

The Ski Glissade
Even the most wacky skiers will stop and think twice before attempting a slope that seems to be too dangerous for turning. Such a slope doesn't necessarily have to be an almost vertical wall. The combination of blue ice, 20° chute, and cliffs or crevasses below, for example, can be much more threatening than a 50° open slope filled with soft corn snow.

The technique for such situations is the ski glissade, basically sideslipping with one pole acting as a brake and outrigger. Place the poles together, basket to grip, and hold them with one hand close to the braking basket, the other a bit higher. Dig the point of one pole into the slope, and lean on it. By distributing the weight evenly over the two skis and the pole tip, you should be able to sideslip on very bad breakable crust.

The ski glissade.

Mountain Skiing

Vic Bein
1982; 192 pp.

$9.95

postpaid from:
The Mountaineers/Books
306 Second Avenue W.
Seattle, WA 98119
or Whole Earth Access

• Start your young'uns early and safely.
Teaching Children to Ski: Asbjorn Flemen & Olav Grosvold, translated by Michael Brady, 1983; 176 pp.; **$9.95** ($10.70 postpaid) from Leisure Press/Human Kinetics Publishers, Inc., P. O. Box 5076, Champaign, IL 61820 (or Whole Earth Access).

• See "First Aid," page 214.

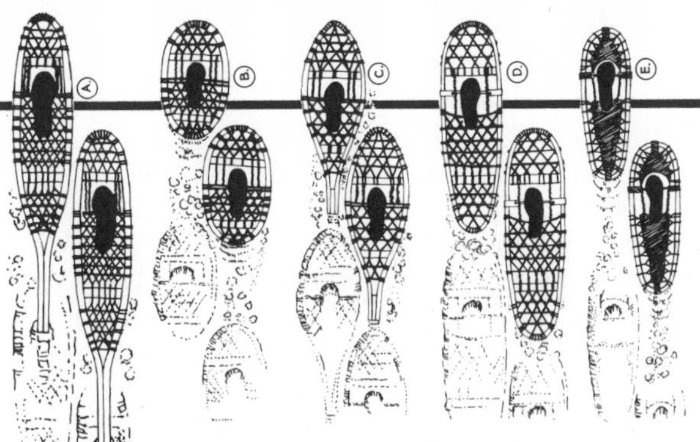

Types of snowshoes: A, Yukon; B, bearpaw; C, beavertail; D, modified bearpaw and its offspring; E, the Western.

Traversing usually develops two trails, one above the other.

Snowshoeing

Bigfooting gracelessly along on snowshoes seems mightily slow at first, especially when compared to swoopy skiing. Matter of fact, snowshoeing is even slower than dry-ground hiking. But then again you're unlikely to lose control on a steep slope, and you can plod your way through terrain and brush that would entangle or otherwise dismay a skier. You can snowshoe right over tough stuff that would stop a summer hiker. You can stay afloat in all but the fluffiest deep snow — silently, privately, and inexorably. This compleat book tells you how. —JB

Snowshoeing
Gene Prater
1980; 176 pp.
$7.95
postpaid from:
The Mountaineers/Books
306 Second Avenue W.
Seattle, WA 98119
or Whole Earth Access

Ramer/Alpine Research, Inc.

Ramer ski bindings and poles are considered by many people to be the best available. I agree. Ramer also offers a passel of other high-quality snowgoer's equipment, some of it from Europe. The classy catalog is also used as an information exchange for a Backcountry Network intended to further the sport of backcountry skiing — a great idea. —JB

Ramer adjustable poles are available with several grips, including this Self Arrest model; brakes for steep stuff.

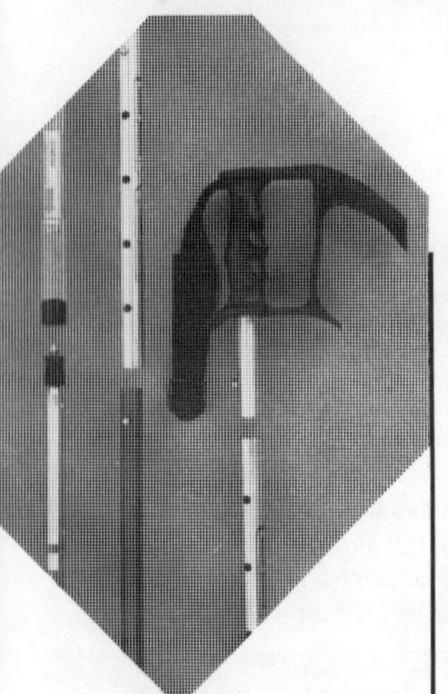

Ramer
Catalog **free** from:
Alpine Research, Inc.
1930 Central Avenue
Suite F
Boulder, CO 80301

Sherpa Snow-Claw Snowshoes

These designs in aluminum and neoprene may not look right if you love the traditional wood and rawhide, but they sure do work well. They work well in summer too: no rot, no porcupine damage, and no need to varnish. A built-in claw for slick conditions is a boon in the boondocks. The slim style and light weight reduces the dreaded mal d'raquette, the severe pain caused by walking with legs a-spraddle. After a few miles, you'll consider their looks as functional elegance. —JB

Sherpa Snow-Claw Snowshoes
$107-$144

Information **free** from:
Sherpa, Inc.
2222 Diversey
Chicago, IL 60647

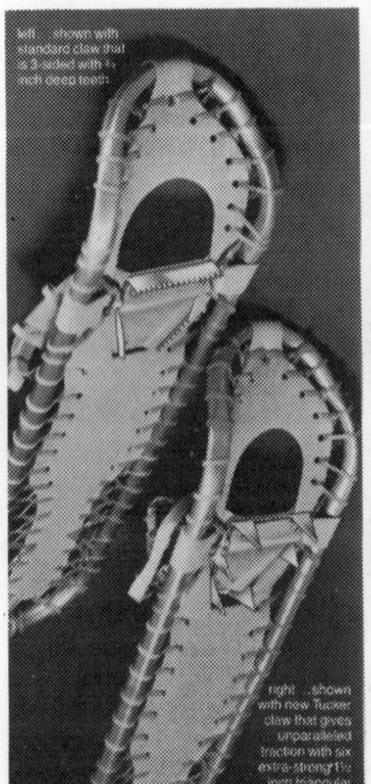

Avalanche Safety

The best, clearest and most practical explanation of avalanches and avalanche safety I've read. Stresses understanding mountain weather, topography, and snow structure leading to avalanches so one can learn to avoid hazardous areas and travel safely on snow-covered mountains. It goes on to cover rescue and first aid procedures in detail and has a fine section on the use of avalanche rescue beacons. Dramatic photographs and excellent diagrams make this sometimes complex subject easy to understand. Frequent anecdotes make for interesting reading. Read it before heading out next winter; it could save your life. —Lance Alexander

•

What to do if avalanched:
Shout out so your companions know you are in trouble.
Throw away your ski poles; you should already be free of the wrist loops.
Kick off your skis.
Grab at trees or rocks.
Wriggle free of your pack.
Swim.
Shut your mouth.
Get into a sitting position facing downhill, with your legs out in front and together.
Make a last desperate effort to pop yourself out if you're below the surface when the slide starts to slow down.
Make a breathing space in front of your nose and mouth with one hand and push the other one towards where you think the surface is.

These photographs of a skier-released avalanche are excellent examples of quick slab release. Note how the snow fractures, cracks and starts moving all at the same time.

Avalanche Safety
(For Skiers and Climbers)
Tony Daffern
1983; 172 pp.
$9.95
($10.95 postpaid) from:
Alpenbooks
P. O. Box 27344
Seattle, WA 98125
or Whole Earth Access

IT'S JUST YOU AND THE WATER and a simple, silent, responsive craft. That's not news: people have been paddling for thousands of years. The news is imaginative designs made possible by modern materials. Kayaks weigh half what they did ten years ago. Same for canoes, and the better brands — Mad River* is a good one — have adapted sophisticated shapes that have finally left the birchbark look behind. Whitewater canoes are now nearly indestructible; I've criminally abused my Blue Hole* 16-footer for years and it still works fine. Rowing boats used to be so fragile that only a few specially-trained people could use them. Now anyone can join the fun. We're not showing a bunch of boats here, because there are literally hundreds of 'em, each adapted to certain uses. Check *Canoe* magazine or your local dealer for advice. I'd advise against buying by mail unless you are pretty sure of what you want. It's best to paddle first.

—JB

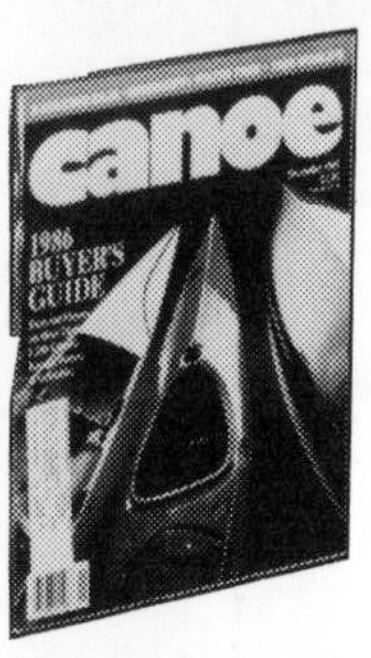

Canoe
George I. Thomas, Editor
$15/year
(6 issues) from:
Canoe
P. O. Box 10748
Des Moines, IA 50349

Canoe

After a bit of struggle, this magazine now serves all canoers and kayakers, and quite nicely too. ***Canoe****'s December issue features a Buyer's Guide that's the only place you can compare (on paper) all available brands.* —*JB*

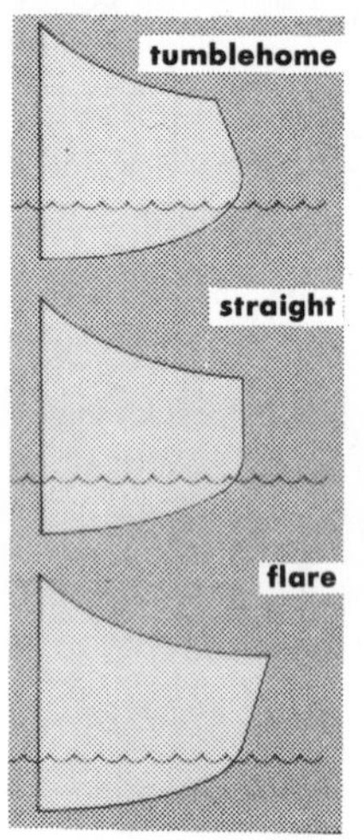

•
Flare in the bow will help keep water from rolling into the boat as it heads into waves and spray.

A slight amount of tumblehome may be desirable at the paddling stations on tandem canoes to give better access to the water. In "sit-n-switch" solo canoes, this tumblehome is even more important, since the overall width can be a hindrance for a sitting paddler.

Canoeing Handbook
Geoff Good, Editor
1983; 349 pp.
$18.75
postpaid from:
Sea Trek
Schoonmaker Point —
Foot of Spring Street
Sausalito, CA 94965

Canoeing Handbook

Paddle power is what this book is about: canoes and kayaks of every sort used for touring, racing, and frolic. What makes the book special is the inclusion of lesser-known subjects such as sea and surf kayaks, sailing canoes, and instruction for disabled folks. If your arms work OK, you can probably go boating. Design, equipment choice, technique, and training are all discussed for the many kinds of boats and water conditions. "Comprehensive" would be a fair description here. The British viewpoint and word use is useful and not a hindrance.
—*JB [Suggested by Will Nordby]*

A rocking exercise to train the paddler to stay in an inverted canoe.

The Entry-Level Guide to Canoeing & Kayaking

The editors of ***Canoe*** *magazine publish this guide once a year. It's especially good for helping you decide what equipment you need (the ads are pure catnip) and encouraging you to use it well. There are articles on elementary technique, renting, and places to learn. But it's the adventure stories, tantalizingly illustrated with calendar photographs, that are gonna getcha . . .* —*JB*
[Suggested by Will Nordby]

An improvised spritsail rig. ►

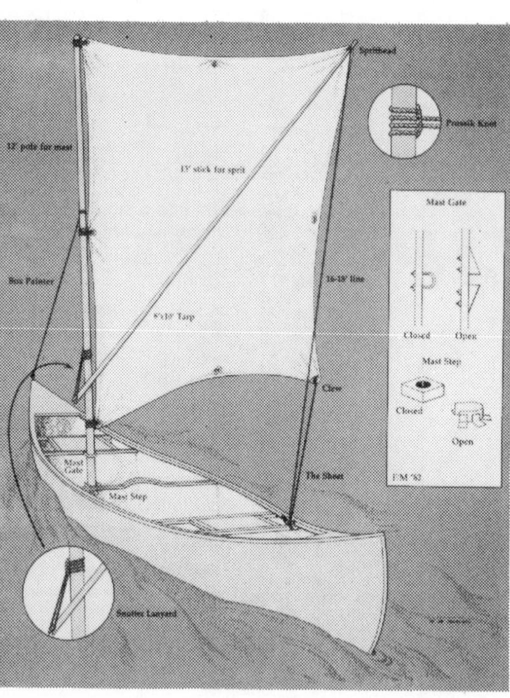

Solo canoeing lets you choose how, when and where you want to paddle. Ah, independence!

The Entry-Level Guide to Canoeing & Kayaking
John Viehman, Editor
$3.95/year
(annual) from:
Canoe
P. O. Box 597
Camden, ME 08483

***Mad River Canoes:** information **free** from P. O. Box 610W, Mad River Green, Waitsfield, VT 05673.
***Blue Hole Canoes:** information **free** from The Blue Hole Canoe Co., Sunbright, TN 37872.

THINK OF KAYAKING one of those pristine rivers you see in Alaska magazines. Nice, but how do you get a boat there? Or, more prosaically, wouldn't it be nice to have a boat with you on your vacation? Except you have to worry about it being stolen from your roof rack. The answer is a portable boat. They come in three basic types: skeleton-with-skin, sectional take-apart, and inflatable. I can tell you from happy experience that a portable will expand your horizons. They'll store in a closet, too. Here are five examples of the breed. —JB

Klepper

Heavy-duty and tough enough for an Atlantic crossing (someone did it!), the Klepper nonetheless stows in a pair of dufflebags. Assembly of the elegantly crafted parts is easy, but it takes patience and discipline to assure that sand is not being trapped in the precision joints — sand-jammed joints can make disassembly a bear. The frame might well win a prize in a sculpture exhibit. —JB

Klepper "Aerius"
$2,000 (approx.)
Information **free** from:
Klepper America
35 Union Square West
New York, NY 10003

Feathercraft

Here we're talking more bird than boat: the Feathercraft weighs less than 40 pounds, making it the lightest of its size available. The aluminum-tubing frame is shock-corded together in the manner often seen in backpacking tents. The unassembled boat fits into one carrying bag equipped with padded shoulder straps. That's about as portable as you can get. —JB
[Suggested by Will Nordby]

Feathercraft
$2,190-$2,798
Catalog **free** from:
Feathercraft Kayaks Ltd.
1334 Cartwright Street
Vancouver, BC
Canada V6H 3R8

Folbot

These well-proven domestic craft look a tad crude compared to a Klepper, but they work well enough. Most come in kit form, bringing the already low price within reach of just about anyone. The folding/unfolding procedure doesn't seem to be particularly finicky, but I notice that most Folbots I've seen are on roof racks, assembled. —JB

SUPER Specifications:

17½ feet	**length**
37 inches	**width**
18 inches	**maximum height**
10 inches	**side height**
79 lbs.	**net weight**
720 lbs.	**safe capacity**
Cockpit size: (Space for 2 to 4 people)	**96" long, 23" wide**

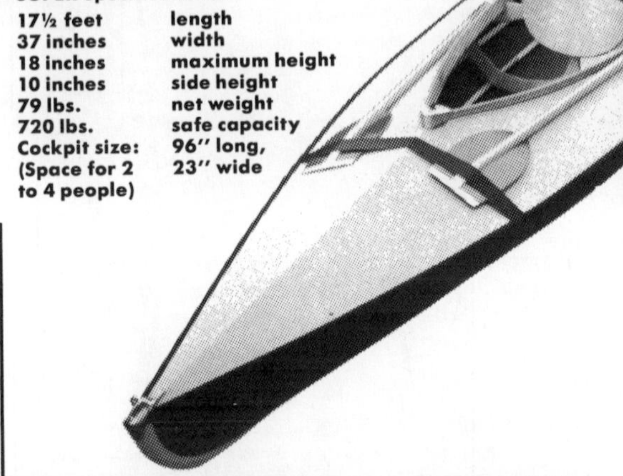

Folbot
$395-$950
Catalog **$2** from:
Folbot, Inc.
P. O. Box 70877
Charleston, SC 29405

Nimbus Seafarer Take-Aparts

Certain conventional hard-shell models of the Nimbus line of kayaks can be had broken down into two, three, or more (as required) screw-together watertight sections. They're available as kits too. —JB
[Suggested by Will Nordby]

The Nimbus sectional sea kayak.

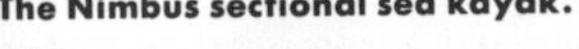

Nimbus Seafarer Take-Aparts
$1,795
Information **$1** from:
Nimbus Kayak Specialists
#6-2330 Tyner Street
Port Coquitlam, BC
Canada V3C 2Z1

• See "Portable Bikes" (p. 267).

Metzeler Inflatables

These inflatables are more rigid than most others and are famous for taking a beating that would trash a folding kayak. Pull the plug, and they whup down to a 2½x2x1' wad that's tidy but no lighter than a kayak. Payloads can be as much as 900 pounds! Inflatables tend to be annoyingly or even impossibly skittish on windy, open water. —JB

Metzeler Inflatable Boats
$495-$2,995
Information **free** from:
Leisure Products
Marketing Systems, Inc.
1044 Northern Blvd.
Roslyn, NY 11576

Derek C. Hutchinson's Guide to Sea Kayaking
Derek C. Hutchinson
1985; 122 pp.
$12.95
($14.45 postpaid) from:
Pacific Search Press
222 Dexter Ave. North
Seattle, WA 98109
or Whole Earth Access

Sea Kayaker

AFTER YEARS of obscure cult status, sea kayaking is fast becoming mainstream (so to speak). With a sea 'yak you can go where no other boat dares venture — fjords, narrow inlets, tiny islands, or estuaries — yet you can confidently scoot across open sea. The low windage and center of gravity make them far more seaworthy than more imposing craft. As with any relatively new sport, there's an unruly variety of equipment available, accompanied by rousing controversy. Right now there are two basic types of sea kayak: pointy, English, high-performance designs that are fast and maneuverable but lacking in cargo space; and large volume, stable American designs that carry a lot and cope with conditions found along North American shores. Test-paddling before you buy is highly recommended. A firm grip on your wallet is also recommended when you're looking at those enticing photographs of sea kayakers cavorting amongst the whales in Baja or silently navigating among the icebergs at the foot of an Alaskan glacier.

Confession: I'm going to buy one soon. There's a kind of purity to sea kayaking that's irresistible. —JB

Sea Kayaking • Sea Kayaking

Sea Kayaking
(A Manual for Long-Distance Touring)
John Dowd
1983; 240 pp.
$8.95
($10.45 postpaid) from:
University of Washington Press
P. O. Box C50096
Seattle, WA 98145
or Whole Earth Access

Why note two books on the same subject? Both authors are among the most experienced sea kayakers in the world. Both want you to join them, to gain the skills, to be safe, and to share the adventure. But they disagree on equipment and technique, sometimes taking opposing views (I was about to say opposite tacks) on critical matters such as self-rescue. Sea kayaking is a young sport. It's hard to say who is right — perhaps both are. In any case, it's you who is going to be out there braving the elements. I'd read everything available. —JB
[Suggested by Will Nordby]

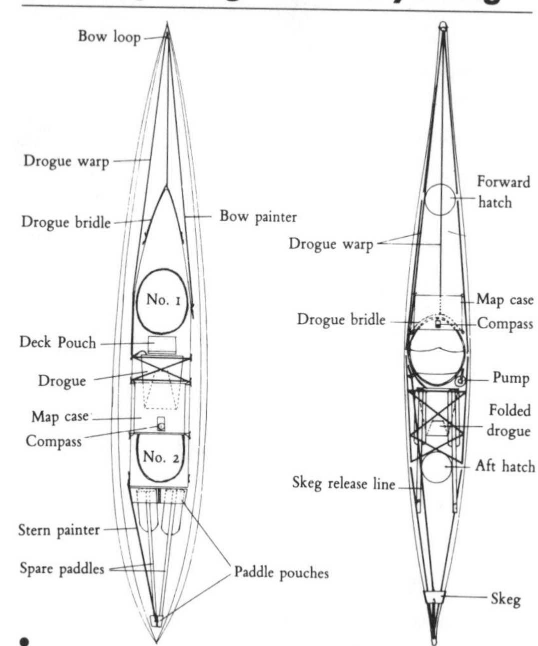

A contrast in design philosophy: Pacific Northwest (left) double is stable, buoyant, voluminous — well suited to poking around fjords and islands. West Greenland or English style (right) is fast, sporty, good in rough seas, but can't hold much and is demanding.
—*Sea Kayaking (A Manual for Long-Distance Touring)*

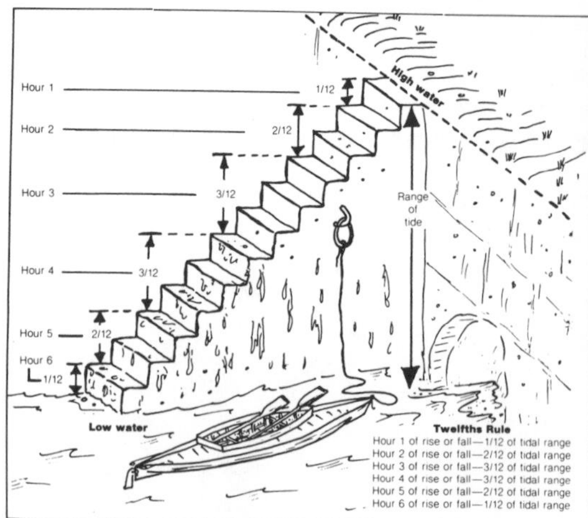

Sea Kayaker

Sea Kayaker
John Dowd, Editor
$10/year
(4 issues) from:
Sea Kayaker
6327 Seaview Ave. NW
Seattle, WA 98107

Equipment, adventures, latest techniques (usually discovered the hard way), and the wonder of it all are well served in this quarterly.
—JB *[Suggested by Will Nordby]*

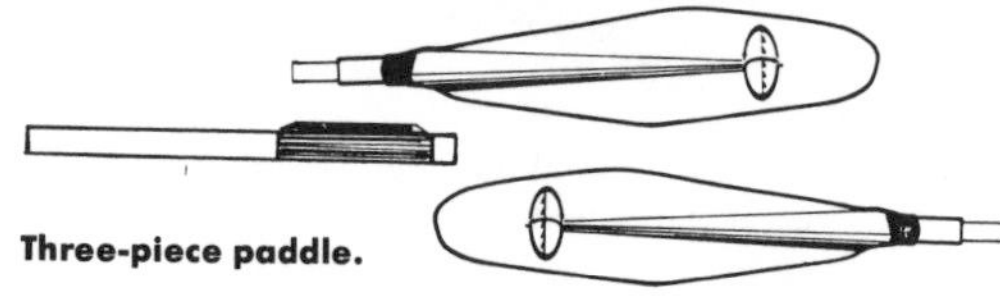

Three-piece paddle.

Take me to your dealer

We don't often feature dealers. But in a young, relatively undeveloped endeavor, a dealer carrying the products of a number of small manufacturers is often the only widely experienced expert around. Herewith are some dealers of good repute. —JB

Ecomarine Ocean Kayak Centre: Catalog **$2**; 1668 Duranleau Street, Granville Island, Maritime Market, Vancouver, BC Canada V6H 3S4.

Great River Outfitters: Catalog **free**; 3721 Shallow Brook, Bloomfield Hills, MI 48013.

Sea Trek: Catalog **$2**; Schoonmaker Point — Foot of Spring Street, Sausalito, CA 94965.

Canoecraft

A person of modest means and skills can actually build one of these "stripper" canoes by following the extraordinarily complete procedures in this book. The authors lead you through the scary parts, never assuming you already know how to "trim the remaining tips flush with the inner stem." There's none of the subtle snobbery found in so many boatbuilding books. Complete parts lists and sources are provided along with the advice. Who can resist the cover shot? Next winter's work awaits you. . . . —JB

◄ Continue planking up one side only once you have covered the stems, extending the strips over the keel-line.

Canoecraft
Ted Moores
and Marilyn Mohr
1983; 145 pp.
$14.95
($15.95 postpaid) from:
Harrowsmith
The Creamery
Charlotte, VT 05445
or Whole Earth Access

Rowing Boats

These needlecraft are a far cry from the traditional seaworthy workboats that have graced our shores for centuries. You can still get the older styles, some in modern materials. But lately there has been a great surge of creativity in long, thin shells that practically fly over the water. Rowing is great aerobic training too, incomparably more aesthetic than (ugh) rowing machines. These two dealers carry a variety of equipment. Their expertise is boundless. —JB

Small Craft Inc.: brochure **free**; Box 766, Baltic, CT 06330.
Rowing Crafters: brochure **$1**; 520 Waldo Point, Sausalito, CA 94965.

Rowing Crafters

Canoe Poling
Al, Syl and Frank Beletz
1974; 148 pp.
$6.95
postpaid from:
A. C. Mackenzie
River Press
P. O. Box 9301
Richmond Heights
Station
Richmond Heights,
MO 63117
or Whole Earth Access

Canoe Poling

Canoe UPstream for a change, even in whitewater. Edge your way down streams that would be impossible to paddle. Sneak along through mangrove swamps. That's what poling technique can make possible. This book is scruffily produced, but it has everything you need to know and is well illustrated. The same folks will sell you a fine aluminum pole. I have one and it works better than you'd believe. —JB

• This book on the joys, terrors, and paddling technique of open canoeing is remarkably good — it'd be hard to do it better. It's the photographs that do it. They're so clear you'd think they were taken by a nearby fish. As one who regularly participates in canoe madness, I rate this instruction, and spirit thereof, A+.

Path of the Paddle: Bill Mason, 1984; 200 pp. **$18.95** postpaid from Firefly Books Ltd., 3520 Pharmacy Avenue/Unit 1-C, Scarborough, Ontario M1W2T8 (or Whole Earth Access).

Yakima Racks

Lemme see . . . an ideal rack would be sturdy, lockable, adaptable to any load (boats, bikes, skis, luggage, or plywood), and fit any car, including the new ones without rain gutters. You got it! —JB

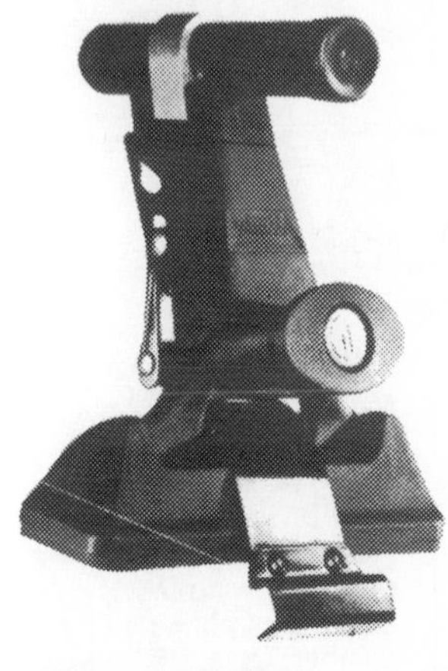

Yakima Racks
Brochure **free** from:
Yakima Racks
P. O. Drawer 4899
Arcata, CA 95521

Open Water Sport Diver Manual
Jeppesen
1984; 289 pp.
$9.78 postpaid from:
Jeppesen Sanderson
55 Inverness Drive East
Englewood, CO 80112
or Whole Earth Access

Undercurrent
Ben Davison, Editor
$28/year
(11 issues) from:
Undercurrent
Atcom Bldg.
2312 Broadway
New York, NY 10024-4397

DAN
Membership **$15**/year
(Includes *Underwater Diving Accident Manual*, *Alert Diver* newsletter, and membership card and tank decals showing DAN emergency phone number) from:
DAN
P. O. Box 3823
Duke University
Medical Center
Durham, NC 27710

AT FIRST GLANCE, a scuba diver must seem like some kind of masochist: swathed in neoprene; harnessed to a cylinder of compressed gases; festooned with hoses, regulators & gauges; 20-some-odd pounds of lead strapped around the waist, like middle-age spread gone wild. Dip below the surface of the water, though, and that encumbrance melts into the background. Diving is as close as most of us will ever come to the weightlessness of space, in an environment as alien as can be found on this planet.

People today are diving in just about any body of water that happens to be handy: from the warm tropics to the frigid north, in lakes, rivers, caverns, and quarries. All that's necessary is reasonably good health and physical ability, completion of a course of instruction by one of the recognized certification agencies, and a collection of the above mentioned equipment. Although equipment can be easily rented, you'll eventually want to buy your own. Get on the mailing lists of several dive shops in your area. Most offer reasonable sale prices, and you should be able to try out some of the gear in their pool before you buy.

—David Burnor

Open Water Sport Diver Manual

Of the courses available, I'm most impressed with Jeppesen's. It is currently taught by the YMCA, NAUI, SSI, PDIC, NASE, and many PADI instructors, and meets the requirements of all other diving certification agencies. They have a good manual that emphasizes the development of safe diving habits, a thorough understanding of diving principles, and a respect for the underwater environment. They're also on top of the latest research. Using the findings from recent ultrasound bubble detection tests, they've revised their dive tables to show much more conservative no-decompression limits than the U.S. Navy tables in common use. —*David Burnor*

•

After a dive like this, your "bottom time" is 30 minutes at 50 feet, even though you actually spend only 15 minutes at 50 feet. Bottom time, in other words, refers to the *total* time of the dive from the beginning of the descent to the beginning of the direct ascent. The depth of the dive always refers to the deepest point of the dive, no matter how briefly you stay at that depth.

•

It is important to note that even though the No-Decompression Limits Table indicates that you can dive as long as you wish at depths of 30 feet or less, it is best to avoid extreme exposures even at shallow depths and, as a general rule, to be more conservative than the table, especially if you fall into any of the categories listed.

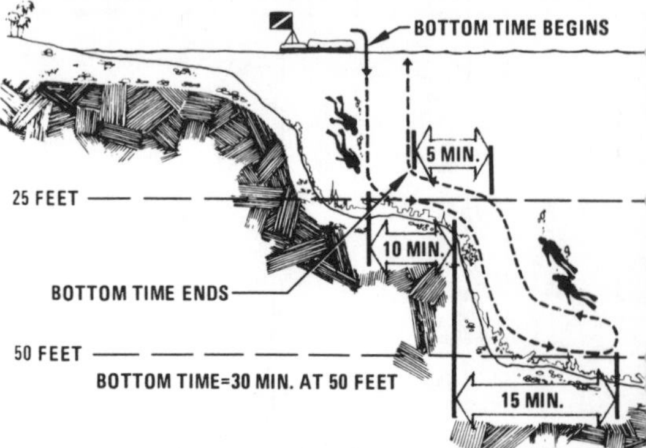

Undercurrent

There are a number of slick diving magazines available, but each month I look forward to a slim newsletter called ***Undercurrent****. It's like a* ***Consumer Reports*** *of the diving industry. With no paid ads, they're not beholden to anyone. Like restaurant reviewers, their critics visit diving resorts anonymously — getting the same treatment that you will — and present a full report, warts and all. Unbiased equipment evaluations, practical consumer advice, and sound safety tips round out each issue.*

—*David Burnor*

•

Equipment
Not only must all gear be in good working order, but the diver must also be familiar with the specific gear to be used. New or unfamiliar gear should be tried first in a swimming pool, not in open water. All scuba equipment should be overhauled or serviced by a certified scuba specialist at least once a year. Additionally, divers should understand the basic mechanical principles of the scuba equipment.

Perhaps the most important area of responsibility is the physical and psychological well-being of the diver about to enter the water. To avoid excessive stress the diver should maintain physical fitness, overlearn skills through practice and repetition, know his physical limitations and practice buddymanship.

DAN

Given good instruction and equipment, and a clear head, diving is a safe sport. However, there are certain dangers not found on dry land. Air embolism and decompression sickness are the most severe problems and immediate recompression treatment may be necessary to prevent serious, permanent injury. ***DAN****, the Divers Alert Network, maintains a 24-hour emergency telephone line (919/684-8111) staffed by physicians trained in all aspects of diving medicine. They, and their network of regional coordinators, work with the injured diver and the physician on the scene to insure the proper diagnosis and treatment of dive-related problems. Their* ***Alert Diver*** *newsletter, available to members, reports on the latest findings in diving medicine and safety.* —*David Burnor*

•

Do not attempt in-water recompression!
In-water recompression of the diver usually ends with the diver forced to the surface by cold or inadequate air supply. This causes incomplete treatment and further nitrogen uptake by the diver. If a victim has mild signs and symptoms of decompression sickness, the usual result is a much more seriously injured diver. If the initial symptoms are serious, the result is usually disastrous. In-water recompression should never be attempted.

—*Underwater Diving Accident Manual*

WindRider

Advanced technique, competition, product tests, interesting ads, and, oh MY, stunning color photographs of people doing exuberantly drastic maneuvers. YUM! —JB

WindRider
Terry Snow, Publisher
$11.97/year
(7 issues) from:
WindRider
P. O. Box 183
Mt. Morris, IL 61054

Boardsailing

Unlike other high-speed sports that intimately pit you against the laws of physics, boardsailing (windsurfing) carries no threat of death or maiming. But you still have to know what you're doing or no thrills — just disconsolate swimming. The authors of this book remember what it feels like to be a beginner. The pictures and instructions are just what you need to get started. Figure on getting wet. —JB

Sailing in a straight line

Tilting the rig back turns the board towards the wind

Tilting the rig forwards turns the board away from the wind

Boardsailing
Charles Wand-Tetley and John Heath
1986; 48 pp.
$6.95
($8.95 postpaid) from:
International Marine Publishing Company
21 Elm Street
Camden, ME 04843
or Whole Earth Access

The Essential Knot Book

Just the knots you're likely to actually need; diagrammed, photographed, and untangled. —JB

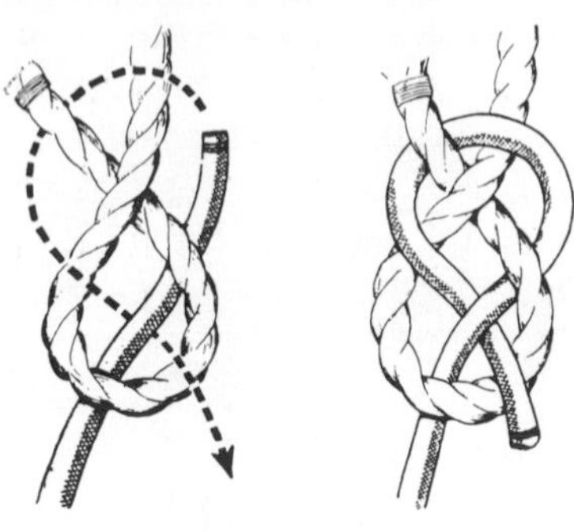

Carrick Bend: This is an excellent knot for joining two lines together whatever their material or relative diameters.

When drawn tight the knot capsizes leaving the bitter ends together and parallel.

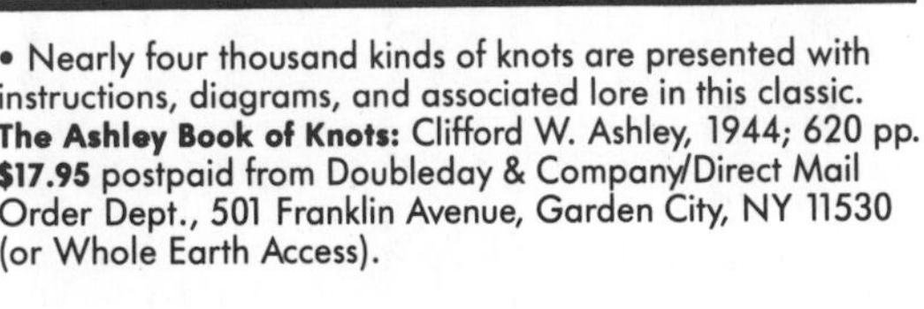

• Nearly four thousand kinds of knots are presented with instructions, diagrams, and associated lore in this classic. **The Ashley Book of Knots:** Clifford W. Ashley, 1944; 620 pp. **$17.95** postpaid from Doubleday & Company/Direct Mail Order Dept., 501 Franklin Avenue, Garden City, NY 11530 (or Whole Earth Access).

The Essential Knot Book
Colin Jarman
1984; 85 pp.
$8.95
(10.95 postpaid) from:
International Marine Publishing Company
21 Elm Street
Camden, ME 04843
or Whole Earth Access

—Chapman Pi

BOATS, I'M abundantly convinced, are better for building competence and mental health than any other toy — skis, airplanes, performance cars, or interactive graphic computers. It has something to do with operating on the wildly various interface between the two fluids, water and air. It takes balance — whether you're in a kayak or a 75-foot sailboat — and real or threatened dunkings drive the lessons of balance into your fibre.

And beyond that, if they're lived with, boats teach aesthetics. They can't help it. —Stewart Brand

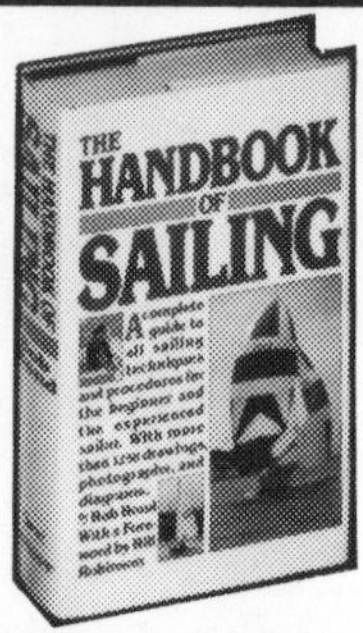

The Handbook of Sailing
Bob Bond
1980; 352 pp.
$22.50
($23.50 postpaid) from:
Random House
Order Dept.
400 Hahn Road
Westminster, MD 21157
or Whole Earth Access

The Handbook of Sailing

"This is the hull" is where the instruction starts; utterly Level One. But you won't stay there long, because it goes on to include the underlying logic of the moves, encouraging you to make them part of your thought process. Basic sailing technique is illustrated with small open boats (including catamarans) of the sort most often used by learners. The drawings and photographs are exceptionally good, detailed enough to show such fine points as preferred body English. More advanced technique is presented applied to ocean-going craft. Comprehensive and free of jargon, the information is easily available to the most lubberly of landlubbers. —JB [Suggested by John Hall]

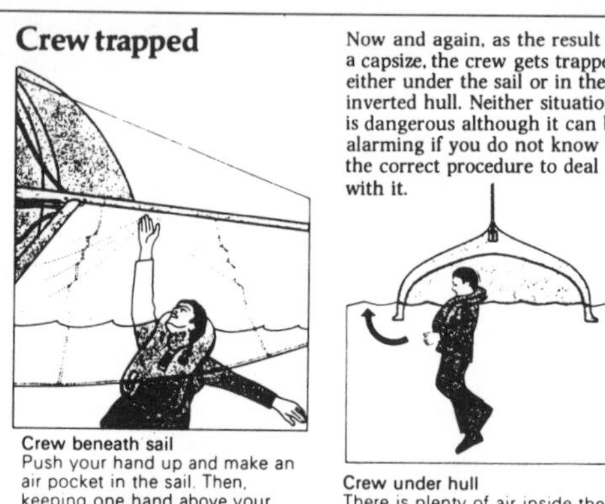

Crew trapped
Now and again, as the result of a capsize, the crew gets trapped either under the sail or in the inverted hull. Neither situation is dangerous although it can be alarming if you do not know the correct procedure to deal with it.
Crew beneath sail
Push your hand up and make an air pocket in the sail. Then, keeping one hand above your head to push the sail, work your way, using a seamline to guide you, to the outside edge.
Crew under hull
There is plenty of air inside the hull. Swim to an outer edge and push yourself under the side decking to get out.

Chapman Piloting
Elbert S. Maloney
1985; 624 pp.
$24.50
($26 postpaid) from:
William Morrow
Publishing Company
6 Henderson Drive
West Caldwell, NJ 07006
or Whole Earth Access

Chapman Piloting

For reference on board stick by "Chapman's." In print since 1922, now in its 57th edition, this is the only available one-volume complete introduction to running a boat — from its excellent intro to nautical terminology through navigation, rules of the road, flag bloody etiquette, weather, electronics, boat trailering, the whole wet gamut. That it is not at all restricted to sailboats helps broaden and inform the otherwise narrow windblown mind.
—Stewart Brand

▲ Boats that must cross a bar with breaking waves must avoid "pitchpoling" — being thrown end over end if caught driving down the face of a steep sea, burying the bow. This double-ended fisherman just misses being caught on the forward face of a breaker. This is no place for pleasure boats.

Weather Warning Signals

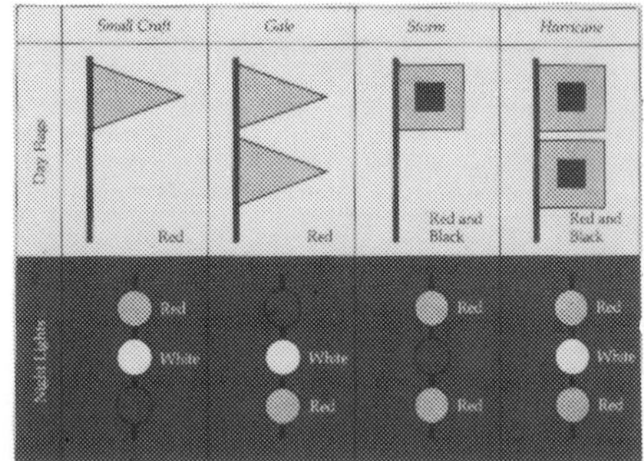

Sailing on a Micro-Budget
Larry Brown
1984; 163 pp.
$14.95 postpaid from:
Simon and Schuster
Mail Order Sales
200 Old Tappan
Old Tappan, NJ 07675
or Whole Earth Access

Sailing on a Micro-Budget

Yachtsmen may blanch at the very title of this book, but statistics don't lie; there is a ratio between boat size and how often it gets used — the bigger, the lesser. What's available in smaller (mostly trailerable) boats and what one may expect from them is examined here in sprightly fashion — enough to make you think mad thoughts. If you can't sail that $300,000 dreamboat to Bora Bora, then perhaps you might consider a weekend at Lake Tehatchapoocoo? Indeed! Hold on a minute while I get my sneakers and suntan oil. —JB

•

The Dovekie by Edey & Duff boatbuilders, Mattapoisett, Massachusetts is a 21-foot vessel. Leeboards are simple, efficient, and they open up the cabin interior where a centerboard trunk would be a major nuisance. The Dovekie draws only four inches with leeboards raised and so it will go anywhere. The cockpit melts into a partially enclosed "cabin" that has several generous molded in skylights. Canvas panels close up the "cabin" and cockpit at night into a spacious sheltered area. The whole boat weighs only 600 pounds.

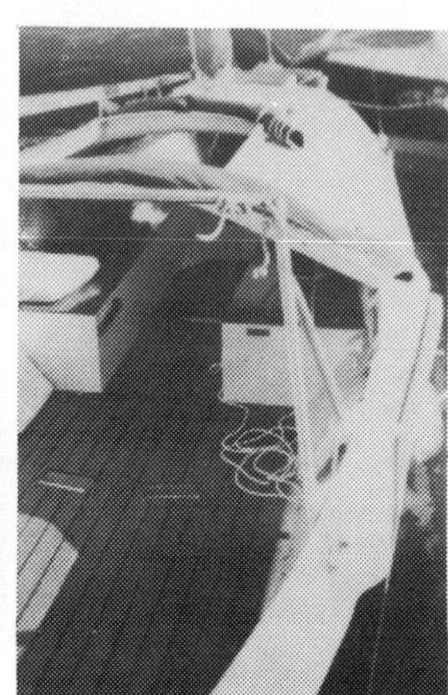

The enormous interior of the Dovekie 21.

Landfall on San Miguel, Azores. '. . . as we approached it took shape, the volcanic peaks, the dark green areas of trees, a patchwork of tiny fields . . . gathered colour and substance'.

Cruising Under Sail

*The hardcore **Whole Earth** readership must chaff whenever they see a book called essential or "must reading," but dammit you can't know too much about a boat at sea if you're going to be on one. Hiscock has spent his entire adult life on them (three boats of his own named Wanderer), sailed all seas, and kept his eyes, mind, and friendship open the whole while. His books are technically complete, redolent with examples, and filled with the blood of shared experiences — at least half his wisdom comes from the next boat over. Which is another thing: there is a kind of fifth world out there sailing, a populous, mobile society making the world its neighborhood and with the self-consciousness and gossip (from the German for God's family) to cover it all. —George Putz*

•

There is one golden rule for the beginning charterer: Be honest about your sailing experience both with yourself and the charter company. It is only fair for both of you. Self-deception is bound to catch up with you.

Cruising Under Sail
Eric Hiscock
1981; 551 pp.
$19.95
($22.95 postpaid) from:
International Marine
Publishing Company
21 Elm Street
Camden, ME 04843
or Whole Earth Access

Bare-Boating

Put your bathing suit back on; this is about how to go sailing without owning a boat (or having it own you). There are a lot of sailors who'd like to spend their once-a-year vacation at sea, but can't afford to keep a boat the rest of the time. Bare-boat charters are for them (us). At first, the prices asked seem outrageous, but they're not if you are honest about what it really costs to keep a boat in the family. Moreover, if you have some friends (they'd better be good ones), you can share the costs down to a more reasonable size. This very complete book will help you decide what sort of boat you need, how to get it, how to get familiar with it, and where to sail it. Reading this is the first step to that Bahamas dream. —JB

Bare-Boating
Brian M. Fagan
1985; 276 pp.
$34.95
($37.95 postpaid) from:
International Marine
Publishing Company
21 Elm Street
Camden, ME 04843
or Whole Earth Access

Owning a large yacht makes no sense unless you plan to sail at least two months a year. You can round the Fastnet Rock off southern Ireland in a bareboat, too.

Living Aboard

If you want to keep your simplicity voluntary, there's nothing like a small mobile home on a large mobile environment to enforce it. This is a dense practical guide to boat living, the best of its kind. —Stewart Brand

•

In Florida and California, it is common to see sailboats with air conditioners. In the North, our air conditioner has always attracted attention when we have used it. Most of our other luxuries and comforts can be tolerated by the sailboat purists, whose usual attitude is: they can have it on *their* boat, but I wouldn't have it on *mine*. Use of the air conditioner, however, seems to infuriate some of these purists, and they speak curtly to us — that is, if they speak to us at all. They seem to feel that by installing an air conditioner in a sailboat we have done something to besmirch the grand old tradition of yachting. Too bad. Anyone who isn't a stuffed shirt about sailboats realizes how sensible it really is.

•

Since we want our boat to be just as much a sailboat as any weekender's boat, we arrange her so that we can go for a sail whenever the mood strikes us. When we are at dockside, everything below deck is always stowed where it would be stowed if we were under sail. Unless we are taking the engine apart or painting, we can be underway in 15 minutes, no matter how long we have been tied up — and can encounter gale-force winds with nothing falling out of place. It has taken us nearly three years to achieve this state. We don't ever want to be like the live-aboard couple who had been in a marina for over a month and said, "We need a couple of days to get everything stowed, then we will be on our way again."

Living Aboard
Jan and Bill Moeller
1977; 305 pp.
$22.50
($25.50 postpaid) from:
International Marine
Publishing Company
21 Elm Street
Camden, ME 04843
or Whole Earth Access

- You can learn sailing on tall ships. See Sail Training (p. 374).
- One ot the all-time nautical adventures is the **Hornblower** series depicting British Empire naval adventures at their best. **The Hornblower Saga:** (Volumes 1-6), C.S. Forester, 1966-1978; 300 pp. **$7.95** each ($9.45 each postpaid) from Little, Brown and Company, 200 West Street, Waltham, MA 02254.

Build the New Instant Boats
Harold H. Payson
1984; 144 pp.
$19.95
($22.95 postpaid) from:
International Marine Publishing Co.
21 Elm Street
Camden, ME 04843
or Whole Earth Access

Instant Boat Plans
Catalog **$3** from:
Harold H. Payson
Pleasant Beach Road
South Thomaston, ME 04858

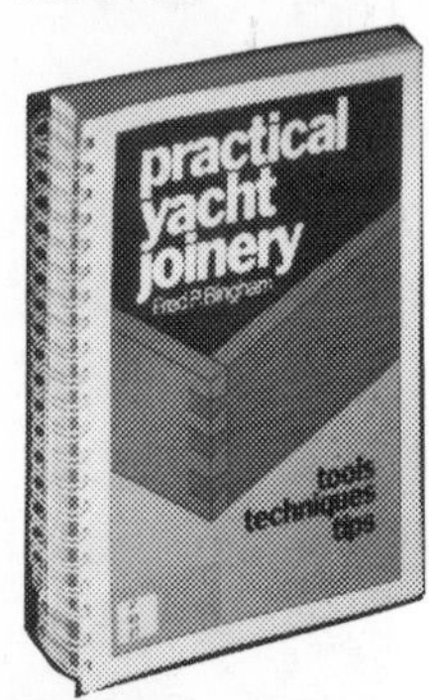

Practical Yacht Joinery
Fred P. Bingham
1983; 274 pp.
$35
($38 postpaid) from:
International Marine Publishing Co.
21 Elm Street
Camden, ME 04843
or Whole Earth Access

ONE OF LIFE'S true pleasures is the moment when you first step aboard a boat you've made. As with most such victories, there is a price: an enervating time delay between start and launch, a worrisome drain on finances, and a statistically high probability that the project will take so much time that your friends and even your mate will turn to more interesting companionship. Nonetheless . . .

—J. Baldwin

Tacking on the bottom panel. The stern transom is stiffened temporarily with a batten, and an oar holds up the forward end of the bottom panel while the after end is tacked.

Build the New Instant Boats

Boatbuilder "Dynamite" Payson and naval architect Philip Bolger — a resourceful and clever cahoots if there ever was one — would have us believe that you can make a perfectly good boat without lofting, jigs, or exotic technique, out of lumberyard wood, quickly. The actual time involved depends on how much experience you have and which of the 11 designs you choose, but several can reasonably be completed in one weekend. Cheap, too; a nifty little sailboat just right for beginners and kids can be had for about $50 and two days' work. That's about as instant as you are likely to get. I can vouch that it can be done.

Mr. Payson sells plans, too. —*JB*

•

Basically, Tack-and-Tape begins with the cutting out of plywood panels, like the planks in plank-on-frame building. These are shaped to fit together, edge to edge, and are temporarily fastened in place with tacks — which, for my choice, are light 18-gauge nails. The outside seams are filled with glass putty. The nails are then easily removed and replaced by long strips of fiberglass tape, which function as the chine logs. So far you've been working bottom up, but once this assembly is stiff enough you turn it right side up and fill and tape the interior seams.

Practical Yacht Joinery

How to put that yacht together so it stays together and looks nice whilst doing so. It is assumed that you are reasonably smart, and that you have some skill, and that you speak a bit of yacht-talk. The whole yacht-builder's toolbox is discussed in great detail before getting to actual woodworking. The woodworking is discussed in such detail that anyone, including a longtime professional, is likely to find many useful tricks of the trade. Some of the details will be useful to landlubbing greenhouse builders who wish to delay Dreaded Rot by clever water-shedding joints, something not covered in carpentry books. The text is terse and encourages one to appreciate the finer things in yacht-construction subtleties. As you'd expect, illustrations and photos make things easier to see. Much more of this and pros will be a dime a dozen! —*JB*

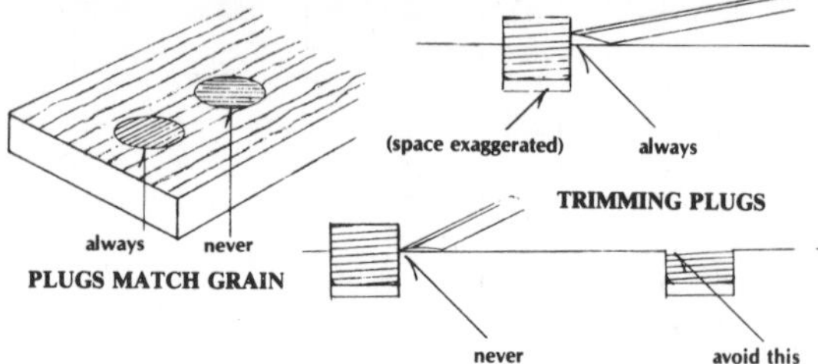

•

After a plug has been tapped in lightly with a small mallet (never to the bottom of the hole, for it may expand and then protrude), it must be cut off carefully after the binder has set. Use a slick or a fairly heavy chisel. Hold the tool blade bevel down with the cutting edge 1/16 to 1/8 inch above the surface, as shown.

Building Classic Small Craft

*For those who wish to build in the smaller size — rowing boats, small daysailers, utilities — **Building Classic Small Craft** by John Gardner is the book. The author is an experienced builder with a solid reputation for skill and the ability to make all processes easy to understand. Though he favors boats of traditional design, he has the good sense to adapt today's materials and techniques where applicable. One is able to have, with a clear conscience, one's cake and eat it too. There's now a Volume 2; more of same.* —*Peter Spectre*

•

Nail one end securely, and then use the length of the board as a lever to spring the board down in place gradually, nailing securely as you proceed, both through the cross cleats of the bottom and through the side edges. Boards several feet longer than the bottom should be used in order to gain leverage and to get the other end down into place. When the planks are securely nailed, the excess is sawed off. ►

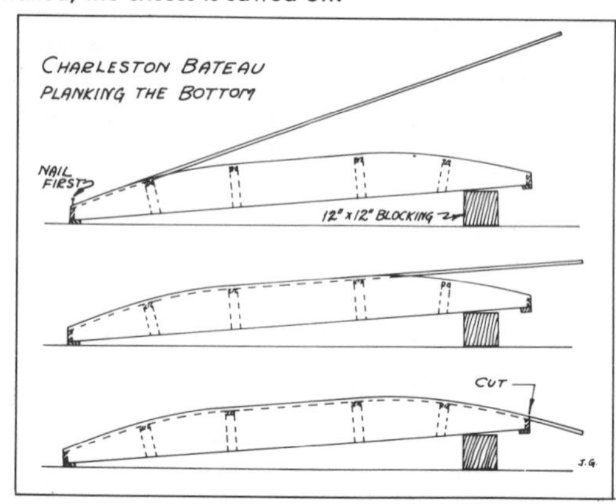

Building Classic Small Craft
John Gardner
Volume 1
1977; 300 pp.
$30 ($33 postpaid)
Volume 2
1984; 241 pp.
$35 ($38 postpaid)
Both from:
International Marine Publishing Co.
21 Elm Street
Camden, ME 04843
or Whole Earth Access

• See also **The Gougeon Brothers on Boat Construction** (p. 162).

• Every imaginable sort of boat damage is put right in this book. It's uncommonly excellent in every way. **The Boat Repair Manual**; George Buchanan, 1985, 312 pp. **$29.95** postpaid from ARCO Publishing, Prepaid Dept., 215 Park Avenue South, New York, NY 10003.

The forepeak is a feast of brightwork — mahogany ply bulkheads and an inner hull layer of cedar.

WoodenBoat
Jonathan Wilson, Editor
$18/year
(6 issues) from:
WoodenBoat
P. O. Box 956
Farmingdale, NY 11737

WoodenBoat

It's easy to use the phrase "lovingly crafted" when looking at a wooden boat in good shape. This magazine is done in the same spirit. It celebrates wooden boatbuilding and the mindwork that applies thereto. Technique, attitude, inspiration, humor (and occasionally lying) are all attended to in traditional-yet-not-stodgy articles adorned with classy photos and drawings. The advertisements are classy too — they're a great source of rare tools and materials. —JB

Defender Industries • Goldbergs' Marine

These arch-rivals are the largest of the mail-order marine supply houses. Goldbergs' has the fancier catalog and the largest variety if you count the clothing section. Defender's more modest publication has few clothes but stocks extensive fiberglass supplies not found with its competitor. Prices and sales fluctuate; I shop both when I want something.

Note that these catalogs are a lode of hardware not found in local stores or even Sears. With a bit of imagination, marine hardware can be adapted to uses undreamed of by the manufacturer. Lots of 12-volt stuff; lots of kerosene lamps; lots of nifty fittings, skylights, vents, and tools. I shop here often and I don't own a boat. —JB

[L136-4] STORM PROOF
Paper Waterproofing for
Charts and Blueprints

Impregnates and protects paper in clear coating that does not stiffen paper and allows erasures. Dries in seconds and no more crumpled charts and maps — read charts in the rain! Dramatically Improves Durability!!
½ Pint . . . $3.95 SP-1   1 Pint . . . $5.95 SP-2

—Defender Industries 1986 Catalog

LVM – AEROGEN GENERATORS

[L122-1]

Keeps batteries charged for off shore and cruising use.

Output up to 7 Amperes!
12V
LVM-25
List $418.00
Net $299.95
LVM-50
List $603.00
Net $399.95

A fair breeze is all that is required to keep refrigerator or running lights or batteries operating.

—Defender Industries 1986 Catalog

• The best selection of high quality books on things boatish is International Marine Publishing Co. Catalog **free** from International Marine Publishing Co., 21 Elm Street, Camden, ME 04843.

Small Boat Journal

This pleasing magazine deals with all small craft and isn't fussy about what they're made of. Articles are well-researched. For instance, the March 1986 issue has the most extensive presentation of rowing boats I've ever seen. Lots of product testing, too. —JB

Small Boat Journal
Thomas Baker, Editor
$15/year
(6 issues) from:
Small Boat Journal
P. O. Box 400
Bennington, VT 05201

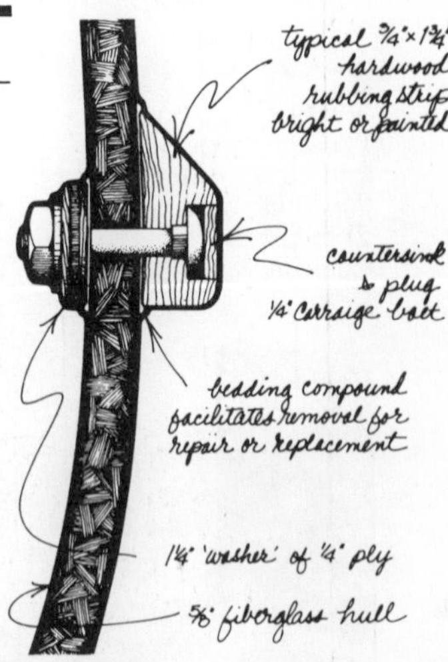

[L48-16]
HELMSMAN FOLDING SEATS
No. 568
Solid hardwood on cast bronze. Yields tremendous cockpit space. 10" diameter.
7 lb.
Goldbergs' Exclusive
List . . . $106.15 Net . . $68.95

—Defender Industries 1986 Catalog

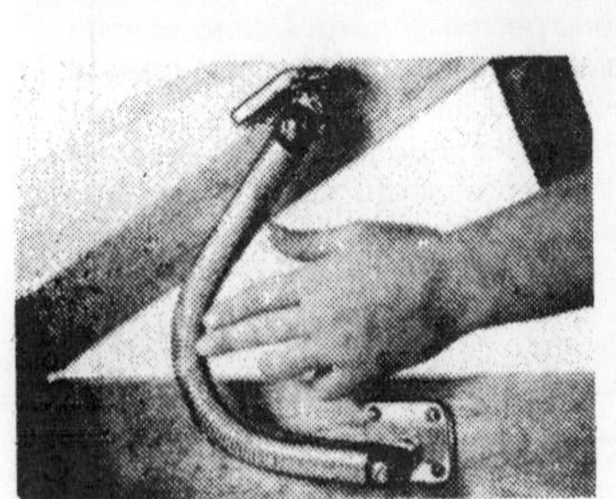

D **GIANT STAINLESS STEEL HOLDER FOR LARGE HATCHES**

This stainless steel holder is designed to keep even the largest hatches from opening "too much" or "not enough". This unit is so strong, it will safely hold even the largest hatches open. And with a simple finger touch, the hatch will easily lower. It comes with a black anodized aluminum end fitting. No. 0115-1.

R51354-148 SH. WT. 4 LB.—MFG. LIST 31.08 . . . . Only **26.66**

—Goldberg's Marine

9" TALL

G

—Goldberg's Marine

Glen-L Boat Plans • Luger Boat Kits

Glen-L is a good source of plans for all sorts of boats, including ski and house. Patterns are full size like a gift from heaven. Luger makes boat kits — by far the easiest way to build your own craft, and possibly the cheapest. —JB

Glen-L Boat Plans: Catalog **$3** from Glen-L Marine Designs, 9152 Rosecrans, Bellflower, CA 90706.
Luger Boat Kits: Catalog **free** from Luger Boats, Inc; P. O. Box 1398, St. Joseph, MO 64502.

Defender Industries

Catalog **$1.25** from:
Defender Industries, Inc.
P. O. Box 820
255 Main Street
New Rochelle,
NY 10802-0820

Goldbergs' Marine

Catalog **$2** from:
Goldbergs' Marine
202 Market Street
Philadelphia, PA 19106

Celestial Navigation Step By Step
Warren Norville
1984; 250 pp.

$21.95
($24.95 postpaid) from:
International Marine Publishing Co.
21 Elm Street
Camden, ME 04843
or Whole Earth Access

Celestial Navigation Step By Step

There are scores of navigation books in print today. They can be divided into two neat categories — those that teach both theory and practice and those that try to simplify things by teaching practice alone. Being a person who believes that understanding the why is as important as understanding the how, I don't think much of the simplified books. What I do like are books that teach me to think my way through a problem. One that does that is **Celestial Navigation Step By Step.** *It's filled with examples and problems, with solutions, and is written with style, which is unusual for this type of book.*

—Peter Spectre

•

Finding Greenwich time and date can be a real brain twister if you let it. Yet the problem is quite simple if you keep in mind that in east longitude you subtract the zone description from the local time, and in west longitude you add the zone description to the local time to get Greenwich time. If the time change at Greenwich passes through midnight, the Greenwich date will change too.

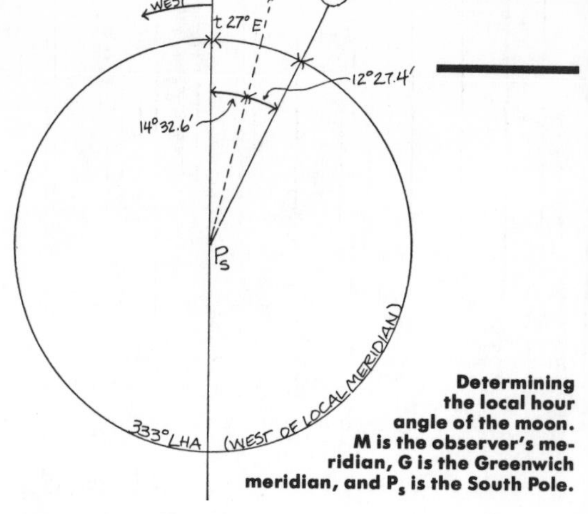

Determining the local hour angle of the moon. M is the observer's meridian, G is the Greenwich meridian, and P_s is the South Pole.

We can sum the problem up with a memory aid that will appear frequently in different ways as long as you study celestial navigation:

When longitude is east
Greenwich time is least
When longitude is west
Greenwich time is best

One Day Celestial Navigation
Otis S. Brown
1984; 133 pp.

$6.95
($7.95 postpaid) from:
Liberty Publishing
50 Scott Adam Road
Cockeysville, MD 21030
or Whole Earth Access

One Day Celestial Navigation

What if you miss Hawaii? It's just that sort of fear that drives folks to involve themselves with the traditional weighty volumes and complex worksheets that make Hegel seem simple by comparison. But you needn't fret. This skinny book gives you what you need to know to fetch Diamond Head, though you may have to do a bit of unprofessional dog-legging to do so. You'll be successful, which is more than you can be sure of using more complex techniques you don't fully understand. The methods shown here are simple enough, but you will have to make that "one day" a disciplined one. Two people learning together will help, and that'll give you the advantage of having more than one person aboard with navigation skills — a useful safety factor. The author also takes you through the steps for checking the accuracy of the ship's compass, and what to do if your clock stops. If you're going out of sight of land, all this is stuff you need to know. This book is about as simple a course as you're likely to find.

—JB

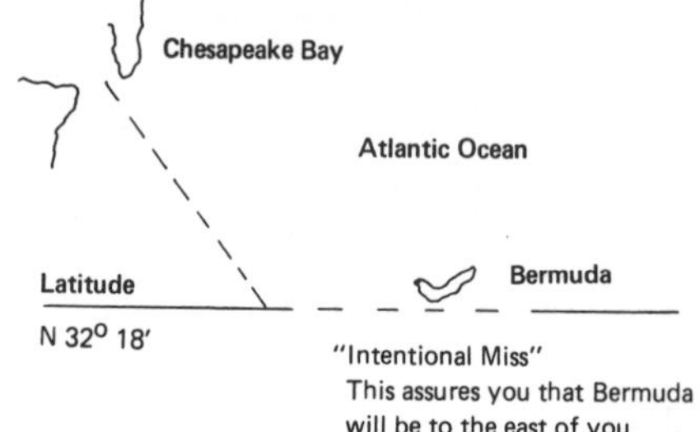

•

Strategy: If you can *only* obtain an accurate latitude, you must modify the approach to your island. You sail down (or up) to the latitude of the island. You intentionally miss it to the west (or east) by sixty miles. This is a dog leg, or "landfall" technique. Upon arrival at the island's latitude you will know in which direction to turn to arrive at the island. You will not know exactly how far you are from the island, but you will be *certain to hit the island.*

Weather for the Mariner
William J. Kotsch
1983; 315 pp.

$16.95
($19.95 postpaid) from:
U. S. Naval Institute Press
Attn.: Customer Service
2062 Generals Highway
Annapolis,
MD 21401-6780
or Whole Earth Access

Weather for the Mariner

I've been watching weather books since I was an obsessive teen. This one surpasses all the others as far as I'm concerned. It's sufficiently and fascinatingly technical without interrupting the comprehensive clarity that makes it so unique. It is a working text for people who live or die by the weather. No reason to limit its use to mariners.

—Stewart Brand

BEAUFORT FORCE 10. Wind speed 48-55 kt, mean 52 kt. Sea criterion: Very high waves with long overhanging crests. The resulting foam, in great patches, is blown in dense white streaks along the direction of the wind. On the whole, the surface of the sea takes on a white appearance. The tumbling of the sea becomes heavy and shocklike. Visibility affected.

•

When the wind backs
And the weatherglass falls,
Then be on your guard
Against gales and squalls.
—Source unknown

•

No weather is ill
If the wind be still.
—W. Camden, 1623

• Of course, if you *really* want to know *everything* about navigation, there's the four-inch-thick tome known world over as "Bowditch."

American Practical Navigator: Nathaniel Bowditch. Volume 1 (1984, 1386 pp.) **$18** postpaid. Volume 2 (1981, 716 pp.) **$13** postpaid; both from DMAODS, Attn.: DDCP, Washington, DC 20315-0020. Make check payable to "Treasurer of the U.S."

FOR THOSE WHO'VE NEVER TRIED IT, flying may seem one of those unreachables that only "other people" do. Hogplop! The idea of learning to fly may seem bigger than your ability, but it's a self-imposed limitation. The truth is that most folks who drive a car could learn to fly a plane.

Learning to fly is an excellent opportunity to take charge of your own life and to acquire a skill that's enjoyable and practical. From the air, the endless drudgery of highway driving changes to an amazing, mile-high view of Nature's creation. And you get to your destination in half the time.

Altho' the sky, like the sea and the mountains, doesn't come easy, mastering flight gives a reward that equals the challenge. Where does one begin? The most likely spot is your local airport. Check out the dealers offering flight instruction, and gamble some dollars on a single flying lesson. The key factor is deciding to *do it.* If you stay with it, you'll end up with a private pilot's license after logging some 50+ hours and leaving at least $2,000 behind.
—Dick Fugett

The Aviation Consumer Used Aircraft Guide
Richard B. Weeghman, Editor
1985; 279 pp.
$21.95
postpaid from:
The Aviation Consumer (Books)
1111 East Putnam Avenue
Riverside, CT 06878

The Aviation Consumer Used Aircraft Guide

When I consider how much learning went into this book, not to mention parts and labor, I'm staggered as well as gratified that it wasn't me who had to pay the bills for all the experience.

The amount of information is incredible, and far surpasses those glossy, surface-level summaries of factory specs and marketing department photos that are normally passed off as "The Compleat Airplane Review." ***Aviation Consumer*** *tells that happy stuff, but also gets down to the guts of the matter and will as soon produce a scoop on Bonanza airframe failures as go into detail regarding Cessna Cardinal RG landing gear problems. Everything is culled from somebody's real flying experience, and by the time you've finished reading the five-page rap on each of 47 airplanes, from J-3 Cub to Citation jet, you'll be closer to understanding the machines than many of the owners are.* —Dick Fugett

◄ Optional cargo pod increases luggage capacity but cuts speed of Cessna 185.

Trade-A-Plane
$10/6 months
(18 issues) from:
Trade-A-Plane Subscriptions
Box 929
Crossville, TN 38555

Trade-A-Plane • Aviation Consumer

There may come a time when one of those flying machines is yours, and when you finally own the sky you'll meet many of the realities of flight. You won't need help with the fun ones, but there are harsh realities too, based on the universal principle about free lunches. You'll run into them when that scratchy old radio packs up and dies, and the guy in the shop starts quoting replacement prices, or when your mechanic strokes his chin and calmly announces that it's time to major your engine, and you faint.

Limited assistance is available. First of all there's our old friend ***Trade-A-Plane****: in addition to all the used aircraft they have good listings on services, as well as equipment, both discounted and used. There's also a relatively unknown magazine called* ***The Aviation Consumer****. It is to pilots what* ***Consumer Reports*** *is to the rest of the world. They evaluate products, conduct reader surveys to find out the owners' opinions, and have used airplane guides that range from Cubs to jets. Since they carry no advertising they are able to step on a lot of toes that other publications avoid. If you have any major expenses coming up, this little journal could save you a bundle.*

If $60 sounds stiff for a magazine, wait till you get that bill for the engine overhaul. —Dick Fugett

The Aviation Consumer
Richard B. Weeghman, Editor
$60/year
(24 issues) from:
The Aviation Consumer Subscriptions
P. O. Box 972
Farmingdale, NY 11737

—Trade-A-Plane

Cessna Skyhawk, the universal Everyman's airplane, reigns as the safest of the four-seaters. Like the 150, it has low landing speed, gentle stall, strut-braced wing and simple fuel system. —*Aviation Consumer*

• Best would-be pilot's book learning.
The Student Pilot's Flight Manual: William K. Kershner, 1979; 281 pp. **$17.95** ($19.45 postpaid) from Iowa State University Press, 2121 South State Avenue, Ames, IA 50010 (or Whole Earth Access).

The Kolb FireStar, piloted by Homer Kolb. —*Ultralight Flying!*

Ultralight Flying!
Michael Bradford, Editor
$24/year
(12 issues) from:
Ultralight Flying!
P. O. Box 6009
Chattanooga, TN 37401

Ultralight Airmanship
Jack Lambie
1984; 144 pp.
$10.95
($13.90 postpaid) from:
Ultralight Publications
P. O. Box 234
Hummelstown, PA 17036

ULTRALIGHTS WERE SPAWNED when a flatland, midwestern hang glider pilot, desperate for lack of launch sites, attached a snowmobile engine to his kite and took off under power. Being airborne without dependency on thermals was a delight, and as news of the feat spread, others began making similar devices. They were not always as airworthy as they were creative.

The FAA had watched hang gliding develop and found it to be a self-disciplined group that knew its place and presented no major menace to the public, so no seriously restrictive regulations were imposed. Ultralights, at first indistinguishable from hang gliders, benefited from this freedom and rediscovered what had been lost back in the primeval 1920s — powered flight without legal restraints.

The sky was available to Everyman, and the considerable discipline and effort required to master hang gliding or earn a private pilot's license were unnecessary. Free wine on skid row would have had no warmer welcome, and as demand skyrocketed backyard builders became manufacturing tycoons. Glorious optimism and the future of ultralights were synonomous.

But alas, that movement is now better compared to the Bataan death march, for booming sales and effervescent predictions have been reduced to disappearing customers and bankrupt factories. Rapacious manufacturers, scofflaw pilots, and too many dingbats falling out of the sky are bringing this form of aerial joy to a painful transition. Perhaps flight that hasn't been earned with effort is too easy. Too bad, for ultralights generated some of the most creative ideas in aviation design.

The FAA issued serious regulations that resulted in the demise of ultralights as unlicensed, powered hang gliders. Small, licensed aircraft known as ARVs (Aerial Recreation Vehicles) will be the next step. Unregulated flight will conclude, leaving behind nought but a few old-timers telling war stories about that time the engine in their Weedhopper quit and . . .

The shifting fortunes of the ultralight movement are best reflected in the oldest magazine, *Ultralight Flying!*, known for years as *Glider Rider*. As for books, Jack Lambie continually puts out the best stuff, and his *Ultralight Airmanship* is worthwhile reading for any aviation enthusiast.

—Dick Fugett

•

If very high in a thermal, perhaps over 14,000 feet, you will find it is almost impossible to tell the effect of oxygen starvation because the brain is the first organ to be affected. How can you comprehend what's going on if you can't think? Some experts say, "Look at your fingertips to see if the color under the nails is turning bluish, to indicate lack of air." This sounds fine except you can't think well enough to decide whether they are blue or not and to what degree.

The effects of altitude vary between people. I get an uneasy feeling of impending doom called "Dreads" while others have the same symptoms as being "Drunk." I notice my peripheral vision pulls in about 30 degrees so it seems as if I can only see clearly straight ahead. The sound of the wind becomes very quiet and the cold of high altitude is not so noticeable. I see little "blips," like the stars you see if you bump your head. Little dots pop up in front of my eyes and disappear.

A good way to check your condition is by doing what the Navy calls "Grunt Breathing." Take a deep breath, holding your mouth closed, and grunt to pressurize your lungs. You will immediately hear better and the vision out of the corner of your eyes will clear. The effect lasts only a few seconds but by grunt breathing you can see how much you change immediately after pressurizing your lungs. —*Ultralight Airmanship*

An example of wind with no lift.

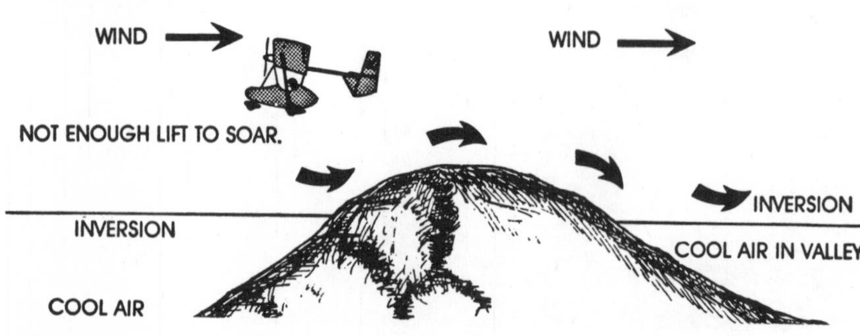

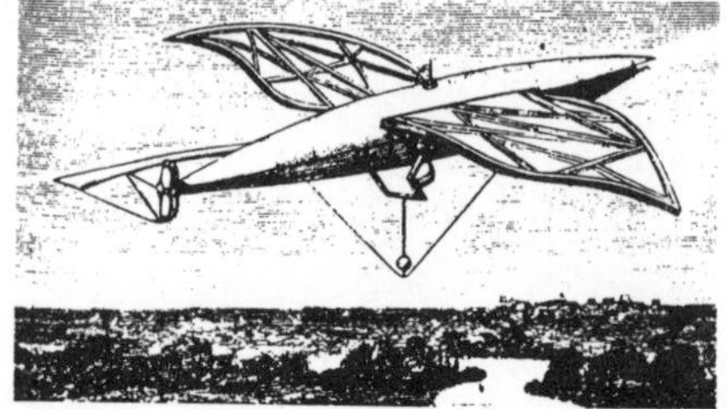

ALTHOUGH THE GENERAL aviation manufacturers back in Wichita, Kansas (which is to airplane manufacturers what Detroit is to carmakers) are in danger of withering away, another segment of the flying population is quite robust — those who make their own machines. Initially, building your own plane might mean acquiring a $100 set of plans or thousands of dollars worth of boxes just unloaded in your workshop.

The Cozy — a 108 hp engine gives 185 mph cruise.

There are some 11,000 registered homebuilts now, and the boom is understandable: superior speed, better economy, and a lower price tag are hard to beat. Early homebuilts were constructed of either steel tubing and aluminum or of wood and fabric. But ever since Bert Rutan introduced his epochal EZ, composite construction utilizing foam and fiberglass has been most popular.

These new machines are strong and light and cruise in the 200-mph range at nearly 30 mpg — all for an outlay of $20,000 or thereabouts, half the price and twice the speed of a plodding, new Cessna 152. The current favorite designs include the Glassair and Cozy.

Of course, one extra input is required — effort. Building your own plane is a project for those who have overcome that mental block that announces itself with the thought, "I couldn't possibly . . ." But if that barrier is behind you, and you've previously demonstrated staying power during periods of long-term challenge, consider a highly rewarding project that will take perhaps 2,000 hours of work — some two to three years of your spare time.

There's a bundle of designs to choose from. Investigate by joining the Experimental Aircraft Association, which includes a subscription to their magazine, *Sport Aviation.* It's loaded with real-life experience, as well as occasional excesses of optimism, for some of the stories are written by people pushing their products. —Dick Fugett

Cockpit of Ulrich and Linda Walter's modified (160hp) ► Cozy — the product of 2,200 hours of work.

Sport Aviation
Jack Cox, Editor
$30/year
(with membership) from:
Experimental Aircraft Association
Wittman Airfield
Oshkosh, WI 54903-3086

Aircraft Spruce & Specialty

When you get past the fantasy level and decide it's time for nuts and bolts (or epoxy and foam), then you'll make acquaintances with AS & S; they've been supplying home builders for nearly three decades. Their hefty catalog gives pictures, prices, and descriptions of everything from the materials and tools required to build a plane, to the instruments and engine you'll have to buy before the project finally takes off.

What lifts this volume above the competition is the descriptive commentary. Windowshopping changes into education, and what began as a simple catalog ends up as a reference book. —*Dick Fugett*

• Aeroquip Firesleeve was specially developed to meet the fire resistance requirements of FAA TSO-C53a or TSO-C75. It may be used for all fuel, oil, hydraulic, fire extinguisher and propeller feathering lines.

"Fire-proof" hose lines as defined by FAA must withstand a direct flame for fifteen minutes under specified flow conditions without failure. "Fire-resistant" lines must withstand a five minute exposure under these conditions. "Fire-proof" hose lines are obtained when the proper size Aeroquip Firesleeve is selected and properly assembled.

Aircraft Spruce & Specialty Company
Catalog **$5** from:
Aircraft Spruce & Specialty Company
P. O. Box 424
Fullerton, CA 92632

• Anyone who wants to build something with the same characteristics as an airplane — light, strong, dependable, immune to vibration, round — should check out Airparts' catalog. It can be had for $1 from Airparts, Inc., 301 North 7th Street, Kansas City, KS 66101.

Airman's Invitational Hang Gliding Meeting, Telluride, Colorado —*Hang Gliding*

Hang Gliding
Gil Dodgen, Editor
$29/year*
(12 issues) from:
United States Hang Gliding Association, Inc.
P. O. Box 66306
Los Angeles, CA 90066.
*Full membership in USHGA (including subscription): $39/year.

Hang Gliding According to Pfeiffer
Rich Pfeiffer
with Maggie Rowe
1984; 238 pp.
$9.95
($10.95 postpaid) from:
Publitec Editions
P. O. Box 4342
Laguna Beach, CA 92652
or Whole Earth Access

Ballooning
Mary Woodhouse, Editor
$25/year
(BFOA membership includes 4 issues) from:
Balloon Federation of America
P. O. Box 264
Indianola, IA 50125

Hang Gliding

They don't get you there as fast as powered flight, and the rush is a shade less than parachuting, but if you truly love the sky, then hang gliders do it best. The hang glider people gave birth to the ultralight movement, and have watched it self-destruct. Meanwhile, they keep concentrating on doing just what the hawks and eagles do — catching thermals.

*Effective self-regulation has kept the FAA off their backs, the machines are debugged and certified now, and the gradual self-elimination of the crazies is producing a healthy sport. Training sites that offer one-day intros can be found, along with all the current happenings, in **Hang Gliding** magazine. If you're getting serious, the most readable book is **Hang Gliding According to Pfeiffer.***
—Dick Fugett

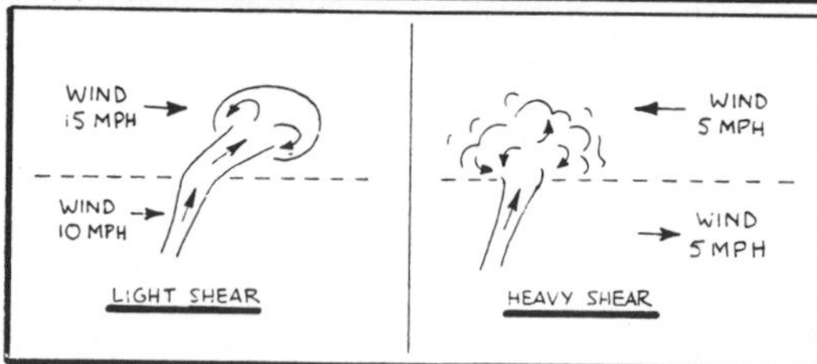

When a thermal encounters a wind shear, it either leans or drifts with the newly-encountered wind or becomes disrupted, depending on the relative strength of the shear and the thermal. In general, a shear involving a wind speed difference of 3-4 mph is sufficient to totally disrupt a thermal, at least in terms of supporting a hang glider.
—Hang Gliding According to Pfeiffer

Balloons

There's yet another way to get airborne. It's big, fat, slow, and fragile, as well as the oldest form of human flight. Altho a gas balloon recently crossed the Pacific, the sample cruise you'll have (for about $100) in a hot air balloon will be noticeably calmer. If the high-energy extremes of other forms of flight are a bit more than you need, consider meandering thru the skies with the clouds, your destination decided by the winds.

*The traditional champagne bottle that awaits your landing dates back centuries to the earliest French flights; it was originally brought along to reassure potentially excitable peasants that the creatures from the sky were friendly. Or so say traditionalists. Another theory goes that balloonists just like to get snockered now and then, so who knows? **Ballooning** covers all the events, and the Balloon Federation of America is in charge.* *—Dick Fugett*

Balloons touch down on Farmington Lake, New Mexico. ►

▼ **America's Freedom Balloon Fest, Provo, Utah.**

HANG ON — spinning, bouncing, flapping, creaking. Don't mess with Mother Nature — just ride it out. Down we go again. Oh, to be bored again, my headache is gone. Descending at 700'/min., this time we *are* going to land (I hope). Hook up landing light, can't see diddly squat; stow it. Out of the thundercloud again. Ah, land, ieee, we're scooting along, at 300' from ground. Can't worry about night high wind landing. We've got to set down. . . .

The ground. We've landed. We're down. We're alive.
—Ballooning

Sailplanes

You may question the serenity of sailplanes if the thermals are cooking and your pilot, after coring one with endless, tight 360s, asks if you're gonna barf. But that's how it is with most rewarding, high-energy situations — there's always a price.

To sample their silent flight all you need is a rural airport with a sign out by the highway that says "GLIDER RIDES." For roughly the same painful price you'll pay for a one-day introduction to anything these days, you can sample the freedom of unpowered flight.

*A glider rating can be added to a private pilot's license for maybe $500. If you've never flown at all, then legal flight could run four times that amount. Decent used machines start around $5,000. The long-time journal of record is **Soaring Magazine**, put out by the Soaring Society of America. They also market a nice book on soaring basics, **The Joy of Soaring**. —Dick Fugett*

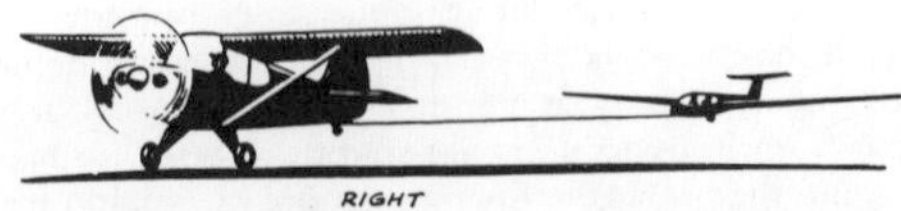

—Joy of Soaring

—Joy of Soaring

Soaring
Robert Said, Editor
$28/year
(12 issues included in SSoA membership) from:
Soaring Society of America
Box 66071
Los Angeles, CA 90066

The Joy of Soaring
(A Training Manual)
Carle Conway
1969; 134 pp.
$17
($18.19 postpaid) from:
Aviation Book Company
1640 Victory Blvd.
Glendale, CA 91201

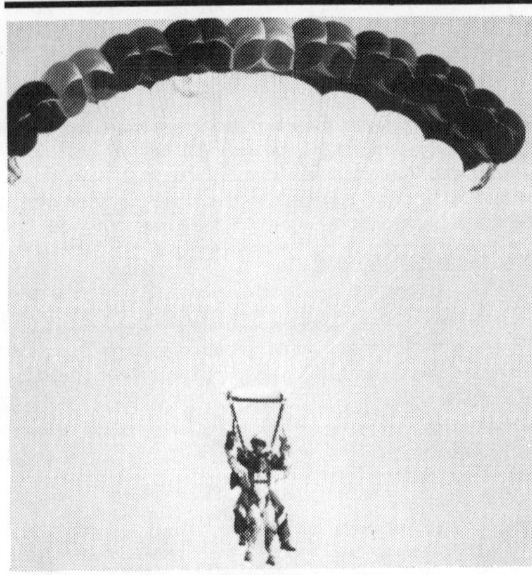

Tandem skydiving: one instructor and one student — and only one parachute. (Photo by Kurt Rodgers.)

Skydiving

For maximum pucker factor there's skydiving, which has undergone major changes in the last decade. No more heavy boots, bulky 50-pound gear, or even round canopies. Jumpers now wear a compact harness and container, light shoes, and come down gently under a steerable, ram-air, square canopy that's actually an airfoil. The old, ankle-busting, 16-foot-per-second descent rate is gone, along with the need for traditional, high jump boots of paratroop legend.

The latest advance, tandem skydiving, has opened the sport to those who'd prefer some experienced company while going out the door. The student and jumpmaster are basically wearing a single harness. After exiting they freefall together under the jumpmaster's control, until he opens the canopy, which the student then guides down.

Whether you choose tandem, or the traditional static line first jump, the day's activities including basic instruction will run about $100. Should you get serious and go for the student training program, plan on spending about $1,000, plus at least that much more for equipment. The days when you could go out to a jump site, borrow someone's chute, and pay $7 for a lift in a Cessna 172 to begin teaching yourself skydiving are long gone.

*For more information and the location of your nearest jump center, try the United States Parachute Association's magazine, **Parachutist**. —Jane Ferrell*

•

What About Accidents?

In 1984, there were 33 fatalities, which occurred at about the rate of one per 61,000 jumps logged and one per 3,528 participants. This further breaks down to one fatality in each 300,000 student jumps.

Viewed in this context, it is perfectly reasonable to tell your whuffo friends that despite 33 fatalities in 1984, ours is statistically not a dangerous sport.

Most skydivers are less prone to die from accidents than the population as a whole; and skydiving itself is a lot less dangerous than driving to and from the drop zone.

Parachutist
Larry Jaffe, Editor
$21.50/year
(12 issues) from:
United States
Parachute Association
1440 Duke Street
Alexandria, VA 22314

INFORMATION: any difference which makes a difference.
—Gregory Bateson

Godel, Escher, Bach
Douglas Hofstadter
1979; 777 pp.
$13.95
($14.95 postpaid) from:
Vintage Books
Random House
Order Dept.
400 Hahn Road
Westminster, MD 21157
or Whole Earth Access

The Mind's I
Douglas R. Hofstadter
and Daniel C. Dennett
1981; 501 pp.
$12.95
($14.45 postpaid) from:
Bantam Books
414 East Golf Road
Des Plaines, IL 60016
or Whole Earth Access

Godel, Escher, Bach • The Mind's I

The subject of the first book — and the frequent preoccupation of its deities, mathematician Kurt Godel, artist M.C. Escher, composer J.S. Bach, and writer Lewis Carroll — is self-reference, what the author calls "strange loops" or "tangled hierarchies." It is the domain of extreme paradox, where math, art, religion (lots of zen in the book, honestly employed), and epistemology collide. It is the fearless exploration of black holes of the mind.

Hofstadter set out to make Godel's Incompleteness Theorem accessible to the lay thinker, and happily he succeeds in that. Along the way he illuminates a world of music, mathematics, computer intelligence (and gossip), and philosophy. The book confirms the suspicion I've had for years that perhaps the most adventurous and fruitful human frontier we have these days is the hall of mirrors, Lewis Carroll's looking glass. —Stewart Brand

Hofstadter's second volume, **The Mind's I**, *is an anthology of essays he co-edits that circles through the apparent paradoxes of consciousness. Round it goes through children, ant colonies, and large computers. Parable and fiction lurk in the book, about the only animals that can keep a tentative grip on the circulating elusiveness of self-consciousness.* —Kevin Kelly

•

A strikingly beautiful, and yet at the same time disturbingly grotesque, illustration of the cyclonic "eye" of a Tangled Hierarchy is given to us by Escher in his *Print Gallery*. What we see is a picture gallery where a young man is standing, looking at a picture of a ship in the harbor of a small town, perhaps a Maltese town, to guess from the architecture, with its little turrets, occasional cupolas, and flat stone roofs, upon one of which sits a boy, relaxing in the heat, while two floors below him a woman — perhaps his mother — gazes out of the window from her apartment which sits directly above a picture gallery where a young man is standing, looking at a picture of a ship in the harbor of a small town, perhaps a Maltese town —

What!? We are back on the same level as we began, though all logic dictates that we cannot be. Let us draw a diagram of what we see.

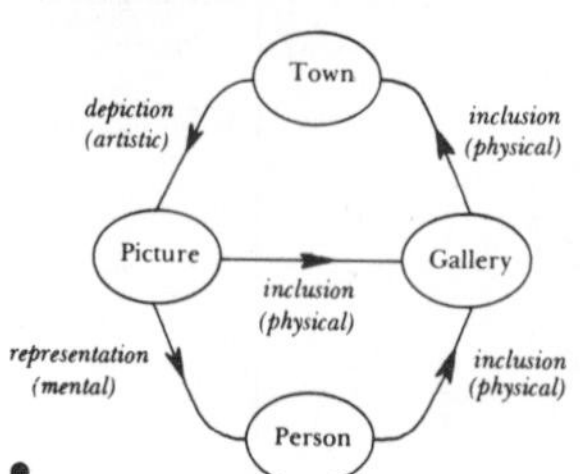

What this diagram shows is three kinds of "in-ness." The gallery is *physically in* the town ("inclusion"); the town is *artistically in* the picture ("depiction"); the picture is *mentally* in the person ("representation"). . . .
—*Godel, Escher, Bach*

•

Examples of memes are tunes, ideas, catch-phrases, clothes fashions, ways of making pots or building arches. Just as genes propagate themselves in the gene pool by leaping from body to body via sperms or eggs, so memes propagate themselves in the meme pool by leaping from brain to brain via a process which, in the broad sense, can be called imitation. If a scientist hears, or reads about, a good idea, he passes it on to his colleagues and students. He mentions it in his articles and his lectures. If the idea catches on, it can be said to propagate itself, spreading from brain to brain. —*The Mind's I*

Grammatical Man
Jeremy Campbell
1982; 319 pp.
$9.95
postpaid from:
Simon & Schuster
Mail Order Sales
200 Old Tappan Road
Old Tappan, NJ 07675
or Whole Earth Access

Grammatical Man

In the age of information it is shocking that there is so little useful information about information — how it behaves, what its economics are, indeed, what it is. A good book on the subject would have to talk about the primary domains of information: evolution, genetics, computer programming, entropy, whole systems, and human language. This book does. It is the only one to encompass the whole natural ecology of information in a readable way. —Kevin Kelly

•

Redundancy makes complexity possible. . . . The more complex the system, the more likely is it that one of its parts will malfunction. Redundancy is a means of keeping the system running in the presence of malfunction. Redundancy, von Neumann declared,

> is the only thing which makes it possible to write a text which is longer than, say, ten pages. In other words, a language which has maximum compression would actually be completely unsuited to conveying information beyond a certain degree of complexity, because you could never find out whether a text is right or wrong. And this is a question of principle. It follows, therefore, that the complexity of the medium in which you work has something to do with redundancy.

•

In a now famous paper published in 1969, the American biologists Jack Lester King and Thomas Jukes wrote, "We cannot agree . . . that DNA is the passive carrier of the evolutionary message. Evolutionary change is not imposed upon DNA from without; it arises from within. Natural selection is the editor, rather than the composer, of the genetic message."

The Infinite World of M. C. Escher

Geometry set at its own throat via the images of dreams. The subjective frontier. —Stewart Brand

The Infinite World of M.C. Escher
M.C. Escher
and J.L. Locher
1985; 152 pp.
$14.98
($16.48 postpaid) from:
Harry N. Abrams, Inc.
Attn.: Cash Sales
100 5th Avenue
New York, NY 10011
or Whole Earth Access

Art and Illusion

So much art criticism is so much a vapid waste of time that a book like this one is thoroughly a surprise. Every page yields fresh information (did you know that the comic strip was singlehandedly invented by a Swiss gent named Topfler in the 1820s?) and worthwhile hypotheses about how art and artists gradually teach themselves energies of effect. —*Stewart Brand*

•

Only in the realm of dreams has the artist found full freedom to create. I think the difference is well summed up in the anecdote about Matisse. When a lady visiting his studio said, "But surely, the arm of this woman is much too long," the artist replied politely, "Madame, you are mistaken. This is not a woman, this is a picture."

•

True, we can switch from one reading to another with increasing rapidity; we will also "remember" the rabbit while we see the duck, but the more closely we watch ourselves, the more certainly we will discover that we cannot experience alternative readings at the same time. Illusion, we will find, is hard to describe or analyze, for though we may be intellectually aware of the fact that any given experience must be an illusion, we cannot, strictly speaking, watch ourselves having an illusion.

•

But no tradition of art had a deeper understanding of what I have called the "screen" than the art of the Far East. Chinese art theory discusses the power of expressing through *absence* of brush and ink. "Figures, even though painted without eyes, must seem to look; without ears, must seem to listen . . . There are things which ten hundred brushstrokes cannot depict but which can be captured by a few simple strokes if they are right. That is truly giving expression to the invisible." The maxim into which these observations were condensed might serve as a motto in this chapter: *"i tao pi pu tao* — idea present, brush may be spared performance."

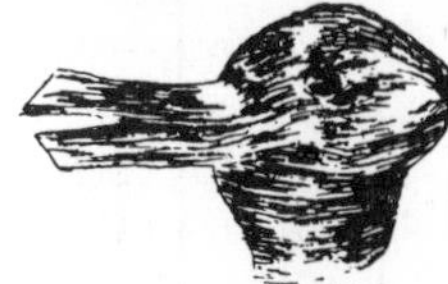

Rabbit or duck?

Art and Illusion
Ernst H. Gombrich
1961; 466 pp.

$14.50
postpaid from:
Princeton University Press
3175 Princeton Pike
Lawrenceville, NJ 08648
or Whole Earth Access

The Image

This book is by an economist enchanted with cybernetics. He's after the organizing principle in life, the image that everything comes together through. He scarcely mentions the brain, and he's right. It ain't the brain. —*Stewart Brand*

•

The meaning of a message is the change which is produced in the image.

•

The gene is a wonderful teacher. It is, however, a very poor learner.

•

I have never been to Australia. In my image of the world, however, it exists with 100 percent certainty. If I sailed to the place where the map makers tell me it is and found nothing there but ocean I would be the most surprised man in the world. I hold to this part of my image with certainty, however, purely on authority. I have been to many other places which I have found on the map and I have almost always found them there. It is interesting to inquire what gives the map this extraordinary authority, an authority greater than that of the sacred books of all religions. It is not an authority which is derived from any political power or from any charismatic experience. As far as I know it is not a crime against the state nor against religion to show a map that has mistakes in it. There is, however, a process of feedback from the users of the maps to the map maker.

•

A guess may be hazarded that one of the important conditions for the initiation of technological change is the development of rather isolated and perhaps somewhat persecuted subcultures within the larger society. It is in the "nonconformist" subcultures that images are most likely to be sensitive and subject to change.

The Image
Kenneth E. Boulding
1956; 175 pp.

$6.95
($8.45 postpaid) from:
University of
Michigan Press
839 Greene Street
Ann Arbor, MI 48106
or Whole Earth Access

Number Words and Number Symbols

Suppose you want to help human communication to re-understand itself. So much of that understanding is wrapped up in numbers that if you penetrate the one you may have a foothold to tweak the other one onto a new course. Invent language and you invent humans.

This book penetrates numbers. —*Steward Brand*

The *chimpu* of the Peruvian and Bolivian Indians, a descendant of the *quipu*. This one shows the number 4456.

◄ **The Mayan "named" place-value notation. The heads are rank levels which are numbered by units from 1 to 19. The vertical beams are 5-groups; curiously enough, there was no decimal grouping.**

▲ **Albrecht Durer's year dates. In writing the dates of the years around 1495, Durer illustrated the development of the 4 into its present form. From three of his drawings dated in successive years.**

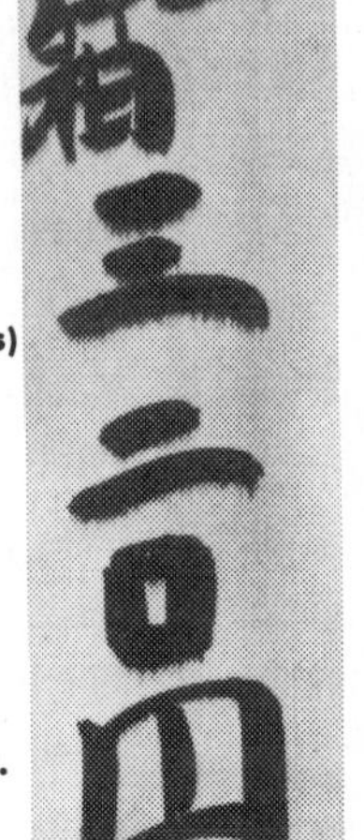

► **"I box 320 yen": a pricetag (for Mandarin oranges) from a fruit store.**

▲ **Old Chinese numerals for 10, 50, and 100.**

Number Words and Number Symbols
Karl Menninger
OUT OF PRINT
The M.I.T. Press

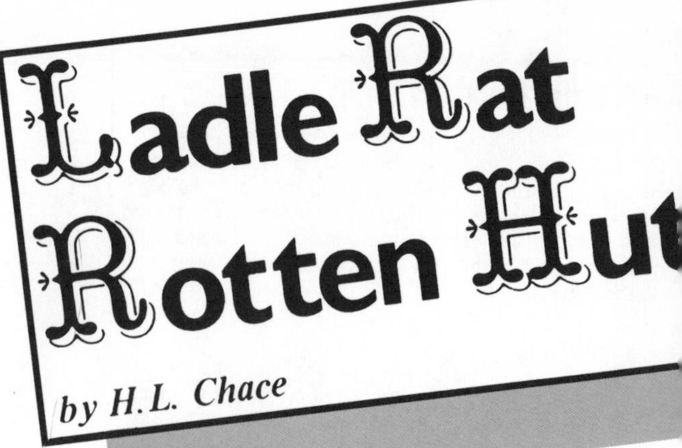

WANTS PAWN TERM, dare worsted ladle gull hoe lift wetter murder inner ladle cordage, honor itch offer lodge, dock, florist. Disk ladle gull orphan worry putty ladle rat cluck wetter ladle rat hut, an fur disk raisin pimple colder Ladle Rat Rotten Hut.

Wan moaning, Ladle Rat Rotten Hut's murder colder inset.

"Ladle Rat Rotten Hut, heresy ladle basking winsome burden barter an shirker cockles. Tick disk ladle basking tutor cordage offer groin-murder hoe lifts honor udder site offer florist. Shaker lake! Dun stopper laundry wrote! Dun stopper peck floors! Dun daily-doily inner florist, an yonder nor sorghum-stenches, dun stopper torque wet strainers!"

"Hoe-cake, murder," resplendent Ladle Rat Rotten Hut, an tickle ladle basking an stuttered oft.

Honor wrote tutor cordage offer groin-murder, Ladle Rat Rotten Hut mitten anomalous woof.

"Wail, wail, wail!" set disk wicket woof, "Evanescent Ladle Rat Rotten Hut! Wares are putty ladle gull goring wizard ladle basking?"

"Armor goring tumor groin-murder's," reprisal ladle gull. "Grammar's seeking bet. Armor ticking arson burden barter an shirker cockles."

"O hoe! Heifer gnats woke," setter wicket woof, butter taught tomb shelf, "Oil tickle shirt court tutor cordage offer groin-murder. Oil ketchup wetter letter, an den – O bore!"

Soda wicket woof tucker shirt court, an whinny retched a cordage offer groin-murder, picked inner windrow, an sore debtor pore oil worming worse lion inner bet. Inner flesh, disk abdominal woof lipped honor bet, paunched honor pore oil worming, an garbled erupt. Den disk ratchet ammonol pot honor groin-murder's nut cup an gnat-gun, any curdled ope inner bet.

Inner ladle wile, Ladle Rat Rotten Hut a raft attar cordage, an ranker dough ball. "Comb ink, sweat hard," setter wicket woof, disgracing is verse.

Ladle Rat Rotten Hut entity bet rum, an stud buyer groin-murder's bet.

"O Grammar!" crater ladle gull historically, "Water bag icer gut! A nervous sausage bag ice!"

"Battered lucky chew whiff, sweat hard," setter bloat-Thursday woof, wetter wicket small honors phase.

"O Grammar, water bag noise! A nervous sore suture anomalous prognosis!"

"Battered small your whiff, doling," whiskered dole woof, ants mouse worse waddling.

"O Grammar, water bag mouser gut! A nervous sore suture bag mouse!"

Daze worry on-forger-nut ladle gull's lest warts. Oil offer sodden, caking offer carvers an sprinkling otter bet, disk hoard-hoarded woof lipped own pore Ladle Rat Rotten Hut an garbled erupt.

MURAL: Yonder nor sorghum-stenches shut ladle gulls stopper torque wet strainers. ■

Anguish Languish

"Ladle Rat Rotten Hut" is often attributed to Anonymous, but it was actually written by H. L. Chace. He was a professor of French at Miami University in Oxford, Ohio, and retired in 1965. I talked to him by phone about the story of the story.

"I wrote it about 1940," he said. "It was going to be part of a little article I was writing. It was in the days of rationing during the war and I thought about what would happen if we had to ration language. If our vocabulary were cut in half, we'd have to get along with other words. Consequently, I thought I'd see how you'd get along with the other half. I've never written that article, but I've always thought of doing it.

"I taught French, and I used the story in my class to show the importance of intonation in learning a foreign language. You see, if you take these English words and put them in columns like a spelling book and just read them, they have no meaning. However, if you read them with the proper intonation, the meaning appears for certain people. For other people the meaning never does appear.

"I never submitted it to anybody, but it got spread some way or other. It's one of those things that got completely out of control. I showed it to a few friends and to a book salesman who came to see me. He liked the thing because it had to do with words. I think I may have given him a copy, and he must have given it to someone else. It first appeared in print in the Merriam Company's magazine ***Word Study.*** *I think it got in* ***Stars and Stripes*** *[U.S. Army newspaper] because I heard from people in Baghdad, Sweden, all over the world.* ***Sports Illustrated*** *found it in another publication and gave me $1000 for it. Arthur Godfrey found it in* ***Sports Illustrated,*** *and he broadcast it and very generously told any readers that wanted a copy they could have one by sending me postage. To my surprise, I mailed about five thousand of them. After that episode, Prentice Hall asked me to write a series of stories for a book, which I did. [****Anguish Languish*** *was published by Prentice Hall in 1955.]*

"The book sold fairly well for that sort of thing. It went through four printings I think, maybe 14,000 copies total. It's used now a good deal in textbooks to demonstrate the phonetic structures of English. The book has been used by some psychologist to determine the ability of people to understand sound, to study the limit of distortion that can be comprehended. That varies from person to person.

"People who like it best are language people, teachers, lawyers, and doctors. That's almost all the people who are interested in it. And children, strange to say. I've had a lot of letters from them."

The book, ***Anguish Languish,*** *is out of print and very hard to find. Chace himself only has one copy. Dover or somebody should reprint it.*

—Anne Herbert

Standing by Words

I cannot imagine a better English teacher than farmer, essayist, poet, novelist Wendell Berry. His writing and his thinking are hard liquor, the kind that makes you go "whooh!" with savor and respect. His subject this time is language, and the model is not far off. His writing (and speaking, if you get the chance to hear it) is his own best example.

*More even than his works on agriculture (**The Unsettling of America** [see p. 61], etc.), this book of essays goes to the center of a wide and terrible malaise that is obscured from our view by its very size. When the land weakens, when the use of language weakens, nothing else can be truly strong.*

Berry wrote elsewhere once, "I stand for what I stand on." This book is about that kind of precision.
—Stewart Brand

•

Two epidemic illnesses of our time — upon both of which virtual industries of cures have been founded — are the disintegration of communities and the disintegration of persons. That these two are related (that private loneliness, for instance, will necessarily accompany public confusion) is clear enough. And I take for granted that most people have explored in themselves and their surroundings some of the intricacies of the practical causes and effects; most of us, for example, have understood that the results are usually bad when people act in social or moral isolation, and also when, because of such isolation, they fail to act.

•

One of the uses of poetry is to reveal and articulate and make and preserve the necessary connections between the domestic and the wild. It is one of the ways we may, with hope of return, get out of our minds (our own and other people's) into the world of creatures, forms, and powers that we did not make. Access to that world is sanity. To be trapped in one's own mind is insanity. To be trapped in another person's mind — by political or technological tyranny — is imprisonment.

Standing by Words
Wendell Berry
1983; 213 pp.
$10.50
($12 postpaid) from:
North Point Press
850 Talbot Avenue
Berkeley, CA 94706
or Whole Earth Access

Etc.

*General Semantics is the art and science of thinking about symbols instead of swallowing them whole and unexamined. **Etc.** is the quarterly magazine put out by the International Society for General Semantics, and it prints smart, scholarly articles about the dangers of loose thinking and fuzzy talk. It's a good antidote for face value. Your subscription also gets you a monthly collection of additions called **Glimpse.*** *—Anne Herbert*

•

Clarity and precision are what one tries to strive for in achieving semantic health. In other words, clarity and precision foster communication. But oddly, perhaps even paradoxically, it is ambiguity that fosters communication in aesthetic experience. To the extent that a work of art is unambiguous, precise, and as clear in its meaning as one could hope for, to that extent, it is not art at all.

•

The greatest changes involve not a transformation of the form of language use but a diminishing of the very role that language itself plays within the culture. With radio and other audio media dealing primarily in music, and visual media using images, music, and sound effects, at the expense of even spoken language, a great part of our public discourse is being conducted in symbolic forms which are less amenable to conscious reasoning and whose semantics have barely begun to be studied.

Etc.
Russell Joyner, Editor
$25/year
(4 issues, includes membership) from:
International Society for General Semantics
P. O. Box 2469
San Francisco, CA 94126

Maledicta

*The last taboos in our culture — obscenity, insults, and completely tasteless ethnic and racial slurs — are boldly investigated by these forbidden-word connoisseurs, basking in the thrill of the verboten. If the language in this journal was any filthier you would have to scrub it out with Comet. For you halfwit gutter throats with a deficient vocabulary, we're not only talking about four-letter words. Recent issues of **Maledicta** compare a list of obscenities printed or left out in 20 different dictionaries, then go on to explore all the euphemisms for farting, report on colorful verbal abuse by the rich and famous, track down bathroom graffiti, dirty jokes, and kakologia, categorize high school sex slang, and so on. Much of it is legitimate academic studies, although always done tongue-in-toilet.*
—Kevin Kelly

•

Little Jimmy, four years old, was bugging his mother. So she told him to go across the street to watch the construction workers and learn something. After two hours he came back inside, and mother asked him what he had learned.

"Well, first you take a goddamn door and you try to fit it into the fucking doorway. But if the son-of-a-bitch doesn't fit, you have to take the cocksucker down again. Then you take a cunt-hair off on both sides and put the motherfucker back up again."

Jimmy's mother was shocked by his language. "You just wait till your father comes home! I want you to repeat that for your father!"

When Jimmy's dad came home, mother told him to ask Jimmy what he had learned across the street.

Jimmy told dad the whole story. His dad was furious and told him, "Son, go outside and get me a switch!"

"Fuck you!" replied Jimmy. "That's the fucking electrician's job!"

•

Who knocked off more Indians than John Wayne?
— *Union Carbide.*

What's Union Carbide's newest product?
— *Dot remover.*

"I assume you don't want to put a wreath on the front door either."

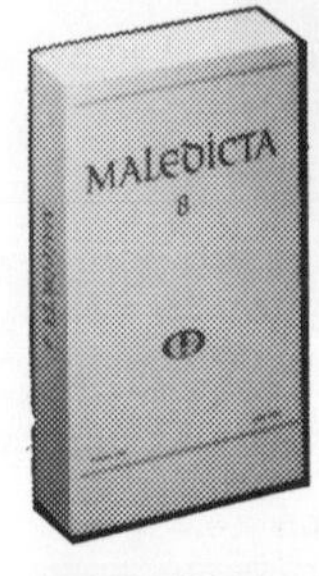

Maledicta
Reinhold Aman, Editor
$19 (annual) from:
Maledicta Press
331 South Greenfield Ave.
Waukesha, WI 53186

THANK YOU
FOR NOT
FARTING

A Maledicta Card

Elements of Style
William Strunk, Jr.
and E. B. White
1979; 92 pp.
$3.50 postpaid from:
Macmillan Publishing Co.
Order Dept.
Front and Brown Streets
Riverside, NJ 08075
or Whole Earth Access

Elements of Style

A thin volume that teaches and demonstrates the virtues of brevity. And clarity. And how good writing is inseparable from common sense. "Strunk and White," as everyone calls it, is fewer than 100 pages, but those pages last a lifetime. —Steven Levy

•

Use the active voice. The active voice is usually more direct and vigorous than the passive:

I shall always remember my first visit to Boston.

This is much better than

My first visit to Boston will always be remembered by me.

The latter sentence is less direct, less bold, and less concise.

•

Write with nouns and verbs. . . . not with adjectives and adverbs. The adjective hasn't been built that can pull a weak or inaccurate noun out of a tight place.

•

Do not overstate. When you overstate, the reader will be instantly on guard, and everything that has preceded your overstatement as well as everything that follows it will be suspect in his mind because he has lost confidence in your judgement or your poise.

•

Use definite, specific, concrete language. Prefer the specific to the general, the definite to the vague, the concrete to the abstract.

A period of unfavorable weather set in.	*It rained every day for a week.*
He showed satisfaction as he took possession of his well-earned reward.	*He grinned as he pocketed the coin.*

•

Keep related words together. The position of the words in a sentence is the principal means of showing their relationship. Confusion and ambiguity result when words are badly placed. The writer must, therefore, bring together the words and groups of words that are related in thought and keep apart those that are not so related.

He noticed a large stain in the rug that was right in the center.	*He noticed a large stain right in the center of the rug.*

Writing Without Teachers
Peter Elbow
1973; 196 pp.
$5.95 postpaid from:
Oxford University Press
16-00 Pollitt Drive
Fairlawn, NJ 07410
or Whole Earth Access

Writing Without Teachers

I "taught" college composition for three years, and was continually amazed at how intelligent, articulate people froze up when it came to committing themselves to paper. Peter Elbow has a solution: freewriting, best done in a class set up by and for people who want to write better. —Steven Levy

According to Peter Elbow, writing is sculpted from a rocky mass that you've generated freely, rather than wrought from an agony of cerebral ozone. His advice on how ranges from the specific to the sublime. Read the book literally — you'll write. Then read **Writing** *as a metaphor and just enjoy his wisdom.* —Stephanie Mills
[Suggested by Jim Moore]

•

As we write we edit unacceptable thoughts and feelings, as we do in speaking. In writing there is more time to do it so the editing is heavier: when speaking, there's someone right there waiting for a reply and he'll get bored or think we're crazy if we don't come out with *something*. Most of the time in speaking, we settle for the catch-as-catch-can way in which the words tumble out. In writing, however, there's a chance to try to get them right. But the opportunity to get them right is a terrible burden: you can work for two hours trying to get a paragraph "right" and discover it's not right at all. And then give up.

Editing, *in itself*, is not the problem. Editing is usually necessary if we want to end up with something satisfactory. The problem is that editing goes on *at the same time* as producing. The editor is, as it were, constantly looking over the shoulder of the producer and constantly fiddling with what he's doing while he's in the middle of trying to do it. . . . It's an unnecessary burden to try to think of words and also worry at the same time whether they're the right words.

•

Trying to get the beginning just right is a formula for failure — and probably a secret tactic to make yourself give up writing. Make some words, whatever they are, and then grab hold of that line and reel in as hard as you can. Afterwards you can throw away lousy beginnings and make new ones. This is the quickest way to get into good writing.

On Writing Well
William Zinsser
1985; 246 pp.
$9.50
($11 postpaid) from:
Harper and Row
2350 Virginia Avenue
Hagerstown, MD 21740
or Whole Earth Access

On Writing Well

The fact that William Zinsser revised his excellent **On Writing Well** *a mere four years after its first publication says more about writing well than anything I can think of. Writing, to be good, cannot be writ as if in stone, not even by a professor of it. It's got to be honest, responsive, current, and above all mindful of the reader's impatient intelligence.*

If you are serious about communicating with your readers, this book belongs on your shelf right next to Strunk and White's **Elements of Style** *and the dictionary of your choice.* —Stephanie Mills

•

Two paragraphs of the final manuscript of this chapter. Although they look ► like a first draft, they have already been rewritten and retyped — like almost every other page — four or five times. With each rewrite I try to make what I have written tighter, stronger and more precise, eliminating every element that is not doing useful work, until at last I have a clean copy for the printer. Then I go over it once more, reading it aloud, and am always amazed at how much clutter can still be profitably cut.

The writer must therefore constantly ask himself: What am I trying to say? ~~in this sentence?~~ (Surprisingly often, he doesn't know.) ~~And~~ Then he must look at what he has ~~just~~ written and ask: Have I said it? Is it clear to someone encountering ~~who is coming upon~~ the subject for the first time? If it's not, ~~clear,~~ it is because some fuzz has worked its way into the machinery. The clear writer is a person ~~who is~~ clear-headed enough to see this stuff for what it is: fuzz.

I don't mean ~~to suggest~~ that some peoplc are born clear-headed and are therefore natural writers, whereas others ~~other people~~ are naturally fuzzy and will ~~therefore~~ never write well. Thinking clearly is a ~~an entirely~~ conscious act that the writer must force ~~keep forcing~~ upon himself, just as if he were embarking ~~starting out~~ on any other ~~kind of~~ project that requires ~~calls for~~ logic: adding up a laundry list or doing an algebra problem. ~~or playing chess.~~ Good writing doesn't ~~just~~ come naturally, though most people obviously think it does. ~~it's as easy as walking.~~ The professional

Becoming a Writer

Dorothea Brande makes not one mention of technique, her tacit assumption being that once a writer has gotten past the "root" problems, a style manual should be easy to find. Instead she offers exercises for learning to see innocently, harnessing the flow of the subconscious, and reckoning with grittier concerns such as writer's block. "Her whole focus," observes John Gardner in the foreword, "is on the writer's mind and heart." That single-mindedness of focus is the glory of this wise and useful little book. —Teresa Carpenter

•

If you find yourself groping for a theme you may take this as a fair piece of advice, simple as it sounds: "You can write about anything which has been vivid enough to cause you to comment upon it." If a situation has caught your attention to that extent, it has meaning for you, and if you can find what that meaning is you have the basis for a story.

•

The conclusion should be plain. If you want to stimulate yourself into writing, amuse yourself in wordless ways. Instead of going to a theater, hear a symphony orchestra, or go by yourself to a museum; go alone for long walks, or ride by yourself on a bus-top. If you will conscientiously refuse to talk or read you will find youself compensating for it to your great advantage.

Becoming a Writer
Dorothea Brande
1961; 186 pp.
$5.95
($7.20 postpaid) from:
St. Martin's Press
Cash Sales
175 Fifth Avenue
New York, NY 10010
or Whole Earth Access

The Art of Fiction

The late John Gardner was an accomplished novelist with a passionate concern in promoting a literary ethic of conservatism and high standards. This book, "designed to teach the serious beginning writer the art of fiction," is a thoughtful consideration of the techniques and pitfalls of that art. It manages to maintain a critical rigorousness that demystifies the work of world-class fiction without dampening the enthusiasm of novices, who can benefit mightily from the pragmatic discussion herein. —Steven Levy

•

No ignoramus — no writer who has kept himself innocent of education — has ever produced great art. . . . All great writing is in a sense imitation of great writing. Writing a novel, however innovative that novel may be, the writer struggles to achieve one specific large effect, what can only be called the effect we are used to getting from good novels. However weird the technique, whatever the novel's mode, we say when we have finished it, "Now *that* is a novel!"

•

In great fiction we are moved by what happens, not by the whimpering or bawling of the writer's presentation of what happens. That is, in great fiction, we are moved by characters and events, not by the emotion of the person who happens to be telling the story. Sometimes, as in the fiction of Tolstoy or Chekhov — and one might mention many others — the narrative voice is deliberately kept calm and dispassionate, so that the emotion arising from the fictional events comes through almost wholly untinged by presentation; but restraint of that kind is not an aesthetic necessity. A flamboyant style like that of Faulkner at his best can be equally successful. The trick is simply that the style must work in the service of the material, not in advertisement of the writer.

The Art of Fiction
John Gardner
1983; 224 pp.
$4.95
($5.95 postpaid) from:
Random House
Order Dept.
400 Hahn Road
Westminster, MD 21157
or Whole Earth Access

Writer's Market • The International Directory of Little Magazines and Small Presses

When I was beginning a career as a free-lancer, I thumbed the hell out of ***Writer's Market.*** *It has the addresses, editors' names, story requirements, and payment fees for almost anywhere you'd want to sell your work, and a lot of places you wouldn't care to. Don't make the mistake, though, of using it as an exclusive reference — before you send anything out, you must get hold of the actual publication to see if it's right for your idea. But for addresses alone, it's worth its price.* ***The International Directory,*** *covering the small press world, does an even better job. A great resource for placing fiction and poetry, it's also a spiritual road map of the independent publishing movement. And since it clues you in on thousands of fascinating publications you never heard of, it's almost as valuable for readers as it is for writers.* —Steven Levy

CHICAGO READER, Box 11101, Chicago IL 60611. (312)828-0350. Editor: Robert A. Roth. 80% freelance written. "The *Reader* is distributed free in Chicago's lakefront neighborhoods. Generally speaking, these are Chicago's best educated, most affluent neighborhoods—and they have an unusually high concentration of young adults." Weekly tabloid; 128 pages. Circ. 117,000. Pays "by 15th of month following publication." Buys all rights. Byline given. Phone queries OK. Photocopied submissions OK. Computer printout submissions acceptable; prefers letter-quality to dot-matrix. SASE. Reports "very slow," up to 1 year or more.
Nonfiction: "We want magazine features on Chicago topics. Will also consider reviews." Buys 500 mss/year. Submit complete ms. Length: "Whatever's appropriate to the story." Pays $50-675.
Photos: By assignment only.
Columns/Departments: By assignment only.

—**Writer's Market**

CLINTON ST. QUARTERLY, David Milholland, Co-Editor; Jim Blashfield, Co-Editor; Lenny Dee, Co-Editor; Peggy Lindquist, Co-Editor, Box 3588, Portland, OR 97208, 503-222-6039. 1979. Fiction, articles, cartoons, interviews, satire, non-fiction. "The *CSQ* features an eclectic blend of writing on politics, art, and the times we live in. We are especially interested in writing which explores intense presonal experience and offers ways for others to understand and relect on it. Most of ur writers come from or live in the Western U.S. though we're looking for the best work we can obtain from any source. We don't give a hoot about credentials—july talent" circ. 50M. 4/yr. Pub'd 4 issues 1984; expects 4 issues 1985, 4 issues 1986. sub. price: $6; per copy: $2; sample: $2. Back issues: all issues after first year available for $2 each. 48pp; 11 × 17; of. Reporting time: 2 weeks-2 months. Payment: range is from $40-$150. Copyrighted, reverts to author. Pub's reviews: 8-10 in 1984. §Contemporary political issues, sex and sexism, writing about the Western U.S., small/med. press novels, humor, U.S. involvements abroad. Ads: $500/$300/write for ad rates and contract discounts.

—**International Directory of Little Magazines and Small Presses**

Writer's Market
Paula Deimling, Editor
1986; 1,043 pp.
$19.95
($21.95 postpaid) from:
Writer's Digest Books
9933 Alliance Road
Cincinnati, OH 45242
or Whole Earth Access

The International Directory of Little Magazines and Small Presses
Len Fulton and
Ellen Ferber, Editors
1986; 702 pp.
$20.95
($24.95 postpaid) from:
Dustbooks
P. O. Box 100
Paradise, CA 95969
or Whole Earth Access

GOOD WRITING USUALLY MEANS REWRITING. You gradually nudge your sentences closer and closer to the image you have in mind. Nothing helps that process like a computer or electronic typewriter (with memory). Yes, you can produce equally fine writing with a regular typewriter or quill pen, but it is a much more difficult, less rewarding process. As psychologist-turned-software-evaluator Charles Spezzano wrote, "A good word processing program can change your whole attitude toward writing, while pens and paper keep you stuck in your old compulsive habits."

When you type on a computer or electronic typewriter, your words go into the computer's memory. You can move them around. You can fix errors. You can revise, rethink, restretch your imagination. When you have it the way you want it, you can print it out. If you discover an error after printing, fix it and print it out again.

Three types of writing computers now exist for individuals. —Art Kleiner

The arrangement of the menu screen for PC-WRITE niftily mirrors the arrangement of function keys on the PC keyboard. The left three columns reflect the three rows of gray shift and "F" keys; the gray shift and white cursor pad keys are on the right. This map, then, tells you what each key does. The seven other menu screens are equally thrifty and compact.

```
                  Press arrow keys to select topics:
Quick summary, Cursor movement, Simple editing, Marked blocks, Search/replace
Saving/switching files, Ruler/windows, Simple formats, Printer fonts/commands
Legend:        ^ means with Ctrl key      * means with Shift key
F1  FILES       |F2  RULER        |Esc      |<-Bksp  |NumLock          |Scroll Lock
        save.   | reset margin,   | un-del  | delete | switch keys     | entered text
  switch files. | split screen.   |*R swap  |*L swap | from cursor     | overwrite or
 ^page breaks   |^read Ruler.     |^del wd  |^del wd | to numbers.     | pushright old
F3  COPY        |F4  DELETE       |TAB      |<Enter  |Home  7|Up     8|PgUp  9|Search-
 mark, mark,    | mark; delete    |to stop  | create | left M| a line |scroll |to beg
  copy marked.  | to hold area.   |*back-   | a line |*start |*to top |*screen|*go end
 ^insert file.  |^insert hold.    |* wards  | break, |^isbook|        |^paragr|
F5  CLEAR       |F6  MOVE         |Ctrl     | start  |Left  4|       5|Right 6|Search+
     text       | mark, mark,     |^means   | line.  |cursor |        |cursor |to end
   marked       | move marked     |^Ctrl    |*align  |*side  |        |*side  |search
 ^mark entire.  |^mark to file.   |^  key   |^del ln |^word  |        |^word  |for
F7  REFORMAT    |F8  CASE         |Shift    |PrtSc   |End   1|Down   2|PgDn  3|Find
    paragraph,  | change case,    |*means   | replay |rightM | a line |scroll |text
     marked.    | or marked.      |*Shift   |*print  |*end ln|*bottom |*screen|set
 *reform mode.  |*center line.    |*  key   |^reset  |^tobook|        |^paragr|using
F9  FIND        |F10 REPLACE      |Alt      |Ins            0|Del            .|F9 be-
                | search and      | enters  | insert space,   | delete text    |
                | replace once.   | font    | push right.     | pull right.    |
```

Electronic Typewriters

($150 - $500) Model numbers change too rapidly to recommend, but we hear consistently good reports about Canon and Brother. The most important feature is amount of memory, measured in K or KB (both abbreviations for the same thing, "kilobytes;" one K holds about 150 words of text, or a half a double-spaced page). Get 8K or more.

Some typewriters have cartridges where you can store old documents until you want to use them again. Also look for lift-off correction (fixes errors even after they're put on the page), pitch selection (gives you italic or boldface), and interchangeable print wheels (for different fonts, if you care). —Art Kleiner

Dedicated Word Processing Computers

These sell for $400 - $1,000. Smith-Corona makes one. We don't recommend them, because they're priced almost as high as personal computers, which are much more versatile — even just for writing. —Art Kleiner

PC-WRITE: $10 ($75 with registration) from Quicksoft, 219 1st Avenue North, #224, Seattle, WA 98109.

Microsoft Word: $450; information **free** from Microsoft Corp, 16011 Northeast 36th, Box 97017, Redmond, WA 98073-9717.

Word Proof II: $65; information **free** from IBM, Entry Systems Division, P. O. Box 1328, Boca Raton, FL 33432.

Hayden:Speller: $39.95 from Spinnaker-Hayden Software, 1 Kendall Square, Cambridge, MA 02139.

Punctuation + Style: $125; information **free** from Oasis Systems, 6160 Lusk Blvd., Suite C 206, San Diego, CA 92121.

Turbo Lightning: $95 from Borland International, 4585 Scotts Valley Drive, Scotts Valley, CA 95066 ($69.95 from Whole Earth Access).

Personal Computers With Word Processing Programs

We prefer either an IBM PC-compatible or Apple Macintosh (see pp. 352-353). Whichever you choose, shop around in person. Test-drive as many keyboards and screens as possible. Choose one that feels comfortable. Especially with IBM PC-compatibles, you will have many keyboard and screen choices. More important than the machine is which word processing software you use.

We suggest two:

PC-Write, a "shareware" program for IBM PC and compatibles, is a great versatile tool and a great bargain. It costs $10. The manual is on disk — you print it out. For $75 you can register it which entitles you to a slick manual and telephone support should you need it. You probably won't. PC-Write has all the basic word processing goodies, it's blazingly fast, and it blends sweetly with other programs like spelling checkers, telecommunication programs, and especially other public domain (inexpensive) programs. Some of the editors at Whole Earth use it in preference to the hundreds of other programs we have around.

Microsoft Word, from one of the major computer companies, is our favorite powerhouse writing tool. It permits automatic indexes, multiple files on the screen for cross-checking, and many other features. It presents all these features considerately (what other programs call "macros," Word calls a "glossary"). On both the Mac and PC, Word excels with a mouse, the pointing device that you move with your hand to locate your position on the screen.

For word processing on other computers, see the ***Whole Earth Software Catalog*** *(p. 354).*

Beyond elementary "typewriting" programs are writer aids. Word Proof II (PC/compatibles) and Hayden: Speller (Macintosh) scour through your finished computerized text. When they don't recognize a word's spelling, they suggest alternatives or let you add the word to their "dictionary." Punctuation + Style (PC/compatibles) does the same for compositional usage — it checks your words against a list of punctuation, abbreviation, and capitalization conventions, and even monitors for cliches and overused phrases. Turbo Lightning (PC/compatibles) checks spelling immediately while you type (it signals a misspelling), and includes a thesaurus: if you think a word isn't quite right, Lightning will suggest synonyms and replace the old word with the new word automatically.

Used with a critical eye (for instance, sometimes there are better synonyms than the suggestions from Turbo Lightning), these can gradually improve your writing. —Art Kleiner

• Word processing carried just a bit further and you're doing desktop publishing. What you need to know is on p. 316.

• The best source for buying electronic typewriters by discount mail order is J & R Electronics (p. 348).

• There is nothing like precise language to cure the lazy babblings possible with a word processor. See **Standing by Words** by Wendell Berry (p. 297) for inspiration and example.

BOOKS RECORDED ON TAPE are a kind of jui-jitsu. In one swift motion they flip a wasted half-hour car commute over into an eagerly awaited 30 minutes with a great novelist, thinker, or storyteller. Cheap Walkman-like gadgets bestow the same powers to bus and train commuters. Mowing the front lawn, doing piecework on an assembly line, or jogging all become somewhat bearable while listening to Ray Bradbury read his science fiction classic *The Martian Chronicles*, or while immersed in 70 hours of *War and Peace.* An unexpected bonus is that books heard are often remembered far more vividly than books read. Generally cassettes are rented for 30 days. But you shouldn't have to buy or rent these; demand that your local public library stock a shelf-full (many do already).

—Kevin Kelly

One of Whole Earth's editors, Ted Schultz embarks on his one-hour, twice-daily commute. He begins the review of 31 cassettes of "The Biography of Peter the Great" (Books on Tape), about a month's work.

Books on Tape

The pioneer source is Books on Tape, now sporting over 1,000 titles. They issue 20 new ones a month. Their wide, pleasing selection is particularly strong in biographies, sea adventures, journals of early travelers, mysteries, contemporary nonfiction, and those acclaimed, long historical works by the likes of Churchill, Theodore White, etc. that you always wanted to get to. These books are read in their full length by trained, easy-to-hear narrators. For rent or sale. —KK

Books on Tape: Catalog **$5** from P. O. Box 7900, Newport Beach, CA 92660.

•

The Age of Discontinuity by Peter F. Drucker: Order rental book (1337) $15.50. 11 1½-hour cassettes. Read by Michael Prichard.

Peter Drucker, management consultant and noted business and economic philosopher, analyzes the major forces at work during the third quarter of the twentieth century.

Listen for Pleasure

About 100 popular (mostly recent) books read by famous British and American actors, some reading stories that became movies they starred in: for instance Tom Courtenay narrating **The Loneliness of the Long Distance Runner**. *A couple of tapes feature famous authors reading their own: John le Carre retelling his* **Smiley's People**, *which is outstanding. Every book is abridged* **Reader's Digest** *style to fit onto two cassettes — two to three hours' listening time. The voices are vigorous and of superb quality. For sale only ($14 each).* —KK

Listen for Pleasure: Catalog **free** from 1 Columbia Drive, Niagara Falls, NY 14305.

Recorded Books

Slim but well-chosen collection of old favorites, new nonfiction, and (thank you) some overlooked minor classics. These are word-for-word recordings by expert narrators. For rent or sale. —KK

Recorded Books: Catalog **free** from 6306 Aaron Lane, Clinton, MD 20735.

Caedmon

The fountainhead of poetry on tape. Originally founded 30 years ago to record modern poets on 78-RPM records. An illustrious pantheon of great poets and novelists perform their own masterpieces, or those of their mentors. Other great and fascinating literature is memorably recorded by spoken-word artists. Unfortunately most of the offerings are selections and abridgements. Tape quality varies due to the age of some of the recordings. For sale only. —KK

Claire Bloom reads Guy de Maupassant and Jane Austen on Caedmon recordings.

Caedmon: Catalog **free** from 1995 Broadway, New York, NY 10023; 800/223-0420.

On Cassette

Bingo! What a gold mine! This handy reference lists every nonmusic audio cassette known to be around (about 11,500 of them). In it you can find out if that wonderful book you wish they had on tape is made or not. It'll tell you its price and who to order it from. You can look it up by title, author, or subject. It covers plays and poetry, too. And interviews, radio shows, seminars, speeches, and language instruction. I'd be flabbergasted if you had trouble convincing your library to buy this book. —KK

Dostoyevsky, Fyodor. The Brothers Karamazov. 2 cass. (Running Time: 120 min.) (Fiction Ser.). 1985. 14.95 (ISBN 0-87188-194-2). Warner Audio Pub.
--Crime & Punishment. unabr. ed. Read by Walter Zimmerman. (Running Time: 1 hr. 30 min. per cass.) 1984. Part I, 8 cass. rental 13.50 (9120-A); Part II, 8 cass. rental 13.50 (9120-B). Bks on Tape.
Raskolnikov, a student in St. Petersburg, murders an old woman, a money-lender, & her sister to prove his theory that violence purifies the strong. But no sooner is the deed done than Raskolnikov's remorse lays siege to his resolve.
--Crime & Punishment. Tr. by Constance Garnett. Performed by James Mason. 1 cass. LC 81-740216. 8.98 (CDL5 1691). Caedmon.
Excerpts.
--Notes from the Underground. unabr. ed. 4 cass. (Running Time: 5 hrs.) 1984. 24.00 (C-34); rental 5.00. Jimcin Record.
The book relates the experiences of a singular young man who spurns the rule of God & man. The problem he faces is that of all nihilists, which is to deny authority while simultaneously explaining order.
--The Thief. unabr. ed. Incl. The Wedding; The Long Exile. Tolstoy, Leo. 6.95 (N-52). Jimcin Record.

On Cassette
Ernest Lee, Editor
1985; 658 pp.
$63.45
postpaid from:
R. R. Bowker
205 East 42nd Street
New York, NY 10017

The Mind's Eye

This audience is children, all ears, wide-eyed. Some 150 fairy tales, ghost stories, vintage Dickens, and books your mother read to you on her lap. The stories are frisky, hearty dramatizations with sound effects and a cast of hundreds when needed. All this commotion is crammed onto one or two cassettes each (with exceptions: the breathless **Lord of the Rings** *on twelve tapes). For sale only.* —KK

The Mind's Eye: Catalog **free** from 4 Commercial Blvd., Suite 2, Novato, CA 94947.

Norwood XLP Cassette Recorder

This cassette recorder takes standard-sized cassettes, but can record and play at one-fourth normal speed, and also can record on two different tracks (one track at a time). Thus you can record or play back 12 hours on a C-90 cassette normally good for 1½ hours: that means you can fit 8X as much time on each cassette. The sound quality is good enough for voice and reading of books, though music wouldn't sound great. —Warren Hatch

Norwood XLP Cassette Recorder: $134 postpaid from Norwood Industries, 3828 South Main Street, Salt Lake City, UT 84115.

How to Read a Book
Mortimer J. Adler and Charles Van Doren
1972; 426 pp.
$9.95
($10.95 postpaid) from:
Simon and Schuster
200 Old Tappan Road
Old Tappan, NJ 07675
or Whole Earth Access

How to Read a Book

Authors Adler and Van Doren propose a reexamination of the much-overlooked idea that there are techniques for reading books, just as there are techniques for driving in the rain and playing soccer. They've resurrected and present here a collection of rules and instructions of the sort used in the Middle Ages as part of the trivium of logic, grammar, and rhetoric. Few people could read then, but the ones who could usually read very well. The authors believe that with this rhetorical tool kit and a lot of hard work, most people can do the same.

I spent 6½ years in college. My best intellectual happening there was coming across this book. —T. Durso

•

Analytical reading is thorough reading, complete reading, or good reading — the best reading you can do. If inspectional reading is the best and most complete reading that is possible given a limited time, then analytical reading is the best and most complete reading that is possible given unlimited time.

The analytical reader must ask many, and organized, questions of what he is reading. We do not want to state these questions here, since this book is mainly about reading at this level: Part Two gives its rules and tells you how to do it. We do want to emphasize here that analytical reading is always intensely active. On this level of reading, the reader grasps a book — the metaphor is apt — and works at it until the book becomes his own. Francis Bacon once remarked that "some books are to be tasted, others to be swallowed, and some few to be chewed and digested." Reading a book analytically is chewing and digesting it.

•

What you can learn from the title of a book

In 1859, Darwin published a very famous book. A century later the entire English-speaking world celebrated the publication of the book. It was discussed endlessly, and its influence was assessed by learned and not-so-learned commentators. The book was about the theory of evolution, and the word "species" was in the title. What was the title?

Probably you said *The Origin of Species*, in which case you were correct. But you might not have said that. You might have said that the title was *The Origin of the Species*. Recently, we asked some twenty-five reasonably well-read persons what the title of Darwin's book was and more than half said *The Origin of the Species*. The reason for the mistake is obvious; they supposed, never having read the book, that it had something to do with the development of the human species. In fact, it has little or nothing to do with that subject, which Darwin covered in a later book, *The Descent of Man*. *The Origin of Species* is about what its title says it is about.

The Reader's Adviser
Sarah L. Prakken, Editor
$75 each*
($78.75 postpaid);
$194 3-volume set
($204.75 postpaid)
All from:
R.R. Bowker Company
205 East 42nd Street
New York, NY 10017

The Reader's Adviser

If you throw darts at a world map and go where they point, you'll have a much more interesting vacation than anything the travel bureau can offer. Likewise if you throw one of these hefty volumes at a bed, examine the open pages and read in the direction indicated, your mind will meet minds a bookstore dare not carry. Every goddamn page (2616 all told) has fascinating people and works that I've never heard of in my high rent liberal education, warmly and searchingly remarked upon, with all the access information you need to waltz cheerfully through library procedures to the goods. —Stewart Brand

*Volume I: The Best in American and British Fiction, Poetry, Essays, Literary Biography, Bibliography and Reference

Volume II: The Best in American and British Drama and World Literature in English Translation

Volume III: The Best in the Reference Literature of the World

•

Walton, Izaak. 1593-1683. ***The Compleat Angler***, one of the most famous books in English, was written by a self-educated ironmonger. Walton wrote it for his own pleasure as well as that of others; it not only describes the technique of angling, but is a contemplative essay on the peace and quietude attained by the fisherman. After its first appearance in 1653 there were frequent revisions adding new material during the author's lifetime. George Saintsbury called Walton's style one of a "singular and golden simplicity." In spite of Walton's background he became recognized as a "gentleman" of cultured tastes and learning. An Anglican and Royalist, he was overjoyed with the Restoration. In his own time, Walton was known as a biographer, author of the *Lives of John Donne, Sir Henry Wotton, Richard Hooker, George Herbert and Robert Sanderson*. Kenneth Rexroth wrote a charming essay on *The Compleat Angler* in the *Saturday Review* of Sept. 16, 1967, which catches the secret of its enduring appeal and that of its author shining through it: "Izaak Walton, above all other writers in English, owes his enormous popularity to his virtues as a man, and these virtues are what condition his style and give his work its fundamental meaning. Millions have read him with joy who have never caught a fish since childhood, if at all. Indeed, . . . in America at least, most of the kinds of fish he talks about are left to small boys. The second half of *The Compleat Angler* was added in the late editions and written by Charles Cotton as a guide to trout fishing in rough water. Those who want to know how to catch fish can learn most from Cotton's additions. We read Izaak Walton for a special quality of soul . . . for his tone, for his perfect attunement to the quiet streams and flowered meadows and bosky hills of the Thames valley long ago. . . . It may sound outrageous to say that Izaak Walton wrote one of the Great Books — and that about catching fish — because he was a saint, but so it is. —*Volume III*

The Pushcart Prize IX
Bill Henderson
1984; 588 pp.
$9.95
($10.95 postpaid) from:
Avon Books
P. O. Box 767
Dresden, TN 38225
or Whole Earth Access

The Pushcart Prize

Printing good (and bad) writing is easy and cheap these days, but getting it to where people can buy it is still complicated and expensive. That hurts small, worthy presses, and it also hurts you since you're missing a lot, no matter how many bookstores you go to.

Here is a way to miss less of what's being published by groups smaller than Time, Inc. and ***Mother Jones. The Pushcart Prize*** *is a collection of good writing nominated annually from hundreds of small press publications. Strange good things by people you wouldn't otherwise see. And it lists where the pieces were originally published so you can use it as a guide to small magazines you might be interested in. —Anne Herbert*

• A catalog of the best remaindered books at discount prices. **Daedalus Books:** Catalog **free** from 2260 25th Place NE, Washington, DC 20018.

Lord of the Rings, etc.

*think no other fictional world matches the depth of olkien's. This children's tale (**The Hobbit**) seized the Oxord mythologist and ancient languages scholar Tolkien and hurled him and us into a saga so vast that he never did encompass it all. The three-volumed **Lord of the Rings** s the central masterpiece — the journey of the hobbits, nen, and elves, and wizard Gandalf to destroy the Ring of Power of the dark Lord Sauron. It is a tale of surprising nvention, subtlety, and insight.* —Stewart Brand

•

'Hold it up!' said Gandalf. 'And look closely!'

As Frodo did so, he now saw fine lines, finer than the finest penstrokes, running along the ring, outside and inside: lines of fire that seemed to form the letters of a flowing script. They shone piercingly bright, and yet remote, as if out of a great depth.

'I cannot read the fiery letters,' said Frodo in a quavering voice.

'No,' said Gandalf, 'but I can. The letters are Elvish, of an ancient mode, but the language is that of Mordor, which I will not utter here. But this in the Common Tongue is what is said, close enough:

One Ring to rule them all, One Ring to find them,
One Ring to bring them all and in the darkness bind them.

It is only two lines of a verse long known in Elven-lore:

Three Rings for the Elven-kings under the sky,
Seven for the Dwarf-lords in their halls of stone,
Nine for Mortal Men doomed to die,
One for the Dark Lord on his dark throne
In the Land of Mordor where the Shadows lie.
One Ring to rule them all, One Ring to find them,
One Ring to bring them all and in the darkness bind them
In the Land of Mordor where the Shadows lie.'

He paused, and then said slowly in a deep voice: 'This is the Master-ring, the One Ring to rule them all. This is the One Ring that he lost many years ago, to the great weakening of his power. He greatly desires it — but he must *not* get it.'

Frodo sat silent and motionless. Fear seemed to stretch out a vast hand, like a dark cloud rising in the East and looming up to engulf him. 'This ring!' he stammered. 'How, how on earth did it come to me?'

—*The Fellowship of the Ring*

The Hobbit
J.R.R. Tolkien
1938

The Lord of the Rings
J.R.R. Tolkien
1955 (3 volumes)

The Hobbit and the Lord of the Rings
(Paperback boxed set)
$24.45
($28.45 postpaid) from:
Houghton-Mifflin
Mail Order Dept.
Wayside Road
Burlington, MA 01803
or Whole Earth Access

The Once and Future King

*One of the most popular story books around (**Camelot**, good play, so-so movie), this four-volumes-in-one tragedy of King Arthur is more about learning than any other fiction I can think of. Young Arthur learns the ways of the wide world by being magicked into the personae of various animals by Merlyn — a fish, a hawk, an ant, and grandest of all, a migrating goose. "Where did T.H. White get that?" Gregory Bateson kept asking, certain that it was borrowed from some tribe or other. Best of all, the learning doesn't stop with being crowned or being married, as most stories conveniently do. The hard lessons of full maturity, even of civilization itself growing up, are the simultaneous working and the burden of the tragedy.*

*Twice in reading **The Once and Future King**, end of the first book and end of the fourth, I have dripped salt tears and been unable to go on reading aloud. No other book has managed that.* —Stewart Brand

•

"Come, sword," he said. "I must cry your mercy and take you for a better cause.

"This is extraordinary," said the Wart. "I feel strange when I have hold of this sword, and I notice everything much more clearly. Look at the beautiful gargoyles of the church, and of the monastery which it belongs to. See how splendidly all the famous banners in the aisle are waving. How nobly that yew holds up the red flakes of its timbers to worship God. How clean the snow is. I can smell something like fetherfew and sweet briar — and is it music that I hear?"

It was music, whether of pan-pipes or of recorders, and the light in the churchyard was so clear, without being dazzling, that one could have picked a pin out twenty yards away.

"There is something in this place," said the Wart. "There are people. Oh, people, what do you want?"

Nobody answered him, but the music was loud and the light beautiful.

"People," cried the Wart, "I must take this sword. It is not for me, but for Kay. I will bring it back."

There was still no answer, and Wart turned back to the anvil. He saw the golden letters, which he did not read, and the jewels on the pommel, flashing in the lovely light.

"Come, sword," said the Wart.

The Once and Future King
T.H. White
1985; 639 pp.
$4.95
($5.70 postpaid) from:
Berkley Publishing Group
390 Murray Hill Pkwy.
East Rutherford, NJ 07073
or Whole Earth Access

Manas

An anonymously produced philosophical humanist journal. A weekly thoughtful delight, these are the good thoughts that lead to and emerge from good actions. It's also one of the few places you hear about old books used in renewed ways — Gandhi, Ortega y Gasset, Tolstoy — and new and promising activities and publications. —Stewart Brand

•

In short, some arguments with some people cannot be won, even by the most skilled and devoted of advocates. Socrates lost in his attempt to persuade the Athenians to interest themselves in his ideas about education, although he went on arguing to his dying breath. So with his imitators and followers, of whom E.F. Schumacher was one. He said:

> There is no doubt . . . the need to transmit know-how, but this must take second place, for it is obviously somewhat foolhardy to put great powers into the hands of people without making sure that they have a reasonable idea of what to do with them. At present, there can be little doubt that the whole of mankind is in mortal danger, not because we are short of scientific and technological know-how, but because we tend to use it destructively, without wisdom. More education can help us only if it produces more wisdom.

Manas
$10/year
(41 issues) from:
Manas Publishing Company
P. O. Box 32112
El Sereno Station
Los Angeles, CA 90032

The Sun

***The Sun** tries to print the truth. Not the news or the latest, but the truth, Mr. Truth, the Queen of All Our Dreams.*

And it does. Not, for me, with every word or every story, but in every issue my mind is truly boggled by something in a way it was hungry for. The means used are interviews with people poetic and spiritual, stories about the mundane and exhilarating details of trying to live a good (not hedonistic — good) life, and the best quotations page I've ever seen.
—*Anne Herbert*

The Sun
Sy Safransky, Editor
$28/year
(12 issues) from:
The Sun
412 West Rosemary Street
Chapel Hill, NC 27514

—Love and Rockets

ARE COMICS SOLELY "KID'S STUFF"? If you ask your average citizens this pressing question, they'll likely answer with an adamant "Yes!" — though a few fans of Doonesbury and Garfield may point to the funnies page in the daily paper as an exception to the rule.

'Twas not always thus. The first comic strips at the turn of the century were aimed almost exclusively at adults. *Mutt and Jeff,* one of the earliest strips, got its start in the *S.F. Chronicle*'s sports pages with jokes about horse racing. One-panel political and gag cartoons grew up in the 19th century in non-juvenile humor magazines like *Punch, Judge,* and *Life.* More recently, when comic books as we know them got off the ground at the start of the 1940s, they found their largest audience in WWII servicemen.

It was only with the advent of television and the baby boom that comics increasingly came to rely on kids as their staple readers. This situation held for most of the '50s and '60s until the counterculture spawned the subgenre of underground comix aimed at hip adults. Undergrounds foreswore the voluntary censorship that kept other comic publishers locked into preadolescent markets. The results were, by turns, creative, jarring, entertaining, and offensive, and a significant number of underground artists and publishers have continued to produce unique works right up to the present. However, because of their emphasis on taboo-breaking, undergrounds have never captured a mass audience and likely never will.

—Nexus

It was left for a new wave of comics publishers — variously called alternative or independent — to yank comics up a notch in status. *Heavy Metal* magazine initiated the process in the mid '70s with its slick-paper reprints of comic stories from France (where comics have always had a large adult audience). Independent publishers such as First Comics, Eclipse Comics, and Fantagraphics have kept the momentum going with "graphic novels" (book length, softbound color comics) and a new spate of adventurous comic books especially aimed at comic collectors. These latter comics often closely ape the mainstream (juvenile) comics from publishers like Marvel and DC; the biggest sellers continue to be superhero stories. However, there are also a significant number of exceptions to the rule, the best independent comics being fully mature fare with no apologies.

The listings that follow are unavoidably incomplete. Given the turnover in new titles and in artists assigned to books, outstanding comics often have all-too-brief lifespans. Here are some that are flourishing as I write.

—Jay Kinney

Fantagraphics Books

Catalog **free** from 4359 Cornell Road, Agoura, CA 91301.

One of the smallest independent publishers and one of the most willing to take risks. Fantagraphic's leading publication, ***Comics Journal****, has been arguing the case for better comics for years. Now with a growing line of unusual titles, publisher Gary Groth is putting his money where his mouth is.*

Love and Rockets

Arguably the finest regular comic now being published. Written and drawn by the Hernandez brothers, ***Love and Rockets*** *combines classic comic art with scripts worthy of Gabriel Garcia Marquez. Plus it has the best female characters in comics today. Seek this one out!*

Neat Stuff

Peter Bagge's gross, slapstick, and — yes — insightful comic strips about childhood and ne'er-do-wells.

Journey

An epic tale of frontiersman Wolverine MacAllistaire in the wilds of Michigan. William Messner-Loebs' complex and unique personal statement.

The Comics Journal

Gary Groth, Editor. **$18**/year (9 issues) from Fantagraphics (see address on left).

The only essential journal of news and criticism for the comics industry. Good coverage of both mainstream and alternative comics and creators.

First Comics

Newsletter **free** from 435 N. LaSalle, Chicago, IL 60610.

Of all the independents, this publisher is closest to Marvel Comics in product: lots of superheroes and several titles outlasting the departure of their original creators.

Nexus

As good a science fiction universe as you are likely to find in comics; superior art and writing by Mike Baron and Steve Rude.

Shatter

When it initially appeared, this title scored piles of publicity as the first comic book drawn on a computer (a Macintosh). With originator Michael Saenz now gone, it isn't the same, but it's still worth a look.

American Flagg!

For its first two years this was the finest comic being published by First — a blistering, dystopian future vision written and drawn by Howard Chaykin. Graphic novel reprints of its best episodes (such as ***Hard Times****) are worth obtaining.*

—Alien Encounter

Kitchen Sink Comix

Catalog **free** from 2 Swamp Road, Princeton, WI 54968.

Kitchen Sink has one foot in the underground camp and one foot in the independent camp. Reprints of classic material by Milton Caniff and Will Eisner rub shoulders with new science-fiction comics and a full-fledged underground or two. Some new 3-D comics, also.

—Death Rattle

Eclipse Comics

Catalog **free** with SASE from P. O. Box 199, Guerneville, CA 95446.

These folks straddle a lot of territory with their comics. Their superheroes (such as **DNA Agents***) are pretty standard fare, but they've got other items such as a mini-series from P. Craig Russell that stands above the herd. Recently, Eclipse has been in the forefront of the 3-D comic revival, with nicely produced 3-D editions of several of their titles.*

Seduction of the Innocent

This series is named after the sensationalist 1950s book of the same name that led the witch-hunt against comic books for corrupting our nation's children. The vintage comic strips reprinted here are those that originally caused PTAs to quake in their pumps.

Scout

A grim future a la **Road Warrior***, an American Indian hero, and good strong art and writing from Timothy Truman.*

Alien Encounters • Tales of Terror

Two anthology comics presenting short science fiction and horror strips; various artists and writers, most of them good.

Last Gasp Comics

Catalog **$1** from 2180 Bryant St., San Francisco, CA 94110.

This is one of the original underground comic publishers. Last Gasp still publishes many comix and distributes even more.

Weirdo Magazine

Robert Crumb founded this quarterly anthology of cartoon strangeness; it remains one of the least predictable publications in America.

—Weirdo

Steve Canyon Magazine

Nicely produced reprints of Milton Caniff's famous mix of patriotism and the exotic.

The Spirit

Reprints of Will Eisner's beloved suspense strip from the 1940s.

Death Rattle

Anthology comic of new science fiction and horror comics.

Lonely Nights

Frank confessions from the flabbergasting psyche of Dori Seda. Very funny and uninhibited.

Anarchy Comics

Antiauthoritarian political cartooning from both the U.S. and Europe.

—Weirdo

—Raw Magazine

Raw Books

Flyer **free** from 27 Greene Street, New York, NY 10013.

If comics have an avant garde, Raw is it.

Raw Magazine

Giant-format comics-as-art magazine, edited by Art Spiegelman and Francoise Mouly. Exquisitely designed.

X by Sue Coe

The latest of the Raw "one-shots," this small 32-page hardcover combines fiery paintings and words to roast the American Dream. Makes Kathe Kollwitz seem like Grandma Moses.

—American Splendor

Russ Cochran

P. O. Box 469, West Plains, MO 65775.

This small publisher has been reprinting the complete run of the infamous EC comics from the early 1950s in beautiful hardcover editions. These were the best comic books ever produced. Period.

American Splendor

Information **free** with SASE from Harvey Pekar, P. O. Box 18471, Cleveland Heights, OH 44118.

Harvey has been chronicling his "ordinary" life in Cleveland for years now. He writes the strips and hires a variety of cartoonists to illustrate them. All true, all deadpan, always entertaining.

"Libraries will get you through times of no money better than money will get you through times of no libraries." —Anne Herbert

JUST AS CHURCHES can be sanctuaries for live human bodies, libraries should be revered as sanctuaries for live human thoughts and feelings. Libraries also provide a free way to read any book in this Catalog — if it isn't in that branch, most libraries have excellent inter-library loan methods for finding just about anything (given enough time). As Anne Herbert wrote, "I've known people who would call 17 bookstores to find a book and never go down the street to the library. At the library, it doesn't matter if the books are out of print. They're there, and the price is right."

Three librarians helped us gather these four pages on libraries, research and reference: Steve Cisler (Pinole Valley), Mary Richardson (Sausalito), and Kay Roberts (Bay Area Reference Center). —Art Kleiner

Finding Facts Fast
Alden Todd
1979; 123 pp.
$3.95
($4.95 postpaid) from:
Ten Speed Press
P. O. Box 7123
Berkeley, CA 94707
or Whole Earth Access

Finding Facts Fast

A basic handbook for laypeople. It has beautiful two- and three-page descriptions of how to treat hundreds of problems in research from very elemental to very advanced levels. From "finding the right library" to "government as an information source" to "oral history collections" and "obtaining out-of-print books." Every time I get lost in the world of information I use Todd to ground me.
—Richard Green

Yup. Still unsurpassed after 14 years. This is where you learn research common sense. Also see ***The Independent Scholar's Handbook*** *(p. 378) and* ***The Reporter's Handbook*** *(p. 105).*
—Art Kleiner

•

Another starting point is with companies, organizations and associations, through which you can find the specialists who would know their own trade press. The researcher can then go directly to his target by asking the specialized craftsman, or professional, or businessman: "What trade journals do you read? Which ones do your colleagues read? Which are your best printed sources of information?" and, "Do you have copies of them?"

The World Almanac
Hana U. Lane, Editor
$5.95
($7.45 postpaid) from:
World Almanac Publications
Box 984
Cincinnati, OH 45201
or Whole Earth Access

The World Almanac

When I was ten I remember being given two thick paperbacks: the ***Johnson Smith Novelty Catalog*** *(p. 364) and the 1952* ***World Almanac****. I spent a long time leafing through each of them, but the* ***World Almanac*** *had more staying power. Now, as a librarian, I find it one of the most useful reference works available. The print is a bit small, and the maps are just so-so. Published each November, current through October. Use the detailed index in the front, or the one-page Quick Reference index in the back.*
—Steve Cisler

Answers Online
(Your Guide to Informational Data Bases)
Barbara Newlin
1985; 370 pp.
$16.95
postpaid from:
McGraw Hill
Retail Center
P. O. Box 400
Hightstown, NJ 08520
or Whole Earth Access

Answers Online

Deep specialization sometimes requires deep research. The very deepest these days takes place via computer network and modem. Instead of plowing for hours through reference books, you dial into the bowels of highly exclusive data banks, where they charge by the second and no one can afford to browse. Thus, you must carefully narrow down your focus before you ever turn on your computer terminal. This book tells how to do it, when to do it, what to look for, and when to go to the library instead.
—Art Kleiner

Magazine Index
Information **free** from:
Information Access Co.
11 Davis Drive
Belmont, CA 94002

Magazine Index (on Microfilm)

By far the best index for finding magazine articles is this self-contained microfilm display available for use in most libraries. It's the size of a regular microfiche reader but with only one filmstrip roll, which the libraries update monthly or bimonthly. Unlike the ***Reader's Guide to Periodical Literature****, it's a one-stop magazine index — you don't have to keep going from volume to volume. It indexes 400 magazines back six years, with supplements on fiche going back to 1977.*
—KK

Library Journal

Simply the best periodical for books in America. Best reviews, widest coverage, least nonsense. To stay current in any field I'd call it essential.
—Stewart Brand

•

Van Doren, Charles: The Joy of Reading.
Veteran critic and editor Van Doren offers the fruits of decades as a constant reader. Speaking directly to general readers, he aims to bestow the same gift he received from his father, poet Mark Van Doren: "to be acquainted with all kinds of books and not to be afraid of or reluctant to try to read any particular kind." His 210 selections for discussion are unabashedly personal, ranging across centuries, subjects, and genres. All, from the *Orestia* to *Charlotte's Web*, are books he loves and rereads, in which "the author has something important to say about something important." *—Starr E. Smith, Georgetown Univ. Lib., Washington, D.C.*

Science Books & Films • Current Contents

For keeping up with the flow of scientific verbiage. ***Current Contents*** *is, in Kevin Kelly's words, "nothing more than the reproduced tables of contents from the several thousand best scientific journals. The scientists I know use it for connecting with the 200 papers that will do them any good, while weeding out the thousands of redundant ones and the other million or so that have nothing to do with them."* ***Science Books & Films****, from the publishers of* ***Science*** *(p. 26), reviews new science-oriented books and films, right on down to a kindergarten age level, with high standards and gritty detail.*
—Art Kleiner
[Suggested by Kevin Kelly and John Lord]

•

de DUVE, CHRISTIAN. *A Guided Tour of the Living Cell, Vols. 1 & 2.* (Illus. by Neil O. Hardy.) NY: Scientific American Books (dist. by Freeman), 1985.
. . . Although somewhat expensive, the contents of this two-volume set make it a bargain. If public and academic libraries can purchase only one cell biology book for the year, they could not make a better choice. *—James C. McDonald, Wake Forest Univ., Winston-Salem, NC*
—Science Books & Films

Yellow Pages

No reference book matches the practical currency of the ***Yellow Pages*** *in your local telephone directory. On any subject you can browse, call, inquire, ask who else would have information, and proceed to the heart of any matter.*
—Stewart Brand

Once a year I check out a ***Manhattan Yellow Pages*** *(now available in two editions: the* ***New York County Business-to-Business Directory*** *and the* ***Manhattan Consumer Yellow Pages****) from the local university library. They contain whole categories not found in local* ***Yellow Pages****.*
—JB

You can order any far-flung phone book through your local phone company business office.
—Art Kleiner

RESEARCH NEED NOT BE DULL. Any of these reference books is grist for hours of dreamy browsing — and they can provide surprisingly simple shortcuts to answering tough questions. You probably need not buy them — even small libraries have most of them.

GREAT REFERENCE BOOKS

by Art Kleiner and Steve Cisler

Library Journal
John N. Berry III, Editor
$64/year
(20 issues) from:
R. R. Bowker Company
Subscription Department
P. O. Box 1427
Riverton, NJ 08077

Science Books & Films
Kathleen S. Johnston, Editor
$25/year
(5 issues) from:
American Association for the Advancement of Science
P. O. Box 465
Hanover, PA 17331

Current Contents
Beverly Bartolomeo, Editor
$272/year
(52 issues) from:
Institute for Scientific Information
3501 Market Street
Philadelphia, PA 19104

Manhattan Consumer Yellow Pages
$11.60 postpaid;
New York County Business-to-Business Directory
$12.95 postpaid.
Order by phone from your local telephone company business office.

Encyclopedia of Associations

First stop for finding any organization or group. These are, by and large, accessible groups willing to help you research thousands of fast-moving topics that books can't keep up with. Plus hilariously obscure pursuits like barbed wire collecting.

Encyclopedia of Associations (National Organizations of the United States, Vol. I): Katherine Gruber, Editor. Annual (Vol. I is in three books); 2,290 pp. **$199.50** postpaid from Gale Research Company, Book Tower, Detroit, MI 48226.

Statistical Abstract of the United States

Tells how many of who's doing what where this year. How many unemployed teachers, National Park visitors, or new housing projects. Exhaustive and inexpensive.

Statistical Abstract of the United States (National Data Book and Guide to Sources): annual; 1,019 pp. **$19** postpaid (stock no. 003-024-06135-0) from Superintendent of Documents, U.S. Government Printing Office, Washington, D.C. 20402.

Statesman's Yearbook

Descriptions and great bibliography about every country on the planet. Compiled in Britain.

Statesman's Yearbook: John Paxton, Editor. Annual; 1,749 pp. **$45** postpaid from St. Martin's Press, 175 5th Avenue, New York, NY 10010.

Chase's Annual Events

Lists what happened in past years for any day of the year. A bit silly, but great fodder for disk jockeys ("Marlon Brando was born this day, and pizza invented") and other compulsive talkers.

Chase's Annual Events: William D. Chase and Helen M. Chase. Annual; 224 pp. **$16.95** postpaid from Contemporary Books, 180 North Michigan Avenue, Chicago, IL 60601.

Current Biography Yearbook

They rewrite news stories into biographical sketches of anyone who's been important in the news. Especially good for historical biographies, back to 1940.

Current Biography Yearbook: Charles Moritz, Editor. 11 issues/year, cumulated into hardbound annual. 35 vols. (1940-1985) **$35** each from H. W. Wilson Company, 950 University Avenue, Bronx, NY 10452.

The Art Index

Says J. Baldwin, "It's the Reader's Guide to Periodical Literature for magazines architectural or visual."

The Art Index: price information from H. W. Wilson Company, 950 University Avenue, Bronx, NY 10452.

Whole Again Resource Guide

Listings and descriptions of the vast alternative press. Includes independent newsletters and magazines you won't see in most mainstream directories. Just revised (1986).

Whole Again Resource Guide: Tim Ryan, 1986/87; 300 pp. **$26.95** postpaid from Sourcenet, Box 6767, Santa Barbara, CA 93160 (or Whole Earth Access).

National Five-Digit Zip Code and Post Office Directory

Tells how to get in touch with that corporation that you know is "somewhere in the Midwest . . ."

National Five-Digit Zip Code and Post Office Directory: United States Postal Service. Annual; 2,310 pp. **$9** postpaid from Superintendent of Documents, U.S. Government Printing Office, Washington, DC 20402-1575.

Science Citation Index • Social Science Citation Index

Who's influencing whom in science and academia. If you've ever been published, find the articles that footnoted you. Trace the path of an idea down its paper trail of citations. In Kevin Kelly's words: "Information is a communicable disease."

Science Citation Index and **Social Science Citation Index:** information from Institute for Scientific Information/Fulfillment Services, 3501 Market Street, Philadelphia, PA 19104.

Harvard Encyclopedia of American Ethnic Groups

Where we all came from and how we got here. Erudite, fascinating, candid. Includes some surprising enclaves, like the Kalmyks — Mongolian Buddhists in Pennsylvania.

Harvard Encyclopedia of American Ethnic Groups: Stephan Thernstrom, Editor. 1980; 1,102 pp. **$72** postpaid from Harvard University Press, 79 Garden Street, Cambridge, MA 02138. ■

• See **Information U.S.A.** (p. 103), **Thomas Register** (p. 189), and **Sweet's Files** (p. 119).

• Some of this stuff might be handy for a home library, too. **Gaylord Library Supplies:** catalog **free** from Box 4901, Syracuse, NY 13221-4901.

American Heritage Dictionary
1983; 896 pp.
$9.95
($10.70 postpaid) from:
Dell Books
P. O. Box 1000
Pinebrook, NJ 07058-1000
or Whole Earth Access

American Heritage Dictionary of the English Language

Six years ago, Stewart Brand researched dictionaries with the help of a meta-dictionary called the ***Dictionary Buyer's Guide****. His conclusion:* ***American Heritage*** *is "the most interesting and usable English dictionary in print." We still agree, only more so. Perhaps best known for its inviting line-drawn illustrations in the margins, the* ***American Heritage*** *dictionary is complete and intelligent enough to impress even librarians, who'd say "****Webster's*** *has a place in our hearts."*

Dictionaries may well be the most essential books in this whole Catalog; they make all the other books accessible.
—Art Kleiner

radio wave *n.* A radio-frequency electromagnetic wave.
rad·ish (răd'ĭsh) *n.* **1.** A plant with a thickened, edible root. **2.** The pungent root of the radish plant. [< Lat. *radix*, root.]

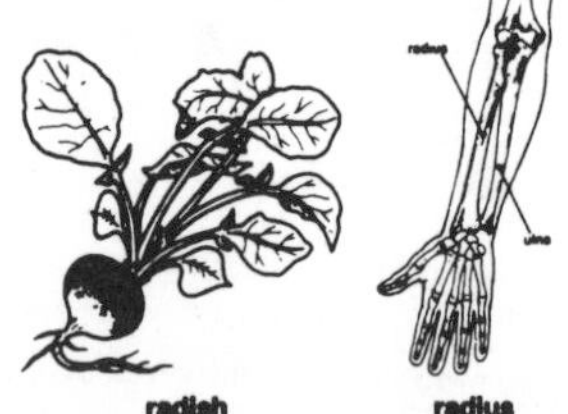

ra·di·um (rā'dē-əm) *n.* *Symbol* **Ra** A rare, white, highly radioactive metallic element,

rag·lan (răg'lən) *n.* A garment with slanted shoulder seams and sleeves extending in one piece to the neckline. [< 1st Baron *Raglan* (1788–1855).]
ra·gout (ră-gōō') *n.* A meat and vegetable stew. [< Fr. *ragoûter*, to renew the appetite.]
rag·time (răg'tīm') *n.* A style of jazz in which a syncopated melody is played against a steadily accented accompaniment. [Perh. < *ragged time*.]
rag·weed (răg'wēd') *n.* Any of several weeds whose profuse pollen is one of the chief causes of hay fever.
raid (rād) *n.* A surprise attack, invasion, or forcible entry. *—v.* To make a raid on. [< OE *rād*, ride.] **—raid'er** *n.*
rail[1] (rāl) *n.* **1.** A horizontal bar or timber supported by vertical posts, as in a fence. **2.** A bar used as a track for a vehicle, such as a railroad car. **3.** A railroad: *transported goods by rail.* *—v.* To enclose or supply with a rail. [< Lat. *regula*, rod.]
rail[2] (rāl) *v.* To complain bitterly or abusively.

Brewer's Dictionary of Phrase and Fable

A dangerously seductive encyclopedic reference to the maddeningly obscure phrase, the curiously opaque line, and the abstruse story. ***Brewer's*** *is a necessity for reading books your grandfather read, explaining the vernacular that was part of his language but is, alas, lost to us poor solemn birds. This book, taken with an infusion of Bret Harte's and Damon Runyon's filigreed stories, is guaranteed to bring color to your language and whimsy to your correspondence.*
—Jan Adkins

•

Mayonnaise. A sauce made with pepper, salt, oil, vinegar, the yolk of egg, etc., beaten up together. When the Duc de Richelieu captured Port Mahon, Minorca, in 1756, he demanded food on landing; in the absence of a prepared meal, he took whatever he could find and beat it up together — hence the original form *mahonnaise*.

Brewer's Dictionary of Phrase and Fable
E. Cobham Brewer;
revised by Ivor H. Evans
1981; 1,248 pp.
$26.45
($27.95 postpaid) from:
Harper & Row
2350 Virginia Avenue
Hagerstown, MD 21740
or Whole Earth Access

The Oxford-Duden Pictorial English Dictionary

A useful book that proceeds from the premise that you may not know the name of something but you certainly know what it looks like. If you are wondering what to call those pointy shoes Renaissance men wore, you look up a page illustrating costumes and find that the name is crackowes. That a hat with brim turned up to form three sides is a tricorn. That an aglet is the plastic tip of a shoelace.
—Joseph Hold [Suggested by Wayne Curtis]

38. woman of Nuremberg [ca. 1500]
39. shoulder cape
40. Burgundian [15th Cent.]
41. short doublet
42. piked shoes (peaked shoes, copped shoes, crackowes, poulaines)

The Oxford-Duden Pictorial English Dictionary
Edited by John Pheby
1984; 820 pp.
$12.95
postpaid from:
Oxford University Press
16-00 Pollitt Drive
Fair Lawn, NJ 07410
or Whole Earth Access

World Book Encyclopedia

As a librarian, I am frequently asked "Which encyclopedia should I buy?" by parents who want to ensure that their children will do well in school. (Like computers, many encyclopedias are bought by anxious parents for kids who end up not using them.) If you need an encyclopedia, I recommend ***The World Book****. It has the kinds of questions kids ask, the price is fair, the indexing is simple, and at our library we could not live without it. I use it way more than any other set. Even reference librarians reluctantly agree that it is more useful than academic encyclopedias, especially as a starting point. As one librarian said, "Here's where you find the answers for real questions that real people ask!"*
—Steve Cisler

World Book Encyclopedia
A. Richard Harmet,
Executive Editor
Annual; 14,000 pp.

$499-$599
($528-$628 postpaid) from:
World Book, Inc.
Merchandise Mart Plaza
Chicago, IL 60654

• For a word processing program that includes a built-in thesaurus see **Turbo Lightning** (p. 302).

• Used encyclopedias are often seen at very low prices in newspaper classifieds, fleamarkets, and garage sales. For most purposes, they won't be excessively out of date.

Scott, Foresman Beginning Dictionary

This children's dictionary stands out for its conceptual grace, graphic liveliness, and wit. —Stewart Brand

•

nerve (nerv), **1** fiber or bundle of fibers connecting the brain or spinal cord with the eyes, ears, muscles, and glands. **2** mental strength; courage. See picture. **3** rude boldness. *They had a lot of nerve to say that we were talking too loud.* noun.

nerve (definition 2) — It takes great *nerve* to hang by one hand from an airplane.

***neglect* (definition 5) — her room showed weeks of neglect.**

Scott, Foresman Beginning Dictionary
Clarence L. Barnhart, Editor
1983; 718 pp.

$15.48
($16.41 postpaid) from:
Scott, Foresman and Co.
1900 East Lake Avenue
Glenview, IL 60025
or Whole Earth Access

Bartlett's Familiar Quotations

Endlessly and instantly entertaining. Its chronological format gives it an order of contemporaries, and its brief entries remind a writer of the power in the short, terse statement. It has a truly useful index and the best cast of characters in publishing. —Jan Adkins

Bartlett's Familiar Quotations
John Bartlett
15th Ed. 1980; 1,540 pp.

$29.45
($30.95 postpaid) from:
Little, Brown and Company
200 West Street
Waltham, MA 02154
or Whole Earth Access

•

I like a bit of a mongrel myself, whether it's a man or a dog; they're the best for every day.
—*Misalliance [1910] episode I*
George Bernard Shaw

If parents would only realize how they bore their children!
Ib.

•

A good marriage is that in which each appoints the other guardian of his solitude.
—Rainer Maria Rilke, *Letters*

•

Late on the third day, at the very moment when, at sunset, we were making our way through a herd of hippopotamuses, there flashed upon my mind, unforeseen and unsought, the phrase, "Reverence for Life."
—Albert Schweitzer, *Out of My Life and Thought [1949]*

The Synonym Finder

The word you have in your head is usually not the word you need on the page. A thesaurus takes you from here to there. Ideally every dictionary would incorporate a thesaurus, but since they don't, the best we've seen (thousands of entries, 1.5 million synonyms, organized alphabetically, easiest to use) is not Roget's, not Webster's, not even Random House's, but Rodale's. —Art Kleiner
[Suggested by Joel Russ]

•

essential, *adj.* **1.** indispensable, necessary, requisite, vital, important; fundamental, constitutional, characteristic, inherent, basic, intrinsic; indigenous, inward, organic, ingrained; absolute, cardinal, principal, leading, main, capital; substantial, material, *Sl.* nitty-gritty.

—*n.* **2.** fundamental, rudiment, cornerstone; indispensable, element, chief point, main ingredient, primary constituent, vital part; crux, *Sl.* nitty-gritty, brass tacks, bare bones, bottom line; quality, attribute, characteristic, peculiarity, trait, feature, mark.

The Synonym Finder
J. I. Rodale; revised by Laurence Urdang
1978; 1,361 pp.

$19.95
postpaid from:
Rodale Press, Inc.
33 East Minor Street
Emmaus, PA 18049
or Whole Earth Access

Origins

This classic dictionary of word origins is so standard a text among professional and amateur wordcrafters that it is usually referred to personally — "Partridge." —Stewart Brand

•

whole, whence **wholly** — cf **whole cloth (out of)**, **wholemeal**, **wholesale**, **wholesome**; **hail**, v, and **hale**, adj; **heal** (whence **healer** and pa, vn **healing**) — **health**, whence **healthful**, **healthless** (obs), **healthy** (whence **healthiness**).

1. The n *whole* derives from the adj *whole*, ME *hole (hoole)*, earlier *hale*, OE *hal*, sound (complete), healthy: cf OFris *hel*, OS *hel*, OHG-MHG-G *heil*, Go *hails*, MD *hiel*, MD-D *heel*, ON *heill*, syn OSI *celu*, OP *kailustikan*, health, Gr *koilu*, the beautiful (prop, neu adj). The OGmc etym is **khailaz;* the IE, **koilos;* the IE r, **kail-, *koil-*.

2. From *whole cloth*, a (large) uncut piece of cloth, derives (of a story, a lie) 'made *out of whole cloth*' — a sheer fabrication; *whole meal*=*meal* (grain coarsely ground) of *entire-wheat; wholesale*, goods sold in large quantities, hence the corresp adj, whence the sense 'both extensive and undiscriminating or indiscriminate. . . .'

Origins
(A Short Etymological Dictionary of Modern English)
Eric Partridge
1977; 972 pp.

OUT OF PRINT
MacMillan Publishing Co.
Front and Brown Streets
Riverside, NJ 08075

SEVERAL TIMES A YEAR, I reserve an entire day to peruse the stock of a large magazine store. I snoop into everything from *Modern Hair Styles* to *Supermarket Manager's Monthly, Battles of World War II, CB, Kung-fu, Jack & Jill, People, Motor Trend, Four Wheel Drive, Orchid Raising, Consumer Reports, Playboy* and *Playgirl, Woman's Day, Art News, Modern Camera, Ski, Vogue Patterns, Field & Stream, Dogs, Cats, Horses* . . .egad! Snoop-reading gives me a cross-section of what is going on in this vast country. Perhaps it's a bizarre idea, but I have found over the years that the habit really does seem to reveal trends. I usually make peace with the magazine store by buying one now and then as the day progresses. I am limited, finally, by curvature of the spine, clatter from the mental storage-retrieval system, and squint.

This game can also be played in the periodical room of a big library. If it is a university library, you will soon be into things you have never even *heard* of, let alone suspected that there were enough people interested in to make possible a specialized magazine. Most universities admit anyone at all to the periodical room without an ID, and furnish you with good light and a nice chair too. Whenever I get to feeling provincial, I hie me to the nearest one and settle in for a spell. I've found that a significant number of the successful ideas and good times of my life have come rather directly from being able to say, "I remember reading about some people that were . . ." Specialist periodicals are also the best place to establish access to further knowledge in that field, not so much from facts given in the feature articles, but in the *ads.* Advertising has reduced the theory to practical usefulness, if that's what you need. That's where I find new catalogs, too.

—J. Baldwin

Wall Street Journal
Robert Bartley, Editor
$114/year
(260 issues) from:
Wall Street Journal
200 Burnett Road
Chicopee, MA 01021

The Wall Street Journal

The only daily NEWSpaper. Perhaps because it's harnessed to real events (namely price changes, the relatively uncontrollable democracy of the market), **The Wall Street Journal** *has an honesty. Having an honesty it has an originality (maybe those qualities are not separable). I know that if I were restricted to two periodicals for all my news, I would take* **Science** *(p. 26) and* **The Wall Street Journal**.

—*Stewart Brand*

•

One procedure that has long disturbed animal activists is the LD50 test. Widely used since the 1920s, the test involves force-feeding products to 40 or more animals, usually rodents, until half of them die. The lethal dose for 50% of the population establishes the product's ranking of an index of acute toxicity. Over the years, rats at P&G have been force-fed the ingredients of Tide detergent, Prell shampoo and Downy fabric softener, among others.

•

Why is a truly accurate artificial chocolate flavor so hard to come up with? "Chocolate is one of Mother Nature's best-kept secrets," says James F. Echeandia, a candy consultant in Orlando, Fla. Only the flavors of coffee and sizzling meat are harder to reproduce.

•

Man himself has become a limiting factor in jet-fighter technology. "In terms of performance, I'd say the plane

right now is ahead of its human pilot," says William Lowe, a test pilot at McDonnell Douglas Corp. "It can dish out more than we can take, both physically and mentally."

In fact, when General Dynamics Corp. designed the F-16, now the military's principal attack jet, it engineered the plane right up to the pilot's usual physical limits for enduring G-forces, a measure of acceleration defined by gravity . . .

One result of all this is a widening debate within the military concerning the design of future jets. If pilots can't endure much more abuse than current jets require, one argument goes, then perhaps combat fighters, as now used, will soon become obsolete.

Utne Reader
Eric Utne, Editor
$18/year
(6 issues) from:
Utne Reader
P. O. Box 1974
Marion, OH 43305

Utne Reader

Handy idea, handy result. A magazine offering "The best of the alternative press" — a **Reader's Digest** *for New Age types. The press represented varies in its alternativity from* **Esquire, Savvy,** *and* **Harper's,** *to* **In These Times, ChurchWorld, The Progressive** *(some good stuff, makes me want to check out the source publication),* **The Guardian,** *and* **Dissent.** *(Those and more are in one issue.) There're full articles, edited articles, glosses, and magazine reviews by subject area (a bunch on renewable energy, a bunch on American Indians).*

By and large any issue is bound to stop scanners and force them to read two to six times — that's better than **Esquire** *or* **New Age Journal** *are managing these days. If you're cutting back on your magazine exposure, probably a healthy practice in the excessively pop culture going on, the* **Utne Reader** *might be a good tool for tapering off.*

—*Stewart Brand*

•

When the male lodge takes the form of a men's talk-group, it can become a context for the naming of male wounds — wounds that often fester because men don't talk about them. Another power of the male lodge — whether as actual physical place, mythic motif, mode of conversation and presence, or simple pleasures of friendship — is that it allows men to develop feeling judgments and values of their own, and to establish patterns of relationship unconstrained by the notion that women are the rightful arbiters of what constitutes feeling.

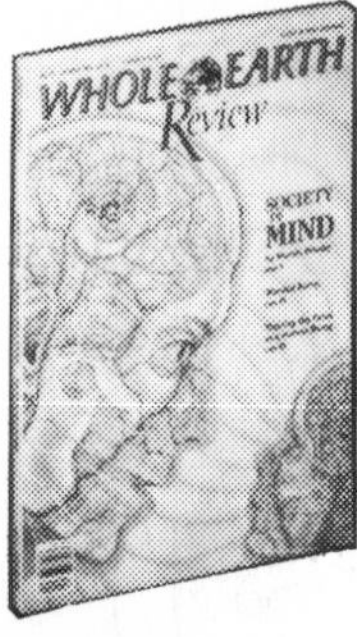

Whole Earth Review
Kevin Kelly, Editor
$18/year
(4 issues) from:
Whole Earth Review
P. O. Box 15187
Santa Ana, CA 92705

Whole Earth Review

All the wonderful things we don't have room to explore here we print in our magazine of unorthodox cultural and technical news. See inside front cover of this **Catalog** *for more explanation.*

—*Kevin Kelly*

Understanding Media

That media are extensions of our senses — telephone for ears, computers for mind — and that these new media are forces in themselves, the main event, regardless of what they bother to say ("the medium is the message"), are insights originating from McLuhan. That the media immediately engulfed McLuhan's ideas, and made them at once obvious and degrees more consequential, is part of his message. —Kevin Kelly

Everybody talks about McLuhan, and everybody does something about him, and that makes it subjectively harder to get at him. He's got other insights than what you hear about, so it's worth the trouble to track him down. The primest McLuhan is **Understanding Media.** —Stewart Brand

•

The electric light ended the regime of night and day, of indoors and out-of-doors. But it is when the light encounters already existing patterns of human organization that the hybrid energy is released. Cars can travel all night, ball players can play all night, and windows can be left out of buildings. In a word, the message of the electric light is total change. It is pure information without any content to restrict its transforming and informing power.

•

Man the food-gatherer reappears incongruously as information-gatherer. In this role, electronic man is no less a nomad than his paleolithic ancestors.

•

Everybody experiences far more than he understands. Yet it is experience, rather than understanding, that influences behavior, especially in collective matters of media and technology, where the individual is almost inevitably unaware of their effect upon him.

•

It is a principal aspect of the electric age that it establishes a global network that has much of the character of our central nervous system. Our central nervous system is not merely an electric network, but it constitutes a single unified field of experience. As biologists point out, the brain is the interacting place where all kinds of impressions and experiences can be exchanged and translated, enabling us to *react to the world as a whole.*

Understanding Media
Marshall McLuhan
1964; 320 pp.
$4.95
($5.95 postpaid) from:
New American Library
120 Woodbine Street
Bergenfield, NJ 07621
or Whole Earth Access

Culture Is Our Business

McLuhan's best format. Each pair of pages has a reprint of an ad on the right, and fresh McLuhan aphorisms, quotes, and misquotes on the left. The resulting energy across the spread is economic and multi-directional — i.e., you make it.

This book should be restored to print. His news stays news. —Stewart Brand

•

One of the many flips of our time is that the electric information environment returns man to the condition of the most primitive prober and hunter. Privacy invasion is now one of our biggest knowledge industries.

•

The great corporations are new tribal families. It was the tribal and feudal family form that was dissolved by "nationalism."

•

In the sixteenth century religion went inward and private with Gutenberg hardware. Liturgy collapsed. Bureaucracy boomed. Today liturgy returns. Bureaucracy fades.

When the evolutionary process shifts from biology to software technology the body becomes the old hardware environment. The human body is now a probe, a laboratory for experiments. In the middle of the nineteenth century Claude Bernard was the first medical man to conceive of le milieu intérieur. He saw the body, not as an outer object, but as an inner landscape, exactly as did the new painters and poets of the avant garde.

•

Invention is the mother of necessity.

Culture Is Our Business
Marshall McLuhan
OUT OF PRINT
McGraw-Hill Book. Co.

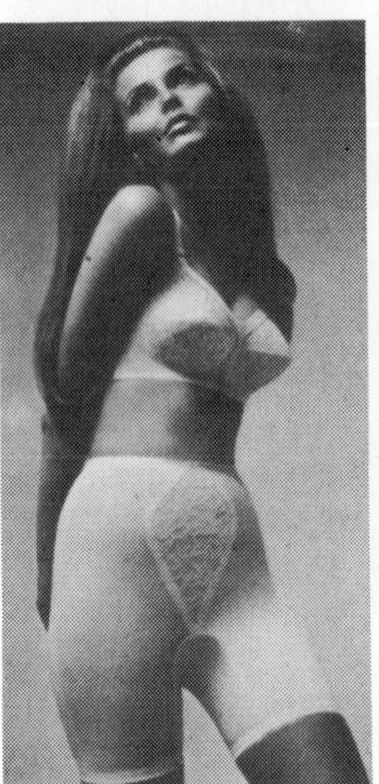

If nature didn't, Warner's will.

No Sense of Place

TV, telephones, and movies explode. The Earth shrinks. Social behavior alters. Childhood, a recent invention, disappears again. All heroes die. Places become events. The rest of this show, hinted at early by McLuhan, is rehearsed here in this analytical book. The news is not new; the comprehensible and comprehensive evidence is. —Kevin Kelly

•

In contrast to print, television does not allow control over what is "expressed" along with what is "communicated." Television news programs, for example, cannot escape presenting a wide range of personal expressions in addition to "objective facts." Rather than attempting to fight this aspect of television news, producers have taken the parts of the back region that are difficult to hide and thrust them into the show itself. This is especially true of local news programs. Backstage expressiveness, personal feelings, informal interaction, and ad-libbed jokes have become an important aspect of the performance. Similarly, many television quiz and talk shows have abandoned attempts to hide microphones, camera operators, "applause" signs, and cue cards.

•

We cannot select uses for new media that advance old goals without often altering the social systems out of which the goals developed. We cannot, for example, "buy the wife" a television set to ease her boredom with housework without changing her sense of place in the world. We cannot use television to "educate" our children without simultaneously altering the functions of reading and the structure of the family and the school. . . . We cannot have mediated intimacy with our political leaders, in the hope of getting closer to greatness, without losing a belief in heroes. And if we use media to teach many different groups about each other, we also change the lines of social association and the perimeters of group identities.

No Sense of Place
Joshua Meyrowitz
1985; 416 pp.
$24.95
postpaid from:
Oxford University Press
16-00 Pollitt Drive
Fair Lawn, NJ 07410
or Whole Earth Access

• A weekly insider's view of advertising and mainstream magazine publishing can be found in **Advertising Age: $57**/year (52 issues) from 965 East Jefferson, Detroit, MI 48207.

• See **Media Law** (p. 205).

Small Press

Small Press
Michael Coffey, Editor
$19.95/year
(6 issues) from:
Meckler Publishing
11 Ferry Lane West
West Port, CT 06880

New York is not publishing. Small presses are. Most of the hundreds of thousands of books published each year are put out by thriving small-time publishers, not by Madison Avenue. Most of these folks are new and specialized. They produce technical books, how-to manuals, slim volumes of poetry, large gorgeous handmade tomes, corporate reports, or regional guides and cookbooks. ***Small Press*** *is for them. Done with the graphic care a fine book would be, this magazine profiles successful small presses, and it stresses both fine bookmaking and fine bookkeeping — the technical details of publishing as a small business and craft. Computers make small-time publishing sensible and powerful, and this journal wisely tracks that gigantic revolution.* —Kevin Kelly

•

If you're going to do a lot of foreign-language work and don't want to mess around with remembering the codes for special characters, you may want to look into some of the word processors designed specifically for working with foreign languages. Available programs include *Select Bilingual* (Select Information Systems, $395), *Electric Pencil Professional* (Blue Cat, $249.95), *Proofwriter* (Image Processing Systems, $250), and *Multi-Lingual Scribe* (Gamma Productions, $149.95). Most work by providing you with "alternate keyboards." By pressing some key or key combination, the keyboard is reconfigured so, for instance, the question mark becomes an upside-down question mark for working in Spanish.

The Self-Publishing Manual

The Self-Publishing Manual
Dan Poynter
1986; 352 pp.
$14.95
($15.95 postpaid) from:
Para Publishing
P. O. Box 4232-500
Santa Barbara, CA 93140
or Whole Earth Access

No other book tells you how to print, copyright and sell your own book with as much practical experience as this one. Heed what it says. Heed what it does as well — it is profitably self-published, along with another ten books, by the author. —Kevin Kelly

•

Initial press runs should normally be limited to the number of books one can reasonably estimate will be sold in the first year. Unless you have a substantial number of prepublication sales, it is a good idea to limit the first printing to no more than 5,000. No matter how diligently you proofread, some errors will not surface until they appear in ink. Also, once you see the book in its final state, you will wish you had done some things differently. By printing a smaller number, you can use the next few months to catch your errors and make some design changes. Then you will be much happier about the revised second edition.

▲

As a small publisher, it makes more sense to market your book like breakfast food or soap. Develop your product, pour on the promotion, carve a niche in the market and then continue to sell at the same level for years. This can be done with a non-fiction book which is revised at each printing.

Editing by Design

Editing by Design
Jan V. White
1982; 248 pp.
$29.95
($33.45 postpaid) from:
R. R. Bowker Company
Book Order Department
201 East 42nd Avenue
New York, NY 10017
or Whole Earth Access

Outstanding book on design — using the image and images of the page to carry a message with pure clarity. This one book, heeded, could cure the rotten design of most amateur publishing. —Stewart Brand

•

Very few pictures are so clearly focused on a subject that words become superfluous. It is very risky to run pictures without them. Pictures are not the universal panacea; having a good shot or two does not mean that the problems of presentation have been solved for that story.

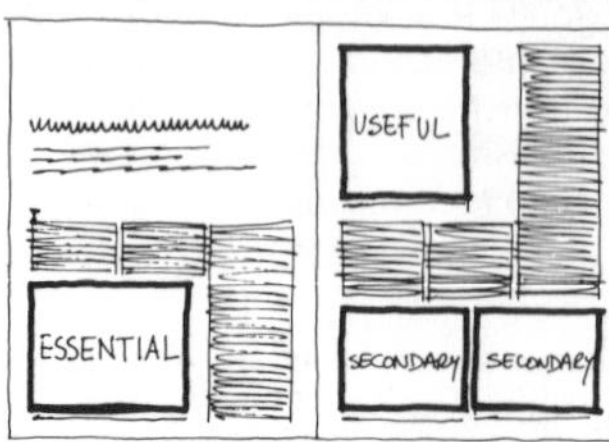

The size of each picture does not reflect the relative importance of each in the story. So the reader has to discover it through thought and analysis and hard, slow work.

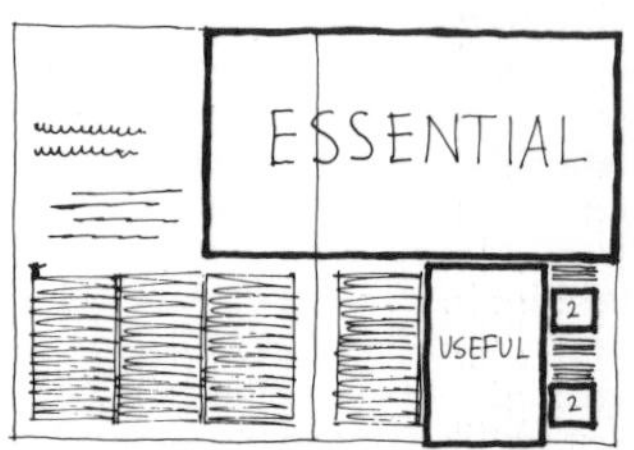

There can be no question in anyone's mind about which picture the editors deemed most important. Not only does the spread communicate more clearly and faster, but it looks better and more dynamic. Yet all the type is in this scheme that was shown in the scheme above.

•

Making the spread appear wider: Use tricks to make the spread appear wider than it is. The simplest example of this is, of course, the full-bleed two-page picture which can create an impression of enormous size.

A single picture is wide enough, but splitting the space horizontally emphasizes the width even more.

• The first **Whole Earth Catalog** was self-published in 1968. It probably couldn't have been done any other way; established publishers will rarely take on something without precedent.

How to Do Leaflets, Newsletters and Newspapers

There's no leverage like local publishing — it's cheap, fast, relatively easy, and outrageously effective if done well. In this manual are all the instructions you need to do it well. (Technically, at least; the rest is character.) The book is its own best demonstration. I wish I'd had it when we started. —*Stewart Brand*

Getting the line spacing right.

•

What makes a good headline? . . . Make it active, not passive. Tell what's *happening*, not just what *is*. Instead of "Dental Plan Highlights," say something like: "You Have New Dental Benefits" or "We Won Free Dental Visits!"

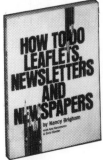

How to Do Leaflets, Newsletters and Newspapers
Nancy Brigham with Ann Raszmann and Dick Cluster
1982; 144 pp.
$4.95
($6.20 postpaid) from:
Kampmann and Company
9 East 40th Street
New York, NY 10016
or Whole Earth Access

How to Produce a Small Newspaper

I can't imagine why anyone would dream of starting a small restaurant or a small bookstore when it's possible to start or take over or work for a small newspaper. As art and news media go, nothing else can give you as much freedom, creativity, responsibility, effectiveness, contact, and home-town audience. —*Stewart Brand*

How to Produce a Small Newspaper
Editors of the Harvard Post
1984; 158 pp.
$9.95
($11.20 postpaid) from:
Kampmann and Company
9 East 40th Street
New York, NY 10016
or Whole Earth Access

For Two Celebrity Reps, It's a War of Nerves

Thrown together in a new legislative district, Frank and Noble are voicing mutual admiration — but are still trying to psych each other out of the race

Just as Elaine Noble is quick to support a potential Barney Frank bid for Congress, so he is quick to support a possible run by Noble for the Boston School Committee.

PROVINCETOWN ADVOCATE

Reads Chief's Critique

Benson Bares Fire Fault Report

SCRAM Suit In Hearing Monday

Local Rule Soon Nationwide

Nude Ban Demonstration Saturday

◄

The newspaper at left chooses a large, bold headline style, and breaks up the type page by use of subheads and excerpts from the article set in a smaller display type. This is a useful alternative when pictures are lacking. At right, a good example of how to use one traditional type style imaginatively in headlines to keep a varied but unified appearance.

•

"Experts" may tell you that no newspaper averaging less than 65 percent advertising can survive, but the Harvard Post has been doing quite well enough with about 40 percent. When we go over a certain amount of advertising dollars in an issue, we prefer to add four more pages rather than to crowd the paper with ads.

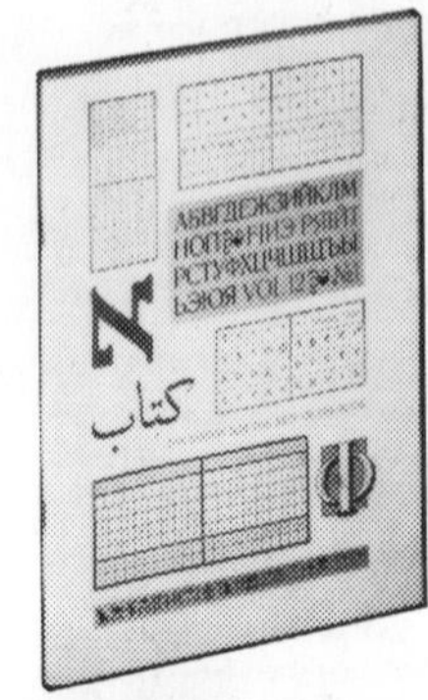

Fine Print
Sandra Kirshenbaum, Editor
$48/year
(4 issues) from:
Fine Print
P. O. Box 3394
San Francisco, CA 94119

Fine Print

It's probably a sign of advancing age, but I am coming to honor the well made book. If you're a similar anachronism, this precise publication on "the Arts of the Book" will hone your intolerance fine. —*Stewart Brand*

Drawing of Wang Chen's wooden movable type printing process, ca. 1300. At right, typesetting with characters in compartments arranged by rhymes; and left, printing by brushing on the back of paper from the type frames.

Pocket Pal

This tasty book has been around since 1934 and has been continually revised as the printing biz evolved. **Pocket Pal** *will teach you the language you need to know to keep your local printer from bullshitting you overmuch. You will also learn a healthy respect for his art and the myriad events which transpire in a complicated printing job.* —*E. Todd Ellison*

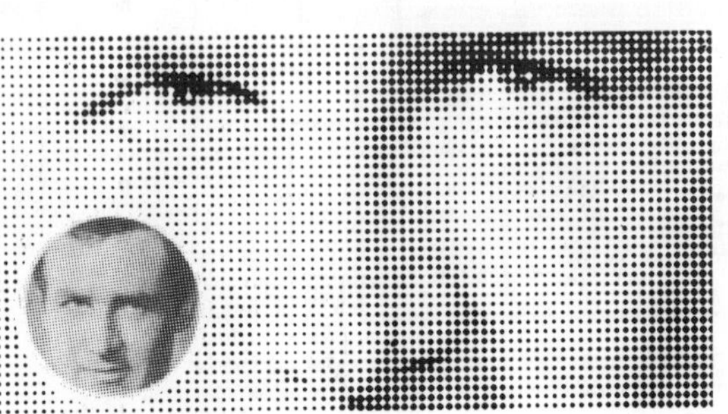

Halftone dots enlarged.

Pocket Pal
(A Graphic Arts Production Handbook)
1983; 216 pp.
$4.25 postpaid from:
International Paper Co.
Attn.: Pocket Pal
P. O. Box 100,
Church Street Station
New York, NY 10046
or Whole Earth Access

Personal Publishing
Terry Ulick, Editor
$30/year
(12 issues) from:
Personal Publishing
P. O. Box 390
Itasca, IL 60143

PageMaker
Version 1.2.
Copy-protected.
$495
Macintosh external disk drive required; hard disk recommended.
Information **free** from:
Aldus Corporation
411 First Avenue, Suite 200
Seattle, WA 98104.

ESKTOP PUBLISHING — using a personal computer to write, typeset, design and publish a newsletter, magazine, or book — represents a tremendous advantage for small publishers. Tasks that used to take a handful of specialists days have been compressed into page-makeup programs that enable a jack-of-all-trades publisher to directly control the whole process. For the megalomaniacs among us this is indeed good news. However, it is a mixed blessing for everyone else.

For example, desktop publishing plays havoc with clearcut job descriptions. Once you have a single software program that lets you specify page layout formats, choose typefaces and point sizes, "pour in" word processed copy, and manipulate illustrations in quick succession, you have a program which practically begs for a new breed of multi-talented publishing workers. Where does this leave the editor who can't design, the art director who can't spell, or the typesetter who merely wants to typeset? Good question.

At this juncture, the tools for desktop publishing seem best suited to modest tasks such as producing an 8-page newsletter or knocking out an ad sheet or flyer in a day's time. Full-scale book or magazine publishing on your PC can be done; it is still likely to call for more skills than most single humans possess. Desktop publishing is about efficiently chewing what you've already bitten off, *not* about using your computer to bite off more than you can sanely chew.

—Jay Kinney

PageMaker

This software program used in conjunction with a Macintosh has my vote for the best hardware/software combo for desktop publishing. While there are several other competing programs available (some geared for the IBM PC), there are none with the intuitive design and ease of use that PageMaker provides. Earlier versions of this program had a tendency to freeze up or bomb out at unexpected moments, but most of those bugs have been ironed out by now. If you are considering publishing you should investigate PageMaker. —Jay Kinney

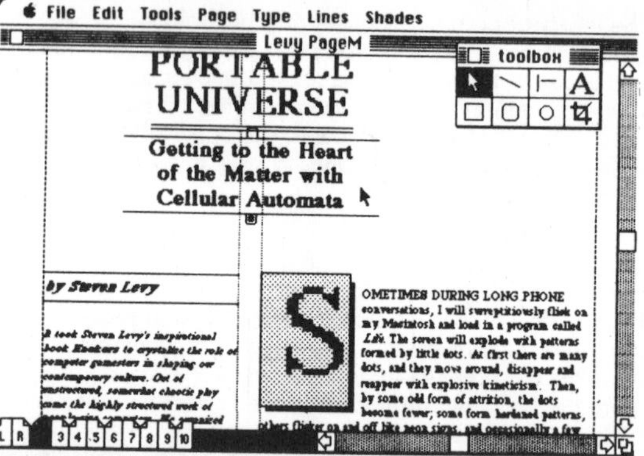

What you see on the Macintosh screen is not always what is finally printed out. Shown here are column guides which help shape the columns of type but do not print themselves. The headline and body copy look somewhat crude onscreen, but are later tightened up by the POSTSCRIPT language embedded in the LaserWriter printer.

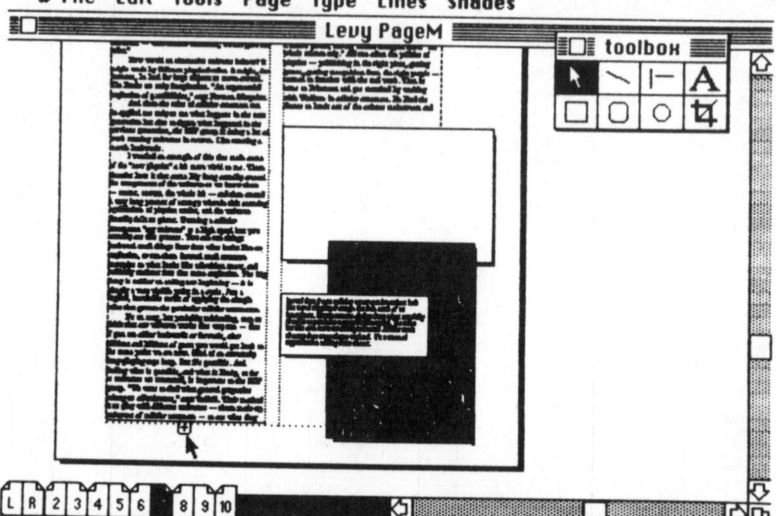

PAGEMAKER allows views of page layouts at several sizes: 50% (as above), 70%, actual size, 200%, and a "fit in window" size. Type can be continued from column to column and page to page by clicking the mouse on the tab at the foot of a column of type.

Personal Publishing

This monthly magazine is geared to those who are just starting out in desktop publishing and is strong on explaining and illustrating the fundamentals of the field. Almost entirely staff-written, the magazine is opinionated, partisan (it favors the Mac over any other PC), and inspirational. It's a Macintosh and LaserWriter production — one of the handsomest such publications I've seen.

—Jay Kinney

Illustration Number 7. A banner for the text is started. A simple rectangle is chosen for type, because in MacDraw you can not arch type. The rectangle is filled with white, given a black rule, and filled with upper case Times Roman type. The positioning of the rectangle is important. Any lower, and it would look funny, but any higher, it would cover up the serifs.

Illustration Number 8. To create a banner effect, i imagined that the rectangle is part of "ribbon" that bends has dimension. This makes the lettering appear to be c long banner that is raised above the "V" where needed. T is a standard graphic device, found in many illustrations older type treatments.

Illustration Number 9. The left "tail" of the banner is copied, then pasted on the right side of the banner. Here, the logo takes on its final shape. The arrow, the "V" and the banner are all in place. All that is left is detail work.

Illustration Number 10. Detail work consists of giving simple black and white elements some shading. This important to give the feeling of the banner floating abc the "V" and having a 3-dimensional quality. MacDra polygons are created and filled with line patterns.

Illustration Number 11. The last element is placed: The type that will identify the number of the article. Here, the cover version is created, with the word VICTORY in place of a number. Notice the type is light, and extra spaces have been added between the letters.

Illustration Number 12. The final logo. A heavy rule ha been added beneath the word VICTORY for emphasis and f added detail. The finished logo has all of the elements w wanted, put together very effectively and in a very short tim using the power of a drawing program such as MacDraw GEM Draw.

• As we go to press, PC World Communications, Inc., has announced another magazine on desktop publishing to be called **Publish!** Judging from their other publications, this one will bear watching!

(Far left) Mountain scenes created with fractal surfaces.

(Left) A computer-generated strawberry, showing both diffuse and specular reflection.

Fundamentals of Interactive Computer Graphics

For those who dream of flying not as an airplane flies but as a bird flies, or dream of trekking across alien landscapes, here at last is an exhaustive prescription for making the visual dimension of these dreams concrete.

***Fundamentals** sketches out the techniques for generating realistic visual images from computer models. It actually shows how to do it. [Programming skills are mandatory —KK.] Hardware, software techniques, actual code (in PASCAL) — it's all presented with an unusual and refreshing concern for convenient, intuitive user controls (currently fashionable buzz phrase: "human factors engineering").*

You can get a good long look at one state-of-the-art application of these techniques in the NASA Jet Propulsion Laboratory documentary on the Voyager Saturn fly-by. This movie includes several minutes of computer-simulated outer planet fly-bys. —Ken Crossen

•

Shadow algorithms for point light sources are identical to hidden-surface algorithms! The hidden-surface algorithm determines which surfaces can be seen from the viewpoint, and the shadow algorithm determines which surfaces can be "seen" from the light source. The surfaces that are visible both from the viewpoint and from the light source are not in shadow. Those that are visible from the viewpoint but not from the light source are in shadow. This logic can easily be extended to multiple light sources.

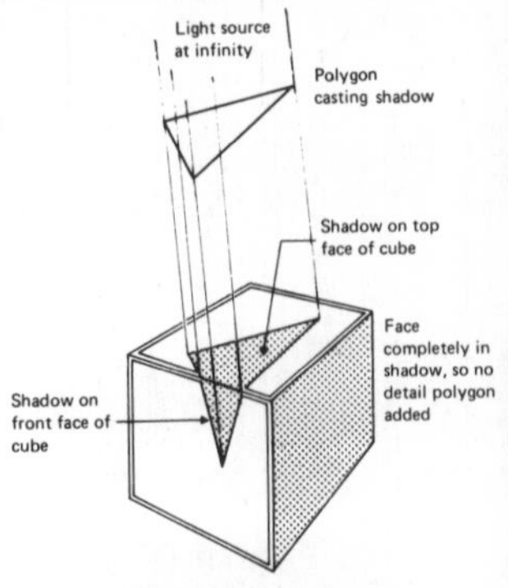

Polygons added to cube to show parts illuminated by light source.

Fundamentals of Interactive Computer Graphics
J. D. Foley and A. Van Dam
1982; 674 pp.
$42.95
($44.15 postpaid) from:
Addison-Wesley Publishing Company
1 Jacob Way
Reading, MA 01867
or Whole Earth Access

AutoCAD • Generic CADD • EASY3D

Good uses for computer graphics: jobs that demand constant alterations, pictures constructed with numerical precision, designs built solely from data, and graphics that make use of repeating template patterns. The best computer aided design (CAD) program for personal computers: AutoCAD.

This well-proven program has earned a remarkably good reputation for being fast, versatile, and agreeable with hundreds of customized peripherals (like color printers and digitizing tablets) that let it do practical work. It can rotate objects through 3D, scale up or down size, and "freeze" particular features of the design that you don't want to change. A typical application would be to draw an engineering or architectural project assembled out of standard components, compile a list of materials, and then amend the whole drawing to fit a substituted, smaller part. Ughhh. If you need to do this more than once, buy a computer slave.

AutoCAD is an expensive professional system. You can get an abbreviated jolt by plugging in Generic CADD, a $100 clone that similarly sketches, but without 3D rotation. The best performer on the Macintosh is EASY3D, which does. Picture processing, like word processing, will make a bad design quickly bad, or a good design quickly over. —Kevin Kelly

AutoCAD: $300-$2,750 from Autodesk, Inc., (415) 331-0356.

Generic CADD: $99.95 from Generic Software, (206) 885-5307.

EASY3D: $104 from Enabling Technologies, (312) 427-0408.

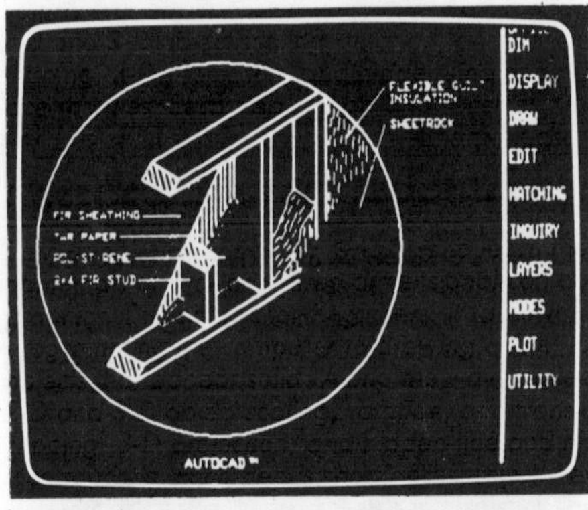

Both these drawings were created with AutoCAD, showing the program's versatility. Although it looks as if the entire drawing is on one layer, in both cases, various pieces are actually drawn on separate layers.

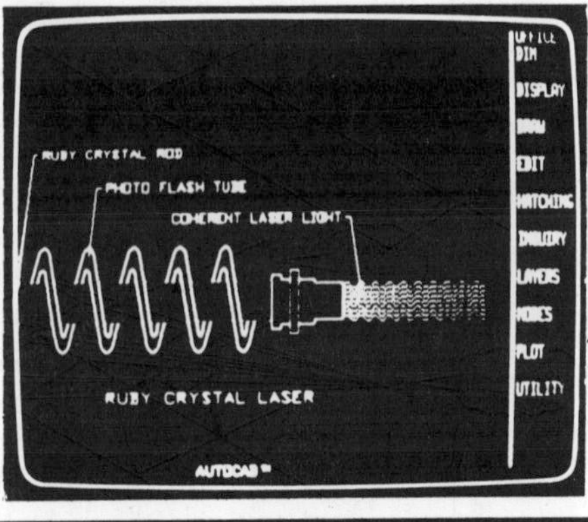

Microcomputer Graphics

*I am using **Microcomputer Graphics** to learn the fundamentals of two- and three-dimensional computer graphics. This book is for beginners. It takes you from programming the computer to drawing a line, to drawing objects that appear solid. Along the way you learn about 2-D and 3-D object scaling, rotation, and translation; line clipping; 3-D projection; and hidden-line and hidden-surface routines. Each step is short and succinctly explained with lots of illustrations.* —Charlie Richardson

►
To obtain a two-dimensional (screen) representation of a three-dimensional object we'll next develop a method for projecting each point of the object onto a plane. . . .

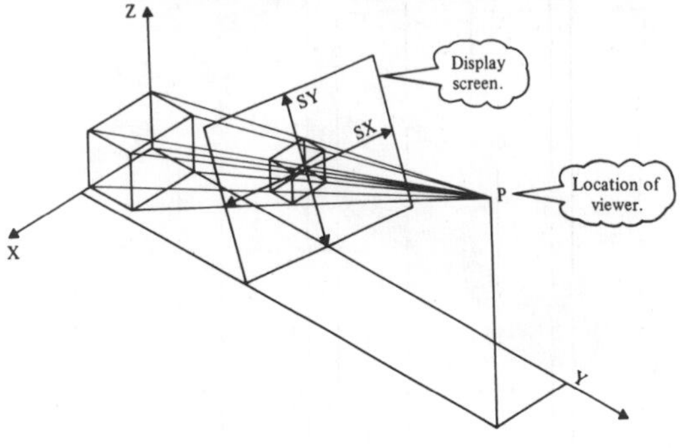

Microcomputer Graphics
Roy E. Myers
(for the Apple Computer)
1982; 282 pp.
(for the IBM PC)
1984; 268 pp.
$14.38 each (postpaid)
from:
Addison-Wesley Publishing Co.
1 Jacob Way
Reading, MA 01867
or Whole Earth Access

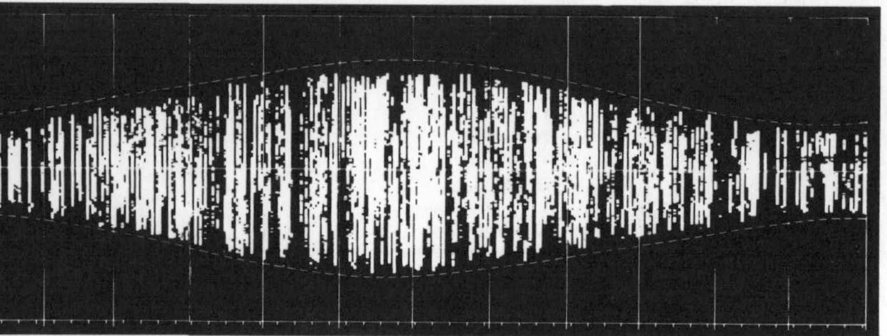

An annual sunshine record reports about 1,000 numbers per square inch (160 per square centimeter). The visual metaphor corresponds appropriately to the days when the image is reversed, so that the light areas are the times when the sun shines.

The Visual Display of Quantitative Information

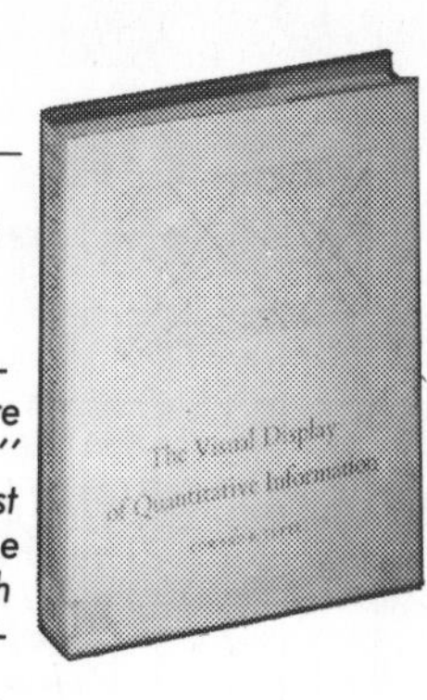

THE visual style book. Turn a page in this finely printed volume and you'll be treated to another ingenious chart that is at once simple, telling, and beautiful. Flamboyant graphs, particularly those dressing up insensible data, are bad craft: "If the statistics are boring, then you've got the wrong numbers." The rules are like writing well — do it honest and clear. Tufte gives memorable, handsome examples of how to display information with integrity and clarity. The book is a good example. It's one that you return to dip into before you pick up graph paper. —Kevin Kelly

The Visual Display of Quantitative Information
Edward R. Tufte
1983; 197 pp.

$32
postpaid from:
Graphics Press
P. O. Box 430
Cheshire, CT 06410
or Whole Earth Access

Forget All the Rules . . .

As he was being taken away by the police, acrobat Philippe Petit explained why he had walked a rope between two of the world's tallest buildings: "I see three oranges, I have to juggle. I see two towers, I have to walk."

Seeing unique aspects in commonplace things is also what makes for original graphic design. In this inspiring book, Bob Gill showcases a hundred of his toughest design problems with his wittiest solutions. According to Gill, to arrive at a unique solution you need to define a unique problem. However, the complete title of the book is **Forget all the rules you ever learned about graphic design. Including the ones in this book.** *—David Jouris*

•

I wanted to do something that was original. But I kept thinking of ideas based on images I had already seen. Then I realized that it was inevitable that my ideas *had* to be based on previous experiences. What else could possibly be in my consciousness *but* previous experiences?

I would have to go *outside of my head* to look for an original idea. I decided that getting involved with the new problem was the most likely way of going outside. Of having a new experience.

If I could express the uniqueness of what the problem was trying to communicate with an image which was valid *only* for that problem, then I would have invented a unique image.

In other words, defining a unique problem would inspire a unique solution.

Original problem: Logo for the Broadway musical *Dancin'*. It has no plot but many styles of dancing.

Redefined: How can one image give the impression of many styles of dancing?

Forget All the Rules
Bob Gill
1981; 168 pp.

$17.95
($19.95 postpaid) from:
Watson Guptill Publishers
P. O. Box 2013
Lakewood, NJ 08701
or Whole Earth Access

Writing & Illuminating & Lettering

Continuously in print since its initial publication in 1906, this is the text that anyone involved in the lettering arts ought to have. It has held an undisputed position as the best book on the craft of lettering for 80 years.

Through his study of medieval manuscripts in the British Museum, Edward Johnston rediscovered the dynamic properties of the square cut pen as the essential letter making tool. Single-handedly he revived an art that had been killed by the invention of printing in the 15th century. Though somewhat dated in appearance, this book's thinking remains sound; its spirit is pervasive: "All things — materials, tools, methods — are waiting to serve us and we have only to find the 'spell' that will set the whole universe a-making for us." —John Prestianni

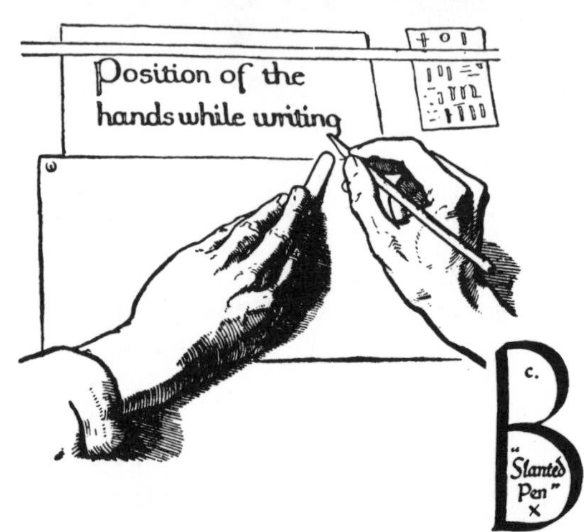

Writing & Illuminating & Lettering
Edward Johnston
1977; 439 pp.

$11.95
($12.95 postpaid) from:
Taplinger Publishing Co.
132 West 22nd Street
New York, NY 10011
or Whole Earth Access

◄ **Four dummy covers suggested for *Time's* July 29, 1985 special issue. —*How . . .***

How . . .
Philip Smith, Editor
$27/year
(6 issues) from:
How Magazine
6400 Goldsboro Road
Bethesda, MD 20817

Step-by-Step Graphics • How . . .

The current trend in graphics magazines is the how-to genre. Two have successfully entered the marketplace this year, indicating a growing hunger for nitty-gritty studio tips on tools and techniques.

***Step-by-Step Graphics** is a good entry-level introduction, offering solid advice on such basics as copy-fitting, trouble-shooting the airbrush, or simple techniques for adding color to black and white line art. The emphasis is on the creative process rather than the finished result, with lots of large, clear photos showing each stage of a project. Readers are encouraged to participate by sharing short cuts and case studies of their own. Though a bit pricey at $7.50 a copy, the information is often worth it.*

***How . . .** is geared more for the graphic arts professional, focusing as much on business tips as studio techniques. Each issue offers advice from top-level art buyers on developing and presenting your portfolio. The how-to features include the evolution of concepts as well as the steps involved in their execution. Close-up articles feature graphics heavyweights such as Milton Glaser. The magazine itself is quite attractively designed.*
—Rebecca Wilson

•
Once the background was dry, Conge applied the remaining hues with several different Percy Baker brushes. The colors are all Peerless mineral-base watercolor dyes. "I like their intensity," he says. "If you took a quart, which would last a lifetime, and poured it into a swimming pool, it would change the color of the water in the whole pool. It's incredible." Next, it was off to the printer, whose first chromalin was "quite unsatisfactory," Conge says. "The whites were dirty and the overall colors heavy and deep." —How . . .

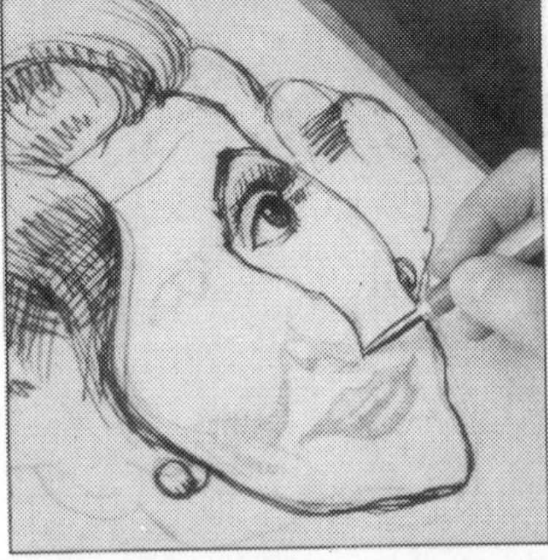

Gersten works in layers of tissue paper until he reaches a point where he is satisfied with the relationships between characteristics — eyes to nose, nose to mouth and so on. He continually refines his sketch by placing a new piece of tissue paper directly on top of the previous one. —*Step-by-Step Graphics*

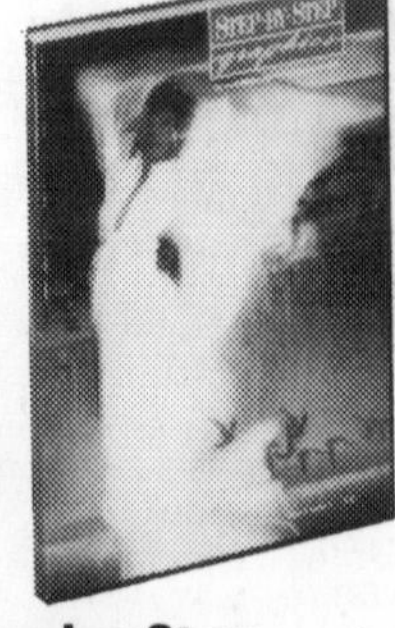

Step-by-Step Graphics
Nancy Aldrich-Ruenzel, Editor
$39/year
(6 issues) from:
Step-by-Step Graphics
6000 N. Forest Park Drive
Peoria, IL 61614-3592

• Here's assistance in visualizing 3-D objects onto 2-D paper. **Rapid Viz** (A New Method for the Rapid Visualization of Ideas): Kurt Hanks and Larry Belliston, 1980; 149 pp. **$9.95** ($11.45 postpaid) from William Kaufmann, 95 1st Street, Los Altos, CA 94022 (or Whole Earth Access).

Dot Pasteup Supplies

The kind of things you need to put together brochures, draft architectural plans, paste up newsletters, make advertisements, and put ideas into permanence. Sturdy, versatile tools for a paper society.
—Kevin Kelly

0.70 CERANOMATIC DRAFTING PRO SRP Pentel JAPAN

PENTEL CERANOMATIC TECHNICAL PEN

LINE WIDTHS
0.13
0.18
0.25
0.35
0.50
0.70
1.00

Dot Pasteup Supplies
Catalog **free** from:
Dot Pasteup Supply Co.
P. O. Box 369
Omaha, NE 68101

TRANSPARENT FLEXIBLE CURVES

One side is divided in millimeters; the other side is graduated in inches. The first two inches are subdivided in thirty-seconds and the remainder in sixteenths. The raised portion permits ink drawing.

30 cm long . .	$5.00
40 cm long . .	6.00
50 cm long . .	7.00

Charrette

This is an excellent catalog for browsing — it's the most complete graphic supplier I've seen. The prices are not discounted, but Charrette carries items that are difficult to find or are simply not found in this country. My favorite items are the metal stencils from France with letters that Le Corbusier used and the Caran'd Ache Fixpencil from Switzerland that has fat leads for sketching (6B).
—Lawrence Kasparowitz

Charrette
Catalog
$3.50 from:
Charrette
31 Olympia Avenue
Woburn, MA 01888

▲**Clear Cubes** Four different designs of the same size are provided on one cube with two surfaces free for handling. Order by number and size.

Mini—3/8"	$10.25
Small—½"	$11.25
Medium—1"	$13.00

►
Charrette MC-150 Scale Model Camera with Quartz Halogen Light. For architects, designers, modelmakers. Scale models aid in visualizing, rendering, and presenting design concepts. Everything in the scene — from 2½" to infinity — is in focus. $765.00.

The Photographer's Handbook
John Hedgecoe
1982; 352 pp.
$18.95
($19.95 postpaid) from:
Random House
Order Dept.
400 Hahn Road
Westminster, MD 21157
or Whole Earth Access

The wallpaper effect of the print is achieved using one negative. One exposure was made in the center of the paper and developer applied to the area with a cotton swab. Once the image had emerged, successive images were positioned, exposed and developed — about 30 in all.

The Photographer's Handbook

I was a photogger before I was a catalogger, and long I've deplored the dearth of practical/comprehensive books on photography. The one book I long relied on, Feininger's **Total Picture Control**, *has now been surpassed by this beautiful, newly revised book. It's quite wonderful to use, rewarding the browser as well as the photographer who has a special problem. I went to sleep on the subject of photography years ago. This book makes me think about waking up and trying some of its myriad ideas and techniques.*

The book replaces about eight others I might have reviewed.
—Stewart Brand

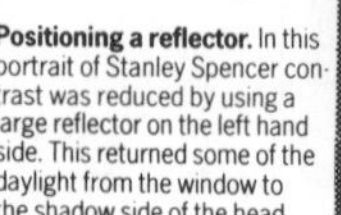

Positioning a reflector. In this portrait of Stanley Spencer contrast was reduced by using a large reflector on the left hand side. This returned some of the daylight from the window to the shadow side of the head.

◄ **An excessively fast shutter speed may sometimes destroy the feeling and excitement of speed events. . . . The picture simulates a spectator's impression as the participants flash past. It was shot at a relatively slow shutter speed, panning and zooming.**

Competitive Camera

The best discount mail order prices on the full spectrum of photo and related gear that we've been able to find. Far surpasses prices at your local camera shop. Usually, but not always, beats the discount competition (which you should check anyway: 47th Street Photo, catalog **$2**, *36 East 19th Street, NY, NY 10003).* *—Stewart Brand*

You'll find the absolute rock-bottomest prices for extremely popular 35mm cameras in crowded ads in photo magazines. Shop at Competitive Camera for a far greater range of goods: top quality low-cost cameras, lenses, tape recorders, binoculars, projectors, tripods, flash gear, darkroom supplies, etc. My experience in ordering photo equipment by mail leans toward satisfaction. The procedure: Know exactly what you want, down to the minutiae of model numbers; know what you don't want; call in on the 800 number and order with a credit card (do NOT pay by check). I've tried other ways, but this one is the most rewarding.
—Kevin Kelly

Competitive Camera
Catalog **free** from:
Competitive Camera
363 Seventh Avenue
New York, NY 10001

American Photographer

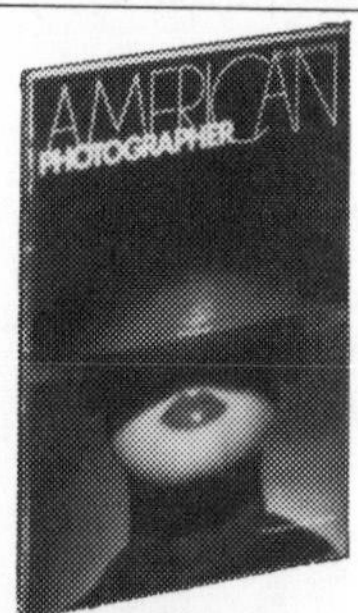

American Photographer
Sean Callahan, Editor
$19.98/year
(12 issues) from:
American Photographer
P. O. Box 2833
Boulder, CO 80302

A photography magazine that doesn't pander to the unquenchable greed for bright, ever-new gadgets with ever-more-amazing bells and whistles. Rather, it focuses on developing practical techniques for dedicated amateurs and creative professionals. It generously gives lots of full-page space to inspirational photo essays. I find that it's the only photo mag that teaches me something with each issue. *—Kevin Kelly*

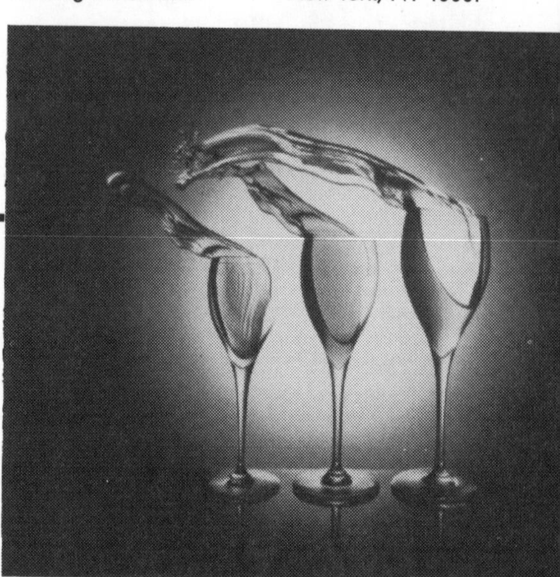

After mounting three Baccarat wine-glasses on one end of a 2 x 3-foot Formica board and fastening a 4 x 5 Toyo view camera onto the other end, Collins mounted the entire assembly on a turntable, which he would pivot suddenly to propel the liquids out of their glasses.

If we could slide the scale around on the print it would be obvious to the eye which picture areas match what scale tones.

The New Zone System Manual

The manual for highest quality black and white photos, with details in the black and in the white areas. The key is previsualization, which is looking at reality through an accurately imagined photographic print, then knowing how to make the calculations and mechanical and chemical adjustments so the print has what you saw, plus any divine grace that happened by. —Stewart Brand

•

"What zone values do I want to render the cloth in?" That is the question! The essence of that question underlies all photography whether the photographer knows how to get it into the print or doesn't. The snapshooter is satisfied with anything the camera gives; the professional only with what he or she can make it yield. In between stands the student who thinks he is "supposed" to want something, and wonders what.

The New Zone System Manual
Minor White,
Richard D. Zakia,
Peter Lorenz
1976; 140 pp.
$18.95
($20.95 postpaid) from:
Morgan & Morgan, Inc.
145 Palisade Street
Dobbs Ferry, NY 10522
or Whole Earth Access

Pinhole Journal • The Hole Thing

Photography minus equipment. Looks like fun.
—Stewart Brand

★ VARIOUS PINHOLE CAMERAS ★

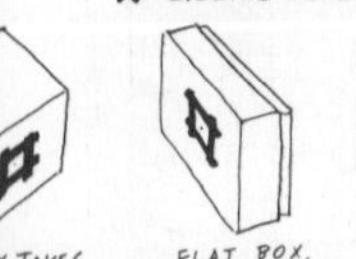
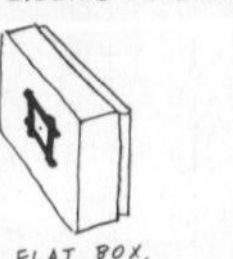

—The Hole Thing

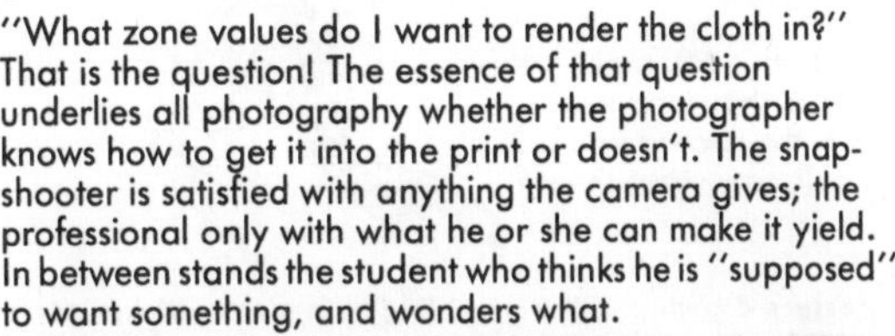

David Pugh "Pig on Manhole Cover," November 1982 PinZip photo f/110, 4 sec. Newark, Del. of a 3" high brass piggy bank standing on a manhole cover which is on a 4 foot high concrete structure on the edge of a swamp. The PinZip was placed directly on the manhole cover. The raised letters (part of the word "SALISBURY") are about 1/8" high; the square bumps are about 1/4" high. 6¼" x 8½"
—Pinhole Journal

Pinhole Journal
Eric Renner, Editor
$32.50/year
(3 issues) from:
Pinhole Resource
Star Route 15, Box 1655
San Lorenzo, NM 88057

The Hole Thing
(A Manual of Pinhole Fotografy)
Jim Shull
1974; 64 pp.
$5.95
($7.45 postpaid) from:
Morgan & Morgan
145 Palisades Street
Dobbs Ferry, NY 10522
or Whole Earth Access

Holography Handbook

How to make holographs in your basement. You'll need a basement to hold the one-ton plywood sandbox that serves as a vibration-free table. It's got to be dark, too. The sand allows you to stick in and adjust optical components glued to sharpened plastic pipes. About as low-rent high-tech as you'll ever see. Making holograms is modern alchemy. Use the formulas in this great, masterful book.
—Kevin Kelly

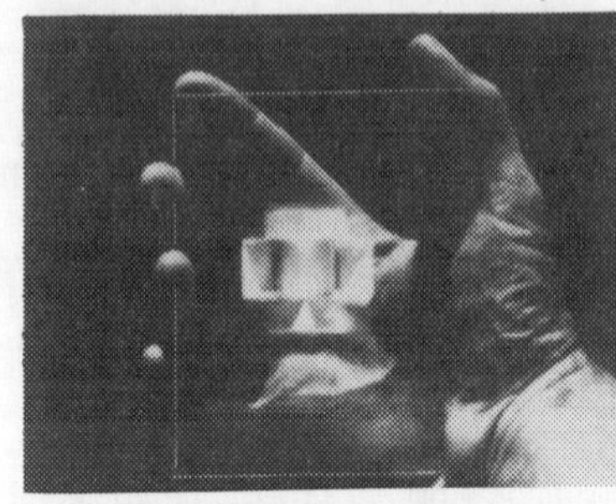

"Cubes" Dichromate hologram by Fred Unterseher and Bob Schlesinger, 1980.

Here I am making an innertube sandwich using plenty of carpet pieces for bread. There is carpet between the concrete floor and the concrete blocks, between the blocks and the wood base, between the wood and the inner tubes, and on top of the tubes. I used 6 inch size inner tube, the type used in forklift tires.

Holography Handbook
Fred Unterseher,
Jeannene Hansen, and
Bob Schlesinger
1982; 408 pp.
$16.95
($17.95 postpaid) from:
Ross Books
P. O. Box 4340
Berkeley, CA 94704
or Whole Earth Access

• All the specialized photography books you'll ever need are stocked by Light Impressions. Books by famous gallery artists, alternative photo processes, studio tricks, shooting slide shows, darkroom methods, making a career, etc. **Light Impressions:** Catalog **free** from 439 Monroe Avenue, Rochester, NY 14603.

The Natural Way to Draw
Kimon Nicolaides
1975; 221 pp.
$8.95
($9.95 postpaid) from:
Houghton Mifflin Co.
Mail Order Dept.
Wayside Road
Burlington, MA 01803
or Whole Earth Access

The Natural Way to Draw

This classic work by an outstanding art teacher is not only the best how-to book on drawing, it is one of the best how-to books we've seen on any subject. —Stewart Brand [Suggested by Roy Sebern]

•

The sooner you make your first five thousand mistakes, the sooner you will be able to correct them.

A gesture drawing is like scribbling rather than like printing carefully — think more of the meaning than of the way the thing looks.

Think of the whole form, the surface of which can be seen only if you walk all the way around the model.

In contour drawing you touch the edge of the form.

In gesture drawing you feel the movement of the whole.

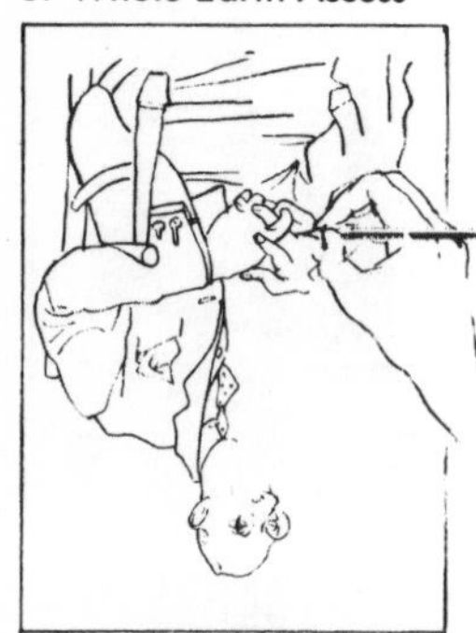

Drawing on the Right Side of the Brain • Drawing on the Artist Within

If you've always wanted to draw, but lacked the "talent," Betty Edwards' simple exercises can help you turn your stick figures into real drawings. ***Drawing on the Right Side of the Brain*** *gives the basics on how to see and how to put what you see onto paper.*

Once you've learned to draw what you can see you'll want to draw what you imagine. Her new book, ***Drawing on the Artist Within****, helps you to add expressiveness and innovation, turning your drawings into art.*

—Kathleen O'Neill

◄

Inverted drawing. Forcing the cognitive shift from the dominant left-hemisphere mode to the subdominant right-hemisphere mode. —*Drawing on the Right Side of the Brain*

►

In the first drawing, the student had great difficulty reconciling his stored knowledge of what the objects were "supposed to look like" with what he saw. Notice in the drawing that the legs of the cart are all the same length, and a symbol is used for the wheels. When he switched to R-mode drawing, using a viewfinder and drawing only the shapes of the negative spaces, he was far more successful. The visual information apparently came through clearly; the drawing looks confident and as though it were done with ease. And, in fact, it was done with ease, because the left hemisphere had been tricked into keeping quiet.

—Drawing on the Right Side of the Brain

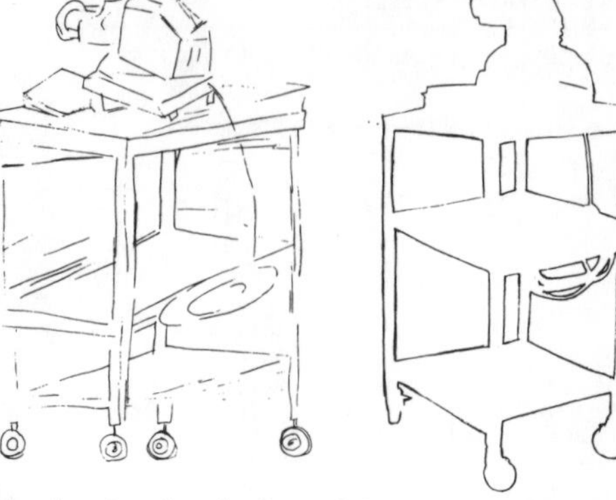

Drawing on the Right Side of the Brain
Betty Edwards
1979; 207 pp.
$9.95
($11.20 postpaid) from:
St. Martin's Press
175 5th Avenue
New York, NY 10010
or Whole Earth Access

Drawing on the Artist Within
Betty Edwards
1986; 240 pp.
$18.95
postpaid from:
Simon and Schuster
Mail Order Sales
200 Old Tappan Road
Old Tappan, NJ 07675
or Whole Earth Access

R.F.'s three drawings over a three-week period.

◄

A casual observer viewing R.F's three drawings might conclude that he had "learned to draw" in the three weeks. But that wasn't it at all: R.F. had learned to see "differently" — that is, to "see" information which was out there all the time, but which was at first simply rejected because of quick closure and premature, preprogrammed conclusions. *—Drawing on the Artist Within*

Thinking with a Pencil

Good title, wonderful book — an inviting pragmatic introduction to the full range of image-representation. Nelms makes it look easy and great fun. —Stewart Brand

Thinking with a Pencil
Henning Nelms
1981; 347 pp.
$8.95
($9.95 postpaid) from:
Ten Speed Press
P. O. Box 7123
Berkeley, CA 94707
or Whole Earth Access

322. WHEELS ON DIFFERENT AXES
The short-axis rule applies, no matter which way the axle slants.

•

Practical drawings are mental tools. Once you have learned to make them, you will find that they are as useful in solving problems as saws and hammers are useful in carpentry.

•

Omitting the useless is as important as including the essential. Aristotle stated a fundamental truth when he said that everything which does not add will detract.

151. DISTINGUISHING SEVERAL POSITIONS OF THE SAME OBJECT BY DOTTED LINE
Also note use of a dotted line to indicate the path of the ball

e in Japan from kozo and sulphite pulp, aper represents one of the great decora- evements in Japanese papermaking. It is weight white paper with real maple leaves d in the sheet. Silky fibers also decorate

Daniel Smith Inc.

Here is an immense selection of absolutely first rate art supplies, as well as a wonderfully prompt and efficient mail order house. Their goods are discounted, generally 20-30 percent off retail, and are interestingly and informatively laid out in the illustrated (photos) yearly catalog, supplemented by intermittent special sale catalogs. In terms of sheer care and knowledgeability, no other art supplier I have found even comes close.

The fine artist is at home here. Unlike most of the other large art supply houses like Flax, Pearl, etc., they focus on fine arts and secondarily on graphic arts.

Daniel Smith has grown from a small manufacturer of fine etching and lithographic inks to their present just described stature, without sacrificing one bit of integrity; one couldn't ask for more.

And they still make those wonderful inks. —*Garta Hodge*

SENNELIER SOFT PASTELS

Sennelier is a third generation family company that has been supplying France's best known artists since the turn of the century. Their pastels are still handmade and enjoy a strong following.

Product Number		List Price	Our Price
6112051	50 Color Portrait	118.00	**94.40**
6112052	50 Color Landscape	118.00	**94.40**
6112172	172 Color Set	376.00	**263.20**

"Fine" Quality Japanese Hake Brushes

This is the classic flat brush used by Japanese artists for blending or painting large areas. The hake brush is comprised of white goat hair and features a smooth, natural wood handle. We offer this brush in sizes from ⅝" to 6". It is excellent for water colors, gouache and sumi.

Daniel Smith Inc.
Catalog
$4 from:
4130 1st Avenue South
Seattle, WA 98134

The Artist's Handbook of Materials and Techniques
(4th Edition)
Ralph Mayer
1981; 733 pp.
$24.95
($26.20 postpaid) from:
Viking Penguin
299 Murray Hill Pkwy.
East Rutherford, NJ 07073
or Whole Earth Access

The Artist's Handbook of Materials and Techniques

Part of becoming a Rembrandt or Da Vinci is creating art work that lasts for several hundred years. Cracking, peeling, fading, or darkening colors are usually the result of poor technique.

This book thoroughly covers traditional media from pigment to finishing (the section on fresco sounds enticingly difficult). The new sections on polymers and synthetic organic pigments rounds it out.

No illustrations — make your own. —*Kathleen O'Neill*

•

Handling the Tempera Paint

When painting with egg, plenty of water should be used, and the brush should be dipped into water frequently. When the amount of egg is in proper relation to that of pigment, a large amount of water may be added to the paint; inexperienced painters often have difficulty in handling the tempera medium through not introducing enough water. When too much egg is used, the paint will dry too rapidly and brush out with difficulty; when not enough egg is used in relation to the amount of pigment, the resulting film will be weak and powdery. To test the paint film it should be brushed out and allowed to dry on a sheet of glass. If it can be peeled off in a continuous, tough film with a knife, there is enough egg to bind it; if it powders or flakes off there is not enough. Some pigments, as will be found by experience, require a little more egg than others.

•

Red Sable Watercolor Brushes. The one source of hair for the finest brushes is the tail of the kolinsky (known also as Siberian mink or red Tartar marten). No other hair has the same springiness, durability, and combination of desirable properties.

Ylem
Fred Stitt, Editor
$15/year
(4 issues) from:
Ylem
P. O. Box 749
Orinda, CA 94563

Leonardo

Most art books and magazines are about the product of art, with lots of four-color pictures to wow you. ***Leonardo*** *is the opposite. It's pure process, pure tool — TECHNIQUE — of the most advanced, most refined, most modern of arts. (The news stays the same in this world; only science and technology change, and art chases them.) I view this publication with the same contemporary fascination as* ***Science*** *or* ***New Scientist*** *(p. 26). They announce the present (i.e., future).*

Not cheap, not for browsing. Lay out the bucks and make the magazine earn it back in your work or settle it all at your library. —*Stewart Brand*

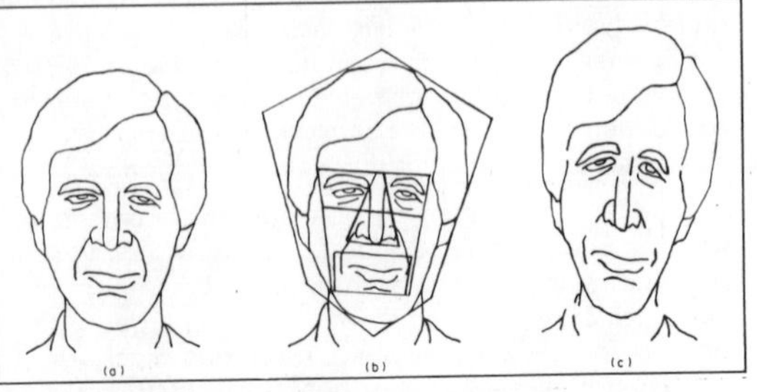

A computer-assisted caricature made by stretching and squashing areas in a line drawing on a frame buffer; by the authors, 1981.

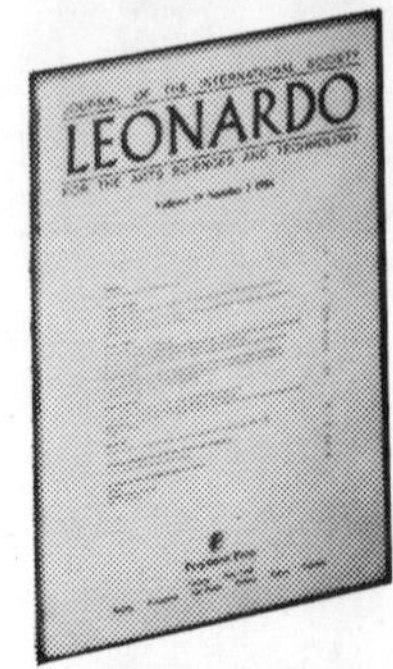

Leonardo
Roger F. Malina, Editor
$30/year
(4 issues) from:
Pergamon Press
Journals Dept.
Maxwell House
Fairview Park
Elmsford, NY 10523

Ylem

Along every breaking edge of technology there are a few artists wedged into the nicks figuring out creative mis-uses for new-fangled things, immediately enlarging everyone's scope. Our culture has bred a gang of artists hanging around Xerox machines, lasers, geodesics, Polaroid devices, video, and, of course, computers. Their art makes technology better, which makes them better artists. Some of their latest ideas and exhibit events can be found in this newsletter compiled by and for "artists using science and technology." —*Kevin Kelly*

• Artists are geniuses at finding new uses for old tools. Some promising catalog sources: Jerryco (p. 161), Brookstone (p. 159), Edmund Scientific (p. 389), and Cerulean Blue, Ltd. (p. 181, from **The Fiberworks Source Book**). Don't forget your local office supply store or the mail order sources on p. 195.

Continuous closed form organized by six different views. The trajectory changes direction in the centre, crossing to another spatial situation. This crossing is repeated six times before return to the point of origin. The 'impossible' form is organized by six three-dimensional rectangles.

—**Celtic Art, The Methods of Construction from Dover.**

Stage 3

MAPLE Seeds, The Anatomy of Nature. Medusa, Treasury of Fantastic and Mythological Characters. Letter "M" Special Effects Alphabets. Letter "A", Fantastic Alphabets. All from Dover

Art Reference

"What do you do when you run out of ideas?" my civil servant Dad asked when he worried about me working as an artist. Use picture archives, that's what.

A working artist needs pictorial reference as a tool for inspiration, for seeing visual connections not made before, or for models to draw from. Inventing images, drawing constructions out of the blue, is helped if you've got a few aids.

My bookshelves are lined with field-tested books that I crib from while working in the studio. I use them as creative inspiration. Small books will do. Like any postage stamp book. Mine cost me 25 cents at a street sale. Stamps in general give good art-ref; they're very graphic and basic, these vignettes and symbols of the world.

An example of a good photo resource book is the paperback **Best of Life**. *The world's best photographers, out on the beat, bringing it all home. These are the images many of us (I) culled our (my) view of "real" from.*

Big picture books, encyclopedias, and reference tomes are expensive and often out of print. Since art reference is often used as found art, this is reflected in their purchase — a bit of an old encyclopedia is quite useful in a found-art context. So I buy my books at street sales, the flea market, and jumble sales when I can. This means that much of my collection is quite fortuitous — a random lot. Keep looking around the stalls and you'll find them cheap.

By far the most useful source for in-print copyright-free material is the fascinating collection from Dover pictorial archives — very cheap books crammed with old, odd, wonderful reference pictures, weird typefaces, classy etchings, vintage photographs, and off-beat scientific treatises. Their free catalogs are a trip in themselves.

—David Wills

The Best of Life: David E. Scherman, Editor, 1973; 303 pp. **$14.95** ($15.95 postpaid) from Avon Books, P. O. Box 767, Dresden, TN 38225 (or Whole Earth Access).

The Complete Dover Fine Art Catalog, The Complete Dover Art Instruction Catalog, The Complete Dover Pictorial Archive Catalog: Catalogs **free** from Dover Publications, Inc., 31 East 2nd Street, Mineola, NY 11501.

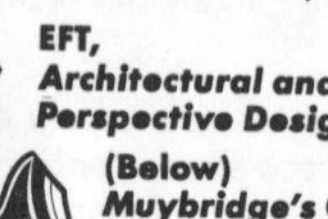

LEFT, Architectural and Perspective Designs.

(Below) Muybridge's Complete Human and Animal Locomotion (a real deal, 3 volumes, 1600 pages, cloth bound for $100). All from Dover.

(Right) phone booth stuffing, 1960. —Best of Life

Letter "L" above: Bizarre & Ornamental Alphabets.

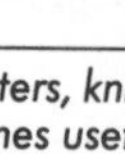

BABOON, 1800 Woodcuts of the Bewick School. Letter "B", Special Effects Alphabets, both from Dover.

Stage 2

Designer's Guide to Color

Anybody who designs with color — house painters, knitters, graphic types, etc. — will find these two volumes useful. They show the effect of thousands of two- and three-color combinations, and how perceived colors change in relation to their neighbors. The charts will lead you to thoughtful and often surprising color combinations.

Volume One shows many possible dual color combinations, with one hue constant per page. Volume Two deals with pastels and brights, and includes more three-color combos. Each color is broken down into percentages of stock printing tints: yellows, magenta, cyan, and black, for graphic-arts folks. Most color books costs hundreds; these have gobs of color, few words, and are very affordable.

—Kathleen O'Neill

754

Designer's Guide to Color
(Volume One)
1983; 135 pp.

Designer's Guide to Color
(Volume Two)
1984; 128 pp.

$9.95 each
($11.45 postpaid) from:
Chronicle Books
One Hallidie Plaza
Suite 806
San Francisco, CA 94102
or Whole Earth Access

Book of Kells. Stage 1

Bizzaro

Crazy, wild, fun rubberstamps for those important times in life.

—Kevin Kelly

Bizzaro
Catalog **free** from:
Bizzaro Inc.
Box 126
Annex Station
Providence, RI 02901

Thanks
#464
$4.95

Keep Sn
#428
$3.50

Exhibits for the Small Museum

I used to work in exhibit design and can affirm that this is a right handy little book for the friendly task of making stuff visible, interesting, understandable, and protected. Great primer for a first-time museum. (Don't tear down that old building. Do this book to it.) —Stewart Brand

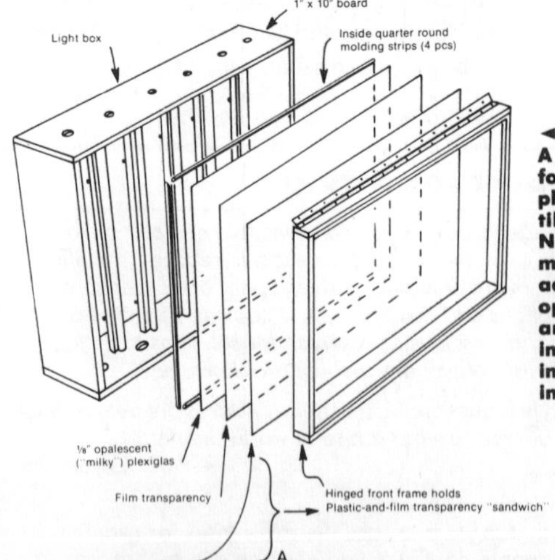

◄ **A light box is used for backlighting photographs, textiles, prints, etc. Note: a layer of mylar film should be added between the opalescent Plexiglas and the material being exhibited. This increases the filtering of UV rays.**

◄ **Railing heights provide "mini-rest" opportunity.**

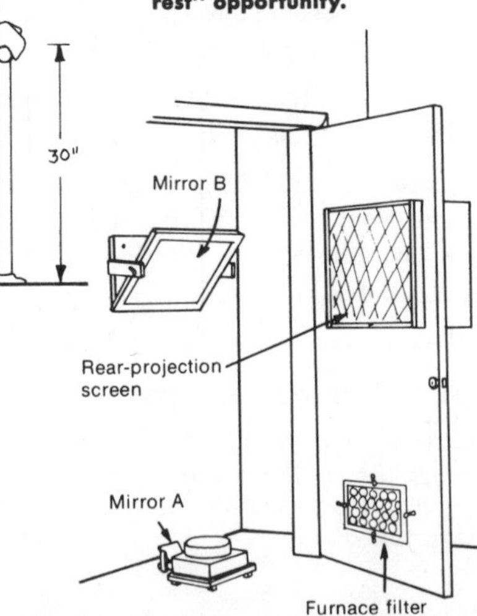

A closet with a slide projector, mirrors, and translucent rear-projection screen can be a useful set-up. By "bending" the projector's beam with mirrors, it is possible to get the equivalent of a 6'9" projection distance in a closet that is only 30" deep.

Exhibits for the Small Museum
Arminta Neal
1976; 169 pp.

$11 postpaid from:
American Association for State and Local History
172 2nd Avenue N
Suite 102
Nashville, TN 37201
or Whole Earth Access

A Conference and Workshop Planner's Manual

The best conferences are on new subjects by new people. The worst conferences are by new people who don't know what they're doing. This straightforward text — it's basically a well-experienced checklist — can make the difference. —Stewart Brand

•

After the resource person [speaker] has confirmed his or her willingness to participate according to the terms of the contract, you should send a follow-up letter. In this letter, you will provide the resource person with the following:

— A current agenda, including names of other speakers and their topics
— Information on housing, meals, airport pickup arrangements, directions, and maps
— Information on the design of the assigned meeting room
— Feedback from the planning committee on information the resource person sent regarding the design, required materials, or other requests
— Information on any pre-event or post-event activities
— Any required registration procedures
— Information on whether a member of the program committee or a facilitator has been assigned to him or her and how contact will be made

•

Decide on when the exhibits will be open, keeping in mind the following:

—Exhibit hours should be the equivalent of from one-third to one-half of the total conference time
—At least one-third of the time scheduled for exhibits should not compete with other conference or workshop programs

Sample Floor Plan

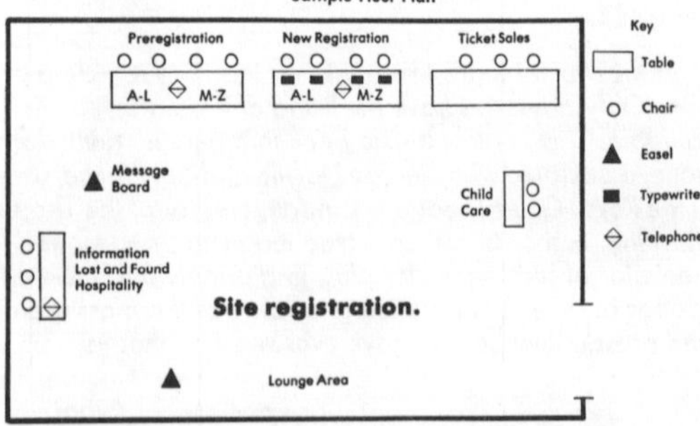

A Conference and Workshop Planner's Manual
Lois B. Hart and Gordon Schleicher
1979; 150 pp.

$15
($16.95 postpaid) from:
Leadership Dynamics Inc.
P. O. Box 320
Lyons, CO 80540
or Whole Earth Access

Organizing and Operating Profitable Workshop Classes

It's sort of shocking that ALL you need to know to turn your skill into a class can be compressed into so small and blithe a booklet. —Stewart Brand

•

TEACHING ADULTS

An informative, informal approach is successful with adults. They are your peers who share an interest with you, and some of them may become your good friends. They will, at first, regard you with a critical eye. It is important that you be well-organized and self-confident.

The old adage stands: be yourself. If you are bouncy and bubbly, don't try to be austere and dignified. If you are reserved, don't try to become a comedian. If you are slightly messy and tend to have ink on your fingers most of the time, don't start getting a weekly manicure just to impress your students.

Being well-organized and self-confident comes from knowing your material and knowing what you want your students to learn. You will then teach well, and your students will be satisfied.

Organizing and Operating Profitable Workshop Classes
Janet Ruhe-Schoen
1981; 31 pp.

$2.50
($3.50 postpaid) from:
Pilot Books
103 Cooper Street
Babylon, NY 11702
or Whole Earth Access

• See **How to Make Meetings Work** (p. 104).
• The little booklet **P.R.** (p. 194) has hints for publicity and the books on p. 315 have simple instructions for publishing brochures and flyers that any conference or museum requires.

IDENTITY IS A FRAME; death is a curtain; we are all actors. Those who "act" the identity of others are directly connected to the lineage of Paleolithic shamans; first transformers; first knowers that identity is mutable.

That their magic is fundamental is proven time and time again by the power available to even the puffiest bourgeois theatrical when it brushes this charged ground.

A study of the following books will put stretch in your sense of self, aid the development of penetrating observation, and do for your human interactions what jogging does for the cardiovascular system. Become your own transformer. Practice throwing your own switches. You'll be surprised what your little electric train can do.

—Peter Coyote

An Actor Prepares
Constantin Stanislavski
1964; 295 pp.
$14.95
($15.89 postpaid) from:
Theatre Arts Books
153 Waverly Place
New York, NY 10014
or Whole Earth Access

An Actor Prepares

The Source Text. Stanislavski's studies of the techniques of the best actors of his day are the basis of all subsequent teachings. His dedication and worship of nature are an inspiration. —*Peter Coyote*

•

Never lose yourself on the stage. Always act in your own person, as an artist. You can never get away from yourself. The moment you lose yourself on the stage marks the departure from truly living your part and the beginning of exaggerated false acting. Therefore, no matter how much you act, how many parts you take, you should never allow yourself any exception to the rule of using your own feelings. To break that rule is the equivalent of killing the person you are portraying, because you deprive him of a palpitating, human soul, which is the real source of life for a part.

•

When you speak to the person who is playing opposite you, learn to follow through until you are certain your thoughts have penetrated his consciousness. Only after you are convinced of this and have added with your eyes what could not be put into words, should you continue to say the rest of your lines.

Respect for Acting
Uta Hagen with
Haskel Frankel
1973; 227 pp.
$13.95 postpaid from:
Macmillan Publishing Co.
Order Dept.
Front and Brown Streets
Riverside, NJ 08075
or Whole Earth Access

Respect for Acting

Uta Hagen's book is an indispensable companion to Stanislavski's. A consummate actress and teacher, she offers precise methodologies for developing one's intuitions, perceptions and responses, and coaxing open the doors of the subconscious as reservoir for solutions to acting problems. (Which are real-life problems, no?)

Her style is passionate, and her standards are demandingly high, offered to what is best in world theater.
—*Peter Coyote*

•

A great danger is to take the five senses for granted. Most people do. Once you become aware that the sources which move in on you when you truly touch, taste, smell, see and hear are endless, you must also realize that self-involvement deadens the senses, and vanity slaughters them until you end up playing all alone — and meaninglessly.

•

Overacting, as it is usually thought of, means that the actor is playing to the gallery instead of with the other characters on stage. Or that he is hanging onto his own sensations or wallowing in false emotion. Underacting is primarily an empty imitation of nature, the actor playing in the ''manner'' of naturalness, unrelated to the roots of the given *reality*.

Impro
Keith Johnstone
1979; 208 pp.
$14.95
($15.89 postpaid) from:
Theatre Arts Books
153 Waverly Place
New York, NY 10014
or Whole Earth Access

Impro

Most theater texts are like books on learning to ride a bike. Only after you have the hang of it are they valuable. This book is a rare peek into genius. Keith Johnstone, associated with George Devine and Tony Richardson of the Royal Court Theatre in London, creator of the Theatre Machine, comes across as a true magician, an inspired innovator of techniques for plugging people into the wellsprings of their own imaginations. One of the most useful and provocative books I have ever read on theater.
—*Peter Coyote*
[Suggested by Pat Ryan]

•

'Try to get your status just a little above or below your partner's,' I said, and I insisted that the gap should be minimal. The actors seemed to know exactly what I meant and the work was transformed. The scenes became 'authentic', and actors seemed marvellously observant. Suddenly we understood that every inflection and movement implies a status, and that no action is due to chance, or really 'motiveless'. It was hysterically funny, but at the same time very alarming. All our secret manoeuvrings were exposed. If someone asked a question we didn't bother to answer it, we concentrated on why it had been asked. No one could make an 'innocuous' remark without everyone instantly grasping what lay behind it. Normally we are 'forbidden' to see status transactions except when there's a conflict. In reality status transactions continue all the time. In the park we'll notice the ducks squabbling, but not how carefully they keep their distances when they are not.

Norcosto • Mutual Hardware

Low-cost theater equipment, costumes, makeup, etc. for school-size productions. I can't imagine opening a new wave nightclub or restaurant without some of these toys.
—*Stewart Brand*

Fig. 9005
COBWEB MACHINE

Fig. 9005 Cobweb Machine is used to produce authentic cobwebs which even fools a spider. Useful in setting the scenes in mysteries, comedies and dramas. Web is produced by the spraying of Fig. 9006 Cobweb Juice from the juice holder in machine.

—*Mutual Hardware*

• Good coverage of national and regional theater plus the complete text of one play per issue.
American Theater: Jim O'Quinn, Editor. **$24**/year (11 issues) from Theater Communications Group, 355 Lexington Avenue, New York, NY 10017.

• America's giant of play publishers offers a catalog organized by special interest — Chinese plays, Monologues, Black plays, etc. — and indexed by author and title.
French's Basic Catalogue of Plays: **$2** from Samuel French, Inc., 45 West 25th Street, New York, NY 10010.

The Small Theatre Handbook

All the practical steps to take in creating a new theater and maintaining it are covered by this good-humored handbook: from budgets, funding, and legal requirements to choosing plays, managing actors, and touring productions. Written with such love of small theatre, it still points out where stresses are sure to arise and tells how to work through them.

Green emphasizes the importance of keeping that critical balance of respect and responsibility between the artistic and administrative staffs.

The book should be a little longer in the fundraising area, but there's an excellent bibliography. —Annette Rose
Antenna Theater

•

Don't count on selling tickets. Do your best at publicity, and keep your fingers crossed. The price of a ticket should not be so small that the audience feels that it — and the experience of the theatre itself — is inconsequential. Nor should it be so high that the audience fears that nothing could possibly be worth this much money. You may be tempted not to set a price at all, but to ask for ''donations at the door.'' Resist. Accept responsibility for setting, if not a value on the two hours you ask someone to spend with you, than at least a monetary metaphor for it.

The Small Theatre Handbook
Joann Green
1981; 163 pp.
$8.95
($10.20 postpaid) from:
Kampmann and Company
9 East 40th Street
New York, NY 10016
or Whole Earth Access

Stage Makeup

This is one art that would require a hell of a book to put across with the printed page alone. ***Stage Makeup*** *does it. Step-by-step close-up photos, in color where needed, make it easy enough to try, and when you find it isn't easy, the photos help you learn where you went wrong. Not all the tricks of the trade are here, but enough to get you work.* —*Stewart Brand*

◄

There are two major illusions which need to be created in the extreme stout technique: (1) all wrinkles and folds of flesh will be shaped as horizontally as possible to make the face seem wider. This will apply also to the use of wig, mustache, and beard. (2) We will create the illusion that the face is larger than it actually is by making many features appear smaller than they actually are. Therefore, carrying the facial lines horizontally, making the features smaller, plus creating specific optical illusions of roundness, will contribute to the extreme stout effect we seek.

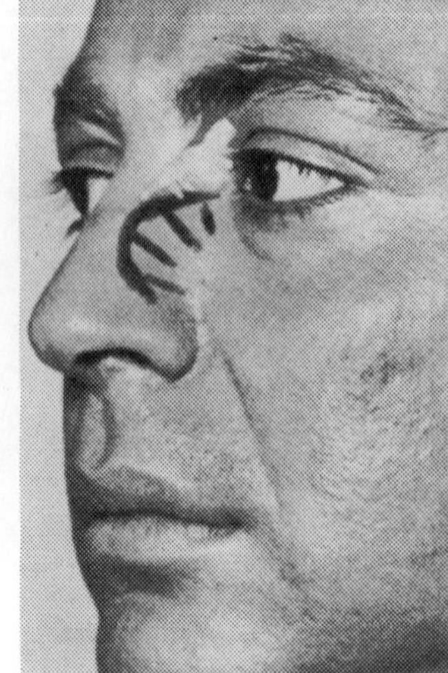

To make the bridge of the nose shorter and wider, carry the shadow from the corner of the eye onto the bridge in an arc, moving down to the nostril. Apply a strong highlight in the corner of the eye.

rosco fog and smoke system
rosco
Fog/Smoke Machine
N806 Series III Fog Machine 565.00/Discount Code H
N804 Water Base Fog (1 liter) 12.95/Discount Code E
N805 Water Base Fog (1 Gal.) 49.00/Discount Code E

Rosco's Fog and Smoke system is the first developed specially for the performing arts. The system produces safe, realistic smoke that is non-toxic and does not irritate eyes, skin or throat. The machines are sturdy and designed for remote operation. The fluid leaves no oily residue and emits no unpleasant odors. Available for 120 or 240 volt operation and comes with 25' remote controller.
—Norcosto

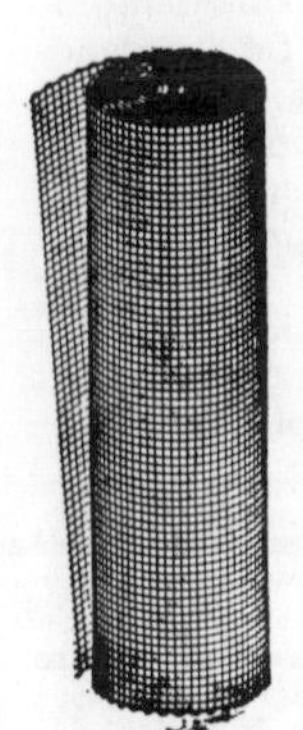

▲
A pliable soft black wire, woven but not welded, used for making all types of scenery shapes.
Size, width, inch: 36''. Length, feet: 100'. $190
Size, width, inch: 48''. Length, feet: 100'. $260
—Mutual Hardware

—Norcosto

Stage Makeup
Herman Buchman
1971; 191 pp.
$27.50
($29.50 postpaid) from:
Watson-Guptill Publications
1695 Oak Street
Lakewood, NJ 08701
or Whole Earth Access

• This set designer's magazine puts out a remarkable book, too.
Theater Crafts: Patricia MacKay, Editor. **$24**/year (10 issues) from Theater Crafts, P. O. Box 630, Holmes, PA 19043.

Theater Crafts How-To: Theater Crafts Magazine, Editors, 1984; 168 pp. **$9.95** ($11.20 postpaid) from Drama Book Publishers, 821 Broadway, New York, NY 10003.

Catalog for the Performing Arts: **$2** from Norcosto, 3203 North Highway, #100, Minneapolis, MN 55422.

Theatrical Equipment and Supplies Catalog: **$2** from Mutual Hardware Corp., 5-45 49th Avenue, Long Island City, NY 11101.

Independent Filmmaking
Lenny Lipton
1983; 445 pp.
$9.95 postpaid from:
Simon & Schuster
Mail Order Sales
200 Old Tappan Road
Old Tappan, NJ 07675
or Whole Earth Access

The Steadicam. Expensive and cumbersome, it is the last word in smooth hand-held cinematography, and has been used to good effect on many features. (Cinema Products)

Independent Filmmaking

My quick survey of film schools shows Lipton's book still the favorite how-to. After more than ten years in print and some 110,000 copies sold, it's become a kind of institution. Video freaks may find Lipton's views condescending, but he has added a useful section called "Video for the Filmmaker." This book remains technically astute and entertaining to read. —*Tom Schneider*

•

It's usually quite easy to produce smooth motion on the screen hand-holding a camera with a lens half the *normal* focal length, say 5 to 7 millimeters for 8mm and super 8, or 10 millimeters for 16mm. Short focal lengths also help to take the place of a tripod you're trying to hold steady, with no intended motion. With practice, it's very nearly possible to reproduce the steadiness of a dolly or tripod mounted camera. Accomplishing this is really no great feat. To help hold a motionless shot steady, you can lean against anything available, a wall for example, but really, this isn't necessary.

Why use a tripod, if it doesn't matter? The traditional advice for filmmaking is to use a tripod whenever possible. My practice is to avoid using a tripod whenever possible.

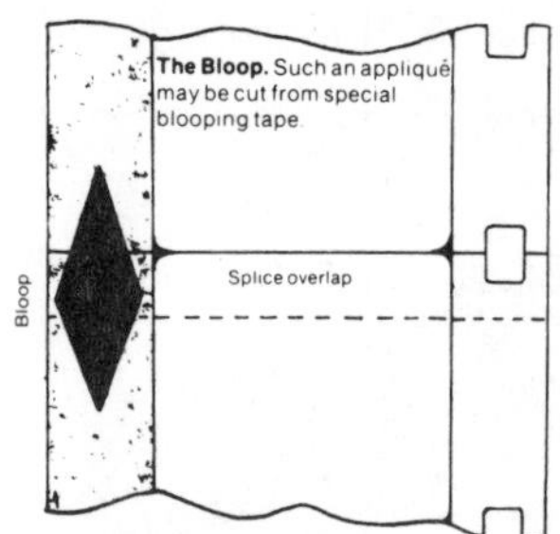
The Bloop. Such an appliqué may be cut from special blooping tape.
Splice overlap
Bloop

◄ Spliced optical track often makes a popping sound at the splice point. The way to eliminate this is called *blooping*. You make a small oval or wedge shape over the splice with ink. This makes an inaudible sound that covers the sound of the splice. You can use especially formulated *blooping ink*, or you can try metallic blooping tape, cut to the shape of a flat parallelogram, and pressed directly over the splice.

When the Shooting Stops. . . the Cutting Begins
Ralph Rosenblum and Robert Karen
OUT OF PRINT
Penguin Books

When the Shooting Stops. . . the Cutting Begins

This book is undeservedly out of print. Here is an engaging history of film editing told by Rosenblum, an editor who seems to have been in many historically important editing rooms. He started in the forties, assisting Helen Van Dongen, the stoic cutter who (this book reveals) took director Robert Flaherty's stream-of-consciousness cinematography and carved it into cogent films like ***The Louisiana Story.***

The tale is spiced by eavesdropping on privileged conversations. Behind the editing room door famous directors confess their secret insecurities. In exchange for this confidence, the editor/father/analyst accepts an unspoken contract: No matter how much the footage is reworked and "saved in the editing room," all the credit will remain with the director.

*We are a fly on the wall as Woody Allen and Marshall Brickman learn that the most brilliant comic writing (****Annie Hall****) sometimes falls flat on the screen, and that the biggest laugh comes at the most unexpected point. Even a director as experienced as Sydney Lumet (****The Pawnbroker****) turns to Rosenblum to solve problems never foreseen in the shooting script.*

Every film craft should have a book this good written about it. —*Tom Schneider*

•

As a director of live TV shows Sidney [Lumet] had to make fast editorial choices, pushing buttons in his booth to select the best camera angle from those available on his monitor screens. As a filmmaker, the editing impulse has remained. He is the only director I've worked with who could tell me cut-for-cut what he wanted in a scene and even come up with tricks I had never considered. An example arose during the editing of *Long Day's Journey.* I had always cut dialogue scenes by carefully choosing whether to focus on the speaker or the listener. Lumet came up with an alternative approach, "mathematical cutting," in which we cut back and forth from one actor to the other in evenly matched but progressively shorter snippets of film, totally ignoring who was talking and who was listening, and markedly increasing the tension. Clearly, if a picture needed astute editorial consideration, Sidney was the director to handle it.

American Cinematographer
George Turner, Editor
$22/year
(12 issues) from:
American Cinematographer
P. O. Box 2230
Hollywood, CA 90078

Millimeter
Peter Caranicas, Editor
$45/year
(12 issues) from:
Millimeter
P. O. Box 95759
Cleveland, OH 44101

American Cinematographer • Millimeter

You can be an insider for the price of a subscription. ***American Cinematographer*** *is where you'll find out how it's done when you can hire ten experts and all the equipment you need to produce three perfect minutes on screen.* ***Cinematographer*** *has taken more interest lately in the history of American filmmaking, besides front-line reports on the latest marriages of film and video.*

Millimeter*, "The Magazine of the Motion Picture and Television Production Industries," is the journal that's making the marriage work. Its attitude is let's get on with it: Film or tape, television or cinema, what's the difference, as long as there's money to be made. Sometimes it's hard to tell the ads from the editorial material, but to take the pulse of the film industry, East Coast, West Coast, and in between, this is the one.* —*Tom Schneider*

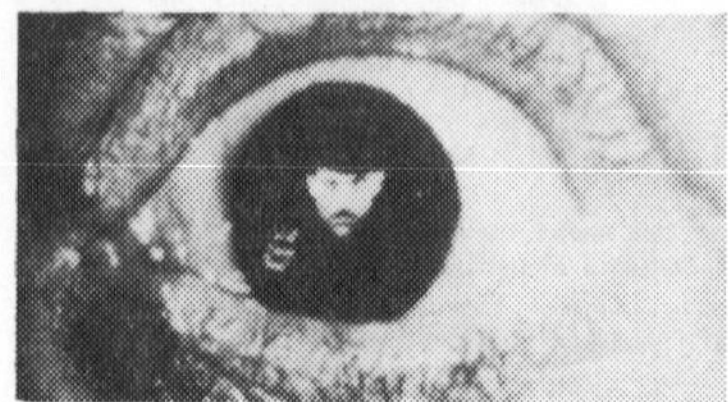

The glowing face of a murderer, Boris Karloff, is reflected in the victim's eye in "The Invisible Ray" (1936). —American Cinematographer

• Our reviewer for these pages is Tom Schneider, a filmmaker, and author of one of our favorite books, **The Moveable Nest** (p. 141) and its syndicated newspaper column version.

Cinefex

It is evidence of film's magic that what happens behind the scenes has always been as entertaining as the show up front, and sometimes more.

When monsters slobber and spaceships hurtle across the screen, I believe it. But when the scene is flipped and I'm shown how the most convincing special effects are done, I find it unbelievable, yet altogether spellbinding. Hundreds of people work years to construct incredibly elaborate illusions out of latex, tiny models and winking computers — each a secret of fine craftsmanship waiting to be told. This amazing magazine (scads of color pictures, no advertising) is what some folks around here sneak off to a corner with and read for hours. —Kevin Kelly

Cinefex
Don Shay, Editor
$15/year
(4 issues) from:
Cinefex
P. O. Box 20027
Riverside, CA 92516

◄
For maximum control, Dream Quest dismissed the possibility of using actual cloud footage in favor of creating their own on stage. Experimentation led to the employment of polyester fiber fill glued onto pieces of plexiglass. . . An inverted camera and snorkel lens were used to obtain cloud imagery that appeared to be whizzing by on either side of the thermopod cockpit. Gioffre makes minor adjustments to the simulated cloud formations.

▲
An army of technicians prepare to orchestrate Falkor's multitudinous cables. The 43-foot-long mechanical creature was capable of various head movements and facial expressions, including the ability to form words.

►
One of the more ingenious innovations in the film *Temple of Doom* was the employment of a modified Nikon — only slightly larger than a standard 35mm still camera — to photograph the mine car chase. Without the Nikon, the miniature cave sets would have had to have been twice as large, just to accommodate ILM's smallest VistaVision camera. Mounted on a specially designed car, the camera had full pan and tilt capability.

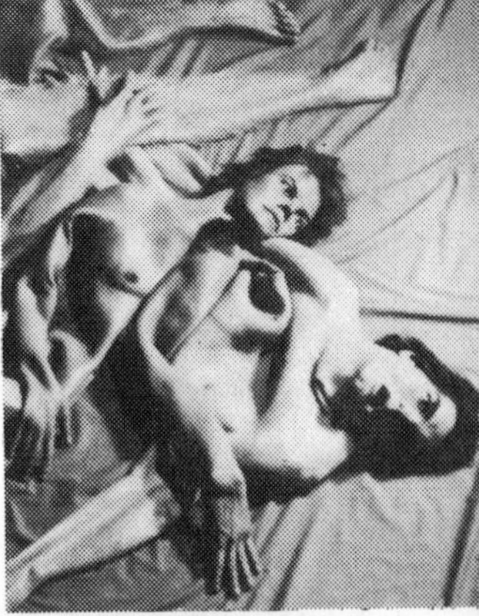

To produce the alien husks, full head casts and sectional body casts were taken of the three Antarean-portraying actors, eventually resulting in one-piece fiberglass molds. Skinflex was then injected to create the basic husk shapes.

The Dark Side of Genius: The Life of Alfred Hitchcock

There are plenty of powerful directors whose lives and work are documented and worth studying: Huston, Ford, Kurosawa, Truffaut. The advantages of examining Hitchcock are that so much is known about him; that most of his films are available for rental on video cassette, and that his methods are rather obvious. It's no detraction from his genius to observe that Hitchcock was only a few steps ahead of the state of the art; consequently, the world was ready for his innovations and took to them immediately. When you look at one of his films now (try watching it two or three times to get past being taken in by the story), it's like a textbook demonstration of how to create suspense, develop a story, reveal a character's inner thoughts, etc.

Dark as some of his themes were, and much of his life, the man sure knew how to tell a good story.

His life would have made one of his most macabre films. —Tom Schneider

•
The fantasies Hitchcock spun and that his screenwriters gave structure to were always geared to cinematic realization. His films depended on the emergence, from deep within him, of mysterious images — images that were often violent, at times tender. From his own secret longings and vivid imagination there came the small germs of stories — sometimes fearful and erotic, sometimes quietly comic or dreamlike. But the plots and the characters would always be subordinate to the power of the images — just as in dreams, the narrative is never quite logical or clear and is always subordinate to the images. Similarly, the residue of feelings left by dreams, like the impression left by Hitchcock's images, is more important than any half-remembered "plot."

Directing for Film and Television

You can't learn directing from a book. The author makes this clear from the start, then goes on to bring a remarkable amount of his considerable experience into nearly proving himself wrong. This is not just for beginners. Open the book anywhere and find a generous serving of truth from a working director who has passion, wit, and a rare talent for teaching.

Put this on your shelf next to **When the Shooting Stops***. . . . you'll have the core of a very good library on film craft.* —Tom Schneider

•
One of the most exciting kinds of script writing is the kind that places us right in the *midst* of a scene. We see the lovers quarreling, but we don't know why — yet. The scene has reached a point of tension; we have to fight to keep up; they know so much more than we do, but it's exciting precisely because the scene has momentum. Conversely, a script in which dialogue *starts* as we dissolve to the scene, though we know that the characters have been with each other for two hours, limps along. A script in which every scene crackles with accepted facts that we perceive rather than receive, is a good script. A script that crackles, in general, that leads us from scene to scene, enticing us to want to see more, is a good script.

Directing for Film and Television
Christopher Lukas
1985; 193 pp.
$11.95 postpaid from:
Doubleday & Company
Direct Mail Order
501 Franklin Avenue
Garden City, NY 11530
or Whole Earth Access

The Dark Side of Genius
(The Life of Alfred Hitchcock)
Donald Spoto
1983; 665 pp.
$4.95
($5.95 postpaid) from:
Random House
Order Dept.
400 Hahn Road
Westminster, MD 21157
or Whole Earth Access

The Home Video Handbook
Charles Bensinger
1982; 392 pp.

$13.95
($16.45 postpaid) from:
Howard W. Sams & Co.
Department DM
4300 West 62nd Street
Indianapolis, IN 46268
or Whole Earth Access

The Home Video Handbook

An excellent overview of consumer cameras and recorders (VHS and Beta), how to hook them up and how to use them to shoot your own home videos. Well illustrated, as up-to-date as can be, and full of useful tips for beginners. —Fabrice Florin

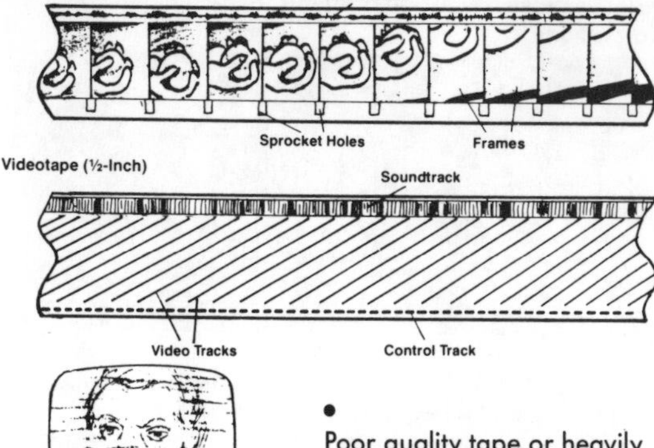

One Clogged Head

Two Clogged Heads

•

Poor quality tape or heavily used or damaged tape can completely clog one or both video heads. Half the picture may disappear or perhaps the whole picture may disappear, but sometimes these symptoms will soon clear up as the tape continues to play.

Good lighting.

•

The camera, in particular must *never* be pointed at the sun or any unusually bright light source. Otherwise, the camera tube will immediately be *burned*. A *burn* means that excessive amounts of light have destroyed the photosensitive surface of the tube and eliminated its ability to respond to changes in light. A black spot or streak will appear in the picture which, in the case of a severe burn, will remain there permanently.

Use of External Mic.

The Video Production Guide
Lon McQuillin
1983; 382 pp.

$28.95
($31.45 postpaid) from:
Howard W. Sams & Co.
4300 West 62nd Street
Indianapolis, IN 46268
or Whole Earth Access

The Video Production Guide

If you're serious about getting involved in the technical side of video production, here is the most up-to-date and comprehensive introduction to the field from the people who brought you the more consumer-oriented ***Video Guide****. This thorough overview of the production process gets down to the nuts and bolts of planning, shooting, and editing a videotape or television program. The book outlines most of what you need to know about video, from how professional equipment works to how to get a job. A definitive textbook of the video craft.* —Fabrice Florin

The complete audio/video man.

•

McQ's Rule No. 3: Always figure you'll spend more than you figured!

•

Another matter of importance is *lighting continuity*. Just as continuity of action and camera perspective are crucial, so is lighting. The lighting director must understand the scene and design lighting that is optimal to create the desired dramatic effect for each camera angle. When these shots are cut together they should appear to have the same lighting throughout the entire scene. This is not an easy job.

•

Study commercials with the sound turned off, and you'll be better able to examine the camera and lighting techniques used without the distraction of the audio. If you have a video tape recorder (VTR) available to you, record some commercials and study them with and without the sound.

•

Television is a two-dimensional medium, so any *depth* in the picture is an illusion. The creation of an illusion of depth is aided by the use of planes within the image. Foreground and background, when used properly to offset and highlight the main subject, can heighten the illusion. . . . Lighting is another major factor in creating a feeling of depth.

UNIVERSAL VIDEO "GAFFER GRIP" LIGHT MOUNTS
Heavy duty spring loaded grip clamps to any surface up to 2½" wide. Equipped with 3" long stud, and is pre-drilled to accept an extra stud allowing you to mount two lights. Rubber cleats prevent marring.

DLQ-5320N	Grip with ⅜" Mount	$24.95
DLQ-1202N	Grip with ⅝" Mount	$24.95

Universal Video

Catalog **free** from:
Universal Video
195 Bonhomme Street
P. O. Box 488
Hackensack, NJ 07602

Universal Video

This impressive catalog of video accessories, supplies, and equipment offers a whole range of useful products, from cable adaptors to VCR cleaning kits. Professionals and amateurs alike will find some nifty gizmos that would be hard to get in a store. —Fabrice Florin

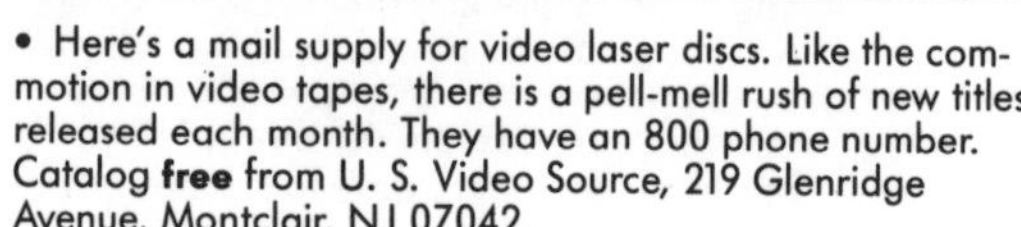

• Here's a mail supply for video laser discs. Like the commotion in video tapes, there is a pell-mell rush of new titles released each month. They have an 800 phone number. Catalog **free** from U. S. Video Source, 219 Glenridge Avenue, Montclair, NJ 07042.

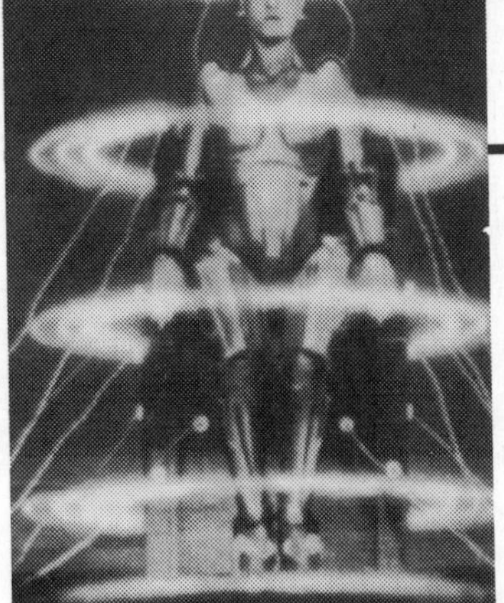

(Above) The transformation of a robot into human form in *Metropolis*.

(Right) Fred Allen nearly escapes injury in the wacky comedy *It's in the Bag*.

Video Times

There doesn't seem to be anywhere to turn except to **Video Times** *for lively, intelligent reviews of material on video tape. In the evenhanded way* **Library Journal** *reviews all kinds of books, this earnest magazine is tackling anything on tape. Video cassettes transform TV and Hollywood material into personal theater (you choose what and when you watch), bestowing a relaxed intimacy to an otherwise harrying and manipulative medium. The magazine's broad reviews and groupings (drama, horror, documentary, experimental, etc.) reflect an emerging sense of video literature.* —KK

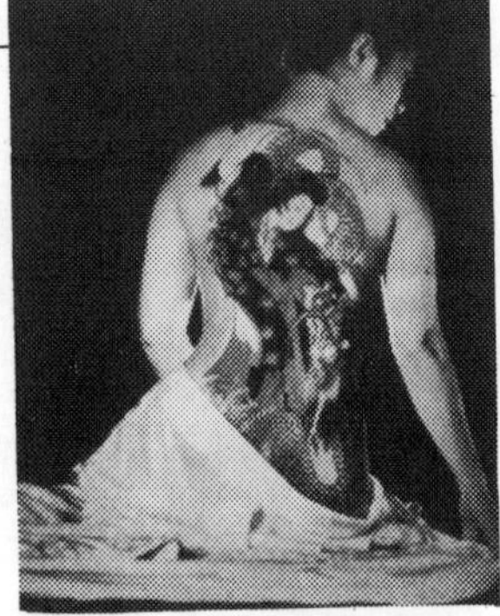

▲ The artist's handwork is displayed on his subject's back in *Irezumi* (1982), C, Director: Yoichi Takabayashi. Subtitled. Pacific Arts, $59.95.

Video Times
Laurie Fortman and Amy Tao, Editors
$19.95/year
(12 issues) from:
Publications International
3841 West Oakton Street
Skokie, IL 60076

•

It's in the Bag: Once in a while, a Hollywood studio would turn out a really demented comedy, and this is one of them. I used to catch this early on Sunday mornings on channel 9 in L.A., but now it must be something of a cult item because it seldom shows up anywhere. Fred Allen plays Fred Floogle, owner of Floogle's Flea Circus, who inherits a fortune stuffed into the lining of one of 12 chairs. He spends the movie tracking down that chair, running into all sorts of oddball characters in the process, including Jack Benny.

The Video Schoolhouse

How-to books, even the best, only guide you so far. At some point a how-to video tape, even a mediocre one, will open up better visual understanding (oh, so that's how it goes!) so that the skill moves from your head to your hand quicker. Someone has finally rounded up all the how-to video tapes available for sale (over 1,000) into a fat mail order catalog. They seem to include everything, poor to fair to excellent: sports coaching, health care material, dancing lessons, and the brightest of the Saturday morning TV do-it-yourself instruction. Self-education rewinds. —KK

•

How to Rebuild Your VW Engine: Video documentary, includes how to check for cracks, check case, warpage, align 40 hp rods, check cam and lifters, check deck height, do end play, assemble crank, assemble "bottom end," how to use a torque wrench, proper ring and piston placement, and much more. (2 hours)
AM022 $49.00

•

Celestial Navigation Simplified: William F. Buckley is your dapper host on this comprehensive tape designed to help sailors navigate by the stars. (60 min.)
BT011 $69.95

•

Quick Dog Training: Barbara Woodhouse demonstrates and explains techniques she uses in her wildly successful dog training classes. (90 min.)
PA022 $59.95

The Video Schoolhouse
Catalog **$2** from:
Video Schoolhouse
2611 Garden Road
Monterey, CA 93940

Leonard Maltin's TV Movies

The boom in home video has spawned its own guidebook industry. Everyone from Pauline Kael to Roger Ebert has a book of reviews designed to help the viewer find his way through the video marketplace. The standby in my house has always been **Leonard Maltin's TV Movies.** *This $5 volume lists over 16,000 films, making it the most comprehensive guide available. Videophiles, late-night TV addicts, 8- and 16mm collectors, and those lucky enough to have a neighborhood repertory house will find Maltin's capsule reviews and 4-star rating system right on target.* —David Burnor

Monster of Piedras Blancas, The (1958) **71m.** *½ D: Irvin Berwick. Les Tremayne, Forrest Lewis, John Harmon, Frank Arvidson, Wayne Berwick. Sluggish chiller with crustacean terror thirsting for blood on a deserted seacoast; obvious and amateurish.
Monster on the Campus (1958) **76m.** **½ D: Jack Arnold. Arthur Franz, Joanna Moore, Judson Pratt, Nancy Walters, Troy Donahue. Above-par chiller involving discovery of prehistoric fish whose blood turns a college professor into rampaging beast.

Leonard Maltin's TV Movies
(1985-1986 Edition)
Leonard Maltin
1984; 1,021 pp.
$4.95
($5.95 postpaid) from:
New American Library
Cash Sales
120 Woodbine Street
Bergenfield, NJ 07621
or Whole Earth Access

Four Arguments for the Elimination of Television

Former adman Jerry Mander denounces the inherent dangers of a system where information is controlled by commercial interests and distorts our perception of reality. Food for thought if you're trying to kick the TV habit. —Fabrice Florin

•

A majority of adults, nearly as high a percentage as children, use television to learn how to handle specific life problems: family routines; relationships with fellow workers; hierarchical values; how to deal with rebellious children; how to understand deviations from the social norm, sexually, politically, socially and interpersonally. The overall fare of television situation-comedies and dramatic programs is taken as valid, useful, informative, and, in the words of the report, "true to life."

Most viewers of television programming give the programming concrete validity, as though it were not fictional. When solving subsequent, similar problems in their own families, people report recalling how the problem was solved in a television version of that situation. They often make similar choices.

•

Even if a given subtle emotion can be conveyed from time to time on TV, you could never build an entire program on it as you could on violent emotions. In signal-to-noise terms the entire program would become indistinct in comparison with the background of more aggressive, expressive and efficient action shows.

Four Arguments for the Elimination of Television
Jerry Mander
1978; 371 pp.
$7.95
($9.45 postpaid) from:
William Morrow
Publishing Company
6 Henderson Drive
West Caldwell, NJ 07006
or Whole Earth Access

INTERACTIVE VIDEO

by Fabrice Florin

INTERACTIVE VIDEO will give you a good reason to turn your TV back on. Rather than watching passively, slumped in an armchair, you drive this video software like a computer program. At the touch of buttons you scan through a storehouse of images and sounds much as you would flip through the pages of a book. With the help of a microcomputer you can rearrange the display of sound and images in a new order, or have it branch in alternative paths for a teaching lesson or game. Like a good book, it encourages multiple readings.

The heart of the new machine is a videodisc, the same glimmering plastic laser videodiscs that play popular movies and, in compact size, music. Each disc becomes an extremely durable visual encyclopedia with up to 54,000 color pages per disc side. A slide collection that large would cost four or five times the price of the disc. It's also the equivalent of several 16mm films, which could justify the purchase of both a player and a disc. Some of the better discs have dual sound tracks. The initial one is for beginners; then you graduate and go through the same images with the advanced sound track. The largest drawback so far is that you cannot *record* images or sounds — you can only play and reorder the prerecorded component images.

Here's where to find some of the best:

Shuttle Reports (NASA).

NASA Space Discs: *Highlights of the Apollo and Space Shuttle missions, with breathtaking spacewalks, spectacular lunar landscapes and some really gorgeous pictures of the Earth from outer space. Half a dozen different discs are available.* **$45.50** each postpaid from Optical Data Corporation, 66 Hanover Rd., Florham Park, NJ 07932.

◄ **King Kong.**

Criterion Collection: *Citizen Kane* ($91.45 postpaid), ***King Kong* ($76.45** postpaid), *and other cinematic milestones, reproduced from the finest prints, with production stills, storyboards and rare outtakes, as well as informative text and audio commentaries.* From Voyager Company, 2139 Manning Ave., Los Angeles, CA 90025.

Discount Videodiscs: *A fine laserdisc mail order house, with thousands of movie titles in stock, as well as dozens of interactive video programs, many at discount prices. Be sure to ask for their useful quarterly newsletter* ***The Laser Beam.*** Catalog **free** from Starship Industries, 605 Utterback Store Rd., Great Falls, VA 22066.

Discount Videodisc Players: *Although this dealer specializes in industrial videodisc equipment, consumers can find some pretty good deals on reconditioned players or brand new models at wholesale prices. Ask for referrals if they don't have what you need.* Catalog **free** from American Technology Resources, 1245 Providence Road, Media, PA 19063.

Interactive Video

Interactive Video
Signe Hoffos and the EPIC team, Editors
1983; 290 pp.

$19.95
($22.95 postpaid) from:
The Videodisc Monitor
P. O. Box 26
Falls Church, VA 22046
or Whole Earth Access

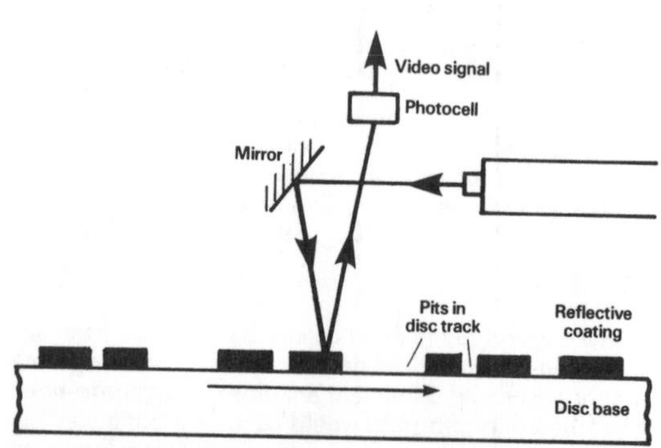

The inner workings of a Philips LaserVision videodisc player.

If you want to learn more about interactive video, this plain-vanilla paperback is the best introduction to the field I know. It is well organized and offers an intelligent overview of how interactive systems work, from consumer to industrial applications. It is marketed in the U.S. by the publishers of ***The Videodisc Monitor,*** *the trade rag of interactive video, and is an excellent source of serious information.* —Fabrice Florin

• Two of several just-hatched newsletters for laser disc (movies, mostly) aficionados. Can't tell which is the better one yet. Try **Disc Deals: $20**/yr. (12 issues) from P. O. Box 391, Pine Lake, GA 30072. Or **Laser Disc Newsletter: $25**/yr. (12 issues) from Suite 428, 496 Hudson St., New York, NY 10014.

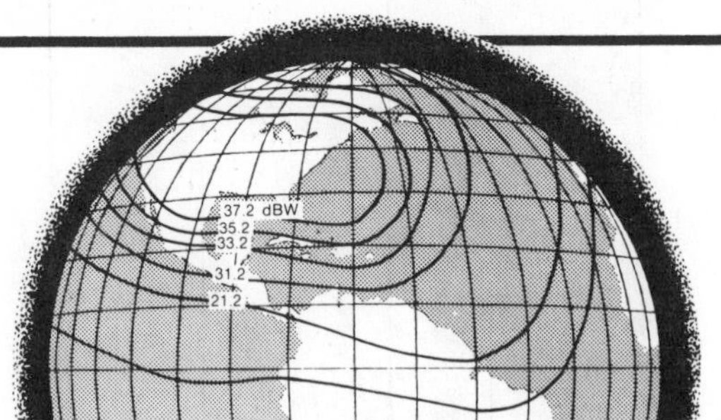

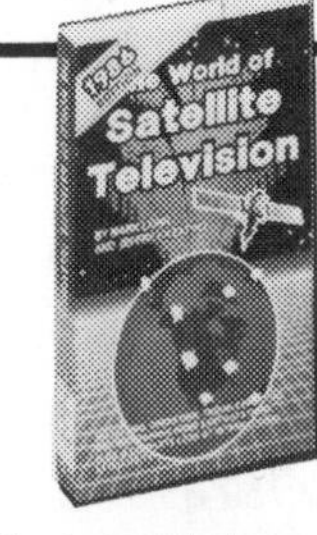

The World of Satellite Television
Mark Long and
Jeffrey Keating
1983; 224 pp.
$10.95
($12.95 postpaid) from:
Quantum Publishing, Inc.
P. O. Box 310
Mendocino, CA 95460
or Whole Earth Access

The World of Satellite Television

The big dummy's guide to installing, operating and maintaining a backyard satellite dish. A basic, sensible, essential initiation to a precision tool. —Kevin Kelly

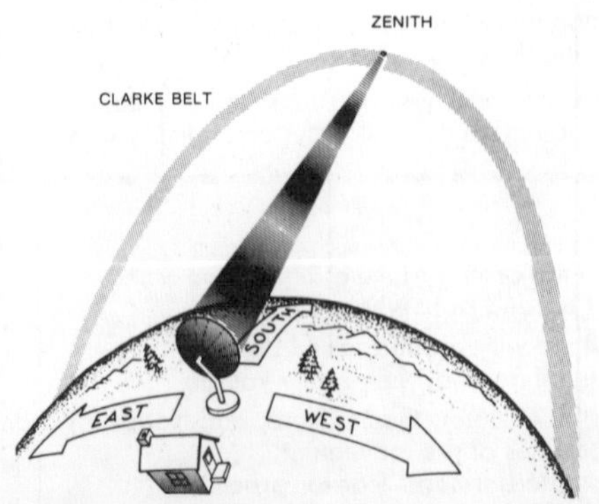

P-611 Satellite Antenna

Build your own backyard earth station antenna entirely from materials available from your local hardware store, lumber yard, and welding shop. The plans are for a strikingly handsome (for a change) and adequately large, 11-foot redwood "dish" with a galvanized steel cloth mesh. Depending on how good a scavenger you are, it'll cost between $300 and $600. If you have to buy the hardware fittings, this company's kit would probably save you money: they ship (via UPS) the cables, bolts, mesh, and feedhorn you need for $435. All this does not include the electronic amplifiers also required. The folks are very helpful. —Kevin Kelly

P-611 Satellite Antenna Plans
$25 postpaid

P-611 Satellite Antenna Kit III
$435 postpaid

Information **free** from Ghost Fighters Inc., 2762 Highway 93, Victorville, MT 59870.

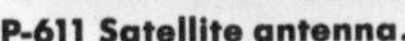
P-611 Satellite antenna.

Home Satellite TV

There's more of a sense of honest revolution here than in the other dozen home-satellite periodicals in print. Sign up and get involved with grassroots crankiness (kidnapping commercial satellites) and hands-on inventiveness that pushes the technological limits of backyard dishes. —Kevin Kelly

•

It is imperative that your dealer check for interference and reception before the actual installation. Microwave interference can come from nearby telephone relay equipment or airport radar, and the result on your set can range from mild to total obstruction of your picture. The cost for filtering out the interference can be prohibitive, so be sure that if, for some unknown reason, your dealer does not check for interference, he gives you a written guarantee that your system will not suffer from this problem.

◄ *In the heart of the city:* A tiny 2½-foot Ku band antenna peers through a plate glass window and just over Manhattan's Chrysler building skyline to see football from across the country. The owner successfully switched to the Ku band system when his apartment house demanded a $100 million insurance policy to allow a C-band dish on the roof.

Home Satellite TV
Bob Wolenik, Editor
$12/year
(6 issues) from:
Miller Magazines
2660 East Main Street
Ventura, CA 93003

Satellite TV Week

Decidedly the best listings for figuring out which program to watch when there are 18 satellites, each delivering three channels on average, in four time zones, beaming down 24 hours a day. Many other contenders' listings are muddled and unwieldy (they come out monthly or fortnightly; this arrives weekly). It has the neatest movie index, which notes every place and every time a particular movie will show. Can't miss it. —Kevin Kelly
[Suggested by Vince Kelly]

"SPLASH" *** (1984, Comedy) Tom Hanks, Daryl Hannah. A New York bachelor without much success at love falls for a beautiful girl who literally washes up on shore, unaware at first that she's the mermaid he saw as a child. 'PG' (CC) (Adult Themes, Brief Nudity) (1 hr., 51 min.)
Sun. *13 [F3] 10:00 pm; 23 [G1] 7:00 pm*

"THE STAR CHAMBER" ** (1983, Drama) Michael Douglas, Hal Holbrook. A dedicated young judge becomes involved with a secret panel of justices directing

"TESTAMENT" *** (1983, Drama) Jane Alexander, William Devane. The aftermath of nuclear holocaust -- from not knowing who launched the attack or why, to the horrors of slow death b radiation poisoning -- and its effects on a northern California family. 'PG' (Adult Situations) (1 hr., 29 min.)
Sun. *10 [G1] 3:30 pm; 13 [F3] 11:00 am, 11:55 pm; 14 [G1] 6:30 pm; 23 [G1] 8:00 am, 8:55 pm*
Thu. *13 [F3] 2:00 pm; 23 [G1] 11:00 am* ***Sat.*** *10 [G1] 10:00 am, 11:45 pm; 14 [G1] 1:00 pm, 2:45 am*

• The rock-bottom lowest prices on satellite dishes — about $1,000 complete.
Jake's Discount Center: P. O. Box 593, 17 South 500 West, Brigham City, UT 84302.

Satellite TV Week
John Ponce, Editor
$48/year
(52 issues) from:
Satellite TV Week
P. O. Box 308
Fortuna, CA 95540

International Folk Dancing U.S.A.
Betty Casey
1981; 363 pp.
$11.25
($12.75 postpaid) from:
Betty Casey
59 Hilltop Drive
Kerrville, TX 78028
or Whole Earth Access

International Folk Dancing U.S.A.

Betty Casey traveled 25,000 miles while researching international folk dancing as practiced in the United States. Her book covers the folk dance scene better than any I've seen. Illustrated with 157 photographs and line diagrams, it contains information about folk dancing history, pioneer leaders in the folk dance movement, guidelines for setting up a group, and descriptions of over 150 dances from 30 different countries and areas worldwide.

The section on folk dance camps and organizations is a helpful guide to finding local folk dance groups. Since most groups tend to stick together for quite a while, chances are that most of those mentioned are still in existence. —Denise Partida

•

Folk dance enthusiasts sometimes bring back differing choreography or music — from the same country. Also, the same dance taught by one teacher may be presented differently by another. How can this happen? Who is right? Perhaps everyone is right.

Dick Crum, noted researcher and choreographer, told of researching dances in a Balkan village where two brothers in the same dance line were doing different steps. How could he write up an instruction sheet? Include both sets of steps and let the dancers decide? Make a selection himself and note that there were also other authentic steps? . . .

"Improvisation permeates most dance traditions beyond the imagination of most American folk dancers."

Aman dancers.

The Complete Book of Square Dancing
Betty Casey
1976; 192 pp.
$12.50
postpaid from:
Doubleday & Company
Direct Mail Order
501 Franklin Avenue
Garden City, NY 11530
or Whole Earth Access

The Complete Book of Square Dancing

Swing your partner just like your grandparents did; square dancing is a uniquely American tradition. In recent years, the 85 basic moves, known as "mainstream," have been standardized so you can dance without ineptitude anywhere there's a group squarin' up. The moves, plus a bit about calling them, are nicely diagrammed, photographed, and explained so you can get a head start on learning or bone up for teaching. Round dancing is explained, too. Yee HAH! —JB

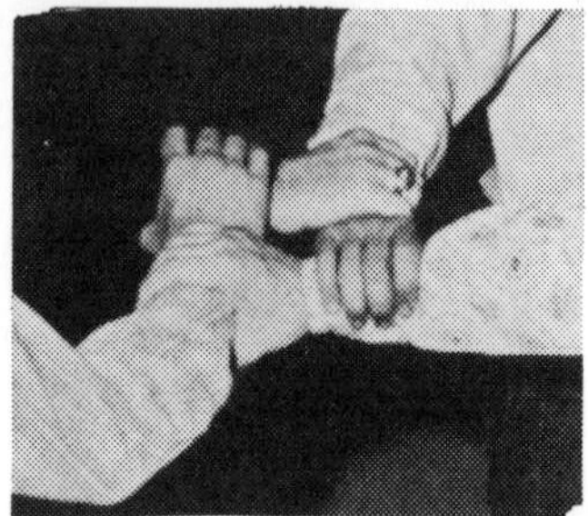

"Pack saddle" star.

•

Call:
*All** to the center, *Make a Right-hand Star*†
Turn it around right where you are
Go all the way around, don't be slow
Dance full around, then home you go.

*Substitute *Ladies, Gents, Sides,* and *Heads* for practice in other uses of the movement.
†Substitute *Left-hand Star* for practice.

Viltis
Vytautas F. Beliajus, Editor
$15/year
(6 issues) from:
Viltis
P. O. Box 1226
Denver, CO 80201

Viltis

Lively and eclectic, **Viltis** *is considered by many to be the folk dancing magazine. Along with the news and views, you get recipes and travel stories from folks bringing back new dances from afar.* **Viltis** *is one of those rare labors of love, and looks it. Editor Vytautas F. Beliajus has been at it since 1942.* —Denise Partida

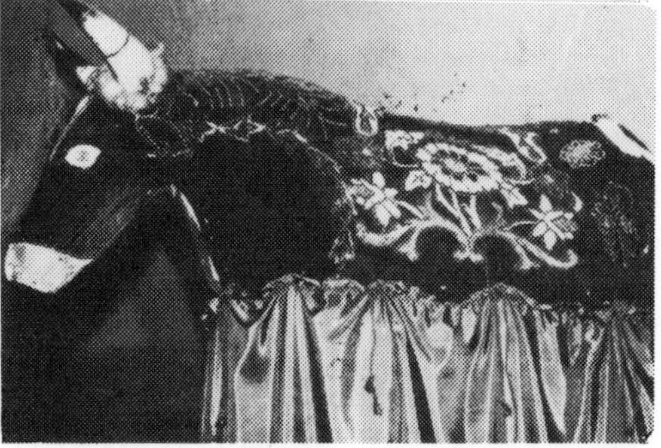

A "bull" costume for folk dance.

Folkraft Records

The catalog for Folkraft Records lists over 700 records (7", 45 rpm) for folk dances from all over the world. Margin notes tell you what each dance is; for example, D'Hammerschmiedsgselln *is a Bavarian mixer for two couples or four men, while* Szatmari Karikaza *is a Hungarian circle dance for women. You get the idea . . .*

Each record is mailed out with accompanying instructions for the dance or dances on it. The Folkraft label also has records for square and contra dances, rhythm studies, and exercise and fitness music. Dance Record Distributors, Ltd. can obtain the recordings of every other record company worldwide for teachers and libraries. —Denise Partida

Folkraft Records
$3-$4.50
Catalog **free** from:
Dance Records Distributors
P. O. Box 102
Florham Park, NJ 07932-0102

•

Ibo — Africa	*DB115
In The Green Meadow — Czech	1168
Itik Itik — Philippine	M517
Jove Male Mome — Bulgaria (line)	1526
Limbo Rock — Caribbean	1523
Little Blacksmith (mixer) — Baltic	1418
Little Brown Gal — Hawaii	M60151
Lott Is Dead (mixer) — Baltic	1419

Records are 7" 45 RPM. *$3.25 **$3.50

• See 'Music by Mail" (p. 342-343).

• For fancy ethnic clothing, see Folkwear (p. 147).

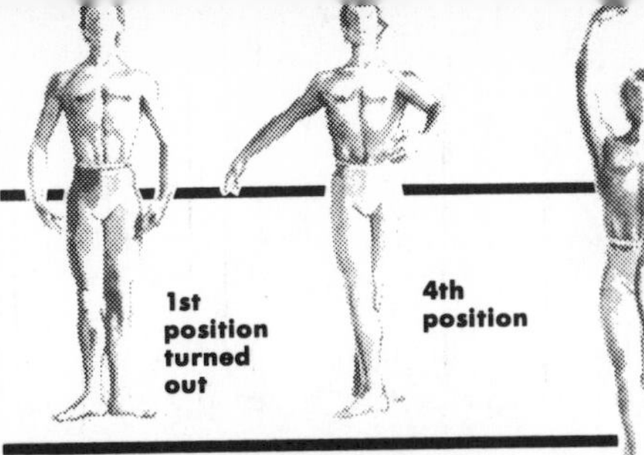

The Dance Workshop • On the Count of One: Modern Dance Methods

I love to dance. Since the age of five I've been moving to music aided and encouraged by my mother, who shares my love. I was hesitant to review books on dance because there is no music and you are sitting on your butt instead of moving about. But I remembered spending hours staring at my mother's book on ballet — copying over and over the different positions the stick figures were doing. ***The Dance Workshop*** *can be used in the same way. It starts off with warm-up exercises (very important if you want to spare yourself lots of pain) and progresses to positions, steps, and movements basic to all forms of dance. Instead of stick figures there are graceful drawings of people doing the movements step by step.*

If you know the basics and really want to leap into the subject, modern dance in particular, then ***On the Count of One: Modern Dance Methods*** *is the book you want. A very thorough and technical look at dance, discussing music, vocabulary, technique, and the teaching of modern dance.*

The best thing to do is to take a dance class at your local JC, dance studio, or park recreation department, move with the music and use these books to help you further understand and enjoy this marvelous art.
—Susan Erkel Ryan [Suggested by David Jouris]

•

All artistic expression is based on craft, the technical control of a given instrument of expression. In dance, the instrument is the human body, and the craft is inseparably connected with science, which, in this case, is a thorough knowledge of anatomical structure and the principles of kinesiology. This science is needed to ensure the dancer's safety and effectiveness of movement.
—*On the Count of One*

▲ *The Basic Positions of Dance*
In order to exercise well, it is important to know exactly where your body is in a given space. The body positions shown here are basic to dance all over the world, because they are basic to our body shape and function. It is important to learn them well since it is easier to execute any movement with care and precision if you have a formal position to start from and return to. The positions known as 1st and 2nd can be done either with the legs turned out or with the legs parallel.
—*The Dance Workshop*

Side Stretches ►
All dancers must acquire, and then maintain, a high degree of flexibility in the hip sockets. The more flexible you are, the easier it is to move. No matter how stiff you may feel, everyone is capable of improving their ability to stretch. All you need is the right mental approach and plenty of practice.
—*The Dance Workshop*

—Dance Workshop

The Dance Workshop
Robert Cohan
1986; 192 pp.
$9.95
postpaid from:
Simon & Schuster
Mail Order Sales
200 Old Tappan Road
Old Tappan, NJ 07675
or Whole Earth Access

On the Count of One
(Modern Dance Methods)
Elizabeth Sherbon
1982; 284 pp.
$16.95
($18.95 postpaid) from:
Mayfield Publishing Co.
285 Hamilton Ave.
Palo Alto, CA 94301
or Whole Earth Access

Dancing entails a different kind of focus.

Dancing

Dance may not be something to learn from a book, but this book serves as a great introduction to those of us who are beguiled and yet intimidated by the idea of dancing. Addressed both to the hesitant adult beginner who prances around the house when nobody's looking and to the young adult considering a career in dance, ***Dancing*** *cuts through a lot of the mystique and mistaken glamour with practical, specific advice: choosing a style of dance, finding a good teacher and getting the most out of a class, preventing injury, and even viewing dance.*

A real aid for parents who want to get their youngsters started off on the right foot — both daughters and sons (plenty of photos of men dancing, though most of the pronouns are "she"). Competent directory of dance resources around the country, with special emphasis on New York.

Dancing *does what no elegant dance picture book can do: makes it plain that you can dance even if you don't look like a Capezio ad.* *—Nancy E. Dunn*

•

A good class has a thorough warm-up with adequate time to establish alignment and placement. The teacher should be constructive and inspiring, and should push you beyond your limits physically by increasing your range of movement and strength; and mentally, by breaking through barriers of fear. Avoid an inhibiting atmosphere in which too much discipline prevents you from making mistakes and learning from them; a frustrated, negative teacher; overcrowded classes, and rushed classes, especially the warm-up.

Dancing
Ellen Jacob
1981; 350 pp.
$11.95
($13.20 postpaid) from:
Variety Arts
305 Riverside Drive
Suite 4A
New York, NY 10025
or Whole Earth Access

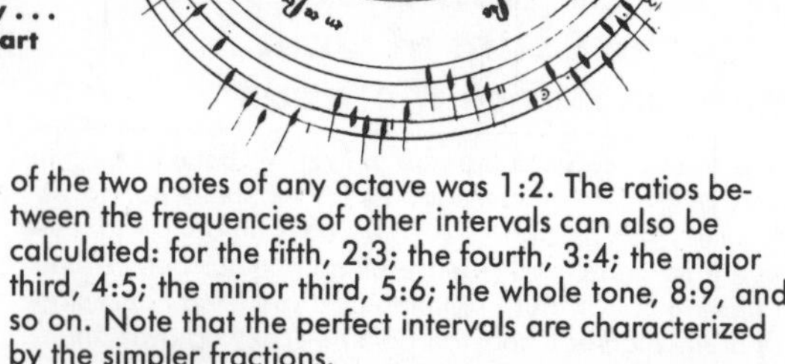

Introducing Music
Otto Karolyi
1965; 175 pp.

$4.95
($5.95 postpaid) from:
Viking Penguin Books
299 Murray Hill Pkwy.
East Rutherford, NJ 07073
or Whole Earth Access

Introducing Music

Limpidly clear introduction to reading and understanding music. —*Stewart Brand*

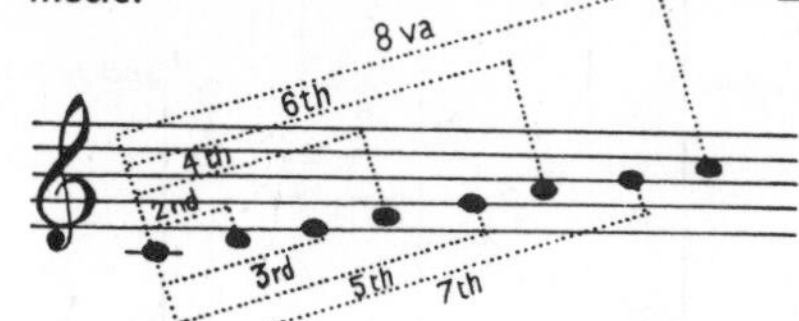

If only the whole world could feel the power of harmony . . . —Mozart

▲

Perfect intervals are the unison, fourth, fifth, and octave. The remaining intervals such as the second, third, sixth, and seventh are *major intervals*. If a major interval is reduced by a semitone we get a *minor interval*; thus C to E is a major third, but C to E♭ is a minor third; C to D is a major second, but C to D♭ is a minor second; and so on. We have seen that the ratio between the frequencies of the two notes of any octave was 1:2. The ratios between the frequencies of other intervals can also be calculated: for the fifth, 2:3; the fourth, 3:4; the major third, 4:5; the minor third, 5:6; the whole tone, 8:9, and so on. Note that the perfect intervals are characterized by the simpler fractions.

Musics of Many Cultures
Elizabeth May, Editor
1980; 434 pp.

$19.95
($21.45 postpaid) from:
University of
California Press
2120 Berkeley Way
Berkeley, CA 94720
or Whole Earth Access

Musics of Many Cultures

As much as can be put down on paper, here is the music springing from human life on Earth. This book speaks about structure, role in culture, and history of ethnic musics around the world, and gives a thoroughly handy film bibliography and album discography so you can dip to one corner of the world, get comfortable, and become lost in the stirring songs others make. Comes with three floppy records to get you started. —*Kevin Kelly*

A *bonang barung* of a gamelan.

The Tuning of the World
R. Murray Schafer
1977; 301 pp.

$13.95
postpaid from:
University of
Pennsylvania Press
Blockley Hall
418 Service Drive, Floor 13
Philadelphia, PA 19104
or Whole Earth Access

The Tuning of the World

One of the most remarkable books on sound around. The author charts the geography and history of our sonic environment — our soundscape. No type of noise, roar, clatter, hiss, twang, vibration, or audible rhythm escapes his notice. For instance, he discovered European towns hum at harmonies of G sharp (50 hertz power supply), while America drones at B natural (60 hertz). He divides our surroundings into dominant tonal patterns, mapping out the evolution of sound on Earth. Other topics discussed: Sacred sounds, the concert hall as a substitute for outdoor life, the intent of Muzak, sounds of water creatures, sound imperialism, ceremonies about silence, and taboo sounds. A marvelous, awakening book. —*Charlie Bremer.*

•

The rhythms of all poetry and recited literature bear a relationship to breathing patterns. When the sentence is long and natural, a relaxed breathing style is expected; when irregular or jumpy, an erratic breath pattern is suggested. Compare the jabbing style of twentieth-century verse with the more relaxed lines of that which preceded it. *Something* has happened between Pope and Pound, and that something is very likely the accumulation of syncopations and offbeats in the soundscape. And the perceptible jitteriness in Pound's verse begins after he has moved from rural life in America to the big city of London. Just as human conversational style is abbreviated by the telephone bell, contemporary verse bears the marks of having dodged the acoustic shrapnel of modern life. Car horns punctuate modern verse, not bubbling brooks.

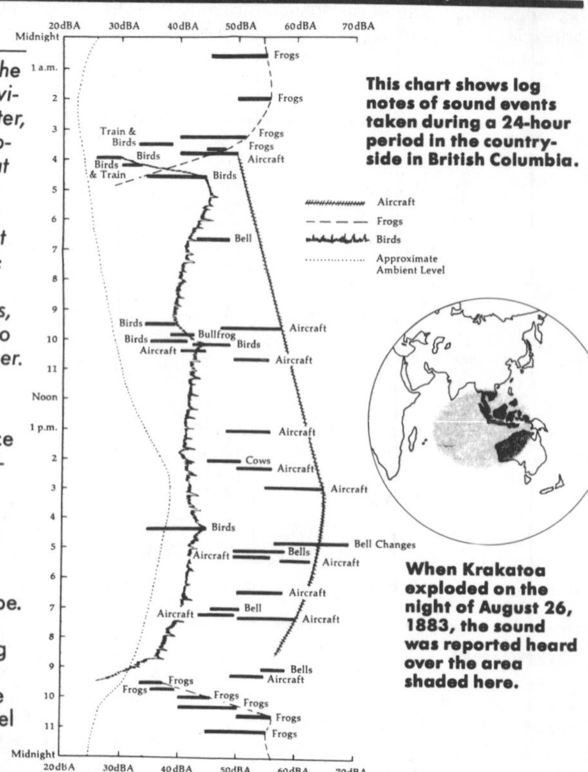

This chart shows log notes of sound events taken during a 24-hour period in the countryside in British Columbia.

When Krakatoa exploded on the night of August 26, 1883, the sound was reported heard over the area shaded here.

1 2 3

At the base of the keyboard are three numbered arrows. One of them covers exactly an octave on the keyboard; the other two do not. Which arrow points out an octave?

Basic Concepts in Music

An interesting and useful programmed text designed to accommodate both the absolute ignoramus and the person with any degree of musical experience. Covers basic components of music notation; notational components of rhythm and melody; harmonic structure of basic intervals and chords; major and minor scales, chords and keys; and the basic structure of music. The child who can read can progress through the book at his own rate; the parent with a piano or penny-whistle and some sheet music at his disposal can learn much to pass on to the children.
—Carol Van Strum

Even if two white keys do not have a black key between them, the two keys are still a half step apart.

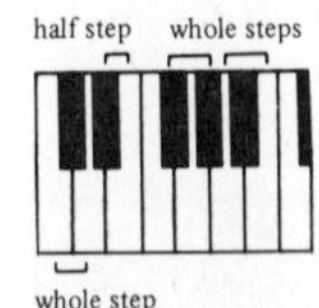
half step
whole steps
whole step

The mathematical relationship of music notes is illustrated on the right. Observe the two ways of writing eighth and sixteenth notes shown in the chart—with flags or with connecting beams. There is absolutely no difference in time value between the two ways of writing eighth notes.

or
or

Traditional American Folk Songs

For 40 years, starting in 1938, Anne and Frank Warner collected folk songs along the rural backroads of the Eastern Seaboard. Frank was a poor folk singer himself and so was able to win the confidence of wary mountain folk like F. Proffitt, who first sang them "Tom Dooley." The Warners did angelic work. For the 200 songs they transcribed in this bountiful book, they record the players' own story of how they learnt the song and where they think it came from. The Warners reprint personal, fascinating correspondence with the artists and often a snapshot of the scene. They clearly portray the songs they received as gifts from the makers to the listeners. What we are given: music as community.
—Kevin Kelly

Her old father came this to know,
That his daughter loved me so.
He cursed, he swore among them all,
He swore he'd use the cannon ball.

He come home so late in the night,
Inquirin' for his heart's delight.
Upstairs he run, the door he broke,
He found her hung by her own bed rope.

Out with his knife, and he cut her down,
All in her bosom a letter he found,
Said, "Dig my grave both deep and wide,
And bury sweet William by my side."

"All on my breast a snowy white dove
To show to the world I died for love."

Composing Music

This takes a pragmatic approach to teaching composition. It begins with no rules and few instructions, assumes you can read and write a tiny bit, and hands you a very simple composition assignment. Gently, by chapters, it presents traditional composing concepts, including easy work on harmony, melody structure, use of motifs, and so on. The beauty of this approach is that there is no right or wrong, no correct results — it is for you to try your wings.

The second half of the book deals with writing for instruments available to you with techniques in popular music, and with a look at a few concepts from modern "serious" music. This is a wonderful book for anyone who is developing improvising skills or who would like a fun way to explore music.
—Jim Stockford

•

Get in touch with your voice and your ear. Sing as you compose and find the tones through what you sing. Playing the piano (or some other instrument) will, of course, help develop your ear, but your main aim should be to get the music in your ear and voice as well as in your mind and fingers. Learn to sing, tone by tone, what you compose, *while* you are composing it. You should also be able to sing the *completed* series of tones.

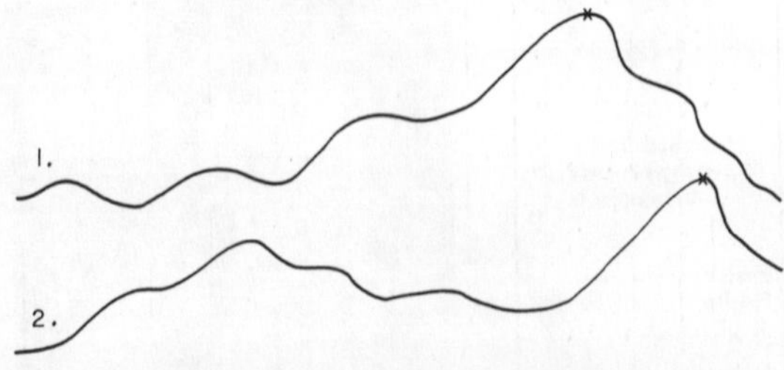
1.
2.

Picture music includes all music that is written without actual tones. Sometimes this type of music looks more like a drawing than a piece of music, as you will see later in this chapter.

When writing two or more simultaneous melodies, make sure that they do not have identical curves.

Try to have melodies that have *different* shapes — that reach their peaks at different points.

A RUDE AND RAMBLING BOY

A rude and a ram - bling boy I am, A rude and ram - bling boy — I'll
be. I'd give this world, I am but sure, If I knew she loved me so.
• 1st verse

Nathan Hicks, luthier, and his family. Valle Crucis, NC (1938).

Basic Concepts in Music
Gary M. Martin
1980; 288 pp.
$21.75 postpaid from:
Wadsworth Publishing Co.
7625 Empire Drive
Florence, KY 41042
or Whole Earth Access

Composing Music
William Russo
with Jeffrey Ainis
and David Stevenson
1983; 230 pp.
$12.95 postpaid from:
Prentice-Hall Inc.
Mail Order Sales
200 Old Tappan Road
Old Tappan, NJ 07675
or Whole Earth Access

Traditional American Folk Songs
Anne Warner
1984; 501 pp.
$25.95
($27.45 postpaid) from:
Syracuse University Press
1600 Jamesville Avenue
Syracuse, NY 13244-5160
or Whole Earth Access

• An exemplary guide to a versatile musical instrument — even veteran players will pick up a net tip or two.
The Guitar Owner's Manual: Will Martin, 1983; 107 pp. **$6.95** postpaid from W. W. Norton, 500 Fifth Avenue, New York, NY 10110.

• The original and best folksong periodical in print. It retains the folksy spirit of Pete Seeger, who helped to start it.
Sing Out: $11/year (4 issues) from P. O. Box 1071, Easton, PA 18042.

Sound Designs • Vibrations

"That's not REAL music," whispered an elderly woman to her companion as they watched my friend play exotic drums. "He's just making it up."

Not only that, ladies, he made up the instruments. They were slit drums — oblong wooden boxes with slits on top that formed tuned bars. You'll find slit drum designs, and other fanciful instruments, in these two books. Musical instruments can be created out of almost anything, and making them up is the most exemplary music education there is, especially for kids. Many of the designs discussed here started out as simple folk instruments somewhere else in the world. They are adapted, improved, and presented with directions for constructing them out of modern materials, store-bought or scrap. They make real music. ***Sound Designs****, the stronger of the two books, emphasizes instruments that you strike, while* ***Vibrations*** *tackles a few that you pluck.* —Kevin Kelly

Sound Design
Reinhold Banek
and Jon Scoville
1980; 209 pp.
$8.95
($9.95 postpaid) from:
Ten Speed Press
P. O. Box 7123
Berkeley, CA 94707
or Whole Earth Access

Vibrations
David Sawyer
1977; 102 pp.
$12.95 postpaid from:
Cambridge
University Press
510 North Avenue
New Rochelle, NY 10801
or Whole Earth Access

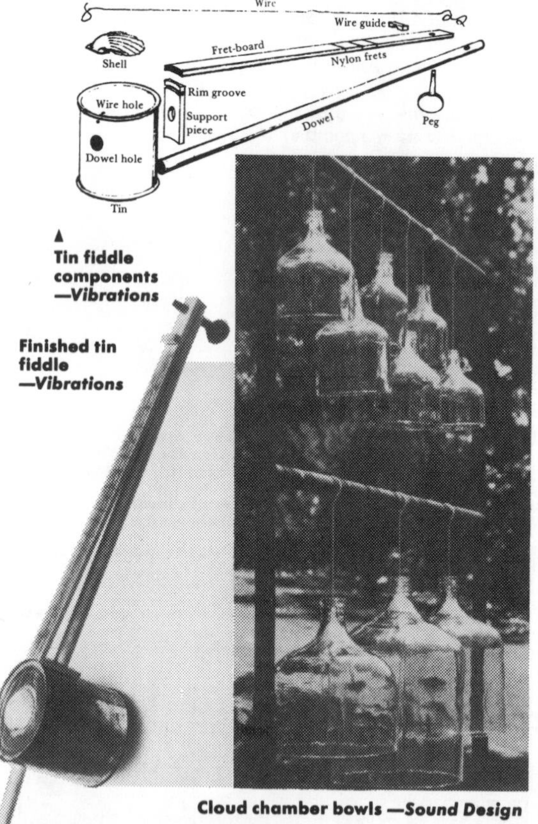

▲ **Tin fiddle components —*Vibrations***

Finished tin fiddle —*Vibrations*

Cloud chamber bowls —*Sound Design*

Thumb piano —*Sound Design*

Experimental Musical Instruments
Bart Hopkin, Editor
$20/year
(6 issues) from:
Experimental Musical
Instruments
P. O. Box 784
Nicasio, CA 94946

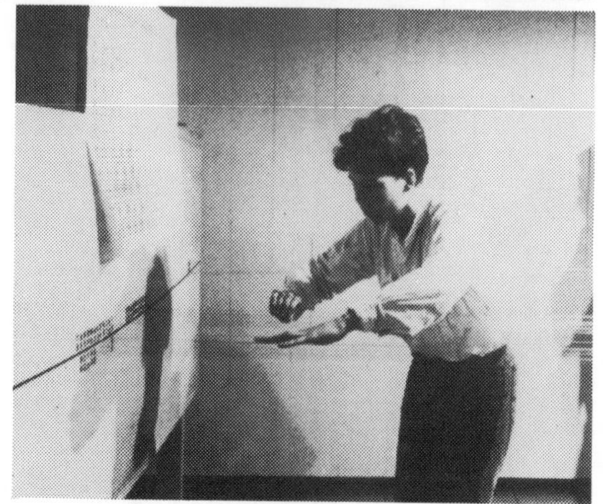

◄ **Ellen Fullman plays the Long String Instrument. The most recent manifestation of the instrument has fourteen strings in two groups of seven. Their full length is ninety feet. At one end the strings are attached to some stable surface, such as a wall. At the opposite end the strings are secured to a rectangular soundboard, eight inches by fifty-nine inches, made of spruce.**

Musical Instruments of the World

With sufficient cleverness I daresay you could cobble together some damned interesting instruments just by close attention to the illustrations, profuse (4,000) and detailed as they are, in this absorbing survey of the world's noise-makers. —Stewart Brand

Musical Instruments of the World
Ruth Midgley, Editor
1980; 320 pp.
$14.95 postpaid from:
Facts on File
460 Park Avenue South
New York, NY 10016
or Whole Earth Access

Experimental Musical Instruments

The next step following a successful revolution is to build new kinds of tools to overthrow the next success. After the acceptance of far-out music, here come radically insurgent instruments — harps 50 feet long, steel cellos, drums that float on water, and devices that amplify the natural micro-sounds of a fly heartbeat or a seedling sprouting. All are discussed in this fascinating newsletter with great emphasis on trying out newly invented apparati that make musical sounds. —Kevin Kelly
[Suggested by Roger Hoffman]

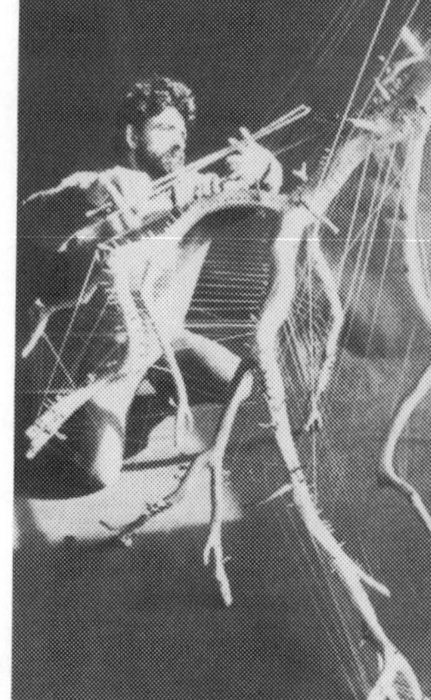

► **The Semi-Civilized Tree**

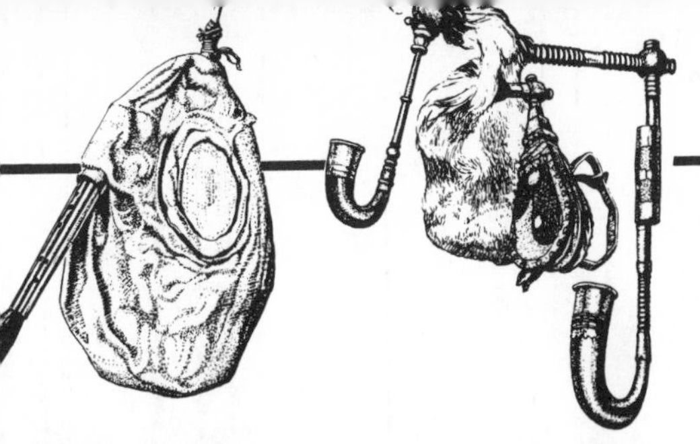

(Left to right) Bagpipes: Arab, Tunisian, Yugoslavian, Russian, Bohemian.—*Musical Instruments of the World*

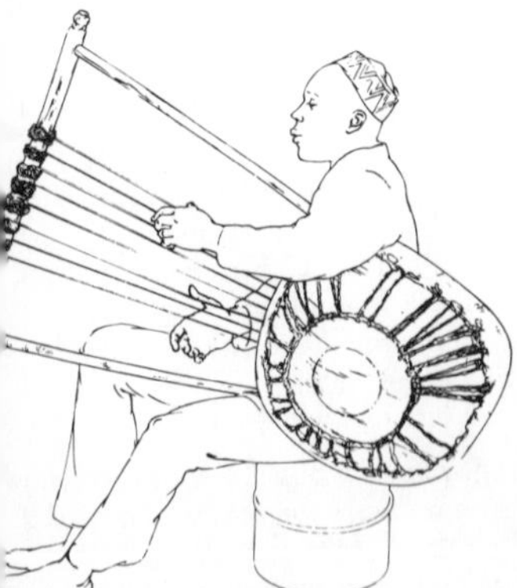

A Kenyan musician playing the obukano, a large bowl-shaped lyre that has been described as "the double bass of East Africa." This instrument has eight strings, tuned by adjusting the rings on the crossbar. It is played with the fingers. Smaller lyres are also widely found in Kenya.

Elderly Instruments

If the Lord came down and told me She was going to zap all guitar stores into oblivion except for one and that I should name the sole survivor, I guess I would have to name Elderly Music. They sell just about any stringed instrument you'd want — guitars, dobros, mandolins, banjos, and so on, with spare parts, accessories, and gizmos — and Elderly is the only place I know of that sells used instruments by mail. Each of their four catalogs is thick, with small print. They have the biggest, best selection of American folk music books and records that I've seen, and I used to wholesale the stuff.
—James Stockford
[Suggested by Warren Allen]

•

Anglo (or German) Concertinas produce 2 different notes on the same button (push-pull). The Anglo is used often by singers and to play Morris dance tunes.

Elderly Instruments
Instrument Catalog,
Book Catalog,
Record Catalog
$2 each
Electric Guitars and Accessories Catalog
$1 from:
Elderly Instruments
1100 North Washington
P. O. Box 14210
Lansing, MI 48901

The Luthier's Mercantile
Catalog
$3 from:
P. O. Box 774
412 Moore Lane
Healdsburg, CA 95448

Musical Saw

I play saw. It's the easiest instrument to learn except maybe for kazoo — you can get into it in a week or two well enough to show off. People generally eat it up: "Hey look . . . he's playing a SAW!" What I like best is being able to sit in on some good bluegrass (the slow numbers). Hank Williams tunes are just right. You can get together with other saw-ers and do barbershop harmony too. Yes, you can probably play the saw you have hanging in the garage, but even the best of them (Sandvik or Disston) will only give you an octave or so. This professional saw gets a good two octaves and sounds fine wailing along as harmony with a fiddle. No particular skill needed except you have to be able to carry a tune. *—JB*

The Luthier's Mercantile

Materials, tools, supplies, and advice for the lofty craft of building traditional stringed instruments. Slightly more than a catalog, this publication also has articles on workshop tips and luthier tool techniques. *—Doug Roomian*

Rosette: black, white, brown, red. Largest ring width of any rosette we carry. Inside diameter 93mm. Ring width 24mm.

European classic style machine heads — mechanically identical to EMG but brass hand engraving on "gun metal" black background. Pearloid buttons, plastic rollers, with lyre. Post hole spacing 70mm.

Homespun Tapes

You've had your fiddle long enough to play a few songs, but you really wonder how those Irish players get that certain sound. Well, Irish fiddle master Kevin Burke might not be available for private lessons, but you can get the next best thing — his lessons on tape. You choose the time and place, and you will never be embarrassed by not having practiced enough for your next lesson.

Six 60-minute tapes and accompanying sheet music take you from simple hornpipe tunes to elaborate reels with ornamenting grace notes and rolls. The tapes play each song slowly, naming notes and repeating sections, so even if you don't read music you can follow along.

In addition to songs there are lots of helpful playing hints, encouragement, and information on where to hear other versions of the material. *—Kathleen O'Neill*

•

Blues Harmonica
taught by John Sebastian and Paul Butterfield
John Sebastian starts at the beginning, teaching on the first three tapes the rudiments of playing, concentrating on the mechanics: tonguing, breathing, reed bending, vibrato, etc. In an amusing, informal manner, he shows a number of licks and instrumentals while providing you with the tools to go on to more advanced playing.

Paul Butterfield picks it up where John leaves off, and on tapes 4-6 you'll discover the way a great bluesman thinks about his music and his instrument. Paul discusses the finer points of technique, including some advice about electric harp.

Price: $12.95 each. $65 for the entire series of six, plus postage.

Paul Butterfield, John Sebastian

Homespun Tapes
Catalog
$1 from:
Homespun Tapes
P. O. Box 694
Woodstock, NY 12498

• Basic, specific, conservative, sympathetic, relaxed and condensed.
The Guitar Owner's Manual: Will Martin, 1983; 107 pp.
$6.95 ($7.95 postpaid) from W. W. Norton, 500 Fifth Avenue, New York, NY 10110.

Tenor Musical Saw
$38.45 postpaid
Kit (with mallet, bow, case, etc., in addition to saw):
$63 postpaid
Information **free**
All from:
Mussehl and Westphal
130 South 4th Street
Delavan, WI 53115

Yamaha DX-7
$2095
Information **free** from:
Yamaha International Corporation
P. O. Box 6600
Buena Park, CA 90622

Casio CZ-101
$349
Information **free** from:
EMP
2915 South 160th Street
New Berlin, WI 53151

MIDI for Musicians
Craig Anderton
1986; 105 pp.
$14.95
($16.45 postpaid) from:
Music Sales Corp.
Distribution Center
P. O. Box 572
Chester, NY 10918
or Whole Earth Access

Electronic Music

There are two clear winners among the many, many electronic musical instruments on the market: Casio's CZ-101 and Yamaha's DX-7. If your budget allows, buy both. If not, buy the first one, then the other later when you can afford it. I recommend these partly because they are very capable instruments with a wide variety of sound possibilities and partly because these are the most widely purchased instruments in the market.

Each offers customizable sound capabilities. Each lets you play several different sounding noises at the same time (polyphonic). Each has many preset sounds, so you can play right away without having to create your own tones. The differences? The more expensive DX-7 has more buttons and a bigger, heftier keyboard while the CZ-101 has fewer control buttons and that "inexpensive" feel. Both create their sounds using the FM synthesis method, yet each has its characteristic albeit subtle color.

Both the DX-7 and CZ-101 are tremendously popular. The former has single-handedly deposed the lead guitar from the limelight role in popular music — most serious musicians own or have access to a sturdy DX-7. The CZ-101 offers FM synthesis for a small fraction of the DX-7's price and is generally available from mass merchandisers at a discount or on a time-payment basis. If recommending the two most ubiquitous instruments seems to be superficial, let me reassure you that the reverse is true. Machines should be as transparent as possible. The machine should allow possibilities, not limit them. The best computerized machine (and you can't walk into a music store any longer to play a keyboard unless it is connected to a computer) is that which has the most and the best software written for it. If you want the greatest flexibility, you must choose the machine which hosts the greatest amount of software development — the most popular machine.

This monopolist philosophy makes it possible for developers to pour in money to create software imitations of a grand piano, a bassoon, or the sound of the sea. Both of these keyboards let you pick and choose among the latest sounds of session musicians working in the big studios for the big record labels. Simply put, the DX-7 and CZ-101 offer you the widest choices for synthesized music.
—Jim Stockford

All the features and functions of the CZ-1000 in a mini keyboard configuration. Battery powered operation allows full portability.
■ DIMENSIONS: 676(W) × 208(D) × 70(H) mm (26⁵/₈"(W) × 3³/₁₆"(D) × 2³/₄"(H)) ■ WEIGHT: 3.2 kg (7.1 lb) INCLUDING DRY CELLS

Yamaha DX-7 (inset: Casio C2-101).

MIDI for Musicians

Electronic technology has recently given musicians several powerful tools: synthesizers, sound samplers (devices which store sounds as digital information), sequencers, and editors (devices which store sequences of sounds and give the musician the power to delete or add notes or parts, to play passages at various speeds, to change the order of parts, and to write compositions in step time and then play them back in real time. However, for many years each manufacturer had a different standard. A Yamaha sequencer, for example, might not work properly to sequence a part played on a Roland synthesizer. In order to allow various musical instruments and computers to work with each other regardless of the manufacturer, a standard format was developed called MIDI, Musical Instrument Digital Interface. This is a brand new technology (it's only been around since 1983). It gives musicians tremendous power to compose and record. This is the book that best explains what MIDI is and does.
—Rob Griffin

•

Due to the rapid rate of technological change, instruments often became obsolete within a few months after their introduction. Eventually keyboard players were almost afraid to buy anything because they felt that a newer, better version would be introduced soon. Although MIDI hasn't put an end to this problem, it has certainly helped extend the useful life of a piece of equipment by making it compatible with newer devices.

Computer Music Journal
Curtis Roads, Editor
$26/year
(4 issues) from:
MIT Press Journals Dept.
28 Carleton Street
Cambridge, MA 02142

Computer Music Journal

The international experts cover everything about computer music in this quarterly. Upcoming symposiums and scholarly dialogue on the latest systems and techniques. Good reviews of the newest products and publications. Sometimes includes a special soundsheet or flexi-disc with examples of some wonderful music. There is no more authoritative place to get information on the subject.
—Tim Ennis

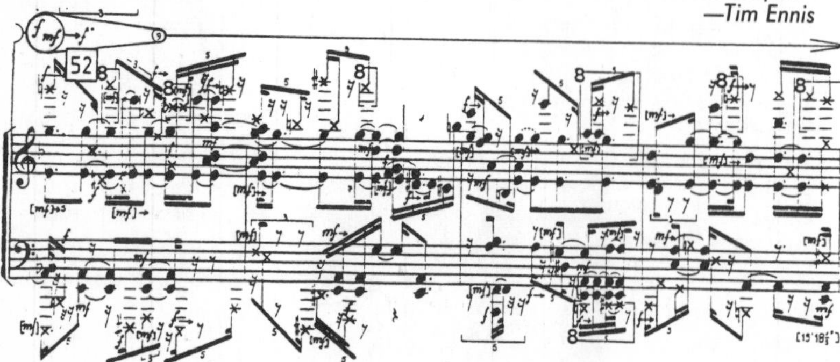

Excerpt from the score of *Cogluotobusisletmesi* by Clarence Barlow.

•

The robot is designed to track a human singer who sings into a microphone connected to the system. The robot plays the organ along with the human, with tempo regulated in part by the vocalist. For pitch analysis, a system of five narrowly tuned bandpass filters is used to derive a fundamental frequency every 30 msec. If the singer is out of tune, the organ player can adjust the tuning of the organ for a more euphonious ensemble effect. Ironically, the robot musician cannot hear its own performance.

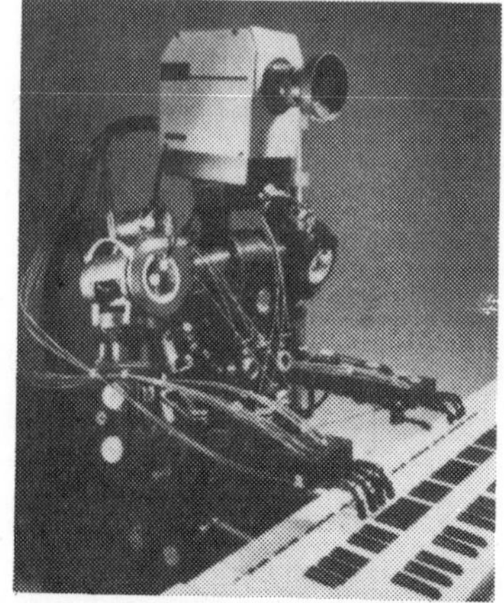

Unsound

There is something going on here, but I don't know what it is, do I, Mr. Jones? Whatever it is, it's happening in that twilight between music, theatre, visual art, and American pop technology. Bands play "industrial noise" (metal grating, endless loops of screeching rhythms stolen from other recorded music). They advertise their performances with the instant litter of xerox leaflets, and produce home-brewed cassette tapes in uninhibited innovation. Sizzling through this magazine is the raw, urban energy of hardware culture art.
—Kevin Kelly

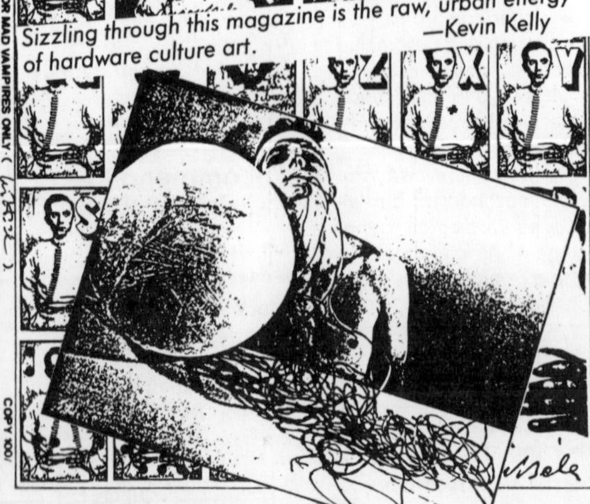

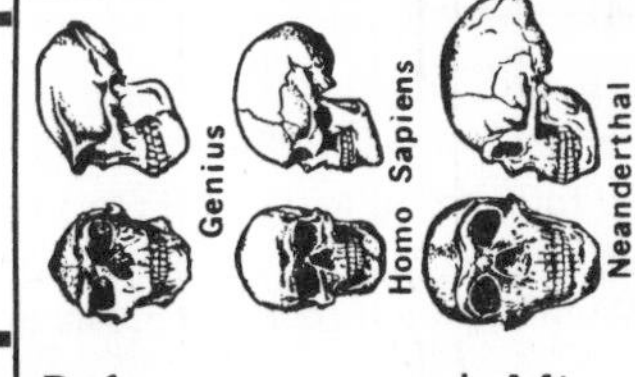

OPtion

The most interesting service of this funky magazine is that it candidly reviews zillions of small-label cassettes of weird new musics like "trance" sounds, experimental acoustics, amplified rants, noise tapes, and just plain wacky music. Almost all of these grassroots recordings are only available via mail, so the complete addresses of the artists are given. With high-quality recording gear so affordable, any garage can become a center for never-before-heard sounds, dilating our narrow idea of music.

Besides unflinching reviews of independent tapes, this fairly hefty magazine pays attention to unusual commercial releases and exotic ethnic recordings.
—Kevin Kelly

MOSTLY OCEAN Interesting and enjoyable acoustic (and some electric) guitar improvisations in cyclic structures, with diagrams instead of names, plus some ensemble music (with percussion, bass, keyboard, vocals). (172 Murray St., Binghampton, NY 13905, C46, $6)

MINOY: "Lunar Eclipse/Chinese Reflecting Pool" "Lunar Eclipse" maintains the sensation of overcrowding and paranoia for over 20 minutes. "Chinese Reflecting Pool" is a bit more sparse and pentatonic. The synths could be wooden flutes. Well-recorded on chrome tape. (923 W. 232 St., Torrance, CA 90502, $6 postpaid)—MS

37 PINK: Corrective Justice The thing I like about noise bands is that they force listener participation. Like, is the noise coming out of my speakers what the band recorded on the tape or is it the sound of my cassette deck going berserk and shredding the tape? 37 Pink is a hardcore noise band. Rhythmic, pulsing white noise static combines with high-pitched oscillations to form a spacy industrial background, upon which muffled vocals and tape loops are sometimes overlaid. If you're curious about noise bands, this is a good and inexpensive place to start. (Box 55502, Tucson AZ 85703-5502, C45, $4)—BM

JUSTIN SARAGOZA: Ode to Sammy Davis Jr. This eccentric (but nice) tape was "recorded as an improvisation for any instrument and a prepared tape." Basically, it's a lot of noodling and experimentation with a solo electric guitar. What the tie-in with Sammy Davis Jr. is, I'm not sure of, since the music here bears no resemblance to his, but this tape makes for pleasant listening. No price listed, so it seems this might be a good contact for all the tape swappers out there (but write first). (4855 W. Warm Springs, Las Vegas, NV 89118, one-sided C60) BM

OPtion
Scott Becker, Editor
$12/year
(6 issues) from:
Sonic Options Network
P. O. Box 491034
Los Angeles, CA 90049

Unsound
William Davenport, Editor
$12/year
(4 issues) from:
Unsound
801 22nd Street
San Francisco, CA 94107

Sound Choice

Another offshoot of the defunct OP journal, Sound Choice, like OPtion, is a slightly scruffy but very fun magazine devoted to widening the distribution of independently-produced records and audio cassettes; emphasis on punk, electronically synthesized music, found sound, poetry, and ambient noise. Lots of reviews, source addresses, and ads for off-beat hearables.
—Robert Horvitz

These guys are a little more out on the fringe, pushing the envelope of acceptability. Recent articles cover clandestine radio, mail art, and the burgeoning underground of tape swapping. Gritty cultural news.
—Kevin Kelly

•

Cassettes are a whole new kind of garage sale, old sounds often very carefully produced and elaborately displayed. Cassettes are variously scrapbooks, operas, entertaining companions, books, manifestos, noise experiments, all kinds of rock and roll, lots of eccentricity, practice tapes and finely lacquered years-in-the-making treasures. Audio wild cards. They can be almost anything.

•

Literate people presuppose that most of us are the lonely crowd in our alienated society; and the Walkman, according to this view, should be a sign, an ikon, for self-enclosure. Instead, it's an instrument for effecting visible historical change, an absolute collective, for the simple reason that sound unifies. Sight isolates, sound incorporates. Whereas sight situates the observer outside what he views, at a distance, sounds pour into the hearer. By contrast with vision, the dissecting sense, the auditory ideal is harmony, a putting together.

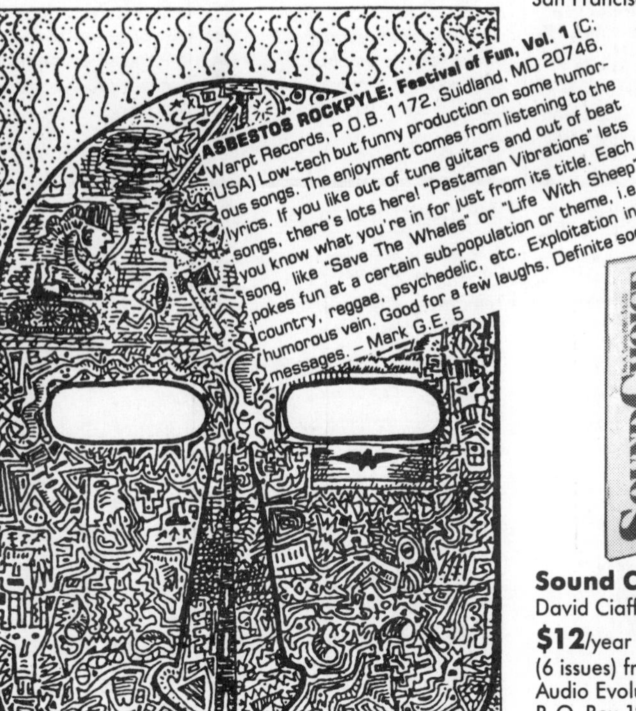

ASBESTOS ROCKPYLE: Festival of Fun, Vol. 1 (C: Warpt Records, P.O.B. 1172, Suidland, MD 20746, USA) Low-tech but funny production on some humorous songs. The enjoyment comes from listening to the lyrics. If you like out of tune guitars and out of beat songs, there's lots here! "Pastaman Vibrations" lets you know what you're in for just from its title. Each song, like "Save The Whales" or "Life With Sheep" pokes fun at a certain sub-population or theme, i.e., country, reggae, psychedelic, etc. Exploitation in a humorous vein. Good for a few laughs. Definite social messages. —Mark G.E. 5

Sound Choice
David Ciaffardini, Editor
$12/year
(6 issues) from:
Audio Evolution Network
P. O. Box 1251
Ojai, CA 93023

—Ear Magazine

LIKE ANY OTHER MASS MEDIUM, the music business prefers the homogenized blockbuster popular hit. Even at the lower end of the mainstream's sales figures, diversity and individual expression are rare, smothered by the need to move units (records) by appealing to the largest percentage of consumers. This means offending the smallest number of consumers. Thus large, diversified conglomerates provide sugar-coated notes-by-numbers that pass for music and pop culture in the Billboard society.

Away from the roar of the main highway, however, is a network of smaller independent record labels providing a sense of the real diversity of music being made today. Distribution to stores is a major difficulty for most, since there is a vicious chicken-and-egg circle of radio play and the stores' willingness to stock the records. That leaves smaller independent and specialist stores, which are relatively few and far between, and our old friend, the mail order business. Broadly speaking, there are three types of mail order distributor: larger companies offering a variety of musics and labels, distributors specializing in one musical field, and a few labels who make an extra effort to make their own releases available directly to individuals.

by Jonathan E.

Specialists

Jaybee Jazz

Box 24504, Creve Coeur, MO 63141.

Jazz classics, European and Japanese reissues, good prices. Catalog **free.**

First Edition Records

Box 1138, Whittier, CA 90609.

Jazz classics, out of print. Catalog **free.**

Andy's Front Hall

P. O. Box 307/Wormer Road, Voorheesville, NY 12186.

A wide range of folk records, songbooks, instructional materials, and some instruments. Catalog **$1.**

Musical Heritage Society

1710 Highway 35, Ocean, NJ 07712.

Classical records and tapes. Membership **$1***; includes a monthly magazine. Catalog* **$2***. [Suggested by Jay D. Eckert]*

AudioSource

1185 Chess Drive, Foster City, CA 94404.

Audiophile recordings of European classical music and Japanese-pressed classic rock and jazz. Catalog **$1.**

RAS Records

P. O. Box 42517, Washington, DC 20015.

The catalog is a virtual history of Jamaican music and has some records not offered elsewhere including Jamaican 7'' singles. Catalog **free.**

Sterns African Records

116 Whitfield Street, London W1P 5RW, U.K.

A wide and current selection of African pop from all over. Catalog **free.**

Midnight Records

P. O. Box 390/Dept. W, Old Chelsea Station, New York, NY 10011.

A wide range of rock, both old and new, over- and underground. Out-of-prints and collectables catalog **$1***; current in-print records catalog* **$1***. Catalogs updated four times yearly.*

CRI

170 West 74th Street, New York, NY 10023.

(Composer's Recordings, Inc.) Avant-garde music, with a large selection of electronic music. Catalog **free.**

Original Music

R. D. 1/Box 190, Lasher Road, Tivoli, NY 12583.

Their offerings are rapidly expanding and now include video. A good selection of African and Latin plus other music from around the world, intelligently described. Their own label is the most concise and inclusive introduction to the range of African music. Also a good book selection. Catalog **free.**

African Record Center

1194 Nostrand Avenue, New York, NY 11225.

Mostly older recordings from western and central Africa. Catalog **$1.**

The Record One-Stop

P. O. Box 547, Kenner, LA 70063.

Oldies and New Orleans R&B. Catalog **$2.**

Shanachie Records

Dalebrook Park, HoHoKus, NJ 07423.

Specializing in reggae and Irish folk, they also offer some African and a range of traditional musics. Catalog **free.**

Recommended Records

387 Wandsworth Road, London SW8, U.K.

Modern music from the experimental end of the continuum. Expert notes with a sense of humor. Catalog **free** *with International Reply Coupon.*

Hearts of Space

P. O. Box 31321, San Francisco, CA 94131.

A range of music from the relaxing, unfrantic end of the musical spectrum. Catalog **$1.**

Wide Range

Down Home Music

10341 San Pablo Avenue, El Cerrito, CA 94530.

A wide range: vintage rock 'n' roll; country; blues and gospel; bluegrass; American folk; vintage jazz; ethnic music; British, Irish and European folk; magazines and books. Honest descriptions of records offered along with track listings. Catalog **free.**

Roundup Records

P. O. Box 154, North Cambridge, MA 02140.

Their mag, ***The Record Roundup****, offers the latest releases with lengthy and unflinching reviews. Over 10,000 titles from 350 labels are arranged by artist in their Artist Catalog.* ***The Record Roundup*** *plus Artist Catalog:* **$5***/year. Artist Catalog alone:* **$2.**

Moby Music

14410 Ventura Boulevard, Sherman Oaks, CA 91423.

Specializes in imports and new American releases. Catalog **free.**

New Music Distribution Service

500 Broadway, New York, NY 10012.

"The New Music Distribution Service distributes all independently produced recordings of new music, regardless of commercial potential or personal taste." A wide range of music is offered in their informative catalog. Catalog **free.**

Ladyslipper

P. O. Box 3130, Durham, NC 27705.

A selection of musical offerings whose only common denominator is that they are created by women. Witty descriptions. Catalog **free.**

Schwann Record Catalog

535 Boylston Street, Boston, MA 02116.

Not a mail order source, but a listing of all albums available through record stores. Includes jazz, classical, pop, language study, aerobics and international. 500 pages. Catalog **$4.95.**

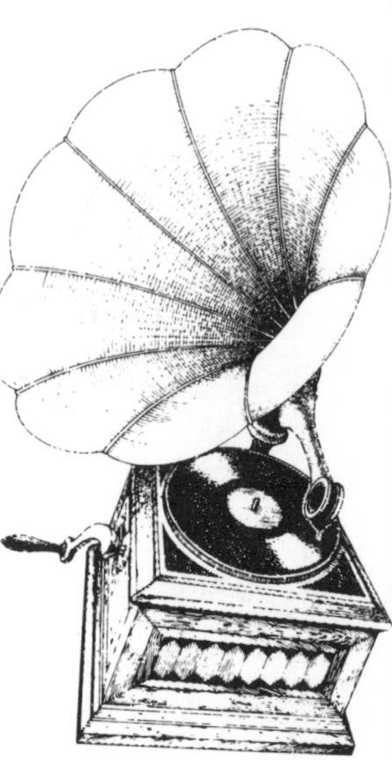
—Reggae and African Beat

Own-Label Mail Distributors

Alligator Records

P. O. Box 60234, Chicago, IL 60660.

The leading blues label and one of the reggae contenders. Their own catalog of records plus posters, T-shirts and video. Catalog **free.**

Off Centaur Publications

P. O. Box 424, El Cerrito, CA 94530.

Mostly cassettes of Filk music, "the particular and peculiar music of science fiction fans." Also some folk, and songbooks, and other esoterica. Catalog **free.**

Folk-Legacy Records

Sharon Mountain Road, Sharon, CT 06069.

Traditional and contemporary folk music from the northeastern U.S. and the British Isles. Catalog **free.**

Giorno Poetry Systems Institute

222 Bowery, New York, NY 10012.

New York poetry, performance art, and avant garde recordings. Big names but not for the faint of heart. Brochure **free.**

Paredon Records

P. O. Box 11260, Oakland, CA 94611.

Music reflecting the political struggles for peace, justice and national liberation around the world, including recordings from the USA's New Song Movement. Catalog **free.**

—Reggae and African Beat

Folkways Records

632 Broadway, New York, NY 10012.

The widest range of (mostly) traditional musics, including American Indian. They reputedly never allow their titles to go out of print. Catalog **free** *(see p. 334).*

ROIR Cassettes

611 Broadway/Suite 725, New York, NY 10012.

Records on cassette, that is. Music from the radical end of the spectrum in several styles. Many early works and live shows by an eclectic assortment of artists. Catalog **free.**

Music of the World

P. O. Box 258, Brooklyn, NY 11209.

Their own line of cassettes from leading musicians of various musics, both traditional and contemporary, from around the world. Catalog **free.**

Music Magazines

WARD Report

David Bassin and Kevin Berger, Editors. $45/year (24 issues) from WARD, 405 Schrader Street, San Francisco, CA 94117.

Published by the Western Association of Rock Disk Jockeys, a dance-rock DJ pool, this is the one I work on. We attempt to improve the quality of sounds heard in discos and on college radio by reviewing the most worthy current releases, with an emphasis on independent-label rock. My own One World Beat column is the most regular and wide-ranging coverage of reggae, Caribbean, and African musics that I know of (muted trumpet).

Maximum Rock'n'Roll

$9 for 6 issues from Maximum Rock'n'Roll, P. O. Box 288, Berkeley, CA 94701.

Politically aware punk. Enthusiastic and critical coverage of records, concerts and currents.

down beat

Art Lance, Editor. $18/year (12 issues) from down beat, 180 West Park Avenue, Elmhurst, IL 60126.

In its 53rd year, this jazz-based glossy covers a range of serious contemporary musics. A good blend of well-established and up-and-coming artists.

Ear

Carol Tuynman, Editor. $12/year (5 issues) from Ear Magazine, 325 Spring Street/Room 208, New York, NY 10013.

Discussion and articles covering the progressive new music spectrum. Occasional special issues on topics such as revolutionary song or the summer solstice.

Rock and Roll Confidential

Dave Marsh, Editor. $18/year (12 issues) from Rock and Roll Confidential, P. O. Box 1073, Maywood, NJ 07607.

The social conscience of rock'n'roll. Insider news and brief reviews of selected current releases.

Goldmine

Trey Foster, Editor. $35/year (26 issues) from Krause Publications, 700 East State Street, Iola, WI 54990.

Packed with eye-straining ads for serious vinyl collectors and record junkies, along with pieces on music greats and some reviews and news on current happenings.

JazzTimes

Mike Joice, Editor. $10/year (12 issues) from JazzTimes Magazine, 8055 13th Street/Suite 301, Silver Spring, MD 20910.

News and reviews from the jazz world. Grass-roots feel and full of information.

Living Blues

Jim O'Neal, Editor. $18/year (6 issues) from Living Blues Magazine, University of Mississippi Center for the Study of Southern Culture, University, MS 38677.

Strictly blues, lots of record reviews, interviews with blues survivors, and obituaries.

Puncture

Katherine Spielmann, Editor. $12 for 6 issues from Puncture, 1674 Filbert Street #3, San Francisco, CA 94123.

Fanzine spirit on nice paper. Record, tape and show reviews of the rock underground with a sprinkling of reggae and African.

Reggae and African Beat

C. C. Smith, Editor. $9.95/year (6 issues) from Bongo Productions, P. O. Box 29820, Los Angeles, CA 90029.

Committed to the spirit behind the music as well as to the form of the music. Heavy on features and comment, erratic on reviews. ■

Philip Glass. **Laurie Anderson.**

—Ear

AudioCraft
Randy Thom
1982; 183 pp.
$15
($17 postpaid) from:
National Federation of Community Broadcasters
1314 14th Street NW
Washington, DC 20005
or Whole Earth Access

AudioCraft

Last winter I began producing occasional news features for Radio Netherlands' Media Network program. This book has been a tremendous help. Clearly written and presuming no technical expertise, it gives good basic advice on how to do broadcast-quality audio production on a limited budget, without putting a lot of you-can't-do-that cramps on your creativity. Covers situations relevant to newsgathering, concert "remotes," radio dramas, interviews, documentaries, recording sessions, promotional "spots," etc. Intended primarily for community radio stations and sound artists, it should also benefit film- and video-makers (author Thom won an Oscar for his sound work on ***The Right Stuff****).* —Robert Horvitz

•

Whenever possible, monitor the "PLAYBACK" ("REPRODUCE") signal while recording, instead of the "INPUT" ("SOURCE") signal. Remember that with the meter-and-output switch in the "PLAYBACK" position you will hear the actual signal that has been put on the tape, so that you can hear any technical problems, such as dropout, improperly threaded tape, or electronic problems *as they occur,* rather than later (when it may be too late). . . .

During recording, the technician should occasionally switch back and forth between the "INPUT" and "REPRODUCE" positions. If the "REPRODUCE" signal sounds significantly different from the "INPUT" signal, something is wrong.

Since most tape recorders transport the tape from left to right, this is actually the way the sounds get put on the tape itself. Think about it. Most tape editing is simply a matter of physically cutting out unwanted words or phrases, and joining the remaining pieces with adhesive tape.

•

A problem occurs when two microphones are positioned so that a single sound causes the element of one mike to vibrate out of phase with the element of the other. For this reason, it is a good idea to mix into one channel the outputs of all the mikes in a *multi-mike* setup (*sum* the mikes) one by one and listen for a drop in level or change in frequency response (tone quality) as each mike is added. If such a change occurs, you know that the last mike is significantly out of phase with at least one of the others.

The Craft of Interviewing
John Brady
1976; 244 pp.
$5.95
($6.95 postpaid) from:
Random House
Order Dept.
400 Hahn Road
Westminster, MD 21157
or Whole Earth Access

The Craft of Interviewing

Not a brilliant book, but plenty competent enough to vastly improve the level of most dumb-question-dumb-answer published conversation. It also helps if interviewers have studied and done a bit of field anthropology.

If you find yourself being an interviewee, these skills are even more important, since it's your ass on the line. —Stewart Brand

•

"I think it is very important for a person to do his homework," explains Manchester. "There's nothing more insulting than to ask a man, like a President of the United States, a question that he's answered many times before. Then he's quite likely to dismiss you. So what you want to ask are the questions he's never been asked before, questions that show that you have a great familiarity with his life. And then he's likely to respect you and be interested in the exchange, the colloquy." In preparing for his initial interview, Manchester went through a list of the appointments that President Kennedy had made with special assistants and cabinet advisers. He found that over 80 percent of them were within a few years of the President's age. So he asked Kennedy if he were a "generation chauvinist." "Now, he'd never thought of this," says Manchester, "but he liked the idea and he played with it, and it was entertaining for him. A really first-rate interview with an articulate man can be fascinating for him. And if he is fascinated, then it will go on and you will learn more from him. It all depends on how much time you spend in advance."

The ARRL 1986 Handbook
Mark Wilson, Editor
1985; 1,170 pp.
$18 postpaid from:
American Radio Relay League
225 Main Street
Newington, CT 06111
or Whole Earth Access

The ARRL 1986 Handbook

The largest and oldest national organization of ham radio operators, the American Radio Relay League, publishes a wide variety of excellent books, learning aids, and how-to guides, designed to serve absolute beginners as well as advanced experimenters. Their annual ***Handbook*** *is a comprehensive reference, finely honed over the years to explain radio theory and practice in the clearest, most accurate, hands-on terms. Includes many construction projects. Don't order it without asking about their other goodies.* —Robert Horvitz

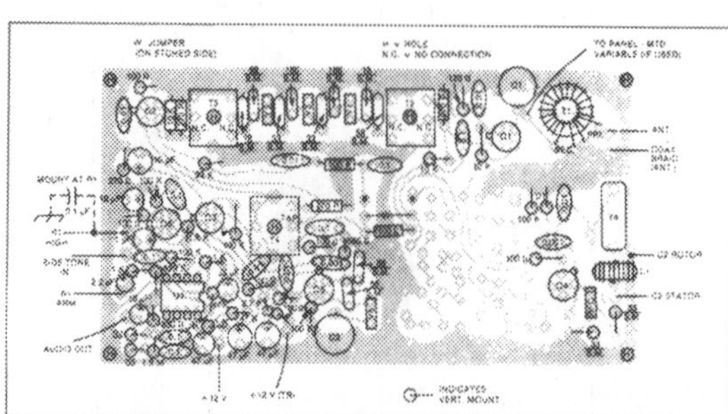

Parts-placement guide for the CW-receiver PC board. The component side is shown with an X-ray view of the foil. This guide shows the VXO layout.

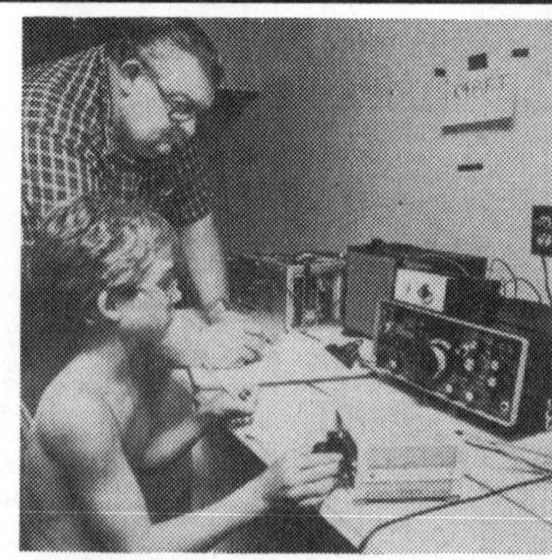

Bill Christian, K41KR (left) and Tim Dionne, KB4BDG, operate in the 1983 Field Day. During this annual, two-day event, thousands of radio amateurs around the U.S. set up and operate portable, emergency-powered stations.

• For the passionate radio amateur.
QST: Paul L. Rinaldo, Editor. **$25**/year (12 issues) from American Radio Relay League, 225 Main Street, Newington, CT 06111.

Hy-Gain HF antennas —EGE

TH7DX

A SHORT-WAVE RADIO receiver gives you direct access to broadcasts from around the world: news and opinion, musics too diverse to catalog, a front-row-center seat on international affairs. Channels in this band can be noisy and variable in loudness, so you have to concentrate(earphones really help), but the content of short-wave transmissions amply rewards the extra effort.

—Robert Horvitz

Sony ICF-2002

Short-Wave Receivers

*Like personal computers, short-wave receivers have been evolving at such a feverish pace that any radio still tops in its class two years after introduction qualifies as a classic. The **Sony ICF-2002** and the **Icom IC-R71A** are two such classics, designed for different requirements. It's possible that improved versions or successor models will be introduced after we go to press, but you won't go wrong with these proven winners.*

*The **Icom** is for the serious explorer, someone who wants to hear as many different stations as he can. Its tuning system is wonderfully flexible: you can use the digital keypad, if you know the frequency you want to listen to; the rotary knob, if you want to browse; or the 32-channel programmable memory, if you've entered the sought frequency ahead of time. A variable pass-band filter, as well as impulse and notch filters, clean away noise, and the overall sound quality (through headphones) is superior. The **Icom** is compact enough to carry around, though it isn't a true portable.*

Icom IC-R71A

*If portability is an important requirement, the **Sony ICF-2002** offers the best performance and easiest tuning in the smallest package — about the size of a paperback book. Frequency coverage is 153 to 29,995 kHz (AM, SSB), plus 76 to 108 MHz (FM). While designed for travel use, the **2002** is good enough to double as a home station if you add a wire antenna in place of the built-in whip. (Note: outside the US, this radio is called the **ICF-7600D.**)*

—Robert Horvitz

Icom IC-R71A: $849; information **free** from Icom America, 2380 116th Avenue NE, Bellevue, WA 98004.

Sony ICF-2002: $259.95; information **free** from Sony Corporation, Sony Drive, Park Ridge, NJ 07656.

Publications

*A short-wave radio without schedule and frequency information is sort of like a computer without software: a waste of capability. With thousands of stations on the air, and channel assignments changing seasonally, the **International Listening Guide**, issued four times a year, is indispensable for anyone interested in English-language programming. Over 800 broadcasts beamed to all parts of the globe are listed by time and frequency. At-a-glance inserts focus on news programs in English, schedules of the major "world services" (BBC, VOA, Radio Moscow, Radio Australia), and where to find "DX" programs that give additional tuning guidance.*

*The **World Radio TV Handbook** is an annual directory of broadcasting stations worldwide. Loaded with technical details, maps, addresses, callsigns and format notes, serious short-wave listeners find it very useful.*

*The **Association of North American Radio Clubs** is a consortium of many of the largest and oldest noncommercial listeners' groups in the U.S. and Canada. Primary purpose of the clubs is to share information about radio equipment, ways to improve reception, recent loggings, and events of interest. The **ANARC Club List** gives brief sketches of each club and its newsletter and details about joining.*

—Robert Horvitz

International Listening Guide: Bernd Friedewald, Editor. **$14**/year (4 issues) from International Listening Guide, Merianstr.2, D-3588 Hamberg, West Germany.

World Radio TV Handbook: Jens M. Frost, Editor-In-Chief, 1986; 607 pp. **$21.95** postpaid from Watson-Guptill Publishers, P. O. Box 2013, Lakewood, NJ 08701.

Association of North American Radio Clubs: Information 25¢ plus legal-size SASE from ANARC Club List, P. O. Box 180403, Austin, TX 78718-0403.

```
----------------------------------
17815 kHz
----------------------------------
   CAIRO      AU 1000-1100 A
S* DW       w ME 0800-0850 Pd
W           v AS 1330-1420 In
   MOROCCO    AF 1100-1400 A
              AF 1700-1900 A
W  MOSCOW     AS 0300-1000 C,R,W
S             AS 0300-1000 C/R
              AS 1000:1230V,Kh,V
              AS 1100-1200 Th,La
 * V.ISRAEL   EU%1000-1030 R
 *            EU 1400-1455 R
 *            EU 1455-1525 Z,Ge
 *            EU 1630-1740 R,Yi
   Cultura,Bz.  0900-0500 P
----------------------------------
```

—International Listening Guide

TONGA (Kingdom of)

L.T: UTC + 13h — **Pr.L:** Tongan, English — **E.C:** a/c 50, 240V.

TONGA BROADCASTING COMMISSION

ADDR: P.O. Box 36, Nuku'alofa. **Te:** 21-555. **Cable:** BROADCOM.
L.P: Gen.Mgr: S.T. Fusimalohi. Contr.N: S.H. Fonua; Contr.Prgrs: M. Heimuli; Contr.Tech.Sces: Siale Fetu'ufuka; Accountant: S. Taunisila.
STATION: (G.C: 175.10W/21.08S) A3Z 1017kHz 10kW.
D.PRGR: 1800-1000. **N. in Tongan:** 1845, 0200, 0800, 1145.
N. in English: 1800(BBC), 1900(R.Aust), 0900 (R.Aust), 0055(VOA).
ANN: E: "This is the Call of The Friendly Islands A3Z Nuku'alofa of the Tonga Broadc. Commission". T: "Ko e Ui 'E ni 'a e 'Otu Felenite, mei he A3Z Nuku'alofa 'a e Komisoni Fakamafolalea Tonga" — **INT-SIG:** Tongan Noseflute — **FI:** Revenue from adv. **F.PL:** FM Sce.

—World Radio TV Handbook

• Covers the exciting areas of cellular radiotelephony, paging, mobile satellites, and new radio services generally, from the users' perspective.

Personal Communications Technology: Ben Kobb, Editor. **$25**/year (12 issues) from Horizon House, Circulation Dept., 685 Canton Street, Norwood, MA 02062.

Equipment Suppliers

Although short-wave equipment is more widely available than it used to be, you may not have a store nearby that carries a good selection. Mail order is still a convenient way to shop, and the prices are generally less than you'd pay in a store. These are some of the leading mail order suppliers of short-wave equipment.

—Robert Horvitz

EGE: Catalog **$1** from 13646 Jefferson Davis Hwy., Woodbridge, VA 22191.

Universal Shortwave Radio: Catalog **$1** from 1280 Aida Drive, Reynoldsburg, OH 43068.

Radio West: Catalog **$1** from 3417 Purer Road, Escondido, CA 92025.

Electronic Equipment Bank: Catalog **free** from 516 Mill Street, NE, Vienna, VA 22180

Grove Enterprises: Catalog **free** from P. O. Box 98, Brasstown, NC 28902.

TELEX HEADSETS

Procom 350/352-IC ultra-light headset with boom mike, and Procom 250 extra-padded ear pieces with boom mike.

—EGE

Using Your Meter
Alvis J. Evans
1985; 128 pp.
$3.95
($6.45 postpaid) from:
Radio Shack — 018344
Mail Order Dept.
900 Terminal Road
Ft. Worth, TX 76106
or Whole Earth Access

Using Your Meter

I bought several copies of this book recently: a couple for friends and two for myself. For $3.95 I got a complete course in electronics along with various instructions and tips on how to use meters around the house and inside electronic circuitry. I also learned how to buy meters, what features to look for, what kind of meters to use in what applications. So did my friends.

The text is clear although the information is very dense. Evans moves right along in 128 pages, covering all the electronics I studied in all the high school and college physics courses I ever took and also how to use that information practically. This is the kind of book you should read three times. The very basic stuff is in the middle. Tips on troubleshooting washers and dryers, heating and cooling systems, record players, automobile alternators, and other familiar equipment is in the back. Right in the front you learn about types of meters and how they operate. ***Using Your Meter*** *offers an amazing value of information.* —James Stockford

•

When the bell doesn't ring: Assume that the bell does not operate when the button switch is pushed. The two most common problems are a bad switch or a bad bell. To track down the trouble, measure the voltage across the push button switch. With the switch open, 10 volts should appear across the open switch. There is no current in the circuit and thus no voltage across the bell (M_3). When the switch is closed, meter M_1 should read zero. If a voltage appears across the switch even when it is closed, this indicates that the circuit is not operating properly. Check the contacts to see if they are corroded or broken. The switch can possibly be repaired by simply scraping and cleaning the contacts. However, it may have to be replaced. If 10 volts appears across the bell when the button is pushed and the bell does not ring, the bell is probably defective. Disconnect it and check its resistance to see if it has an open coil.

Function	Meter	Button Not Pushed	Button Pushed
Voltage	M_1	10V	0V
	M_2	10V	10V
	M_3	0V	10V
Resistance	M_1	4-7Ω	0
	M_2	1-2Ω	0-1
	M_3	2-5Ω	0-1

The Art of Electronics
Paul Horowitz and Winfield Hill
1980; 716 pp.
$32.50 postpaid from:
Cambridge University Press
510 North Avenue
New Rochelle, NY 10801
or Whole Earth Access

The Art of Electronics

Extremely good book. As a practicing digital-electronics technician with no formal training (my major in college was cultural anthropology), I've hunted high and low for good electronics textbooks. This one is the best, bar none. No extraneous math, lots of insider's information on the peculiarities of circuit design, and a huge range of topics covered clearly and thoroughly. So well written that I've had difficulty putting it down! Has a good index and bibliography and works well as a stand-alone reference book. As an introduction and workbook on today's electronics it has no peer. —Bud Spurgeon

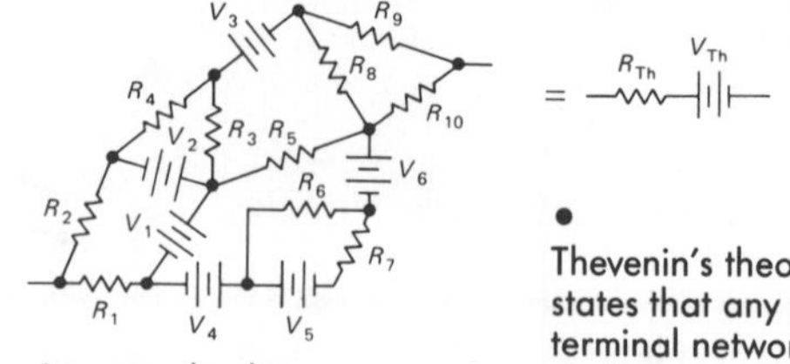

•

Thevenin's theorem states that any two-terminal network of resistors and voltage sources is equivalent to a single resistor *R* in series with a single voltage source *V*. This is remarkable. Any mess of batteries and resistors can be mimicked with one battery and one resistor.

Don Lancaster's Cookbook Library

These books provide the home-brew tinkerer with a, um, grounding in the basics of micro circuits — with which you can build your own calculators, amplifiers, meters and terminals, and get a start on building your own computer. Each book deals with a different type of component. CMOS circuits are building-block electronic switch circuits out of which computer choice pathways are woven. TTL circuits are simpler, more often used to build clocks, meters, and peripherals. Getting through TTL is a good step towards learning CMOS. Active filters are useful in amplifying or controlling sound frequencies. Lancaster takes pride in teaching you to make things that are more useful and versatile — more artistic, really — than what you can buy commercially. You'll need some electronics experience, or lots of time, or both. —Art Kleiner

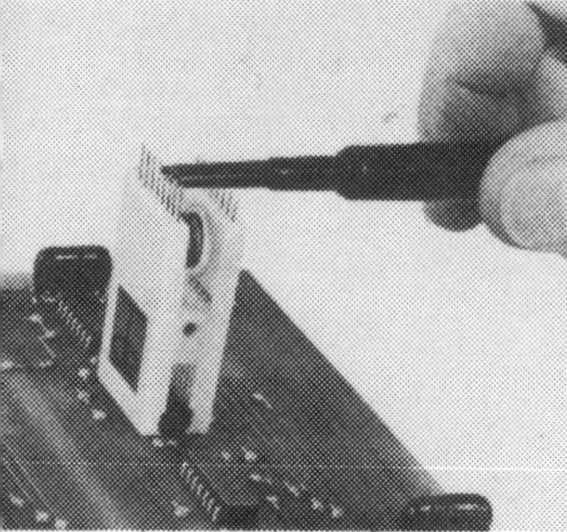

◄ **API Glomper Clip** —*TTL*

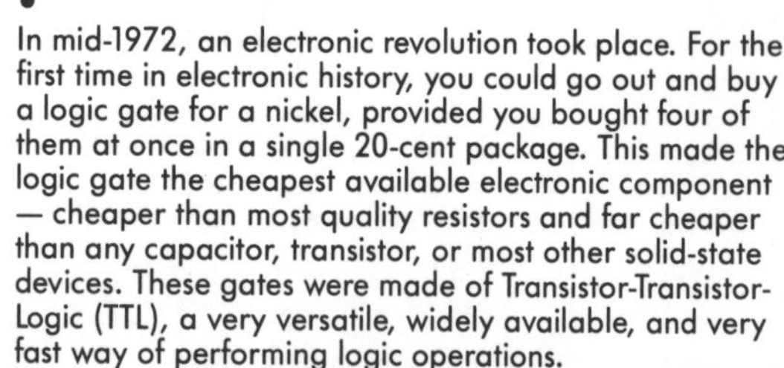

•

In mid-1972, an electronic revolution took place. For the first time in electronic history, you could go out and buy a logic gate for a nickel, provided you bought four of them at once in a single 20-cent package. This made the logic gate the cheapest available electronic component — cheaper than most quality resistors and far cheaper than any capacitor, transistor, or most other solid-state devices. These gates were made of Transistor-Transistor-Logic (TTL), a very versatile, widely available, and very fast way of performing logic operations.

The extremely low cost did two things. First and foremost, it opened up a fantastic number of still expanding applications for digital circuitry. At long last, doing things digitally was not only better than using traditional analog circuits, but now it was often cheaper as well.
—*TTL Cookbook*

•

An *active filter* is some combination of integrated-circuit operational amplifiers, resistors, and capacitors that does things that normally could be done only with expensive inductor-capacitor passive filter combinations. Active filters are versatile, low-cost items that are easy to design and easy to tune. They have gain and have a number of other benefits. Active filters are well suited for most subaudio, audio, and ultrasonic filtering or equalizing applications. Important areas of use for active filters include many other areas.

This book is about active filters. It is user-oriented. It tells you everything you need to know to build active filters, and does so with an absolute minimum of math or obscure theory. —*Active-Filter Cookbook*

Active Filter Cookbook
Don Lancaster
1975; 240 pp.
$15.95
($18.45 postpaid)

CMOS Cookbook
Don Lancaster
1977; 416 pp.
$14.95
($17.45 postpaid)

TTL Cookbook
Don Lancaster
1977; 416 pp.
$14.95
($17.45 postpaid)

All from:
Howard W. Sams & Co.
Department DM
4300 West 62nd Street
Indianapolis, IN 46268
or Whole Earth Access

Electronic Buyers Club (EBC)

If over a year's time you're buying much in the way of electronic supplies, this place is well worth knowing about. EBC is the only supplier I've found that beats Mouser's prices. The catch is you have to buy a membership for $35. For that you get your own membership number and a thick, very well laid-out catalog. The catalog alone may be worth the membership cost for the search time you can save (no specs, tho'). EBC's selection of active and passive components, tools, and supplies is fairly broad, though limited to a few manufacturers, a problem if exact replacement is an issue. Their digital IC selection is very broad. I'm a member. —James Stockford

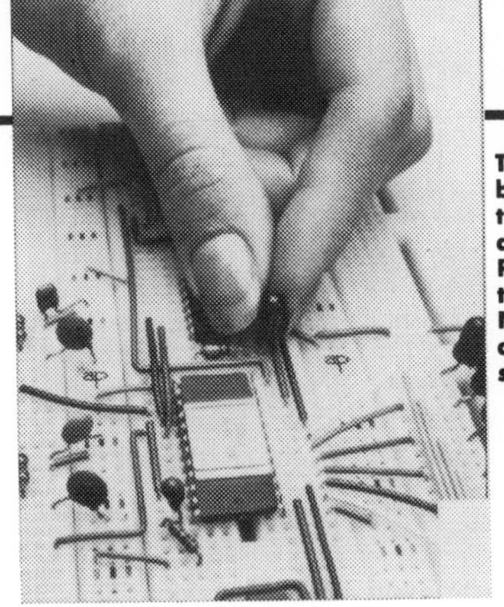

The solderless breadboard: With the lead spacing of all sizes of DIPs. Push them in; pull them out. No solder. No bent leads. No damaged parts. No special tools.

Electronic Buyers Club
Membership **$35**
(includes catalog and updates) from:
Electronic Buyers Club
P. O. Box 617
Columbia, MO 65205

Mouser Electronics
Catalog **free** from:
Mouser Electronics
P. O. Box 839
Mansfield, TX 76063

Mouser Electronics

Mouser Electronics is the best all-purpose supplier of electronic components and supplies I've found. Of all the standard mail order sources of electronic passive and active devices, hardware, and tools, Mouser's prices are lowest, often by 20-30 percent. Their selection is very broad, especially for switches, connectors, LEDs, and capacitors. They even have a good selection of printed circuit board supplies, grommets and stand-offs, computer interface panels, and drafting aids. Perfect for hobbyists, prototype designers, and electronic repair shops. —James Stockford

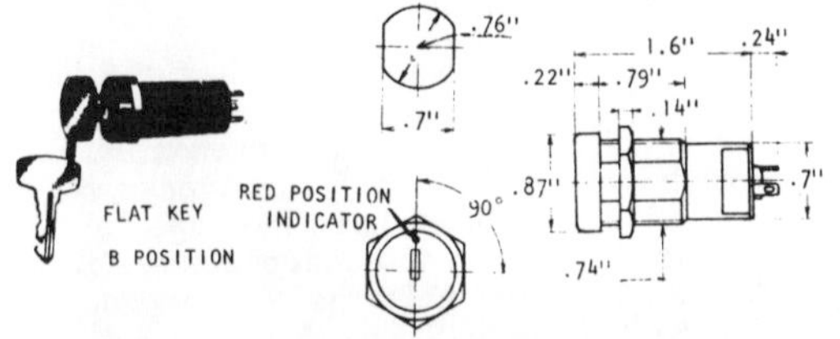

SECURITY KEY SWITCHES

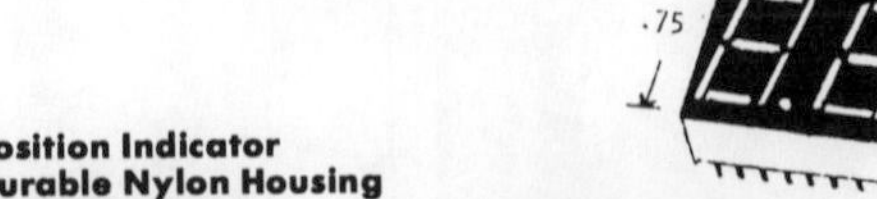

- **Position Indicator**
- **Durable Nylon Housing**
- **Solder Terminals**
- **Complete With 2 Keys and Mounting Hardware**

- **Electrical Life: 15,000 Operations**
- **Mechanical Life: 30,000 Operations**

- **Rating: 1A, 125VAC** • **Contact Res: 20 MilliOHMS**
- **Volt, Breakdown, 1000VAC 1 Min**
- **Insulation Resistance: 100 MegOHMS @ 500VDC**

RADIAL LEADS X SERIES

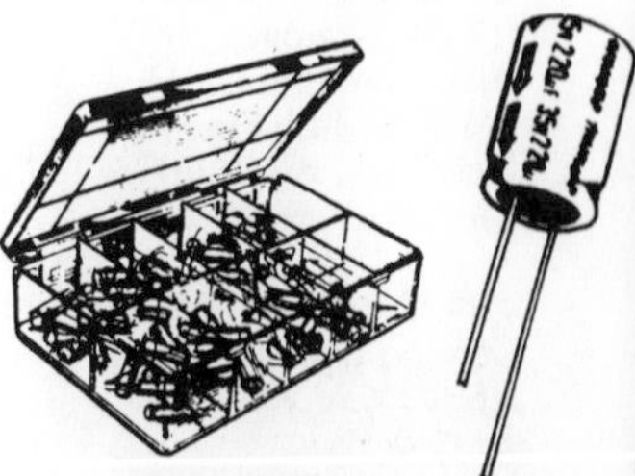

STOCK NO.	WV	QTY	PRICE EACH
37-20PK-1	25	30	7.95
37-20PR-1	50	30	8.50

◄ **2 digit LED displays: .600" pin row spacing.**

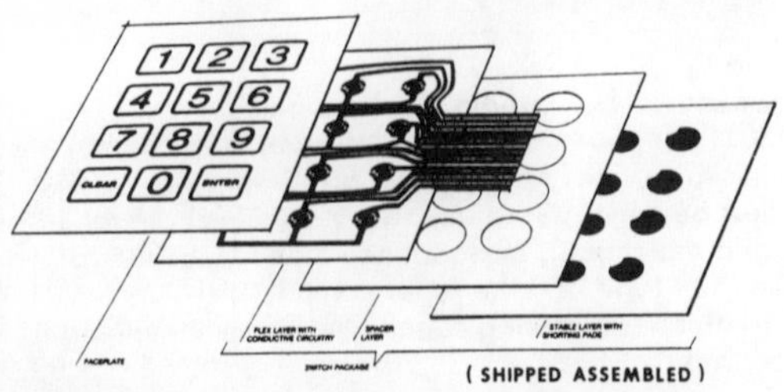

Xymox Membrane Switches

IEEE Spectrum

Here is the hard poop on the latest in electronic technology. It has astonishing and bewildering tech reports for the hard-core, but what distinguishes it is an emphasis on social and political ramifications (a special issue on technology in war and peace won a Pulitzer last year). Other distinctions include crisp writing and intriguing ads. Here I have read about new video-game techniques; prospects for high-definition TV standards; "smart" credit cards with built-in integrated circuits; New York's new fuel-cell power plant; issues in technology-transfer controls; the first realistic discussion of who-knew-what-when about the doomed jetliner KAL007. Every library should get this magazine. —Steve Upstill

IEEE Spectrum
Donald Christiansen, Editor
$67/year
(12 issues) from:
IEEE Service Center
445 Hoes Lane
Piscataway, NJ 08854

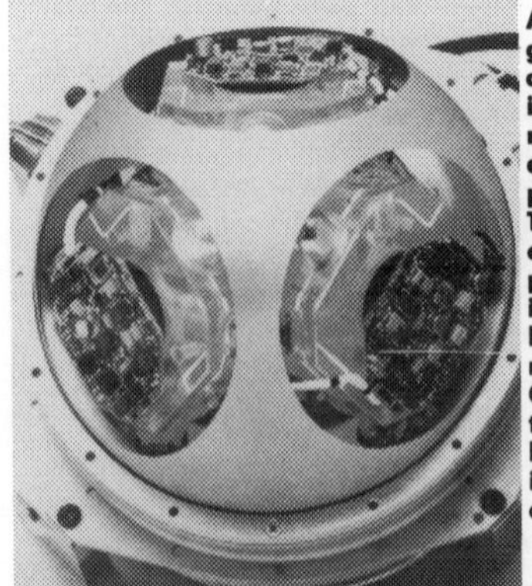

A ring laser gyroscope system consists of three individual gyros that measure rotation about three mutually perpendicular axes. The glowing gas discharge in each gyro provides the pumping for the ring laser. This system, made by Litton Guidance and Control Systems, Woodland Hills, Calif., is used in commercial aircraft.

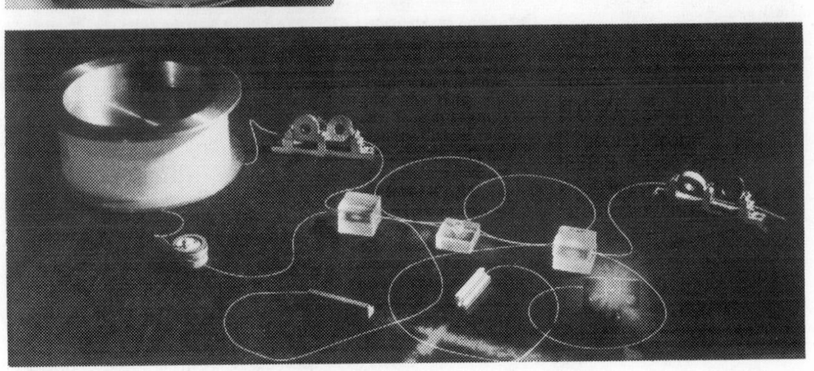

► **The first all-fiber-optic gyro, with fiber-optic components (directional couplers, a polarizer, phase modulator, and polarization controllers) on an unbroken strand of single-mode fiber, was built at Stanford University in 1981. Electronic signal processing and sinusoidal optical-phase modulation are used to achieve digital output and linear response.**

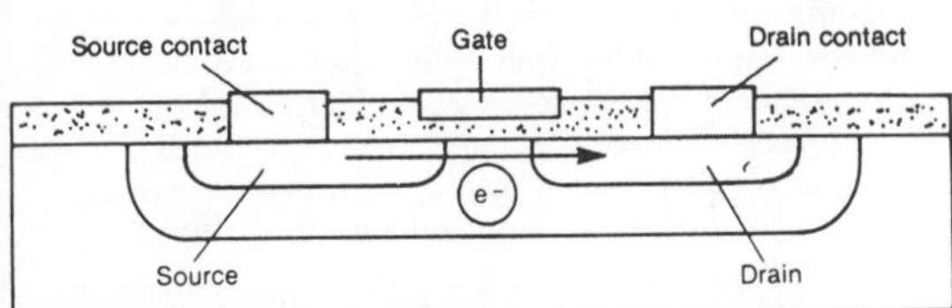

Typical horizontal transistor (insulating-gate field-effect transistor)

GADGET

Gadget
George Arthur, Editor
$15/year
(12 issues) from:
A.G. Consultants, Inc.
116 West 14th Street
New York, NY 10011

J & R Music World
Catalog **free** from:
J & R Music World
23 Park Row
New York, NY 10038

Wisconsin Discount Stereo
1-800-356-9514

GUIDE TO
ELECTRONICS
IN THE HOME

Consumer Reports Guide To Electronics In The Home
Editors of Consumer Reports Books
with Monte Florman
1986; 224 pp.
$6.95
($9.10 postpaid) from:
Consumer Reports Books
540 Barnum Avenue
Bridgeport, CT 06608
or Whole Earth Access

Gadget

This "newsletter for grown-up kids" features highly subjective user reports of the latest technological te..ıpta-tions available to the American consumer. The tests are in marked contrast to the pickynit documented programs of ***Consumer Reports*** *(p. 150).* ***Gadget****'s total criticism might consist of a laconic "nobody on our staff liked it." This is thin soup, considering that* ***Consumer Reports*** *costs $3 less per year. But* ***Gadget*** *reports on products as soon as they appear. Sometimes they show something that has only been on the market a matter of weeks. This can be an advantage if you value being the first on your block to have the latest equipment, or if you are into electronic devices which obsolete themselves quickly.* ***Gadget*** *has no ads.* —JB

▼

The smallest microwave oven we've seen is the *Half-Pint,* a 13" cube that fits into recreational vehicles, college dorm rooms, vacation homes and dens with ease. This attractive unit from *Sharp (10 Sharp Plaza, Paramus, NJ 07652)* holds a 10" dinner plate, has a 15-minute dial timer, a see-through door and 400 watts of power. An easy-to-clean acrylic interior makes the Half-Pint perfect for meals or snacks. Price: $149.

Half-Pint

FM STEREO

Toshiba RP-30 FM Receiver

SenDEC

NEC Cellular Telephone

▲

Do you need a simple, self-contained electronic door access system that doesn't use keys or security cards? Check out SenDEC, a combination-code lock that's easy to install and operate. The correct code combination unlocks the door in three to five seconds, and the combination is easy to change. A product of *Mountain West Alarm Supply (4215 N. 16th St., P. O. Box 10780, Phoenix, AZ 85064),* SenDEC is useful for residential, industrial or military applications. Price: Contact company.

▲

NEC Cellular Telephone (Model TR5E800-8A). Manufactured by: NEC America, Inc., 4936 Rosecrans Ave., Hawthorne, CA 90250. Price (uninstalled): $2,995.

It's a Japanese firm, NEC, which has marketed a cellular telephone which is perhaps the best *Gadget* has tested. Portable (the bulky transceiver box, usually mounted in the car trunk, is done away with), the *NEC TR5E800-8A* actually worked in the *Gadget* office.

That's probably not the acid test for mobile communications, but the NEC instrument is the first we've tested that did function from within our walls.

◄

Toshiba RP-30 FM Stereo Receiver
Manufactured by: *Toshiba, 82 Totowa Rd., Wayne, NJ 07470.* Price: $64.95. A demonstration of the limitations of miniaturization. Although we admitted it was "the smallest personal stereo unit we've seen" (about the size of a matchbox), performance didn't measure up . . . While the sound and the super-compact size . . . are remarkable, its receiving capabilities leave something to be desired.

J & R Music World • Wisconsin Discount Stereo

Mail order can offer major savings over local retail. Unlike most mail order consumer electronics stores, J & R offers three comprehensive catalogs — on computers, stereos, and videotapes. Between them you'll find home security devices, musical keyboards, telephones, blank tapes, copiers, watches, and shavers. Wisconsin Discount Stereo is often less expensive but has no catalog. For both, first visit a store near you and get familiar with the features — then compare prices and shop mail order via their 800 number. —Saul Feldman

While comparing prices, check Whole Earth Access, which also discounts consumer electronics. —Art Kleiner

$69.95
Sony PS-LX240 Semi-Automatic Belt-Drive Turntable •Semi-automatic operation with end-of-play return. •P-mount plug-in cartridge connector design. •Straight low mass tonearm. •Belt-drive motor. •Includes moving magnet cartridge. •Sony Bulk Molding Compound (SBMC) base.
SON PSLX240 . . . Retail $89.95 . . . **Your Cost $69.95**

$329.95
Panasonic PV-1360 VHS HQ Video Recorder •Front loading design •14-position tuner •Wireless remote control •14 day/2 event timer •Multi-function display •One touch recording •Still frame/advance, slow motion and search in SLP
PAN PV1360 . . . . Retail $499.95 . . . **Your Cost $329.95**

Large-screen color TV sets: Brand repair index

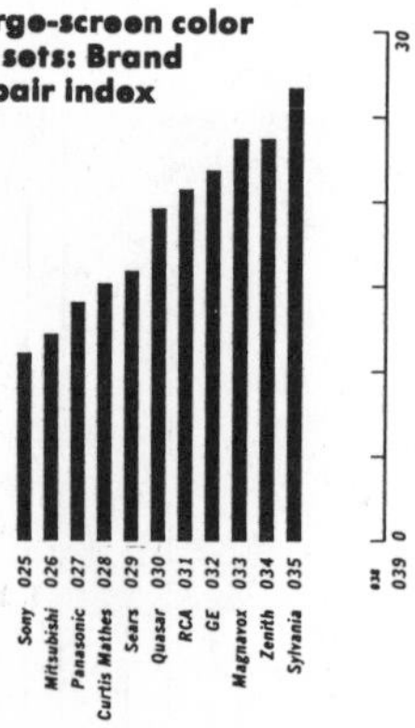
0
30
Sony
Mitsubishi
Panasonic
Curtis Mathes
Sears
Quasar
RCA
GE
Magnavox
Zenith
Sylvania

Guide to Electronics in The Home

The more antiquated among us sometimes find it difficult to deal with things electronic. Which devices are useful? Which of those are best? ***Consumer Reports*** *(p. 150), at its best here, explains it all as it reviews home computers, TVs, hifis, radios, tape decks, phones, and alarms. As is their custom, the Consumers Union folks don't comment on every model of every brand. They make up for this by educating you in the basics so you can, for instance, make sense out of specification sheets and salesman hype. This is the best general introduction to electronic gadgetry this side of the nearest teenage hacker.* —JB

◄

The graph compares the reliability of eleven brands of large-screen TV sets, as reported by some 50,000 readers who had bought TV sets between 1980 and 1985. The bars in the graph represent an index showing the frequency with which the sets in each brand have needed repairs; the longer the bar, the more frequent the need for repair.

•

There's no extra benefit in using expensive tapes in a portable cassette recorder. It lacks the electronic refinements necessary for getting the best out of a tape. Bargain-priced tapes, however, could increase the risk of an exasperating tape tangle or cassette misfit. You probably won't go wrong if you follow a middle course and buy the lowest-priced brand-name Type I (ferric) tape available.

UNLIKE PERSONAL COMPUTERS, robots have not become a popular consumer item — despite such prototypes as Heathkit's "Hero" and Nolan Bushnell's "Topo." The personal robots that exist today are like the primitive personal computers of a decade ago. They show a great deal of promise, but they are sort of useless novelty items now. As costs shrink, that will change. Sometime soon, many a small industrial workshop and school will find it worthwhile to buy a robot. Families will follow suit later. In the meantime, robotics has become the most intriguing, involving, gripping field of inquiry for home electronics experimenters.

As one robot-maker, Maris Ambats, described the scene, "Robotics is at an early stage, and an independent experimenter can make substantial original contributions without a large budget or elaborate equipment."
—Art Kleiner

The Frank, Jr. arm and mobile base made from Automat components and Designatronics electronic parts.
—The Robot Experimenter

Basic Robotic Concepts

Generally agreed upon as the best overall technical book. It's designed to educate people about the various problems in robotics — balancing the machine, vision systems, motors, torque curves, wheels versus legs, and programming the intelligence. *—Art Kleiner*
[Suggested by Richard Prather]

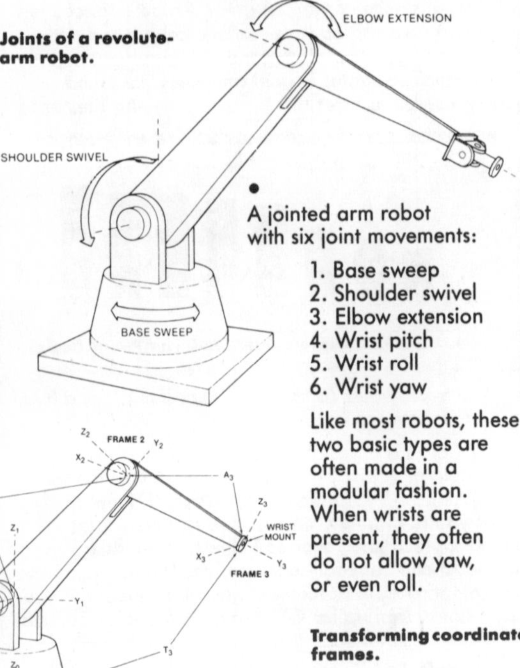

Joints of a revolute-arm robot.

•

A jointed arm robot with six joint movements:

1. Base sweep
2. Shoulder swivel
3. Elbow extension
4. Wrist pitch
5. Wrist roll
6. Wrist yaw

Like most robots, these two basic types are often made in a modular fashion. When wrists are present, they often do not allow yaw, or even roll.

Transforming coordinate frames.

Basic Robotic Concepts
John M. Holland
1983; 270 pp.
$19.95
($22.45 postpaid) from:
Howard W. Sams & Co.
4300 West 62nd Street
Indianapolis, IN 46268
or Whole Earth Access

The Robot Experimenter

The only regular source of information, besides ***Radio Electronics*** *magazine, for people who are building their own robots. It deserves to survive and thrive.*
—Richard Prather (Homebrew Robotics Club)

Robot Experimenter
Raymond Cote, Editor
$24/year
(12 issues) from:
Robot Experimenter
P. O. Box 458
Peterborough, NH
03458-0458

Robotics

Edited by an artificial intelligence pioneer, this anthology covers all the bases: the history of automatons, artificial common sense, sensors, human-machine partnerships (cyborgs), industrial robots, and the effects of robots on society. Here is the best starting point for a non-tinkerer who wants to know what robotics is about, and how it might change the world. *—Art Kleiner*

•

At some point in the future someone would go to work by slipping on a comfortable jacket lined with a myriad of sensors and musclelike motors. Each motion of his arm and fingers would then be reproduced at another place by mobile, mechanical hands. Light, dexterous, and strong, those remote mechanical hands have their own sensors, which will transmit what's happening back to the worker so that he will seem to feel whatever the remote hands may touch. The same will be done for the motions of the head and eyes, so that the operator will seem to see and sense what's happening in the other workplace. Once we can do such things, it will be another simple step to give those remote presences different strengths and scale of size. These remote bodies can have the brute capacity of a giant or the delicacy of a surgeon. And, using these information channels, an operator could be anyplace — in another room, another city, another country, even out on a space station orbiting the Earth.

•

A 1980 census of robots, taken by Bache Halsey Stuart Shields, Inc., showed that the United States had 3,000 of them. . . . The entire Soviet Union had only 25, and these were evidently experimental devices, but Poland had 360. . . . The true homeland of the robot appears to be Japan, with 10,000 in the census, more than the rest of the world combined.

Robotics
Marvin Minsky, Editor
1985; 317 pp.
$19.95
postpaid from:
Doubleday and Company
Direct Mail Order
501 Franklin Avenue
Garden City, NY 11530
or Whole Earth Access

Man-controlled machines, like the rifle-armed Ro-Veh, can be made to rush in where wise men would never go.

This intelligent prosthetic arm, from the University of Utah, converts fine muscle contractions into delicate limb movement.

BEGINNING 100 YEARS AGO, the telephone industry changed a nation of remote outposts into a vast interwoven network of sense, nonsense, business, motion, and emotion. The 1982 divestiture decision prompted a flood of change in telephones and telephone services. When the waters subside, the entire infrastructure of our culture will be new.

Meanwhile: Answering machines have revamped our habits of courtesy. New models let you retrieve messages from any faraway touchtone phone, or even forward messages to another phone. The consumer electronics catalogs on p. 348 carry them. Panasonic is the most consistently reliable brand. Cellular phones ("car phones") are revamping the morning commute. They vary so much locally that you should shop locally — don't even rely on national gossip sources.

—Art Kleiner

The Complete Guide to Lower Phone Costs
Robert Krughoff and staff of Consumer's Checkbook
1985; 71 pp.
$6.95 postpaid

Consumer's Checkbook Long-Distance Cost Comparison
$10 - $75
Information **free**
All from:
Consumer's Checkbook
806 15th Street, NW
Suite 925
Washington, DC 20005
or Whole Earth Access

Installing Your Own Telephones

If you want a phone extension — for home or business — you should probably install it yourself. This how-to guide is excellent — full of diagrams, written clearly, and organized for scanning.

—*Art Kleiner*

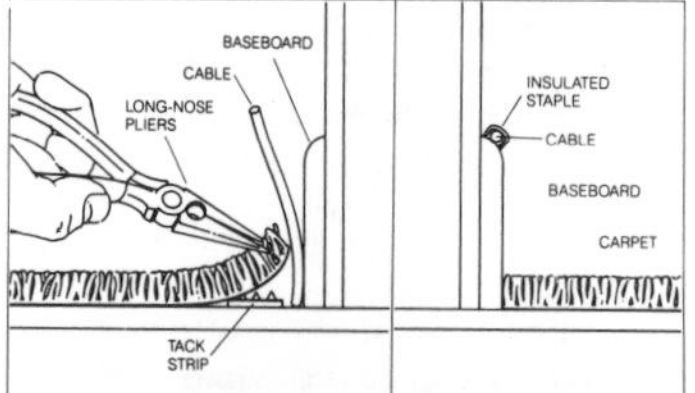

One of the neatest ways to run the cable without exposing it is to run it along the baseboard under the carpet. The carpet is pulled up with a long nose pliers without pulling the carpet away from the tack strip. At the doorway, the cable runs under the metal strip that finishes the carpet in the doorway.

•

Your local telephone company only guarantees to supply a finite amount of ringing power — usually for five telephones. Each standard ringing power unit is a REN. If the telephones that you install add to more than 5 REN, then the amount guaranteed by the telephone company has been exceeded, and your telephone may not ring. It will depend on how far you are from the central office. Standard telephones take 1 REN to ring. Many electronic telephones take much less than 1 REN so more of them can be connected to the line.

Installing Your Own Telephones
Master Publishing, Inc.
1986; 170 pp.
$9.95
postpaid from:
Prentice-Hall Company
Mail Order Sales
200 Old Tappan Road
Old Tappan, NJ 07675
or Whole Earth Access

The Complete Guide to Lower Phone Costs • Consumer's Checkbook Long-Distance Cost Comparison

Most of us will be victims, not consumers, of long-distance phone companies (AT&T, Allnet, MCI, etc.) — the options are too complex and change too rapidly. For $10 - $75, depending on your monthly bill, Consumer's Checkbook will computer-analyze your phone bill and suggest the best long-distance carriers. A great service — priced low enough to save you back its cost in a couple of months. You can also get their more general, masterful ***Complete Guide*** *which evaluates in print amenities like sound quality, as well as rates.*

—*Art Kleiner*

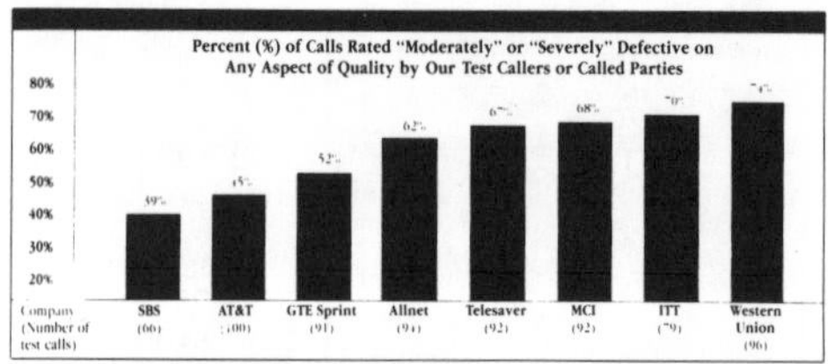

—The Complete Guide to Lower Phone Costs

•

Q. Which is the best company if I expect to place a lot of calls when traveling?

A. GTE Sprint is a good bet. It charges the same for calls originating away from your home city as for calls you make from your home phone. Also, GTE Sprint allows you to originate calls from a relatively large number of locations (over 350 cities). If you find a lower-cost company for calls from your home phone but that company does not have a good travel feature, you may want to sign up for GTE Sprint as a backup service to be used when traveling — so long as you'll call enough each month to meet GTE Sprint's $5 minimum usage requirement.

—*The Complete Guide to Lower Phone Costs*

Teleconnect
Andy Moore, Editor
$15/year
(12 issues) from:
Teleconnect
12 West 21st Street
New York, NY 10010

Which Phone System Should I Buy?
1985; 316 pp.
$39.95
($43.95 postpaid) from:
Telecom Library, Inc.
12 West 21st Street
New York, NY 10010
or Whole Earth Access

Teleconnect • Which Phone System Should I Buy?

One of the most viciously irreverent, smart, and unpretentious trade magazines around — covering telephones and the telephone industry. They also publish books. If you run a small business, their ***Which Phone System Should I Buy?*** *answers exactly that question. No one else will, adequately, not even high-priced consultants.*

—*Art Kleiner*

•

To save money, the White House has changed the Moscow Hot Line to a low-cost long distance carrier.

The White House has discovered an extra benefit. There'll never be another War. The superpowers are spending their lives bitching at each other about the quality of the line and whose fault it is.

—*Teleconnect*

From answering machine to "personal call management system." Sony's IT-A600 is tops. Especially check out "message transfer:" the machine calls you to tell you there's a message. Around $230 - $260.

—Teleconnect

Probably the oldest continuously made phone, the "500" single line rotary (dial) telephone set. This is the classic electro-mechanical telephone. It will work fine behind most PBXs. It will last a zillion years. The wallphone version is called the 554.

—Which Phone System Should I Buy?

SOMEDAY EVERYONE WILL COMMUNICATE this way. Now, only a small number of lucky pioneers do. Me, for instance. Without leaving home, I work 20 hours a month for a company 8,000 miles away in London. I've exchanged detailed (sometimes heartfelt) thoughts with dozens of people I would never have otherwise met — including several distant contributors to this *Catalog.* There is no more immediate, involving way to initiate a project between a group of far-flung people. Computer networks may make it possible to join the 1990s equivalent of the vibrant cultural life of Paris-in-the-20s through any computer in any small town.

Computer networkers type words into their machines. The words travel across phone lines to other computers, where they appear as private mail or public messages (readable by anyone else with a computer). Many computer networks are like universities without schedules, where members sign in at their own convenience to take part in wide-ranging, overlapping conversations on a variety of topics.

Whole Earth editors became so enamored of computer networks that we started our own — *the WELL (Whole Earth 'Lectronic Link).* Like all such networks, you pay by the minute — in our case, $3/hour plus $8/month plus (if you're not local) $4/hour for national transmission carrier. You pay by credit card. To check in, dial (415) 332-6106 and at the log in prompt, type (in lower case): *newuser* and press the enter key or carriage return.

If you've ever sat waiting by the mailbox, you should consider this technology. Being on computer networks is like having new mail show up several times a day. —Art Kleiner

The Complete Handbook of Personal Computer Communications
Alfred Glossbrenner
1985; 512 pp.
$14.95
($16.45 postpaid) from:
St. Martin's Press
175 Fifth Avenue
New York, NY 10010
or Whole Earth Access

The Complete Handbook of Personal Computer Communications

Only book you need. All the lore on how to set up your computer for networking, find the particular networks you need, and connect your computer to someone else's typesetting equipment or directly to another computer. Now in its extensively revised second edition, this book resounds with enthusiasm and clarity. —*Art Kleiner*

•

Industry newsletters of the sort found on NewsNet are really more like private, expert consultations. Most contain "the inside dope" on what's going on in a particular field. And most can tell you what's likely to take place six months from now, what your competition is doing, how national and world events are likely to affect the industry as a whole, and so on. In many cases there will also be commentary and analysis, interviews with key people, advice, tips, and other information — all of it gathered, selected, and filtered through the expertise and experience of the newsletter's creator or editor.

This is the kind of information the general press will never carry. . . . More than 80% of all newsletters on the NewsNet system are transmitted directly to the company's Prime computers from the personal computers and communicating word processors of their creators. As a result, you can be reading a newsletter within *hours* of the time it left its creator's floppy disk.

•

One of the important features offered by a system like MCI Mail is the option to have your message printed out and delivered by U. S. mail. This is important because it lets you send letters to people who do not have access to a personal computer.

Link-Up
Loraine Page, Editor
$22/year
(11 issues) from:
Learned Information, Inc.
143 Old Marlton Pike
Medford, NJ 08055

Link-Up

A tabloid with personal writing that keeps track of new computer networks, information services, terminal software, and anything else you need to telecommunicate effectively via personal computer. Some articles pick a topic (investing, psychology, detective work, religion) and describe everything online that's related. Link-Up is also beginning to cover some of the legal and social ramifications of the new telecom technology. —*Art Kleiner*

•

The University of the Pacific's School of Pharmacy offers doctors and psychiatrists drug information via a private service, Drug.Info, on Source Telecomputing. The University's staff reviews most major publications to provide an up-to-the-minute digest of important drug developments. You can quickly scan articles and choose those that appear most significant to your practice. You can then forward the article to your associates via electronic mail.

•

Before you decide to meet a CompuServer or attend a CompuServe CB party in some faraway city, check out the pix in the CB database. If you are using CompuServe's Vidtex communications software, you can download and print digitized pictures of other CompuServers. To get into the database, you send CompuServe a good, sharp 5" x 7" or 8" x 10" black and white photo of your head and shoulders.

• Many of the editors and contributors of this catalog host on-line conferences on The WELL, Whole Earth's own regional network. Jay Kinney runs the Spirituality conference; Dick Fugett, Politics; Kevin Kelly, Travel; Art Kleiner, Telecommunications; and James Stockford, Music. There are 120 other conferences going on, too. Experts are encouraged to start their own topics.

Software from Hallmark enables Apple and Commodore owners to compose greetings offline, then send them via CompuServe.

There is usually a half-hour or more to look over the items that will be sold before a scheduled auction starts. —*Before You Buy a Used Computer*

By Art Kleiner

PERSONAL computers are tools for 1. capturing and playing back dreams, 2. simulating real-life situations without real-life consequences, 3. automating clerical work. Your computer becomes a symbiotic mental environment, irrevocably customized and wedded to your own habits of thought.

How to decide if you really want a computer? Visit a friend who has used one for more than six months. Watch them at work. See how intrigued you become.

Unfortunately, reliable shopping information is scarce. It's too hard for even the most dedicated evaluators to keep up with the rapidly changing gold-rush-style computer industry. "No matter what you buy," says Woody Liswood, "the first person you meet after your purchase will tell you that you should have purchased something different."

Here are our preferred computer choices — current for summertime 1986. Prices mentioned are "street price" — what you'd pay at a discount store (see p. 354).

David Jouris

Editor Art Kleiner's IBM-clone setup at home.

Generic (no-brand-name) IBM PC-Compatible, $1400-$1800. 640K memory, one-two floppy drives, 20-megabyte hard disk, Hercules-compatible monochrome monitor.

Least expensive, most versatile, full-computing system. Because so many IBM PCs and "compatibles" (computers that work similarly) exist, you can find well-crafted software packages to do just about anything.

Beginning in 1985, independent dealers began buying components, assembling them, and selling PC-compatibles without brand names. I paid $1,500 for such a "generic clone" — the equivalent brand-name IBM-PC would have cost $2,800. If generic computers make you nervous, Zenith and others have clones at in-between prices. Prices continue to drop and choices to multiply. Before you buy, get the self-published, frequently updated *IBM XT Clone Buyer's Guide* — filled with detailed advice and user-group lore. Also, buy your clone locally — it's not uncommon for any computer to have parts that need replacing in the first week or so. Disadvantages: PC-compatibles aren't as intuitively obvious as Macintoshes, Atari STs, or Amigas — they require more struggling and futzing. Frequently, PC-compatible programs don't work together, and may, in the wrong combination, unexpectedly freeze up your machine. You learn to ameliorate that. A book on using the computer is essential — we recommend *Introducing PC-DOS and MS-DOS.*

Essentials: A 20-megabyte hard disk (about $450 extra) gives you a single permanent storage place for all your programs and data. A hard disk is such a great convenience that if you can't afford one, consider the Atari 1040ST instead. Since hard disks fail, you need a back-up program to restore lost material. We recommend DMS PC Intelligent Backup ($130). Also get 1Dir ($70), for mapping and navigating your hard disk territory.

We recommend PC-Write ($10) for writing (see p. 302). For telecommunicating, pfs:Access ($95, easier) or ProComm ($50, more versatile). For number work, the VP Planner spreadsheet ($70). SideKick ($54) pops up extra tools — calculator, notepad, phone dialer — on your screen anytime. Also Managing Your Money (see p. 202). Though color is not essential, if you have any interest in graphics you'll want an EGA (Enhanced Graphics Adapter) color board and monitor ($1,175 extra).

Having a PC-compatible means never running out of bewildering choices. *PC* is the most consistently useful magazine for keeping up. Even more than with other computers, buy slowly, buy as little as possible, and plug into the gossip channels of a nearby user's group.

DMS PC Intelligent Backup: $130 ($150 list), Sterling Software, (800) 554-8677.

1Dir: $70 ($95 list), Bourbaki, Inc., (208) 342-5849.

PC-Write: $10 ($75 with technical support), Quicksoft, (206) 282-0452.

pfs:Access: $95 ($140 list), Software Publishing Corp., (415) 962-8910.

ProComm: $50, PIL Software Systems, Columbia, MO.

VP Planner: $70 ($100 list), Paperback Software International, (415) 644-2116.

SideKick: $54 ($85 list), Borland International, (408) 438-8400.

EGA color board: $450 ($525 list); **EGA monitor: $725** ($849 list); both from IBM Personal Computer Customer Relations, P. O. Box 2910, Delray Beach, FL 33444.

Editor Jay Kinney's home office with the Mac ImageWriter (lower left) and Laser Printer behind it.

512K Macintosh with upgrade, or Mac Plus ($1700-$2900), with either two 800K disk drives, or one 800K drive and a hard disk.

Apple's Macintosh was the first popularly priced computer to meet human beings halfway. It engages us — it presents a visual "desktop" on the screen, a mental landscape where you travel by moving an electronic "mouse" across the surface of your real desk. The Mac's smaller "stiff disks" have more capacity and durability than the IBM PC-compatible "floppy disks."

Macintosh software usually feels intuitively correct, with images built into the fabric of nearly everything you see onscreen. And it all works together. You can draw pictures on your spreadsheet image, or fit a piece of text into a "wine cellar" drawing in

David Jouris

Whole Earth Software Catalog editor Richard Dalton's home workstation with Atari ST.

your graphic file cabinet. The Mac has been a magnet for creative designers; often the most interesting new software appears here first. That's especially true for "desktop publishing" (see p. 316).

Disadvantages: It's more expensive than our other choices (though more durably made). Accessories, like hard disks, are particularly high-priced. It can only produce black-and-white images (so far). And it's s-l-o-w — except for the new MacPlus. You can find shops that "upgrade" the 512K Mac, for faster speed. If the difference between an upgraded 512K and a Plus is $400 or less, we recommend getting the Plus.

Essentials: Apple's own ImageWriter II Printer ($595). MacWrite ($125), the word processor, no longer comes free with the machine, but it should. FullPaint ($80) is a refinement of the groundbreaking MacPaint ($125) drawing program. Switcher ($20) "wipe-dissolves" (like a cinema transition) from one program to another, smoothly and quickly. OverVUE ($230) manages lists and files easily. Excel ($265) is the best spreadsheet (see p. 195). MicroPhone ($60) is our favorite communications program. *Macworld* is less flashy than the other good magazine, *MacUser,* but it has more depth.

ImageWriter II Printer: $595; MacWrite: $125; MacPaint: $125; Switcher: $20; all from Apple Computer, (800) 538-9696.

FullPaint: $80 ($100 list), Ann Arbor Softworks, (313) 996-3838.

OverVUE: $230 ($295 list), ProVue Development Corp., (714) 969-2431.

Excel: $265 ($395 list), Microsoft Corp., (800) 426-9400.

MicroPhone: $60 ($75 list), Software Ventures, (415) 644-3232.

Atari 1040 ST with color monitor and one disk drive ($1100)

The price-buster. The ST is as inviting as the Mac (which it blatantly copied), but it runs much faster. It has colors (although only 4-16 can appear on the screen at one time), excellent music capabilities, a growing legion of users, a fast-expanding community of software (public domain and commercial), and a street price under $1100 (including monitor). Get the better value, the 1040 ST, not its clumsier predecessor, the 520 ST.

Disadvantages: Not as well constructed as the Mac, or as adaptable as the PC, and has less software available than either. Forthcoming systems to run PC or Mac software aren't available yet. Unlike the Mac, Atari ST software will not necessarily all work together easily.

Essentials: First Word, the writing program that comes with the computer. A painting/drawing program, like Degas ($35, easier) or EasyDraw ($150, more complex). ST-Term ($40) for telecommunicating. Since the ST is exalted by a color printer, consider the inexpensive Okimate-20 ($220). There is no great ST magazine yet, but generally Atari-oriented *Antic* covers most new innovations.

Degas: $35 ($40 list), Batteries Included, (416) 881-9819.

EasyDraw: $150, MiGraph, (206) 838-4677.

ST-Term: $40, Commnet Systems, (408) 745-2367.

Okimate-20: $220 ($270 list), Oki-Data, (609) 235-2600.

Other choices:

Commodore Amiga ($1800): To create or use fancy color graphics, to program at the top of your craft, or to meld computers, video, and/or music. Technically, it surpasses most other business computers (it can run several programs at once, a surprisingly useful feature), but the availability of good software is still uncertain.

Radio Shack Model 100 ($400): The size of a three-ring-binder. Bring it with you anywhere; it runs on batteries. Great for note-taking. Still a good deal until other, more capable "laptops" come down in price.

Used computers

Used computers: Great deals and values, some pitfalls. Most used computers work fine, but many only run obsolete software. Read two books first: *The Skeptical Consumer's Guide to Used Computers* (what to buy) and *Before You Buy a Used Computer* (where to buy it).

Cheap home computers: Wait. Major changes are coming during the next year, and the entire industry is poised, holding its breath. If you absolutely can't spend more than $400, and you mostly need a word processor, I'd buy an electronic typewriter. (See "Consumer Electronics," p. 348, for a mail order source.)

IBM XT Clone Buyer's Guide
Edwin Rutsch
1986; 172 pp.
$9.95 postpaid from:
Modular Information System
431 Ashbury Street
San Francisco, CA 94117
or Whole Earth Access

Introducing PC-DOS and MS-DOS
Thomas Sheldon
1985; 374 pp.
$18.95 postpaid from:
McGraw-Hill Order Dept.
Princeton Road
Hightstown, NJ 08520
or Whole Earth Access

PC Magazine
Bill Machrone, Editor
$34.97/year
(22 issues) from:
PC Magazine
P. O. Box 2445
Boulder, CO 80321

MacWorld
Jerry Borrell, Editor
$30/year
(12 issues) from:
MacWorld
Subscription Dept.
P. O. Box 54529
Boulder, CO 80323

MacUser
Steven Bobker, Editor
$27/year
(12 issues) from:
MacUser
29 Haviland Street South
Norwalk, CT 06854

Antic
Nat Friedland, Editor
$28/year
(12 issues) from:
Antic
P. O. Box 1919
Marion, OH 43306

Before You Buy a Used Computer
Dona Z. Meilach
1985; 159 pp.
$10.95
($13.55 postpaid) from:
Publisher's Central Bureau
1 Champion Avenue
Avenel, NJ 07001
or Whole Earth Access

The Skeptical Consumer's Guide to Used Computers
Ed Kahn and John Bear
1985; 306 pp.
$9.95
($10.95 postpaid) from:
Ten Speed Press
P. O. Box 7123
Berkeley, CA 94707
or Whole Earth Access

Whole Earth Software Catalog

Whole Earth Software Catalog
(for 1986)
Stewart Brand,
Editor in Chief
1985; 224 pp.
$15 postpaid from:
Whole Earth Review
27 Gate Five Road
Sausalito, CA 94965
or Whole Earth Access

Tells what to buy. Software, computers, books, magazines — all beloved. Comparative, informal reviews. Current in September '85 — about 20 percent outdated now. Our choices since then appear in the **Whole Earth Review** *(see inside front cover). We made this book; you'd expect us to review it at the expense of its competition. However, there isn't any. We have a number of industry acquaintances who would immediately, gleefully inform us if there were other software review compendiums — worthy or unworthy — with our range and currency. So far, there are none. Reviewing software is hard. This catalog makes your job easier.*
—*Art Kleiner*

For presentation graphics . . .

EXECUVISION

IBM PC/XT/AT (256); copy-protected; $395 (street price $259); IBM color card and Enhanced Graphics Adapter, Tecmar Graphics Master. Input: keyboard only. Output to Epson and IBM graphics dot matrix printers; Polaroid Palette; Lang Videoslide. With E Z Capture Plus option ($125): Output to most dot matrix printers; IBM color printer; Diablo Inkjet C-150 and other color printers; HP 7475A plotter. VCN, 238 Main St., Cambridge, MA 02142; 617/497-4000.

RIK JADRNICEK: EXECUVISION steps beyond the world of basic business graphics with a fantastic set of tools for preparing presentation graphics. You can freely edit the images you create and include them in slideshows. You can cut small sections out of an image, save them in a library on disk and then paste them into other images you create later.

The creators of EXECUVISION sell libraries of graphic shapes you can use, including decorative borders, initials and decorative designs, faces and figures, and maps and international symbols.

The documentation is very thorough and extensively illustrated (even showing the IBM and its keyboard every step of the way). Let the pictures speak for themselves . . .

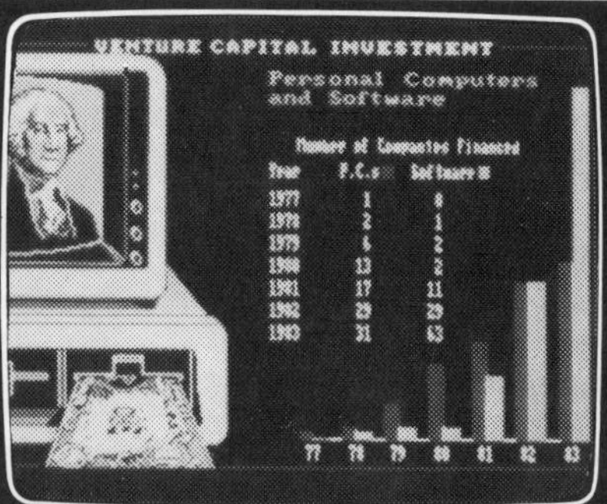

This graph didn't pop up automatically from data. It's entirely hand-drawn, with numbers typed onscreen, using EXECUVISION. With the E Z Capture Plus option, EXECUVISION can use data imported from 1-2-3 (p. 68), SYMPHONY (p. 111), FRAMEWORK (p. 110), or any screen in 320 x 200 resolution.

Hackers

Hackers
Steven Levy
1984; 448 pp.
$4.50
($5.25 postpaid) from:
Dell Books
P. O. Box 1000
Pinebrook, NJ 07058-1000
or Whole Earth Access

Steven Levy is to computer history what Barbara Tuchman is to the 14th Century. He tells how programming changes people, how programmers created a subculture, and how that subculture changed the whole culture.
—*Art Kleiner*

•

Something new was coalescing around the TX-0: a new way of life, with a philosophy, an ethic, and a dream.

The Hacker Ethic:

Access to computers — and anything which might teach you something about the way the world works — should be unlimited and total. Always yield to the Hands-On Imperative!

Hackers believe that essential lessons can be learned about the systems — about the world — from taking things apart, seeing how they work, and using this knowledge to create new and even more interesting things. They resent any person, physical barrier, or law that tries to keep them from doing this.

All information should be free.

Mistrust Authority — Promote Decentralization.

The best way to promote this free exchange of information is to have an open system, something which presents no boundaries between a hacker and a piece of information or an item of equipment that he needs in his quest for knowledge, improvement, and time on-line. The last thing you need is a bureaucracy.

Hackers should be judged by their hacking, not bogus criteria such as degrees, age, race, or position.

You can create art and beauty on a computer.

Computers can change your life for the better.

How to Get Free Software

How to Get Free Software
Alfred Glossbrenner
1984; 432 pp.
$14.95
($15.20 postpaid) from:
St. Martin's Press
Cash Sales
175 Fifth Avenue
New York, NY 10010
or Whole Earth Access

No one we know has a more comprehensive knowledge of software then Alfred Glossbrenner. His new book, ***How to Get Free Software****, has chapter and verse on the subject. The major problem with public domain programs is finding out about them and finding where to get them. He takes care of both. (The minor problems are dealing with the sheer volume of choices and working without manuals.)*
—*Stewart Brand*

•

Once you get "plugged in," you'll discover that there is an informal network of users groups across the continent. Many groups regularly exchange newsletters and information, and many share their member-contributed free software.

In almost all users groups there will be a "software librarian" who has taken the responsibility for organizing, building, and maintaining the group's free software collection. Frequently, the librarian and assisting members will bring the entire library to the group's monthly meeting. And either before, after, or during the meeting, members will be free to pick up any programs they want. If you bring your own blank disks, there will usually be a copying charge of about $1 to help maintain the library. But often a club will be able to provide you with a disk at a discounted price. (If you do bring your own floppies, try to format them beforehand.)

•

Indeed, if you are interested in programming, free software can provide a wonderful learning experience. Unlike most commercial software, the vast majority of public domain programs are "listable." That means you can print out and review the program itself and see how its author accomplished (or failed to accomplish) a particular goal. This can alert you to interesting techniques or save you from making similar mistakes. And in some cases it can teach you more about BASIC, Pascal, assembler, and other languages than many textbooks can.

Software by Mail

Substantial deals here. 800-SOFTWARE offers free help after the sale — sometimes better than what you get from the software manufacturer. They have a crack team of advisors, and a really good newsletter. You pay a little more money for this. LOGIC-SOFT discounts deeply — they offer to beat any cheaper price you find by $10. I and others have had good luck with them. They ship every order over $100 by Purolator Courier, free. COMPUTER MAIL ORDER has the widest range. At reasonable prices, they sell software for just about any type of computer.
—*Saul Feldman*

800-SOFTWARE: (800) 225-9273
LOGIC-SOFT: (800) 645-3491
COMPUTER MAIL ORDER: (800) 233-8950

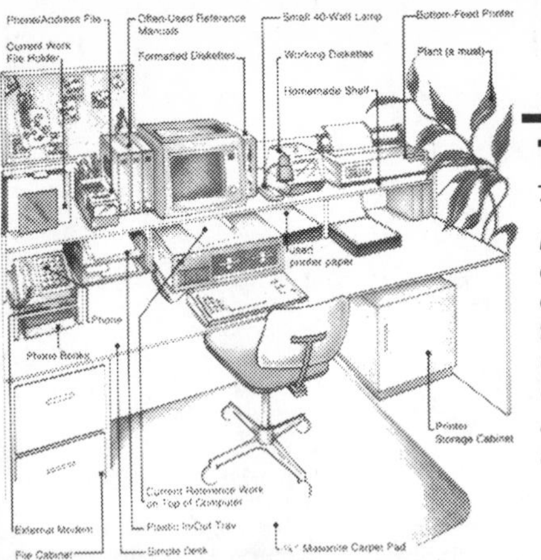

Through the MicroMaze

This is the introductory computer book I've been waiting for. Its subject is the setting up of your personal computer scene — that two-week obstacle that keeps the almost-ready-to-jump from jumping. How to lay out your work area, how to hook everything up, how to get fluent in the fundamentals of your computer's operating system. With color pictures, clear diagrams, and really sensible advice, this book is a comfort and a blessing. —*Stewart Brand*

This drawing shows how to get all your hardware and storage needs organized for convenient use.

Through the MicroMaze
Wayne Creekmore and Stephanie Behasa
1984; 64 pp.
$9.95
($11.95 postpaid) from:
Ashton-Tate
Publication Group
20101 Hamilton Avenue
Torrance, CA 90502
or Whole Earth Access

INSIDE A FLOPPY DISKETTE DRIVE

Disk hub....
Index emitter (works with index detector below disk)
Write-protect switch
Disk spindle
D.C. Stepper motor
D.C. Drive motor
Head assembly and band drive
Index detector

The Plain English Repair and Maintenance Guide for Home Computers

For fiddling with your hardware, get this cheerful, excellent guide. Detecting a problem in your mysterious computer and fixing it is a coming-of-age, a departure from helplessness. —*Stewart Brand*

IBM PC-compatible owners should get the special edition targeted for them. —*Art Kleiner*

One sick chip can infect all others that are logically connected to it "downstream."

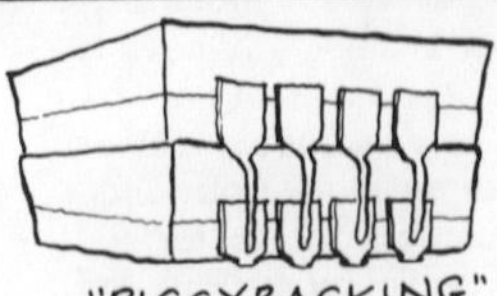

◄ *Substitution of ICs without removing originals.*

If you suspect that a chip is defective, you can simply press another of the same type over it. This is called "piggybacking" (big surprise!) and is a handy trouble-shooting technique if you have a stock of chips on hand. Here's how to do it:

a. Turn off power.
b. Carefully bend the new chip leads in slightly so that each will contact its mate on the original chip.

The Plain English Repair and Maintenance Guide for Home Computers
Henry F. Beechhold
1984; 265 pp.
IBM PC version:
Henry F. Beechhold
1985; 258 pp.
$14.95 each postpaid
Both from:
Simon & Schuster
Mail Order Sales
200 Old Tappan
Old Tappan, NJ 07675
or Whole Earth Access

Computer Magazines

For learning about fast-changing computers, magazines are essential. ***InfoWorld****, the traditional microcomputer industry bible, is declining slowly but definitely from a finder for the computer-literate public to a trade gossip sheet. We still recommend it — for now.* ***Computer Shopper*** *is like hunkering down at a computer swap meet — gritty, technical, hacker-ish, and full of tiny ads. It lists all the known active user groups and computer bulletin boards in each state. It's about the only place that talks about "orphaned" computers, discontinued models such as the Timex Sinclair that are still being widely used.* —*Art Kleiner*

•

According to the report, which compiled the results of tests and surveys from 123 various research groups worldwide, a person takes 20 percent to 30 percent longer to read text from a computer screen than to read the same text on paper, despite improvements in the design and resolution of screens. The report also concludes that users are less able to detect typographical errors on a computer screen, said Carol Mills, director of the Usability Test Laboratory for the Institute. —*InfoWorld*

Bulletin Boards: Iowa
ABBS Apple-Med., Iowa City, IA 319-353-6528
COMPUCENTER IOWA 319-338-2750 300/1200 Baud Upload/Download
COMPUCENTER 319-338-2750 300/1200 BAUD *24
THE COMPUTER CELLAR Cedar Falls, IA 319-277-0646
DICK DAVIN REALTY Iowa City, IA 319-338-3947: 300/1200 BAUD *24
IBM PC Cedar Rapids, IA 319-363-3314 *24
SUNSHINE BBS/EXCHANGE, DUBUQUE, IA 319-557-9659 *24

•

Several Tucson cave divers have put me onto the ultimate mouse working surface.

Besides being cheap and easy to get, it beats just about all the commercial products whiskers down.

So, run down to your friendly neighborhood divers supply or scuba shop, and get yourself some 1/8 inch or 1/4 inch nylon *wetsuit material*.

Cost is around a dollar per square foot, and you use it fuzzy side up. It even comes in decorator colors. You can cut it with plain old scissors. —*Computer Shopper*

• The largest all-computer bookstore in the land is **Computer Literacy Bookshop**, 520 Lawrence Expressway, Suite 310, Sunnyvale, CA 94086; (408) 730-9955. They carry over 9,000 titles, many of them for professional computerists.

Computer Shopper
Stan Veit, Editor
$18/year
(12 issues) from:
Patch Publishing Co., Inc.
P. O. Box F
Titusville, FL 32781-9990

InfoWorld
Jonathan Sacks, Editor
$39/year
(51 issues) from:
InfoWorld
P. O. Box 1018
Southeastern, PA 19398

The Amazing Newborn

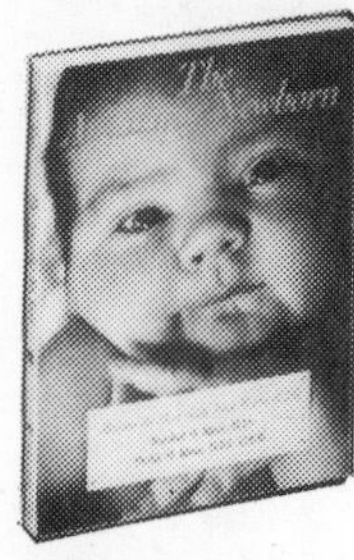

The Amazing Newborn
Marshall Klaus, M.D., and Phyllis Klaus, M.Ed., C.S.W.
1985; 145 pp.
$10.53
postpaid from:
Addison-Wesley Publishing Co.
1 Jacob Way
Reading, MA 01867
or Whole Earth Access

Become immersed in the world of the newborn. All the photographs in this book are of babies less than ten days old and illustrate well "each of the special and often newly discovered capacities with which human beings begin life."

I am troubled by the idea of experimentation with newborns and some of the text is based on it. But this is mostly overshadowed by observations of infant behavior in real life. **The Amazing Newborn** *is sensitive, revealing, inspirational, and transforming in adding appreciation and understanding of the newborn as real humans.*
—Peggy O'Mara McMahon

Right after birth, within the first hour of life, normal infants have a prolonged period of quiet alertness, averaging forty minutes, during which they look directly at their mother's and father's face and eyes and can respond to voices. It is as though newborns had rehearsed the perfect approach to the first meeting with their parents. In this state, motor activity is suppressed and all the baby's energy seems to be channeled into seeing and hearing.

A young infant imitating Professor Meltzoff protrudes his tongue, opens his mouth, and purses his lips. Each gesture was done at a different time.

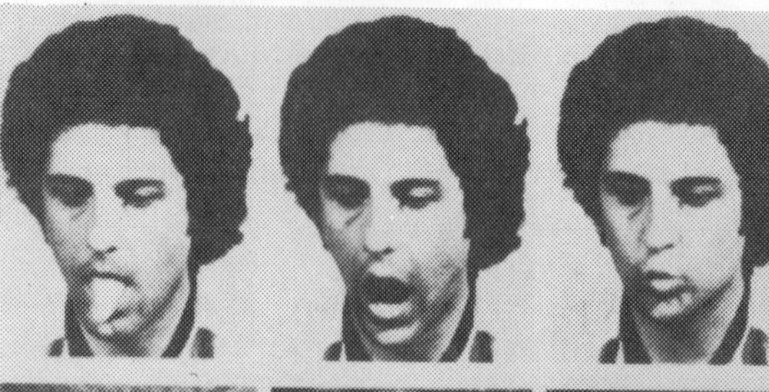

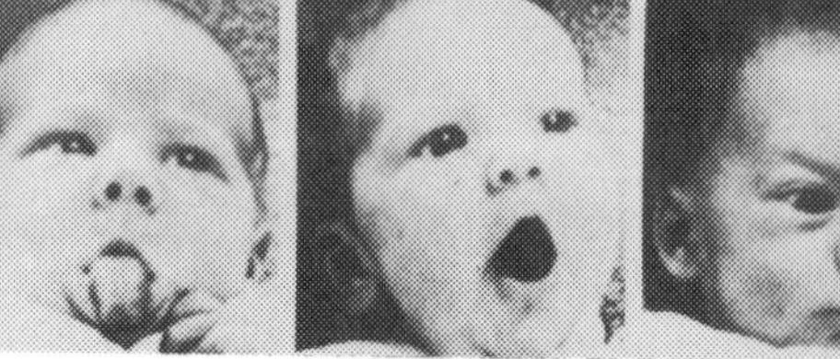

The Womanly Art of Breastfeeding

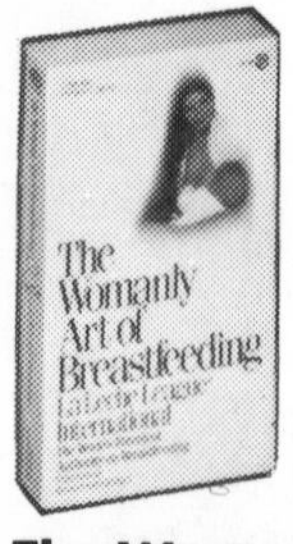

The Womanly Art of Breastfeeding
La Leche League International
1981; 368 pp.
$7.95
($9.45 postpaid) from:
New American Library
120 Woodbine Street
Bergenfield, NJ 07621
or Whole Earth Access

We have La Leche League International to thank for reversing the trend away from breastfeeding that was prevalent 25 years ago; today over 50 percent of women choose breastfeeding (90 percent in some areas). Thirteen years ago, when I was pregnant with my first child, I kept this book in the bathroom and read it over and over again and again to gain the confidence to breastfeed. **The Womanly Art of Breastfeeding** *reassures you that everyone can breastfeed and tells you everything you need to know for success. A traditional view of mothering is emphasized because the authors — seven founding mothers of La Leche League — have found that many traditional values help insure the physical closeness and contact necessary for breastfeeding. First published in 1958 and updated over the years, this book has become the breastfeeding bible.* *—Peggy O'Mara McMahon*

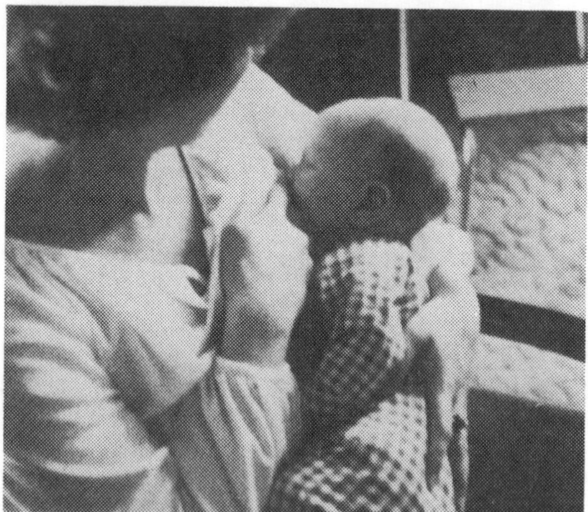

Becky Herbin holds her son Michael close with his body facing her, and uses her fingers to shape her nipple so he can grasp it properly.

•

Breastfeeding while sitting up is basically the same as when lying down. Baby should be held facing your breast with head up close, yet tilted back slightly. Baby should be looking up at you. Cup your breast in your hand and press down on the areola with your thumb. This should point your nipple out and upward. Again, baby should get your nipple and part of the areola well into his mouth. He will be able to grasp the nipple well if you hold him close to you. If baby chews only on the end of the nipple, he may develop a style of nursing described by one mother as the "cliff-hanger." Baby won't get as much milk, and mother is likely to get sore nipples. As your baby grows older and holds his head well, you won't have to take such careful notice of angle and position; he'll get where he want to go, all on his own.

Crying Baby, Sleepless Nights

Crying Baby, Sleepless Nights
Sandy Jones
1983; 293 pp.
$7.95
($8.95 postpaid) from:
Warner Books
P. O. Box 690
New York, NY 10019
or Whole Earth Access

One of the adjustments of new parenthood is the reality of nighttime parenting. New babies don't know about day and night right away, and they need frequent feedings and close contact. Sandy Jones gives you many suggestions on how to determine if baby's night waking is normal night waking, or if there really is something you can do about it. Mothers with babies with colic will love this book and be reassured by it. It's also good for expectant parents wanting to know what to expect from a new baby. The book includes 100 tips for the "less-than-perfect" mother, a directory of support groups for parents, and information on finding the right pediatrician.
—Peggy O'Mara McMahon

•

What's the secret of knowing one baby cry from the other? Most mothers use their inner sense of their babies' daily schedule to help them, along with observing baby behavior in its everyday context.

If the baby's been asleep for three and a half hours and he wakes up crying, he's probably hungry. If the baby's been up for three hours and he seems fitful and keeps batting at his ear and mildly fussing, he's probably ready to nurse off to sleep. If he wakes up in the middle of the night with a loud, piercing scream, he's probably in pain from a diaper pin pressing into his side, a string from his sleeper wrapped around his toe, a bubble of gas trapped in his stomach, or some other inner or outer pain.

Baby Supplies

You really don't need as much paraphernalia for a new baby as some would make you think. Here are the only things I have found really necessary with four babies: Four or five dozen 100 percent cotton diapers. Can be found easily at local department stores. Prefolded Curity diapers are my favorite. Disposable diapers are expensive, ecologically unsound, and rough and uncomfortable on baby's skin; natual fiber cotton or wool diaper covers (3 or 4 pair). They're cool and breathable for baby's skin. Try Happy Baby Bunz; babies love 100 percent cotton, versatile, long-wearing clothing. Check used clothing stores and catalogs, but Hanna Anderson and Biobottoms are a sure bet; a Snugli. My second child needed a lot of physical contact and he practically lived in his Snugli baby carrier for his first six months. Being able to put him happily in the Snugli meant that I could do some work around the house while he slept peacefully — a plus for us both. —Peggy O'Mara McMahon

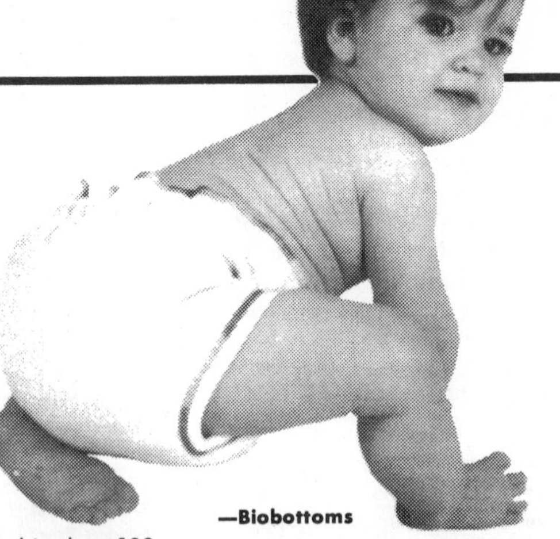

—Biobottoms

Snugli baby carrier.

Nikky Diaper Covers: **$6.50-10.75.** Information **free** from Happy Baby Bunz, P. O. Box 745, Carmichael, CA 95609.

Hanna Anderson: Catalog **$2** from Hanna Anderson, 422 Northwest 8th, Portland, OR 97209.

Biobottoms: Catalog **free** from Biobottoms, P. O. Box 1060, Petaluma, CA 94953.

Snugli Baby Carrier: **$22-60.** Brochure and dealer list **free** from Snugli, Inc., 12980 West Cedar Drive, Lakewood, CO 80228-1903.

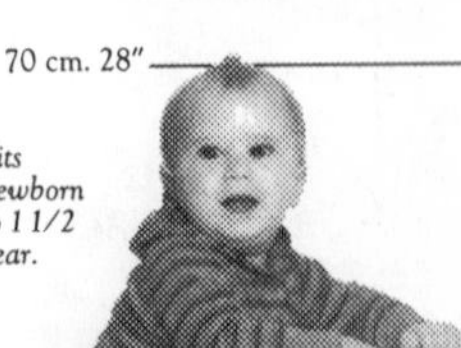

Cotton Coverups.
For spring our little hooded model comes in bright new colors and the ever popular white. Each has the drawstring hem, 4 button front and ribbed cuffs. You will find lots of uses for this little snuggler. Imported.
No. 2202 Crayon yellow and white.
No. 2205 Pure, almost formal white.
No. 2200 Just right red with white.
No. 2231 Just right red/Swedish blue.

—Hanna Anderson

The Affordable Baby

Having a baby costs money. Some expenses are inevitable (like diapers). Others are optional. What you spend depends on knowing what your choices are and how to shop around. Bundy provides a complete consumer guide to costs and comparisons for parents-to-be, from health care (what does yours cover?) to writing a will. She also tells you the advantages and disadvantages of various options (disposable diapers are convenient but costly; cloth are economical but time-consuming) that allow you to make decisions based on your own values, needs, and lifestyle. A good book to get if you're even thinking about having a baby. —Cindy Craig

•

How to Care for Cloth Diapers

This section could equally be titled "disadvantages of cloth diapers." Yes, cloth diapers will save you money — some estimates are savings of $800 or more over two and a half years of diapering — but they cost time and effort. If you're considering cloth, be sure you know what's involved in caring for them.

Diaper stains are difficult to remove, so to help prevent permanent staining, soiled diapers must be rinsed in the toilet as soon as they're taken off. Then they must be wrung out and put in a pail containing water with a teaspoonful of Borax to deodorize and kill ammonia-producing bacteria. Before laundering, the water must be wrung out. Diapers must be washed within a day or two of being soiled and they must be washed separately from the rest of the laundry. Wash them in a good-quality detergent, using the hottest cycle on your washing machine. As detergent residue can cause diaper rash, it's best to put diapers through two rinse cycles. Diapers must be thoroughly dried — in the sun is best. Then they must be folded and stored.

The Affordable Baby
Darcie Bundy
1985; 289 pp.

$6.95
($8.45 postpaid) from:
Harper and Row
2350 Virginia Avenue
Hagerstown, MD 21740
or Whole Earth Access

The Family Bed

Just mention the family bed concept and you encourage heated discussion. Even in a society such as ours where co-family sleeping is discouraged strongly, large numbers of people find that it beautifully fulfills their parenting needs. Tine Thevenin contends that babies need to sleep with their parents, that this arrangement assures the type of physical closeness so crucial to bonding and human development.

As a veteran of twelve years of various arrangements of co-family sleeping, I have suggested this book to many new parents and every one has thanked me profusely. Even if you have not contemplated the family bed, or you fear it will ruin your sex life, spoil your children, and scandalize your relatives, you too deserve to gain a perspective on nighttime parenting and broaden your understanding of what really is "normal." —Peggy O'Mara McMahon

If we could do it all over again, we would buy a king-size bed at the time of our marriage. —Mother, St. Paul, MN

The Family Bed
Tine Thevenin
1976; 195 pp.

$9.95
($10.95 postpaid) from:
Tine Thevenin
P. O. Box 16004
Minneapolis, MN 55416
or Whole Earth Access

• The foibles of baby-having and -raising are satirized with rare wit and exceedingly funny drawings.
Babies and Other Hazards of Sex: Dave Barry, 1984; 96 pp. **$4.95** postpaid from Rodale Press Inc., 33 East Minor Street, Emmaus, PA 18049 (or Whole Earth Access).

Whole Child, Whole Parent
Polly Berrien Berends
1983; 360 pp.

$10.95
($12.45 postpaid) from:
Harper and Row
2350 Virginia Avenue
Hagerstown, MD 21740
or Whole Earth Access

Whole Child, Whole Parent

I read the original version of this classic spiritual and practical guide to parenting during a panic period when my first child was one year old. It helped me regain the larger purpose of my mothering and gave me practical ways for putting my ideals into practice. I've been dipping into it ever since.

I especially love the book suggestions; this book alone helped me choose books for my first child.
—Peggy O'Mara McMahon

•

Choosing what toys to buy is a small matter compared with the overall task of discerning from moment to moment how to respond to our children in an intelligently loving way. When buying a toy seems called for, here are some things to consider: . . .

Toys to avoid.
Terrific but too temporary. Some beautiful, well-made, and educationally sound toys that are valuable in a preschool may be almost worthless at home because the child learns what they offer in a few minutes. At least in the beginning, children are not interested in the having of toys (possessiveness is acquired), but in what they can learn from them. As soon as the child has learned all he can from a toy, he will lose interest in it. If he can learn everything in one sitting, he will be through in one sitting. Glenn Doman estimates that the average toy designed for the average eighteen-month-old holds interest for about 90 seconds. . . .

Rectal temperature.

Creative Parenting
William Sears, M.D.
1982; 512 pp.

$10.95
($12.45 postpaid) from:
Dodd, Meade and Co.
P. O. Box 141000
Nashville, TN 37214
or Whole Earth Access

Creative Parenting

I usually don't recommend comprehensive "baby books" because reading the book can imply a tacit agreement that the author is the expert and the parent is not. Since I believe that the parents are the experts, it is good to have the welcome voice of Dr. Sears, who is a father of five and brings his personal experience to the ideas he discusses in the book. Topics covered are thorough: pregnancy, birth, early time of parenting, the newborn, father feelings, infant feeding and nutrition, fussy baby, sleep habits, mother-baby separation, developmental stages, common childhood illnesses, child safety and first aid, and special situations. ***Creative Parenting*** *will help you regain your perspective as parents with wisdom and practicality.*
—Peggy O'Mara McMahon

•

Adolescents are themselves going through an identity crisis, and are particularly vulnerable to the effects of a divorce. The adolescent can think abstractly and is even more prone to fantasize about marriage in general. The adolescent may become very judgmental about who is at fault and may wonder what kind of people his parents are. The behavioral problems of the adolescent are more likely to involve his peer relationships and minor delinquencies. Sexual gratification and sudden love affairs may occur. Adolescents are particularly judgmental about the possible sexual activities of the parents, and both the mother and the visiting father should exercise some discretion about their sexual pursuits. Do not count upon your adolescents to welcome a household free of marriage conflicts and tensions because, unless there has been excessive physical violence during the marriage, children do not usually view divorce as something which improves the family situation.

Birth & Life Bookstore

Hundreds, no thousands, of in-print books on children, birthing, adoption, toilet training, and so on. They stock nine books alone on the topic of twins. Longish, detailed reviews fill the front of their newsletter/catalog evaluating the latest mothering/fathering/babying books. They are far more up to date than we could ever be. —Kevin Kelly

Imprints
Catalog **free** from:
Birth & Life Bookstore
7001 Alonzo Avenue NW
P. O. Box 70625
Seattle, WA 98107-0625

How To Talk So Kids Will Listen & Listen So Kids Will Talk
Adele Faber
and Elaine Mazlish
1980; 242 pp.

$5.95
($6.95 postpaid) from:
Avon Books
P. O. Box 767
Dresden, TN 38225
or Whole Earth Access

How To Talk So Kids Will Listen & Listen So Kids Will Talk

*Reading Adele Faber and Elaine Mazlish's first book (**Liberated Parents/Liberated Children**) changed my life. It was the first time I read about accepting and speaking from feelings. It took the idea of personal responsibility and translated it into action.* ***How to Talk*** *makes the information about accepting feelings, talking about feelings, engaging cooperation, alternatives to punishment, encouraging autonomy, praise, and freeing children from playing roles accessible through its liberal use of cartoons, and realistic dialogue. All of these ideas do much to help our children attain a positive self-image and to reduce disharmony in the home. This is tangible stuff you can read and use. —Peggy O'Mara McMahon*

I. DESCRIBE.
Describe what you see or describe the problem.

Instead of

It's hard to do what needs to be done when people are telling you what's wrong with you.

Describe

It's easier to concentrate on the problem when someone just describes it to you.

II. GIVE INFORMATION.

Instead of

Give information

Information is a lot easier to take than accusation.

Taking Care of Your Child

A companion volume to Vickery and Fries' ***Take Care of Yourself: A Consumer's Guide to Medical Care*** *(p. 206),* ***Taking Care of Your Child*** *includes decision charts — clinical algorithms — for the 96 most common childhood medical problems. Additional brief, solid chapters on pregnancy, birth, physical and psychological development, school problems, and immunizations. Includes a log for recording your child's immunization records.*

The best available home medical guide for parents.
—Tom Ferguson, M.D.

•

Nausea/Vomiting Home Treatment
Avoid solid foods. Frequent, small feedings of clear liquids should be given instead. A tablespoon of clear fluid every few minutes will usually stay down. Often, Popsicles or iced fruit bars will work if nothing else will stay down. As the condition improves, larger amounts of fluids and then jello and applesauce may be given. Sometimes, sucking on hard candy or chewing ice chips helps. In younger children you may wish to give commercially available electrolyte solutions (Pedialyte, Lytren). These are effective in keeping children from becoming dehydrated but are of very little caloric value.

Taking Care of Your Child
Robert H. Pantell, M.D.
James F. Fries, M.D.
Donald M. Vickery, M.D.
1984; 444 pp.
$14.95
postpaid from:
Addison-Wesley Publishing Company
1 Jacob Way
Reading, MA 01867
or Whole Earth Access

Mothering

I've watched ***Mothering*** *evolve from a warm, visually attractive, down-home and relatively unsophisticated new publication to a warm, visually attractive, down-home, broader and more professional alternative "family" magazine. While the mechanical quality has improved,* ***Mothering*** *has retained a special feeling of intimate communication with and between its readers.*

Mothering *is a quarterly publication about the "art of nurturing." Regular feature sections include: The Art of Mothering, Family Health, A Child's World, Pregnancy and Birth, Midwifery, Choices in Education, and Family Living. Each issue also offers articles on home cooking , fathering, breastfeeding and family centered business, as well as an ongoing dialogue between readers, comprehensive reviews of related books, and unique black and white photography throughout.* *—Katy Addison-Peet*

•

War toy sales have increased 600 percent over the past three years.

The typical war cartoon averages 41 acts of violence per hour with an attempted murder every two minutes.

An attempted murder is a standard act of violence in cartoon monitoring and is, by far, the most common act of violence.

The average American child will see 800 advertisements promoting war toys on TV this year and about 250 episodes of war cartoons produced to sell these toys. This is the equivalent of 22 days of classroom instruction.

Mothering
Peggy O'Mara McMahon, Editor
$15/year
(4 issues) from:
Mothering
P. O. Box 8410
Santa Fe, NM 87504

Festivals, Family and Food • The Alternate Celebrations Catalogue

We can spend so much time thinking about our children and our parenting. This book helps us find new and meaningful ways to be with our children and our loved ones. ***Festivals, Family and Food*** *contains poems, inspirational sayings, recipes, activities, and historical perspective for celebrating lots of new holidays and adding meaning to the "regulars." The authors of the book are British and the holidays mentioned reflect this, and some recipes will have to be adapted by those using whole wheat flour and minimizing sweeteners, and only Christian holidays are included. But used along with* ***The Alternate Celebrations Catalogue*** *we can begin to create new, vibrant and personal traditions in our families.*
—Peggy O'Mara McMahon

•

The theme of this book is a simple but bold suggestion; that if rituals and festivals have traditionally contributed to the integration and stability of communities and societies, then in the modern context they may do the same for our personal integration and for a healthy social ethos. 'Family' today may be in new forms, with single parents or single individuals joining together or with couples and their children. . . . Even if we manage only once a year to gather with friends or relatives in celebration of one festival or occasion, this is time well spent.

•

All Souls' Day
November 2 is by tradition the Day of All Souls, and it was long believed that the unhappy souls of the dead would return to their former homes. On the eve of All Souls it was customary to keep kitchens warm and leave food on the table overnight for the visiting spirits. Until 1850 the following 'Shropshire Soul Cakes' were distributed on All Souls' Day, and there is a similar 'souls cake' tradition in Belgium, Bavaria and the Tyrol.

Shropshire Soul Cakes

3 lbs plain flour
8 oz softened butter
8 oz sugar
1 oz yeast
2 eggs
1 teaspoon allspice
milk

Sift the flour and work in the slightly softened butter. Cream the yeast with a teaspoon of the sugar. Mix flour with the eggs, yeast and enough milk to make a light dough. Leave to rise, covered, in a warm place for about thirty minutes. Then work in the sugar and spice and form into flat bun shapes. Let rise for fiteen minutes, then bake at 425°F (Reg 7) for fifteen minutes.
—Festivals, Family and Food

Festivals, Family and Food
Diana Carey and Judy Large
1982; 216 pp.
$12.95
($15.95 postpaid) from:
Hearthsong
P. O. Box B
Sebastopol, CA 95472

The Alternate Celebrations Catalogue
Milo Shannon-Thornberry
1982; 192 pp.
$8.95
($10.45 postpaid) from:
Pilgrim Press
132 W. 31st St./15th Floor
New York, NY 10001
or Whole Earth Access

Parents Without Partners Sourcebook

Parents Without Partners Sourcebook
Stephen L. Atlas
1984; 192 pp.
$8.95
($9.95 postpaid) from:
Running Press
Book Publishers
125 South 22nd Street
Philadelphia, PA 19103
or Whole Earth Access

A good place to begin when you are still picking up the pieces. Covers everything from holidays and school conferences to gay parents, starting to date, and recovering as a widow or widower. The book offers an appendix of referral sources for specific needs, and bibliographies under several subjects. —*Sallie Tisdale*

•

It's easy for a single parent to become defensive and anticipate rejection by a minister or by church members. "I often wonder," Dr. Manning muses, "if we singles let ourselves feel *too* alienated — almost paranoid — if we're not welcomed specifically as singles. We *will* probably be welcomed if we put ourselves forward as individuals who can help in real ways — participate on committees, for instance — and thus gain credibility when we propose programs for single people and their children.

•

For children from divorced homes, the public schools of Andover, Massachusetts, have developed a peer support program that has the cooperation and endorsement of the superintendent and assistant superintendent of schools. The heart of the Andover program consists of support groups, run by mental health personnel and trained Peer Counselors, motivated and caring teenagers who devote time and energy to helping others. Groups are limited to youngsters from stepfamilies or single-parent homes. Thus, children hear about the program through announcements in the school newspaper, newsletters, and sometimes letters to parents. Children sometimes recruit their friends, though parental permission is always required for a child to participate.

•

Child Abuse

Parents Anonymous, National Office, 2230 Hawthorne Boulevard, Suite 208, Torrance, CA 90505. Toll-free: (800) 421-0353, (in California:) (800) 352-0386.

Parents Anonymous helps parents deal constructively with anger, frustration, and other negative feelings toward their children. The group is supportive, charges no dues, and has chapters in each state. Each state has a 24-hour hotline, and each chapter has weekly meetings, where baby-sitting is usually provided free.

•

Fathers

Coalition of Free Men, P. O. Box 129, Manhasset, NY 11030. (516) 482-6378.

This nonprofit clearinghouse for men's rights and fathers' rights organizations can recommend groups and other resources for single fathers in all areas of the United States.

A national clearinghouse for resources and organizations for unmarried fathers is being coordinated by:

Fathering Support Services, 3248 N. Racine, Chicago, IL 60657. (312) 327-3752.

The Difficult Child

The Difficult Child
Stanley Turecki, M.D.
and Leslie Tonner
1985; 224 pp.
$15.95
($17.45 postpaid) from:
Bantam Books
414 East Golf Road
Des Plaines, IL 60016
or Whole Earth Access

I wish I'd had this book five years ago; I might have been able to spare both my son and me many painful arguments. Turecki, a child psychiatrist, asserts that more than 10 percent of children are born "difficult" by temperament: highly sensitive, poorly adaptable, negative in mood, or disorganized. Such children can be extremely frustrating to rear. Turecki speaks from experience; he began the research that led to this book after years of trouble with one of his own children. This is a straightforward, practical approach to understanding your child and regaining your authority as a parent, free of guilt. —*Sallie Tisdale*

•

The problem is that difficult children *provoke* ineffective discipline. Their behavior is often bewildering to the parents, who then become more and more tentative in their response. What should the parent do? The messages the child is giving out are ambiguous; there seems to be no reason for the child's behavior. The parent then looks for motives in an effort to understand what is going on. Often this leads to a descent to the child's level, to a power struggle that no one wins. The parent ends up feeling victimized, exhausted, and incapable of coping. On to the next round.

•

You are trying here to interfere with your customary gut responses to your child. Therefore, stop to think, and hold back from your previous automatic responses to his behavior: the immediate "no," the threats, the screaming. Try to disengage *your* feelings from this process and replace them with the attitude of a professor studying his subject. Aim for as cool an attitude of detachment as you can manage.

On Being Father

On Being Father
Frank Ferrara
1985; 175 pp.
$7.95 postpaid from:
Doubleday and Company
Direct Mail Order
501 Franklin Avenue
Garden City, NY 11530
or Whole Earth Access

At last, an unapologetic, middle-of-the-road male perspective on divorce and giving up custody of the children. Ferrara freely shares not only his own experiences, mistakes, and solutions, but the residual anger he still struggles to control. He makes no attempt to be a 'new age' man or father — Ferrara settles for being a good man and father. The book covers living arrangements, visits, changes in parent-child relationships as the child grows, and issues of sex and remarriage. —*Sallie Tisdale*

•

Competitiveness arises when you have a need to "prove" that the divorce wasn't your fault, that she was the one really to blame for the failure of the marriage. So you try to show — to her, to the children, to your friends, and most of all to yourself — that you're a better person and a better parent than she is. You try to be both a better father *and* a better mother than your ex-wife. You're always comparing yourself to her, using her as a sort of measuring rod for yourself as you play your game of one-upmanship.

•

To put it bluntly, being a parent showed me my failings. Or rather, being a *single* parent showed me. I never would have learned this lesson if my wife and I had stayed together and gone on as we were. It was only in becoming a single parent that I saw how much I had to learn and was kicked into trying to improve myself. It was painful. And frightening.

• **Don't Shoot the Dog** (p. 225) has some good strategies for reducing family squabbling.

• The insight in this classic parenting book is still helpful. **Liberated Parents, Liberated Children:** Adele Faber and Elaine Mazlish, 1974; 237 pp. **$3.95** ($4.95 postpaid) from Avon Books, P. O. Box 767, Dresden, TN 38225.

Creative Publications

This catalog is intended for math and science teachers, but is a fantastic resource for home-schoolers and a really interesting catalog for others, too. They have a unique selection of books, workbooks, software, and materials — all of very high quality. I've used their materials with my own children and also in a month-long exhibit at a children's museum where over 1,200 children played with them. The children loved everything we ordered from Creative Publications, notably the Pattern Blocks and the Rubber Stamps. The nicest thing is that they believe that children (yes, even children) deserve nice graphics, beautiful photographs, and quality materials. This catalog is a treat. —Jeanne Finan

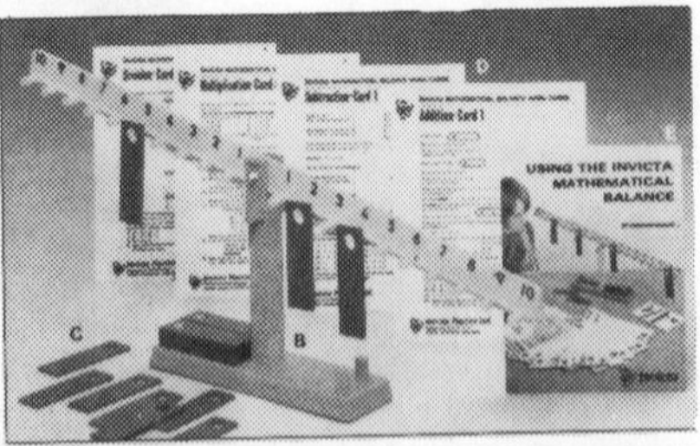

•

Math Balance with Masses. Sturdy 8½″ high balance allows the child to deal with abstract mathematical ideas by manipulating a physical model. Encourages exploration of the fundamental operations, solves simple algebraic equations, and demonstrates the commutative and associative laws. $20.95

Constructive Playthings

Lotsa toys, nursery gear, and learning stuff for younger children. Especially handy for home teaching (p. 381) or stocking a neighborhood day care center. —Stewart Brand

Constructive Playthings
Catalog
$2 from:
Constructive Playthings
1227 E. 119th Street
Grandview, MO 64030

LACING MOUSE
Lacing the wooden mouse with a rope tail through the eyes of the wooden swiss cheese house is fun but it also teaches little ones eye-hand coordination as they play. House is 4½″ high. Ages 2-3.
No. NAT-A21T $7.95

GIANT TINKERTOY
An exciting dimension in creative construction in a big way! The 53 colorful plastic rods and spools are 16 times the size of standard Tinkertoy so children can build a 5 ft. robot or anything they want, indoors or out. Instructions included. Ages 4-10.
No. GAB-30090T $51.95

• You can still get *real* Flexible Flyer sleds (spring steel runners!) and the best coaster wagons with auto-type steering from Lehman's Hardware (p. 143).

Child Life Play Specialties

Beautiful, institutional-quality outdoor play equipment for children! The whole gamut from baby swings to a fantastic "super chief" swing set with enough stuff on it to be a playground in itself. They have a 60-day return policy and a good warranty. Spare parts and hardware are available. The stuff isn't cheap, but it looks like you get what you pay for. —Andrea Sharp
[Suggested by Charlie Teswood]

►

Fireman's Gym Complete, with frame in Kit form: $350. The optional 8 ft. Slide can be attached to any of the four sides. It has a durable plastic bonded surface that is cool in the sun.

All structural frames are constructed of pressure treated (Wolmanized) Douglas fir, western hemlock and Sitka spruce or Alaskan yellow cedar.

Kits are sold unpainted but always include a proper supply of lead free paint for customer application. The special non-slip surface on our ladder rungs gives a secure and safe climbing grip.

Community Playthings

Solid, long-lasting, great-looking toys — quality goods. The catalog includes a variety of furniture and toys for disabled kids. Everything has a one-year warranty. These toys are the products and income of the Rifton, New York, Bruderhof Community. It shows. —Stewart Brand

Community Playthings
Catalog **free** from:
Community Playthings
Rifton, NY 12471

Wagon. Solid maple box 35″ x 15″ x 4″. Heavy steel chassis. 8″ diam. wheels and solid steel axles. $145.

Educational Teaching Aids

Fat catalog of institutional-strength classroom materials. Impressive range of self-directed and Montessori-type learning aids. I'd go here if I was outfitting a primary school. —Kevin Kelly

00-1005 STACK COTS
Sanitary, non-absorbent, polypropylene bed requires only a damp cloth to clean. Cots stack one on top of the other, ready for use. 22″×52″×12″ high. **Each Cot, 32.95**

Child Life Play Specialties
Catalog **free** from:
Child Life Play
Specialties, Inc.
P. O. Box 527
Holliston, MA 01746

Creative Publications
Catalog **free** from:
Creative Publications
1101 San Antonio Road
North, Suite 104
Mountain View, CA 94043

Montessori Dressing Materials

—Educational Teaching Aids

00-2946 ETA "U" FILM KIT
35mm filmstrip material upon which you may write, type or draw, then erase and use again. Includes a 25-ft. roll of "U" Film, 4 colored markers, 10 plastic storage cans and labels, one splicer, splicing tapes, and manual.
Kit, 36.95
00-2949 25 Foot Roll "U" Film 13.95

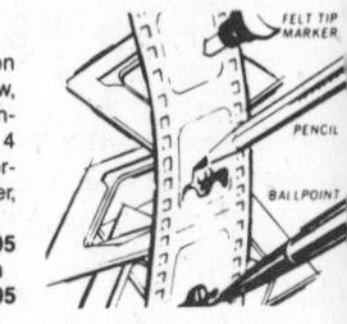

—Educational Teaching Aids

Educational Teaching Aids
Catalog
$1 from:
ETA
199 West Carpenter Ave.
Wheeling, IL 60090

Games Magazine
R. Wayne Schmittberger
Editor
$15.97/year
(12 issues) from:
Games Magazine
P. O. Box 10147
Des Moines, IA 50340

Games

By games they mean brain games — puzzles and pencil games and board games that require cogitation. Some of the magazine is about games — a report on the Fourth National Wargaming Convention and a play-by-play analysis of a championship Scrabble game. But mostly it is games — good games that you can play alone or with others. A crossword puzzle with two sets of clues — very hard and very easy, non-math logic puzzles, a 554-dot connect the dot puzzle, endless mindboggling word games and on and on. Also reader participation contests that make the ones in other magazines seem tame, and detailed reviews of new board games. The super slick, super graphic presentation seems appropriate in this case — hooks you right into playing as you leaf through.

The games are consistently original and fun and funny.
—Anne Herbert

•

Where in the Whorl?

If you find prints charming, you'll enjoy this maze. Start at the arrow in the lower left corner, then journey to the center of the whorl by the shortest possible path. Your route may not go outside the thumbprint.

1. CRYPTOON
V RUYM EUJ FMIW: SLC VFWLCUFZM NKUF JSMWF'D ZSYMC UFQ NCMWZCVNDVSFW SDRMC DRUF MQM SA FMID UFJ IVFB SA EUD.

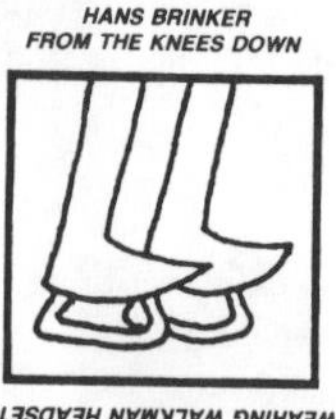

HANS BRINKER
FROM THE KNEES DOWN
TWO TURKEYS
WEARING WALKMAN HEADSETS

Children's Games In Street and Playground
Iona and Peter Opie
1969; 371 pp.
$9.95
postpaid from:
Oxford University Press
16-100 Pollitt Drive
Fair Lawn, NJ 07410
or Whole Earth Access

Children's Games in Street and Playground

Suppose you were trying to replace war. Would you be interested in "games in which children may deliberately scare each other, ritually hurt each other, take foolish risks, promote fights, play ten against one, and yet in which they consistently observe their own sense of fair play" (dust jacket blurb)? The games are not learned from adults but passed on through the generations of children. This study comes from England, which looks to have a much richer game cycle than American kids usually experience. A product of ten years' research, the book thoroughly describes the rules of play and the popularity of more than a thousand fascinating games.
—Stewart Brand

•

Sardines

'Sardines', played indoors or out, is the most popular of the games consisting purely of hiding and finding. One person goes off to hide while the others shut their eyes and count to the agreed number. The seekers split up, and search independently of each other. Indeed, if one of the seekers finds the hider he is careful not to let the others know, but slips into the hiding-place when they are not looking. Ideally the hiding-place should be somewhere that will accommodate all the players; but it seldom is, and as further players find it, and crowd in, the silent squeeze becomes tighter and more suffocating, players sometimes having to lie on top of each other. Those who are still searching gradually become aware that their fellow searchers are disappearing, and rush to the places where they were last seen, thinking they will be near the hidy-hole. When the last person arrives he is sometimes chased back to the starting-place, but more often than not there are just sighs of relief as the sardines extract themselves from their cramped positions, and complain of their stiffness and the length of time they have been waiting.

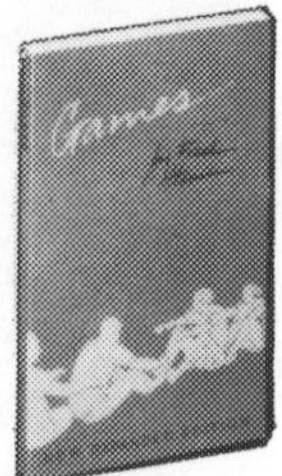

Games
Frank W. Harris
1982; 84 pp.
$6.95
($7.95 postpaid) from:
Frank W. Harris
2129 Rose Street
Berkeley, CA 94709
or Whole Earth Access

Games

Some fun old games (and some new) that work well for groups playing inside in a gymnasium-sized room. You're It!
—Kevin Kelly

•

Johnny on the Pony (Buck, Buck)

The first player in the standing team runs, places both hands on the back of one of the players bent over and jumps on top. Each succeeding player does the same until all players are astride the bent-over team.

If any player sitting astride touches the ground in any way the other team stands and takes their turn. If all players of the second team succeed in staying astride without touching the ground they then call out in unison "Johnny on the pony, one, two, three" and simultaneously bounce up and down.

If any of them slip off while doing this, or touch the ground, the other team goes. If anyone on the bent-over team buckles or caves in the first team goes again.

According to Hoyle

The Hoyle that folks want everything to be according to is this official rule book for most card, dice and other gambling games (e.g., Mah Jongg); board games such as Chess and Backgammon; plus a selection of parlor games. No more arguments.
—JB

According to Hoyle
Richard L. Frey
1970; 285 pp.
$3.50
($4.50 postpaid) from:
Random House
Order Dept.
400 Hahn Road
Westminster, MD 21157
or Whole Earth Access

New Games

The idea of New Games, back when we were involved in starting them at the First New Games Tournament in 1973, was to encourage the meta-game of always inventing new and more interesting rules, livelier and more interesting games. The New Games Foundation carried on that scheme through innumerable workshops, crystalizing into these two books. Together they describe 126 wild and wooly new contact sports — Hunker Hawser, Slaughter, Earthball, The Mating Game, Prui, Snake-in-the-Grass, etc. The reader-player is given encouragement and guidance to invent further.

Another part of the original idea was to help get people so used to improving rules all the time that changing the rules of war to something manageable would seem natural to do. More new games, please. —Stewart Brand

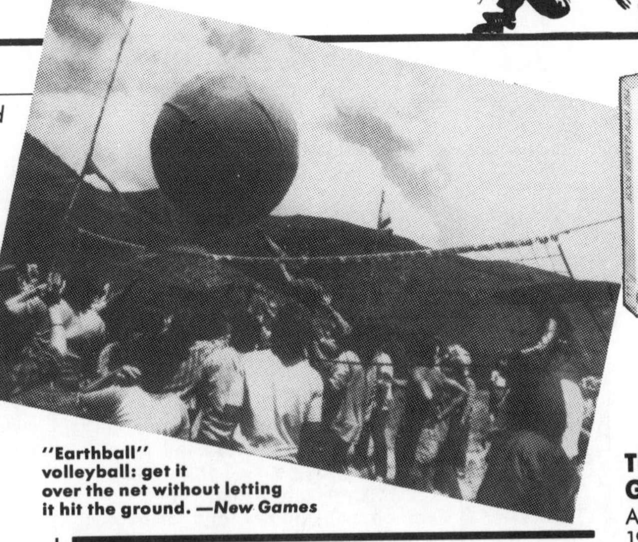

"Earthball" volleyball: get it over the net without letting it hit the ground. —New Games

The New Games Book
Andrew Fluegelman, Editor
1976; 193 pp.
$7.95 postpaid

More New Games
Andrew Fluegelman, Editor
1981; 190 pp.
$7.95 postpaid

both from:
Doubleday and Company
Direct Mail Order
501 Franklin Avenue
Garden City, NY 11530
or Whole Earth Access

•

Tweezli-Whop

You'll need two burlap sacks filled with straw and a wooden rail perched high enough to keep your feet from touching the ground. The area beneath the rail should be generously cushioned — a minor haystack will do. You and your partner straddle the rail, face-to-face, and have a go at "whopping" each other with the sacks until one (and frequently both) fall off.

•

Keep an eye out for spectators. Most people who stand around watching a game really want to be playing with you. Invite them.

•

Crab Grab

We assume the classic crab position — bellies up, elbows and knees bent, bodies elevated on hands and feet. We must maintain this position — supported by at least three extremities — while each of us tries to make the other touch his rear end to the ground.

The rest of the rules are for us to create. We can allow players to make contact only with their feet, or we can allow hand-to-hand or foot-to-hand or perhaps body-to-body contact too. It all depends on whether we want the game to be very active, extremely active, or totally exhausting.

Boffers

You can hit each other endlessly with Boffers and it never hurts, but it does make a very loud, cracking sound (known as a boff). It's a safe way to vent your hostility, with shades of Errol Flynn.

Sword-play games, from Three Musketeers to Star Wars, are what Boffers are all about. They are not for clubbing, but for dueling and also swatting (as in Swat Tag).

Boffers are white foam swords. They come in a set containing two swords and two eye-and-ear guards.
—New Games Foundation

Boffers
$19 postpaid
Information **free** from:
Grand Dance
Boffer Company
P. O. Box 02301
Portland, OR 97202
or Whole Earth Access

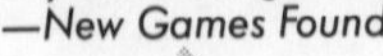

► **Boffing in *The World According To Garp.***

Playfair

Two rules: no competition and no equipment. When you get a crowd of people involved in these imaginative body routines, EVERYBODY has fun. (Try Octopus Massage or Amoeba Tag.) Because the goal is to laugh and holler your way to cooperation, they're great for warming up a large group project — or a memorable party. Blows grumpiness and boredom right out of the water. Never fails. —Kevin Kelly

•

Going out dancing is wonderful, but there's one thing wrong with it — you always have to keep your eyes on your partner, and you never get to check out all the other people who are whirling around you on the dance floor. So we're going to do a dance now that is the opposite of that — this time you're going to get to look at everybody *but* your own partner!

Playfair
Matt Weinstein
and Joel Goodman
1980; 249 pp.
$9.95
($11.20 postpaid) from:
Impact Publishers
P. O. Box 1094
San Luis Obispo, CA 93406
or Whole Earth Access

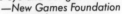

• Develop your courage and balance with games involving ropes used in challenging ways.
Cow's Tails and Cobras: $10.50 ($12.75 postpaid) from Project Adventure, P. O. Box 100, Hamilton, MA 01936.

• See also the game in **The Evolution of Cooperation** (p. 94).

Animal Town Game Company

Friendly, organic, educational, enjoyable board games about small farms, whales, bees, beavers, chickens, etc. Cooperation wins. Also children's books, Earthballs, etc.
—Stewart Brand

◄ *Nectar Collector.* The object is to move your bee (marker) around the board and gather "nectar" (beads), fill your honeycomb and enter the Queen Bee's Royal Chamber. Players collect nectar — and sometimes lose it, by landing on spaces depicting possible events in a bee's life cycle. A player might even land on spaces like "Bee-In-Need", which enables him/her to help another bee. Although there is a single winner, winning is not the main object, but rather learning how important cooperation is among bees and, on a larger scale, among all creatures. You will gain a sense of unity and sharing playing the game. Two to four players, ages 8 on up. Younger ones will enjoy playing if they have help. Board (19" x 19"), bee markers, "honey drops", magic ring, die, community apiary, beekeeper button, rules, information booklet and muslin bag. One game provides 20 to 30 minutes of fun. Beekeepers love it.

Animal Town Game Company
Catalog **free** from:
Animal Town
Game Company
P. O. Box 2002
Santa Barbara, CA 93120

—Animal Town Game Company

World Wide Games

This small woodworking company makes and sells games, mostly wooden; some expensive ones (up to $130); mostly inexpensive ($1 to $15). About half of their games are American (old and new); the others originated overseas. For the games they make, they sell replacement parts. The woodworking is clean, smooth, and solid.

Our family has been buying these inexpensive games for several years. Their mail-order service is fast. Their catalog is free.
—R. W. Radl

World Wide Games
Catalog **free** from:
World Wide Games
Norwich Avenue
Colchester,
CT 06415

● Table Cricket provides lots of action and fun for all ages. Each team tries to hit the ball through goal to the left. This game, for 2-8 players, has solid oak sides and ends, hardwood plywood bottom, birch rods with red plastic grips, cloth goal bags, 2 wooden balls and rules. Size 18" x 40" — 25 lbs.

The Johnson Smith Catalog

If you were ever a kid, you remember Johnson Smith. But you may have forgotten just how relevant Johnson Smith could be to your present happiness, not to mention your spiritual development.

They've been around for 72 years. Remember the lists you used to make of all the things you wanted? Well, surprise! You'll still want the same things: secret agent pen radio, juggling kits, X-ray Spex, Magic Money Maker, joy buzzers and, of course, VENTRILO ("BOYS! BOYS! BOYS! Learn Ventriloquism and Apparently THROW YOUR VOICE! Into a trunk, under the bed, under a table, back of the door, into a desk at school, or anywhere"). Yes, Johnson Smith is alive and well, and unchanged. But what about you? Get with it, kids! *—Robert Goldman*

The Johnson Smith Catalog
Catalog **free** from:
Johnson Smith
4514 19th Ct. East
Bradenton, FL 34203

Deluxe Joy Buzzer

Just wind, then hide this devilish device in your hand just before you shake hands. Handshake pressure causes spring to unwind so fast it produces a very shocking experience for your victim. All time classic pocket practical joke. No batteries. Not electric. All metal. Made in U.S.A.
☐ **2529 Joy Buzzer** **$2.49**

SUCKER CANDY
Tastes great at first, then WOW! Your friends (ex-friends?) won't suspect a thing. Horrible tasting centers. Great tasting outer coating slowly melts away then lookout!
☐ **2099 Sucker Candy** **$1.20**

Comic Bald Head Mask

Change in seconds to "shiny" bald head. Fits over head above eyebrows, over forehead, around ears & back down to neck.
☐ **4620 Bald Head Mask, $3.98**

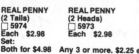

GIANT BALLOONS
Super-size balloons. Easy to inflate with vacuum cleaner, or fill with helium to give it **tremendous lifting power when soaring into the air.** Lift signs, objects. Do entertaining stunts, advertising effects, attract crowds. See for miles. Smaller balloon inflates up to 8-ft. high & 2-ft. around. Big balloon inflates up to 15-ft. & almost 50-ft. around. With instructions.
☐ **3010 8' Diameter (24' Around)..$12.98**
☐ **3082 15' Diameter (50' Around). $39.95**

Pottery Head With Growing Green Hair
Plant grass seed on head, fill with water, watch green "hair" grow in days. Amusing, comical man's head, attractively made of porous pottery. Hair grows in few days. Use over and over. 4½" high. With seeds & instructions. Guaranteed to grow.
☐ **5005 Growing Head** **$8.98**

REAL PENNY (2 Tails) ☐ **5974** **Each $2.98**
REAL PENNY (2 Heads) ☐ **5973** **Each $2.98**
Set: Both for $4.98 **Any 3 or more, $2.25 ea.**

Both sides are the same. Either 2 heads or 2 tails. Finest quality. So carefully made from genuine coins they appear to be right from mint. **Sold only for magic, trick or joke use. Legal for fun use; illegal for fraudulent use**

Mail-Order Fireworks

For those of us who like to celebrate year-round events like birthdays, New Year's Eve, or the end of a wonderful day with fireworks, here are three mail-order sources offering some really great Chinese- and U.S.-made fireworks. Blue Angel is generally the cheapest, though Neptune and Olde Glory undersell them on particular items. Olde Glory has a small selection, but they're geared toward smaller lots on individual items. Shop around — the full-color catalogs are nearly as dazzling as silver sparklers. *—Ted Schultz*

Blue Angel Fireworks: Catalog **free** from Blue Angel Co., P. O. Box 26/12900 Canfield Road, Columbiana, OH 44408.

Neptune Fireworks: Catalog **free** from Neptune Fireworks Co., P. O. Box 398/1300 Stirling Road #3A, Dania, FL 33004.

Olde Glory Fireworks: Catalog **free** from Olde Glory Fireworks, P. O. Box 2863, Rapid City, SD 57709.

—Neptune Fireworks

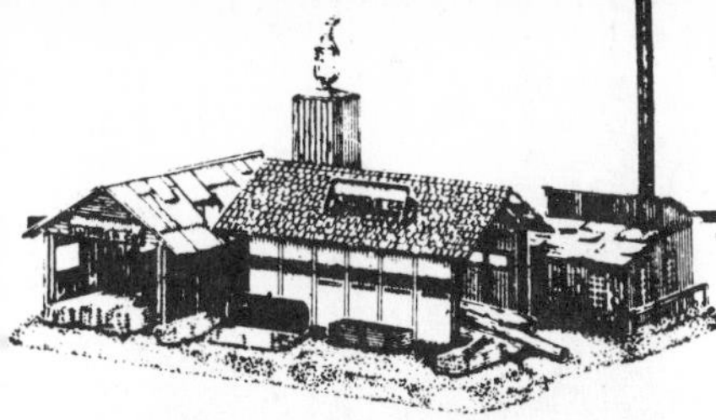

7788 SAWMILL and LUMBER YARD **13.95**

TK17 Shag Bark 3½" (3/Kit)........................ 2.98

—HO Gauge Model Railroads

America's Hobby Center

A legendary outfit. They have to publish a separate catalog for each type of ware they stock (model trains, planes, boats, and cars), because their inventory is overwhelmingly huge. Making models can involve the same kind of destiny-controlling creativity as writing a good story. My own obsession once was model trains; now I cry out with nostalgia and sheer covetousness when I look through their train catalog. Prices are low, sale prices are amazingly low, and service is always good. —Art Kleiner

SQUARE BRASS TUBING

12"

149	1/16 Sq.	.45
150	3/32 Sq.	.50
151	1/8 Sq.	.55
152	5/32 Sq.	.65
153	3/16 Sq.	.75
154	7/32 Sq.	.85
155	1/4 Sq.	.95

—Model Cars

MUFFLERS

No. 2630 for .049 & .051 **4.35**

No. 2640 for .09 Engines **5.55**

PEE WEE .020 (.327cc) No. 100 **19.10**

2 in 1 PEANUT SCALE MODELS

P-1 S.E.5a PLUS 13" Wingspan — FOKKER D-8 13" Wingspan — Both for **6.95**

P-2 CITABRIA PLUS 13" Wingspan — 13" Span — Both for **6.95**

P-3 WACO S.R.E. PLUS 13" Wingspan — MONOCOUPE — INTERSTATE CADET 13" Wingspan — Both for **6.95**

Rubber Motor WINDER — 5 to 1 Gear Ratio **4.95**

—Catalog of Models

Catalog of Models
$2.50

HO and N Gauge Model Railroads
Catalog
$2

Wood and Plastic Ships
Catalog
$1.50

Model Cars
Catalog
$1.50

All from:
America's Hobby Center
146 West 22nd Street
New York, NY 10011

The Modelmaker's Handbook

An inspiring book that revels in those added touches of finesse — the highlighted rivet, the shadowed canopy, the flattened wheel with realistic bulge. The authors have obviously dribbled enough glue to not let it mar their realistic weathered finishes. They are able to pass on their persnickety ways in a clear, well-drawn manner. —David Wills

There are utilitarian applications here (making a model of a landscape you're designing, for instance), but the real purpose of this craft is love of country — the imaginary miniature country you give life to with these methods. Also covers ships, planes, trains, and cars. —Art Kleiner

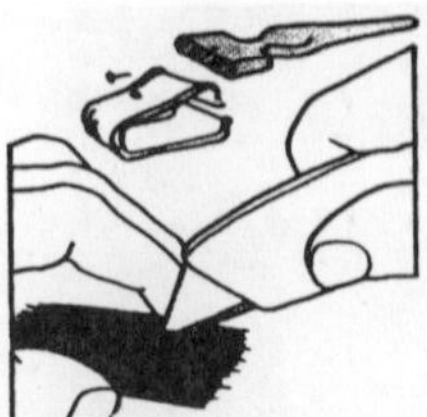

Making reeds, rushes and coarse grass Break off the handle of a brush and split the resin to separate the clumps of bristles. Cut to size allowing ¼ inch (5 mm) for planting. Dip ends in cyanoacrylate glue to secure them.

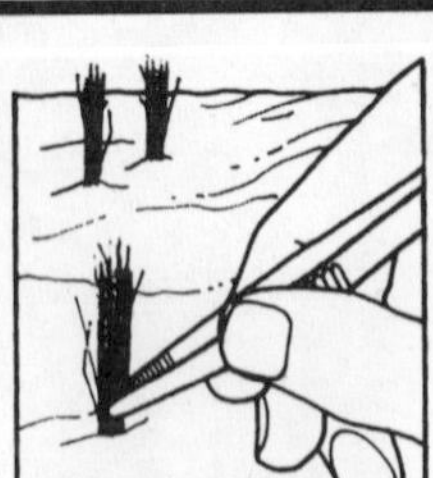

Holding a clump in tweezers, glue it in a hole drilled in the baseboard or push it into the soft ground. Position the clumps of bristles in several irregularly spaced groups.

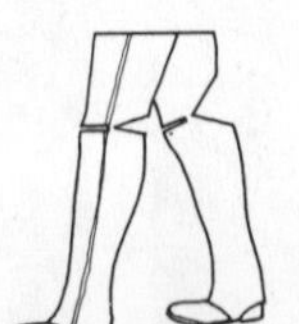

Bending a leg Cut a wedge from behind the knee. Make a straight cut in front.

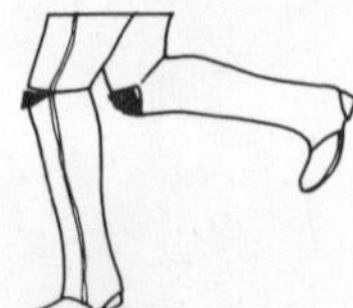

Bend the leg into position. Secure it with glue, then reshape with filler.

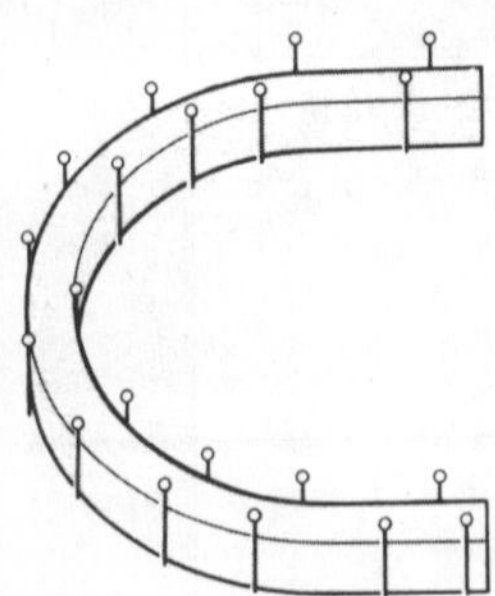

Pinning a wet balsa strip Secure the strip on the building board with straight pins to hold it in shape while it dries.

The Modelmaker's Handbook
Albert Jackson and David Day
1981; 352 pp.

$21.95
($22.95 postpaid) from:
Random House
Order Dept.
400 Hahn Road
Westminster, MD 21157
or Whole Earth Access

The Complete Dollmaker

By no means complete, these instructions will get you going on a variety of homemade dolls, both stuffed ones (soft) and the sculptured kind (hard, as in porcelain or wax). —Kevin Kelly

•

A combination of polyester and sawdust makes a hard stuffing if it is tightly compressed. Whatever the material, a doll is not properly stuffed unless it is as firm as it can be without the seams bursting. Most stuffed dolls benefit from the insertion of a dowel or wire in the neck area to maintain the position of the head.

Working diagram of a doll in progress.

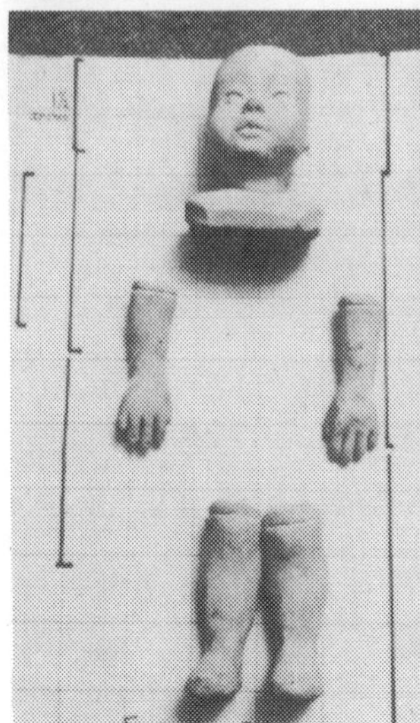

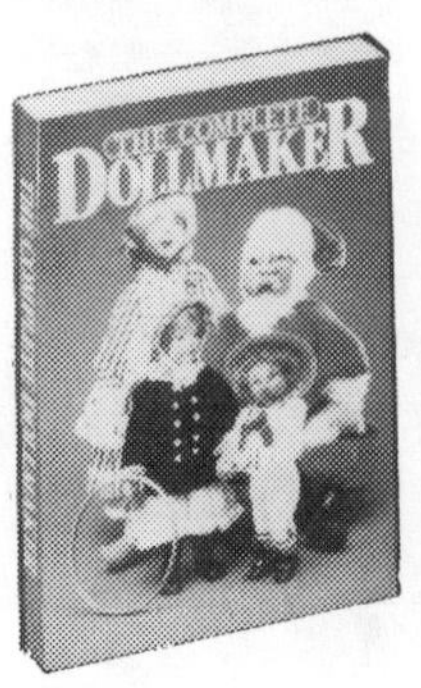

The Complete Dollmaker
Alice D. Weiner
1985; 192 pp.

$12.95
($14.45 postpaid) from:
Sterling Publishing Co.
2 Park Avenue
New York, NY 10016
or Whole Earth Access

• This snazzy new magazine serves those who would miniaturize the world. **Scale Woodcraft: $14.95** (4 issues) from Scale Woodcraft, P. O. Box 840, Peterborough, NH 03458-9956.

• One of the best suppliers of modelers' tools is **Micro Mark:** catalog **free** from Box 5112-215-24, 24 East Main Street, Clinton, NJ 08809.

Boomerang
Benjamin Ruhe
and Eric Darnell
1985; 95 pp.
$9.95
($11.95 postpaid) from:
Workman Publishing
One West 39th Street
New York, NY 10018
or Whole Earth Access

Boomerang

Undocumented observation confirms that there is a little latent boomeranger in all of us, but it won't be latent long if this book crosses your path; being a closet boomeranger just isn't practical. ***Boomerang*** *tells you how to throw and catch, gives a bit of history of the sport, and presents very good plans for making your own, which you don't have to do because an excellent boomerang is included with the book.*
—JB

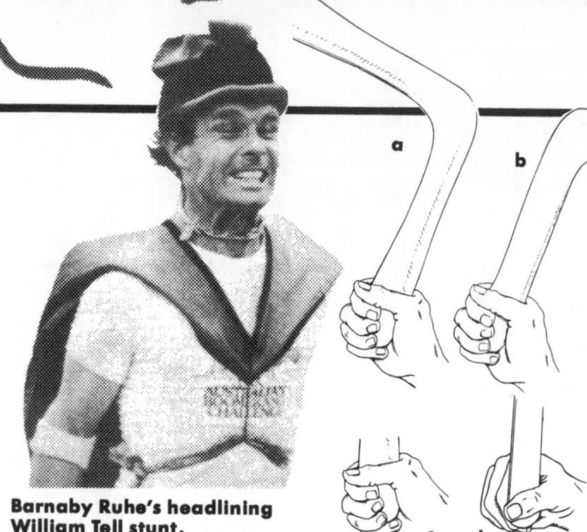

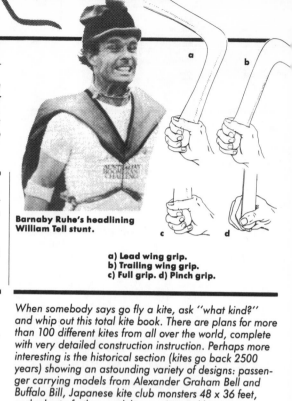

Barnaby Ruhe's headlining William Tell stunt.

a) Lead wing grip.
b) Trailing wing grip.
c) Full grip. d) Pinch grip.

Many Happy Returns

Boomerangers keep up with things in ***Many Happy Returns****, the newsletter that comes with membership in the U.S. Boomerang Association.* *—JB*

Many Happy Returns: $10/year (4 issues, membership included) from U. S. Boomerang Association, P. O. Box 182, Delaware, OH 43015.

The Penguin Book of Kites
David Pelham
1976; 224 pp.
$9.95
($10.95 postpaid) from:
Viking Penguin Books
299 Murray Hill Pkwy.
East Rutherford,
NJ 07073
or Whole Earth Access

Kitelines
Valerie Govig, Editor
$11/year
(4 issues) from:
KiteLines
7106 Campfield Road
Baltimore, MD 21207

The Penguin Book of Kites • Kitelines

When somebody says go fly a kite, ask "what kind?" and whip out this total kite book. There are plans for more than 100 different kites from all over the world, complete with very detailed construction instruction. Perhaps more interesting is the historical section (kites go back 2500 years) showing an astounding variety of designs: passenger carrying models from Alexander Graham Bell and Buffalo Bill, Japanese kite club monsters 48 x 36 feet, and a host of other models amazing and bizarre.

The nicely produced ***Kitelines*** *magazine will keep you up with the latest ideas, contest dates, and purveyors of kitish products.* *—JB*

▲ **The kite used to raise the aerial for Marconi's first transatlantic wireless reception.**
—*The Penguin Book of Kites*

Peter Lynn's Dragonfly. —*Kitelines* ►

Paper Flight
Jack Botermans
1984; 120 pp.
$9.95
($10.95 postpaid) from:
Henry Holt & Co.
521 Fifth Avenue, 12th floor
New York, NY 10175
or Whole Earth Access

Paper Flight

Take one sheet of paper and make your choice of 48 different designs of aircraft, flying saucers, helicopters, reproductions of real aircraft, birds, and insects.

My favorites are the flies and the French Mirage. Flypaper at its best!

Note to libraries: The plans are shown in a way that does not invite tearing out the pages.
—Joe Eddy Brown

Flies will not bother you if they're made of paper.

Sherlock Special.

Woodworking with Kids

I haven't found a more inspiring book about teaching kids in general or about learning woodworking in particular. That it does both well is a surprise, but no accident. It is clear, inventive, and extremely wise. A book like this in sewing, cooking, and all the sciences would make a school that worked. —Kevin Kelly

•

When kids think about woodworking, they often imagine boxes or boxlike objects, such as birdhouses, benches and cabinets. Here's an easy way for young children to make boxes using only a square, pencil, saw and hammer. The trick is to build the box from the bottom up. The bottom determines the size of the first side, the bottom and first side determine the size of the second side, and so on; this method is forgiving of the inaccuracies likely to occur when young kids use a saw. It's also a good way to help children understand right angles and rectangles, without having to resort to geometry.

◄ Amy bored ¼-in. holes about 1 in. deep into the apron ends to take the dowels. She placed them about ¾ in. from the edges, centered between the faces of the apron. The straighter the hole the better, though ¼-in. dowels are flexible enough to forgive small errors.

After boring, Amy put an apron, end up, in the vise and inserted a dowel center in each hole. (Dowel centers allow you to mate holes accurately in two pieces of wood.)

•

Expect some surprising answers when you ask a child "What do you want to make?" Little kids commonly ask for a horse, dog or man, projects that make us think of sculpture rather than woodworking. But don't discourage a child who has these ideas, because almost anything can be expressed in wood once you know the basic woodworking language.

Woodworking with Kids
Richard Starr
1982; 205 pp.
$19.95
postpaid from:
W.W. Norton
500 5th Avenue
New York, NY 10110
or Whole Earth Access

Toy Book

Want to make a waterscope and magnifier, or a hexaflexagon, or a rope machine (that makes real rope)? Here's simple instructions for these and 48 other toys and games, with plenty of photos and diagrams. Make your own discovery toys, pretending toys, games, building toys, action toys and design toys without spending much (if any) money. All the toys were designed and tested on a whole herd of children by a professional designer and toy consultant who helped design the Boston Children's Museum. For kids age 1 through 11 and parents of all descriptions. —Sylvia Jacobs

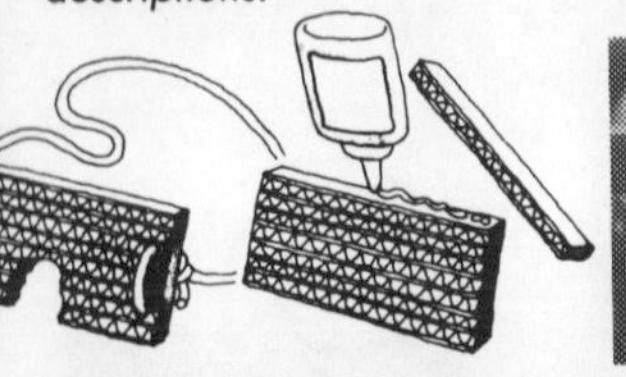

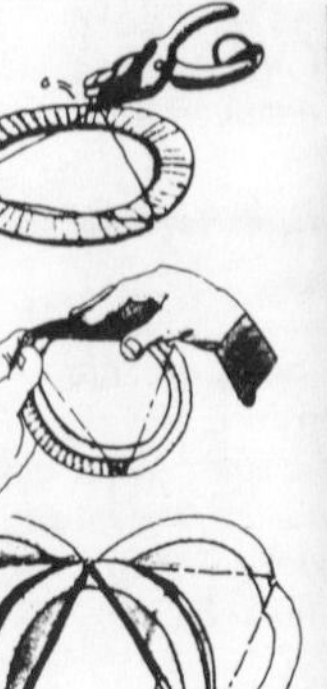

▲ *Building Circles* is a modular construction toy. The pieces fit together in any direction, and there are no rules as to what you can make. With a batch of folded paper plates and some rubber bands, you can build hundreds of different forms and patterns — towers, gloves, hats, mobiles, or whatever. The circles are easily connected with rubber bands, and they come apart easily to be used over and over again.

Toy Book
Steven Caney
1972; 175 pp.
$6.95
($8.95 postpaid) from:
Workman Publishing
One West 39th Street
New York, NY 10018
or Whole Earth Access

Cherry Tree Toys

Old-timey hardwood parts (and kits) for making wooden toys. —Kevin Kelly

Cherry Tree Toys
Catalog **$1** from:
Cherry Tree Toys
P. O. Box 369
408 South Jefferson
Belmont, OH 43718

Small Train. Plan, kit or toy; parts required in plan: (1) #6, (2) #7, (12) #14, (6) #17, (1) 1/4" x 12" dowel, (3) 3/8" x 12" dowels, (1) 1" x 12" dowel. Size: 22" long.

Making Things

A few ideas on how to turn odds and ends into instructive toys. Perfect if you need to mind a gang of young'uns and you've forgotten what you did at that age. —Kevin Kelly

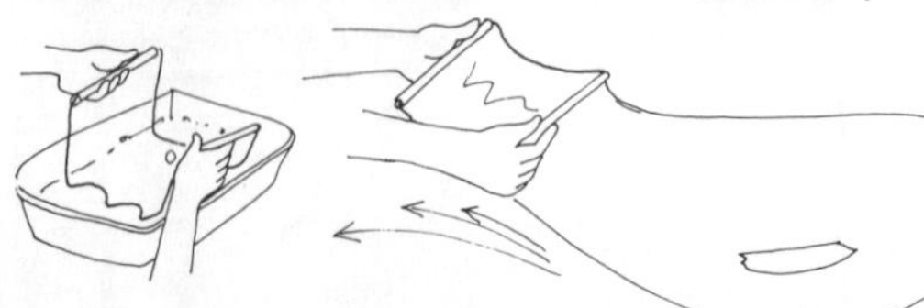

But best of all and biggest are bubbles made with glycerine & soap on a plastic straw and string frame.

Gather a film across the strings, pull the straws apart to stretch the film open. Pull upwards filling the film with air gently. Relax the contraption and snap the bubble free of the frame. FANTASTIC!

Making Things
Ann Wiseman
1973; 164 pp.
$8.95
($10.45 postpaid) from:
Little, Brown & Company
Order Dept.
200 West Street
Waltham, MA 02254
or Whole Earth Access

The Read-Aloud Handbook

The value of this book is in its practical and simple approach — if we want to we can have children who want to learn to read, and to think. We need only give them our time. Trelease makes convincing and hopeful arguments on how to reverse the increasing illiteracy in America. His chapter about television's effects on kids is downright scary, but he gives parents workable suggestions on how to control its influence. From picture books to novels, more than 300 titles are synopsized, and there are references to hundreds of other good books.
—Lindi Wood

•

More than half a century ago there was a poor Quaker woman who took in a foundling child and began reading Dickens to him every night. Surely she could not have dreamed the words and stories would have such an enormous impact; the boy, James Michener, would write his first book at age 39 and his thirty-second at 78. In between there would be bestsellers translated into fifty-two languages, selling more than 60 million copies, and enjoyed by countless millions of readers.

•

Start with something simple like *Bennett Cerf's Books of Animal Riddles* or *Bennet Cerf's Book of Laughs*. The child will love memorizing jokes from these books and trying them out on family and friends. Nothing builds self-confidence like a well-told and well-received joke.

The Read-Aloud Handbook
Jim Trelease
1985; 243 pp.
$6.95
($7.95 postpaid) from:
Penguin Books
299 Murray Hill Pkwy.
East Rutherford, NJ 07073
or Whole Earth Access

The Horn Book Magazine

This is where librarians learn what's new, and particularly what's good in the world of children's literature. It is also where publishers advertise their children's books. Although articles are included in this very literate journal, the heart of each issue is the dozens of detailed reviews of new children's books. *—Richard Nilsen*

The Horn Book
Anita Silvey, Editor
$30/year
(6 issues) from:
The Horn Book, Inc.
Park Square Building
31 St. James Avenue
Boston, MA 02116-4167

•

In a world in which we use the word *gentle* to describe everything from laxatives to scouring powder, Molly Bang has restored dignity to the word with her truly gentle tale of *The Paper Crane*. The classic folk-tale motif of an act of kindness being rewarded by a magical gift has a contemporary setting.

Molly Bang, Author-Illustrator
— The Paper Crane **Greenwillow 1985.**

The World Treasury of Children's Literature

Now in his early eighties, Clifton Fadiman adds a nice turn to a distinguished career and considers children's literature. "Grandparents and grandchildren, the enders and the beginners, are not rivals but natural friends," says he. Volumes I and II are for kids aged four to eight and are in fact one book divided in two to give small hands a better chance at holding on. Volume III is for ages nine through fourteen, but with Fadiman's interesting commentaries and catholic taste it makes little sense to put age brackets on these selections. He is also careful to refer young readers to the full length versions of the books he chooses from. Here are Jonathan Swift, A.A. Milne and Maurice Sendak, but also Sylvia Plath, Lennon-McCartney and Yevgeny Yevtushenko.
—Richard Nilsen

•

The Panther
The panther is like a leopard,
Except it hasn't been peppered.
Should you behold a panther crouch,
Prepare to say Ouch.
Better yet, if called by a panther,
Don't anther.

The Eel
I don't mind eels
Except as meals
And the way they feels.
—Ogden Nash

MAXINE W. KUMIN

Snail

No one writes a letter to the snail.
He does not have a mailbox for his mail.
He does not have a bathtub or a rug.
There's no one in his house that he can hug.
There isn't any room when he's inside.

And yet they say the snail is satisfied.

The World Treasury of Children's Literature
(Volume I & II)
Clifton Fadiman, Editor
1984; 629 pp.
$40
($42 postpaid)
(Volume III)
1985; 634 pp.
$29.95
($31.45 postpaid)
both from:
Little, Brown & Company
Attn.: Order Dept.
200 West Street
Waltham, MA 02254
or Whole Earth Access

From *Paris, Pee Wee, and Big Dog* (© Caroline Binch).

National Association for the Preservation and Perpetuation of Storytelling

The best single resource for storytellers. Yearly $20 dues include subscriptions to the **National Storytelling Journal**, *a quarterly magazine dealing with issues in the story-telling movement, and the* **Yarnspinner**, *a monthly national calendar of storytelling performances, workshops and festivals. You also get a national* **Directory of Storytelling** *which gives access to storytellers across the country, and a free* **Catalog of Storytelling** *which offers books and recordings. They also sponsor a festival, a conference, and an ongoing school of storytelling. —Robin Moore*

NAPPS
Membership **$20**/year
Information **free**
from:
National Association for the Preservation and Perpetuation of Storytelling
P. O. Box 309
Jonesborough, TN 37659

The Original Bert and I
Marshall Dodge and Robert Bryan

Nineteen hilarious tall tales and anecdotes told in the traditional language and accent of the Down-Easters. **Album F129A $8.95. Cassette F129C $8.95.**

Iphat Mujury from Zimbabwe, Africa told ageless stories from his homeland that frequently contained songs accompanied by the mbira, an African instrument hundreds of years old.

World Tales

This is a rare and magical book, beautiful to look at and impossible to put down. Each story is more wondrous than the last, embellished — adorned, really — with extravagant pictures by a variety of artists in the tradition of the illustrated book or illuminated manuscript. Idries Shah's tales about each tale, showing where and when each story has unaccountably occurred in widely diverse cultures over vast reaches of time, are as mysterious and wonderful as the tales themselves. —Carol Van Strum

•

The two brothers were fighting at that moment as to who was the true owner of the pouch. As it went from one to the other, it fell on the ground. In came the rat and snatched it between his teeth. . . . They beat the rat with sticks, but still it held on. Then, from the sky swooped a falcon, the one which Ahmad had released, and took the pouch in its beak. The rat escaped and ran away.

Soon the pouch was laid at Ahmad's feet by the falcon. As soon as the pouch was in his fingers Ahmad wished that his village could be returned to him with all it contained. No sooner were the words out of his mouth than he heard the lowing of his cattle, and his pretty wife came towards him, with laughing eyes. But the two false brothers came to Ahmed with false smiles on their faces, and pretended that they knew nothing about the matter of the village being spirited away.

Ahmed looked at them, and saw them for what they were. He knew that if they remained there, trouble would always be in the air.

World Tales
Collected by Idries Shah
OUT OF PRINT
Harcourt Brace Jovanovitch

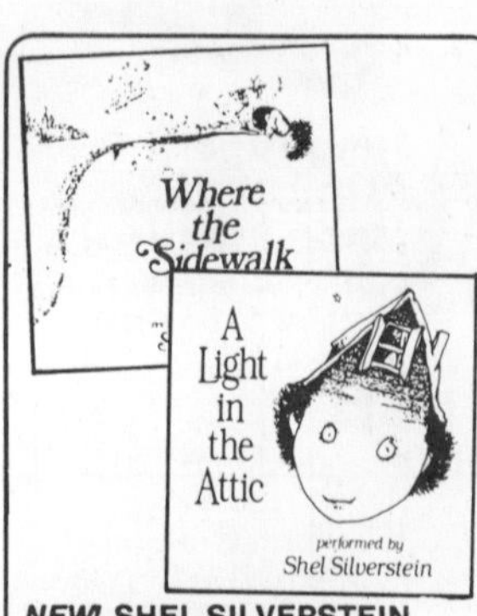

***NEW!* SHEL SILVERSTEIN**
LIGHT IN THE ATTIC
Now, performed by the author, the award-winning book that spent 140 weeks on the N.Y. Times Best Seller List is a sound recording. Ages 5-up.
2CB 4021 LP or Cassette $8.98

WHERE THE SIDEWALK ENDS
From *Captain Hook* to the *Crocodile's Toothache*, sheer enjoyment. Grammy winner, Shel Silverstein, is magnificient. Ages 5-adult.
2CB 3941 LP or Cassette $8.98

• Many consider Garrison Keillor to be the state-of-the-art contemporary storyteller. "A Prairie Home Companion," his weekly radio show, airs on some 260 PBS affiliate stations nationwide. Tapes are available from Minnesota Public Radio, Dept. GB, 45 E St., St. Paul, MN 55101. —Robin Moore

Educational Record Center

On long car and plane trips with our kids, I've found nothing beats a pair of headphones and a cassette player loaded with tapes from a source like this. The Educational Record Center covers the world of children's literature with records and cassettes, readalongs (book plus recordings), filmstrips and videos. —Andrea Sharp

MARTIN LUTHER KING, JR. SPEAKS
These albums capture 3 of Dr. Kings' famous speeches:
MARCH TO FREEDOM **2MC 906**
Detroit Freedom Rally 6/23/63
MARCH ON WASHINGTON **2MC 908**
I Have a Dream... 8/28/63
FREE AT LAST (Memphis) **2MC 929**
I've been to the mountaintop! 6/3/68
SAVE! 2MC 99K 3 LPs or 3 Cass $22.00
EACH LP or Cass $7.98

Educational Record Center
Catalog **free** from:
Educational Record Center
472 East Paces Ferry Rd.
Atlanta, GA 30305

The Use and Training of the Human Voice
Arthur Lessac
1967; 320 pp.
$12.50
($13.75 postpaid) from:
Drama Book Publishers
821 Broadway
New York, NY 10003
or Whole Earth Access

The Use and Training of the Human Voice

Everything you need to understand, train, improve, and enjoy your voice is here in this wonderful book. Lessac's method is uncomplicated and precise . . . a basic system for actors, speakers, singers, everyone who uses the voice as an instrument beyond simple communication.

One of the best features of Lessac's approach is the way he relates the voice to general health and the total person. Many people who never get near a stage or a microphone can use the book to make real gains in self-awareness and well-being.

Best of all, perhaps, the book is designed for self-teaching. It takes nothing for granted, but exposes every vital aspect of the use and training of the voice. —Scott Beach

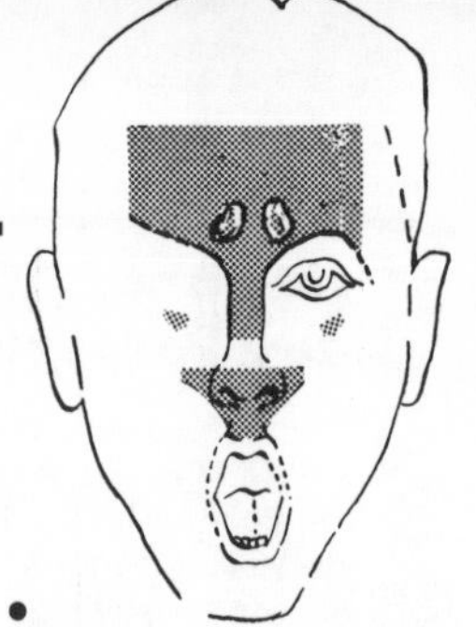

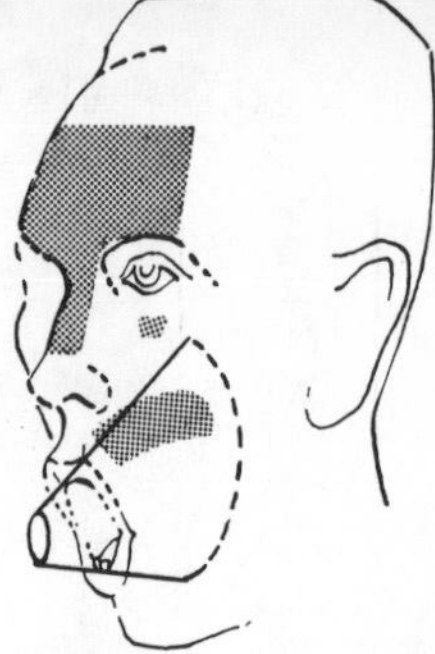

•

When the voice is properly used, the tones are consciously transmitted through the hard palate, the nasal bone, the sinuses, and the forehead. Some of the sound waves continue on through the frontal sinuses, cranial bone, spine, and ribs, to produce chest resonance, but the conscious action takes places in these four areas of the head and the more tonal action felt in these structures, the greater the chest resonance. When sound is transmitted in this way, we feel the vibratory-tonal actions.

Language Acquisition Made Practical
E. Thomas Brewster and Elizabeth S. Brewster
1976; 384 pp.
$12
postpaid from:
Lingua House
135 North Oakland
P. O. Box 91
Pasadena, CA 91182
or Whole Earth Access

Language Acquisition Made Practical

This superb handbook trains you to learn any language in the world on your own, in the language's home turf.

The trick is to teach native speakers to teach you to learn their language. Comprende? It's done slowly, naturally, and playfully — the way you learned English. Your assistant doesn't even have to dig your jive. You begin conversing with one word, trying to make as many mistakes as you possibly can, entertaining the folks in the marketplace or anywhere else they'll put up with your blabberings. This well-tested program shows you how to construct your own exercises that fit the language you are after and later how to discover its grammar by yourself. The goal is multiculturalism, inseparable from multilingualism. Like realizing that you don't need a degree in anything to build your own house, learning that you can become fluent in another language without schools is deliciously radical. —Kevin Kelly

•

By using these sentence patterns you can get extra drill on new vocabulary while talking with people. You can touch an object and ask "What is this?" They may answer, "This is a Kefala." You can then touch a similar object and ask "Is this a Kefala?" and they will answer positively or negatively.

If you are talking with children, this can become quite a game and give you lots of practice with new words. Children will often catch on, and participate with you in the game. First, you can ask the questions while they answer. Then you can trade roles and let them ask the questions while you try to answer. If you enter into the spirit of the game, everybody can have fun while you practice vocabulary.

•

To prepare for a Comprehension drill, you need to plan a list of related activities and have Kino make up a 3 x 5 card with the activities written in his language. The activities for the first day might include sit, stand, squat down, clap your hands, scratch your leg, stretch your arms. In the drill, Kino will instruct you *in his language* to do an activity; for example, "stand up." He will stand up and you observe and then mimic the action by standing yourself. Do not say what he says. Kino then introduces the second item, performing the activity while giving the verbal instructions. You mimic the activity — for example, "sit down." Kino then again gives the first instruction, "stand up," and you respond by standing. Then Kino can give the instructions without acting them out himself — "sit down," "stand up," and you respond to his verbal directions. When doing comprehension drills, respond rapidly without hesitation and make a distinct robust response with your body.

The Overnight Guide to Public Speaking
Ed Wohlmuth
1983; 128 pp.
$9.95
($10.95 postpaid) from:
Running Press
125 South 22nd Street
Philadelphia, PA 19103
or Whole Earth Access

The Overnight Guide to Public Speaking

You can read this book overnight. Ed Wohlmuth's advice, delivered in a breezy, optimistic style, will help your speech. His approach is a bit "show biz," but you can modify that element to your own taste. When I had to give a three hour class recently I followed his suggestions, which included revising my remarks into a more informal style, consciously inserting some "signals" into the presentation and corraling a friend into letting me practice my talk on him the night before. Result: The class went well and everyone enjoyed themselves, including me. This book works. —Jay Kinney

•

Once your facts are assembled, their method of *presentation* becomes crucial. People have a great interest in *people*, not things. The black musician's name was James Reese Europe, and he probably invented the style of popular music we call the fox-trot. I think that's certainly more interesting than the name of the library where I found his concert booklet. Try to relate *your* facts to actual individuals, living or dead. Always tell what the person did in terms that describe *action*. He *invented* that musical style. She *discovered* that chemical element. That's the stuff that'll involve your audience.

Audio-Forum

Don't expect to learn a language by listening to tapes. The best you can expect from cassettes is tireless practice, at your convenience, of what you learn from a class or tutor. Audio-Forum has the best selection of courses, including a well respected crash course called "Language/30." Some of the full-length courses were originally developed by the U.S. Foreign Service Institute. All come with a text book (essential) in a cacophonous selection of languages: Zulu, Xhosa, Serbo-Croatian, eight dialects of Arabic, Urdu, Khmer, and of course, good ole Spanish and French. —Kevin Kelly

Audio-Forum
Catalog
free from:
Audio-Forum
96 Broad Street
Suite A-30
Guilford, CT 06437

KIDS AND COMPUTERS take naturally to each other. Unlike other electronic babysitters, a well-crafted software package, "educational" or "game," engages and challenges the people who use it. Kids test themselves against the machine, and come away with:

A new skill. *Typing Tutor III*, for instance teaches the most fundamental computer skill, maybe better than a person could. It automatically rewards your progress by giving you new challenges, and patiently repeats the typing combinations that give you the most trouble. There's no other typing program better, even for adults;

New knowledge. *Robot Odyssey I* teaches the physics of electronics by plunging you into an imaginary city-full of workshops, where you can design and operate your own working "robots";

Participation in an impossible world. *Hitchhiker's Guide to the Galaxy* retells the well-known Douglas Adams story, complete with wry aliens and misanthropic robots — but you play the main character. Make the wrong move and you end the game prematurely;

Participation in a hard-to-experience part of the real world. *Balance of Power* makes you United States President in a tense, sobering simulation of the Cold War. Make the wrong move and you end the game for everybody;

Or all of the above. *Flight Simulator II* offers the knowledgeable, skillful experience of steering an airplane through a simulated landscape. More than just an amazingly visual game, this will actually drill you in flying techniques.

Flight Simulator II

Most of the best learning and playing software runs on the Apple IIe and IIc computers — computers which we do not recommend you buy *unless* your main need is educational. More and more games are becoming available for the computers we recommend on pp. 352-353 — the Macintosh, IBM PC/compatibles, and Atari 1040ST. Kids will find some of the best software on their own. Word of mouth on this subject is reliable. —Art Kleiner

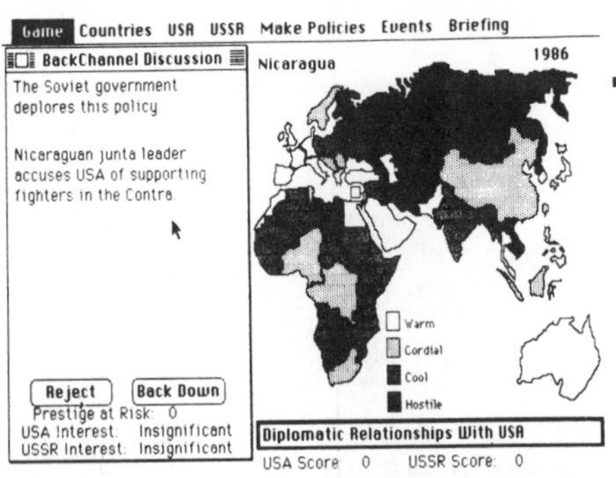

—Balance of Power.

Typing Tutor III: $40-$60 from Simon and Schuster, Electronic Publishing Group, 800-624-0023.

Robot Odyssey I: $50 from The Learning Company, 415-328-5410.

Hitchhiker's Guide to the Galaxy: $35-$40 from Infocom, 617-492-6000.

Balance of Power: $50 from Menu International, 303-482-5000.

Flight Simulator II: $34-$50 from SubLOGIC Corp., 217-359-8482.

Publications

We also trust five printed sources: *The Educational Software Preview Guide* ($10, annual, from San Mateo County Office of Education, 333 Main Street, Redwood City, CA 94063). Twenty computer savvy educators meet once a year to decide what programs to recommend to teachers and parents. They put the resulting comments in this book.

Family Guide to Educational Software free from Garvinghouse, P. O. Box 1717, Middletown, CT 06457). A complete (80 pages), illustrated, informative, wholesome, up-to-date mail order catalog for games and learning programs. Updated quarterly.

Family Computing (Claudia Cohn, Editor. $19.97/year (12 issues) from Family Computing, P. O. Box 2886, Boulder, CO 80322.) The best general computers-for-learning magazine. The tiredest question in the business is, "What use do computers have in the home?" Every month this magazine comes up with 50 pages of answers.

Games Magazine (p. 362) and the *Whole Earth Software Catalog* (p. 354) both review and evaluate game software.

—Art Kleiner, Kevin Kelly, Stewart Brand, Steven Levy, Robert Scarola, Gerri Sinclair

Logo

I remember my vivid fascination with math as a teenager. Not school math, but my own dreamy reveries of, say, patterns of interlocking hexagons. This quiet, playful fascination gradually helped me understand the patterns of my own puzzle-solving thoughts. Playing with *Logo* years later, I recognized the same feeling.

Logo is a computer programming language deliberately designed to spark creativity and self-awareness. As its MIT inventor Seymour Papert says: *"Logo* is not programmed learning; it's for learning how to program in learning." At first, you use *Logo* to define relationships between shapes on a computer screen. Then you invent your own commands and rules for executing commands: Make a box. Move the "turtle" on the screen (the fancy name for *Logo*'s graphic cursor). Take a list of words and sort it. You build fancy commands from simple commands. You make programmed patterns that must wait for cues from your friends at the screen before the patterns can spin themselves out.

There's a whole tribe of *Logo* variations on the market. We recommend *Logo Writer* for an Apple IIe computer with 80 column card, and plain *Apple Logo* for earlier Apple IIs. The choice for IBM users is *PC Logo*, which does best with a color graphics card. You can also get *Atari Logo, Amiga TLC Logo*, and *Macintosh (Mac Logo)* versions. For new *Logo* products see *The Educational Software Preview Guide* (above). —Art Kleiner

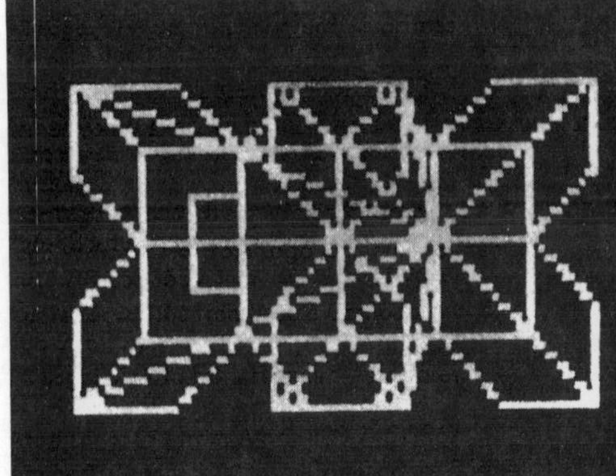

Salt crystals, grown in Apple Logo.

Logo Writer: $395 from Logo Computer Systems, Inc., 213-258-1559.

Apple Logo: $100 from Apple Computer, 408-996-1010.

PC Logo: $149.95 from Harvard Associates, 617-492-0660.

Atari Logo: $50 from Atari, 408-745-2367.

Amiga TLC Logo: $100 from Commodore Business Machines, 1200 Wilson Drive, West Chester, PA 19380.

Mac Logo: $124.95 from Microsoft Corp., 206-828-8080.

How to hold two clubs.

The Juggling Book

I've found juggling to be a sport/meditation-in-action/training superbly suited for the balancing act and juggling of energies required for staying aloft. When I juggle I am either focused and centered or I drop me balls. Simple as that. Instant bio-feedback. If I'm ON I can step back and watch my hands put out continuing displays of patterns and form change.

*With **The Juggling Book**, it should only take you 30 minutes to an hour at the beach or on a large grassy area (saves on furniture) to get started. If you don't know anyone who juggles, Carlo's book seems lucid and thorough enough to do the trick. There's a wealth of material here, some nice advanced stunts — the progression from three- to four-ball juggling is clear and logical — and the emphasis on inner states and mindset is right on. My only complaint is not enough pictures.* —Jon Scoville

•

Once learned, the ability to juggle is never lost or forgotten, no matter how young or old you are when you learn or how many years intervene. In my teaching experience I have never found anyone unable to learn because of any so-called lack of coordination. This is a myth that conveniently covers up a real desire to learn, embarrassment, or some other kind of mental block. If you can throw and catch a ball, you can learn how to juggle.

The Juggling Book
Carlo
1974; 102 pp.
$6.95
($7.95 postpaid) from:
Random House
Order Dept.
400 Hahn Road
Westminster, MD 21157
or Whole Earth Access

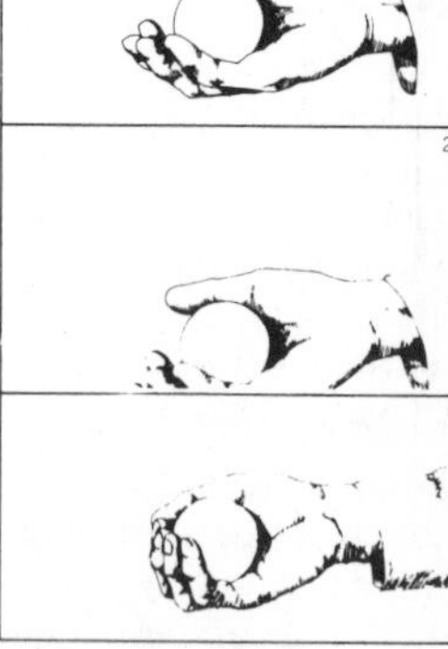

Popping the ball.

Clown

This is the most accessible book I've found for the closet clown. It has sections on make-up, movements, and prop building, and sequence photos of six (count 'em) six classic routines that even a kid can comprehend. Time-tested at Camp Winna Rainbow. Yes, you too can learn to slap, take, slow burn, blow off and add a little laughter to this sometimes weary world. —Wavy Gravy

Clown
Mark Stolzenberg
1981; 160 pp.
$8.95
($10.45 postpaid) from:
Sterling Publishing
2 Park Avenue
New York, NY 10016
or Whole Earth Access

The clown who is getting slapped should clap his hands and throw his head abruptly to the side in the upstage direction — or away from the hand that is slapping. This staccato movement of the head gives the illusion of impact. If you clap your hands exactly when the slapper's hand arrives, it will look and sound as though you've really been hit.

•

Remember: all your slaps and falls should have a comic feeling, and you always need to let the audience know that you haven't been hurt.

When you do a fall, always land facing the audience, if possible. If you want to land in profile, or at an angle to the audience, make sure you let the audience see your face and your reaction.

•

Staying in Character
It's important to perform your slaps and falls as your character would do them. One character might get angry after a fall. Another might cry or laugh. One clown might get up slowly; another might jump right back up to his feet. Your slapstick skills should not stand out awkwardly from your character.

Louis Tannen's Catalog of Magic • Hank Lee's Catalog of Magic

Hank Lee has nice stuff for young magicians and parties. Louis Tannen has the biggest magic catalog around, with all manner of tricks, equipment, and work plans for larger gear. —Stewart Brand

Louis Tannen's Catalog of Magic
1985; 828 pp.
$8 postpaid from:
Louis Tannen, Inc.
6 W. 32nd Street, 4th Floor
New York, NY 10001

Hank Lee's Catalog of Magic
Catalog
$5 from:
Hank Lee's Magic Factory
125 Lincoln Street
P. O. Box 1359
Boston, MA 02205

◄ *Two Goblets*

The latest in the Masters of Magic series. A brilliant, crisp, well-constructed treatment of the Cups and Balls.
All of the traditional weaknesses have been eliminated through the marvelous handling.
– At no time do you have an extra ball palmed!
– At no time do you perform a false transfer!
– Uses only 2 Cups from a 3 Cup COMBO SET
This is a two cup, one ball routine, which is very easy for the audience to follow. One ball penetrates, vanishes, appears, and transposes. For the finale, three HUGE balls appear!!
To create this new effect, some clever new moves and dodges were invented. All are very easy, yet very strong. The entire routine runs about 3 minutes. More than 75 photos along with the clearly written text explain every moment of the routine. A super cups and balls routine!!
$12.50 (10.130) no cups supplied...see COMBO CUPS above)

—*Hank Lee's Catalog of Magic*

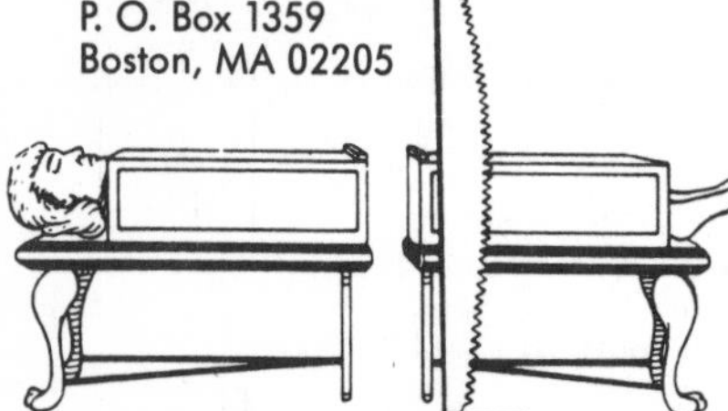

1375—SAWING A LADY IN TWO—New Thin Model

The performer's lady assistant is placed in the box with her feet and ankles projecting from one end and her head from the other. Her feet and head are then secured with stocks which slide down in metal grooves at each end of the box. By means of an ordinary cross-cut saw, the box is then cut exactly in half, after which the two sections of the box are separated and moved some distance apart.

With our version of this baffling effect, only one lady is used and the box is easily reconstructed for performing this effect over and over.

Superior Professional Model, made to order....................
Osborne Workshop Plans.................... $25.00

—*Louis Tannen's*

• Most jugglers recommend Dube. Their "airflite" clubs are the classic affordable, high-quality clubs. Unicycles, top hats, balls, rings, torches, etc.
Dube Juggling Equipment: catalog **free** from Brian Dube, Inc., 25 Park Place, New York, NY 10007.

The Book of Massage

Better than medicine, a caring touch can heal and restore. Learning how is mere good manners. There are several approaches, some from the East and some from the West (both illustrated well in this soothing book). All begin with a comfortable mat and hands pressing knowingly. Get the knowing from this excellent guide. —Kevin Kelly

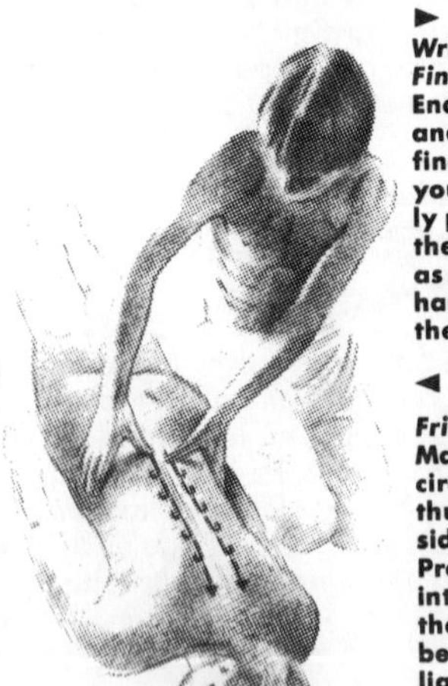

► ***Wringing off the Fingers*** **Enclose the thumb and each of the fingers in turn in your hand and gently pull them, stretch them and twist them as you slide your hand down and off the tip.**

◄ ***Friction along Spine*** **Make short deep circles with your thumbs up either side of the spine. Press them briefly into the hollows at the base of the skull, before sweeping lightly back down.**

Take the foot halfway back to release the knee. Then bring it over to the opposite buttock, as far as it will comfortably go. Bounce it up and down a little to increase the stretch.

The Book of Massage
Lucinda Lidell
1984; 192 pp.

$9.95 postpaid from:
Simon & Schuster
Mail Order Sales
200 Old Tappan Road
Old Tappan, NJ 07675
or Whole Earth Access

Tai Chi — Ten Minutes to Health

As the title promises, this book is less a philosophical tome to this taoist exercise than a handy manual designed to instruct the reader in step-by-step detail. The book employs 590 photographs and 295 diagrams in illustrating Tai Chi's 44 moves and positions — enough for any beginner to quickly familiarize himself with Tai Chi's graceful calisthenics —Ken Conner

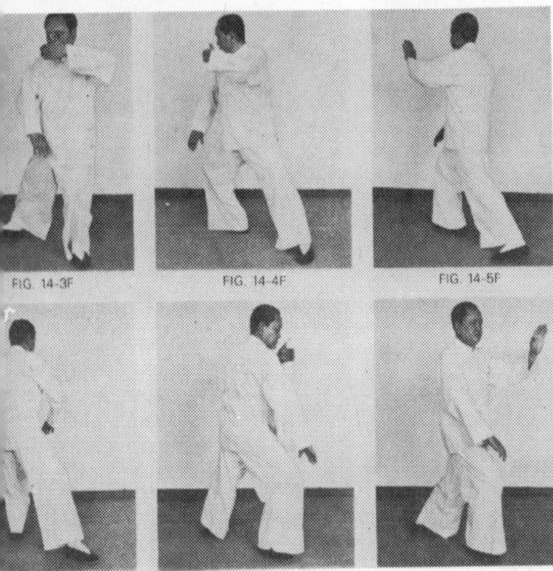

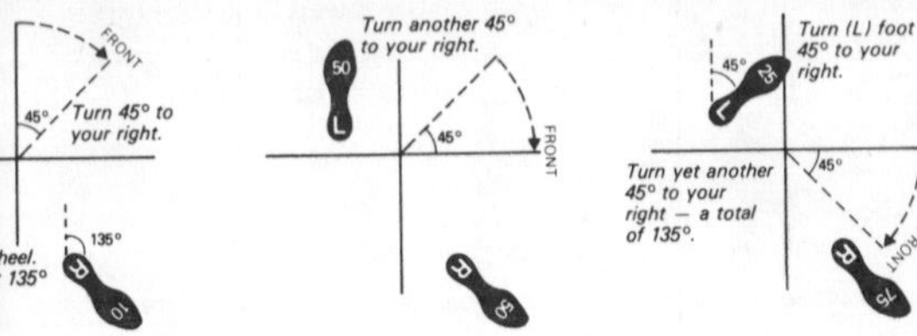

Bao hu gui shan **— "embrace tiger and return to mountain."**

• See also **Stretching** (p. 238).
• See also "Dance" (p. 335).
• See also Esalen workshops (p. 377).

Tai Chi
(Ten Minutes to Health)
Chia Siew Pang
and Goh Ewe Hock
1985; 131 pp.

$12.95
($13.89 postpaid) from:
CRCS Publications
P. O. Box 20850
Reno, NV 89515
or Whole Earth Access

Dolan's Sports

I've dealt with many of the martial arts mail order houses and this is the best I've seen. Wide range of equipment and books from many different arts. All the equipment I've ordered from them (they manufacture much of what they sell) has been sturdy, well made, and worth its price. There's some garbage, of course, but far less than the other sources I've seen. They have a wonderful and rare (for this field) 30-day no-questions-asked refund/exchange policy. —John Michael Greer

"Break-Up rebreakable boards save you money . . . can be used indefinitely!" $21.95 ea.

Face Guard: A unique combination of maximum protection and visibility. Fits over the head and closes under the chin with a velcro strap for a secure fit.
No. 741 Red **. $32.95**
No. 742 Black **. 32.95**

Focus Glove: professional all leather training aid. Firm pad provides a target for kicking and punching. $22.95.

Dolan's Sports
Catalog **free** from:
Dolan's Sports
P. O. Box 26
Farmingdale, NJ 07727

The beam on ropes course.
—Outward Bound

Outward Bound

Now 25 years old, Outward Bound continues to offer challenging courses in such skills as rock climbing and whitewater running. If you're a chickenheart (or think you are), the instruction is just what you need — emphasis is on building self-confidence and leadership. Special courses are arranged for executives, folks with substance-abuse problems, cancer patients unwilling to give up, and victims of domestic violence (and even the perpetrators thereof!). I personally know a number of people who returned from Outward Bound courses noticeably changed for the better. —JB

Outward Bound
Courses **$675-1500**
Information **free** from:
Outward Bound
National Office
384 Field Point Road
Greenwich, CT 06830

The National Outdoor Leadership School

In simple terms, the NOLS goal is this: to teach you the skills necessary to survive in the wilderness — whether it's kayaking in Alaska, mountain climbing in the Rockies, or backpacking in Africa — and to pass through that wilderness without leaving any trace of your having been there. Unlike Outward Bound, NOLS is not into character development or proving yourself. Instead, it teaches only those skills directly related to the wilderness experience.

Both styles have their merits. The fundamental difference, I think, is between self-command and harmony. Me, I'll take harmony. —Joe Kane

•

ADVENTURE COURSE
AGE: 14-15 only
DURATION: 24 days
LOCATION: Absaroka and Bighorn Ranges (Wyoming) and Uinta Range (Utah)
The Adventure Course is an adaption of the NOLS Wilderness Course to the needs of young adults. If you are 14 or 15 years old, this expedition has been designed to meet your level of energy and curiosity. Many of our most outstanding graduates, including quite a few NOLS instructors, began their outdoor training with an Adventure Course.

The National Outdoor Leadership School
Courses **$900-4000**
Catalog **free** from:
National Outdoor Leadership School
P. O. Box AA, Dept. W.E.
Lander, WY 82520

Directory of Sail Training Ships and Programs

For anyone who yearns for the sailing life, for the romance and adventure of "a tall ship and a star to steer her by," this is a directory full of photos and statistics about a number of ships still sailing in the traditional way. What's traditional? you may ask. When the captain shouts "All hands on deck!" and you're asked to go aloft, up the ratlines in the rigging to the yards to furl the topsails, and you're balanced up there 50 feet high, hung out over the yard gathering in sail — that's traditional. (Working aloft is not mandatory, however.) Traditional sailing is also an attitude about the sea and the tall ships who grace her waters. It is an understanding of the natural ways of travelling through the water; the combination of wind, waves, and manpower that keep a ship moving.

The American Sail Training Association, founded in 1973, is an organization devoted to three purposes: promoting sail training as an educational and character-building experience for young people, bringing together the sail training ships of the world in a spirit of friendship and international goodwill, and educating our young people in the values of our maritime traditions.

While many of the ships in the directory offer sail training only for young people, there is still a large number of them who offer cruising opportunities in East Coast waters and the Pacific for those with a free spirit and time to travel. —Merlyn Storm

•

Gaff Topsail Schooner
LOA: 93'6" *LWL 86'2"*
Beam: 24'3" *Draft: 8'4"*
Tons: 98
Sail Area: 7,400 sq. ft.
Rig Height: 106'

Waters: Coastal California, Pacific
Season: Year round
Contact: Nautical Heritage Society
24532 Del Prado
Dana Point, CA 92629
(714) 661-1001
Cost: $700 for 11-day cruise

The Californian is a hand-hewed re-creation of the Lawrence, a 19th century Coast Guard cutter. The founders of the Nautical Heritage Society have developed the Californian Sail Training Program out of a dedicated belief that traditional sail training is a unique and valuable form of education.

Directory of Sail Training Ships and Programs
Nancy Richardson, Editor
Catalog
$5 from:
American Sail Training Association
Newport Harbour Center
365 Thames
Newport, RI 02840

Kibbutz Aliya Desk

If you're between the ages of 15 and 35, this outfit can arrange an involvement with a kibbutz. You should be Jewish and ready for hard work. Some programs require that you study Hebrew while at the kibbutz. There are programs for temporary workers, summer stays, University semesters, and even permanent residence. I know several people who have participated in this sort of thing, and they say it's a combination of inspiring and disillusioning. Real, in other words, and very much worth the time and money. —JB

•

Project Discovery

This is a unique program, co-sponsored by Kibbutz Aliya Desk and the archaeologist Dr. Adam Zertal. It includes three weeks on a kibbutz, one week of participation in archaeological excavations, and a week of a "follow the Bible" tour.
DATES: Mid-June, 1986 COST: $1680
The program cost includes round-trip airfare (New York — Tel Aviv — New York); registration fee; airport transfer; kibbutz residence (includes meals and laundry); the excavation; the 7-day tour; and an insurance policy.

Kibbutz Aliya Desk
Information **free** from:
Kibbutz Aliya Desk
27 West 20th Street
New York, NY 10011

International Youth Exchange

You go there and stay with a family, or they come here and stay with a host family. Our government is encouraging (with grants) the many private organizations that carry out such programs. This booklet tells you how to be student or host, and provides a list of the organizations involved — plus a bit of chat that will enable you to make a good choice. Looks like the bureaucrats have done it right this time. —JB

•

Should I become an exchange student?

To help you decide whether or not you want to become an exchange student, ask yourself questions such as these:

Do I want to learn to speak another language? Can I keep up in a school that may make unfamiliar academic demands on me?

Can I handle day-to-day challenges and frustrations? Cope with occasional loneliness? Tolerate attitudes, ideas and values that are different from my own?

Am I willing to compromise? Make more decisions on my own? Laugh at myself when I do or say something others may think is silly or inapproriate?

Can I be a friend and a part of a host family without acting like a "guest" in a foreign country?

•

To help you decide if hosting is right for your family, an experienced exchange organization may ask you the following questions:

• Do you enjoy having people in your home?

• Do you like the intensity, spontaneity and unpredictability of teenagers?

• Are you prepared for the expenses related to hosting?

• Can your family's values, attitudes and behavior stand up to questioning by a student eager to learn more about American culture?

• Would you have the time and patience to talk to someone learning your language?

International Youth Exchange
Catalog **free** from:
Youth Exchange
Pueblo, CO 81009

Experiment in International Living
Information **free** from:
Experiment in
International Living
Kipling Road
Brattleboro, VT 05301

Audubon Expedition School
$6800/year (Sept.-May)
Information **free** from:
National Audubon Society
Expedition Institute
Northeast Audubon
Center, Route 4
Sharon, CT 06069

Experiment in International Living

Over 100,000 young people have participated in the programs of the Experiment in International Living since the action commenced in 1932. "Homestay" — living with a family and engaging in whatever it is that they do in normal life — is the backbone of this enterprise. It's probably the best way to learn about folks different than yourself. There are adult programs, too.

School For International Training is their academic division, offering coursework in subjects chosen to enhance intercultural relationships. Credit can usually be arranged at your base college or university. When you hear people say "my semester abroad," it's often this program.

The word experiment is well retained in the organization name; new things are being tried all the time (one reason for the Experiment's long life). There is a growing program involving Elderhostel (p. 216), and a lively one, International Students of English, intended to bring foreigners' English to a level sufficient to permit enrollment at an American university. The Experiment also has taught English to thousands of refugees. Yes, the Experiment is included in the International Youth Exchange noted elsewhere on this page. —JB

•

Can I go with a friend?

This often-asked question gets a positive "no." The reason? It is a drawback to making new friends and getting to know your host country. By the end of the first day you will have made many new friends.

How can my parents and friends contact me while I'm abroad?

Your family and friends may write to you in care of the local Experiment representative who knows your whereabouts at all times. To insure your total immersion in the culture, we strongly discourage visits and phone calls from family and friends.

Audubon Expedition School

One of the more tempting education opportunities around is this schoolbus load of students that travels all around the country each year from September through May. The bus stops at such diverse locations as wilderness areas, Native American communities, and my own turf until recently, The New Alchemy Institute. Students don't stay in the bus, either. They hike, ski, bike, boat, and participate in the action of the areas they study, for graduate, undergraduate or even high school credit. Praise for this school is high and I can see why: There's that indefinable feeling of reality that is missing from so much classroom instruction. They have scholarships, summer expeditions, and a degree program through Lesley College. —JB

[Suggested by Jim Swan]

• Also see Peace Corps (p. 90) and **Globe** (p. 254).

• Outward Bound graduates tell it like they did it.
Outward Bound U.S.A.: Joshua L. Miner and Joe Boldt, 1981; 374 pp. **$8.95** ($10.45 postpaid) from William Morrow Publishing Co., Wilmor Warehouse, 6 Henderson Drive, West Caldwell, NJ 07006 (or Whole Earth Access).

• See Earthwatch, (p. 258).

Helping Out in the Outdoors

When people volunteer everybody is winning. Needed jobs get done (cheerfully!), and the volunteers go home with more than they gave. Like to partake? Our parks could use your help. Wanted are fire lookouts, craft instructors, trail crews, campground hosts, surveyors, and tree planters. Experience accepted, willingness preferred. Some jobs pay no money, others furnish groceries or lodging or gas money, or work clothes, and some even pay meagerly. Look over this quarterly directory, decide who to give your love to, and write to them early. —Kevin Kelly

•

Timber technician: Do you want to get into the tall timber? If you like the odor of pine, you will like this position. Three hardy men or women are needed to use forestry tools to fell trees, buck logs, and spread seed-bearing branches so that a new forest can be created. Your efforts will be seen for 150 years. We will give you the know-how. Dates: June through October. Benefits: Work days and hours are negotiable, housing, transportation to the work site. Requirements, 18 or older.

Lesley College National Audubon Society
Catalog **free** from:
Lesley College National
Audubon Society
Attn.: Outreach
29 Everett Street
Cambridge, MA 02238

Helping Out in the Outdoors
Published in February and August
$3/issue or
$12/2 years
(4 issues) from:
Washington Trails
Association
16812 36th Avenue West
Lynnwood, WA 98037

ORMULA for an interesting life: acquire skills and use them. The more skills, the more interesting. —Stewart Brand

Getting Skilled
Tom Hebert
and John Coyne
1980; 145 pp.
$1.50 postpaid
or Whole Earth Access

Handbook of Trade and Technical Careers and Training
National Association of Trade and Technical Schools
1985-86; 80 pp.
free
Both from:
NATTS
2251 Wisconsin Ave., NW
Room 200
Washington, DC 20007

Getting Skilled • Handbook of Trade and Technical Careers

*One of the encouraging signs I see in our society these days is that there are many young people NOT going to college, nor planning to. Having made that decision, many just diddle around waiting for something to happen, which it often doesn't. There is a hunger to be good at something. A so-called "trade-school" can be a good answer, and it fortunately is an answer that is rapidly losing a second-best reputation. OK. How do you find out about trade schools? **Getting Skilled** is the best I've seen on the subject by far. If you counsel students it will help you a lot. It also lists many schools in a huge appendix. The authors are well in tune with coming trends, too; this isn't a rehashed 1938 text.* —JB

*A very useful **Handbook of Trade and Technical Careers and Training** indicates the range of skills that trade schools teach, which schools, and how to reach them. NATTS (National Association of Trade and Technical Schools) has other career training booklets too. The price is right: free.* —Stewart Brand

Skill	Term
Actor	150 weeks
Air Conditioning and Refrigeration Technician	12-73 weeks
Appliance Repairer	12-72 weeks
Architectural Engineering Technician	60-100 weeks
Artist, Commercial	52-136 weeks
Artist, Fine	104-152 weeks
Auto Body Repairer	26-52 weeks
Automotive Mechanic	14-50 weeks
Aviation Maintenance Technician	33-84 weeks
Baker	18 weeks
Bank Teller	32 weeks
Barber/Hairstylist	32-52 weeks
Bartender	2 weeks
Blueprint Reader	3-40 weeks
Brickmason	102 weeks
Broadcaster	13-48 weeks
Broadcasting Technician	10-92 weeks
Building Maintenance Technician	52-60 weeks
Cabinetmaker	60 weeks
Carpenter	102 weeks
Civil Engineering Technician	18-104 weeks
Coin-Operated Machine Repairer	26 weeks
Computer Service Technician	30-120 weeks
Construction Technologist	32-104 weeks
Cosmetologist	52 weeks
Data Processor	21-100 weeks
Dealer	4-16 weeks
Dental Assistant	12-50 weeks
Dental Laboratory Technician	26-72 weeks
Diamond Cutter and Grader	26-40 weeks
Diesel Mechanic	10-48 weeks
Dietetic Technician	13-52 weeks
Diver	8-15 weeks
Drafter	17-88 weeks
Dressmaker and Designer	3-88 weeks
Electrician	21-104 weeks
Electrologist	52 weeks
Electronics Technology	24-108 weeks
Emergency Medical Technician	28-34 weeks
Engraver	12 weeks
Fashion Designer	33-96 weeks
Fashion Illustrator	52-136 weeks

—NATTS

The Informed Performer's Directory of Instruction for the Performing Arts
Kat Smith
1981; 254 pp.
$9.95
($10.95 postpaid) from:
Avon Books
P. O. Box 767
Dresden, TN 38225
or Whole Earth Access

The Informed Performer's Directory of Instruction for the Performing Arts

After catching your breath from reading the title, you'll find a rousing collection of schools and coaches for acting, dance, speech, voice, and a variety of other bits like mime and stage combat, where the action is. Mostly in New York and California —JB

PROGRAM:	Stage Dialects, Stage Speech
INSTRUCTOR:	Gordon A. Jacoby
ESTABLISHED:	1964
REGISTRATION FEE:	None
CLASS FEE:	$225 per term
SCHEDULE:	2 1¾-hour sessions per week, 12 weeks
AUDITING:	Not usually permitted
AUDITING FEE:	$10
ENTRANCE REQUIREMENTS:	Interview
CANCELLATION POLICIES:	Refunds and make-ups available
SCHOLARSHIPS:	Not available
REQUIRED MATERIALS:	None
NUMBER OF STUDENTS PER CLASS:	10
STUDENT BREAKDOWN:	50% female, 50% male; 50% 18–25, 40% 26–35, 10% 36–45; 10% under 6 months, 40% ½–1 year, 40% 1–2 years, 10% 2–3 years
VOCAL CASSETTES:	Students are permitted to record exercises at class.

Ringling Bros. and Barnum & Bailey Clown College
Information
free from:
Ringling Bros. and Barnum & Bailey Clown College
P. O. Box 1528
Venice, FL 33595

WoodenBoat School

*If messing about in boats is good for the soul, think of the salutary effects of making a boat, from wood, yourself, from scratch. Boatbuilding is a bit different from other crafts in that the penalty for unskilled or even uninspired praxis tends to include unintended swimming. Nature as art critic. There are a number of woodenboat-making schools. This one has a good reputation with people we know well. For other equally worthy schools, see the advertisements in **WoodenBoat** magazine (p. 289).* —JB

WoodenBoat School
Information
free from:
WoodenBoat School
P. O. Box 78
Brooklin, ME
04616

Ringling Bros. and Barnum & Bailey Clown College

Run away and join the circus. No kidding. Free tuition, you pay for room, board, and makeup. Nine-week course begins every September. —Stewart Brand

•

Q. What subjects are taught at clown college?

A. Clowning, Clown Makeup, Comedy Acrobatics, Fundamental Gymnastics, Acrobatableaux, Juggling, Equilibrium (unicycle riding, rolling cylinder, stilt walking), Mime, Comedic Movement, Pantomime, Arenaction, Elephant Riding, Web-sitting, Clown Props Building, Clown Costuming (Design, Cutting and Draping). Lectures on: Famous Clowns of the Past; Origins of Clowning; The Mechanics of Visual Comedy; History of the Big Tops; Arena Circuses; Circus Jargon; Transportation and Logistics; Production Clowning; Engagement and Performance Direction; Circus Promotion, Publicity and Public Relations; Animal Training and Care; Circus Bands and Music; Thrill Acts.

• See also the Owner Builder Center, p. 121.
• For crafts schools check under specific craft, pp. 170-183.

The Esalen Catalog

Though you can't get a seminar at the Esalen Institute hot springs on the California Big Sur coast through the mail, you can get their catalog, survey the offerings along several dimensions of humanistic psychology, and go to Big Sur for one hell of a weekend. Since 1962 Esalen has been the stage where new acts and new actors try out the Human Potential big time. —Stewart Brand

•

Approaches to Christian Mysticism
Brother David Steindl-Rast

Awareness of Eastern mysticism makes many people ask: what of the mystical tradition in the West? Is it still alive? Can one find meaning in it today? Brother David has spent more than 30 years in both Eastern and Western monasteries exploring the roots of mysticism in the human heart. He will lead participants in discovering these roots in their own life experience. We shall ask what the pursuit of the path of the heart demands from each one personally, and how it can be practiced in one's daily life.

Like Thomas Merton, his late fellow monk and friend, Brother David is a bridge-builder between East and West. The focus of this weekend, however, will be on the Christian tradition and on our need to wrestle with it. Input and question periods will alternate with silent time for guided experience.

Naropa Institute

In Boulder, Colorado, a robust and innovative school has grown up around Chogyam Trungpa. Theater, music, dance, science, martial arts, poetry, calligraphy, and psychology are some of the courses. Leading artists, philosophers, and spiritual teachers regularly hold forth. Impressive operation. —Stewart Brand

Naropa Institute

Catalog **$4** from:
Naropa Institute
2130 Arapahoe Avenue
Boulder, CO 80302

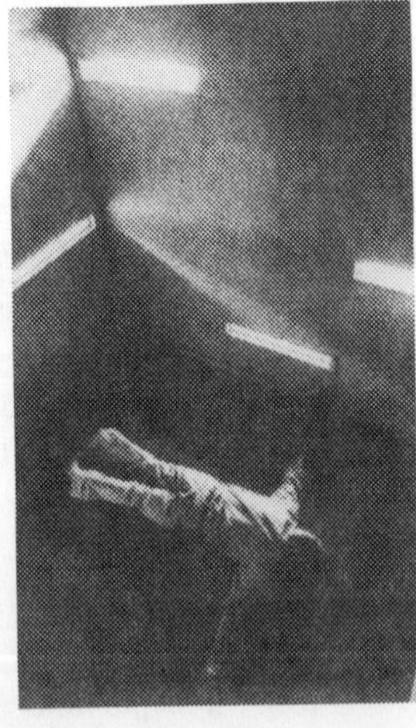

•

Space Awareness Practice

Five specially designed rooms of different architecture, color, lighting, and emotional quality are the setting for this practice. The purpose of the practice is to become more precise about the continuous interaction between one's environment, one's body sensibilities, and one's state of mind.

The Esalen Catalog

Catalog **free;** subscription **$10** (3 issues plus other mailings) from:
Esalen Institute
Big Sur, CA 93920

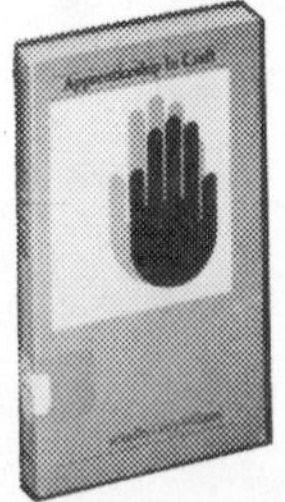

Apprenticeship in Craft

Both craftspeople considering taking on apprentices and those thinking of apprenticing themselves to a master craftsperson to learn a craft should read this thoughtful book before taking another step. It will give you a sense of all that is involved in the apprentice-master relationship. Detailed information is given on the pros and cons of apprenticeships as well as on contracts, payments, work arrangements, evaluation, termination, and other facets of apprenticeships. The book is a series of musings by 45 craftspeople, administrators, and educators who have been personally involved in apprenticeships. It sounds like the truth. —Marilyn Green

Sam Maloof, furniture maker, with apprentice Jerry Marcotte.

•

I am direct about what I have to offer in the way of studio time and materials. In fact, I once wrote lists of "what I expect" and "what I offer," to clarify these areas for myself. I now show these lists to prospective apprentices. I've lost a few promising people by using such a direct approach, but I'm convinced it was for the best.

During the interview, I look for maturity (which seems to have little correlation with age), a sense of commitment to clay, and motivation. I also look for some kind of positive chemistry. An apprentice becomes an important part of my life. I have to feel free to be myself and to work with someone who will fit into my lifestyle.

Perhaps more important, I look for the ability to take initiative and solve problems. The apprentice should have the ability to function independently and add to the workings of the studio. He should be able to institute better ways of doing things. I always hope to learn as I teach, and I consider any new idea a "payoff."

Apprenticeship in Craft

Gerry Williams, Editor
1981; 215 pp.

$9.50

postpaid from:
Studio Potter Books
Box 65
Goffstown, NH 03045
or Whole Earth Access

The Tracker School

Tom Brown, Jr., grew up in the desolate New Jersey Pine Barrens. He was schooled mercilessly but compassionately in woodlore and survival by his best friend's father, a Navajo tracker named Stalking Wolf. With a consummate storyteller's skill (perhaps that of his coauthor) he entices the rest of us by telling how he exchanged his small-town-boy's self-centeredness for the cunning, observant care, and sheer goodheartedness of a tracker. The result is a masterpiece of lore about how to see and how to learn: two books (with more coming soon). ***The Tracker*** *was the first and is, so far, the most powerful.* ***The Search*** *is its sequel. It includes the thoughts that led to the founding of The Tracker School. The school emphasizes the increasing of your sensitivity to what's going on around you. It is claimed that an apt student will be able to sneak up to deer close enough to touch one. From what we've heard, the course work is a good antidote to our lack of education in the ways of nature.*
—Art Kleiner, Becca Herber, and JB

• Tom Brown's newest book is **Tom Brown's Guide to Wild Edible and Medicinal Plants:** Tom Brown, Jr., 1985; 234 pp. **$7.95** ($8.70 postpaid) from Berkley Publishing Group, 390 Murray Hill Pkwy., East Rutherford, NJ 07073.

• Tom Brown also has a series of field guides on wilderness and urban survival and various nature observation skills.

The Tracker*

Tom Brown, Jr. and William Jon Watkins
1978; 229 pp.

$3.50

($5 postpaid)

The Search*

Tom Brown, Jr. and William Owen
1980; 219 pp.

$6.95

($8.45 postpaid)

The Tracker School

Courses $465-515
Catalog **free**

All from:
The Tracker, Inc.
P. O. Box 173
Ashbury, NJ 08802
*or Whole Earth Access

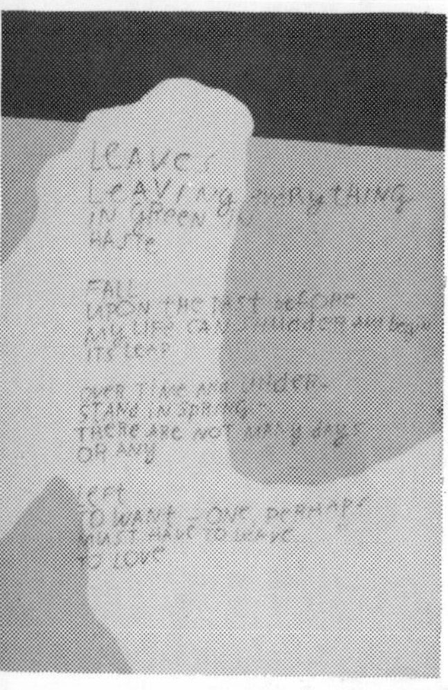

—Corita Kent

The Independent Scholar's Handbook
Ronald Gross
1982; 261 pp.
$10.95
postpaid from:
Addison-Wesley Publishing Co.
1 Jacob Way
Reading, MA 01867
or Whole Earth Access

Tutorial Study Program
Catalog
$5
information
free
from:
International College
1019 Gayley Avenue
Los Angeles, CA 90024

Some rules and hints for teachers and students.

RULE ONE: Find a place you trust, and then try trusting it for awhile.

RULE TWO: General duties of a student — pull everything out of your teacher; pull everything out of your fellow students.

RULE THREE: General duties of a teacher — pull everything out of your students.

RULE FOUR: Consider everything an experiment.

RULE FIVE: Be self-disciplined — this means finding someone wise or smart and choosing to follow them. To be disciplined is to follow in a good way. To be self-disciplined is to follow in a better way.

RULE SIX: Nothing is a mistake. There's no win and no fail, there's only make.

RULE SEVEN: The only rule is work. If you work it will lead to something. It's the people who do all of the work all of the time who eventually catch on to things.

RULE EIGHT: Don't try to create and analyze at the same time. They're different processes.

RULE NINE: Be happy whenever you can manage it. Enjoy yourself. It's lighter than you think.

RULE TEN: "We're breaking all the rules. Even our own rules. And how do we do that? By leaving plenty of room for X quantities." (John Cage)

HINTS: Always be around. Come or go to everything. Always go to classes. Read anything you can get your hands on. Look at movies carefully, often. Save everything — it might come in handy later. —Corita Kent

Tutorial Study Program

So sensible you wonder what's taken it so long to reappear. A system of apprenticeship, internship, to an international guild of tutors. For a period of time like eight months you live near and work with a master the likes of Anna Halprin, Elisabeth Mann Borghese, Ravi Shankar and Yehudi Menuhin. They offer B.A., M.A. and Ph.D. degrees. Nine month's tuition is $4,600.
—Stewart Brand [Suggested by Gregory Bateson]

The Independent Scholar's Handbook

Ever talk about Plato at four in the morning in a doughnut shop with a well-read blue-collar stranger? That's the feeling this book evokes. The author doesn't describe the ways to get accreditation, academic legitimacy, or even intellectual power. He tells how to find out the things that would change your life if you took the trouble to learn them, how to tell other people about them, and how to support yourself meanwhile. The methods include reporting and cultivating experts, but mainly forming the kind of relationship with libraries that master chefs have with their food suppliers. The book is full of anecdotes about independent researchers like Eric Hoffer that make you want to follow up everything they ever wrote; but more important, it's full of solid advice, the kind that will be news even to people who have pursued this particular path with a heart for years. This **Catalog***'s best contributors always seem to work this way. —Art Kleiner*

•

As your interests, feelings, curiosity, enthusiasm, and concerns begin to converge on a particular topic, it will be well to draft, purely for your own use at first, a brief statement of your plans. I have never known an independent scholar who did not discover, at the end of an hour or two of work on such a one-page statement, that he or she had sharper goals.

•

By making the process of browsing a bit more self-conscious, you can conduct your own informal "reconnaissance" of the terrain of learning. All you have to do is follow these three rules:

1. Pick the best places.
2. Keep moving.
3. Keep a list.

•

Eric Hoffer said: Listen, suppose you come to San Francisco looking for a person whose address you don't know. You can trace him by research. You look in the telephone directory, you go to City Hall; if he's a workman, you go to the unions; if he's a doctor, you go to the medical associations, and so on. This is not my way! My way is to stand on the corner of Powell and Market and wait for him to come by. And if you have all the time in the world and you are interested in the passing scene, this is as good a way as any; and if you don't meet him, you are going to meet someone else. That's how I do research. I go to the library, I pick up the things that interest me, I use whatever comes my way. And I believe that if you have a good theory, the things you need *will* come your way. You'll be lucky. You know what Pasteur said: Chance favors the prepared mind.

The Lifetime Reading Plan

Will reading the best works of Plato, Marcus Aurelius, Chaucer, Shaw, Dickens, Voltaire, Thoreau, Freud, Nabokov, Borges, etc., make you a better person?

Yes.

Will this book help you DO IT? Also yes. The selection is fine, the 1-page introductions to each author by Fadiman are inviting, not daunting. —Stewart Brand

The Lifetime Reading Plan
Clifton Fadiman
1960, 1978; 256 pp
$15.45
($16.95 postpaid) from:
Harper and Row
2350 Virginia Avenue
Hagerstown, MD 21740
or Whole Earth Access

•

The books here discussed may take you fifty years to finish. They can of course be read in a much shorter time. The point is that they are intended to occupy an important part of a whole life, no matter what your present age may be. Many of them happen to be more entertaining than the latest best-seller. Still, it is not on the entertainment level that they are most profitably read. What they offer is of larger dimensions. It is rather like what is offered by loving and marrying, having and rearing children, carving out a career, creating a home. They can be a major experience, a source of continuous internal growth. Hence the word Lifetime. These authors are life companions. Once part of you, they work in and on and with you until you die. They should not be read in a hurry, any more than friends are made in a hurry.

Bear's Guide to Finding Money For College

We have two major self-esteem rites-of-passage in our culture, and a good book for each. What the indispensable **What Color Is Your Parachute** *(see p. 187) does for landing a job, this does for landing an education.*

It's about how to approach the financing of your learning as creatively as you choose what to learn. The book wisely counsels not paying so much in the first place (even Ivy League schools will bargain on tuition if you don't call it that), and provides excellent, clever, unconventional means of digging up what money you do need. Use these strategies for any kind of degree. —Kevin Kelly

•

Thousands of corporations have programs in which they will pay for all or part of their employees' school expenses. Based on what the corporations say they would have done, over six billion dollars in tuition and fee reimbursement goes unclaimed each year, simply because no one asked for it. This is partly because school-attending employees were unaware of the reimbursement plan, and partly because not enough employees chose to attend school in their spare time.

•

Some schools encourage currently enrolled students or alumni to help promote the school to others in their community, business, etc. For each student who enrolls as a result of their efforts, they are paid a fee or commission, which can range from just a few dollars to many hundreds of dollars. Many students have been able to reduce their own tuitions to zero by this method.

Wishcraft

The obstacles which held up my life always seemed to be mysterious, invisible things — ghosts. The spell for release is in two parts: 1) The wish. Trying to change yourself and trying to deny yourself are equally futile. The only power that will ever make you really go comes from your own deep wishes, interests, and desires. 2) The craft. If you don't have practical techniques: for problem-solving, planning, getting your hands on information and contacts; for coping with human feelings that aren't going to go away; for getting the emotional support risk-taking requires; and for figuring out what your wishes really are, your desires will dissipate like steam without an engine. So, with the lessons of **Wishcraft**, *no more ghosts. Real wishes. Real problems. Real solutions. Real changes.* —David Finacom

•

It's a common assumption that if you really try your hardest to get something and don't get it, you'll be shattered — so it's safer not to risk going all out. That is totally false. The exact opposite is true. . . . *You never feel really bad when you've given something your best shot.* You may be disappointed, but you don't blame yourself. But if you haven't given it your best shot, you feel terrible. Because you never really know whether you could have done better . . . but you do know you could have done more. Win or lose, all-out efforts leave you feeling clean and good about yourself.

• For superb career guidance see **What Color Is Your Parachute?** (p. 187).
• See also "Adventure Travel" (p. 258) for life-changing learning.

Non-Traditional College Degrees

Education and accreditation have parted ways. For job opportunity, get some easy degrees. For an interesting life, get some hard education. I can see good argument for getting them separately — you don't cross your purposes or narrow your possibilities so much. This intelligent, practical book will tutor you in the non-traditional course. —Stewart Brand

•

The philosophy behind "credit for life experience" can be expressed very simply: Academic credit is given for what you know, without regard for how, when, or where the learning was acquired. . . .

The most common error people make when thinking about getting credit for life experience is to confuse time spent with learning. Being a regular church-goer for thirty years is not worth any college credit, in and of itself. But the regular church-goer who can document that he or she has taught Sunday school classes, worked with youth groups, participated in leadership programs, organized community drives, studied Latin or Greek, taken tours to the Holy Land, or engaged in lengthy philosophical discussions with a clergyman, is likely to get credit for those experiences.

•

In my counseling practice, I regularly hear from people who are distressed, often devastated, to have discovered that some project on which they have been working for many months was really not what their faculty advisor or school had in mind, so they are getting little or no credit for it.

Indeed, I went through a similar sort of event myself. After I had worked nearly two years on my Doctorate, one key member of my faculty guidance committee died, and a second transferred to another school. No one else on the faculty seemed interested in working with me, and without a binding agreement of any sort, there was no way I could make it happen. I simply dropped out.

Young Person's Guide To Military Service

Historically, a stint in the military has held fascination for brute and poet alike. To serve or not isn't an easy question and never has been. This book won't help you much with the moral aspects, but it does a fair job of helping you decide which service branch to join and what life will be like there. It's not like in the movies. —JB

•

Unlike in the Navy, where women are barred from serving on combat vessels, it is possible for women in the Coast Guard to serve on or even command the largest ships.

•

How do you feel about nuclear weapons? Would you be comfortable working in a missile silo or servicing a B-52 that carries nuclear bombs? You might be willing to defend the United States, but how would you feel about fighting insurgents in Central America? If you served in a National Guard unit, would you have any objection to halting a riot in an American city? Or protecting strikebreakers in a labor dispute?

Young Person's Guide to Military Service
Jeff Bradley
1983; 175 pp.
$8.95
($10.20 postpaid) from:
Kampmann and Co.
9 East 40th Street
New York, NY 10016
or Whole Earth Access

Bear's Guide to Finding Money For College
John Bear, Ph.D.
1984; 157 pp.
$5.95
($6.95 postpaid)

Bear's Guide to Non-Traditional College Degrees
John Bear, Ph.D.
1985; 265 pp.
$9.95
($10.95 postpaid)

both from:
Ten Speed Press
P. O. Box 7123
Berkeley, CA 94707
or Whole Earth Access

Wishcraft
Barbara Sher
with Annie Gottlieb
1979; 278 pp.
$6.95
($7.95 postpaid) from:
Random House
Order Dept.
400 Hahn Road
Westminster, MD 21157
or Whole Earth Access

Aa Bb Cc Dd Ee Ff Gg Hh Ii Jj Kk Ll Mm

Aa Bb Cc Dd Ee Ff Gg Hh Ii Jj Kk

nan nbn ncn ndn nen nfn ngn nhn nin njn nkn

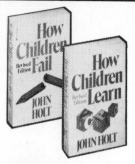

How Children Fail • How Children Learn

How Children Fail
John Holt
1982; 298 pp.
$5.99 postpaid

How Children Learn
John Holt
1983; 303 pp.
$7.95 postpaid
Both from:
Delacorte Press
501 Franklin Avenue
Garden City, NY 11530
or Whole Earth Access

What makes John Holt's contributions to learning and educational reform so useful is that his whole approach was grounded in humility. He was a keen observer — always watching the action on at least two levels — and he constantly experimented and learned from his failures. But it was humility that allowed him to see that small children learn naturally and that teaching that talks down to them will inevitably make them stupid.

This pair of books have been changing educators since they appeared in the 1960s. Each was significantly expanded in a revised edition in the 1980s. The additions are set off in indented type and provide a gloss on the original text that amplifies and deepens the insights.
—Richard Nilsen

•

It took me a long time to learn, as a classroom teacher, that on the days when I came to class just bursting with some great teaching idea, good things rarely happened. The children, with their great quickness and keenness of perception, would sense that there was something "funny," wrong, about me. Instead of being a forty-year-old human being in a room full of ten-year-old human beings, I was now a "scientist" in a room full of laboratory animals. . . . In no time at all they fell back into their old defensive and evasive strategies, began to give me sneaky looks, to ask for hints, to say "I don't get it." I could see them growing stupid in front of my eyes.
—How Children Fail

•

All I am saying in this book can be summed up in two words — Trust Children. Nothing could be more simple — or more difficult. Difficult, because to trust children we must trust ourselves — and most of us were taught as children that we could not be trusted.
—How Children Learn

The Big Book of Home Learning

When kids are home they learn at home.

Teaching at home means: be prepared to learn at home, quicker than your kids. To stay ahead, I recommend this enormous treasurehouse of tools for home learners and home teachers. It evaluates home-style curricula, goes deep into computer software, considers graduate testing, points to ongoing home school magazines, recommends books, and closes with advice for starting up your own minischool. It deserves kudos for honorable work. This big book supersedes the four others we were going to recommend.
—Kevin Kelly
[Suggested by Judy Wilson]

•

The first commonly used method of home schooling is to make home into a school. Mom becomes Teacher, the kids pupils. A room is set up complete with desks, wall maps, ticking clock (to record when one "period" ends and another begins), storage cabinets, and bookcases. Each subject is handled in one-hour chunks.

Following the typical classroom method, Teacher lectures all subjects. Pupils must raise their hands for permission to speak. Teacher decides what is to be learned and when and enforces her will on the students.

People who strictly follow this method rarely last long as home schoolers. They burn out from trying to imitate, for the sake of maybe four students, a ritual designed to cope with hundreds. The children also become dissatisfied, finding that the home environment is not much freer than their old classrooms.

•

Palmer Method Handwriting is based on the so-true idea

Deschooling Society

Deschooling Society
Ivan Illich
1971; 181 pp.
$5.95
($7.45 postpaid) from:
Harper & Row
2350 Virginia Avenue
Hagerstown, MD 21740
or Whole Earth Access

*Illich gives a devastating analysis of the ways in which educational institutions act to minimize learning and maximize conformity and social stratification. Are his solutions practical, or in fact real, given the current state of education? **Deschooling Society** clarifies many of the problems, but if readers are anxiously looking for ready answers, they should look elsewhere.* *—Diane and Eddie Grayson*

•

School teaches us that instruction produces learning. The existence of schools produces the demand for schooling. Once we have learned to need school, all our activities tend to take the shape of client relationships to other specialized institutions. Once the self-taught man or woman has been discredited, all nonprofessional activity is rendered suspect.

The Paideia Proposal

The Paideia Proposal
Mortimer J. Adler
1982; 96 pp.
$3.25 postpaid from:
Macmillan Publishing Co.
Front and Brown Streets
Riverside, NJ 08075
or Whole Earth Access

This is a brief and serious attempt to make the big American educational system actually work. Not abolish it, not home schooling, not start our own school, but how to change public schooling so that the system of universal education produces citizens capable of maintaining democracy. *—Richard Nilsen*
[Suggested by Sheldon Drance]

•

At the very heart of a multitrack system of public schooling lies an abominable discrimination. The system aims at different goals for different groups of children. . . .

The one-track system of public schooling that *The Paideia Proposal* advocates has the same objectives for all without exception.

These objectives are not now aimed at in any degree by the lower tracks onto which a large number of our underprivileged children are shunted — an educational dead end. It is a dead end because these tracks do not lead to the result that the public schools of a democratic society should seek, first and foremost, for all its children — preparation to go on learning, either at advanced levels of schooling, or in adult life, or both.

The Same Course of Study for All

	COLUMN ONE	COLUMN TWO	COLUMN THREE
Goals	ACQUISITION OF ORGANIZED KNOWLEDGE	DEVELOPMENT OF INTELLECTUAL SKILLS – SKILLS OF LEARNING	ENLARGED UNDERSTANDING OF IDEAS AND VALUES
	by means of	by means of	by means of
Means	DIDACTIC INSTRUCTION LECTURES AND RESPONSES TEXTBOOKS AND OTHER AIDS	COACHING, EXERCISES, AND SUPERVISED PRACTICE	MAIEUTIC OR SOCRATIC QUESTIONING AND ACTIVE PARTICIPATION
	in three areas of subject-matter	in the operations of	in the
Areas Operations and Activities	LANGUAGE, LITERATURE, AND THE FINE ARTS MATHEMATICS AND NATURAL SCIENCE HISTORY, GEOGRAPHY, AND SOCIAL STUDIES	READING, WRITING, SPEAKING, LISTENING CALCULATING, PROBLEM-SOLVING OBSERVING, MEASURING, ESTIMATING EXERCISING CRITICAL JUDGMENT	DISCUSSION OF BOOKS (NOT TEXTBOOKS) AND OTHER WORKS OF ART AND INVOLVEMENT IN ARTISTIC ACTIVITIES e.g., MUSIC, DRAMA, VISUAL ARTS

THE THREE COLUMNS DO NOT CORRESPOND TO SEPARATE COURSES, NOR IS ONE KIND OF TEACHING AND LEARNING NECESSARILY CONFINED TO ANY ONE CLASS t Uu Vv Ww Xx Yy Zz 0 1 2 3 4 5 6 7 8 9

p Qq Rr Ss Tt Uu Vv Ww Xx Yy Zz

n nqn nrn nsn ntn nun nvn nwn nxn nyn nzn

hat handwriting practice should be handwriting prac-ice, not poetry-composing time or puzzle-solving time. f the learner has to concentrate on language arts at the ame time as practicing his handwriting, obviously his ask will be complicated. As they say, "Handwriting lass should be to teach 'how' to write so the rest of the day may be used to teach 'what' to write." The method s over a hundred years old, and is still the company's only product. The handwriting produced is a very lovely cursive hand. Students are encouraged to cleave to the norm rather than to invent their own style. Workbooks are less than $3 in all grades, and teacher's editions are under $10.

•

Along with traditional and classic schooling, "unschool-ing" is one of the most popular home school formats. To avoid confusion, I should mention that the word "un-schooling" is used for two separate things. Some people refer to the act of removing one's children from the schools, or refusing to enroll them, as "unschooling." But "unschooling" also describes a very popular home schooling philosophy: that children learn better from doing real things than made-up exercises.

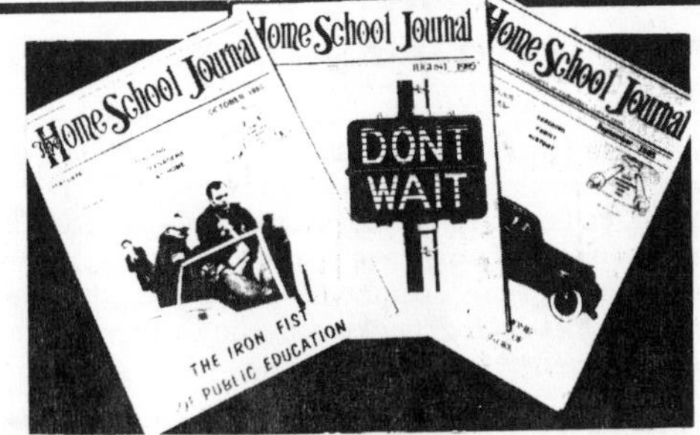

***Home School Journal*. Warren Rushton, editor. Free. Donations are requested; $18/year meets printing costs.**

•

Coming at you directly from the People's Republic of Nebraska, this "Magazine of Christian Conviction" is a folksy, grass-roots effort. Written by real, live home schoolers, it's a cut above the usual state newsletter, but not on a par (professionally) with the best national magazines except for the legal reporting, which is the best I've seen. Straight from the trenches, the *Journal* is a *war* journal of little folk against the Establishment, of Christians versus lions, full of fighting spirit, and thus not as spiffy and manicured as a peacetime production.

The Big Book of Home Learning
Mary Pride
1986; 348 pp.
$17.50
($18.50 postpaid) from:
Good News Publishers
9825 West Roosevelt Road
Westchester, IL 60153
or Whole Earth Access

Growing Without Schooling • John Holt's Book and Music Store

***Growing Without Schooling** is a newsletter begun by John Holt about not sending children to school. Letters from people who are doing it, advice about what to do and not do with kids at home, the latest legal news, and a directory of unschoolers. The **Book and Music Store** is a mail order catalog of books and tools for younger and older children, parents, and educators.* —*Anne Herbert*

QUADRO CONSTRUCTION SETS. Each set contains different lengths of plastic pipes and a large variety of corner pieces, plus square panels that can be inserted to create walls, floors, slides, seats, etc. The finished models will support up to 220 lbs. The sets come with instructions for building all sorts of structures: houses, slides, parallel bars, tunnels, shelves, tables and chairs, beds; all kinds of climbing structures and frames.

•

By Herge: Popular cartoon adventures of a resourceful boy detective. Great mixture of slapstick and suspense. More actual *reading* than many children's books.

Black Island	$5.95
The Calculus Affair	$5.25
The Castafiore Emerald	$5.95
Cigars of the Pharoahs	$5.25
The Crab with the Golden Claws	$5.25
King Ottokar's Sceptre	$5.25
Prisoners of the Sun	$5.25
Red Rackham's Treasure	$5.95
The Seven Crystal Balls	$5.95
Tintin in Tibet	$5.95

—*John Holt's Book and Music Store*

•

"You had a late reader, didn't you?"

"Yes, my oldest son didn't start reading until he was 8½."

"How did he do the last time he was tested?"

"His reading level was 11th grade, plus." He was 10 at the time. "It's the most reassuring thing that ever could have happened."

He likes to read the *Wall Street Journal* and other financial news, and is writing to mining companies about stock. The TinTin comic books were responsible for Ronnie's sudden interest in reading.

—*Growing Without Schooling*

Growing Without Schooling
Donna Richoux, Editor
$15/year
(6 issues) from:
Growing Without Schooling
729 Boylston Street
Boston, MA 02116

John Holt's Book and Music Store
Catalog free
with SASE from:
John Holt's Book and Music Store
729 Boylston St.
Boston, MA 02116

Better Than School

*After watching their lively, intelligent son wither in the classroom for over a year, Nancy and Bob Wallace took him out of school to teach him at home. **Better Than School** is one family's experience with home schooling. It is as much a tale about bureaucratic oppression as it is a chronicle of constant experimentation, excitement, mistakes, and triumphs as the entire family is caught up in the adventure of learning.*

This is not an instruction manual for home teaching, but a book of inspiration and encouragement to parents wishing to educate their children — and themselves — in their own unique ways. For educators and other "experts," it offers a rare glimpse of the extraordinary capabilities lurking in the most ordinary — or even learning disabled — child. —*Carol Van Strum*

•

As usual, the school board ranted. They seemed primarily to be disgusted that Ishmael was doing so well. "You must push Ishmael too hard," one board member accused, and others seemed to be outraged that we allowed Ishmael to make choices about what he wanted to learn. We just sat there.

They did finally grant us permission to teach Ishmael at home for another year. They knew they had no other choice. It wouldn't have looked good to say, "Ishmael has been learning so much and appears to be so happy at home that we have decided to deny him permission to learn at home again next year."

Better Than School
Nancy Wallace
1983; 256 pp.
$10.95
($12.45 postpaid) from:
Larson Publications
4936 Route 414
Burdett, NY 14818
or Whole Earth Access

How to learn things: A handy tip

If you're starting to learn about a field that you know nothing about, go to the children's library and get some fifth, sixth, seventh grade books about it before you go into grownup books. Basic books for grownups tend to be aimed at college freshmen taking required courses — and everybody knows that they're supposed to suffer, including the people who write the books. Basic books for kids are aimed at kids browsing in libraries who don't have to be there and could leave anytime. The books have colors and pictures and a will to sell the subject; the good ones assume you know nothing without being condescending. You can get some vocabulary and feel for the shape of the subject before you get into the stuck-up real books. Kids' books can also help you if you are one of those freshmen in one of those required courses.
—Anne Herbert

Super-Learning
Sheila Ostrander,
Lynn Schroeder and
Nancy Ostrander
1985; 342 pp.
$4.50
($5.25 postpaid) from:
Delacorte Press
1 Dag Hammarskjold Plaza
245 East 47th Street
New York, NY 10017
or Whole Earth Access

Super-Learning

A gee-whiz tour through some of the most innovative methods for accelerated learning becoming available, including suggestology. The data supports the author's contention that it is possible for normal people to learn mental and physical skills five to ten times faster, with better retention and with less effort using the techniques described.

Lots of exercises, lots of cheery confidence. Feels like one of the steps to overcoming our determination to maintain an educational system geared to work as slowly as possible. Read it and upgrade the schools in your town.
—Jim Fadiman

•

As the class members shuffled through pages of material, the teacher started reading French phrases in different intonations. Then, stately classical music began in the background. The fifteen men and women leaned back, closed their eyes, and embarked on developing hypermnesia, more easily called supermemory. The teacher kept reciting. Sometimes her voice was businesslike as if ordering work to be done, sometimes it sounded soft, whispering, then unexpectedly hard and commanding.

Shadows began to darken in the room, it was sunset, yet the teacher kept on, repeating in a special rhythm French words, idioms, translations. Finally, she stopped. They weren't through yet; they still had to take a test. At least the class members weren't as keyed up. Somehow during the session their anxiety had been smoothed, the usual kinks relaxed. But they still didn't hold much hope for decent test scores.

Finally the teacher told them, "The class average is ninety-seven percent. You learned one thousand words in a day!"

The Memory Book
Harry Lorayne and
Jerry Lucas
1974; 206 pp.
$3.95
($4.95 postpaid) from:
Random House
Order Department
400 Hahn Road
Westminster, MD 21157
or Whole Earth Access

The Memory Book

I almost forgot to mention this compact paperback which concisely outlines methods to improve your recall. They truly work. My dad taught me these when I was a kid and I still rely on them. At first the methods seem to be gimmicky, but soon become habit. One of the authors is the guy who memorizes phone book listings as a stunt on late night talk shows. The techniques are well proven (a couple are thousands of years old) and will benefit anyone. Imagine how much more efficient you'd be if your memory was just five percent better, and how much easier your life would be if everyone else's improved.
—Kevin Kelly

•

Here's a basic memory rule: You Can Remember Any New Piece of Information if It Is Associated to Something You Already Know or Remember. . . .

Very few people can easily remember the shape of Russia, or Greece, or any other country — except Italy, that is. That's because most people have been told, or have read, that Italy's shaped like a boot. There's that rule again — the shape of a boot was the something already known, and the shape of Italy *could not be forgotten* once that association was made.

•

As you reach for the phone, you place the pencil behind your ear, or in your hair. The phone call is finished — that took only a few minutes — but now you waste time searching for the pencil that's perched behind your ear. Would you like to avoid that aggravation? All right, then; the next time the phone rings and you start to place the pencil behind your ear, make a fast mental picture in your mind. Actually "see" the pencil going *into* your ear — all the way.

The idea may make you shudder, but when you think of that pencil, you'll know where it is. That silly association of seeing the pencil go into your ear *forced* you to think of two things in a fraction of a second: 1) the pencil, and 2) where you were putting it. Problem solved!

Rules of Thumb
Tom Parker
1983; 148 pp.
$5.70
($6.70 postpaid) from:
Houghton Mifflin Co.
Mail Order Dept.
Wayside Road
Burlington, MA 01803
or Whole Earth Access

Rules of Thumb

Accumulated knowledge, dehydrated for storage. Author-editor-illustrator Tom Parker collected this bunch from his readers. It's a varied lot, presented in no particular order, but indexed by subject. In an earlier day, many of these would have been part of an oral tradition passed down by elders and storytellers.
—JB

•

Erecting a telephone pole: One fifth of the length of a telephone pole should be planted in the ground. —*Ron Bean, mechanics of materials student, Madison, Wisconsin.*

•

Digging a grave: When digging a grave by hand, haul away seventeen wheelbarrow loads of dirt and pile the rest by the hole. You will have just the right amount to backfill. —*Randall Lacey, wind-power engineer.*

•

Choosing a woodstove: If you are trying to decide what size woodstove you need you can start by figuring 2.5 cubic feet of firebox per 1000 square feet of living space. —*Dan Hoffman, city council alderman.*

•

Ann Landers' pencil test: To determine whether you need to wear a bra, place a pencil under your breast. If the pencil falls to the floor, you don't need to wear a bra; if it stays, you need one. —*Ann Landers, advice columnist.*

• Keep track as the limits of human performance — silly and serious — are explored.
Guinness Book of World Records: Norris McWhirter, 1986; 709 pp. **$4.50** ($6 postpaid) from Bantam Books, 414 East Golf Road, Des Plaines, IL 60016.

Foxfire

Foxfire *is a quarterly publication concerned with researching, recording and preserving Appalachian folk art, crafts and traditions. A typical issue contains articles on quilting, chairmaking, soap making, home remedies, mountain recipes, feather beds and home-made hominy, plus regional poetry and book reviews. One issue was devoted entirely to log cabin building. These are not superficial ''feature'' articles, but definitive, detailed treatments of traditional skills and crafts that have come close to dying out of our culture.*

Foxfire *would be a credit to a group of professional folklorists. But when you consider that it is edited and published by high school kids at the Rabun County High School in Clayton, Georgia, it becomes impressive indeed. The thing I like most about it is the way these kids are looking immediately around them for their inspiration, instead of taking cues from New York and California. In their own way, these people are as hip and sophisticated as any young people putting out a magazine on either coast. More so, even. They're cooler, more adult.* **Foxfire's** *editors and writers (and some excellent photographers) seem to me as aware of what's wrong with the world as anyone. The thing that distinguishes them from their shrill counterparts in the cities is the absence of fad, slogan and cliche as they set out to improve the world. These kids in Georgia are living in a real world, studying real things, and in consequence they are creating a wonderfully real publication in* **Foxfire.**

—Gurney Norman

Since Gurney wrote this review in 1969 **Foxfire** *has grown and deepened with the years into a flat-out landmark of American education and folklore technique. It's been widely copied, always to good effect. Try it in your area. The old-timers tell things to youngsters they wouldn't say to anybody else.* *—Stewart Brand*

Foxfire
Elliot Wigginton, Advisor
$8/year (4 issues)

The Foxfire Book — Hog dressing, log cabin building, mountain crafts and foods, planting by the signs, snake lore, hunting tales, faith healing, moonshining, and other affairs of plain living. 1972. **$9.95** postpaid.

Foxfire 2 — Ghost stories, spring wild plant foods, spinning and weaving, midwifing, burial customs, corn shuckin's, wagon making and more affairs of plain living. 1973. **$9.95** postpaid.

Foxfire 3 — Animal care, banjos and dulcimers, hide tanning, summer and fall wild plant foods, butter churns, ginseng, and still more affairs of plain living. 1975. **$10.95** postpaid.

Foxfire 4 — Fiddle making, spring houses, horse trading, sassafras tea, berry buckets, gardening, and further affairs of plain living. 1977. **$10.95** postpaid.

Foxfire 5 -- Ironmaking, blacksmithing, flintlock rifles, bear hunting, and other affairs of plain living. 1979. **$10.95** postpaid.

Foxfire 6 — Shoemaking, 100 toys and games, gourd banjos and songbows, wooden locks, a water-powered sawmill and other affairs of just plain living. 1980. **$10.95** postpaid.

Foxfire 7 — Southern Appalachian religious heritage: baptizing, camp meetings, faith healing, snake handling. 1982. **$10.95** postpaid.

Foxfire 8 — Southern folk pottery from pug mills, ash glazes, and groundhog kilns to face jugs, churns, and roosters; mule swapping and chicken fighting. 1984. **$10.95** postpaid.

And there should be a **Foxfire 9** in fall of 1986.

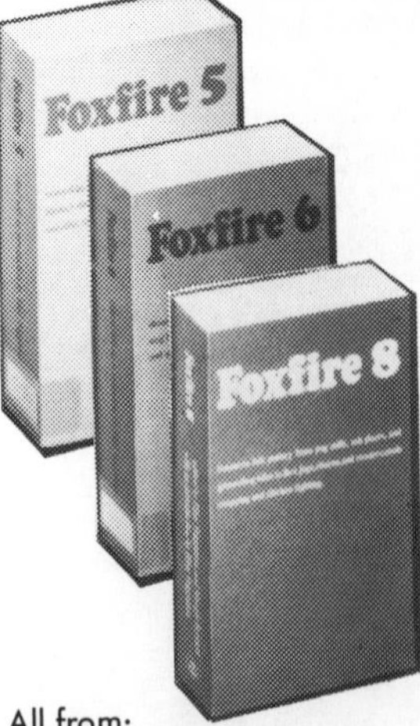

All from:
The Foxfire Fund, Inc.
P. O. Box B
Rabun Gap, GA 30568
or Whole Earth Access

The Brown Paper School Books

Appealing exploration of omnipresent subjects — body, weather, thinking, games, stars, local history. There is approximately no way to read these books and just sit there. Try this, notice that, well what about the other.
—Stewart Brand

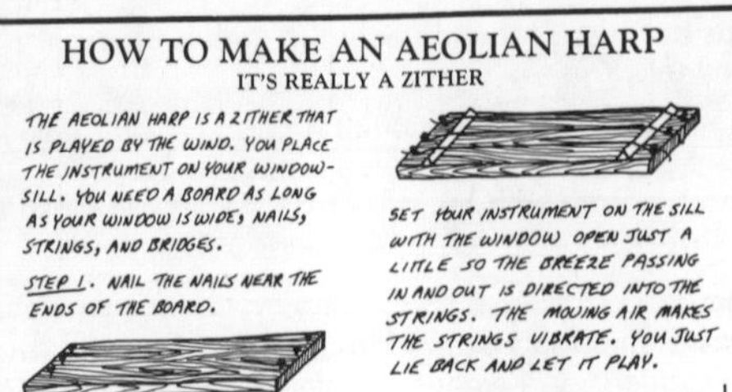

HOW TO MAKE AN AEOLIAN HARP
IT'S REALLY A ZITHER
THE AEOLIAN HARP IS A ZITHER THAT IS PLAYED BY THE WIND. YOU PLACE THE INSTRUMENT ON YOUR WINDOW-SILL. YOU NEED A BOARD AS LONG AS YOUR WINDOW IS WIDE, NAILS, STRINGS, AND BRIDGES.
STEP 1. NAIL THE NAILS NEAR THE ENDS OF THE BOARD.
SET YOUR INSTRUMENT ON THE SILL WITH THE WINDOW OPEN JUST A LITTLE SO THE BREEZE PASSING IN AND OUT IS DIRECTED INTO THE STRINGS. THE MOVING AIR MAKES THE STRINGS VIBRATE. YOU JUST LIE BACK AND LET IT PLAY.
STEP 2. STRETCH MONOFILAMENT OR WIRE STRINGS VERY TIGHT FROM THE NAILS ON ONE END TO THE NAILS ON THE OTHER.

STEP 3. SLIP THE BRIDGES UNDER THE STRINGS INSIDE THE NAILS AT BOTH ENDS. THE BRIDGES HELP STRETCH THE STRINGS AND LIFT THEM SO THEY CAN VIBRATE FREELY.

YOU CAN MAKE A LONG, NARROW SOUND BOX THAT WILL FIT YOUR WINDOW. WHEN THE AEOLIAN HARP HAS A SOUND BOX, IT PLAYS EVEN LOUDER.
EYE SCREWS
SOUND HOLES

—Make Mine Music!

•

My Backyard History Book
The I Hate Mathematics Book
The Reason for Seasons (The Great Cosmic Megagalactic Trip, Without Moving from Your Chair)
Blood and Guts (A Working Guide to your Own Insides)
The Book of Think (Or How to Solve a Problem Twice Your Size)
Everybody's a Winner (A Kid's Guide to New Sports and Fitness)
The Night Sky Book (An Everyday Guide to Every Night)
I Am Not a Short Adult (Getting Good at Being)
This Book Is About Time
Good for Me (All About Food in 32 Bites)
Beastly Neighbors (All About Wild Things in the City or Why Earwigs Make Good Mothers)
Make Mine Music!
The Book of Where (How to Be Naturally Geographic)
Gee, Wiz! (How to Mix Art and Science or the Art of Thinking Scientifically)
Math for Smarty Pants
Only Human (Why We Are the Way We Are)
Word Works (Why the Alphabet Is a Kid's Best Friend)

•

Get old inner tubes from a company that sells truck tires. (Car tires are mostly tubeless these days.) Stage a tube race by having contestants sit on the tubes and try to make them move. Touching the ground directly with feet or hands is not allowed.

•

Get a 10-by-20-foot sheet of plastic from a hardware or builder's supply store (about $4.50). Unroll it on the ground, flood it with water from a garden hose, and you've got a dandy Super Slide.
—Everybody's a Winner

The Brown Paper School Books
$7.95 each
($8.55 each, postpaid)
All from:
Little, Brown & Co.
200 West Street
Waltham, MA 02254
or Whole Earth Access

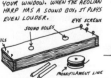

Super slide.

Brain/Mind Bulletin
Marilyn Ferguson, Editor
$35/year
(17 issues) from:
Interface Press
P. O. Box 42211
Los Angeles, CA 90042

Brain/Mind Bulletin

Easily the handiest way to stay current with news and gossip on the soft psychology frontier. Despite success and a burgeoning of the subject matter, editor Marilyn Ferguson has admirably kept the bulletin's format to a terse, packed four pages. —*Stewart Brand*

•

A startling new finding: Not only do the brain hemispheres switch dominance every 90 to 120 minutes throughout the day, but the sides of the *body* switch regularly in their dominance of sympathetic tone.

Researchers sampled nervous-system transmitters by taking blood from both arms every 7.5 minutes for periods of three to six hours. They found that the catecholamines — dopamine, norepinephrine, epinephrine [adrenaline] — were more concentrated on one side or the other every two to three hours.

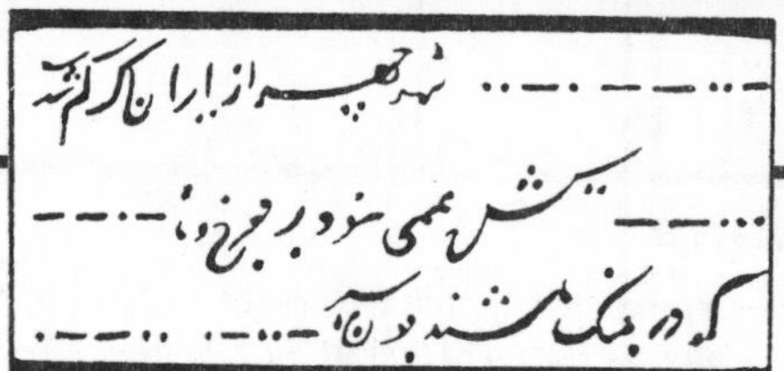

•

Pickering showed Persian real words and nonsense anagrams to English-speaking undergraduates who later drew them from memory. Neither subjects nor experimenters knew which Persian character strings were real words until after the data had been collected and analyzed.

Subjects guessed the meaning of each word and rated their confidence in each guess. They reported feeling more confident in their guesses when they were viewing the true words, and their confidence ratings were twice as strong for high-frequency as compared to low-frequency words.

Brain & Psyche
Jonathan Winson
1985; 300 pp.
$16.95 postpaid from:
Doubleday & Co.
Direct Mail Order
501 Franklin Avenue
Garden City, NY 11530
or Whole Earth Access

Brain & Psyche

Like most mammals, we dream. The few mammals that don't dream, like the egg-laying echidna, appear to integrate experience with memory as they plod along in real time. Winson's new theory of dreams says that the rest of us, with more to think about than leaf mold and ants, save the day's news and take several runs at folding it into the rest of our memories during the night. We process the day's input of information while we sleep, in batches which we perceive as dreams. —*Hank Roberts*

•

I hypothesize that the complex function of assimilating new information, associating it with memories of past experiences, and formulating a plan to govern new behavior adaptively during the waking state required a very large prefrontal cortex in this early mammal. It is clear that had the evolution of the brain proceeded along this line, higher mammals and man as we know them would never have been. For what occurred was that the new line of marsupial and placental mammals — lower-order animals like the echidna — had very small prefrontal cortices. As higher mammalian forms evolved, more and more cortical tissue was added culminating in the brain of man, and this additional neural machinery provided many additional sensory, motor, and associative capabilities. Even with this evolutionary growth, man's prefrontal cortex did not grow to be as large a proportion of total cortex as it was in the echidna. Thus, should the organization of man's brain have been similar to the echidna's, he might have needed a wheelbarrow to carry it around. In short, man would not have evolved.

What was the scheme that nature hit upon in marsupial and placental mammals? I propose that . . . . the task of associating recent events to past memories and evolving a neural substrate to guide future behavior was accomplished when the animal was asleep.

The Teachings of Don Juan
Carlos Castaneda
1968; 196 pp.
$5.95
($7.45 postpaid) from:
University of California Press
2120 Berkeley Way
Berkeley, CA 94720
or Whole Earth Access

A Separate Reality
Carlos Castaneda
1971; 263 pp.
$4.95 postpaid from:
Simon & Schuster
Mail Order Sales
200 Old Tappan Road
Old Tappan, NJ 07675
or Whole Earth Access

The Teachings of Don Juan • A Separate Reality

Astounding books exploring the mind's perception of reality using the methods of a Mexican Indian sorcerer, "don Juan." Harsh, humorous, told with shocking adroitness, the truths here have been confirmed by others who have worked with native shamans or explored the nether reaches of sundry mystical paths. Unfortunately Castaneda's later books (there are now 6 total), though they are interesting, fictionalize ever farther away from his extraordinary field experience in the mountains of Mexico. The ideas in these two books have entered the American language to stay. —*Stewart Brand*

•

"I say it is useless to waste your life on one path, especially if that path has no heart."

"But how do you know when a path has no heart, don Juan?"

"Before you embark on it you ask the question: Does this path have a heart? If the answer is no, you will know it, and then you must choose another path."

"But how will I know for sure whether a path has a heart or not?"

"Anybody would know that. The trouble is nobody asks the question; and when a man finally realizes that he has taken a path without a heart, the path is ready to kill him. At that point very few men can stop to deliberate, and leave the path."

"How should I proceed to ask the question properly, don Juan?"

"Just ask it."

"I mean, is there a proper method, so I would not lie to myself and believe the answer is yes when it really is no?"

"Why would you lie?"

"Perhaps because at the moment the path is pleasant and enjoyable."

"That is nonsense. A path without a heart is never enjoyable. You have to work hard even to take it. On the other hand, a path with heart is easy; it does not make you work at liking it." —*The Teachings of Don Juan*

•

There was a question I wanted to ask him. I knew he was going to evade it, so I waited for him to mention the subject; I waited all day. Finally, before I left that evening, I had to ask him, "Did I really fly, don Juan?"

"That is what you told me. Didn't you?"

"I know, don Juan. I mean, did my body fly? Did I take off like a bird?"

"You always ask me questions I cannot answer. You flew. That is what the second portion of the devil's weed is for. As you take more of it, you will learn how to fly perfectly. It is not a simple matter. A man *flies* with the help of the second portion of the devil's weed. That is all I can tell you. What you want to know makes no sense. Birds fly like birds and a man who has taken the devil's weed flies as such [*el enyerbado vuela asi*]."

"As birds do? [*Asi como los pajaros?*]."

"No, he flies as a man who has taken the weed [*No, asi como los enyerbados*]." —*The Teachings of Don Juan*

Zen and the Art of Motorcycle Maintenance

Philosophical practicality. Practical philosophy. Harsh realism. Lofty aspiring. With Pirsig on the motorcycle road with his disturbed son Chris, the apparent contradictions kick each other into robust life. A kickstart of a book for anyone. —*Stewart Brand*

•

When he brought his motorcycle over I got my wrenches out but then noticed that no amount of tightening would stop the slippage, because the ends of the collars were pinched shut.

"You're going to have to shim those out," I said.

"What's shim?"

"It's a thin, flat strip of metal. You just slip it around the handlebar under the collar there and it will open up the collar to where you can tighten it again. You use shims like that to make adjustments in all kinds of machines."

"Oh," he said. He was getting interested. "Good. Where do you buy them?"

"I've got some right here," I said gleefully, holding up a can of beer in my hand.

He didn't understand for a moment. Then he said, "What, the can?"

"Sure," I said, "best shim stock in the world."

I thought this was pretty clever myself. Save him a trip to God knows where to get shim stock. Save him time. Save him money.

But to my surprise he didn't see the cleverness of this at all. In fact he got noticeably haughty about the whole thing. Pretty soon he was dodging and filling with all kinds of excuses and, before I realized what his real attitude was, we had decided not to fix the handlebars after all.

As far as I know those handlebars are still loose. And I believe now that he was actually offended at the time. I had had the *nerve* to propose repair of his new eighteen-hundred-dollar BMW, the pride of a half-century of German mechanical finesse, with a piece of old *beer* can!

•

The purpose of scientific method is to select a single truth from among many hypothetical truths. That, more than anything else, is what science is all about. But historically science has done exactly the opposite. Through multiplication upon multiplication of facts, information, theories and hypotheses, it is science itself that is leading mankind from single absolute truths to multiple, indeterminate, relative ones. The major producer of the social chaos, the indeterminacy of thought and values that rational knowledge is supposed to eliminate, is none other than science itself. And what Phaedrus saw in the isolation of his own laboratory work years ago is now seen everywhere in the technological world today. Scientifically produced antiscience — chaos.

•

I tell him getting stuck is the commonest trouble of all. Usually, I say, your mind gets stuck when you're trying to do too many things at once. What you have to do is try not to force words to come. That just gets you more stuck. What you have to do now is separate out the things and do them one at a time. You're trying to think of what to *say* and what to say *first* at the same time and that's too hard. So separate them out. Just make a list of all the things you want to say in any old order. Then later we'll figure out the right order.

"Like what things?" he asks.

"Well, what do you want to tell her?"

"About the trip."

"What things about the trip?"

He thinks for a while. "About the mountain we climbed."

"Okay, write that down," I say.

He does.

Then I see him write down another item, then another, while I finish my cigarette and coffee. He goes through three sheets of paper, listing things he wants to say.

"Save those," I tell him, "and we'll work on them later."

"I'll never get all this into one letter," he says.

He sees me laugh and frowns.

I say, "Just pick out the best things." Then we head outside and onto the motorcycle again.

Zen and the Art of Motorcycle Maintenance
Robert M. Pirsig
1974; 412 pp.

$7.95
($9.45 postpaid) from:
William Morrow Publishing Co.
6 Henderson Drive
West Caldwell, NJ 07006
or Whole Earth Access

Against Method • The Structure of Scientific Revolutions

These two books aren't new, but they remain among the best papers examining what constitutes scientific "truth." Kuhn's book shows the advancement of science to be irregular and subject to highly nonlogical processes. Mr. Feyerabend argues that science is but one ideology out of many, and that truth is most likely to be found in an intellectual environment that encourages the proliferation of many theories and ideologies.

Fortunately, both books are easily read, though you'll probably have to stop and ponder now and then as your logic base is assailed. —*JB*

•

Aristotle's *Physica*, Ptolemy's *Almagest*, Newton's *Principia* and *Opticks*, Franklin's *Electricity*, Lavoisier's *Chemistry*, and Lyell's *Geology* — these and many other works served for a time implicitly to define the legitimate problems and methods of a research field for succeeding generations of practitioners. They were able to do so because they shared two essential characteristics. Their achievement was sufficiently unprecedented to attract an enduring group of adherents away from competing modes of scientific activity. Simultaneously, it was sufficiently open-ended to leave all sorts of problems for the redefined group of practitioners to resolve.

Achievements that share these two characteristics I shall henceforth refer to as 'paradigms,' a term that relates closely to 'normal science.'
—*The Structure of Scientific Revolutions*

•

The consistency condition which demands that new hypotheses agree with accepted *theories* is unreasonable because it preserves the older theory, and not the better theory. Hypotheses contradicting well-confirmed theories give us evidence that cannot be obtained in any other way. Proliferation of theories is beneficial for science, while uniformity impairs its critical power. Uniformity also endangers the free development of the individual.

•

There is no idea, however ancient and absurd, that is not capable of improving our knowledge. The whole history of thought is absorbed into science and is used for improving every single theory. Nor is political interference rejected. It may be needed to overcome the chauvinism of science that resists alternatives to the status quo.

•

No theory ever agrees with all the *facts* in its domain, yet it is not always the theory that is to blame. Facts are constituted by older ideologies, and a clash between facts and theories may be proof of progress. It is also a first step in our attempt to find the principles implicit in familiar observational notions. —*Against Method*

Against Method
Paul Feyerabend
1975; 339 pp.

$9.95
($10.95 postpaid) from:
Schocken Books, Inc.
62 Cooper Square
New York, NY 10003
or Whole Earth Access

The Structure of Scientific Revolutions
Thomas S. Kuhn
1970; 210 pp.

$6.95
($7.45 postpaid) from:
University of Chicago Press
11030 South Langley
Chicago, IL 60628
or Whole Earth Access

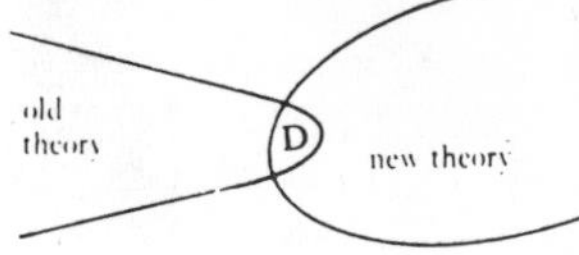

Sharing Nature with Children
Joseph Bharat Cornell
1979; 143 pp.
$6.95
($8.90 postpaid) from:
Ananda Publications
14618 Tyler Foote Road
Nevada City, CA 95959
or Whole Earth Access

Sharing Nature with Children

Smelling, feeling, listening, watching, guessing — imagining yourself to be a part of nature. Taking joy in it. That's what this extraordinary book is about. It's a far cry from the obedient line of kids marching along to the chirping of a bored teacher on a "nature walk." This is absolutely the best awareness-of-nature book I've ever seen. It works for adults, too. —JB

The 40 activities in this book are easy to use — for family or class outings. Kids actually like them. ***Sharing Nature with Children*** *was the most helpful book I found when doing research for a bioregional curriculum guide — Joseph Cornell knows how to talk about nature to kids without talking down to them.* —Jeanne Carstensen

•

A tree is a living creature. It eats, rests, breathes and circulates its "blood" much as we do. The heartbeat of a tree is a wonderful crackling, gurgling flow of life. The best time to hear the forest heartbeat is in early spring, when the trees send first surges of sap upward to their branches, preparing them for another season of growth.

Choose a tree that is at least six inches in diameter and has thin bark. Deciduous trees are generally better for listening to than conifers, and certain individuals of a species may have a louder heartbeat than others. Press a stethoscope firmly against the tree, keeping it motionless so as not to make interfering noises. You may have to try several different places on the tree trunk before you find a good listening spot.

Children will want to hear their own heartbeat. Listen also to the heartbeats of mammals and birds — the variety in sounds and rhythms is fascinating.

Ranger Rick
Trudy Farrand, Editor
$14/year
(12 issues) from:
National Wildlife Federation
8925 Leesburg Pike
Vienna, VA 22180

Zoobooks
John Wexo, Editor
$14/year
(10 issues) from:
Wildlife Education, Ltd.
930 West Washington St.
Suite 14
San Diego, CA 92103

Ranger Rick • Zoobooks

Gorgeous pictures of animals, good articles on wildlife and ecology, good magazine for parents and teachers and kids to have around. Aimed at people 6 to 12 years old — direct without being condescending.
—Anne Herbert [Suggested by E. Gerald Bishop]

Zoobooks *are aimed at an audience a little more sophisticated than Ranger Rick's; it's all super photographs and easy reading but without cute stories for the little kids.*

A choice between these magazines would be hard to make, so we show 'em both. —JB

◄ **Cougars hide their cubs in caves, rock piles, and thickets. If another animal discovers her nursery, the mother moves her young — one at a time — to a new den. —Ranger Rick**

◄ As the predator tries to catch her, the mother killdeer moves farther and farther away from her young. She appears to be hurt, but she always stays one step ahead of the enemy. At the last minute, the "crippled" killdeer suddenly flies into the air, leaving the predator behind. —Ranger Rick

► **A mother sea turtle comes ashore long enough to lay her eggs and cover them up. Then she returns to the sea. Sea turtles are very awkward on land. They can only move by dragging their heavy bodies over the sand, leaving an unusual trail behind them. —Zoobooks**

Nature at Work

The subtle connections, cycles, and energy flows of ecology are wonderfully elucidated in this superior primer. Students and teachers will revel in it. —JB

We can study an ecosystem in terms of trophic levels and pyramids. If we measure the amount of energy stored at each trophic level over a year, we can build up a pyramid of energy.

Nature at Work
1978; 84 pp.
$9.95 postpaid from:
Cambridge University Press
Attn.: Order Dept.
510 North Avenue
New Rochelle, NY 10801
or Whole Earth Access

• Holling Clancy Holling has written many adventure stories laced with nature lore and anthropology. They've been hard to put down since 1941. **Paddle-to-the-Sea** — the voyage of a tiny handcarved canoe — is my favorite.
Paddle-to-the-Sea: Holling Clancy Holling, 1969; 58 pp. **$5.70** ($6.40 postpaid) from Houghton Mifflin Company, Mail Order Department, Wayside Road, Burlington, MA 01803 (or Whole Earth Access).

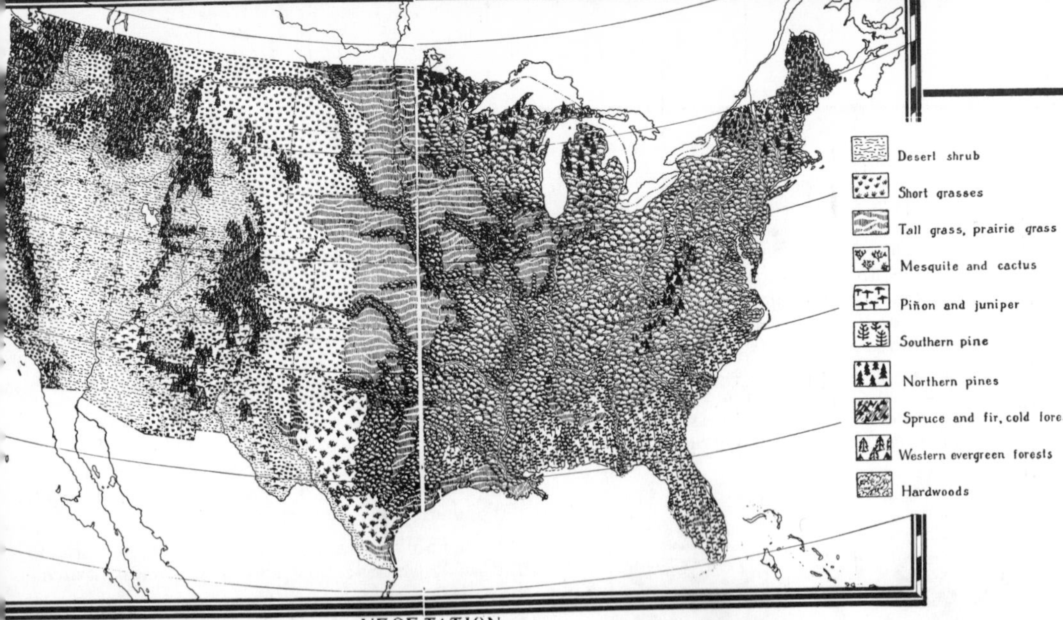

VEGETATION

Man In Nature
Carl Sauer
1975; 285 pp.
$9.95
($10.95 postpaid) from:
Turtle Island Foundation
2845 Buena Vista Way
Berkeley, CA 94708
or Whole Earth Access

Man In Nature

This book is exactly as subtitled: "America Before the Days of the White Man," and "A First Book on Geography." No other book (for kids or adults) spells out North American bioregional life like **Man in Nature.** *It creates "locale" like Thoreau or John Muir. Read it to a child for your own pleasure.* —Peter Warshall

•

Making a new field was a good deal of work. These people had no plows, no animals for pulling, and no good tools for cutting wood. But they had a very good way of making a new field.

The men took their stone axes and cut or broke the bark around green trees. Captain Smith calls it bruising the bark. Actually, nothing more was necessary than to beat the bark to pieces, so that the sap could no longer flow to the branches and leaves.

If this was done in summer the trees usually died over winter. The next spring they stood bare and leafless.

Girdling trees.

That was all that was necessary for the first planting. The sun then could shine through the dead tree trunks on the ground. The ground was rich with dead and rotten leaves. Such ground was fine for corn and beans and pumpkins.

Golden Guides
$2.95 each
($3.95 postpaid) from:
Western Publishing Co.
Attn.: Dept. M
1220 Mound Avenue
Racine, WI 53404
or Whole Earth Access

Golden Guides

Competence, color, intelligent editing, and a reasonable price make any one of the Golden Guide series a good — perhaps the best — place to start. Handy pocket size makes them easy to tote along on your explorations. —JB

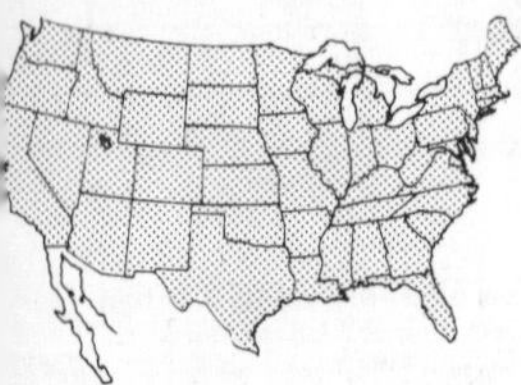

Scarlet Pimpernel, *Anagallis arvensis*, suspected of being somewhat poisonous to livestock, is the only species in its genus in the U.S. It belongs to the primrose family, Primulaceae.

—A Golden Guide to Weeds

Care of the Wild Feathered and Furred
Mae Hickman and
Maxine Guy
1973; 143 pp.
$9.95
($11.45 postpaid) from:
Michael Kesend Publishing, Ltd.
1025 5th Avenue
New York, NY 10028
or Whole Earth Access

Care of the Wild Feathered and Furred

A good way to graduate from bunny love to rabbit understanding is to take care of one that is injured. It takes more than a good heart and regard for God's creatures, it takes knowledge and skill. Here's where to get plenty of both; how to feed 'em, house 'em and make repairs. —JB

•

A helpful feeding device is a 25-watt night light placed 6 inches from the floor of the pen. The light attracts many insects needed for food by healing or growing birds.

Bind the gauze over the sutured area with two long strips of tape, continuing the tape around the bird's body so the gauze will remain firmly in place.

Physics

To have no understanding of basic physics in an industrial society is to be ignorant in a debilitating way; even if you don't like science and technology, there's no point in being blind. But learning physics is tough if you aren't adept at calculus. Until now. These three books are marvels of clarity — entirely free of author ego-brandishing that so often clouds explanatory writing. ***Conceptual Physics*** *is the whole bit right up to a nibble at quantum physics.* ***Thinking Physics*** *is a set of fun and maddening questions that force you to use your noodle (and what you've learned in the first book).* ***Relativity Visualized*** *is just that, and a good job of it, too. You're unlikely to find an easier way to learn this stuff.* —JB

Conceptual Physics
Paul G. Hewitt
1985; 650 pp.
$31.75
($33.25 postpaid) from:
Little, Brown & Co.
Attn.: Order Dept.
200 West Street
Waltham, MA 02254
or Whole Earth Access

Thinking Physics
Lewis C. Epstein
1986; 565 pp.
$17.95
($19.95 postpaid) from:
Insight Press
614 Vermont Street
San Francisco, CA 94107
or Whole Earth Access

Relativity Visualized
Lewis C. Epstein
1985; 200 pp.
$12.95
($14.95 postpaid) from:
Insight Press
614 Vermont Street
San Francisco, CA 94107
or Whole Earth Access

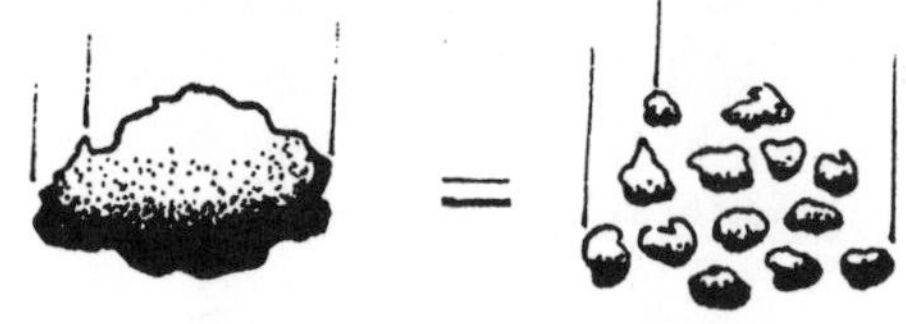

•

Galileo's explanation: The following is Galileo's explanation of why large and small masses (disregarding air resistance) fall at the same rate.

The acceleration of a large falling rock is the same as the acceleration of a small falling rock because a large rock is just a bunch of small rocks falling together.

This explanation is occasionally reinvented by people who think about these things. Though not the first to think this way, they walk in the footprints of the old master! —*Relativity Visualized*

•

Battleship floating in a bathtub

Can a battleship float in a bathtub?* Of course, you have to imagine a very big bathtub or a very small battleship. In either case, there is just a bit of water all around and under the ship. Specifically, suppose the ship weighs 100 tons (a very small ship) and the water in the tub weighs 100 pounds. Will it float or touch bottom?

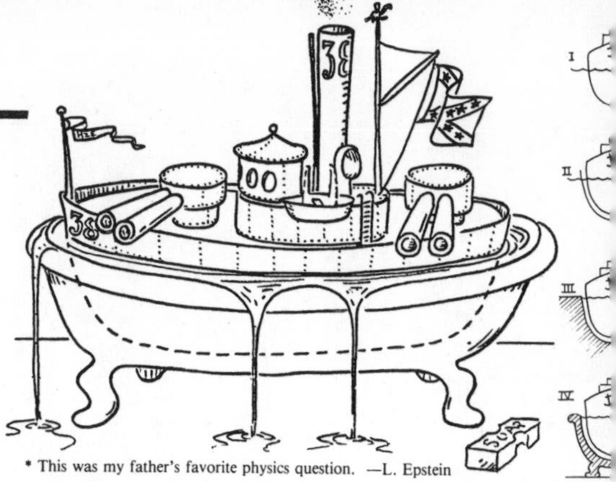

* This was my father's favorite physics question. —L. Epstein

a) It will float if there is enough water to go all around it
b) It will touch bottom because the ship's weight exceeds the water's weight

The answer is: a. There are a lot of ways to show why. This way was suggested by a student. Consider the ship floating in the ocean (sketch I). Next, surround the ship with a big plastic baggie — this is actually done sometimes with oil tankers — (sketch II). Next, let the ocean freeze except for the water in the baggie next to the ship (sketch III). Finally, get an ice sculptor to cut a bathtub out of the solid ice and you have it (sketch IV).

This question points out the danger of thinking in words, rather than thinking in pictures and ideas. If you just think in words you might reason: "To float, the battleship must displace its own weight in water. Its own weight is 100 tons, but there is only 100 pounds of water available — so it cannot float." But if you picture the idea you will see the displacement refers to the water that would fill the ship's hull if the inside of the ship's hull were filled to the water-line. And this displacement is 100 tons.

Don't rely on words, or equations, until you can picture the idea they represent. —*Thinking Physics*

The Exploratorium

In San Francisco, you don't say, "Let's go to the science museum," you say, "Let's spend the day at the Exploratorium." It's a place of discovery where you learn about light and sound and physics and biology and computers and whatever is being shown at the time of your visit, and whatever is being built for future shows (the workshop is visible so you can watch exhibits being made). Visitors are encouraged to poke, grab, and wiggle as they explore the amazing variety of fascinating stuff in the enormous space. It's what a "museum" should be. Even the store is wonderful. And you can book parties there if you're a member!

The Exploratorium publishes nifty items too: Posters, exhibit catalogs, ***What's Going On*** *newsletter, and* ***The Exploratorium Quarterly.*** *Most interesting: two (and soon three)* ***Exploratorium Cookbooks*** *that tell you how to make your own exhibits. The whole bit is carried off with imagination, sass and humor in a way that makes most other museums of any sort seem sort of sad by comparison.* —JB

Exploratorium
Membership **$30**/year
Publications list **free**

Exploratorium Cookbook I
1984; 180 pp.
$60

Cookbook II
1980; 180 pp.
$40

Individual Cookbook recipes **$1**
All from:
The Exploratorium
3601 Lyon Street
San Francisco, CA 94123

Magnetic lines of force can be seen and felt using a large magnet and several pounds of black sand (magnetite) or iron filings. The sand follows the magnetic lines of force and can be made to form images of the magnetic field. The sand, (without dirtying one's hands) provides a very pleasant and unusual tactile sensation because of its attraction to the magnet. Magnetic "castles of sand" can also be built.
—Exploratorium Cookbook II

• Some of the best textbooks for kids are adult textbooks. Precocious students should check the books on math (p. 25), and science magazines (p. 26). The diagrams in **Scientific American** are amazingly fascinating and accessible to interested kids.

THIS EXPLAINS HOW YOU CAN GET "INTO" OR "OUT OF" A CIRCLE ON THE SPHERE, WITHOUT CROSSING IT. JUST THINK OF THE CIRCLE AS BEING MADE OF ELASTIC, SLIDING ABOUT LIKE A RUBBER BAND ON A BILLIARD BALL.

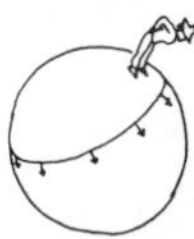
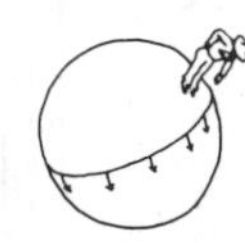

—*Here's Looking at Euclid*

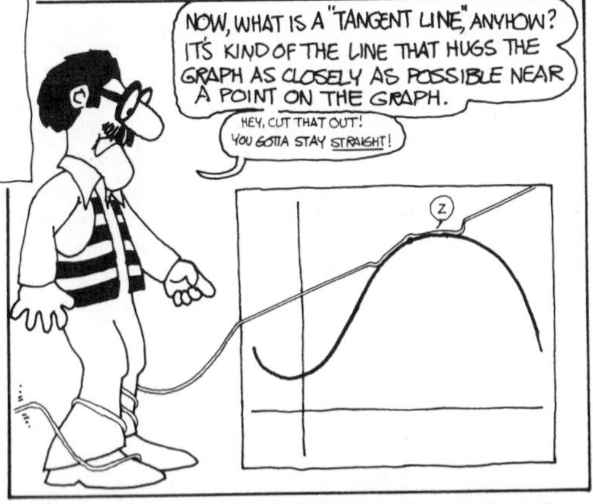

NOW, WHAT IS A "TANGENT LINE," ANYHOW? IT'S KIND OF THE LINE THAT HUGS THE GRAPH AS CLOSELY AS POSSIBLE NEAR A POINT ON THE GRAPH.
HEY, CUT THAT OUT! YOU GOTTA STAY STRAIGHT!
Z

—*Prof. E. McSquared's Calculus Primer*

Mathematics

Is numberwork your nemesis? ***Mathematics*** *is an utterly crap-free and glittery-clear math textbook that makes the work fun and interesting. Not a stamp or coin problem in sight.* ***Here's Looking at Euclid*** *does the same for geometry, particularly the spherical kind that has been the downfall of so many of us. It's in comic book form, and it does the deed — even geodesics are served in a way that should present no problem for a 12-year-old, let alone an adult.* ***Prof. E. McSquared's*** *also uses comics to teach calculus. If the intricacies of that subject have eluded you or filled you with paralyzing hatred, you might give this sugar-coated text a look. All these books require discipline, but at least they aren't boring or creepy.* —JB

•

Three golfers named Tom, Dick, and Harry are walking to the clubhouse. Tom, the best golfer of the three, always tells the truth. Dick sometimes tells the truth, while Harry, the worst golfer, never does. Use deductive reasoning to figure out who is who and explain how you know.

—*Mathematics*

THE GUY IN THE MIDDLE IS TOM
I'M DICK
THE GUY IN THE MIDDLE IS HARRY

Mathematics
Harold R. Jacobs
1982; 649 pp.
$19.95
($21.45 postpaid) from:
W. H. Freeman & Co.
4419 West 1980 South
Salt Lake City, UT 84104
or Whole Earth Access

Here's Looking at Euclid
Jean-Pierre Petit,
translated by Ian Stewart
1985; 63 pp.
$7.95
($9.45 postpaid) from:
William Kaufmann, Inc.
95 First Street
Los Altos, CA 94022
or Whole Earth Access

Prof. E. McSquared's Calculus Primer
Howard Swann and
John Johnson
1977; 214 pp.
$10.95
($12.45 postpaid) from:
William Kaufmann, Inc.
95 First Street
Los Altos, CA 94022
or Whole Earth Access

Edmund Scientific • Nasco Science

Wondrous goodies abound in these catalogs. Edmund's, recovered from an unseemly dalliance with New Age gadgets, is back to their best thing: optical stuff, and a huge selection of equipment and hardware aimed at the intelligent amateur, including kids. (Their bargain basement is an associated company, Jerryco, p. 161.) Nasco is a professional lab supply company. To get their extensive catalog or to buy from it, you have to have a "legitimate" letterhead such as a school or research firm. That's easily arranged, and well worth the trouble if you are in need of such merchandise. —JB

Edmund Scientific: Catalog **free** from 101 East Gloucester Pike, Attn.: Catalogue Entry, Barrington, NJ 08007.
Nasco Science: catalog **free** from 1524 Princeton Avenue, Modesto, CA 95352.

TAKE A TRIP INTO TIME
True-scale replicas of six dinosaurs: stegosaurus, woolly mammoth, tyrannousaurus, triceratops, brontosaurus and pteranodon. 5" to 20". **F34,704 $34.95**

NINE OUNCE MAGNET LIFTS 95 POUNDS!
Two ceramic magnets are sandwiched between steel plates. Mounted metal handle features dent for attachment of retrieval line. Ideal for picking up ferrous objects. Palm-size.
95 Pound Lift Magnet F42,095 $14.95

EASY-TO-CUT TRANSPARENT FILTERS
Heat resistant 0.0005 to 0.01 inches in thickness. Colors are vibrant & fine for striking photographic effects. Booklets and separate sheets available. Order sheets by number.
F82,010 Gold Amber; F82,039 Dk. Urban Blue; F82,031 Daylight Blue; F82,034 Dk. Med. Blue; F82,038 Lt. Med. Blue; F82,000 Frost; F82,040 Light Green; F82,041 Med. Green; F82,043 Yellow Green; F82,004 Med. Lemon; F82,012 Orange; F82,029 Med. Purple; F82,015 Med. Red.
20" × 24" Filter Sheets **$8.95 each.**
Book of 44 Filters (each a different color)
5" × 8" **F60,403 $32.95**
8" × 10" **F70,638 $49.95**
1½" × 3¼" **F40,675 $5.95**
Book of 6 Filters (red, green, blue, cyan, magenta, yellow)
8" × 10" **F60,373 $14.95**
2" × 2" **F40,676 $3.95**
Book of Spectral Curves (for all above filters) **F9081 $3.95**

SCOPE LIGHT
Illuminates microscope from surface level. Adjustable arm, sturdy circular base. 4½" high. Black w/silver trim. W/ bulb. Permits more detailed studies from any scope.
F34,769 $29.95
Spare Bulb F34,770 $2.95

—*Edmund Scientific*

The Science Book

Lots of interesting, various science experiments that invite willing participation by avoiding the sappy condescension usually found in books of this sort. The examples are taken from everyday life, making it all much more real than lab simulations do. —JB

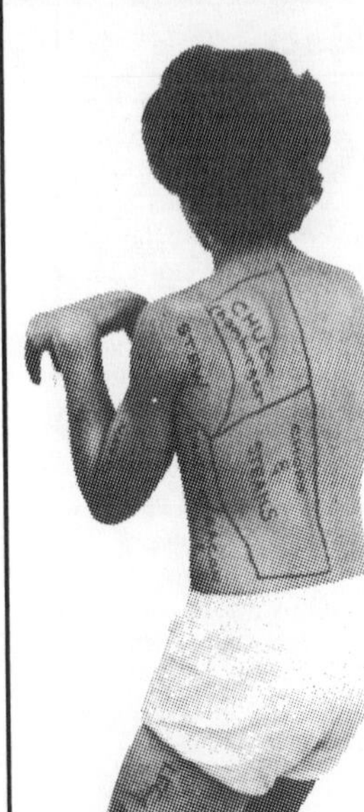

A butcher's view of you

This photograph shows where such meat as chops, spareribs, bacon, and ham would come from on you.

Your own anatomy is not so different from a lamb, cow or pig. Here you can see the same cuts of meat outlined and labelled.

The Science Book
Sara Stein
1980; 288 pp.
$7.95
($9.95 postpaid) from:
Workman Publishing Co.
1 West 39th Street
New York, NY 10018
or Whole Earth Access

Fortean Times
Richard J. M. Rickard and Paul R. A. de G. Sieveking, Editors
$12/year
(4 issues) from:
BM-Fortean Times
96 Mansfield Road
London NW3 2HX
England

Fortean Times

This quarterly exudes a delightful sense of humor and a healthy excitement for all things strange and wonderful. It carries on in the tradition of Charles Fort, an eccentric American writer who in the '20s and '30s produced four books of mysterious occurences combined with whimsical cosmic philosophy. Highlighted by entertaining editorial commentary, **FT** *features mind-boggling surveys of weird events culled from the newspapers of the world, in categories like rains of frogs, sea serpents, strange fires, religious miracles, out-of-place animals, ice meteors, phantom cats, etc. In addition,* **FT** *offers eccentric columnists, odd comic strips, and elegant shoestring design. Great fun to read, and a continuing testament to the strangeness of our world.* —Ted Schultz

•

The Death of a Wolf Boy
According to the United News of India (UNI), a wolf boy called Ramu died in Prem Nivas, Mother Theresa's Home for the Destitute and Dying in Lucknow on 18 (or 20?) February 1985. He had developed cramps two weeks earlier and had not responded to treatment. The report said that he had been captured in a forest in 1976, aged about 10, in the company of three wolf cubs. He was on all fours, had matted hair, nails like claws, and his palms, elbows and knees were calloused like the pads of a wolf's paws. He ate raw meat, and after his capture he would sneak out and attack chickens. He learned to wash and wear clothes, but never to speak.
(AP) Houston (TX) *Chronicle*, 23 + 27 Feb. 1985.

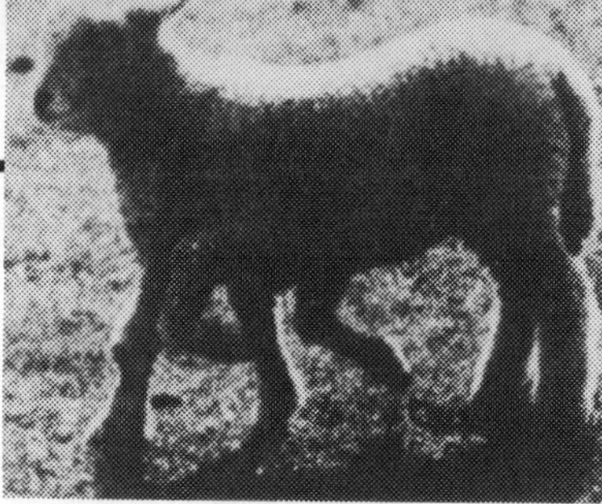

Six-legged lamb born on a West Wales farm sent in to *Amateur Photographer* (Aug. 31, 1985) by O. G. Jeremy of Manselton, Swansea

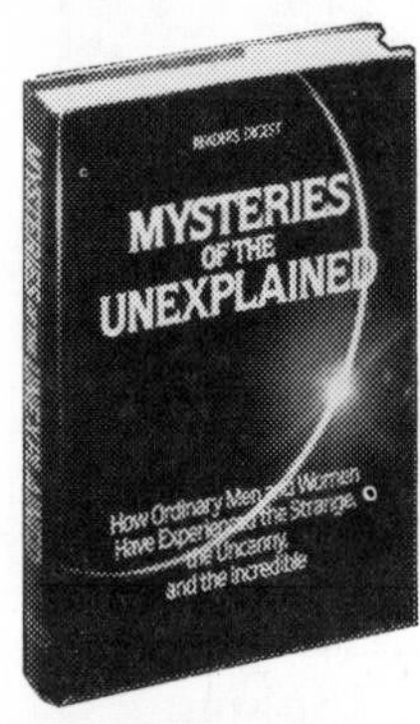

Mysteries of the Unexplained
The Editors of *Reader's Digest*
1982; 320 pp.
$19.95
($21.89 postpaid) from:
Reader's Digest
Attn.: Order Entry
Pleasantville, NY 10570
or Whole Earth Access

Mysteries of the Unexplained

Thank God not everything in the universe is explained. Some of life's weirdness will someday be understood, some will never be known, and some (probably most) mysteries will turn out to be illusory. The wonder of not knowing for sure is what is celebrated in this Reader's Digest compendium of curious and spooky marvels. It's given me the dubious pleasure of being perplexed by mysteries I wasn't even aware of, like spontaneous human combustion (a human bursts into flames unaccountably and the body consumes itself by its own heat), or stigmata (an affliction that causes people to bleed in the manner of Christ's wounds on certain holy days). Not to mention UFOs and ball lightning and the usual oddities. —Kevin Kelly

A peerless browse, this collection of fascinating photos and sufficiently brief accounts of still-half-understood goings-on will give any reader an itchy mind. —Stewart Brand

•

An eight-inch globe of ball lightning — about as bright as a 10-watt bulb, and giving off no perceptible heat — emerged from the pilot's cabin and floated down the aisle of an airliner on a New York-to-Washington flight on March 19, 1963, just after lightning had struck the plane. Passenger R. C. Jennison was especially struck by its perfect symmetry and "almost solid appearance." (*Nature*, 224:895, November 29, 1969)

A Japanese fishing trawler hauled the decomposing body of an unidentified sea creature, its long neck dangling, from the waters off New Zealand in 1977.

The Sourcebooks
William R. Corliss, Editor
$11.95-$18.95
postpaid;
information **free** from:
The Sourcebook Project
P. O. Box 107
Glen Arm, MD 21057

The Sourcebook Project

The **Sourcebooks** *are the* **Encyclopedia Brittanica** *of the unexplained. For over 13 years, physicist and science writer William R. Corliss has systematically searched the pages of a century's backlog of scientific journals, extracting every report of the bizarre or inexplicable in an exhaustive effort to "catalog what is not known." His ever-expanding database currently encompasses over 30,000 items, some of which he's managed to catalog in his 13-volume* **Sourcebook** *series; over 20 more volumes are planned. The volumes bear titles like* **Rare Halos, Mirages, Anomalous Rainbows, and Related Electromagnetic Phenomena; Tornados, Dark Days, Anomalous Precipitation, and Related Weather Phenomena;** *and* **The Sun and Solar System Debris.** *The books are subdivided into a very well-planned categorization scheme that is the first cross-referenced taxonomy of anomalies. Individual anomaly types are rated in two ways: once for reliability of the reports, and once for "anomalousness," the extent to which the phenomenon, if real, violates currently accepted scientific theory. Clearly, the* **Sourcebooks** *are the ultimate reference tool for the strange-phenomena connoisseur.*

The tireless Mr. Corliss also publishes a newsletter, **Science Frontiers,** *sent free for the asking.* —Ted Schultz

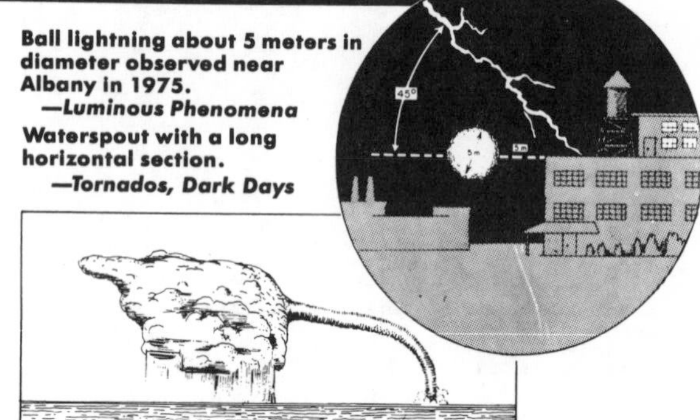

Ball lightning about 5 meters in diameter observed near Albany in 1975.
—*Luminous Phenomena*

Waterspout with a long horizontal section.
—*Tornados, Dark Days*

• Ice Falls or Hydrometeors
Description. Chunks of ice that fall from the sky that are substantially larger than the largest recognized hailstones; that is, more than five inches in diameter or weighing more than 2 pounds. The ice pieces may fall from a clear sky or they may descend after a powerful stroke of lightning. The chunks may be clear ice, or layered structures, or aggregations of small hailstones. This diversity of structure and meteorological conditions suggests that ice falls may have several different origins.
—*Tornados, Dark Days*

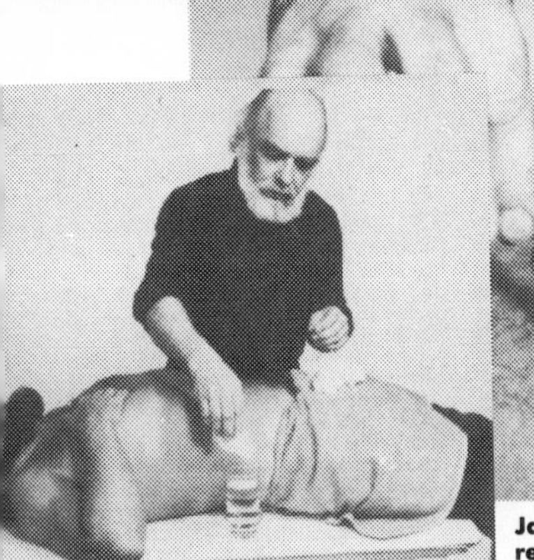

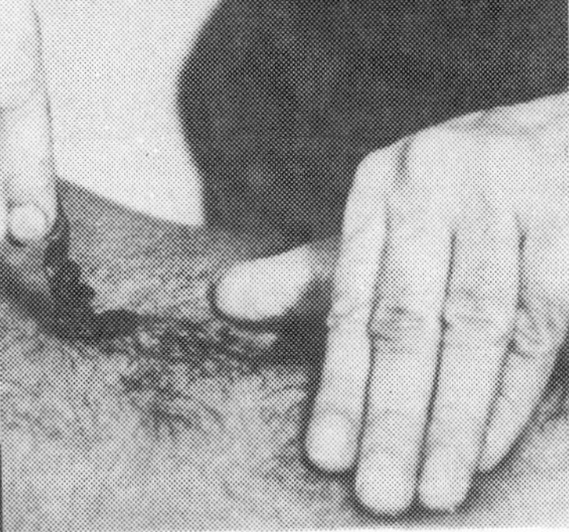

James Randi simulates a psychic healer removing a supposed tumor.

Science and the Paranormal

If you just wanted to read one book skeptical of the paranormal, this would have to be it. Twenty experts, most of them scientists, take the time to study the evidence for various paranormal claims within their areas of expertise. Botanist Arthur Galston discusses the failures to replicate "plant consciousness" research published in the sensationalistic **Secret Life of Plants**. *Astronomer Carl Sagan examines the Biblically-inspired catastrophist reinterpretation of solar system history proposed in Immanuel Velikovsky's* **Worlds in Collision**. *Surgeon William Nolen reports on his extensive investigation of psychic healing. The magician James "The Amazing" Randi demonstrates his duplications of psychic "miracles." The lyrical closing chapter by M.I.T. physicist Philip Morrison redirects the reader to the genuine fountains of wonder that are the basis of all great science. This book is an intelligent, informed analysis of some of the most widely held paranormal beliefs, and a lesson in critical thinking to boot.*

—Ted Schultz

•

As an experienced surgeon I immediately recognized what I had previously suspected from viewing the films: These so-called operations were simply feats of legerdemain. I managed to persuade Joe Mercado, one of the best-known psychic surgeons, to operate on me, explaining that I had high blood pressure (true) and that high blood pressure might be caused by kidney disease (also true). He operated on me while I stood by the side of the altar in his church (at six foot one I was too tall to lie down on the altar on which he operated on most of his patients). Looking down on his hands, I could easily see as he began the "operation" that he had palmed the intestines and fat of a small animal. I watched him carefully as he pushed against me and it was apparent, both visually and from the way his hands felt as they pressed on my abdominal musculature, that he had not penetrated my abdominal wall. When he "removed" the fatty tissue, he held it up for all the spectators to see and said, "Evil tissue." He immediately tossed it into a can of flaming alcohol kept behind the altar.

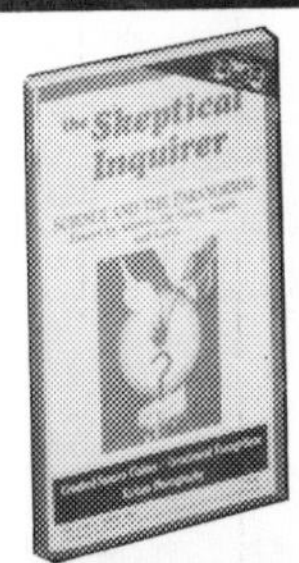

The Skeptical Inquirer
Kendrick Frazier, Editor
$20/year
(4 issues) from:
The Skeptical Inquirer
Box 229
Buffalo, NY 14215-0229

Fads and Fallacies in the Name of Science

Martin Gardner is a well-known science writer who for years authored the "Mathematical Games" column in **Scientific American**. *First published in 1952, this volume is THE classic of skeptical literature. Gardner displays some of the best qualities of a skeptical author: good writing, good research in an area fraught with obscurity, and genuine fascination for pseudoscience and crankery of all kinds. His book is a parade of eccentric people and eccentric theories: hollow and flat Earth, bizarre physics, Lysenkoism, the Bates vision-correction system, Reich's orgonomy, general semantics, parapsychology, medical quackery (always a fertile field). You'd have to spend years haunting libraries and writing away for pamphlets to assemble half of the histories and biographies that Gardner presents here in a thoroughly sane, good-humored style.* —Ted Schultz

•

Nor is Henry [the dowser] likely to try the blindfold test with which he was once challenged by a wise professor at the University of Massachusetts. This test is even simpler. Let Henry find a spot where his rod dips strongly. Then let him be blindfolded securely and led about over the area to see if his stick dips repeatedly when he walks across the same spot. Could anything be fairer?

•

The Great Pyramid of Egypt was involved in many medieval and Renaissance cults, especially in the Rosicrucian and other occult traditions, but it was not until 1859 that modern Pyramidology was born. This was the year that John Taylor, an eccentric partner in a London publishing firm, issued his *The Great Pyramid: Why was it Built? And Who Built it?*

Taylor never visited the Pyramid, but the more he studied its structure, the more he became convinced that its architect was not an Egyptian, but an Israelite acting under divine orders. Perhaps it was Noah himself.

The Skeptical Inquirer

For years paranormalists complained: "Why don't scientists investigate this?" Scientists do, and their reports regularly take up the challenge in the pages of the **Skeptical Inquirer**. *For a decade, this journal of the Committee for the Scientific Investigation of Claims of the Paranormal has been a lone voice in a sea of irrationality. High-quality articles with plenty of references thoroughly survey and analyze all kinds of paranormal claims. Sure, there's plenty of debunking — usually right on target. Anyone who reads from the extensive literature of the paranormal has to read the* **Skeptical Inquirer**, *if only for balance. I recently purchased a complete set of back issues; you can't get this information anywhere else.* —Ted Schultz

•

When UFO commentator and gadfly James Moseley shocked and upset many readers of his newsletter, *Saucer Smear*, by announcing that he was "losing the faith," the well-known UFO and Fortean researcher Jerome Clark suggested that he might regain some of his lost "faith" if he were to look into a really excellent UFO case, such as Rendlesham. Moseley did, and the result eroded his confidence in UFOlogy even further. He found that two British researchers from the Swindon Centre for UFO Research and Investigation made a brief preliminary investigation and found five major discrepancies in the published reports.

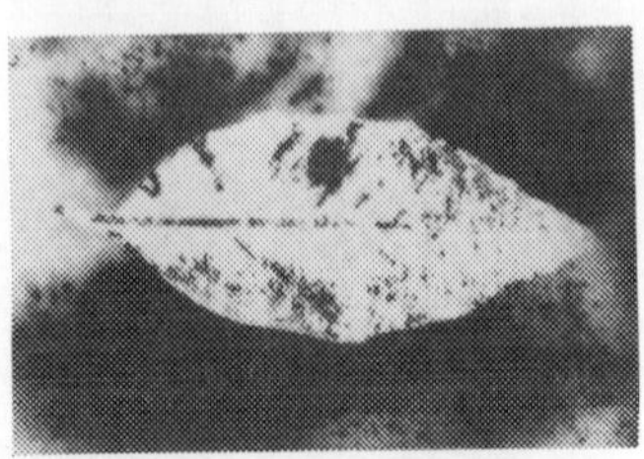

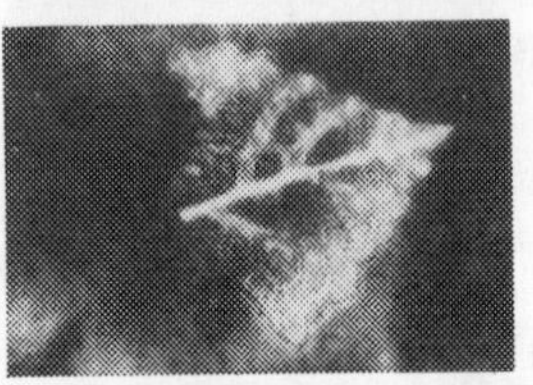

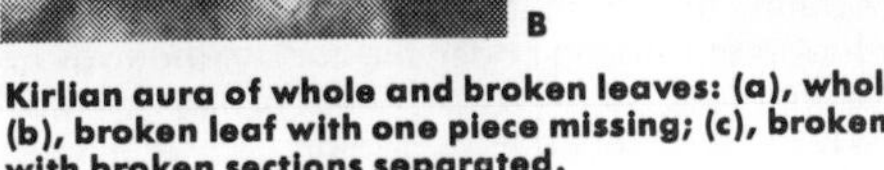

Kirlian aura of whole and broken leaves: (a), whole leaf; (b), broken leaf with one piece missing; (c), broken leaf with broken sections separated.

Fads and Fallacies
Martin Gardner
1957; 363 pp.
$5.95
($6.60 postpaid) from:
Dover Publications
31 E. Second Street
Mineola, NY 11501
or Whole Earth Access

Science and the Paranormal
George O. Abell and Barry Singer, Editors
1981; 414 pp.
$12.95 postpaid from:
Macmillan Publishing Co.
Order Dept.
Front and Brown Streets
Riverside, NJ 08075
or Whole Earth Access

None of our photographs demonstrated the phantom-leaf effect. In no case was an aura detected in the region of the missing leaf or around its boundary.

Pantheon Fairy Tale and Folklore Library
Titles include:
African Folktales **$10.95**
American Indian Myths & Legends **$11.95**
Irish Folktales **$19.95**
Afro-American Folktales **$11.95**
Russian Fairy Tales **$8.95**
Eighty Fairy Tales: Hans Christian Anderson **$7.95**
Norwegian Folk Tales **$6.95**
British Folktales **$7.95**
An Encyclopedia of Fairies **$8.95**
Italian Folktales **$10.95**
The Norse Myths **$7.95**
Catalog **free**
All from:
Pantheon Books
Order Dept.
Random House
400 Hahn Road
Westminster, MD 21157
or Whole Earth Access

The Vanishing Hitchhiker
Jan Harold Brunvand
1981; 208 pp.
$6.95
($7.65 postpaid)

The Choking Doberman
Jan Harold Brunvand
1984; 240 pp.
$13.95
($14.90 postpaid)
Both from:
W. W. Norton
500 Fifth Avenue
New York, NY 10110
or Whole Earth Access

Pantheon Fairy Tale and Folklore Library

This series of books offers attractively designed and illustrated collections of folktales, myths, and fairytales from around the world. African, Irish, Norse, Italian, Russian, Chinese tales, and more, provide insights into different cultures and genuine entertainment. —*Jay Kinney*

•

The Four Champions

The Horny Head champion, the Penis champion, the Farting champion, and the Testicles champion set off on a journey together. They came to a town, where they lodged in the compound of the chief. Bundles of corn were sent to feed them from the chief's storehouse — but the town had nowhere to thresh it!

Then the Horny Head said, "May the chief's life be prolonged! Here we are and yet they're looking for a place to thresh. Let them come and do it on my head!" So they came and undid the bundles on Horny Head's noggin.

But then they had to find a piece of wood with which to thresh the corn so Penis said, "May the chief's life be prolonged! Here we are now, and yet they're looking for something to thresh with! Just give me a bit of room and you'll see!" And pulling out his penis, he began threshing, and presently the corn was threshed.

But there was no wind, and word was brought to the chief that, though the corn was threshed, there was no wind and so could be no winnowing. Then said the Wind Breaker, "May the chief's life be prolonged! Here are we, and in spite of that they're still looking for wind!" And he unveiled his anus, and let rip. And all the chaff was blown away, leaving just the grain.

But they had no bag to put the grain in. So Testicles said, "May the chief's life be prolonged! Here are we, and inspite of what we've done, they're still looking for a sack to catch the grain!" And opening his scrotum, he said, "Bring me the grain and pour it in here." And they did it, and he carried the corn home.

All right, among the four of them that exercised his special gift, who was the champion?

—*Hausa, African Folktales*

The Vanishing Hitchhiker • The Choking Doberman

This lady came in from the rain, and her miniature poodle was wet and shivering. So she put him into the microwave to dry him off. He exploded. She was so horrified she had a heart attack and died.

I've told that one. I thought it was true. It is, but a different kind of true. It's a modern urban legend, a gripping, bizarre, often moralistic tale that goes the rounds as a factual account — "It happened to a friend of a friend of mine"; "I read it in the newspaper." Hundreds are in circulation at any time, and many do get picked up in newspapers. Vanishingly few have factual origins.

But they are wonderful stories, living for decades and often reappearing after centuries in new guises. A major collector of these modern folk tales is Jan Harold Brunvand in two riveting books, ***The Vanishing Hitchhiker*** *(1981) and* ***The Choking Doberman*** *(1984). He collects, tells, compares versions, tests factuality, and interprets. How many can you recognize just from his titles? . . . "The Death Car," "The Killer in the Back Seat," "The Kentucky Fried Rat," "Alligators in the Sewers," "The Solid Cement Cadillac," "The Economical Car," "Cruise Control," "The Bump in the Rug," "The Stuck Couple," "Superglue Revenge," "The Image on Glass," and scores more. Many have to do with new technologies, many have to do with racism (the doberman is choking on black fingers) and fear of foreigners.*

Either book will give you a new angle on your civilization, but I'd get both. The stories ring in your mind for years. That's what keeps them alive. —*Stewart Brand*

•

A girl managed to wrap her hair into a perfect beehive. Proud of her accomplishment, she kept spraying it and spraying it, never bothering to wash it again. Bugs began to live in her hair. After about six months, they ate through to her brain and killed her.

—*The Vanishing Hitchhiker*

•

The lady came home from the grocery store, and she saw her husband working under the car. All that was exposed were his legs, so in passing she reached down, unzipped his zipper, chuckled to herself, and went into the house. Immediately she saw her husband sitting in the easy chair reading a newspaper. She cried, "Who is *that* under the car?" and her husband replied, "My mechanic." She told her husband what she'd done, and they went outside to find the mechanic lying unconscious, in a pool of blood, because when the lady unzipped his pants he was so startled he sat up and clobbered his head under the car.

—*The Vanishing Hitchhiker*

•

Her true story was about a jogger in Central Park in New York City. He had been running along early one morning at his customary pace and surrounded by streams of others out getting their prework exercise, when suddenly another jogger passed by him on the path and bumped him rather hard. Checking quickly, the jogger discovered that his billfold was missing from his pocket, and he thought, "This can't happen to me; I'm not going to let it happen." So he upped his speed a bit, caught up to the other jogger, and confronted him. "Give me that billfold," he snarled, trying to sound as menacing as possible, and hoping for the best. The other jogger quickly handed it over, and our hero turned back toward his apartment for a shower and a quick change of clothes. But when he got home, there was his own billfold on the dresser, and the one he had in his pocket belonged to someone else.

I hated to tell her that this was just a new aerobic variation on an old commuter theme. How old? For starters, here's a version from the "My Favorite Jokes" section of *Parade* magazine, 3 September 1972, as told by comic Gus Christie:

This is supposed to be a true story. A man, we'll call him Mr. Jones, is riding to work on the subway in New York City and there's a guy who keeps bumping into him. After a while Jones gets apprehensive and thinks, "This can't be what I think it is!" He checks his wallet — and it's gone. "That's it! Nine o'clock in the morning and I get mugged in the subway. Things are really getting bad." He grabs the guy, shakes him hard, and says, "All right, cough up, give me that wallet!" The guy is petrified and he hands over a wallet. So Jones goes off to work and when he gets to his office his wife calls and says, "Honey, you left your wallet on the bureau this morning." —*The Choking Doberman*

Parabola

Underground rivers of juice flow in this magazine of myth. The major players in the subject play here, with a graphic excitement never seen in academic publications.
—Stewart Brand

•

It is not by chance that we speak of a "pride of lions," for those old collective words often expressed a salient quality in the beasts or birds they described. The lion is felt by man to be a king among beasts. His pride is very different from the human sin of usurping a merit not his own; it is a natural pride which is the quality of being absolutely true to oneself. A lion who turns man-eating when unable through injury to catch his natural prey becomes a pariah, cast out of his pride, for he is untrue

to his lion nature, no longer a proud king among beasts. It is interesting to remember how Laurens van der Post writes in *The Heart of the Hunter* of the Bushman's feeling for the lion, and of his own observations. He says the lion is by far the most individual of the wild animals in Africa. Every lion you encounter will act in a different way and you can never predict his behavior as you can with almost all the other species.

Parabola
Lorraine Kisly, Editor
$18/year
(4 issues) from:
Parabola
656 Broadway
New York, NY 10012

Primal Myths

Any extensive exploration of mythology will reveal how incredibly heterogeneous human culture is. I know of no book that shows this better than Barbara C. Sproul's **Primal Myths.** *Sproul has collected the creation myths of every corner of the world. From the Yao of northern Mozambique we learn how "the gods were driven off the face of the earth by the cruelty of man." The Jains and Buddhists of India give us rarified discussions of why there are no creators at all. The Maidu of California tell us that the world was created from the dirt under turtles' fingernails.*

Rich with plot and character, they can be read as beguiling stories, or pondered as philosophical verities. Each myth is preceded by a concise paragraph or two that helps explain it, and places the people in geographical context. There is enough charm and truth in this book to allow you to fall in love with humanity again.
—David Kennedy

•

Mundurucu: The People Climbed Out

Karusakaibo had made the world but had not created men. One day Dairru, the armadillo, offended the creator and was forced to take refuge in a hole in the ground. Karusakaibo blew into the hole and stamped his foot on the earth. Daiiru was blown out of the hole by the rush of air. He reported that people were living in the earth. He and Karusakaibo made a cotton rope and lowered it into the hole. The people began to climb out. When half of them had emerged, the rope broke and half remained underground, where they still live. The sun passes through their country from west to east when it is night on the earth; the moon shines there when the earth has moonless nights.

Primal Myths
Barbara C. Sproul
1979; 352 pp.
$9.95
($11.45 postpaid) from:
Harper & Row
2350 Virginia Ave.
Hagerstown, MD 21740
or Whole Earth Access

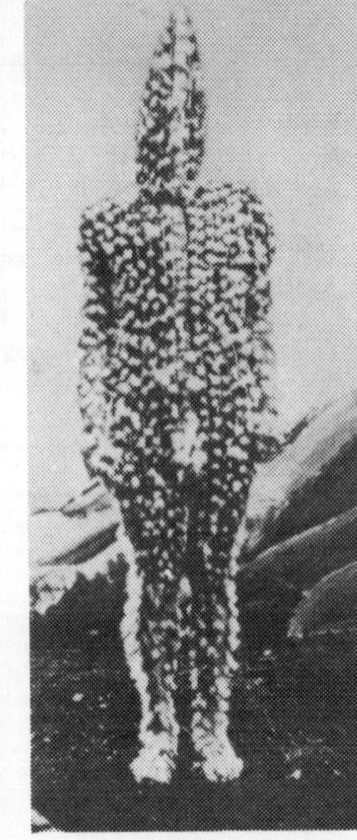

The Way of the Animal Powers

This formidable work of art and scholarship concerns the myths of the first peoples — the hunter-gatherers of our ancestry and of today. Their images, their beliefs, are deeply sophisticated and as troubling and inspiring as the reader will let them be. The medium, arch-mythologist Joseph Campbell, is welcoming you to a long night's journey. This is Volume I of an **Historical Atlas of World Mythology.** *Maps abound, along with some of the best reproductions yet of mythic creatures both famous and heretofore little known.*
—Stewart Brand

◄

The male initiation rites of the Ona were conducted in a special lodge of the men's society, the *kloketen*, from which women were excluded; and associated with the mystifications of this institution were a number of such Hallowe'en spooks as we see here. These apparitions would appear from time to time, ranging through the bush of areas about the men's house, and any woman or child seeing one or more of them was to suppose that they were the inhabitants of the *kloketen* with whom the men held converse in their meetings. An important moment in the initiations of a boy took place when he was compelled to get up and wrestle with one of these characters, who would let the youngster put him down, after which the masquerade was uncovered, and the boy turned into a man. There was a legend of the *kloketen* having been originally of the women, but taken and kept from them by the men.

The Way of the Animal Powers
Joseph Campbell
1983; 304 pp.
$75
($78 postpaid) from:
Alfred Van Der Marck Editions
Harper & Row
2350 Virginia Avenue
Hagerstown, MD 21740
or Whole Earth Access

• Also see Joseph Campbell's **Hero with a Thousand Faces** (p. 401).

• Learn how to record and create some of your own stories and myths from **At a Journal Workshop** (p. 400).

ASK someone what yoga is all about and their most likely response will have to do with people doing hea stands and other physical stuff. It's an interesting case of the tail wagging the dog, for way back when i all began the physical postures, or asanas, were only a small part of the main affair. Some two millenn ago Patanjali, whose work marks the first clear beginning of what is known today as yoga, produce the yogic sutras, a series of short aphorisms which formulate ashtanga, or eight limbed yoga. The asanas, or hatha yoga, are just one limb, and not one that received much of the founder's attention.

Patanjali's sparse aphorisms were intended to be memorized and handed down verbally by teachers who would then amplify with their own comments; thus, in a book they are always accompanied by an interpretation. The most available volume is *How to Know God* by Christopher Isherwood and Swami Prabhavananda, and it's a good introduction to what yoga is all about, which is much more than headstands.

The word "yoga" comes from the same Sanskrit base that gives us our word "yoke," and implies a union or harnessing of energies, in this case a discipline or technique for investigating and developing the Self. A look at the literature reveals a fully developed philosophy, a way of explaining the world around us and wh we're here. You might say it's similar to the Buddhist approach, but a bit less ethereal. Or it could be compared to some of the basic tenets of Hindu thinking, but since pinning down Hinduism with words and logic is like trying to put a puffy white cloud into a plain brown wrapper with a small plastic fork we are left with our curiosity, a few source documents like Patanjali, and whatever conclusions we reach on our own after going through the commentary and collating it with personal experience.

Interesting, you say, but perhaps you're hot to do headstands and perfect that lotus. Let's get on with it.

—Dick Fugett

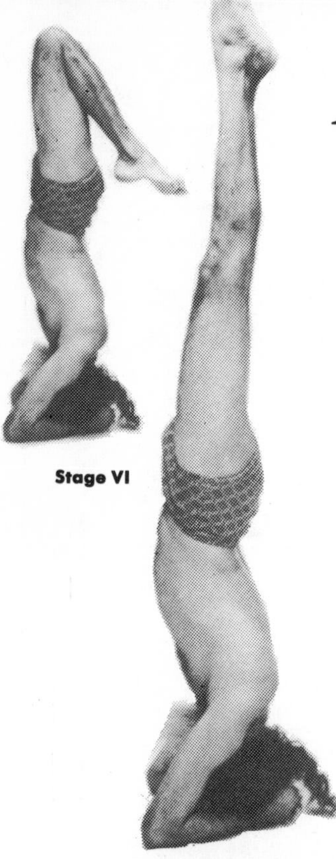

Stage VI

Sirshasana — Stage VII —*Integral Yoga Hatha*

Integral Yoga Hatha
Yogiraj Sri
Swami Satchidananda
1970; 189 pp.
$9.95
($11.95 postpaid) from:
Henry Holt & Co.
521 Fifth Avenue, 12th floor
New York, NY 10175
or Whole Earth Access

Light On Yoga
B. K. S. Iyengar
1976; 544 pp.
$12.95
($13.95 postpaid) from:
Schocken Books
62 Cooper Square
New York, NY 10003
or Whole Earth Access

How to Know God

How to Know God
(The Yoga Aphorisms of Patanjali)
Translated by Swami Prabhavananda and Christopher Isherwood
1981; 224 pp.
$6.95
($8.45 postpaid) from:
Vedanta Press
1946 Vedanta Place
Hollywood, CA 90068-3996
or Whole Earth Access

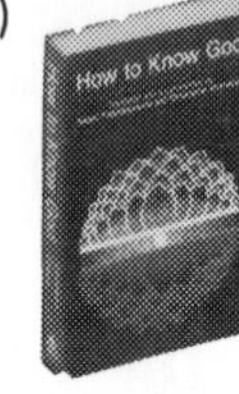

Integral Yoga Hatha • Light on Yoga

The practice of hatha yoga acquaints us with our bodies in a slow, precise manner that no sport can offer. Diligent pursuit will reward us with a new physical well-being, a clearer mind, and most importantly, an inner calm unknown before. Hatha is an invaluable tool for developing ourselves, one that we can take with us wherever we go, like meditation.

Because it can become more than just an exploration of the physical package, a teacher, especially at the beginning, can give insights that the purely self-taught person may miss. A few classes or a retreat can produce rewards that more than justify the money spent.

When it comes to books on the topic there's a bushel, but two could be said to be standards. ***Integral Yoga Hatha*** *has probably started more people then any other, it's simple, clear and well illustrated, and each asana, or posture, is also described in writing. If you'd like a closer look, there are numerous Integral Yoga institutes around the country offering classes in hatha and related topics.*

If you've reached advanced levels and enjoy new challenge (Beware of Egofeed — hey look, I did a Lotus!) then check out ***Light on Yoga.*** *Iyengar is a master of the art, and the pictures in the book illustrate his talent. They could also be discouraging for the beginner, so don't worry about whether you'll ever be that loose, just appreciate the incredible possibilities inherent in the human structure, and wonder why the rest of us don't develop them. The book also has a superior introduction to the entire yogic philosophy.* —*Dick Fugett*

Yoga Journal

Yoga Journal *began 12 years ago as a small, regional magazine devoted completely to hatha yoga, but its growth and diversification have made it the best known voice of the movement. YJ still emphasizes hatha, but articles can range from body work and acupuncture to nutrition and martial arts.*

There are also good interviews with people making the news, book reviews, and event announcements — which are interesting for anyone looking for new directions.

—*Dick Fugett*

Yoga Journal
Stephan Bodian, Editor
$15/year
(6 issues) from:
Yoga Journal
P. O. Box 15203
Santa Ana, CA
92705-0203

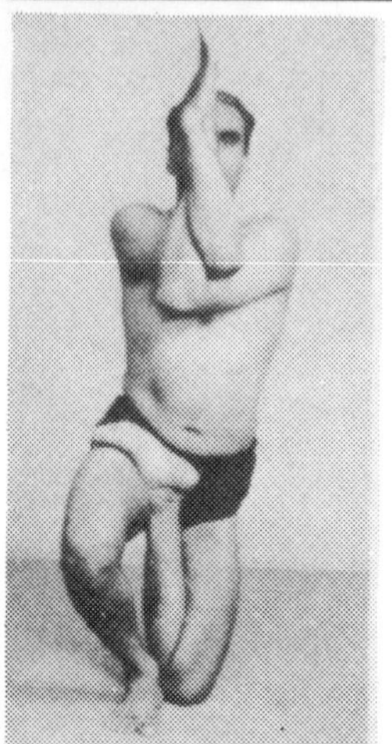

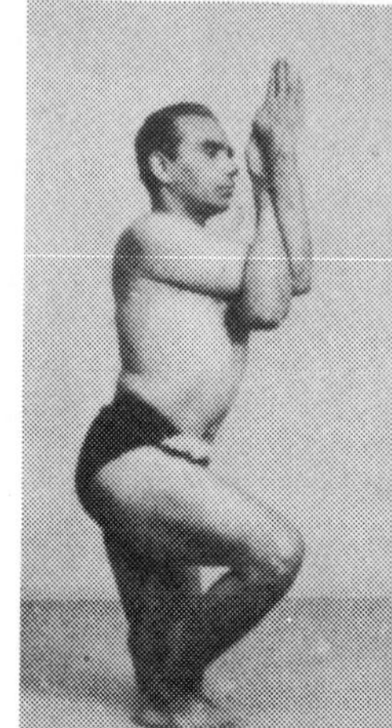

Vatayanasana Eleven: Vatayana means a horse. The pose resembles a horse's face; hence the name.

—Light On Yoga

ooks on Buddhism

ddhism is a nontheistic world view ıd meditative endeavor which has lped millions of individuals and ızens of societies live in clarity and acefulness. According to Nancy 'ilson Ross, nearly one-fourth of the ople on earth are followers of this ay of life and thought.

e main teachings of Buddhism are terdependence, that nothing exists parate of everything else; nondual- , that correct perception requires ecoming one with the object; non- olence, which springs from this npathetic understanding; and joy, which arises from aintaining awareness of what is actually happening, ven as it changes. The root "buddh" means to be awake, aware, and the most important practice in Buddhism is wareness of what is going on: in your body, your mind, our feelings, and the world around. The many schools nd sects of Buddhism — including Zen (meditation), betan, Vipassana (insight), and Shin (devotion) — all erive from these fundamental teachings of Shakyamuni uddha, who lived 2,500 years ago in northern India.

or the past century, and particularly the past 30 years, sian teachers have brought these meditation practices nd understandings to Westerners, and a generation of Vestern Buddhist practitioners is now making these teach- gs available throughout the U.S., Canada, Europe, and ustralia. In addition, many universities now have pro- rams in Buddhist studies. A complete directory of Buddhist enters is available from Snow Lion Publications.

here are many excellent books, journals, newsletters, nd tapes on Buddhism in English. The three books I ecommend most highly are **The Miracle of Mindfulness**, y Thich Nhat Hanh, **Zen Mind, Beginner's Mind**, by hunryu Suzuki, and **Meditation in Action**, by Chogyam rungpa. They all speak clearly, simply, and directly bout Buddhist understanding from within the tradition. fourth book, **Taking the Path of Zen**, by Robert Aitken, rovides an excellent how-to manual for someone en- ering Zen practice.

wo other introductory books, **Buddhism: A Way of Life nd Thought**, by Nancy Wilson Ross, and **What the Buddha aught**, by Walpola Rahula, elucidate Buddhist philo- ophy and history in clear, nonacademic terms. For further eading, see the bibliography in Nancy Wilson Ross's ook. For further information or meditation instruction, ontact one of the centers listed in the **International uddhist Directory**.

—Arnold Kotler

—The Miracle of Mindfulness

•

The conception of *dukkha* may be viewed from three aspects: (1) *dukkha* as ordinary suffering *(dukkha-dukkha)*, 2) *dukkha* as produced by change *(viparinama-dukkha)* and (3) *dukkha* as conditioned states *(samkhara-dukkha)*.

All kinds of suffering in life like birth, old age, sickness, death, association with unpleasant persons and conditions, separation from beloved ones and pleasant conditions, not getting what one desires, grief, lamentation, distress — all such forms of physical and mental suffering, which are universally accepted as suffering or pain, are includ- ed in *dukkha* as ordinary suffering (*dukkha-dukkha*).

—*What the Buddha Taught*

•

Breath counting: Zazen is a matter of just doing it. However, even for the advanced Zen student, work on the meditation cushions is always being refined. It is like learning to drive a car. At first everything is mechanical and awkward. You consciously depress the clutch and shift into low, then release the clutch gradually while depressing the gas pedal, steering to stay within the white lines and to avoid other cars. There are so many things to remember and to do all at once, that at first you make mistakes and perhaps even have an accident. But when you become one with the car, you are more confident. And you become a better and better driver with experience.

—*Taking the Path of Zen*

•

The purpose of studying Buddhism is not to study Buddhism, but to study ourselves. It is impossible to study ourselves without some teaching. If you want to know what water is you need science, and the scientist needs a laboratory. In the laboratory there are various ways in which to study what water is. Thus it is possible to know what kind of elements water has, the various forms it takes, and its nature. But it is impossible thereby to know water in itself. It is the same thing with us. We need some teaching, but just by studying the teaching alone, it is impossible to know what "I" in myself am. Through the teaching we may under- stand our human nature. But the teaching is not we our- selves; it is some explanation of ourselves. So if you are attached to the teaching, or to the teacher, that is a big mistake. —*Zen Mind, Beginner's Mind*

•

During its long centuries of quiet pilgrimage by land and sea, much of Buddhism's powerful influence may have had its source in the deliberate avoidance of claims to exclusive Truth, adherence to inflexible dogma, or the authority of any final, sacrosanct, theocratic hierarchy. The "Come and see for yourself" attitude of the original Great Teacher, Siddhartha Gautama, who became the Buddha, the Enlightened One, his pragmatic insistence on "Don't take my word for it. Try it yourself!" the unswerving challenge of his famous aphorism, "Look within, *thou* art the Buddha" — all this served to lower the resistance that so often attends the arrival of a new and unfamiliar faith. —*Buddhism*

•

Buddha never claimed that he was an Incarnation of God, or any kind of Divine Being. He was just a simple human being who had gone through certain things and had achieved the awakened state of mind. It is possible, partially at least, for any of us to have such an experience. —*Meditation in Action*

Taking the Path of Zen
Robert Aitken
1982; 149 pp.
$9.50
($11.00 postpaid) from:
North Point Press
850 Talbot Avenue
Berkeley, CA 94706
or Whole Earth Access

Meditation In Action
Chogyam Trungpa
1969; 74 pp.
$4.95
($5.95 postpaid) from:
Shambhala Publications
P. O. Box 308
Boston, MA 02117
or Whole Earth Access

The Miracle of Mindfulness
(A Manual on Meditation)
Thich Nhat Hanh
1976; 108 pp.
$7.95
($9.95 postpaid) from:
Beacon Press
Order Dept.
25 Beacon Street
Boston, MA 02108
or Whole Earth Access

Buddhism
Nancy Wilson Ross
1980; 208 pp.
$6.95
($7.95 postpaid) from:
Random House
Order Dept.
400 Hahn Road
Westminster, MD 21157
or Whole Earth Access

Zen Mind, Beginner's Mind
Shunryu Suzuki
1970; 138 pp.
$5.95
($6.95 postpaid) from:
Charles E. Tuttle Co., Inc.
28 South Main Street
Rutland, VT 05701
or Whole Earth Access

International Buddhist Directory
Compiled by Tushita
Meditation Centre
1985; 120 pp.
$8.95
($10.45 postpaid) from:
Snow Lion Publications
P. O. Box 6483
Ithaca, NY 14850
or Whole Earth Access

What the Buddha Taught
Walpola Rahula
1974; 151 pp.
$8.95
($10.45 postpaid) from:
Grove Press
Order Dept.
10 East 53rd Street
New York, NY 10022
or Whole Earth Access

Back to the Sources

This book is an ambitious introduction and guide to the process of Jewish study. There are sections in this 448-page anthology covering Bible narratives and Bible law, Rabbinic folklore and Rabbinic law, medieval philosophy and mysticism, the teachings of the Hasidic Masters and the Hebrew prayerbook itself. Through it all is a sense of tradition as something organic and growing, an art which invites us to participate and make our own contribution once we have grasped the fundamentals.

***Back to the Sources** comes out of an informal "school" of people who have been privately involved for years in Jewish spiritual renewal, but professionally have been part of the university community.*

The authors go to great lengths to supply the background information and give the reader choices of interpretation. There is warmth in this book, and the kind of wry humor that comes of an intelligence aware of its own limitations.
—*Ya'qub ibn Yusuf*

•

We tend nowadays to think of the Jewish sermon as a modern invention, something borrowed perhaps from our Protestant neighbors. But in fact, sermons have been preached throughout much of Jewish history. In rabbinic times, sermons were so popular that people would flock from miles around to hear the Sabbath or Festival address of some renowned preacher.

The preacher would enter dramatically after his assistants had "warmed up" the audience, and as he spoke, an underling — acting as a kind of primitive "living loudspeaker" — would repeat his words so that all could hear. We do not have an actual transcript of an ancient sermon in its entirety, but fragments of these ancient sermons, reworked and polished by later editors, form the core of one major type of midrashic literature. Reasonably enough, this body of literature is called *homiletical* Midrash, since it is based, at least in essence, on the homilies preached by the ancient sages.

Back to the Sources
Barry W. Holtz, Editor
1984; 448 pp.
$10.95
Postpaid from:
Simon and Schuster
Mail Order Sales
200 Old Tappan Road
Old Tappan, NJ 07675
or Whole Earth Access

Holy Qur'an • The Koran Interpreted

The Qur'an is The Book revealed from Allah (God) through His prophet Muhammad (on whom be blessings and peace!) over a period of 23 years. Unlike the Torah, the Psalms, or the Gospels, it has been handed down unchanged since the time of its revelation. Consequently, its text has not been "improved," "clarified" or "interpreted." It remains exactly what Muhammad (who was illiterate) recited to the early Muslims.

As the Qur'an itself states, it is a book of guidance "to those who guard against evil, who believe in the Unseen" and like any book of guidance, it must be approached with respect and openness. This can be difficult for non-Muslims since the Qur'an abounds with images and thoughts that are both sublime, inspiring, and beautiful, as well as (often simultaneously) mystifying, violent, and terrifying. On first reading, it may strike you as a very peculiar and upsetting — yet compelling — book. Second readings and beyond get even more interesting.

Ideally, the Qur'an should be read or listened to in the original Arabic, as it was revealed, for there is much beauty and even greater emotional and spiritual power in its sounds. However, Arabic is a difficult language to learn, so most of us will have to settle, initially at least, for translations.

The two English translations included here have each been chosen for different reasons.

***The Holy Qur'an**, translated by A. Yusuf Ali, a Pakistani Muslim, has language which tends to be stilted, flowery, and archaic. However, it also includes extensive footnotes and commentary which are quite helpful and insightful.*

***The Koran Interpreted** comes from Arthur J. Arberry, a great Orientalist, but not — at least publicly — a Muslim. This translation has several shortcomings, including a puny index and no footnotes, yet Arberry conveys some of the poetry, cadence and grandeur of the Arabic. He has captured something ineffable from the original that no other translation has even touched.*
—*Latifa and Micha 'Abd al-Hayy Weinman*

The Holy Qur'an
Abdullah Yusuf Ali
1983; 1,862 pp.
$20
($21 postpaid) from:
International Book Centre
P. O. Box 295
Troy, MI 48099

The Koran Interpreted
Arthur J. Arberry
1955; 358 pp.
$13.95
postpaid from:
MacMillan Publishing Co.
Order Dept.
Front and Brown Streets
Riverside, NJ 08075
or Whole Earth Access

Ideals and Realities of Islam

A very clear presentation of the doctrines and beliefs of Islam by one of the most distinguished Muslim thinkers in the West. Includes a glossary and listings of additional readings the reader can investigate. —*Jay Kinney*

•

For nearly fourteen hundred years Muslims have tried to awaken in the morning as the Prophet awakened, to eat as he ate, to wash as he washed himself, even to cut their nails as he did. There has been no greater force for the unification of the Muslim peoples than the presence of this common model for the minutest acts of daily life. A Chinese Muslim, although racially a Chinese, has a countenance, behaviour, manner of walking and acting that resembles in certain ways those of a Muslim on the coast of the Atlantic. That is because both have for centuries copied the same model. Something of the soul of the Prophet is to be seen in both places. It is this essential unifying factor, a common *Sunnah* or way of living as a model, that makes a bazaar in Morocco have a 'feeling' or *ambiance* of a bazaar in Persia, although the people in the two places speak a different language and dress differently. There is something in the air which an intelligent foreign observer will immediately detect as belonging to the same religious and spiritual climate. And this sameness is brought about firstly through the presence of the Quran and secondly, and in a more immediate and tangible way, through the 'presence' of the Prophet in his community by virtue of his *Hadith* [sayings] and *Sunnah*.

Ideals and Realities of Islam
Seyyed Hossein Nasr
1985; 188 pp.
$6.95
($8.45 postpaid) from:
Allen and Unwin
Order Dept.
8 Winchester Place
Winchester, MA 01890
or Whole Earth Access

• The effect of religious beliefs on the design and ornament of buildings is shown brilliantly in **Traditional Islamic Craft in Moroccan Architecture** (p. 116).

Good News Bible

*The **Bible** doesn't say what you think it says no matter what you think. It's older, stranger, and longer than will fit into anyone's second hand summaries — and that's all most of us have of it since most editions preserve 16th century book design as well as language and are very hard for modern eyes to read.*

*This edition of the **Bible** is actually easy to read so you can get right to the strangeness of the stories. The things it has that most **Bibles** don't have are a clear typeface, well-placed white space, lots of headings to tell you when a new story starts, lots of pictures integrated into the text, readable maps, and an easy-to-use index (done by page number, not chapter and verse).*

The translation itself is clear conversational English. It was originally done by the American Bible Society for people in other countries who speak English as a second language.

*If you've ever tried to read the **Bible** cover to cover, be advised it's a bad idea. The **Bible** was written by a lot of different people at a lot of different times, so it should be read more like a magazine than a book. Flip around, see what looks interesting, skip the boring parts. The individual stories are tightly written and short so it really isn't a big deal to read any one of them. And the way the **Good News Bible** is set up makes it easy to tell where one story stops and another begins. (Some good easy short stories to start on are Ruth, Esther, and Jonah.)*

—Anne Herbert

Good News Bible
American Bible Society
1976; 408 pp.
$2 postpaid from:
American Bible Society
P. O. Box 5656
Grand Central Station
New York, NY 10164

•

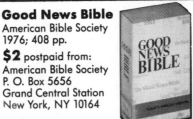

Elijah and Elisha stopped by the river, and the fifty prophets stood a short distance away. Then Elijah took off his cloak, rolled it up, and struck the water with it; the water divided, and he and Elisha crossed to the other side on dry ground. There, Elijah said to Elisha, "Tell me what you want me to do for you before I am taken away."

"Let me receive the share of your power that will make me your successor," Elisha answered.

"That is a difficult request to grant," Elijah replied. "But you will receive it if you see me as I am being taken away from you; if you don't see me, you won't receive it."

They kept talking as they walked on; then suddenly a chariot of fire pulled by horses of fire came between them, and Elijah was taken up to heaven by a whirlwind. Elisha saw it and cried out to Elijah, "My father, my father! Mighty defender of Israel! You are gone!" And he never saw Elijah again.

"I am the Lord, and I do not change." (3.6)

Mere Christianity
C. S. Lewis
1952; 175 pp.
$4.95 postpaid from:
Macmillan Publishing Co.
Order Department
Front and Brown Streets
Riverside, NJ 08075
or Whole Earth Access

Mere Christianity

*Read this book for an idea of the intellectual arguments in favor of Christianity. What began as an informal radio talk 40 years ago has become a perennial best seller (2 million copies) that imaginatively puts forth the gist of Christianity with common sense reasoning. It's written for the modern skeptic by the Cambridge don of Middle English who also wrote the classic **Chronicles of Narnia**, a sophisticated children's fairy tale. In presenting the case for Christianity, C. S. Lewis avoids religious jargon. He deserves sainthood for that.*

—Kevin Kelly

•

Christianity asserts that every individual human being is going to live for ever, and this must be either true or false. Now there are a good many things which would not be worth bothering about if I were going to live only seventy years, but which I had better bother about very seriously if I am going to live for ever. Perhaps my bad temper or my jealousy are gradually getting worse — so gradually that the increase in seventy years will not be very noticeable. But it might be absolute hell in a million years: in fact, if Christianity is true, Hell is the precisely correct technical term for what it would be.

The Living Testament

*Christianity as we know it is much more than just the **Bible** and millions of believers. It is also the product of several dozen key theologians, saints, and renegades who exerted unusual influence on both their own and subsequent generations. **The Living Testament** gathers together the writings of many of these church leaders, such as St. Jerome, St. Bernard, St. Augustine, Martin Luther, John Wesley, Mother Teresa, and even Billy Graham in one big compendium. John Bunyan's **Pilgrim's Progress** is here as is Jonathan Edwards' seminal **Sinners in the Hands of an Angry God**. There's plenty in this book to both inspire and horrify anyone.* *—Jay Kinney*

•

St. Francis of Assisi: from The Canticle of the Sun

1 Most high, most great and good Lord, to You belong praises, glory and every blessing; to You alone do they belong, most high, and no one is worthy to name You.
2 Bless You, my Lord, for the gift of all Your creatures and especially for our brother sun, by whom the day is enlightened. He is radiant and bright, of great splendour, bearing witness to You, O my God.
3 Bless You, Lord, for our sister the moon and the stars; you have formed them in the heavens, fair and clear.

The Living Testament
M. Basil Pennington,
Alan Jones and
Mark Booth
1985; 382 pp.
$14.95
($16.45 postpaid) from:
Harper and Row
2350 Virginia Avenue
Hagerstown, MD 21740
or Whole Earth Access

Sojourners

*One of the surprises about the peace movement of the '80s has been the presence (and central organizing significance) of evangelical Christians — a category usually pigeonholed as diehard conservative. One of the most influential such groups has been the Sojourners Fellowship, a Washington, D.C., religious community which is active in peace actions and publishes **Sojourners** magazine monthly. This is a handsome, intelligent journal whose coverage extends from the sanctuary movement to Christian feminism to South Africa. **Sojourners** is decidedly ecumenical, drawing upon a multi-denominational pool of contributors, including Catholic priest Henri Nouwen, writer Gary Wills, and even economist Gar Alperovitz. This is a vital representation of Christianity active in the "real world."* *—Jay Kinney*

"The Way of the Cross," a 320-kilometer pilgrimage in Nicaragua that traveled for two weeks, marching for peace.

Sojourners
Jim Wallis, Editor
$18/year
(11 issues) from:
Sojourners
Subscription Manager
P. O. Box 29272
Washington, DC 20017

The Other Bible
Willis Barnstone
1984; 742 pp.
$14.95
($16.45 postpaid) from:
Harper and Row
2350 Virginia Avenue
Hagerstown, MD 21740
or Whole Earth Access

The Other Bible

For my money this is the most significant sourcebook for exploring an alternative Western spirituality since the English translations of the gnostic Nag Hammadi Library were published. The ancient texts presented here — selections from the Dead Sea Scrolls, apocryphal scriptures, kabbalistic and hermetic texts, and some of the Nag Hammadi scriptures themselves — have been previously scattered in at least a dozen books of varying degrees of availability. In collecting these together and writing short introductions for each of the 88 subsections of material, editor Willis Barnstone has made it immeasurably easier to obtain an overview of the diverse spiritual currents at play in the days before orthodox Christianity took hold in the West.

Possession of a mere fraction of the 742 pages of material collected here would have led to burning at the stake during the Inquisition. It is one of the ironic blessings of our secular age that books like this are now freely available in inexpensive, paperback editions.
—Jay Kinney

•

The Gospel of Thomas
These are the secret sayings which the living Jesus spoke and which Didymos Judas Thomas wrote down.

(1) And he said, "Whoever finds the interpretation of these sayings will not experience death."

(2) Jesus said, "Let him who seeks continue seeking until he finds. When he finds, he will become troubled. When he becomes troubled, he will be astonished, and he will rule over the All."

Gnosis
Jay Kinney, Editor
$15/2 years
(4 issues) from:
Gnosis Magazine
P. O. Box 14217
San Francisco, CA 94114

The Classics of Western Spiritualty

I can't praise this series of books too highly. In an ecumenical move transcending that of any other religious publisher I can think of, Paulist Press has committed itself to publish the most important writings of the key figures of western religion. They've made it an ongoing series that will ultimately comprise as many as eighty volumes. These classics include both the famous and the relatively obscure, not only in Christian spirituality, but in Jewish, Islamic, and Native spiritualities as well. The authors' writings are preceded by a knowledgeable introduction giving some biographical information and placing the texts in the context of the writers' times and other works.

As might be expected with an encyclopedic project such as this, each volume is not going to be of equal interest to everyone. What's important is that Origen, Julian of Norwich, Sharafuddin Maneri, Menahem Nahum, and several dozen other mystics and spiritual masters are now easily accessible and accorded equal stature. The books are all attractively designed, nicely printed, and modestly priced, and available individually or by subscription. The series, which is now up to fifty volumes, has been going for several years at the pace of approximately one book a month. If your local library isn't already acquiring the series as they appear, I'd suggest they catch up: books such as these are what libraries are for. —Jay Kinney

•

And in this he showed me something small, no bigger than a hazelnut, lying in the palm of my hand, as it seemed to me, and it was as round as a ball. I looked at it with the eye of my understanding and thought: What can this be? I was amazed that it could last, for I thought that because of its littleness it would suddenly have fallen into nothing. And I was answered in my understanding: It lasts and always will, because God loves it; and thus everything has being through the love of God.
—from *Julian of Norwich: Showings*

The Classics of Western Spirituality
John Farina, Editor-in-Chief
$11.95
average postpaid price from:
Paulist Press
997 MacArthur Blvd.
Malwah, NJ 07430

Gnosis

Gnosis is the kind of knowledge you get when you meet God. Truth. Western spiritual traditions are full of mystics who sought this gnosis, this direct experience of the divine. But their teachings — Alchemy, Gnosticism, the Kabbalah, Mysticism, Magic, Sufism, to name but a few — aren't widely known due to frequent persecution by orthodox religious authorities. What is known tends to make these traditions seem like strange, primitive islands.

Former **Whole Earth Review** *editor Jay Kinney has founded a magazine called* **Gnosis** *to help bring western inner traditions back into the light. Westerners in search of spiritual growth and illumination need not borrow the path from other cultures; we can look in our own back yard. Each issue of* **Gnosis** *roots expertly through one theme (e.g. Gnosticism, Magic and Tradition) with academic and ecstatic voices speaking side by side. I love the feeling of guided ferment on these pages; the reader is prodded into complex learning as the variations and controversies within each tradition are allowed to educate about its essence. The letters section is packed with impassioned and erudite debate. These 50-page texts are meaning in the making.* *—Jeanne Carstensen*

•

Given that most aspects of the magical mythos are quite unprovable to the skeptical inquirer, there is a strong temptation to write off the whole worldview as a swamp of delusion, and some historians of the occult, such as James Webb and Ellic Howe, have taken this approach.

At least two factors lead me to suggest that readers withhold judgement until engaging in further study themselves. First, the worldview and symbolic universe of Western Magic is fundamentally the same as that of other forms of Western esotericism: Hermeticism, Alchemy, esoteric Freemasonry, Theosophy, and Rosicrucianism. While details and metaphors may differ from system to system, they share the same teachings far more often than not. If the reader has a working familiarity with one of those disciplines — and sees value in it — chances are that further investigations of High Magic will find value there as well.

Second, as we have come to learn more about Eastern paths in recent decades, it has become apparent that the same general worldview — including notions of planes of consciousness, four (or five) basic elements, discarnate teachers, and so on — applies there as well. Indeed the main difference in Eastern and Western esoteric approaches may not be one of details so much as one of attitude: the East tends to consider such inner realms as distractions on the way to Enlightenment, while Western esoteric traditions are devoted to their exploration and utilization as an integral part of the same spiritual journey.

Mysticism

The mystical event is to occupy ONE. Every time it happens it is a life enhancer and a history enhancer. Evelyn Underhill wrote this classic to gather and map the full range of Western mystical experience — Greek, Catholic, Protestant — and yours if you care to follow the steps. Each of those ONEs is unique. Each is the same. That seems pat, but this book approximately proves it. —Stewart Brand

•

Where the philosopher guesses and argues, the mystic lives and looks; and speaks, consequently, the disconcerting language of first-hand experience, not the neat dialectic of the schools. Hence whilst the Absolute of the metaphysicians remains a diagram — impersonal and unattainable — the Absolute of the mystics is lovable, attainable, alive.

•

"All mystics," said Saint-Martin, "speak the same language, for they come from the same country." The deep undying life within us came from that country too: and it recognizes the accents of home, though it cannot always understand what they would say.

•

To go up alone into the mountain and come back as an ambassador to the world, has ever been the method of humanity's best friends.

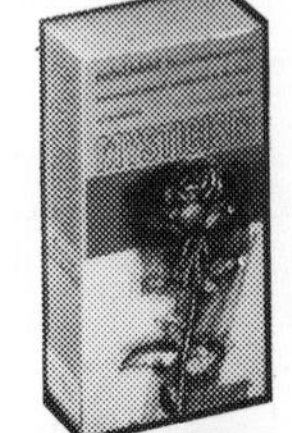

Mysticism
Evelyn Underhill
1911, 1983; 519 pp.
$11.95
($13.45 postpaid) from:
New American Library
120 Woodbine Street
Bergenfield, NJ 07621
or Whole Earth Access

Breakthrough

At first glance Meister Eckhart, the great Dominican mystic of the thirteenth century, seems an unlikely resource for anyone immersed in current struggles for social justice. The sermons of Eckhart which have survived the centuries are absolutely giddy with a sense of unity with the divine; moreover, it's a contagious giddiness that can leave the reader swooning. But behind that ecstasy was a disciplined mind which had some important points to make.

With these new translations of 37 sermons and accompanying commentaries, Dominican author Matthew Fox does a yeoman's job of making Eckhart accessible. Fox makes clear Eckhart's love for the world and shows how it culminates in a compassionate concern for justice. This is a polemical reading of Eckhart to be sure — Nazi ideologue Alfred Rosenberg liked to cite Eckhart in support of wholly different notions — but Fox's reading seems both fair and true to Eckhart's own intentions.

Meister Eckhart was branded a heretic by his own church shortly after he died and he slipped into historical obscurity until fairly recently. This book is a significant attempt to reclaim him for our own time. —Jay Kinney

•

The just person does not seek anything with his work, for every single person who seeks anything or even something with his or her works is working for a why and is a servant and a mercenary. Therefore, if you wish to be conformed and transformed into justice, do not intend anything in your work and strive for no why, either in time or in eternity. Do not aim at reward or blessedness, neither this nor that. For such works are truly fully dead. Indeed, I say that even if you take God as your goal, all such works which you do with this intention are dead and you will spoil good works. —Meister Eckhart

Breakthrough
Matthew Fox
1980; 579 pp.
$9.95
postpaid from:
Doubleday and Company
Direct Mail Order
501 Franklin Avenue
Garden City, NY 11530
or Whole Earth Access

Drawing Down the Moon • Circle Network News

Drawing Down the Moon *is an intelligent, sensitive, well-researched, thorough, critical study of the modern witchcraft scene. It does an excellent job of dealing with subjects which are often misunderstood and misrepresented. There is a new generation of practicing pagans attempting to identify a spiritual tradition linked to their continuing personal and social concerns.* ***Circle*** *is the best way to contact them. —Martha Burning*

•

So perhaps the best way to begin to understand the power behind the simple word *witch* is to enter that circle in the same spirit in which C. G. Jung consulted the I Ching before writing his famous introduction to the Wilhelm-Baynes translation. Do it, perhaps, on a full moon, in a park or in the clearing of a wood. You don't need any of the tools you will read about in books on the Craft. You need no special clothes, or lack of them. Perhaps you might make up a chant, a string of names of gods and goddesses who were loved and familiar to you from childhood myths, a simple string of names for earth and moon and stars, easily repeatable like a mantra. —*Drawing Down the Moon*

Drawing down the moon: one of the few known depictions of this ancient ritual, from a Greek vase probably of the second century B.C. —*Drawing Down the Moon*

Drawing Down the Moon
Margot Adler
1986; 608 pp.
$14.95
($16.95 postpaid) from:
Beacon Press
Attn.: Order Dept.
25 Beacon Street
Boston, MA 02108
or Whole Earth Access

Circle Network News
Dennis Carpenter, Editor
$9/year
(4 issues) from:
Circle
P. O. Box 213
Mount Horeb, WI 53572

Hanuman carrying the Gods Siva and Parvati in his heart. —*Circle Network News*

Memories, Dreams, Reflections

Memories, Dreams, Reflections
C.G. Jung
1963; 430 pp.
$6.95
($7.95 postpaid) from:
Random House
Vintage Books
Order Dept.
400 Hahn Road
Westminster, MD 21157
or Whole Earth Access

I think there is no more remarkable autobiography in this century. Dream power and intellectual power collided in Jung's life, merged finally, and carried him pilot-and-passenger on a psychic Gulf Stream, far and strange. He took 20th Century science with him. —Stewart Brand

•

At the beginning of 1944 I broke my foot, and this misadventure was followed by a heart attack. In a state of unconsciousness I experienced deliriums and visions which must have begun when I hung on the edge of death and was being given oxygen and camphor injections. The images were so tremendous that I myself concluded that I was close to death. My nurse afterward told me, "It was as if you were surrounded by a bright glow." That was a phenomenon she had sometimes observed in the dying, she added. I had reached the outermost limit, and do not know whether I was in a dream or an ecstasy. At any rate, extremely strange things began to happen to me.

It seemed to me that I was high up in space. Far below I saw the globe of the earth, bathed in a gloriously blue light. I saw the deep blue seas and the continents. Far below my feet lay Ceylon, and in the distance ahead of me the subcontinent of India. My field of vision did not include the whole earth, but its global shape was plainly distinguishable and its outlines shone with a silvery gleam through that wonderful blue light. In many places the globe seemed colored or spotted dark green like oxidized silver. Far away to the left lay a broad expanse — the reddish-yellow desert of Arabia; it was as though the silver of the earth had there assumed a reddish-gold hue. Then came the Red Sea, and far, far back — as if in the upper left of a map — I could just make out a bit of the Mediterranean. My gaze was chiefly directed toward that. Everything else appeared indistinct. I could also see the snow-covered Himalayas, but in that direction it was foggy or cloudy. I did not look to the right at all. I knew that I was on the point of departing from the earth.

Later I discovered how high in space one would have to be to have so extensive a view — approximately a thousand miles! The sight of the earth from this height was the most glorious thing I had ever seen.

Symbol of the sacred in a ring of flames floating above the world of war and technology. Painted in 1920, it was inspired by a dream Jung had had on 22 January 1914, anticipating the outbreak of war in August 1914.
—Word and Image

C.G. Jung: Word and Image

C.G. Jung: Word and Image
Aniela Jaffe, Editor
1979; 238 pp.
$16.50
postpaid from:
Princeton University Press
41 William Street
Princeton, NJ 08540
or Whole Earth Access

If not nothing, then Jung is surely image. This collection by an old collaborator of his takes his lifelong caterpillar-crawl of thought and gives it colorful flight and new life. Jung's biography is visible, as well as the things he saw that moved him, the archetypal images he recognized, and his own bizarre beautiful paintings, carvings, buildings. He lived with beautiful care. The book is bright and clear and not the slightest bit slick. —Stewart Brand

►

Tree-man, by a thirty-five-year-old woman. Image of neurotically delayed development caused by psychic disturbances in childhood. Difficulties centered around developing a will of her own.

At a Journal Workshop

At a Journal Workshop
Ira Progoff
1975; 320 pp.
$9.95
($11.70 postpaid) from:
Dialogue House Library
80 East 11th St., Suite 305
New York, NY 10003
or Whole Earth Access

Progoff, a former protege of psychologist Carl Jung, has devised an innovative way of keeping a psychological journal.

Like most Jungian psychologists, Progoff feels that each of us possesses self-directing, self-healing capacities which are not always accessible to our day-to-day consciousness. Persons seeking to get in touch with these capabilities have usually required professional guidance. The Intensive Journal method was developed to allow people to use journal-writing to gain entry to those capacities. (Progoff and his associates also teach his journal method through a series of weekend and week-long workshops. For information about workshops in your area, write to the address below).

Progoff writes of "going down our own well until we reach the underground stream . . . . We do not go down that well by analyzing or by any effort of will. Rather we focus ourselves inward, relax the analytical mind, and allow phrases, images, and memories to arise on their own." —Tom Ferguson, M.D. [Suggested by Brad Smith]

•

Each person must be aware of his own tendencies, and they are different in this respect for each individual. We have found it often to be the case that when a person writes on and on in the Period Log, his extended verbalization tends to lead him away from the basic factuality of his life. Educated people may especially be seduced into quasi-literary writing instead of basic, unvarnished statements of their inner experience.

•

At the point where we read back to ourselves the continuity of dreams that we have collected in our Dream Log, a further step that extends our experience becomes possible. Our purpose in *feeding back* these dreams to ourselves in their consecutive movement is not to enable us to interpret their movement, nor to "understand" them, nor to analyze their "pattern." Our purpose rather is to place ourselves back into the movement of our dream process as a whole so that the process can now freely extend itself. Having come this far, where else do our dreams wish to go? What else are they reaching for? What else do they wish to say to us?

Isis Giving Bread and Water to the Soul.

The Hero With A Thousand Faces

Myths and man's dreamworld have, for the past fifty years or so, been the objects of various alchemical attempts at synthesis. The hero with a thousand faces is one of those syntheses. It's about the mono-myth. Campbell traces his hero right out into the void. —J.D. Smith

•

The Chinese tell of a crossing of the Fairy Bridge under guidance of the Jade Maiden and the Golden Youth. The Hindus picture a towering firmament of heavens and a many-leveled underworld of hells. The soul gravitates after death to the story appropriate to its relative density, there to digest and assimilate the whole meaning of its past life. When the lesson has been learned, it returns to the world, to prepare itself for the next level of experience. Thus gradually it makes its way through all the levels of life-value until it has broken past the confines of the cosmic egg. Dante's *Divina Commedia* is an exhaustive review of the stages: "Inferno," the misery of the spirit bound to the prides and actions of the flesh; "Purgatorio," the process of transmuting fleshly into spiritual experience; "Paradiso," the degrees of spiritual realization.

The Hero With A Thousand Faces
Joseph Campbell
1949; 416 pp.
$9.95
postpaid from:
Princeton University Press
41 William Street
Princeton, NJ 08540
or Whole Earth Access

Life After Life

Truth is qualitative but proving something requires numbers. The author has investigated the experience of over 100 people who clinically have died and then recovered. They all had a similar experience, and none had further fears of death. That may be sufficient proof for you to relax now about dying. Or you can wait for the truth.
—Stewart Brand

•

What is perhaps the most incredible common element in the accounts I have studied, and is certainly the element which has the most profound effect upon the individual, is the encounter with a very bright light. Typically, at its first appearance this light is dim, but it rapidly gets brighter until it reaches an unearthly brilliance. Yet, even though this light (usually said to be white or "clear") is of an indescribable brilliance, many make the specific point that it does not in any way hurt their eyes, or dazzle them, or keep them from seeing other things around them (perhaps because at this point they don't have physical "eyes" to be dazzled).

Despite the light's unusual manifestation, however, not one person has expressed any doubt whatsoever that it was a being, a being of light. Not only that, it is a personal being. It has a very definite personality. The love and warmth which emanate from this being to the dying person are utterly beyond words, and he feels completely surrounded by it and taken up in it, completely at ease and accepted in the presence of this being. He senses an irresistible magnetic attraction to this light. He is ineluctably drawn to it.

•

The reason why death is no longer frightening, as all of these excerpts express, is that after his experience a person no longer entertains any doubts about his survival of bodily death. It is no longer merely an abstract possibility to him, but a fact of his experience.

•

Many persons report being out of their bodies for extended periods and witnessing many events in the physical world during the interlude. Can any of these reports be checked out with other witnesses who were known to be present, or with later confirming events, and thus be corroborated?

In quite a few instances, the somewhat surprising answer to this question is "yes." Furthermore, the descriptions of events witnessed while out of the body tend to check out fairly well. Several doctors have told me, for example, that they are utterly baffled about how patients with no medical knowledge could describe in such detail and so correctly the procedure used in resuscitation attempts, even though these events took place while the doctors knew the patients involved to be "dead."

Life After Life
Raymond A. Moody, Jr., M.D.
1975; 187 pp.
$3.95
($5.45 postpaid) from:
Bantam Books
414 East Golf Road
Des Plaines, IL 60016
or Whole Earth Access

The I Ching

Gregory Bateson remarked once to his secretary, Judy Van Slooten, "I am going to build a church some day. It will have a holy of holies and a holy of holies of holies, and in that ultimate box will be a random number table." Check Bateson's ***Mind and Nature*** *(reviewed on p. 22). All originality, he says, whether in evolution or in human learning, comes from "raids on the random."*

The ancient Chinese Taoists who made this oracle may have had a similar idea, or they may have stumbled on it or coevolved into it, but obviously it served them. And it serves us. It profoundly served the generation that emitted the original ***Whole Earth Catalog.*** *Ending with this review is a piece of homage to that time and those people, both passing rapidly, both remembered too easily for superficial and dismissable things rather than for the real risks taken with real clarity in the face of overwhelming opposition.*

Clink clink go the tossed pennies. How about a statement for the end of the ***Essential Whole Earth Catalog,*** *ancient random number table . . . Hm, 51, The Arousing.*
—Stewart Brand

•

51. *Chên / The Arousing (Shock, Thunder)*

above CHÊN THE AROUSING, THUNDER
below CHÊN THE AROUSING, THUNDER

The hexagram Chen represents the eldest son, who seizes rule with energy and power. A yang line develops below two yin lines and presses upward forcibly. This movement is so violent that it arouses terror. It is symbolized by thunder, which bursts forth from the earth and by its shock causes fear and trembling.

The Judgment
Shock brings success.
Shock comes — oh, oh!
Laughing words — ha, ha!
The shock terrifies for a hundred miles,
And he does not let fall the sacrificial spoon
and chalice.

The shock that comes from the manifestation of God within the depths of the earth makes man afraid, but this fear of God is good, for joy and merriment can follow upon it.

When a man has learned within his heart what fear and trembling mean, he is safeguarded against any terror produced by outside influences. Let the thunder roll and spread terror a hundred miles around: he remains so composed and reverent in spirit that the sacrificial rite is not interrupted. This is the spirit that must animate leaders and rulers of men — a profound inner seriousness from which all outer terrors glance off harmlessly.

The I Ching
Richard Wilhelm and Cary F. Baynes, Translators
1977; 740 pp.
$17.50
postpaid from:
Princeton University Press
41 William Street
Princeton, NJ 08540
or Whole Earth Access

GENESIS

Whole Earth Catalog
Fall 1970
$3

by Stewart Brand

THE *WHOLE EARTH CATALOG* got started in a plane over Nebraska in March 1968. The sun had set ahead of the plane while I sat reading *Spaceship Earth* by Barbara Ward. Between chapters, I gazed out the window into dark nothing and slipped into a reverie about how I could help my friends who were starting their own civilization hither and yon in the sticks. The L. L. Bean Catalog of outdoor stuff (p. 274) came to mind, and I pondered upon Mr. Bean's service to humanity over the years. So many of the problems I could identify came down to a matter of access: Where to buy a windmill. Where to get good information on beekeeping. Where to lay hands on a computer.

Shortly, I was fantasizing access service. A truck store, maybe, traveling around with information and samples of what was worth getting and information on where to get it. A catalog, continuously updated, in part by the users. A catalog that owed nothing to the suppliers and everything to the users. It would be something I could put some years into.

Amid the fever I was in by this time, I remembered R. Buckminster Fuller's admonition that you have about ten minutes to act on an idea before it recedes back into dreamland, so I started writing on the end papers of Barbara Ward's book (never did finish reading it).

One of the main things that drove me into business was ignorance. A liberally educated young man, I hadn't the faintest idea how the world worked. Bargaining, distribution, mark-up, profit, bankruptcy, lease, invoice, fiscal year, inventory — they were all a mystery to me and were usually depicted as sordid. I noticed that great lengths were gone to in order to prevent "consumers" from knowing that part of the purchase price went to the retailer. It seemed exquisitely insane to me. You sell deception and buy mistrust to no advantage. The retailer in fact earns his 25-40 percent by tiresome work, but the prevailing attitude makes him out a clever crook. Ignorance institutionalized. Would you mind leaving the room? We're talking about money.

At the time, in fact, finances were not particularly on my mind. How To Make Money was not the design problem. (I'd heard and bought Ken Kesey's advice that you don't make money by making money: you have that in mind early on, but then you forget it and concentrate entirely on good product; the money comes to pass.) The problem was How to Generate a Low-Maintenance, High-Yield, Self-Sustaining, Critical Information Service.

Easy. You name what you know is good stuff and indicate exactly where to get it. You do this on newsprint, which costs half of the next-higher paper stock. Low overhead at every step. Employ stone amateurs with energy and enthusiasm. Build furniture out of scrap doors, light tables out of scrap plywood, work in whatever space you have. Pay your pros $5/hour (no raises) and the beginners $2/hour with $.25/hour raises every couple months. Employees fill out their own time sheets. If they get dishonest about that — or anything that hurts service — fire them. Spread responsibility as far as it will go, credit too.

What you're trying to do is to nourish and design an organism that can learn and stay alive while it's learning. Once that process hits its stride, don't tinker with it; work for it, let it work for you. Make interesting demands on each other.

By June 1969, we were being mentioned in a lot of underground papers such as the *East Village Other.* And then Nicholas von Høffman wrote a full piece on the *Whole Earth Catalog* that got syndicated all over the U.S. We were caught. We were famous.

Of all the press notices we eventually got, from *Time* and *Vogue* to *Hotcha!* in Germany to a big article in *Esquire,* nothing had the business impact of one tiny mention in "Uncle Ben Sez" in the Detroit *Free Press,* where some reader asked, "how do we start a farm?" and Uncle Ben printed our address. We got hundreds and hundreds of subscriptions from that.

We hired more people. Deposits at the bank were more frequent. The bank officers got more polite.

In September 1969, as I was driving up the hill to work, it suddenly hit me that I didn't want to. Instead of golden opportunity, the publication was becoming a grim chore. I considered the alternatives of taking my medicine like a good boy or setting about passing my job to somebody else. I'm sure I sighed unhappily. And then this other notion glimmered. Keep the job, finish the original assignment, and then stop. Stop a success, and see what happens. Experiment going as well as coming. We printed in the September 1969 Supplement that we would cease publication with a big Catalog, *The Last Whole Earth Catalog,* in Spring of 1971.

MEANWHILE, business was still growing. The morning mail was a daily, heavy Santa Claus bag.

Our stopping was primarily an economic experiment. Rather than do the usual succession things, we preferred to just cease supply and let demand create its own new sources. Our hope was that those sources would be more diverse and better than we had been, or could have been if we had continued.

So, in June 1971, we had the Demise Party celebrating the self-termination of the *Whole Earth Catalog,* and all in all it was a rout. Fifteen hundred people showed up. San Francisco's Exploratorium staff had their museum weirding around us full steam. At midnight, Scott Beach announced from the stage that these here two hundred $100 bills, yes, $20,000, were now the property of the party-goers, just as soon as they could decide what to do with them.

"Flush them down the toilet!" "No, don't!" "Give it to the Indians!" "Bangladesh!" "Our commune needs a pump or we'll all get hepatitis!" And so on. The debate lasted till nine o'clock the next morning, when a dozen remaining hardcore party-goers turned the remaining $15,000 ($5,000 had been distributed to the crowd at one wild point) over to Fred Moore, dishwasher. He later gathered people for other group decidings over what to do with the money. That worked out damn well. Most of the story, *Rolling Stone's* account, is in *The Seven Laws Of Money* (p. 202).

My reasons for perpetrating? Pure curiosity. Some of the surprises were: 1) The money kept trying to come back — innumerable suggestions involved the Portola Institute (Whole Earth's fiscal agency) as the recipient; 2) Handling of more than a pocketful of power was new to most, upsetting, educational; 3) Ideas were mostly busy — unoriginal, guilt-ridden; 4) People who focused on the process of deciding had a much better time than those who focused on the money; 5) "Free money" is crazy.

In 1971 we had ceased making *Whole Earth Catalogs* forever, sincerely expecting that someone would quickly come along and fill the niche better than we did. Well, they didn't. *The Last Whole Earth Catalog* won the National Book Award in 1972 and continued to sell 5,000 copies a week with increasingly outdated information. We updated it in 1973 and 1975 and added what amounted to Volume II in 1974: *The Whole Earth Epilog.* Then the North American economy began to lose its mind, putting more people in need of tools for independence and the economy as a whole in need of greater local resilience.

AFTER BURNING our bridges, we reported before the Throne to announce, "We're here for our next terrific idea." The Throne said, "That Was It."

"It" became a journal called the *CoEvolution Quarterly* (*CQ*). I had been wanting to call it "The Never Piss Against The Wind Newsletter," or perhaps "Making Circuit." I did have a formula in mind: we would print long technical pieces on whatever interested us — the opposite of the predigested pap in, say, *Intellectual Digest.* So the Spring 1974 *CQ* had Paul Ehrlich on coevolution, Roy Rappaport and Howard Odum on energy and culture, Sam Keen on spiritual tyranny, and a nice reception from readers. We had printed 5,000 copies of the 96-page Spring *CQ* and sold them all. The Summer *CQ* sold out 10,000 copies immediately; we had another 7,000 printed.

By Winter 1979, we had put out 24 issues of *CQ.* For years, we resisted the standing temptation to do a new version of the *Catalog* because of the sheer labor involved. Then Art Kleiner, a University of California/Berkeley journalism graduate, indicated that he would like to work with us.

In the brutal/apologetic tones you would use asking someone to scrub the toilets, I said, "Art, how would you like to handle the compiling of a new *Whole Earth Catalog*? That includes working on the distribution deal and production and printing, as well as contacting all of the old listees for their recent information and making final sense out of the doubtless-conflicting evaluation messages from the editors."

"Sure," he said.

If Art was that brave, I guessed we could be. Then began the sift through everything in the *Whole Earth Catalog,* the *Whole Earth Epilog,* and 24 issues of *CoEvolution Quarterly* to identify, update, and assemble the best. New prices, new addresses, new covers, new excerpts (from catalogs and magazines), and often new reviews.

Called *The Next Whole Earth Catalog,* it had 608 folio-size pages, reviewed 3,907 items, and weighed 5½ pounds. Before the ink was dry on the first 1980 edition, work began on a second edition that appeared in 1981.

All told, more than 2.5 million *Whole Earth Catalogs* have been sold since we started in 1968, and that doesn't count the *Whole Earth Software Catalogs* of 1985 and 1986 or the *Catalog* you're presently holding. There's more on the way. ■

BUSINESS

POINT is a nonprofit organization charged to encourage and organize innovative educational projects. One of POINT's primary activities is the occasional publication of *Whole Earth Catalogs* and continuing publication of *Whole Earth Review.* Previous *Whole Earth Catalogs* paid their way as service publications, and we expect this one will too. The habit of publishing our real costs and real returns within each *Catalog* is one aspect of our goal to make processes transparent. Our business is dealing in useful information. In a world of fast-decaying news, useful means current, which means expensive. The quicker, the costlier. Production of this *Catalog* began in earnest on January 1, 1986 and was completed on schedule on August 1, 1986; it took a short seven months to construct a book that would ordinarily take at least a year.

Doubleday advanced us $120,000 against future royalties of the book to get the project rolling. We pay 15 percent ($18,000) of that on commission to John Brockman Associates for engineering the deal with Doubleday. POINT was paid $50,000 at the start, with the remainder given upon delivery of the finished negatives. In addition, Doubleday paid us $30,000 for production costs because unlike most books, all the production work was done at our editorial offices in Sausalito. As you can see below, the $30,000 covers only a portion of those costs.

Essential Whole Earth Catalog Expenses

Editorial salaries*	$ 41,356
Production salaries*	51,442
Research salaries*	26,600
Contributors	12,000
Production supplies	4,316
Negatives for printer	7,500
Telephone/postage	7,428
Rent	1,400
Total	$152,042

* Everyone gets a flat $10 an hour. Let's see, looks like about 12,000 hours went into preparing this incarnation of the *Catalog.* That works out to be an average 28 hours' work per page, twenty-eight hours includes all researching, gathering, writing, editing, designing, typesetting, pasting-up, proofing, and the massive organizing needed for each step. For comparison, in 1980 the staff put 17,500 hours into the 608-page *Next Whole Earth Catalog,* also averaging about 28 hours per page.

Whole Earth Catalog Income

(What happens to your $15, thank you.)

$ 6.90	to Doubleday
.67	to book wholesaler
6.30	to bookstore
.17	to John Brockman Associates
.96	to us, POINT
$ 15.00	

Figuring that our royalty switches from 7.5 percent to 10 percent after sales of 100,000, we need to sell 122,000 copies of the *Essential Whole Earth Catalog* to begin earning money beyond our advance from Doubleday. Deducting our production costs of $152,042 and agent's fees of $18,000, the *Catalog* will have to sell 136,000 before we make a "profit." Anything above that is gratefully ploughed back into *Whole Earth Review* or the next POINT project. —*Kevin Kelly*

Tree Budget

Here's an estimate of the number of trees it takes to produce the *Essential Whole Earth Catalog.* We'll assume a "printing" of 100,000 copies, each copy weighing 2½ pounds. That's 250,000 pounds of paper. We grossly estimate that an average pulpwood tree grown on a tree farm weighs about 250 pounds and, after processing, yields about 125 pounds of paper. This means that each printing of this *Catalog* requires 250,000 pounds @ 125 pounds/tree, or 2,000 trees.

Let's change trees into forest. Most pulpwood is planted on 6- to 10-foot centers. To make this calculation easier, let's assume 10-foot centers, or 100 square feet per tree. The 2,000 trees will take up 200,000 square feet. It's easier to think about that in acres. There's about 44,000 square feet per acre, so that works out to be about 4½ acres of trees per printing of 100,000 *Catalogs.*

If only 3 percent of Catalog buyers plant a tree (and take care of it), there will be net tree gain. Otherwise, loss.

Long live tree flesh and responsible tree people.

—*Peter Warshall and Stewart Brand*

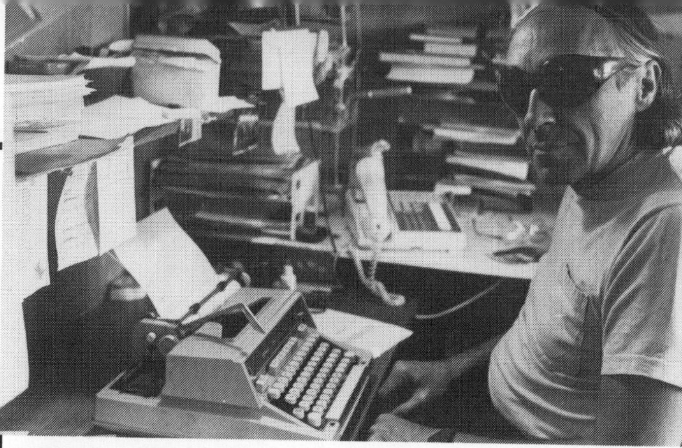

Sporting his volleyball-deflection glasses, J. Baldwin composes reviews between games. He eschews word processors in favor of his trusty and reparable 1950s manual typewriter.

A

B

Jeanne Carstensen trucks pages-in-progress between our waterfront editorial office and nearby production studio.

C

D

Access yeoman David Finacom models a prosthetic shark schnozz as he leaves Whole Earth to become a part-time Alaskan salmon packer.

G

H

This index is just one benefit of the Whole Earth database, compiled by red-eyed David Burnor using SMART, an integrated software package for the IBM PC.

I

J

Fifi Rat critiques James Donnelly's quasimeticulous paste-up as they take a break from typesetting, while Alan Born (with back to camera) keyboards.

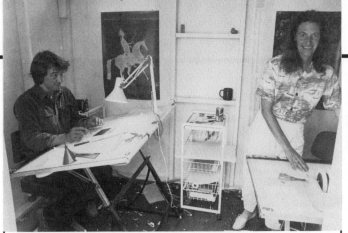

Out in the "doghouse" — a temporary office/hovel in our courtyard that J. Baldwin built for $350 — Steve Lipke and Jerri Linn paste up pages. Steve is a Whole Earth reader who arrived with the right skills at the right time. Jerri is a fabric designer and boat restorer who also helped with layout designs on some pages in the Catalog.

N

O

Each two-page spread's worth of review material is kept in order in a dishwashing tub. The one spread/one bucket approach kept us relatively sane in dealing with the multiplicity of items reviewed. Here, Dorothy Houser wrestles down a latecomer so she can confirm access information on its contents.

Proofreader by day, World Beat dj by night, frenetic Briton Jonathan E. eludes pursuit on Susan Erkel's mountain bike.

S

Deep in the stack of Whole Earth's highly evolved library, Don Baker gathers the best of what's there for comparison to the best of the new.

T

Jay Kinney evaluates the classics of contemporary comics, paying particular attention to the 3-D effects.

U

V

W

Seen through a jungle of fennel outside his window, Dick Fugett monitors the heavens through his short-wave unit while adroitly resolving Whole Earth Review subscription complaints.

Eco-poet/wild man Peter Warshall disembarks from the dry-docked, 35-foot shrimp trawler beached in our garden that served him as his office.

Mashed into typical foetal position, Art Kleiner solicits expert contributions to the Catalog.